lonely planet

Brazil

John Noble
Andrew Draffen
Robyn Jones
Chris McAsey
Leonardo Pinheiro

LONELY PLANET PUBLICATIONS
Melbourne • Oakland • London • Paris

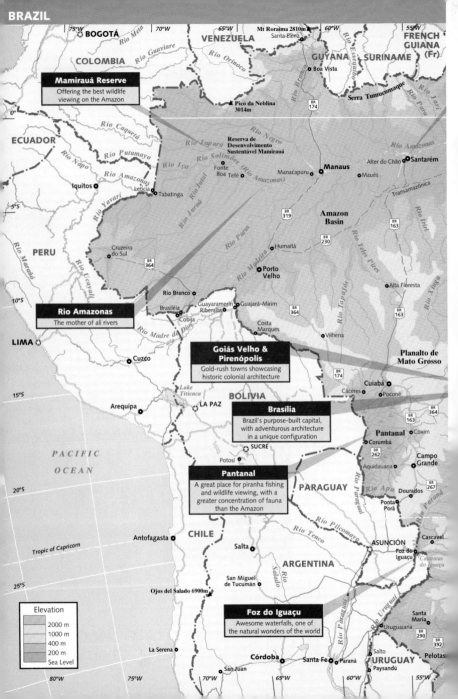

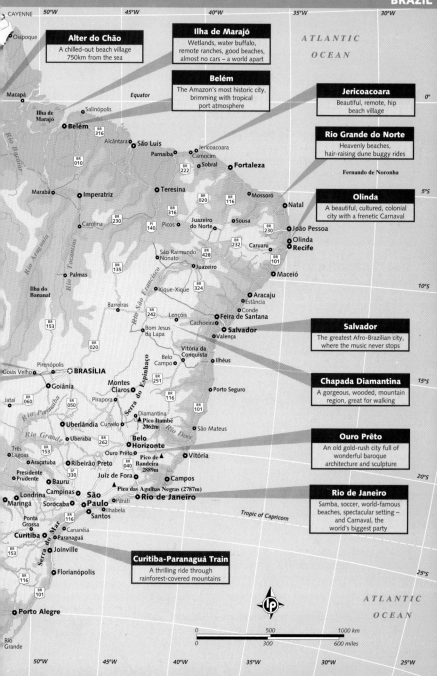

BRAZIL

Alter do Chão
A chilled-out beach village 750km from the sea

Ilha de Marajó
Wetlands, water buffalo, remote ranches, good beaches, almost no cars – a world apart

Belém
The Amazon's most historic city, brimming with tropical port atmosphere

Jericoacoara
Beautiful, remote, hip beach village

Rio Grande do Norte
Heavenly beaches, hair-raising dune buggy rides

Olinda
A beautiful, cultured, colonial city with a frenetic Carnaval

Salvador
The greatest Afro-Brazilian city, where the music never stops

Chapada Diamantina
A gorgeous, wooded, mountain region, great for walking

Ouro Prêto
An old gold-rush city full of wonderful baroque architecture and sculpture

Rio de Janeiro
Samba, soccer, world-famous beaches, spectacular setting – and Carnaval, the world's biggest party

Curitiba-Paranaguá Train
A thrilling ride through rainforest-covered mountains

ATLANTIC OCEAN

ATLANTIC OCEAN

Brazil
5th edition – January 2002
First published – August 1989

Published by
Lonely Planet Publications Pty Ltd ABN 36 005 607 983
90 Maribyrnong St, Footscray, Victoria 3011, Australia

Lonely Planet Offices
Australia Locked Bag 1, Footscray, Victoria 3011
USA 150 Linden St, Oakland, CA 94607
UK 10a Spring Place, London NW5 3BH
France 1 rue du Dahomey, 75011 Paris

Photographs
Many of the images in this guide are available for licensing from
Lonely Planet Images.
W www.lonelyplanetimages.com

Front cover photograph
Sunset on the Pantanal (John Maier Jr)

ISBN 1 86450 146 4

text & maps © Lonely Planet Publications Pty Ltd 2002
photos © photographers as indicated 2002

Printed by SNP SPrint (M) Sdn Bhd
Printed in Malaysia

Contents

THE SOUTHEAST

RIO DE JANEIRO CITY

CARNAVAL

RIO DE JANEIRO STATE

ESPÍRITO SANTO

MINAS GERAIS

THE NORTH

PARÁ, AMAPÁ & TOCANTINS

AMAZONAS & RORAIMA

RONDÔNIA & ACRE

LANGUAGE

GLOSSARY

THANKS

INDEX

REGIONS

GUADELOUPE (Fr)
DOMINICA
MARTINIQUE (Fr)
BARBADOS

NETHERLANDS
ANTILLES
ST LUCIA
ST VINCENT
GRENADA

TRINIDAD &
TOBAGO

ATLANTIC

OCEAN

VENEZUELA

GUYANA

FRENCH
GUIANA (Fr)

COLOMBIA

SURINAME

Equator

The North
page 620

The Northeast
page 456

PERU

The Central West
page 401

BOLIVIA

The Southeast
page 169

PARAGUAY

Tropic of Capricorn

CHILE

The South
page 344

ARGENTINA

URUGUAY

PACIFIC

OCEAN

0   500   1000 km

0   300   600 miles

The Authors

John Noble

John comes from the Ribble Valley in northern England, where it rains even more than in the Amazon rainforest but isn't quite so warm. A degree in philosophy somehow led John into a career in newspaper journalism, but increasing interruptions for travel to various bits of the globe saw him eventually leave Fleet Street for a Lonely Planet trail that has seen him cover, at the last count, 19 countries from Russia to Mexico, Indonesia to Lithuania and Australia to Andorra. He has been the coordinating author of many editions of multi-author titles, including *Mexico*, *Spain*, *Russia,Ukraine & Belarus* and now *Brazil*. Taking on Brazilian Amazonia for this edition, as well as writing the new Natural Brazil section and updating the book's introductory chapters, amounted to one of his most exciting and challenging tasks yet. John is based in Spain, together with his wife and co-author Susan Forsyth and their children, Jack and Isabella.

Andrew Draffen

Australian-born Andrew has traveled and worked his way around Australia, Asia, North America and the Caribbean. He has been coming to Brazil to update this book since its 2nd edition and is also author of Lonely Planet's *Rio de Janeiro* city guide. He now lives in Melbourne and divides his time between writing, coaching other writers and guiding tours to Brazil. He also spends an excessive amount of time daydreaming about Ipanema sunsets.

Robyn Jones

As a teenager Robyn traded farm life in rural Victoria, Australia, for a year as an exchange student in the Brazilian megalopolis of São Paulo. While studying for a degree in architecture, she tripped around Australia and Europe. Later, she returned to Brazil with Leonardo to live in Rio de Janeiro for a while and to meet her future in-laws. She covered the northern region of Brazil for the 3rd and 4th editions of Lonely Planet's *Brazil* and the 7th edition of *South America*, co-wrote *Fiji* and the 5th edition update, wrote the Fiji and Tuvalu chapters of the 1st edition of *South Pacific* and contributed to the 2nd edition of *Travel With Children*. In between travels Robyn works as an architect in Melbourne, where she lives with Leonardo and their two sons, Alex and Nicholas.

Chris McAsey

After being weeded out of law school, Chris bounced around for several years, dabbling in hospitality, professional football and the rag trade. A short holiday in Greece whetted his appetite; he left his dead-end job to travel through Eastern Europe, Asia and the US, study Russian in Moscow and work in Japan. He returned home to complete a BA in professional writing and to write a guide to Australia for Japanese travelers before setting off on his first LP job in Indonesia. After traveling solo for 15 years, he looks forward to adventures with partner Gina and their children, Eden and Fischer.

Leonardo Pinheiro

Leonardo was born and raised in Rio de Janeiro, Brazil. At 15, curious to roam further than Rio city, he jumped on a bus to the Northeast coast. From then on, he traveled throughout Brazil as much as his pocket money and time would allow. After training in agricultural science, Leonardo headed for Sydney to do post-grad studies and to check out the Australian surf. He met Robyn and moved to Melbourne, where they now live with their two sons, Alex and Nicholas. Leonardo also worked on the 3rd and 4th editions of Lonely Planet's *Brazil*, the 7th edition of *South America*, the rewrite of *Fiji* and the 5th edition update, co-wrote the Fiji and Tuvalu chapters of the 1st edition of *South Pacific* and contributed to the 2nd edition of *Travel With Children*. He is currently studying for his PhD in biochemistry.

FROM THE AUTHORS

From John Noble So many people helped me get to grips with the enormity of Amazonia and this project in general that there is only room for a list of some of the names. Thank you Divaldo, Stefano, Juana, Rosana, Jilvan, Andrey and the rest of the Ecológica crew; Deanna Swaney; Marcia (Princetur, Porto Velho); staff at SEBRAE, IBAMA and Setur in Porto Velho; Elias Mansour Macedo; management and staff at the Hotel Rio Branco, Rio Branco; Nelissa Peralta and all at Mamirauá; Chris, Christopher and Liz Wright; Doug and Nancy Trent; the Federação Brasileira dos Albergues da Juventude; Marcos and Tiago at Paratur, Belém; Lourdes Figueiredo; Leonie Mugavin, Didier Buroc, Rachel Suddart and Gabrielle Knight; Mike Astor; Isabella Noble; Axel Antoine-Feill, Marcela Torres and all at Palmari; Sophie Coyaud; Steven Alexander; Waldinor Mota; Frank Coe; Jean-François Le Cornec; the British embassy in Brasília; David and Fiona in Atalaia do Norte; David Cleary; and Nelsí Sadeck. Finally, extra special thanks to Susan Forsyth, Andrew Draffen, Chris McAsey, Robyn Jones, Leonardo Pinheiro, John Maier, Elaine Merrill, Annette Olson, Maria Donohoe and Mariah Bear, whose assistance and encouragement I truly could not have done without! Thanks again everybody – hope you'll think the end product made it worthwhile.

From Andrew *Muito obrigado* to the following for their support, advice and insider tips: John Maier, Mike, Ivandy and Nicholas Astor; Denise and Gabriel Werneck; Paulo Celani; Marcelo Armstrong (Rio); Vera, Arnauldo, Iara, Ivana and Portuga (Sao Paulo); Toursbahia, Luca, Bia (Salvador); David, Cacao (João Pessoa); Francisco, Tia Helena (Natal); Toby (Canoa Quebrada); Ricarte (Paraiba).

From Chris McAsey Thanks to Helvia Angeli (Sematur, Alto Paraíso); the World Wildlife for Nature (Alto Paraíso); the Swedish journos for making me their mascot; Rogério de Souza Dias (Pirenópolis); Dr Sebastião (Cuiabá); the helpful crew at Sebrae (Campo Grande); Fabio Oranges D'Alessandro Viana and Lidiane Cássia Zanini (Foztur, Foz do

Iguaçu); Bethany Patterson (Bute, Australia) for proving that adventurous Aussies are still out there; Douglas Trent (Focus Tours); Ashley and Ola for their wonderful hospitality in Tribeca; Paul and Rosemary Hearnden; Jen, Ross and Jodie.

At home – all my love to Gina, Eden and Fischer – I'll never travel lonely again.

From Robyn & Leo The following people deserve special thanks: an *abraço bem apertado* to Sil, Arnaldo and Raquel for their hospitality in São Paulo; the Arruda family for hints in Sampa – great to see you all again; Laire for babysitting in Rio; Emmanoel for year's end celebrations; Liane and Cassio for hints on Minas and the fun wedding; Leá Barreto Leite for spoiling us as usual; Luisa for sharing her toys and Marcelo for professional advice; Peta & Ian for the new study space; Trich, Keegan & Bree for house-sitting; Mum for again paying our bills; and to Alex and Nicholas for being such happy and healthy co-travelers.

Thanks also to Edgard Bittencourt (Campos do Jordão, SP), Oscar Araripe & family (Tiradentes, MG), Janaina (Iporanga, SP), Adriano (Penedo, RJ), José Isabel Silva & Walter Amaro Silva (Ouro Prêto, MG) and Ana Barbosa Olinto at INFAN (Tiradentes, MG). To the understanding policeman at Belo's rodoviária – we appreciate your not towing us away or locking Leo up! Thanks to the state and municipal tourist officials, including: Carla Bastos (Vitória, ES), Simone (Caxambu, MG), Ana Carolina at Belotur and Luciane at Turminas (Belo Horizonte, MG), Luis Bentes and team (Saquarema, RJ), Renan Wanderlay (Parati, RJ), Marcio André Fernandes (São João del Rei, MG).

This Book

The 1st edition of *Brazil* was written by Mitchell Schoen & William Herzberg. The 2nd edition was written by Andrew Draffen, Deanna Swaney and Robert Strauss. The 3rd edition was written by Andrew Draffen, Chris McAsey, Robyn Jones and Leonardo Pinheiro. The 4th edition was written by Nick Selby, Andrew Draffen, Chris McAsey, Robyn Jones and Leonardo Pinheiro.

FROM THE PUBLISHER

This 5th edition of *Brazil* is a product of Lonely Planet's US office in Oakland, California. A large cast of characters contributed time, talent and energy in putting this one together. Elaine Merrill and Wendy Smith edited the book. They could never have stayed the course without extensive assistance from Wade Fox, Susan Shook Malloy, Vivek Waglé and China Williams. Senior editor Maria Donohoe oversaw the whole process with grace and fortitude, stepping aside only briefly mid-project to get married (talk about multitasking), allowing David Zingarelli to fill her shoes in the interim in his typical excellent way. Kate Hoffman and Mariah Bear provided invaluable supervision. Ken DellaPenta indexed the book.

Dion Good, lead cartographer, skillfully mapped his way from Roraima to Rio Grande do Sul, with the fine assistance of Carole Nuttall. Cartographers Patrick Bock, Justin Colgan, John Culp, Matt DeMartini, Rachel Driver, Lee Espinole, Patrick Huerta, Brad Lodge, Sara Nelson, Don Patterson and Eric Thomsen also helped with mapping. Kimra McAfee wrote the mapping brief. Cartographic technical support was provided by Molly Green, Tim Lohnes and John Spelman. Senior cartographer Annette Olson, relieved for a short time by Sean Brandt, oversaw the entire mapmaking operation. The whole crew worked under the direction of Alex Guilbert.

Designers Josh Schefers and Andreas Schueller took the book masterfully through layout, with the help of Shelley Firth. Beca Lafore created the color sections, and Henia Miedzinski did the cover. Illustrations were contributed by artists Hugh D'Andrade, Hayden Foell, Jun Jalbuena, Rini Keagy, Justin Marler, Henia Miedzinski, Hannah Reineck, Jennifer Steffey, Jim Swanson, Alan Tarbell and Mick Weldon. Art director Susan Rimerman oversaw the entire design process.

Tomi Warren greatly facilitated the delivery of sundry batches of maps and texts to and from all parts of the globe.

Lastly, thank you to all the authors for their hard work. And a special *muito obrigada* to coordinating author John Noble, whose unflagging enthusiasm and meticulous devotion to every aspect of the book went beyond the call of duty. Now it's time for some *caipirinhas*.

Foreword

ABOUT LONELY PLANET GUIDEBOOKS

The story begins with a classic travel adventure: Tony and Maureen Wheeler's 1972 journey across Europe and Asia to Australia. Useful information about the overland trail did not exist at that time, so Tony and Maureen published the first Lonely Planet guidebook to meet a growing need.

From a kitchen table, then from a tiny office in Melbourne (Australia), Lonely Planet has become the largest independent travel publisher in the world, an international company with offices in Melbourne, Oakland (USA), London (UK) and Paris (France).

Today Lonely Planet guidebooks cover the globe. There is an ever-growing list of books, and there's information in a variety of forms and media. Some things haven't changed. The main aim is still to help make it possible for adventurous travelers to get out there – to explore and better understand the world.

At Lonely Planet we believe travelers can make a positive contribution to the countries they visit – if they respect their host communities and spend their money wisely. Since 1986 a percentage of the income from each book has been donated to aid projects and human-rights campaigns.

Updates Lonely Planet thoroughly updates each guidebook as often as possible. This usually means there are around two years between editions, although for more unusual or more stable destinations the gap can be longer. Check the imprint page (usually following the color map at the beginning of the book) for publication dates.

Between editions up-to-date information is available in two free newsletters – the paper *Planet Talk* and email *Comet* (to subscribe, contact any Lonely Planet office) – and on our Web site at www.lonelyplanet.com. The *Upgrades* section of the Web site covers a number of important and volatile destinations and is regularly updated by Lonely Planet authors. *Scoop* covers news and current affairs relevant to travelers. And, lastly, the *Thorn Tree* bulletin board and *Postcards* section of the site carry unverified, but fascinating, reports from travelers.

Correspondence The process of creating new editions begins with the letters, postcards and emails received from travelers. This correspondence often includes suggestions, criticisms and comments about the current editions. Interesting excerpts are immediately passed on via newsletters and the Web site, and everything goes to our authors to be verified when they're researching on the road. We're keen to get more feedback from organizations or individuals who represent communities visited by travelers.

> Lonely Planet gathers information for everyone who's curious about the planet – and especially for those who explore it firsthand. Through guidebooks, phrasebooks, activity guides, maps, literature, newsletters, image library, TV series and Web site we act as an information exchange for a worldwide community of travelers.

Research Authors aim to gather sufficient practical information to enable travelers to make informed choices and to make the mechanics of a journey run smoothly. They also research historical and cultural background to help enrich the travel experience and allow travelers to understand and respond appropriately to cultural and environmental issues.

Authors don't stay in every hotel because that would mean spending a couple of months in each medium-size city and, no, they don't eat at every restaurant because that would mean stretching belts beyond capacity. They do visit hotels and restaurants to check standards and prices, but feedback based on readers' direct experiences can be very helpful.

Many of our authors work undercover; others aren't so secretive. None of them accept freebies in exchange for positive write-ups. And none of our guidebooks contain any advertising.

Production Authors submit their manuscripts and maps to offices in Australia, the USA, UK or France. Editors and cartographers – all experienced travelers themselves – then begin the process of assembling the pieces. When the book finally hits the shops, some things are already out of date, we start getting feedback from readers and the process begins again...

WARNING & REQUEST

Things change – prices go up, schedules change, good places go bad and bad places go bankrupt – nothing stays the same. So, if you find things better or worse, recently opened or long since closed, please tell us and help make the next edition even more accurate and useful. We genuinely value all the feedback we receive. A well-traveled team reads and acknowledges every letter, postcard and email and ensures that every morsel of information finds its way to the appropriate authors, editors and cartographers for verification.

Everyone who writes to us will find their name listed in the next edition of the appropriate guidebook. They will also receive the latest issue of *Planet Talk*, our quarterly printed newsletter, or *Comet*, our monthly email newsletter. Subscriptions to both newsletters are free. The very best contributions will be rewarded with a free guidebook.

We may edit, reproduce and incorporate your comments in all Lonely Planet products, such as guidebooks, Web sites and digital products, so let us know if you don't want your comments reproduced or your name acknowledged.

Send all correspondence to the Lonely Planet office closest to you:

Australia: Locked Bag 1, Footscray, Victoria 3011
USA: 150 Linden St, Oakland, CA 94607
UK: 10a Spring Place, London NW5 3BH
France: 1 rue du Dahomey, 75011 Paris

Or email us at: talk2us@lonelyplanet.com.au

For news, views and updates, see our Web site: www.lonelyplanet.com

HOW TO USE A LONELY PLANET GUIDEBOOK

The best way to use a Lonely Planet guidebook is any way you choose. At Lonely Planet, we believe the most memorable travel experiences are often those that are unexpected, and the finest discoveries are those you make yourself. Guidebooks are not intended to be used as if they provided a detailed set of infallible instructions!

Contents All Lonely Planet guidebooks follow roughly the same format. The Facts about the Destination chapters or sections give background information ranging from history to weather. Facts for the Visitor gives practical information on issues like visas and health. Getting There & Away gives a brief starting point for re-searching travel to and from the destination. Getting Around gives an overview of the transport options when you arrive.

The peculiar demands of each destination determine how sub-sequent chapters are broken up, but some things remain constant. We always start with background, then proceed to sights, places to stay, places to eat, entertainment, getting there and away, and getting around information – in that order.

Heading Hierarchy Lonely Planet headings are used in a strict hierarchical structure that can be visualized as a set of Russian dolls. Each heading (and its following text) is encompassed by any preceding heading that is higher on the hierarchical ladder.

Entry Points We do not assume guidebooks will be read from beginning to end, but that people will dip into them. The tradi-tional entry points are the list of contents and the index. In addi-tion, however, some books have a complete list of maps and an index map illustrating map coverage.

There may also be a color map that shows highlights. These highlights are dealt with in greater detail in the Facts for the Visitor chapter, along with planning questions and suggested itin-eraries. Each chapter covering a geographical region usually begins with a locator map and another list of highlights. Once you find something of interest in a list of highlights, turn to the index.

Maps Maps play a crucial role in Lonely Planet guidebooks and include a huge amount of information. A legend is printed on the back page. We seek to have complete consistency between maps and text and to have every important place in the text captured on a map. Map key numbers usually start in the top left corner.

Although inclusion in a guidebook usually implies a recommen-dation, we cannot list every good place. Exclusion does not necessarily imply criticism. In fact there are a number of reasons why we might exclude a place – sometimes it is simply inappropriate to encourage an influx of travelers.

Introduction

No country ignites the Western imagination as Brazil does. For hundreds of years it has symbolized the great escape into a primordial, tropical paradise. From the mad passion of Carnaval to the vastness of the dark Amazon, Brazil is a country of mythical proportions.

Roughly the size of the US (excluding Alaska), Brazil is a huge country encompassing nearly half of South America, and bordering most of the continent's other nations – Ecuador and Chile are the exceptions. After 40 years of internal migration and population growth, Brazil is also an urban country; four out of every five Brazilians live in a city. São Paulo, with more than 17 million inhabitants, is the world's second most populous city.

Brazil's population is clustered along the Atlantic coast, and much of the country,

including the massive Amazon Basin, remains scarcely populated and hard to access.

For most, the Brazilian journey begins in Rio de Janeiro. For some it goes no farther. One of the world's great cities, Rio has developed a highly advanced culture of pleasure. It revolves around the famous beaches of Copacabana and Ipanema, and is fueled by the music and dance of samba, the beauty of Corcovado and Pão de Açúcar (Sugar Loaf Mountain), the athleticism of soccer, the delight of an ice-cold *cerveja* (beer), the camaraderie of *papo* (chitchat) and the cult of the body beautiful. This hedonism reaches its climax every February or March, during the big bang that is Carnaval – five days of revelry, unrivaled by any other party on the globe.

Rio de Janeiro state is blessed with some of the country's best beaches: from the world-renowned Búzios to the undeveloped Ilha Grande. Inland, the coastal mountains rise rapidly from lush, green, tropical forest, culminating in spectacular peaks. The mountains are punctuated by colonial cities and national parks where you can enjoy Brazil's best hiking and climbing.

The Amazon jungles are the world's largest tropical rainforest, fed by the world's largest river, and home to the richest and most diverse ecosystem on earth – a nature lover's ultimate fantasy! Though threatened by rapid deforestation, Brazilian Amazonia still offers years of exploration for the adventurous traveler.

Far to the south of Amazonia, in the center of the continent, is the Pantanal, the world's largest wetland and home to the greatest concentration of fauna in South America. When the flood waters recede in March, the Pantanal becomes an ornithologist's playground, with more than 200 bird species strutting their stuff: Macaws, parrots, toucans, rheas and jabiru storks are just a few of the more exotic species to be seen. Alligators, deer, capybaras, anteaters, anacondas, river otters and the rare jaguar also thrive in the Pantanal, although several of these species are threatened by poaching.

The Foz do Iguaçu, at Brazil's border with Argentina and Paraguay, may be the country's most dazzling spectacle. These mighty waterfalls are one of the natural wonders of the world, and are superior in size and grandeur to both Niagara and Victoria.

Wherever you go in Brazil, from the standing-room-only crowds of Copacabana to the quieter white-sand beaches along the banks of the Amazon, you'll see Brazilians at their beaches playing. The beach is the national passion – everything and everyone ends up there. Fortunately, with over 8000km of coastline, there is an incredible number of superb beaches, so you should have little problem finding your own tropical hideaway.

The mixing of races in Brazil – Indian, black and white – is most pronounced in the historic Northeast. Racial diversity and the tenacity of a traditional way of life have created a unique and wonderful civilization, with much of Brazil's most exciting music, dance and art, and a series of fascinating 16th and 17th century cities like Recife, Olinda, São Luís and, of course, Salvador.

Once the capital of Brazil and one of the richest cities of the New World, Salvador is today the center of Afro-Brazilian culture. Against a backdrop of 17th century colonial houses, gilded churches and lively beaches, Salvador da Bahia breathes Africa: the rhythms of *afoxé*; the dance-cum-martial-art of *capoeira*; the spirituality of Candomblé, the Afro-Brazilian religion; and the many colorful pageants and festivals, particularly from December to Carnaval.

Brazil may not be the paradise on Earth that many travelers once imagined, but it is a land of often unimaginable beauty. There are still stretches of unexplored rainforest, islands with pristine tropical beaches, and endless rivers. And there are the people themselves, who delight the visitor with their energy, fantasy and joy.

Facts about Brazil

HISTORY
Original Settlers
Archaeologists have dated the human presence in the Rio de Janeiro area and the Serra da Capivara in northeast Brazil to about 50,000 years ago, among the earliest dates in the whole American continent. It's generally believed that the pre-Hispanic inhabitants of the Americas arrived from Siberia in waves of migration between about 60,000 and 8000 BC, crossing land now submerged beneath the Bering Strait, then making their way gradually southward.

Archaeological Findings Brazil's size, climate and impenetrable jungles have all hampered archaeologists' efforts to unravel its prehistory. Brazilian Indians never developed a highly advanced, centralized civilization like the Inca or Maya. They left little for archaeologists to discover; chiefly pottery, trash mounds and some skeletons.

Rock paintings attest to the presence of hunter-gatherers near Monte Alegre, about 700km upstream from the mouth of the Amazon, about 12,000 years ago. Settled societies with thousands of members, cultivating maize and manioc and producing well-made pottery, probably emerged a few centuries BC on the Ilha de Marajó at the river's mouth and in other areas around the lower Amazon. Farther south, at Lagoa Santa in Minas Gerais, the ancient bones of a human being have been linked with a mammoth slaughtered for food as early as 10,000 BC.

The most aesthetically exciting objects excavated in Brazil, elaborate burial urns of the Marajoara culture of about 400–1350 AD, were found on the Ilha de Marajó.

Indigenous Societies in 1500 Estimates of the number of people living in what's now Brazil when the Portuguese arrived in 1500 range from about 2 million to 6 million. The population was probably composed of more than 1000 tribes, ranging from nomadic hunter-gatherers to more settled, agricultural societies. Many probably lived in long communal huts and every couple of years would pack up the village and move to new hunting grounds. Women did most of the 'domestic' work, while the men, who were magnificent archers and fishermen, hunted and went to war. Music, dance and games played a very important role in the culture. Little surplus was produced and they had very few possessions.

This lifestyle, which came to symbolize the ideal of the noble savage in European minds and inspired social thinkers such as Rousseau and Defoe, was punctuated by frequent tribal warfare and ritual cannibalism. In many tribes, captured enemies were ceremonially killed and eaten after battle.

The peoples along the coast at the time of the Portuguese arrival fall into three main groups: the Guarani, the Tupi and the Tapuia. The Guarani occupied the coast south of São Paulo and the Paraguai and Paraná basins inland. The Tupi (also called Tupinambá) occupied most of the rest of the coast. Categorized together because of their similarities of language and culture, these two groups are known as the Tupi-Guarani. A European adaptation of the Tupi-Guarani language spread throughout colonial Brazil and is still spoken by some people in Amazonia. Tapuia was the name given by the Tupi and Guarani to all the different peoples who inhabited shorter stretches of coast in among the Tupi and Guarani.

Early Colonization
The Cabral Expedition In 1500 Pedro Cabral sailed from Lisbon, ostensibly bound for Asia, with 13 ships and 1200 crew. Following Indies trailblazer Vasco da Gama's directions, he sailed his fleet on a south-westerly course in order to exploit the favorable westerly trade winds in the Southern Hemisphere. But after passing the Cape Verde Islands the fleet headed west.

Whether its slow ships were pushed west by the strong equatorial current, or South America was Cabral's secret destination all along, is still a matter of debate.

Cabral landed near present-day Porto Seguro on April 22, 1500. He and his crew were greeted by some of the many Indians living along the coast. Staying only a few days, the Portuguese built a cross and held the first Christian service in the land they dubbed Terra da Vera Cruz (Land of the True Cross). The Indians watched with apparent amazement and then, complying with the exhortations of their guests, knelt before the cross. But it wasn't Catholic ritual that grabbed their attention. It was the construction of the cross. The Indians, living in a Stone Age culture, had never seen iron tools.

Brazilwood Cabral sailed on, leaving behind two convicts to learn the Indians' ways and taking some *pau brasil* (brazilwood) logs, which produced a red dye. Subsequent Portuguese expeditions were disappointed by what they found in Brazil. They had little interest in colonization; instead they sought riches like those of India and Africa, where they established trading stations to obtain spices and ivory. But the Brazilian Stone Age culture produced nothing for the European market, and the land was heavily forested, barely passable and very wild.

However, the red dye from brazilwood provoked the interest of a few Portuguese merchants, and the king granted them the rights to the brazilwood trade. They began sending a few ships each year to harvest the trees. This trade depended entirely on Indian labor exchanged for metal axes and knives – objects that are still used as peace offerings by Brazilians contacting Indians unknown to them.

Brazilwood remained the region's only exportable commodity for the first half of the 16th century. During this time the colony changed its name from Terra da Vera Cruz to Brazil, an act that later, as reports of Brazilian godlessness reached superstition-ridden Portugal, was interpreted as the work of the devil. But the brazilwood trade, which had never been terribly profitable, was soon in jeopardy. The most accessible trees had been rapidly depleted. French competition for the wood intensified, causing fighting to break out, and the Indians stopped volunteering their labor.

Early Settlers In 1531 King João III sent the first settlers to Brazil. Martim Afonso de Sousa was placed in command of five ships with a combined crew of 400. After exploring the coastline he chose São Vicente, near the modern port of Santos in São Paulo state, as the first settlement. Soon after, in an attempt to ward off the ambitions of other European countries, the king divided the Brazilian coast into 15 captaincies, each with 50 leagues (about 250km) of coastline and parallel borders extending westward. These territories were awarded to their *donatários* (donatary captains), mostly *fidalgos* (minor gentry) who then passed the land on to their descendants. The king's plan was designed to secure the long coastline at minimal cost, through settlement. (Ultimately the captaincies were all bought back by the crown by the mid-18th century.)

The settlers were hampered by the climate, hostility from the Indians and competition from the Dutch and French. One donatário, Duarte Coelho, wrote to the king, 'We are obliged to conquer by inches the land that your Majesty has granted us by leagues.' Four captaincies were never settled and four were destroyed by Indians. Only Pernambuco and São Vicente were profitable.

In 1549 the king sent Tomé de Sousa to be the first governor of Brazil, to centralize authority and to save the few remaining captaincies. The king chose for Sousa's base what is now the state of Bahia: the Baía de Todos os Santos (Bay of All Saints) was one of Brazil's best bays, and was surrounded by good land, even though the Indians had recently driven the Portuguese from the area.

Ten ships and 1000 settlers arrived safely. On board were Portuguese officials, soldiers, exiled prisoners, New Christians (converted Jews) and the first six Jesuit priests. Caramuru, a Portuguese living among the

Indians and married to a chief's daughter, selected a spot on high ground for Salvador da Bahia, the new capital of Portuguese Brazil. Salvador remained Brazil's capital until 1763, when Rio de Janeiro took over.

Sugar & Slaves

The colonists soon discovered that the land and climate were ideal for growing sugarcane. Sugar was coveted by a hungry European market, which used it initially for medicinal purposes and as a condiment for almost all foods and even wine. To produce the sugarcane, all the colonists needed were workers. The Portuguese attempted to enslave the Indians to work for them.

Indian Slavery Up and down the coast, the Indians' response to the Portuguese was similar. First, they welcomed the strangers and offered them food, labor and women in exchange for iron tools and liquor. They then became wary of the whites, who abused their customs and beliefs and took the best land. Finally, when voluntary labor became slavery and the use of land became wholesale displacement, the Indians fought back and won many battles.

The capture and sale of Indian slaves became Brazil's second largest enterprise. Expeditions from São Paulo hunted the Indians into the Brazilian interior, exploring and claiming vast lands for the Portuguese and making fortunes supplying the sugar estates with slaves. The members of these expeditions were called *bandeirantes* (flag-bearers) after the *bandeiras* (flags) carried by each group. Their bravery was exceeded only by their brutality.

The Jesuit priests went to great lengths to save the Indians. In their sermons they inveighed against the evils of Indian slavery (though they said little about black slaves). They pleaded with the king of Portugal and set up *aldeias* (missions) to settle, protect and Christianize the Indians. One Brazilian statesman wrote, 'Without the Jesuits, our colonial history would be little more than a chain of nameless atrocities.'

But the monarchy was ambivalent about Indian slavery and too weak to do anything

about it. Most of the Indians not killed by bandeirantes' guns or by the work on the sugar plantations died from introduced European diseases and the alien life in the missions.

African Slavery By the 1550s wealthier sugar barons began to buy African slaves instead of Indians. The Africans were better workers and less susceptible to European diseases. Soon tremendous profits were being made by merchants in the African slave trade. An infamous triangular commerce carried slaves and elephant tusks from Africa, sugar, sugarcane liquor and tobacco from Brazil, and guns and luxury goods from Europe.

By the end of the 16th century, about 30,000 Portuguese settlers and 20,000 black slaves lived in isolated coastal towns surrounded by often hostile Indians. There were about 200 prosperous sugar mills, mostly in Pernambuco and Bahia.

While the legendary gold of El Dorado remained elusive, sugar was extremely lucrative. The sugar trade depended on rich coastal soil and access to European markets, so the Portuguese settled almost exclusively at the mouths of rivers on navigable bays. They avoided moving inland where the forests were dense, the rivers were wild and the Indians were hostile. Wherever sugarcane grew – mainly Bahia, Pernambuco and Rio de Janeiro – so did the fledgling colony. The sugar trade succeeded where the captaincy system had failed, making the Portuguese colonization of Brazil possible. And later, as Portugal's Asian empire declined, tax revenue from the sugar trade kept the Portuguese ship of state afloat.

The sugar plantations were self-sufficient enclaves. They were geared to large-scale production, which required vast tracts of land and specialized processing equipment. This meant a plantation owner typically needed 100 to 150 slaves, both skilled and unskilled, and a fair amount of capital.

Throughout the 17th century, blacks replaced Indians on the plantations. From 1550 to the final abolition of the slavery in

Brazil in 1888, about 3.5 million African slaves were shipped to Brazil – 38% of the total that came to the New World. Those who didn't die on the slave ships generally had short and brutalized lives. Labor on the plantations was hard and tedious, with slaves working 15 to 17 hours a day during the busy season. But the conditions rather than the amount of work were largely responsible for the high mortality rate. Disease was rampant, and many slaves succumbed to dysentery, typhus, yellow fever, malaria, syphilis, tuberculosis or scurvy.

The plantation owners dominated colonial Brazil. Their control over free whites who worked as sharecroppers was almost total, and over slaves it was absolute. Some slave masters were kind, but most were cruel and often sadistic. Families were routinely broken up and tribal groups were intermixed to prevent collective rebellion. The culturally sophisticated slaves from Islamic Africa were particularly feared by the white masters.

Resistance to slavery took many forms. The misery of some slaves manifested itself in *banzo,* the longing for Africa, which culminated in what effectively became slow suicide. Documents of the period refer to the desperation of the slaves who starved themselves to death, killed their babies or fled. Sabotage and theft were frequent, as were work slowdowns, stoppages and revolts.

Those who survived life on the plantations sought solace in their African religion and culture through dance and song. The slaves were given perfunctory indoctrination into Catholicism and, except for among the followers of Islam, a syncretic religion rapidly emerged. Spiritual elements from many African tribes, such as the Yoruba, Bantu and Fon, were preserved and made palatable to the slave masters with a facade of Catholic saints and ritual objects. These are the roots of modern Macumba and Candomblé, both of which were prohibited by law until not long ago (see the Religion section later in this chapter).

Many slaves managed to escape from their masters. *Quilombos* (communities of runaway slaves) were common during the entire colonial period, scattered throughout the countryside. The quilombos ranged from *mocambos* (small groups) hidden in the forests to the most famous, the republic of Palmares, which survived through much of the 17th century.

Palmares covered a broad tract of lush tropical forest straddling the border of Alagoas and Pernambuco states. At its height, 20,000 people lived under its protection. Most were black, but there were also Indians, mulattos (people of mixed black and European parentage), *mestiços* (of mixed European and Indian parentage) and bandits. They lived off the land, growing mostly corn. Agriculture was collective, and productivity was higher than on the slave plantations.

Palmares was really a collection of semi-independent quilombos united under one king to fight off the Portuguese. Led by Zumbí, who had been a king in Africa, the citizens of Palmares became pioneers of guerrilla warfare and defeated many Portuguese attacks. Fearing Palmares' example, the government desperately tried to crush it. Between 1670 and 1695 the rebel region was attacked (on average) every 15 months, until it finally fell to a force of bandeirantes from São Paulo.

As abolitionist sentiment grew in the 19th century, the quilombos received more support and ever-greater numbers of slaves fled the plantations. Only abolition itself, which came about in 1888, stopped the growth of quilombos. More than 700 black villages that began life as quilombos remain in Brazil today. Some were so isolated that they remained completely out of contact with white Brazilians until the last couple of decades.

Ethnic Melting Pot Portugal was not an overpopulated country and not a place where the peasants had much need to leave their land. Consequently, immigrants to Brazil typically came by choice in the hope of garnering untold riches. These settlers were notoriously indisposed to work; even poor whites had a slave or two.

The sugar barons lived on their plantations part-time and escaped to their second houses in the cities, where they often kept *mulata* mistresses. The white women led cloistered lives inside the walls of the *casa grande* (big house). Secluded from all but their family and servants, they married young – usually at 14 or 15 years of age – and often died early.

Sexual relations between masters and slaves were so common that a large mulatto population soon emerged. Away from the plantations there was a shortage of white women, so many poorer settlers lived with black and Indian women. Prostitution was widespread; it was the only way many of the free mixed-race women could survive. Brazil was famous for its sexual permissiveness, and by the beginning of the 18th century it became known as the land of syphilis – a disease that wrought devastation, even in the monasteries.

The church was tolerant of any coupling that helped populate the colony, and even many Catholic priests got away with having mistresses and illegitimate children.

In poorer regions such as Pará, Maranhão, Ceará and São Paulo, where settlers could not afford black slaves, Indian slaves were more common. Indian-white interracial sex was more prevalent than sex between blacks and whites, as is evident in the racial mix in those states today. As in the rest of the colony, sexual relations were rather licentious. As the Bishop of Pará put it, 'the wretched state of manners in this country…makes me think that I am living in the suburbs of Gomorrah, very close indeed, and in the vicinity of Sodom.'

Colonial Rivals

Spain and Portugal had divided the New World exclusively between themselves at the Treaty of Tordesillas in 1494: Portugal was to get everything east of a north-south line 370 leagues west of the Azores Islands – running roughly from the mouth of the Amazon to the modern state of Santa Catarina – while Spain was to rule west of that line. Over the centuries that followed, not only did the Portuguese ignore this imaginary line whenever possible, but rival European powers – principally France and Holland – wanted slices of the pie too.

The French Threat France successfully operated trading stations in Brazil in the first half of the 16th century and had friendly relations with many Indians, who saw them as a lesser evil than the Portuguese. In 1555 three boatloads of French settlers, led by Admiral Nicolas Durand de Villegagnon, landed on a small island in Baía de Guanabara. They intended to add to their empire a large part of southern Brazil, which was to be called Antarctic France.

The Portuguese expelled the French a few years later, after some bloody battles, and founded the city of Rio de Janeiro on the bay. In 1612 the French set up a colony called Equinoctial France in the Northeast but were driven out in 1615 by the Portuguese, who founded São Luís on the site. As a safeguard against further foreign incursions, the Portuguese went on to found Belém, later the stepping stone for their exploration of Amazonia.

The Dutch Threat Holland posed a more serious challenge to Portuguese Brazil. Dutch merchants had profited from the Brazilian sugar trade for many years, but during the period of Portuguese union with Holland's traditional enemy Spain (1580–1640), peaceful trade collapsed. The Dutch set up the Dutch West Indies Company to occupy Brazil's sugar-producing regions and take control of the slave trade. A large Dutch expedition took Bahia in 1624, but a year later, after bloody and confused fighting, the Portuguese retook the city.

Next, in 1630 the Dutch conquered Pernambuco, and from there went on to take control of a major part of the Northeast from the mouth of the Rio San Francisco to Maranhão. They called their territory New Holland and ruled it from Recife. With their superior sea power, the Dutch sailed to Africa and captured part of Portuguese-held Angola to supply slaves for their new colony. In 1637 a Dutch prince, Maurice of Nassau, took over as the governor of New

Holland. An enlightened administrator, he was successful in increasing the number of sugar plantations, creating large cattle farms and re-establishing the discipline of his troops and civil administrators. Hospitals and orphanages were founded, and freedom of worship was guaranteed in an attempt to win over the local population.

But Nassau was undermined by a lack of support from Holland, and when he returned home in 1644, the rot set in. The Pernambucan merchants funded black and Indian soldiers, who fought the Dutch on land. The Portuguese governor of Rio de Janeiro and Angola, Salvador de Sá, sailed from Rio and expelled the Dutch from Angola. Finally, when provisions failed to arrive from home, the Dutch troops mutinied and returned to Europe. A peace treaty was signed in 1654.

Bandeirantes

Throughout the 17th and 18th centuries, bandeirantes from São Paulo continued to march off into the interior to capture Indians. Many bandeirantes were born of Indian mothers and Portuguese fathers. Many others were actually enslaved Indians for whom warfare was less humiliating than slave labor. The bandeirantes generally spoke both Tupi-Guarani and Portuguese, knew the survival skills of the Indians and the use of European weaponry, and wore heavily padded cotton jackets that deflected arrows. Traveling light in bands that ranged from a dozen to a couple of hundred, they would go off for months or years at a time, living off the land and plundering Indian villages. By the mid-17th century they had traversed the interior as far as the Andes, and from there to the mouth of the Amazon. These superhuman exploits secured huge areas west of the Tordesillas line for Portuguese Brazil.

The Jesuits sought desperately to protect their flock of Indians in missions in the remote interior, near the present-day borders with Paraguay and Argentina. They even armed the Indians for defense against the bandeirantes, and desperate battles took place; the bandeirantes were slowed but they were never stopped. Finally, with the collusion of the Portuguese and Spanish crowns, the missions fell and the Jesuits were expelled from Brazil in 1759.

Gold

El Dorado and other South American legends of vast deposits of gold and precious stones clouded European minds and spurred on the roving bandeirantes. Eventually, in the 1690s, bandeirantes discovered a magical luster in the rivers of the Serra do Espinhaço, Brazil's oldest geological formation, in an inaccessible and unsettled region inland from Rio de Janeiro.

People dropped everything to go to what is now south-central Minas Gerais. Unaware of how hazardous the journey was, many died on the way. In the orgy to pan, no one bothered to plant, and in the early years terrible famines swept through the gold towns. The price of basic provisions was always outrageous, and the majority suffered. But the gold was there – more than seemed possible.

When gold was first discovered, there were no white settlers in the territory of Minas Gerais. By 1710 the population was 30,000, and by the end of the 18th century it was half a million. Brazilian gold caused major demographic shifts in three continents. Paulistas (inhabitants of São Paulo state) left their homes, followed by other Brazilians who had failed to strike it rich in commercial agriculture. Some 600,000 Portuguese arrived in Brazil between 1700 and 1760, many headed for the goldfields. Countless slaves were stolen away from Africa to dig and die in Minas.

Old-time Brazilians, particularly the combative Paulistas, resented the flood of new Portuguese immigrants who were cashing in on their gold discoveries. The recent arrivals, numerically superior, loathed the favorable treatment they saw the Paulistas receiving. Gold stakes were more often settled by guns than by judges, and armed confrontations broke out in 1708. The colonial government was faced with a virtual civil war, which lasted over a year before government intervention slowed the hostilities, and saw miners carrying pans in one hand and guns in the other.

Most of the actual mining was done by black slaves. An estimated one-third of the two million slaves who reached Brazil in the 18th century went to the goldfields, where their lives were worse than in the sugar fields. Most slave owners put their workers on an incentive system, allowing the slaves to keep a small percentage of the gold they found. A few who found great quantities of gold were able to buy their own freedom, but for the majority disease and death came quickly.

Wild boomtowns arose in the mountain valleys: Sabará, Mariana, São João del Rei and the greatest, Vila Rica de Ouro Prêto (Rich Town of Black Gold). Wealthy merchants built opulent mansions and employed a class of educated artisans to create architecturally stunning baroque churches. But crime, gambling, drinking and prostitution ruled the streets. The scarcity of white women yielded many mulatto offspring.

The gold did little to develop Brazil's economy, create a middle class, or better the common workers. Most of the wealth went to Portuguese merchants and the king, until it was ultimately traded for English goods.

By 1750 the mining regions were in decline, the migration to the interior was ending and coastal Brazil was returning to center stage.

Settlement Patterns

Apart from some public works and many beautiful churches, the main legacy of Brazil's gold rush was a shift in population from the Northeast to the Southeast. Some stayed in Minas Gerais and raised cattle on its rich lands, but settlement there, as in the Mato Grosso and Goiás farther west, was chiefly in isolated pockets where precious metals had been found. Many people, however, ended up settling in Rio de Janeiro, where the population and economy grew rapidly as gold and supplies passed through the city's ports.

At the beginning of the 19th century there were about three million people in Brazil, not including the Indians, and roughly one million of them were African slaves. In the poorer areas there were fewer black slaves, more poor whites and more Indians.

The inland area with the most settlers was the *sertão*, the arid northeastern interior, where the Rio São Francisco had formed the axis of cattle-based settlement since the 17th century. The sertão was unable to sustain much agriculture, but cattle could graze and survive. It was a poor business, constantly threatened by drought, but the hardy *sertanejos* (sertão inhabitants) – often of mixed Portuguese and Indian extraction – were able to eke out a living.

Most settlers in the South, who were chiefly farmers from the Portuguese Azores, could not afford slaves. The Indians had been clustered in the Jesuit missions far to the west to save them from the bandeirantes. The South was, and remains, Brazil's most European region.

Dom João VI

In 1807 Napoleon's army marched on Lisbon. The Portuguese prince regent (later known as Dom João VI) immediately decided to transfer his court to Brazil. Forty ships carrying his entire entourage and bureaucracy – 15,000 people in all – set sail under the protection of British warships. When the prince regent arrived in Rio his Brazilian subjects celebrated wildly, dancing in the streets. He immediately took over rule of Brazil from his viceroy.

As foreigners have been doing ever since, Dom João fell in love with Brazil. An avid admirer of nature, he founded Rio's botanical gardens and introduced the habit of sea bathing to the water-wary inhabitants of Rio. Expected to return to Portugal after Napoleon's Waterloo in 1815, he stayed in Brazil. The following year his mother, mad Queen Dona Maria I, died, and Dom João VI became king. He declared Rio the capital of the United Kingdom of Portugal and Brazil, thus making Brazil the only New World colony ever to have a European monarch ruling on its soil.

Independence, Empire & Republic

In 1821 Dom João VI finally bowed to political pressures and returned to Portugal, leaving his son Pedro in Brazil as prince regent.

According to legend, in 1822 Pedro pulled out his sword and yelled 'Independência ou morte!' ('Independence or death!'), making himself Emperor Dom Pedro I. Portugal was too weak to fight its favorite son, not to mention the British, who had the most to gain from Brazilian independence and would have come to the aid of the Brazilians. The Brazilian Empire was born, attaining independence without bloodshed, and Dom Pedro I became the first emperor. But from all accounts he was a bumbling incompetent who scandalized even the permissive Brazilians by siring a string of illegitimate children. He was forced to abdicate after nine years, paving the way for his five-year-old son to become emperor.

Until Dom Pedro II reached adolescence, Brazil suffered a period of civil war under the rule of a weak triple regency. In 1840 the nation rallied behind the emperor, and his 50-year reign is regarded as the most prosperous period in Brazilian history. He nurtured an increasingly powerful parliamentary system; went to war with Paraguay; interfered in Argentine, Paraguayan and Uruguayan affairs; abolished slavery and encouraged mass immigration. Ultimately, he forged a nation that would do away with the monarchy forever.

In 1889 a military coup, supported by the coffee aristocracy and a popular wave of republican sentiment, toppled the antiquated Brazilian Empire. The emperor went into exile in Paris, where he died a couple of years later.

A military clique ruled Brazil for the next four years until elections were held, but because of ignorance, threats, and land and literacy requirements, only about 2% of the adult population voted. Little changed, except that the power of the military and the now influential coffee growers increased, while it diminished for the sugar barons.

Coffee

Popular legend has it that the coffee bean was introduced to Brazil in the early 18th century by Francisco de Mello Palheta, an officer from Maranhão who went to Cayenne in French Guiana to settle a border dispute. He reputedly won the heart of the governor's wife, who put some coffee beans into his cup as a parting gift. On his return to Brazil, he planted them.

The international sugar market began a rapid decline in the 1820s. The sugar planters had depleted much of their best soil and were unable to compete with the newly mechanized sugar mills in the West Indies. As rapidly as sugar exports fell, coffee production rose. Coffee flourished on the low mountain slopes of northeastern São Paulo state. As these lands were snatched up, the coffee plantations moved westward into Minas Gerais and western São Paulo.

Coffee production was labor-intensive. Because of the large investment needed to employ so many workers, production excluded small farmers and favored large enterprises using slave labor. The master-slave sugar plantation system, complete with the big house and slave quarters, was reproduced on the coffee *fazendas* (ranches or farms) of São Paulo and Minas Gerais.

By 1889 coffee accounted for two-thirds of Brazil's exports, and profits soared with mechanization and the building of Brazil's first railways. The modernization of production eased the coffee plantations' transition to a free labor force when slavery ended in 1888. During the next decade 800,000 European immigrants, mostly Italians, came to work on the coffee fazendas.

Rio, with a million people by 1890, and São Paulo were the main beneficiaries of the coffee boom. Brazil was still a rural society – only 10% of the population lived in cities – but the cities were growing rapidly. Millions more immigrants – Japanese, German, Spanish and Portuguese – flooded into the cities between 1890 and 1916.

Slave Revolts & Abolition

Slavery in Brazil was not abolished until 1888, 25 years after it ended in the US and

80 years after Britain freed its slaves. Resistance by slaves grew throughout the 19th century, and the specter of Haiti – the site of the first successful slave revolt – haunted the Brazilian planters who, as a result, became more brutal toward their slaves.

Several urban insurrections took place in Bahia. Most were led by Muslim blacks – both those who were free and those in slavery. The 1807 uprising was carefully planned so that slaves from the sugar plantations would be able to meet up with the city slaves at the entrance to the city of Salvador and together attack the whites, seize ships and flee to Africa. However, the plot was betrayed and the leaders killed.

The following year, a similar plan was carried out, but the blacks were defeated in battle. In Minas Gerais, 15,000 slaves congregated in Ouro Prêto and 6000 in São João do Morro, demanding freedom and a constitution. The last big slave revolt in Bahia was in 1835 and was almost successful.

Other Insurrections

With its settlements separated by enormous distances, few communication links, and an economy oriented toward European markets, the Brazilian nation was disunited and lacked a sense of identity. Throughout the 19th century it was plagued by revolts, chiefly by local elites demanding greater autonomy from the central government, or even fighting to secede. Rio Grande do Sul was torn by a civil war between 1835 and 1845 called the Guerra dos Farrapos. There were insurrections in São Paulo and Minas Gerais, and others swept through the North and Northeast during the 1830s and 1840s.

Cabanagem War The bloodiest and most radical revolt was the Cabanagem War of 1835–40, a popular rebellion in the northern state of Pará. The rebels laid siege to the state capital, Belém, appropriating and distributing supplies. They held the city for a year before being defeated by a large government force. The peasants fled to the jungle with the army in pursuit, and eventually 30,000 of the state's 150,000 people were killed.

The most serious insurrections, like the Cabanagem, spread to the oppressed peasants and urban poor. The government always struck back and the revolts failed, in part because the upper and middle classes who led them feared the mobilized poor as much as they feared the government.

Canudos The 19th century was also an era of messianic popular movements among Brazil's poor. Most of these happened in the economically depressed backlands of the Northeast. The most famous was that of Canudos. Its leader, Antônio Conselheiro, had wandered for years through the backlands preaching and prophesying the appearance of the Antichrist and the end of the world. He railed against the new republican government, and in 1893 eventually gathered his followers (who called him the Counsellor) in Canudos, a settlement in the interior of Bahia.

The government sensed plots in Canudos to return Brazil to the Portuguese monarchy. Miraculously, the rebels first defeated a force of state police, and then two subsequent attacks by the federal army. Hysterical demonstrations in the cities demanded that the republic be saved from the rebels. A federal force of 4000 well-supplied soldiers took Canudos after ferocious, hand-to-hand, house-to-house fighting. The military suffered heavy casualties and was disgraced and the federal government embarrassed, but Canudos was wiped out. The soldiers killed every man, woman and child, and then burned the town to the ground to erase it from the nation's memory.

The epic struggle has been memorialized in a masterpiece of Brazilian literature, *Os Sertões* (Rebellion in the Backlands) by Euclides da Cunha. More recently, Mario Vargas Llosa wrote of Canudos in *The War of the End of the World*.

Rubber

In the last decades of the 19th century and the first of the 20th, the Amazon region was the scene of Brazil's next economic boom. The cause was *Hevea brasiliensis* (the rubber tree), a native of the American tropics.

Things started to inflate in 1842 with the invention of vulcanization, which turned rubber into an important industrial material. Demand really increased in 1890 with the invention of the pneumatic tire and the expansion of the fledgling automobile industry in the US. The price of rubber skyrocketed, bringing huge wealth and rapid progress to the main Amazonian cities of Belém, Manaus and Iquitos (Peru), as well as a large population increase in the region. Rubber production reached its peak in 1912, when exports of 42,000 tonnes of latex brought in nearly 40% of Brazil's export revenue.

Then the puncture happened. Unfortunately for Brazil, in 1876 rubber tree seeds had been smuggled out of Amazonia to Kew Gardens in England (see the boxed text 'Henry Wickham – Executioner of Amazonas'). Seedlings quickly found their way to the British colonies in Southeast Asia, where large rubber plantations were established. These plantations started to yield in 1910 and proved to be extremely efficient. The price of latex plummeted on the world market. The Brazilian rubber boom became a blowout.

In the world economy, Brazil remained an exporter of agricultural commodities and importer of manufactured goods. Some seeds of modernization had been planted, but there was no leap forward.

Henry Wickham – Executioner of Amazonas

The man who punctured the Brazilian rubber boom was Henry Alexander Wickham, a classic English Victorian character.

The idea of establishing rubber plantations in the British colonies in Ceylon and Malaya was one that had not escaped the attention of Britain's botanists, but they believed that the seeds or seedlings of *Hevea brasiliensis* would never survive the long journey from Brazil.

In 1876 Wickham, who had been drifting through South America for some time, made a deal with Sir Joseph Hooker at Kew Gardens, who assured him he'd get £10 for every 1000 rubber seeds he could provide.

As luck would have it, on March 1 that year, the 1000-tonne SS *Amazonas* had its entire cargo stolen from the docks in Manaus. Wickham chartered the empty ship and instructed the captain to sail at once and meet him in Santarém. Wickham himself went upriver by canoe to a spot already chosen for the large numbers of rubber trees that grew there.

For the next week he and his Indian helpers collected seeds by listening for the sharp crack of the exploding seed capsules, which scatter their contents up to 50m from the tree. He then packed the precious cargo between dried banana leaves and stored them in cane baskets. When he boarded the *Amazonas* in Santarém, he had 70,000 rubber tree seeds with him.

As they reached Belém, near the mouth of the Amazon, the captain held the ship in the harbor under a full head of steam while Wickham visited the customs officials, declaring, 'All we have here are exceedingly delicate botanical specimens specially designated for delivery to Her Majesty's own Royal Gardens of Kew.'

Wickham arrived at Kew Gardens at 3 am one morning to waken a surprised Sir Joseph Hooker, who sent a goods train to Liverpool to meet the *Amazonas* and ordered workers to clear the hothouse of its other tropical plants in anticipation of the shipment.

The speed of the whole operation succeeded in bringing live rubber seeds to England, and, in August of the same year, the first seedlings were shipped to Ceylon – thus ensuring the collapse of the Brazilian rubber industry.

Wickham was nicknamed the 'Executioner of Amazonas' by the Brazilian rubber barons. He went off to spend his £700 trying to grow tobacco and coffee in northern Queensland, Australia. In 1920 he was knighted by King George V for services to the rubber industry.

The Vargas Era

Coffee was king until the bottom dropped out of the coffee market during the global economic crisis of 1929, badly damaging the Brazilian economy. The São Paulo coffee growers who controlled the government were severely weakened. An opposition alliance formed around the elites of Minas Gerais and Rio Grande do Sul and nationalist military officers. When their presidential candidate, Getúlio Vargas, lost the 1930 election, the military took power by force and then handed the reins to Vargas.

Vargas proved to be a gifted maneuverer who would dominate the political scene for 20 years, skillfully playing off one sector of the ruling elite against another while being careful not to alienate the military. He gained popular support for instituting a smattering of social reform combined with large slabs of demagoguery and nationalism.

In 1937, on the eve of a new election, Vargas sent in the military to shut down congress, as he took complete control of the country. His regime was inspired by the fascist governments of Mussolini in Italy and Salazar in Portugal: He banned political parties, imprisoned political opponents and censored the press. In WWII, Vargas sided with the Allies, but afterward, the contradiction between fighting for democracy in Europe while operating a quasi-fascist state at home became too glaring, and Vargas was forced by the military to step down.

Vargas remained popular, and in 1951 he was legitimately elected president. The world war had afforded Brazil the economic opportunities to begin its fitful march toward industrialization and urbanization. A large network of state corporations, including petroleum and steel companies, was established, the first minimum wage was set and peasants flocked to the cities in search of a better life.

But the Vargas administration was plagued by corruption. The press, especially a young journalist named Carlos Lacerda, attacked him viciously, and the military withdrew its support. In 1954 the chief of Vargas' presidential guard organized an attempt to murder Lacerda. The gunman only lightly wounded Lacerda but killed an air force major who was with him. In the resulting scandal, the military demanded Vargas' resignation. He responded melodramatically by shooting himself in the heart. Popular reaction proved extremely sympathetic to the dead president. Antigovernment newspapers were burned, and the US embassy was attacked. Lacerda was forced into exile, but later returned to become a dynamic governor of Rio.

Juscelino Kubitschek

Juscelino Kubitschek, popularly known as JK, a former state governor of Minas Gerais, was elected president in 1956. His motto was '50 years' progress in five.' His critics responded with '40 years' inflation in four.' The critics were closer to the mark, although industrial production did increase by 80% during Kubitschek's five years.

The dynamic Kubitschek was the first of Brazil's big spenders. Deficit spending and large loans funded roads and hydroelectric projects. Foreign capital was encouraged to invest, and Brazil's automotive industry was started. Kubitschek built Brasília, a new capital that was intended to be the catalyst for the development of Brazil's vast interior.

In the 1961 elections, former São Paulo governor Janio Quadros won the presidency on a wave of public euphoria. He gained 48% of the vote, the highest percentage ever. Quadros had huge plans for political reform, but a moralistic streak had him trying to prohibit the wearing of swimsuits at beauty contests, bikinis on the beaches and the use of amyl nitrate at Carnaval – an uphill battle indeed. After six months in office, he decorated Che Guevara in a public ceremony in Brasília, a move that upset the right-wing military, who started to plot. A few days later Quadros resigned, claiming that 'occult forces' were at work.

Military Dictatorship

João 'Jango' Goulart, Quadros' vice president and formerly Vargas' labor minister, took over the presidency. Opposition to Goulart's leftist policies led to his overthrow by the military in 1964. Within hours of the coup, US President Lyndon Johnson cabled the new government his warmest wishes, and suspicions ran deep that the US had masterminded the coup.

Much of the middle class welcomed the Revolution of 1964, as it was first called.

Lampião

Every country has infamous outlaws somewhere in its history: The US has its bandits, the UK its highwaymen, Australia its bushrangers, and Brazil has its *cangaceiros*. The most famous cangaceiro was Lampião, who terrorized the sertão for more than 20 years.

Lampião was a cowboy, until his parents were killed by a cruel landowner. He and his brothers swore revenge and headed for the sertão to join the roaming bands of outlaws.

Within two years, around 1920, Lampião became head of his own gang. He gained his nickname, 'the Lamp,' because of the bright flashes given off by his rifle when he fought the police. Unlike other cangaço leaders, who were generous to the suffering people of the sertão, Lampião was cruel.

With his band, which numbered between 15 and 50, he roamed the backlands of Pernambuco, Paraíba, Alagoas and Ceará. His fame grew as stories and songs telling of his deeds spread throughout the Northeast.

In 1929 Lampião met Maria Bonita, who became his lover and the first woman to join the cangaço. For another nine years Lampião remained a thorn in the side of the state and federal governments. Protected by the frightened populace and scared landowners, the cangaceiros became careless. One night in July 1938, they were surrounded by a group of military police from Sergipe. Lampião and Maria Bonita, along with nine other gang members, were killed. Their heads were cut off and for almost 30 years remained on display in the Salvador Medical Institute. They were finally buried in 1969.

The last surviving member of Lampião's band, Corisco, who was also the last cangaceiro of all, was killed in 1940.

Brazil's military regime was not as brutal as those of Chile or Argentina; repression tended to come and go in cycles. But at its worst, around 1968 and 1969, the use of torture and the murder of political opponents were widespread. For almost 20 years political parties were outlawed and freedom of speech was curtailed.

Borrowing heavily from international banks, the generals benefited from the Brazilian economic miracle; year after year in the late 1960s and early 1970s the economy of the country grew by more than 10%. The transformation into an urban and semi-industrialized country continued to accelerate.

In the absence of any effective rural land reform, millions came to the cities, where *favelas* (shantytowns) filled the open spaces. The middle class, the bureaucracy and the military all grew.

More mega-projects were undertaken to exploit Brazil's natural resources and to divert attention from much needed social reforms. The greatest of these was the opening up of the Amazon region, which has brought great wealth to a few but little to most Brazilians.

The military regime's honeymoon didn't last. Opposition first burgeoned in 1968 as students, and then many in the Catholic Church (which had been generally supportive of the coup), began to protest against the government. Inspired by liberation theology, the Church had begun to examine Brazilian misery. Church leaders were appalled by the military's flagrant abuse of human rights, and established communities among the poor to fight for social justice.

In 1980 a militant working-class movement centered around the São Paulo automotive industry exploded onto the scene with a series of strikes under the charismatic leadership of Luíz Inácio ('Lula') da Silva, the workers' champion.

With the economic miracle petering out and popular opposition picking up steam, the military announced the so-called *abertura* (opening): a slow and cautious process of returning to civilian rule.

Civilian Rule Again

Sarney & Collor A presidential election was held in 1985 under an electoral college system designed to ensure the victory of the military's candidate. Surprisingly, the opposition candidate, Tancredo Neves, was elected. Millions of Brazilians took to the streets in an outburst of joy at the end of military rule. Tragically, Neves died of heart failure before he could assume the presidency. His vice-presidential candidate José Sarney, a relative unknown who had supported the military until 1984, took office.

During Sarney's term the economy was hampered by runaway inflation, and by 1990 Brazil had run up a US$115 billion foreign debt. In 1988 the congress did manage to hammer out a new, more liberal constitution that theoretically guaranteed human rights.

The first properly democratic presidential election since the military takeover was held in 1989. The charismatic Fernando Collor de Mello, ex-Brazilian karate champion and former governor of the small state of Alagoas, narrowly gained victory over Lula da Silva, running for the Workers' Party (PT). Lula's campaign was killed off by the powerful Globo TV network which, a few days before the election, screened his ex-lover revealing that he had offered her money for an abortion 16 years before.

Collor took office promising to reduce inflation and fight corruption, but by the end of 1992 he had been removed from office and indicted for corruption – accused of being the leader of a gang that used extortion and bribery to suck more than US$1 billion from the economy.

'Collorgate' at least proved to the Brazilian people that the constitution of their fragile democracy was capable of removing a corrupt president without military interference. Many were disappointed that Collor escaped going to prison: He was found not guilty of 'passive corruption' by the Supreme Court in 1994.

Fernando Henrique Cardoso Vice President Itamar Franco became president in 1992 after Collor's resignation. Considered provincial and unprepared for office, Franco surprised his critics with an honest and competent administration. His greatest achievement was to stabilize the economy with the introduction of a new currency, the *real*. The Plano Real (Real Plan) produced an immediate economic boom when introduced in 1994 (for more on the effects of the Plano Real, see the Economy section later in this chapter).

The early favorite in the 1994 presidential election was Lula, back for a second attempt. His downfall was the Plano Real, which he had criticized early. His opponent, the architect of the plan, Franco's finance minister Fernando Henrique Cardoso, rode its success all the way to a landslide victory.

A former left-wing sociology professor from São Paulo, FHC (as he's known in the press – the people call him Fernando Henrique) was now a centrist social democrat, aiming simultaneously to encourage economic growth and tackle Brazil's social problems.

Through the mid-1990s, Cardoso presided over a Brazil with a growing economy, a stable currency, low inflation and record foreign investment. He was able to persuade the congress to change the constitution so that he could stand for a second term of office. He defeated Lula again in 1998 – just before the real had to be devalued, ushering in a year or so of economic belt-tightening – and by 2000 the economy was growing again.

But economic growth doesn't necessarily mean social justice, especially in a country of such incredible extremes of wealth and poverty as Brazil. Over 50 million Brazilians remain truly poor – many of them desperately so. Under Cardoso, some improvements were at least made in education (see the Education section later in this chapter), a start was made on land reform (see the Economy section and the boxed texts 'The Cricket in the Box' and 'Sem Terra,' all later in this chapter), and new welfare programs seemed at least to be stopping the poorest from getting poorer.

But Brazil began the 21st century with a sickly health system, serious urban overcrowding, widespread rural landlessness

The Cricket in the Box

The impeachment of President Collor in 1992 gave Brazilians the confidence to start standing up to the country's corrupt strongmen. The media, young lawyers, members of congress and local citizens' groups all became more assertive against the social cancer of corruption.

In the late 1990s congress set up commissions of investigation into organized crime and into corruption in the judiciary. The crime commission toured the country holding highly publicized hearings, and in late 2000 called for the indictment of 500 people, including many powerful politicians. Three deputies and one senator were expelled from congress over corruption allegations. Although initially opposed to these investigations, President Cardoso's government was embarrassed into backing them.

On a local level, citizens gained the courage to challenge the cynical political orthodoxy encapsulated in the dictum *'Rouba mas faz'* ('He steals, but he gets things done'). Between 1994 and 2000, 112 of the 467 mayors in the state of Rio Grande do Sul were expelled from office.

One particularly pervasive and pernicious form of Brazilian corruption is *grilagem,* the illegal registration of land to transfer it from public to private ownership, often with governmental collusion. This practice has been going on since at least the early 19th century, and, by government estimates in 2000, nearly 1 million sq km – more than 10% of Brazil – is illegally held in this way, the majority of it in the North. In 2001, Raul Jungmann, President Cardoso's ex-Communist agrarian reform minister, characterized many of Brazil's land registry offices, where most grilagem is perpetrated, as 'mints of corruption.'

Grilagem has been part and parcel of the creation of many *latifundia,* the huge landholdings that dominate much of the countryside. Consequences of grilagem include the violent expulsion of informal, landless settlers and of traditional indigenous populations, as big landowners seek to enforce their hold. In 2000, as part of a campaign to strip large landholders of properties obtained through forged titles, the government asked 3065 of them to provide proof of ownership. Raul Jungmann subsequently cancelled the deeds to 1900 latifundia, covering 620,000 sq km, that were not supported by the right papers. The government hopes to redistribute some of this huge amount of property to the landless. Jungmann has said, however, that court challenges could tie up the process for years, even decades.

The word grilagem translates literally as 'cricketing' and refers to an old practice of placing a cricket in a box of newly faked documents: After a while, the cricket's excrement and the effect of its moving about inside the box would make the documents look convincingly old and genuine.

and ongoing environmental abuse. Corruption remained a way of life despite the beginnings of attempts to tackle it, and violent crime – much of it related to drugs or rural land disputes – was rife. In the late 1990s the murder rate was running at 700 a month in greater São Paulo, which thus joined Rio de Janeiro, Washington, DC and the cities of Colombia as the most violent urban centers on Earth. Far too much crime is still committed by the police, who – like most other criminals – are rarely brought to justice. Brazil still has some way to go before it can shake off the jibe that 'it's the land of the future – and always will be.'

GEOGRAPHY

Brazil is the world's fifth largest country (after Russia, Canada, China and the US). It borders every country in South America except Chile and Ecuador, and its 8.5 million sq km occupy almost half the continent. The distance from one side of Brazil to the other is greater than the distance between Brazil and Africa.

A lot of this enormous expanse is inaccessible and inhospitable to humans. Some

36% of the nation's territory is in the Amazon Basin, which, along with the enormous Mato Grosso to its south, has large regions with population densities of less than one person per sq km. Most of this land was not thoroughly explored by Europeans until the 20th century. New rivers and new Indian tribes are still being discovered.

Geographical Regions

Brazil's has four primary geographical regions.

Coastal Band The narrow, 7408km-long coastal band lies between the Atlantic Ocean and the coastal mountain ranges, and stretches all the way from the Uruguayan border to the state of Maranhão. From Rio Grande do Sul to Bahia, the mountains often come right down to the coast. These sheer mountainsides, known as the Great Escarpment, make rivers impossible to navigate. Especially in Rio de Janeiro and Espírito Santo states, the *litoral* (coastal region) is rocky and irregular, with many islands, bays and sudden granite peaks such as Pão de Açúcar in Rio. South of Rio the coastal mountains are called the Serra do Mar.

North of Bahia, the coastal lands are flatter and the transition to the highlands more gradual. Rounded hills signal the beginning of the central plateau. There are navigable rivers and the coast is smooth and calm, well protected by offshore reefs.

Planalto Brasileiro The Planalto Brasileiro (Brazilian Plateau) is an enormous area that extends over most of Brazil's interior south of the Amazon Basin and covers a part of almost every Brazilian state. Averaging 500m in altitude, it is sliced by several large rivers and punctuated by several small mountain ranges that reach no more than 3000m – the highest of these are centered in Minas Gerais.

From Minas Gerais the Planalto descends slowly to the north. The great Rio São Francisco, which begins in the mountains of Minas, follows this northerly descent. Several other rivers cut across the Planalto.

The large tablelands or plains between the river basins are called *chapadões*.

Amazon Basin From the Planalto Brasileiro to the south, the Andes to the west and the Guyana shield to the north, the waters descend to the huge Amazon Basin. In the far west the basin is 1300km wide; in the east, between the Guyana shield and the Planalto Brasileiro, it narrows to 100km.

More than half the length of the 6275km Rio Amazonas is in Peru, where it rises. In Brazil, the river is known as the Rio Solimões from the Peruvian border down to its confluence with its biggest tributary, the Rio Negro, near Manaus. With its estimated 1100 tributaries, the Amazon carries about 20% of the world's fresh water, and the Amazon forest contains 30% of the remaining forest in the world. Large areas of the forest are under water for up to half the year.

Pico da Neblina (3014m) on the Venezuelan border is the highest peak in Brazil.

Paraná-Paraguai Basin In the South, the Paraná-Paraguai Basin, less low-lying than the Amazon, extends into neighboring Paraguay and Argentina and includes the large wetland area known as the Pantanal. It's characterized by open forest, low woods and scrubland. Its two principal rivers, the Paraguai and the Paraná, run south, passing through Paraguay and Argentina into the Rio de la Plata.

Political Divisions

For political and administrative purposes (and for the purposes of this guidebook), Brazil is generally divided into five regions: the Southeast, the South, the Central West, the Northeast and the North.

Southeast The Southeast is developed, urban Brazil. The states of Rio de Janeiro, São Paulo, Minas Gerais and Espírito Santo make up 10% of the national territory but have 43% of the population and contribute some 60% of industrial production.

South Brazil's South has a more European feel than the rest of the country. It comprises

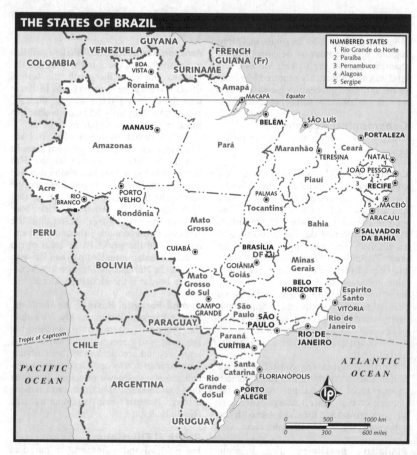

THE STATES OF BRAZIL

NUMBERED STATES
1 Rio Grande do Norte
2 Paraíba
3 Pernambuco
4 Alagoas
5 Sergipe

the prosperous states of Paraná (the location of the magnificent Foz do Iguaçu), Santa Catarina with its very visible German presence, and Rio Grande do Sul.

Central West In the old days, until well into the 20th century the Central West was called the *mato grosso* (thick forest). It comprises the states of Goiás, Mato Grosso, Mato Grosso do Sul and the federal district of Brasília: a total of 22% of the national territory. Only recently opened to road transport, economically this is Brazil's fastest growing region.

Northeast The Northeast, Brazil's poorest region, has retained much of the country's colonial past. It's also the region where the African influence is most evident. It contains 18% of Brazil's area and comprises, moving up the coast, the states of Bahia, Sergipe, Alagoas, Pernambuco, Paraíba, Rio Grande do Norte, Ceará, Piauí and Maranhão. These states are basically divided into the *zona da mata* (bushland just in from the coast) and the sertão.

North The North is the Amazon Basin, encompassing 42% of Brazil's land and including the states of Amazonas, Pará, Rondônia, Acre, Tocantins, Amapá and Roraima. This is Brazil's least populated region and contains most of the country's Indian people. The two major cities are Manaus and Belém, the former on the Rio Negro and the latter near the mouth of the Rio Amazonas.

CLIMATE

Though it's true that only the South has extreme seasonal changes like those of Europe and much of the US, most of the country does have noticeable seasonal variations in rainfall, temperature and humidity. In general, as you go from north to south, the seasonal changes are more defined.

The Brazilian winter lasts from June to August. While much of the country enjoys moderate temperatures all year long, average winter temperatures in the southern states of Rio Grande do Sul, Santa Catarina, Paraná and São Paulo run between 13°C and 18°C. A few towns can even get snow, which seems strange to those Brazilians who sweat every day of their lives.

The summer season is from December to February. With many Brazilians on vacation at this time, travel is difficult and expensive, and from Rio southward the humidity can be oppressive. But it's also the most festive time of year, when Brazilians escape their small, hot apartments and take to the beaches and streets. School holidays run from mid-December to Carnaval, usually in late February.

In summer, Rio is hot and humid. Temperatures in the high 30s (Celsius) are common and they sometimes reach the low 40s. Frequent, short rain showers cool things off a bit, but it's the humidity that is uncomfortable. The rest of the year, Rio's temperatures are generally in the mid-20s, sometimes reaching the low 30s. If you're in Rio in the winter and the weather's lousy (the rain can continue nonstop for days), or you want more heat, head to the Northeast.

The Northeast coast gets about as hot as Rio during the summer, but due to a wonderful tropical breeze and less humidity, it's rarely stifling. Generally, from Bahia to Maranhão, temperatures are a bit warmer

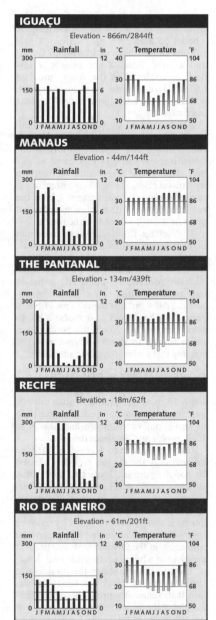

year-round than in Rio, rarely far from 28°C. All in all, it would be hard to imagine a better climate.

The Planalto areas such as Minas Gerais and around Brasília are usually a few degrees cooler than the coast, and less humid. Here summer rains are frequent, while along the coast the rains tend to come intermittently.

Although there are variations in rainfall levels throughout Brazil, rain is a year-round affair. The general pattern is for short, tropical showers that come at any time. These rains rarely alter or interfere with travel plans. The sertão is a notable exception to the general pattern – here the rains fall heavily within a few months, and periodic droughts devastate the region.

The Amazon Basin receives the most rain in Brazil, and Belém is one of the most rained-on cities in the world, but the refreshing showers are usually seen as a godsend. Actually, Amazonia is not nearly as hot as most people imagine – the average temperature is 27°C – but it *is* humid. From June to August the heat tends to decrease a bit. In some parts of the North the period from about January to March is known as winter because that's when the most rain falls.

GOVERNMENT & POLITICS

Brazil slowly returned to democracy in the 1980s. The new constitution, written in 1988, guaranteed freedom of speech and the right to strike, outlawed torture and also gave 16-year-olds and illiterates the vote.

In 1995, Fernando Henrique Cardoso became only the second president elected by popular vote in 32 years to take office. Building on the success of his Plano Real economic program, he persuaded congress to change the constitution to allow presidents, state governors and city mayors *(prefeitos)* to stand for re-election, and he won again in the October 1998 elections, at the head of a broad center-right coalition.

The constitution allows the president to choose ministers of state and initiate legislation. It also names the president commander-in-chief of the armed forces and gives him or her the power of total veto. These executive powers are balanced by a bicameral legislative congress, consisting of an 81-seat senate and a 513-seat chamber of deputies.

Presidential, vice-presidential and congressional elections are held concurrently every four years. Deputies, like the president and vice-president, serve four years; senators serve eight years, with alternately one-third and two-thirds of seats open at each election.

The parties with most seats in the 1999–2002 Congress – and the main components of the Cardoso coalition – were Cardoso's own PSDB (Brazilian Social Democracy Party), the free-market PFL (Liberal Front Party) and the PMDB (Brazilian Democratic Movement Party), a collection of regional bosses. Other major parties are the left-wing PT (Workers' Party) and the conservative PPB (Brazilian Progressive Party).

Brazil is the only genuinely federal country in Latin America, with substantial economic and political power invested in its 26 state governments and 5656 municipalities. In the municipal elections of 2000, the PT won control of 17 of the 62 biggest cities, including São Paulo, where anticorruption campaigner Marta Suplicy, a sexologist by profession, became mayor.

Elections are colorful affairs, regarded by many Brazilians as yet another excuse for a party. Posters cover every available wall space, and convoys of cars cruise through the cities creating as much noise as possible in support of their favored candidate.

Politics remain largely the preserve of the wealthy or those with strong party backing. Electoral candidates not infrequently have to drop out because of costs. Bribes are common, and corruption is still rife at all levels, though less at the top since 'Collorgate' (see 'Civilian Rule Again' in the History section earlier).

ECONOMY

Brazil is a land of scarcely credible economic contrasts. Production techniques that have barely changed since the colonial era dominate many parts of the Northeast and Amazonia, while São Paulo's massive, high-tech automobile, steel, arms and chemical industries successfully compete on the world market. Wealthy Brazilians live closed, first-world existences in luxurious houses behind high walls protected by dogs and armed guards, and head out to luxurious beach resorts or huge country estates for their holidays. Poor Brazilians live in the slums or on the streets of the same cities where the rich live, or try to eke out a subsistence existence from the land or waters around simple rural homes.

The Brazilian economy is the ninth largest in the world. While it's called a developing country, tremendous development has already occurred. Brazil has a workforce of about 75 million people (about a third of whom are women). Of those with jobs, 27% work in industry (a quarter of which is clustered in São Paulo) and 31% in agriculture. Brazil is the world's largest producer of coffee and biggest exporter of sugar and orange juice, the second largest of soya and third largest of beef and chicken. Brazil also is home to a large number of peasants living at subsistence level, and millions who have no land at all. Some 30 million people migrated to the cities between 1970 and 1990.

Cheap labor and underemployment abound. Middle-class families commonly hire two or more live-in maids, people are hired just to walk dogs or watch cars, and five-year-olds who will never go to school sell chewing gum or shine shoes.

In a country where 1% of landowners own nearly half the cultivable land, and around 40% of that land is not cultivated, land redistribution is seen as a solution – but the powerful *fazendeiros* (estate owners), apart from the occasional token gesture, are not interested in parting with their property. Some use extreme violence to keep hold of or expand what they have. Following a notorious massacre of landless people by police in 1996, the Cardoso governments made attempts at land reform, and President Cardoso claimed to have settled 370,000 families by 2000. Opponents, however, charged that the concentration of land ownership in the hands of the few had

actually intensified since 1996. The killing of peasant leaders, trade unionists and church workers involved in land disputes and strikes continues. (See the boxed texts 'Sem Terra' and 'The Cricket in the Box' for more on the subject of land reform.)

Instead of reforming the landholding pattern, successive governments have tried to open up more territory through agricultural and mining development in the Amazon region. Roads were built into Amazonia to encourage settlement by the rural poor from elsewhere in Brazil. But after cutting down the forest and opening up the land, the peasants found the mineral-poor Amazonian soil impossible to farm. Many handed over their land to cattle ranchers. Grandiose plans for development of Amazonia keep on coming: The Cardoso government's 'Avança Brasil' (Advance Brazil) economic program for the years 2000 to 2007 envisages some 8000km of newly-paved or new roads, a dozen new or expanded ports, four new or expanded airports, two gas pipelines and several new electricity-generating plants.

The Plano Real

Brazilian economists call the 1980s the 'Lost Decade.' Wild boom-and-bust cycles decimated the country's economy. Inflation ran at over 100% for most of the decade, and at times exceeded 10,000%. Until 1994, the only certainty in the economy was uncertainty. Then came the Plano Real, devised by the then Finance Minister (later President) Fernando Henrique Cardoso. A stable new currency, the *real*, backed by healthy international reserves, began life on a one-for-one parity with the US dollar. Inflation that had corroded earnings came down to a couple of percentage points, and prices of manufactured goods fell. Foreign investment (encouraged by privatizations) reached record levels, the economy was opened to foreign competition, Brazilian business started modernizing, people had more money to spend and consumption boomed. People dared to wonder, would Brazil finally cease to be the 'country of tomorrow'?

Sem Terra

The Movimento dos Trabalhadores Rurais Sem Terra (MST) (Landless Rural Workers' Movement) is the latest in a long Brazilian tradition of peasant grassroots movements. Arising in 1985 from a Catholic Church group in Rio Grande do Sul, Brazil's southernmost state, the MST has gained momentum and popular support as it has struggled for land reform, using a high media profile and its trademark invasions of unused farmland.

It has developed into a highly organized network with an ideological mix of the ideas of Nicaraguan Sandinistas, Mexican Zapatistas and liberation theology. Led by the intellectual João Pedro Stedile and the charismatic José Rainha, the movement has resettled 200,000 families and created more than 80 agricultural cooperatives. In 1995 the MST received an education award from UNICEF for creating 'public schools of quality education in settlement areas.'

More than 1000 people have died in rural violence in Brazil since 1990, and the killers have rarely been brought to trial. The most publicized deaths came during the massacre of 19 landless by military police in Eldorado dos Carajás, Pará in April 1996.

In a well-publicized long march on Brasília in April 1997, about 2000 landless, carrying farm tools and revolutionary-looking red flags, converged on the capital to demand land reform and justice for the killers of their dead peers.

The government responded by speeding up its long-awaited land reform program, creating a ministry for agrarian reform, raising taxes on unused land and offering more credit to new settlers. But, by 2001, the real culprits had still not been tried.

In 2000 and 2001 the MST suffered from a lack of leadership and struggled with accusations of large-scale corruption within the organization. The rate of invasions slowed, but with the acquittal in 2001 of José Rainha (on appeal) of a murder he didn't commit, things looked sure to get more lively within the movement.

For more information about the MST, visit its Web site at www.mst.org.br. There's a summary page about the organization in English and lots of articles in Portuguese. Other interesting pages include www.christusrex.org/www2/mst, in English, and you'll find some memorable black and white photographs by Sebastião Salgado at www.nytimes.com/specials/salgado/home.

But in the wake of the 1997 Asian money markets crisis, capital fled Brazil in anticipation of devaluation, which came about in January 1999. The real was freed to float to its own level. Accompanying austerity measures managed to return the economy to growth in 2000, though unemployment was still above 1994 levels.

The Plano Real showed that Brazil's economy has great potential. All the ingredients for progress are here: a large labor force, the means of production, transport systems and markets for the products. The question is whether or not they can be coordinated efficiently. Meanwhile, theory apart, the social reality remains that at least 55 million Brazilians live in poverty.

Social Conditions

Brazil is one of the world's most unequal countries. The richest 10% of Brazilians receive about 50% of the nation's income; the poorest 10% receive less than 1%. Some 40 million people still have no main water supply and 60 million have no sewerage. Brazil, with its dreams of greatness, has squalor that compares with the poorest countries in Africa and Asia.

As always, these ills hit some groups much harder than others. If you are a black, an Indian or from the North or Northeast, the odds against escaping poverty are high. Income in the northeastern states of Maranhão and Piauí is, on average, one-seventh of income in the Distrito Federal (the district containing Brasília, the capital). The sertão, the arid northeastern interior, is home to some 10 million subsistence farmers. Here infant mortality in the 1990s, at 84 per 1000 births, was three times the national average.

The Cardoso governments elected in 1994 and 1998 introduced antipoverty measures designed to benefit 26 million people in one way or another. But one Brazilian in three still lives in poverty, according to a definition used by many Brazilian analysts. And, according to a 1999 World Bank report, 35 million people earn less than US$40 a month, not enough to eat adequately. The official minimum wage hovers around US$75. One third of the women employed in Brazil work as maids and nannies, and most earn less than the minimum wage.

Recent research at least indicates that the number of *meninos da rua* – homeless children living rough on city streets – is far lower than the 'millions' that some people claimed in the wake of the 1993 Candelaria massacre, when eight such children were murdered by off-duty police in Rio de Janeiro. In 2000 researchers carrying out a comprehensive sweep of São Paulo counted 609 children among the total 8704 homeless.

POPULATION & PEOPLE

According to the 2000 census Brazil's population was 170 million, making it the world's fifth most populous country. There were 14 million Brazilians in 1890, 70 million in 1960, 119 million in 1980 and 147 million in 1991. The birth rate has dropped – from 3.5 children per woman in 1984 to 2.1 in 1997.

Brazil is one of the least densely populated nations in the world, averaging only 20 people per sq km. The US averages 28 people per sq km. The Brazilian population is concentrated along the coastal strip and in cities. There are 13 million people in the enormous expanses of the North and less than 12 million in the Central West, but over 72 million in the Southeast and 48 million in the Northeast. Greater São Paulo has more than 17 million residents, greater Rio more than 10 million.

Some 500 years ago when Pedro Cabral visited Brazil, he left two convicts behind who subsequently married natives. Such colonization through interracial reproduction was how the Portuguese managed to control Brazil. This 'strategy' was pursued, often consciously, for hundreds of years. First between Portuguese and indigenous people, then between the Portuguese and their black slaves and finally between Indians and blacks, interracial sex thoroughly mixed the three groups.

Brazil has had several waves of voluntary immigration. After the end of slavery in 1888, millions of Europeans were recruited to work in the coffee fields. The largest contingent was from Italy, but there were also many Portuguese and Spaniards, and smaller groups of Germans and Russians. Japanese immigration began in 1908, and today São Paulo has the largest Japanese community outside of Japan.

During the 1970s some 50,000 Portuguese from Portugal's newly independent African colonies, and Latin Americans fleeing military dictatorships in Argentina, Chile, Uruguay and Paraguay settled in Brazil.

Today there are literally dozens of terms to describe Brazilians' various racial compositions and skin tones, but those considered white still hold most of the power in government, business and property. Nonwhites are poorer and find it harder to get jobs, even when they have similar qualifications.

Indians

In 1500, when the Portuguese arrived, there were perhaps 5 or 6 million people in what has since become Brazil, grouped in probably more than 1000 tribes. These indigenous people's descendants today number no more than 350,000, in around 200 tribes (including some 50 who remain uncontacted by white or black people). Customs and beliefs vary widely from tribe to tribe – as do the strengths of these traditions in the face of expulsion from traditional lands, declining numbers, missionary activity and other influences. Brazil's largest groups of Indian peoples include the Tikuna on the upper Rio Solimões (numbering 20,000 or more), the Yanomami in northwestern Amazonia (over 11,000), and the 30,000 or so Guarani in the Central West and South.

After centuries of genocidal attacks, slavery, dispossession and death from imported diseases, Brazil's Indian population is now finally growing again, but still faces a host of problems. Most Indians live in the Amazon rainforest, and the threats that the rainforest faces – logging, mining, ranching, farming, roads, settlements, dams, hydroelectric schemes – also threaten the Indians whose way of life depends on it.

Indian Policy During the 20th century, the general thrust of official policy on the Indians and their lands was toward pacification, integration, and dispossession. About 50 tribes were extinguished during that period.

In 1910 Marechal Cândido Rondon (1865–1958), who favored a humane and dignified Indian policy, founded the SPI (Serviço de Proteção ao Índio) to protect the Indians against massacres and land dispossession. His aim was assimilation of Indians into mainstream Brazilian culture. Unfortunately, Rondon's good intentions

The Yanomami

The Yanomami, who inhabit a remote area straddling the borders of Brazil's Roraima and Amazonas states and Venezuela, are one of the most numerous and also one of the most recently contacted indigenous peoples of Amazonia. Literally a Stone Age people, living a seminomadic life with stone implements, pottery, animal hides and plants, they were dragged abruptly into the late 20th century.

The Yanomami probably had first contact with outsiders in the 1950s, but such contact remained slight until the mid-1970s when Hwy BR-210 was cut westward across Roraima and into their lands. Yanomami mixed with the construction workers and died from measles, influenza and venereal diseases. Several villages were wiped out.

In the mid-1980s a gold rush sent prospectors swarming into Yanomami territory, polluting rivers and destroying forest. By 1989 the miners' numbers had reached an estimated 40,000. As a result, in the period 1986–93, nearly 20% of the Yanomami population died, chiefly from malaria and other introduced diseases. In 1988 an absurd plan to create 19 separate pockets of land for the Yanomami, depriving them of 70% of their territory, was initiated by the Sarney government and FUNAI. The agency's president at the time was Romero Jucá, a friend of Sarney who encouraged the garimpeiros (prospectors), and considered selling off timber and minerals from Indian lands to be part of his job. Two years later, growing international and national criticism of the genocide being perpetrated on the Yanomami forced the authorities to designate only a handful of zones open for mining.

In 1991 the Venezuelan government officially recognized the Yanomami territory in Venezuela as a special Indian reserve; a few months later President Collor defied opposition and followed suit on the Brazilian side, creating the 96,650 sq km Terra Indígena Yanomami, Brazil's largest single Indian territory. The Brazilian military continues to oppose Collor's decision, arguing that the border areas should be developed and settled to discourage possible foreign intrusions.

The gold prospectors have never truly left Yanomami lands, and many mining companies are itching to get in there. In 1996 five Brazilian gold miners were convicted of genocide for the 1993 murder of 16 Yanomami at Haximú in Venezuela.

The Yanomami are a slight people, with typical Amerindian features. The center of each community is the yano, a large round timber-and-thatch structure where each family has its own section facing onto an open central area used for communal dance and ceremony. Each family arranges its own area by slinging hammocks around a constantly burning fire that forms the center of family life.

were swept aside, and the SPI became notorious for corruption, greed and the killing and expulsion of Indians.

In 1967 the SPI was replaced by FUNAI (the Fundação Nacional do Índio), which was given the ambitious and controversial tasks of protecting Indian communities and their traditional lands, addressing their medical and educational needs, promoting research, and contacting and pacifying hitherto unknown tribes.

FUNAI has been criticized for adopting a patronizing attitude toward Indians and

for manipulating against Indian interests in favor of other claims to Indian land. It's difficult to see how this grossly underfunded and understaffed organization, however many well-intentioned people there may be in its ranks, can escape contradictions. It is simultaneously supposed to represent Indians and development-minded governments with inevitable links to local strongmen, politicians and generals who see Indians chiefly as obstacles to their own pursuit of wealth and power. FUNAI presidents, some of whom have acted in direct

The Yanomami

Intertribal visits are an opportunity to eat well – if the hunt has been successful everyone gets to eat monkey, which is a delicacy. Otherwise tapir, wild pig and a variety of insects provide protein, which is balanced with garden fruits, yams, bananas and manioc. Once the garden soils and hunting grounds are exhausted, the village is dismantled and moves on to a new site.

The Yanomami hold elaborate ceremonies and rituals and place great emphasis on intertribal alliances. The latter are intended to minimize feuds or violence. Intertribal hostility is thought to manifest itself in disease that comes from evil spirits that are sent by the shamans (medicine men) of enemy tribes.

Disease is cured with shaman dances, healing hands and various herbs. Sometimes the village shaman will enlist good spirits to fight evil spirits by using *yakoana* (a hallucinogenic herbal powder).

When a tribe member dies, the body is hung from a tree until dry, then burned to ashes. The ashes are mixed with bananas, which are then eaten by friends and family of the deceased to incorporate and preserve the spirit. Mourning rituals are elaborate.

There has long been a widespread notion that the Yanomami are an aggressive people who live in a state of chronic warfare. This view stems largely from the influential work of US anthropologist Napoleon Chagnon, who first encountered the Yanomami in the 1960s and whose book *The Fierce People* became an academic best-seller. Chagnon's theories were strongly challenged in 2001 in the book *Darkness in El Dorado*, by Patrick Tierney, and are also challenged by Survival, the respected international organization that campaigns for tribal peoples. In 2001 Survival characterized the Yanomami as 'a generally peaceable people who have suffered enormous violence at the hands of outsiders,' adding that the image Chagnon created had done a great deal of damage to Yanomami interests over the previous 30 years.

opposition to Indian interests, come and go as rapidly as football coaches.

Right into the 1990s, Indians such as the Yanomami in northwestern Amazonia were suffering massacres by miners and dying in the thousands from new (to them) diseases such as malaria. The Makuxi people of the Raposa-Serra do Sol area in northeast Roraima, whose land rights are contested by ranchers, miners and their own state government, suffer sporadic violence and killings. New roads and settlement schemes in the 1960s, 1970s and 1980s displaced many Indians, with disastrous results. The Kaiowá, a large subgroup of the Guarani living in Mato Grosso do Sul, close to the borders with Bolivia and Paraguay, have suffered a wave of suicides provoked by loss of lands and profound alienation. Between 1985 and 2000, more than 300 Kaiowá, many of them children or young adults, killed themselves.

Brazil's 1988 constitution recognizes Indians' rights to their distinct way of life and to the use of their traditional lands (but not to the ownership of them, for legally Indians are still considered minors). The government set a target year of 1993 for settling the boundaries of all the 900,000 sq km of Indian land *(terra indígena)*, about 11% of Brazil's territory. But such demarcation – an important stage in the process of establishing Indians' legal rights to their land – is a long, laborious process, usually facing plenty of opposition, and by 2000, one-third of Indian land remained undemarcated. Even demarcation doesn't necessarily guarantee protection from illegal invasion or from annulments of demarcation decisions.

Indian Resistance Indian rights are defended by organizations such as the CIMI (Indian Missionary Council), ISA (Socio-Environmental Institute) and CCPY (Pro-Yanomami Commission) – and by more than 100 organizations of Indians themselves that have emerged since the 1970s. Indian consciousness and the will to defend Indian rights is gradually growing. In 1980, nearly 1000 Xavante Indians, tired of FUNAI inactivity, started marking the boundaries of their reserve in Mato Grosso state. When a fierce

conflict with encroaching ranchers arose, 31 Xavante leaders paid a surprise visit to the president of FUNAI in Brasília and demanded immediate boundary demarcation. In 1982, over 200 Indian leaders met in Brasília to debate land ownership at the First National Assembly of Indigenous Nations.

Subsequent years saw a spate of hostage-takings and confiscations by Indians, who were thereby able to force rapid decisions from the government. In 1989 the first meeting of the Indigenous Nations of Xingu included a huge cast of Brazilian Indians, foreign environmentalists, and even the rock star Sting. Two Kayapó chiefs, Raoni and Megaron, accompanied Sting on a world tour to raise funds for the preservation of the Amazon rainforest.

In the 1990s attention focused on efforts to save the Yanomami of far northwestern Brazil (see the boxed text 'The Yanomami'), but many Indian peoples around the country were becoming more assertive. In 2000, a diverse group of Indians marked the 500th anniversary of the Portuguese arrival in Brazil with a protest, gathering at Coroa Vermelha, Bahia, site of the Portuguese landing in 1500. The same year Indians occupied at least two national parks – Araguaia in Tocantins and Monte Pascoal in Bahia – claiming that these lands were traditionally theirs.

Further Information Survival International (☎ 020-7242 1441), 11-15 Emerald Street, London WC1N 3QL, UK is a good source of information on Brazilian Indians. Survival International was founded in 1969 in response to British press reports on the treatment of Brazil's Indians, and now campaigns for tribal peoples in several countries. On its useful Web site, www.survival.org.uk, you can buy the booklet *Disinherited – Indians in Brazil,* a brief introduction to the topic, published by the group in 2000.

The Brazilian NGO Instituto Socioambiental (☎ 0xx11-3825-5544, socioamb@ax.apc.org), Avenida Higienópolis 901, 01238-001 São Paulo, is another informative organization working in Indian interests. On its informative Portuguese-and-English Web site, www.socioambiental.org, you can order some interesting maps, which they will mail to other countries.

COIAB (Coordenação das Organizações Indígenas da Amazônia Brasileira; ☎ 0xx92-233-0548, coica-dh@buriti.com.br), Avenida Ayrão 235, Presidente Vargas, 69025-290 Manaus, Amazonas, is a coordinating and support body for more than 60 independent Indian organizations in northern Brazil, and can supply contact details for over 100 more Indian organizations in all parts of the country. COIAB also works in the field of indigenous health.

The Centro de Preservação das Artes Indígenas (☎/fax 0xx91-527-1176, cpci@netsan.com.br), Rua Dom Macêdo Costa 500, 68109-000 Alter do Chão, Pará, an excellent museum of Brazilian Indian art, has a good library on Indian subjects and is endeavoring to develop an autonomous indigenous university. Staff at the center can answer questions in English, but the few workers are very busy, so give them time. Or check out the Web site at www.pamiriwi.hpg.com.br. Other Web sites worth looking at include those of Rio de Janeiro's Museu do Índio (www.museudoindio.org.br, in English and Portuguese); CIMI (www.cimi.org.br); CCPY (www.uol.com.br/yanomami) and FUNAI (www.funai.gov.br).

Visiting Indigenous Lands The official procedure for applying to visit Indian territory is not straightforward. In fact, in 2001 FUNAI was reviewing the whole subject and had suspended tourist visits to Indian territories completely, pending consultations with indigenous groups and research into ecotourism possibilities. Scientists and researchers were being required to work through Brazilian academic institutions. In this procedure, the institution writes to the science research council of Brazil's Ministry of Science & Technology supporting the research proposal, which must be worked out in detail, and the ministry confers with FUNAI which, with luck, says yes. FUNAI's head office (☎ 0xx61-313-3500, fax 0xx61-226-7480) is at Setor de Edifícios Públicos Sul 702/902,

Edifício Lex, Bloco A, 70390-025, Brasília, Distrito Federal.

In practice, the formal procedures are not always followed. A friendly chat with someone at FUNAI headquarters might open up procedural shortcuts. In some areas ecotourism outfits and local FUNAI offices may be able to set up tourist visits to Indian villages and lands. NGOs and local FUNAI offices may be able to help researchers. Much depends on the situation locally and any contacts you may have. If you're considering visiting Indian territory, think of the effects *you* will have on those you visit, and go with a good guide. Ill-advised and ill-prepared contacts can be dangerous for both sides.

EDUCATION

Education in Brazil is based on class. Public schools are improving, but are still pretty bad, so anyone with the means sends their children to private schools. Almost all university students are from private schools, so very few poor children reach university, and the poverty cycle keeps getting renewed. This also means that white Brazilians tend to get better educations than others.

One improvement in recent years has been a rise in the number of children attending primary school. In 2000, 96% of seven-to-14-year-olds were enrolled (up from 67% in 1970). This increase has been thanks to Brazil's falling birthrate, government efforts to create more places for children in schools (at both existing and newly built facilities) and welfare payments in several cities and states to poor parents whose children attend school instead of being sent out to work or beg.

Even so, according to the *The Economist* magazine, in 1999 there were 736,000 seven-to-14-year-olds still working on farms or in workshops instead of going to school. Many children (60% by some estimates) do not complete primary school.

Teaching standards are low: Half the country's 1.5 million primary school teachers have had no higher education, and in some areas the proportion is much higher (93% in Maranhão state). Teachers' pay levels do not attract many highly-educated professionals. Most primary school teachers, for example, need to take second jobs to make ends meet.

Officially, Brazil's literacy rate is over 80%, but this includes many who can do little more than write their names and sound out a few words.

About one-third of Brazilian children attend secondary school (the rate has doubled since 1990). The number of university places has grown too, but demand for them now far exceeds supply. About 5% of 18-to-21-year-olds are in further or higher education. Brazil spends more of its GDP than most countries on higher education, but has a lower-than-average percentage of young people in higher education. This is because most of the money goes to fund free public universities run by federal, state or city governments. Since the mid-1990s the government has encouraged the foundation of private universities, but these are hard for poor students to get into.

ARTS

Brazilians are among the most musical people on the planet, and music is undoubtedly the most highly developed art form here. Wherever you go, you'll find people playing, singing and dancing. Perhaps because of its African roots, Brazilian music is a collective community act, a celebration, a *festa*, and is virtually inseparable from dancing. Genres like *pagode, samba, frevo, forró* and *lambada* all have their corresponding dances.

Music & Dance

Shaped by the mixing of varied influences from three continents, Brazilian popular music has always been characterized by great diversity. The *samba canção* (samba song), for example, is a mixture of Spanish bolero with the cadences and rhythms of African music. *Bossa nova* was influenced by

Carmen Miranda

samba and North American music, particularly jazz. *Tropicalismo*, in the 1960s and 1970s, mixed influences ranging from bossa nova and Italian ballads to blues and North American rock. Brazil is still creating new and original musical forms today.

If you want to dig into some Brazilian music before you head off to Brazil (and you surely will when you get back), two good places to start are the Web sites www.allbrazilianmusic.com and www.slipcue.com/music/brazil/brazillist. The latter reviews many recordings available outside Brazil. See Shopping in the Facts for the Visitor chapter for information on buying recordings in Brazil.

Samba & Pagode *Tudo dá samba:* everything makes for a samba. This most popular Brazilian rhythm originated among black Bahians in Rio de Janeiro and is generally considered to have been first performed at the Rio Carnaval in 1917, though its roots go back much further. It's intimately linked with African rhythms, notably the Angolan tam-tam, which provided the basis for samba's music and distinctive dance steps. Samba caught on quickly after the advent of radio and records, and has since become a national symbol. It is the music of the masses.

The 1930s are known as the Golden Age of Samba. By then, samba canção had also evolved, performed by small groups with European melodies laid over the African percussion – as had *choro*, a romantic, improvised, samba-related music with a ukulele or guitar playing off against a recorder or flute.

The most famous 'Brazilian' singer of this period, perhaps of all time, was Portuguese-born Carmen Miranda. A star of many Hollywood musicals of the period, she was known for her fiery Latin temperament and her 'fruity' costumes.

Samba was pushed out of favor by other styles in the 1950s, 1960s and early 1970s. Then pagode – informal, backyard-party samba, the kind of music that can be made by a small four-string *cavaquinho* guitar along with a few beer cans and tables to bang on – emerged in Rio. It's relaxed, rhythmic and melodic and, throughout the country, possibly now the most popular musical genre of all. Pioneers were singers Beth Carvalho (also the queen of samba canção), Jorge Aragão and Zeca Pagodinho, and the group Fundo de Quintal, who introduced the banjo and replaced the heavy floor tom-tom (drum) with the *repinique,* a tiny tambourine played with plastic drumsticks. Bezerra da Silva invented the *sambandido* (gangsta samba) style, long before American gangsta rap. By the 1990s the name pagode was being applied to more commercial, pop and rock-influenced samba. But 'pure pagode' pioneers such as Carvalho (who launched the 21st century on Copacabana), Aragão and Pagodinho are still going very strong.

Bossa Nova When bossa nova was invented in the 1950s, the democratic nature of Brazilian music was challenged. Bossa nova was modern and intellectual and became internationally popular. The middle class stopped listening to the old interpretations of samba and other regional music like the forró of the Northeast.

Bossa nova initiated a new style of playing and singing. The more operatic, florid style of singing was replaced by a quieter, more relaxed sound; remember the soft, smooth *The Girl from Ipanema,* composed by the late Antônio Carlos (Tom) Jobim and Vinícius de Moraes. Guitarist João Gilberto, bossa nova's super-cool founding father, is still playing, although other leading figures, such as guitarist and composer Baden Powell and singers Nara Leão and Elis Regina, are no longer with us. João Gilberto's daughter, Bebel, has sparked a new wave of popularity for bossa nova rhythms with her crossover lounge/world music albums.

Bossa nova was associated with Brazil's rising urban, university-educated middle class. It was a musical response to other modernist movements of the 1950s and 1960s such as Cinema Novo and the Brazilian modern architecture of Oscar Niemeyer et al.

Tropicalismo At the end of the 1960s the movement known as tropicalismo burst onto the scene. Tropicalismo provoked a kind of general amnesty for all the forgotten musical traditions of the past. The leading figures – Gilberto Gil, Caetano Veloso, Rita Lee, Maria Betânia and Gal Costa (all of whom are still around, with Veloso the most consistently innovative) – believed that all musical styles were important and relevant. All the styles and traditions in Brazilian music, plus North American rock and pop, could be freely mixed. This led to innovations like the introduction of the electric guitar and the sound of electric samba. Tropicalismo had its political dimension, and figures such as Veloso and Gil spent time in jail and exile during the military dictatorship.

Música Popular Brasileira (MPB) Paralleling, overlapping with and at times blending the aforementioned musical movements since the 1970s has been the music known as MPB (Brazilian Popular Music). This nebulous term covers a range of styles from innovative jazz- and bossa nova-influenced stuff to some pretty sickly pop.

Early MPB stars were Chico Buarque de Hollanda, mixing traditional samba with a more modern, universal flavor, and Jorge Ben, playing an original pop samba without losing the black rhythms of the Rio suburbs he came from.

Milton Nascimento, from Minas Gerais, has long been famous in Brazil for his fine voice, stirring anthems and ballads that reflect the spirituality of the *Mineiro* (someone from Minas). He's also jazz-influenced, and has kept his innovative touch longer than most early MPB names. Roberto Carlos, the composer of many early MPB classics and once a fiery rock-'n'-roller, has turned to schmaltzy ballads, sung in Spanish instead of Portuguese, but still somehow manages to occupy more shelf space in Brazilian music shops than anyone else.

Brazilian Rock Derived more from English than American rock, this is the least Brazilian of all Brazilian music. Pronounced, of course, 'hock,' it's very popular. Groups like Kid Abelha, Legião Urbana (who led a wave of punk-driven bands from Brasília), and the reggae-based Skank and Cidade Negra are worth a listen. The versatile and original Ed Motta, from Rio, injects soul, jazz, traditional Brazilian music and more into rock. He's well worth seeking out, and his 2000 album, *As Segundas Intençoes do Manual Prático*, is probably his best. Heavy metal band Sepultura, from Minas Gerais, achieved fame among headbangers worldwide in the 1990s.

Racionais MCs, from São Paulo, have led Brazilian rap since the late 1980s with their hard-edged lyrics about life in the favelas and jails. Their 1998 album *Sobrevivendo no Inferno* (Surviving in Hell) sold over a million copies, a record for independent releases in Brazil. Another rap star is Gabriel O Pensador, a white middle-class Carioca who directs a biting wit at…white middle-class Cariocas. Members of the Rio rock/rap band Planet Hemp campaign actively for marijuana legalization and get into a lot of legal trouble as a result. Some very boring funk, emanating chiefly from Rio, has received huge TV exposure. Hopefully, juvenile bands like O Bonde do Tigrão will vanish as fast they appeared.

Regional Music Samba, tropicalismo and bossa nova are all national musical forms, but wherever you go in Brazil you'll hear regional specialties.

The Northeast has perhaps the most regional musical and dance styles. The most important is forró, a lively, syncopated music centered on the accordion and the *zabumba* (an African drum). Though a few artists such as Luiz Gonzaga and Jackson do Pandeiro achieved national status, forró was long disdained as hick by the urbane inhabitants of Brazil's more southerly cities – as is neatly encapsulated by the title of one good compilation available internationally, *Forró: Music for Maids and Taxi Drivers*. Lately, however, forró has surged in popularity nationwide and at the same time returned from electrification to its roots – accordion, zabumba, triangle – with a big helping hand from the film *Eu, Tu, Eles* (Me, You, Them). The movie features lots of *pé-de-serra* (foot of the hills) down-home forró, including tropicalismo veteran Gilberto Gil singing the hit *Esperando na Janela*. São Paulo forró group Falamansa – with only one Northeasterner in their ranks – sold 800,000 copies of their first album *Deixe Entrar* in the seven months after it was released in 2000.

Another type of distinctive regional music is the wonderful Bumba Meu Boi festival sound from São Luís, Maranhão. There is also frevo, a frenetic, samba-related, Carnaval-based music specific to Recife and neighboring Olinda.

The *trio elétrico*, also called *frevo baiano*, began more as a change in technology than in music. It started as a joke when, during Carnaval in Salvador in the 1950s, Dodô, Armandinho and Osmar got on top of a truck and played frevo with electric guitars. The trio elétrico is not necessarily a trio, but it's still the backbone of Salvador's Carnaval, when trucks piled high with speakers – with musicians perched on top – drive through the city surrounded by dancing mobs. It was popularized during the tropicalismo era, when Caetano Veloso began writing songs about the trio elétrico. Another important element of Carnaval on the streets of Salvador is the *afro bloco*, or Afro-Brazilian percussion group. Filhos de Gandhi and Grupo Olodum are the most famous of these – Filhos have deep African roots and are strongly influenced by Candomblé (Afro-Brazilian religion); Olodum invented samba-reggae.

Mangue Beat, from Recife, combines folkloric and regional styles with international influences as diverse as hip-hop, neo-psychedelic and tejano. The early leaders of the genre were Chico Science e Nação Zumbi – the title of whose 1996 masterpiece, *Afrociberdelia*, kind of summed up what their music was about. Chico Science died in a 1997 car crash, but Nação Zumbi has gone forward without him, and other bands such as Mestre Ambrósio and Mundo Livre S/A continue to carry the Mangue torch.

Axé is a label for the profuse samba/pop/rock/reggae/funk/Caribbean fusion music that emerged from Salvador in the 1990s. Taking its cue from Salvador's older Carnaval forms, axé was popularized by the powerful, flamboyant Daniela Mercury. Other exponents include the groups Ara Ketu and Chiclete com Banana. At its best it's great, superenergetic music (hear Daniela sing *Toda Menina Baiana* (Every Bahian Girl), but some bands overcommercialized it at the end of the 1990s.

The influence of Brazilian Indian music was absorbed and diluted, as was so much that derived from Brazil's indigenous cultures. The *carimbó* music of the Amazon region (where the majority of Indians live today) is influenced primarily by the blacks of the coastal zones.

Other Styles Lambada, a dance style influenced by carimbó and by Caribbean rhythms like rumba, merengue and salsa, became popular in Brazil in the late 1980s and caught on briefly in Europe and the US. The most successful lambada artist was Beto Barbosa with her group Kaoma.

Also hugely popular is *sertanejo*, a kind of Brazilian country & western music, a favorite with truck drivers and cowboys. It's characterized by soaring harmonies and lyrics about broken hearts, life on the road etc. Exponents like to pair off in duos, such as Milionário e José Rico, Chitãozinho e Xororó, and Leandro e Leonardo.

Painting & Sculpture

The first colonial painters were the Jesuit and Benedictine missionaries, who painted their churches and sacred objects in a European baroque style. The 17th century Dutch invasion in the Northeast brought with it some important Flemish artists, such as Frans Post, who painted the flora and fauna in their tropical surroundings.

Brazilian baroque art peaked in the 18th century, when the wealth provided by the gold rush allowed talented artists to realize their full potential. The acknowledged genius of this period was the sculptor and architect Antônio Francisco Lisboa (1730–1814), better known as Aleijadinho (see the Minas Gerais chapter for information on his life and works).

In the 19th and 20th centuries, Brazilian artists followed international trends such as neoclassicism, romanticism, impressionism, academicism and modernism. Internationally, the best known Brazilian painter is Cândido Portinari (1903–62). Early in his career he made the decision to paint only Brazil and its people. Strongly influenced by the Mexican muralists like Diego Rivera, he managed to fuse native, expressionist influences into a powerful, socially conscious and sophisticated style.

To immerse yourself in Brazilian art, head for São Paulo, which has the country's greatest concentration of major art museums.

Indigenous Crafts

Fundamentally, Indian artwork is created for utilitarian or religious purposes, but after the first contacts with Europeans, Indians were soon visited by traders who perceived native artifacts as valuable, tradable goods. Items were acquired by bartering and then sold as curiosities or collectibles in Brazil and abroad. Today many Indians produce artistic handicrafts for sale as tourist curios – the income helps to pay their keep on the margin of a society that has destroyed much of their environment and way of life, leaving little other purpose for their art. The Wai Wai of western Pará state adeptly produce a range of for-sale crafts.

Colorful seeds and the plumage of forest birds are used in the making of necklaces, bracelets, earrings, headdresses and blankets. The Tumucumaque of northern Amapá and Pará make some of the finest headdresses. Some tribes pluck feathers from a bird such as a macaw, then smear the plucked area of the bird's skin with a vegetable dye that changes the color of the new plumage.

Ceramic arts were a specialty of the Marajoara, Tapajoara and other cultures that flourished in eastern Amazonia centuries before the arrival of the Portuguese. Today the Karajá tribe in Tocantins is known for its skillfully painted figurines. Grasses, leaves and bark from the forests are used in highly developed Indian handicrafts such as weaving and basketry. The Tumucumaque and the Kaxinawá of Acre are especially skilled at producing woven bags and baskets to transport or store forest foods.

Architecture

In recent years Brazil's fine architectural heritage has finally started to receive the attention and money it needs if it is not to decay into oblivion. Several outstanding collections of buildings are on the UNESCO World Heritage list, including the historic centers of the Northeastern cities of Salvador, Olinda and São Luís.

Salvador, capital of colonial Brazil from 1549 to 1763, has managed to preserve many outstanding Renaissance and baroque buildings. A special feature of its old town, where more than 600 buildings and monuments have been restored since 1992, are the many brightly colored houses, often decorated with high-quality stucco

Olinda is essentially an 18th-century city. Its architectural wealth and unique atmosphere stem from its 20 baroque churches and many convents, chapels and brightly colored houses with red tile roofs. In São Luís, the entire street plan of the late-17th-century heart of the city survives, along with many historic buildings, including fine mansions with colorful tiled facades.

The 18th-century mining towns of Minas Gerais harbor further colonial architectural riches. The jewel in the crown is Ouro Prêto, the focal point of the 18th-century gold rush, adorned with the greatest concentration of fine baroque buildings in Brazil, many of them designed or embellished by the genius of Brazilian baroque, Aleijadinho. Lovely Ouro Prêto is joined on the World Heritage list by Diamantina, founded by 18th-century diamond hunters. Other Minas towns, such as Santa Bárbara and São João del Rei, also enjoy treasures of baroque architecture.

Brazil's architecture in the 19th and early 20th centuries was much influenced by French styles. Neoclassical tastes yielded grandiose, monumental constructions such as Rio de Janeiro's Museu Nacional de Belas Artes and Amazonian rubber-boom entertainment palaces such as Manaus' Teatro Amazonas and Belém's Teatro da Paz. Art nouveau style arrived around the turn of the 20th century: An outstanding example in Rio is the interior of the Confeitaria Colombo.

The 1930s was the era of art deco, as exemplified by Rio's central railway station and statue of Christ the Redeemer, and, on a humbler scale, Belém's Hotel Central, a longtime travelers' favorite. The 1930s also saw the emergence of a new generation of Brazilian architects, led by Oscar Niemeyer and influenced by the modernist ideas of Le Corbusier, who would develop the functional style, with its extensive use of steel and glass and its lack of ornamentation. The Catedral Metropolitana and Museu de Arte Moderna in Rio de Janeiro, Niemeyer's spaceship-like Museu do Arte Contemporânea in nearby Niterói, and the Museu de Arte de São Paulo (by Lina Bo Bardi) are all good examples of modern Brazilian architecture.

But the outstanding creation of the 20th century is the city of Brasília, the new national capital created in the 1950s and 1960s from scratch by Niemeyer, urban planner Lúcio Costa and landscape architect Burle Marx. Some love Brasília, some hate it, but none can deny the daring of its very concept, of its airplane-shaped street plan, of the crown-shaped cathedral or the Santuário dom Bosco (with its beautiful stained glass), or of the way arches and water are used in government buildings such as the Palácio de Itamaraty and Palácio de Justiça. Brasília is another World Heritage site.

Literature

Since the mid-1990s Brazilians have been buying books in record numbers, and good Brazilian novels are increasingly being translated into English.

Best-selling author Paulo Coelho, whose dozen titles have sold approaching 10 million books in Brazil alone, is Latin America's second most read novelist (after Gabriel García Márquez). Coelho's more recent efforts, such as *Veronika Decides to Die*, about a writer committed to a mental hospital after a suicide attempt, and *The Fifth Mountain*, a fictionalized tale about the prophet Elijah, are more sophisticated than the new-age spiritual fables with which he sprang to fame in the mid-1990s, such as *The Alchemist* and *The Pilgrimage*.

Joaquim Maria Machado de Assis (1839–1908) is widely regarded as Brazil's greatest writer. The son of a freed slave, Assis worked as a typesetter and journalist in late-19th-century Rio. A tremendous stylist with a great sense of humor and irony, Assis had an understanding of human relations that was subtle and deeply cynical. Look for Gregory Rabassa's good late-1990s translations of *Quincas Borba* and *The Posthumous Memoirs of Bras Cubas* (previously published as *Philosopher or Dog?* and *Epitaph of a Small Winner* respectively). Machado's other major novel was *Dom Casmurro*.

Brazil's most famous writer is Jorge Amado, who died in August 2001. Born near Ilhéus in 1912, and a longtime resident of Salvador, Amado wrote colorful romances of Bahia's people and places. His early work was strongly influenced by Communism. His later books are lighter in subject, but more picturesque and intimate in style. The two most acclaimed are *Gabriela, Clove and Cinnamon*, which is set in Ilhéus, and *Dona Flor and her Two Husbands*, whose antics occur in Salvador. *Tent of Miracles* explores race relations in Brazil, and *Pen, Sword and Camisole* laughs its way through the petty worlds of military and academic politics. *The Violent Land* is an early Amado classic. *Shepherds of the Night*, three short stories about a group of Bahian characters, first inspired one of the authors of this guidebook to visit Brazil.

Without a word wasted, Graciliano Ramos (1892–1953) tells of peasant life in the sertão in his best book, *Barren Lives*. The stories are powerful portraits – strong stuff. Read anything you can find by Mário de Andrade (1893–1945), a leader of the country's 1920s artistic renaissance. His comic *Macunaíma*, which pioneered the use of vernacular language in Brazilian literature and was a precursor of magical realism, could only take place in Brazil.

The writings of the existentialist-influenced, Ukrainian-born Clarice Lispector (1925–77) are more subjective, focusing on human isolation, alienation and moral doubt, and conveying a deep understanding of women's feelings. The short story collections *Family Ties* and *Soulstorm* are among her best works.

Themes of repression and violence gained prominence starting in the late 1960s with the advent of military dictatorship. The bizarre and brutal *Zero*, by Ignácio de Loyola Brandão, had the honor of being banned by the military government until a national protest helped lift the prohibition. *Tower of Glass*, five stories by Ivan Ângelo, is all São Paulo: An absurdist 1970s look at big-city life where nothing that matters, matters. João Ubaldo Ribeiro's *Sergeant Getúlio* is a story of a military man in Brazil's Northeast. No book tells better of the sadism, brutality and patriarchy that run through Brazil's history. Ribeiro's *An Invincible Memory* (which, like *Sergeant Getúlio*, was translated into English by the author himself) is a hugely popular 400-year saga of two Bahian families from opposite ends of the social spectrum.

Márcio Souza is a modern satirist based in Manaus. His biting humor captures the frightening side of the Amazon, and his imaginative parodies of Brazilian history reveal the stupidity of personal and official endeavors to conquer the rainforest. Do your best to obtain *Mad Maria* (a historical novel about the Madeira-Mamoré Railway) and *Emperor of the Amazon* if you're going to Amazonia.

Dinah Silveira de Queiroz's *The Women of Brazil* is about a Portuguese girl who goes to 17th-century Brazil to meet her betrothed. Another author of interest is Joyce Cavalcante, who emerged in the 1990s as a writer able to express the experience of women in modern Brazil as well as the enduring social problems of the Northeast. Her *Intimate Enemies* is a tale of corruption, violence, polygamy – and humor.

Cinema

It was the cinema that opened the world's ears to bossa nova, by way of Marcel Camus' romantic *Black Orpheus* (1958), set amid Rio's Carnaval. In the 1960s, the Cinema Novo movement, led by Glauber Rocha with films like *Black God, White Devil* (1963), forged a polemical national style using Afro-Brazilian traditions in conscious resistance to the influences of Hollywood.

The military dictatorship didn't exactly encourage creative cinematography. Hector Babenco's *Pixote* (1981), the tale of a street kid in Rio, did win the best film award at Cannes, however.

Since the end of the dictatorship, Brazil has enjoyed a film renaissance, even though all the big money and much of the talent these days goes into *telenovelas* (TV soap operas). *Carlota Joaquina – Princesa de Brasil* (1994), the first film directed by Brazilian actress Carla Camuruti, is a hilarious blend of fairy tale, satire and historical drama about a Spanish princess married to the Portuguese prince regent (later Dom João VI) when the Portuguese court fled to Brazil to escape Napoleon.

Bruno Barreto's Oscar-nominated *O Que É Isso Companeiro* (1998; released as *Four Days in September* outside Brazil) is based on the 1969 kidnapping of the US ambassador to Brazil by leftist guerrillas. Walter Salles' *Central do Brasil* (1998; released as *Central Station* outside Brazil), another Oscar nominee, is the touching story of a middle-aged woman who works in the Rio railway station writing letters for illiterate people and ends up accompanying a young boy on a search for his father deep into the real, unglamorized Brazil. At the time of writing, film fans were waiting with bated breath for *Me, You, Them,* the English-subtitled version of *Eu, Tu, Eles,* Andrusha Waddington's 2000 movie about a Northeasterner with three husbands, which contributed hugely to the recent wave of popularity for that funky Northeastern music, forró.

SOCIETY & CONDUCT

Brazilian culture has been shaped not only by the Portuguese, who provided its language and main religion, but also by native Indians, black Africans, and other settlers from Europe, the Middle East and Asia.

Indian culture, though often ignored or denigrated by urban Brazilians, has helped shape modern Brazil and its legends, dance and music. Many indigenous foods and beverages, such as tapioca, manioc, potatoes, *mate* and *guaraná* have become staples. The indigenous people also gave the colonists numerous objects and skills that are now in daily use, such as hammocks, dugout canoes and thatched roofing.

The influence of African culture is also very powerful, especially in the Northeast. The slaves imported by the Portuguese brought with them their religion, music and cuisine, all which have profoundly influenced Brazilian identity.

All these elements have combined to produce a nation of people well known for their spontaneity, friendliness and lust for life. Though every generalization has its exceptions, few visitors would disagree that Brazilians at large rank among the planet's more friendly, helpful and relaxed people. Time is not one of the major factors here, it's difficult to underdress, and you'll find Brazilians make you smile a lot.

The diverse population mix yields many regional differences and perceptions. One of the funniest examples of this is the rivalry between the citizens of Rio de Janeiro and São Paulo. Paulistas (inhabitants of São Paulo state) will tell you that Cariocas (inhabitants of Rio) are hedonistic, frivolous and irresponsible. Cariocas think of Paulistas as materialistic, neurotic workaholics. Meanwhile, both Paulista and Carioca agree that the Nordestinos (Northeasterners) do things more slowly and simply, and are the worst drivers! Mineiros, from the state of Minas Gerais, are considered the thriftiest and most religious of Brazilians – Cariocas claim they're saving up for their tombs!

Kiss Kiss

The standard Brazilian greeting for members of the opposite sex is a kiss on each cheek. To get it right, always start by going to *their* right cheek – you lunge to your left. Kiss once, then switch cheeks. If you're close, or wishing luck or marriage on the person you're kissing, throw in a third kiss back on the first cheek (kiss, kiss, kiss).

In Brazil, time is warped. The cities and their 21st-century urban inhabitants exist only a short distance from fisherfolk, cattle herders and forest dwellers whose simple lifestyles have changed little in 300 years. And deep in Brazil's Amazon jungles there are still an estimated 50 uncontacted nomadic or seminomadic Indian groups – people who have had no contact with white or black Brazilians.

Brazilians have an excellent sense of humor and adore telling 'Portuguese' jokes, just as some of the less politically correct Americans tell Polish jokes and Australians and Britons tell Irish jokes.

If you manage to get a grasp of the language, listen to Brazilians when a group of them gets together on the beach or in a corner bar. If you can get past the fact that they all talk at once, you'll discover that the conversation almost always turns to soccer, criticism of the government, family matters or the latest twist in a current soap opera.

The Portuguese language, love of soccer, Carnaval and the sound of samba unify Brazilians. Observe their expressive way of communicating; go to a soccer game and watch the intensity and variety of emotions, both on the field and in the stands; experience the bacchanalia of Carnaval and attempt to dance the samba – and you may begin to understand what it is to be Brazilian.

RELIGION

Officially, Brazil is a Catholic country and claims the largest Catholic population of any country in the world. But Brazil is also noted for the diversity and syncretism of its many sects and religions, which offer great flexibility to their followers. For example, without much difficulty you can find churchgoing Catholics who feel no contradiction about attending spiritualist gatherings or appealing for help at a *terreiro de umbanda* (the house of one of the Afro-Brazilian cults).

Brazil's principal religious roots have been the animism of the indigenous people, Catholicism, and African cults brought by the blacks during the period of slavery. The colonists prohibited slaves from practicing their religions, just as they forbade music and dance for fear that they would reinforce the group identity of the captives. Religious persecution led to religious syncretism: To avoid persecution the slaves gave Catholic names and identities to all their African gods. This was generally done by finding the similarities between the Catholic images and the *orixá* (gods) of Candomblé (see Afro-Brazilian Cults later in this section). Thus, the slaves worshipped their own deities behind the representations of the Catholic saints.

In the 19th century, Brazil wrote freedom of religion into its constitution, but the African cults continued to suffer persecution for many years. Candomblé was seen by the white elites as charlatanism that displayed the ignorance of the poorest classes. However, the spectrum of religious life was gradually broadened by the addition of Indian animism to Afro-Catholic syncretism, and by the increasing fascination of whites with the spiritualism of Kardecism (see Kardecism later in this section).

Today large numbers of converts are being attracted to evangelical Christianity, to the Afro-Brazilian cults, and to spiritualist or mystic sects.

Christianity

Catholicism retains its status as Brazil's official religion, but is declining in popularity. Many people now merely turn up at church for the basics: baptism, marriage and burial. Evangelical Christianity, however, is booming. All over Brazil, especially in the poorer areas where people are most desperate, you will come across simple, recently built churches full of worshipers. Sometimes there will be two or three rival evangelical churches on the same street, going by names such as the Assembléia de Deus (Assembly of God), Igreja Pentecostal Deus é Amor (God is Love Pentecostal Church) and even the Igreja do Evangelho Quadrangular (Church of the Quadrangular Gospel). In one they may be moaning, groaning and speaking in tongues, in another they'll simply be listening to the stern words of a preacher.

Note: In this book you will find the abbreviation NS used for 'Nossa Senhora' (Our Lady) or 'Nosso Senhor' (Our Lord), eg, NS do Pilar.

Afro-Brazilian Cults

These cults do not follow the ideas of major European or Asian religions, nor do they use doctrines to define good and evil. One of the things most shocking to Europeans in their first contact with African images and rituals was the cult of Exú. This entity was generally represented by combined human and animal images, with a horn and an erect penis. Seeking parallels with their own beliefs, Europeans identified Exú as the devil. For Africans, however, Exú represents the link between the material and the spiritual worlds.

In the rituals of Candomblé, Exú acts as a messenger between the gods and human beings. Ultimately, his responsibility is the temporal world. Everything related to money, love, and protection against thieves comes under the watchful eye of Exú.

Candomblé This is the most orthodox of the many cults that were brought from Africa by the Nago, Yoruba, and Jeje peoples. Candomblé, an African word denoting a dance in honor of the gods, is a general term for the cult in Bahia. Elsewhere in Brazil the cult has different names: In Rio it's Macumba; in Amazonas and Pará it's Babassuê; in Pernambuco and Alagoas it's Xangô; in Rio Grande do Sul it's Pará or Batuque; in Maranhão, the term Tambor is used. For suggested reading on

Candomblé, see the Books section in the Facts for the Visitor chapter.

Afro-Brazilian rituals are practiced in a *casa-de-santo* or *terreiro* and directed by a *pai* or *mãe de santo* (literally saint's father or mother – the Candomblé priests). This is where the initiation of novices takes place as well as consultations and rituals. The ceremonies are conducted in the Yoruba language. The religious hierarchy and structure is clearly established and consistent from one terreiro to the next. Not all ceremonies are open to the public.

If you attend a Candomblé ceremony, it's best to go as the invited guest of a knowledgeable friend or commercial guide. If your request to visit is declined, you should accept the decision. Some ceremonies are only open to certain members of a terreiro, and there is also sometimes genuine concern that visitors, not knowing the customs involved, may interrupt the rituals.

Although Candomblé ceremonies do not have rigid rules, some general points apply to most. If in doubt, ask the person who has taken you to the ceremony. Dress can be casual, but shorts should not be worn. White is the preferred color; black, purple, and brown should be avoided. Hats should not be worn inside the terreiro; and if you wish to smoke, you should only do so outside.

On arrival at the terreiro, make sure you do not stand blocking the doorway. Usually someone inside is responsible for directing people to their seats – men are often seated on the right, women on the left. The seating pattern is important, so make sure you only sit where directed. Watch respectfully and follow the advice of your friend or guide as to what form of participation is expected of you. Sometimes drinks and food are distributed. Depending on the ritual involved, these may be intended only as offerings, or they may be intended for consumption. No offense will be taken if you don't eat or drink what's offered. For a description of a visit to a Candomblé ceremony, see the boxed text 'An Evening of Candomblé,' in the Bahia chapter.

According to Candomblé, each person has an orixá (god) that attends to the needs of an individual from birth and provides protection throughout life. The orixá for each person is identified after a pai or mãe de santo makes successive throws with a handful of *búzios* (shells).

Shells also figure in the divination ritual known as the *Jogo dos Búzios* (Casting of Shells), in which the position of the shells is used to interpret your luck, your future and your past relation with the gods. The Jogo dos Búzios is a simple version of the ceremony in which the orixá Ifa is invoked to transmit the words of the deities to the people. The mãe de santo casts 16 seashells on a white towel. She interprets the number and arrangement of face-up and face-down shells to predict the future. The Jogo dos Búzios is a serious, respected force in Bahia and is even used by politicians to foretell election results. In Salvador, visitors can consult a mãe de santo for this Candomblé-style fortune-telling any day of the week except Friday or Monday – Thursday is best!

Like the gods in European classical mythology, each orixá has a personality and particular history. Power struggles among them are part of the history of Candomblé.

Although orixá are divided into male and female types, there are some that can switch from one gender to the other. One such is Logunedé, son of two male gods, Ogun and Oxoss. Another is Oxumaré, who is male for six months of the year and female for the other months. Oxumaré is represented by the rainbow or by the river that runs from the mainland to the sea. These androgynous gods are generally, but not necessarily, the gods of homosexuals. Candomblé is very accepting of homosexuality.

To keep themselves strong and healthy, followers of Candomblé always give food to their respective orixá. In rituals, Exú is the first to be given food because he is the messenger who contacts the orixá. Each orixá has its preferred offerings. Exú likes *cachaça* and other alcoholic drinks, cigarettes, cigars, strong perfumes and meat. To please Iemanjá, the goddess of the sea, one should give perfume, white and blue flowers, rice and fried fish. Oxalá, the greatest god and owner of the sun, eats cooked white corn. Oxúm, god of fresh waters and waterfalls, is famous for his vanity. He should be honored with earrings, necklaces, mirrors, perfumes, champagne and honey.

Each orixá is worshipped at a particular time and place. For example, Oxósse, god of the forests, should be revered in a forest or park, but Xangô, the god of stone and justice, receives his offerings in rocky places.

In Bahia and Rio, followers of Afro-Brazilian cults turn out in huge numbers to attend a series of festivals at the year's end – especially those held during the night of December 31 and on New Year's Day. Millions of Brazilians go to the beach at this time to pay homage to Iemanjá. Flowers, perfumes, fruits and even jewelry are tossed into the sea to please the mother of the waters, or to gain protection and good luck in the new year.

Umbanda & Quimbanda Umbanda, or white magic, is a mixture of Candomblé and spiritualism. It has Angolan/Bantu and other various roots, but in its present form is a religion native to Brazil. The ceremony, conducted in Portuguese, incorporates figures from all the Brazilian ethnicities: *preto velho* (the old black slave), *o caboclo* and other Indian deities, *o guerreiro* (the white warrior), and so on. Umbanda is less organized than Candomblé, and each pai or mãe de santo modifies the religion.

Quimbanda is the evil counterpart to Umbanda. Its rituals involve lots of blood, animal sacrifice and nasty deeds. Quimbanda is technically illegal.

Kardecism

During the 19th century, Allan Kardec, the French spiritual master, introduced spiritualism to Brazilian whites in a palatable form.

Kardec's teachings, which incorporated some Eastern religious ideas into a European framework, are now followed by large numbers of Brazilians. Kardecism emphasizes parlor seances, multiple reincarnations and speaking to the dead. Kardec's writings on his teachings include *The Book of Spirits* and *The Book of Mediums*.

Other Cults

A few Indian rites have become popularized among Brazilians without being incorporated into Afro-Brazilian cults. The cults União da Vegetal (in Brasília, São Paulo and the South) and Santo Daime (centered in Acre and Amazonas states) are both based on consumption of the hallucinogenic drink *ayahuasca*. Made from stems of the vine *Banisteriopsis caapi* and leaves of the bush *Psychotria viridis,* ayahuasca has been used for centuries by some indigenous peoples of South America. Ayahuasca apart, these cults are very straight, dictating that hierarchy, moral behavior and dress follow strict codes. The government tolerates the use of ayahuasca in the religious ceremonies of these cults, and tightly controls its production and supply.

The cult of Santo Daime was founded in 1930 in Rio Branco, Acre, by Raimundo Irineu Serra, a rubber tapper who had been initiated into ayahuasca by Indians on the Acre-Peru border. In visions he received instructions to set up a base near Rio Branco to spread the doctrine of ayahuasca. The name Santo Daime comes from the wording of the cult's prayers, *'Dai-me força, dai-me luz…'* ('Give me strength, give me light…'). Santo Daime and União da Vegetal together have between 10,000 and 20,000 members, including, in Santo Daime's case, notable Brazilian figures such as flamboyant singer Ney Matogrosso and cartoonist Glauco. Santo Daime's two major communities are Ceú do Mapiá in Amazonas and Colônia Cinco Mil near Rio Branco, Acre.

The Brasília area, believed by some to be specially propitious for supernatural contact, has become a virtual capital of new religions. You can visit syncretic cults both in the city and near it, in places such as Vale do Amanhecer (Valley of the Dawn) and Cidade Eclética (Eclectic City) – see the boxed text 'Brasília – Capital of the Third Millennium,' in the Distrito Federal chapter.

LANGUAGE

Brazilians speak Portuguese. If you know some Spanish it will certainly help you to read Portuguese straightaway, and you can use it to make yourself understood, but coming to grips with spoken Portuguese takes a little longer. English-speaking Brazilians are genuine rarities.

See the Language Guide at the end of this book for an introduction to Brazilian Portuguese, which has some important differences (especially in pronunciation) from the Portuguese spoken in Portugal. Even if you never understand a word Brazilians say, you'll certainly come to enjoy the mellifluous musicality with which they speak – a quality exhibited par excellence by TV soccer commentators, who can keep up an unbroken stream of passionate poetry for 90 minutes.

When the Portuguese arrived in 1500, an estimated 700 indigenous languages were spoken by Brazil's Indian peoples. About 180 survive, 130 of them being considered endangered because they have fewer than 600 speakers.

NATURAL BRAZIL

Brazil is justly celebrated for the incredible abundance and variety of its fauna and flora. From the fearsome jaguar to the quaint pink river dolphin, and from the mighty mahogany to the hundreds of different orchids, Brazil is a natural cornucopia unrivaled on the planet. It has more known species of plants (55,000), freshwater fish (3000) and mammals (520-plus) than any other country in the world. It ranks second for the number of amphibians (517), third for birds (1622) and fifth for reptiles (468) – not to mention the 10 to 15 million insect species that fly, hop, crawl and wriggle their lives away here too. Some 131 of the mammals, 294 of the amphibians and 172 of the reptiles are endemic. New species are being discovered all the time, including several previously unknown small primates identified in the 1990s.

Unhappily, Brazil is also renowned for the destruction of this natural abundance. Amazonia, which harbors a high proportion of the country's biological diversity, has long been among the world's most critical environmental crisis zones. Less widely known is that all of Brazil's other major ecosystems are also threatened. Even as new species are being discovered, others are becoming extinct. The last known wild spix macaw, a beautiful iridescent blue bird, disappeared from its haunts in Bahia state in 2000. More than a hundred other Brazilian birds and more than 70 mammals are considered endangered.

The human assault on natural Brazil has gone on more or less unfettered since Europeans arrived in 1500. But since the 1990s an awakening of environmental consciousness among Brazilians – and even among some of the country's politicians – means that attitudes are at last slowly starting to change. One aspect of the increased environmental consciousness is an awareness that untrammeled natural environments attract tourists (and their dollars). The accessibility of Brazil's natural wonders is increasing quickly. This section serves as an introduction to what's where in natural Brazil, how it's faring in conservation terms, and how you can get to see it.

For recommended field guides and further reading matter, see the Books section in the Facts for the Visitor chapter.

Ecosystems

Brazil has five principal ecosystems: Amazon rainforest, Atlantic rainforest, the arid *caatinga,* the central *cerrado* savanna, and the wetlands of the Pantanal.

AMAZON RAINFOREST

Covering nearly all of Brazil's North region plus parts of Mato Grosso and Maranhão states – a total of 3.6 million sq km, about 42% of Brazil – and a further 2.4 million sq km in neighboring countries, the Amazon rainforest is the largest tropical forest in the world, and the planet's most biologically diverse ecosystem. The Amazon is home to around 20% of the world's bird species, 20% of plant species, 10% of

NATURAL BRAZIL

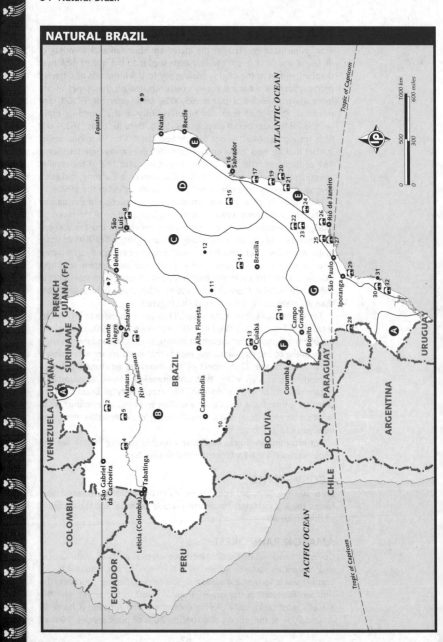

NATURAL BRAZIL

ECOSYSTEMS
A Grasslands
B Amazon Rainforest
C Cerrado
D Caatinga
E Atlantic Rainforest
F Pantanal
G Former Atlantic Rainforest

NATURAL DESTINATIONS
1 Pico da Neblina
2 Reserva Xixuaú-Xipariná
3 Rio Javari
4 Reserva de Desenvolvimento
Sustentável Mamirauá
5 Parque Nacional do Jaú
6 Floresta Nacional do Tapajós
7 Ilha do Marajó
8 Parque Nacional dos Lençóis
Maranhenses
9 Fernando de Noronha
Archipelago

10 Rio Guaporé
11 Ilha do Bananal
12 Jalapão
13 Parque Nacional da Chapada
dos Guimarães
14 Parque Nacional da Chapada
dos Veadeiros
15 Parque Nacional da Chapada
Diamantina
16 Praia do Forte
17 Eco Parque da Una
18 Parque Nacional das Emas
19 Parque Nacional de Monte
Pascoal
20 Parque Nacional Marinho de
Abrolhos
21 Parque Estadual de Itaúnas
22 Parque Nacional da Serra do
Cipó
23 Parque Natural do Caraça
24 Parque Nacional de Caparaó
25 Parque Nacional do Itatiaia

26 Parque Nacional da Serra dos
Órgãos
27 Parque Nacional da Serra da
Bocaina
28 Parque Nacional do Iguaçu
29 Parque Nacional do Superaguí
30 Parque Nacional de Saõ
Joaquim
31 Praia da Rosa
32 Parque Nacional de Aparados
da Serra & Parque Nacional
da Serra Geral

mammal species and some 2000 to 3000 species of fish (in contrast, Europe has about 200). The forest still keeps many of its secrets: To this day, major tributaries of the Amazon River are unexplored, and thousands of species have not yet been classified.

Unfortunately, humanity has been destroying the Amazon forests so quickly (see the boxed text 'Advance Brazil?' for some figures) that countless animal and plant species are likely to be extinguished before they're even known to us.

Rainforests can occur wherever more than 2000mm of rain falls annually and where this rainfall is spread over the whole year. The Amazon basin averages between 130 and 250 rainy days a year, depending

Why the Rainforest Matters

The two main reasons the Amazon rainforest is important to the future of humanity and the planet Earth are its biodiversity (biological diversity) and its effect on the climate.

Biodiversity Tropical forests have a far greater concentration of different plant and animal species than most other ecosystems. For example, of the 250,000 species of higher plants known to science, 90,000 are found in tropical Latin America (and that's triple the number known in tropical Africa). The Amazon rainforest alone contains an estimated one-fifth of all the planet's bird and plant species. This fund of genetic diversity is a vital source of food, medicines and chemicals used worldwide. About a quarter of the medicines used in the developed world contain elements extracted from tropical forests. The Amazon rainforest has already given us rubber, manioc and cocoa, as well as antimalarial drugs, cancer drugs and hundreds of other medicinal plants. Some 1300 of the Amazon's plants have acknowledged medicinal value, and more are being discovered all the time. Simply put, a cure for AIDS (or breast cancer or the common cold) might be lurking in forest flora or fauna. The destruction of such a storehouse would be an incalculable loss.

Climate The greenhouse theory, in simple terms, is this: Solar heat reaching the Earth returns to space as infrared radiation. But carbon in the atmosphere, in the form of carbon dioxide (CO_2) or methane (CH_4), reflects some of this radiation back to the Earth, heating up the planet. The more carbon in the atmosphere, the hotter the Earth gets, with unpredictable and very probably undesirable consequences. The gases that reflect the radiation back to earth are known as greenhouse gases because they have, like a greenhouse, the effect of trapping heat.

By day, trees absorb carbon dioxide and release oxygen; by night, they absorb oxygen and release carbon dioxide. In a mature forest, the consumption and release of these two gases is in balance. But growing trees absorb more carbon dioxide than they release, and burning or dead trees release carbon dioxide without absorbing any at all. So when tree-dense

where in the system you are. About half the rain comes from damp trade winds blowing in from the Atlantic Ocean. The rest results from vapor released by Amazonia's own soil and trees – much of that vapor itself being recycled rain. Humidity is always greater than 80%, and temperatures range fairly constantly between 22°C by night and 31°C by day.

Floodplain & Dry Land
Seasonal rainfall patterns mean that the water levels of the Amazon River and its hundreds of tributaries rise and fall in an annual rhythm. This produces dramatic alterations in the region's geography. Water levels routinely vary between low and high by 10m to 15m; during

Why the Rainforest Matters

areas are burned or otherwise deforested, levels of carbon in the atmosphere increase and, as a result, the Earth gets hotter.

Another source of carbon in the atmosphere is the burning of fossil fuels by motor vehicles, industrial processes and so on. In 1997 the world's rich countries, which emit much more carbon than the poorer countries, signed the Kyoto Protocol, by which they agreed to, by about 2010, cut their emissions of greenhouse gases by around 5% from 1990 levels.

At the time of writing, the Kyoto deal was near collapse because first the signatories failed to agree on how to implement their agreement, and then George W Bush, a firm opponent of the whole thing, somehow got himself installed as president of the US. However, some of the ideas that have spun off from the protocol are likely to linger, even if the deal itself doesn't survive. And some of these ideas are potential goldmines for countries with rainforest, as the rich countries have come up with schemes to pay other countries to make carbon-emission cuts, instead of making the all their cuts themselves.

For example, if an Amazonian state in, say, Brazil undertakes to plant more trees, or even just stall the destruction of trees it had been planning to destroy (meaning that less carbon would be released into the atmosphere), it could 'sell' this commitment to a rich-country company that was being required to reduce carbon emissions but was reluctant to make the reduction in its own operations. A future global market in such 'carbon credits' is foreseen, and researchers in Brazil and elsewhere have even been trying to figure out ways to measure exactly how much carbon is 'sequestered' (locked away) by different types of trees in different situations.

Another climatic effect of the Amazon rainforest is its release of large quantities of water vapor into the air, which contributes greatly to rainfall both as it falls on the rainforest and on nearby areas. As the area that is rainforest shrinks, rainfall is likely to diminish in the northern half of South America, which in turn may have an effect on the rainfall and climates in other regions.

high-water periods, areas totaling at least 150,000 sq km (about the size of England and Wales together) are flooded. The high waters link rivers, creeks and lakes that are otherwise unconnected, providing river travelers with numerous shortcuts. The seasons are not the same everywhere in the Amazon basin: High water on the Amazon itself and its major northern tributary, the Rio Negro, is in June; while high water on the southern tributaries such as the Madeira, Agaguaia and Tocantins takes place in March.

The regularly inundated floodplains of the 'white-water' (actually creamy-brown) rivers flowing down from the Andes are known as *várzea* and generally sustain forests no more than 20m tall. Many of the trees have elevated roots. *Igapó*, a name used for a flooded forest, more often refers to areas flooded by the darker waters of the Rio Negro basin. It's particularly fascinating to boat through a flooded forest because you move along at treetop level and can get closer to the wildlife.

Forests on *terra firme* (higher land, not subject to flooding) typically grow to 30m in height. Here are found the Brazil nut tree and valuable hardwoods such as mahogany, all of which prefer a drier environment.

On the waters themselves live aquatic plants such as the giant *Vitória regia* water lilies (named after Britain's Queen Victoria) and even floating islands with amphibious grasses.

Forest Layers

The rainforest is stratified into layers of plant and animal life. Most of the animal activity takes place in the canopy layer, 20 to 30m above ground, where trees compete for sunshine and the butterflies, sloths and the majority of birds and monkeys live. Here hummingbirds hover for pollen, and macaws and parrots seek out nuts and tender shoots. The dense foliage of the canopy layer blots out the sunlight at lower levels. A few tall trees reaching up to 40m, even 50m, poke above the canopy and dominate the forest skyline. These 'emergent trees' are inhabited by birds like the harpy eagle and toucan and, unlike most other rainforest plants, disperse their seeds by wind.

Below the canopy is the understory. Epiphytes ('air plants') hang at mid-levels, and below them are bushes, saplings and shrubs that grow up to 5m in height. Last is a ground cover of ferns, seedlings and herbs – plants adapted to very little light. Down here live ants and termites, the so-called social insects. The *saubas* (leaf-cutter ants) use leaves to build underground nests for raising fungus gardens, while army ants swarm through the jungle in huge masses, eating everything that happens to be in their path. Insects, fungi and roots fight for access to nutrients, keeping the forest floor quite tidy. At ground level it's cooler than in the canopy, averaging about 28°C, but humidity is higher, at about 90%.

The forest's soils are typically shallow. Many trees have buttress roots that spread over wide patches of ground to gather more nutrients.

Threats to Amazonia

In the 1970s, Brazil's military government attempted to tame Amazonia with the ambitious Plano de Integração Nacional. Long roads, like the 2000km of the Transamazônica from Aguiarnópolis (Tocantins state) to Labrea (Amazonas), were cleared through the jungle. The roads were intended to be safety valves to ease the social tensions and land hunger of Brazil's drought-stricken Northeast. Thousands left the Northeast to build homesteads in the newly cleared forest. Most of these hopeful settlers failed to establish a foothold and abandoned the land for the favelas of Amazonia's growing cities. Along the roads also came loggers, who cleared further great tracts of jungle, and cattle ranchers, who took over cheap lands abandoned by settlers.

During the 1980s, Brazil treated the forests as assets that could be used to pay back the international debt incurred during the 20 years of military dictatorship. Encouraged by the International Monetary Fund and the World Bank, the government provided large incentives to coax multinational timber and mining firms to exploit the Amazon.

A turning point of sorts was the 1988 assassination of Chico Mendes, a leader among the rubber tappers and a prominent opponent of rainforest destruction, in Xapuri (Acre state) by a hostile landowner. (See the boxed text 'Chico Mendes & His Legacy' in the Rondônia & Acre chapter). The incident sparked an international reaction, and in the 1990s, foreign governments and international institutions increasingly made environmental policies a condition of aid or loans.

Farming & Ranching The lushness of the Amazon jungle is deceptive. Only about 17% of Amazonia is suitable for sustained agriculture or livestock raising. Most of the soil is too thin and too lacking in calcium, phosphorus and potassium to be suitable for crops. The jungle ecosystem recycles most organic matter before it can even be absorbed into the soil.

Slash-and-burn agriculture seems to have worked well for the traditional indigenous populations, who would fell small areas of trees and burn off remaining material. The resulting ash would support a few years of varied crops: squash, corn, manioc, plantains and beans. After a few seasons, the Indians would move on. The clearings were small in size and number and the land was left fallow long enough for the jungle to recover.

By contrast, the agricultural techniques of modern settlers have generally proved inappropriate. Settlers who burned off small plots found that their fertility was exhausted after a few years. Even as pasture, the land often ceases to be useful after 15 or 20 years of continuous use. With all its nutrients exhausted, such land takes a long time to recover.

Hydroelectricity & Mining Further damage to the Amazonian environment and its indigenous human population has been caused by hydroelectric schemes (which in flat Amazonia flood unusually large areas of forest) and mining.

Garimpeiros (wildcat miners, usually seeking gold) have a hand in deforestation and erosion and use mercury separation to extract gold from ore. Large quantities of highly poisonous mercury are washed into the rivers, where they become a major health hazard. At the other end of the mining spectrum is the vast Provincia Mineral de Carajás in the southeast of Pará state, with its huge workings of iron and other minerals, its own railway to the coast at São Luís and its own purpose-built hydroelectric station at Tucuruí.

Advance Brazil?

By the year 2000, about 14% of the Brazilian Amazon rainforest had been completely destroyed, amounting to a loss of around 550,000 sq km, an area about the size of France, virtually all since 1970. Deforestation was continuing at a rate approaching 20,000 sq km a year, meaning that since then at least 10,000 sq km more land has had its best trees extracted and then been abandoned.

The Cardoso government's national economic program Avança Brasil (Advance Brazil), unveiled in 1999, envisaged a raft of new infrastructure projects for Amazonia in the years 2000–07. These were summarized in the respected Brazilian current-affairs magazine Veja, in November 2000, as follows:

- Paving or construction of 8000km of roads
- Opening or expansion of more than a dozen river ports and four airports
- Opening of two gas pipelines
- Building three new thermal power stations
- Opening of the second stage of the giant Tucuruí hydroelectric project on the Rio Tocantins, and constructing a new hydroelectric project at Belo Monte on the Rio Xingu
- Opening of hidrovias (aquatic freeways for river traffic) along the Madeira, Araguaia and Tocantins rivers, totaling 3300km in length
- Putting in a new 1400km stretch of the Ferrovia Norte-Sul freight railroad
- Adding thousands of kilometers of new electric power lines

Environmental scientists inside and outside of Brazil predict some very dire consequences from Avança Brasil. They base their forecasts on the effects of past infrastructure projects in Amazonia, especially construction of roads. Roads make it easy for not only loggers but also cattle ranchers, miners and small farmers to move in and clear forest, increasing the risk of fires.

One group, made up of researchers from the Woods Hole Research Center in the US, and IPAM and ISA in Brazil, looked back at three roads paved during the 1960s and 1970s. The group reported that by 1991, 55% of the vegetation had been destroyed within 50km on either side

Fire Fire is used by ranchers and small farmers to clear virgin forest, to burn off land that is already partly cleared, to clear away secondary forest growth and to burn cattle pastures to encourage grass growth. Fires often get out of control, and the problem becomes particularly acute when the annual rains do not come as expected after the August-September burning season.

The extended Amazonian dry season of late 1997 and (north of the equator) early 1998, associated with a strong El Niño, brought a dramatic

Advance Brazil?

of the Brasília-Belém highway, 40% within 50km of the parallel Hwy PA-150 (the 'timber corridor' of southeast Pará), and 33% within 50km of Hwy BR-364, the Cuiabá-Porto Velho road. The researchers predicted that, with the implementation of Avança Brasil, by about 2030 the total deforested area in Brazilian Amazonia could amount to about 1.3 million sq km – more than a third of the existing rainforest area.

Another group, led by American biologist William Laurance of the Smithsonian Tropical Research Institute, forecast that by the year 2020 somewhere between 1.05 and 1.6 million sq km of rainforest would be completely devastated or heavily degraded. And these figures did not include other areas that would be damaged to a lesser degree. In the worst case, the team calculated, a further 1.2 million sq km would be moderately degraded, 1 million sq km lightly degraded, and less than 200,000 sq km would remain in its pristine state.

One of the roads due to be paved under Avança Brasil is Hwy BR-163 from Cuiabá to Santarém. The towns of Novo Progresso and Moraes de Almeida on this road (which already exists but was still mostly unpaved in 2001) were Amazonia's latest logging hub at the start of the 21st century. Logging operations move from one zone to another over the course of time as timber supplies become exhausted, and the number of sawmills in Novo Progresso and Moraes de Almeida jumped from fewer than 15 in 1997 to more than 100 in 2000. According to Veja, Laurance reckoned the swath of destruction straddling a paved Hwy BR-163 could reach a width of 200km.

Not surprisingly, the Brazilian government challenged the findings of Laurance and others, stating that Avança Brasil was guided by principles of environmental preservation and sustainable development, and that improving the living standards of the generally poor Amazonian population would discourage deforestation. Cardoso's Environment Minister, José Sarney Filho, said that infrastructure projects could still be modified in the light of environmental-impact studies. The government also argued that important factors had changed since the building of the 1960s and 1970s highways: Incentives to settlement in Amazonia had been removed, and new measures to protect the Amazon forest meant that today's infrastructure projects were less destructive than those of years past.

increase in fires. And fires and drought one year – even ground fires that don't touch the forest canopy – increase the danger of fires in subsequent years by drying out the upper layers of soil, making it hard for the forest to retain the moisture that provides a natural barrier against fire. Researchers fear that a new drought could produce truly catastrophic fires. The risk is greatest in southern and eastern Amazonia.

Searching for Solutions It's easy for foreigners to complain about destruction of the Amazon environment and forget that some 14 million Brazilians are trying to make a living in it. What's more, foreign governments and international institutions have in the past actively encouraged destructive development schemes in Amazonia. Any viable solution to Amazonia's problems has to address the aspirations of its inhabitants, who are mostly poor and lacking in adequate education, medical care and sanitation.

The rancher-landowner-agribusiness lobby is very powerful in Brazilian politics and generally opposes attempts to conserve the environment. Even when governments legislate to protect Brazil's forests, enforcement is poor, largely because of a shortage of funds. Illegal logging is rife in Amazonia. Even some Amazonian national parks are encroached upon with near impunity by loggers or settlers. The arrival in Brazil in the 1990s of many Asian logging companies, in search of new timber sources now that they have exhausted their own forests, does not increase Amazonia's conservation prospects. The logging industry is the third-largest employer in Amazonia (after agriculture and fishing) but has in the past been conducted inefficiently, with heavy wastage. It was once estimated that for every 27 trees felled in the state of Pará only one actually arrived at a timber mill.

The environmental initiatives that seemingly offer the best prospects of success are those that make conservation act in the interests of the local populace – such as extractive reserves, sustainable development reserves (see the Conservation Units section later in this special section for an elaboration of these terms), fish-farming, fishing tourism and community ecotourism projects. Unfortunately, most of these are alarmingly small-scale compared with the size of the Amazonian population and the amount of destruction that is being wreaked throughout the region's ecosystem.

Politicians, even when sympathetic to environmental causes, tend to respond more readily to proposals for development and economic growth than plans for conservation. During research for this edition, environmentalists were raising the alarm about a wave of planned infrastructure schemes in Amazonia (see the box 'Advance Brazil?'), and putting up stiff resistance to proposed changes to Brazil's 1965 Forest Code, which would reduce the amount of forest that has to be preserved on Amazonian rural properties from 80% to 25%.

Hopes for more rational logging practices have been raised by international certification schemes such as that of the Forest Stewardship Council. This council seeks to certify timber that has been produced by sustainable methods, something that is increasingly demanded by domestic and international consumers of Brazilian timber. This type of consumer demand encourages reduced-impact logging, a practice that began to take off in Brazil in the 1990s, whereby forestry areas are divided into blocks to be exploited on a rotating basis and given sufficient time to regenerate. At the same time, the largest specimens of valuable tree species are left standing in order to reseed the block, and care is taken to minimize damage to trees that are not being felled.

ATLANTIC RAINFOREST

When Europeans arrived in 1500, Brazil's 'other' tropical rainforest, the Mata Atlântica (Atlantic Forest) extended right along the country's southeast-facing coast from Rio Grande do Norte to Rio Grande do Sul. It formed a band that gradually widened toward the south, where it reached a width of up to 800km. Atlantic forest covered about 1 million sq km in all.

If you travel along the coast, you'll have plenty of opportunities to experience the Mata Atlântica, even though no more than 7% of the original forest remains. Today, three-quarters of Brazil's population and all its main industrial cities are located in what used to be Mata Atlântica. Brazilwood extraction, sugarcane and coffee cultivation, farming, ranching, logging, fires and acid rain have also taken their toll of the forest.

Nevertheless, what remains of the Atlantic rainforest – dozens of separate fragments – is incredibly luxuriant, and some areas boast what may be the highest biodiversity levels on earth. The Mata Atlântica is older than the Amazon forest and has evolved independently. Though it shares many animal and plant families with other Brazilian ecosystems, it also contains many unique species – 17 of its 21 primate types are found only here, as are more than 900 of its 2000-plus kinds of butterflies, and many of its more than 600 bird species.

Many species are also endangered, including the four types of lion tamarin (handsome small monkeys) and the woolly spider monkey (the largest primate in the Americas).

The Atlantic forest's distinctive flora – more than half of its tree species exist nowhere else – includes many large trees such as brazilwood, ironwood, Bahian jacaranda and cedar, as well as a number of rare tree ferns.

The conservation effort received a boost in 1999 when UNESCO placed 33 separate areas in Paraná, São Paulo, Espírito Santo and Bahia states, totaling 5820 sq km, on the World Heritage List.

CAATINGA

Caatinga is the natural vegetation of much of the interior of the Northeast region plus bits of Minas Gerais state, totaling some 11% of Brazilian territory – although less than one-tenth of this is in its natural state. Caatinga is semi-arid, with vegetation composed mainly of cacti and thorny shrubs adapted to lack of water and extreme heat.

Rainfall (300 to 800mm a year) is irregular, and often torrential when it comes, but when it does rain, the trees break into leaf and the ground turns green.

Wildlife tends to be nocturnal or subterranean, and much of it – anteaters and armadillos, for example – has been severely depleted by

hunting and habitat destruction. The handsome laughing falcon is a typical sight in caatinga skies, but the last known wild spix macaw, a beautiful, iridescent blue bird, disappeared from its haunts near Curaçá, Bahia, in 2000. The demise of the last spix leaves another caatinga denizen, the Lear's macaw, as the world's rarest macaw, with about 150 left.

Wood and coal from the caatingas are a primary energy source for many of the region's 20 million inhabitants. Wood and coal also fuel 30% of the Northeast's industries, generating many jobs and contributing 15% of the income on rural properties. Centuries of cattle ranching, and more recent ill-advised attempts at irrigated, pesticide-aided agriculture, have devastated large areas of caatinga. Studies have predicted that continued destruction at the present rate will see the caatingas disappear in Paraíba in about 25 years, in Pernambuco in 35 years, in Ceará in 45 years and in Rio Grande do Norte in 60 years.

CERRADO

Cerrado covers the central high plains of Brazil – 2 million sq km in a rough triangle from southern Minas Gerais to Mato Grosso to southern Maranhão. Typical cerrado is open savanna grasslands dotted with trees, though it can edge into scrub or palm stands or even fairly thick gallery forest. Plant diversity is great – an estimated 10,000 species, of which 44% are found nowhere else in the world, and which are used to produce cork, fibers, oils, handicrafts, medicines and food. Medicinal plants native to cerrado include arnica and golden trumpet.

More than half the original cerrado vegetation has already been cleared, and less than 2% is under environmental protection. In the past the major problem was mining, which contaminated rivers with mercury and caused erosion and serious silting of streams. But, since the mid-20th century, intensive farming and cattle ranching, along with an accompanying wave of human settlement, have posed even greater dangers to the natural balance. Intensive farming over large areas, often done with single crops such as soybeans, rice, maize or wheat, has depleted soils and contaminated water and soils with pesticides and fertilizers.

From the cerrado, rivers flow north to Amazonia, south to the Pantanal and east to the coast, meaning that agrotoxics from here can have an effect over a very wide range of Brazilian regions. Proposals for

Left: Armadillo

Butterfly, Iguaçu Falls

Caiman, the Pantanal, Mato Grosso

Fox, the Pantanal

Lion tamarin and baby

Puma cub

White-necked heron, the Pantanal

Crested caracara

Toucan, a treetop-dweller

Macaw, at risk from poachers

Tropical vegetation

Rainforest flora

Cane toad *(Bufo marinus)*

hidrovias – aquatic freeways for the export of products such as soybeans, made by dredging and straightening existing rivers so that they can take large river traffic year-round – threaten yet further ecological interference, including disruption to vital seasonal flood and drainage patterns.

None of this bodes well for such rare and mostly endangered cerrado inhabitants as the maned wolf, giant anteater, giant and three-banded armadillo, pampas deer and the largest bird in Brazil, the non-flying rhea.

PANTANAL

The Pantanal is a vast wetland in the center of South America. It is about half the size of France – 230,000 sq km spread across Brazil, Bolivia and Paraguay. It's the largest inland wetland on earth, and 140,000 sq km of it lies in Brazil, in the states of Mato Grosso and Mato Grosso do Sul.

During the rainy season, from October to March, the waters from the higher surrounding lands run into the Pantanal, inundating as much as two-thirds of it for half the year. The Pantanal, though 2000km upstream from the Atlantic Ocean, is only 100 to 200m above sea level and drains very slowly. Its chief outlet is the Rio Paraguai, which ultimately drains into the Atlantic Ocean via the Rio de la Plata. Waters reach their highest levels, up to 3m above dry-season levels, around March in the northern Pantanal, but not until about June in the south.

This seasonal flooding has made systematic farming impossible and severely limited human incursions into the area. The Pantanal is still one of Brazil's wildest and least explored regions. It's also an enormously rich feeding ground for wildlife, and, if your priority is viewing wildlife, the Pantanal offers greater visible numbers and at least as large a variety of creatures as Amazonia, with which it has many species in common.

The flood waters replenish the soil's nutrients, the waters teem with fish, and the ponds provide excellent ecological niches for many animals and plants. Birds fly in flocks of thousands and gather in enormous rookeries. Six different species may nest on a single tree branch.

With cerrado to the east, Amazon rainforest to the north and spots of Atlantic rainforest to the south, Pantanal vegetation – 1700 plant species – is a mishmash of savanna, forest, meadows and even, on some of the highest points, caatinga. In the dry season the lagoons and marshes dry out and fresh grasses emerge on the savanna, while hawks and alligators compete for fish in the shrinking ponds.

The environment supports about 650 bird species – including kites, hawks, herons, woodpeckers, ibises, storks, kingfishers, hummingbirds, parakeets, toucans and macaws. The Pantanal's substantial number of nesting birds settling like snow in the birds of prey reflects its abundance of food sources. Snails, inse 260 fish species form the basis of the diet of the numerous Pantanal.

A mere list can't do justice to the color of a flock o or the clumsiness of the jabiru stork, the me scarlet-collared symbol of the Pantanal, no of nesting birds settling like snow in the ing flock of rheas. Listen for the c quero-quero (I want, I want) in Brazil for its distinctive call. If you're very lucky you'll see the endangered hyacinth macaw.

The Pantanal is also a haven for some 50 reptile and 80 mammal species, including anacondas (though snakes on the whole are not common), iguanas, jaguars, ocelots, pumas, maned wolves, pampas and marsh deer, giant and collared anteaters, four species of armadillo, black

Poaching & Pollution in the Pantanal

Poachers are doing more damage to the Pantanal than to any other region in Brazil, including Amazonia. Although game-hunting has been illegal here since 1967, considerable poaching continues. It's difficult to determine the number of animals killed each year, but estimates start at 500,000.

Animals are smuggled into Bolivia and Paraguay, where poaching is also illegal but the relevant laws are not enforced in even a token manner. The Brazilian government has done little to stem the slaughter, although efforts have improved marginally in recent years. A poorly funded Institute of Environmental Poaching & Control exists in Mato Grosso do Sul, but few prosecutions have been made. In February 1999, authorities uncovered an attempt to smuggle 24 eggs of the endangered hyacinth macaw from São Paulo to the US – the value of each eggs was estimated at US$10,000.

The slow and fearless alligator is easily shot at short range. An alligator skin commands a price of up to US$500, but only the supple, small-scaled skin of the jacaré's flanks is used (to make fashionable wallets, belts, purses and shoes). The rest of the carcass is discarded.

Just as poachers supply the fashion industry with skins, they supply American pet shops with rare tropical fish and birds. A hyacinth macaw, for example, will sell in the US for US$6000 to US$12,000 – though a person involved in the early stages of poaching actually receives very little of this money.

In addition to the damage caused by poachers, the Pantanal faces a range of other threats, from hydroelectric plants to indiscriminate farming in the surrounding uplands that results in erosion and silting in the wetlands.

Tourism is booming – the industry hoped for 1 million visitors to the Pantanal in 2001 – but is at least starting to be regulated with a modicum of efficacy. And a plan to deepen and straighten the Rio Paraguai into a massive hidrovia (aquatic freeway) through the Pan-tanal, from Cáceres in the north to Uruguay in the south, was shelved by ...azilian government in 2001. Subsequent attempts to detach ...astructure projects from the overall hidrovia plan, including ...rge port at Morrinho south of Cáceres, were put on hold ...onmental-impact study. The central purpose of the ...rport Mato Grosso soybeans via the Rio de la ...ould damage the Pantanal's seasonal water-

howler and brown capuchin monkeys, tapirs, opossums, crab-eating raccoons, crab-eating foxes – and somewhere between 10 and 35 million alligators.

The capybara, the world's largest rodent, is the most visible mammal in the Pantanal, with a population of about 600,000. It's often seen in family groups or even large herds.

The giant river otter has been hunted almost out of existence here. The marsh deer, down to about 35,000 in number, is also at risk. Both anteater species and the maned wolf are endangered and not easily seen: Local people prize anteater meat. The killing of anteaters has led to an increase in ants and termites, and many *fazendas* (ranches) use dangerous pesticides to destroy the mounds.

With thousands of alligators sunning themselves on the edge of each and every body of water, it's hard to believe that they are endangered by poachers (see the boxed text 'Poaching & Pollution in the Pantanal'). Alligators feed mainly on fish, and are the primary check on the growth of the piranha population, which has been growing rapidly as a result of alligator slaughter. The size of an adult alligator is determined by the availability of food: Those on the river's edge are often a lot bigger than those that feed in small ponds.

Cattle live pretty much in harmony with the wildlife, grazing during the dry season and gathering on the little islets that form during the wet. Though some jaguars eat only their natural prey, such as capybara and tapir, others will attack sick or injured cattle, and the occasional big cat goes on a rampage, killing healthy cattle. These rogue jaguars (and, unfortunately, sometimes others) are then killed by cattle ranchers. Jaguars are also killed for their skins and are threatened with extinction in the Pantanal.

OTHER VEGETATION ZONES

The mountainous regions of southern Brazil were once covered by coniferous forests dominated by the prehistoric-looking, 30- to 40m-high araucaria (Paraná pine) tree. The araucaria forests have been decimated by timber cutters and now survive only in scattered areas such as the Aparados da Serra, São Joaquim and Serra da Bocaina national parks and the Parque Estadual Horto Florestal in São Paulo state, generally at altitudes above 500m.

Apart from the cerrado, grasslands occur chiefly in Brazil's far north (northern Roraima) and far south (Rio Grande do Sul). Unlike the cerrado, which has a consistent scattering of medium to tall trees, the Roraima grasslands or savannas have only low trees and bushes, while the *campos do sul* on the rolling southern plains (*pampas*) generally have no trees except where interspersed with patches of woodland.

Wildlife

The richness and diversity of Brazilian fauna are astounding. The following brief portraits cover a selection of the most exciting and most frequently seen species. Many of them are widely distributed around the country. Portuguese names and (in italics) scientific names are included to help identification: The Portuguese names are often the only ones local guides know.

MAMMALS
Edentates

This order covers anteaters, sloth and armadillos. Edentate means toothless, but that's not strictly true of sloth.

The giant anteater (tamanduá bandeira; *Myrmecophaga tridactyla*) can grow well over 2m long: Its Portuguese name, which means 'flag

anteater,' refers to its long, hairy tail, which waves like a flag as the creature forages for ants and termites, tearing open their nests with its sharp claws and eating 35,000 a day with its long, sticky tongue. You're most likely to see the giant anteater in cerrado savanna habitat. Its meat is prized in some areas of Brazil, and it's a threatened species. The collared or lesser anteater (tamanduá mirim or tamanduá colete; *Tamandua tetradactyla*), up to 1.4m long, is yellow and black, mainly nocturnal and often climbs trees.

Sloths (preguiças), true to their name, move very slowly. And they're not, by the look of it, too bright. They hang upside down from branches by strong arms and legs, feeding on leaves, sleeping up to 18 hours a day and descending to the ground to excrete just once a week. Surprisingly, they're good swimmers. You have a good chance of seeing some if you get a bit off the beaten track in Amazonia: From a moderate distance they look like clumps of vegetation high in trees. The species you're most likely to see is the brown-throated three-toed sloth (preguiça de três dedos; *Bradypus variegatus*).

Brazil's several species of armadillo (tatu) are mainly nocturnal and rarely seen. Two of them are endangered.

Primates

About 75 of the world's 250 primate species are found in Brazil, many of them unique to the country. Some are hunted for their meat. On an Amazon jungle trip you're very likely to see groups of monkeys moving through trees.

The most common primate in Amazonia is the little squirrel monkey

Left: Giant Anteater

(macaco-de-cheiro or mico-de-cheiro; *saimiri sciureus*), with its pale face, dark nose area, big ears and long tail. It moves in small, noisy groups. The black spider monkey (macaco prêto or macaco aranha; *Ateles paniscus*), up to 1.5m long (60% tail) and with long, thin limbs and prehensile tail, is fairly common in parts of Amazonia where it isn't hunted. The woolly spider monkey (muriqui or mono-carvoeiro; *Brachyteles arachnoides*) is not a true spider monkey, and it has thicker, brown fur. It's the largest primate in the Americas, and is endangered: The Parque Nacional da Serra da Bocaina is its main stronghold.

Howler monkeys (guariba, bugio or barbado in Portuguese) are much easier heard than seen: Their roar (not really a howl) carries over many kilometers. They're stocky, up to 1.25m long (half tail), and live in groups of up to 20 that are led by a single male, usually 10 to 20m high in trees. In Amazonia you're most likely to encounter the red howler *(Alouatta seniculus)*. Farther south, including in the Pantanal, the black howler *(A. caraya)* is the local species. The brown howler monkey *(A. fusca)* inhabits Mata Atlântica.

Capuchin monkeys are named for the hair atop their heads, which resembles a monk's cowl. They're widely dispersed – found in Amazonia, the Pantanal, the cerrado and the Mata Atlântica (even Rio de Janeiro's Tijuca forest) – living in groups of up to 20 led by one male. The usual species is the brown capuchin (macaco-prego; *Cebus apella*), measuring up to 1m (half tail).

The two types of uakari monkey, black-headed and bald, inhabit Amazonian flooded forest. The bald uakari (uacari or bicó; *Cacajao calvus)* has a red or pink bald head and thick, shaggy body fur ranging from chestnut-red to white (giving rise to the popular names red uakari and white uakari). The monkey's red complexion and baldness has earned it the nickname *macaco-inglês* (English monkey) – for its resemblance to sunburned, drunken English people! Uakaris are endangered, but if you happen to visit the Mamirauá reserve you stand a good chance of seeing the very distinctive white uakari.

Around 20 species of marmosets and tamarin, small – often very small – primates, are found in Brazil. In Portuguese they're generally called sauim, saguim, sagui or soim. Scientifically the marmosets belong to the genera *Cebuella, Callithrix* and *Callimico,* and the tamarins to *Leontopithecus* and *Saguinus.* Some are fairly common, but the four species of lion tamarin (mico-leão; genus *Leontopithecus),* inhabitants of the Atlantic rainforests with a resemblance to miniature lions, are all endangered. The golden lion tamarin (mico-leão-dourado; *L. rosalia)* exists only in the Reserva Biológica Poço das Antas in Rio de Janeiro state (within earshot of the interstate Hwy BR-101). A conservationists' campaign to save this species – a squirrel-sized creature with a brilliant orange-gold color – has, amazingly, brought it back from near-extinction. Its population, down to about 100 in the 1970s, passed the 1000 mark in 2001, and the golden lion tamarin has become a symbol of the whole struggle to save the remaining Atlantic rainforests.

Carnivores

Everyone dreams of sighting a wild jaguar (onça pintada; *Panthera onca)*, but few see one. This biggest American feline – yellow with black spots – is widely but thinly distributed in Brazil, occurring in Amazonia, the Pantanal, the cerrado and such easterly national parks as Caparaó, Ilha Grande, Monte Pascoal, Chapada Diamantina and Chapada dos Veadeiros. A male jaguar can grow 2.5m long including tail, and weigh 120kg (females, up to 90kg). The black panther (onça preta), found in Amazonia, is simply an all-black jaguar.

Jaguars hunt at night, covering large distances. They prey on a wide variety of animals, in trees, water and on the ground, including sloths, monkeys, fish, deer, tapirs, capybaras and agoutis – but rarely people. They're generally solitary and, unusually among cats, good swimmers.

Brazil's five other wild cats are also widely but sparsely distributed, and endangered and rarely seen. The puma (suçuarana or onça parda; *Felis concolor)*, almost as big as the jaguar, is the same beast as North America's cougar or mountain lion. As well as feeding on deer, it's known to attack herds of domestic animals such as sheep or goats. Three smaller cats have markings similar to the jaguar's: The largest of them (up to 1.4m with tail, and 15kg) is the ocelot (jaguatirica or gato-maracajá; *F. pardalis)*; next largest in size is the margay (jaguatirica or gato-maracajá or gato-do-mato-grande; *F. wiedii)*; and then the oncilla (jaguatirica or gato-do-mato-pequeno; *F. tigrina)*. Probably more often seen than any other Brazilian feline, because it's active by day, is the jaguarundi (gato-mourisco; *F. yaguaroundi)*. It's similar in size to the margay, and has a uniformly colored coat, which may be black or any shade of brown or gray.

The widespread coati (quati; *Nasua nasua)* is one of the creatures you're most likely to come across – possibly as a pet, for it's easily tamed. It's furry and cute, the size of a small or medium-sized dog, with a long brown-and-yellow-ringed tail, and a long, flexible snout that it uses to nose around for food on the ground or up in trees.

Scientifically the coati is a procyonid – one of the raccoon family. Its distant relative, the crab-eating raccoon (guaxirim or mão-pelada; *Procyon cancrivorus)*, has a ringed tail and black eye mask, like the North American raccoon. It's found in Amazonia, the Pantanal and in between, always near water, where it finds its diet of crabs, fish, mollusks and small amphibians.

The giant otter (ariranha; *Pteronura brasiliensis,* can measure 2m from nose to tip of tail. It inhabits lakes and calm rivers in forests from Amazonia to the Pantanal, usually in family groups of six to eight. The Alta Floresta district and Reserva Xixuaú-Xiparíná are two areas where visitors regularly see giant otters. This species sometimes eats snakes, birds and even small alligators, as well as fish. The smaller southern river otter (lontra; *Lutra longicaudis)* is also widely dispersed.

The maned wolf (lobo guará; *Chrysocyon brachyurus)* inhabits cerrado and the Pantanal. It's russet-colored, fox-faced and long-legged, about 1m long (plus tail) and has a mane of darker hair on the back of the neck. It's hunted, and is another threatened species. Other Brazilian members of the dog family include the crab-eating fox (lobinho or cachorro do mato; *Cerdocyon thous)* and the bush dog (cachorro do mato vinagre; *Speothos venaticus),* both present in cerrado and Pantanal. You'd be lucky to see any of these three.

Ungulates

Though no longer used in formal classification, the term ungulate generally refers to hoofed quadrupeds.

The Brazilian tapir (anta; *Tapirus terrestris)* occurs in most forested parts of the country but is shy and nocturnal. Related to the horse and about the size of stocky pony (it can weigh 300kg), the tapir has a long snout that helps it forage for leaves, fruit and roots. It rarely strays far from mud, which it uses to keep cool and control parasites.

Peccaries – similar to wild boars – are fairly widely distributed in forests. They live in groups, are active by day, and consume a diet of fruit, roots, carrion and small animals. The collared peccary (cateto or caititu; *Pecari tajacu),* around 1m long and weighing 20kg, is named for the light-colored semicircle below its neck and is found in groups of 10 to 50. The slightly bigger white-lipped peccary (queixada or porco-do-mato; *Tayassu pecari)* travels in groups of 50 or more.

In the Pantanal, most people see at least a few deer. The biggest, which is active by day, is the marsh deer (cervo-do-pantanal; *Blastocerus dichotomus),* with antlers that can grow to 60cm. Other species – some found as far north as Amazonia – include the pampas deer (veado-campeiro; *Ozotoceros bezoarticus),* which lives more out in the open than most other deer, and the small (60 to 70cm long) gray brocket deer (veado-catingueiro; *Mazama gouazoubira)* and the red brocket deer (veado-mateiro; *M. americana).*

Rodents

The widespread capybara (capivara; *Hydrochaeris hydrochaeris)* is the world's largest rodent, 1m long and up to 70kg in weight. It has a guinea-pig-like face and a bulky, hairy body but no tail. It's vegetarian and at home on land or in water. Herds of up to 40 may be seen

in the Pantanal. Smaller rodents – but still up to 60 or 70cm long – include the paca (paca; *Agouti paca)* and various species of agouti (cutia; genus *Dasyprocta).* You can distinguish the paca by its rows of white spots. Porcupines (ouriço or porco-espinho) are rodents too: Brazil has several tree-dwelling species.

Right: Capybara

Aquatic Mammals

On many rivers in the Amazon basin you should catch glimpses of the pink dolphin (boto or boto cor-de-rosa; *Inia geoffrensis*). One of the world's five freshwater cetaceans, it lives only in the Amazon and Orinoco rivers and their tributaries – and it really is pink! It's most often seen where tributaries meet larger rivers, and is most active in early morning and late afternoon. Sightings are tantalizing – and getting good photos virtually impossible – as the dolphin surfaces unpredictably, for just a second or so at a time, to breathe. Often they don't even lift their heads above the surface – but now and then, they do! The pink dolphin has a lumpy forehead, a long beak, no dorsal fin (just a ridge), and tiny eyes – it's almost blind but has a highly evolved sonar system. Adults are 1.8 to 2.5m long, weighing 85 to 160kg.

Amazonian rivers are also home to the gray dolphin (tucuxi; *Sotalia fluviatilis*), a bit smaller than the pink but often found together with it. Unlike the pink dolphin, the gray also inhabits the sea, in coastal waters from Florianópolis to Panama. When it surfaces it usually lifts its head and part of its body out of the water.

Larger than the dolphins is the Amazon manatee (peixe-boi; *Trichechus inunguis*), a slow-moving vegetarian that is illegally hunted for its meat by riverbank-dwellers, and consequently in danger of extinction. Prospects are even poorer for the marine West Indian manatee (peixe-boi-marinho; *T. manatus*), just 400 of which are left in coastal waters north of the mouth of the Amazon.

Seven whale species occur off the coasts of Brazil. The country's first dedicated whale sanctuary was declared along 130km of the Santa Catarina coast in 2000, to protect the southern right whale (baleia franca do sul; *Eubalaena australis*), once the abundant raw material of a Brazilian whaling industry but now down to a world population of about 7000. Mothers and calves can be seen from Praia de Rosa beach between June and October.

Another rare whale, the humpback (baleia jubarte; *Megaptera novaeangliae*), breeds in the same months in the Parque Nacional Marinho de Abrolhos, off the coast of southern Bahia. Arraial do Cabo, Rio de Janeiro state, is another good humpback-watching spot.

The Fernando de Noronha archipelago, off Natal in Northeast Brazil, is a good site for observing the spinner dolphin (golfinho rotador; *Stenella longirostris*), a small marine dolphin less than 1.8m long.

REPTILES
Snakes

The general Brazilian word for snake is *cobra*. The infamous anaconda (sucuri; *Eunectes notaeus* or *E. murinus*) can grow up to 10m long and weigh 200kg. It kills its victims by coiling around them to crush and suffocate, then eats them whole. On *extremely* rare occasions, an anaconda gets a person. It's not poisonous but can bite viciously. Generally an olive-brown color with black patterning, anacondas can live in water or on land and are considered common in the Pantanal.

Other constrictor snakes – using the same cheerful coil-crush-suffocate technique – include the boa constrictor (jibóia; *Boa constrictor*), which is 3 to 5m long with mostly brown patterning and lives off small animals in varied and widespread habitats; and the handsome green-and-yellow emerald tree boa *(Corallus caninus)*. A number of other snakes live in trees but most are harmless.

Venomous snakes don't pose major problems to humans, but Brazil has quite a few species of them, including rattlesnakes (cascavel), vipers (vibora, peçonhenta or cobra covinha) and coral snakes (cobra coral). The most dangerous in the Pantanal is Wied's lancehead (jararaca-pintada or boca-de-sapo; *Bothrops neiwiedi*), a gray, black and white patterned viper up to 70cm long that sometimes hides in houses and has a bite that can be fatal if not treated quickly. Also to be steered clear of is the Brazilian coral snake (cobra coral; *Micrurus frontalis*), with its rings of red, black and white. It lurks under rocks or logs and only bites when it feels threatened – but it's very poisonous when it does. The false coral snakes (cobra falsa-coral; genus *Atractus*) are, lucky for them, nearly impossible to distinguish from the real thing.

Alligators

Brazil has five species of alligator or caiman (jacaré). They eat fish, amphibians, crustaceans and some birds. In the Pantanal, the most common is a subspecies called the Paraguayan caiman (jacaré-do-Pantanal; *Caiman crocodilus yacare*). Amazonia has four species. The biggest is the black caiman (jacaré açu; *Melanosuchus niger*), which

Don't Roll with the Alligators

Although they eat young or injured animals, alligators rarely attack people, and capybaras and many birds mingle with them in peace and harmony.

But you must be careful walking in the water. The reptiles will usually swim away before you get close, but if stepped on, they will grab the offending leg and roll. This has probably never happened to a tourist, and rarely does a local Brazilian suffer this unpleasant fate, but even so, the odd alligator attack is used as an excuse by Pantaneiros to justify slaughtering the big creatures.

If this million-to-one nightmare should happen to you, and if, against all the odds, you retain a modicum of composure, it's said that clouting the thing on the nose should make it open its mouth.

reaches up to 6m long and is endangered because it's hunted for its skin and meat. The most common Amazonian alligator – the one you'll probably get to handle on nighttime alligator expeditions – is the spectacled caiman (jacaré tingá; *C. crocodilus*), which can grow up to 2.3m long. Alligator eggs, in nests of leaves and stalks, and are vulnerable to predators such as coatis and lizards; the hatched young are prey to herons and storks.

Turtles

Brazil's five species of sea turtle (tartaruga marina) are all under effective official protection (see the boxed text 'The TAMAR Project to Save Sea Turtles' in the Bahia chapter), though here and there shells are still sold and eggs eaten. There are also several species of river turtle (quelônio).

FISH

Amazonia is home to at least 2000 freshwater fish species, and the Pantanal to 260 species.

The monarch of Amazonian fish is the beautiful and enormous pirarucu (*Arapaima gigas*), which can grow to 3m long and weigh well over 100kg. Its red and silvery-brown scale patterns are reminiscent of Chinese paintings. The pirarucu is a voracious hunter of other fish, and good food for humans. To try to preserve its shrinking population, it's forbidden to catch them if they are less than 1.5m in length or during the October-to-March spawning season.

The pirarucu quite often comes to the river surface to breathe. It's a member of the primitive *Osteoglossiformes* order, characterized by a bony tongue, and rear fins that almost join the tail. The male protects the young for up to the first six months of their lives.

Another Amazonian osteoglossiform, which also has good meat, is the aruanã (*Osteoglossum bicirrhosum*). Up to 1m long, it can leap 2m in the air for fruit or insects. The adult males nurture the young inside their mouths.

The most important food fish of central Amazonia is the little jaraqui (genus *Semaprochilodus*), which swims in shoals of thousands. Two further food fish – the pirapitinga (*Piaractus brachypomus*) and the tambaqui (*Colossoma macropomum*) – are of the same family (Serrasalmidae) as piranhas. The rotund tambaqui can reach 1m in length and weigh up to 25kg. Normally it lives on nuts (which it can crack with its jaws) and seeds, but when the waters recede it turns carnivore.

Amazonia harbors at least 100 species of catfish, named for the long barbels (whiskers) that help them search for food on river bottoms. One catfish, the piraíba or filhote (*Brachyplatystoma filamentosum*), is the biggest of all Amazonian fish, growing up to 3m long and weighing as much as 200kg. It's an aggressive creature and will even attack water birds. The dourado (*B. flavicans*), growing up to 1m long and with pale gold sides, is common in the Pantanal as well as in Amazonia, and is probably the best-tasting catfish. Its diet consists of other fish.

The piramutuba *(B. vaillanti)* lays its eggs on the upper Rio Solimões, then descends in big shoals to mature at the mouth of the Rio Amazonas. It can grow to more than 1m long and is heavily fished on the lower Amazonas.

You will probably hear about the candiru in Amazonia. There are many species of these small catfish of the Trichomycteridae family, most of them pretty obnoxious. The really infamous type of candiru is one of the *Vandellia* genus, about 5cm long. This little charmer normally lives inside the gills of other fish to suck their blood, but is attracted to urine and reputedly able to wriggle up humans' urinary tracts, where it lodges itself with sharp spines and can only be removed by surgery. The belief that it can actually swim up a stream of urine to get inside you is almost certainly false, but it's probably not a good idea to urinate in Amazonian waters! Locals wear clothing to exclude the candiru in areas where it's known.

Other best-avoided inhabitants of Brazilian fresh waters include the stingray (arraia; *Potamotrygon motoro)* and the electric eel (poraquê; *Electrophorus electricus).* The stingray lives on river floors, and if you should step on it can inflict deep, painful cuts with barbs in its tail. To avoid this, slide your feet along the bottom as you walk. The electric eel,

Piranha Lunch

People eat piranhas a billion times more often than piranhas eat people, and the fish is reasonably tasty, if a bit small and bony. On an Amazon jungle trip you'll very likely find yourself trying to catch your own piranha lunch. You'll be taken by canoe to some propitious spot, with a simple fishing rod constructed of cane, line and hook, and a supply of small chunks of meat for bait. Pop a piece of bait onto the hook, dangle it into the water, and – hey, presto – free lunch! For the piranhas, that is, who will deftly nibble bait after bait off your hook without biting once.

Your local companions, however, will land half a dozen of the ugly little snappers without even trying – and these will be *your* lunch.

A piranha is not just a piranha, of course. It could be any of about 50 species of the *Serrasalmus* genus. Piranhas are found in the basins of Amazon, Orinoco, Paraguai and São Francisco rivers and in the rivers of the Guianas. Some live on seeds and fruits, some on other fish (some little blighters eat just the scales or fins of other fish), and only a handful of species are potentially a risk to larger creatures. These types are at their least amiable when stuck in tributaries, meanders or lakes that get cut off from main rivers in the dry season. When they have eaten all the other fish, the piranhas will attack more or less anything, including wounded mammals entering their waters. The scent of blood or bodily fluids in the water can whip a shoal into delirium. Confirmed accounts of human fatalities caused by piranhas are *extremely* few and far between, but plenty of Amazonia river folk have scars or missing fingers to testify just how sharp and vicious those little triangular piranha teeth are.

up to 2.75m long, is capable of a 600-volt discharge to stun its prey and could kill a human with a volley of electric pulses.

A fish that, by contrast, is very much sought after in Amazonia – both for its delicious taste and its famous fighting qualities as a sport fish – is the peacock bass or tucunaré *(Cichla monoculus)*. Growing to 50cm or more, it has a peacock-like 'eye' spot on its tail. Also sought – for home aquariums the world over – are the tiny but brightly colored tetra fish (genus: *Hyphassobrycon*). They come from the murky flooded forests *(igapós)* of Amazonia, where they would doubtless go unseen if more demurely pigmented.

BIRDS

Almost everywhere in Brazil, birds form a major proportion of the observed wildlife. The bird life is amazingly colorful, plentiful and varied – the stronger your binoculars, the better!

The biggest Brazilian bird is the flightless rhea (ema; *Rhea americana)*, found in the cerrado and Pantanal. It grows to 1.4m tall and weighs around 30kg.

Waterfowl

Widely seen freshwater fishing birds include a couple of types of cormorant (biguá; genus *Phalacrocorax)* and the similar anhinga (biguatinga or carará; *Anhinga anhinga)*. You can often see them standing on waterside branches, their wings spread out to dry.

The *Ciconiiformes* order comprises herons (garça or socó), egrets (garça or garcinha), storks (cegonhas), ibises (curicaca) and their relatives. They're mostly large, highly visible birds, often seen flapping inelegantly along waterways or standing motionless in shallows or on branches just above the water ready to jab for fish with their long beaks. Many species are found in the Pantanal and Amazonia. The tiger heron (socó-boi; *Tigrisoma lineatum)*, with its brown and black stripes, is particularly distinctive. Hundreds of snowy egrets (garcinha; *Egretta thula)* gather by in waterside rookeries, looking like a sudden blooming of white flowers in the treetops.

Of the storks, the tall (1.40m) black-headed and red-necked jabiru (tuiuiú or jaburu; *Jabiru mycteria)* has become a symbol of the Pantanal and is also found in Amazonia. In the Pantanal, also look for the similarly-sized maguari stork (tabuiaiá; *Ciconia maguari)*, mainly white with a pinkish face, and the smaller wood stork (cabeça-seca; *Mycteria americana)*, with its black head and beak with a curved end. The beautiful pink roseate spoonbill (colhereiro; *Platalea ajaja)* is another Pantanal inhabitant of this order. Brazil's most spectacular ibis is the scarlet ibis (guará; *Eudocimus ruber)*, which is very pink, 50cm long and found living in flocks on the Ilha do Marajó at the mouth of the Amazon.

Kingfishers (martim-pescador or ariramba in Portuguese) are among the most visible birds along many of Brazil's waterways, flying across or along rivers as boats approach. There are several species, the biggest being the 42cm-long ringed kingfisher (martim-pescador-matraca, martim-pescador-grande or ariramba-grande; *Ceryle torquata*), which is predominantly bright turquoise with a rust-colored underside.

Birds of Prey

Brazil has around 40 species of eagles, hawks, falcons, kites, caracaras and kestrels, some quite common, and they're generally not easy to tell apart. The word gavião is used for almost any of them; águia means eagle and falcão means falcon.

The crested caracara (caracará or carcará; *Polyborus plancus*) is common in many areas: It's 50 to 60cm long with a 1.2 or 1.3m wingspan. Its broad diet includes fish dying for lack of oxygen as Pantanal ponds dry up, and animals that have been run over on roads or burnt in forest fires. Also common in Amazonia and the Pantanal are the yellow-headed caracara (gavião-pinhé or carrapateiro; *Milvago chimachima*), about 40cm long, and the black-collared hawk (gavião-belo; *Busarellus nigricollis*), a reddish-brown fish-catcher about 45cm long, with a white head and chest. The osprey (aguia pescadora; *Pandion haliaetus*), or fishing eagle, is bigger (55 to 60cm; wingspan 1.45 to 1.7m), with a darker brown body.

Brazil's most emblematic bird of prey is the ferocious, very large (and rare) harpy eagle (águia real or harpia; *Harpia harpyja*), found chiefly in Amazonia, where it enjoys a diet of monkeys, sloths and other large animals (see the boxed text 'The Harpy Eagle's Fight for Survival' in the Mato Grosso & Mato Grosso do Sul chapter).

Macaws & Parrots

These are the kind of birds people travel intercontinentally to see, and there are dozens of different species. The general Brazilian word for macaw is arara; for parrot, it's papagaio or maracanã; for parakeet, periquito. These birds have strong, curved beaks that they use to break open seeds and nuts.

Macaws, the biggest of these birds, grab most of the glamour. You can distinguish them by their dead-straight body shape when flying, and straight-as-an-arrow trajectory. They often go in pairs and make a lot of raucous noise. They travel up to 25km a day foraging for food.

The name of scarlet macaw (arara vermelha) is given to two large, gloriously colored species – *Ara chloroptera*, also called the red-and-green macaw, 90 to 95cm long with blue-and-green wings and a red-striped face,

Right: Macaws

Not a Fossil

The hoatzin (cigana; *Opisthocomus hoazin*) is a turkey-sized, clumsily flying Amazonian bird with a tatty crest, large blue rings around its bright eyes and a bad smell caused by its slow digestive processes. The young have claws on their wings, which were once thought to be evidence that the hoatzin descended from the archaeopteryx, a prehistoric bird. In fact, the chicks use these claws to climb back up to the nest after they have jumped out to escape predators. The hoatzin may be most closely related to the cuckoo. But it's still enough of a freak to be the unique member of its family, the Opisthocomidae.

and *A. macao*, a bit smaller, with blue-and-yellow wings. The latter bird is restricted to Amazonia, but the red-and-green also inhabits other regions, including the Pantanal, cerrado and even the caatinga. The blue-and-yellow macaw (arara-amarela or arara-canindé; *A. ararauna)*, about 85cm long, is also widely distributed. The yellow covers its underside, the blue its upper parts.

Unfortunately, the beautiful plumage of the macaws makes them a major target for poachers. Poaching has contributed greatly to the decline of the hyacinth macaw (arara-azul; *Anodorhynchus hyacinthinus)*, the world's largest parrot (1m long), which is endemic to the Pantanal. This gorgeous bird, deep blue with splashes of bright yellow on the face, is down to a population of about 3000, and conservationists are struggling to bring it back from the verge of extinction.

Hummingbirds

These beautiful little birds, with their dazzling iridescent colors, may be seen all over Brazil, including cities. They beat their wings up to 80 times a second, which allows them to hover while extracting pollen from flowers – making a light humming noise as they do so. They flit rapidly, almost insect-like, from one spot to the next, and can even fly backward. The poetic Brazilian name for them is beija-flor *(flower-kisser)*. There are many dozens of species (family Trochilidae*)*.

Trogons

This family of medium-sized, brightly colored, sometimes iridescent birds with long tails – called surucuá or saracuá in Portuguese – includes the celebrated quetzals. You may see them perching and flying at medium height in tropical forests. Amazonia has at least seven species, including the pavonine quetzal (surucuá açu; *Pharomacrus pavoninus)*. The blue-crowned trogon (surucuá-de-coroa-azul; *Trogon curucui)* also inhabits the Pantanal.

Toucans

Among the most emblematic and colorful groups of Latin American birds, toucans have huge beaks, sometimes as long as their bodies, which enable them to reach berries at the end of branches. But the beak is light and almost hollow, allowing the birds to fly with a surprising agility. They live at forest treetop level and are often best seen from boats. In Portuguese, some are called tucano, others araçari.

Brazil's biggest is the toco toucan (tucanuçu or tucano; *Ramphastos toco*), with habitats ranging from Amazonia to the cerrado to the Pantanal. The bird is around 55cm long, including its bright orange beak, and its plumage is black except for a white neck area. In Amazonia you may see the white-throated toucan (tucano-assoviador; *Ramphastos tucanus*) or the yellow-ridged toucan (tucano-rouco or tucano pequeno de papo branco; *R. culminatus*). Both of these birds are fairly large, with black beaks.

Conservation Units

Much of Brazil is, officially at least, under environmental protection. Over 350 areas throughout the country, covering more than 300,000 sq km (more than 5% of Brazil), are protected in a confusing variety of conservation units, ranging from national parks and national forests to extractive reserves and sustainable development reserves. Some of these are run by the federal government, some by state governments and some by private individuals or nongovernmental organizations.

Unfortunately, the degree of protection the units actually receive is also variable and in some cases practically nonexistent. The federal government's environmental agency, IBAMA (Instituto Brasileiro do Meio Ambiente e dos Recursos Naturais Renováveis; Brazilian Institute of the Environment & Renewable Natural Resources) has a minuscule budget and is even unable to protect many of the 40 national parks from illegal logging, ranching, settlement and poaching.

Permits, or at least an official guide, are needed to visit many conservation units legally. Wherever possible, regulations of this type are cited in this book.

The categories Parque Nacional (PARNA; National Park), Parque Estadual (PES; State Park), Estacão Ecológica (ESEC; Ecological Station), Reserva Biológica (REBIO; Biological Reserve), and Reserva Ecológica (RESEC; Ecological Reserve) are classified as *de Uso Indireto* (Indirect Use). This means that their ecosystems are supposedly under total government protection.

Flora and fauna may not be consumed, collected, damaged or destroyed. National and state parks and ecological stations are also designated exclusively for scientific research. In national and state parks, recreational uses and ecological tourism are also permitted.

The categories Área de Protecão Ambiental (APA; Environmental Protection Area), Área de Relevante Interesse Ecológico (ARIE; Area of Ecological Interest), Floresta Nacional (FLONA; National Forest), Floresta Estadual (FES; State Forest), and Reserva Extrativista (RESEX; Extractive Reserve) are all *de Uso Direto* (Direct Use), meaning their resources can be exploited or managed in ways compatible with nature conservation. National and state forests are areas of predominantly native forest, geared to sustainable exploitation and scientific research. Extractive reserves are areas with human populations dependent on traditional extractive activities – such as rubber tapping, fruit or nut collecting or fishing – in conjunction with subsistence agriculture. Extractive reserves are dedicated to protecting these peoples' ways of life while ensuring the sustainable use of reserve resources.

Any of these conservation units can be run at either the state or federal level (except, of course, for national and state parks, and national and state forests, which are run at federal or state level as their titles indicate).

Three more state-level categories – Reserva de Desenvolvimento Sustentável (REDS; Sustainable Development Reserve), Floresta Estadual de Rendimento Sustentável (FERS; Sustainable-Yield State Forest) and Floresta Estadual Extrativista (FEEX; State Extractive Forest) – aim to combine sustainable exploitation, research into resource management, and improved living standards for local populations.

Private owners can also create nature reserves under the title Reserva Particular Patrimônio Natural (RPPN; Private Natural Heritage Reserve).

Terras Indígenas (Indigenous Lands) occupy about 11% of Brazilian territory. Though these are not explicitly dedicated to nature conservation, their Indian inhabitants tend to use them with minimal environmental impact.

Where to Go

In many regions, national parks offer the best opportunities for getting close to nature. See the regional chapters for much more detail.

Two of the best things you can take with you on any nature trip are strong binoculars and a good guide – both will reveal things you'd otherwise never guess at. For further tips on what to take, see the Pantanal section in the Mato Grosso & Mato Grosso do Sul chapter, the introduction to the North section, and Photography & Video in the Facts for the Visitor chapter.

SOUTHEAST

In Rio de Janeiro itself, the **Parque Nacional da Tijuca** offers magnificent panoramic views and walks in lush Mata Atlântica. The mountainous Parque Nacional do Itatiaia, 150km northwest of the city, is a favorite with walkers and climbers – its big attraction is the Agulhas Negras (2787m) peak. Some 400 bird and 67 mammal species have been recorded here. Another climbing mecca is the Parque Nacional da Serra dos Órgãos, 86km northeast of Rio. As well as spectacular peaks, it offers some great walks, with plenty of trails. These last two parks both possess a well-developed visitor infrastructure.

The **Parque Nacional da Serra da Bocaina** is where the coastal escarpment meets the sea, and the Atlantic rainforest quickly changes to araucaria forest as you move up from the coast. The varied and plentiful wildlife includes the endangered woolly spider monkey. The park is not easily accessible but has many walking trails.

The **Iporanga** area of São Paulo state is one of the least disturbed zones of Atlantic forest, and it is of international importance for its biodiversity.

The **Parque Nacional de Caparaó** contains Brazil's third-highest peak, **Pico da Bandeira** (2890m), where you can reach the summit in a day hike from campsites in the park or accommodations just outside it.

The **Parque Nacional da Serra do Cipó**, northeast of Belo Horizonte, is a beautiful area of mountains, waterfalls and cerrado, noted for its many flower species. You can camp in or near the park or stay in a nearby pousada. Also in Minas Gerais is the **Parque Natural do Caraça**, a beautiful transition area between Mata Atlântica and wild mountain vegetation, with easily accessible hiking trails and creeks that form waterfalls and natural swimming pools.

SOUTH

More than 340 bird and 40 mammal species have been recorded in the forests of the **Parque Nacional do Iguaçu**, on the Brazilian side of the famous Iguaçu Falls, but for those interested in fauna and flora, the Argentine Parque Nacional del Iguazú on the far side of the falls is actually better.

On the coast of Paraná is the **Parque Nacional do Superaguí**, with one of the largest remaining tracts of Mata Atlântica, offering hiking, beaches and pousadas in the village of Vila do Superaguí. The park's abundant wildlife includes the rare black-faced lion tamarin, a small primate only discovered in the 1990s (numbering about 400), and the endangered purple-faced parrot. Also notable is the huge number of wild orchids.

Brazil's first whale sanctuary was declared in 2000 along part of the coast of Santa Catarina state. The beautiful bay of **Praia da Rosa** is a breeding ground for southern right whales: Mothers and calves can be seen from the beach from June to October. In Santa Catarina's Serra do Mar, where it even snows sometimes, the **Parque Nacional de São Joaquim** contains rare araucaria forests and dramatic rock formations, but has no infrastructure for visits.

Brazil's southernmost state, Rio Grande do Sul, contains the unforgettable **Parque Nacional de Aparados da Serra**, with the 700m-deep Cânion do Itaimbezinho. This park has trails for day hikes and a visitors' center. The adjoining **Parque Nacional da Serra Geral**, where there is another stunning fissure in the earth, the Cânion da Fortaleza, has no infrastructure, but camping is allowed.

CENTRAL WEST
Pantanal

If you're looking to see animals in the wild, don't miss the Pantanal, which has the greatest concentration of fauna in the New World. In the Amazon, the animals hide in the dense foliage, but in the open spaces of the Pantanal, wildlife is visible to the most casual observer. There are three main access cities for the Brazilian Pantanal – Cuiabá to the north,

Campo Grande to the east and Corumbá to the west.

Basically there are four ways to visit the Pantanal (prices given here include meals): First, you can make your own way along the Transpantaneira, the rough road leading into the northern Pantanal from Poconé, south of Cuiabá. This requires driving or hitchhiking. Accommodations start around US$35/70 a night for singles/doubles, though you can camp here and there.

Second, it is possible to take a safari with a small tour operator from Cuiabá, staying on farms. The approximate cost is US$50 a day.

The third option is to take a cheap three- to four-day tour from Corumbá or Campo Grande, staying in tent or hut camps along Estrada Parque, a 117km dirt road looping through the southern Pantanal. This costs approximately US$30 to $40 a day.

Last, you can base yourself at a *hotel-fazenda* (ranch-style hotel) or pousada and take trips out from there. Many have horses and boats for hire, with room prices between US$35/70 and US$100/170 for singles/doubles, usually including transportation by 4WD, boat or small plane from and back to Corumbá or Cuiabá.

Near the southern Pantanal is the small town of **Bonito**, which has become popular for wetsuit swimming in rivers teeming with fish, and snorkeling and diving in lakes.

If possible, visit the Pantanal during the dry season, which is from April/May to September/October. The best months to watch birds are July to September – but reservations are definitely needed for all accommodations in July.

National Parks

The **Parque Nacional da Chapada dos Veadeiros**, 200km north of Brasília, contains rare fauna and flora, as well as spectacular waterfalls and canyons in a sublime landscape. You need to enter with a guide but this is easy and not too costly to arrange. There are accommodations in the nearby village, São Jorge, and town, Alto Paraíso.

In southwest Goiás is the remote **Parque Nacional das Emas**, the best preserved tract of savanna-like cerrado in Brazil, with abundant visible wildlife including the emas (rheas) for which it's named. Go with a guide from one of the nearby towns. There are no accommodations or camping in the park.

Near Cuiabá is the popular **Parque Nacional da Chapada dos Guimarães**, with its waterfalls, huge valleys and strange rock formations – best visited in a hire-car or on an excursion from nearby Chapada dos Guimarães town, which has accommodations.

NORTHEAST

In Bahia, the **Parque Nacional da Chapada Diamantina** has a network of trails offering great hiking to peaks, waterfalls and rivers. It's easily accessible from the attractive old mining town of Lençóis.

On the southern Bahia coast, the **Parque Nacional de Monte Pascoal**, with ecosystems ranging from Atlantic rainforest to mangroves and reefs, has a visitors' center reachable by taxi from the town of Itamaraju. Guides will accompany you along the park's trails, including up Monte Pascoal itself, which was the first piece of Brazil seen by Portuguese eyes. It's also possible to enter the park from the coastal villages Caraiva and Corumbau, which have accommodations.

The **Eco Parque da Una**, 45km south of Olivença, is a private Atlantic forest reserve where guides will lead you on a two-hour trail to see such rare species as the golden-headed lion tamarin.

Approximately 80km off the southernmost stretch of the Bahia coast is **Parque Nacional Marinho de Abrolhos**. Its attractions are coral reefs, whale-watching and the marine and bird life of the numerous reefs and islets. Access is by organized boat trips, chiefly from Caravelas.

Projeto TAMAR, a government-backed project to save Brazil's five sea turtle species, has 21 stations on the coasts. The headquarters, which you can visit, is at **Praia do Forte** in Bahia. Other stations open to visits are in the **Parque Estadual de Itaúnas** in Espírito Santo, and on the **Fernando de Noronha archipelago**, 350km out into the Atlantic from Natal. The marine and bird life and the diving and snorkeling at Fernando de Noronha are outstanding. Access is by plane from Recife or Natal, and you can go independently or by organized tour from either city. There are plenty of accommodations on the islands.

In Maranhão state, the **Parque Nacional dos Lençóis Maranhenses** has spectacular beaches, mangroves, dunes and lagoons and interesting fauna. You can arrange for access by boat from the town of Barreirinhas, or take a tour from Barreirinhas or São Luis.

NORTH
The Amazon region is trying hard to realize its ecotourism potential and to offer more visitors a richer experience than is available in the immediate vicinity of Manaus. A government program called Proecotur, with funding from the Inter American Development Bank, aims to create 10,000 new jungle-lodge-type beds by 2006 in environmentally protected areas of Amazonia. It's to be hoped this will be done in a small-scale, low-impact way, with community involvement.

On the large **Ilha de Marajó**, in the mouth of the Rio Amazonas, you can stay on a fazenda and explore a unique wetland ecosystem with varied wildlife. In Tocantins state, the **Ilha do Bananal**, a 20,000 sq km island between two branches of the mighty Rio Araguaia, forms a transition zone between cerrado, wetlands and Amazon rainforest. The island and nearby areas are rich in wildlife, and there is lodging available in several nearby spots. In eastern Tocantins, the unique, sparsely populated **Jalapão** district combines cerrado, rivers, lakes and desert-like areas with sand dunes, and can be visited in tours from Palmas city.

Upstream on the Amazon, possibilities in the Santarém region include riverboat excursions to take you through the floodplains and creeks from **Monte Alegre** and **Santarém** itself, and visits to the **Floresta Nacional do Tapajós**.

Manaus is the nature-tourism capital of Brazilian Amazonia. Several jungle lodges are within a few hours of the city by road and/or river. In a stay at one of these – typically costing around US$100 per day in total, including transportation from and back to Manaus – you'll do things like jungle walks, piranha fishing and nighttime alligator spotting. An alternative is to take a tour or river cruise with one of the numerous Manaus agencies. Budget operators cater to backpackers for US$30 to $40 a day, staying a couple of nights in rustic cabins with maybe a night or two camping in the jungle and with many of the same activities as you'd do at a jungle lodge.

At the other end of the price scale, you could take a customized expedition of two weeks (or even longer) to distant tributaries in search of, say, jaguars or rare macaws, for US$150 to $200 per person per day using a reasonably comfortable riverboat. The farther you get from sprawling, urban Manaus, the more wildlife you're likely to see. On a trip of less than five days from Manaus you will probably see pink and gray river dolphins, alligators, piranhas, a fair variety of birds and a few monkeys, but it won't be the teeming jungles you might have imagined.

One of the very best places for wildlife-spotting in Amazonia is the **Reserva de Desenvolvimento Sustentável Mamirauá**, between the Solimões and Japurá rivers, about halfway from Manaus to the Colombian border. Accessible by a couple of hours' motorboat ride from the town of Tefé (which is reachable by plane or riverboat from Manaus or Tabatinga), this floodplain reserve runs a very professional ecotourism program in which you are sure to see plenty of monkeys, sloths, river dolphins, alligators and birds, for an all-inclusive price starting around US$80 a day per person.

Dedicated nature-lovers could consider a trip to the Reserva Xixuaú-Xipariná, $1\frac{1}{2}$ days' boat trip north from Manaus, which has ecotourism facilities and a great abundance and diversity of wildlife. The Parque Nacional do Jaú, in the Rio Negro basin northwest of Manaus, is the world's biggest piece of protected tropical rainforest, very rich in biodiversity. If you have a boat at your disposal, you can enter the park with a permit from IBAMA in Manaus, but visitor facilities are nonexistent. Another area the adventurous and well-funded might head for is the upper Rio Negro, where there's a good lodge in the remote settlement of São Gabriel da Cachoeira. From here it's even possible to mount an expedition up Brazil's highest peak, Pico da Neblina (3014m), on the Venezuelan border. Neblina is in the remote Parque Nacional do Pico da Neblina, which lacks any kind of standard tourist infrastructure.

The contiguous towns of Tabatinga (Brazil) and Leticia (Colombia), in the triple-frontier area where Brazil, Colombia and Peru meet, are jumping-off points for several good ecotourism destinations, including some reasonably priced lodges along the **Rio Javari**, which forms the Brazil-Peru border. Relatively untouched jungle areas are easier to reach here than from Manaus.

In the state of Rondônia, an interesting-looking ecotourism program is being set up along the **Guaporé Valley** and there's a very good

German-run ecolodge, the Hotel Fazenda Rancho Grande, near Ca-caulândia. On the southern edge of the Amazon rainforest in the north of Mato Grosso state, the area around **Alta Floresta** offers some of the best wildlife viewing in all Brazilian Amazonia. Accommodations include the good Cristalino Jungle Lodge.

ORGANIZED TOURS

Plenty of firms inside and outside Brazil are eager to organize an entire nature-oriented trip for you. All will doubtless use the buzz-word 'eco-tourism' somewhere in their blurb. This term has about as many inter-pretations as people who utter it, but those who give thought to such matters consider true ecotourism to mean something more specific than just 'nature tourism.' The real thing should incorporate such elements as education, conservation, sustainable development and benefits to (and involvement with) local communities. It's worth keeping these notions in mind when selecting a tour company. For your own satisfac-tion, you should also look into what equipment the company provides to help you observe fauna and flora (such as a telescope and a tape recorder with playback), what reference materials are available (ask for species lists before the trip) and what qualifications and experience their guides have (look for professional naturalists).

Operators specific to single localities are covered in the regional chap-ters in this book. The following are among the companies offering a wider range of trips.

Focus Tours (☎ 505-466-4688, focustours@aol.com), 103 Moya Rd, Santa Fe, NM 87505-8360, USA, is a highly rated birding and nature tour firm using English-speaking naturalist guides. It uses tape recorders to record and play back calls, encouraging wildlife to come into view. It's active in conservation too. Destinations include the Pantanal, Chapada dos Guimarães, Alta Floresta, the Emas and Itatiaia national parks, Foz do Iguaçu and the Parque Natural do Caraça. Focus' owner, Doug Trent, has been running ecological tours to Brazil since before the word 'ecotourism' was coined, and what he doesn't know about birds isn't worth knowing. Have a look at Focus' very interesting Web site, www.focustours.com.

There's also Brazil Eco Travel Center (☎ 0xx21-2512-8882, info@ ecotravelcenter.com.br), Rua Visconde de Pirajá 572, 7th floor, Ipanema, Rio de Janeiro, which is a dedicated and professional firm offering trips to a complete range of Brazil's best natural destinations, including the Pantanal, national parks in the cerrado and Mata Atlântica. The center offers Amazon lodge and river trips, ascents of the Pico da Neblina and visits to emblematic conservation projects such as Projeto TAMAR in Bahia and the Reserva Biológica Poço das Antas in Rio de Janeiro state. The Web site is www.ecotravelcenter.com.br.

Two very well-established US-based birding tour operators, both vis-iting several different areas of Brazil, are Field Guides (☎ 512-263-7295, toll-free ☎ 800-728-4953), 9433 Bee Cave Rd, Building 1, Suite 150, Austin, TX 78733 (www.fieldguides.com), and Victor Emanuel Nature

Tours (☎ 512-328-5221, toll-free ☎ 800-328-8368), Box 33008, Austin, TX 78764 (www.ventbird.com).

Discover The World (☎ 01737-218802), 29 Nork Way, Banstead, Surrey, SM7 1PB, UK, offers whale-watching stays in Santa Catarina state, with surfing and dolphin-watching thrown in for those who wish. The Web site is www.discover-the-world.co.uk.

Ecotour Expeditions (☎ 401-423-3377, toll-free ☎ 800-688-1822), PO Box 128, Jamestown, RI 02835-0128, USA, does Pantanal lodge trips and boat-based Amazonia trips. The Web site is www.naturetours .com. Forum International (☎ 925-671-2900, toll-free ☎ 800-252-4475), 91 Gregory Lane No 21, Pleasant Hill, CA 94523, USA, offers Amazon river trips, Alta Floresta birding and Pantanal lodge visits. The Web site is www.foruminternational.com.

Environmental Organizations

The Brazilian conservation movement has recently enjoyed some political successes, and the level of environmental awareness in the country is slowly increasing. But there are a great many battles still to fight, not least against the 'megaproject' mentality, which looks to large-scale human interference in nature as the way forward for Brazil's economy. Such interference takes the form of construction of long-distance roads through the rainforest, flooding of large areas for hydroelectricity, the dredging of hundred of kilometers of river for shipping freeways, and the planting of vast areas of bush with chemically fertilized soybeans. In the 1990s, a few environmentalists attained political power – such as Marina Silva, a federal senator from Acre; state governors João Alberto Capiberibe (of Amapá) and Jorge Viana (of Acre); and Mary Allegretti, appointed Amazonia Secretary in the Environment Ministry in 1999. But the 'mega' mentality remains prevalent in most circles of Brazilian government.

The following organizations are among those working actively to protect Brazil's environment. Strategies range from campaigns to save single animal or plant species to lobbying in Brasília and pressuring institutions to stop financing destructive projects. A few groups concentrate primarily on research. Many of their Web sites are in English as well as Portuguese.

Australia
Friends of the Earth (☎ 03-9419-87000), PO Box 222, Fitzroy 3065, Victoria; www.foe.org.au
Greenpeace (☎ 1800-815-151), GPO Box 2622, Sydney, NSW 2001; www.greenpeace.org.au

Brazil
Amigos da Terra – Amazônia Brasileira (Friends of the Earth – Amazonia Program; ☎ 0xx11-3887-9369, fax 0xx11-3884-2795), Rua Bento de Andrade 85, 04503-010 São Paulo. The Web site, at amazonia.org.br, has a good English-language environmental news section.

Conservation International (☎ 0xx31- 3441-1795, info@conservation.org.br), Avenida Antônio Abrahão Caram 820, Conjunto 302, 31275-000 Belo Horizonte, Minas Gerais; www.conservation.org.br. This one is a branch of a large international field-based organization working for biodiversity and sustainable development, in Brazil it's involved in grassroots conservation projects and national policy initiatives.

Ecológica (☎ 0xx 63-215-4333, travel@bananalecotour.com.br), Rua SO 11, Quadra 103 Sul, Conjunto 03, Lote 28, 77173-020 Palmas, Tocantins; www.bananalecotour.com.br. This one's a dynamic institute involved in carbon sequestration research, climate change consultancy, environmental education and ecotourism.

Greenpeace (☎ 0xx11-3066-1155, greenpeace.brazil@dialb.greenpeace.org), Rua dos Pinheiros 240, conjunto 32, 05422-000 São Paulo; visit its Web site (www.greenpeace.org.br) for information.

Instituto do Homem e Meio Ambiente da Amazônia (IMAZON; ☎ 0xx91-235-0122, imazon@imazon.org.br), Caixa Postal 5101, 66613-397 Belém, Pará; www.imazon.org.br. This research organization promotes sustainable development.

Instituto de Pesquisa Ambiental da Amazônia (IPAM; ☎/fax 0xx91-276-3576, ipam@amazon.com.br) Caixa Postal 8520, 66080-970 Belém, Pará. This environmental research institute and pressure group is dedicated to sustainable development in Amazonia; has funding from the Woods Hole Research Center, a US ecological research institute; organizes courses for environmentalists around Brazil and is trying to form alliance of naturalist/environmentalist professionals.

Instituto Socioambiental (ISA; ☎ 0xx11-825-5544, fax 0xx11-825-7861), Avenida Higienópolis 901, 01238-001 São Paulo; www.socioambiental.org. This group campaigns and lobbies for Brazil's environment and indigenous peoples, and publishes a journal, maps etc.

Projeto TAMAR (☎ 0xx71-876-1113, protamar@e-net.com.br), Caixa Postal 2219, 40210-970 Salvador, Bahia; www.tamar.com.br. This is the project to protect sea turtles along Brazil's coasts.

SOS Mata Atlântica (☎ 0xx11-3887-1195, smata@ax.apc.org), Rua Manoel da Nóbrega 456, 04001-001 São Paulo; www.sosmatatlantica.org.br. SOS is one of the few Brazilian NGOs with money; it carries out political pressure work and environmental education, chiefly in defense of the Atlantic rainforest.

The Nature Conservancy (☎ 0xx61-468-4819), SHIN Centro de Atividades 05, Conjunto J Bloco B, Salas 301-309, 71503-505 Brasília, DF; nature.org. This is the Brazil office of a US-based organization geared to protecting fragile ecosystems and endangered species; in Brazil it works with local partner organizations to preserve ecosystems and promote compatible development.

WWF Brasil (☎ 0xx61-364-7400, panda@wwf.org.br), SHIS EQ QL 06/08, conjunto E 2° andar, 71620-430 Brasília, DF; www.wwf.org.br

Canada

Greenpeace (☎ 416-597-8408) 250 Dundas St W, Suite 605, Toronto, Ontario M5T 2Z5; www.greenpeacecanada.org

UK

Friends of the Earth (☎ 020-7490 1555, info@foe.co.uk), 26-28 Underwood St, London N1 7JQ; www.foe.co.uk

Greenpeace (☎ 020-7865-8100), Canonbury Villas, London N1 2PN; www.greenpeace.org.uk

Rainforest Foundation UK (☎ 020-7251-6345, rainforestuk@rainforestuk.com), Suite A5, City Cloisters, 196 Old St, London EC1V 9FR; www.rainforestfoundationuk.org. This organization helps indigenous and traditional rainforest populations protect their environment and at the same time obtain their rights.

USA

Chico Mendes Sustainable Rainforest Campaign (☎ 212-505-2100, contact@environmentaldefense.org), Environmental Defense, 257 Park Ave S, New

York, NY 10010; www.environmentaldefense.org/programs/International/chico

Conservation International (☎ 212-912-1000, toll-free ☎ 800-406-2306), 1919 M St NW, Suite 600, Washington, DC 20036; www.conservation.org

Greenpeace (☎ 800-326-0959), 702 H St NW, Washington DC 20001; www.greenpeaceusa.org

Rainforest Action Network (RAN) (☎ 415-398-4404, rainforest@ran.org), 221 Pine St, Suite 500, San Francisco, CA 94104; www.ran.org. RAN works to protect rainforests and support inhabitants' rights through education, grass-roots organizing and nonviolent direct action.

Rainforest Alliance (☎ 212-677-1900, canopy@ra.org), 65 Bleecker St, New York, NY 10012; www.rainforest-alliance.org

Rainforest Foundation USA (☎ 212-431-9098, rffny@rffny.org), 270 Lafayette St, Suite 1107, New York, NY 10012; www.savetherest.org

The Nature Conservancy (toll-free ☎ 800-628-6860, comment@tnc.org), 4245 N Fairfax Drive, Suite 100, Arlington, VA 22203-1606; nature.org

Facts for the Visitor

HIGHLIGHTS

Brazil offers an awful lot more than Carnaval, beaches and Amazon River trips. The following are some suggestions for you to explore and enjoy the country.

Historic Cities & Architecture

Ouro Prêto is the crowning jewel in a diadem of spectacular baroque historic cities in Minas Gerais, including Tiradentes, Diamantina and São João del Rei. Historic coastal cities with a wealth of well preserved (or restored) architecture include Salvador, Olinda, São Luís and Belém.

In the state of Goiás, the old gold towns of Goiás Velho and Pirenópolis are filled with 18th-century colonial architecture and impressive churches and museums.

Museums

Visit the fascinating Museu Emílio Goeldi (Belém) for a study of the peoples and development of Amazonia; check out anthropology and herbal/indigenous medicine at the Museu do Homem do Nordeste, Recife; learn about Indian art and culture at the Centro de Preservação das Artes Indígenas in Alter do Chão, Pará; or see the bizarre sculptures of the Olaria de Brennand near Recife.

For imperial splendors of the past, visit the Museu Imperial in the 19th-century palace of Brazil's emperors at Petrópolis.

São Paulo has the country's greatest concentration of major art museums, though Rio, with the Museu Nacional de Belas Artes and a couple of others, certainly shouldn't be ignored. Also in Rio, don't miss the folk arts and crafts at the excellent Museu Folclorico Edson Carneiro.

Beaches

Brazil has so many glorious beaches. The following are just some of the brightest stars in a crowded constellation.

Southeast Rio de Janeiro's great beaches include Pepino and Barra. Elsewhere in Rio state try not to overlook the small, idyllic beaches around Parati or the rainforest-backed strands of Ilha Grande.

South Praia do Santinho, an uncrowded open surf beach backed by sand dunes, is one of the many great beaches on Ilha de Santa Catarina, near Florianópolis. Praia da Rosa, also in Santa Catarina state, is a sweeping bay with pumping surf framed by forested hills; you may see calving whales from June to October. Praia Ponta do Bicho on Ilha do Mel, Paraná, is another beautiful, sweeping bay, this one with calm water.

Northeast Bahia has almost endless mesmerizingly beautiful beaches. Choose between the hip scene at Arraial d'Ajuda, Trancoso and Caraiva (south of Porto Seguro), the gorgeous beaches of Morro

de São Paulo and quieter Boipeba, or the breathtaking, unspoiled and hard-to-reach Peninsula do Maraú – among many others!

Farther north, Alagoas state has many fishing villages with fabulous palm-shaded beaches. The excellent beach of Porto de Galinhas, Pernambuco, curves along a pretty bay lined with coconut palms, mangroves and cashew trees. The Tibaú do Sul area in Rio Grande do Norte has many lovely little rocky beaches. The Ceará coast is lined with almost 600km of glorious beaches, with the dune- and palm-lined strands of Jericoacoara ranking high with travelers and hip Brazilians.

North Alter do Chão (Pará) is the loveliest of the many Amazonia river beaches. Algodoal, Joanes and Salinópolis have good estuary or ocean beaches near the mouth of the Amazonas.

Celebrations

Carnaval in Rio is probably the world's most famous party. Some Brazilian cities go, if possible, even crazier at Carnaval: Try Salvador, or Recife and neighboring Olinda, or Porto Seguro. The Micareta at Feira de Santana in inland Bahia is Carnaval in all but name, held two months after Carnaval itself. So is Carnatal in Natal in the first week of December.

New Year's Eve is another big party time, above all on Copacabana beach (Rio de Janeiro).

Some northern towns stage festivals around the theme of the death and reincarnation of a bull that are highly colorful and musical: Hundreds of thousands of people descend on São Luís for the Bumba Meu Boi events between mid-June and mid-August, and on the Amazonas town of Parintins for the Boi-Bumbá festival (three days in late June).

Major religion-based celebrations include the Círio de Nazaré in Belém in mid-October, when hundreds of thousands accompany an image of the Virgin through the streets; Semana Santa (Holy Week) in Goiás Velho; and the three-day Festa da NS da Boa Morte in Cachoeira, Bahia, a fascinating Candomblé (Afro-Brazilian religion) event in mid-August.

For three days at the Festa do Divino Espírito Santo, 45 days after Easter, Pirenópolis, Goiás, returns to the Middle Ages with a series of medieval tournaments and dances known as the Cavalhada. See the Public Holidays and Special Events section later in this chapter.

Accommodations

Amazonian jungle lodges provide some of Brazil's most exotic places to stay. Two of the best, for architectural adventurousness, ambiance and the general experience, are Reserva Natural Palmari on the Rio Javari (Amazonas state) and Canguçu Lodge/Research Center on the Rio Javaés (Tocantins). Among the many attractive *fazenda* (ranch) hotels and lodges in the Pantanal, the stilt-built Pousada Passo do Lontra and the Hotel Sesc Porto Cercado on the Rio Cuiabá stand out.

At the Hospedaria do Colégio Caraça (Santa Bárbara, Minas Gerais), you can sleep in a former monastery, eat spectacular natural food and watch the nightly feeding of wolves.

The Hotel Solar da Ponte (Tiradentes, Minas Gerais) is a lovingly re-created colonial mansion. In Espírito Santo, the Aroso Paço Hotel, with stunning views of Pedra Azul, is a definite winner.

The same Brazilian-Belgian couple runs two of the best little travelers' pousadas in the country, some distance apart: Pousada Ventania do Rio-Mar in Joanes, Ilha de Marajó (Pará) and Pousada São Francisco in Ouro Prêto (Minas Gerais). Also notably friendly is the Pousada dos Prazeres, on a sweeping bay on Ilha do Mel in Paraná, with a seafood bar and views across to the Parque Nacional do Superaguí.

Music & Dance

Every Tuesday and Sunday night huge musical parties take over the Pelourinho area of Salvador, the capital of most of Brazil's many African-based musical forms. Carnaval bands and dancers carry out live street rehearsals these and other nights – the action hardly ever stops.

Rio de Janeiro is the capital of samba: Here you can visit Carnaval samba schools in rehearsal or go to several good samba clubs with live bands. Rio and São Paulo have club/disco scenes to rival the scene in New York or Ibiza. Porto Seguro, Fortaleza and Recife are not exactly dull on this score either, with some vast and original dance spaces – Recife's Fun House has nine different sections, each with a different rhythm and ambiance.

The exciting, folky, *forró* music and dancing from the Northeast is popular just about everywhere in Brazil these days. Near its home territory, the cities of Fortaleza, Natal and João Pessoa all have some pretty hot forró spots. São Luís is Brazil's reggae capital.

Natural Wonders

With its vast rainforests, wetlands, coastal mountain ranges and huge variety of plant and animal life, Brazil in its entirety could be classed as one of the world's natural wonders. See the Natural Brazil special section for more on this natural heritage.

The country has hundreds of beautiful waterfalls, but none more awesome than the Foz do Iguaçu on the borders with Argentina and Paraguay. This is one of the natural wonders of the world, superior in size and grandeur to both Niagara and Victoria.

Spectacular mountain areas here include the Chapada dos Guimarães in Mato Grosso, Chapada dos Veadeiros in Goiás and Chapada Diamantina in Bahia. All of these, plus the bizarre needle-like peaks of the Serra dos Órgãos outside Rio de Janeiro and several other mountain areas in the Southeast and South, are part of Brazil's national park network. The Parque Nacional de Aparados da Serra in Rio Grande do Sul contains the Cânion do Itaimbezinho, a fantastic narrow canyon with waterfalls and sheer 600 to 720m escarpments.

Canoeing in the flooded forests and along the *igarapés* (jungle creeks) of Amazonia is a wonderful experience. You can get a close-up view of piranha dental work by piranha fishing at the same time.

Other Highlights

Attending a big soccer game at Rio's Maracanã stadium is something fans the world over dream of doing.

In Minas Gerais, hit the hippy-dippy mountainside town of São Tome Das Letras to check out the UFOs, and take the half-hour steam train ride between São João del Rei and Tiradentes.

Check out dune-buggy rides on the coasts of Rio Grande do Norte and Ceará. Strip down at the nudist beach at Tambaba (near João Pessoa), and take a catamaran excursion from São Luís to Alcântara. Experience something otherworldly at a Candomblé ritual in Salvador.

Don't miss the four-hour scenic train ride from Curitiba to Paranaguá (Paraná).

SUGGESTED ITINERARIES
One Week

Why only a week? Brazil deserves much more! Pick a city and stay put: either **Rio de Janeiro**, the *cidade maravilhosa*, or vibrant, exciting **Salvador**. Going anywhere else, unless you've got friends, business or an adventure destination in mind, is a waste of time if you only have a week. In both cities there's lots of music, and both offer short, interesting side trips.

In Rio state, there are four national parks within a few hours of the city for great hiking in the lush Atlantic rainforest; fantastic beaches along the coast toward the colonial gem, Parati; and great surf at Rio itself and at Saquarema. Búzios, the beach resort for Rio's beautiful people, is a couple of hours to the northeast.

Close to Salvador there are some great beaches, and the Recôncavo region, with its colonial towns, is also close by.

Two to Three Weeks

An extra couple of weeks means you can move a little more and really start to enjoy Brazil. A Brazilian air pass allows you up to five flights in 21 days, and you can add on extra flights for US$100.

If you don't mind moving around a bit, travel light and have some fun. In 14 to 21 days, your itinerary could include the following.

Rio de Janeiro Rio is a good starting and finishing point for any trip. You could easily spend 14 to 21 days in Rio state and never be bored. Instead of buying an air pass, you could rent a car and tour the state. There's lots of variety, from beaches to mountains (see the one-week itinerary).

Minas Gerais Belo Horizonte has some great nightlife, and it's a good base from which to explore the rich baroque churches of the colonial towns set among Minas' hills. **Ouro Prêto** and **Tiradentes** are the most beautiful, but there are others close by, like **Mariana** and **Diamantina**.

Foz do Iguaçu A sight not to be missed in the southern state of Paraná, these falls should be included on any itinerary for a minimum of two days.

Florianópolis Partly located on the island of Santa Catarina, Florianópolis is the capital of the southern state of Santa Catarina. Rent a car for a couple of days and explore a lovely island with some great beaches and surf.

Pantanal The Central West cities of Cuiabá, Campo Grande and Corumbá are the gateways to the fascinating Pantanal wetlands with their teeming wildlife. A three- or four-day tour is not hard to set up and can be inexpensive. If you go to Cuiabá you can also visit **Chapada dos Guimarães**.

Salvador Try to spend at least a week here, in what's truly the black Rome. There is so much African heritage here, yet it's so Brazilian too. A must for music lovers.

Recife There are good beaches here and the colonial town of **Olinda** is next door. You could easily spend three days here.

Fortaleza This lively city is a good base for the Northeastern beaches. A few hours' bus ride will take you to **Canoa Quebrada** or hip **Jericoacoara**, where all you have to do is lie among the dunes and get down to a bit of forró music after dark.

Manaus Manaus is the capital of the northern state of Amazonas. Three or four days here could easily include an introductory jungle trip. The city itself has some historical attractions such as the opera house and market.

Ninety Days or More

Now you're talking. Ninety days is the maximum duration before you need to leave the country or get an extension of your time. You'll be able to move at a sane pace and get a good feel for the variety that Brazil offers. Many travelers with this much time will be including Brazil in a larger South American tour. It's advisable to spend the last part of your tour in Brazil, because once here, you won't want to leave!

A classic overlander's route is to enter through Paraguay or Bolivia at **Corumbá**, spend some time exploring the **Pantanal** and **Bonito**, then move east through **Foz do Iguaçu**, **São Paulo** and **Rio**, check out Rio city and state, and head north into **Bahia**, lying on the beach at one of the hip resorts like **Arraial d'Ajuda**, **Trancoso**, **Morro de São Paulo** or **Boipeba**. The city of **Salvador** is on this route and it's definitely worth a good chunk of your time. From Salvador you won't regret a venture inland to the **Chapada Diamantina** mountains, where you'll find some of Brazil's best trails.

Many travelers move on through the Northeast region, with its multitude of **beaches** and lively cities such as **Recife**, **Fortaleza** and **São Luís**, before arriving in **Belém**, where a good side trip can be made to the **Ilha de Marajó**, a large island in the mouth of the **Rio Amazonas**. From Belém you can travel up the Amazonas to **Santarém** and **Manaus**, taking in a jungle trip or lodge or two en route, then head out to Peru, Venezuela or Bolivia.

Ending your Brazil trip with a 21-day air pass is a good way to take in some of the out-of-the-way places you may have missed.

If you have six months for traveling, spend two to four weeks in Rio (from the start of February until Carnaval would be ideal). Spend December or January at the hip beaches in the Northeast – you'll meet lots of Brazilians on vacation (then you can go and visit them later!).

Try to fit in not just Foz do Iguaçu but also other highlights of the South, such as Itaimbezinho canyon, the beaches and surf of Santa Catarina state, and whale-watching at Praia da Rosa. Spend two weeks in Salvador, two in the Pantanal, another two in Amazonia, three days at Foz do Iguaçu and at least two weeks in Minas Gerais. Travel through the Northeast for a month or so.

Of course, you may want to stop and stay put for a while. That's the best thing about traveling for long periods. You'll have a great time.

PLANNING
When to Go

See the Climate section in the Facts about Brazil chapter for details of seasonal factors that may influence your decision on when to visit the country. There are few regions that can't be comfortably visited all year round.

What Kind of Trip

Brazil's diversity means that you can choose exactly the type of trip you'd like; from mountain climbing and hot-air ballooning to an off-the-beaten-track adventure, from Amazon river trips to just lolling about on one of the country's luscious beaches for a month – Brazil just can't disappoint.

Because distances are so great, every bit of predeparture planning helps you enjoy your time on the ground.

Maps*

Given the size of Brazil, it's essential to be armed with decent maps that give a clear idea of scale. It's easy to underestimate distances and the time required for travel, particularly if you plan to visit several regions using roads rather than airports.

Decent maps for general planning include Bartholomew's *Brazil & Bolivia World Travel Map* (1996), GeoCenter's *Brazil, Bolivia, Paraguay, Uruguay* and the South America sectional maps published by International Travel Map Productions (ITM). Coverage of Brazil is provided in ITM's *South America Southern* (1993), *South America North East* (1994), *South America North West* (1993) and *The Amazon Basin* (1992). At least some of these can be obtained from Internet bookstores.

Omni Resources (☎ 336-227-8300), 1004 South Mebane St, PO Box 2096, Burlington, NC 27216, USA is a good source of Brazil

maps. They ship worldwide, and you can order online (www.omnimap.com). Also see the Useful Organizations section later in this chapter.

Brazilian-published maps are harder to get outside Brazil, but once you get here it's easy to obtain the very useful publications in the Quatro Rodas series from newsstands and some bookstores. These include *Guia Rodoviário*, a compact book of maps covering individual states, the *Atlas Rodoviário* road atlas (larger but it fits into a backpack), and excellent street atlases for Rio de Janeiro, São Paulo, Belo Horizonte and Fortaleza. Each costs between US$10 and US$16.

Good topographical maps at various scales are published by the IBGE, the government geographical service, and the DSG, the army geographical service. They cost around US$6 and US$15, respectively, per sheet. Availability is erratic, but IBGE offices in most state capitals sell IBGE maps. Office locations can be found on the IBGE Web site (www.ibge.net) – look for the IBGE/DIPEQ addresses under 'Locais de Atendimento.' One of the country's best sources of DSG and IBGE maps is Editora Geográfica Paulini in Rio de Janeiro (see the Maps section in the Rio City chapter).

Searchable street maps of 128 Brazilian cities are online at www.terra.com.br/turismo. Street maps from tourist offices are a matter of potluck. But telephone directories in many states include excellent city maps as well as phone numbers.

What to Bring

The happiest travelers are those who can slip all their luggage under their plane seats. Pack light. Backpacks with detachable daypacks make a versatile combination. Use small padlocks to secure your pack, particularly if you have to leave it unattended in one of the more down-market hotels. For more details about security, refer to the Dangers & Annoyances section in this chapter.

What you bring will be determined by what you do. If you're planning a river or jungle trip, read the Amazonas & Roraima chapter ahead of time. If you're traveling cheap, a cotton sheet sleeping sack will come in handy.

With its warm climate and informal dress standards, you don't need to bring many clothes to Brazil. Except for in the South and Minas Gerais, where it gets cold in the winter, the only weather you need to contend with is heat and rain, and whatever you're lacking you can purchase while traveling. Buying clothes is easy and has the added advantage of helping you appear less like a tourist.

Most clothing is not particularly cheap in Brazil, but shoes are. You can get some good deals on leather shoes. Tennis shoes are the norm in Brazil, as are light jeans. Bring a pair of comfortable shorts and a light rain jacket. Bring your smallest bathing suit – men and women – but a *maiô* (Brazilian suit) is easy to find. There are many funny T-shirts that are practical garments to buy along the way and are also good souvenirs.

You don't need more than a pair of shorts, trousers, a couple of T-shirts, a long-sleeved shirt, bathing suit, towel, underwear, walking shoes, flip-flops or sandals and some rain gear. Quick-drying, light cotton clothes are the most convenient. Sun-protection cream is readily available in Brazil, as are most other toiletries.

Usually, one set of clothes to wear and one to wash is adequate. It's probably a good idea if one set of clothes is presentable or could pass at a good restaurant or club. While dress is informal, many Brazilians are very fashion conscious and pay close attention to their own appearance and yours.

For information regarding compiling a basic medical kit, see the Health section in this chapter.

RESPONSIBLE TOURISM

Most places you'll go in Brazil welcome tourism as a money maker, but be sensitive to local ways of doing things – especially with indigenous peoples who have some delicate traditions and unique beliefs. Many are very wary about having their photo taken – only snap them if you're sure (probably having asked them) that they won't mind.

As for Brazil's environment, we all have an obligation to protect it. You can do your bit by using environmentally friendly tourism services wherever possible (for brief comments on this, see Organized Tours in the Natural Brazil section). As the saying goes, take only photos, leave only footprints (but don't leave footprints on the coral). Using the services of local community groups and enterprises – as guides, hosts, artisans or whatever you need – helps to ensure that your money goes direct to those who are working to help you, as does buying crafts and other products directly from the artisans or from their trusted representatives.

In the end, a responsible tourist is one who treats the visited place with as much respect as if it were home.

TOURIST OFFICES
Local Tourist Offices

Most tourist offices in Brazil are sponsored by individual states and municipalities. In many places, they have shoestring budgets that are chopped or maintained according to the whims (or feuds!) of regional and local politicians. Some tourist offices clearly function only as a sinecure for politicians' relatives; others have dedicated, knowledgeable staff who care about tourism in their locality and are interested in providing information. Some offices are conveniently placed in the center of town; others are so far out of range that you'll spend an entire day getting there. Keep your sense of humor, prepare for potluck and don't expect too much!

Embratur, the Brazilian Tourist Board, has its headquarters in Brasília, but maintains an office in Rio de Janeiro (☎ 0xx21-2509-6017) at Rua Uruguaiana 174, 8th floor. In Brasília, the board office is at Embratur, Setor Comercial Norte, Quadra 2, Bloco G, 70712-907 Brasília, DF (☎ 0xx61-429-7777). Embratur's Web site is at www.embratur.gov.br.

Tourist Offices Abroad

Brazilian consulates and embassies are able to provide limited tourist information, and the embassy in the UK actually has a dedicated tourist information section (see Embassies & Consulates in this chapter for contact details). Several Brazilian embassies and consulates provide useful tourist information on their Web sites. Riotur, the Rio de Janeiro city tourist board, maintains offices in the US at 3601 Aviation Blvd, Suite 2100, Manhattan Beach, CA 90266 (☎ 310-643-2638, rio@myriad.cc) and 554 Fifth Ave, 4th floor, New York, NY 10036 (☎ 646-366-8164, rio@myriad.cc).

VISAS & DOCUMENTS

Everyone needs to carry a passport and obtain an entry/exit card on arrival. Many nationalities also need to obtain a visa beforehand. Depending on where you are coming from you may also need a yellow fever vaccination certificate. On your arrival in Brazil, immigration officials may ask to see your onward or return ticket and/or proof of means of support such as credit card or traveler's checks.

Visa regulations change from time to time, and you should always get the latest information from your local Brazilian embassy or consulate (many have Web sites containing current requirements – see the Embassies & Consulates section).

Passport

By law you must carry a passport with you at all times, but many travelers opt to carry a photocopy (preferably certified) when tripping around town and leave their passport securely locked up at their hotel. It's convenient to have extra passport photos for any documents or visas you might need to acquire in Brazil.

Entry/Exit Card

On entering Brazil, all tourists must fill out a *cartão de entrada/saida* (entry/exit card); immigration officials will keep half, you keep the other. They will also stamp your passport and, if for some reason they are not granting you the usual 90-day stay in Brazil, the number of days will be written beneath the word *Prazo* on the stamp in your passport.

When you leave Brazil, the second half of the entry/exit card will be taken by immigration officials. Make sure you don't lose your card while traveling around Brazil, or your departure could be delayed until officials have checked your story.

Visas

At the time of writing, Brazilian visas were necessary for tourists who were citizens of countries that required visas for visitors from Brazil. Australian, Canadian, New Zealand and US citizens were required to have visas; citizens of the UK, Ireland, France, Germany, the Netherlands, South Africa, Portugal, Spain, and Scandinavian countries were not.

Tourist visas are issued by Brazilian diplomatic offices and are valid for a traveler's arrival in Brazil within 90 days of issue and then for a 90-day stay. The processing fee depends on your nationality and where you are applying. US citizens, Canadians and Australians usually pay about the equivalent of US$35 to US$50.

In many Brazilian embassies and consulates it takes only a couple of hours to issue a visa if you go in person (it's instant in some places), but the processing can take a couple of weeks or more if you do it by mail. You will normally need to present a passport valid for at least six months, a passport photograph, and a roundtrip or onward ticket or a photocopy of it or a statement from a travel agent that you have it. If you don't have the ticketing requirements, proof of means of support such as credit cards or bank statements may be acceptable.

Extensions to Entry/Exit Cards & Visas

These are handled by Brazil's Polícia Federal, which has offices in the state capitals and border towns. You must apply before your entry/exit card or visa lapses, and don't leave it until the last minute. Tourist offices can tell you where the nearest Polícia Federal office is. When you go, dress nicely! Some Fed stations don't take kindly to people in shorts.

In most cases an extension seems to be pretty automatic, but sometimes you may not be given the full 90 days. The police may well require that you have a ticket out of the country and proof of sufficient funds, though this seems to be at the discretion of the officer. You may be told to complete a DARF form (US$1), which you have to buy from vendors outside the police station or from a *papelaria* (stationery shop). After filling it out, you must go to a bank and pay a fee of about US$40. You then return to the Polícia Federal with the DARF form stamped by the bank. The extension should then be routinely issued.

If you opt for the maximum 90-day extension and then leave the country before the end of that period, you cannot return until the full 90 days have elapsed.

Young Travelers

People under 18 years of age traveling to Brazil without their parents or legal guardians, or with only one of them, or applying for a visa to do so, must have a notarized letter of authorization from the non-accompanying parent(s) or guardian(s), or from a court. Check with a Brazilian consulate well in advance about the bureaucratic procedures you'll have to go through.

Travel Insurance

A travel insurance policy to cover theft, loss and medical problems is a good idea. Some policies offer lower and higher medical-expense options; the higher ones are chiefly for countries such as the US, which has extremely high medical costs. There is a wide variety of policies available so check the small print.

Some policies specifically exclude 'dangerous activities,' which can include scuba diving, motorcycling, even trekking. A locally acquired motorcycle license is not valid under some policies.

You may prefer a policy that pays doctors or hospitals directly rather than stipulating that you pay on the spot and file a claim later. If you are going to claim later, make sure you keep all documentation. Some companies ask you to telephone collect to a center in your home country where an immediate assessment of your problem is made.

Check that the policy covers an ambulance ride or an emergency flight home.

Driver's License & Permits

Your home-country driver's license is valid in Brazil, but because local authorities probably won't be familiar with it, it's a very good idea to carry an International Driver's Permit (IDP) as well. This gives police less scope for claiming that you are not driving with a legal license. IDPs are issued by your national motoring association and usually cost the equivalent of about US$10. The ideal thing is to get your license translated by an officially recognized translator, then stamped and approved by Detran (the Department of Transportation). This doesn't cost much – except in time.

To rent a car you must be at least 21 (older with some rental firms), have a credit card in your name and your valid driver's license from your home country (not just an IDP).

All vehicles in Brazil must carry the registration document and proof of insurance.

To take a vehicle in or out of Brazil, you might need a *carnet de passage en douane,* which is kind of a vehicle passport, or a *libreta de pasos por aduana,* which is a booklet of customs passes, which in practice are not often required. Contact your local automobile association for details about all documentation.

Hostel Card

An HI (Hostelling International) membership card is very useful if you plan to stay in the 50-odd *albergues da juventude* (youth hostels) of the Federação Brasileira dos Albergues da Juventude (FBAJ). Most hostels will let you in without one, but will charge you about 50% more. See Hostels in the Accommodations section later in this chapter for how to obtain one.

Student, Youth & Seniors' Cards

The International Student Identity Card (ISIC) is practically useless in Brazil, where in larger cities on good days it might get you a US$0.50 discount to a major museum but usually not even that. If you've got one, bring it, but don't make a special trip to get one for Brazil. Seniors in Brazil get some discounts for things like public transport and museums: your passport will prove your age, but you might as well also bring along any seniors' cards you have.

Vaccination Certificates

At the time of writing a yellow fever vaccination certificate was required for travelers who within three months prior to arriving in Brazil (or applying for a Brazilian visa) had been in Bolivia, Colombia, Ecuador, French Guiana, Peru, Venezuela or any of about a dozen African countries. The list of countries can vary, so you should check with a Brazilian consulate. The card is indeed often demanded when you enter Brazil from these countries. At some Brazilian borders there are vaccination posts where you can have the jab and get the certificate immediately, but it's sensible to get your card in advance.

Children between three months and six years old are required to have a polio vaccination certificate.

Copies

All important documents (passport data pages and visa pages, credit cards, travel insurance policy, air/bus/train tickets, driver's license, essential contact addresses and numbers) should be photocopied before you leave home. Leave one copy with someone at home and keep another with you, separate from the originals. Once you're in Brazil, it's wise to make a photocopy of your entry/exit card and keep this in a safe place, separate from your passport.

It's also a good idea to store details of your vital travel documents in Lonely Planet's free online Travel Vault in case you misplace the photocopies or can't be bothered with them. Your password-protected Travel Vault is accessible online anywhere in the world – create it at www.ekno.lonelyplanet.com.

EMBASSIES & CONSULATES
Your Own Embassy

It's important to realize what your own embassy – the embassy of the country of which you are a citizen – can and can't do to help you if you get into trouble. Generally speaking, it won't be much help in emergencies if the trouble you're in is remotely your own fault. Remember that you are bound by the laws of the country you are in. Your embassy will not be sympathetic if you end up in jail after committing a crime locally, even if such actions are legal in your own country.

In genuine emergencies, you might get some assistance, but only if other channels have been exhausted. If you need to get home urgently, a free ticket home is exceedingly unlikely – the embassy would expect you to have insurance. If all your money and documents are stolen, it might assist you with getting a new passport, but a loan for onward travel is out of the question.

Some embassies used to keep letters for travelers or have a small reading room with home newspapers, but these days most of the mail-holding services have been stopped and even newspapers tend to be out of date.

Brazilian Embassies & Consulates

There are Brazilian diplomatic posts in the following countries:

Argentina
Consulate (☎ 011-4394-5255) Carlos Pellegrini 1363, 5° Piso, 1011 Buenos Aires; www.brasil .org.ar/consulado/index.asp
Consulate (☎ 03757-21348) Avenida Guaraní 70, Puerto Iguazú (open 8 am to 2 pm, Monday to Friday)

Australia
Embassy (☎ 02-6273-4837) 19 Forster Crescent, Yarralumla, ACT 2600; http://brazil.org.au

Bolivia
Embassy (☎ 02-440202) Calle Capitán Ravelo 2334, Edificio Metrobol, La Paz; Web site www .embajadabrasil.org.bo
Consulate (☎ 03-344400) Avenida German Busch 330, Santa Cruz
Consulate Avenida General Rene Barrientos, Cobija (open 8 am to 1 pm, Monday to Friday)
Consulate (☎ 0855-3766) Avenida 24 de Septiembre, Guayaramerín (open 9 am to 1 pm and 3 to 5 pm, Monday to Friday)

Canada
Embassy (☎ 613-237-1090) 450 Wilbrod St,

Ottawa, Ontario K1N 6M8
Consulates in Toronto (☎ 416-922-2503) www
.consbrastoronto.org, and Montreal (☎ 514-499-
0968)

Colombia

Embassy (☎ 091-218-0800) Calle 93 No 14-20,
Piso 8, Bogotá 8; www.geocities.com/secombra
Consulate (☎ 091-218-0800) Calle 13 No 10-31,
Leticia (open 8 am to 2 pm Monday to Friday)

France

Embassy (☎ 01 45 61 63 00) 34 Cours Albert, 1er,
75008 Paris; www.bresil.org

French Guiana

Consulate (☎ 29-6010) 444 chemin Saint-Antoine,
97337 Cayenne; www.nplus.gf/~cbrascay

Germany

Embassy (☎ 030-726280) Wallstrasse 57, 10179
Berlin-Mitte; www.brasilianische-botschaft.de

Guyana

Embassy (☎ 02-57970) 308 Church St, Queens-
town, Georgetown

Ireland

Embassy (☎ 01-475-6000) Harcourt Centre,
Europa House, 5th Floor, Harcourt St, Dublin 2

Netherlands

Embassy (☎ 070-302 39 59) Mauritskade 19,
2514 HD, The Hague

New Zealand

Embassy (☎ 04-473-3516) 10 Brandon St, Level
9, Wellington 1

Paraguay

Consulate (☎ 021-448084) General Díaz 523 at
14 de Mayo, 3° Piso, Asunción; Web site www
.embajadabrasil.org.py
Consulate (☎ 061-500984) Calle Pampliega 205,
Ciudad del Este (open 7 am to noon, Monday to
Friday)

Peru

Embassy (☎ 01-421-2759) Avenida José Pardo
850, Miraflores, Lima 100

Spain

Embassy (☎ 91 700 4650) Calle Fernando El
Santo 6, 28010 Madrid

UK

Consulate (☎ 020-7930-9055) 6 St Alban's St,
London SW1Y 4SQ; www.brazil.org.uk

Uruguay

Consulate (☎ 02-900-6282) Convencion 1343, 6°
Piso, Montevideo; www.brasmont.org.uy

USA

Embassy (☎ 202-238-2700) 3006 Massachusetts
Ave NW, Washington, DC 20008; www.brasilemb
.org
Consulates in Boston (☎ 617-542-4000),

www.consulatebrazil.org; Chicago (☎ 312-464-
0244); Houston (☎ 713-961-3063), www.brazil-
houston.org; Los Angeles (☎ 323-651-2664);
Miami (☎ 305-285-6200), Web site www
.brazilmiami.org; New York (☎ 917-777-7777),
www.brazilny.org; and San Francisco (☎ 415-981-
8170), www.brazilsf.org

Venezuela

Embassy (☎ 02-261-7553) Calle Los Chag-
uaramos at Avenida Mohedano, Centro Geren-
cial Mohedano, Piso 6, La Castellana 1060,
Caracas
Consulate (☎ 088-951262) Avenida Gran
Mariscal, Santa Elena de Uairén (open 8 am to
noon, Monday to Friday)

Embassies & Consulates in Brazil

Embassies are all in Brasília, but many
countries have consulates in Rio and São
Paulo, and often other cities too. It's a good
idea to register with your embassy or consulate if spending a long time in a remote or
unstable area.

Generally speaking, your embassy won't
be much help in emergencies if the trouble
you're in is remotely your own fault. Remember that in Brazil you are bound by
Brazilian laws. Your embassy will not be
sympathetic if you end up in jail after committing a crime locally, even if such actions
are legal in your own country. In genuine
emergencies you might get some assistance
from your embassy, but only if other channels have been exhausted. For example, if
you need to get home urgently, a free ticket
home is exceedingly unlikely – the embassy
would expect you to have insurance. If you
have all your money and documents stolen,
it might assist with getting a new passport,
but a loan for onward travel is out of the
question.

The following is a selective list of embassies and consulates in Brazil. Consulates
in Rio and São Paulo generally open during
normal office hours from Monday to Friday
(see Business Hours later in this chapter),
but may have shortened hours for visa applications. In addresses in Brasília, SES
stands for Setor de Embaixadas Sul.

Argentina

Embassy (☎ 0xx61-365-3000) SHIS, Q L-2, conj
01, casa 19, Lago Sul, Brasília; www.embarg.org.br

Consulate (☎ 0xx21-2553-1646) Praia de Botafogo 228, Sobreloja 201, Botafogo, Rio de Janeiro
Consulate (☎ 0xx11-284-1355) Avenida Paulista 1106, 9° andar, São Paulo
Consulate (☎ 0xx45-574-2969) Travessa Eduardo Branchi 26, Foz do Iguaçu (open 10 am to 2:30 pm, Monday to Friday)
Consulate (☎ 0xx51-321-1360) Rua Coronel Bordini 1033, Porto Alegre

Australia
Embassy (☎ 0xx61-248-5569) SHIS, Q I-9, conj 16, casa 1, Brasília
Consulate (☎ 0xx21-3824-4734) Avenida Presidente Wilson 231, 23rd floor, Centro, Rio de Janeiro

Bolivia
Embassy (☎ 0xx61-364-3362) SHIS, Q L-10, conj 01, casa 06, Lago Sul, Brasília
Consulate (☎ 0xx21-2551-1796) Avenida Rui Barbosa 664, Apt 101, Botafogo, Rio de Janeiro
Consulate (☎ 0xx68-546-3595) Rua Major Salinas 205, Brasiléia (open 8 am to noon, Monday to Friday)
Consulate (☎ 0xx67-231-5605) Rua Antônio Maria Coelho 881, Corumbá (open 8:30 am to 1:30 pm, Monday to Friday)
Consulate (☎ 0xx69-541-5876) Avenida Beira Rio 505, 1° andar, Guajará-Mirim (open 8 am to 1:30 pm, Monday to Friday)

Canada
Embassy (☎ 0xx61-321-2171) SES, Avenida das Nações, Q 803, lote 16, Brasília; Web site www.dfait-maeci.gc.ca/brazil
Consulate (☎ 0xx21-2543-3004) Rua Lauro Müller 116, sala 2707, Botafogo, Rio de Janeiro
Consulate (☎ 0xx11-5509-4321) Avenida Nações Unidas 12901, 16° andar, São Paulo

Colombia
Embassy (☎ 0xx61-226-8902) SES, Avenida das Nações, Q 803, lote 10, Brasília
Consulate (☎ 0xx21-2552-6248, fax 553-1563) Praia do Flamengo 284, No 101, Rio de Janeiro
Honorary Consulate (☎ 0xx92-412-2597) Avenida da Amizade 2205, Tabatinga

France
Embassy (☎ 0xx61-312-9100) SES, Avenida das Nações, Q 801, lote 04, Brasília; www.ambafrance-br.org.br
Consulate (☎ 0xx21-2210-1272) Avenida Presidente Antônio Carlos 58, 6°, andar, Rio de Janeiro
Honorary Consulate (☎ 0xx91-224-6818) Rua Aristides Lobo 651, Belém
Honorary Consulate (☎ 0xx96-223-7554) Rua Jovino Dinoa 1693, Macapá (open 9 am to noon, Monday, Tuesday, Thursday, Friday)

Note: French honorary consulates do not issue visas for French Guiana or France

Germany
Embassy (☎ 0xx61-443-7330) SES, Avenida das Nações, Q 807, lote 25, Brasília; www.embaixada-alemanha.org.br
Consulate (☎ 0xx21-2553-6777) Rua Presidente Carlos de Campos 417, Laranjeiras, Rio de Janeiro

Guyana
Embassy (☎ 0xx61-326-9269) SBN, Q 02, Edifício Paulo Mauricio, 13° andar, sala 1310, Brasília

Ireland
Honorary Consulate (☎ 0xx21-2501-8455) Rua 24 de Maio 347, Riachuelo, Rio de Janeiro

Netherlands
Embassy (☎ 0xx61-321-47 69) SES, Avenida das Nações, Q 801, lote 05, Brasília
Consulate (☎ 0xx21-2552-9028) Praia de Botafogo 242, 10° andar, Rio de Janeiro

New Zealand
Consulate (☎ 0xx11-288-0307) Alameda Campinas 579, 15° andar, São Paulo

Paraguay
Embassy (☎ 0xx61-244-9449) SES, Avenida das Nações, Q 811, lote 42, Brasília
Consulate (☎ 0xx21-2553-2294) Praia de Botafogo 242, 2° andar, Rio de Janeiro
Consulate (☎ 0xx45-523-2898) Rua Bartolomeu de Guzmão 738, Foz de Iguaçú (open 8:30 am to 8 pm, Monday to Friday)

Peru
Embassy (☎ 0xx61-242-9435) SES, Avenida das Nações, Q 811, lote 43, Brasília
Consulate (☎ 0xx21-2551-9596) Avenida Rui Barbosa 314, 2° andar, Flamengo, Rio de Janeiro

Spain
Embassy (☎ 0xx61-244-2121) SES, Avenida das Nações, Q 811, lote 44, Brasília
Consulate (☎ 0xx21-2543-3200) Rua Lauro Müller 116, salas 1601/12, Torre Rio Sul, Botafogo, Rio de Janeiro

UK
Embassy (☎ 0xx61-225-2710) SES, Avenida das Nações, Q 801, lote 08, Brasília; www.reinounido.org.br
Consulate (☎ 0xx21-2555-9600) Praia do Flamengo 284, 2° andar, Rio de Janeiro
Consulate (☎ 0xx11-816-2303) Rua Fereira de Arauja 741, Pinheiros, São Paulo
Consulate (☎ 0xx71-243-7399) Avenida Estados Unidos 18B, 8° andar, Comércio, Salvador

Uruguay
Embassy (☎ 0xx61-322-1200) SES, Avenida das Nações, Q 803, lote 14, Brasília; Web site

www.emburuguai.org.br)
Consulate (☎ 0xx21-2553-6030) Praia de
Botafogo 242, 6° andar, Rio de Janeiro
Consulate (☎ 0xx51-224-3499), Rua Siqueira
Campos 1171, Porto Alegre

USA
Embassy (☎ 0xx61-321-7272) SES, Avenida das
Nações, Q 801, lote 3, Brasília; Web site www
.embaixada-americana.org.br
Consulate (☎ 0xx21-2292-7117) Avenida Presi-
dente Wilson 147, Rio de Janeiro; www
.consulado-americano-rio.org.br/rio5.htm
Consulate (☎ 0xx11-3081-6511) Rua Padre João
Manoel 933, Cerqueira César, São Paulo;
www.consuladoamericanosp.org.br
Consular Agency (☎ 0xx71-345-1545) Rua Per-
nambuco 51, Pituba, Salvador

Venezuela
Embassy (☎ 0xx61-322-1011) SES, Avenida das
Nações, Q 803, lote 13, Brasília
Consulate (☎ 0xx21-552-6699) Praia de Botafogo
242, 5° andar, Botafogo, Rio de Janeiro
Consulate (☎ 0xx95-623-9285) Avenida Ben-
jamin Constant 525E, Boa Vista (open 8 am to
noon, Monday to Friday)
Consulate (☎ 0xx92-233-6004) Rua Ferreira
Pena 179, Centro, Manaus

CUSTOMS
Travelers entering Brazil are allowed to
bring in one radio, tape player, typewriter,
notebook computer and video and still
camera each. Plants and seeds must be declared on arrival. Apart from clothes,
books, periodicals and other personal articles for domestic or professional use or
consumption, goods that have cost more
than US$500 (US$150 if you are arriving by
land, river or lake) are subject to 50%
import duty.

MONEY
Currency
Brazil's currency is the *real* (pronounced
'hay-ow,' often written R$); the plural is
reais ('HAY-ice'). One real is made up of
100 centavos. The real was introduced on a
one-for-one parity with the US dollar in
1994 but had declined bit by bit to a value of
around US$0.50 by 2001.

Banknotes are easy to distinguish from
each other, as they come in different colors.
There's a green one-real note, a blue/purple
five, a red 10, a brown 50 and a blue 100.

Many of the coins are frustratingly
similar. Their denominations are one, five,
10, 25 and 50 centavos, and one real (as well
as the one-real note).

There is a chronic shortage of change
(*troco* or *miúdo*) all over Brazil, especially
in the Northeast. When you change money,
ask for lots of small notes – and take very
few notes in denominations larger than the
equivalent of US$5.

Although the change shortage genuinely exists, it is also commonly used as an
excuse to simply retain a tip. If you're un-
willing to go along with this, insist that the
seller find change and hang around until it
is procured.

To find out if the seller has change –
preferably *before* you purchase – ask '*tem
troco?*' (do you have change?). If you want
to convey that you don't have change,
saying '*não tem troco*' makes it clear that
you neither have change nor have been able
to find any in the vicinity – thus heading off
the seller's inevitable request that you hunt
around the vicinity! Sweets are sometimes
used instead of small change.

Exchange Rates
Exchange rates are written up every day on
the front page and in the business section of
the major daily papers: *O Globo, Jornal do
Brasil* and the *Folha de São Paulo*, and are
announced on the evening TV news.

Exchange rates as of press time were as
follows:

country	unit		reais
Argentina	P$1	=	R$2.23
Australia	A$1	=	R$1.14
Bolivia	B$1	=	R$0.38
Canada	C$1	=	R$1.44
European Union	€1	=	R$1.98
Japan	¥100	=	R$1.97
New Zealand	NZ$1	=	R$0.92
Paraguay	₲1	=	R$0.0006
Peru	S/1	=	R$0.74
UK	UK£1	=	R$3.20
US	US$1	=	R$2.23
Uruguay	Ur$1	=	R$0.19
Venezuela	1Bs	=	R$0.003

Exchanging Money

It's best to take a combination of international credit and/or debit card(s), US$ traveler's checks and US$ cash. Each form of money has its pros and cons and having all three gives you maximum flexibility.

Cash & Traveler's Checks Even if you are relying mainly on credit or debit cards as your source of funds, it's a good idea to take a little cash and a few traveler's checks too. You can change these in banks or in *casas de câmbio* (exchange offices). Banks have slower, more bureaucratic procedures but on the whole give better exchange rates (an exception being Banco do Brasil which charges US$20 commission for every traveler's check transaction). You'll usually get a 1% or 2% better exchange rate for cash than for traveler's checks. Checks, of course, have the advantage of being replaceable if lost or stolen.

Both cash and traveler's checks should be in US dollars, and American Express is easily the most recognized traveler's check. Thomas Cook, Barclays and Citibank traveler's checks are less widely accepted, but you should be able to cash them in large cities.

American Express has offices in 16 Brazilian cities. American Express card holders can purchase US-dollar traveler's checks at these offices.

Learn in advance how to get refunds from your traveler's check company. Leave a copy of the serial numbers somewhere safe, and keep the record of serial numbers separate from your checks on the road. Keep a close, accurate and current record of your traveler's check expenditures. This speeds up the refund process. Guard your traveler's checks – they are valuable to thieves even without your countersignature.

Credit & Debit Cards A credit card saves your having to carry much cash or many traveler's checks. You can use it to pay for many purchases and to make cash withdrawals from ATMs and over-the-counter at banks. Visa is the most widely accepted credit card, followed by MasterCard. Amer-

ican Express and Diners Club cards are useful too. Cirrus debit cards can be used for ATM withdrawals in many cities.

If you put your traveling money into your card account before you leave, you won't have to worry about getting someone at home to pay your bills.

Unfortunately, it can be hard to find an ATM that accepts your particular card. Only some ATMs accept cards from outside Brazil, and there is little logic to which ones will and which won't honor your card. You can usually resort to an over-the-counter withdrawal – Visa cash advances are widely available, even in small towns that have no other currency exchange facilities. For that you'll need your passport, and the process can be time-consuming, especially at the ubiquitous but super-bureaucratic Banco do Brasil. In Brazilian banks generally, it's preferable to deal with machines than to try to make contact with human beings. The insides of banks are characterized by people standing in long motionless lines, signs instructing you not to speak to the security guards and the complete absence of anyone else who looks available to be asked anything at all.

Many Banco do Brasil branches have ATMs plastered with Visa stickers, but it's a matter of trial and error to find one that will accept *your* Visa card. One of our authors on this edition rarely had problems getting cash with his Bank of Melbourne Visa card from Bradesco Dia e Noite (Day & Night) or Banco do Brasil ATMs with the Visa logo; another had a success rate of about 2% with a British Barclaycard Visa in the same banks. The ATMs at branches of HSBC banks – there's at least one in most cities – are generally good for Cirrus withdrawals.

Credit card fraud is widespread, so be careful. Keep your card in sight at all times – do not give it to waiters and let them take it away. The online credit card receipts do not have carbon paper inserts and offer protection against misuse. Most places now use them. If you do sign an older-style receipt, you should ask for the carbon inserts and destroy them after use.

Use these toll-free numbers to report lost or stolen credit cards: American Express (☎ 0800-785050), Diners Club (☎ 0800-784444), MasterCard (☎ 0800-784411) and Visa(☎ 0800-784556).

International Transfers Transferring money from a bank back home to you in Brazil is either cheap and problematic or easy and expensive. Assuming you don't have an account in a Brazilian bank, the best course is to ask your bank at home for the name of the Brazilian bank they have a correspondent relationship with, and ask them for the best possible way to transfer money. Citibank, with branches throughout the world including in some Brazilian cities, is a good bet. The Brazilian American Cultural Center (BACC), which has offices in the US and Brazil, provides a special remittance service for members. For details see the Useful Organizations section in this chapter.

The fastest way to get money to Brazil is through Western Union, a service available at many Banco do Brasil branches. Western Union has 80,000-odd branches worldwide. A fee of US$15 to US$20 is charged for transfers from the US to Brazil, and it can take as little as 15 minutes for the money to be available for pick-up. You can organize transfers online at www.westernunion .com, which also details agency locations worldwide.

Security

The first rule is to carry on your person only what you immediately need. Try to use only ATMs that are inside buildings. When using any ATM, always be aware of those around you, including when you walk outside. The same goes for banks and exchange offices in general. Robbers sometimes watch these places looking for targets. See the Dangers & Annoyances section later in this chapter for more safety information.

Costs

The devaluation of the real in 1999 made Brazil cheaper for foreign travelers than it had been for a long, long time. Prices rose a bit afterward, but Brazil should remain

cheaper than North America or Europe for at least several years.

If you're pretty frugal, you can travel on about US$35 to US$40 a day – up to US$10 for accommodations, the same for food and drink, the same for bus travel, admission to sights and the occasional entertainment, and the rest for the odd special excursion or special purchases. If you just plan to lie on a beach for a month, eating rice, beans and fish every day, US$15 to US$25 should be enough. If you want reasonably comfortable rooms, a touch of quality in what you eat, a couple of drinks most nights, and the occasional taxi ride (sometimes advisable for security), you could easily spend twice as much. If you're consistently staying in good mid-range hotels, eating in at least one good restaurant a day, and taking the odd flight, rental car and guided excursion, you're probably looking at US$100 a day.

Bear in mind that during the December to February holiday season accommodations costs generally increase by around 25% to 30%.

Brazil is not among the kinder destinations for solo travelers. If you share rooms and meals with someone else, you can shave maybe 20% off the above budgets.

Tipping

Workers in most services get tipped 10%, and as they make the minimum wage – which is not enough to live on – you can be sure they need the money. In restaurants the service charge will usually be included in the bill and is mandatory. If a waitperson is friendly and helpful you can give more. When the service charge is not included, a 10% tip is customary.

There are many places where tipping is not customary but is a welcome gesture. The local juice stands, bars, coffee corners, street and beach vendors are all tipped on occasion. Parking assistants receive no wages and are dependent on tips, usually the equivalent of US$1. Gas station attendants, shoe shiners and barbers are also frequently tipped. Most people round taxi fares up to the nearest *real,* but tipping is not expected.

Bargaining

'Quem não chora não mama.'
(Those who don't cry, don't suckle.)

– Brazilian saying to justify bargaining

A little bargaining for hotel rooms should become second nature. Before you agree to take a room, ask for a better price. *'Tem desconto?'* ('Is there a discount?') and *'Pode fazer um melhor preço?'* ('Can you give a better price?') are the phrases to use. It's also possible to reduce the price if you state that you don't want a TV, private bath, or air conditioning.

There's often a discount for paying *á vista* (cash) or for staying during the low season *(baixa estação* or *época baixa)*. If you're staying longer than a couple of days, ask for a discount. Once a discount has been quoted, make sure it is noted on your bill at the same time – this avoids 'misunderstandings' at a later date. You should also bargain when shopping in markets and riding in unmetered taxis.

POST & COMMUNICATIONS

The telephone system is efficient in some places but an exercise in frustration in others. Public Internet services exist in every medium-sized city and many smaller places. Postal services are pretty good: Most mail seems to get through.

Post

A postcard or letter weighing up to 20g costs US$0.75 to the US, US$0.85 to Europe and US$1 to Australia.

There are mailboxes on the street, but it's safer to go to a post office *correios* (pronounced 'ku-HEY-ush'). Most post offices are open from 9 am to 6 pm Monday to Friday, and Saturday morning. Air mail letters to the US and Europe arrive in a week or so. For Australia, allow about two weeks.

Brazilian postal codes are five numbers followed by three; the first five are the base code for the city, the others specify the location. In this book we list the base code for each city.

For receiving mail, the *posta restante* system seems to function reasonably well.

Post offices hold mail for 30 days. A reliable alternative for American Express customers is to have mail sent to one of its offices.

Telephone

International Calls To phone Brazil from abroad, dial your international access code, then 55 (Brazil's country code), then the city code (omitting the initial 0xx), then the number.

The cost of international calls from Brazil depends on where you call from, but expect it to be about US$1 a minute to the US or Canada, and US$1.75 a minute to Europe or Australia. Prices are about 20% lower during *hora reduzida,* which is typically from 8 pm to 6 am daily and all day Sunday.

To make an international call at your own expense, ordinary card pay phones – nicknamed *orelhões* (big ears; you'll understand why as soon as you see one) – are of little use unless you have an international calling card. For one thing, most pay phones are restricted to domestic calls only. For another, even if they are enabled for international calls, 30-unit Brazilian phone cards (often the only denomination available) may last less than a minute on an international call, and there's no facility for switching cards in mid-call.

If you have an international calling card, or if you only have to talk for less than a minute, you need to find a phone that will make international calls. Every town has a telephone office *(posto telefônico),* and international calls should be possible on at least some of its phones. Some phones in airports and on the streets of the bigger cities will also make international calls. They may be marked *'Este aparelho faz ligações internacionais'* ('This apparatus makes international calls') – or they may not be identified in any way at all.

Without an international calling card, your best option is to find a telephone office with some phones that don't require a card, where you pay in cash after you have finished talking (don't forget to establish the cost per minute before you call). Normally you'll be directed to a booth and will dial the call yourself. Country codes include the following: US and Canada ☎ 1, UK ☎ 44, Australia ☎ 61, New Zealand ☎ 64, France ☎ 33, Germany ☎ 49, Argentina ☎ 54, Peru ☎ 51, Paraguay ☎ 595, Colombia ☎ 57, Bolivia ☎ 591 and Venezuela ☎ 58.

You can also make calls from your hotel or a private phone, but in hotels it's essential

Brazilian City Codes & Carriers

Brazil has several rival long-distance telephone carriers. When making an international or intercity call, you have to select a carrier and include its two-digit code (código de prestadora) in the number you dial. Brazilian city codes are commonly quoted with an xx representing the carrier code – eg, ☎ 0xx21 for Rio de Janeiro or ☎ 0xx71 for Salvador. You'll find city codes listed in this way beneath each city heading in this book.

Different carriers cover different areas of the country, and you have to use one that covers both the place you are calling from and the place you're calling to. The carriers are as follows:

Carrier	Code	Area of Coverage
Brasil Telecom	14	Distrito Federal, states of Mato Grosso, Mato Grosso do Sul, Acre, Goiás, Tocantins, Rondônia, Santa Catarina, Paraná (except Sercontel area) and Pelotas, Capão do Leão, Morro Redondo & Turuçu (Rio Grande do Sul)
Canbrá	85	States of Rio de Janeiro, Minas Gerais (except CTBC areas), Espírito Santo, Bahia, Sergipe, Alagoas, Pernambuco, Rio Grande do Norte, Ceará, Piauí, Maranhão, Pará, Amapá, Roraima, Amazonas
Ceterp	16	Guatapará & Ribeirão Preto (São Paulo state)
CRT	51	Rio Grande do Sul (except Brasil Telecom area)
CTBC Telecom	12	Some areas of São Paulo, Minas Gerais, Mato Grosso do Sul & Goiás states
Embratel	21	All of Brazil & international calls
Intelig	23	All of Brazil & international calls
Sercontel	43	Londrina & Tamarana (Paraná state)
Telefônica	15	São Paulo state (except CTBC and Ceterp areas)
Telemar	31	Same as Canbrá (above)
Vésper	89	São Paulo state (except CTBC and Ceterp areas)

This may look complicated, but in practice it's straightforward. For one thing, you can use Embratel (☎ 21) or Intelig (☎ 23) for any call; for another, other major carriers usually have their names and codes widely displayed in their localities, so you absorb them unconsciously.

For example, to call from Rio de Janeiro to Fortaleza (city code 0xx85) in the state of Ceará, you dial 0 followed by 21 or 23 or 31 or 85 (the codes of the four carriers that cover both Rio and Ceará), followed by 85 for Fortaleza, followed by the number.

For an international call, dial 00 followed by 21 or 23 (the international carriers), followed by the country code, city code and number.

There appears to be little appreciable difference between the carriers, but at least the system gives you alternatives if the lines on your initial choice always seem to be busy.

to try to establish beforehand what it will cost you. Hotels often add a markup.

For international collect *(a cobrar)* calls, try dialing ☎ 000107 from any phone, although this only works to some countries. Or try dialing the local operator (☎ 100) and asking to be transferred to an international operator *(telefonista internacional)*. Failing that, you need to locate a phone that can do international calls (see above). Home Country Direct services get you through to an operator in the country you're calling (or at least an interactive recorded message there) which will connect the collect call for you. For most Home Country Direct services, dial ☎ 00080 followed by the country code (for North America, instead of the country code use ☎ 10 for AT&T, ☎ 12 for MCI and ☎ 16 for Sprint; for Australia, dial 0008006112). Alternatively, you can get a Brazilian international operator by dialing ☎ 000111. They usually speak English, but if not, you could experiment with some of the following phrases:

I would like to make an international call to…
   Quero fazer uma ligação internacional para…
I would like to reverse the charges.
   Quero fazê-la a cobrar.
I am calling from a public (private) telephone (in Rio de Janeiro).
   Estou falando dum telefone público (particular) no Rio de Janeiro.
My name is…
   Meu nôme é…
The area code is…
   O código é…
The number is…
   O número é…

If you're having telephone troubles, staff at reception desks at larger hotels can be helpful.

Be careful with services advertised by stickers on some phones announcing free calls to multilingual operators who can get you collect calls to the US or international credit-card calls. Make sure you establish the costs of any call before making it.

eKno Communication Service Lonely Planet's eKno global communication service provides low-cost international calls – for local calls, you're usually better off with a local phone card. eKno also offers free messaging services, email, travel information and an online travel vault, where you can securely store all your important documents. You can join online at www.ekno.lonelyplanet.com, where you will find the local-access numbers for the 24-hour customer-service center. Once you have joined, check the eKno Web site for the latest access numbers for each country and for updates on new features.

One caveat: In Brazil, eKno cannot be used from just any phone. You can only get through to the eKno access numbers from a phone that makes international calls, and this counts out a substantial number of street pay phones.

Domestic Calls You can make domestic calls – intercity or local – from normal card pay phones on the street and in telephone offices. The telephone cards you need are sold for US$1.40 per 30 units at telephone offices and for around US$2 by vendors, newsstands and anywhere else where you see advertising for *cartões telefônicos*. The most common denomination is 30 units, but 20-, 60- and 90-unit cards are sometimes available.

For calls within the city you're in, just slide the card into the phone, check the readout to see if it's given you proper credit, and dial the number (nearly always seven or eight digits – and many of the seven-digit ones are in process of being changed to eight). Local calls cost only one or two units. For information, call ☎ 102.

For calls to other cities, you need to precede the number with 0, then the code of your selected carrier (see the boxed text 'Brazilian City Codes and Carriers'), then the two or three digits representing the city. City codes are therefore usually given in the format 0 x x digit digit, with the two x's representing the carrier code. A long-distance call usually eats up between five and 10 phone card units per minute.

You need to include the city code (0 x x digit digit) when calling to another city even if that city has the same city code as the one you're calling from.

To make an intercity collect call (*chamada a cobrar*), stick a 9 in front of the 0xx. To make a local collect call dial 9090 and then the number. A recorded message in Portuguese will ask you to say your name and the name of the state where you're calling from, after the beep.

You will easily recognize toll-free numbers in Brazil, which are usually made up of 0800 followed by six digits.

Mobile phones in Brazil are known as cellular phones (*celular* in Portuguese, often shortened to *cel*). They have eight-digit numbers starting with a 9, and calls to them run through your phone-card units much faster than calls to regular numbers. Mobiles have city codes just like normal phone numbers (0 x x digit digit), and if you're calling from another city you have to use them.

Fax

Larger post offices have fax services. International faxes cost about US$5 per page.

Email & Internet Access

As lovers of all things modern, Brazilians have taken to the Internet in large numbers. You can find Internet cafés and other public Internet services in just about any town of medium-size and above. With a free Web-based email account (available from sites such as www.hotmail.com and www.yahoo.com) you can use the Internet and email as much as you like, as long as you can afford the typical price of US$2.50 or US$3 an hour.

Post offices are starting to install Internet terminals, and the communications company Telemar is launching public Internet terminals operable with telephone cards.

DIGITAL RESOURCES

The World Wide Web is a rich resource for travelers. You can research your trip, hunt down bargain air fares, book hotels or chat with locals and other travelers about the best places to visit (or avoid!).

A good place to begin your Web explorations is at the Lonely Planet Web site (www.lonelyplanet.com). You'll find succinct summaries on traveling to most places on Earth, postcards from other travelers, and the Thorn Tree electronic bulletin board where

you can ask questions before you go or give advice when you return. You can also find travel news and updates to many of Lonely Planet's most popular guidebooks, and the subWWWay section, which links you to useful travel resources elsewhere on the Web.

The following are among the best general Web sites on Brazil. You'll find more specialized sites recommended throughout this book in the sections covering specific areas.

http://lanic.utexas.edu/la/brazil
    Brazil site at the University of Texas, the best collection of Brazil links to be found

www.terra.com.br/turismo
    Portuguese-language travel site with, among other things, searchable street maps of 128 Brazilian cities and up-to-date what's-on guides for 50 of them

www.brazilmax.com
    The self-proclaimed hip gringo's guide to Brazilian culture and society; good, selective articles and links

www.brazil.org.uk
    Site of the Brazilian embassy in London, with comprehensive information on many aspects of the country, including practical information for tourists and links to dozens of local tourism sites in Brazil

www.southamericadaily.com
  Brazil news from several sources and links to BBC and CNN TV and BBC radio
www.oneworld.org/sejup/
  News on social justice and environmental issues

BOOKS

Most books are published in different editions by different publishers in different countries. As a result, a book might be a hardcover rarity in one country while it's readily available in paperback in another. Your local bookstore or library can search by title or author and advise you on the availability of the recommendations in this section.

For recommended Brazilian literature, refer to the Literature section in the Facts about Brazil chapter.

Lonely Planet

Lonely Planet publishes an excellent *Brazilian phrasebook*, which covers practically anything you'd ever need to say in Portuguese down here. *Healthy Travel – Central & South America*, by Isabelle Young, is a handy little companion with a wealth of practical advice on how to deal with (and if possible avoid) everything from hay fever to tarantulas.

Lonely Planet country guides cover all South American countries except the Guianas, while *South America on a shoestring* covers all countries on the continent plus the Falkland Islands. If your travels are focusing on Rio, LP's *Rio de Janeiro* city guide is penned by one of the authors of this book, long-time Brazil expert Andrew Draffen.

The French-language Lonely Planet Guides de Voyage publishes *Brésil*.

Guidebooks

Quatro Rodas publishes the best all-around series of Brazil guides. They're in Portuguese, but easy to follow. The bigger sellers are readily available at most newsstands and all are available in Brazilian bookshops.

The flagship title is *Quatro Rodas: Guia Brasil*, with detailed listings of accommodations and restaurants in more than 900 cities

and towns, plus some information on transportation and sights and useful little local maps. It comes with an excellent foldout map of the country. The only field it doesn't cover, unfortunately, is budget.

Other good Quatro Rodas titles include *Guia de Praias*, geared toward beach freaks on driving tours, with great aerial photos plus information on hotels, campsites, ecological parks and some maps; and *Turismo Ecológico no Brasil*, with practical details for about 80 nature and activity tourism destinations, heavily weighted toward the Southeast, with cross-referenced indexes for everything from trekking to caving. There's also *Guia de Rio de Janeiro*, which is quite inexpensive. See Maps, earlier in this chapter, for further Quatro Rodas publications.

Two other very nice Portuguese-language guides to have, but more expensive, are *Parques Nacionais Brasil* (Brazil National Parks) and *Pantanal & Bonito*, both in the Guias Philips series. They're packed with attractive photos, lots of fauna and flora data and some practical information.

Travel

Travelers' Tales Brazil, edited by Lonely Planet author Scott Doggett and Annette Haddad, is a fine anthology of tales of travel and life in Brazil. Writers include Steven Berkoff, Joe Kane, Petru Popescu and Alma Guillermoprieto, who present a series of glimpses of Brazilian experiences as varied and riveting as the country itself.

Peter Fleming's *Brazilian Adventure* is about the young journalist's expedition into Mato Grosso in the 1930s in search of vanished explorer Colonel Fawcett. At the time this area was the world's last, vast unexplored region. What Fleming found is less important than the telling, written with the humor of the disenchanted Briton. Travel adventures don't get any funnier than this – highly recommended.

Then again, maybe they do get funnier: It's not exactly about Brazil (though the author does pass through), but Redmond O'Hanlon's *In Trouble Again: A Journey Between the Orinoco and the Amazon* is one of the most hilarious true travel tales ever written. See if you don't squirm as he describes the *candiru* toothpick fish that lodges itself in your... well, just read it and see.

Also not solely about Brazil is Peter Matthiessen's *The Cloud Forest,* an account of a 30,000km journey across the South American wilderness from the Amazon to Tierra del Fuego. It's well worth a read. Matthiessen is a master at describing his environment.

Moritz Thomsen's *The Saddest Pleasure: A Journey on Two Rivers* (1990) is a highly recommended book – skip the sickly introduction – about the author's experiences in South America, including journeys through Brazil, along the Amazon and into his own tormented soul.

Running The Amazon by Joe Kane is the story of the 10 men and one woman, who in 1986 became the only expedition ever to cover the entire length of the Rio Amazonas, from the Andes to the Atlantic, on foot and in rafts and kayaks.

History & Politics

The 500th anniversary of the arrival of the Portuguese in Brazil finally prompted the appearance of a couple of decent, 300-page English-language surveys of Brazil's fascinating and fantastic past: *A Concise History of Brazil,* by Boris Fausto, and *Brazil: Five Centuries of Change,* by Thomas E Skidmore. Fausto's book is the drier, but apart from its treatment of the 20th century (which is Skidmore's specialty), is probably more balanced and accurate. *A History of Brazil,* by E Bradford Burns, is a more in-depth look at the country's story up to 1993. For readers who like their history with a dose of fiction, *Brazil,* by South African novelist Errol Lincoln Uys, traces the history of two Brazilian families from pre-Cabral times to the founding of Brasília.

John Hemming's books on the Indians of Brazil (see the Indians section, next) cover that fascinating slice of Brazilian history comprehensively.

The best books on colonial Brazil are mostly hard to get: Try to track down Caio Prado Jr's *The Colonial Background of Modern Brazil,* Charles R Boxer's excellently written *Golden Age of Brazil, 1695-1750* and Gilberto Freyre's *The Masters & the Slaves: A Study in the Development of Brazilian Civilization.* Freyre's social history of his country revolutionized Brazilians' notions of Brazil when it appeared in 1933. For one thing, it recognized the contribution of blacks to Brazilian culture – and many still consider it a key to understanding the place, even though some of the author's attitudes seem old-fashioned today. He has been rebuked by academics for contributing to the myth of racial democracy in Brazil.

One of the best treatments of 19th-century Brazil is Emília Viotti da Costa's essay collection *The Brazilian Empire: Myths & Histories.* The revised paperback edition of 2000 has a new chapter on women in 19th-century Brazil.

The unbelievable late-19th century mystics' rebellion in Canudos was immortalized in *Rebellion in the Backlands,* by Euclides da Cunha (1902), a sort of meditation on Brazilian civilization that mixes history, geography and philosophy, and is considered a masterpiece of Brazilian literature. The story of da Cunha and the rebellion is told by Mario Vargas Llosa in his novel *The War of the End of the World,* which is light, entertaining reading for the traveler.

Thomas Skidmore's *Politics in Brazil, 1930-1964* and *The Politics of Military Rule in Brazil, 1964-1985* are informative accounts of the mid-20th century.

Indians

Claude Levi-Strauss' *Tristes Tropiques* (1955), a study of a number of Indian peoples of the Brazilian interior, was an anthropological milestone. It is also a beautifully written travelogue and a reflection on Western culture and the author's own background as a Jewish fugitive from Nazi Europe.

The first and last word on the destruction of the Brazilian Indians is provided by *Red Gold* and *Amazon Frontier* by John Hemming, mammoth works covering the period up to 1760 and the years 1760-1910 respectively. A post-1910 sequel is on the way from Hemming, an eloquent campaigner for Indian rights.

Before the Bulldozer: The Nambiquara Indians and the World Bank, by David Price (1989), is the story of an anthropologist's attempt to defend a small society from the development of a 1600km highway.

A brief introduction to the contemporary Indian situation in Brazil can be found in the Survival International booklet *Disinherited – Indians in Brazil,* written by Fiona Watson, Caroline Pearce and Stephen Corry. Many books have been written about the Yanomami people of far northwest Amazonia since the outside world hit them in the 1970s. One of the most stimulating recent accounts is *Darkness in El Dorado,* by Patrick Tierney (2000), which lambastes the self-serving nature of many scientists' and journalists' dealings with the Yanomami. See the Indians section under Population & People in the Facts about Brazil chapter for more on these two books.

Amazonia (1991), by the renowned explorer and photographer Loren McIntyre, records in magnificent images the gradual demise of the region and its original inhabitants. To learn more about McIntyre's many journeys in search of the source of the Amazon and his extraordinary psychic experiences with indigenous tribes, track down a copy of *Amazon Beaming* (1991), by Petru Popescu.

Music

The Brazilian Sound, by Chris McGowan and Ricardo Pessanha, is a well illustrated, very readable introductory history of Brazilian popular music incorporating social analysis and interviews with the famous. An updated edition was published in 1998. *Samba,* by Alma Guillermoprieto, describes a year in the life of Mangueira, one of the most traditional Rio samba schools. The author joined the school and went on to parade with them. It's an excellent read.

Environment, Flora & Fauna

Amazon Watershed, by British environmental investigative journalist George Monbiot, delves – at some personal risk to the author – into the root causes of the destruction of the Amazon forests, from rapacious loggers and the Yanomami gold rush to the migration of poor settlers expelled from lands elsewhere in Brazil and the negative influence of the US, UK, IMF and World Bank. Though published in 1991 it's still an absorbing and relevant read.

Henry Walter Bates' *The Naturalist on the Rivers Amazon,* a classic journal of plant, animal and human life in Amazonia in the 1850s, is now available as an e-book (available at www.amazon.com among other places). In traditional paper form, you may be able to find secondhand copies of George Woodcock's *Henry Walter Bates, Naturalist of the Amazons* (1969), a fascinating account of Bates' investigations and travels.

The most captivating of more modern naturalist books on Amazonia is Sy Montgomery's *Journey of the Pink Dolphins* (2000). In lively and moving prose the author recounts some magical experiences during her studies of these amazing inhabitants of Amazonian waterways. *Andes to Amazon,* by Michael Bright, a lavishly illustrated hardback accompanying a recent BBC TV series on South American natural history, includes two excellent chapters on the Amazon and a section on the Pantanal.

A Field Guide To Medicinal And Useful Plants Of The Upper Amazon by James L Castner, Stephen L Timme and James A Duke, published in 1998, combines clear photos, accurate description, and interesting information on how Amazonia's huge wealth of medicinal plants is used locally. This fine field guide is a telling argument for the preservation of biodiversity. So is *Tales of a Shaman's Apprentice,* by Mark Plotkin. For 15 years Plotkin devotedly tracked down Amazonian witchdoctors in order to understand some of their encyclopedic and indispensable knowledge of medicinal plants. His account is a travelogue and an adventure story too – an excellent read.

A good field guide to the animals of tropical Brazil is *Neotropical Rainforest Mammals,* by Louise Emmons. *Aves Brasileiras,* by Johan Dalgas Frisch, is the classic Brazilian bird identification guide, with names in Portuguese, Latin, English and Spanish – but unfortunately is not very easy to obtain.

Birders in the Amazon region of Brazil often use field guides for adjacent countries – many species overlap. *A Guide to the Birds of Colombia,* by Steven L Hilty and William L Brown, *A Guide to the Birds of Venezuela,* by Raadolphe de Schauensee and William Phelps, and *South American Birds: A Photographic Aid to Identification,* by John S Dunning are all very useful.

Readers with special interest in the battle for the rainforest should look for *The World is Burning,* an account of the Chico Mendes story by Alex Shoumatoff (see the boxed text 'Chico Mendes' in the Randônia & Acre chapter in the section The North). *The Fate of the Forest: Developers, Destroyers, and Defenders of the Amazon,* by Susanna Hecht and Alexander Cockburn (1989), is one of the best analyses of the complex web of destruction, complete with ideas on ways to mend the damage, while Augusta Dwyer has written a fierce indictment of corruption and mismanagement titled *Into the Amazon: The Struggle for the Rain Forest.*

Religion

The strength and cultural richness of Candomblé has attracted a number of perceptive Western authors, several of whom are converts. One of the most recent nonacademic books on the subject is *Sacred Leaves of Candomblé,* by Robert A Voeks (1997), which focuses on how plants are used in the spiritual and medicinal practices of Candomblé. For light reading, try Jorge Amado's novel *Dona Flor and Her Two Husbands. The African Religions of Brazil,* by the French anthropologist Roger Bastide, is a scholarly look at the social forces that shaped Candomblé. Ruth Landes' *The City of Women* is about Candomblé in Bahia. These last two books are out of print but findable.

Other Books

The Brazilians, by Joseph A Page, is readable and anecdotal but also as penetrating a portrait of the country and its people as you're likely to find. Page looks back into the past to illuminate modern popular cultural manifestations such as Carnaval, soccer and *telenovelas,* as well as the country's unnerving tendency toward violence. It's good on the regions as well as the main cities.

Jan Rocha's *Brazil in Focus* is a good, brief introduction to contemporary people, politics and culture in Brazil. Another successful overall portrait of the country is *Brazil: The Once and Future Country,* by Marshall C Eakin.

Eat Smart in Brazil: How to Decipher the Menu, Know the Market Foods & Embark on a Tasting Adventure, by Joan and David Peterson, is a good and handy paperback guide to, well, food in Brazil.

Carolina Maria de Jesus lived and wrote in the slums of São Paulo in the 1950s. Her book *Child of the Dark* is strong and compelling. It was published in the UK and Australia under the title *Beyond All Pity.*

If you're spending any time in Rio (and even if you're not), buy a copy of Priscilla Ann Goslin's hilarious *How to Be a Carioca – The Alternative Guide for the Tourist in Rio.* It's a lot of laughs, and Goslin's insights into the Rio lifestyle are right on the mark.

NEWSPAPERS & MAGAZINES

Brazil's media industry is concentrated in the hands of a few organizations. The company that owns the major TV network, Globo, also controls some leading publications.

In English, *Time* and *Newsweek* and the daily *International Herald Tribune* are available fairly widely. European and US newspapers are sold at some newsstands in tourist and business areas of Rio and São Paulo, but they are expensive.

In Portuguese, the *Folha de São Paulo* and Rio's *Jornal do Brasil* are both fine newspapers, with good national and international coverage and a socially liberal stance. *O Estado de São Paulo* and Rio's *O Globo* are a little more comprehensive in their coverage and also more conservative. All these papers are available nationwide.

The weekly *Veja* is one of the best things about Brazil – a truly excellent current-affairs magazine, somewhat in the *Time/*

Newsweek style but with more range, depth, irreverence and penetrating analysis. In seven or eight major cities it comes with a *Vejinha* (Little Veja), which is a good pull-out guide to what's happening locally. *Isto É* and *Época* are rival news mags. Brazilian magazines such as *Terra* and *Expedicão Eco Turismo* have good articles on off-the-beaten-track travel destinations.

Every medium-sized town in Brazil has its own daily newspaper. These can be useful for transport and entertainment information. You'll find links to the Web sites of over 300 Brazilian newspapers at www .zonalatina.com/Zlpapers.htm.

TV

Major hotels and some bars and restaurants have pay-TV with CNN and occasionally other English-language programs, but that's about as much as you should expect.

Brazilian TV is mostly game shows, soccer, *telenovelas* (soap operas) and bad American films dubbed into Portuguese. News programs like to dwell on disasters and accidents, and show detailed diagrams of the diseased interiors of the bodies/corpses of well known people who are ill or have died.

Hotel rooms of decent budget standard and above generally have a TV that will show somewhere between two and eight channels, a high proportion of which (especially in the provinces) are devoted to Christian evangelism. One channel (though it may go by different local names in some areas) will nearly always be Globo, put on by the country's most powerful TV empire. Globo's logo is a circle inside a slightly warped rectangle inside a circle.

The telenovelas bring the country to a halt at key moments. They're aired at various times between 6 and 9 pm Monday to Saturday (Globo squeezes in three during those hours). If you only switch the box on late at night you will probably settle on *Programa do Jô*, a talk show (with musical interludes) hosted by the intelligent, likeable and large Jô Soares (on Globo, of course). Jô speaks six languages, and occasionally interviews foreigners in English (shown with sub-

titles). The other guy worth looking out for is Otávio Mesquita, who makes his living going around with TV cameras and a small band of comically uniformed musicians trying to annoy pompous people in authority. Sílvio Santos, who among other things hosts the Brazilian version of *Who Wants to Be a Millionaire?*, is a much-hyped 'TV personality' with a voice, smile and quiff of hair so smooth they make the flesh crawl. Another big face is Xuxa, a former child bubblegum pop star who has grown into a coquettish TV presenter who always wears a sickly-sweet smile.

Pay-TV, here as everywhere, has some good stuff, but you're highly unlikely to see it, except for MTV, which does find its way onto some hotel-room screens.

VIDEO SYSTEMS

Brazilian video and television operates on the PAL image registration system, like Australia and most of western Europe. French (SECAM) and US (NTSC) video machines and prerecorded tapes are incompatible with PAL tapes and machines. Many of the videos made for tourists in Brazil are available in NTSC as well as PAL, however.

PHOTOGRAPHY & VIDEO
Film & Equipment

Cameras will suffer on the road and they may get broken, lost or stolen. But there are so many good shots in Brazil that you'll kick yourself if you don't bring a camera along on your travels.

Your choice of camera will depend on your photographic requirements. Automatic 35mm rangefinders will suffice for standard portraits and landscapes. For general wildlife shots, a single-lens reflex camera with a 200mm or 300mm zoom lens is essential. Photographers who are after close-up shots of wildlife prefer a 400mm or 500mm telephoto with a fixed focal length lens.

If you're nervous about losing your expensive camera, disposable ones are readily available in most large cities.

Kodak and Fuji print film are sold and processed almost everywhere, but for high-quality results you should use a large lab in

Rio city or São Paulo. If you're shooting professional-quality print film or slides it's best to bring film with you. Slide film is expensive in Brazil (around US$15 a roll, not including processing) and high-ISO slide film is only obtainable in a few cities.

For camera repairs in Rio, Camera Service Miyazaki (☎/fax 0xx21-2522-4894) at shop 214, Rua Djalma Ulrich 110, Copacabana is recommended (enter via Avenida NS de Copacabana 1063).

Heat and humidity can ruin film, so remember to keep it in the coolest, driest place available. Use a lead film bag to protect film from airport X-ray machines. This is especially important for the sensitive high-ISO films. Useful accessories include a cable release, polarizing filter, lens-cleaning kit, plenty of silica-gel packs, and a bean bag or clamp or monopod. Don't carry a flashy camera bag – it may attract the attention of thieves – and make sure your equipment is insured.

Video cameras are no longer a big deal in Brazil so you won't get any weird stares as you shoot.

Technical Tips & Restrictions

Photography in the rainforest requires attention to the dimness of the light. You'll have to experiment with a combination of fast film (400 ISO and upward), a tripod, flash unit, and cable release. When exposed to the forest's humid conditions for an extended period, your cameras and lenses may have their functioning impaired by fungus growth. The standard preventative measure is to keep your gear sealed in plastic bags together with silica-gel packs.

When shooting on beaches, remember to adjust for the glare from water or sand. Don't take a camera to a beach unless it will be closely guarded – see the Dangers & Annoyances section in this chapter.

Some Candomblé temples do not permit photography. Avoid taking photographs or video in banks or near military bases or other sensitive areas.

Respect the wishes of the locals and be sure to ask their permission before taking a photo or video of them.

TIME

Brazil has four time zones. Brasília time, which is GMT/UTC minus three hours, covers the whole of the Southeast, South and Northeast regions, plus, in the Central West section, the Distrito Federal (including Brasília) and the state of Goiás, and in the North the states of Tocantins, Amapá and the eastern half of Pará.

The remainder of the Central West (Mato Grosso and Mato Grosso do Sul states) and the rest of the North (except Acre and far southwest Amazonas state) are one hour behind Brasília time (GMT/UTC minus four hours). Acre and southwest Amazonas (southwest of a line drawn between Tabatinga and Porto Acre, which is on the Amazonas/Acre border just north of Rio Branco) are two hours behind Brasília time (GMT/UTC minus five hours). The Fernando de Noronha archipelago, out in the Atlantic Ocean 350km off Natal, is one hour *ahead* of Brasília time (GMT/UTC minus two hours).

Thus when it's noon in London and 7 am in New York, it should be 9 am in most of Brazil but 10 am in Fernando de Noronha, 8 am in Mato Grosso and most of the North, and 7 am in Acre. We say 'should be' because daylight saving means that it usually isn't. Brazilian daylight saving time runs from mid-October to mid-February, during which period clocks are advanced one hour – but only in the Southeast, South and Central West and the states of Bahia and Tocantins! And of course Northern Hemisphere daylight saving happens in the other half of the year, so in reality the time difference between Rio and New York is three hours in December and one hour in July. And the time difference between Rio and Manaus is three hours from October to February but two hours otherwise. Got that clear then?

Not surprisingly, Brazilians as well as foreign travelers sometimes don't know what time of day it is, and a lot of travelers have a few tales to tell about connections missed due to temporal ignorance.

Even when they do know the time, Brazilians are not noted for respecting it. Don't be surprised, or angry, if they arrive a couple of hours later than expected. To them it is acceptable, and they always have the most inventive reasons for it.

ELECTRICITY

Electrical current is not standardized in Brazil and can be almost anywhere between 110V and 220V, so it's a good idea to carry a converter if you can't travel without your hair dryer.

In Rio de Janeiro and São Paulo, the current is mostly 110 or 120V, 60Hz AC, though some hotels have 220V. Check before you plug in.

The most common power outlets have two sockets and most will take both round and flat prongs.

WEIGHTS & MEASURES

Brazil uses the metric system. There is a metric conversion table inside the back cover of this book.

The Brazilian system indicates decimals with commas and thousands with points (so a thousand bucks would be written US$1.000,00).

LAUNDRY

Oddly, washing clothes isn't cheap here, at least if you send them out. Most Brazilians wash their own clothes or have domestic help do it. If you don't want to wash your own, inquire at your hotel: Housekeepers will often wash clothes at home to make a few extra reais. Some coin laundries exist in larger cities. They generally cost about US$2.50 to wash and the same to dry.

TOILETS

Public toilets are not common but they exist at every bus station and airport and somewhere else in most cities and towns; there's usually an entrance fee around US$0.50. Brazilians are quite nice about letting you use toilets in restaurants and bars. As in other Latin American countries, toilet paper isn't flushed. There's usually a nice smelly basket next to the toilet to put it in.

HEALTH

Travel health depends on your predeparture preparations, your daily health care while traveling and how you handle any medical problem that develops. While the potential dangers can seem quite frightening, in reality few travelers experience anything more than upset stomachs.

Predeparture Planning

Immunizations Plan ahead for your vaccinations: Some of them require more than one injection, while some should not be given in combination. Some should not be given during pregnancy or to people with allergies – discuss this with your doctor. It's recommended you seek medical advice at least six weeks before travel.

Talk about your requirements with your doctor. Carry proof of your vaccinations, especially yellow fever, as this is often needed to enter Brazil and neighboring countries (see the Visas & Documents section earlier in this chapter). Vaccinations you should consider getting for this trip include the following:

Diphtheria & Tetanus Vaccinations for these two diseases are usually combined and are recommended for everyone. After an initial course of three injections (usually given in childhood), boosters are necessary every 10 years.

Everyday Health

Normal body temperature is up to 37°C (98.6°F); more than 2°C (4°F) higher indicates a high fever. The normal adult pulse rate is 60 to 100 per minute (children 80 to 100, babies 100 to 140). As a general rule, pulse increases about 20 beats per minute for each 1°C (2°F) rise in fever.

Respiration (breathing) rate is also an indicator of illness. Count the number of breaths per minute: Between 12 and 20 is normal for adults and older children (up to 30 for younger children, 40 for babies). People with a high fever or serious respiratory illness breathe more quickly than normal. More than 40 shallow breaths a minute may indicate pneumonia.

Polio Everyone should keep up to date with this vaccination, which is normally given in childhood. A booster every 10 years maintains immunity.

Hepatitis A Hepatitis A vaccine (eg, Avaxim, Havrix 1440 or VAQTA) provides long-term immunity (possibly more than 10 years) after an initial injection and a booster at six to 12 months.

Alternatively, an injection of gamma globulin can provide short-term protection against hepatitis A – two to six months, depending on the dose given. It is not a vaccine, but is a ready-made antibody collected from blood donations. It is reasonably effective and, unlike the vaccine, is protective immediately. Because it is a blood product, however, there are current concerns about its long-term safety.

Hepatitis A vaccine and hepatitis B vaccine are available in a combined form called Twinrix. Three injections over a six-month period are required, the first two providing substantial protection against hepatitis A.

Hepatitis B Travelers who should consider vaccination against hepatitis B include those on a long trip, as well as those visiting countries where there are high levels of hepatitis B infection, where blood transfusions may not be adequately screened or where sexual contact or needle sharing is a possibility. Vaccination involves three injections, with a booster at 12 months. More rapid courses are available if necessary.

Meningococcal Meningitis Vaccination is recommended for travelers to certain parts of Brazil. A single injection gives good protection for three years against the major epidemic forms of the disease. Protection may be less effective in children under two years of age.

Typhoid Vaccination may be required if you are travelling for more than a couple of weeks in most parts of Central or South America. It is available either as an injection or in capsule form.

Yellow Fever This is the only vaccine that is a legal requirement for entry into certain countries. Brazil and several neighboring countries are among these, but the requirement only applies if you are coming from certain countries (see Visas & Documents earlier in this chapter). But vaccination is recommended in any case for travel in most lowland tropical areas of South America – including, at the time of writing, the Brazilian states of Acre, Amapá, Amazonas, Bahia, Distrito Federal, Goiás, Maranhão, Mato Grosso, Mato Grosso do Sul, Minas Gerais, Pará, Rondônia, Roraima and Tocantins. You may have to go to a special yellow fever vaccination center to get the inoculation.

Rabies Vaccination should be considered by those who will spend a month or longer in a country where rabies is common, especially if they are cycling, handling animals, caving or traveling to remote areas, and for children (who may not report a bite). Pretravel rabies vaccination involves having three injections over 21 to 28 days. If someone who has been vaccinated is bitten or scratched by an animal, they will require two booster injections of vaccine; those not vaccinated require more.

Malaria Medication Antimalarial drugs do not prevent you from being infected, but kill the malaria parasites during a stage in their development and significantly reduce the risk of becoming very ill or dying. Expert advice on medication should be sought, as there are many factors to consider, including the area to be visited, the risk of exposure to malaria-carrying mosquitoes, the side effects of medication, your medical history and whether you are an adult or child or pregnant. Travelers to isolated areas in high-risk countries might like to carry a treatment dose of medication for use if symptoms occur. At the time of writing malaria was a risk in the states of Acre, Amapá, Amazonas, Pará, Rondônia, Roraima, Tocantins and western Maranhão and northern Mato Grosso. But you should check the latest available information.

Health Insurance Make sure that you have adequate health insurance. See Travel Insurance under Visas & Documents, earlier in this chapter.

Travel Health Guides Lonely Planet's *Healthy Travel – Central & South America,* by Isabelle Young, is handily pocket-sized and packed with useful information including pretrip planning, emergency first aid, immunization and disease information, and tips on what to do if you get sick on the road. *Travel with Children,* from Lonely Planet, includes advice on travel health for younger children.

There are a number of excellent travel health sites on the Internet. From the Lonely Planet Web site there are links at www.lonelyplanet.com/weblinks/wlheal.htm to the World Health Organization and the US Centers for Disease Control & Prevention.

Other Preparations Make sure you're healthy before you start traveling. If you are going on a long trip make sure your teeth are OK. If you wear glasses take a spare pair and your prescription.

If you require a particular medication, take an adequate supply, as it may not be available locally. Taking part of the packaging showing the generic name rather than the brand will make getting replacements easier. To avoid any problems, it's a good idea to have a legible prescription or letter from your doctor to show that you legally use the medication.

Basic Rules

Food There is an old colonial adage: 'If you can cook it, boil it or peel it, you can eat it…otherwise forget it.' Vegetables and fruit should be washed with purified water or peeled, when possible. Beware of ice cream that is sold in the street or anywhere it might have melted and been refrozen; if there's any doubt (eg, a power cut in the last day or two) steer well clear. Shellfish, such as mussels, oysters and clams, should be avoided, as well as undercooked meat, particularly if it is ground. Steaming does not make shellfish safe for eating.

If a place looks clean and well run and the vendor also looks clean and healthy, then the food is probably safe. In general, places that are packed with travelers or locals will be fine, while empty restaurants are questionable. The food in busy restaurants is cooked and eaten quite quickly with little sitting around and has probably not been reheated.

Water The number one rule is *be careful of the water,* especially ice. Most Brazilian urban tap water is in fact heavily treated, which should make it safe to drink (if unpleasant to taste), but if you don't know for certain that the water is safe, assume the worst. Reputable brands of bottled water or

Nutrition

If your diet is poor or limited in variety, if you're traveling hard and fast and therefore missing meals, or if you simply lose your appetite, you can soon start to lose weight and place your health at risk.

Make sure your diet is well balanced. Cooked eggs, tofu, beans, lentils and nuts are all safe ways to get protein. Fruit you can peel (bananas, oranges or mandarins, for example) is usually safe and a good source of vitamins. Melons can harbor bacteria in their flesh and are best avoided. Try to eat plenty of grains (including rice) and bread. Remember that although food is generally safer if it is cooked well, overcooked food loses much of its nutritional value. If your diet isn't well balanced or if your food intake is insufficient, it's a good idea to take vitamin and iron pills.

In hot climates, make sure you drink enough – don't rely on feeling thirsty to indicate when you should drink. Not needing to urinate or voiding small amounts of very dark-yellow urine is a danger sign. Always carry a water bottle on long trips. Excessive sweating can lead to loss of salt and therefore muscle cramping. Salt tablets are not a good ideas as a preventative, but in places where salt is not used much, adding salt to food can help.

soft drinks are generally fine, although sometimes bottles may be refilled with tap water. Only use water from containers with an unbroken serrated seal – not tops or corks. Take care with fruit juice, particularly if water may have been added. Milk should be treated with suspicion as it is often unpasteurized, though boiled milk is fine if it is kept hygienically. Tea or coffee should also be OK, since the water should have been boiled.

The simplest way of purifying water is to boil it thoroughly. Vigorous boiling should be satisfactory; however, at high altitude water boils at a lower temperature, so germs are less likely to be killed. Boil it for longer in these environments.

Consider purchasing a water filter for a long trip. There are two main kinds of filter. Total filters take out all parasites, bacteria and viruses, and make water safe to drink. They are often expensive, but can be more cost effective than buying bottled water. Simple filters (which can even be a nylon mesh bag) take out dirt and larger foreign bodies from the water, so that chemical solutions work much more effectively; if water is dirty, chemical solutions may not work at all.

It's very important when buying a filter to read the specifications, so that you know exactly what it removes from the water and what it doesn't. Simple filtering will not remove all dangerous organisms, so if you cannot boil water it should be treated chemically.

Chlorine tablets will kill many pathogens, but not some parasites like giardia and amoebic cysts. Iodine is more effective in purifying water and is available in tablet form. Follow the directions carefully and remember that too much iodine can be harmful.

Medical Problems & Treatment

Self-diagnosis and treatment can be risky, so you should always seek medical help. An embassy, consulate or five-star hotel can usually recommend a local doctor or clinic. Drug dosages given in this section are for emergency use only. Correct diagnosis is vital. Medication names given are generic –

check with a pharmacist for brands available locally.

Antibiotics should ideally be administered only under medical supervision. Take only the recommended dose at the prescribed intervals and use the whole course, even if the illness seems to be cured earlier. Stop immediately if there are any serious reactions, and don't take a medication at all if you are unsure that it is the correct one. Some people are allergic to commonly prescribed antibiotics such as penicillin; carry this information (perhaps on a bracelet) when traveling.

Environmental Hazards

Heat Exhaustion Dehydration and salt deficiency can cause heat exhaustion. Take time to acclimatize to high temperatures, drink sufficient liquids and do not do anything too physically demanding.

Salt deficiency is characterized by fatigue, lethargy, headaches, giddiness and muscle cramps; adding extra salt to your food may help remedy this condition.

Heatstroke This serious, occasionally fatal condition can occur if the body's heat-regulating mechanism breaks down and the body temperature rises to dangerous levels. Long, continuous periods of exposure to high temperatures and insufficient fluids can leave you vulnerable to heatstroke.

The symptoms are feeling unwell, not sweating very much (or at all) and a high body temperature (39–41°C or 102–106°F). Where sweating has ceased the skin becomes flushed and red. Severe, throbbing headaches and lack of coordination will also occur, and the sufferer may become confused or aggressive. Eventually the victim will be delirious or convulse. Hospitalization is essential, but in the interim get victims out of the sun, remove their clothing, cover them with a wet sheet or towel and then fan continually. Give fluids if they are conscious.

Jet Lag Jet lag is experienced when a person travels by air across more than three time zones. When we travel long distances rapidly, our bodies take time to adjust to the 'new' time of our destination, and we may experience fatigue, impaired concentration, disorientation, anxiety, insomnia and loss of appetite. These effects will usually be gone within three days but, to minimize the impact of jet lag, try the following:

- Rest for a couple of days before departure.
- Try to select flight schedules that minimize sleep deprivation; arriving late in the day means you can go to sleep soon after you arrive. For very long flights, try to schedule a stopover.
- Avoid excessive eating (which bloats the stomach) and alcohol (which causes dehydration) during the flight. Instead, drink plenty of noncarbonated, nonalcoholic drinks such as fruit juice or water.
- Avoid smoking.
- Wear loose-fitting clothes and perhaps bring an eye mask and ear plugs to help you sleep.

Motion Sickness Eating lightly before and during a trip will reduce the chances of motion sickness. If you are prone to motion sickness try to find a place that minimizes movement – near the wing on aircraft, close to amidships on boats, near the center on buses. Fresh air usually helps; reading and cigarette smoke don't. Commercial motion-sickness preparations, which can cause drowsiness, have to be taken before the trip commences. Ginger (available in capsule form) and peppermint (including mint-flavored sweets) are natural preventatives.

Prickly Heat Prickly heat is an itchy rash caused by excessive perspiration trapped under the skin. It usually strikes people who have just arrived in a hot climate. Keeping cool, bathing often, drying the skin and using a mild talcum or prickly heat powder or resorting to air-conditioning may help.

Sunburn In the tropics, the desert or at high altitudes you can get sunburned surprisingly quickly, even through clouds. Use a sunscreen, a hat, and a barrier cream for your nose and lips. Calamine lotion or a commercial after-sun preparation are good for mild sunburn. Protect your eyes with good quality sunglasses.

Medical Kit Checklist

The following is a list of items you should consider including in your medical kit – consult your pharmacist for brands available in your country.

- ☐ **Aspirin or paracetamol** (acetaminophen in the USA) – for pain or fever
- ☐ **Antihistamine** – for allergies, (eg, hay fever); to ease the itch from insect bites or stings; and to prevent motion sickness
- ☐ **Cold and flu tablets, throat lozenges and nasal decongestant**
- ☐ **Multivitamins** – consider for long trips, when dietary vitamin intake may be inadequate
- ☐ **Antibiotics** – consider including these if you're traveling well off the beaten track; see your doctor, as they must be prescribed, and carry the prescription with you
- ☐ **Loperamide or diphenoxylate** –'blockers' for diarrhea
- ☐ **Prochlorperazine or metaclopramide** – for nausea and vomiting
- ☐ **Rehydration mixture** – to prevent dehydration, which may occur, for example, during bouts of diarrhea; particularly important when traveling with children
- ☐ **Insect repellent, sunscreen, lip balm and eye drops**
- ☐ **Calamine lotion, sting relief spray or aloe vera** – to ease irritation from sunburn and insect bites or stings
- ☐ **Antifungal cream or powder** – for fungal skin infections and thrush
- ☐ **Antiseptic (such as povidone-iodine)** – for cuts and grazes
- ☐ **Bandages, Band-Aids (plasters) and other wound dressings**
- ☐ **Water purification tablets or iodine**
- ☐ **Scissors, tweezers and a thermometer** – note that mercury thermometers are prohibited by airlines
- ☐ **Syringes and needles** – in case you need injections in a country with medical hygiene problems; ask your doctor for a note explaining why you have them

Infectious Diseases

Diarrhea Simple things like a change of water, food or climate can all cause a mild bout of diarrhea, but a few rushed toilet trips with no other symptoms are not indicative of a major problem.

Dehydration is the main danger with any diarrhea, particularly in children or the elderly, as dehydration can occur quickly. Under all circumstances *fluid replacement* (at least equal to the volume being lost) is the most important thing to remember. Weak black tea with a little sugar, soda water, or soft drinks allowed to go flat and diluted 50% with clean water are all good.

With severe diarrhea, a rehydrating solution is preferable to replace minerals and salts lost. Commercially available oral rehydration salts (ORS) are very useful; add them to boiled or bottled water. In an emergency you can make up a solution of six teaspoons of sugar and a half teaspoon of salt dissolved in a liter of boiled or bottled water.

You need to drink at least the same volume of fluid that you are losing in bowel movements and vomiting. Urine is the best guide to the adequacy of replacement – if you have small amounts of dark, concentrated urine, you need to drink more. Keep drinking small amounts often. Stick to a bland diet as you recover.

Gut-paralyzing drugs such as loperamide or diphenoxylate can be used to bring relief from the symptoms, although they do not actually cure the problem. Only use these drugs if you do not have access to toilets (eg, if you *must* travel). Note that these drugs are not recommended for children under 12 years.

In certain situations antibiotics may be required: diarrhea with blood or mucus (dysentery), any diarrhea with fever, profuse watery diarrhea, persistent diarrhea not improving after 48 hours, and severe diarrhea. These suggest a more serious cause of diarrhea, and gut-paralyzing drugs should be avoided. In these situations, a stool test may be necessary to diagnose what bug is causing your diarrhea, so you should seek medical help urgently. Where this is not possible the recommended drugs for bacterial diarrhea (the most likely cause of severe diarrhea in travelers) are norfloxacin 400mg twice daily for three days, or ciprofloxacin 500mg twice daily for five days. These are not recommended for children or pregnant women. The drug of choice for children would be co-trimoxazole, with dosage dependent on weight. A five-day course is given. Ampicillin or amoxycillin may be given during pregnancy, but medical care is necessary.

Two other causes of persistent diarrhea in travelers are giardiasis and amoebic dysentery. Giardiasis is caused by a common parasite, *Giardia lamblia*. Symptoms include stomach cramps, nausea, a bloated stomach, watery, foul-smelling diarrhea and frequent gas. Giardiasis can appear several weeks after you have been exposed to the parasite. The symptoms may disappear for a few days and then return; this can go on for several weeks.

Amoebic dysentery, caused by the protozoan *Entamoeba histolytica,* is characterized by a gradual onset of low-grade diarrhea, often with blood and mucus. Cramping, abdominal pain and vomiting are less likely than in other types of diarrhea, and fever may not be present. It will persist until treated and can recur and cause other health problems.

You should seek medical advice if you think you have giardiasis or amoebic dysentery, but where this is not possible, tinidazole or metronidazole are the recommended drugs. Treatment is a 2g single dose of tinidazole or 250mg of metronidazole three times daily for five to 10 days.

Fungal Infections Fungal infections occur more commonly in hot weather and are usually found on the scalp, between the toes (athlete's foot) or fingers, in the groin and on the body (ringworm). You get ringworm (which is a fungal infection, not a worm) from infected animals or other people. Moisture encourages these infections.

To prevent fungal infections, wear loose, comfortable clothes, avoid artificial fibers, wash frequently and dry carefully. If you do get an infection, wash the affected area at least daily with a disinfectant or medicated soap and water, and rinse and dry well. Apply an antifungal cream or powder like tolnaftate. Try to expose the infected area to air or sunlight as much as possible and wash all towels and underwear in hot water, change them often and let them dry in the sun.

Hepatitis Hepatitis is a general term for inflammation of the liver. It is a common disease worldwide. There are several different viruses that cause hepatitis, and they are transmitted in different ways. The symptoms are similar in all forms of the illness, and include fever, chills, headache, fatigue, feelings of weakness and aches and pains, followed by loss of appetite, nausea, vomiting, abdominal pain, dark urine, light-colored feces, jaundiced (yellow) skin and yellowing of the whites of the eyes. People who have had hepatitis should avoid alcohol for some time after the illness, as the liver needs time to recover.

Hepatitis A is transmitted by contaminated food and drinking water. If you contract it, you should seek medical advice, but there is not much you can do apart from resting, drinking lots of fluids, eating lightly and avoiding fatty foods. **Hepatitis E** is transmitted in the same way; it can be particularly serious in pregnant women.

There are almost 300 million chronic carriers of **hepatitis B** in the world. It is spread through contact with infected blood, blood products or body fluids; for example, through sexual contact, unsterilized needles and blood transfusions, or contact with blood via small breaks in the skin. Other risks include having a shave, tattoo or body piercing with contaminated equipment. The symptoms of type B may be more severe than hepatitis A, and the disease may lead to long-term problems. **Hepatitis C** and **D** are spread in the same way as hepatitis B and can also lead to long term complications.

There are vaccines against hepatitis A and B, but there are currently none against the other types of hepatitis. Following the basic rules about food and water (hepatitis A and E) and avoiding risky situations

(hepatitis B, C and D) are important preventative measures.

HIV & AIDS Infection with the human immunodeficiency virus (HIV) may lead to acquired immune deficiency syndrome (AIDS), which is a fatal disease. In 2000 Brazil had 544,000 cases of HIV, one-third of the Latin American total, according to its Health Ministry, and about 180,000 notified AIDS cases, with about 20,000 new ones each year.

Any exposure to infected blood, blood products or body fluids may put an individual at risk. The disease is often transmitted through sexual contact or dirty needles – vaccinations, acupuncture, tattooing and body piercing can potentially be as dangerous as intravenous drug use. HIV/AIDS can also be spread through infected blood transfusions; some developing countries cannot afford to screen blood.

If you do need an injection, ask to see the syringe unwrapped in front of you, or take a needle and syringe pack with you. Fear of HIV infection should never preclude treatment for serious medical conditions.

Intestinal Worms These parasites are most common in rural, tropical areas. The different worms have different ways of infecting people. Some may be ingested in food such as undercooked meat (tapeworms, for instance) and some enter through your skin (eg, hookworms). Infestations may not show up for some time, and although they are generally not serious, if left untreated some can cause severe health problems later. Consider having a stool test to check for these when you return home, and then determine the appropriate treatment.

Meningococcal Meningitis This serious disease can be fatal. There are recurring outbreaks in Brazil, notably in the São Paulo area.

A fever, severe headache, sensitivity to light and neck stiffness that prevents forward bending of the head are the first symptoms. There may also be purple patches on the skin. Death can occur within a few hours, so urgent treatment is required.

Treatment is large doses of penicillin given intravenously, or chloramphenicol injections.

Schistosomiasis Also known as bilharzia, this disease is carried in water by minute worms. They infect certain varieties of freshwater snails found in rivers, streams, lakes and particularly behind dams. The worms multiply and are eventually discharged into the water.

The worm enters through the skin and attaches itself to your intestines or bladder. The first symptom may be a general feeling of being unwell, or a tingling and sometimes a light rash around the area where it entered. Weeks later a high fever may develop. Once the disease is established abdominal pain and blood in the urine are other signs. The infection often causes no symptoms until the disease is well established (months to years after exposure) and damage to internal organs irreversible.

The main method of preventing the disease is avoiding swimming or bathing in freshwater where bilharzia is present. Even deep water can be infected. If you do get wet, dry off quickly and dry your clothes as well.

A blood test is the most reliable way to diagnose the disease, but the test will not show positive until a number of weeks after exposure.

Sexually Transmitted Diseases HIV/AIDS and hepatitis B can be transmitted through sexual contact – see the relevant sections earlier in this chapter for more details. Other STDs include gonorrhea, herpes and syphilis; common symptoms are sores, blisters or rashes around the genitals, and discharge or pain when urinating. In some STDs, such as wart virus or chlamydia, symptoms may be less marked or not observed at all, especially in women. Chlamydia infection can cause infertility in men and women before any symptoms have been noticed. Syphilis symptoms eventually disappear, but the disease continues and can cause severe problems later. While abstinence from sexual contact is the only 100%

effective prevention, using condoms is also effective. Antibiotics are used to treat gonorrhea and syphilis. The different sexually transmitted diseases each require specific antibiotics.

Typhoid Typhoid fever is a dangerous gut infection caused by contaminated water and food. Medical help must be sought.

In its early stages sufferers may feel they have a bad cold or flu on the way, as early symptoms are a headache, body aches and a fever that rises a little each day until it is around 40°C (104°F) or more. The victim's pulse is often slow relative to the degree of fever present – unlike a normal fever where the pulse increases. There may also be abdominal pain, vomiting, constipation or diarrhea.

In the second week the high fever and slow pulse continue and a few pink spots may appear on the body; trembling, delirium, weakness, weight loss and dehydration may occur. Complications such as pneumonia, perforated bowel or meningitis may develop.

Insect-Borne Diseases

For information on Chagas' disease, filariasis, leishmaniasis, typhus and yellow fever (all insect-borne illnesses), see the Less Common Diseases information at the end of this Health section.

Malaria This serious and potentially fatal disease is spread through mosquito bites. If you are traveling in endemic areas, it is extremely important to avoid mosquito bites and to take tablets to prevent this disease. Symptoms can range from fever, chills and sweating, abdominal pains, headache and diarrhea to a vague feeling of ill health. Seek medical help immediately if malaria is at all suspected. Without treatment malaria can rapidly become more serious and can be fatal.

If medical care is not available, malaria tablets can be used for treatment. You need to use a different malaria tablet from the one you were taking when you contracted malaria, and at the same time continue taking the preventive dose. The standard *treatment dose* of mefloquine is two 250mg tablets and two more six hours later. With Fansidar, it's a single dose of three tablets. If you were previously taking mefloquine and cannot obtain Fansidar, alternatives are Malarone (atovaquone-proguanil; four tablets once daily for three days), halofantrine (three doses of two 250mg tablets every six hours) or quinine sulphate (600mg every six hours). There is a greater than normal risk of side effects with these dosages if they are used with mefloquine, so medical advice is preferable. Halofantrine is no longer recommended by the WHO as emergency standby treatment, because of side effects, and should only be used if no other drugs are available.

Travelers are advised to prevent mosquito bites at all times. The main messages are as follows:

- Wear light-colored clothing.
- Wear long trousers and long-sleeved shirts.
- Use mosquito repellents containing the compound DEET on exposed areas (prolonged overuse of DEET may be harmful, especially to children, but its use is considered preferable to being bitten by disease-transmitting mosquitoes).
- Avoid perfume or aftershave.
- Use a mosquito net impregnated with mosquito repellent (permethrin) – it may be worth taking your own.
- Wear clothing impregnated with permethrin, which will effectively deter mosquitoes and other insects.

Dengue Fever This viral disease transmitted by mosquitoes is fast becoming one of the top public health problems in the tropical world. Unlike the malaria mosquito, the *Aedes aegypti* mosquito, which transmits the dengue virus, is most active during the day, and is found mainly in urban areas, in and around human dwellings.

Signs and symptoms of dengue fever include a sudden onset of high fever, headache, joint and muscle pains, nausea and vomiting. A rash of small red spots sometimes appears three to four days after the onset of fever. Dengue may be mistaken for other infectious diseases, including malaria

and influenza. It may progress to the potentially fatal dengue hemorrhagic fever (DHF), which is characterized by heavy bleeding, but this usually affects residents of the country rather than travelers. Recovery even from simple dengue fever may be prolonged, with fatigue lasting for several weeks.

Seek medical attention just as soon as possible if you think you may be infected. There is no specific treatment and no vaccine. The best prevention is to avoid mosquito bites by covering up, and using insect repellents containing the compound DEET and mosquito nets – see the Malaria section earlier for more on avoiding mosquito bites.

Cuts, Bites & Stings

See Less Common Diseases for details on rabies, which is passed through animal bites.

For any cut, bite or sting, wash well and treat any cut with an antiseptic such as povidone-iodine. Where possible avoid bandages and Band-Aids, which can keep wounds wet.

Bedbugs live in various places, but particularly in dirty mattresses and bedding, evidenced by spots of blood on bedclothes or on the wall. Bedbugs leave itchy bites in neat rows. Calamine lotion or a sting relief spray may help.

All lice cause itching and discomfort. They make themselves at home in your hair (head lice), your clothing (body lice) or your pubic hair (crabs). You catch lice through direct contact with infected people or by sharing combs, clothing and the like. Medicated powder or shampoo treatment will kill the lice, and infected clothing should then be washed in very hot, soapy water and left in the sun to dry.

Bee and wasp stings are usually painful rather than dangerous. However, in people who are allergic to them, severe breathing difficulties may occur and require urgent medical care. Calamine lotion or a sting relief spray will give relief, and ice packs will reduce the pain and swelling.

Leeches may be present in damp rainforest conditions; they attach themselves to your skin to suck your blood. Trekkers often get them on their legs or in their boots. Salt or a lighted cigarette end will make them fall off. Do not pull them off, as the bite is then more likely to become infected. Clean and apply pressure if the point of attachment is bleeding. An insect repellent may keep them away.

You should always check all over your body if you have been walking through a potentially tick-infested area, as ticks can cause skin infections and other more serious diseases such as typhus. If you find an attached tick, press down around its head with tweezers, grab the head and gently pull upward.

To minimize your chances of being bitten by snakes, always wear boots, socks and long trousers when walking through undergrowth where they may be present. Don't put your hands into holes and crevices. Snakebites do not cause instantaneous death, and antivenins are usually available. Immediately wrap the bitten limb tightly, as you would for a sprained ankle, then attach a splint to immobilize it. Keep the victim still and seek medical help. Tourniquets and sucking out the poison are now comprehensively discredited.

Women's Health

Antibiotic use, synthetic underwear, sweating and contraceptive pills can lead to fungal vaginal infections, especially in hot climates. Fungal infections are characterized by a rash, itch and discharge and can be treated with a vinegar or lemon-juice douche, or with yogurt. Nystatin, miconazole or clotrimazole suppositories or vaginal creams are the usual treatment. Maintaining good personal hygiene and wearing loose-fitting clothes and cotton underwear may help prevent these infections.

Sexually transmitted diseases are a major cause of vaginal problems. Symptoms include a smelly discharge, painful intercourse and sometimes a burning sensation when urinating. Medical attention should be sought and male sexual partners must also be treated. For more details see the earlier section on Sexually Transmitted Diseases. Besides abstinence, the best thing is to practice safe sex using condoms.

It is not advisable to travel to some places while pregnant, as some vaccinations normally used to prevent serious diseases are not advisable during pregnancy. In addition, some diseases (eg, malaria) are quite serious for pregnant women and may increase the risk of stillbirth.

Most miscarriages occur during the first three months of pregnancy. Miscarriage, although not uncommon, can occasionally lead to severe bleeding. The last three months should also be spent within reasonable distance of good medical care. A baby born as early as 24 weeks stands a chance of survival, but only in a good, modern hospital. Pregnant women should avoid all unnecessary medication, but vaccinations and malarial prophylactics should still be taken where needed. Additional care should be taken to prevent illness, and particular attention should be paid to diet and nutrition. Alcohol and nicotine, for example, should be avoided.

Less Common Diseases

The following diseases pose a small risk to travelers, and so are only mentioned in passing. Seek medical advice if you think you may have any of them.

Chagas' Disease In remote rural areas of South and Central America, this parasitic disease is transmitted by a bug that hides in crevices in the walls and thatched roofs of mud huts and on palm fronds. It bites at night, and a hard, violet-colored swelling appears in about a week. Chagas' disease can be treated in its early stages, but untreated infection can lead to death some years later.

Cholera This is the worst of the watery diarrheas, and medical help should be sought. Outbreaks of cholera are generally widely reported, so you can avoid such problem areas. *Fluid replacement is the most vital treatment* – the risk of dehydration is severe, as you may lose up to 20L a day. If there is a delay in getting to a hospital, begin taking tetracycline. The adult dose is 250mg four times daily. It is not recommended for children under nine years nor for pregnant women. Tetracycline may help shorten the illness, but adequate fluids are required to save lives.

Filariasis This mosquito-transmitted parasitic infection is found in many parts of South America, especially the Atlantic coast. Possible symptoms include fever, pain and swelling of the lymph glands, inflammation of lymph drainage areas, swelling of a limb or the scrotum, skin rashes and blindness. Treatment is available to eliminate the parasites from the body, but some of the damage may already not be reversible. Medical advice should be obtained promptly if the infection is suspected.

Leishmaniasis This is a group of parasitic diseases transmitted by sandfly bites, occurring in many parts of Brazil. Cutaneous leishmaniasis affects the skin tissue, causing ulceration and disfigurement; visceral leishmaniasis affects the internal organs. Seek medical advice, as laboratory testing is required for diagnosis and correct treatment. Avoiding sandfly bites is the best precaution. Bites are usually painless, itchy and yet another reason to cover up and apply repellent.

Rabies This fatal viral infection is found in many countries. Many animals can be infected (such as dogs, cats, bats and monkeys), and it is their saliva which is infectious. Any bite, scratch or even lick from an animal should be cleaned immediately and thoroughly. Scrub with soap and running water, then apply alcohol or iodine solution. Medical help should be sought promptly to receive a course of injections to prevent the onset of symptoms and death.

Tetanus This disease is caused by a germ which lives in soil and in the feces of horses and other animals. It enters the body via breaks in the skin. The first symptom may be discomfort in swallowing, or stiffening of the jaw and neck; this is followed by painful convulsions of the jaw and whole body. The disease can be fatal. It can be prevented by vaccination.

Tuberculosis (TB) Tuberculosis is a bacterial infection usually transmitted between people by coughing, but which may be transmitted through consumption of unpasteurized milk. Milk that has been boiled is safe to drink, and the souring of milk to make yogurt or cheese also kills the bacilli. Close household contact with an infected person is usually required to pass on the disease.

Typhus This disease is spread by ticks, mites or lice. It begins with fever, chills, headache and muscle pains followed a few days later by a body rash. There is often a large painful sore at the site of the bite and nearby lymph nodes are swollen and painful. Typhus can be treated under medical supervision. Seek local advice on areas where ticks pose a danger, and always check your skin carefully for ticks after walking in a danger area such as a tropical forest. An insect repellent can help, and walkers in tick-infested areas should consider having their boots and pants impregnated with benzyl benzoate and dibutylphthalate.

Yellow Fever This viral disease is transmitted by mosquitoes. The initial symptoms are fever, headache, abdominal pain and vomiting. Seek medical care urgently and drink lots of fluids.

WOMEN TRAVELERS
Attitudes Toward Women

Depending on where they travel in Brazil, women traveling alone will experience a range of responses. In São Paulo, for example, where there are many people of European ancestry, foreign women without traveling companions will scarcely be given a sideways glance. In the more traditional rural areas of the Northeast, where a large percentage of the population is of ethnically mixed origin, blonde-haired and light-skinned women, especially those without male escorts, will certainly arouse curiosity.

Although *machismo* is an undeniable element in the Brazilian social structure, it is less overt than in Spanish-speaking Latin America. Perhaps because attitudes toward sex and pornography are quite liberal in

Brazil, males feel little need to assert their masculinity or prove their prowess in the eyes of peers.

Flirtation – often exaggerated – is a prominent element in Brazilian male/female relations. It goes both ways and is nearly always regarded as amusingly innocent banter; no sense of insult, exploitation or serious intent should be assumed.

Safety Precautions

If you encounter unwelcome attention, you should be able to stop it by merely expressing displeasure.

Although most of Brazil is nearly as safe for women as for men, it's a good idea to keep a low profile in the cities at night and to avoid going alone to bars and nightclubs if you'd rather not chance your behavior being misinterpreted.

Similarly, women should not hitchhike alone or even in groups (even men or couples should exercise caution when hitching). Most important, the roughest areas of the north and west, where there are lots of men but few local women, should be considered off limits by lone female travelers.

What to Wear

Once you've spent an hour in Copacabana or Ipanema, where some women run their errands wearing *fio dental* (dental floss – the famous skimpy bikini) you'll be aware that in some parts of Brazil, the dress restrictions aren't as strict as in others. What works in Rio will probably not be appropriate in a Northeastern city, or a Piauí backwater. It seems largely a matter of personal taste, but it's still best to blend your clothing in to meet local standards.

GAY & LESBIAN TRAVELERS

Brazilians are pretty laid back when it comes to most sexual issues, and homosexuality is widely accepted in most larger urban areas. Bisexuality is condoned, if not winked at. Especially in Rio, Salvador and São Paulo, the gay bars are all-welcome affairs attended by fun loving GLS (*Gays, Lesbians e Simpatizantes*) crowds of heterosexuals,

homosexuals and who-gives-a-sexuals – people are far more concerned with dancing and having a good time than determining your sexual preference. That said, the degree to which you can be out in Brazil varies greatly by region, and in some smaller towns flamboyance is not appreciated.

There is no law against homosexuality in Brazil. The age of consent is 18 years, the same as for heterosexuals. Rio and São Paulo have the largest and liveliest gay scenes. See the chapters on those cities for information on locales.

In Rio, Sun Line Turismo is a travel agency specializing in gay and lesbian tourism and operating a 24-hour helpline. See the Rio City chapter for details. Rio's Arco Iris Association (☎ 0xx21-9293-5322) is a gay lobbying group that assists and informs the local gay and lesbian community. In Salvador, the Grupo Gay da Bahia can be reached at ☎ 0xx71-322-2552.

The Rio Gay Guide at www.riogayguide .com is an excellent resource for gay and lesbian tourists in Rio. Another informative site that was lots of good links is www .pridelinks.com/Regional/Brazil.

DISABLED TRAVELERS

Travelers in wheelchairs don't have the easiest of times in Brazil, but in the large cities there is a concerted effort to keep people mobile. Problems you'll encounter include immensely crowded public buses and restaurants with entrance steps. It pays to plan your trip through contact with some of the organizations listed here.

Organizations

In Australia, try ACROD (☎ 02-628 24333), ACROD House, PO Box 60, Curtain, ACT, 2605. ACROD´s Web site at www.acrod .org.au has excellent links, among them the highly useful www.independentliving.org. In the UK, RADAR (☎ 020-7250-3222, radar@ radar.org.uk), 250 City Rd, London ECIV 8AF, is run by and for disabled people. Its Web site at www.radar.org.uk is very together, and, although travel is not a feature, there are travel-specific links to good sites such as www.holidaycare.org.uk.

In the US, Twin Peaks Press (☎ 360-694-2462, fax 360-696-3210), PO Box 129, Vancouver, WA 98666-0129, publishes some useful material, including the *Disability News You Can Use* newsletter with a travel section in each issue. Cost is US$49 annually, US$65 outside the US. Check out their Web site at www.pacifier.com/~twinpeak. Other useful organizations in the US include the following:

Access-able Travel Source (☎ 303-232 2979), PO Box 1796, Wheatridge, CO 80034 (www.access-able.com)

International Association for Medical Assistance to Travelers (☎ 716-754 4883), 417 Center Street, NY 14092 (www.sentex.net/~iamat)

Mobility International USA (☎ 541-343-1284), PO Box 10767, Eugene, OR 97440 (www.miusa.org) – advises disabled travelers on mobility issues, runs an exchange program and publishes the quarterly *Over the Rainbow* newsletter

Moss Rehabilitation Hospital (☎ 215-456-5995) – Web site at www.mossresourcenet.org; offers an online travel information service with a disability fact sheet

SENIOR TRAVELERS

If you're over 65 years old, you can expect to receive some discounts at such places as museums and tourist attractions, but at nowhere near the level you would at home. The American Association of Retired Persons (AARP; toll-free ☎ 800-424-3410) 601 E St NW, Washington, DC 20049 (www.aarp.org), is an advocacy and service group for Americans 50 years and over and a good resource for travel bargains. Membership for one/three years is US$8/20.

Elderhostel (toll-free ☎ 877-426-8056), 75 Federal St, Boston, MA 02111 (www.elderhostel.org), for people 55 and older and their companions, arranges some trips to Brazil.

Grand Circle Travel (☎ 617-350-7500), geared to the over-50 traveler, offers escorted tours and travel information in a variety of formats and distributes a useful free booklet titled *Going Abroad: 101 Tips for Mature Travelers*. Contact them at 347 Congress St, Boston, MA 02210 or at www.gct.com.

TRAVEL WITH CHILDREN

Brazilians generally love children, and children are welcome at nearly all hotels, cafés and restaurants. Many hotels let children stay free, although the age limit varies. Babysitters are readily available, and most restaurants have high chairs. The common bond shared by all parents of all nationalities will often bring you that welcome extra personal contact and attention from Brazilians.

Apart from the obvious attractions for children of beaches, coasts and swimming pools in Brazil, you can also find excellent special attractions in many areas, such as amusement parks, zoos, aquariums and train and boat rides.

Bear in mind that children, younger ones especially, don't like traveling all the time – they're happier if they can settle into places for a little while, make friends and do some of the familiar things they are used to doing back home.

Children are likely to be more affected than adults by heat and disrupted sleeping patterns. They need to be given time to acclimatize and extra care to avoid sunburn. Be sure to replace fluids if a child gets diarrhea (see the Health section earlier in this chapter).

Check carefully with your doctor before departure about immunizations and other medical aspects of taking children to Brazil. Children between three months and six years old are required to have a polio vaccination certificate. Diapers are widely available in Brazil, but you may not easily find creams, baby foods or familiar medicines outside larger cities.

See the Visas & Documents section in this chapter for information on special bureaucratic requirements for some travelers under the age of 18.

Children under two years old generally fly for 10% of the adult fare. Those between two and 12 usually pay 50% on international flights and 67% on Brazilian domestic flights. Lonely Planet's *Travel with Children* contains lots of practical advice on this subject, as well as firsthand stories from many parents who have done it.

USEFUL ORGANIZATIONS

South American Explorers (☎ 607-277-0488), 126 Indian Creek Rd, Ithaca, NY 14850, USA is a club providing services, information and support to mountaineers, scientific researchers, explorers and travelers. It also sells a wide range of books, guides and maps for South America. Its Web site alone (www.samexplo.org) is informative enough, but membership is quite a bargain considering the benefits offered – such as discounts, help and advice in planning trips and expeditions, and access to libraries, maps, an electronic bulletin board and clubhouses in Peru and Ecuador.

The Brazilian American Cultural Center (BACC; toll-free ☎ 800-222-2746), 16 W 46th St, New York, NY 10036, USA, is a tourism organization and travel agency which offers members discounted flights and tours. It also sells discounted air passes and other air tickets for travel within Brazil. Members receive a monthly newspaper and can send money to South America using BACC's remittance service. BACC also has an office in Rio de Janeiro (☎ 0xx21-2523-2499).
Web site: www.idainc.org/bacc

DANGERS & ANNOYANCES
Security

Brazil receives a lot of bad press about its violence and high crime rate. We feel that the dangers to travelers, while they do exist, get exaggerated. Nevertheless this section has been written in detail to heighten awareness, as many readers may not have previously experienced the type and extent of crime evident in Brazil (or other Latin American countries). It is not, however, a compendium of things that will or are even likely to happen to you. It is neither necessary nor helpful to become paranoid.

By using common sense, there are many things travelers can do to reduce their risks.

Predeparture Precautions If you work on the elements of vulnerability, you can be significantly safer. For starters, take with you only things that you are prepared to lose or replace. Travel insurance is essential for the replacement of valuables, and the cost of a good policy can help prevent anything from a minimal disturbance to the abrupt termination of your travel plans. Loss through petty theft or violence is a stressful experience that can be reduced if you think ahead – the less you have, the less you can lose.

Don't bring jewelry, and if you have to wear a watch, use a cheapie worth a few dollars and keep it in your pocket.

Make copies of your passport and important documents (see Visas & Documents earlier in this chapter). A passport is worth a lot of money to some people, so keep a close eye on it. If you do lose it, the photocopies described earlier and a copy of your birth certificate usually speed up the issuing of a new passport at embassies and consulates.

Make sure you know the number to call if you lose your credit card and be quick to cancel it if lost or stolen – and see the money section earlier in this chapter for some sensible precautions to take in regard to credit cards.

Security Accessories A thick backpack cover or modified canvas sack improves protection against pilfering, planting of drugs and general wear and tear. Double zippers on your daypack can be secured with safety pins, which reduce the ease of access favored by petty thieves. A small, padlockable bag is useful for enclosing items that you are leaving in a safe, and a medium-size combination lock or padlock is good for replacing the padlock on your hotel door. Rubber wedges are handy to prevent access to doors or windows. To deter thieves operating with razors, you can line the inside of your daypack (and even your backpack) with lightweight wire mesh.

Don't keep all your valuables together: Distribute them about your person and baggage to avoid the risk of losing everything in one fell swoop.

Various types of money belt are available to be worn around the waist, neck or shoulder, and leather or cotton material is more comfortable than synthetics. Such belts are only useful if worn *under* clothing – pouches worn outside clothing are easy prey and attract attention. Determined thieves are wise to conventional money belts, and some travelers now also use cloth pouches sewn into trousers or attached inside with safety pins. Other methods include belts with a concealed zipper compartment, and bandages or pouches worn around the leg.

If you wear glasses, secure them with an elastic strap to deter petty theft.

Finally, the extra pair of eyes provided by a traveling companion are an obvious asset.

Security Precautions in Brazil There are certain key things you can do to reduce attention from criminals. Start by dressing down: Your clothes should be casual and preferably something that blends in – inexpensive clothes bought in Brazil are an obvious choice.

Most travelers carry a daypack. Whether you're in a bus station, restaurant, shop or elsewhere, whenever you have to put your daypack down, *always* put your foot through the strap. It makes things more difficult for furtive fingers and bag-slashers.

If you're carrying a camera, never wander around with it dangling over your shoulder or around your neck – keep it out of sight as much as possible. It's also unwise to keep it in a swanky camera bag, which is an obvious target. A plastic bag from a local supermarket is not a bad thing to carry a camera in – it won't *look* valuable.

Get used to keeping small change and a few banknotes in a pocket so you can pay for bus tickets and small expenses without displaying large amounts of money. This easily accessible money is also useful to rapidly appease a mugger. If you carry a wallet, keep it thin, keep it in your front pocket and don't use it on public transport or in crowded places where it might attract unwelcome attention and be easily snatched.

Before arriving in a new place, make sure you have a map or at least a rough idea of the area's orientation. Try to plan your schedule so you don't arrive at night, and use taxis – hang the expense – if necessary to avoid walking through risky areas. Be observant and alert and learn to look like a street-smart local. Walk purposefully. Don't wander round touristy areas in a jet-lagged state soon after your arrival in Brazil; you'll be an obvious target.

If you consider your hotel to be reliable, place valuables in its safe and get a receipt. Package your valuables in a small, padlockable bag, or use a large envelope with a signed seal that will easily show any tampering. Count your money and traveler's checks before and after retrieving them from the safe – this should quickly identify any attempts to extract single bills or checks that might otherwise go unnoticed.

Check the door, door frame, and windows of your room for unsecured access or signs of forced entry. If your hotel provides a padlock, it's recommended to use your own combination lock (or padlock) instead. A hotel padlock obviously increases the number of people with access to your room. Don't leave anything valuable lying around the room. It's just too much of a temptation to cleaners and other hotel staff.

Scams & Robbery Techniques Distraction is a common tactic employed by street thieves in Brazil and elsewhere around the world. The aim is to throw potential victims off guard so that they're easier prey. It may be something as simple as asking you for a cigarette or a light so that you slow down in your walk and take your attention off other people around you.

If you're suspicious or uneasy about someone or some situation for any reason – or even for no reason that you can put your finger on – don't hesitate to make excuses and leave, change your route or do whatever else is needed to extricate yourself.

Techniques are continually being developed, and imported or exported across national borders, to relieve the unwary of their belongings. Keep abreast of new scams by talking to other travelers. Theft and security are sources of endless fascination and stories; some are true, some are incredible and some are taller than Corcovado!

Accept the fact that you might be mugged, pickpocketed or have your bag snatched in Brazil. If you only carry the minimum on your person, and don't try to resist those who try to take it from you, you won't come to any real harm.

Cream A classic distraction method is the 'cream technique,' common the world over, including in Brazil. You're walking down the street or standing in some public place, when someone surreptitiously sprays a substance on your shoulder, your daypack or anything else connected with you. The substance can be anything from mustard to chocolate or even dog shit. An assistant (young or old, male or female) then taps you on the shoulder and amicably offers to clean off the mess…if you'll just put down your bag for a second. The moment you do this, someone makes off with it in a flash.

The golden rule is to ignore any such attempt or offer, and simply endure your mucky state until you can find a safe place, such as your hotel, where you can wash.

Diversion Another technique involves people working to divert you or literally throw you off balance. This usually happens when you're standing in the street or somewhere busy like a bus station. One or more characters suddenly ask you a question, bump into you or stage an angry discussion or fight around you, and while you are off balance or diverted, there'll be an attempt to pick your pockets or grab your gear. Assume that any and all public brawls, arguments, large acrimonious altercations and other colorful street spectacles are conspiracies designed to rob *you* personally.

Money Changing Never change money on the street; ignore itinerant money changers who whisper favorable rates into your ear as you pass; and never follow any of these types into a side street for a transaction. *Never*.

Drugging There have also been reports of druggings. Spiked drinks are one danger area. While you're temporarily unconscious or semiconscious as a result of some noxious substance slipped into your beverage, you're powerless to resist thieves. There have even been reported cases of rape in such circumstances. If you start to

feel unaccountably dizzy, disoriented, fatigued, or just mentally vacant not long after imbibing, your drink may have been spiked.

Exercise *extreme* caution when someone you don't know and trust offers you a drink of *any* kind or even cigarettes, sweets etc. If the circumstances make you suspicious or uneasy, the offer can be tactfully refused by claiming stomach or other medical problems.

In the Northeast, male travelers have reported that 'good-time' ladies at beach bars make friendly advances over spiked drinks. The semiconscious traveler is then accompanied back to his hotel, where the woman explains to the desk clerk that she needs the key to help her 'drunken friend' to his room – where she cleans out all his valuables and then makes a quick exit.

On the Beach Don't take anything to city beaches except just enough money for lunch and drinks. No camera, no bag, no jewelry. Wear your bathing suit and bring a towel. That's it. If you want to photograph the beach, go with a friend, then return the camera to your room before staying on the beach. Don't hang out on deserted city beaches at night. See the Dangers & Annoyances section in the Rio city chapter for more tips.

On the Street Thieves watch for people leaving hotels, car-rental agencies, American Express offices, tourist sights – places with lots of foreigners – then they follow their targets. If you notice you are being followed or closely observed, it helps to pause and look straight at the person(s) involved or, if you're not alone, simply point out the person(s) to your companion. This makes it clear that the element of surprise favored by petty criminals has been lost.

Don't advertise the fact that you're a foreigner by flashing big bills or wearing jewelry. After dark, don't walk along empty or nearly empty streets or into deserted parks. Don't wander into *favelas* (slums) any time. If an area you're heading into gets grungier and grungier, till you start to feel uneasy, turn round and go back.

Never carry any more money than you need for the specific outing you're on, and keep it discreetly stashed away in a money belt, money sock, secret pocket or shoe. But always have enough money on hand to appease a mugger (about US$2 to US$5). There have been stories of certain tourists, fresh from military training, disarming would-be muggers and breaking all their fingers, but we do not recommend resistance. There have been other reports of tourists shot dead while pursuing muggers – obviously an absurd price to pay for loss of cash or valuables.

Buses When you take city buses, have your change ready before boarding. You are less of a target once you have passed through the turnstile inside, or if you're standing near the conductor. Avoid super-crowded buses. If you talk out loudly, it's easier for thieves to single you out. If you're carrying valuables, take a taxi.

Long-distance bus travel is usually well organized. If you hand over luggage to be placed in the baggage compartment, make sure you receive a receipt. Two or more items can be padlocked together. Try to take your pack inside and put it on the overhead luggage racks. If you have to place baggage on the roof, secure it with a padlock.

Taxis Although taxi drivers' tricks with fares can be irritating (see the Getting Around chapter), taxis pose minimal danger of outright theft.

If you keep a passenger door open during the loading or unloading of luggage, it reduces the ease with which a taxi can drive off with your luggage and without you! Watch your luggage (slip your foot or arm through a strap) while you're standing outside a taxi discussing fares or arranging baggage. Opportunistic thieves can quickly make off with your items while you're thus distracted.

Always question the presence of any unexplained characters accompanying the driver, and don't hesitate to take another taxi if you feel uneasy. If there are mechanical or orientation problems en route, don't allow yourself to be separated from your luggage. When you arrive at your destination, *never* hand over your luggage to a person who tries to help you out of the car and offers to carry something, unless you are quite positive about their identity. Otherwise, it can be a case of 'May I take your bags? Thanks!'

Boats Passengers on local boats, particularly in northern Brazil, are targets for thieves who take advantage of crowded conditions, long journeys and unsecured baggage – particularly at night. It's best not to entrust your baggage to anyone, before or after departure. We've heard of bogus 'officials,' even wearing uniform and issuing receipts, who have made off with baggage entrusted to them before departure.

Once on board, make sure you keep all valuables on your person, and never flash your money or camera around. Double zippers on your baggage should be padlocked, and it's important that any baggage you are not carrying on your person is secured to a fixture on the boat. Thieves prefer to rifle through unsecured and unobserved baggage, extract valuables and then simply dump the rest overboard. A bicycle padlock or chain is useful for securing your baggage. Some travelers use a large eyelet hook and a rope to suspend baggage from the ceiling next to their hammock. Do not assume that cabins can be securely locked.

Plumbing

Much Brazilian plumbing is poorly installed and can pose problems to the uninitiated. Hot, or at least tepid, showers are usually provided by a deadly-looking device that attaches to the shower head and electrically heats the water as it passes through. Wires that are often bare run into the shower head or just dangle from the ceiling. The dangling variety indicates that the device is broken. Don't bother getting undressed if this is the case.

Most of these heaters are activated by the flow of water. In some cases it's a simple case of the less water, the hotter. Other devices have three temperature settings on the head.

If you want to avoid electric shocks, it's not a good idea to change the setting while the shower is on – nor indeed to touch the heating device at all while it's operating. Don't touch the water controls again until you've dried off and have your footwear on.

EMERGENCIES
Emergency telephone numbers are the same all over Brazil, and you can call them free, without a phone card: Police (☎ 190), Ambulance (☎ 192) and Fire (☎ 193).

LEGAL MATTERS
Police
If something is stolen from you, you can report it to the police. No big investigation is going to occur, but you will get a police report to give to your insurance company. However, the police aren't always to be trusted. Brazilian police are known to plant drugs and sting gringos for bribes. The bribes are like pyramids: The more people are involved, the bigger the bribe becomes.

Drugs
The military regime had a pathological aversion to drugs and enacted stiff penalties, which are still in force. Drugs provide a perfect excuse for the police to get a fair amount of money from you, and Brazilian prisons are brutal places.

Police checkpoints along the highways stop cars and buses at random. Police along the coastal drive from Rio to São Paulo are notorious for hassling young people and foreigners. Border areas are also dangerous.

A large amount of cocaine is smuggled out of Bolivia and Peru through Brazil. Be very careful with drugs. If you're going to buy, don't buy from strangers and don't carry anything around with you.

Marijuana is plentiful in Brazil, and very illegal. Nevertheless, it's widely used, and, like many other things in Brazil, everyone except the military and the police has a rather tolerant attitude toward it. Bahia seems to have the most open climate. But because of the laws against possession, you won't bump into much unless you know someone or go to an 'in' vacation spot with the young and hip, such as Arraial d'Ajuda, Morro de São Paulo or Jericoacoara, or at groovy hippie hangouts like São Tome de las Letras in Minas.

There are some wild hallucinogenic substances in Amazonia. The best known is ayahuasca or yagé, which comes from a jungle vine and has ritual uses among certain tribes and cults. For more details about the cults see the Religion section in the Facts about Brazil chapter.

If you're coming from one of the Andean countries and have been chewing coca leaves, be especially careful to clean out your pack before arriving in Brazil. One reader who entered Brazil with all of 17.7 grams of coca leaves was sentenced to four years in jail – fortunately for him, he skipped the country before the trial happened.

There's a lot of this around, and because of the stiff penalties involved with possession or apparent possession (a little planted coke goes a long way to locking you up), we advise you to stay away from it in any form.

BUSINESS HOURS
Most shops and government services (including post offices) are open from 9 am to 6 pm Monday to Friday and 9 am to 1 pm Saturday. Shopping malls usually stay open till 10 pm Monday to Saturday, and often even open on Sunday. Because many Brazilians have little free time during the week, Saturday morning is usually spent shopping.

Banks, always in their own little world, are generally open from 9 or 10 am to 2 or 3 pm.

HOLIDAYS
The official national holidays are as follows:

New Year's Day January 1 – officially, the Day of Universal Confraternization

Carnaval February/March – the two days before Ash Wednesday, which falls 46 days before Easter Sunday

Good Friday & Easter Sunday March/April

Tiradentes Day April 21 – In honor of Tiradentes, an 18th-century Brazilian nationalist martyr

May Day/Labor Day May 1

Corpus Christi Late May/June – 60 days after Easter Sunday

Independence Day September 7

Day of NS de Aparecida October 12 – holiday of Brazil's religious patron

All Souls' Day November 2

Proclamation of the Republic Day November 15

Christmas Day December 25

April 19, the Dia do Índio (Indian Day), is not a national holiday, but it's marked by festivities in Indian villages around the country.

Most states have several additional local holidays, when everyone goes fishing.

CULTURAL EVENTS

Highlights of Brazil's festivals include the following; see the regional chapters for details of these and many other events.

January

New Year's Eve and New Year's Day Festa de Iemanjá; Rio de Janeiro
Procissão do Senhor Bom Jesus dos Navegantes; Salvador, Bahia

Lavagem do Bonfim Second Thursday in January; Salvador, Bahia

Bom Jesus dos Navegantes Four days after the second Sunday in January; Penedo, Alagoas

Festa de Santo Amaro January 24 to February 2; Santo Amaro, Bahia

February

Festa de Iemanjá February 2; Salvador, Bahia

Shrove Tuesday and **Carnaval** February or March depending on the Easter date and the locale; the famous fat Tuesday celebration and the days preceding it

March

Semana Santa The week before Easter, in March or April; celebrations in Congonhas, Ouro Prêto, Goiás Velho

April

Micareta In April or early May; Feira de Santana, Bahia

May

Festa do Divino Espírito Santo In May or June, 40 days after Easter; Parati, Rio de Janeiro

Cavalhada Held 45 days after Easter; Pirenópolis, Goiás

Festa do Divino The first Sunday after Ascension Day; Alcântara, Maranhão

June

Festas Juninas Celebrated throughout June in Rio state and much of the rest of the country

Festival Folclórico do Amazonas Manaus, Amazonas

Festa de São João Held June 22–24; Cachoeira, Bahia

Boi-Bumbá Three days in late June; Parintins, Amazonas

Bumba Meu Boi From late June to the second week of August; São Luís, Maranhão

July

Regata de Jangadas Second half of July; Fortaleza, Ceará

Festival de Dança Joinville, Santa Catarina

Carnaval Fora-de-Época Last week of July; Fortaleza, Ceará

August

Festa da NS de Boa Morte Held in mid-August; Cachoeira, Bahia

Festa de Iemanjá Held August 15; Fortaleza, Ceará

Festa de NS d'Ajuda Also August 15; Porto Seguro, Bahia

Folclore Nordestino In late August; Olinda, Pernambuco

September

Festa de NS de Nazaré On September 7–8; Saquarema, Rio de Janeiro

Festa de NS dos Remédios On September 8; Parati, Rio de Janeiro

Festa do Çairé Second Week of September; Alter do Chão, Pará

Jubileu do Senhor Bom Jesus do Matosinhos Takes places September 7–14; Congonhas, Minas Gerais

October

Círio de Nazaré Starts the second Sunday in October; Belém, Pará

Festa de NS Aparecida Held October 12; Aparecida, São Paulo

Oktoberfest The middle two weeks in October; Blumenau, Santa Catarina

NS do Rosário Second half of October; Cachoeira, Bahia

October 23–25; Ouro Prêto, Minas Gerais

Rio Jazz Festival Varying dates in October; Rio de Janeiro

November

Festa do Padre Cícero Held November 1–2; Juazeiro do Norte, Ceará

December

Carnatal First week of December; Natal, Rio Grande do Norte

Festa de Santa Barbara Celebrated December 4–6; Salvador, Bahia

Maceió Fest Held December 7–10; Maceió, Alagoas

ACTIVITIES

Brazilians are seeking out ever more 'radical' ways to spend their time, so opportunities for fresh-air adventure are on the rise. The Quatro Rodas guide *Turismo Ecológico no Brasil* (see the Books section earlier in this chapter) and the Web sites 360 Graus (www.360graus.com.br) and Guia Verde (www.guiaverde.com.br) cover a host of activities from canyoning, paragliding, kitesurfing or wakeboarding to rafting, surfing, trekking, diving or mountain climbing. They're in Portuguese, but need little translation.

Hiking

Hiking in Brazil is highly popular. It's best during the cooler months, April to October. During the summer, the tropical sun heats the rock to oven temperatures and turns the jungles into steamy saunas.

There are lots of great places to hike in Brazil, both in the national and state parks and along the coastline, and especially in the Southeast and South. Plenty of good hikes are mentioned in the regional chapters. Outstanding areas include the national parks of Chapada Diamantina (Bahia), Serra dos Órgãos and Itatiaia (Rio de Janeiro), Chapada dos Veadeiros (Goiás) and Caparaó (Minas Gerais), as well as Marumbi state park (Paraná), the Serra de São José near Tiradentes (Minas Gerais) and the Canela area (Rio Grande do Sul).

Contact some of the local hiking and rock-climbing clubs (see the Rio de Janeiro City chapter), which have details of trekking options.

Climbing

Climbing in Brazil is also best from April to October. The best thing about rock climbing in Brazil is that one hour you can be on the beach, and the next on a world-class climb 300m above a city. Brazil has lots of fantastic climbs, ranging from beginner level to routes yet to be conquered. Within 40 minutes of central Rio de Janeiro, the hub of Brazilian climbing, are some 350 documented climbs. The national parks of Serra dos Órgãos and Itatiaia (Rio de Janeiro) and Caparaó (Minas Gerais) have some particularly good climbs.

Climbing Vocabulary Although most Brazilians in the clubs know a little English, it helps to know a little Portuguese to smooth the way.

equipment *equipamento*
bolt *grampo*
rope *corda*
carabiner *mosquetão*
harness *baudrie*
backpack *mochila*
webbing *fita*
chalk powder *pó de magnésio*
rock *rocha*
summit *topo/cume*
crack *fenda*
route *via/rota*
a fall *queda*
to be secured *estar preso*
a hold *uma agarra*
to belay *dar segurança*
to make a stupid mistake and fall *tomar uma vaca*

Surfing

Surfing is very popular, and several Brazilian professionals are usually to be found in the top 20 of the world rankings.

There's surf virtually all along the coast, with particularly good waves in the South. The best surf beaches are in Santa Catarina state, and the Brazilian championships are held at Praia da Joaquina on Ilha de Santa Catarina. São Francisco do Sul (Santa Catarina), Ilha do Mel (Paraná) and Ubatuba, Ilhabela, Maresias and the Boiçucanga area (all São Paulo state) all serve up good waves.

In Rio state, Saquarema has the best surf. Búzios and Itacoatiara beach in Niterói are also popular breaks. There's plenty of surf close to the city of Rio, where an annual round of the professional World Championship Tour takes place at Barra da Tijuca beach. The waves are best in the Brazilian winter (from June to August).

On other surf beaches, even in Espírito Santo state with its breaks of only 1-3m, surfing is still a way of life, and boogie boarding is popular as well. Rentals of boogie boards and surfboards are easy to arrange right on the beach wherever you go.

Farther north, Itacaré and Sítio (Bahia) and Porto de Galinhas and Fernando de Noronha (Pernambuco) are among the better spots.

A curious event is the national pororoca surf championship held at São Domingos do Capim, Pará state, at the time of the full moon nearest the March equinox. The waves here are formed by the tidal bore *(pororoca)* on a tributary of the Rio Amazonas, a long way from the ocean. Waves can reach a few meters.

Surfing Vocabulary Despite their reputation for aggressiveness in the water, once on land Brazilian surfers become very interested in foreign surfers and their travels. They are also reasonably willing to lend you their boards if you ask politely.

surfer *surfista*

wave *onda*

wind *vento*

surfboard *prancha*

boogie board *body board*

to break *quebrar*

Are there any waves? *Tem ondas?*

Could I borrow your board please? *Pode me emprestar sua prancha por favor?*

Let's go surfing. *Vamos pegar ondas.*

Windsurfing

Windsurfing has caught on in Brazil. In Rio you can rent equipment at Barra da Tijuca, but there are better conditions, and again equipment to rent, at Búzios in eastern Rio state. In São Paulo state there's good windsurfing at Ilhabela, around Boiçucanga and even at Santos. But Brazil's hardcore windsurfing mecca is much farther north, along the Ceará coast northwest of Fortaleza, where constant, regular, strong trade winds blow from July to December. Jericoacoara and the small fishing village of Icaraizinho are the most popular spots.

Other Water Sports

As you would expect in a place with such a long coastline and so many beach lovers, all water sports are popular. And as you would expect in a place with such a large gap between rich and poor, they're restricted to those who can afford them. What this means to the traveler is that in order to rent the equipment needed for any of these activities you need to go to established resorts.

Sailing is big at Búzios in Rio state and the larger resorts along the coast. Diving *(mergulho* in Portuguese) doesn't match the Caribbean, but is worthwhile if you're keen. Arraial do Cabo is a good spot in Rio state. Sites elsewhere include the Reserva Biológica do Avoredo near Porto Belo, Santa Catarina; Boipeba, Bahia; Ponta de Seixas near João Pessoa; Paraíba; and Fernando de Noronha, Pernambuco.

Don't miss inner-tubing down the Rio Nhundiaquara (Morretes, Paraná).

Fishing in the interior of Brazil is fantastic. The Rio Araguaia in Goiás and Tocantins is known as a fishing paradise with a large variety of fish including the pintado, dourado and tucunaré (peacock bass). The legendary fighting qualities of the tucunaré attract sports fishers from far and wide to the Araguaia and other Amazonian rivers. Fishing for piranha is not undertaken by serious anglers, though it's good fun. Fishing is brilliant in the Pantanal too, and is allowed from February to October (see the Pantanal section of the Mato Grosso chapter for information on permits and more).

Horseback Riding

In Minas Gerais you can ride stretches of the old gold road, the Estrada Real, or take a five-day horse trek from the state capital, Belo Horizonte, to its most famous historic town, Ouro Prêto. The Pantanal is another attractive riding area.

Hang Gliding & Paragliding

It's easy – and fantastic – to hang glide *duplo* in Rio – see the Rio City chapter. Paragliding *(parapente)* can be set up, too. Another place you can double hang glide is Rio da Barra, near Trancoso, Bahia.

LANGUAGE COURSES

There are lots of ways to learn Portuguese in Brazil. It's easy to arrange classes through branches of the IBEU (Instituto Brazil Estados Unidos), where Brazilians go to learn English. Rio de Janeiro offers the most opportunities for classes (see the Language Courses section in the Rio City chapter). However, there will be a language institute in each large city. The Web site www.1stop-language.com has a database of Portuguese language schools in Brazil. The National Registration Center for Study Abroad (☎ 414-278-0631), PO Box 1393, Milwaukee, WI 53201, USA, has information on Portuguese language schools in some Brazilian cities.

Web site: www.nrcsa.com.

WORK

Brazil has high unemployment, and tourists are not supposed to take jobs. However, it's not unusual for foreigners to find language-teaching work in language schools in the bigger cities. Pay is not great (around US$10 an hour), but if you can work for three or four days a week you can live on it. For teaching work it's helpful to be able to speak some Portuguese, although some schools insist that only English be spoken in class. Private language tutoring may pay a little more, but you'll need to allow enough time to get some students: Look for 'Professor de Ingles' or 'English Teacher' in the newspaper classified ads, or ask around at the language schools.

Volunteer Work

Action Without Borders (☎ 212-843-3973), 350 Fifth Ave, Suite 6614, New York, NY 10118 USA, lists Brazilian volunteer openings on its Web site (www.idealist.org). Also look at www.istc.umn.edu, the site of the International Study and Travel Center (☎ 612-626-4782), 94 Blegen Hall, 269 19th Ave S, Minneapolis, MN 55455, USA.

Earthwatch (toll-free ☎ 800-776-0188), 3 Clock Tower Place, Suite 100, Box 75, Maynard, MA 01754, USA (also with offices in Britain and Australia), runs environmental and archaeological projects in Brazil that you pay to take part in (usually US$1500 to US$2000 for 10 to 15 days). Its Web site is at www.earthwatch.org.

A little door-knocking can help you find volunteer work with welfare organizations in Brazil. One traveler reported walking up to the front door of a Catholic home for abandoned children in Recife and asking if there was anything he could do. The priests gave him a bed and he spent two months helping with the cooking, getting the children out of jail, telling them stories and breaking up knife fights. He said it was the highlight of his trip.

International NGOs (nongovernmental organizations) work in all sorts of fields in Brazil, including environmental, medical and social welfare projects. If you have some particular interest or skill, try contacting relevant organizations to volunteer your services. In Amazonia while researching this edition, we met young foreign volunteers with varied skills providing medical care to isolated Indian settlements, observing the habits of pink river dolphins in a jungle nature reserve, and studying the carbon-sequestration properties of trees at a remote ecological research center.

ACCOMMODATIONS

Brazilian accommodations are simple, yet usually clean and reasonably safe.

Reservations

In tourist centers, especially Rio, reservations are a good idea during July and from Christmastime to Carnaval. This is true for mid-range or top-end hotels, and for the most popular budget ones as well. The same goes for any vacation mecca (eg Búzios) on weekends, and anywhere at any time that has a major festival going on. Try to contact the hotel a few days ahead: Most upper mid-range places, at least, should have someone who'll understand some English or Spanish on the phone. For prime peak times (eg, Carnaval in Rio or Salvador), try to make contact a few weeks ahead. Online booking is not yet widespread, but in Places to Stay sections you will find some places where you can book this way. The Web site www.cade.com.br lists Brazilian hotels where you can book online.

At any time, a straightforward phone call from the bus station or airport can establish whether your preferred hostelry has an available room.

Be wary of taxi drivers, particularly in Rio, who know just the hotel for you. You may find yourself being taken to an expensive hotel which pays the cabbie a commission. Cabbies may also claim that the hotel you want to go to is full. Think about it: How would they know?

Another good reason for making a reservation in mid-range or top-end hotels is that the price may be up to 30% cheaper than the 'rack rate' you get if you just walk in off the street. If your language skills aren't up to it, get a travel agent to do it for you.

In summer, it's not a bad idea to travel during the week and stay put, usually in a city, during the weekends, when the locals are making their pilgrimages away from the cities.

Camping

Camping is popular in Brazil and is a viable alternative in many parts of the country for travelers on limited budgets or those who want to explore some of the national or state parks – as long as you're prepared to carry a tent and the other necessary gear.

The Camping Clube do Brasil (☎ 0xx21-2210-3171), Rua Senador Dantas 75, 29º andar, 20037-900 Centro, Rio de Janeiro, has 48 sites as far apart as Fortaleza and Porto Alegre. There's full information on them at www.campingclub.com.br.

Minimum-Impact Camping The following guidelines are recommended for those camping in wilderness or other fragile areas of Brazil:

- Select a well-drained campsite and, especially if it's raining, use some type of waterproof groundsheet to prevent having to dig trenches.
- Along popular routes, camp in established sites.
- Carry as little packaging in as possible, and carry out all your rubbish.
- Use established toilet facilities if available. Otherwise, select a site at least 100m from water sources and bury wastes in a small hole about 15cm deep. If possible, burn used toilet paper or bury it well.
- Use only biodegradable soap products (you'll probably have to carry them from home). Disperse waste water at least 50m from watercourses.
- Try to select an established site for fires, and keep them as small as possible. Use only fallen dead wood and make sure the fire is fully extinguished before leaving.

Dormitórios

A *dormitório* is dorm-style sleeping with several beds to a room. These are usually the cheapest places in town, often costing as little as US$2 a head per night. Obviously, security is not always the greatest in such places.

Hostels

Youth hostels in Brazil are called *albergues da juventude*. The Federação Brasileira dos Albergues da Juventude (FBAJ) has more than 50 hostels in 14 states, including many in state capitals and popular travel destinations. Quality varies but many hostels are excellent, and the cost is very reasonable. They're great places to meet young Brazilians.

A dormitory bed in an FBAJ hostel costs between US$7.50 and US$16 per person. Non-HI members usually pay 50% extra, but you can buy an HI guest card for US$15 at many hostels and at youth hostel association offices in Brazil.

The FBAJ's headquarters (☎ 0xx21-2286-0303, info@hostel.org.br) is at the

Albergue da Juventude Chave Rio de Janeiro, Rua General Dionísio 63 in Rio's Botafogo district.

The FBAJ's English-and-Portuguese Web site (www.hostel.org.br) lists all FBAJ hostels, often with links to the hostels' own sites. Booklets listing the hostels and describing how to reach them (in Portuguese) are available free at hostels, hostel offices and travel agents.

There are also a few dozen non-FBAJ hostels around the country, many of which are also fine.

Pousadas

Most budget travelers stay at *pousadas* (small guesthouses) where a room without a bathroom can go for as little as US$7 per person. The small scale of pousadas, and the personal touch this often brings, can make

---

Motels

Motels are a Brazilian institution and must never be confused with hotels! They have names like Alibi, Ilha do Capri, Sinless, L'Amour and Wet Dreams. Rented by the hour, the motel room is Brazil's solution to the lack of privacy caused by overcrowded living conditions. Used by adults who still live with their parents, kids who want to get away from their parents and parents who want to get away from their kids, they are an integral part of the nation's social fabric, a bedrock of Brazilian morality, and are treated by Brazilians with what most outsiders consider to be incredible nonchalance.

The quality of motels varies, reflecting their popularity with all social classes. Most are away from the city center, with walled-in garages for anonymity. Rooms have circular vibra-beds with mirrors overhead, adult movies, and room service with a menu full of foods and sometimes sex toys (with instructions).

Motels can be fun if you're traveling as a couple. If you're having trouble finding accommodations, they're not too expensive.

---

them some of the most pleasant places to stay in Brazil.

Rooms with communal bathrooms down the hall are called *quartos*. Similar rooms with a private bathroom are called *apartamentos*, and cost a few dollars more.

Not that all pousadas are cheap: They run the spectrum of comfort and price, and at some you could even pay US$100 for a double room.

Breakfast is usually included in the price of a pousada.

Hotels

Brazil has good, modern, luxury hotels and old, shabby, moldy hotels, and everything in between. A decent hotel with clean, comfortable, air-conditioned rooms, but no frills, can cost as little as US$20 to US$30 a double per night, including private bathroom and – in all but the cheapest hotels – breakfast. At the top end of the scale, the best superluxury hotels in Rio cost US$300 or so per night.

A very cheap hotel can cost as little as US$5/7 for single/double quartos – like pousadas, hotel rooms may be quartos (with shared bathrooms) or apartamentos (with private bathroom). For that kind of bargain price expect a bare, shabby room with nothing but a bed and maybe a fan. The walls *may* reach up to the ceiling and the sheets *may* have been changed since the previous occupant. The door will probably be lockable and the room will probably be swept daily.

At more expensive places, taxes of 10% or more are often added to the basic price. The price you're initially quoted normally includes all taxes, but it does no harm to check. Prices are in fact often flexible. Many mid-range and top-end hotels will give you a discount of up to 30%, occasionally even 40%, from their posted prices, just for the asking *('Ha algum desconto?')*, especially if business is slow. Sometimes the discount is available only if you pay cash, or if you stay a few days; sometimes it's available to anyone who asks for it. Hotels in tourist areas often raise prices during the high seasons. Hotels in business-oriented cities such as Goiânia, Curitiba, Porto Alegre and Brasília readily give discounts on weekends.

Sometimes good hotels have a few quartos or cheaper rooms that are not advertised. It pays to ask about these, as they allow you to use all the facilities of the hotel while paying considerably less than the other guests.

It's always a good idea to look at a room before deciding to take it. Check the shower, the bed, the fan or air-con and the lock on the door. Three big sleep killers in Brazil are mosquitoes, heat and, in rural areas, roosters. Fans do wonders against the first two, but you can't do much about the third – and, unfortunately, visualizing yourself with your hands around the rooster's neck doesn't help!

Many medium-priced and expensive hotels have safes at the front desk that you can use with confidence as long as you get a receipt.

There are a few games played by hotel clerks to get you into a more expensive room. If you want a single room there are only doubles; if you want a quarto, there are only apartamentos. Don't say yes too quickly – if you feign a desire to look for alternative lodging, they will often remember that there is a cheaper room after all. In reality, some hotels don't have singles. It is generally much cheaper to travel with someone else, as rooms for two are nowhere near twice as expensive as rooms for one.

Rental Accommodations

It's possible to rent vacation or short or long-term apartments through a number of sources. Real estate agencies in most large cities will be able to provide information on rentals for foreigners. The best bet is to speak to other foreigners in Brazil to get an idea of current prices, which vary from city to city. In the classified real estate sections of newspapers, apartments are usually listed under *temporada* or *apartamentos para aluguel*. If you just want a room in someone else's house or apartment, look under *vaga* or *quarto*. Generally, an apartment that runs US$200 per week in Belo Horizonte will cost you two to three times that in Rio or São Paulo.

Accommodations in Remote Areas

If you're traveling where there are no hotels – as in parts of Amazonia and the Northeast – a hammock and mosquito net are essential. With these basics (inexpensively bought in almost any town) and friendly locals, you can get a good night's rest anywhere. Most fishing villages along the coast have seen an outsider or two and will put you up for the night. If they've seen a few more outsiders, they'll probably charge you a couple of dollars.

Another type of remote-area accommodation is the jungle lodge – a hotel catering to tourists in or on the edge of the forest. These usually have all the amenities of a mid-range or even top-end hotel, with considerably more exotic setting and architecture (they're usually made of wood and often stand on stilts).

FOOD

Brazilian eateries serve some of the biggest portions on the planet. It's hard to go hungry here, even on a modest budget.

The basic Brazilian diet revolves around *arroz* (white rice), *feijão* (black beans) and *farinha* (manioc flour). It's possible to eat these every day, and in some places it's hard not to. The tasty black beans are typically cooked in bacon. The white rice is often very starchy. Manioc (cassava, *mandioca* in Portuguese) root, the staple of the Indians, slaves and Portuguese for hundreds of years, is a hardy root that grows everywhere. It's a bit of an acquired taste for some palates. It often comes gently toasted and mixed with tiny bits of onion or bacon, under the name *farofa*.

From the rice-bean-flour core, meals go in one of three directions: meat *(carne)*, chicken *(galinha* or *frango)*, or fish *(peixe)*. One of these, plus maybe a bit of salad, goes to make up the typical Brazilian meal that is called *prato feito* (set meal) or *refeição*. Servings are usually large and prices low (US$2 to US$4), but after a while *prato feito* can become a trifle monotonous. If quantity is your thing, you can live like a king.

Meat, chicken and fish are, well, cooked, and that's about it. It's generally good quality meat, chicken or fish, but Brazilians don't do much with it. Steak, big and rare, is the national passion. The best cut is *filé*. Sausage is *lingüiça*. Chicken is usually grilled, sometimes fried. Fish is generally fried.

Where to Eat

A *lanchonete* is a snack bar typically serving *sanduíches, pasteis* (crumbed hors d'oeuvres) and other *tira-gostos* and *petiscos* (snacks). The term *sanduich* covers a multitude of inexpensive and usually hot sins from the *X-tudo* (hamburger with everything) to the very dependable *misto quente* (toasted ham and cheese sandwich).

Restaurantes serve proper sit-down meals, ranging from cheap *prato feito* and por-quilo buffets (see Meal Times below) to expensive à la carte choices off the menu *(cardápio)*. Your average main dish from the menu costs around US$5 to US$10. In some places, the portions are *doble,* specifically intended for two people. In others, they're not for two, but they're gigantic anyway.

In the cities you can get many of the dishes that you like back home. *Pizzarias* are almost a dime a dozen now. Most of them serve *massa* (pasta) too. There's also fine dining. For US$10 to US$15 you can have a superb Japanese or Indian dinner in Rio or São Paulo. *Churrascarias* bring you all the barbecued meat you can eat and a variety of other goodies for a fixed price (around US$20 in Rio). They must be tried – vegetarians who can stand the carnage will have no problem filling up at the salad bar.

Rodízio is a name for the serving system typical of churrascarias where they come round offering you item after item till you can eat no more. Rodízios are especially good in the South. Occasionally you come across rodízios of other types of food such as pizza and pasta.

Meal Times

Breakfast is called *café da manhã,* often shortened to *café,* which is also the word for coffee. Most people eat it some time between 6 and 8:30 am. It's included in your room price at most hotels, and at mid-range places is often a sizable buffet of coffee, juice, fruit, breads, cheese, ham, pastries, cereal, and maybe yogurt or eggs.

Lunch *(almoço)* is the main meal for Brazilians. They tend to eat it early – some time between 11:30 am and 1:30 pm.

Many restaurants offer *por quilo* (per-kilogram) lunch buffets. These are a convenient option for travelers, as you don't have to decipher a *cardápio* (menu) or try to communicate with a waiter. You serve yourself what you want, they weigh it and give you a check (bill). A typical price is around US$7 per kg, and most people will eat around half a kilo. Waiters come to your table to take your drink order, which they add to your check, and later you can serve yourself some of the tempting desserts *(sobremesas),* which also get weighed and added to the check. Pay when you leave. Go early for por quilo: Many places start serving around 11:30 am, and by 2 pm what's left may be looking a little unappetizing.

Restaurants in Rio will often bring you a *couvert* (appetizer) whether you ask for it or not. This is optional, so you are perfectly within your rights to send it back. The typical couvert is a ridiculously overpriced and tedious basket of bread, crackers, pheasant eggs and a couple of carrot and celery sticks. Most restaurants will still bring bread with your soup at no extra charge.

Dinner *(jantar)* doesn't vary much from lunch, unless you go to a better restaurant. Dishes are often intended to be divided between two people, and are priced accordingly (if you can't eat it all ask for a *embalagem* (doggie bag) and give it to someone on the street).

In much of the country you can eat dinner any time from about 7 pm to midnight. People wander into restaurants in an erratic trickle all evening. In the big cities, Brazilians dine late. Restaurants in Rio and São Paulo don't get busy until 10 pm at weekends.

The Check (Bill)

A 10% tip is generally included in the check. If not, it's customary to leave at least 10%.

Overcharging is standard procedure in many restaurants frequented by tourists. If a check isn't itemized, don't hesitate to ask the waiter: *'pode discriminar?'* ('can you itemize?'). Also, take your time and count your change – shortchanging is common. It's all part of the game. They good-naturedly overcharge and you can good-naturedly hassle them until the check is fixed. They're used to it.

Brazilian Dishes

Despite much sameness, there are regional differences among cuisines. The cooking in the Northern interior *(comida do sertão)* shows a heavy Indian influence, using many special, traditional tubers and fruits. The Amazon region offers some unique and tasty varieties of fish (including piranha!). The *comida baiana* of the Northeastern coast has a distinct African flavor, using peppers, spices and the delicious oil of the *dendê* palm. The slaves introduced greater variety into the preparation of meat and fish, and dishes like *vatapá* and *caruru*.

Minas Gerais is the home of *comida mineira*, a heavy but tasty cuisine based on pork, vegetables like *couve* (a spinach-like leaf) and the bean-like *quiabo*, and *tutú*, a kind of refried bean paste.

In the South, Rio Grande do Sul's *comida gaúcha* revolves around meat, meat and more meat. This cuisine has the most extensive vocabulary for different cuts of meat you're ever likely to hear.

The following are some common Brazilian dishes:

Acarajé – this is what the baianas, Bahian women in flowing white dresses, sell on street corners throughout Bahia. The baianas are an unforgettable sight, but you're likely to whiff the wonderful-smelling dendê oil they use before you see them. Acarajé is made from peeled brown beans mashed in salt and onions and then fried. Inside these delicious fried balls is vatapá, dried shrimp, pepper and tomato sauce. Dendê oil is strong stuff. Many stomachs can't handle it, and North Americans believe it will cause instant heart disease.

Angú – a cake made with very thin cornmeal, called fubá, and mixed with water and salt

Barreado – a mixture of meats and spices cooked in a sealed clay pot for 24 hours, served with banana and farofa – the state dish of Paraná

Bobó de camarão – manioc paste cooked and flavored with dried shrimp, coconut milk and cashew nuts

Camarão á paulista – unshelled fresh shrimp fried in olive oil with lots of garlic and salt

Canja – a big soup made with chicken broth. More often than not it's a meal in itself

Carangueijada – a kind of crab cooked whole and seasoned

Carne do sol – a tasty, salted meat, grilled and served with beans, rice and vegetables

Caruru – one of the most popular Brazilian dishes brought from Africa. This is made with okra or other vegetables cooked in water. The water is then drained, and onions, salt, shrimp and malagueta peppers are added, mixed and grated together with the okra paste and dendê oil. Traditionally, a sea fish such as garoupa is then added.

Casquinha de carangueijo or *siri* – stuffed crab. The meat is prepared with manioc flour.

Cozido – a stew, usually with more vegetables (eg, potatoes, sweet potatoes, carrots and manioc) than other Brazilian stews

Dourado – scrumptious freshwater fish found throughout Brazil

Empadão – a tasty meat, vegetable, olive and egg pie, typical of Goiás

Feijoada – the national dish of Brazil, a meat stew served with rice and a bowl of beans, traditionally eaten for Saturday lunch. There are many variations, depending on what animal happens to be walking through the kitchen while the chefs are at work. Orange peel, peppers and flour accompany the stew

Frango ao molho pardo – chicken pieces stewed with vegetables and then covered with a seasoned sauce made from the blood of the bird

Moqueca – a kind of sauce or stew and a style of cooking from Bahia. The moqueca sauce is defined by its heavy use of dendê oil and coconut milk, often with peppers and onions. Fish, shrimp, oyster, crab or a combination can all be done moqueca-style. A moqueca must be cooked in a covered clay pot.

Moqueca capixaba – a moqueca from Espírito Santo, cooked using lighter urucum oil instead of dendê oil

Pato no tucupi – roast duck flavored with garlic and cooked in the tucupi sauce, made from the juice of the manioc plant and jambu, a local vegetable. This is a very popular dish in Pará.

Peixada – fish cooked in broth with vegetables and eggs

Peixe a delícia – broiled or grilled fish, usually made with bananas and coconut milk, particularly delicious in Fortaleza.

Pirarucu ao forno – a preparation of the most famous fish from the rivers of Amazonia, in which the fish is oven-cooked with lemon and other seasonings

Prato de verão – literally 'summer plate.' This is basically a fruit salad – served at many juice bars in Rio.

Tacacá – an Indian dish of dried shrimp cooked with pepper, jambu, manioc and much more

Tutu á mineira – a black-bean feijoada often served with couve (a type of kale) – typical of Minas Gerais

Vatapá – a seafood dish with a thick sauce made from manioc paste, coconut and dendê oil. This is perhaps the most famous Brazilian dish of African origin.

Xinxim de galinha – pieces of chicken flavored with garlic, salt and lemon. Dendê oil and shrimp are often added.

Vegetarian Fare

Vegetarianism is very much a minority activity in Brazil. Many Brazilian waiters consider *sem carne* (without meat) to include such 'vegetable' groups as chicken, pork and animal fats, so be very clear when ordering in restaurants. Beware especially the typical black bean dishes, which almost always include or are flavored with meat.

Por quilo restaurants (see Meal Times, earlier in this section) are good for vegetarians – they usually offer at least half a dozen different salad, vegetable and bean dishes. Most cities now have vegetarian restaurants that serve salads, casseroles, brown rice etc. Their food might be healthy, but you need a bit of luck for it to be tasty too.

Fruit, Vegetables & Ice Cream

From the savory nirvana of *graviola* to the confusingly clinical taste of *cupuaçú*, Brazil's fruits, ice creams (*sorvetes*) and juices (see Drinks, later in this chapter) are a highlight.

Many fruits of the Northeast and Amazonia have no English name, so there's no sense in attempting to translate them: You'll just have to taste *ingá, abiu, marimari, pitanga, taperebá, sorva, pitamba, uxí, pupunha, seriguela, bacuri* and *jambo*. The taste descriptions in the following partial list of Brazilian fruits and veggies are unashamedly subjective: Be bold with your choices and enjoy!

Abacate – avocado

Abacaxi – pineapple

Açaí – gritty, forest-berry taste and deep purple color. Ground up with crushed ice, it makes a great, ice-cold sorbet-like food to which you can add granola, ginseng, honey etc.

Acerola – wonderful cherry flavor; a megasource of vitamin C

Alface – lettuce

Alho – garlic

Ameixa – plum, prune

Bacaba – Amazonian fruit used in wines and syrups

Betarraba – beetroot

Biribá – Amazonian fruit eaten plain

Buriti – a palm-tree fruit with a mealy texture and a hint of peach followed by an odd aftertaste. Also used in ice cream and for wine.

Cacau – pulp from cocoa pod; tastes wonderfully sweet and creamy. It's nothing like cocoa, which is extracted from the bean.

Caja – has a pear-like taste

Cajú – fruit of cashew (the nut is enclosed in an appendage of the fruit). It has a tart taste, like a cross between lemon and pear.

Carambola – starfruit, which has a tangy, citrus flavor

Cenoura – carrot

Chuchu – chayote; looks like a wrinkly avocado

Cupuaçú – cool taste, strangely clinical. It's best with milk and sugar.

Fruto-do-conde – green, very popular sugar-apple fruit

Gengibre – ginger; commonly drunk as atchim (a mixture of lemon and ginger)

Genipapo – tastes like curdled cow piss – not everyone's favorite! It's better as a liqueur.

Goiaba – guava

Graviola – custard apple – creamy and aromatic, with an exquisite taste

Jaca – large fruit of the jackfruit tree

Laranja – orange

Limão – lime or lemon

Maçã – apple

Mamão – papaya (pawpaw)

Manga – mango

Mangaba – has a tart flavor, similar to pear

Maracujá – passion fruit

Melancia – watermelon

Melão – honeydew melon

Morango – strawberry

Murici – mealy fruit with vague caramel taste

Pera – pear

Pêssego – peach

Pupunha – a fatty, vitamin-rich Amazonian fruit taken with coffee

Repolho – cabbage

Sapoti – has a gritty, semisweet Worcestershire-sauce taste. Brits may even recognize a hint of Marmite. Rather confusing for a fruit!

Tamarindo – pleasantly acidic, plum-like

Tangerina – mandarin orange, tangerine

Tapereba – has a gritty texture. The flavor is a cross between acerola and sweet potato.

Uva – grape

DRINKS
Nonalcoholic Drinks

Sucos (juices) in Brazil are divine. They vary by region and season (the Amazon has fruits you won't believe). Every town has plenty of juice bars, often offering 30 or 40 different varieties, usually at around US$1 for a good-sized glass.

The juices may be made from fresh fruit and vegetables or from pulp. Request them *sem açúcar e gelo* or *natural* if you don't want sugar and ice. Juices often have water mixed in; this is almost certain to be purified but if you're worried about it, you can ask for juices mixed with orange juice (*suco de laranja*) instead of water, or for a *vitamina*, which is juice with milk. Orange juice is rarely adulterated and mixes well with papaya, carrot and several other fruits.

There is an incredible variety of fruits and combinations, so you should spend some time experimenting.

Caldo de cana is a tasty juice extracted directly from lengths of sugarcane, usually while you wait. The machine that does the crushing is a noisy, multi-cogged affair that has to be cranked up every time someone wants a drink. Brazilians often like to nibble pasteis (small pastries) while they drink caldo.

Few liquids slip better down a thirsty throat than the juice of a cold coconut *(coco)*, sold just about everywhere there are people and it's hot. When you've drunk it dry, ask the vendor to split the husk open and slice off a couple of slivers for you to scoop out the flesh.

Brazilians take their coffee as strong as the devil, as hot as hell, and as sweet as love. They call it *cafezinho* and drink it as an espresso-sized coffee without milk and cut with plenty of sugar. Cafezinho is taken often and at all times. It's sold in stand-up bars and dispensed free in large thermoses in restaurants, at hotel reception desks and in offices to keep the workers perky. Brazilians have been known to take one to bed with them to go to sleep. If you don't like the sugar, hunt around for a café with *espresso*. They're easy to find in cities and large towns. *Café com leite* is coffee with hot milk, usually drunk for breakfast.

Chá, tea, is not nearly as important a drink as coffee, except in the state of Rio Grande do Sul, where the gaúchos drink *mate*, a strong tea drunk through a silver straw from a hollow gourd.

Soft drinks *(refrigerantes)* are found everywhere and are cheaper than bottled water. Guaraná 'champagne,' a Brazilian soft drink made from the berry of an Amazonian plant, is about as popular as Coke and has all sorts of supposedly marvelous properties (see the boxed text 'Guaraná: Fountain of Eternal Youth' in the Amazonas & Roraima chapter). It's pretty refreshing: cold, carbonated, sweet – and you can tell yourself it's healthy too!

Alcoholic Drinks

'Para que nossas mulheres não fiquem viúva.'
(May our wives never be widows.)
- Brazilian drinking toast

Cachaça is found everywhere – even in the most miserable frontier shantytowns. Bottled beer usually follows the introduction of electricity to a region. Found at the pinnacle of Brazilian civilization is *chopp* (see the following section), which is only available in large and prosperous economic centers with paved roads and electricity.

Beer Brazilians, like most civilized people, enjoy their beer served icy cold *(bem gelada)*. A *cerveja* is a 600ml bottled beer. A *cervejinha* is 300ml of bottled or canned beer. Cans are more expensive than bottles. Of the common brands, Antártica (say 'ant-**okt**-chee-kah') is the best, followed by Brahma (although some Brazilians argue that Brahma is better in Rio). The best beers are the regional ones, like Bohemia from Petrópolis, Cerpa from Pará, Cerma from Maranhão and the tasty Serramalte, which comes from Rio Grande do Sul. Bavaria is a tasty pilsner, which only comes in 300ml bottles and is found in the more upmarket bars. Caracu is a stout-like beer, also only available in 300ml bottles. Xingu is a sweet black beer from Santa Catarina. Hunt around for it – you won't be sorry. Antarctica and Brahma breweries both do a decent dark 'malzbier.'

Chopp (pronounced 'shope' with a little 'pfff' at the end, 'shope-fff') is a pale blond pilsner draft, lighter and far superior to canned or bottled beer. Antarctica and Brahma produce the two most widespread versions. In big cities you may even find *chopp escuro*, a kind of light stout. Key phrase: '*Moço, mais um chopp!*' ('Waiter, another chopp!').

Cachaça Also called *pinga* or *aguardente*, cachaça is a high-proof sugarcane alcohol produced and drunk throughout the country. It ranges from excrementally cheap to as dear as whisky, and yes, price definitely signals a difference in taste and effect (and aftereffect!). Cachaça literally means 'booze.' Pinga (which literally means 'drop') is considered more polite. The production of cachaça is as old as slavery in Brazil. The distilleries grew up with the sugar plantations, which were the first to

---

Cocktail of the Gods

There are as many individual variations on how to concoct a caipirinha as there are caipirinha concocters. You can't go far wrong following these basics:

Ingredients
2 limes (lemon is an acceptable substitute)
16 ice cubes
4 teaspoons sugar
300ml cachaça (the better the cachaça, the better the caipirinha)

Cool your glasses in the fridge beforehand. Cut the limes into chunks or eighths, and mix the sugar with them. Splinter the ice and mix it with the lime-sugar mix and the cachaça. Shake it all together in a cocktail shaker (if you lack one of those, stir well in a jug). Serve, sit back and watch the sun go down.

---

supply local consumption and then to export to Africa to exchange for slaves.

There are well over 100 brands of cachaça. A cheap one can cut a hole in the strongest stomach lining. Velho Barreiro, Ypioca, Pitú, Carangueijo, and São Francisco are some of the better labels. Many distilleries will allow you to take a tour and watch the process from raw sugar to rotgut and then sample some of the goodies. The smaller distilleries usually make a much smoother cachaça than the commercial brands.

The caipirinha is the unofficial Brazilian national drink. The ingredients are simple: cachaça, lime, sugar and crushed ice, but a well-made caipirinha is a work of art, sublime when sipped in the cool of an evening. If you'd like to make your own divine concoction, see the boxed text 'Cocktail of the Gods' for a straightforward caipirinha recipe.

A *caipirosca* is a caipirinha with vodka replacing cachaça. *Caipirissima* is still another variation, with Bacardi rum instead of cachaça. *Batidas* are wonderful mixes of cachaça, sugar and fruit juice.

ENTERTAINMENT
Clubs

There are major clubs in the major cities, as you'd expect. São Paulo and Rio especially have concentrations of clubs, but other cities like Belo Horizonte, Porto Alegre, Salvador, Recife, Fortaleza and São Luís have hot nightlife too. Nothing much gets going in the clubs before midnight. In this book we list selected clubs as well as what's-on guides and listings magazines. Club admission in the large cities ranges from US$5 to US$15. Some smaller discos/clubs may be called *danceteria* or *boite* (pronounced 'bwachy'). Like some larger clubs, these may or not have professional ladies present. Some are striptease joints.

Live Music

The best places to hear live music are generally pubs and bars. Most towns and cities of any size have a quite a choice of venues. Rio and São Paulo of course are hubs of the musical arts, with heaps going on, but the Pelourinho district of Salvador has probably the highest concentration of spots where you can regularly hear great live music. In fact if you're staying in the area, it can be hard to get to sleep for the music. See the regional chapters for venue information and the Arts section in Facts about Brazil for some of the many musical styles and artists to listen for in this intensely musical country. Places with live music often levy a small cover charge.

Other Live Entertainment

Most big cities have a busy venue or two for classical music, opera, theater and ballet. Rio and São Paulo, however, dominate the 'cultural' scene. See the Rio City chapter and the São Paulo City section of the São Paulo State chapter for details.

Bars & Pubs

Brazilian pubs and bars are congenial, friendly places, and there's no telling where they'll turn up. Rio and São Paulo have highly competitive, sophisticated drinking spots, and other cities have a strange mix of places. Check the various sections on cities for bars, but also look in local papers and magazines for new venues, which open all the time.

Cinemas

There are cinemas in almost every town of any size. They show mainly foreign films, including all the big Hollywood releases and many European films, in the original language with subtitles. Showings run from the afternoon to night, and a ticket usually costs around US$5.

Rio has many film aficionados and many special events. The prestigious Brazilian Film Festival takes place in Gramado, Rio Grande do Sul, in August. See the Cinema section under Arts in the Facts about Brazil chapter for information on some of the best Brazilian-made films.

SPECTATOR SPORTS
Soccer

Soccer, or football as it's also called (*futebol* to Brazilians), was introduced in the 1890s when a young student from São Paulo, Charles Miller, returned from studying in England with two footballs and a rule book and began to organize the first league. It quickly became the national passion, and Brazil is the only country to have won four World Cups (1958, 1962, 1970 and 1994). The rest of world acknowledges that Brazilians are the best footballers, and Brazilians are, to put it mildly, psycho about the game.

No one goes to work on big international game days, a situation that the government – which is prepared to spend whatever it takes to win the World Cup – laments. When Brazil unexpectedly lost to France in the 1998 World Cup final, millions cried on the streets and depression gripped the country for weeks. Since then some of the shady business that goes on behind the soccer scenes has started to come to light, and parliamentary commissions have investigated corruption in football. The fans may criticize the way football is run, but nothing dims their insane passion for the game itself.

They know their football, too. Each good move is rewarded with superlatives. A fancy dribble past an opponent receives a

Brazilian Football: Facts for Fans

If proof were needed that Brazilians love their soccer, you could cite the fact that it never really stops. Apart from a couple of short breaks for the Christmas–New Year holiday and Carnaval, professional club competitions go on all year, and the games can be played on any day of the week (though Saturday, Sunday and Wednesday are favorites).

What follows is a brief breakdown of what titles are played for and when. There is also a listing of Brazil's main clubs, so that if the TV shows red, green and white stripes confronting black and red hoops a few days before Christmas, you'll understand why everyone around it is so emotional.

An excellent Web site for results, schedules and league tables is www.netgol.com (in Portuguese, but not hard to decipher).

The Competitions Brazil's football year is divided into two *semestres*. The premier competition is the **Campeonato Brasileiro** (Brazilian Championship), played in the second semester. Between about late July and mid-November, 20-odd top clubs play each other once each in a league (three points for a win, one for a draw). At the end, the top eight enter a *mata-mata* (sudden-death) knockout phase, culminating in a two-leg final in mid-December to decide the national champion. From the competition's inception in 1971 up to 2000, Flamengo has won the most titles (five), followed by Vasco da Gama and Palmeiras (four each), and São Paulo, Corinthians and Internacional (three each).

The other main second-semester event, held between August and December, is the **Copa Mercosul** (Mercosur Cup), contested by the best teams from Brazil, Argentina, Uruguay, Paraguay and Chile.

The first semester revolves chiefly around **state and regional championships**. Each of Brazil's 26 states holds its own championship, usually from January till June. The regional tourneys (Torneio Rio-São Paulo, Copa Sul-Minas, Copa Nordeste etc), during the first few months of the year involve most of the same teams as the state championships. The Campeonato Carioca (the Rio state championship) has a uniquely complicated format comprising two different competitions, the Taça Guanabara followed by the Taça Rio, with the two *taça* winners playing off for the state championship.

Concurrent with the state and regional championships are the **Copa do Brasil** (Brazil Cup), **Copa dos Campeões** (Champions' Cup) and **Copa Libertadores** (Liberators' Cup or, as it's known in Brazil, Taça dos Libertadores). The Copa do Brasil is Brazil's version of England's FA Cup, a sudden-death competition, which starts out with 64 teams in March and ends in a two-leg final in July.

The Copa dos Campeões, contested by the eight winners of the year's major regional and state championships, is another sudden-death event, running from late June to late July. Its winners,

Brazilian Football: Facts for Fans

along with the winners of the Copa do Brasil and the two finalists of the Campeonato Brasileiro, comprise the four Brazilian representatives in the following year's Copa Libertadores, Latin America's premier club competition, played between February and June/July. Brazilian clubs won the Libertadores 11 times between 1960 (its first year) and 2000.

The most important competitions entered by Brazil's national team, with their famous yellow shirts and blue shorts, are the **World Cup** and the **Copa América**. The South American qualifying contest for the World Cup has recently taken the form of a full home-and-away league involving the top 10 South American soccer nations. The Copa América takes place around July in odd-numbered years, in a different South American country each time, and is contested by the South American nations.

The Clubs The major Brazilian clubs are as follows:

Club	Home City	Stadium (Capacity)	Shirt Colors
Bahia	Salvador	Fonte Nova (96,000)	white
Botafogo	Niterói (Rio de Janeiro)	Caio Martins (15,000)	black & white stripes
Corinthians	São Paulo	Pacaembu (40,000)	white; black collar
Cruzeiro	Belo Horizonte	Mineirão (90,000)	blue
Flamengo	Rio de Janeiro	Maracanã (120,000)	red; black hoops
Fluminense	Rio de Janeiro	Laranjeiras (10,000)*	red, green & white stripes
Grêmio	Porto Alegre	Olímpico (55,000)	blue, black & white stripes
Internacional	Porto Alegre	Beira-Rio (80,000)	red
Palmeiras	São Paulo	Parque Antarctica (28,000)	green
Santa Cruz	Recife	Arruda (80,000)	white; black & red hoops
Santos	Santos	Vila Belmiro (26,000)	white
São Paulo	São Paulo	Morumbi (65,000)	white; red & black hoops
Sport	Recife	Ilha do Retiro (50,000)	red & black hoops
Vasco da Gama	Rio de Janeiro	São Januário (40,000)	white; black slash

* Fluminense play most of their home games at the Maracanã.

A Few Technical Terms

atacante – striker
cartão amarelo/vermelho – yellow/red card
Clube dos 13 – Club of 13 (a grouping of Brazil's 20, yes 20, most powerful clubs)
craque – star
goleiro – goalkeeper
juiz – referee
lateral-direito – right back
lateral-esquerdo – left back

meia – attacking midfielder
técnico – coach
time – team
torcedor – fan
volante – defensive midfielder
zagueiro – center back

Spanish bullfight *olé;* a goal results in delirium. And radio and TV announcers stretch the word 'goal' for at *least* 20 seconds (GOOOOOOOOOOOOOL!) – an astounding bit of audio even before it's enhanced by a wah-wah reverb effect.

Brazilians play the world's most creative, artistic and thrilling style of soccer. They are lousy defenders, but who cares when they attack so excitingly? Most of the best players leave Brazil for lucrative contracts with European clubs, but that hardly matters when so many gifted kids are waiting to replace them. You'll see tiny children playing skilled, rough matches in the streets, on the beaches, just about anywhere.

Go to a game. It's an intense spectacle, one of the most colorful pageants you'll ever see. Crowds are very rumbustious, but no more prone to violence than in, say, Italy, Spain or England. Don't tempt pickpockets inside or outside the stadium by carrying anything you don't need. Ticket prices vary according to your place in the stadium – typically they're between US$3 and US$10. To get away relatively easily

Pelé

Brazil's most famous international personality is undoubtedly Pelé. Any other country would be happy to have produced just one footballer as talented as Brazilians Garrincha, Didi, Gerson, Tostão, Jairzinho, Carlos Alberto, Socrates, Romário, Juninho or Ronaldo (to name just a few), but in the history of Brazilian soccer all these play second fiddle to Pelé. And he's not just a legendary footballer who has won several 'player of the 20th century' awards: He was also Brazil's first black government minister (for sport, from 1995 to 1998) and has even been knighted by Britain's Queen Elizabeth II.

The lad has come a long way since he was born Édson Arantes do Nascimento in Três Corações, Minas Gerais, on October 23, 1940. His public image remains impeccable. He's never smoked, never been photographed with a drink in hand and has NEVER been involved with drugs.

In a 22-year career, the teams on which Pelé played gained 53 titles, including three World Cups (in Sweden in 1958, Chile in 1962 and Mexico in 1970), dual world club championships (with Santos in 1962 and 1963), two South American championships, 11 Paulista state championships and four Rio–São Paulo tournaments.

Pelé retired from the Brazilian team in 1971 and from Santos in 1974. In 1975 the New York Cosmos coaxed him north to the US, where he played until 1977, when the team won the American championship. He finally retired at the end of that year, after a game between the Cosmos and Santos in which he played the first half for the Cosmos and the second half with Santos.

In 1363 games (112 for the Brazilian team), he scored 1282 goals. When he scored his 1000th goal in 1969, he dedicated it 'to the children of Brazil.' Pelé called getting the goal 'one of the greatest blessings a man could ever expect to receive from God.'

In Brazil, Pelé is known simply as O Rei (The King).

after the game, try walking half a kilometer or so to escape the thickest crowds, then catching a taxi. See the boxed text 'Brazilian Football: Facts for Fans' for the information you need in order to understand the basics of who's playing who, where, when and for what.

Volleyball

Volleyball is Brazil's second sport. A natural for the beach, it's also a popular spectator sport on TV. A local variation you'll see on Rio's beaches is volleyball played without hands (futvolei). It's quite fun to watch but it's bloody hard to play.

Motor Racing

Brazilians love speed. Taxi drivers may give you a hint of it, and since the early 1970s Brazilian drivers have won more Formula One world championships than any other nationality. Emerson Fittipaldi was world champion twice in the 1970s, Nelson Piquet won his third world championship in 1987, and the late great Ayrton Senna took it out three times. The Brazilian Grand Prix at Interlagos, São Paulo, usually takes place in March, one of the first of the Formula One season.

Tennis

Tennis is increasingly popular, especially in the Southeast and South. Brazil's tennis hero is the highly popular Gustavo 'Guga' Kuerten from Florianópolis. French Open champion in 1997 and 2000, in the latter year Guga also became the first South American to be ranked first in the world.

SHOPPING

Smart souvenir hunters can do well in Brazil, provided they know a little about Brazilian culture. Many people find the best souvenirs to be recorded music, musical instruments, local crafts (Indian and otherwise) and artwork.

Glitzy, air-conditioned shopping malls – imaginatively called *shoppings* – are a feature of every self-respecting medium-sized city, and São Paulo has hundreds of them. Browsing the many markets and

small streetside stores yields, for better or worse, less predictable results.

Music

Brazilian music is sure to evoke your most precious travel memories. The best music stores are in the big malls. Regional music enthusiasts should check out the selection at the Museu Folclorico Edson Carneiro in Rio. New-release CDs cost around US$15 in stores, but compilation albums of a star's best songs, such as those in the *Pérolas* and *XXI Vinteum* series, are about half that price and can be a good value. Tapes (called K7 – 'ka-sete') cost around US$8. Street stalls sell bootleg CDs for around US$6 and tapes for about US$2.

Brazil's many varieties of percussion, wind and string instruments make fun souvenirs and presents. You can often find inexpensive ones at craft markets as well as in music stores.

Art & Crafts

Although nearly everything can be found in Rio and São Paulo, there is a premium for moving craft and art pieces from the hinterland into the fancy stores of the big cities. The inexpensive exceptions include the 'hippie' fairs at Ipanema and Praça 15 de Novembro in Rio, the Artíndia stores of FUNAI (the government Indian agency) and museum gift shops.

Most of the Indian crafts in FUNAI stores are inexpensive, but quality generally matches price. Museum gift shops, on the other hand, stock some very worthwhile souvenirs. They're good for artisanry and prints of local art. The Carmen Miranda museum in Rio sells T-shirts of the great lady herself, complete with her famous fruit headdress.

Outside the two big cities, your best bets for craftwork are artisan fairs – held on Saturday and Sunday in many cities – cooperative stores, and government-run shops. The Northeast has a rich assortment of artistic items. Salvador and nearby Cachoeira are notable for their rough-hewn wood sculpture. Artisans in Fortaleza and the southeastern coast of Ceará specialize in fine lace.

The interior of Pernambuco, in particular Caruaru, is famous for its wildly imaginative ceramic figurines.

Some Amazonian Indian peoples now make artifacts such as bows, arrows, baskets, feather headdresses, carvings, pottery and beads specifically as commodities to sell (see Indigenous Crafts in the Arts section in the Facts about Brazil chapter). Some are very attractive even if not quite the genuine article.

Gemstones
Gemstones are the most famous souvenir/luxury items from Minas Gerais. But if you're in the market for fine jewelry and precious stones, wait until you return to the big cities to make your purchases. Buy from a large and reputable dealer like Amsterdam Sauer or H Stern in Rio. Stern is an international dealership based in Ipanema, and its reputation for quality and honesty is beyond reproach. It isn't a discount store – in fact it has a checkin desk where you have to get an identity tag before you can enter – but its jewelry is less expensive in Brazil than at its outlets in other parts of the world.

Leather
Brazilian leather goods are moderately priced, but the leather isn't particularly supple. The better Brazilian shoes, belts, wallets, purses and luggage are sold in the upmarket shops of Ipanema and Copacabana. Shoes are extremely good value, but many of the best are reserved for export, and larger sizes are difficult to find. Good quality, cheap, durable, leather soccer balls with hand-stitched panels are sold all over Brazil in sporting-goods stores. Inflated soccer balls should not be put in the cargo hold of a plane.

In interior Pernambuco, the *sertanejos'* curious traditional leather hats appeal to some travelers.

Other Purchases
Functional and decorative hammocks are available in cities throughout Amazonia. These string, mesh or cloth slings are fixtures in most Brazilian homes. They're indispensable for travelers and make fine, portable gifts. A typical one-person hammock costs around US$8 to US$10; a large *casal* (double) hammock might run US$20.

Coffee-table picture books on Brazil, videotapes of Carnaval and of highlights of the Brazilian national football team and Pelé in various World Cup matches are hawked in the streets of Copacabana, and available in stores too. Guaraná powder, a stimulant (said to be an aphrodisiac) derived from an Amazonian fruit, is sold by health stores and pharmacies around the country. Especially in the Amazon region itself, there are plenty of shops and market stalls devoted to herbal and other natural medicinal preparations – oils, powders, infusions – just name your ailment.

A Brazilian 'dental floss' bikini is fun to have. If nothing else, you can prove to people back home just how little Brazilians really do wear on the beach. Plenty of stores sell very brief beachwear.

Candomblé stores are a good source of curios. They range from magical incense guaranteed to bring good fortune and increase sexual allure, wisdom and health to amulets and ceramic figurines of Afro-Brazilian gods.

If you're in Brazil during Carnaval, make sure you pick up a copy of the Carnaval edition of *Manchete* magazine.

Getting There & Away

Most travelers start their Brazilian odyssey by flying down to Rio, but this is only one of many ways to arrive. The country has several other gateway airports and land borders with every other country in South America except Chile and Ecuador. So while some travelers are in the air en route to Rio, others will be busing in from Uruguay in the south or Venezuela in the north, and yet others may be arriving by the *trem da morte* (death train) from Bolivia or coming in by boat along the Amazon from Peru.

AIR

Cheap deals on air travel are volatile and you always need to put in some work to find the best deal for your needs.

Airports & Airlines

The most popular international gateways are Aeroporto Galeão in Rio de Janeiro and São Paulo's Aeroporto Guarulhos. From both these airports, connecting flights to airports throughout the country leave regularly. Farther north, Salvador and Recife receive a few direct scheduled flights from Europe. Recife, Fortaleza, Belém, Manaus and Belo Horizonte receive some direct scheduled flights from the US.

Varig, Brazil's international airline, flies in from Miami, New York, Los Angeles, Mexico City and nine European and 11 South American cities. From the US, other carriers serving Brazil are Continental Airlines, Delta Airlines, American Airlines, Japan Airlines (JAL), United Airlines and the Brazilian carriers TAM and TransBrasil; from Europe, Air France, Alitalia, British Airways, Iberia, KLM, Lufthansa, Swissair, TAP Air Portugal, TAM and TransBrasil; and from Australia, Qantas and Aerolineas Argentinas.

Some Brazil air passes, for flights within Brazil, can only be bought in conjunction with an international ticket on specified airlines (see the Getting Around chapter).

Buying Tickets

An air ticket can gouge a great slice out of anyone's budget, but you can reduce the cost by finding discounted fares. Passengers flying economy can usually manage some sort of discount.

Lower fares are often also available by traveling midweek or taking advantage of short-lived promotional offers. Generally you'll pay less for a round-trip ticket if you come back within 90 days.

For high-season travel – which basically means flying to Brazil in December, January or between mid-June and mid-August – you should book as far ahead as possible as seats, especially cheap seats, fill up early.

When looking for bargain airfares, go to a travel agent rather than directly to airlines. From time to time, airlines do have promotional fares and special offers, but generally they only sell fares at the official listed price. An exception to this is booking on the Internet. Some airlines offer excellent fares to Web surfers. They may sell seats by auction or simply cut prices to reflect the reduced cost of electronic selling.

Many travel agents have Web sites too, which can make the Internet an easy way to compare prices, a good start for when you're ready to start negotiating with your favorite travel agency. Online ticket sales work well for a simple one-way or round-trip on specified dates. But they're no substitute for a travel agent who knows about special deals and can offer advice on many other aspects of your flight and trip.

The days when some travel agents would routinely fleece travelers by running off with their money are, happily, almost over. Paying by credit card generally offers protection, as most card issuers provide refunds if you can prove you didn't get what you paid for. Similar protection can be obtained by buying a ticket from a bonded agent, such as one covered by the Air Transport Operators License (ATOL) program in the UK. Agents who only accept cash should hand

Air Travel Glossary

Cancellation Penalties If you have to cancel or change a discounted ticket, there are often heavy penalties involved; insurance can sometimes be taken out against these penalties. Some airlines impose penalties on regular tickets as well, particularly against 'no-show' passengers.

Courier Fares Businesses often need to send urgent documents or freight securely and quickly. Courier companies hire people to accompany the package through customs and, in return, offer a discount ticket which is sometimes a phenomenal bargain. However, you may have to surrender all your baggage allowance and take only carry-on luggage.

Full Fares Airlines traditionally offer 1st class (coded F), business class (coded J) and economy class (coded Y) tickets. These days, so many promotional and discounted fares are available that few passengers pay full economy fare.

Lost Tickets If you lose your airline ticket, an airline will usually treat it like a traveler's check and, after inquiries, issue you with another one. Legally, however, an airline is entitled to treat it like cash: if you lose it, it's gone forever. Take good care of your tickets.

Onward Tickets An entry requirement for many countries is a ticket out of the country. If you're unsure of your next move, the easiest solution is to buy the cheapest onward ticket to a neighboring country or a ticket from a reliable airline that can later be refunded if you do not use it.

Open-Jaw Tickets These are return tickets that permit you to fly into one place but return from another. If available, these tickets can save you backtracking to your arrival point.

Overbooking Because almost every flight has some passengers that fail to show up, airlines often book more passengers than they have seats. Usually excess passengers make up for the no-shows, but occasionally somebody gets 'bumped' onto the next available flight. Guess who it is most likely to be? The passengers who check in late.

Promotional Fares These are officially discounted fares, available from travel agencies or direct from the airline.

Reconfirmation If you don't reconfirm your flight at least 72 hours prior to departure, the airline may delete your name from the passenger list. Call to find out if your airline requires reconfirmation.

Restrictions Discounted tickets often have various restrictions – for example, they may need to be paid for in advance, or altering them may incur a penalty. Other restrictions include minimum and maximum periods you must be away.

Round-the-World Tickets RTW tickets give you a limited period (usually a year) in which to circumnavigate the globe. You can go anywhere the carrying airlines go as long as you don't backtrack. The number of stopovers or total number of separate flights is decided before you set off, and these tickets usually cost a bit more than a basic return flight.

Transferred Tickets Airline tickets cannot be transferred from one person to another. Travelers sometimes try to sell the return half of a ticket, but officials can ask you to prove that you are the person named on the ticket. On an international flight, tickets are compared with passports.

Travel Periods Ticket prices vary with the time of year. There is a low (off-peak) season and a high (peak) season, and often a low-shoulder season and a high-shoulder season as well. Usually the fare depends on your outward flight – if you depart in the high season and return in the low season, you pay the high-season fare.

over the tickets straightaway. After you've made a booking or paid your deposit, call the airline and confirm that the booking was made. It's generally not advisable to send money (even checks) through the mail unless the agent is very well established – some travelers have reported being ripped off by fly-by-night mail-order ticket agents.

You may decide to pay more than the rock-bottom fare and opt for the safety of a better known travel agent. Firms such as STA Travel, which has offices worldwide, Council Travel in the US and Usit Campus (formerly Campus Travel) in the UK are not going to disappear overnight, and they do offer good prices to most destinations.

If you purchase a ticket and later want to make changes to your route or get a refund, you need to contact the original travel agent. Airlines only issue refunds to the purchaser of a ticket – usually the travel agent who bought the ticket on your behalf. Many travelers change their routes halfway through their trips, so think carefully before buying a ticket that is not easily refunded.

Student & Youth Fares Full-time students and people under 26 have access to better deals than other travelers – cheaper fares and/or more flexibility to change flights or routes. You have to show a document proving your date of birth or a valid International Student Identity Card when buying your ticket and boarding the plane.

Air Passes If you're combining travels in Brazil with other countries in southern South America, you might look into the Mercosur Airpass, valid for flights within Argentina, Brazil, Chile (except Easter Island), Uruguay and Paraguay. The pass has to be bought before you travel to South America and is available to holders of an international round-trip ticket from outside South America to Argentina, Brazil, Chile, Uruguay or Paraguay. The pass gives you up to two stopovers in each country (plus your starting and finishing points) in one month, and its price depends on how many miles you're going to fly: 1901–2500 miles, for example, costs US$285; 4201–5200 miles

is US$530; and more than 7200 miles is US$870. If you're interested, ask your travel agent.

For information on air passes for flights solely within Brazil, see the Getting Around chapter.

Courier Flights Courier flights are a great bargain if you're lucky enough to find one. A New York-Rio round-trip ticket, for example, could be yours for US$200. Air-freight companies expedite delivery of urgent items by sending them with you as your baggage allowance. You are permitted to bring along a carry-on bag, but that's all. In return, you get a steeply discounted ticket. Courier tickets are sold for a fixed date, and schedule changes can be difficult to make. Arrangements usually have to be made a month or more in advance.

Courier flights are occasionally advertised in the press, or you could contact airfreight companies listed in the phone book. You may even have to go to their offices – staff aren't always keen to give out information over the phone. *Travel Unlimited* (PO Box 1058, Allston, MA 02134 USA) is a monthly travel newsletter which publishes many courier flight deals from airports worldwide. A 12-month subscription costs US$25 (US$35 outside the US). The US$45 membership fee for the International Association of Air Travel Couriers gets members a bimonthly update of aircourier offerings and access to daily last-minute specials: Contact IAATC in the US at ☎ 561-582-8320 or UK ☎ 01305-216920, or visit its Web sites, www.courier.org or www.aircourier.co.uk.

Travelers with Special Needs

Most international airlines can cater to people with special needs – travelers with disabilities, people with young children and even children traveling alone.

If you have special dietary preferences (vegetarian, kosher etc) you can request appropriate meals with advance notice. If you are traveling in a wheelchair, most international airports can provide an escort from the check-in desk to the plane where needed, and ramps, elevators, toilets and phones are generally available and accessible.

Departure Tax

The airport tax for international departures from Brazil is a hefty US$36. This may be included in the price you pay for your ticket. If it's not, you have to pay it in cash in US dollars or in *reais* at the airport before or at check-in, so remember to keep that amount of cash in reserve. If your ticket price included the tax, it may be shown in the taxes section at the bottom of your ticket by the letters BR following the amount – but to be certain, you should ask the agent when you buy the ticket.

The USA

Discount travel agents in the US are known as consolidators (although you won't see a sign on the door saying 'consolidator'). San Francisco is the ticket-consolidator capital of America. Good deals can also be found in Los Angeles, New York and other big cities. Consolidators can be located through the telephone yellow pages or the major daily newspapers. The *New York Times, Los Angeles Times, Chicago Tribune* and *San Francisco Chronicle* all produce weekly travel sections in which you'll find a number of travel agency ads. Good Web sites for discount airfares to Brazil include www.onetravel.com, www.wonderlink.com and www.brol.com.

Council Travel, the largest student travel organization in the US, has around 60 offices. Its head office (toll-free ☎ 800-226-8624) is at 205 E 42nd St, New York, NY 10017. Its Web site is www.counciltravel.com. STA Travel (toll-free ☎ 800-777-0112) has offices in Boston, Chicago, Miami, New York, Philadelphia, San Francisco and other major cities or check its Web site at www.statravel.com.

The Brazilian American Cultural Center (BACC; see the Useful Organizations section in the Facts for the Visitor chapter) offers members some flights that are extremely good bargains – for example, New York-Rio round-trip for under US$400. Its Web site is www.idainc.org/bacc.

The major US departure cities to Brazil are New York, Miami and Los Angeles. If you don't want to arrive in Rio or São Paulo, there are direct flights to some other cities including Manaus and Belém (both of which are halfway between Miami and Rio), and Fortaleza and Recife. Where there is no direct flight you'll usually have to connect in one of the 'big two' cities, and your fare will reflect that you have taken a second flight. Flying to Salvador, for instance, usually costs 10% to 20% more than flying to Rio.

Discounted fares from the US to Brazil are generally for a maximum of four months. From Miami to Rio de Janeiro, São Paulo or Recife, fares can go as low as US$520 round-trip midweek in low season. From New York to Rio or São Paulo you're looking at US$600, and from Los Angeles US$650. Add about US$50 for high-season travel and US$50 for travel on Saturday and Sunday. Student fares are similar.

Discounted round-trip fares from Miami to Manaus, using the weekly direct flights of Varig and Lloyd Aereo Boliviano, are in the US$700 region. If you're heading for the north of Brazil consider going via Venezuela: Miami-Caracas round-trip fares have at times been as low as US$200 and you can bus it from Caracas to Santa Elena on the Brazilian border for about US$30 or to Manaus for about US$70. At the time of writing the Venezuelan airline Aéropostal was offering Manaus-Miami round-trip fares, changing planes in Caracas, starting at US$529.

Nondiscounted fares in general are less expensive if you come back within three months. Low-season round-trip fares to Rio or São Paulo start around US$1300/1870 for under/over three months' stay from New York; US$990/1800 from Miami, and US$1570/2375 from Los Angeles.

If your Brazil trip is going to be short – say, three weeks or less – and you can accept fixed dates, try asking travel agents about charter flights. These often have good prices.

Canada

Canadian discount air ticket sellers are also known as consolidators, and their fares tend to be about 10% higher than fares sold in the US. The *Globe & Mail, Toronto Star, Montreal Gazette* and *Vancouver Sun* carry travel agents' ads and are good places to look for cheap fares. Airlines flying between Canada and Brazil include Canadian Airlines and Air Canada, but many routings are with US airlines, involving a change of planes in the US.

Travel CUTS (toll-free ☎ 800-667-2887) is Canada's national student travel agency and has offices in all major cities. Its Web address is www.travelcuts.com.

The UK

Airline ticket discounters are known as bucket shops in the UK. Despite the name, there is nothing under-the-counter about them. Advertisements for many agencies appear in the travel pages of the weekend papers, such as the *Independent* on Saturday and the *Sunday Times*.

For students or travelers under 26, popular travel agencies include STA Travel (☎ 020-7361-6161), which has an office at 86 Old Brompton Rd, London SW7 3LQ, and 38 other branches, mainly in university cities. Visit its Web site at www.statravel.co.uk. Usit Campus (☎ 0870-240-1010), 52 Grosvenor Gardens, London SW1WOAG, has about 50 branches throughout the UK (Web site: www.usitcampus.co.uk).

An excellent place to start your fare inquiries for Brazil is Journey Latin America (JLA; ☎ 020-8747-3108), 12 & 13 Heathfield Terrace, Chiswick, London W4 4JE (Web site: www.journeylatinamerica.co.uk). Another recommended agency is Trailfinders (☎ 020-7938-3939), 194 Kensington High St, London W8 7RG, with branches in Bristol, Birmingham, Manchester and Newcastle-upon-Tyne (Web site: www.trailfinders.co.uk).

Three-month round-trip airfares from London to Rio or São Paulo start around £400, and with the cheapest fares you're probably looking at changing planes before you leave Europe. For direct flights, with British Airways or Varig, you'd be lucky to pay much under £500. The cheapest fares to Brazil's Northeast coast are often on TAP Air Portugal, using that airline's direct flights

from Lisbon to Salvador and Recife. In 2001, flights on TAP to those two cities, bought through an agency such as Journey Latin America, were around £320/440 one-way/round-trip. London-Manaus or London-Belém is likely to be via Rio or São Paulo and you're looking at £430/670 one-way/round-trip. One-year round-trips in all these cases cost £75 to £150 more.

For short trips (usually not more than three weeks) charter flights are worth looking into. In 2001, charter flights began from London to Salvador (by Airtours, ☎ 0870-400 1200), and to Recife and Natal (by Unijet, ☎ 0870-600 8009). Unijet two-week round-trips from London to Natal began at £419 and to Recife at £489; you can check fares online at www.unijet.com.

Continental Europe

A variety of European and Brazilian airlines fly direct to Rio and São Paulo. The only scheduled direct flights to other Brazilian cities are by TAP Air Portugal from Lisbon to Salvador and Recife. Normally you have to change in Rio or São Paulo to fly to other Brazilian cities. There are charter flights to Salvador, Recife, Fortaleza and Natal but on these you usually have to come back within about three weeks.

Fares are pretty similar from starting points across western Europe. You're looking at discounted or student three-month round-trip fares to Rio or São Paulo for US$500 to US$750, and usually a couple of hundred dollars more for most other destinations.

Many travel agencies in Europe have ties with STA Travel and sell student, youth and other cheap tickets. They include Voyages Wasteels (☎ 08 03 88 70 04), 11 rue Dupuytren, 756006 Paris (Web site: www.voyages-wasteels.fr); STA Travel (☎ 030 311 0950), Goethestrasse 73, 10625 Berlin; and Passaggi (☎ 06-474 0923), Stazione Termini FS, Galleria Di Tesla, Rome.

France has a network of student travel agencies which can supply discount tickets to travelers of all ages. OTU Voyages (☎ 01 40 29 12 12) has a central Paris office at 39 Ave Georges Bernanos (5e) and another

37 offices around the country. The Web address is www.otu.fr. Acceuil des Jeunes en France (☎ 01 42 77 87 80), 119 rue Saint Martin (4e), Paris, is another popular discount travel agency.

A general travel agency with some of the best services and deals is Nouvelles Frontières (☎ 08 25 00 08 25), 5 Ave de l'Opéra (1er), Paris, with dozens of other offices around France and a Web site at www.nouvelles-frontieres.com. An interesting Web site for fares from France, Switzerland or Belgium is www.degriftour.com.

If you're heading for northern Brazil, look into TAT European Airlines which flies from Paris to Cayenne (French Guiana) from around US$200/400 one-way/round-trip From Cayenne you can fly into Brazil at Macapá or Belém with the Brazilian regional airline Penta, for a total fare from Paris of about US$400/650, or you can reduce costs by doing at least part of the Cayenne-Brazil leg overland.

Belgium, Switzerland and the Netherlands are also good places for buying discount air tickets. In Belgium, Acotra Student Travel Agency (☎ 02-512 86 07) at rue de la Madeline, Brussels, and WATS Reizen (☎ 03-226 16 26) at de Keyserlei 44, Antwerp, are both well-known. Also try the Web site www.airstop.be. In Switzerland, SSR Voyages (☎ 01-297 11 11) specializes in student, youth and budget fares. SSR has a branch at Leonhardstrasse 10, Zurich, and others in most major Swiss cities. Its Web address is www.ssr.ch.

In the Netherlands, the official student travel agency, NBBS Reizen, is at Rokin 66, Amsterdam (☎ 020-624 09 89), and there are several other agencies around the city. Another recommended travel agent in Amsterdam is Malibu Travel (☎ 020-626 32 30) at Prinsengracht 230.

In Italy, the student travel agency CTS has branches all over the country including at Via Genova 16, off Via Nazionale, Rome (☎ 06-462 04 31). Its Web site is www.cts.it. In Spain, Halcón Viajes (902-300 600) is a reliable nationwide travel agency with over 500 branches and respectable fares; TIVE, the youth and student travel organization,

has its Madrid office at Calle Fernando El Católico 88 (☎ 91 543 7412).

Australia

Quite a few Australian travel agencies specialize in discount air tickets. Some, particularly smaller ones, advertise cheap airfares in the weekend newspapers, such as the *Age* in Melbourne and the *Sydney Morning Herald*. Two well-known agents for cheap fares are STA Travel and Flight Centre. STA Travel (☎ 03-9349 2411) has its main office at 224 Faraday St, Carlton, VIC 3053, and offices in all major cities and on many university campuses. Call ☎ 131 776 Australiawide for the location of the nearest STA branch or visit the Web site at www.statravel.com.au (also good for fares). Flight Centre (☎ 131 600 Australiawide) has a central office at 82 Elizabeth St, Sydney, and dozens of offices throughout Australia. Its Web address is www.flightcentre.com.au. Another good Web site for fares is www.travel.com.au.

If you fly between mid-December and the end of February, expect to pay A$200 to A$500 more than the fares quoted here. Qantas flies twice a week from Sydney, via Auckland, to Buenos Aires, where you can connect with an Aerolineas Argentinas flight to Rio de Janeiro. Round-trip fares start around A$2150. Doing the whole route with Aerolineas Argentinas costs marginally more.

For those who want to combine Brazil with other American countries, Aerolineas Argentinas flies from Sydney to Cancún, Miami and New York via Buenos Aires, where you can stop over and detour into Brazil, for around A$2600. Qantas and Varig fly to Los Angeles and New York, with a stopover in either Rio de Janeiro or Buenos Aires; 60-day round-trip fares start at A$2290. United Airlines flies Sydney-Auckland-Los Angeles-New York-Rio for A$2269 round-trip.

Aerolineas Argentinas is part of the Global Explorer network with, among others, British Airways, Qantas, American Airlines, Cathay Pacific and LanChile, providing almost endless options for a Round-the-World ticket taking in Brazil. RTW fares from Sydney start from A$2550. Varig is part of the Star Alliance, with Air Canada, Ansett, Lufthansa, Mexicana, Lauda, Air New Zealand, SAS, Singapore Airlines, Thai and United. Star Alliance RTW fares from Australia start around A$2700.

Another option is a Circle Americas fare, where travel must be in a circle via Auckland, Buenos Aires, North America and the Pacific. Offered by Aerolineas Argentinas and Air New Zealand, Circle Americas fares from Australia start at A$2750.

New Zealand

The *New Zealand Herald* has a travel section in which travel agents advertise fares. Flight Centre (☎ 09-309 6171) has a large central office in Auckland at National Bank Towers (corner of Queen and Darby Sts) and many branches throughout New Zealand. STA Travel (☎ 09-309 0458) has its main office at 10 High St, Auckland, and has offices in Hamilton, Palmerston North, Wellington, Christchurch and Dunedin. The Web address is www.statravel.com.au. Another good Web site for fares is www.travel.co.nz.

Auckland-Rio round-trip flights via Buenos Aires with Aerolineas Argentinas start at NZ$2579. Air New Zealand, Qantas and LanChile fly from Auckland to Los Angeles via Rio de Janeiro, with round-trip fares from NZ$2370 (45-day) or NZ$2520 (90-day). Also consider a Circle Americas fare (see the Australia section earlier in this chapter). RTW fares from New Zealand start from NZ$2930.

If you fly between mid-December and the end of February, fares rise between about NZ$200 and NZ$500.

South America

In addition to flights between South American capitals and the major Brazilian cities, shortish cross-border flights provide alternatives to some overland routes into or out of Brazil.

Surinam Airways flies between Belém and Cayenne (French Guiana), Paramaribo (Suriname) and Georgetown (Guyana).

One-way/round-trip fares starting from Belém are US$202/260 to Cayenne, US$266/340 to Paramaribo and US$318/407 to Georgetown. Penta, a Brazilian regional airline, flies between Belém, Macapá and Cayenne (Belém-Cayenne costs US$212/284 one-way/round-trip).

If you can get the connections right, it's cheaper to fly with Air Guyane between Cayenne and St Georges on the French Guiana-Brazil border (US$30 one way; daily) and then between Oiapoque, on the Brazilian side of the same border, and Macapá with Penta (US$99; Monday to Friday).

The Venezuelan airline Aéropostal flies between Caracas and Barcelona in Venezuela, and Boa Vista and Manaus in Brazil. Manaus-Caracas one-way/round-trip fares start at US$360/380. Other international flights into Manaus are with Lloyd Aéreo Boliviano (LAB) from Santa Cruz, Bolivia; and with Ecuatoriana from Guayaquil and Quito, Ecuador.

From Iquitos, Peru, there's a flying boat service to Tabatinga on the Rio Amazonas on the Brazil/Peru/Colombia triple frontier. From Bogotá, Colombia you can fly to Leticia, the Colombian town at the triple frontier, then take a combi or taxi or walk across the border into Brazil.

The Bolivian towns Cobija, Guayamerín and Puerto Suárez, across the border from the Brazilian towns of Brasiléia, Guajará-Mirim and Corumbá, respectively, can all be reached by domestic flights from several cities inside Bolivia.

Farther south, you can fly from Asunción (Paraguay) to Ciudad del Este (across the border from Foz do Iguaçu, Brazil) and from Buenos Aires to Puerto Iguazú (also opposite Foz do Iguaçu), Porto Alegre, Curitiba or Florianópolis.

See city sections of this book for further information on all these flights.

In Caracas, IVI Tours (☎ 02-993 60 82), Residencia La Hacienda, Piso Bajo, Local 1-4-T, Final Avenida Principal de las Mercedes, often has a range of good fares. ASATEJ (☎ 011-4511 8700), Argentina's student travel agency, has an located office at Florida 835, 3° piso, oficina 320 (1005), Buenos Aires. It has 15 other offices in Argentina and also offices in Montevideo, Santiago de Chile and Mexico City. Its Web site is www.asatej.org.

A good Web site for researching online airfares and reservations from Argentina, Brazil, Chile, Mexico, Uruguay or Venezuela is www.viajo.com.

Approximate round-trip fares on Varig from other South American capitals to Rio or São Paulo include Buenos Aires US$270, Montevideo US$400, Asunción US$265, Santiago US$420, La Paz US$505, Lima US$625, Caracas US$785 and Bogotá US$700. Other airlines on these routes, with roughly similar fares, include Swissair (Buenos Aires and Santiago), TAM and LanChile (Santiago), Aerolineas Argentinas and TransBrasil (Buenos Aires), Pluna (Montevideo) and Avianca (Bogotá). You can also fly from Buenos Aires to Salvador and Recife.

Flights from Brazil

Rio de Janeiro is Brazil's most popular international gateway, and there is no shortage of travel agents. For student fares try the STB (Student Travel Bureau), which has some 30 branches around the country including at Rua Visconde de Pirajá 550, Ipanema (☎ 0xx21-2512-8577). Its Web site is at www.stb.com.br. Discount agencies in São Paulo include US Tour (☎ 0xx11-3813-1308); the Web site is www.ustour.com.br. Other Web sites to search for cheap flights include www.passagembarata.com.br and www.viajo.com.br. See the Information sections under individual cities in this book for some other recommended travel agencies.

LAND

There's direct land access to Brazil from nine countries. Several border towns can also be reached by air or river – see the Air and River sections elsewhere in this chapter.

Car & Motorcycle

See Visas & Documents in the Facts for the Visitor chapter for information on the documents you need to carry if taking a vehicle

into Brazil. At the border you will be asked to sign a bond (*termo de responsabilidade*) containing the owner's identification details and home address, destination, and description of the vehicle (make, model, year, serial number, color and tag number). You will also be asked to pay a bank guarantee (to be determined by customs) and sign a statement agreeing that if you stay for more than 90 days you will contact customs in the area where the entry was registered to apply for an extension for the permit. This must be presented to customs at the time of departure. If your vehicle overstays its permitted time in Brazil, it is liable to be seized and the bank guarantee forfeited. It's illegal to sell the vehicle in Brazil.

Travelers planning to take their own vehicles need to check in advance what spare parts and gasoline are likely to be available. Unleaded gas is not on sale across Brazil, and neither is every little part for your car. (Brazil does have plenty of Volkswagen parts.)

Bicycle

You don't see many long-distance cyclists in Brazil. Crazy drivers who only respect vehicles larger than themselves, lots of trucks on the main roads spewing out unfiltered exhaust fumes, roads without shoulder room and the threat of theft are just some of the reasons for this. Long-distance cycling in Brazil is not recommended; it's a dangerous thing to do.

If you're still determined to tackle Brazil by bike, go over your bike with a fine-tooth comb before you leave home and fill your repair kit with every imaginable spare part.

Bicycles can travel by air. If you simply wheel your bike to the check-in desk, it should be treated as a piece of baggage. You may have to remove the pedals and turn the handlebars sideways so that it takes up less space in the aircraft's hold; confirm with the airline well in advance that this is possible, preferably before you pay for your ticket.

Border Crossings

Argentina The main border point used by travelers is Puerto Iguazú/Foz do Iguaçu, a 20-hour bus ride from Buenos Aires (see the Foz do Iguaçu section in the Paraná chapter for more information). Farther south, you can cross from Paso de los Libres (Argentina) to Uruguaiana (Brazil), which is also served by buses from Buenos Aires in Argentina.

Direct buses run between Buenos Aires and Porto Alegre (20 hours, US$64), Florianópolis, Curitiba, São Paulo and Rio de Janeiro (42 hours, US$141).

Bolivia Brazil's border with Bolivia is its longest. Most of it runs through remote wetlands and lowland forests, and it's much used by smugglers. The main crossings are at Corumbá, Cáceres, Guajará-Mirim and Brasiléia.

Corumbá, opposite the Bolivian town of Quijarro, is the busiest crossing point. Corumbá is a good access point for the Pantanal and has bus connections with São Paulo, Rio de Janeiro, Campo Grande and southern Brazil. The Bolivian train service between Quijarro and Santa Cruz is known as the Death Train (because of what happens to some of those who attempt to ride free on the roof), but it's a beautiful ride.

For more information, see the Corumbá section in the Mato Grosso & Mato Grosso do Sul chapter.

The Bolivian border town of San Matías is 115km southwest of Cáceres in Mato Grosso, Brazil. Cáceres has several daily bus connections with Cuiabá, 215km east. A daily bus runs between Cáceres and Santa Cruz, Bolivia, leaving Cáceres daily at 6 am (US$24, 24 hours). The Cáceres–San Matías trip takes 4½ hours, for US$10.

Guajará-Mirim in Rondônia, Brazil is a short boat ride across the Rio Mamoré from Guayaramerín, Bolivia. Guajará-Mirim has daily bus connections with Porto Velho (5½ hours), and buses run between Guayaramerín and the Bolivian towns of Riberalta, Cobija, Trinidad, Santa Rosa, Reyes, Rurrenabaque and La Paz. From late December to late February, rains can make the roads very difficult. See Guayaramerín in the Rondônia & Acre chapter for details.

Brasiléia, a 4½-hour bus ride from Rio Branco in Brazil's Acre state, stands opposite Cobija, Bolivia, which has bus connections to Riberalta, Guayaramerín and La Paz (see Cobija in the Rondônia & Acre chapter for details). This route is less direct than the Guayaramerín-Guajará-Mirim route between Bolivia and Brazil, and buses face the same wet-season difficulties.

Chile Chile does not share a border with Brazil, but direct buses run between Santiago and Brazilian cities such as Porto Alegre (US$116, 36 hours), Curitiba (US$120, 52 hours), São Paulo (US$120, 56 hours) and Rio de Janeiro (US$130, 62 hours).

Colombia Leticia, on the Rio Amazonas in far southeast Colombia, is contiguous with Tabatinga, Brazil. You can cross the border by foot, combi or taxi. From within Colombia, Leticia is only really accessible by air. Tabatinga is a quick flight (or a several-day Amazon boat ride) from Manaus or Tefé. See the Triple Frontier section in the Amazonas & Roraima chapter for more details.

French Guiana The Brazilian town of Oiapoque, a rugged 560km bus ride north of Macapá (US$30, 12 to 24 hours depending on weather conditions), stands across the Rio Oiapoque from St Georges, French Guiana. An unpaved road from St Georges to Régina, about halfway to the French Guiana capital of Cayenne, was expected to open in 2001. At the time of writing it was already reportedly possible to get a truck ride along the road for around US$30. Taxi-buses between Régina and Cayenne cost around US$10. St Georges–Cayenne flights cost US$30 (see the Air section earlier in this chapter).

Guyana Lethem in southwest Guyana and Bonfim in Brazil's Roraima state are a short boat ride apart. You can travel between Lethem and the Guyanese capital of Georgetown by plane or truck. The latter takes between two days and two weeks depending on weather conditions. Bonfim is a two-hour bus ride from Boa Vista, the Roraima state capital. See the Boa Vista and Bonfim sections in the Amazonas & Roraima chapter.

Paraguay The two major border crossings are Foz do Iguaçu/Ciudad del Este and Ponta Porã/Pedro Juan Caballero. Use the latter if you're going to or from the Pantanal. See the Foz do Iguaçu section in the Paraná chapter and the Ponta Porã section in the Mato Grosso chapter for details. Direct buses run between Asunción and such Brazilian cities as Curitiba (US$40, 18 hours), São Paulo (US$50, 20 hours) and Rio de Janeiro (US$69, 28 hours).

Peru Peru and Brazil share a long border in the Amazon basin, but the only land route across it is a fairly adventurous one at its far southeast end. Iñapari, Peru is a 10-hour minibus or truck ride north of Puerto Maldonado, Peru. You have to wade across the Rio Acre between Iñapari and the small Brazilian town of Assis Brasil, which is a three to four-hour bus or 4WD trip from Brasiléia. See the Assis Brasil & Iñapari section in the Rondônia & Acre chapter.

Suriname It isn't possible to travel overland between Suriname and Brazil without first passing through either French Guiana or Guyana.

Uruguay The crossing most used by travelers is at Chuy (Uruguay)/Chuí (Brazil). This is actually one town with the international border running down the middle of the main street. See the Rio Grande do Sul chapter for details.

Heading west along the border there are other crossings at (Uruguayan towns first): Río Branco/Jaguarão, Isidoro Noblia/Aceguá, Rivera/Santana do Livramento, Artigas/Quaraí and Bella Unión/Barra do Quaraí. Buses link Jaguarão with Pelotas and Santana do Livramento with Porto Alegre.

Buses run between Montevideo and Brazilian cities such as Porto Alegre (US$58, 12 hours), Florianópolis (US$62, 20 hours), Curitiba, São Paulo and Rio de Janeiro (US$130, 39 hours).

Venezuela Roads from northern Venezuela lead southeast through Ciudad Bolívar and Ciudad Guayana to Santa Elena de Uairén, across the border from Pacaraíma, Brazil. From the border a paved road heads south to Boa Vista (215km) and Manaus (990km). Buses run to Manaus and Boa Vista from as far north as Puerto La Cruz on Venezuela's coast. Santa Elena has bus services to/from Caracas. See the Amazonas & Roraima chapter for more details.

RIVER
Bolivia
From Trinidad in Bolivia you can reach Brazil by a boat trip of about five days down the Río Mamoré to Guayaramerín, opposite the Brazilian town of Guajará-Mirim. You can even start from Puerto Villarroel on the Río Ichilo, a tributary of the Mamoré. See Guayaramerín in the Rondônia & Acre chapter for more details.

Paraguay
Passenger boat services on the Rio Paraguai between Corumbá (Mato Grosso do Sul) and Asunción (Paraguay) have been discontinued. You might be able to travel this route using a sequence of cargo and/or naval boats, but it would necessitate asking around and taking potluck.

Peru
Fast passenger boats make the 400km trip along the Rio Amazonas between Iquitos (Peru) and Tabatinga (Brazil) in eight to 10 hours for US$40 to US$50. From Tabatinga you can continue 3000km down the river to its mouth. See the Triple Frontier section in the Amazonas & Roraima chapter for more information.

ORGANIZED TOURS
If you just want an introduction to the main attractions of Brazil, staying in mid-range or top-end hotels, there are plenty of group-tour options and a few budget- and adventure-minded options. The following are examples of the tours offered by some companies.

For tours focusing on ecotourism, see the Natural Brazil special section.

One company offering small-group trips with interesting itineraries is Explore Worldwide. Its head office is in Aldershot,

England (☎ 01252-76 00 00), but it has agencies in many countries around the world. Its Web site is at www.explore.co.uk.

The US

Brazil Nuts (toll-free ☎ 800-553-9959), 1854 Trade Center Way, Naples, FL 34109, offers various tour packages to Brazil, including Amazon and Pantanal trips, Carnaval trips, Salvador-based trips and the 'Brazil like a Native' 12-day tour, which takes in Rio, Salvador and the Amazon for between US$1745 and US$1845 from Miami. The Brazil Nuts Web site is www.brazilnuts.com.

Forum International (toll-free ☎ 800-252-4475), 91 Gregory Lane, Pleasant Hill, CA 94523, covers Rio, Salvador, an Amazon lodge and Foz do Iguaçu in its small-group 'Best of Brazil' tour for US$1560 plus flights. Web site: www.foruminternational.com

Adventure Center (toll-free ☎ 800-228-8747), 1311 63rd St, Suite 200, Emeryville, CA 94608, offers a number of more adventurous budget trips, often combining Brazil with neighboring countries. One is the 45-day 'Trans Amazonia,' which takes in most of Brazil's most exciting spots plus Venezuela's Gran Sábana plateau, camping about half the time, for US$2250 to US$2330 plus flights. They're online at www.adventure-center.com.

For information on a variety of Brazil trips, visit the Web site at www.infohub.com.

The UK

Trips with Journey Latin America (JLA; ☎ 020-8747-3108) include the nine-night 'Ibis/Brazil in Brief' (Rio, Salvador, Foz do Iguaçu, Ouro Prêto) for £2222 to £2370 from London, with an optional Amazon extension for a further £578. Other JLA tours combine highlights of Brazil and other South American countries. Web site: www.journeylatinamerica.co.uk

Austral Tours (☎ 020-7233-5384) does a 14-day tour taking in Rio, Salvador, Manaus and Amazonia, plus four days at an ecological beach resort north of Salvador. Cost varies seasonally from £2525 to £2680. Web site: www.latinamerica.co.uk

Destination South America (☎ 01285-885 333) has a 14-day tour to Rio, Salvador, Amazonia, Foz do Iguaçu and Praia do Forte for £2125. Visit the Web site: www.destinationsouthamerica.com.

Exodus (☎ 020-8675-5550) offers a nine-week 'Amazon Expedition,' mainly camping, which goes to Rio, Bahia, the Pantanal, Amazonia, Venezuela and Colombia for £1680 plus food and flights. Web site: www.exodus.co.uk

Also worth looking at is South American Experience (☎ 020-7976-5511), with a good Web site at www.sax.mcmail.com/SouthAmerican.htm.

Australia

Inca Tours (toll-free ☎ 1800-024955, ☎ 02-4351-2133, fax 02-4351-2526), 3 Margaret St, Wyong, NSW 2259, specializes in travel to South America. Lew Pullbrook, who runs it, has been visiting the continent for years and really knows his way around. Lew organizes trips for small or larger groups and he's happy for backpackers to call for a bit of advice. Try the Inca Tours Web site at www.southamerica.com.au.

Warning

The information in this chapter is particularly vulnerable to change: prices for international travel are volatile, routes are introduced and canceled, schedules change, special deals come and go, and rules and visa requirements are amended. Airlines and governments seem to take a perverse pleasure in making price structures and regulations as complicated as possible. You should check directly with the airline or a travel agent to make sure you understand how a fare (and any ticket you may buy) works. In addition, the travel industry is highly competitive, and there are many lurks and perks.

The upshot of this is that you should get opinions, quotes and advice from as many airlines and travel agents as possible before you part with your hard-earned cash. The details given in this chapter should be regarded as pointers and are not a substitute for your own careful, up-to-date research.

Getting Around

AIR

Flying in Brazil is not cheap, but with the seemingly endless expanses of *sertão* (backlands), Amazonia and Pantanal between many destinations, the occasional flight can be a necessity. Even if you don't use it, having extra money for flights can add flexibility to your travel plans. If you intend to take more than just a couple of flights, a Brazil Airpass will probably save you a lot of money.

By and large, Brazilian air services operate efficiently, though routings can be tiresome: Planes flying along the coast may stop at every city on the way, so if you're going from Rio de Janeiro to Fortaleza you might stop at Salvador, Maceió, Recife and João Pessoa. Many flights to or from the North, Central West or Northeast touch down at Brasília, and you may even have to change planes there. A flight from Brasília to Manaus (2¼ hours if direct) might go via Porto Velho and Rio Branco and take 6½ hours. It pays to get the most direct routings. Least desirable is having to use more than one airline to get from point A to B; the connections will probably be bad and you won't get any through-ticket discounts.

Nonstop flights from Rio de Janeiro take about one hour to São Paulo, 1½ hours to Brasília, two hours to Salvador and 2¾ hours to Recife. Rio to Foz do Iguaçu with one stop is three hours; Rio to Manaus with one stop is about 4½ hours.

Book as far ahead as practical for busy travel times – from Christmas to Carnaval, Easter, July and August. Flights out of 'working' cities such as São Paulo and Brasília to places where people prefer to spend weekends are often heavily booked on Fridays.

It's always important to reconfirm your flights.

Airlines

Brazil has four major national carriers and many smaller regional airlines. The biggies are Varig, TAM, TransBrasil and VASP. At least one of these flies to every major city. Varig, Brazil's biggest airline, has two affiliates – Nordeste and Rio Sul – which fly to some smaller cities.

Here are the destinations served at the time of writing by the four major airlines:

Varig/Rio Sul/Nordeste Altamira, Aracaju, Araguaína, Barreiras, Belém, Belo Horizonte, Boa Vista, Brasília, Campina Grande, Campinas, Campo Grande, Campos, Carajás, Cascavel, Caxias do Sul, Chapecó, Criciúma, Cuiabá, Curitiba, Fernando de Noronha, Florianópolis, Fortaleza, Foz do Iguaçu, Goiânia, Governador Valadares, Ilhéus, Imperatriz, Ipatinga, Itajaí, João Pessoa, Joinville, Juazeiro do Norte, Juiz de Fora, Lages, Lençóis, Livramento, Londrina, Monte Dourado, Montes Claros, Natal, Navegantes, Palmas, Parnaíba, Passo Fundo, Pelotas, Petrolina, Porto Alegre, Porto Seguro, Porto Velho, Recife, Ribeirão Preto, Rio Branco, Rio de Janeiro, Salvador, Santarém, Santo Ângelo, São José do Rio Preto, São José dos Campos, São Luís, São Paulo, Tabatinga, Tefé, Teresina, Toledo, Trombetas, Tucuruí, Uberaba, Uberlândia, Una, Uruguaiana, Vitória, Vitória da Conquista

TAM Aracaju, Araçatuba, Bauru, Belém, Belo Horizonte, Brasília, Cabo Frio, Campinas, Campo Grande, Caxias do Sul, Comandatuba, Corumbá, Criciúma, Cuiabá, Curitiba, Florianópolis, Fortaleza, Foz do Iguaçu, Goiânia, Ilhéus, Imperatriz, Iquique, Ji-Paraná, João Pessoa, Joinville, Juiz de Fora, Londrina, Macapá, Maceió, Manaus, Marabá, Marília, Natal, Navegantes, Palmas, Porto Alegre, Porto Seguro, Porto Velho, Presidente Prudente, Recife, Ribeirão Preto, Rio de Janeiro, Salvador, São José do Rio Preto, São José dos Campos, São Luís, São Paulo, Sorocaba, Teresina, Uberaba, Uberlândia, Vilhena, Vitória

TransBrasil Bauru, Belém, Blumenau, Brasília, Campinas, Cascavel, Chapecó, Cuiabá, Curitiba, Florianópolis, Fortaleza, Foz do Iguaçu, Goiânia, Joinville, Londrina, Maceió, Manaus, Maringá, Natal, Navegantes, Porto Alegre, Porto Velho, Recife, Ribeirão Preto, Rio de Janeiro, Salvador, São José do Rio Preto, São Luís, São Paulo, Uberlândia, Vitória

VASP Aracaju, Belém, Belo Horizonte, Brasília, Campinas, Campo Grande, Cuiabá, Curitiba,

Florianópolis, Fortaleza, Foz do Iguaçu, Goiânia, Ilhéus, João Pessoa, Londrina, Macapá, Maceió, Manaus, Natal, Porto Alegre, Porto Seguro, Porto Velho, Recife, Ribeirão Preto, Rio Branco, Rio de Janeiro, Salvador, São José do Rio Preto, São Luís, São Paulo, Teresina, Vitória

Smaller airlines include Fly, linking Fortaleza, Recife, Natal, Rio de Janeiro and São Paulo; Trip, serving places such as Rio de Janeiro, Natal, Fernando de Noronha, Recife, Cuiabá and Curitiba; Gol, flying to Rio, São Paulo, Salvador, Brasília, Belo Horizonte, Florianópolis and Porto Alegre; and a host of regional carriers in and around Amazonia such as Penta, TAVAJ, Rico and Meta.

The main airlines have national telephone numbers for reservations and reconfirmations. They also have Web sites where you can often reserve flights:

Varig
☎ 0800-997000; www.varig.com.br

TAM
☎ 0800-123100; www.tam.com.br

TransBrasil
☎ 0800-151151; www.transbrasil.com.br

VASP
☎ 0800-998277; www.vasp.com.br

Fly (Rio de Janeiro)
☎ 0xx21-2533-7605; www.voefly.com.br

Gol
☎ 0800-7892121; www.voegol.com.br

Trip
☎ 0800-7018747; www.airtrip.com.br

Air Taxis Many areas, especially Amazonia, feature air-taxi companies that will fly you anywhere their small planes can reach. These flights are expensive, but they might be affordable if there are enough passengers to share the cost – sometimes you can bargain.

Fares
Ordinary one-way fares are high, and round-trip fares are usually barely (if at all) less than two one-way fares. That's why it can pay to get an air pass even if you're taking only three flights in Brazil (see the Air Passes section).

In general Varig and TAM are the most expensive airlines, followed by TransBrasil, with VASP the cheapest of the big four. But the more expensive airlines sometimes offer discounts, so it's worth going to a travel agent to find the cheapest deals. As a rule you get what you pay for: The extra money you pay Varig may save you several hours by giving you a nonstop flight instead of a flight with connections or a 'milk run.' The smaller airlines such as Fly, Trip and Gol sometimes undercut the majors.

From Rio de Janeiro Here are some one-way fares from Rio at the time of writing:

destination	Varig	VASP
Belém	US$305	US$210
Brasília	US$165	US$120
Fortaleza	US$300	US$170
Foz do Iguaçu	US$195	US$130
Manaus	US$335	US$200
Recife	US$255	US$150
Salvador	US$195	US$110
São Paulo	US$95	US$50

From Belém These one-way fares from Belém indicate the levels of fares between provincial cities:

destination	Varig	VASP
Brasília	US$230	US$160
Fortaleza	US$190	US$130
Manaus	US$205	US$140
Salvador	US$290	US$200

Air Passes
A Brazil Airpass is a very wise investment for anyone who is going to take more than a couple of flights in Brazil. Each of the four major Brazilian airlines – Varig, TAM, TransBrasil and VASP – offers a version of the Brazil Airpass, giving you five flights on its domestic routes within a limited period for a total price that can be as low as US$440. Up to four additional flights can usually be added for US$100 each. Check the lists of each airline's destination cities earlier in this chapter to see which ones suit you best.

You have to buy the pass before you go to Brazil, and to do so you must also have an international round-trip ticket to Brazil. The agent who sells you your international ticket will normally be able to sell you the air pass too. You have to book your air pass itinerary at the time you buy it, and there are usually penalties for changing reservations. Details of each airline's air pass rules change from time to time, so you should go into them with your agent. Common rules are that you're not allowed to visit the same city twice and that you can't use the air pass on the Rio–São Paulo shuttle (between the downtown airports of the two cities). If an airline has no direct flight between two cities, a route involving connections will usually count as just one flight, provided there are no overnight stays en route. Air pass prices do not include domestic departure taxes.

Varig The Varig Brazil Air Pass is valid for 21 days and must be bought in conjunction with an international ticket on Varig or other specified airlines (eg, United, Continental, American or Delta from the US; British Airways from Britain). It can be used on Varig, Nordeste and Rio Sul flights. The minimum price, for five domestic flights, is US$530. There's a US$30 penalty each time you change a reservation.

TAM TAM's Brazil Airpass can be bought in conjunction with an international ticket on any airline. Like Varig's, it's valid for 21 days and costs US$530 for five flights.

TransBrasil The TransBrasil Airpass is valid for 30 days and costs US$440 for five flights if your international ticket is with Trans-Brasil, US$600 if it's with another airline.

VASP The VASP Brazil Airpass, valid for 21 days, costs US$440 for five flights. You can buy it in conjunction with an international ticket on any airline. Dates can be changed at no cost, but destination changes cost US$50.

If for any reason you do not fly on an air pass flight you have reserved, you should reconfirm all your other flights. Travelers have sometimes found that all their air pass reservations had been scrubbed from the computer after they missed, or were bumped from, one flight.

Domestic Departure Tax

Embarkation tax on domestic flights ranges between US$2.50 and US$6 depending on the airport (the bigger the airport, the bigger the tax). If it isn't already included in the price of your ticket, you have to pay it in cash reais at check-in. The check-in clerks *never* have any change. If your ticket has included the tax, it will probably be shown in the taxes section at the bottom of your ticket by the letters 'BR' following the amount paid, in whatever currency you paid for your ticket in.

BUS

Except in the Amazon Basin, buses are the primary form of long-distance transportation for the majority of Brazilians and many foreign travelers. Bus services are generally excellent. Departure times are usually strictly adhered to, and most of the buses are clean, comfortable and well-serviced Mercedes, Volvos and Scanias. The drivers are good, and a mechanical governor limits their wilder urges to 80km/h.

All major cities are linked by frequent buses – one leaves every 15 minutes from Rio to São Paulo during peak hours – and there are a surprising number of long-distance buses. It's rare that you will have to change buses between two major cities, no matter what the distance.

'Progress is roads,' goes a Brazilian saying. And wherever there is a road in Brazil, no matter what condition it's in, there is a bus that travels it. Authors of one edition of this book will never forget the bus that rescued them on an almost deserted peninsula out near Ponta do Mutá – a place where few people go, and no one seems to have heard of. How they got there is hard to explain; how the bus got there is impossible to explain. The 'road' was more like a wide footpath, impassable by normal car and apparently unknown to Brazilian cartographers. But the bus came and eventually delivered our authors to a humble fishing village of no more than a hundred people.

Bus service and road conditions do vary by region. The South has the most and the best roads. Coastal highways are usually good; Amazonia and the sertão are another story. Some roads in these regions alternate every few hundred meters between dirt (which is better) and pothole-infested sealed road (which is much worse). This pattern conforms to no obvious geographical or human design, and forces constant speeding up and slowing down. The Quatro Rodas *Atlas Rodoviário,* a very useful road atlas for any traveler, helpfully marks the worst stretches of road with lines of large X's and classifies them as *estradas precárias.*

In Amazonia road travel is in fact not generally a practical option, with a few exceptions such as the good paved road from Manaus north to Boa Vista and Venezuela and a few shorter stretches around the cities. Several of the ambitious long-distance roads cut across the region in the 1970s and 1980s have been effectively reclaimed by the jungle, although there are plans for bulldozers to try to win back some of them for carbon monoxide.

Departure and fare information for buses from Rio de Janeiro and Salvador is available on the Web site www.novorio .com.br. Most of Brazil's other main cities are due to be added to this site, which will also supposedly offer an online booking facility too.

Classes

There are three main classes of long-distance bus. The ordinary *comum* or *convencional* is the most common. It's fairly comfortable and usually has a toilet on board. An *executivo* is more comfortable (often with reclining seats), costs about 25% more and stops less often. A *leito* can cost twice as much as a comum and is exceptionally comfortable. It has spacious, fully reclining seats with blankets and pillows, air-conditioning, and more often than not, a steward serving sandwiches, coffee, soda and *água mineral.* If you don't mind missing the scenery, a leito can get

you there in comfort and save you the additional cost of a hotel room.

With or without toilets, buses generally make pit stops every three or four hours. These stops are great places to meet other passengers, buy bizarre memorabilia and wish you were back home eating a healthy vegetarian quiche.

Air-conditioning on buses is quite strong; carry a light sweater or jacket to keep warm.

Reservations

Usually you can go down to the bus station and buy a ticket for the next bus out. Where this is difficult (for example, in Ouro Prêto) this book tries to let you know. In general, though, it's a good idea to buy a ticket at least a few hours in advance or, if it's convenient, the day before departure. On weekends, holidays and from December to February, advance purchase is always a good idea.

Aside from getting you on the bus, buying a ticket early has a few other advantages. First, it gets you an assigned seat – many common buses fill the aisles with standing passengers. Second, you can ask for a front-row seat, with extra leg space, or a window seat with a view and the side of the bus to lean on (ask for a *janela*), and you can steer clear of the rear seats near the toilet, which can get smelly.

You don't always have to go to the bus station to buy your bus ticket. Selected travel agents in the major cities sell tickets for long-distance buses. This can save you a long trip out to an often chaotic bus station; in addition, the price is usually the same *and* the agents are more likely to speak some English and be less rushed.

Costs

Bus travel throughout Brazil is very cheap (fares average around US$2.50 per hour in comum). For example, the six-hour trip from Rio to São Paulo costs US$16 comum or US$32 leito, and the 20-hour trip from Rio to Florianópolis is US$45 comum or US$80 leito. The 36-hour Rio-Recife ride costs US$88 comum, and for US$117 you could even take a 60-hour ride from Rio to Belém.

Bus Stations

Every big city, and most small ones, has one main long-distance bus station *(rodoviária,* pronounced 'ho-do-vi-**ah**-ri-ya'), often located on the outskirts. Some are modern, comfortable stations. All have restaurants, newsstands and toilets, and some even have post offices and long-distance telephone facilities. Most importantly, all the long-distance bus companies operate out of the same place, making it easy to find your bus.

Inside the rodoviária you'll find ticket offices for the various bus companies. They usually post bus destinations and schedules in their windows; occasionally the schedules are printed on leaflets, but sometimes you just have to get in line and ask the teller for information. This can be difficult if you don't speak much Portuguese and the teller is in a highly agitated state after the 23rd *cafezinho* or speaks with an accent from the interior of Ceará. The best strategy is probably to have a pen and paper handy and ask the teller to write down what you need to know.

When you find a bus company that goes to your destination, don't assume it's the only one; there are often two or more, and the quality may vary.

TRAIN

Brazil's passenger-train services have been scaled down to almost nothing in recent years, as the railways became more and more debt-ridden. There are still over 30,000km of track, but most trains carry only cargo. Rail enthusiasts should not quite despair, however, as there are still a couple of great rides. The outstanding one is the trip from Curitiba to Paranaguá, descending the coastal mountain range, with some unforgettable views. The Belo Horizonte-Vitória run, via Santa Bárbara and Sabará, is cheaper and far more pleasant than the bus ride.

A steam train is affectionately known in Brazil as a *Marias Fumaça* (Smoking Mary), and a couple still run as leisure attractions. One is the 13km ride from São João del Rei to Tiradentes in Minas Gerais – great fun. Another is a 7km stretch of the old Madeira-Mamoré 'Death Railway' through the Ama-

zonian jungles near Porto Velho. Another pleasant short trip, this time by electric train, is the ride through the Serra da Mantiquera of São Paulo state from Campos do Jordão to Santo Antônio do Pinhal, the highest stretch of track in the country.

CAR & MOTORCYCLE

Especially in Rio, the anarchic side of the Brazilian personality emerges from behind the driver's wheel as lane dividers, one-way streets and sidewalks are disregarded. The police take little interest in road safety. Authors of an earlier edition of this book were once given a lift by police on a highway north of Salvador. The police car, running at its top speed of about 140km/h, was passed by several other cars at speeds of over 150km/h. As each car passed, the police simply shook their heads and sighed *'Não respeito'* (No respect).

Car

The number of fatalities caused by motor vehicles in Brazil is estimated at 80,000 per year. The roads can be very dangerous, especially the busy highways such as the Rio-São Paulo corridor. In general the driver is king of the road and likes to demonstrate it; other motorists are treated as gate-crashers, and pedestrians are shown little mercy and no courtesy. Car wrecks are piled up at the police checkpoints that dot the highways, and you'll see some horrible ones.

Road Rules A red light in Brazil does mean 'stop' – officially. In practice, this has been modified to 'Maybe we'll stop, maybe we'll slow down – but if it's night we'll probably do neither.' Drivers use their horns without restraint, and buses, which have no horns, rev their engines instead. One of the craziest habits is driving at night without headlights. This is done, it seems, so that the headlights can be flashed to warn approaching vehicles.

Many drivers are racing fans and tend to imagine that they are Ayrton Senna, finding it impossible to slow down to anyone else's pace. The worst are the Rio bus drivers, or maybe the São Paulo commuters, or maybe the São Paulo-Curitiba truck drivers, or maybe…anyway, you get the idea. This cult of speed is insatiable; its only positive aspect is that, unlike more sedate drivers in other areas, these drivers tend to be very alert and rarely fall asleep at the wheel.

Driving at night is particularly hazardous because other drivers are more likely to be drunk and, at least in the Northeast and the interior, the roads are often poor and unreliable. Like malaria, potholes are endemic. Poorly banked turns are the norm.

The Brazilian speed-bump industry must be one of the world's largest. Its products are large too, and often well nigh invisible until it's far too late. They're known variously as *quebra-molas* (spring-breakers), *lombadas* (over which your car will *lambada*), *ondulações* or *sonorizadores*. Always slow down as you enter a town.

In big cities, keep your windows closed and doors locked when stopped: São Paulo has the worst reputation for robbery of motorists at stoplights. Further headaches for the driver in Brazil are posed by poor signposting; impossible one-way systems; tropical rainstorms; drivers overtaking on blind corners; flat tires (very common, but luckily there are *borracheiros* – tire repairers – at frequent intervals along the roads); cyclists going the wrong way along any kind of road (especially at night, without lights); and, of course, the police (see the boxed text 'Unfair Cops').

All that said, driving can still be a convenient way to get around Brazil, and it's certainly an experience. It has all the advantages of flexibility and easier access to out-of-the-way places as in any other country. Just drive very, as they say, defensively. And for security, choose hotels with off-street parking; most in the mid-range and above offer this option.

In the Northeast, everything happens more slowly, and that holds true for driving too. Many trucks and buses in this area help you pass at night with their turn signals (indicators). A flashing right signal means it's clear to go; a flashing left means that a vehicle is approaching from the opposite direction.

Rental A small four-seat car costs around US$40 a day with unlimited kilometers (about US$50 with air-con). If you take a car for five days you will often get a sixth and seventh day for no extra cost. In addition, you will probably be offered a variety of insurance options, and it's probably wise to take as much insurance as you can get (about US$20 a day). Ordinary gasoline *(combustível* or *gasolina)* costs around US$1.20 per liter, which works out to approximately US$0.08 per kilometer.

If you can share the expense with friends, renting a car is a great way to explore some of the many remote beaches, fishing villages and back roads of Brazil. Several familiar multinationals dominate the car rental business in Brazil, and getting a car is safe and

---

Unfair Cops

Brazil's multifarious varieties of police all perform their own *fiscalização* (checks) on drivers in search of supplements to their meager wages. Make sure all your papers are in order (see the Visas & Documents section in the Facts for the Visitor chapter and the Car & Motorcycle section in the Getting There & Away chapter), and still be prepared for some very creative ways of extracting money from you – eg, 'It's our commandant's birthday and he's having a party. How 'bout a couple of dollars for beer?'

Less amusingly, two of the authors researching this edition were hit with a US$300 fine for doing 80km/h in a 60km/h zone. To avoid giving the cops that kind of excuse to fleece you, all you can do is avoid violating any rule or regulation of the road (not that you necessarily need to have broken any rule to be fined).

Keep in mind that the police you meet on the roads are a mixed bunch. Once when one of us was stopped for speeding, the cop proved very friendly. He said he didn't want Australians to get the idea that Brazilian police officers were bastards. Only some of them are, it seems.

easy if you have a driver's license (carteira de habilitação), credit card and passport, and are over the minimum age (21 with some firms, including Avis; 25 with others). You should also carry an international driver's permit, though it's not actually required by rental companies.

There is little price variation among the major rental companies except for occasional promotional deals. Fiat Unos are the cheapest cars to rent, followed by the Volkswagen Gol, Ford Fiesta, Opel Corsa and similar vehicles. Sometimes a rental company will claim to be out of these cheaper models; if this is the case, don't hesitate to shop around.

When looking at the contract, pay close attention to any theft clause that appears to load a large percentage of any loss onto the renter. Another tricky clause you may encounter stipulates that if you have an accident and get a police statement, you won't have to pay for the damage. But you will have to pay 70% of the daily rental for the number of days it takes the rental company to fix the car!

The big companies have offices in most cities; they are always out at the airport and often in the center of town as well. In the phone book, look under autolocadoras or locadoras de automóveis.

Motorcycle

Unless you're a very competent rider, it's not a good idea to motorcycle around Brazil. There are road laws, but no one obeys them, so anything goes. Motorcycling can, however, be a rewarding experience. Brazil is a beautiful country, but try to keep your eyes on the road.

A road/trail bike is ideal because of its versatility. Smaller bikes are OK for the cities, but on the Brazilian highways, with heavy truck traffic and pollution, it's wise to have a larger one.

Renting a bike is as expensive as renting a car. For those who want to buy a bike, Brazil manufactures its own, but they are expensive. The most powerful we saw was 600cc.

Motorcycles are popular in Brazil, especially in and around the cities. Theft is a big problem; you can't even insure a bike

because theft is so common. Most people who ride keep their bike in a guarded place, at least overnight. For the traveler this can be difficult to organize, but if you can maneuver around the practical problems, for you Brazil may turn out to be a great place to have a motorcycle.

BICYCLE

You don't see many long-distance cyclists in Brazil. We wouldn't recommend cycling there, as conditions are dangerous. See the Land section in the Getting There & Away chapter.

HITCHHIKING

Hitchhiking is never entirely safe in any country in the world, and is not recommended. Travelers who decide to hitchhike should understand that they are taking a small but potentially serious risk. People who do choose to hitchhike will be safer if they travel in pairs and let someone know where they are planning to go.

Hitchhiking in Brazil, with the possible exception of the Pantanal and a few other areas where it's commonplace among local folk, is difficult. The word for a lift in Portuguese is carona, so ask 'Pode dar carona?' ('Can you give us a lift?'). The best way to hitch – practically the only way if you want rides – is to ask drivers when they're not in their vehicles, for example by waiting at a gas station or a truck stop. But even this can be difficult.

BOAT

The Amazon region is probably the last great bastion of passenger river travel in the world. Rivers still perform the function of highways throughout much of Amazonia, with passenger-carrying vessels of many shapes and sizes putt-putting up and down every river and creek that has anyone living near it. For information on river travel in the Amazon region, see the North section.

River travel in the rest of Brazil has decreased rapidly due to the construction of a comprehensive road network, but it's still possible to travel by boat along the lower reaches of the Rio São Francisco (see the Propriá and Penedo sections of the Sergipe & Alagoas chapter).

Boat is also the only – or at least, the most interesting – way of getting around many parts of the Pantanal and to many islands and beaches along the Atlantic coast.

LOCAL TRANSPORTATION
Bus

Local bus services tend to be pretty good in Brazil. Since most Brazilians take the bus to work every day, municipal buses are usually frequent and their network of routes is comprehensive. They are always cheap and nearly always crowded.

In most city buses, you get on at the back and exit from the front, though occasionally the reverse is true. Usually there's a money collector sitting at a turnstile just inside the entrance, with the price displayed nearby. If you're unsure if it's the right bus, it's easy to hop on the back and ask the money collector if the bus is going to your destination – *'você vai para ...?'* If it's the wrong bus no one will mind if you hop off, even if the bus has gone a stop or two.

You'll have difficulty getting bulky luggage through the narrow turnstile – a backpack would be touch and go.

Crime can be a problem on buses. Rather than remain behind the turnstile, it's safer to pay the fare and go through the turnstile. Try to avoid carrying valuables if you can. If you must take valuables with you then keep them well hidden. See the Dangers & Annoyances section in the Facts for the Visitor chapter for more information.

Jumping on a local bus is one of the best ways to get to know a city. With a map and a few dollars you can tour the town and maybe meet some of the locals.

Taxi

Taxi rides are reasonably priced, if not cheap, but you should be aware of various tricks used by some drivers to increase the charges. We have met plenty of superb, friendly, honest and knowledgeable Brazilian taxi drivers. However, we have also met rogue cabbies with unsavory characteristics.

Taxis in the cities usually have meters that start showing around US$1.50 on the meter and rise by something like US$1 per kilometer. Unless you have agreed separately on a fare that you are unequivocally happy with, you should always make sure the driver turns on the meter when you start off. Otherwise the odds are the driver will try to overcharge you. There is very rarely any good reason why a meter should not be used, and you are not obliged to pay anything other than what it shows, except in the rare circumstance that there has been a recent official rise in taxi rates and the meter has not yet been adjusted (in which case the price shown by the meter will be converted to something higher by use of a chart known as a *tabela*).

As a general rule, there's a standard taxi rate that applies from approximately 6 am to 10 pm Monday to Saturday, and a higher rate that applies outside these hours, on holidays and outside city limits. Sometimes there is a standard charge, typically for the trip between the airport and the city center. Some airports and bus stations now have a system for you to purchase a fixed-price taxi ticket from a *bilheteria* (ticket office). At a few such places it's much cheaper to go onto the street outside and find a cab that will take you for the meter fare or sometimes even less. In this book we've indicated places where this is the case. If you are carrying valuables, however, the special airport taxi, or a radio taxi, can be a worthwhile investment. These are probably the safest taxis on the road.

If a taxi has no meter, you must agree on the price beforehand, and make sure there is no doubt about it. Learn the numbers in Portuguese. If the driver hesitates for a long time or starts using fingers instead of talking to you about numbers, you may find the price has been grasped from imagination rather than being the normal rate. You don't want to have an argument at the end of the ride – it's not worth it, even if you win.

If the driver claims to have no change, hold firm and see if this is just a ploy to extract more from you. We often found that change mysteriously appeared out of the driver's pocket when we said we'd be happy to wait in the taxi until change could be found. You can avoid this scenario by carrying change.

If possible, orient yourself before taking a taxi, and keep a map handy in case you find yourself being taken on a wild detour – even following the route on the map during the ride isn't a bad idea, and it's an effective way of orienting yourself. Never use taxi touts – an almost certain rip-off. Deal directly with the taxi driver at the taxi rank, or with the taxi company.

The worst place to get a cab is where the tourists are. Don't get a cab near one of the expensive hotels. In Rio, for example, walk a block away from the beach at Copacabana to flag down a cab.

For more tips on security and taxi travel see the Dangers & Annoyances section in the Facts for the Visitor chapter.

The Southeast

The Southeast region, known in Brazil as the Sudeste, comprises almost 11% of the country and is home to a whopping 44% of Brasileiros – 90% of whom live in cities. The region is made up of the states of Rio de Janeiro, Espírito Santo, São Paulo and Minas Gerais.

The Southeast is the economic power-house of Brazil and contains 60% of the industry of the country. This wealth attracts migrants from all over Brazil, who flock to the three largest cities – São Paulo, Rio de Janeiro and Belo Horizonte – in search of something better.

Geographically, the Southeast contains the most mountainous areas of the Planalto Brasileiro: the Serras da Mantiqueira, do Mar and do Espinhaço, making it popular with hikers and climbers. Most of the region was once covered by lush Mata Atlântica (Atlantic Rainforest), but this has been devastated since the arrival of the Portuguese. Inland Minas Gerais also contains areas of *cerrado* and *caatinga*. Two great rivers begin in the mountains of the Southeast: the south-flowing Paraná, formed by the Paranaíba and Grande Rivers, and the north-flowing São Francisco, which begins in the Serra da Canastra in Minas.

The attractions of the Southeast include the *cidade maravilhosa,* Rio de Janeiro; his-

toric colonial towns (Parati, Ouro Prêto and, in Minas, many others); national parks (Serra dos Órgãos, Itatiaia and Caparaó); and the people themselves – the hard-working Paulistas (from São Paulo state), the fun-loving Cariocas (from Rio), the strong-willed Capixabas (from Espírito Santo) and the spiritual Mineiros (from Minas Gerais).

THE SOUTHEAST

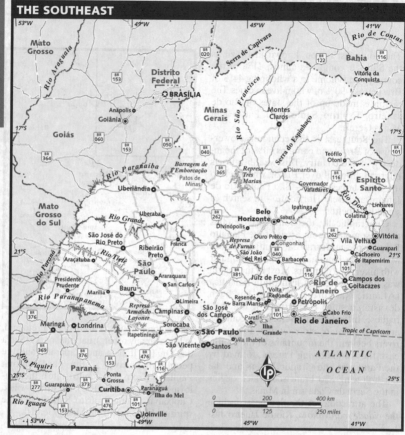

Rio de Janeiro City

☎ 0xx21 • postcode 20000-000
• pop 7 million

Rio is the *Cidade Maravilhosa* (Marvelous City). Seven million Cariocas, as the inhabitants are called, are jammed into the world's most beautiful city setting – between ocean and escarpment. This makes Rio one of the most densely populated places on earth. This thick brew of Cariocas pursues pleasure like no other people: beaches and the body beautiful, samba and soccer, *cerveja* (beer) and *cachaça* (sugarcane rum).

Rio has its problems, and they are enormous. A third of the people live in the *favelas* (shantytowns) that blanket many of the hillsides. The poor have no schools, no doctors and no jobs. Drug abuse and violence are endemic. Police corruption and brutality are commonplace. Nevertheless, in Rio everything ends with samba – soccer games, weddings, work, political demonstrations and, of course, a day at the beach. There's a lust for life and a love of romance, music, dance and talk that seems to distinguish the Cariocas from everyone else. For anyone coming from the efficiency and rationalism of the developed, capitalist world, this is potent stuff. The sensuality of Carnaval is the best-known expression of this Dionysian spirit, but there are plenty more.

Rio has its glitzy side – the international tourist crowd and the lives of its rich and famous, but happily it's also a good city for the budget traveler. There are plenty of cheap restaurants and hotels. The beaches are free and democratic. There's a lot to explore in the city center and in several other neighborhoods, with their parks and museums. Public transport is fast and easy. And if you can meet some locals – not nearly so hard as in New York, London or Sydney – well, then you're on easy street.

HISTORY

Gaspar de Lemos set sail from Portugal for Brazil in May 1501 and entered a huge bay

---

Highlights

- Watching the sunset from the Sugarloaf and Corcovado
- Hiking through the Atlantic rainforest in the Parque Nacional da Tijuca
- Traveling from Centro to Santa Teresa on the historic little tram
- Going to a soccer game at Maracanã stadium
- Getting hot and sweaty at a samba school rehearsal
- Taking a fascinating favela tour
- Strolling through the magnificent Jardim Botânico
- Hang-gliding off Pedra Bonita (if you're adventurous)
- Lounging on the world-famous beaches of Copacabana and Ipanema

---

in January 1502. Mistaking the bay for a river, he named it Rio de Janeiro.

It was the French, however, who first settled along the great bay. Like the Portuguese, the French had been harvesting brazilwood along the Brazilian coast, but unlike the Portuguese, they hadn't attempted any permanent settlements until Rio de Janeiro.

As the Portuguese colonization of Brazil began to take hold, the French became concerned that they'd be pushed out of the colony. Three ships of French settlers reached the Baía de Guanabara (as Rio's bay is now called) in 1555. They settled on a small island in the bay and called it Antarctic France.

Almost from the start, the town seemed doomed to failure. It was torn by religious divisions and demoralized by the puritanical rule of the French leader, Nicolas de Villegagnon. Antarctic France was weak and disheartened when the Portuguese attacked.

A greater threat to the Portuguese were the powerful Tamoio Indians, who had allied with the French. A series of battles occurred, but the Portuguese were better armed and better supplied than the French, whom they finally expelled in 1560. They drove the Tamoio from the region in a series of bloody battles.

The Portuguese set up a fortified town on the Morro Castelo in 1567 to maximize protection from European invasion by sea and Indian attack by land. They named it São Sebastião do Rio de Janeiro, after King Sebastião of Portugal.

The founding 500 Cariocas built a typical Brazilian town: poorly planned, with irregular streets in medieval Portuguese style. By the end of the century the small settlement was, if not exactly prosperous, surviving on the export of brazilwood and sugarcane, and from fishing in the Baía de Guanabara.

In 1660 the city had a population of 3000 Indians, 750 Portuguese and 100 blacks. It grew along the waterfront and what is now Praça 15 de Novembro (often referred to as Praça Quinze). Religious orders, Jesuits, Franciscans and Benedictines, came and built austere, closed-in churches.

With its excellent harbor and good lands for sugarcane, Rio became the third most important settlement in Brazil (after Salvador da Bahia and Recife-Olinda) in the 17th century. African slaves were brought in and sugar plantations thrived. The owners of the sugar estates lived in the protection and comfort of the fortified city.

The gold rush in Minas Gerais at the beginning of the 18th century changed Rio forever. In 1704 the Caminho Novo, a new road to the Minas gold fields, was opened. Gold poured through the ports of Rio until it began to run out half a century later. Much of the gold was used to repay Portuguese debts to the British. Many of the Portuguese immigrants didn't return to Minas, but stayed on in Rio.

Rio was now the prize of Brazil. In 1710 the French, who were at war with Portugal and raiding its colonies, attacked the city. The French were initially defeated, but a second expedition succeeded and the entire resident population abandoned the city in the dark of night. The French threatened to level the city unless a sizeable ransom in gold, sugar and cattle was paid. The Portuguese obliged. During the return voyage to France, the victors lost two ships and most of the gold in severe storms.

Rio quickly recovered from the setback. Its fortifications were improved, many richly decorated churches were built and by 1763 its population had reached 50,000. That year, with international sugar prices slumping, Rio replaced Salvador de Bahia as the colonial capital.

In 1808 the entire Portuguese monarchy and court – barely escaping the invasion in their homeland by Napoleon's armies – arrived in Rio. Thus the city came to house the court of the Portuguese Empire – or at least what was left of it.

With the court came an influx of money and skills that helped build the city's lasting monuments, such as the palace at the Quinta da Boa Vista and the Jardim Botânico (a pet project of Prince Regent Dom João). The Portuguese court was followed by talented French exiles, such as architect Jean de Montigny and painters Jean-Baptiste Debret and Nicolas Antoine Taunay.

A coffee boom in the mountains of São Paulo and Rio revitalized Brazil's economy. Rio took on a new importance as a port and commercial center, and coffee commerce modernized the city. A telegraph system and gas streetlights were installed in 1854. Regular passenger ships began sailing then to London in 1845, and from Rio to Paris in 1851. A ferry service to Niterói began in 1862.

At the end of the 19th century the city's population exploded with European immigration and internal migration (mostly ex-slaves from the declining coffee and sugar regions). In 1872 Rio had 275,000 inhabitants; by 1890 there were about 522,000, a quarter of them foreign-born. By 1900 the population had reached 800,000. The city spread rapidly between the steep hills, bay and ocean. The first tunnel through the mountains to Copacabana was built in 1892.

[Continued on page 184]

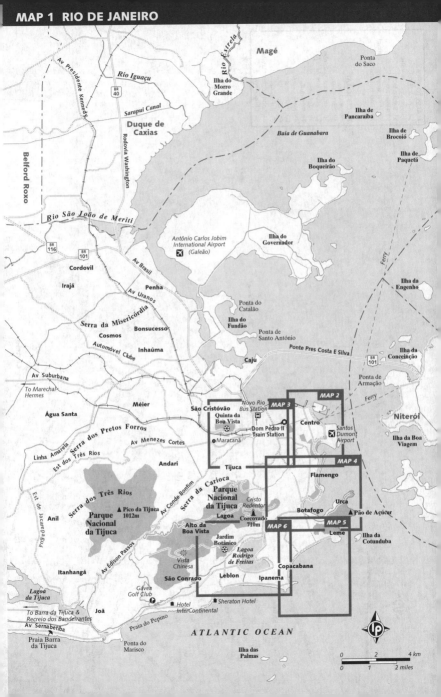

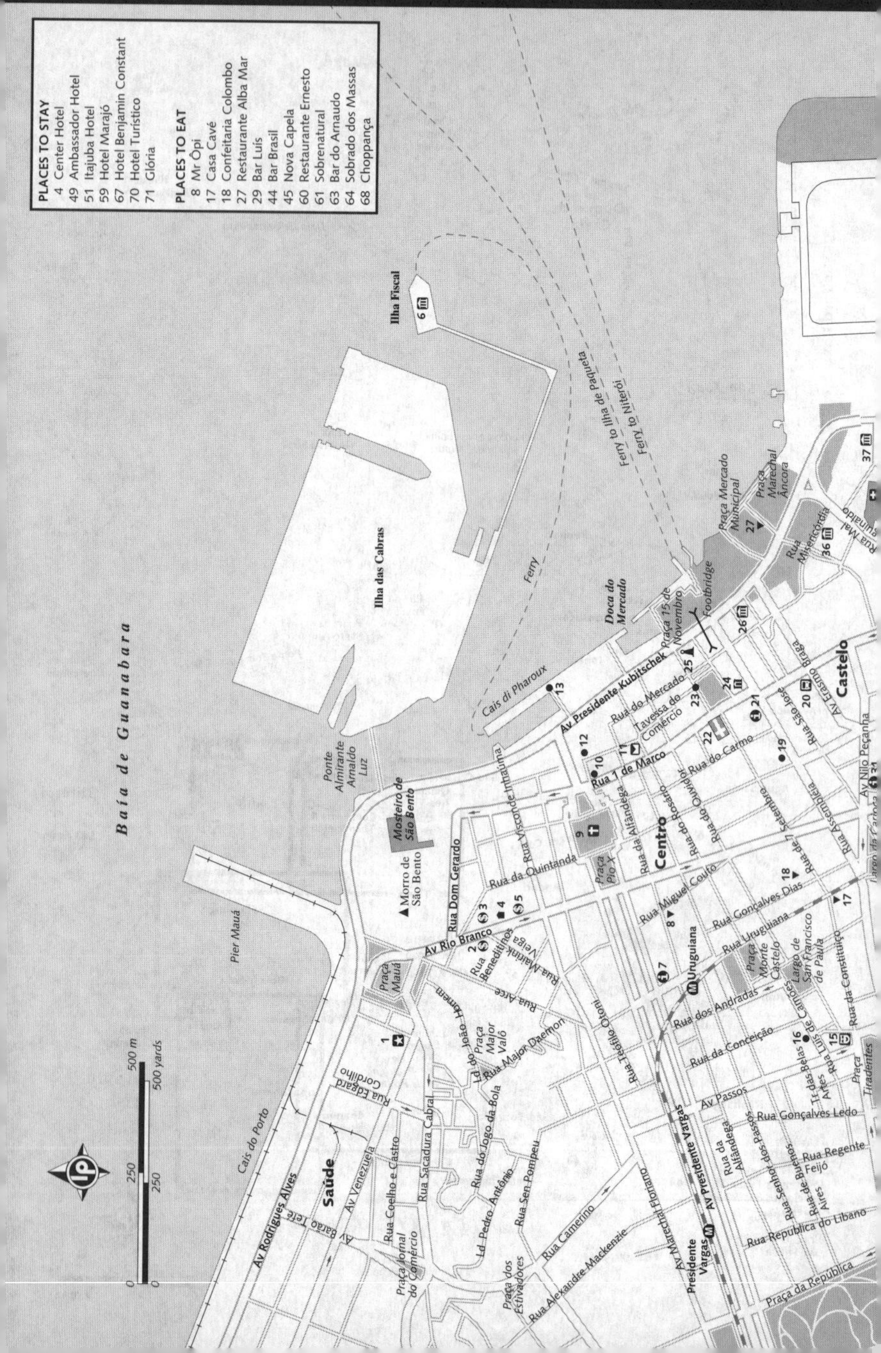

MAP 2 CENTRO

PLACES TO STAY
- 4 Center Hotel
- 49 Ambassador Hotel
- 51 Itajuba Hotel
- 59 Hotel Marajó
- 67 Hotel Benjamin Constant
- 70 Hotel Turístico
- 71 Glória

PLACES TO EAT
- 8 Mr Opi
- 17 Casa Cavé
- 18 Confeitaria Colombo
- 27 Restaurante Alba Mar
- 29 Bar Luís
- 44 Bar Brasil
- 45 Nova Capela
- 60 Restaurante Ernesto
- 61 Sobrenatural
- 63 Bar do Arnaudo
- 64 Sobrado dos Massas
- 68 Choppança

Baía de Guanabara

Ilha das Cabras

Ilha Fiscal
6 ⋒

Ferry to Ilha de Paquetá
Ferry to Niterói

Pier Mauá

Cais do Porto

Ponte
Almirante
Arnaldo
Luz

Cais di Pharoux

Doca do
Mercado

Praça Mercado
Municipal

Praça
Marechal
Âncora

37 ⋒

Praça
Mauá

Saúde

Mosteiro de
São Bento

▲ Morro de
São Bento

Av Rio Branco

Rua Dom Gerardo

Av Presidente Kubitschek

Praça 15 de
Novembro

Footbridge

26 ⋒

27

36 ⋒

Castelo

Centro

Tiradentes

Praça da República

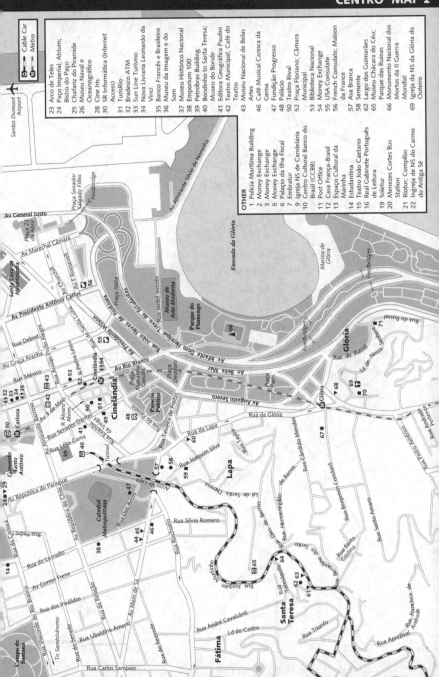

Santos Dumont Airport

Cable Car
Metro

23 Arco de Teles
24 Paço Imperial; Atrium; Bistro do Paço
25 Chafariz do Piramide
26 Museu Naval e Oceanográfico
28 Cine Íris
30 SR Informática (Internet Access)
31 Turistko
32 Bradesco ATM
33 Sun Line Turismo
34 Nova Livraria Leonardo da Vinci
35 Banco Francês e Brasileiro
36 Museu da Imagem e do Som
37 Museu Histórico Nacional
38 Emporium 100
39 Petrobras Building
40 Bondinho to Santa Teresa; Museu do Bonde
41 Editora Geográfica Paulini
42 Teatro Municipal; Café do Teatro
43 Museu Nacional de Belas Artes
46 Café Musical Carioca da Gema
47 Fundição Progresso
48 Palácio
50 Teatro Rival
52 Praça Floriano; Câmara Municipal
53 Biblioteca Nacional
54 Money Exchange
55 USA Consulate
56 French Consulate; Maison da France
57 Asa Branca
58 Semente
62 Largo dos Guimarães
66 Museu Chácara do Céu; Parque das Ruinas
66 Monumento Nacional dos Mortos da II Guerra Mundial
69 Igreja da NS da Glória do Outeiro

OTHER
1 Policia Marítima Building
2 Money Exchange
3 Money Exchange
5 Money Exchange
6 Palacio da Ilha Fiscal
7 Embratur
9 Igreja NS de Candelária
10 Centro Cultural Banco do Brasil (CCBB)
11 Post Office
12 Casa França-Brasil
13 Espaço Cultural da Marinha
14 Estudantina
15 Teatro João Caetano
16 Real Gabinete Português de Leitura
19 Soletur
20 Menezes Cortes Bus Station
21 Riotur; CompRio
22 Ingreja de NS do Carmo do Antiga Sé

MAP 3 SÃO CRISTÓVÃO & MARACANÃ

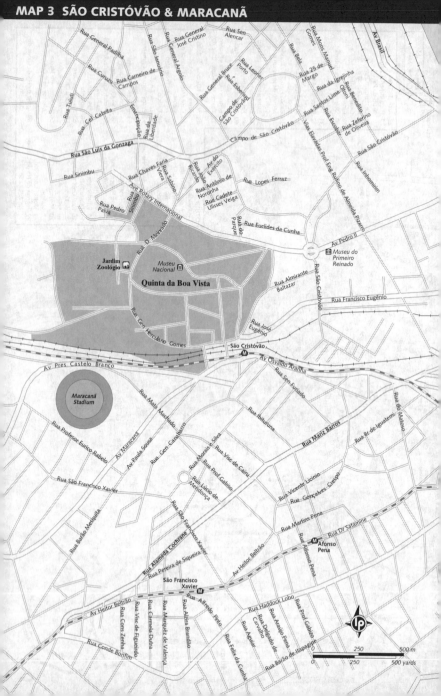

M = Metro
[T] = Tram

Baía de Guanabara

Cais do Porto

Novo Rio Bus Station

Av Rodrigues Alves
Rua da Gamboa
Rua Equador
Av Cidade de Lima
Rua Santo Cristo
Rua Coelho da Crivo
Av Pref Pereira Reis

Praça Marechal Hermes
Santo Cristo
Rua Santo Cristo
Rua Capiteribe
Rua Orestes
Rua Sara
Rua Carlos Gomes
Rua do Pinto
Igreja Santo Cristo
Rua da América
Rua Cardoso Marinho
Rua Vidal Negreiros
Rua Ebroíno Uruguai
Rua da América

Rua Rivadávia Correia
Rua do Propósito
Rua Pedro Ernesto
Praça Cel Assunção
Av Venezuela
Rua Sacadura Cabral
Rua de Livramento
Rua Sousa e Silva

Cemitério dos Ingleses
Rua do Livramento
Rua do Monte
Túnel João Ricardo
Ld do Barroso
Ld do Faria
Ld do Livramento
Praça dos Estivadores
Rua Alexandre Mackenzie

Gamboa
Rua Bento Ribeiro
Rua Barão de So Félix
Rua da Visconda de Gávea
Rua Senador Pompeu

Museu Histórico e Diplomático
Av Marechal Floriano

Rua Senador Pompeu
Rua Nabuco de Freitas
Dom Pedro II Train Station
Central M

Av Francisco Bicalho
Canal do Mangue
Av Francisco Bicalho
Rua General Luís M Morais
Rua Pedro Alves
Rua Moteira Pinto

Rua Pereira Franco
Praça General Pedra
Praça Noronha Santos

see Sambódromo map

Av Presidente Vargas

Campus da Universidade Rio de Janeiro
Rua Central Caldwell
Rua de Santana
Praça da República
Campo de Santana

Feira Nordestina

Av Presidente Vargas
Praça Onze M
Rua Benedito Hipólito
Rua Carmo Neto
Rua Júlio Carmo
Rua Afonso Cavalcanti
Rua Rodrigues Santos
Rua Corrêa Vasques
Rua Sta Maria
Rua Aníbal Benévolo
Rua Neri Pinheiro
Rua Salvador de Sá
Av Salvador de Sá
Rua Machado Coelho
Rua Pref Barroso
Rua Marques do Sapucaí
Viaduto São Sebastião

Cathedral
Rua Marques de Pombal
Rua Frei Caneca
Av Mem de Sá
Rua do Senado
Rua Carlos Sampaio
Praça Cruz Vermelha
Hospital Souza Aguiar

Estácio M
Rua Joaquim Palhares
Rua João Paulo
Rua João Paulo I
Rua Haddock Lobo
Rua Aristides Lobo
Rua Estácio de Sá
Rua Frei Caneca
Cidade Nova
Rua Senhor do Matozinhos
Sambódromo Museu do Carnaval

Av Engenheiro Freyssinet
Estácio
Rua Prof Quintino do Vale
Rua Maia de Lacerda
Rua São Carlos
Rua São Roberto
Rua do Zinco Latuinho Rabelo
Rua São Cláudio
R Major Freitas

Rua Santa Maria
Rua Carolina Reidner
Rua do Catumbi
Rua Van Erven
Rua dos Coqueiros
Rua Itapiru

Fátima
Rua Paula Matos
Rua Washington Luís
Rua do Resende
Túnel Martins da Sá
Rua Progresso
Rua Cardeal Arcoverde
Lagas das Neves
Rua Padre Miguelino
leme
Rua do Oriente

Catumbi
Rua Gonçalves
Cemitério do Catumbi

Rua Dr Agra
Rua Miguel Resende
Rua Monte Alegre
Rua Aarão Reis
Rua Alves

Rio Comprido
Rua Ambiré Calvalcante
Rua Azevedo Lima
Rua Costa Ferraz
Rua Campos da Paz
Rua da Estrela

▲ Morro de Santos Rodrigues

Santa Teresa
Rua Navarro
Rua Elieu Visconti
Túnel Santa Bárbara

MAP 4 FLAMENGO & BOTAFOGO

Rua Cruzeiro

Rua Falet

Rua Falet

Rua Abreu Visconti

Rua Cor João Felipe

Rua Almirante Alexandrino

Rua Prof. João Felipe

Túnel Santa Barbara

▲ Morro da Nova
Cintra 267m

Rua Pedro
Américo

Rua Andrade
Pertence **1**
Rua Silveira Martin
Catete **5** M **6**
8 **7**
9
10
Rua Con
Dutra
15
Rua Arturo
Bernardes **12**
13 **16**
14

Rua Bento Lisboa

Rua Correa
de Maze

Rua Benfa de Baependi

Rua 2 de
Dezembro

Rua Gen Mariante

Parque
Guinle
17

Rua Gago Coutinho

Largo do
Machado

Rua Machado
Assis

Largo do
Machado M **Flameng**

Rua das Laranjeiras

▲ Morro São Judas
Tadeu 246m

Rua Dr Julio Otoni

Tunnel

Rua Baro de Petropolis

●**25**

27
26 **28**
Rua
Cosme Velho

Rua Alice

Rua Alice

Rua Mário Portela

Laranjeiras

Rua das Laranjeiras

Rua Soares Cabral

Praça David
Ben Gurion

Rua Cardoso Junior

Rua General Gliceiro

Rua Prof. Luis Castanheda

Rua Belisário Távora

Rua Couto
Fernandes

Rua Osvaldo
Seabra

▲ Mirante Dona
Marta 363m

Est. Mirante Dona Marta

Parque Nacional
da Tijuca

Rua Pereira da Silva

Rua Efurt

Rua Conde de Baependi

●**19**
Rua Esteves Junir

Rua São Salvador

Praça São
Salvador

Rua Coelho Neto

Rua Passandu

Rua Pinheiro Machado

Rua Juçana

Rua Jaguá

Rua Mundo Novo

▲ Morro Mundo
Novo 128m

Rua Marquês Olinda

Rua Assunção

Rua Bambina

Rua Muniz Barreto

Praça
Radial Sul

Rua Barão de
Lucena

Rua Eduardo
Chnille

Rua Neteira

Rua Paulo IV

Rua Marquês de Abrantes

Flamengo M

Rua Baro do Flamb

Rua Bento
Flamengo **21**
20 **22**

Rua Barão e
Flamengo

Rua S
Vergueir

Rua Bel
de Icara

Av. Osvaldo Cruz

Rua Frei
do Botafogo

Praia do Botafogo

Av. das Nações Unidas

30
31

Rua Prof Alfredo
Gomes

32

33

Av. Reporter Nestor Moreir

Rua São Clemente

Botafogo

Botafogo M

Rua Sorocaba

34
35

Rua da Matriz

Rua Guilherme Guinle

Rua 19 Fevereiro

36

Morro do
Pasmado ▲

Túnel do
Pasmado

Rua Bartolmeu Portela

Humaitá

Rua Alfredo
Chaves

Rua David
Clímaco de
Alvim

Rua Cesário

Rua João Afonso

Rua Viúva
Lacerda

Rua Humaitá

Rua Conde Irajá

Rua Minuano

Rua Martins Ferreira

Rua Miranda
Valverde

Rua Voluntários da Pátria

Rua Henrique
Novaes

Rua Capitão Salomão

39

Rua Visconde de
Caravelas

40

41 **42**

Rua Visconde da Silva

Rua Sorocaba

Rua São João Batista

Rua Mena
Barreto

Rua Dona Mariana

Rua Paulo Barreto

Rua Prof. Fernando

Rua Álvaro Rodrigues

Rua General Polidoro

Cemitério São
João Batista

Rua Álvaro Ramos

Rua Gen Polidoro

Rua Arnaldo
Quintela

Rua Acea
Bueno

Rua Farani

43

Rua Gen Goiás
Monteiro

●**44**

37
Rua General
Severiano

Rua da Passagem

45

Av. Venceslau Bras

Av. Lauro Sodre

Rua Lauro Mü

Morro de São João

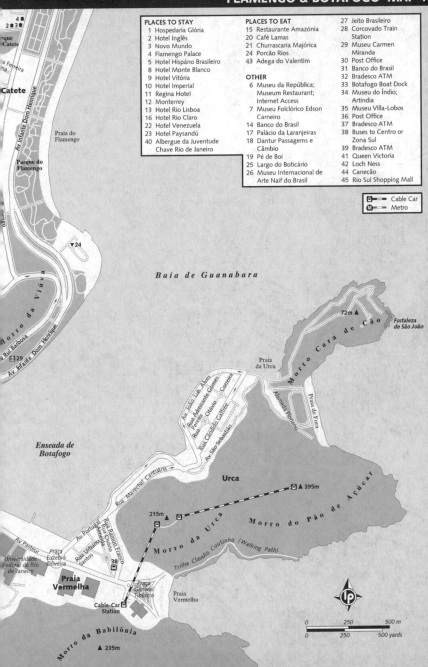

PLACES TO STAY
1 Hospedaria Glória
2 Hotel Inglês
3 Novo Mundo
4 Flamengo Palace
5 Hotel Hispáno Brasileiro
8 Hotel Monte Blanco
9 Hotel Vitória
10 Hotel Imperial
11 Regina Hotel
12 Monterrey
13 Hotel Rio Lisboa
16 Hotel Rio Claro
22 Hotel Venezuela
23 Hotel Paysandú
40 Albergue da Juventude
Chave Rio de Janeiro

PLACES TO EAT
15 Restaurante Amazónia
20 Café Lamas
21 Churrascaria Majórica
24 Porcão Rios
43 Adega do Valentim

OTHER
6 Museu da República;
Museum Restaurant;
Internet Access
7 Museu Folclórico Edson
Carneiro
14 Banco do Brasil
17 Palácio da Laranjeiras
18 Dantur Passagens e
Câmbio
19 Pé de Boi
25 Largo do Boticário
26 Museu Internacional de
Arte Naif do Brasil

27 Jeito Brasileiro
28 Corcovado Train
Station
29 Museu Carmen
Miranda
30 Post Office
31 Banco do Brasil
32 Bradesco ATM
33 Botafogo Boat Dock
34 Museu do Índio;
Artindia
35 Museu Villa-Lobos
36 Post Office
37 Bradesco ATM
38 Buses to Centro or
Zona Sul
39 Bradesco ATM
41 Queen Victoria
42 Loch Ness
44 Canecão
45 Rio Sul Shopping Mall

Cable Car
Metro

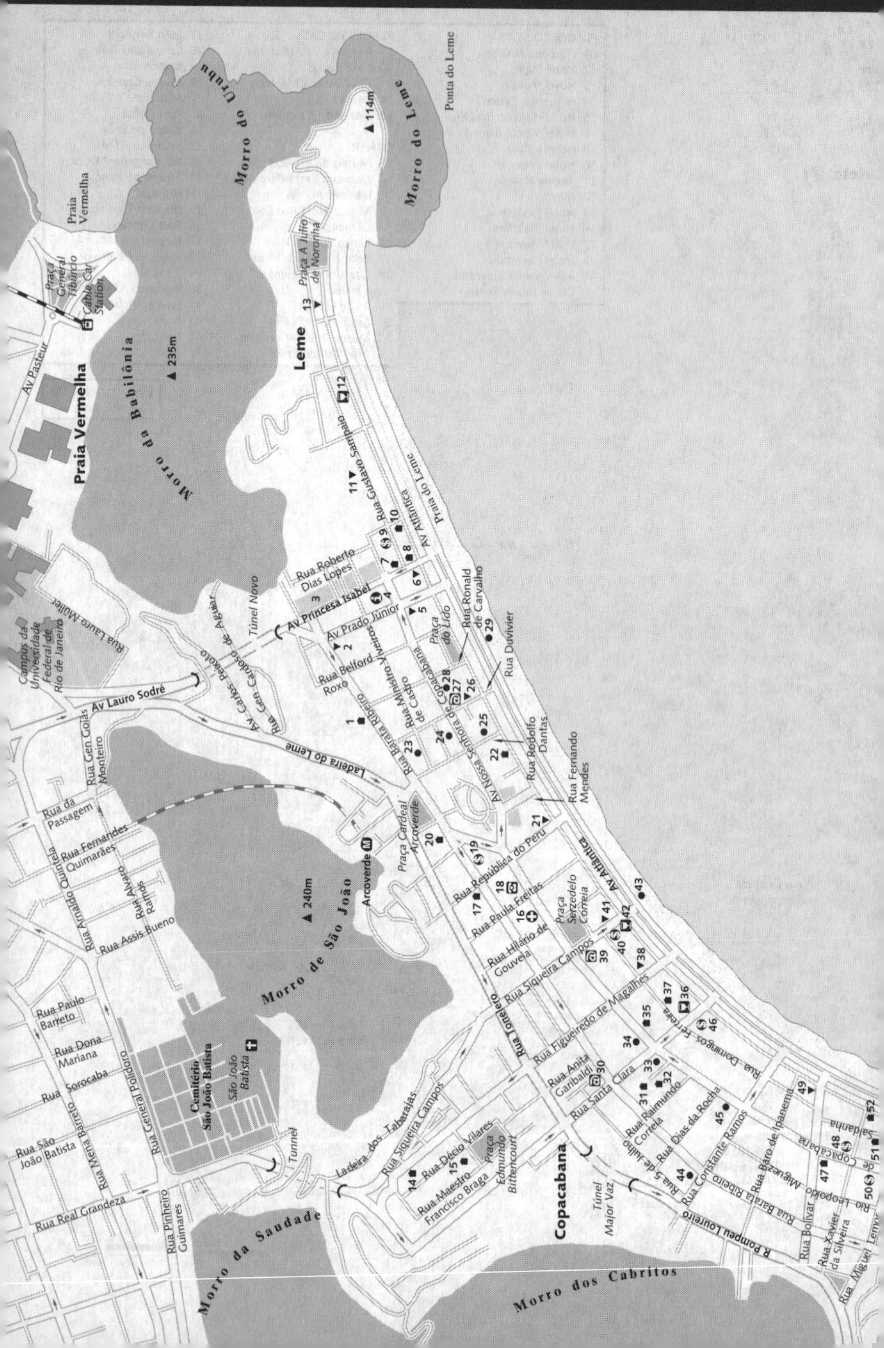

MAP 5 COPACABANA

Morro do Urubu

Morro do Leme

Morro do Leme

▲ 114m

Ponta do Leme

Praia Vermelha

Praça A Júlio de Nordinha

Praça General Tibúrcio

Cable Car Station

Leme

13

Praia Vermelha

Av Pasteur

▲ 235m

Morro da Babilônia

Rua Gustavo Sampaio

11 ▶ 9 ▶ 10

12

Praia do Leme

Rua Roberto Dias Lopes

3

Av Atlântica

7 ▶ 8 ▶
6 ▶

Campus da Universidade Federal do Rio de Janeiro

Rua Lauro Müller

Av Lauro Sodré

Túnel Novo

Av Prado Júnior

Av Princesa Isabel

4

5

Praça do Lido

Rua Ronald de Carvalho

Rua Belford Roxo

2

Rua do Lido

Rua Duvivier

29

Rua Gen Caldwell

Ladeira do Leme

Rua Barata Ribeiro

1

Rua Milton de Castro

23

24

28

27

26

25

Rua Rodolfo Dantas

Rua Gen Goiás Monteiro

Rua da Passagem

▲ 240m

Rua Fernando Mendes

22

Rua Fernandes Guimarães

Túnel

Praça Cardeal Arcoverde

Arcoverde Ⓜ

20

19

21

Av Nossa Senhora

Rua Aldo Rainho

Rua Assis Bueno

17 ▶

18

16

Rua República do Peru

Praça Serzedelo Correia

43

42

Morro de São João

Rua Hilário de Gouveia

Rua Paula Freitas

40

38

39

Av Atlântica

Rua Siqueira Campos

Rua Paulo Barreto

Rua Dona Mariana

Rua Tonelero

37

36

Rua Domingos Ferreira

35

46

Rua Sorocaba

Cemitério São João Batista

São João Batista ✚

Rua Barata Ribeiro

34

30

Rua Anita Garibaldi

41

Rua São João Batista

Rua Mena Barreto

Rua Figueiredo de Magalhães

Rua Santa Clara

31

33

32

Rua General Polidoro

Rua Raimundo Correia

Rua Dias da Rocha

45

49

Rua Maestro Francisco Braga

Rua Décio Vilares

14

15

Praça Edmundo Bittencourt

48

47

50

51

52

Ladeira Jos. Tabasilas

Rua Siqueira Campos

44

Rua Barão de Ipanema

Rua Constante Ramos

Rua Baroneza

Rua Xavier da Silveira

Rua Miguel Lemos

Av Nossa Sra de Copacabana

Rua Pompeu Loureiro

Rua Bolívar

Rua Leopoldo

Túnel Major Vaz

Rua Real Grandeza

Rua Pinheiro Guimarães

Copacabana

Morro da Saudade

Morro dos Cabritos

🚠 ▬ Cable Car
Ⓜ ▭ Metro

PLACES TO STAY
1 Copacabana Holiday (Flat Rental)
7 Acapulco
8 Le Meridien; Cafe de la Paix; Le Saint Itonoré; Le Rond Point Bar
10 Fantastic Rio (Flat Rental)
14 Hotel Santa Clara
15 Copacabana Praia Hostel
17 Apa Hotel
20 Copacabana Hotel Residencia
22 Copacabana Palace Hotel; Cipriani; Pergula; American Express Office
31 Pousada Girassol
32 Hotel Angrense
35 Grande Hotel Canada
37 Hotel Toledo
47 Hotel Copa Linda
51 Biaritz Hotel
52 Rio Othon Palace
55 Hotel Debret
57 Hotel Martinique
67 Yvonne Reiman (Flat Rental)
68 Atlantis Copacabana
70 Sofitel Rio Palace; Le Pré Catalan

PLACES TO EAT
2 Cervantes
5 O Crack dos Galetos
6 Mab's
11 Restaurante Shirley
13 Mániu's
21 Manoel e Joaquim
26 Quick Galetos
38 Arataca
41 Manoel e Joaquim
49 Dom Camillo Restaurante & Pizzaria
58 Restaurante Lucas
64 Copa Rio Galetos
65 Lope's Confeitaria

OTHER
3 Car Rental Agencies
4 Riotur
9 Bradesco ATM
12 Sindicato do Chopp
16 Galdino Campos Cárdio Copa Clinic
18 Telephone Office
19 Bradesco ATM
23 Laundromat
24 VASP
25 Varig
27 Internet House
28 Andesol
29 Bicycle Rental
30 Cyber Place; Clube Israelite & Brasileiro
33 Soletur
34 IBEU
36 Sindicato do Chopp
39 Copa Cybercafe
40 Money Exchange
42 Maxim's Rio
43 Rainbow (Gay Kiosk)
44 Farmácia Piaui
45 Livraria Siciliana
46 Bradesco ATM
48 Convencional Câmbio e Turismo
50 Bradesco ATM
53 Help
54 Money Exchange
56 Money Exchange
59 Laundromat
60 Telerede
61 Sindicato do Chopp
62 Le Boy
63 Bunker 94
66 Blue Angel
69 BASE
71 Museu Histórico do Exército e Forte de Copacabana

ATLANTIC OCEAN

Ponta de Copacabana

Praia de Copacabana

Av Atlántica

Av Nossa Senhra

Rua Sá Ferreira
Rua Souza Lima
Rua Francisco Sá
Rua Júlio de Castilhos

Arpoador

Praça Coronel Eugênio Franco

Praia de Diabo

Rua Francisco Otaviano
Rua Conselheiro Lafaiete
Parque Garota de Ipanema

Praça do Arpoador
Praia do Arpoador

Ponta do Arpoador
🤿 Snorkeling

Rua Raul Pompéia
Rua Bulhões de Carvalho
Av Rainha Elizabeth

Morro do Cantagalo

Rua Joaquim Nabuco

N

0   250   500 m
0   250   500 yards

MAP 6 IPANEMA, LEBLON & GÁVEA

Tunnel

Lagoa

Parque Lage

Rua Jardim Botânico

Rua Miguel Pereira

Rua Capitão Salomão

Rua Visconde da Silva

Rua Real Grandeza

Rua Visconde de Caravelas

Rua General Dionísio

Rua Pinheiro Guimarães

Cemitério São João Batista

Rua Macedo Sobrinho

Rua Humaitá

Rua Enrico Cruz

Av Alexandre Ferreira

Rua Maria Angélica

Rua Frei Leandro

Rua da Fonte da Saudade

Morro da Saudade

▲ 245m

Rua Euclides da Rocha

Rua Siqueira Campos

Rua Figueiredo de Magalhães

Braga Maestro Francisco

Rua Santa Clara

Borges de Medeiros

Machado

Av Epitácio Pessoa

Lagoa Rodrigo de Freitas

Parque Tom Jobim

Morro dos Cabritos

▲ 385m

Copacabana

Túnel Major Vaz

Rua 5 de julho

Rua Dias da Rocha

Rua Constante Ramos

Parque da Catacumba

Av Epitácio Pessoa

Rua Barata Ribeiro

Rua Barão de Ipanema

R Pompeu Loureiro

Rua Xavier da Silveira

Rua Bolívar

Parque do Cantagalo

Av Henrique Dodsworth

Rua Miguel Lemos

Av Rainha

Rua Nossa Senhora de Copacabana

Rua Aires de Saldanha

Ilha dos Caiçaras

Av Epitácio Pessoa

Morro do Cantagalo

▲ 202m

Tunnel

Jardim de Alah

Av Epitácio Pessoa

Rua Garcia D'Ávila

Rua Alberto de Campos

Rua Saint Roman

Rua Sá Ferreira

Av Atlântica

Dumont

Rua Barão de Jaguaripe

Rua Nascimento da Silva

Rua Sousa Lima

Praça Espanha

22 ● 25

Rua Redentor

Rua Vinícius de Moraes

Rua Francisco Sá

Rua Barão da Torre

27 fin

Rua Barões de Castro

Rua Júlio de Castilhos

Rua Visconde de Pirajá

26 28 fin

30 ● 31 32

Praça Nossa Senhora de Paz

● 37 41

38 ● 43 ▼

▲ ▼ 42

44 46 ▼

Rua Teixeira de Melo

Rua Antônio Parreiras 54 ●

53 ▼

Rua Consselheiro Lafaiete

23 ●

24

● 36

39 ● 45 ●

Rua Henrique

Rua Prudente de Morais

Ipanema

33

34 ● ▼ ▼ 39

35

40 ▼

47 ▼

48 ●

50 ▼

49

▼ 51

52

Praça General Osório

Rua Gomes Carneiro

Rua Paul Redfern

Rua Aristides de Mendonça

55 57 ●

56

58 ▼

Rua Maria Quitéria

Rua Joana Angélica

● 59

60 ▼

● 62

63

Rua Rainha Elizabeth

▼ 65

Rua Joaquim Nabuco

Av Vieira Souto

Praia de Ipanema

● 61

Rua Francisco Otaviano

● 66

Arpoador

Parque Garota de Ipanema

Praça do Arpoador

Praia do Arpoador

Praia de Diabo

Ponta do Arpoador

]Continued from page 172]

Twelve years later, the Leme Tunnel was completed. This meant the rich started to move farther out from the center, in a pattern that continues today.

The early 1920s to late 1950s was Rio's golden age. It became a destination for Hollywood celebrities and international high society, who came to gamble at the casinos and perform at the nightclubs.

The city remained the political capital of Brazil until 1960, when the capital was moved to Brasília. During that decade, a hotel building boom along the beaches saw the rise of big hotels like the Sheraton, Rio Palace, and Le Meridien. At the same time, the favelas of Rio were becoming overcrowded with immigrants from poverty-stricken areas of the Northeast and interior. The 'marvelous city' began to lose its gloss, as urban crime and violence began to increase.

The turning point for Rio came when it was chosen as host city for Eco 92, the United Nations Conference on Environment and Development. In the buildup to the conference, major projects, financed by federal grants, were undertaken to upgrade the roads of Rio and restore many old buildings and parks, as well as improve living conditions in the favelas. This trend has continued.

The beautiful people flock to Rio, the 'Cidade Maravilhosa.'

Rio remains the cultural and tourist capital of Brazil. It still sets the fashion and pace for the rest of the nation and should continue to do so for many years to come.

ORIENTATION

Rio is divided into a *zona norte* (north zone) and a *zona sul* (south zone) by the Serra da Carioca, steep mountains that are part of the Parque Nacional da Tijuca. These mountains descend to the edge of the city center, where the zonas norte and sul meet. Corcovado, one of these mountain peaks, offers the best way to become familiar with the city's geography – from here you have views of both zones. The statue Cristo Redentor (Christ the Redeemer), with his outstretched arms, gazes down on the Bahia da Guanabara and the landmark Pão de Açúcar (Sugarloaf). His left arm points toward the zona norte, and his right reaches out toward the zona sul suburbs of Copacabana, Ipanema, Leblon and beyond.

Rio is a tale of two cities. The upper and middle classes reside in the zona sul, the lower class in the zona norte. Favelas cover steep hillsides on both sides of town – Rocinha, Brazil's largest favela with between 150,000 and 300,000 residents, is in Gávea, one of Rio's richest neighborhoods. Most industry is in the zona norte, as is most of the pollution. The ocean beaches are in the zona sul.

Unless they work in the zona norte, residents of the zona sul rarely go to the other side of the city. The same holds true for travelers, unless they head north to the Maracanã soccer stadium or to the Quinta da Boa Vista (the park containing the national museum) or to the international airport on the Ilha do Governador.

Maps

Lonely Planet produces an excellent city map for Rio de Janeiro. The Brazilian maps used by most Brazilian and foreign travelers are produced by Quatro Rodas, which also publishes the essential *Guia Brasil,* a travel guide in Portuguese which is updated annually. The Rio city maps provided in *Guia Brasil* help with orientation. The guides are readily available at newsstands.

Riotur also provides a useful map of the city with detailed street layout. It's available free from Riotur information booths.

For topographic maps of Rio and other parts of Brazil, visit Editora Geográfica Paulini (Map 2; ☎ 2220-0181), at Rua Senador Dantas 75, shops J and K.

INFORMATION
Tourist Offices

Riotur is the very useful Rio city tourism agency. The agency operates a tourist information hotline (☎ 2542-8080) from 8 am to 8 pm daily. The receptionists speak English and more often than not they'll be able to help. The multilingual Web site, at www.rio.rj.gov.br/riotur, is also a good source of information.

The main Riotur office can be found at Rua da Assembléia 10, 9th floor, Centro (Map 2, metro stop Carioca), but the special 'tourist room' is in Copacabana (Map 5, ☎ 2541-7522), Avenida Princesa Isabel 183. In the tourist room there are free brochures (in Portuguese and English) and maps. It's open daily from 8 am to 8 pm.

You can also get these brochures at the Riotur information booths at the main bus station (Rodoviária Novo Rio, open 6 am to midnight daily), Pão de Açúcar (8 am to 7 pm daily); the international airport on the Ilha do Governador (5 am to 11 pm daily); the Corcovado cog train station at Cosme Velho (7 am to 7 pm daily); and also from some hotels.

If you arrive in Rio by bus or plane, the Riotur booths can save you a lot of time by calling around town to find you a vacant hotel and making a reservation. The staff only have lists of the middle- to top-end hotels, but if you give them the phone number of a cheaper one they will be happy to call it.

TurisRio (Map 2, ☎ 2544-7992) is the Rio state tourism agency. Its office is at Rua da Ajuda 5, 6th floor, Centro, and is open 9 am to 6 pm, Monday to Friday. The Web site www.turisrio.gov.br is worth a look too. Embratur (Map 2, ☎ 2509-6017, rio@embratur.com.br) is Brazil's national tourism agency. Their main office is in Brasília, but there's a branch at Rua Uruguaiana 174, 8th floor. For the average traveler, neither of these last two agencies is worth a special trip.

Many hotels have free copies of *Rio this Month,* a useful guide in Portuguese and English to the main attractions.

The Rio Convention & Visitors Bureau (Map 6, ☎ 2259-6165, Rua Visconde de Pirajá 547), operates as a supporting organization for anyone interested in holding their business events in Rio. The Web site www.rioconventionbureau.com.br has lots of useful visitor information in English.

Visa Extensions

One place you can extend your visa or entry/exit card is the Polícia Federal in the Polícia Marítima building (Map 2, ☎ 2291-2142, ext 1378) at Avenida Venezuela 2, Centro, near the far end of Avenida Rio Branco. Extensions are also available from federal police offices at the international airport and the Via Parque shopping mall in Barra da Tijuca.

Money

Changing money in Rio is easy, especially if you have cash. The money exchanges *(casas de câmbio)* should give you close to the bank rate for cash, and a few points less for traveler's checks. Many travel agents also double as câmbios, and this will be written on their sign outside.

In the center of the city, there are several travel agencies/money exchanges on either side of Avenida Rio Branco, a couple of blocks north of the intersection with Avenida Presidente Vargas (Map 2). Be very cautious carrying money in the city center and don't take much to the beach.

The major banks with currency exchange facilities include the following:

Banco do Brasil
    Rua Senador Dantas 105, 11th floor and Rua do Acre 15 in Centro (Map 2); Avenida NS de Copacabana 594, Copacabana (Map 5); and the International Airport, Terminal One, 3rd floor (Map 1)

Banco do Boston
Avenida Rio Branco 110, Centro (American Express Traveler's Checks only; Map 2)
Banerj
Avenida Nilo Peçanha 175 (traveler's checks only; Map 2)
Citibank
Rua da Assembléia 100, Centro (Map 2); Rua Visconde de Pirajá 459A, Ipanema (Map 5)
Banco Francês e Brasileiro
Avenida Rio Branco 193, Centro (Map 2)

In Copacabana, there is a cluster of money exchange places behind the Copacabana Palace Hotel, near the intersection of Avenida NS de Copacabana and Rua Fernando Mendes. Ipanema has several money exchanges scattered around along Rua Visconde da Pirajá.

At the international airport, it's best to change money at one of the exchange booths on the ground floor (arrivals), open 6:30 am to 11 pm. Banco do Brasil, on the third floor, is open 8 am to 10 pm daily, but charges 3% commission, even for cash.

If you're using ATMs as your chief source of cash, the Banco do Brasil ATMs at the international airport work for Visa, and the Banco 24 Horas ATM around the corner from Banco do Brasil works for Cirrus. ATMs at HSBC, Avenida Rio Branco 108, Centro, and some Bradesco ATMs work for Visa. ATMs at Citibank, located at Rua Visconde de Pirajá 459A, Ipanema, work for Visa, Plus, MasterCard and Cirrus cards.

Post

Any mail addressed to Posta Restante, Rio de Janeiro, Brazil, ends up at the post office at Rua Primeiro de Março 64 (Map 2), in the city. They hold mail for 30 days and are reasonably efficient. Post offices usually open 8 am to 6 pm weekdays and until noon on Saturday.

Telephone

Rio is notorious for its inefficient telephone service, and it hasn't improved since privatization, which occurred in the late 1990s. Lines cross and fail with irritating frequency. The only solution is to keep trying.

International phone calls can be made from the following Telemar telephone offices:

Antônio Carlos Jobim International Airport, open 24 hours (Map 1)
Centro, Praça Tiradentes 41, open 24 hours (Map 1); and Rua do Ouvidor 60, open 6:30 am to 11 pm (Map 1)
Copacabana, Avenida NS de Copacabana 540 (upstairs), open 24 hours (Map 5)
Ipanema, Rua Visconde de Pirajá 111, open 6 am to 11 pm (Map 6)
Novo Rio Bus Station, open 24 hours (Map 3)

Fax

Faxes can be sent from any large post office in Rio. The branch at the international airport is open 24 hours.

Email & Internet Access

Most Cariocas have an email address even if they don't have a computer. Getting access to your own phone line is usually only possible at the top-end hotels. At other hotels all the lines go through a switchboard. Remember that local calls are timed rather than flat fee.

Internet access is now widely available in Rio. Larger hotels all provide Internet and email access, as do youth hostels. Access is also available from the following cafés and IT stores. The cost ranges from US$2 to $5 per hour.

Centro (Map 2)
CompRio, Rua da Assembléia 10, basement level
SR Informática, Edifício Avenida Central, 3rd floor
Catete (Map 4)
Museu da República
Botafogo (Map 4)
El Turf Cyber Bar, Rio Sul shopping mall, shop D91
Copacabana (Map 5)
Internet House, Avenida NS de Copacabana 193
CopaCyberCafé, Rua Siqueira Campos 43, shop 901
Cyber Place, Clube Israelita Brasileiro, Rua Barata Ribeiro 489, shop 21
Telerede, Rua Francisco Sá 26, shop B
Ipanema (Map 6)
Livraria Letras & Expressões, post office at

Praça General Osório (15 minutes free)
Estação Ipanema, Rua Visconde de Pirajá, 605
Barra da Tijuca
@Point, Barra Shopping, Avenida das Américas
4666
Web Station, Barra Point Shopping Center,
Avenida Armando Lombardi 350

Internet Resources

There are lots of informative Web sites
about Rio. As well as those mentioned in
the Tourist Offices section, you may like to
have a look at the following:

www.vivabrazil.com.br/riodejaneiro – in English
and Portuguese, with some good photos and
links
www.ipanema.com – with English and German
versions, a good introductory site; includes the
Rio Gay Guide
www.123-rio.com – a multilingual site with lots of
useful information
www.marcelo.botelho.com – images of Rio,
through Marcelo's live cams.

Travel Agencies

Rio has no shortage of travel agencies eager
to give advice, book plane tickets and organize tours. They can also save you unnecessary trips to the bus station by selling bus
tickets in advance. Many agents are brusque
and unhelpful but some are quite the opposite, so it's usually worth walking out on
type one to find type two.

In Copacabana, try Andesol (Map 5;
☎ 2275-4370, fax 2541-0748), at Avenida NS
de Copacabana 209. The staff speaks
English, French, German, Spanish and
Italian, and is very helpful. Close to Copacabana's Rio Othon Palace, Convencional
Câmbio e Turismo Ltda (Map 5; ☎ 2522-
0793, fax 2267-2600, convenci@iis.com.br)
has been recommended by readers as a
good place to change money and find cheap
hotel deals.

In Ipanema, Blumar/Brazil Nuts (Map 5;
☎ 2511-3636, fax 2511-3739, operacao@
blumar.com.br), at Rua Visconde de Pirajá
550, is useful.

Soletur (☎ 2525-5000, fax 2267-6633) is
one of the big operators, and can arrange
tours to anywhere else in Brazil. They have

offices in the center (Map 2) at Rua da Qui-
tanda 20, in Copacabana (Map 5) at Rua
Santa Clara 70, and in Ipanema (Map 6) at
Rua Visconde de Pirajá 351. Dantur Pas-
sagems e Câmbio (Map 4; ☎ 2557-7144), at
Largo do Machado 29, shop 47, is useful if
you're staying in the Catete/Botafogo/Fla-
mengo area.

Sun Line Turismo (☎ 9291-8074, sun
.line@uol.com.br, Avenida Rio Branco 185,
room 602) in Centro, is a travel agency specializing in gay and lesbian tourism. Sun
Line offers a transfer service from the
airport to your hotel for US$15, and can
assist and advise you on anything you need
in Rio. This agency also operates a 24-hour
help line at the above number. Call and ask
for Marco.

Brazil Eco Travel Center (Map 6; ☎ 2512-
8882, Rua Visconde de Pirajá 572, 7th floor),
in Ipanema, is a fine outfit to contact if you
want to set up an organized trip to any of
the exciting ecotourism destinations in
Brazil – see the Natural Brazil special
section for details.

Bookstores

Finding books in English or French is easy
in Rio. Nova Livraria Leonardo da Vinci
(Map 2; ☎ 2533-2237), in Edifício Marquês
do Herval (just past Avenida Rio Branco
185), is Rio's best bookshop; it's one floor
down on the *sobreloja* level. It has largest
collection of foreign books in Rio (including many Lonely Planet guidebooks) and
knowledgeable staff who, for a tidy sum, will
order just about any book you want. It's
open 9 am to 7 pm Monday to Friday, and
9 am to noon on Saturday.

All stores in the Livraria Siciliana chain
have a collection of paperbacks in English.
They are at Visconde de Pirajá 511,
Ipanema (Map 6), and Avenida NS de Copacabana 830, Copacabana (Map 5).

Ipanema has lots of good bookshops.
Livraria Letras & Expressões (Map 6;
☎ 2521-6110), Rua Visconde de Pirajá 276,
stocks many books and magazines in
English. It's open 24 hours. It has another
branch in Leblon (☎ 2511-5085), at the
corner of Rua Dias Ferreira and Avenida

THE SOUTHEAST

Ataulfo de Paiva. Livraria Travessa (Map 6; ☎ 2287-5157), Rua Visconde de Pirajá 462, has a great selection of foreign-language books. Both these bookstores also contain groovy little cafés.

In Leblon, Livraria Argumento Rio (Map 6; ☎ 2259-9398), Rua Dias Ferreira 417, is an excellent bookstore with a cool little café in the back. Here you'll find a good range of books about Rio, as well as a large selection of Lonely Planet guides.

Many of the newsstands on Avenida Rio Branco in Centro and in Ipanema and Copacabana stock large selections of foreign newspapers and magazines.

Libraries

The Biblioteca Nacional (Map 2; ☎ 2262-8255), at Avenida Rio Branco 219, is the largest public library in Latin America. It has an archive of nearly 6 million works, and also houses a café and bookstore. Hours are 9 am to 8 pm Monday to Friday and 9 am to 3 pm Saturday. There are free guided tours at 11 am, 3 pm and 5 pm from Monday to Friday.

Founded in 1837, the Real Gabinete Português de Leitura (Royal Portuguese Reading Cabinet), on Rua Luís de Camões (Map 2), is a beautiful building housing some 350,000 volumes. The archive includes many rare and precious volumes, including manuscripts by Gonçalves Dias and Machado de Assis. It's open 9 am to 5 pm Monday to Friday.

The Instituto Brasil-Estados Unidos (IBEU; Map 5, ☎ 2548-8332), Avenida NS de Copacabana 690, 3rd floor, has an English library with a large fiction collection, many books about Brazil in English, and a good selection of current magazines from the US. To borrow books you have to take classes there or take out a membership, but it's cheap. It's open 8 am to 8 pm Monday to Friday.

Maison de France (Map 2; ☎ 2210-1272), in the French Consulate building at Avenida Presidente Antônio Carlos 58, contains a library with a collection of records, CDs, videos, and 22,000 books – all in French. It's open 10:30 am to 7 pm Tuesday to Friday.

Cultural Centers

The Riotur *Rio Incomparável* guide gives details of exhibitions at the cultural centers. The Centro Cultural do Banco do Brasil (CCBB; Map 2; ☎ 3808-2000), at Rua Primeiro do Março 66, is Rio's finest cultural center. It always has interesting exhibitions and is well worth taking some time for. They often have free lunchtime concerts as well. Hours are Tuesday to Sunday from noon to 8 pm.

Close by, Casa França-Brasil, in the old customs building (Map 2), stages many prominent exhibitions. It's open from 10 am to 8 pm, Tuesday to Sunday. The Paço Imperial, on Praça 15 de Novembro (Map 2), is an important arts space, and even offers cafés, a restaurant and a bookshop. It's open from noon to 6 pm, Tuesday to Sunday. In Ipanema, the Casa da Cultura Laura Alvim (Map 6), at Avenida Vieira Souto 176, has a theater and often puts on interesting exhibitions.

Laundry

There are laundries in Copacabana at Rua Ministro Viveiros de Castro 194 and Avenida NS de Copacabana 1226 (Map 5). In Catete, English is spoken at the laundry at Rua Correia Dutra 16A (Map 4). In Ipanema there's one on Rua Farme de Amoedo close to the intersection with Rua Visconde de Pirajá (Map 6). At these laundries you can do it yourself, or pay a little more and go to the beach while they do it for you.

If you don't want to go to a laundry, inquire at your hotel, as often the housekeepers wash clothes at home to make a few extra reais.

Toilets

Public toilets are scarce in Rio, although they can usually be found in parks. Your best bet is to go into a café or restaurant. At the beach, everybody pees in the water, but there are toilets and showers in the numbered lifeguard posts *(postos)*, where you have to pay a fee (around US$0.50) to enter. The fee for the toilets at the Rio bus station is US$0.50.

Luggage Storage

There are luggage lockers on the 2nd floor of Terminal One in the international airport and a luggage-storage facility at the Novo Rio bus station. Both are inexpensive.

Medical Services

Galdino Campos Cárdio Copa (Map 5; ☎ 2548-9966), at Avenida NS de Copacabana 492, is a 24-hour clinic. Staff here speaks English and French.

There are several 24-hour pharmacies, including branches of Farmácia Piauí at Avenida Ataulfo de Paiva 1283, (☎ 2274-8448) in Leblon (Map 6); Rua Barata Ribeiro 646 and Rua Prado Junior 237 (☎ 2255-6249) in Copacabana (Map 5); and Praia do Flamengo 224, Flamengo (Map 4; ☎ 2284-1548).

Emergency

If you have the misfortune to be robbed, you should report it to the Tourist Police Office (Map 6; ☎ 3399-7170), at Rua Afrânio de Melo Franco 159 in Leblon; it's open 24 hours. No big investigation is going to occur, but you will get a police form to give to your insurance company.

To call emergency telephone numbers in Rio you don't need a phone card. Useful numbers include Radio Police (☎ 190), Ambulance (☎ 193) and Fire (☎ 193).

Dangers & Annoyances

Rio gets a lot of bad international press about violence, the high crime rate, and *balas perdidas* (stray bullets) – but don't let this stop you from coming. Travelers to Rio have as much chance of getting mugged as in any other big city, so the same precautions apply here. The biggest crime of all would be not to visit Rio. By following a few common-sense precautions, you're unlikely to suffer anything worse than sunburn.

Don't bring any jewelry, chains, or expensive watches, and if you must wear a watch, then make it a cheapie worth only a few dollars. Get used to keeping small change and a few banknotes in a shirt pocket so that you can pay for bus tickets and small expenses without extracting large wads.

Better still, carry only the cash you think you'll need. If you have a camera with you, keep it out of sight as much as possible.

If you ride the local buses (which are great fun), have your change ready before boarding. Avoid the super-crowded ones. The air-conditioned buses are more expensive, but more secure. Take one from the airport to save a few dollars on a taxi.

If you consider your hotel to be reliable (as a rough guide, this probably means any place with an Embratur rating three stars or more), place valuables in the safe and get a receipt. Package your valuables in a small, double-zippered bag which can be padlocked, or use a large envelope with a signed seal that will easily show any tampering.

Keep your credit card in sight at all times. Don't give it to waiters and let them take it away. Don't keep it in the hotel safe. Lonely Planet gets letters all the time from readers who are victims of credit-card fraud; when you're the victim, it can feel as if Rio must be one of the capitals of credit-card scams.

The heavy police presence at Copacabana and Ipanema means the beaches are quite safe – but don't go to sleep. Take only the money you need for snacks and drinks.

Apart from the fast grab, one particular beach scam seems to be the favorite: A pair of thieves wait for you to be alone on the beach guarding your gear and that of your friends (because you have decided to take turns going in the water). One thief approaches from one side and asks you for a light or the time. While you're distracted, the thief's partner grabs your gear from the other side.

Another scam at Copacabana is overcharging tourists for drinks on the beach. Always ask the price of the drink before you imbibe.

Distraction is a common tactic employed by street thieves. See the Dangers & Annoyances section in the Facts for the Visitor chapter for information on the so-called cream technique and other methods of distraction, and further tips on security in Brazil (including Rio).

At the time of writing, a number of druggings had recently been reported. Exercise caution when you are offered cigarettes, beer, sweets etc. If you feel at all suspicious or uneasy, the offer can be tactfully refused by claiming stomach or other medical problems.

WALKING TOUR (MAP 2)

The center of Rio, now a potpourri of the new and old, has character and life. Don't miss exploring some of the city's museums, colonial buildings, churches (of course) and traditional meeting places – restaurants, bars, shops and street corners. Here is a suggested walking tour. You could amble round the route in a day, but if you linger in some of the cafés, bars, museums and so on, or take the odd side trip, a day could easily extend to two.

Take a bus or the metro to the Cinelândia stop, and find the main square along Avenida Rio Branco, called **Praça Floriano**; it's the heart of modern Rio. Praça Floriano comes to life at lunchtime and after work when the outdoor cafés are filled with beer drinkers, samba musicians and political debaters. The square is Rio's political marketplace. There's daily speechmaking, literature sales and street theater. Most city marches and rallies culminate here on the steps of the old **Câmara Municipal** (City Hall).

South toward the bay is **Praça Mahatma Gandhi**, where you'll see a monument that was a gift from India in 1964. South beyond the plaza and across several lanes of busy roads is the large **Museu de Arte Moderna**, in the Parque do Flamengo.

On the east side of Avenida Rio Branco facing Praça Floriano is the **Biblioteca Nacional**. Built in 1910 in the neoclassical style, it's open to visitors and usually has an exhibition. The most impressive building on Praça Floriano is the **Teatro Municipal**. Just to the north on Avenida Rio Branco you'll also find the **Museu Nacional de Belas Artes**, housing some of Brazil's best paintings.

Now turn around and head back to the other side of the Teatro Municipal and walk down the pedestrian only Avenida 13 de Maio – on your left are some of Rio's best *suco* (juice) bars. Cross a street and you're in the Largo da Carioca. Up on the hill is

the recently restored **Convento Santo Antônio**. The original church here was started in 1608, making it one of Rio's oldest. The statue here of Santo Antônio is an object of great devotion for many Cariocas in search of a husband. The church's sacristy, which dates from 1745, has some beautiful jacaranda woodcarving and blue Portuguese tiles.

Gazing at the skyline from the convent, you'll notice the **Petrobras** building, which looks rather like a Rubik's cube. Behind it is the ultramodern **Catedral Metropolitana** (the inside is cavernous, with beautiful, huge stained-glass windows.) If you have time for a side trip, consider heading over to the nearby *bondinho* (little tram) that goes up to **Santa Teresa** (see the Santa Teresa section later in this chapter).

Next find the shops along 19th-century-era Rua da Carioca. The old wine and cheese shop has some of Brazil's best cheese, from the Canastra mountains in Minas Gerais. It also has bargains in Portuguese and Spanish wines. Two shops sell fine Brazilian-made instruments, including all the Carnaval percussion, which make great gifts. There are several good jewelry shops off Rua da Carioca, on Rua Ramalho Ortigão.

Stop at the famous **Bar Luis**, Rua da Carioca 39, for a *chopp* (draft beer) and lunch or a snack. Rio's longest-running restaurant, it was opened in 1887 and was called Bar Adolf until WWII. For decades, many of Rio's intellectuals have carried on with their musings here, while eating the best German food in Rio.

At the end of the block you'll pass the **Cinema Iris**, which used to be Rio's most elegant theater, and emerge into the hustle of **Praça Tiradentes**. It's easy to see that this was once a fabulous part of the city. On opposite sides of the square are the **Teatro João Caetano** and the **Teatro Carlos Gomez**, which both show plays and dance performances. The narrow streets in this part of town house many old and mostly dilapidated small buildings. It's worth exploring along Rua de Buenos Aires as far as **Campo de Santana** and then returning along Rua da

Alfândega. Campo de Santana is a pleasant park, scene of the proclamation – re-enacted in every Brazilian classroom – of Brazil's independence from Portugal by Emperor Dom Pedro I, on September 7, 1822. Wander around the park and try to spot some of the agoutis that run wild here.

Back near Avenida Rio Branco, at Rua Gonçalves Dias 30, hit the **Confeitaria Colombo** for a shot of coffee and art nouveau. Offering succor to shopping-weary matrons since 1894, the Colombo is best for (very strong) coffee and desserts.

From here, cross Avenida Rio Branco, go down Rua da Assembléia, stop at Riotur if you want tourist information, then continue to **Praça 15 de Novembro**. In the square are the **Chafariz da Pirâmide** (Pyramid Fountain), built in 1789, and a **craft market**. If you face the bay, on your right is the **Paço Imperial**, which was the Portuguese royal palace and the seat of government. After independence it housed the Department of Telegraphs, but it has been restored and now contains temporary exhibits and a couple of popular cafés.

On the opposite side of the square is the historic **Arco de Teles**, part of an old aqueduct running between two buildings. Walking through the arch into **Travessa de Comércio**, you'll find several bars, restaurants, fishing supply stores and a couple of simple colonial churches. It's a colorful area.

Overlooking Praça 15 de Novembro is the **Igreja de NS do Carmo da Antiga Sé**, which was the metropolitan cathedral until 1976. The most important religious services were held there during imperial times.

From Praça 15 de Novembro, stroll over to the **waterfront**, where ferries leave to **Niterói** and **Ilha de Paquetá**. The ferry to Niterói takes only 15 minutes and you never have to wait long. Consider crossing the bay and walking around central Niterói. If you have some time catch a local bus to the Niterói's unique Niemeyer-designed **Museu do Arte Contemporânea (MAC)**, with its fantastic views. To get to the MAC from the Niterói ferry terminal, turn right as you leave and walk about 50m across to the bus terminal in the middle of the road

and catch a 47B minibus. It will drop you right at the museum door.

Back in Rio, when you're at the ferry docks and facing the bay, you'll see the landmark **Restaurante Alba Mar** a few hundred meters to your right. It's in a green gazebo overlooking the bay. On Saturday the building is surrounded by the tents of the **Feira de Antiguidades**, a strange and fun hodge-podge of antiques, clothes, foods and other odds and ends.

If you want to extend your walking tour, go back through Arco de Teles and follow the street around toward Rua Primeiro de Março. Walk up along the right-hand side and you'll come to the **Centro Cultural do Banco do Brasil** (CCBB). Go in and check out the building and any of the current exhibitions. Most are free. Then have a look behind the CCBB at the **Casa França-Brasil**. From there, you'll be able to see the **Igreja NS de Candelária**. Take a moment to look at the interior of the church, then keep going up Rua Primeiro de Março, through the naval area, to Rua Dom Gerardo, the last street before a hill. The monastery **Mosteiro de São Bento** is on top of the hill. From Rua Dom Gerardo, head back down Avenida Rio Branco, and try to imagine it as it was in 1910: a tree-lined boulevard, with sidewalk cafés – the Champs-Élysées of Rio.

CENTRO

Rio's center *(Centro)* is all business and bustle during the day and absolutely deserted at night and on weekends. It's a working city – the center of finance and commerce.

Centro is the site of the original settlement. Most of the important museums and colonial buildings of the city are here. Small enough to explore on foot, the city center is lively and interesting, and occasionally beautiful, despite the many modern, Bauhaus-inspired buildings.

Two wide avenues cross at the center: Avenida Rio Branco, where buses leave for the zona sul, and Avenida Presidente Vargas, which heads out to the Sambó-dromo and the zona norte. Rio's modern Metrô (subway) follows these two avenues as it burrows under the city. Most banks and airlines have their headquarters and offices on Avenida Rio Branco.

Sightseeing is safer here during the week, because there are lots of people around. On weekends, you stand out much more.

Museu Histórico Nacional (Map 2)

Housed in the colonial arsenal (restored in 1985), this museum is filled with historical relics and interesting displays, one of the best being the re-creation of a colonial pharmacy. The building is near the bay on Praça Marechal Âncora. It's open 10 am to 5:30 pm, Tuesday to Friday, and 2 to 6 pm on weekends. Entry is free.

Museu Histórico e Diplomático (Map 3)

Housed in the restored Palácio Itamaraty (which was home to the presidents of Brazil from 1889 until 1897), the museum has an impressive collection of art, antiques and maps. Located at Avenida Marechal Floriano 196 (☎ 2253-7961), it is a short walk from Presidente Vargas metro station. There are 45-minute guided tours from 1:15 pm to 4:15 pm, on Monday, Wednesday and Friday. To guarantee a tour in English or French, call before you visit.

Museu Nacional de Belas Artes (Map 2)

This is the premier fine art museum of Rio. There are more than 800 original paintings and sculptures in the collection. The most important gallery is the Galeria de Arte Brasileira, where you can see such 20th-century classics as Cândido Portinari's *Café*. There are also galleries with folk art, African art and contemporary exhibits. Taking photos is prohibited. If you'd like a guided tour in English, phone first to make a reservation.

At Avenida Rio Branco 199, the museum (☎ 2240-0068) is open 10 am to 6 pm Tuesday to Friday, and from 2 to 6 pm on Saturday, Sunday and holidays. Take any of the city-bound buses and get off near Avenida Rio Branco, or take the metro to Carioca station. Entry costs US$2, but is free on Sunday.

Museu Naval e Oceanográfico (Map 2)

This museum chronicles the history of the Brazilian navy from the 16th century to the present. It includes an interesting exhibition of model warships, as well as maps and navigational instruments. Close to Praça 15 de Novembro, at Rua Dom Manuel 15, the museum is open noon to 4:30 pm daily. Entry is US$2.

Naval enthusiasts should also visit the nearby Espaço Cultural da Marinha (ECM), on the waterfront near the intersection of Avenida Presidente Vargas and Avenida Presidente Kubitschek. It contains the *Riachuelo* submarine, the *Bauru* (a WWII torpedo boat), and the 19th-century Brazilian imperial family's large rowboat. The ECM is open noon to 5 pm, Tuesday to Sunday. Entry is US$2.

The boat tour to Ilha Fiscal leaves from the docks here (see the Ilha Fiscal section later in this chapter for details).

Sambódromo & Museu do Carnaval (Map 3)

To the west of Centro, close to the Praça Onze metro station, you'll find the epicenter of Rio's Carnaval. Designed by Oscar Niemeyer and completed in 1984, the Sambódromo (sambadrome) is a tiered street (Rua Marquês do Sapucaí) designed for samba parades (see the special section on Carnaval). It also houses the Museu do Carnaval. The museum contains lots of material relating to the history of Rio's samba schools. Empty sambadromes, though, are like empty stadiums – there's not a lot happening. The museum is open 11 am to 5 pm Tuesday to Sunday. Enter through Rua Frei Caneca; admission is free.

ILHA DE PAQUETÁ (MAP 1)

This island in the Baía de Guanabara was once a very popular tourist spot and is now frequented mostly by families from the zona norte. There are no cars on the island. Transport is by foot, bicycle (with literally

Market in the spa town of Caxambu

News in Petrópolis

Bathing suit shopping, Rio

Capoeira performance in the streets of Pelourinho, Salvador

Drumming up a frenzy, Salvador

hundreds for rent) or horse-drawn cart. There's a certain dirty, decadent charm to the colonial buildings, unassuming beaches and businesses catering to local tourism. Sadly, the bay is too polluted for swimming, and the place gets very crowded.

Go to Paquetá for the boat ride through the bay and to see Cariocas at play – especially during the Festa de São Roque, which is celebrated over five days in August. Boats leave from near the Praça 15 de Novembro in Centro. The regular ferry takes one hour and costs US$0.50. The more comfortable hydrofoil is worth taking, at least one way. It gets to the island in 25 minutes and costs US$5. The ferry service goes from 5:30 am to 11 pm, leaving every two to three hours. During the week, the hydrofoil leaves at 10 am, noon, 2 and 4 pm, and returns at 7:40 and 11:40 am and 12:30, 2:30 and 4:30 pm. On the weekend, it leaves every hour on the hour from Rio from 8 am to 3 pm and at 4:30 pm and returns hourly from 8:30 am to 5:30 pm.

ILHA FISCAL (MAP 2)

The lime green, neo-gothic palace sitting in the Baía de Guanabara looks like something out of a fairy tale; it was designed by engineer Adolfo del Vecchio and completed in 1889. Originally used to as a headquarters for supervising port operations, the Palácio Ilha Fiscal is famous as the location of the last imperial ball, held November 9, 1889. It's now open for guided tours, which leave from the dock at the ECM. From April to September tours leave Thursday to Sunday at 1 and 4 pm; from October to March tours leave at 1:30 and 4:30 pm on the same days. The trip and tour cost US$2.

CINELÂNDIA (MAP 2)

At the southern edge of the business district, Cinelândia's shops, bars, restaurants and movie theaters are popular day and night. There are also several decent, reasonably priced hotels. The bars and restaurants get crowded at lunch and after work, when there's often samba in the streets. There's a greater mix of Cariocas here than in any other section of the city. Several gay and mixed bars here stay open until late.

LAPA (MAP 3)

By the old aqueduct (the Arcos da Lapa) that carries the Santa Teresa tram out of the city center is Lapa, the setting for many a Brazilian novel and a gathering place for the bohemians of Rio. After years as a derelict red-light area, Lapa is undergoing a renaissance, with restoration of many old buildings underway. Prostitution still exists here, but there are also several great music clubs, like the Fundação Progresso, Asa Branca, Semente and Café Musical Carioca da Gema. There are also some very cheap hotels (See Places to Stay and Entertainment, later in this chapter). Lapa goes to sleep very late on Friday and Saturday.

The landmark aqueduct, with its 42 arches, dates from 1732. It was built to carry water from the Rio Carioca to the city.

SÃO CRISTÓVÃO (MAP 3)

One of the few zona norte suburbs travelers are likely to visit, São Cristóvão is where you will find the Quinta da Boa Vista, a large park containing the Museu Nacional and the Jardim Zoológico. Also in this area is the Maracanã soccer stadium and the Feira Nordestina, a lively Sunday market. In the 19th century the suburb was the home of the nobility, including the emperors Dom Pedro I and Dom Pedro II themselves. It has since become one of the most populous suburbs in Rio.

Maracanã

This stadium, Brazil's temple of soccer and a colossus among coliseums, easily accommodates more than 100,000 people, and on occasions such as the World Cup final of 1950 or Pelé's last game has squeezed in close to 200,000 crazed fans (although it's now been modified so it holds fewer). If you like sports, if you want to understand Brazil, or if you just want an intense, quasipsychedelic experience, then by all means go see a game of *futebol* – preferably a championship game or one between any two of Rio's big four clubs, Flamengo (Fla), Fluminense (Flu),

Vasco and Botafogo (see the boxed text 'Brazilian Football: Facts for Fans' in the Facts for the Visitor chapter).

There's a sports museum inside the stadium. In it are photographs, posters, cups and the uniforms of Brazilian sporting greats, including Pelé's famous No 10 shirt. There's also a store where you can buy soccer shirts. The museum is open 9 am to 5 pm Monday to Friday. Enter through Gate No 18, which is on Rua Professor Eurico Rabelo.

Quinta da Boa Vista

Quinta da Boa Vista was the residence of the imperial family until the republic was proclaimed. Today it's a large and busy park, with gardens and lakes, which is crowded on weekends with soccer games and families from the zona norte. In the center of the park, the former imperial mansion houses the **Museu Nacional** and **Museu da Fauna**. The **Jardim Zoológico**, Rio's zoo, is 200m away.

To get to Quinta da Boa Vista, from Centro take the metro to São Cristóvão or bus No 472 or 474; from the zona sul take bus No 472 or 474.

SANTA TERESA

This is one of Rio's most unusual and charming neighborhoods. Situated along the ridge of the hill that rises from the city center, Santa Teresa is a beautiful area of cobbled streets, hills and old homes. In the 19th century Rio's upper crust lived here and rode the *bonde* (tram) to work in Centro.

During the 1960s and 1970s many artists and hippies moved into the mansions of Santa Teresa. Just a few meters below them, the favelas spread on the hillsides. There is a lively scene in the bars around Largo dos Guimarães on the weekend. It's necessary to be particularly cautious in this district, especially at night.

Every year in the last weekend of November, local artists open their studios to the public. If you're around don't miss it. Programs are available at Museu do Bonde and the Museu Chácara do Céu.

Santa Teresa Tram (Maps 2 & 3)

The *bondinho* (little tram) goes over the Arcos da Lapa – the old aqueduct – to Santa Teresa from Avenida República do Chile and Rua Senador Dantas in Centro. Catch it at the tram station on Rua Lélio Gama, Centro, behind the Petrobras building downtown. The favelas down the hillsides have made Santa Teresa a high-crime area. Young thieves jump on and off the tram very quickly. Go by all means, but don't take valuables.

You may wonder why people choose to hang onto the side of the tram even when there are spare seats. They're fare-dodgers, trying to avoid having to pay the regular fare of US$0.50.

There's a small but interesting **Museu do Bonde** at the tram depot close to Largo dos Guimarães at Rua Carlos Brant 14, with a history of Rio's tramways since 1865. While you're there, wander down to the fascinating old workshop that houses the trams. Entry to the museum is free and it's open 9 am to 4:30 pm daily.

Museu Chácara do Céu (Map 2)

At Rua Joaquim Murtinho Nobre 93, this is a delightful museum that occupies part of the former mansion of wealthy industrialist and arts patron Raymundo Ottoni de Castro Maya.

It contains antiques and artworks from his private collection, which he bequeathed to the nation. The assorted treasures include works by Vlaminck, Monet, Portinari and Picasso, to name a few of the most prominent. The house is surrounded by beautiful gardens and has a great view of Baía de Guanabara.

It's open noon to 5 pm daily (except Tuesday). Entry is US$5 (free on Sunday).

Parque das Ruinas (Map 2)

Connected to the Chácara do Céu by a walkway, this park contains the ruins of the mansion belonging to Brazilian heiress Laurinda Santos Lobo, and her house was a meeting point for Rio's artists and intellectuals for many years until her death in 1946. The interesting partial renovation includes a café and a stage where free jazz concerts are held every Thursday night. Don't miss the excellent view of Rio from the top floor.

GLÓRIA (MAP 2)

Glória and Catete became desirable suburbs in the mid-19th century, when they were on the outskirts of the city. Many noblemen and merchants built stately homes in this district, including the Barão de Novo Friburgo, who built the Palácio do Catete. By the end of the century, though, the rich had moved farther out as the inner city expanded outward.

Today, many of the former mansions have become hotels, and the area is now a favorite with backpackers.

Igreja de Nossa Senhora da Glória do Outeiro

Looking over the suburb that bears its name, this baroque beauty was the favorite of Dom Pedro II. He was married, and his daughter, Princesa Isabel, was baptized here. The octagonal church, built in 1714, has an altar carved by Mestre Valentim. On August 15 worshippers gather here to celebrate the Festa de NS da Glória do Outeiro.

The church and small museum are open 8 am to noon and 1 to 5 pm Monday to Friday, and from 8 am to noon Saturday and Sunday. There are Sunday masses at 8 am and noon. To get there, take the metro to Glória and climb up the Ladeira da Glória.

CATETE (MAP 4)
Museu da República

The Museu da República, in the Palácio do Catete, at Rua do Catete 153, has been wonderfully restored. Built between 1858 and 1866, and easily distinguished by the bronze condors on the eaves, the palace was home to the president of Brazil from 1897 until 1954, when then-president Getúlio Vargas shot himself here (see the Facts about Brazil chapter for details). The bedroom in which the suicide occurred is on display. The museum has a good collection of art and artifacts from the republican period, and also houses a good lunch restaurant, art-house cinema and book-store. Close to the cinema and the bookstore you'll see a couple of small booths, where Internet access is available. Museum hours are noon to 5 pm Tuesday to Friday, and 2 to 6 pm on the weekend. Admission is US$2, free on Wednesday.

The grounds of the Palácio do Catete are now the Parque do Catete, a quiet refuge from the city. Special performances in the park include concerts, plays and other popular events. Pick up a program from the museum or look in the Riotur booklet.

Museu Folclórico Edson Carneiro

This small museum should not be missed, especially if you're staying in the Catete/Flamengo area. It has excellent displays of folk art – probably Brazil's richest artistic tradition – a folklore library and a small craft shop with some wonderful crafts, books and folk music at very cheap prices.

The museum is on the northeastern edge of the park, with one entrance inside the grounds of the Palácio do Catete, at Rua do Catete 181, and the other next door. The museum is open 11 am to 6 pm Tuesday to Friday, and 3 to 6 pm Saturday, Sunday, and holidays. Entry costs US$1.

FLAMENGO

Flamengo was once Rio's finest residential district, but when the tunnel to Copacabana was completed in 1904, the upper classes began moving out. Flamengo is still mostly residential. The apartments are often big and graceful, although a few high-rise offices have recently been built among them. With the exception of classy waterfront buildings, Flamengo is mostly a middle-class area.

There are fewer nightclubs and restaurants here than in nearby Botafogo or Cinelândia.

Parque do Flamengo (Maps 2 & 4)

The result of a landfill project that leveled the São Antônio hill in 1965, the park spreads out over 1.2 sq km of shoreline. It runs all the way from downtown Rio through

Glória, Catete, Flamengo itself and on around to Botafogo. Designed by famous Brazilian landscaper Burle Marx, Flamengo is a park with loads of fields and a bay for activities and sports.

The park is not considered safe at night, although the sports areas are well lit – take care if you do go to see soccer in the wee small hours.

There are three museums in the park: the Museu de Arte Moderna, the Monumento Nacional dos Mortos da II Guerra Mundial, and the Museu Carmen Miranda.

Museu de Arte Moderna (Map 2)

At the northern end of Aterro do Flamengo, looking a bit like an airport hangar, is the Museu de Arte Moderna (MAM).

The museum was devastated in 1978 by a fire that consumed 90% of its collection. It has worked hard to rebuild, and today is the most important center of contemporary art in Rio. It holds many temporary exhibitions and has a permanent display of more than 11,000 works, including pieces by Brazilian artists Bruno Giorgi, Di Cavalcanti and Maria Martins.

The MAM is open noon to 6 pm Tuesday to Friday and noon to 7 pm on weekends. Entry is US$5 (half-price for students).

Monumento Nacional dos Mortos da II Guerra Mundial (Map 2)

This monument to the soldiers who fought in WWII contains a museum, a mausoleum and the Tomb of the Unknown Soldier. The museum exhibits uniforms, medals and documents from the Brazilian campaign in Italy. There's also a small lake, with sculptures by Ceschiatti and Anísio Araújo de Medeiros close by. The monument is open 10 am to 4 pm, Tuesday to Sunday. Entry is free.

Museu Carmen Miranda (Map 4)

The small Museu Carmen Miranda at the southern end of the Aterro do Flamengo, across the street from Avenida Rui Barbosa 560, is filled with Carmen memorabilia and paraphernalia, including costumes, posters, music and a small exhibit of other personal items. It's open 11 am to 5 pm Tuesday to Friday, and from 10 am to 4 pm on Saturday and Sunday. Entry is free.

Praia do Flamengo (Map 4)

This popular beach is a thin strip of sand on the bay, with a great view. Like the park, it was also part of the Flamengo landfill project. Within an easy walk of most of the budget hotels in Catete/Flamengo, there's a different class of Carioca here than on the luxurious beaches to the south, and it's fun to watch them play. Swimming here, though, is definitely suspect. There always seems to be a lot of rubbish in the water.

BOTAFOGO (MAP 4)

Early development in Botafogo was spurred by the construction of a tram that ran up to the botanical garden, linking the bay and the Lagoa Rodrigo de Freitas. This artery, now used by motor vehicles instead, still plays a vital role in Rio's traffic flow, and Botafogo's streets are extremely congested. There are several palatial mansions here that housed foreign consulates when Rio was the capital of Brazil. This area has fewer high-rise buildings than much of the rest of Rio.

There are not many hotels in Botafogo but there are lots of good bars and restaurants where the locals go to avoid the tourist glitz and high prices of Copacabana.

Museu do Índio

At Rua das Palmeiras 55, the Museu do Índio has a good library with more than 25,000 titles, a map, photo, video and sound archive, and a quiet garden with a Guarani-built mud hut, and native foods and medicinal plants. The displays concentrate on the economic, religious and social lives of the indigenous people of Brazil. There's also a small craft shop. The museum and shop are both open 10 am to 5:30 pm Tuesday to Friday, from 1 to 5 pm on Saturday and Sunday. Entry is free. The museum's Web site, at www.museudoindio.org.br, is a good online resource for information on Indians in Brazil.

Rio's Postcards – Sugarloaf & Christ the Redeemer

The two must-see attractions of Rio for any visitor are its postcard images – the Sugarloaf and the statue of Christ the Redeemer (Map 4).

Pão de Açúcar (Sugarloaf) is dazzling. Seen from its peak, Rio is undoubtedly the most beautiful city in the world. There are many good times to make the ascent, but sunset on a clear day is the most spectacular. As day becomes night and the city lights start to sparkle down below, the view is delightful.

Everyone must go to Pão de Açúcar, but if you can, avoid it from about 10 to 11 am and 2 to 3 pm, which is when most tourist buses arrive. Avoid cloudy days as well.

To reach the summit, 396m above Rio and the Baía de Guanabara, you have to take two cable cars. The first ascends 215m to Morro da Urca. From here, you can see Guanabara Bay and along the winding coastline. On the ocean side of the mountain is Praia Vermelha, in a small, calm bay. Morro da Urca has its own restaurant, souvenir shops, a playground, a helipad and an outdoor theater.

The second cable car goes up to Pão de Açúcar. At the top, you have a wonderful view of the city, Corcovado mountain with the statue of **Cristo Redentor**, and the famous long curve of Praia de Copacabana. There's also a fast-food place and souvenir shops, but the view is the big attraction. Don't rush it – you can stay up here for as long as you want. Take some time to wander around the pathways down below.

The two-stage cable cars leave about every 30 minutes from Praça General Tibúrcio at Praia Vermelha in Urca (Map 4). They operate 8 am to 10 pm daily and cost US$11. Take a bus marked 'Urca' from Centro or Flamengo (No 107), or a No 500, 511 or 512 from the zona sul. The open-air bus that runs along the Ipanema and Copacabana beaches also goes to Pão de Açúcar.

Corcovado (Hunchback) is the mountain and Cristo Redentor (Christ the Redeemer) is the statue upon it. The mountain rises straight up from the city to 710m. At night, the brightly lit statue is visible from all over the city.

The view from the top of Corcovado is a spectacular panorama of Rio and its surroundings. Christ's left arm points toward the zona norte, and Maracanã, the largest soccer stadium in the world, is easily visible in the foreground. You can also see the international airport just beyond and the Serra dos Órgãos mountain range in the far distance. In front of Christ is Pão de Açúcar, in its classic postcard pose. To the right you can see the Lagoa Rodrigo de Freitas, the racetrack, the Jardim Botânico, and over to Ipanema and Leblon.

Corcovado lies within the Parque Nacional da Tijuca. You can get here by car or taxi, but the best way is to go up in the cog train – for the view, sit on the right-hand side going up. The round-trip costs US$12, and the train leaves from Rua Cosme Velho 513 (Map 4). You can either get a taxi there or take a bus marked 'Rua Cosme Velho' – No 184 or 180 from Centro and Glória, No 583 from Largo do Machado, Copacabana and Ipanema, or No 584 from Leblon.

During the high season, the trains, which only leave every 30 minutes, can be slow going. Corcovado and the train line are open 8:30 am to 6:30 pm. If you have some time before the upward train leaves, walk up Rua Cosme Velho toward the tunnel. The first road on your right is known as the Largo do Boticário, a picturesque colonial square featured in many postcards of the city. Also worth a visit is Rio's naif art museum, about 100m up the hill to the left of the train station. If you have a train ticket you can get in here for half-price.

Taxi drivers are quite happy to make a deal to provide return trips with waiting time. The cost (around US$25) for two or more people works out to be cheaper than the train fares.

On the Estrada das Paineiras, halfway to Corcovado, it's worth stopping over at the Dona Marta lookout for the fine view of Baía de Guanabara and Botafogo. The overlook has a helipad.

Museu Villa-Lobos

This museum is in a century-old building and is dedicated to the memory of composer Heitor Villa-Lobos. As well as his personal items, there's also an extensive sound archive. The museum is at Rua Sorocaba 200 in Botafogo, and it's open 10 am to 5:30 pm, Monday to Friday. Entry is free.

Beaches

The **Praia do Botafogo** is a small beach on a calm inlet looking out at Pão de Açúcar. The Rio Yacht Club is next door.

The **Praia da Urca** is another small beach, this one only 100m long. It's right next to the Fortaleza de São João, and is used mostly by military personnel and their families.

Praia Vermelha sits below Morro da Urca, facing the sea. The thick sand here, unlike the sand at any other beach in Rio, gives the beach its name – *vermelha* (red). The water is usually calm because the beach is protected by the headland. There's a nice walking and jogging track behind the beach (see Walking & Jogging later in this chapter).

COPACABANA & LEME (MAP 5)

This is the famous curved beach you know all about. What's surprising about Copacabana is the number of people who live there. Fronted by beach and backed by steep hills, the Copacabana suburb is for the greater part no more than four blocks wide, but crammed into this narrow strip of land are 25,000 people per square kilometer – one of the highest population densities in the world.

Only three parallel streets traverse the length of Copacabana. Avenida Atlântica runs along the ocean. The one-way Avenida NS de Copacabana is two blocks inland, with traffic running in the direction of the business district. One block farther inland, Rua Barata Ribeiro is also one-way, in the direction of Ipanema and Leblon. The names of all these streets change when they reach Ipanema.

Copacabana is undoubtedly the capital of Brazilian tourism. It's possible to spend an entire Brazilian vacation without leaving it, and some people do just that. The majority of Rio's mid-range and top-end hotels are here, and they are accompanied by plenty of restaurants, shops and bars. For pure city excitement, Copacabana is Rio's liveliest theater.

It is also the heart of Rio's recreational sex industry. There are many *boîtes* (bars with strip shows) and prostitutes; anything and everyone is for sale.

Between Christmas and Carnaval, prices here are exorbitant, the hotels are full and restaurants get overcrowded. The streets are noisy and hot.

Museu Histórico do Exército & Forte de Copacabana

This fort was built in 1914, and the original features are preserved, including walls up to 12m thick, defended by Krupp cannons. The museum displays weapons, but one of the best reasons to visit is the fantastic view you'll get of Copacabana. The fort is open 10 am and 4 pm, Tuesday to Sunday. Entry is US$2.

Praia da Copacabana/Leme

The world's most famous beach runs for 4.5km in front of one of the world's most densely populated residential areas. From the scalloped beach you can see the Sugarloaf and the Morro do Leme, those well-known granite slabs that surround the entrance to the bay – a magnificent confluence of land and sea. The last kilometer at the east end, from Avenida Princesa Isabel to Morro do Leme, is called Praia do Leme.

When you visit Copacabana, which you must, do as the locals do: Take only the essentials with you. The area is now heavily policed and is lit at night, so it's OK to walk around during the evening. Avenida NS de Copacabana is more dangerous; watch out on the weekend, when the shops are closed and there are few locals around.

There's always something happening on the beach during the day and on the sidewalks at night: drinking, singing, eating and all kinds of people checking out the scene. You'll find tourists watching Brazilians,

Brazilians watching tourists; the poor from nearby favelas eyeing the rich; the rich avoiding the poor; prostitutes looking for tricks, and johns looking for treats.

The gay section of the beach, known as the Stock or Stock Market, runs between the Copacabana Palace Hotel and Rua Fernando Mendes. Look for the identifying rainbow flag.

JARDIM BOTÂNICO & GÁVEA (MAP 6)

These two well-to-do suburbs lie near the Lagoa Rodrigo de Freitas, Jardim Botânico to the northwest and Gávea to the west. Botânico has some good restaurants and bars, but its main attractions are the parks and gardens. Gávea is next to the Jóquei Clube racetrack, and also has a number of excellent bars and restaurants. Praça Santos Dumont, at the end of Rua Jardim Botânico, gets very lively in the evening outside the bar/restaurant called Hipódromo and Hipódromo Up (upstairs).

The Jardim Botânico garden was first planted by order of the Prince Regent Dom João in 1808. There are more than 5000 varieties of plants on 1.41 sq km. Quiet and serene on weekdays, the botanical garden blossoms with families and music on the weekend. The row of palms, planted when the garden first opened, the Amazonas section, and the lake containing the huge Vitória Régia water lilies are some of the highlights. It's a good idea to take insect repellent.

The garden is at Rua Jardim Botânico 920 and is open 8 am to 5 pm daily. Entry is US$2, and for this you'll receive a map with suggested walks. To get there take a 'Jardim Botânico' bus, or any one marked *via Jóquei*: No 170 from Centro; No 571, 572, or 594 from the zona sul.

The Parque Lage, about 1km from the Jardim Botânico at Rua Jardim Botânico 414, is a beautiful park at the base of Parque Nacional da Tijuca. There are English-style gardens, little lakes and a mansion that now houses the Instituto Nacional de Belas Artes – there are often art shows and sometimes performances here.

It's a tranquil place, with no sports allowed, and a favorite of families with small children. It's open 8 am to 5 pm daily. Take a 'Jardim Botânico' bus.

There's also the Parque da Cidade, a pleasant park that was once a coffee plantation and now contains the Museu Histórico da Cidade. Housed in a two-story 19th-century mansion, the museum has interesting displays of furniture, porcelain, photographs and paintings by well-known artists. It covers the period from the foundation of Rio in 1565 to 1930 and is open 11 am to 5 pm Tuesday to Sunday.

Entry costs US$2. The park itself is open 7 am to 6 pm daily.

IPANEMA & LEBLON (MAP 6)

Ipanema and Leblon are two of Rio's most desirable districts. They face the same stretch of beach and are separated by the Jardim de Alah, a canal and adjacent park. It's largely a residential area, mostly well-to-do and becoming more so as rents continue to rise. Most of Rio's better (and more expensive!) bars, restaurants and nightclubs are here, as well as many of the city's most fashionable boutiques.

Museu H Stern

The headquarters of the famous jeweler H Stern, at Rua Garcia D'Ávila 113, contains a museum. If you're in the neighborhood, you may find the 12-minute guided tour interesting. There is a permanent exhibition of fine jewelry, some rare mineral specimens and a large collection of tourmalines. There is no pressure to buy, but you may not be able to resist. With a coupon, available at the museum desk or from the hotel reception at better hotels, you can get a free cab ride to and from the shop and anywhere in the zona sul.

Hours are 8:30 am to 6 pm Monday to Friday, and 8:30 am to 1 pm Saturday.

Museu Amsterdam Sauer

Next door to H Stern at Rua Garcia D'Ávila 105, this museum also has a collection of precious stones, as well as life-size replica mines. It's open 9:30 am to 5:30 pm,

Monday to Friday, and from 9:30 am to 1 pm Saturday.

Beaches

The beaches along the Ipanema and Leblon strip are really one beach, although it narrows at the Leblon end, which is divided from Ipanema by the canal. The beach of Ipanema, like the suburb, is the richest and most chic of Rio. There isn't quite the frenzy of Copacabana, and the beach is a bit safer

and cleaner. Ipanema is now lit up in the evenings, and many family groups come down with their barbecues and cook on the beach. It's the safest the beach has been at night for many years.

The word *ipanema* is Indian for 'bad, dangerous waters,' and is given to this place for good reason. The waves can get big and the undertow is often strong. Be careful, and swim only where you see the locals swim.

Different parts of the beach attract different crowds. The beach at Posto 9, right off Rua Vinícius de Moraes, is **Garota de Ipanema**. Today it's also known as the Cemetério dos Elefantes because of the old leftists, hippies and artists who hang out there, but it's also popular with the young and beautiful who like to go down there around sunset and smoke a joint. Just to the east, the beach in front of Rua Farme de Amoedo, also called Land of Marlboro and Crystal Palace, is the gay section.

The small beach **Praia do Arpoador** is wedged between Copacabana and Ipanema. There's good surfing here, even at night

(when the beach is lit), and there's a giant rock jutting out into the ocean with a great view, especially at sunset. A lot of people from the zona norte come down here to relax on weekends.

More or less beneath the Sheraton Hotel and the Morro Dois Irmãos, **Praia do Vidigal** has a mix of the hotel patrons and the favela dwellers who were pushed farther up the hill to make way for the Sheraton. Security is good here, with the only entrance under surveillance by hotel staff. It's a quiet beach, with few vendors. Unfortunately, the water's often heavily polluted.

After the Sheraton there is no beach for a few kilometers until **Praia do Pepino** in São Conrado. You can take the Avenida Niemeyer route through the tunnel leading to Barra da Tijuca.

Pepino is a beautiful beach, less crowded than Ipanema. It's also where the hang-gliders hang out when they're not hanging up in the wide blue yonder. Along the beach are two big resort hotels, the Hotel Nacional and the Hotel InterContinental. Behind them, nestled into the hillside, in a nice twist of social irony, is Rocinha, Brazil's biggest favela.

Buses No 591 and 592 go to Pepino from Copacabana/Leme. Don't take valuables, as these buses are frequent targets of robbers. There is also a Real air-conditioned bus that goes along Copacabana and Ipanema beaches to Pepino.

BARRA DA TIJUCA (MAP 1)

Barra is the Miami of Rio – beaches and malls dot the landscape. Like fungi in a rainforest, hundreds of buildings have sprung up wherever there happens to be an open space. Whether a condominium building, restaurant, shopping center or disco, these big, modern structures are, without exception, monstrosities.

Barra da Tijuca is no longer fashionable with Rio's rich and famous. It's too far from anywhere, and suffers huge traffic bottlenecks and a chronic shortage of water. The upper crust is moving back to Ipanema, Leblon, and the traditional Avenida Oswaldo Cruz area of Flamengo. Barra now caters to *emergentes*, the nouveaux riches from the towns west of Rio.

The best thing about Barra is the beach. It's 12km long, with clean, green water. The first few kilometers are filled with bars and seafood restaurants.

The young and hip hang out in front of kiosk No 1 – also known as the *barraca do Pepê* after the famous Carioca hang-gliding champion who died during a competition in Japan in 1991.

The farther out you go the more deserted it gets, and the stalls turn into trailers. It's calm on weekdays and crazy on hot summer weekends.

The Museu Casa do Pontal is owned by French designer Jacques Van de Beuque. It is an impressive collection of over 4500 pieces, one of the best folk art collections in Brazil. The assorted artifacts are grouped according to themes, including music, Carnaval, religion and folklore.

The museum is at Estrada do Pontal 3295. It's open 9 am to 5:30 pm, Tuesday to Sunday. Entry is US$3; children under five get in free. To get there from the zona sul, take a No 175 bus to Barra Shopping and catch a No 702 or 703, which both go past the museum.

BEACHES WEST OF BARRA DA TIJUCA

Although it gets crowded on weekends, the beach **Recreio dos Bandeirantes** is almost deserted during the week. The large rock at the western end acts as a natural breakwater, creating a calm bay. It's popular with families.

Prainha, the next beach along the coast past Recreio, is one of the best surfing beaches in Rio, so it's always full of *surfistas* (surfers.)

The most isolated and unspoiled beach close to the city is **Grumari**, which is quiet during the week and packed on weekends with Cariocas looking to get away from city beaches. It is in a beautiful setting, featuring mountains and natural vegetation. Four kilometers of this stretch have been set aside as an Environmental Protection Area, which should stop its becoming more

cheesecake for the rich. Cinema buffs should note that scenes from the movie *Blame It on Rio* were filmed here.

From Grumari, a narrow road climbs over a jungle-covered hillside toward **Guaratiba**. There's a good view of the **Restinga da Marambaia**, a large spit of land that is closed off to the public by a naval base. Cariocas enjoy eating a seafood lunch at one of the restaurants in the area.

ACTIVITIES
Cycling

Cycling is popular with Cariocas. Currently, there are 74 kilometers of bike paths, including around Lagoa das Freitas, in Barra da Tijuca, and on the oceanfront from Leblon to Leme. This last path also goes all the way to Flamengo and the center. In the Floresta da Tijuca there's a 6km bikeway from Cascatinha to Açude. If you have a bit of road sense and don't mind mixing it with the traffic, a bike is a fun way to get around.

Rio by Bike (☎/fax 2268-0565, ☎ 9985-7540, flycelani@ax.apc.org) offers bilingual guided city tours for beginners and mountain bike tours for advanced riders. They also rent 18-speed mountain bikes for US$18 a day (8 am to 8 pm) and US$12 for half a day (11 am to 8 pm). They will deliver and pick up the bike from your hotel. It's best to call them direct rather than ask your hotel receptionist to make the booking, as you may end up paying commission.

Golf

Rio has two 18-hole golf courses close to the city: Gávea Golf Club (Map 1; ☎ 3322-4141), Estrada da Gávea 800, and Itanhangá Golf Club (☎ 2494-2507), Estrada da Barra 2005. Both of these clubs welcome visitors during the week 7 am to sunset, but on the weekend you need to be invited by a member. Green fees are about US$75 a round, plus club rental of US$25 and caddie fee of US$25.

A cheaper option is Golden Green (☎/fax 434-0696), which has six tricky par-three holes. It's near Barra da Tijuca beach opposite Posto 7. It's open 7 am to 10 pm daily. The green fee is US$20 for 18 holes during the week and US$26 on the weekend. Hiring clubs will cost US$13, and cart rental is an extra US$7.

Surfing

In Rio city, surfing is very popular, with the locals ripping the fast, hollow beach breaks. When the surf is good, it gets crowded. Arpoador, between Copacabana and Ipanema, is where most surfers congregate, though there are some fun beach breaks farther out in Barra, Grumari, Joá and Prainha (considered by many to be the best surf spot in Rio). Boards can be rented in Rio, but they're so cheap that you'd be crazy not to buy one, especially if you've planned a surfing expedition down the coast. Galeria River (pronounced 'heever'), at Rua Francisco Otaviano 67 in Arpoador (Map 6) is an arcade full of surf shops.

Hang Gliding

If you weigh less than 80kg (about 180lb) and have US$80 to spend, you can do the fantastic hang glide off the 510m Pedra Bonita – one of the giant granite slabs that towers above Rio – onto Pepino beach in São Conrado. The winds are reputed to be very safe here and the pilots know what they are doing. Guest riders are secured in a kind of pouch attached to the kite.

Most tandem pilots can provide a wingtip-mounted camera with flash, wide-angle lens, motor drive and a long cable release to take pictures of you in flight. If you want to take pictures yourself, realize that takeoff and landing pictures are impossible, since you can't be encumbered with equipment. Your camera must fit into the pouch in the front of your flight suit. It's a good idea to have the camera strapped around your neck and a lens cover strapped to the lens or you risk losing the equipment and beaning a Carioca at the same time. Flights are usually extremely smooth so it's possible to take stable shots. Hang-gliders themselves make dramatic shots, especially when photographed from above.

Know your exact weight in kilos in advance. Ideally, your pilot should be heavier than you. If you're heavier than the pilot, he or she will have to use a weight belt and switch to a larger glider. If you're over 80kg you may still be able to fly – it depends on the weight of the pilot. You don't need any experience or special training – anyone from 7 to 70 years old can do it.

Flights naturally depend on atmospheric conditions. You can usually fly on all but three or four days per month – more during the winter. If you fly early in the day, there is more flexibility to accommodate weather delays. For the experience of a lifetime, it's not all that expensive: US$80 for anywhere from 10 to 25 minutes of extreme pleasure. This price includes being picked up and dropped off at your hotel.

The cheapest way to arrange a flight is to go right to the far end of Pepino beach on Avenida Prefeito Mendes de Moraes, where the flyers hang out at the Vôo Livre club. During the week, you can probably get a flight for around US$60.

Ruy Marra is an excellent tandem glider pilot and widely regarded as one of the best in Rio. He runs Super Fly Agency (☎ 3322-2286, ☎ 9982-5703) in São Conrado and is also the person to see if you're interested in para-gliding. Paulo Celani and Dehilton Carvalho of Just Fly (☎ 2208-9822, ☎ 9985-7540, flycelani@ax.apc.org) are both highly experienced tandem hang gliding flyers. Paulo is the pilot who was featured in the Lonely Planet Brazil video. The Associação Brasileiro de Vôo Livre (☎ 3322-0266) offers classes in hang gliding.

Ultra-leve (ultralight) flights are more comfortable than hang gliding, but you have to listen to the motor. The trips leave from the Aeroclube do Jacarepaguá. The Clube Esportivo UltraLeves (☎ 2441-1880), north of Barra da Tijuca, has some long-range ultralights that can stay up for more than two hours. Fifteen-minute flights cost around US$30.

Helicopter Flights

Joy flights over the city can be arranged by Helisight (☎ 2511-2141, infohsgt@helisight .com.br). Helisight has four helipads at strategic and scenic locations: Pier Mauá

Flying Over Rio

The drive up to the takeoff point with Paulo the hang gliding pilot was awesome. Pedra Bonita looms over Pepino beach in São Conrado. The road winds up through the lush green Tijuca forest. We were waved through the private entrance to the hang gliding area, and our car's engine whined as we climbed the extremely steep hill.

When we reached the top, Paulo assembled the glider, untangled the cables, tightened the wing nuts, and slipped elastic bands over the wing struts. Up close the glider looked flimsy. We put on our flight suits and practiced a few takeoff sprints near the platform, a 5m-long runway of wooden boards inclined at a 15° downhill angle. We were 550m above sea level and a few kilometers inland from the beach. If I were a rock, it would take me more than 10 seconds to kiss the dirt.

I wore old sneakers for traction and two good-luck charms to amuse the ambulance crew that I anticipated would be searching through the tangled ball of crumpled metal, torn nylon and mangled flesh that would surely end up down below.

With the glider resting at the top of the runway, we clipped ourselves onto it and checked the balance of the craft as we hung side by side. Paulo adjusted his weight belt, all the straps, the leg cuffs and helmet and gave me very brief instructions: Hold on to the cuff of his shorts, keep my hands to myself, resist the temptation to hold the control bar or cables (this can throw the glider), and when he gave the countdown 'um, dois, tres, ja,' run very fast.

We checked the windsocks on either side of the platform, the surface of the sea and the rippling of the leaves to ascertain the direction, speed and flow of the wind. A smooth wind coming inland from a flat sea is best.

'Um, dois, tres, ja!' Four bounding steps and we were flying. It's not the free-fall sinking feeling you get from elevators, but a perfect calm. I closed my eyes and felt as if I was still – the only movement, a soft wind caressing my face.

Miraculously, it seemed, I was suspended between earth and sky. To our left was Rocinha, the most famous of the zona sul's favelas, to the right Pedra Bonita, and below us the fabulous homes of Rio's rich and famous. We floated over skyscrapers and Pepino beach, made a few lazy circles over the water, and before I knew it, it was time for the descent.

To land we stood upright and pointed the nose up. The glider stalled and we touched down on the sand, gentle as a feather.

downtown at the docks; Mirante Dona Marta, just below Cristo Redentor; Lagoa Rodrigo de Freitas; and Morro da Urca, the first cable-car stop as you go up Pão de Açúcar.

Helisight offers nine different flights to choose from. Five minutes aloft cost US$43, and 30 minutes is US$148 per person. Any of these flights make for a definite 'video opportunity.'

Hiking & Climbing

Excellent hiking is possible, and it is surprisingly close to the city. There are three national parks with trail systems in Rio state: Parque Nacional da Tijuca (see the boxed text 'Parque Nacional & Floresta da Tijuca'), Parque Nacional da Serra dos Órgãos and Parque Nacional do Itatiaia (see the Rio de Janeiro State chapter for information on these latter two parks). Rio Hiking (☎ 2245-4036, tours@riohiking .com.br) offers a variety of guided walks, including Pico da Tijuca, the highest point in the Tijuca massif, Pedra da Gávea, the Sugarloaf and Corcovado.

For anyone interested in climbing or hiking, the Rio's hiking and climbing clubs are unbeatable sources of information, as well as the best place to meet like-minded people. The clubs meet regularly and welcome visitors. All of the following are

Parque Nacional & Floresta da Tijuca

The Tijuca is all that's left of the Atlantic rainforest that once surrounded Rio de Janeiro. In 15 minutes you can go from the concrete jungle of Copacabana to the 120-sq-km tropical jungle of the Parque Nacional da Tijuca. A more rapid and drastic transition is hard to imagine. The forest is an exuberant green, with beautiful trees, creeks and waterfalls, mountainous terrain and high peaks. It has an excellent, well-signposted trail system. Candomblistas leave offerings by the roadside, families have picnics, and serious hikers climb the 1012m to the summit of **Pico da Tijuca**.

The heart of the forest is in the Floresta (Forest) da Tijuca, where you'll find several waterfalls (including the 35m-high Cascatinha de Taunay), peaks and restaurants. It's a beautiful spot. It is also home to different species of birds and animals, including iguanas and monkeys. This area offers several good day hikes. Maps can be obtained at the small crafts shop just inside the park entrance, which is open 7 am to 9 pm daily.

The entire park closes at sunset and is rather heavily policed. Kids have been known to wander off and get lost in the forest – it's that big. It's best to go by car, but if you can't, catch a No 221, 233 or 234 bus or take the metro to Sãens Pena and catch a bus going to Barra da Tijuca and get off at Alta da Boa Vista, the small suburb close to the park entrance.

The best route by car is to take Rua Jardim Botânico two blocks past the Jardim Botânico (heading east from Gávea). Turn left on Rua Lopes Quintas and then follow the Tijuca or Corcovado signs for two quick left turns until you reach the back of the Jardim Botânico, where you turn right. Then follow the signs for a quick ascent into the forest and past the **Vista Chinesa** (get out for a good view) and the **Mesa do Imperador**. Turn right when you seem to come out of the forest on the main road and you'll see the stone columns to the entrance of Alto da Boa Vista on your left after a couple of kilometers. You can also drive up to Alto da Boa Vista by heading out to São Conrado and turning right up the hill at the Parque Nacional da Tijuca signs.

---

well organized and have notice boards listing weekend excursions.

Centro Excursionista Brasileira (☎ 2252-9844, ceb@ceb.rg.br), Avenida Almirante Barroso 2, 8th floor, Centro. CEB meets Thursday at 7 pm to discuss the program for the weekend – geared toward trekking and day hikes. CEB also runs a small restaurant, which is open 6 pm Monday to Friday, where people meet informally to plan excursions.

Centro Excursionista Rio de Janeiro, Avenida Rio Branco 277/805, Centro. CERJ offers the greatest diversity of activities, ranging from hikes to technical climbing. CERJ meets on Tuesday and Thursday evening.

Clube Excursionista Carioca, Rua Hilário de Gouveia 71/206, Copacabana. This club specializes in difficult technical climbing. CEC meets on Wednesday and Friday evenings at 8:30 pm.

Tennis

The climate's not ideal for tennis, but if you fancy a game, you can book a court at the InterContinental (☎ 3322-2200) or Sheraton (☎ 2274-1122). Courts are available to nonguests for around US$10 an hour during the day, a bit more at night. In Barra, you can get a game at the Rio Sport Center (☎ 3325-6644) at Avenida Ayrton Senna 2541, opposite the Terra Encantada amusement park.

Walking & Jogging

There are some good walking and jogging paths in the zona sul. If you're staying in the Catete/Flamengo area, Parque do Flamengo has plenty of space and lots of workout stations. Around Lagoa Rodrigo de Freitas are 9.5km of cycling, jogging and walking track. At the Parque do Cantalago here you can rent bicycles, tricycles or quadricycles. Along the seaside, from Leme to Barra da Tijuca, there's a bike path and footpath. On Sunday the road itself is closed to traffic, and is full of cyclists, joggers, roller-bladers and baby strollers.

Closed to bicycles but not to walkers and joggers is the Pista Cládio Coutinho, between the mountains and the sea at Praia Vermelha in Urca. It's open 7 am to 6 pm daily and is very secure because the army maintains guard posts. People in bathing suits aren't allowed in (unless they're running). It's a nice place to be around sunset.

LANGUAGE COURSES

The Instituto Brasil-Estados Unidos (IBEU; Map 4, ☎ 2548-8332) has a variety of Portuguese language classes that start every month or two. The cost for a four-week course held three times a week is about US$500. For information stop by Avenida NS de Copacabana 690, on the 5th floor.

Next door to IBEU is a Casa Matos store which sells the language books for the IBEU courses. It's a good place to pick up a book or dictionaries to study Portuguese on your own. Other places that offer courses include Britannia (☎ 2511-0143), with branches in Leblon and Ipanema, and Berlitz (☎ 2240-6606) in Centro and Ipanema.

ORGANIZED TOURS
City Tours

Most of the larger tour companies, such as Gray Line (☎ 2512-9919, fax 2259-5847), offer sightseeing tours of Rio. Company brochures can be found on the reception desks of most hotels. These tours cover the usual tourist destinations, and the prices are quite reasonable – a four-hour tour covering Corcovado and Tijuca costs around US$25. The down side is that it's possible to spend more time on the bus as it picks up passengers from other hotels than on the actual tour!

A good alternative to this type of tour is the municipal City Tour bus (☎ 0800-258060) Three *very* air-conditioned buses take you to 270 sightseeing spots. Tickets are available from hotel desks or on the buses and cost US$11, $20 or $28 for 24, 48 or 72 hours respectively. Passengers receive a map with route descriptions in English, Spanish, French and Portuguese. The buses also offer audio descriptions (in four languages) on personal earphones. You can

hop on or off the buses anytime you like. They run daily from 8 am to 6 pm at half-hour intervals. Various routes and tickets are available at Riotur or on the buses themselves.

For a more personalized tour, there are several excellent independent Carioca operators, all of whom will pick you up and drop you off at your hotel. It is recommended that you book with them directly. This ensures you get the tour you want at the best price. If you book from your hotel, the desk clerk may decide to add commission, or even place you on an inferior tour, just because there is a kickback from a certain tour operator.

You also might want to try a tour by Luis Amaral (☎ 2259-5532, riolife@travelrio.com). They are a good way to get to know Rio without feeling like a complete tourist, and Luis is a friendly guy who can put together a tour to do whatever you want. Have a look at his Web site (www.travelrio.com) for full details (in English) about his tours.

Pedro Novak of Qualitour (☎/fax 2232-9710, pnovak@trip.com.br) is another recommended operator who offers jeep tours to a variety of destinations within the city and farther out in Rio state. Pedro speaks English, German, French, Hungarian and, of course, Portuguese.

Rio Jeep Adventures (☎ 2208-9822, ☎ 9985-7540, flycelani@ax.apc.org) does fun, four-hour tours of the Tijuca forest for US$35 per person, as well as some to the beaches farther afield such as Prainha and Grumari.

Historic Rio Tours

Run by art historian Professor Carlos Roquette (☎ 3322-4872, ☎ 9911-3829), who speaks English and French as well as Portuguese, these tours bring old Rio to life.

Itineraries include a night at the Teatro Municipal, colonial Rio, baroque Rio, imperial Rio and a walking tour of Centro. Professor Roquette really knows his city, and if you have an obscure question, he seems to welcome the challenge. The professor charges US$50 for a four-hour tour and US$10 for each additional hour.

Naif artist and multilingual tour guide Fabio Sombra (☎/fax 2275-8605, fasombra@ mail.com) offers some excellent cultural tours. His most popular is 'Historical Rio with Santa Teresa,' a four-hour tour that takes you to the ruins of the old port, the historical sites of Praça 15, the monastery of São Bento and the Catedral Metropolitana. It also passes you through Cinelândia and Lapa, and ends in Santa Teresa at Bar do Arnaudo. This tour costs US$70 for four people. Fabio also customizes tours if you want something different. He also enjoys visitors to his studio at Rua Dr Xavier Sigaud 205 (about 10 minutes walk from the Sugarloaf in Urca), where he gives a colorful slide show called 'Rio Folk Experience.' Call in advance before you drop by.

Tram Tours

A couple of interesting and enjoyable tours run on the special tourist trams that leave every Saturday from the tram station downtown on Rua Lélio Gama (Map 2). The *bonde ecológico* (ecological tram) that leaves at 10 am runs through Santa Teresa to the Dois Irmãos stop. The *bonde histórico* (historic tram) leaves at 2 pm and passes through Santa Teresa to the Largo das Neves. The tram drivers are real characters. Both tours cost US$3 each. For more information, call the tram museum (☎ 2222-1003), mentioned earlier in the Santa Teresa Tram section.

Favela Tours

This is one of the most interesting tours in Rio, and is highly recommended. If you want to visit a favela (shantytown), you'd be crazy to do it on your own. Since large amounts of drugs (mostly cocaine) are trafficked through them each week, there are lots of young, heavily armed characters around.

The safest option is to join one of the favela tours that now operate throughout the city. English-speaking Marcelo Armstrong (☎ 3322-2727, ☎ 9989-0074) is the pioneer of favela tourism.

He takes individuals and small groups to visit Rocinha, the largest favela in Rio, and also to Vila Canoas near São Conrado.

These tours include a visit to private houses, a school and a medical center. You will come away with an excellent idea how a favela operates as a social unit.

You can take a camera, but use common sense – it's courteous to ask permission before taking anybody's picture, and for heaven's sake don't even look like you're about to photograph suspicious or armed characters

Marcelo also conducts a variety of other interesting tours – he's a terrific guide who really knows the city.

SPECIAL EVENTS

Carnaval is, of course, Rio's biggest and most famous bash (see the special section following this chapter). There are, however, many other exciting events that take place at other times of year.

Dia de São Sebastião

January 20 – The patron saint of the city is commemorated with a procession carrying his image from the Igreja de São Sebastião dos Capuchinos in Tijuca (Rua Haddock Lobo 266) to the Catedral Metropolitana, where it's blessed in a mass celebrated by the Archbishop of Rio de Janeiro.

Dia da Fundação da Cidade

March 1 – The founding of the city by Estácio de Sá in 1565 is commemorated with a mass in the church of its patron saint, São Sebastião.

Sexta-Feira da Paixão

March or April – Good Friday is celebrated throughout the city. The most important ceremony is a re-enactment of the Stations of the Cross under the Arcos da Lapa, carried out by more than a hundred actors and actresses.

Festas Juninas

June – The June Festival is one of the most important folkloric festivals in Brazil. In Rio, it's celebrated in various public squares throughout the month, primarily on June 13 (Dia de Santo Antônio), June 24 (São João) and June 29 (São Pedro).

Festa da São Pedro do Mar

July 13 – The fishing community pays homage to its patron saint in a maritime procession. Decorated boats leave from the fishing district of Caju and sail to the statue of São Pedro in Urca.

Festa de NS da Glória do Outeiro

August 15 – A solemn mass is held in the Igreja

NS da Glória do Outeiro, ablaze with decorated lights, with a procession into the streets of Glória to mark the Feast of the Assumption. This festa includes music and colorful stalls set up in the Praça NS da Glória. Festivities start at 8 am and continue all day.

Dia de Independência do Brasil
September 7 – Independence Day is celebrated with a big military parade down Avenida Presidente Vargas. It starts at 8 am at Candelária and goes just past Praça Onze, just north of the Sambódromo.

Festa da Penha
October – This is one of the largest religious and popular festivals in the city. It takes place every Sunday in October and the first Sunday in November, at Igreja NS da Penha de França, Largo da Penha 19. It's very lively.

Rio Jazz Festival
October – Dates vary from year to year, but the Rio Jazz Festival is when the beautiful people of Rio all come out together for three nights of great music. Both national and international acts present a wide variety of music – not only jazz.

New Year & Festa de Iemanjá
December 31 – New Year's Eve in Rio is celebrated by millions of people. Tons of fireworks explode in the sky over Copacabana. New Year's Eve coincides with the Festival de Iemanjá, the sea goddess. Wearing white, the faithful carry a statue of Iemanjá to the beach and launch flowers and other offerings into the sea.

PLACES TO STAY

Rio's accommodations give you a choice of the good, the bad or the musty. Hotels are ranked by Embratur, the federal tourism authority, from two-star for the cheaper (musty) ones to five-star for the most luxurious. The cheapest hotels are unclassified, but still regulated.

So what do the stars mean? Well, a five-star hotel has a pool or two, at least two very good restaurants, a nightclub and bar, gym, sauna and a beauty salon. A four-star hotel has a good restaurant, a sauna and a bar. A three-star hotel may have everything a four-star hotel has, but there's something that downgrades it – the furnishings may be a bit beat-up, cheaper, or a bit sparser.

There's a big gap between three stars and two stars. A two-star hotel is usually clean and comfortable (and musty), but that's about all. By the way, all hotels with a star rating have air-conditioning in the rooms, though some of the older models are very noisy. All rated hotels also have a small *frigobar* (refrigerator) in the rooms, either empty, or full of nibbles costing double what they would in the nearby supermarket. Bathrooms also have bidets, a sign of the European influence.

Below two stars there are still plenty of decent places if you're traveling on a tight budget and need a safe place to sleep. Air-conditioning is usually optional (if available), but mostly the rooms have fans.

Breakfast is usually included in room rates but surprisingly, a few of the more expensive places now charge extra. The meal ranges from sumptuous buffets at the top end to a cup of coffee and a bread roll at the bottom. In between there should be fresh juice, good coffee, fresh rolls with a slice each of ham and cheese, as well as plenty of fresh fruit.

Many hotels have a 10% service charge, and will also collect a 5% government room tax. There's even a US$1 to $2 local tourism

The sea goddess Iemanjá

tax charged by some. The cheaper places don't seem to bother with all this.

Reservations are a good idea in Rio, especially if you plan to stay in a mid-range or top-end hotel. Many hotels now offer the option of booking online, but you won't necessarily get a discount that way. In fact the hotel may try and book you into a more expensive room by claiming the cheaper rooms are full at the time you want to stay. Normally you should aim for a discount of around 30% when you book in advance. A couple of Web sites to check for accommodations and for making online reservations are www.ipanema.com and www.riodejaneiro.com.

If you want an ocean view, request it when you make your reservation. It will cost around 20% more. For New Year's Eve and Carnaval, hotel prices go up and everyone gives dire warnings of there being no places to stay. These are not good times to arrive without a reservation, but you should be able to find a room somewhere.

Rates quoted here for mid-range and top-end hotels are for a standard room if you walk in off the street, so you should be able to get the price down a bit by reserving in advance or going through a travel agent.

PLACES TO STAY – BUDGET
Camping
The **Camping Clube do Brasil** (☎ 2490-3400, Estrada do Pontal 5900, Recreio dos Bandeirantes) runs a campground opposite Recreio dos Bandeirantes beach. The price is US$7 per person, but during December and January it's members only.

Hostels
Rio has a couple of quite good youth hostels. The HI hostel **Albergue da Juventude Chave do Rio de Janeiro** (Map 4; ☎ 2286-0303, fax 2286-5652, riohostel@riohostel .com.br, Rua General Dionísio 63) in Botafogo is a model youth hostel. You'll meet lots of young Brazilians here from all over the country. It gets busy, so you need to make reservations. The only problem with this place is its location, but if you get the hang of the buses quickly, it shouldn't hamper you too much. From the Novo Rio

bus station, catch a No 170, 172 or 173 bus and ask the driver to let you off at the Largo dos Leões. Go up Rua Voluntários da Pátria to Rua General Dionísio, then turn left. The hostel charge US$13 for HI members, a bit more during summer. Nonmembers get charged 50% more and can stay only 24 hours. Student-card holders pay US$3 more than members. Breakfast is included.

In Copacabana there is the non-HI hostel **Copacabana Praia** (Map 5; ☎ 2547-5422, Rua Tenente Marones de Gusmão 85), near the Hotel Santa Clara. Although it's a few blocks from the beach, it's still a good value. A relaxed and friendly place, it costs US$13 for dormitory beds and US$40 for apartments with a stove and a refrigerator. These apartments will sleep up to four people. Sheet rental for the dorm beds is an extra US$3.

Hotels
The best area for budget hotels is around Glória, Catete and Flamengo. This used to be a desirable part of the city, and is still quite nice. Many of the places used to be better hotels, so you can get some pleasant rooms at very reasonable prices. These hotels are often full from December to February, so reservations are not a bad idea. At other times, you can usually find a place quite easily.

From Glória to Lapa, on the edge of the business district near the aqueduct (Map 2), there are several budget hotels. Generally, these are barely cheaper than the hotels farther from the city, in Catete, but the Glória to Lapa area is less safe at night. If, however, everything else is booked up, you'll see several hotels if you walk along Rua Joaquim Silva (near the Passeio Público), then over to Avenida Mem de Sá, turn up Avenida Gomes Freire and then take a right turn into Praça Tiradentes. The **Hotel Marajó** (Map 2; ☎ 2224-4134, Rua Joaquim Silva 99) is recommended. Single/double/triple apartamentos are priced at US$15/23/36. An apartamento with two single beds costs US$27.

Glória (Maps 2 & 4) Right near the Glória metro station, the men-only **Hotel Benjamin**

Constant (Map 2; Rua Benjamin Constant 10) is one of the cheapest places around. The rooms are small and dingy, but cost only US$4 per person without breakfast. A bit better is the *Hospedaría Glória* (Map 4; ☎ 2558-8064, Rua do Catete 34), another men-only place with quartos for US$4. Owner Pepe, from Spain, is a veteran traveler.

The best budget place is *Hotel Turístico* (Map 2; ☎ 2557-7698, fax 2558-9388, Ladeira da Glória 30). It's one of Rio's most popular budget hotels, even though the prices are getting a bit high. There are always plenty of gringos staying here. It's across from the Glória metro station, 30m up the street that emerges between two sidewalk restaurants. The rooms are clean and safe, with small balconies. The hotel is often full, but they do take reservations. Single quartos cost US$20 and prices for single/double apartamentos start at US$25/35.

Catete (Map 4) On the quiet Rua Arturo Bernardes are the cheapest hotels in Catete: The *Monterrey* (☎ 2265-9899) and the *Hotel Rio Lisboa* (☎ 2265-9599) are at Nos 39 and 29. At the Monterrey, single/double quartos go for US$10/15 (US$20 for two single beds) and apartamentos cost US$15/20. At the Rio Lisboa, single quartos cost US$8 and apartamentos are US$12/18.

On busy Rua do Catete are several budget hotels worthy of note. The *Hotel Monte Blanco* (☎ 2225-0121), at No 160, a few steps from the Catete metro stop, is reasonably clean and has air-conditioned apartamentos for US$14/22. Ask for a quiet room in the back; they have round beds and sparkling wall paint. Up the stairs at No 172, the *Hotel Vitória* (☎ 2205-5397, fax 2557-0159) is one of the best budget hotels in the area. It has clean apartamentos for US$14/20. The *Hotel Rio Claro* (☎ 2558-5180), a few blocks down at No 233, has musty singles for US$15 and also doubles with air-conditioning, TV and hot shower for US$19.

The *Hotel Hispáno Brasileiro* (☎ 2265-5990, Rua Silveira Martins 135), has big, clean apartamentos. Singles are US$15 and doubles US$25. Facing the Parque do Catete at Rua Silveira Martins 20, the *Hotel*

Inglês (☎ 2558-3052, fax 2558-3447) is a faded but decent two-star hotel, where singles/doubles/triples cost US$26/33/42.

Some hotels in Catete have barred groups of young backpackers because they have gained a reputation for making too much noise and cooking in the rooms. Those that still accept them includes the *Vitória*, *Monte Blanco* and *Hispáno Brasileiro*.

Flamengo (Map 4) Near the Largo do Machado metro station, the elegant Rua Paissandu has two reasonable budget hotels. The *Hotel Venezuela* (☎ 2557-7098), at No 34, is a bit shabby. All the rooms have double beds, air-conditioning, TV and hot water; single/double apartamentos cost US$13/25. The *Hotel Paysandú* (☎/fax 2558-7270), at No 23, is a two-star Embratur hotel with dark and dingy quartos for US$14/28 and apartamentos for US$20/33.

Copacabana (Map 5) The *Pousada Girassol* (☎/fax 2256-6951, Travessa Angrense 25A) offers cheerful, comfortable apartamentos with ceiling fans for US$20/35/45 for a single/double/triple. It's in an excellent location and offers very good value. Next door, at No 25, the *Hotel Angrense* (☎/fax 2548-0509, angrense@antares.com.br) has clean but dreary quartos for US$20/35 and apartamentos for US$25/45. English is spoken here.

Hotel Copa Linda (☎ 2267-3399) has small and basic rooms for US$35 single or double. It's at Avenida NS de Copacabana 956 on the 2nd floor.

PLACES TO STAY – MID-RANGE

If you want to be near the beach, there are several reasonably priced hotels in Copacabana, a couple in Ipanema and even some in Leblon. They all get seriously busy in the high season between Christmas and Carnaval, so it might pay to book ahead.

For roughly the same price as these Copa, Ipanema and Leblon lodgings, you can get a cheerier room in Flamengo or in Centro near Cinelândia (these hotels are also conveniently within range of the airport or bus station). There are also a few places in Barra da Tijuca, but this is a long way out from the action, and you'll be spending a lot of money on taxis or time on buses.

Andesol and Convencional Turismo (see the Travel Agencies section earlier in this chapter) have a good selection of discounted, mid-range hotels available.

Centro (Map 2)

The three star *Center Hotel* (☎ 2233-6781, fax 2283-1689, centerhotel@bigfoot.com, Avenida Rio Branco 33) provides decent single/double apartamentos for US$40/45, plus a 10% service charge. The English-language brochure says, 'The Hotel owns individual safes for guests to keep documents and other worthless objects.'

Cinelândia (Map 2)

The *Itajuba Hotel* (☎ 2210-3163, fax 2240-7461, itahotel@openlink.com.br, Rua Álvaro Alvim 23) is a good base for experiencing the street Carnaval of Rio. It has rooms with refrigerators and is (usually) quiet. Apartamentos are US$27/44. Nearby is the *Ambassador Hotel* (☎ 2297-7181, fax 2220-4783, ambassador@uol.com.br, Rua Senador Dantas 25), with parking and a restaurant. Rooms cost US$35/43, with a discount for cash.

Glória (Map 2)

Behind a beautiful white facade is the five-star *Glória* (☎ 2555-7272, fax 2555-7282, hgloria@iis.com.br, Rua do Russel 632). Once a grand 1920s beachfront hotel, the Glória fell off the pace when the big luxury hotels went up in Copacabana and Ipanema. It even lost its beach to the big landfill of 1965 that created the Aterro do Flamengo. That didn't stop it from maintaining its status as a fine hotel. It was upgraded and renovated in 1990, and it's easily the best hotel close to the city center. Favored by business travelers, package tour groups and politicians, the Glória is a classy place. Singles/doubles start at US$75/85.

Catete & Flamengo (Map 4)

The *Hotel Imperial* (☎ 2556-5212, fax 2558-5815, Rua do Catete 186) is a funky hotel, which provides parking. The quality and prices of the rooms vary, starting at US$35/40 for apartamentos. Some of the rooms have air-conditioning, and all are very clean.

At Rua Ferreira Viana 29, *Regina Hotel* (☎ 2556-1647, fax 2285-2999, hotelregina@hotelregina.com.br) is a respectable mid-range hotel with a snazzy lobby, clean rooms and hot showers. Apartamentos here start at US$40/45.

The three-star *Flamengo Palace* (☎ 2557-7552, fax 2265-2846, Praia do Flamengo 6), next to the Novo Mundo Hotel, has comfortable apartamentos with a view of Pão de Açúcar for US$55/60. Rooms without the view are US$48/55. For all rooms, there's a 10% service charge.

Nearby, the *Novo Mundo* (☎ 2557-6226, fax 2265-2369, reservas@hotelnovomundorio.com.br, Praia do Flamengo 20) was once a luxury hotel, but has slipped a bit. It still provides good service and a great view of Pão de Açúcar at US$75/88 for a standard apartamento.

Leme (Map 5)

The *Acapulco* (☎ 2275-0022, fax 2275-3396, Rua Gustavo Sampaio 854), is a well-located three-star Embratur hotel with apartamentos costing US$40/60. There's no service charge. It's one block from the beach, behind the Meridien Hotel.

Copacabana (Map 5)

The *Hotel Santa Clara* (☎ 2256-2650, fax 2547-4042, reserva@hotelsantaclara.com.br, Rua Décio Vilares 316), is a delightful mid-price option, with single/double apartamentos starting at US$50/60.

The *Grande Hotel Canada* (☎ 2257-1864, fax 2255-3705, hotel.canada@uol.com.br, Avenida NS de Copacabana 687) has apartamentos starting at US$50/60, less in low season. The rooms are modern, with air-con and TV. It's two blocks from the beach, in a busy area.

The *Hotel Martinique* (☎ 2522-1652, fax 2287-7640) combines a perfect location with good rooms at a moderate price. It's on the quiet Rua Sá Ferreira at No 30, one block from the beach at the south end of Copacabana. Clean, comfortable rooms with air-conditioning start at US$44/54, and a few shoebox singles are US$33.

Also one block from the beach is the two star *Hotel Toledo* (☎ 2257-1995, fax 2257-1931, Rua Domingos Ferreira 71). The rooms are as fine as those in many higher priced hotels. Starting at US$50/60, aparta-mentos are a good value, and there are also some tiny singles for US$30.

The *Biarritz Hotel* (☎ 2522-0542, fax 2287 7640) is a small place at Rua Aires de Saldanha 54, close to the beach behind the Rio Othon Palace. Double apartamentos start at US$55, and all rooms have air-conditioning and TV. It also has mini singles for US$30. Also try the *Apa Hotel* (☎ 2548-8112, fax 2256-3628, apa@apahotel.com.br, Rua República do Peru 305) three blocks from the beach and two blocks from the metro. Rooms here are US$45/50. It has friendly, English-speaking staff.

If you want to spend more money and stay on the beachfront, the *Hotel Debret* (☎ 2522-0132, fax 2521-0899, Avenida Atlân-tica 3564) is a traditional hotel in a converted apartment building. It has attractive colonial-style furnishings and rooms from US$49/55. Rooms with a sea view are US$70. The en-trance is on Rua Almirante Gonçalves.

Right on the division of Copacabana and Ipanema, the *Atlantis Copacabana* (☎ 2521-1142, fax 2287-8896, atlantishotel@ uol.com.br, Rua Bulhões de Carvalho 61) is a good deal at US$75 for a double.

Ipanema & Leblon (Map 6)

There are two relatively inexpensive hotels in Ipanema. The *Hotel San Marco* (☎/fax 2540-5032, Rua Visconde de Pirajá 524) is a couple of blocks from the beach. Rooms are small but do have air-conditioning, TV and refrigerator. Single/double apartamentos start at US$45/55. The *Hotel Vermont* (☎ 2521-0057, fax 2267-7046, Rua Visconde de Pirajá 254) also has simple rooms at US$75/80.

You can get a seaside apartment at the *Arpoador Inn* (☎ 2523-0060, fax 2511-5094, arpoador@unisys.com.br, Rua Francisco Otaviano 177). This six-floor hotel is the only one in Ipanema or Copacabana that doesn't have a busy street between it and the beach. The musty beachfront rooms are more expensive than those facing the street, but the view and the roar of the surf make it all worthwhile. Rooms without the view cost US$50/57, with view US$100/115.

The *Ipanema Inn* (☎ 2523-6092, 2511-5094, arpoador@unisys.com.br, Rua Maria Quitéria 27), around the corner from the Caesar Park, may appeal to beach-loving and budget-conscious travelers who don't mind beat-up rooms. TV is an optional extra and the hotel provides umbrellas and towels for the beach. Apartamentos cost US$60/68.

PLACES TO STAY – TOP END
Leme (Map 5)

Le Meridien (☎ 2275-9922, fax 2541-6447, pubrel@domain.com.br, Avenida Atlântica 1020) is modern, luxurious and chic. The Meridien is popular with Europeans and business travelers. Rooms start at US$180/ 200, US$220/240 with a sea view. On New Year's Eve, the hotel turns into a fireworks cascade.

Copacabana (Map 5)

Of the many top hotels in Rio, the 1920s style *Copacabana Palace Hotel* (☎ 2548-7070, fax 2235-7330, business.center@ copacabanapalace.com.br, Avenida Atlân-tica 1702) is favored by royalty and rock stars. It is truly a symbol of the city, and, after a massive facelift, it is a modern luxury hotel as well. With a great pool and excel-lent restaurants, the Copacabana Palace is a wonderful splurge. Standard apartamentos cost US$300/315.

The *Rio Othon Palace* (☎ 2522-1522, fax 2522-1697, rio@othon.com.br, Avenida Atlântica 3264) is another Copacabana landmark. Many US travel agents consider it the best five-star hotel on the beach, so consequently it's a favorite with package tourists. Varig also has a check-in counter in the lobby, so clients don't need to go to the airport so early. Rooms start at US$220; the suites are well appointed.

The *Sofitel Rio Palace* (☎ 2525-1232, fax 2525-1200, Avenida Atlântica 4240) has excellent views and luxurious public areas. It's very popular with US tourists and has a long list of stars who have stayed here – Frank Sinatra once sang in the auditorium. Rooms start at US$230/250, but the hotel often offers a discount. A plus is the Cassino Atlântico shopping center, which is right here.

Ipanema & Leblon (Map 6)

The *Everest Rio Hotel* (☎ 2522-2282, fax 2521-3198, reservas@everest.com.br, Rua Prudente de Morais 1117) is a modern five-star place a block from the beach. The floor-to-ceiling windows are a nice touch. Its suites are good for families, and there's a small playground. Singles/doubles are US$240/264, with a corporate discount of 40%.

The *Sol Ipanema* (☎ 2523-0095, fax 2247-8484, hotel@solipanema.com.br, Avenida Viera Souto 320), on the beachfront, is a quiet hotel opposite Posto 9, where the beautiful people go. It supplies towels, chairs and umbrellas. Double rooms start at US$182, but the view is definitely worth an extra US$40.

The *Caesar Park* (☎ 2525-2525, fax 2521-6000, Avenida Vieira Souto 460), is favored by ex-dictators and businesspeople with large expense accounts. Service is impeccable, and security is tight on the beach in front. Apartamentos begin at US$250.

PLACES TO STAY – LONG-TERM

A relatively inexpensive option in the zona sul is to rent an apartment by the week or the month. Look under *temporada* or *apartamentos para aluguel* in any daily newspaper. If you just want a room in someone's house or apartment, check the listings under *vaga* or *quarto*.

There are loads of rental agencies. You could try *Copacabana Holiday* (Map 5; ☎ 2542-1525, fax 2542-1597, Rua Barata Ribeiro 90A), in Copacabana. They rent apartments for a minimum of three days starting from US$75. The manager, Lúcio, speaks conversational English and is very helpful.

Apartur Imóveis (Map 5; ☎ 2287-5757, Rua Visconde de Pirajá 371 S/204), in Ipanema,

offers similar deals. *Fantastic Rio* (Map 5; ☎ 2541-0615, fax 2543-2667, hpcorr@ hotmail.com, Avenida Atlântica 974, apartment 501), in Leme, rents luxury apartments, from one-bedroom flats to four-bedroom beachfront places. Prices vary according to length of stay, but they're definitely a good value.

Also recommended is multilingual *Yvonne Reimann* (☎ 2267-0054, Avenida Atlântica 4066, apartamento 605), who rents self-contained flats for a week or more. Prices are around US$40 a night for a two-room flat.

There are numerous residential hotels, or *aparthoteis*, which are often more spacious and less expensive than normal hotels. This sector has grown quickly over the last few years, so there are lots of small, modern apartments available. Prices vary from the middle to the top end, and low-season discounts are usually available. Riotur's *Rio Incomparável* guide has a full listing of aparthotels in the various suburbs.

Close to the metro, the *Copacabana Hotel Residência* (Map 5; ☎ 2548-7212, fax 2235-1828, Rua Barata Ribeiro 222) provides serviced apartments for about US$100 a night, or US$1850 a month.

Ipanema Flat Hotel Residência (Map 6; ☎ 2523-1292, fax 2287-9844, Rua Gomes Carneiro 137) has apartamentos with kitchen for US$100 a day and US$1500 a month.

In Leblon *Rio Flat Service* (Map 6; ☎ 2239-4598, fax 2259-2191, Rua Almirante Guilhem 322) has three residential hotels that are more like apartments, with a living room and kitchen. The flat service also offers a swimming pool, and provides breakfast and room service. Apartments start at US$100 a night, or US$1500 a month.

PLACES TO EAT

There's lots of fast food in Rio: You'll see the McDonald's golden arches all over the place, as well as a local version called *Bobs*. There are other chains around the city, like Pizza Hut, Domino's Pizza and Subway Sandwiches. A good budget option with several locations in Copacabana and Ipanema is *Sindicato do Chopp*, which has cheap, decent food and excellent draught beer. Pizzas are a popular Brazilian fast food, and you'll see plenty of pizzerias. Pizzas are standard menu items in most restaurants.

Traditional Brazilian fast food can be found at the juice bars and the *botecos*. Botecos (often called *botequims*) are the local bars of Cariocas. Patrons drop in for a cafezinho and a shot of cachaça before work, and a snack, a caipirinha or a chopp later in the day. Botecos are not known for cleanliness, but nobody seems to mind – not the Cariocas anyway. The quality of food served by botecos varies but can be good. Try such savory delights as a *coxina de galinha* (savory chicken wrapped in dough), a *pastel de palmito* (small pastry with palm heart inside) or a *pão de queijo* (cheese-filled ball of pastry).

The *pratos feitos* (literally, made plates) of meat, beans and rice at the many botecos are big enough to feed two, and the price is only US$4 to $5. For something lighter, and probably healthier, you can eat at a juice bar. Most have sandwiches and fruit salads.

Self-serve per-kilo restaurants are handy for travelers who don't speak much Portuguese. Help yourself to the hot and cold buffets, then get your plate weighed and order a drink, which is brought to your table. Price and quality, though, vary greatly. You usually pay the bill on the way out, so don't lose the ticket.

Galetos are small restaurants serving chicken and steak grilled over the open flame as you sit behind the counter and watch; Cariocas of all kinds sidle up to the counter and dig into a chicken with a couvert of chopped onions, tomato and bread rolls. The whole thing costs around US$5. You'll do plenty of finger lickin'.

Eating in Rio is not expensive unless you want to splurge. Eateries for which no prices are quoted in the following listings are all reasonably cheap.

Make a habit of asking for an *embalagem* (doggie bag) when you don't finish your food. Then wrap it up and hand it to a street person.

Centro (Map 2)

Bar Luis (☎ 2262-6900, *Rua da Carioca 39*) is a Rio institution that opened in 1887. The city's oldest *cervejaria* (pub), on Rio's most venerable street, is a bar-less old dining room serving good German food and the best dark draft beer in Rio at moderate prices. It's open for lunch, and for dinner until midnight from Monday to Saturday.

Another landmark is the **Confeitaria Colombo** (☎ 2232-2300, *Rua Gonçalves Dias 34*), one block west of Avenida Rio Branco on a parallel street. It's a big, ornate, turn-of-the-century coffeehouse and restaurant where you can sit down for a meal, or stand if you're just having a dessert or cake. The Colombo is best for coffee and cake or a snack. Another old-style coffeehouse is **Casa Cavé** (☎ 2221-0533), on the corner of Rua 7 de Setembro and Rua Uruguiana. It has good ice cream and traditional ambience.

Inside the Paço Imperial on Praça 15 de Novembro, the **Atrium** (☎ 2220-0193) and the **Bistro do Paço** (☎ 2533-6353) are both very popular with locals. The Atrium is a classy lunch spot, and the Bistro has a varied French/Swiss menu with daily specials. After lunch you can wander around the exhibitions.

The green gazebo structure near the Niterói ferry is **Restaurante Alba Mar** (☎ 2240-8378, *Praça Marechal Âncora 184*). It looks out on the Baía de Guanabara and Niterói. Go for the view and the seafood. Dishes start at US$20, and the *peixe brasileira* (fish in coconut milk) is recommended.

Café do Teatro (☎ 2262-4164, *Avenida Rio Branco*), under the Teatro Municipal, is a place to recall the good old days. Entering the dark, dramatic Assyrian Room, with its elaborate tilework and ornate columns, is like walking into a Cecil B DeMille film. The 80-year-old restaurant is where the upper crust of Rio used to dine and drink after the theater, and it must be seen to be believed. The café serves lunch only and closes on Saturday and Sunday. It's somewhat expensive and semiformal, but don't be deterred – you can have a drink and light snack by the bar, listen to piano music, and breathe in the Assyrian atmosphere.

A recommended self-serve place downtown is **Mr Ôpi** (☎ 2224-5820, *Rua da Alfândega 91*), where sushi is included in the buffet.

Lapa (Map 2)

Restaurante Ernesto (☎ 2221-4116, *Lago da Lapa 41*) is close to the arch of the viaduct that the tram crosses on the way to Santa Teresa. It's a good place to eat if you've been to a show in the city.

Bar Brasil (☎ 2509-5943, *Avenida Mem de Sá 90*) and *Nova Capela* (☎ 2252-6228, *Avenida Mem de Sá 96*) are two traditional places dating from the beginning of the 1900s. Bar Brasil serves German food with a Brazilian touch, and one plate will easily feed two. Nova Capela is a great late-night place, with good, cheap, traditional Portuguese food. Its bad-tempered waiters are legendary.

Santa Teresa (Map 2)

In picturesque Santa Teresa, the bar/restaurants around Largo dos Guimarães are very lively on weekends. *Bar do Arnaudo* (☎ 2252-9246, *Rua Almirante Alexandrino 316B*) has some of the best Northeastern food in the city and a great view. Try the excellent *carne do sol* (grilled salt meat).

Close by, *Sobrenatural* (☎ 2616-4349, *Rua Almirante Alexandrino 432*) is a casual bar/restaurant with tasty snacks. On the weekend there's live music, and a lot of young people crowd the street outside. *Sobrado dos Massas*, at the Curvelo tram stop down the hill from Largo dos Guimarães, serves Santa Teresa's best *feijoada* every Saturday.

Glória & Catete (Maps 2 & 4)

Choppança (☎ 2557-7847, *Rua do Russel 32B*) has friendly service and good cheap food. Steak and rice is US$6 and pizzas cost US$5. Next door, *Taberna da Glória* (☎ 2265-7835, *Rua do Russel 32A*) is good for Brazilian staple dishes, like the Sunday *cozido*, roast piglet on Thursday and *feijoada* on Saturday.

Restaurante Amazonia (☎ 2557-4569), upstairs at Rua do Catete 234, serves good steak and a tasty grilled chicken with creamed corn sauce, either for about US$9. For a splurge, eat lunch at the *Museum* (☎ 2558-0969, *Rua do Catete 153*), a chic restaurant in the Museu da República. It has excellent food and a nice, relaxed atmosphere.

Flamengo & Botafogo (Map 4)

The popular *Churrascaria Majórica* (☎ 2205-6820, *Rua Senador Vergueiro 11*), in Flamengo, has good meat, reasonable prices and an interior done in gaúcho kitsch.

Café Lamas (☎ 2556-0799, *Rua Marquês de Abrantes 18A*) has been operating in Flamengo since 1874, and is one of Rio's most renowned eateries. It has a lively and loyal clientele, a typical meaty menu and standard prices – try the grilled *linguiça* (sausage), or filet mignon with garlic.

Providing diners with a great view of the Sugarloaf, *Porção Rios* (☎ 2554-8862, *Avenida Infante Dom Henrique*) is an above-average *churrascaria* in a privileged location in Flamengo Park.

Adega do Valentim (☎ 2541-1166, *Rua da Passagem 176*), is a highly recommended Portuguese restaurant. The baked rabbit with spicy rice is excellent, as are the cod dishes. There is a Portuguese dance show on Friday and Saturday night.

Leme (Map 5)

Máriu's (☎ 2542-2393, *Avenida Atlântica 290*) features an all-the-meat-you-can-eat deal for US$20. Many people think this is the best *churrascaria* in Rio, and they may be right. Be prepared to wait during prime time, as there's always a big tourist crowd.

Restaurante Shirley (☎ 2275-1398, *Rua Gustavo Sampaio 610A*) serves the best Spanish food in Rio. It has delicious seafood plates from US$10 to $25. Try the mussel vinaigrette appetizer or the octopus and squid in ink. One dish serves two easily.

The Meridien hotel, at Avenida Atlântica 1020, is home to some fine restaurants and bars. For French food, there is *Café de la Paix*, and one of Rio's best, *Le Saint Honoré* – supervised by Paul Bocuse – with great food and a spectacular view. Then there's the *Le Rond Point Bar*, which is cozy.

Copacabana (Map 5)

For cheap grilled chicken, there are lots of galetos in Copacabana. These include *O Crack dos Galetos* (*Avenida Prado Junior 63*), one block from the beach, and *Quick*

Galetos (Rua Duvivier 28A), near the Hotel Internacional Rio. *Copa Rio Galetos* (Rua Júlio de Castilhos 36) is farther down, toward the Ipanema end of Copacabana. Close by is *Lope's Confeitaria* (Avenida NS de Copacabana 1334), off Rua Júlio de Castilhos, an excellent lanchonete with big portions and small prices for typical Brazilian food.

Restaurante Lucas (☎ 2523-7194, Avenida Atlântica 3744) has reasonably priced seafood and German dishes starting at US$10.

Arataca (☎ 2548-6624, Rua Domingos Ferreira 41) features the exotic cuisine of the Amazon. This place, around the corner from their regular restaurant (also named Arataca), is actually a counter-lunch stand and deli, with the same food for only half the price. In addition to regional dishes such as vatapá and *pato* (duck), they serve real guaraná juice (try it) and delicious sorbets made from Amazonas fruits.

Mab's (☎ 2275-7299, Avenida Atlântica 1140), on the corner of Rua Prado Junior, has excellent seafood soup in a crock for US$10, chock-full of piping hot marine critters.

Cervantes (☎ 2275-6147, Avenida Prado Junior 335B) is the best sandwich joint in Rio, and is also a late-night hangout for a strange and colorful crew. Meat sandwiches come with pineapple (US$5). The beer, steak and fries are excellent.

Dom Camillo Restaurante & Pizzaria (☎ 2549-9958, Avenida Atlântica 3056) is a beachfront Italian place with wonderful seafood pasta and tiramisu to die for.

The *Manoel e Joaquim* (☎ 2549-3550) bar/restaurants are recommended for their good and inexpensive local food. Try the deep-fried cheese prawns on Greek-style rice. Portions are large, and there is an English version of their menu available. The two branches in Copacabana are at Rua Siqueira Campos 12 and at Avenida Atlântica 1936.

The Copacabana Palace Hotel, at Avenida Atlântica 1702, has restaurants worth trying, among them the formal *Cipriani* and the *Pergula*.

The Sofitel Rio Palace, at Avenida Atlântica 4240, is another hotel with a good restaurant, the *La Pré Catalan*.

Ipanema (Map 6)

In Ipanema, two good self-serve lunch places are the small and friendly *Arab* (Rua Gomes Carneiro 131A) (also good for breakfast), and *Jangadeiros* (Rua Visconde de Pirajá 106), which has a tasty, varied menu and a loyal clientele. The photographs of old Rio on the wall of the latter are a nice touch.

Chaika's (Rua Visconde de Pirajá 321) is where the girl from Ipanema really eats. There's a stand-up fast-food bar, and a restaurant in the back with delicious hamburgers, the sweetest pastries and good cappuccinos (a rarity in Rio). Chaika's stays busy late into the night.

Cia da Fruta, at the corner of Farme de Amoedo and Visconde de Pirajá, is a good juice and sandwich bar.

If you want to eat a feijoada and it isn't Saturday, go to *Casa da Feijoada* (☎ 2247-2776, Rua Prudente de Morais 10B) any day of the week with US$20. This place also offers executive lunch specials for US$10, as well as delicious homemade sweets for dessert.

Yemanjá (☎ 2247-7004, Rua Visconde de Pirajá 128A) offers good Bahian food at a reasonable price, something often hard to find in Rio. The seafood moquecas for US$30 are excellent, and portions are large enough for two.

Barril 1800 (☎ 2523-0085, Avenida Vieira Souto 1800) is open late into the night. This popular beach café is for people-meeting and watching. After a day at Ipanema beach, you can stroll over to the *Caffé Felice* (☎ 2522-7749, Rua Gomes Carneiro 30) for terrific ice cream or a healthy sandwich.

Garota de Ipanema (☎ 2523-3787, Rua Vinícius de Moraes 49), has lively open-air dining. There are always a few foreigners checking out the place where Tom Jobim and Vinícius de Moraes were sitting when they wrote 'The Girl from Ipanema.' The appetizers here are delicious – try the famous kibes (meatballs).

New Natural (☎ 2287-0301, Rua Barão da Torre 167) is a very natural health-food restaurant with an inexpensive lunch special that includes soup, rice, veggies and beans for less than US$5. Other good dishes are pancakes with chicken or vegetables.

Via Farme (☎ 2513-4358, *Rua Farme de Amoedo 47*) offers a good plate of pasta at a reasonable price. The four-cheese pasta and the seafood pasta dishes are excellent, and portions are large enough for two. Most dishes are less than US$15.

Porcão (☎ 2521-0999, *Rua Barão da Torre 218*) has steadily been moving up in the churrasco ratings game. It's an all-you-can-eat feast for about US$20 a person. It's popular with soccer players and other macho types.

Zaza Bistro Tropical (☎ 2247-9102, *Rua Joana Angelica 40*) is a stylish, romantic restaurant with fine French and Thai cuisine. The floor cushions in the upstairs dining room add an exotic touch.

The *Restaurante Galani*, at the Caesar Park Hotel at Avenida Vieira Souto 460, serves a legendary *feijoada* on Saturday. The spectacular breakfast views here make for a good start to the day.

Leblon (Map 6)
Fellini (☎ 2511-3600, *Rua General Orquiza 104*) is a popular, high-quality, self-serve lunch spot. *Celeiro* (☎ 2274-7843, *Rua Dias Ferreira 199*) has a fantastic (and expensive) lunchtime salad bar. *Garcia & Rodrigues* (☎ 2512-8188, *Avenida Ataulfo de Paiva 1251*) is an elegant dinner restaurant, open at 8 pm, which serves wonderful French food with a Brazilian flavor.

Gávea (Map 6)
Guimas (☎ 2259-7996, *Jose Roberto Macedo Soares 5*) is highly recommended. It's not cheap, but the prices (US$15 to $30 per person) are fair for the outstanding cuisine you're served. Guimas offers what many restaurants in Rio lack: creative cooking. Try the trout with leeks or the roast duck with honey-and-pear rice. This small but comfortable open-air restaurant opens at noon and gets very crowded later in the evening. If you order one of the boa lembrança (literally, 'good memory') dessert specials, you'll receive an attractive ceramic plate.

Other Areas
In Barra de Guaratiba, *Tia Palmira* (☎ 2410-8169, *Caminho do Souza 18*) serves traditional Brazilian seafood dishes in a great outdoor setting. It can be very crowded at lunchtime on the weekend.

In Vargem Grande, *Barreado* (☎ 2442-2023, *Estrada dos Bandeirantes 21295*) is a charmingly rustic restaurant serving traditional Brazilian dishes. It's a great spot for a long lunch.

ENTERTAINMENT
Any night of the week is a good one for going out and joining Cariocas at what they love: singing or dancing. Cariocas love to go out late in the evening, and you probably won't meet a gringo who would complain about Rio's nightlife.

To find out what's going on, pick up the *Jornal do Brasil* at any newsstand and turn to the entertainment section. On Friday the publication includes an entertainment magazine called *Programa,* which lists the event for the week. The newspaper *O Globo* includes a *Rio Show* magazine on Friday. For even more listings, check the *Veja Rio* pullout section in the weekly *Veja* magazine. The entertainment sections are easy to figure out, even if you don't speak Portuguese.

Nightlife varies widely by neighborhood. Leblon and Ipanema have upmarket, trendy clubs with excellent jazz. Botafogo is the heart of gay Rio. Cinelândia and Lapa, in the center, have a lot of samba and pagode, and there's been a resurgence of nightlife in the nearby historical neighborhood of Santa Teresa. Copacabana is a mixed bag, with some good local hangouts but also a strong tourist influence with a lot of sex for sale.

There are many fine Brazilian actors and playwrights, but there's not much point going to the theater if you don't understand Portuguese. If you fancy a look anyway, there are full listings available in the publications mentioned in the introduction to this Entertainment section.

Dance Clubs
Rio clubs rival those in San Francisco, New York, and Ibiza. Most discos open around 10, but don't get started until well past midnight. Often clubs have theme nights or

special parties – with various DJs spinning different nights of the week. Some discos have multiple dance floors with DJs spinning different mixes in each. Flyers advertising raves and dance parties can be found near the front door of most clubs. Other places to check for rave flyers and ads are in the surf shops in Galeria River by Praia Aproador, between Ipanema and Copacabana and in the hipper clothing stores.

Expect to pay anywhere from US$4 to US$13 to get into most discos. In general, women pay less than men, if at all.

Favorites include *Cine Irís* (Map 2; ☎ 2262-1729, Rua da Carioca 51, Centro), a porn theater by day, disco dance party by night. The club is often the venue for special parties and rave parties, with techno, trance and disco being the music of choice. *Fundição Progresso* (Map 2; ☎ 2220-5070, Rua dos Arcos, Lapa) holds dance parties throughout the summer.

Bunker 94 (Map 5; ☎ 2521-0367, Rua Raul Pompéia 94, Copacabana) has three rooms with different music. You'll find a mix of twenty-something college students and hipsters grooving to techno, British Invasion hits, and New Wave classics.

Around the corner from Bunker 94, in the basement of Shopping Cassino Atlantico, you'll find *BASE* (Map 5; ☎ 2522-0544, Rua Francisco Otaviano 20A). A standard disco playing rock, pop, and the occasional hip hop evening dance party. Busy on the weekends, this club offers a variety of rooms for dancing, eating, or hanging out.

Ritmo Leblon (Map 5; ☎ 2274-4145, Rua Cupertino Durão 173, Leblon) has a bright, colorful bar, a dance floor, and a very comfortable lounge area with cushy sofas. *Hipodromo Up* (Map 5; ☎ 2294-0095, Praça Santos Dumont 108) plays Brazilian popular music and rock standards, with live shows starting around 10 pm.

Help (Map 5; ☎ 2522-1296, Avenida Atlântica 3432) deserves a special mention here. It calls itself the biggest disco in Latin America and no one seems to doubt it. It's full of 'professional' ladies, and lots of drunken gringos seem to get robbed just outside. That doesn't mean you shouldn't go

there – it's definitely an interesting place – but it couldn't hurt to keep the above-mentioned warning in mind.

Samba If you want to see and hear samba, you can go to one of the big tourist productions, or you can head to one of the samba school rehearsals.

The big tourist shows are corny, glitzy, lavish, Vegas-style performances, with plenty of beautiful, topless mulatas who make samba look easy. The most popular is *Plataforma* (Map 6; ☎ 2274-4022, Rua Adalberto Ferreira 32), in Leblon. Shows start around 10 pm. See the Samba Schools & Shows section below for more information.

Bars

A great way to meet Cariocas is to check out one of the popular zona sul *baixos*. Baixos are small concentrations of bars and cafés. Hanging around baixo-style means having a chopp at an outdoor table while standing in the street, and just looking and chatting. Cariocas aren't known for their formality and are quite happy to converse with friendly strangers.

Bar Brasil (Map 2; ☎ 2509-5943, Avenida Mem de Sá 90), in Lapa is an old bohemian hangout and is always lively (it also serves food; see the Places to Eat section earlier in this chapter). Some Cariocas who live in the zona sul only come into the center to go to Bar Brasil. Lapa, along Avenida Mem de Sá, is generally an interesting area to explore at night.

In Copacabana, the beachfront bars are a good place to have a couple of chopps in the early evening, but as the night wears on things get a little seedier, and it might be time to move on. The *Sindicato do Chopp* (Map 5; Avenida Atlântica 3806 and Rua Santa Clara 18) has two branches in Copacabana, and another in nearby Leme. The Copa locations are popular with locals and get pretty noisy.

Two Rio favorites right next door to each other in Ipanema are *Sindicato do Chopp* (Map 6; ☎ 2523-1745, Rua Farme do Amoedo 85) and *Bar Bofetada* (Map 6; ☎ 2522-9526, Rua Farme do Amoedo 87A) with two floors.

Sindicato has a big indoor patio. Bofetada, which boasts that it is the most Carioca place in all Rio, showcases live choró and bossa nova music. There's also a cluster of restaurants and bars on the corner of Rua Prudente de Morais and Rua Paul Redfern.

There's always a crowd at the **Bar Bracarense** *(Map 6; ☎ 2294-3549, Rua José Linhares 85B, Leblon)*, known for the best salgados (savory snacks) in all of Rio. If you're looking to sample the local firewater, cachaça, the **Academia de Cachaça** *(Map 6; ☎ 2239-1542, Rua Conde de Bernadotte 26A, Leblon)* offers the widest variety from all over Brazil. A visit to the Academia is very worth your while. The range of cachaça here is impressive – some of the good stuff is even smooth!

Located on the busy Leblon intersection of Rua Carlos Góis and Avenida Ataulfo de Paiva you'll find **Casa Clipper** *(Map 6; ☎ 2259-0148, Rua Carlos Góis, 219A)*. With a dozen tables on the sidewalk and an active social crowd swilling chopps, you really can't miss it.

A real hotspot in the zona sul is Praça Santos Dumont in Gávea, especially on Monday night. There are lots of bars, and people hanging around in the streets drinking and looking at everyone else. The outdoor kiosks on the Jardim Botânico side of Lagoa Rodrigo de Freitas are pleasant spots for a drink, and they feature live music nightly.

Gay & Lesbian Venues

Rio's gay community is neither out nor flamboyant most of the year, the exception being at Carnaval time, when anything goes. Still, there is a large gay and lesbian scene in Rio. Here are some places to check out.

If you're spending a day on Copacabana Beach, there is a gay-friendly drink stand on the beach, across the street from the Copacabana Palace Hotel. In Ipanema you'll find the same on the beach across from Rua Farme de Amoedo. There are not any specifically gay neighborhoods in Rio, although traditionally Botafogo and Cinelândia have been popular areas. The most popular gay destinations can be found toward the Ipanema end of Copacabana. You won't find an exclusive concentration of gay establishments, but there are many places where gay and lesbian couples can feel at home.

One of the best bars in Copacabana and a secret by day, is the **Blue Angel** *(Map 5; ☎ 2513-2501, Rua Júlio de Castilhos 15)*. Popular with a mixed clientele during the week, the Blue Angel is dominated by a gay male scene on the weekend and includes a shrine to Bette Davis above the bathrooms. It's a cozy bar with not much room to get down in, although there's usually someone getting down during mid-week when the crowd is smaller.

If you're looking for dancing, two blocks away is the best known gay club **Le Boy** *(Map 5; ☎ 2521-0367, Rua Raul Pompeia 94)*, with dancing on the weekends and drag shows during the week. There's an active scene going on outside this club, and after midnight some of it ends up two doors down at Bunker 94 (see Discos & Clubs).

You'll find lots of gay couples after 10 pm at **Caffe Felice** in Ipanema *(☎ 2522-7749, Rua Gomes Carneiro 30)* and at **Bar Bofetada** *(Map 6; Rua Farme de Amoedo 87A)*, also in Ipanema. **Maxim's Rio** *(Map 5; ☎ 2255-7444, Avenida Atlântica 1850, Copacabana)* is popular with the gay scene during Carnaval and with a diverse crowd the rest of the year.

In Botafogo there used to be a high concentration of gay venues near the intersection of Rua Visconde and Rua Real Grandeza, but that's been changing. Here you'll still find **Loch Ness** *(Map 4; ☎ 2537-9291, 22 Rua Visconde da Silva)*, the bar and restaurant where they have good food and a drag show. Down the street, **Queen Victoria** *(Map 4; ☎ 2530-5332, Rua Visconde da Silva 30)* is a pub and sushi restaurant popular with gay men and lesbians.

Don't feel limited to only these places, there are many other places where young gays hang out, and gay couples are welcome almost everywhere in the city.

Concerts & Music Festivals

Rio is a cultural city in its own right but it also attracts a lot of big international acts.

Concertgoers can see Brazilian stars like Gilberto Gil and Milton Nascimento, as well as international stars like U2, Oasis and the Rolling Stones, who make Rio a stop on their world tours. Citywide music festivals include the Free Jazz Festival and January's Rock in Rio Festival.

There are a number of major venues to check out in and around Rio. *Teatro Rival* (*Map 2*; ☎ 2240-4469, *Rua Álvaro Alvim 33-37*) is a Cinelândia club that stages big shows featuring top Brazilian stars. Tickets range from US$10 to $15.

Canecão (*Map 4*; ☎ 2543-1241, *Avenida Venceslau Brás 215*) is near the Rio Sul shopping mall in Botofogo.

One of the largest venues in Barra de Tijuca is *ATU Hall* (*Map 1*; ☎ 2421-1331, *Avenida Ayrton Senna 3000*), previously named the Metropolitan, where you'll usually find large international acts.

Big concerts also take place on the beaches of Copacabana, Ipanema, Botafogo, and Barra de Tijuca. Ipanema's *Posto 10* is a common place for big acts to perform.

Samba Schools & Shows

In the samba schools, things start to heat up in October. That's when, after intense lobbying, the schools finally choose the *samba do enredo*, the samba that their members will defend with blood, sweat and beer in the Sambódromo during Carnaval. Rehearsals are generally open to the public for watching and joining in. Entry costs only a few dollars, and you can really make a night of it. Check with Riotur or the newspaper for schedules and locations. Here is a listing of the samba schools (the best ones for tourists are generally Salgueiro and Mangueira), rehearsal days and contact information; it is best to confirm this information before heading out for the evening.

Beija-Flor (☎ 2791-2866, *Pracinha Wallace Paes Leme 1025, Nilópolis*), Friday 10 pm, free

Caprichosos de Pilares (☎ 2592-5620, *Rua Faleiros 1, Pilares*), Saturday evening, free before midnight, US$2 after

Grande Rio (☎ 2775-8422, *Rua Almirante Barroso 5 & 6, Duque de Caixas*), Saturday 11 pm, US$3

Imperatriz Leopoldinense (☎ 2560-8037, *Rua Barão de Tefé 1, Fundos*), Saturday 11 pm, US$3

Império Serrano (☎ 3359-4944, *Avenida Ministro Edgard Romero 114, Madureira*), Saturday 10 pm, US$1

Mangueira (☎ 2567-4637, *Rua Visconde de Niterói 1072, Mangueira*), Saturday 7 pm, US$8, across the Bay from Rio in Niterói

Mocidade Independente de Padre Miguel (☎ 3332-5823, *Rua Coronel Tamarindo 38, Padre Miguel*), Saturday 10 pm, free for women until midnight, then US$2, men US$3

Paraíso do Tuiuti (☎ 3860-6298, *Campo de São Cristóvão 33, São Cristóvão*), Friday 11 pm, free

Portela (☎ 2489-6440, *Rua Clara Nunes 81, Madureira*), Thursday 8 pm, Friday 10 pm, women US$1, men US$2

Salgueiro (☎ 2238-5564, *Rua Silva Teles 104, Andaraí*), Saturday 10 pm, US$3

Tradição (*Estrada Intendente Magalhães 160, Campinho*), Friday 10 pm, US$3

União da Ilha do Governador (☎ 3396-4951, *Estrada do Galeão 322, Ilha do Governador*), Saturday 11 pm, women free, men US$3

Unidos da Tijuca (☎ 2516-4053, *Clube dos Portuários, Rua Francisco Bicalho 47, Cidade Nova*), Saturday 10 pm, women free until midnight, then US$2, men US$3

Viradouro (☎ 2628-7840, *Avenida do Contorno 16, Barreto, Niterói*), Saturday 10 pm, women free until 11 pm, then US$1, men US$2

There are some excellent samba clubs in the Lapa area. *Emporium 100* (*Map 2*; ☎ 3852-5904, *Rua do Lavradio 100*), is an antique store by day and dance club at night. *Café Musical Carioca da Gema* (*Map 2*; ☎ 2221-0043, *Avenida Mem de Sá 79*) is also highly recommended. Here you'll find lots of roots samba and MPB. The best nights for both are Wednesday to Saturday, and the music and dancing are great.

Estudantina (*Map 2*; ☎ 2232-1149, *Praça Tiradentes 79*) is only open on the weekend and for special parties. The specialty here is live bands that play Brazilian standards; The music starts around 10:30pm. Within view of the Arcos de Lapa you'll find *Asa Branca* (*Map 2*; ☎ 2252-4428, *Avenida Mem de Sá 17*), another traditional club with live samba music and a happy hour dance, which starts around 5pm. Also next to the arches is

THE SOUTHEAST

Semente (Map 2, ☎ 2242-5165, Rua Joaquim Silva 138), a great little place where the action often spills onto the streets. There's live samba, choró and MPB every night from 9 pm.

Strip Clubs

There is a plethora of strip clubs at the top of Copacabana near Leme (Map 5). This area of town arguably has the best, safest strip clubs in Rio. Clubs charge US$10 and up for entrance, which often includes a drink or two. Most clubs cater to men, but some allow couples. You might find some of the top actresses and actors doing a show at a club, as this type of work doesn't have the stigma in Rio that it does in other countries and cultures.

Cinemas

Most movies shown in the theaters are screened in their original language with Portuguese subtitles; consequently there are plenty of films in English. Brazil gets most of the hits from the US, and also many European films.

For a complete listing of cinemas and current films, look in the daily newspapers. If the titles are written in Portuguese, the English translation is usually underneath. Entry to movies is around US$5.

SPECTATOR SPORTS
Soccer

Brazilian soccer is perhaps the most imaginative and exciting in the world. Complementing the action on the field, the stands are filled with fanatical fans who cheer their teams on in all sorts of ways. In addition to the more usual chanting, singing and shouting; waving banners and streamers in team colors, spectators pound huge samba drums. Pyromaniacs detonate firecrackers, Roman candles, and smoke bombs (in team colors), and launch incendiary balloons. Fans also throw toilet paper, beer and even dead chickens – possibly Macumba inspired. The scene, in short, is sheer lunacy.

Games usually take place every Saturday and Sunday and sometimes during the week.

Obviously, you have to be careful if you go to Maracanã, Rio's enormous temple of soccer (see the Things to See & Do section earlier in this chapter). The big question is how to get to and from the game safely. Major hotels offer special trips to games, which cost about US$40. This is a rip-off, but it's a safe and easy way to get to the game. Staff will drop you off and pick you up right in front of the gate and escort you to lower-level seats.

To go by metro, catch a train to Maracanã station and walk along Avenida Osvaldo Aranha. By bus, catch a bus marked 'Maracanã' (from the zona sul, Nos 434, 464 and 455; from Praça 15 in Centro, No 238 and 239) and leave a couple of hours before game time. Returning to your hotel by bus is often a drag – they are very crowded. Taking a cab is a possible alternative, but they can be hard to flag down; the best strategy is to walk away from the stadium a bit.

However you get to the stadium, it's a good idea to buy lower-level seats, called *cadeira*, instead of the upper-level bleachers, called *arquibancada*. While the lower level is not the best perspective for watching the game, it is the safest because of the overhead covering that protects you from descending objects (like cups full of bodily fluids). The ticket price is US$5, unless it's a championship game, when it's more.

Beach Sports

Surprisingly, volleyball is Brazil's second most popular sport. A natural activity for the beach, it's also a popular spectator sport on TV. A local variation you'll see on the beaches of Rio is volleyball played without the hands *(futvolei)*. It's fun to watch but bloody hard to play.

Peteca is a cross between volleyball and badminton, and is played with a peteca, which is similar to, but a little larger than, a shuttlecock. You'll see them being hawked on the beach. Peteca is a particular favorite with older Cariocas who are getting a bit slow for volleyball.

Usually played on the firm sand at the shoreline, *frescobol* involves two players, each with a wooden racquet, hitting a small rubber ball back and forth as hard as possible. Cariocas make it look easy.

Horse Racing

There's a lot to see at the racetrack (Map 6). The *Jóquei Clube,* which seats 35,000, is on the Gávea side of the Lagoa Rodrigo de Freitas at Praça Santos Dumont 31 (take any of the buses that go to Jardim Botânico). It's a beautiful track, with a great view of the mountains and Corcovado. It's rarely crowded and the fans are great to watch – it's a different slice of Rio life. Races are held every Saturday and Sunday afternoon, and Monday and Friday night.

The big horse race of the year is the Brazilian Grand Prix, held on the first Sunday in August.

SHOPPING

Most shops are open Monday to Friday 9 am to 7 pm (some stay open even later). Saturday has half-day shopping, 9 am to 1 pm. The malls are usually open 10 am to 10 pm, Monday to Friday, and 10 am to 8 pm on the weekend.

Gifts & Souvenirs

Pé de Boi (Map 4; ☎ 2285-4395), Rua Ipiranga 55 in Laranjeiras, is a shop that sells the traditional artisan handicrafts of Brazil, Peru, Guatemala and Ecuador. It carries lots of wood, lace, pottery and prints. It's not inexpensive – you have to buy closer to the original source to get a better price – but if you have some extra dollars (at least US$10 to $20), these pieces are the best gifts to bring home: imaginative and very Brazilian. The small shop is worth a visit just to look around. Ana Maria Chindler, the owner, knows what she's selling and is happy to tell you about it.

Artindia (Map 3; ☎ 2286-8899), inside the grounds of the Museu do Índio in Botafogo, has a wide variety of indigenous handicrafts made from straw, wood, clay and feathers. Items include masks, musical instruments, toys, pots, baskets and weapons.

Jeito Brasileiro (☎ 2205-7636), next to the Corcovado train terminal in Cosme Velho,

has a wide selection of handicrafts from all over Brazil, including folk art made by members of the Camucim tribe.

In Santa Teresa, La Vereda, at Rua Almirante Alexandrino 428, sells a good variety of craft items from the rest of Brazil, as well as showcasing lots of the work of artists from Santa Teresa, including wooden miniatures of the yellow trams.

Other places to try are the souvenir shops in Copacabana, on Avenida NS de Copacabana between the Praça do Lido and Rua Paula Freitas.

Kitsch souvenirs abound. They include classic plastic TVs with scenic views, butterfly trays, lacquered piranhas, toucans carved from semi-precious stones and lots of T-shirts

Coffee-table picture books on Brazil, videotapes of Carnaval and videotapes of highlights of the Brazilian national soccer team and Pelé in various World Cup matches are hawked in the streets of Copacabana.

Music

Compilation specials are a good value if you're just starting to build your Brazilian music collection, as some are really cheap. Brazilian music videos are widely available. If you're not familiar with the artist, have a listen to the music on the equipment in the shop.

The largest chain of music shops is Gabriela, with branches in most shopping malls, including Rio Sul. The latest releases can be found cheaper at the large department stores, such as Carrefour and Lojas Americanas.

Casa Oliveira is a beautiful shop at Rua da Carioca 70 – Rio's oldest street, in Centro (Map 2). It sells a wide variety of musical instruments, including all the noisemakers that fuel the Carnaval *baterias* (percussion sections), and a variety of small mandolin-like stringed instruments, as well as accordions and electric guitars. These make great gifts, and it's a fun place to try out playing the instruments even if you don't buy. You'll also find a good selection at the Sunday hippie fair in Ipanema (see Markets, later in this chapter).

Bossa nova fans should check out Toca da Vinícius (Map 6; ☎ 2247-5227) at Rua Vinícius de Moraes 129 for music and books about the genre. This place also has a gallery and bossa nova museum and often hosts music shows.

Shopping Malls

Brazilians, like North Americans, seem to measure progress by shopping malls. They love to shop at these monsters. Rio Sul was the first mall to maul Rio. There are all kinds of shops. The C&A department store has a good range of clothes and is inexpensive. You'll come to Rio Sul right before you enter the Copacabana tunnel in Botafogo (Map 4). There are free buses from Copacabana.

Barra da Tijuca must be the mall capital of Brazil. Barra Shopping, Avenida das Américas, is the big one, on the right as you drive south into Barra and more are under construction. They're hard to miss!

Markets

There are several open-air markets (feiras), where visitors can snap up a bargain, sample some traditional snacks, or just watch Cariocas.

The Feira do Nordestino is held at the Pavilhão de São Cristóvão (Map 3) on the northern side of town every Sunday, near the Quinta da Boa Vista. It starts early and goes until about 3 pm. The fair is very Northeastern in character. There are lots of barracas (stalls) selling meat, beer, cachaça and even magic potions. For entertainment you'll see comedy, capoeira and bands of accordions, guitar and tambourine players performing forró. It's a great scene. Of course there's plenty to buy; besides food, they have lots of cheap clothes, some well-priced hammocks and a few good Northeastern gifts such as leather vaqueiro (cowboy) hats.

If you're ready for adventure, it's best to arrive the night before the market. This is set-up time and also party time. At about 9 or 10 pm the stalls open for dinner and beer. Some vendors are busy setting up, while others are already finished. Music and

dancing starts and doesn't stop until sunrise. It's great fun so long as you're careful and don't carry valuables with you.

In Centro on Saturday is the Feira de Antiguidades, the antique market in the Praça Mercado Municipal (Map 2) next to the Niterói ferry terminal and the Restaurante Alba Mar. It goes from 9 am to 5 pm, and the stalls have a wide assortment of porcelain, glassware, plates, carpets, paintings and jewelry. Bargain hard here.

Also in Centro on Thursday and Friday is a hippie fair, in Praça 15 de Novembro (Map 2). There are more than 300 stalls here, including many selling leather goods. It's not worth a special trip, as most of the items can be found at the hippie fair in Ipanema, but if you're in the area, drop by and browse.

In the zona sul, the most famous market is the Feira de Arte de Ipanema, better known as the hippie fair. There aren't many actual hippies there, but there is a lot of good souvenir material, such as artwork, musical instruments, toys, leather goods and clothing. Held in Praça General Osório (Map 6), the market starts at 9 am and goes to 6 pm every Sunday.

Also in the zona sul is the antique fair every Saturday from 11 am to 6 am in the Shopping Cassino Atlântico, which is under the Sofitel Rio Palace at Avenida Atlântica 4240. It has plenty of porcelain, glassware etc. On Sunday there are two antique markets in Leblon – one takes place in Praça Santos Dumont (Map 6) and another in the Rio Design Center (Map 6).

When Cariocas go to weekend market, they go to the Babilônia Feira Hype, held in the Jóquei Clube (Map 6) every Saturday. The emphasis here is on bright, fashionable clothing, and you won't find the touristy souvenir stuff like at the Ipanema hippie fair. As well as stalls, there are often music and dance performances.

In Copacabana, there's a market with lots of potential souvenirs and gifts held every day between 5 and 9 pm. It's located on the Avenida Atlântica median strip between Ruas Xavier da Silviera and Bolívar, just across from Posto 5.

GETTING THERE & AWAY
Air

From Rio, flights go to all of Brazil and Latin America. Shuttle flights to São Paulo leave from the convenient Santos Dumont airport, located in the city center along the bay. Here you can also catch some flights to a variety of other destinations such as Porto Seguro or Belo Horizonte.

Almost all other flights – domestic and international – leave from Aeroporto Galeão, also called the Antônio Carlos Jobim International Airport, on Ilha do Governador.

Airline offices usually stay open until 1 pm on Saturday. Varig (☎ 2534-0333, ☎ 0800-997000) has its main office at Avenida Rio Branco 277, in Centro. Varig also has branch offices in Copacabana at Rua Rodolfo Dantas 16 (Map 5; ☎ 2541-6343), and in Ipanema at Rua Visconde de Pirajá 351 (☎ 2523-0040). It's worth noting, though that the staffers at the main office are considerably more reliable and knowledgeable than those at the branches.

VASP (☎ 3814-8000) has a city office at Rua Santa Luzia 735. There are also offices at Santos Dumont airport (☎ 3814-7070), Avenida NS de Copacabana 262 (Map 5; ☎ 3814-8094) in Copacabana and (Map 6; ☎ 3814-8098) Rua Visconde de Pirajá 444, in Ipanema.

TAM (☎ 2524-1717, 24-hour ☎ 0800-123100) has a city office at Praça Floriano 19 on the 28th floor. The TAM airport office is in Terminal Two at the international airport.

TransBrasil (☎ 2297-4477, ☎ 0800-151151) is in Centro at Rua Santa Luzia 651. The other offices are Rua Maria Quitéria 77, Ipanema (☎ 521-0300), and Santos Dumont airport (☎ 2262-6061).

Rio Sul/Nordeste (☎ 2221-0079, ☎ 0800-992004) has offices in Centro at Rua Buenos Aires 68 and Avenida Rio Branco 85. They also have a desk at Santos Dumont airport. International airlines with offices or representatives in Rio include the following:

Aeroflot (☎ 2547-8514), Avenida NS de Copacabana 647, Copacabana

Aerolíneas Argentinas (☎ 2292 4131), Rua São José 70, 8th floor, Centro

Air France (☎ 2524-8661), Avenida Presidente Antônio Carlos 58, 10th floor, Centro

Alitalia (☎ 2524-2544), Avenida Presidente Wilson 231, 21st floor, Centro

American Airlines (☎ 2210-3126, ☎ 0800-216176), Avenida Presidente Wilson 165, 5th floor, Centro

Avianca (☎ 2220-7697), Avenida Presidente Wilson 165, No 801, Centro

British Airways/Qantas (☎ 0800-176144), Terminal One, International Airport

Canadian Airlines (☎ 2220-5343), Rua da Ajuda 35, 29th floor, Centro

Continental (☎ 2531-1142, ☎ 0800-544777), Rua da Assembléia 10, No 3710, Centro

Delta Airlines (☎ 0800-221121), Rua do Ouvidor 161, 14th floor, Centro

Iberia (☎ 2282-1336), Avenida Presidente Antônio Carlos 51, 9th floor, Centro

Japan Air Lines (☎ 2220-6414), Avenida Rio Branco 156, No 2014, Centro

KLM (☎ 2524-7744), Avenida Rio Branco 311A, Centro

LanChile (☎ 2220-0299, ☎ 0800-554900) Rua 7 de Setembro 111, No 702, Centro

Lloyd Aero Boliviano (☎ 2220-9548, ☎ 0800-118111), Avenida Calógeras 30A, Centro

Lufthansa (☎ 2217-6111), Avenida Rio Branco 156D, Centro

Swissair (☎ 2297-5177), Avenida Rio Branco 108, 10th floor, Centro

United Airlines (☎ 3804-1200, ☎ 0800-245532), Avenida Presidente Antônio Carlos 51, 5th floor, Centro

Bus

From Rio, there are buses going everywhere. Most arrive and depart from the loud Novo Rio Bus Station (Map 3; ☎ 2291-5151), Avenida Francisco Bicalho in São Cristóvão, about five minutes by bus north of the center. At the bus station you can get information on transport and lodging if you ask at the Riotur desk on the ground floor.

The other Rio bus station is the Menezes Cortes Bus Station (Map 2; ☎ 2224-7577), Rua São José, which handles services to the zona sul and some intrastate destinations. For travelers, there's really no need to come here. All destinations are served by the Novo Rio bus station.

Excellent buses leave the Novo Rio station every 15 minutes or so for São Paulo (US$15, six hours). Most of the major destinations are serviced by very comfortable *leito* buses leaving late at night.

Many travel agents in the city sell bus tickets, but will add a small charge. It's a good idea to buy a ticket a couple of days in advance if you can, especially if you want to travel on weekends or holiday periods.

Buses listed below leave daily from Rio.

bus	duration	cost
International		
Asunción, Paraguay	28 hours	US$69
Buenos Aires, Argentina	42 hours	US$141
Montevideo, Uruguay	39 hours	US$130
Santiago, Chile	62 hours	US$130
National		
Angra dos Reis	3 hours	US$9
Belém	60 hours	US$117
Belo Horizonte	7 hours	US$17
Brasília	18 hours	US$41
Cabo Frio	3 hours	US$8
Curitiba	11 hours	US$32
Florianópolis	20 hours	US$45
Foz do Iguaçu	22 hours	US$48
Goiânia	18 hours	US$48
Ouro Prêto	7 hours	US$18
Parati	4 hours	US$13
Petrópolis	1½ hours	US$5
Porto Alegre	27 hours	US$73
Recife	38 hours	US$88
Salvador	26 hours	US$24
São João del Rei	5½ hours	US$13
Vitória	8 hours	US$20

You can find all the latest information about bus travel from Rio on the bus station's site at www.novorio.com.br. Even though it's in Portuguese, it's pretty easy. Just click on the Horários e Preços (Hours and Prices) button, and plug in your destination city.

GETTING AROUND
To/From the Airports

All international and nearly all domestic flights use Aeroporto Internacional Antônio Carlos Jobim (commonly called Galeão or GIG), 15km north of the city center on Ilha do Governador.

If you come in at the Santos Dumont airport, you can take the same bus as for Galeão airport from the zona sul, or get to the city and take a taxi, or simply walk to the airport from Centro. The Real bus (described below) or a taxi, are the best ways to get to the zona sul from this airport.

There are two routes of air-conditioned buses (known as *frescão* in Carioca slang) operating from the international airport. You can catch these outside the first-floor arrival area of Terminal One, where the bus company – Real Auto Bus (☎ 0800-240850) – has an office and a waiting room. The bus will also pass outside the ground floor of Terminal Two. Both lines run from 5:20 to 12:10 am, every 40 minutes or so. One route goes to Centro and to Santos Dumont airport (US$2.30); the other to the city center, then south through Glória, Flamengo and Botafogo and along the beaches of Copacabana, Ipanema, Leblon, Vidigal, São Conrado and Barra (US$2.70 flat fare). The driver will stop wherever you ask. If you want to catch the metro, ask the driver to let you off right outside the entrance to Carioca metro station. On both routes, you can stop at the Novo Rio bus station if you want to leave Rio immediately by bus.

If you're heading to the airport, you can get the Real bus in front of the major hotels along the beach, but you have to look alive and flag it down. The direction sign should say 'Aeroporto Internacional.'

Taxi drivers going out from the airport may try to rip you off. The safest course, a radio taxi for which you pay a set fare at the airport, is also the most expensive way to go. A yellow and blue common *comum* taxi is about 20% cheaper, if the meter is working and if you pay what is on the fare schedule. A sample fare from the airport to Copacabana is US$20 in a common taxi, US$30 in a radio taxi. Sharing a taxi from the airport is a good idea; taxis will take up to four people. If you're headed to Leblon or Ipanema, the Túnel Rebouças is more direct than the beach route.

Carnaval reveler

Red-hot and blue costumes, Carnaval

A sassy pair

CATHLEEN NAUNDORF

Royalty for a night, Carnaval

GUY MOBERLY

A vision in green

GUY MOBERLY

A vision in plum

A good compromise if you're new to Rio and on a budget is to take a bus to somewhere near your destination and then take a short taxi ride to your hotel.

To/From the Bus Station

If you arrive in Rio by bus, it's a good idea to take a taxi to your hotel, or at least to the general area where you want to stay. Don't try walking into town with all your gear – the bus station is in a seedy area – and traveling on local buses with all your belongings is a little risky. A small booth near the Riotur desk at the Novo Rio bus station organizes the yellow cabs in the rank out front. Tell them where you want to go and they'll write a price on a ticket that you need to give to the driver of the first cab on the rank. You then pay the driver the agreed fare. If you just grab a cab, the driver will try to add a bit extra. Sample fares are US$8 to the center or to Santos Dumont airport, US$15 to the international airport and US$13 to Copacabana or Ipanema.

Local buses leave from the stops outside the Novo Rio bus station. For Copacabana, the best are bus No 127, 128 and 136. The best buses to Ipanema and Leblon are No 128, 172 and 173. The last goes via Túnel Santa Bárbara and passes through Leblon first before heading back through Ipanema. For the budget hotels in Catete and Glória, take bus No 136 or 172. These run along Praia do Flamengo and Praia do Botafogo. If you want the Catete budget hotels, keep an eye out for the baroque Igreja da Glória, perched on a hill to your right. Get out here and walk over to Rua Catete. An alternative is to take any bus that goes along Avenida Rio Branco to the center. Get off near the end of Avenida Rio Branco and hop on the metro. Get off the metro at Catete station, in the heart of the budget hotel area (Map 4).

Bus

Rio buses are a real mixture of the good, the bad and the ugly. The good: They're fast, frequent and cheap and, because Rio is long and narrow, it's easy to get the right bus and usually no big deal if you're on the wrong one. The bad: Buses are often crowded, slowed down by traffic and driven by raving maniacs who navigate as if they were Formula One competitors. The ugly: Rio's buses are the scene of many of the robberies that take place in the city. Locals like to joke that getting on a bus is better than going to an amusement park – you get the toboggan, roller-coaster and haunted train rides all for the one low price.

You get on at the back and exit from the front. Usually there's a money collector sitting at a turnstile at the rear of the bus, with the bus price displayed above the collector's head. If you're unsure if it's the right bus, it's easy to hop on the back and ask the money collector if the bus is going to your destination – *'Você vai para...?'* If it's the wrong bus no one will mind if you get off without paying, even if the bus has gone a stop or two. Rather than remain at the rear of the bus, it's safer to pay the fare and go through the turnstile. If you feel paranoid about something on the bus, get off and catch another.

In addition to a number, buses have the destination of the bus, including the areas they travel through, written on the side. Nine out of 10 buses going south from the center will go to Copacabana, and vice versa. If you're staying in the Catete/Flamengo area and want to take a bus to the beaches, you can walk to the main roadway along Aterro do Flamengo and take any bus marked 'Copacabana.'

Metro

Rio's subway system is an excellent, cheap way to get around. It's open 6 am to 11 pm daily, except Sunday. The two lines are air-conditioned, clean and fast. The main line from Copacabana to Sãens Pena has 16 stops. The first 13, from Copacabana to Estácio, are common to both lines. At Estácio the lines split: The main line continues west toward the neighborhood of Andarai, making stops at Afonso Pena, São Francisco Xavier and Sãens Pena, and the secondary line goes north to São Cristóvão, Maracanã and beyond. The main stops for the Centro district are Cinelândia and Carioca.

THE SOUTHEAST

You can buy singles, returns, or multiple journeys of 10 rides. The price of a basic single is US$0.70, and there's no discount for return or for multiple ride tickets.

Car & Motorcycle

Car rental agencies are mainly in two places, at the airport and clustered together on Avenida Princesa Isabel in Copacabana. Prices vary between US$40 -100 a day, but they go down a bit in the low season. There is a bit of competition between the major rental firms, so it's worth shopping around for promotional deals. If you get prices quoted on the phone, make sure they include insurance, which is compulsory. Most agencies will let you drop off cars in another city without an extra charge.

Motorcycles are popular in Rio, but theft is a big problem – it's so common that you can't even get motorcycle insurance. For this reason, no agencies offer them.

Public transport in Rio stops at midnight, so you'll need a car if you are going anywhere after that time.

Taxi

Taxis in Rio are quite reasonably priced, if you're dividing the fare with a friend or two. Taxis are particularly useful late at night and when you're carrying valuables.

The meters are weighted toward distance not time. This gives the drivers an incentive to drive quickly (for a head rush tell your driver that you are in a bit of a hurry) and travel by roundabout routes. It's illegal for cabs to take more than four passengers. Most people don't tip taxi drivers, although it's common to round off the fare to the next *real*.

The radio taxis (☎ 2260-2022) are 30% more expensive than the ordinary ones, but they will come to you and they are safer.

Minivans

In the last few years, minivans (Cariocas call them *vans)* have become an alternative form of transport in Rio. They are technically illegal (recently a large number of cops were charged with organizing the van concessions) but no one seems to mind. They are much quicker than buses and run along Avenida Rio Branco to the zona sul as far as Barra da Tijuca. The destination is written on a card in the front window. On the return trip, they run alongside the coast almost all the way into the center. They run frequently and charge a flat fee of US$2. They are probably not a good idea if you've got very much luggage.

Walking

For God's sake be careful! Drivers run red lights, drive up on footpaths and stop for no one and nothing.

CARNAVAL

Carnaval, like Mardi Gras, is a holiday with its origins in various pagan spring festivals. During the Middle Ages, these tended to be wild parties, until tamed in Europe by both the Reformation and the Counter-Reformation versions of Christianity. But not even the heavy hand of the Inquisition could squelch Carnaval in the Portuguese colony, where it came to acquire Indian costumes and African rhythms.

People speculate that the word *carnaval* derives from the Latin *carne vale,* 'goodbye meat.' The reasoning goes something like this: For the 40 days of Lent, the nominally Catholic Brazilians give up liver and steak filets, in addition to luxuries such as alcohol and pastries. To compensate for the deprivation ahead, they rack up sins in advance with a deliriously carnal blowout in honor of King Momo, the king of Carnaval.

Officially, Rio's Carnaval lasts five days – from the Friday to the Tuesday immediately preceding Ash Wednesday, which is the beginning of Lent. In reality, the excitement builds all year, and the pre-Lenten revelry begins well before the official start. Around August, rehearsals start at the *escolas de samba* (samba 'schools' or clubs). Rehearsals usually take place in the favelas and are open to visitors. They're fun to watch, but go with a Carioca for safety. Corny tourist Carnaval shows are held year-round at Plataforma in Leblon.

The samba schools are actually predated by *bandas* (marching bands with brass and percussion instruments, amateur equivalents of the samba schools), which are now returning to the Carnaval scene as part of the movement to return Carnaval to the streets of Rio. Riotur has all the information in a special Carnaval guide (see the Tourist Offices section in the Rio de Janeiro City chapter.

Carnaval Balls

Carnaval balls are surreal and erotic events. Breasts are painted, stickered with tattoos, covered with fishnet brassieres or just left bare. Bottoms are spandexed, G-stringed or mini-skirted. At one ball at Scala in Leblon we saw a woman (transsexual?) bare her breasts and offer passersby a suck, while rickety old ladies were bopping away in skimpy lingerie. A young and geeky rich guy was dancing on tables with ladies of the evening past their prime, young models and lithe young nymphets, all in various stages of undress.

More action took place on the stages. One stage had a samba band and the other was crushed with young women. They didn't so much dance as grind their hips and lick their lips to the incessant hypnotic music and epileptic flashing of the floor lights. Throngs of sweaty photographers and video crews mashed up to the stage. Everyone played up for the camera, all vying for space and the attention of the photographers. The Vegas-style headdresses, the pasty-faced bouncers and the rich men in private boxes overlooking the dance floor lent a mafioso feel.

Through Carnaval is theoretically the holiday of the poor, tickets to the balls are not cheap. Some cost more than Rio's monthly minimum wage. Some balls are snooty affairs, like the ones at the Copacabana Palace or in Barra at the ATU Hall. Raunchier parties are held in a variety of Rio neighborhoods – in Leblon at Scala (Avenida Afránio de Melo Franco); in Botafogo at Canecão (☎ 543-1241, Avenida Venceslau Brás 215); and in Cobacabana at Help disco (☎ 522-1296, Avenida Atlântica 3432).

Tickets go on sale roughly two weeks beforehand, and the balls are held nightly for the week preceding and all through Carnaval. For details of all the balls and bandas, buy a copy of *Veja* magazine with the *Veja Rio* insert.

There are three basic laws of Carnaval balls. One: Beautiful, flirtatious and apparently unaccompanied women are either escorted by huge, jealous, cachaça-crazed men wielding machetes, or they are really men dressed up as women. Two: Everything costs several times more within the club than outside. And finally: Don't bring more money than you're willing to lose – the club bouncers are big, but not all that effective.

Sambódromo Glossary

Alas – literally the 'wings.' These are groups of samba-school members responsible for a specific part of the central samba do enredo. Special alas include the Baianas, women dressed traditionally as Bahian 'aunts' in full skirts and turbans. The abre ala of each school is the opening wing or float.

Bateria – the drum section. This is the driving beat behind the school's samba and the 'soul' of the school.

Carnavalescos – the artistic directors of the schools. They are responsible for the overall layout and design of their school's theme.

Carros allegoricos – the dazzling floats, usually decorated with near-naked women. The floats are pushed along by the school's maintenance crew.

Desfile – the procession. The most important samba schools *desfilar* (parade) on the Sunday and Monday night of Carnaval. Each school's desfile is judged on its samba, drum section, master of ceremonies and flag bearer, floats, leading commission, costumes, dance coordination and harmony.

Destaques – the richest and most elaborate costumes. The heaviest ones usually get a spot on one of the floats.

Diretores de harmonia – the school organizers. They are usually dressed in white or in the school colors, and run around yelling and 'pumping up' the wings and making sure there aren't any gaps in the parade.

Enredo – the central theme of each school. The samba do enredo is the samba that goes with it. Themes vary tremendously.

Passistas – a school's best samba dancers. They roam the parade in groups or alone, stopping to show their fancy footwork along the way. The women are scantily dressed and the men usually hold tambourines.

Puxador – the interpreter of the theme song. He (they're invariably male) works as a guiding voice leading the school's singers at rehearsals and in the parade.

Street Carnaval

What do poorer Cariocas do in the afternoon and early evening during Carnaval and the preceding weekends? They dance in the streets behind bandas, which pump out the banda's theme song and other Carnaval marching favorites as they move along. To join in the fun, all you need to do is jump in when you see the banda pass. Bandas are one of the most traditional aspects of Carnaval in Rio.

Banda de Ipanema is a traditional banda that parades on the second Saturday before Carnaval, starting from Praça General Osório in Ipanema. It's full of drag queens and party animals. It starts around 5 pm and goes until around 9 pm. The banda parades again on Carnaval Saturday. Banda Carmen Miranda, with its famous gay icon, is also a lot of fun, not only for gays, but for everyone. It parades through Ipanema streets around 4 pm the Sunday before Carnaval. There are lots of bandas parading in Copacabana before and during Carnaval, too.

The street parades on Avenida Rio Branco in Centro and Boulevard 28 de Setembro in Vila Isabel, both on Carnaval Saturday, are really worth checking out. You won't see many other tourists there, but if you remember to carry only a few dollars in your pocket for beers and a snack, you should have nothing to worry about.

Samba Parades

In the Sambódromo (Sambadrome), a tiered street designed for the samba parades of Carnaval by Oscar Niemeyer and completed in 1984, the Brazilians harness sweat, noise and confusion, and turn it into art. The 14 top-level samba schools prepare all year for their hour of glory.

The whole procession is also an elaborate competition. A handpicked set of judges chooses the best school on the basis of many components, including percussion, the *samba do enredo* (theme song), harmony among percussion, song and dance, choreography, costumes, story line, floats and decorations. The championship is hotly contested, with the winner becoming the pride of both Rio and all of Brazil.

The parades begin in moderate mayhem and work themselves up to a higher plane of frenzy. The announcers introduce the school, the group's theme colors and the number of wings. Far away the lone voice of the *puxador* starts the samba. Thousands more voices join him, and then the drummers kick in, 200 to 400 per school. The booming drums drive the parade. The samba do enredo is the loudest music you're ever likely to hear in your life. Sambas, including the themes for each group, flood the airwaves for weeks before the beginning of Carnaval.

From a distance the procession looks like a single living organism. It's a throbbing beast that slowly comes closer – a pulsing, glittering, Japanese-movie-monster slime-mold threatening to engulf all of Rio in samba and vibrant (not to mention vibrating) *mulatas*.

The parades begin with a special opening wing (the *abre alas*), which always displays the name of the school and the theme of the school. Each school offers some sort of unifying message – social commentary, economic criticism or political statement – but it's usually lost in the glitz.

The abre alas is then followed by the *comissão de frente,* a group of elderly men who greet the crowds. This is the samba school's way of honoring men who have contributed over the years.

Next come the main wings of the school, the big allegorical floats, the children's wing, the drummers, the celebrities and the bell-shaped Baianas twirling in elegant hoop-skirts. The Baianas honor the history of the parade itself, which was brought to Rio from Salvador da Bahia in 1877.

The *mestre-sala* (dance master) and *porta-bandeira* (flag bearer) waltz and whirl. Celebrities, dancers and tambourine players strut their stuff. The costumes are fabulously lavish: 1.5m-high feathered headdresses, long flowing capes sparkling with sequins, and rhinestone-studded G-strings.

The floats gush neo-baroque silver foil and gold tinsel. Sparkling models sway to the samba, dancing in their private processions. All the while the puxador leads the song, repeating the samba do enredo for the duration of the parade.

More than an hour after it began, the school makes it past the arch and the judges' stand. There is a few minutes' pause. TV cranes stop bobbing up and down over the foreign press corps.

Next, garbage trucks parade down the runway, clearing the way for the next school. Sanitation workers in orange jumpsuits shimmy, dance and sweep, gracefully catch trash thrown from the stands and take their bows. It's their Carnaval, too.

The Sambadrome parades start on Friday night with the *mirins* (young samba school members) and continue through Saturday night, when the Group A samba schools strut their stuff. Sunday and Monday are the big nights, when the Grupo Especial – the 14 best samba schools in Rio – parade: seven of them on Sunday night and into the morning, and seven more on Monday night. The following Saturday, in the Parade of Champions, the eight top schools strut their stuff once more.

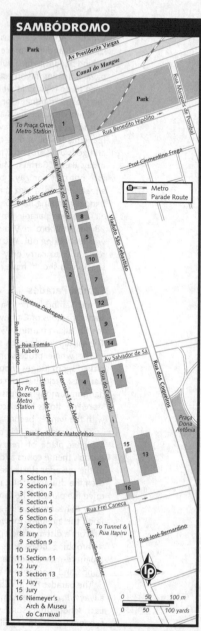

SAMBÓDROMO

1 Section 1
2 Section 2
3 Section 3
4 Section 4
5 Section 5
6 Section 6
7 Section 7
8 Jury
9 Section 9
10 Jury
11 Section 11
12 Jury
13 Section 13
14 Jury
15 Jury
16 Niemeyer's Arch & Museu do Carnaval

Tickets

Getting tickets at legitimate prices can be tough. Many tickets are sold well in advance of the event. Check with Riotur (www.rio.rj.br/riotur) about where you can get them, as the official outlet can vary from year to year. People line up for hours, and travel agents and scalpers snap up the best seats. Riotur reserves seats in private boxes for tourists for US$200, but you should be able to pick up regular tickets for much less from a travel agent or from the Maracanã stadium box office (☎ 2568-9962) for around US$40.

By Carnaval weekend, most tickets will have sold out, but there are lots of scalpers. If you buy a ticket from a scalper (no need to worry about looking for them – they'll find you!), make sure you get both the plastic ticket with the magnetic strip and the ticket showing the seat number. The tickets for different days are color-coded, so double-check the date as well.

Don't fret if you don't get a ticket by either of these means. It is possible to see the show without paying an arm and a leg. The parades last eight to 10 hours each and no one sits through the whole thing. Unless you're an aficionado of a samba school that starts early, show up at the Sambadrome at around midnight, three or four hours into the show. This is when you can get grandstand tickets for about US$10 from scalpers outside the gate.

And if you can't make it during Carnaval proper, there's always the cheaper (but less exciting) Parade of Champions the following Saturday.

If you can possibly avoid it, don't take the bus to or from the Sambadrome. It's much safer to take the metro, which runs round the clock during Carnaval. This is also a great opportunity to check out the paraders commuting in costume.

Dates

Dates for the main samba parade in coming years are:

2002 February 10-11	2003 March 2-3
2004 February 22-23	2005 February 6-7

Do-It-Yourself Carnaval

There's nothing to stop you from actually taking part in a Carnaval parade. Most samba schools are happy to have foreigners join one of the wings. Several Web sites have sprung up that make it possible to choose and buy your costume online before you even get to Rio. One good one with an English version is www.geocities.com/alavaisacudir.

Fantasías (costumes) vary in price according to how elaborate they are, but they usually cost from US$200 to US$300.

If you don't want to buy online, it is always possible to get one by phoning the samba schools directly once you're in Rio, even as little as two weeks before Carnaval. (For information on how to contact the samba schools, see the Entertainment section of the Rio de Janeiro city chapter.) So get out there and samba!

Rio de Janeiro State

The small state of Rio de Janeiro offers much more than just the *cidade maravilhosa* (marvelous city). Within four hours of travel (and often much less) from any point in the state are beaches, mountains and forests that equal any in Brazil. Many of these places offer intimate settings in which to meet Cariocas, who have known about the natural wonders surrounding the city for years. You won't find virgin sites like those in the Northeast – tourism here is fairly developed and prices are higher than in most of Brazil. But if you have only a couple of weeks in Brazil and think that you'll return some day, an itinerary that covers the entire state of Rio would be one of the best possible. For those with all the time in the world, it's easy to pass a month or two here.

Rio de Janeiro state, which lies just above the Tropic of Capricorn, has an area of 43,919 sq km – about the size of Switzerland – and a population of over 14 million. The coast is backed by steep mountains, which descend into the sea around the border with São Paulo and gradually retreat farther inland in the north. This forms a thin strip of land nestled between the lush green mountains and the emerald sea, with beaches that are the most spectacular in Brazil.

Divided by the city of Rio and the giant Baía de Guanabara, with its 131km of coast and 113 islands, are two coastal regions, each with rather different natural characteristics: the Costa Verde (west) and the Costa do Sol (east).

Along the Costa Verde are hundreds of islands, including Ilha Grande and the Restinga de Marambaia, which make for easy swimming and boating. The calm waters and the natural ports and coves allowed safe passage to the Portuguese ships that came to transport sugar, and later gold, to Europe. They also protected pirates, who found a safe haven on Ilha Grande. Beaches wait to be explored, particularly as you get farther away from Rio city; the coastal road stays close to the ocean here and the views

Highlights

- Trekking through the Parque Nacional da Serra dos Órgãos

- Following the old gold route from São José do Barreiro (São Paulo) to Parati, on foot or horseback

- Discovering the colonial architecture of Parati, and exploring its many bays and offshore islands by boat

- Diving at Arraial do Cabo

- Chilling out on Ilha Grande – hiking the beaches, diving, snorkeling or just lazing around in the village of Abraão

- Scaling the peaks of the Prateleiras and the Pico das Agulhas Negras (Parque Nacional de Itatiaia)

- Sun worshipping at the lovely beaches of Saquarema, Arraial do Cabo, Búzios, Ilha Grande – and also around Parati

RIO DE JANEIRO STATE

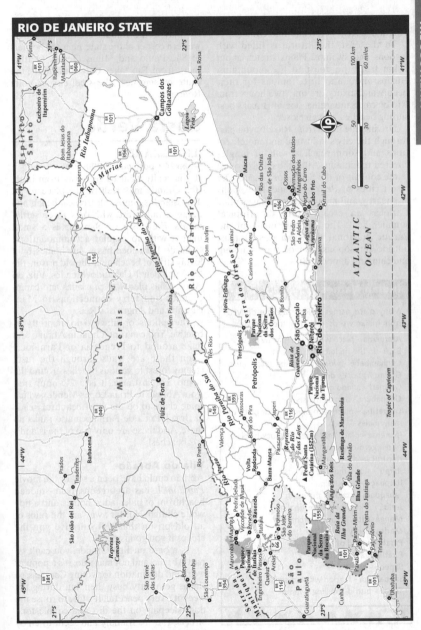

THE SOUTHEAST

are spectacular. The most famous spots are Angra dos Reis, Parati and Ilha Grande.

To the east, the littoral is filled with lagoons and swamps. Plains stretch about 30km from the coast to the mountains. Búzios and Cabo Frio, famous for their beauty and luxury, are only two hours from Rio by car. Saquarema, one of Brazil's best surfing beaches, is even closer.

Driving due north from Rio city, you pass through the city's industrial and motel sections and soon reach a wall of jungle-covered mountains. After the climb, you're in the cool air of the Serra dos Órgãos. The resort cities of Petrópolis and Teresópolis are nearby, and many smaller villages offer Cariocas an escape from the tropical summer heat. The fantastic peaks of the Parque Nacional da Serra dos Órgãos, outside Teresópolis, provide superb hiking and climbing opportunities.

The other mountain region where Cariocas play is the Itatiaia area in the north-western corner of the state, near the borders of São Paulo and Minas Gerais. Getting there from Rio takes only four hours, the route passing near the steel city of Volta Redonda.

Costa Verde

ILHA GRANDE
☎ 0xx24 • postcode 23990-000

If you really want to get away from it all, Ilha Grande may well be the place to go. This island is almost all tropical beach and Atlantic rainforest, with only three settlements. Freguesia de Santana is a small hamlet with no regular accommodations. Praia de Parnaioca has a few homes by a lovely strip of beach near the old prison, the Colônial Penal Can\dido Mendes. Vila do Abraão has plenty of pousadas and camp-grounds and ferry connections to Mangaratiba and Angra dos Reis.

The options for things to do are pretty attractive. You can rent a boat in Abraão and buzz around to Freguesia or Parnaioca. Then there are trails through the lush, steamy forest to various beaches around the island. For instance, it is a 2½-hour trek from Abraão to Praia Lopes Mendes, which some claim to be the most beautiful beach in Brazil. Praia de Parnaioca also ranks up there. And these are only two of the island's 102 beaches!

Vila do Abraão

Abraão could have been a set for the movie *Papillon*. It has a gorgeous, palm-studded beachfront of pale, faded homes, and a tidy white church. Not far away are the ruins of an old prison that will still give you the creeps if you go inside.

As a base on Ilha Grande, you can't go past Abraão, and not many do. It's a popular weekend destination for young Cariocas, so things get pretty busy then, but during the week it's very peaceful. It's OK to rouse the dogs sleeping on the dirt and cobblestone streets. They're friendly and seem to enjoy

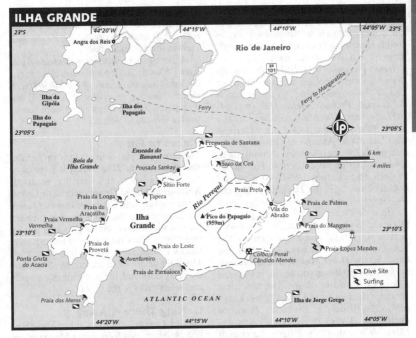

ILHA GRANDE

tramping around the island to the abandoned penitentiary, the beaches, the forest, the hills and the waterfalls.

Orientation & Information

The tourist office in Angra dos Reis (see that section later in this chapter) has information about Ilha Grande, including lodging options. To the left of the dock as you get off the boat in Abraão is the cobbled **Rua da Igreja**, and at the far end of the beach, a trail leads to **Praia de Palmas**, **Praia do Mangues** and **Praia Lopes Mendes**. To the right of the dock are the ferry ticket office, a guesthouse for military police, the road to **Praia Preta** and the trail to the ruined old prison.

It's better to change money before you get here. The top-end hotels and tourist shops may change cash US dollars. Lutz, the German owner of the Pousada Beira Mar, changes traveler's checks, but charges commission.

Activities

The Associação de Barqueiros (☎ 3361-5046) has an information booth near the dock. This outfit organizes day cruises to the northern beaches (from US$15 per person) and from December to March in good weather offers a circumnavigation tour of the island for US$40. Ilha Grande Dive (☎ 9692-2381) on Travessa do Beto organizes dive trips, charging US$65 for a two-tank dive trip.

Places to Stay

Cheap lodging on Ilha Grande is not as easy to come by as it was a few years back. Several pousadas are getting a little more sophisticated and upping their prices. The cheapest option is to camp. There are a couple of campgrounds set back from the beach on Rua Getúlio Vargas. *Camping das Palmeiras* has reasonable facilities and charges US$3 per person. Some locals rent rooms cheaply; just ask around.

Most of the pousadas in Abraão cost between US$30 and US$55 for a double in low season (March to November). Prices double in summer (December to February); those quoted here are for low season.

Beto's Pousada (☎ 3361-5312, Travessa do Beto 63) offers spotless apartamentos for US$20/30 a single/double. A good option is the friendly ***Pousada Beira Mar*** (☎ 3361-5051, beiramar2000@uol.com.br), on the beach 300m from the dock. Lutz, a German who has made Abraão his home, enjoys meeting fellow travelers and showing them his extensive photo collection. He speaks English and charges US$20/40 a single/double. Close by is the ***Pousada Tropicana*** (☎ 3361-5047, pousadatropicana@uol.com.br, Rua da Praia 28). It's a very pleasant place and has apartamentos for US$27/40.

Rua da Igreja, at right angles to the beachfront, features a white church, a few bars and the ***Hotel Mar da Tranquilidade*** (☎/fax 3361-5001) on top of the restaurant Adega do Corsário Negro. The hotel has good apartamentos for US$13/26 weekdays or US$20/40 during weekends. ***Pousada Portal das Borbas*** (☎ 3361-5085, Rua das Flores 4) is a short stroll from the church

along Rua Getúlio Vargas. It has rooms with verandahs facing a nice garden courtyard for US$50 single or double – get one with view to the hill and forest.

A more expensive place is ***Pousada Agua Viva*** (☎/fax 3361-5166), which is close to the dock and has ample suites for US$45/80 with air-conditioning, minibar and cable TV (although it is baffling why anyone would come to Ilha Grande to watch TV).

Places to Eat

The three best places to eat in town are the ***Bar Casarão da Ilha***, which is expensive but serves very high quality seafood; ***Restaurant Minha Deusa*** , with cheap, good home cooking; and ***Café com Banana Internet Café*** next to the creek on Rua Getúlio Vargas, which has reasonably priced snacks and drinks. The café has good atmosphere, videos and Internet access; it is closed on Mondays. There is an ice cream shop near the ferry dock and, in the evenings, a sweets cart often parks in the plaza.

Getting There & Away

Catch a Conerj ferry from either Mangaratiba or Angra dos Reis. From Mangaratiba

VILA DO ABRAÃO

PLACES TO STAY	PLACES TO EAT	OTHER	
6 Pousada Agua Viva	3 Ice Cream Shop	1 Ferry Dock	11 Ilha Grande Dive
7 Pousada Tropicana	5 Bar Casarão da	2 Post Office	14 Telephone Office
8 Pousada Beira Mar	Ilha	4 Associação de	15 Café com Banana
9 Hotel Mar da	13 Restaurant	Barqueiros	Internet Café
Tranquilidade; Adega	Minha Deusa	10 Igreja de São	19 Supermarket
do Corsário Negro		Sebastiao	20 Assembléia de
12 Beto's Pousada			Deus
16 Camping das Palmeiras			
17 Camping Ground			
18 Portal dos Borbas			

To Praia de Palmas, Praia do Mangues & Praia Lopes Mendes

Baía de Ilha Grande

Praia do Canto

Ferry to Angra

Ferry to Mangaratiba

To Praia Preta

Rua da Praia

Plaza

Rua da Igreja

Travessa do Beto

Rua Getúlio Vargas

Rua da Assembléia

Soccer Field

Rua do Bicão

Rua das Flores

Rua do Cemetério

To Colônia Penal

Dirt Paths (walkers only)

0   50   100 m
0   50   100 yards

to Abraão, the ferry leaves at 8 am Monday to Friday, and at 9 am Saturday and Sunday. It returns from Abraão at 5 pm daily.

The ferry from Angra dos Reis to Abraão has daily departures at 3:30 pm and returns from Abraão daily at 10 am. The 1½-hour ride is US$2 during the week and US$6 on weekends.

Enseada do Bananal

Enseada do Bananal is on the northwestern side of the island. Ilha Grande's most stylish hotel, the **Pousada Sankay** (☎ 3365-4065), is here, a 50-minute boat ride from Vila do Abraão. Doubles start at US$85.

ANGRA DOS REIS
☎ 0xx24 • postcode 23900-000
• pop 114,000

Angra dos Reis is a base for visiting nearby islands and beaches, not a tourist attraction in itself. The savage beauty of the tropical, fjord-like coastline along this stretch of Hwy BR-101 has been badly blemished by industrialization. Supertankers dock in Angra's port, a rail line connects Angra to the steel town of Volta Redonda, there's a Petrobras oil refinery and, thanks to the military government and the International Monetary Fund, a controversial nuclear power plant nearby.

The closest beach to Angra is Praia Grande, southwest of the town center. It's a nice beach with trees and a view to Ilha da Gipóia. To get there take the Angra dos Reis municipal bus labeled 'Vila Velha.'

Information

The Centro de Informações Turísticas (☎ 3365-1175, sd@stargate.com.br) is at Avenida Júlio Maria 10. Helpful, English-speaking staff have information about attractions and places to stay in Angra and Ilha Grande. Hours are Monday to Friday from 8 am to 7 pm and weekends from 9 am to 4 pm.

Cambisul Câmbio, Travessa Santa Luzia, changes cash. The Banco do Brasil, Rua do Comércio, will change traveler's checks. Bradesco also has an ATM diagonally opposite its branch office.

The post office is on Praça Lopes Trovão. Long-distance telephone calls can be made from Telemar, Avenida Raul Pompéia 97.

Places to Stay

Pousada Angra Antiga (Rua Arcebispo Santos 162), opposite the town market, is a cheapie with basic, clean single/double quartos for US$10/15 without breakfast. If you want a shower in your room, the best budget bet is the central **Porto Rico** (☎ 3365-0992, Rua Colonel Carvalho 54). Small, clean apartamentos with fan but without breakfast go for US$10/15. The **Pousada da Praia** (☎ 3365-0605, Estrada do Contorno 2940), Praia Grande has a nice courtyard and classy doubles for US$30. To get there take the 'Vila Velha' bus.

The **Palace Hotel** (☎ 3365-0032, fax 3365-2656, Rua Coronel Carvalho 275) is a clean, three-star hotel with TV, air-conditioning, telephone and hot water. Doubles cost about US$44.

Places to Eat

A good seafood place is **Taberna 33**, near the corner of Rua Coronel Carvalho and Rua Raul Pompéia. If your budget doesn't stretch to include seafood, **Fogão de Minas** (Rua Júlio Maria 398), near the market, has very good and cheap self-serve by the kilo. It's popular with locals.

Getting There & Away

Angra dos Reis is almost 150km (three hours) from Rio. Angra's bus station (☎ 3365-1280) is on Largo da Lapa, northeast of the center toward Rio. Buses to Rio leave every hour from 4 am to 10:45 pm (US$9). To Parati, there are six local buses a day, the first leaving at 6 am (US$2, two hours).

PARATI
☎ 0xx24 • postcode 23970-000 • pop 14,000

Oh! Deus, se na terra houvesse um paraíso, não seria muito longe daqui!
(Oh! God, if there were a paradise on earth, it wouldn't be very far from here!)

–Amerigo Vespucci

THE SOUTHEAST

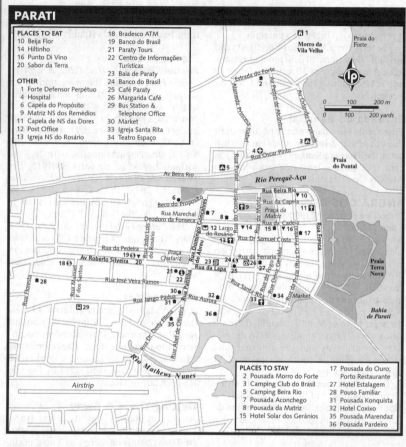

PARATI

PLACES TO EAT
10 Beija Flor
14 Hiltinho
16 Punto Di Vino
20 Sabor da Terra

OTHER
1 Forte Defensor Perpétuo
4 Hospital
6 Capela do Propósito
9 Matriz NS dos Remédios
11 Capela de NS das Dores
12 Post Office
13 Igreja NS do Rosário

18 Bradesco ATM
19 Banco do Brasil
21 Paraty Tours
22 Centro de Informações
   Turísticas
23 Baia de Paraty
24 Banco do Brasil
25 Café Paraty
26 Margarida Café
29 Bus Station &
   Telephone Office
30 Market
33 Igreja Santa Rita
34 Teatro Espaço

PLACES TO STAY
2 Pousada Morro do Forte
3 Camping Club do Brasil
5 Camping Beira Rio
7 Pousada Aconchego
8 Pousada da Matriz
15 Hotel Solar dos Gerânios
17 Pousada do Ouro;
   Porto Restaurante
27 Hotel Estalagem
28 Pouso Familiar
31 Pousada Konquista
32 Hotel Coxixo
35 Pousada Marendaz
36 Pousada Pardeiro

Amerigo was referring to steep, jungled mountains that seem to leap into the sea, a scrambled shoreline with hundreds of islands and jutting peninsulas, and the clear, warm waters of the Baía da Ilha Grande, as calm as an empty aquarium. All this still exists, though no longer in a pristine state, along with one of Brazil's most enchanting settlements – the colonial village of Parati, which Amerigo did not get to enjoy.

Parati is both a great colonial relic, well preserved and architecturally unique, and a launching pad to a dazzling section of the Brazilian coastline. The buildings have simple lines that draw the eye to the general rather than the specific, and earthy colors and textures that magnify, through contrast, the natural beauty that envelops the town. So, while the individual buildings in Parati may well be beautiful, the town, when viewed as a whole, is truly a work of art.

The town – a couple of kilometers off the Rio to Santos highway, in the southwest corner of Rio de Janeiro state – is easy to look around. Just stroll on the *pes-de-moleque* ('street urchins' feet' – the local name for the irregular cobblestone streets), washed clean by the rains and high tides.

Dozens of secluded beaches are within a couple of hours of Parati by boat or bus. There are good swimming beaches close to town, but the best are along the coast toward São Paulo and out on the bay islands.

One of the most popular spots between Rio and São Paulo, Parati is crowded and lively throughout the summer holidays, brimming with Brazilian and Argentine vacationers and good music. That the town is all tourism there is no doubt, proven by the many boutiques and ritzy restaurants. But if you get around these obstacles, Parati is a delight, and there are plenty of beaches to accommodate all visitors. Parati is also renowned for its excellent cachaça.

History

Parati was inhabited by the Guianas Indians when Portuguese from São Vicente, 200km southwest, settled here in the 16th century. With the discovery of gold in Minas Gerais at the end of the 17th century, Parati became an obligatory stopover for those coming from Rio de Janeiro, as it was the only point where the escarpment of the Serra do Mar could be scaled. The precarious road was an old Guianas Indian trail that cut past the Serra do Facão (where the town of Cunha in São Paulo is today) to the valley of the Rio Paraíba, and from there to Pindamonhangaba, Guaratinguetá and then to the mines.

Parati became a busy, important port as miners and supplies headed for the gold mines disembarked, and gold was shipped to Europe. The small town prospered and, as always, the wealthy built churches to prove it. There was so much wealth in Parati that in 1711 Captain Francisco do Amaral Gurgel sailed from Parati to save Rio de Janeiro from a threatened French siege by handing over a ransom of 1000 crates of sugar, 200 head of cattle and 610,000 gold cruzados.

Parati's glory days didn't last long. After the 1720s, a new road from Rio via the Serra dos Órgãos cut 15 days off the journey to Minas Gerais, and Parati started to decline. In the 19th century, the local economy revived with the coffee boom, and now, with the recent construction of the road from Rio, the town's coffers are once again being filled. Until 1954 the only access to Parati was by sea. In that year a road was built through the steep Serra do Mar, passing the town of Cunha, 47km inland. In 1960 the coastal road from Rio, 253km away, was extended to Parati and 330km beyond to São Paulo.

Information

Parati is small and easy to navigate, but street names and house numbers can be confusing. Many streets have more than one name, which is thoroughly perplexing for locals as well as tourists. The numbering system seems to be totally random.

The Centro de Informações Turísticas (☎ 3371-1266, ext 218), on Avenida Roberto Silveira, is open 9 am to 9 pm daily.

Paraty Tours (☎/fax 3371-1327), at Avenida Roberto Silveira 11, just before you hit the colonial part of town, is also useful for information. This company's five-hour schooner cruises are US$15 (US$25 with lunch). It also rents bicycles (US$2 an hour, or US$9 per day).

Banco do Brasil on Avenida Roberto Silveira changes cash and traveler's checks between 9 am and 3pm. It also does Visa cash advances. Another option is Atrium Câmbio e Turismo at Rua do Comércio 26, open every day from 10 am to 7 pm.

The post office is on the corner of Rua Marechal Deodoro da Fonseca (also known as Rua da Cadeia) and Rua Domingo Gonçalves de Abreu. The Telemar office is at the bus station. Internet access is available at Baia de Paraty on Rua da Lapa 245, from 10 am to 10 pm. Margarida Café, Rua Comendador José Luis, also has Internet access.

Churches

Parati's 18th-century prosperity is reflected in its beautiful old homes and churches. Three main churches were used to separate the races.

The **Igreja NS do Rosário e São Benedito dos Homens Pretos** (1725), Rua Dr Samuel Costa, was built by and for slaves. Renovated in 1857, the church has gilded wooden altars dedicated to Our Lady of the Rosary, St Benedict and St John. The pineapple crystals are for prosperity and good luck.

The **Igreja Santa Rita dos Pardos Libertos** (1722), on Rua Santa Rita, was the church for freed mulattos. It has a tiny museum of sacred art and some fine woodwork on the doorways and altars.

Capela de NS das Dores (1800), Rua Fresca, the church of the colonial white élite, was renovated in 1901. The cemetery is fashioned after the catacombs. **Matriz NS dos Remédios** (1787), Praça Monsenhor Hélio Pires, was built on the site of two 17th-century churches. Inside, there is art from past and contemporary local artists. According to legend, the construction of the church was financed by pirate treasure found hidden on Praia da Trindade.

Forte Defensor Perpétuo

The Forte Defensor Perpétuo was built in 1703 to defend from pirate attacks the gold being exported from Minas Gerais. The fort was rebuilt in 1822, the year of Brazil's independence, and was named after Emperor Dom Pedro I. It's on the Morro da Vila Velha, the hill just past Praia do Pontal, a 20-minute walk north of town. The fort houses the **Casa de Artista e Centro de Artes e Tradições Populares de Parati**.

Islands & Beaches

The closest fine beaches on the coast – **Vermelha** and **Lulas** (both northeast of Parati) and **Saco** (to the east) – are about an hour away by boat. Camping is allowed on the beaches. The best island beaches nearby are probably **Araújo** and **Sapeca**, but many of the islands have rocky shores and are private. The mainland beaches tend to be better. These beaches are all small and idyllic; most have *barracas* (stalls) serving beer and fish and, at most, a handful of beachgoers.

Parati has some 65 islands and 300 beaches in its vicinity. Don't limit yourself to the following selection of the most accessible beaches north of town, as there are plenty more. If you do come across any really special beaches and you can bear to share your secret, Lonely Planet would love to know about them. See Getting Around later in this section for information on how to get to the less accessible beaches.

On the other side of the canal, 10 minutes away on foot, is Praia do Pontal – Parati's city beach. There are several barracas and a lively crowd, but the beach itself is not attractive and the water gets dirty.

On the side of the hill, hidden by the rocks, Praia do Forte is the cleanest beach within a quick walk of the city. It is relatively secluded and frequented by a youngish crowd.

Continue on the dirt road north past Praia do Pontal, over the hill, for 2km to Praia do Jabaquara, a big, spacious beach with great views in all directions. There is a small restaurant and a campground that's better than those in town. The sea is very shallow, so it's possible to wade way out into the bay.

Special Events

Parati is known for colorful and distinctive festivals. The two most important are the **Festa do Divino Espírito Santo**, which begins nine days before Pentecostal Sunday (the seventh Sunday after Easter), and the **Festa de NS dos Remédios**, on September 8. The former is planned throughout the year and features all sorts of merrymaking revolving around the *fólios*, musical groups that go from door to door singing and joking.

The **Festas Juninas**, during June, are filled with dances, including the *xiba* (a circle clog dance) and the *ciranda* (a xiba with guitar accompaniment). The festivals culminate on June 29 with a maritime procession to Ilha do Araújo. Parati is a good option for **Carnaval** if you want to get out of Rio for a couple of days.

The Parati region produces excellent cachaça, and in 1984 the town council in its wisdom inaugurated the annual **Festival da Pinga**. The pinga party is held over an August weekend.

Places to Stay

Parati has two very different tourist seasons. From December to February hotels get booked up and room prices double, so reservations are a good idea. Many places require the full amount to be paid in advance – usually placed in their bank account in Rio or São Paulo. This is often nonrefundable.

The rest of the year, finding accommodations is easy and not expensive, the town is quiet and some of the boutiques and restaurants close for the winter. The prices quoted here are low-season rates.

Budget There are a couple of campgrounds on the northern edge of town. Just over the bridge on the left is *Camping Beira Rio* (☎ 3371-1985), and farther along at Praia do Pontal is *Camping Club do Brasil* (☎ 3371-1877).

The *Pouso Familiar* (☎ 3371-1475, Rua José Vieira Ramos 262) is close to the bus station and charges US$15/25 a single/double, including a good breakfast. It's a friendly place, run by Joseph and Lúcia, a Belgian/Brazilian couple. Joseph speaks English, German, French, Spanish and, of course, Dutch, and is very helpful. The pousada also has clothes-washing facilities.

Another recommended place is the homey *Pousada Marendaz* (☎ 3371-1369 pousada-marendaz@uol.com.br, Rua Dr Derly Ellena 9). Run by Rachel and her four sisters, it's more of a family home than a hotel. They charge US$13 per person. Near Marendaz is *Pousada Konquista* (☎ 3371-1308), Rua Jango Pádua 20, offering air-con rooms for US$13/20 single/double. It has a nice terrace with a pool table. *Pousada da Matriz* (☎ 3371-1610, Rua Marechal Deodoro da Fonseca 334) is well located and has basic rooms for US$10 per person without breakfast. Ask to see the better rooms upstairs.

Mid-Range The *Hotel Solar dos Gerânios* (☎/fax 3371-1550), Praça da Matriz (also known as Praça Monsenhor Hélio Pires), is a beautiful old hotel with wood and ceramic sculptures, flat brick and stone, rustic heavy furniture and *azulejos* (Portuguese tiles). Singles/doubles start as low as US$20/30. The *Hotel Estalagem* (☎ 3371-1626) on Rua da Matriz charges US$30/36. Ask for the

room upstairs – it has a great view. *Pousada Aconchego* (☎ 3371-1598, Rua Domingo Gonçalves de Abreu 1) is right on the edge of the old part of the town. It has a nice internal space and swimming pool, and its double fan cooled/air-conditioned rooms are not a bad deal for US$33/40.

For really great vistas of the town and bay, try *Pousada Morro do Forte* (☎ 3371-1211, Rua Orlando Carpinelli 21), up on Morro do Forte. It has comfortable air-con rooms with small balconies opening to gorgeous scenery for US$40/45.

Top End There are three splendid, four-star colonial pousadas in Parati. Owned by a famous Brazilian actor, the *Pousada Pardieiro* (☎ 3371-1370, fax 3371-1139, pp@ pousadapardieiro.com.br, Rua do Comércio 74) has a tranquil garden setting, refined service and impeccable decor. This is one of the best pousadas in Brazil, with single/double rooms from US$80/100. The *Hotel Coxixo* (☎ 3371-1460, fax 3371-1568, Rua do Comércio 362) is just a notch below the Pousada Pardieiro, but it has some standard rooms that are a good deal at US$50. The pousada is cozy and colonial, with beautiful gardens and a pool, and the rooms are simple but comfortable and pretty. To get the US$50 doubles, make reservations early; most doubles go for US$70.

The *Pousada do Ouro* (☎ 3371-1378, fax 3371-1311, ouro@contracthor.com.br, Rua da Praia 145) is the kind of place where you can imagine bumping into Mick Jagger, Sonia Braga or Tom Cruise, especially when you enter the hotel lobby and see photos of them posing in front of the pousada. The hotel has everything – bar, pool and a good restaurant. Doubles cost US$90 to US$130.

Located in the mountains, 16km north of Parati, is the *Hotel le Gite d'Indaiatiba* (☎ 3371-1327, fax 3371-2188). Run by a French guy (if you have any trouble finding the place, ask for *'o hotel do francês'* – everybody knows it), it has small bungalows in a beautiful setting with a great view. You can go horseback riding, trekking or just down to the beach. There's a good library of mostly French books. The cost is US$66 a night for a double during the week, a bit more on weekends. To get there by bus, take the bus labeled 'Barra Grande via Grauna' and get off at the last stop in Grauna. By car, head toward Rio for 12km, then turn off at the Fazenda Grauna road and follow it for 4km.

Places to Eat

Parati has many pretty restaurants, but once your feet touch the cobblestones, prices go up. To beat the inflated prices in the old part of town, try the self-serve at *Sabor da Terra* (*Avenida Roberto Silveira 80*). Of course, the old part of town is much more pleasant. A good option is *Beija Flor* (☎ 3371-1629), on the corner of Rua Dr Pereira and Rua Beira Rio. It is in a pleasant spot in the old part of town and has reasonably priced sandwiches, soups and juices.

One of the best restaurants in the old part of town is *Hiltinho* (☎ 3371-1432, Rua Marechal Deodoro da Fonseca 233). It is expensive, but there's a good menu and portions are ample. Another recommended restaurant is *Punto Di Vino* (☎ 3371-1348) on the same street at No 129 and facing Praça da Matriz. It has wood-fire pizza and excellent pasta dishes. (This street is also known as Rua da Cadeia, which is less of a mouthful.)

Entertainment

Teatro Espaço (☎ 3371-1575, Rua Dona Geralda 327) is a small playhouse which has plays, music and dance performances by the resident theater company 'Contatores de Estórias.' At the time we came past there was an excellent puppet show acclaimed worldwide – really worth watching. It was on twice weekly (Wednesday and Saturday at 9 pm); admission is US$10.

Café Paraty (☎ 3371-1464, Rua do Comércio 253), a popular hangout on the corner of Rua do Comércio and Rua da Lapa, has live music and is good, though now very upmarket. *Margarida Café* (☎ 3371-2820, Rua Comendador José Luis 11), otherwise known as Rua da Ferraria, also has live music every night. Alterna-

tively, just wander the streets and you'll hear some music outside the restaurants by the canal or inside one of the bars.

Getting There & Away

The bus station (☎ 3371-1177) is on Rua Jango Pádua, 500m west of the old town.

There are eight daily buses from Parati to Rio; it's a four-hour trip, with the first bus leaving at 3 am and the last at 9:15 pm. The fare is US$13.

There are 24 buses a day going from Parati to Angra dos Reis, the first leaving at 5 am and the last at 10:30 pm (US$2, two hours).

There are four daily buses (8 am; 12:10, 4 and 9:30 pm) to São Paulo (US$11, six hours). Three daily buses (7:30 am, noon and 6:30 pm) go to Ubatuba; the fare is approximately US$3.

Getting Around

To visit the less accessible beaches, many tourists take one of the schooners from the docks. Departure times vary with the season, but the information is easy to obtain. Tickets cost US$15 per person, with lunch served on board for an additional US$10. The boats make three beach stops of about 45 minutes each.

A more independent alternative is to rent one of the many small motorboats at the port. For US$15 per hour (more in summer), the skipper will take you where you want to go. Bargaining is difficult, but you can lower the cost by finding traveling companions and renting bigger boats – they hold six to 12 passengers. If you figure on a one-hour boat ride and an hour at the beach, you need a boat for at least three hours. Of course, there are even more beautiful beaches farther away.

The strategy of the boat skippers, since they usually can't return to port for another boatload, is to keep you out as long as possible. So don't be surprised if the first beach you go to is out of beer, or the next beach would be much more pleasant if it had cleaner water. These can be very compelling reasons not to return as scheduled, and searching for paradise has a price.

AROUND PARATI
Praia Barra Grande
About 20km north, on the Rio-Santos highway (BR-101), is Praia Barra Grande, an easy-to-reach alternative to the beaches in Baía de Parati. To get there take one of the frequent Parati-Angra buses.

Praia de Parati-Mirim
For accessibility, cost and beauty, this beach is hard to beat. Parati-Mirim is a small town 27km east of Parati. The beach has barracas and houses to rent. From Parati, it's a couple of hours by boat. If you're on a budget,

catch a municipal bus, which makes the 40-minute trip for only US$1. Get the municipal bus to Parati-Mirim from the bus station at 6:30 am, or 12:40 or 5:10 pm.

Praia do Sono
Beaches don't get much prettier than this. Praia do Sono is about 40km southeast of Parati, west of Ponta Negra. It's a four- to five-hour boat ride, and the beach can have rough water and is sometimes difficult to land on. It's much cheaper to catch the bus to Laranjeiras beach, and from there get directions for the 1½-hour walk east to Sono.

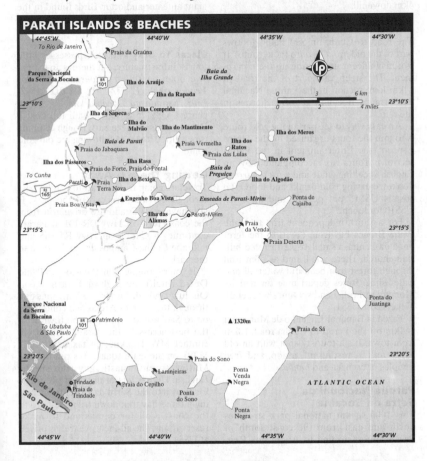

From Parati take the 1040 bus that goes to Laranjeiras beach (ten times daily, US$1 each way). There's food but no formal lodging at the beach. Rough camping is permitted.

Praia da Trindade

About 7.5km west of Sono, this is another beauty. It has lots of simple pousadas so you can stay here for a night or two. The beach is accessible by boat. Alternatively, take the same bus as for Laranjeiras and Praia do Sono and ask the driver to let you off at the entrance to Trindade. From the bus stop, it's 4km downhill.

Inland

The road to Cunha in São Paulo follows part of the old *trilha de ouro* (gold route). It is a magnificent jungle ride up the escarpment. The steep, dirt part of the road (a 14km long section in the Parque Nacional da Serra da Bocaina) gets treacherous in the rain.

An easy way to see part of the gold route is to join the tours organized by the Teatro Espaço (see Entertainment in the Parati section). Tours are accompanied by an English-speaking guide and a *frigo-burro*, a donkey carrying cold drinks and food. The cost is US$15 per person, and an extra US$10 for lunch.

For a short, independent trip, take the Ponte Branca bus from Parati to the Igrejinha da Penha, a small, triple-turreted hillside church. There you'll find a 750m trail through forest to a beautiful waterfall and water slide. Buses depart nine times daily Monday to Friday and six times weekends. Tickets cost US$1.

Fazenda Bananal-Engenho de Murycana is 4km off the Parati to Cunha road, 10km from town. It's a touristy spot with an old sugar mill, a restaurant, a zoo, and free samples of cachaça and *batidas*.

Parque Nacional da Serra da Bocaina

This 1000 sq km national park stretches north and east from the coast south of Parati almost around to Angra dos Reis, reaching into the mountains from Hwy BR-101 to the São Paulo state border and, in some places, into São Paulo state itself. Rising from sea level to the 2132m **Pico da Boa Vista**, the park contains an incredible mixture of vegetation from Mata Atlântica (Atlantic Forest) to Mata Araucária (pine forests) to windswept grassy plateaus in the higher altitudes.

Wildlife is plentiful and includes a large population of the rare woolly spider monkey, as well as other monkeys such as the howler and ring-tailed. Other animals include the tree porcupine, sloth, deer, tapir, giant anteater and otter. Birds found in the park include the harpy, the black-hawk eagle and the black-beaked toucan.

Places to Stay The park possesses little tourist infrastructure, but there is an expensive hotel nearby, the *Pousada Vale dos Veados* (☎ 0xx12-577-1102, fax 0xx12-577-1303, Estrada da Bocaina km 42), which charges US$125 a double with full board. Reservations are necessary. Rough camping is permitted if you're following the old gold route.

Getting There & Away

Travelers going from Parati to Cunha pass through the southern end of the park. If you have a 4WD and are driving in from the coast, turn off Hwy BR-101 at Parati, continue to Cunha on Hwy RJ-165 and take the Cunha-Campos da Cunha road to the park.

If you're coming from the Rio-São Paulo Dutra (multilane highway), turn off at Queluz and drive for 37km, passing through the town of Areias and continuing on to São José do Barreiro, the town with the best access to the park. In São José, contact MW Trekking (☎/fax 0xx12-577-1178), on the main square. It's run by José Milton, an enthusiastic guy who speaks English. He has lots of different programs for trips into the Serra da Bocaina, including a three-day trek down trilha de ouro to the coast. Call for details and to make reservations. The all-inclusive trek is priced at US$120.

Itatiaia Region

The Itatiaia region is a curious mix of Old World charm and New World jungle. The region lies in the Serra da Mantiqueira's Itatiaia massif, in the northwest corner of Rio de Janeiro, and borders the states of São Paulo and Minas Gerais. Penedo and Visconde de Mauá are the towns of most interest to travelers and the Parque Nacional de Itatiaia offers excellent walks and climbing. This idyllic corner of Rio de Janeiro state was settled by Europeans – Penedo by Finns, Itatiaia and Visconde de Mauá by Germans and Swiss – but it is now popular among Brazilians of all ethnic groups. Resende is the regional center.

The climate is Alpine temperate and the chalets are Swiss, but the vegetation is tropical and the warm smiles are pure Brazilian. There are neatly tended little farms with horses and goats, and small homes with clipped lawns and flower boxes side by side with large tracts of dense forest untouched by the machete. This is a wonderful place to tramp around green hills, ride ponies up purple mountains, splash in waterfalls and hike trails without straying too far from the comforts of civilization: a sauna, a fireplace, a soft bed, a little wine and a well-grilled trout! Budget travelers beware – the region is frequented by wealthy Cariocas and Paulistas, so food and accommodations tend to be expensive.

RESENDE

☎ 0xx24 • postcode 27500-000 • pop 97,000
• elevation 407m
Resende, the largest city in the Itatiaia region, is the transport hub for Penedo and Visconde de Mauá. It has no tourist attractions, but is the home of a university and a military academy (the Academia Militar das Agulhas Negras).

Places to Stay & Eat

The military and the university may account for the very cheap hotels in the Campos Elízio part of the city. The best is the *Hotel Presidente* (☎ 3354-5464, *Rua Luis Pistarni 43*), with simple but clean single/double quartos for US$10/15. Double apartamentos are US$26. Lodging doesn't come much cheaper in this part of Brazil. Unless you are camping, you are likely to pay more in Penedo, Visconde de Mauá or the national park, but it's worth paying extra to stay in those places rather than commuting from Resende.

Trem Azul, an eatery close to the main bus station, will give you good value for your money: An all-you-can-eat lunch is US$4.50. Head along Rua da Rodoviaria in the direction of Rio – it's opposite Volkswagen.

Getting There & Away

Buses from Rio de Janeiro and São Paulo go to and from the Resende bus station (☎ 3354-6274), Posto Presidente at the town entrance, several times a day. The Cidade de Aço line runs 20 buses a day to Resende from Rio's Novo Rio bus station, the first leaving at 5:45 am and the last at 9 pm (US$8, 2½ hours).

PENEDO

☎ 0xx24 • postcode 27500-000
• elevation 600m
Finnish immigrants, led by Toivo Uuskallio, settled in the Penedo area in 1929. If the beautiful Scandinavian woodwork doesn't convince you of this, the number of saunas will. The Finns planted citrus groves along the banks of the Rio das Pedras, but when this enterprise failed they turned to preparing Finnish jams and jellies, homemade liqueurs and sauces.

Information

There is a tourist information office (☎ 3351-1876), Avenida Casa das Pedras 766, open 1 to 6 pm during weekdays and 9 am to 6 pm on weekends. Brochures and information are all in Portuguese.

Petiscos Cyber Bar at Avenida das Mangueiras 800 has Internet access as well as snacks and drinks.

Things to See & Do

Penedo's main attractions are the forest and waterfalls. There are three waterfalls worth

THE SOUTHEAST

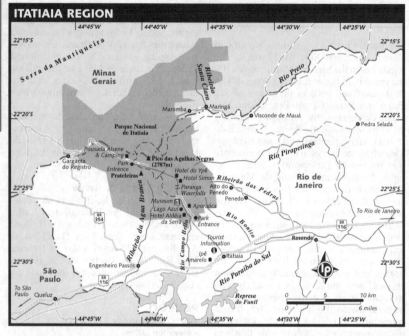

ITATIAIA REGION

visiting: **Três Cachoeiras**, the very pretty **Cachoeira do Roman** which is on private grounds, 10 minutes walk uphill from the Pousada Challenge, and **Cachoeira de Deus** right near the Pousada Challenge.

About one hour of uphill hiking from the end of the asphalt takes you into very dense forest, although there are trails inside. Hopefully you will come across the large bands of big monkeys and steer clear of the wildcats.

You can hire horses at From Penedo (☎ 3351-1380), Rua Finlândia 150 in Penedo, for a guided tour (US$15, 1½ hours).

There is now only a sprinkling of Finns among the assortment of Brazilian people, but they all get together for *letkiss* and *jenkiss* dances every Saturday night at the Clube Finlandês. From 9 pm to 2 am, the Finnish dancers put on Old World togs and do traditional dances. Admission is US$3.

The Sauna Bar and Sauna Finlandesa are near the Clube Finlandês. These sweat shops

are open to the public from early afternoon until 10 pm (later if enough people are interested). Admission is US$4. Otherwise, most of the hotels have their own saunas.

Places to Stay & Eat

Penedo is expensive, due to the large number of weekend tourists who come up from Rio, but the accommodations are well above average, and you'll find that the food is good. Daily rates usually include breakfast and lunch.

The ***Pousada Challenge*** *(☎ 3351-1389, Alameda Áustria 43),* in the hilly suburb of Alto do Penedo, has very clean, prefabricated chalets. Doubles cost US$35, including breakfast and use of the pool and sauna. The ***Apart Penedo*** *(☎ 3351-1204),* close to the end of the paved road, asks US$20/30 for its simple singles/doubles. Nearby, across the creek in a lovely spot, is the ***Hotel Daniela*** *(☎/fax 3351-1151).* It has nicely designed living and breakfast areas, swimming pool and sauna. Doubles go for US$32 during the week and US$47 on weekends.

Palhoça (*Avenida das Mangueiras 2510*) has good and inexpensive meals. Farther down along Avenida das Mangueiras, *Casa do Fritz* at No 518 has reasonable pasta dishes, and *Rei das Trutas* at No 63 is a good place to try some trout.

Casa do Chocolate (*Avenida Casa das Pedras 10*) has sandwiches, 50 different ice cream flavors if it's hot, and hot chocolate if it's cold.

Shopping

Penedo's many small craft shops specialize in jellies, honey, chutneys and preserves, chocolates, cakes and candles. The *Pequena Finlandia* on the corner of Rua das Velas with Avenida das Mangueiras, is a shopping complex with handicrafts and all the other local specialties.

Getting There & Away

There are two buses daily from Rio to Penedo, at 11 am and 5 pm (US$11, 2½ hours). From Resende, it's much easier to get to Penedo and Itatiaia than to Visconde de Mauá. There are 22 Penedo-bound buses daily, from 6 am to 11 pm. The bus services the 3km-long main street and continues to the end of the paved road.

VISCONDE DE MAUÁ
☎ 0xx24 • postcode 27525-000
• elevation 1200m

Mauá is prettier and a little more tranquil than Penedo, and harder to reach. It's a lovely place, with streams, tinkling goat bells, cozy chalets and country lanes graced with wildflowers.

Information

Visconde de Mauá is actually made up of three small villages a few kilometers apart along the Rio Preto. The bus stops first at Mauá, the largest village, and then heads uphill to Maringá, 6km to the west (one side is actually in Minas Gerais). Maromba is farther upstream at the end of the bus route and about 2km west of Maringá. Most travelers stay in Maromba or Maringá.

The tourist information hut is at the entrance to the village of Mauá. Here you'll find information about activities and a list of places to stay, though not the cheapest ones. It's open Tuesday to Sunday from 8 am to 8 pm (closed for lunch).

Things to See & Do

The Santa Clara Cachoeira, the nicest waterfall in the area, is a 40-minute walk north of Maringá on the Ribeirão Santa Clara. Ask the locals for directions. For a bit of a hike, climb up through the bamboo groves on either side of the falls.

The young and the restless can follow the trail from Maromba to the Cachoeira Veu de Noiva in the Parque Nacional de Itatiaia, a full day's hike each way. It's possible to kayak the rapids of the Rio Preto, the cascading river dividing Minas Gerais from Rio state. The river also has small beaches and natural pools.

There are horses for hire by the footbridge in Maringá (US$6 per hour).

Places to Stay

Most pousadas offer full board with lodging; small signposts at each intersection make them easy to find. If you don't want full board, you can bargain the price down quite a bit.

Barragems Camping (☎ 3387-1534) has large grounds by the river in Maringá. Camping is US$5 per person and they also rent chalets for US$30. The *Hotel Casa Alpininha* (☎ /fax 3387-1390) is in Maringá on the Minas side of the river. Doubles cost US$50, including breakfast and lunch.

Maromba is less commercial and has a few cheap pousadas next to the bus stop. The *Pousada Sonhador*, on the right-hand side of the church, charges US$10/20 a single/double, including breakfast. *Casa Bonita Pedra* (☎ 3387-1342) and *Pousada Aguas Claras* (☎ 3387-1241), both next to the cascading river, are very good options. They charge around US$50 a double. *Pousada Moriá* (☎ 3387-1307), opposite the Cachoeira do Escorrega in Maromba, has nice chalets up the hill with views to the valley from US$40.

Places to Eat

Restaurante do Moisés in Maromba has good *prato feito* for US$3. Rua Ponte de Pedestres in Maringá has a couple of good places: *Filho da Truta* has the ubiquitous per kilo; and *Chapeau Noir* has home cooking, often accompanied by live music. *Restaurante Canto do Rio*, next to Bike & Moto in Maringá, has good-value meals in a pleasant location overlooking the river.

Shopping

In Maringá, on the Rio side of the river, you'll see a few hippie stores selling T-shirts, embroidered blouses, natural perfumes and soaps. Casa da Chocolate on the Minas side of the river in Maringá has plenty of home-made goodies.

Getting There & Around

Visconde de Mauá has no bus station. The two main bus stops are at the shops in Maringá and up at the Praça da Maromba in Maromba.

From Resende to Visconde de Mauá, buses leave Monday to Saturday at 2, 4 and 6 pm. It's about 2½ hours up on the winding dirt road and costs US$2. On Sunday there are two buses, at 7 am and 7 pm. Buses leave Maromba for Resende Monday to Saturday at 7:45 and 10 am, and Sunday at 4pm.

From Rio there are direct buses on Friday at 7:30 pm and Saturday at 7:30 am. Direct buses to Rio from Maromba leave on Sunday evening at 4 pm and Monday morning at 7:30 am. The trip takes 4½ hours and the fare is US$13.

If you tire of walking, head to Bike & Moto in Maringá, which rents mountain bikes for US$10 a day and motorcycles for US$10 an hour. Hitchhiking around here is fairly easy and supposedly relatively safe; do it at your own risk.

PARQUE NACIONAL DE ITATIAIA

☎ 0xx24

This national park, established in 1937 to protect 300 sq km of ruggedly beautiful land, contains over 400 species of native birds, and is also home to monkeys and sloths. It features lakes, rivers, waterfalls, alpine meadows and primary and secondary Atlantic rainforests. Don't let the tropical plants fool you; temperatures drop below freezing in June and, occasionally, the park even has a few snowy days! Bring warm clothes, even in summer.

There is a 24-hour tourist information booth in Itatiaia, 1km north of the Via Dutra, on the road to the park's main entrance. The park entrance is about 5.5km north of here.

Museum

The park headquarters and the museum are 3.7km north of the main park entrance, 10km north of the Via Dutra highway (BR-116). The **Lago Azul** (Blue Lake) is a 400m walk from here. The museum, open Tuesday to Sunday from 8 am to 5 pm, has glass cases full of stuffed and mounted animals, pinned moths and snakes in jars.

Activities

Mountain and rock climbing and trekking enthusiasts will want to pit themselves against the local peaks, cliffs and trails. Every two weeks a group scales the **Pico das Agulhas Negras**. At 2787m, it's the highest in the area. For more information, contact the Grupo Excursionista de Agulhas Negras (☎ 9998-0005, fax 24 3352-1734, www.grupogean.cjb.net).

The best access for walks is from Garganta do Registro on the road from Engenheiro Passos to São Lourenço (near the Minas Gerais and Rio de Janeiro state border). The western park entrance is about 15km from Garganta do Registro along a rough gravel road. From here you can see the dramatic pointy range of the **Agulhas Negras** and from a bit farther on, the boulders of the **Prateleiras**. You can hire guides for US$15 a half-day from the Pousada Alsene.

There are simpler hikes on the tamer Itatiaia side of the park, including a 20-minute walk from the main road (6.5km northwest of the main park entrance) to the Poronga waterfalls. Try to get information from the park entrance or the museum.

Places to Stay

Those after an alpine experience should try *Pousada Alsene* (☎ 3363-1773), in a remote location up at 2400m, about 12km east of Garganta do Registro near the western entrance to the park. You need to book in advance and, if you don't have a vehicle, make arrangements to be picked up either from the main road at Garganta do Registro or down at Itatiaia. Dorm beds are US$28 per person and rooms with bathroom are US$38 a double. Prices include breakfast and dinner. You can also camp here for US$5.

Just north of the Via Dutra in Campo Alegre, a suburb of Itatiaia, there is an HI hostel, *Ipê Amarelo* (☎/fax 352-1232, Rua João Mauricio de Macedo Costa 352). Dorm rooms are US$12/15 in high season with/ without a card. The hostel has bicycles for rent and will organize day trips to the park (US$20 including meals and transportation). The hostel is a 15-minute walk west of the bus station (US$2.50 by taxi).

Hotels within the park on the Itatiaia side are mostly expensive, three-star affairs with saunas and swimming pools. The only cheap alternative is the *Aporaóca* (☎ 3352-1423) campground, 4km north of the main entrance to the park, on the way in from Itatiaia and the Via Dutra. The tent sites (US$3 per person) are across the road from the Aporaóca store and the ice-cream shop.

Just 1.6km north of the main park entrance is the reasonably priced *Hotel Aldéia da Serra* (☎ 3352-1152), with chalets for US$53, including breakfast and lunch. The *Hotel Simon* (☎ 3352-1122), 7km north of the main park entrance (12km north of Itatiaia), charges US$100 for a double with full board. The *Hotel do Ypê* (☎/fax 3352-1453, fax 352-1166), about 8.5km north of the main entrance, charges US$100 for doubles in a chalet.

Getting There & Away

Every 20 minutes on weekdays and every 40 minutes on weekends (from 7 am to 11pm), there is a bus from Resende to the town of Itatiaia. However, there are no regular buses into the park. A taxi ride from Itatiaia town to the places to stay within the main section of the park costs between US$8 and US$13. The park entry fee is another US$2.

It takes about an hour by car on the rough gravel road from Garganta do Registro to the park entrance on the northwestern side of the park. A couple of kilometers past the entrance the road deteriorates further and is only passable by 4WD.

North of Rio de Janeiro

PETRÓPOLIS
☎ 0xx24 • postcode 25600-000
• pop 270,000 • elevation 809m

Petrópolis is a lovely mountain retreat with a decidedly European flavor. It's only 60km from Rio de Janeiro, making it an ideal day trip. This is where the imperial court spent the summer when Rio got too muggy, and it's still the home of the heir to the throne, Dom Pedro II's great-grandson Dom Pedro de Orleans e Bragança. Wander around or ride by horse and carriage through the squares and parks, past bridges, canals and old-fashioned street lamps.

Information

Petrotur has a handy information booth on Praça Dom Pedro with brochures and maps. It's open Tuesday to Saturday from 9 am to 5pm. There is also an information office on Avenida Ayrton Senna at the town entrance, and another information booth on Estrada União e Indústria 8764 in Itaipava; both are open daily from 9 am to 7 pm. Most of the museums and other attractions are closed on Mondays.

Walking Tour

This tour is around 4km and takes approximately three hours, including time spent at the attractions. Start at the **Catedral São Pedro de Alcântara**, which houses the **tombs** of Brazil's last emperor, Dom Pedro II, his wife, Dona Teresa, and their daughter, Princesa Isabel.

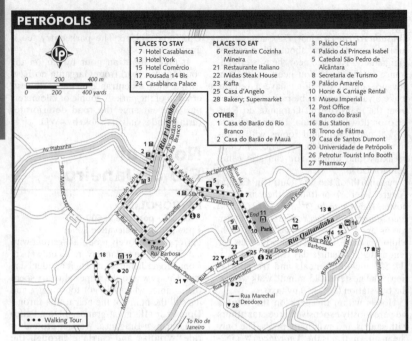

PETRÓPOLIS

PLACES TO STAY
- 7 Hotel Casablanca
- 13 Hotel York
- 15 Hotel Comércio
- 17 Pousada 14 Bis
- 24 Casablanca Palace

PLACES TO EAT
- 6 Restaurante Cozinha Mineira
- 21 Restaurante Italiano
- 22 Midas Steak House
- 23 Kafta
- 25 Casa d'Angelo
- 28 Bakery; Supermarket

OTHER
- 1 Casa do Barão do Rio Branco
- 2 Casa do Barão de Mauá
- 3 Palácio Cristal
- 4 Palácio da Princesa Isabel
- 5 Catedral São Pedro de Alcântara
- 8 Secretaria de Turismo
- 9 Palácio Amarelo
- 10 Horse & Carriage Rental
- 11 Museu Imperial
- 12 Post Office
- 14 Banco do Brasil
- 16 Bus Station
- 18 Trono de Fátima
- 19 Casa de Santos Dumont
- 20 Universidade de Petrópolis
- 26 Petrotur Tourist Info Booth
- 27 Pharmacy

••• Walking Tour

As you leave the cathedral, turn right down Rua 13 de Maio and walk a couple of hundred meters past some crummy shops, until you reach the Rio Piabanha. Cross over the river. Ahead you'll see the **Casa do Barão Rio Branco** and the **Casa do Barão de Maua**. Turn left for the **Palácio Cristal**, an iron and glass structure built in France and imported in 1879 to serve as a hothouse in which to grow orchids. Continue along down Rua Alfredo Pachá. You'll see the Bohemia **brewery** on your right. Sorry, no free samples.

Turn left again onto Avenida Rui Silvera and go down to Praça Rui Barbosa. Cut across the park to the right, and up toward the pink university building with the floral clock in front. Next door, perched up high, is the **Casa de Santos Dumont**, the interesting summer home of Brazil's diminutive father of aviation and inventor of the wristwatch. It's open Tuesday to Sunday from 9 am to 5 pm. Go in and have a look.

As you leave, turn right and start walking uphill, then turn right at the first street on your right. There's a sign advertising the Hotel Margaridas. Keep walking uphill, always taking the right fork, until you reach the **Trono de Fátima**, a 3.5m sculpture of NS de Fátima Madonna, imported from Italy. From here you have a great view of the town and surrounding hills.

Head back down the hill, past the university and through Praça Rui Barbosa (you may want to grab a drink from one of numerous drink stands in the park), then along Avenida Koeller, where you'll pass some fine mansions including the **Palácio da Princesa Isabel**. Turn right at Avenida Tiradentes and make your way up to Petrópolis' main attraction, the **Museu Imperial**, housed in the perfectly preserved and impeccably appointed palace of Dom Pedro II. One interesting exhibit is the 1.7kg imperial crown, with its 639 diamonds and 77 pearls. The museum is open

Tuesday to Sunday from noon to 5:30 pm; admission is US$3. While you're there, you might want to hire a horse and carriage and go for a ride.

Places to Stay
Pousada 14 Bis (☎ 2231-0946, gmobrasil@ pousada14bis.com.br, Rua Santos Dumont 162), near the bus station, is the best option in town. It is in a renovated colonial house decorated with posters depicting the life and feats of Santos Dumont, Brazil's father of aviation. The basement has a bar and games room. Good four-bed dorm rooms cost US$15 per person and single/double apartamentos are US$23/43.

The **Hotel Comércio** (☎ 2242-3500, Rua Dr Porciúncula 56) is directly across from the bus station. It offers basic small rooms for US$10/20. Apartamentos will set you back US$20/30.

If you want to spend a bit more, the **Hotel York** (☎ 2243-2662, fax 2242-8220, Rua do Imperador 78) and the **Casablanca Palace** (☎ 2242-0162, Rua 16 de Março 123) have apartamentos for US$35/53. The York is closer to the bus station. **Hotel Casablanca** (☎ 2242-6662) is next to the grounds of the Museu Imperial and has apartamentos for US$53/66. Yes, the two Casablanca hotels are run by the same group.

There are some beautiful top-end hotels around Petrópolis. **Pousada Alcobaça** (☎ 2221-1240, fax 2221-3390, Rua Agostinho Goulão 298), in the suburb of Corrêas, has a pool, a sauna, a tennis court and lovely gardens crossed by a small river. Doubles go for US$120. The restaurant, which is open to the public, offers excellent main courses for around US$13.

Places to Eat
Rua 16 de Março has lots of eateries, including **Kafta**, the Arab restaurant at No 52, and the **Midas Steak House** at No 170. For good pizza and pasta go to the **Restaurante Italiano** down on Rua João Pessoa near the corner with Rua do Imperador. **Casa d'Angelo**, on the corner of Rua do Imperador and Rua da Imperatriz, is a good place for coffee and toast.

Entertainment
For a drink in elegant surroundings, try **Casa d'Angelo**, on the corner of Rua do Imperador and Rua da Imperatriz. In the suburb of Itaipava, about 20km from the center, there are lots of bars, restaurants and nightspots along Estrada União e Indústria.

Getting There & Away
There are buses back and forth between Rio and the Petrópolis bus station (☎ 2237-6262) on Rua Doutor Porciúcula 75, every half hour, from 5:15 am onward. The trip takes 1½ hours and costs US$5.

VASSOURAS
☎ 0xx24 • postcode 27700-000 • pop 20,000 • elevation 434m

Vassouras, a quiet resort 118km north of Rio, was the most important city in the Paraíba valley in the first half of the 19th century. Surrounded by the huge fazendas of the coffee barons of the time, the town still wears the money they poured into it. They actually were barons, for 18 of them were given titles of nobility by the Portuguese crown. With the abolition of slavery in 1888 and the resulting decline in coffee production, the importance of Vassouras diminished, and this preserved the town.

Museu Chácara da Hera
The beloved grande dame of Vassouras was the aristocratic heiress Eufrásia, who claimed to be devoted to the town despite having palaces in London, Brussels and Paris. Her former home, the Museu Chácara da Hera, is on Rua Dr Fernandes Jr 160, and is open Wednesday to Sunday from 11 am to 5 pm.

Fazendas
There are a few old churches in the town center, as well as old buildings of the schools of medicine, philosophy and engineering, but the real attractions of Vassouras are the coffee fazendas.

Unfortunately, if you don't have a car, you're in for some long hikes. Although the fazendas are protected by the historical preservation institutes, permission must be obtained from the owners before touring the grounds. For more information, ask at the Casa de Cultura (☎ 2471-2765), next to the cinema on Praça Barão do Campo Belo.

If you have a vehicle, take the road from Vassouras to the small town of Barão de Vassouras, 5km away. Pass through the town, and after about 3km you'll see the impressive **Fazenda Santa Mônica** on the banks of the Rio Paraíba. The Fazenda Paraiso and the Fazenda Oriente are farther out on the same road.

Nine kilometers from town is the Fazenda Santa Eufrásia, one of the oldest in the area, dating from the end of the 18th century.

Places to Stay & Eat

The *Pensão Tia Maria*, just up from the bus station at Rua Domingos de Almeida 134, charges US$10 per person, but there are no double beds. Other accommodations options are expensive. The *Mara Palace* (☎ 2471-1993, fax 2471-2524, Rua Chanceler Dr Raul Fernandes 121) charges between US$48 and US$52 a double. The *Hotel Parque Santa Amália* (☎ 2471-1897, fax 2471-3446, Avenida Sebastião Manoel Furtado 526) charges US$50 for doubles, or US$80 with full board.

The *Pensão Tia Maria* and a few other places nearby offer reasonably priced *comida caseira*. But for top restaurants, you are about a hundred years too late.

Getting There & Away

The bus station (☎ 2471-1055) is on Praça Juiz Machado Jr. Frequent buses make the 2½-hour trip to Rio (US$6). The first leaves at 5:15 am, with one leaving every 1½ hours after that. The last one is at 7:30 pm.

TERESÓPOLIS
☎ 0xx21 • postcode 2950-000 • pop 115,000 • elevation 871m

Do as Empress Maria Tereza used to do and escape from the steamy summer heat of Rio to the cool mountain retreat of Teresópolis, the highest city in the state, nestled in the strange, organ-pipe rock formations of the Serra dos Órgãos. The road from Rio to Teresópolis first passes the sinuous curves of a padded green jungle, then winds and climbs past bald peaks which have poked through the jungle cover to touch the clouds.

The city itself is modern, prosperous and dull. The principal attraction is the landscape and its natural treasures, which include the amazing Dedo de Deus visible from the main street; see the Parque Nacional da Serra dos Órgãos section later in this chapter.

Teresópolis is not, however, simply for alpinists: It's a center for sports lovers of all varieties. There are facilities for volleyball, motocross and equestrian activities – many of Brazil's finest thoroughbreds are raised here – not to mention soccer. Teresópolis also bears the distinction of being the training base of Brazil's World Cup squad.

Orientation

Teresópolis is built up along one main street which changes names every few blocks. Starting from the highway to Rio in the Soberbo part of town and continuing north along the Avenida Rotariana (from which a side road leads to the national park) the road is renamed Avenida Oliveira Botelho, Avenida Alberto Torres, Avenida Feliciano Sodré and then Avenida Lúcio Meira. Most of the sites of interest are west of the main drag and up in the hills. The cheap hotels are near the Igreja Matriz de Santa Tereza, Praça Baltazar da Silveira.

Information

The tourist office (☎ 2742-3352) is at Praça Olímpica in the town center. It's open daily from 8 am to 6 pm. The post office is on Avenida Lúcio Meira and the Telemar station is a couple of blocks farther southeast on the same street.

Things to See & Do

The area's main attraction is the Parque Nacional da Serra dos Órgãos. The **Dedo de Deus** (God's Finger) can be seen from the main street, Avenida Feliciano Sodré, however the best place for viewing the peak is the suburb of Soberbo.

The **Mulher de Pedra** (Rock Woman) rock formation, 12km from Teresópolis toward Nova Friburgo, really does look like a reclining woman. **Colina dos Mirantes**, south of the center in the suburb of Fazendinha, is a good place to view the Serra dos Órgãos range and the city. On clear days you can see as far as the Baía de Guanabara. To get there from town, head southeast along Avenida Feliciano Sodré, turn left at Rua Tenente Luiz Meireles and right at Rua Jaguaripe. The Quebra Frascos, the royal family of the Second Empire, had a residence in this neighborhood.

Places to Stay

The cheapest place is the **Hotel Comary** (*☎/fax 2742-3463, Avenida Almirante Lúcio Meira 467*), which has clean quartos for US$7 without breakfast. Double apartamentos are US$20. Have breakfast at the **padaria** (bakery) next door. The **Várzea Palace Hotel** (*☎ 2742-0878, Rua Prefeito Sebastião Teixeira 41/55*) is behind the Igreja Matriz. This grand old white building with red trim has been a Teresópolis institution since 1916. Cheap and classy single/double quartos are US$13/20, apartamentos are US$23/33.

Other hotels nearby include the **Center Residence Hotel** (*☎ 742-5890, Sebastião Teixeira 245*), which has nice apartamentos for US$27/37. The **Hotel Avenida** (*☎/fax 2742-2751, Rua Delfim Moreira 439*), in front of the Igreja Matriz, has overpriced, old apartamentos for US$20/33.

The more expensive hotels are out of town. The **Hotel Alpina** (*☎/fax 2742-5252*) at Km 4 on the road to Petrópolis has apartamentos for US$83 a double. There's a golf club across the road.

Along the Teresópolis to Nova Friburgo road are two hotels. Run by the Hare Krishnas, the **Pousada Vrajabhumi** (*☎/fax 2644-6220*) at Km 6 is in the middle of a forest reserve. There are chalets and natural swimming pools, and rates start at US$88 a double (including all meals, which are vegetarian). The hotel restaurant is open to the public for lunch and dinner. At Km 27, the **Hotel Rosa dos Ventos** (*☎ 2642-8833; fax*

2642-8174) is the only Brazilian hotel in the international Relais & Châteaux chain. It has everything, except that no one under the age of 16 is permitted to stay here. Daily rates, breakfast and lunch included, start at about US$150.

Places to Eat

Restaurante Irene (*☎ 2742-2901, Rua Tenente Luís Meireles 1800*), in the suburb of Bom Retiro, basks in its reputation for providing the best haute cuisine in Teresópolis. It's expensive and reservations are required. **Cheiro de Mato** (*Rua Delfim*

TERESÓPOLIS

PLACES TO STAY	OTHER
5 Hotel Comary	1 Supermarket
7 Hotel Avenida; Pharmacy	2 Gas Station
(24 hours)	3 Tourist Office
9 Várzea Palace Hotel	4 Banco do Brasil
16 Center Residence Hotel	6 Post Office
	8 Igreja Matriz de Santa
PLACES TO EAT	Tereza; ATM (24 hours)
10 Cheiro de Mato	12 Telephone Office
11 Doces Húngaros	14 Bus Station
13 Sand's	
15 Tempero com Arte	

Moreira 140) is a decent vegetarian restaurant. ***Tempero com Arte***, opposite the Center Hotel, is a comfy little place serving some good home cooking. ***Sand's***, on Avenida Almirante Lúcio Meira near the bus station, has a cheap self-serve lunch spread, and ***Doces Húngaros***, which faces the Igreja Matriz, has yummy apple strudel.

Getting There & Away

The bus station is on Rua Primeiro de Maio, off Avenida Tenente Luiz. Buses to Rio depart every half hour from 5 am to 10 pm (US$5, 1½ hours, 95km). There are seven buses to Petrópolis (from 6 am to 7 pm), and four (7 and 11 am, 3 and 7 pm) to Novo Friburgo (US$4, two hours).

PARQUE NACIONAL DA SERRA DOS ÓRGÃOS

☎ 0xx21

Created in 1939, this national park covers 118 sq km of mountainous terrain between Teresópolis and Petrópolis. A distinctive feature of the park are the strangely shaped peaks of the **Pedra do Sino** (2263m), **Pedra do Açu** (2230m), **Agulha do Diabo** (2020m), **Nariz do Frade** (1919m), **Dedo de Deus** (1651m), **Pedra da Ermitage** (1485m) and **Dedo de Nossa Senhora** (1320m). With so many peaks, it's no wonder that this is the mountain climbing, rock climbing and trekking center of Brazil. The region has extensive trails, and it's possible to trek over the forested mountains from Teresópolis to Petrópolis. Unfortunately, most of the trails are unmarked and off the available maps. Hiring a guide, however, is easy and inexpensive. Inquire at the national park entrance (☎/fax 2642-1070), or go with a group organized by one of the hiking and mountaineering clubs in Rio. The best time for walks is from May to October (the drier months).

The main entrance to the national park is at the southern edge of the township of Teresópolis, off Hwy BR-116 from Rio, about 4km from the center. The gate is open Tuesday to Sunday from 8 am to 5 pm (admission US$2). Walking trails, waterfalls, natural swimming pools and tended lawns and gardens make this a very pretty place

for a picnic. There is a visitors center (☎ 2642-1070) and a restaurant up from the main entrance, and, a few kilometers farther uphill, accommodations at the ***Pousada Refúgio do Parque*** (☎ 9221-9147). Rates are US$13 per person including breakfast and soup for dinner. There are also campsites (no shade) for US$4 per person.

From the main entrance, the road extends into the park as far as Barragem Beija Flor. There are several good walks from near here. The highlight is the Trilha Pedra do Sino – a round-trip of about eight hours from the end of the park road. The trail passes Cachoeira Veu da Noiva, the vegetation changes from rainforest to grassland, and the reward is a panoramic view stretching all the way to Rio de Janeiro and the Baía de Guanabara. It costs US$8 to use the trail. For a shorter walk, head up to the Mirante Alexandre Oliveira (1100m), from where there is a good view of Teresópolis – it is about a one-hour round-trip from the park road.

There is another, secondary entrance down in the southeast corner of the national park, off the road from Rio. It also has an information center, walking trails and waterfalls.

Getting There & Away

To get to the park's main entrance from the city center of Teresópolis, take the hourly 'Soberbo' bus (US$0.40). Alternatively, take the more frequent 'Alto' bus and get off at the Praçinha do Alto, from which it's a short walk south to the park's main entrance. A taxi ride from town to the park entrance costs US$10.

NOVA FRIBURGO

☎ 0xx24 • postcode 28600-000
• pop 152,000 • elevation 846m

During the Napoleonic Wars, Dom João VI encouraged immigration to Brazil. At the time, people were starving in Switzerland so, in 1818, 300 families from the Swiss canton of Friburg packed up and headed for Brazil. The passage to Brazil was horrible; many died but enough families survived to settle in the mountains and establish a

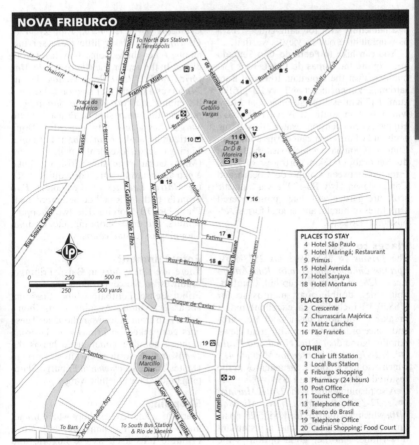

NOVA FRIBURGO

PLACES TO STAY
4 Hotel São Paulo
5 Hotel Maringá; Restaurant
9 Primus
15 Hotel Avenida
17 Hotel Sanjaya
18 Hotel Montanus

PLACES TO EAT
2 Crescente
7 Churrascaría Majórica
12 Matriz Lanches
16 Pão Francês

OTHER
1 Chair Lift Station
3 Local Bus Station
6 Friburgo Shopping
8 Pharmacy (24 hours)
10 Post Office
11 Tourist Office
13 Telephone Office
14 Banco do Brasil
19 Telephone Office
20 Cadinai Shopping; Food Court

small village in the New World. Like Teresópolis and Petrópolis, Nova Friburgo has good hotels and restaurants, as well as many lovely natural attractions: waterfalls, woods, trails, sunny mountain mornings and cool evenings. (It's chilly and rainy during the winter months, from June to August.) The suburb of Cónego is interesting for its Germanic architecture and its apparently perpetually blooming flowers.

Information

The tourist office on Praça Dr Demervel B Moreira (☎ 2523-8000) is open daily from 8 am to 8 pm. As well as maps, it has a complete list of hotels, including the cheapest, with updated prices.

The post office is opposite Praça Getúlio Vargas. The telephone office is on Avenida Alberto Braune.

Things to See & Do

Most of the sights are a few kilometers out of town. Survey the surrounding area from **Morro da Cruz** (1800m). The chairlift to Morro da Cruz runs on weekends and holidays from 9 am to 6 pm. Its station is in the center of town at Praça Teleférico. **Pico da**

Caledônia (2310m) offers fantastic views, and launching sites for hang-gliders. It's a 6km uphill hike, but the view is worth it.

You can hike to **Pedra do Cão Sentado** and explore the **Furnas do Catete** rock formations. Visit the mountain towns of **Bom Jardim** (23km northeast on Hwy RJ-116) or **Lumiar** (25km east of the turnoff at Mury, which is 9km south of Nova Friburgo). Hippies, cheap pensions, waterfalls, walking trails and white-water canoe trips abound in Lumiar. If you have wheels, visit the **Jardim do Nêgo** about 13km northwest of Nova Friburgo, between Campo do Coelho and Conquista on Hwy RJ-130. It's a fantastic sculpture garden with huge moss-covered sculptures of human and animal forms. Admission is US$3.50.

Places to Stay

The **Primus** (☎ 2523-2898, fax 2523-6079, hprimus@hotelprimus.com.br, Rua Adolfo Lautz 128) is up on a steep hill. Comfortable single/double apartamentos go for US$20/35, including an excellent buffet breakfast. The hotel has a pool, pet birds and a nice breakfast room with great views. Another good deal is the **Hotel São Paulo** (☎ 2522-9135, Rua Monsenhor Miranda 41), which also has a pool. Apartamentos in the restored old building are US$30/40.

Also recommended is the **Hotel Maringá** (☎ 2522-2309, Rua Monsenhor Miranda 110), which has quartos for US$15/25, apartamentos for US$25/35, and a restaurant downstairs. Another good option is the **Hotel Montanus** (☎ 2521-1235, Rua Fernando Bizzotto 26), which has simple apartamentos for US$23/30, but you can bargain for a cheaper rate. The **Hotel Avenida** (☎ 2522-9772, Rua Dante Laginestra 89) is a bit cheaper, with quartos for US$20/30 and apartamentos for US$33/40.

A good, mid-range place in the center of town is the **Sanjaya Hotel** (☎ 2522-6052, Avenida Alberto Braune 58). It charges a reasonable US$45/60. The **Hotel Garlipp** (☎/fax 2542-1330) is in Mury, 9km south of town on the road to Niterói, and apartamentos start at US$125 for doubles including full board.

Places to Eat

Crescente (☎ 2523-4616, Rua General Osório 4) is a classy little place serving, among other things, some very tasty trout dishes. In the center, the **Churrascaría Majórica** (☎ 2523-1510, Praça Getúlio Vargas 74) serves a decent filet mignon (US$20) – it's enough for two. **Friburgo Shopping**, a mall on the other side of Praça Getúlio Vargas, has a few bars and cafés. Dona Mariquinha, at the *restaurant* at the Hotel Maringá, serves excellent *comida mineira* (Minas Gerais–style) lunch. You'll feel like a nap afterward for sure. For a quick snack try **Matriz Lanches** or the bakery **Pão Francês**, both on Rua 7 de Setembro, near Praça Dr DB Moreira. The two shopping centers, Friburgo Shopping and Cadinal Shopping, have *food courts*.

Entertainment

There are a few *bars* in Baixo Friburgo, southwest of the center along the front of Friburguense Football Clube Stadium, about 2km along Avenida Conselheiro Julius Arp from Praça Marcilio Dias. These bars get packed on Friday and Saturday nights. Another recommended bar is the **Far West Café** north of the city in Córrego Dantes. There is a *cinema* in Friburgo Shopping on the Praça Getúlio Vargas.

Shopping

Praça do Teleférico has shops where homemade liqueurs and jams are sold. Nova Friburgo bills itself as the lingerie and knitwear capital of Brazil, and there are lots of factory outlets around town.

Getting There & Around

Nova Friburgo is a little over two hours by bus from Rio, via Niterói, on bus line 1001 (US$7). The ride is along a picturesque, winding, misty jungle road.

Novo Friburgo has two long-distance bus stations: the north bus station (Rodoviária Norte, ☎ 2522-6095), 2.5km north of the center at Praça Feliciano Costa, and the south bus station (Rodoviária Sul, ☎ 2522-0400), 4km south of the center at Ponte da Saudade. You'll need to catch a local bus to the central, local bus station just north of Praça Getúlio Vargas. Local buses go to just about all the tourist attractions. Ask for details at the tourist office.

The Rodoviária Norte has bus service for Petrópolis and Teresópolis, and the Rodoviária Sul services for Rio. Buses to Rio leave every 30 to 60 minutes from 5:30 am to 9:30 pm. To Teresópolis there are four buses daily at 7 and 11 am and 3 and 6 pm (US$4, two hours).

An adventurous trip, off the beaten track and heading to the coast, is to catch a bus to Lumiar and from there catch another to Macaé.

East of Rio de Janeiro

SAQUAREMA
☎ 0xx24 • postcode 28990-000 • pop 44,000
After the famous beaches of Rio and the Baía de Guanabara, with their high-rise hotels and bars spilling onto the sands, the quiet, clean beaches east of Rio are a welcome change.

Saquarema, 100km from Rio de Janeiro, was founded near the ocean inlet to the Lagoa de Saquarema, on the narrow stretch of land squeezed between the lagoon and the ocean. Once a series of fishing villages, it has slowly but surely been taken over by low-rise vacation housing developments. However, the weary traveler will find that the town still retains its sleepy character and its charming historical center.

The town's focal point is the gorgeous **church** (1837) perched on the hill near the entrance to the lagoon. From this strategic spot you can survey the long, empty beaches and view the mountains beyond the lagoon. To the west are the beaches of **Boqueirão** a few kilometers away, **Barra Nova** 8km away, and **Jaconé** 15km away. East of the bridge across the inlet is **Praia Itaúna**. It is probably the town's most beautiful beach and is one of the best surf spots in Brazil. An annual surfing contest is held here during the first two weeks of October.

The locals take unusual pride in the natural beauty of their town's setting. Polluting industries are forbidden in the municipality, so it's still possible to find sloths and bands of monkeys in the jungles. Motorboats aren't allowed to muck up the lakes and lagoons, which means the water is still pure, and fish and shrimp are abundant. The long shoreline of fine, white sand beaches and clean water attracts surfers, sports fishers and sun worshippers. Saquarema is a horse-breeding and fruit-growing center; you can visit the orchards and pick fruit, or rent horses or a jeep and take to the hills.

Saquarema hosts mass at NS de Nazaré on September 7 and 8. It attracts around 150,000 pilgrims, second only to the Nazaré celebrations of Belém.

History
On March 17, 1531, Martim Afonso de Sousa founded a Portuguese settlement here and met with the Tamoio Indian chief Sapuguaçu. Nonplussed by de Sousa's five ships and 400 sailors, Sapuguaçu chose to ally the Tamoios with the French. In 1575 Antônio Salema, then Governor of Rio de Janeiro, decided to break the Tamoio-French alliance and, with an army of over 1000 men, massacred the Indians and their French military advisers.

The next big event in Saquarema's history was the slave revolt of Ipitangas, in which 400 slaves took over the plantation mansion and kicked out their master. For a few days the slaves held the town and fought against the cavalry that rode out from Niterói. The town pillory, Bandeque's Post (named after the leader of the slave revolt), was in use as recently as the end of the 19th century.

Information
The Secretaria de Turismo (☎ 2651-2178) at the Prefeitura (City Hall) has friendly staff who can provide useful information. It is open weekdays from 9 am to 8 pm. Try to get hold of Luis, who can speak English and French.

There's a Banco do Brasil on Avenida Saquarema 539. It doesn't have currency exchange, but you can get cash advances using a credit card. The nearest place for exchange is in Cabo Frio.

The post office is close to the bus stop in Praça Oscar de Macedo Soares. The telephone office is at Praça Santo Antonio in Bacaxá, 7km north of Saquarema.

Places to Stay

Prices in Saquarema rise by 30% in high season. Prices quoted here are for low season. The *Hotel Saquarema* (☎ 2651-2275), next to the bus stop on the main praça charges US$13/20 single/double, but stay there only as a last resort. It's OK, but there are better-value accommodations around. The *Pousada da Titia* (☎ 2651-2058, Avenida Salgado Filho 774) is a good alternative, with quartos for US$13 double and apartamentos for US$20.

In town, the *Pousada Canto da Vila* (☎ 2651-1563, Avenida Salgado Filho 52) is a pleasant little place across the road from the beach. Spotless single/double/triple apartamentos cost US$27/40/55.

In Itaúna, *Pousada do Suíço* (☎/fax 651-2203, Rua das Pitangas 580) has air-con rooms for US$35 a double, a good value. The owner speaks German and English. A taxi ride from town should cost about US$3.

There are a few good pousadas right on the beachfront in Itaúna. Surfies will like the *Pousada Itaúna Inn* (☎ 2651-5147): It has an ugly access at the back, but a lovely view to the surf break. Singles/doubles cost US$20/35. The best rooms with sea views are upstairs at the back. *Espuma da Praia* (☎ 2651-2118), which charges US$60 a double, is a converted colonial-style farmhouse with gorgeous and ample frontage facing the beach. It also has a cute swimming pool in the front garden. *Maasai Hotel Beach & Resort* (☎/fax 651-1092) has a good restaurant and swimming pool, and a nice bar and sitting area facing the beach. Comfortable air-con suites (some with spas and sea views) cost US$80 a double.

The *Hotel Fazenda Serra da Castelhana* (☎ 2653-3443 or 2719-5471) about 4km east of town on Rua Latino Melo, charges US$95 an air-con double with three good meals included. It has a swimming pool, sauna, games, horseback rides and other organized activities. A day trip including lunch costs US$13 per person.

Places to Eat

In town, *Restaurante Marisco*, just opposite the bus stop, has good and inexpensive self-serve. *Crepe e Cia* (Avenida Nazareth 160) has delicious crepes. Farther along, *Pizza na Pedra* (Avenida Nazareth 487) has good pizzas and pasta. Just out of the town center and across the bridge, *Lakes Shopping* has a few lanchonetes, a café, and *Jazz Brazil* – the finest bar and restaurant in town.

On Itaúna's beachfront try *Garota da Itaúna* (Avenida Oceânica 165). Also OK is the restaurant at the Maasai pousada, which specializes in seafood dishes. *Le Bistro* (Avenida São Rafael 1134) has quality meals reasonably priced. For per-kilo self-serve meals go to *Restaurante Tropical* (Avenida Vila Mar 17), on the street a block inland from the beachfront kiosks.

Getting There & Around

Buses leave from Rio to Saquarema every hour from 6:30 am to 8 pm. The two-hour trip costs US$5; for an extra US$1 you can go in a bus with air conditioning that departs four times daily (8 and 11 am, 3 and 6:30 pm). To get to Cabo Frio, take a local bus to Bacaxá. From there, buses depart for Cabo Frio every half-hour. The bus stop in Saquarema is on the main praça in the town center.

Walking is the way to get around Saquarema. There are local buses to Jaconé beach, 15km west of the church.

ARRAIAL DO CABO

☎ 0xx24 • postcode 28930-000 • pop 24,000

The village of Arraial do Cabo sits on a corner of the coast, with Cabo Frio 10km due north, and Praia Grande and its continuation Praia Maçambaba stretching 40km due west as far as Itaúna and the entrance to the Lagoa de Saquarema. With four bays, Arraial has beaches that compare with the finest in Búzios, but, unlike Búzios, Arraial is a place where people live and work. The saltworks of the Companhia Nacional de Alcalis, north of town, process both salt and *barrília,* a type of phosphate extracted from the salt.

History

According to Márcio Verneck, a local historian, the Cabo Frio region was inhabited at least 5500 years ago. Before the Portuguese arrived, the warring Tamoio and Goitacazes tribes lived here. In 1503 a Portuguese fleet under the command of Amerigo Vespucci landed at Praia dos Anjos in Arraial do Cabo, and 24 men were left behind to start a settlement, one of the first in the Americas. Fantastic reports about this community became the model for Thomas More's *Utopia.*

The economy of the Portuguese settlement was based on coastal brazilwood, which was felled and shipped back to Europe. Portuguese vessels were at the mercy of Dutch and French corsairs until 1615, when the Portuguese defeated these foes (see also the Cabo Frio section later in this chapter).

Information

There's a tourist office (☎ 620-5039) at the Portal (the town's formal entry portico), about 3km from the center along the Estrada de Arraial do Cabo, where you can get brochures and a map. However, you don't really need a map, as the layout is fairly straightforward and the attractions are the beaches. The post office is at Avenida Getúlio Vargas and the Telemar telephone office is next to the Hotel Praia Grande.

Beaches

'Discovered' many years ago by Amerigo Vespucci, **Praia dos Anjos** has beautiful turquoise water but a little too much boat traffic for comfortable swimming. Nossa Senhora dos Remédios church at the northern end of the beach dates from 1516. Favorite beaches within short walking distance of town are: **Prainha** to the north of town; **Praia do Forno** (accessed by a 1km walking

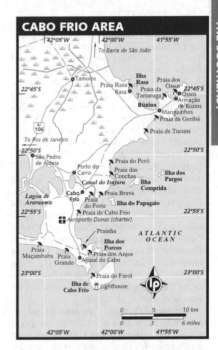

trail from Praia dos Anjos) to the northeast; and the vast **Praia Grande** to the west.

Ilha de Cabo Frio is accessed by boat from Praia dos Anjos. **Praia do Farol** on the protected side of the island is a gorgeous beach with fine white sand. From here there is a 2½ hour walk to the lighthouse. The **Gruta Azul** (Blue Cavern), on the southwestern side of the island, is another beautiful spot. Be alert though: The entrance to the underwater cavern is submerged at high tide. Barracuda Tour (☎ 2622-1340) and Gruta Azul (☎ 2622-1033) have organized boat trips for US$10 per person.

Arrail do Cabo has some of the best diving sites in Rio de Janeiro state. A few dive operators, including Arrail Sub (☎ 2622-1145), rent gear and run diving trips to nearby sites.

Places to Stay

Expect prices to rise by 30% in high season. Prices quoted here are for the low season.

The Camping Club do Brasil has a campground, **CCB – RJ05** (☎ 2622-1023, Avenida da Liberdade 171), near Praia dos Anjos. The charge is US$12 per person. The **Hotel Praia Grande** (☎ 2622-1369, Rua Dom Pedro 41) is a good cheapie in the center of town, with singles/doubles for US$8/15. At Praia dos Anjos, the **Porto dos Anjos** (☎ 2622-1629, Avenida Luis Correa 8) is a house that's been converted into a pousada. Double rooms (US$20) have sea views.

Around Prainha beach, **Pousada da Prainha** (☎ 2622-2512, pousada-da-prainha@ alohanet.com.br, Rua D 90) has simple apartamentos for US$35. Also close to Prainha beach is **Estalagem dos Corais** (☎/fax 2622-2182, Rua E 101), with a pool, sauna and air-conditioned apartamentos for US$40 a double. **Realce Beach Club Pousada** (☎/fax 2622-2633) and **Pousada Orla Mar** (☎ 2622-2410) are both right at the southern end of Prainha beach. Both pousadas have simple, comfortable rooms with sea views starting at US$50.

The **Hotel Pousada Caminho do Sol** (☎/fax 2622-2029, Rua do Sol 50), on Praia Grande, is a pretty resort hotel with a pool and a beautiful view over Praia Grande. Its apartamentos cost from US$50 a double.

Places to Eat

Garrafa de Nansen Restaurante (☎ 2622-1553, Rua Santa Cruz 4) is a classy place for seafood, where you can eat very well for about US$10 per person.

Cheaper eats are available at US$3 per-kilo buffet at **Água na Boca** (☎ 2622-1106), Avenida Litorânea on Praia Grande. Pousada da Prainha also has a good self-serve restaurant. The best restaurant in town is **Todos as Prazeres** (☎ 2622-2365), Rua José Pinto Macedo near the southeastern end of Prainha. It has creative dishes such as fish in orange sauce with coconut farofa for US$10, and apple and gorgonzola soup for US$6; open 1 to 8 pm.

Getting There & Away

There are direct buses daily from Rio to Arraial, the first at 5 am and the last at mid-night (US$10, three hours). An alternative is to catch one of the more frequent buses to Cabo Frio, then take the municipal bus from Cabo Frio (US$0.90), which loops around Arraial and returns to Cabo Frio every 20 minutes. The Arraial do Cabo bus station (☎ 2622-1488) is at Praça da Bandeira in the town center.

CABO FRIO
☎ 0xx24 • postcode 28900-000
• pop 102,000

Santa Helena de Cabo Frio, as it was originally known, was founded in 1615 after the Portuguese had defeated their European foes in the area. The fort of São Mateus was built to protect the lucrative brazilwood trade. In time, the Franciscans joined the settlement and built the Nossa Senhora dos Anjos convent. They were followed by the Jesuits, who settled at Fazenda Campo Novo. By the 1800s, with the brazilwood stands completely destroyed, the economy was geared toward fishing. More recently, tourism, saltworks and chemical industries have become important.

Orientation

The town of Cabo Frio is at the end of the long sweeping beach that extends northward from Arraial do Cabo. Cabo Frio lies to the west of the Canal do Itajuru, which links the Lagoa de Araruama to the Atlantic Ocean. Near the bridge is the town's focal point – a hill with a small white chapel. The town center is east of here, and the bus station is to the west (about 2km from the center) near the end of Avenida Júlia Kubitschek. This road runs almost parallel to the Praia do Forte, named after the fort at its eastern end. There's a small map of Cabo Frio on the wall of the bus station.

Information

There is a tourist information office (☎/fax 647-1689) directly south of the hill, at the end of Avenida João Pessoa on the beachfront at Praça do Contorno, Praia do Forte. It has hotel information and maps; English, Spanish and French are spoken.

There's a Banco do Brasil at Praça Porto Rocha 44 and a Bradesco ATM at Avenida Assunção 904. The post office is at Largo de Santo Antônio 55, in the center, and the Telemar telephone office is on Praça Porto Rocha.

Forte São Mateus

This stone fortress, a stronghold against pirates, was built between 1616 and 1620 to replace the original French-built fort. It is open 10 am to 4 pm Tuesday to Sunday. You will find the fort at the eastern end of Praia do Forte.

Dunes

There are three sand dune spots in and about Cabo Frio. The dunes of **Praia do Peró**, a super beach for surfing and surf casting, are 6km north in the direction of Búzios, near Ogivas and after Praia Brava and Praia das Conchas. The **Dama Branca** (White Lady) sand dunes are on the road to Arraial do Cabo. The **Pontal** dunes of Praia do Forte town beach stretch from the fort to Miranda hill. Robberies can pose a danger at the dunes, so get advice from the locals before you head out to remote beaches and dunes.

Places to Stay & Eat

Cabo Frio is a bit too built up, and it's hard to understand why anyone would want to stay here rather than at Arraial do Cabo or Búzios. If you do enjoy staying in crummy beach cities, both the *Camping Club do Brasil* (☎ 2643-3124) and the *Bosque Club* (☎ 2645-0096), on Rua dos Passageiros at Nos 700 and No 600 respectively, have campsites.

Pousada Costa do Sol (☎ 2644-6596, Rua Maria Duarte de Azvedo 85), in the suburb of Jardim Flamboyant, has simple singles/ doubles for US$12/24. From the bus station, walk three blocks southwest along Rua Inglaterra and turn right.

The cheapest hotels in the town center are located on Rua José Bonifácio. Try the *Atlântico* (☎ 2643-0996, fax 2643-0662) at No 302, where basic apartamentos with fan

are US$30/50, 45% less in low season. There are lots of top end hotels along the water-front, but for the money, you'll have a better time in Búzios.

There are some good eateries around Praça Porto Rocha, in the center. *Bacalhauzinho* at No 27 has excellent bacalhau and a nice atmosphere. For dessert, try *Confeitaria Branca* at No 15.

Getting There & Around

There are regular, air-conditioned buses from Rio de Janeiro and Niterói along Hwy BR-101 (US$8.50 or US$10, three hours). If you're driving, consider taking the old coastal road – it takes longer but provides a beautiful route that winds around foggy green mounds. The bus station (☎ 2643-2291) is 2km west of the center, on Avenida Júlia Kubitschek.

To get to Arraial do Cabo from Cabo Frio, catch a local bus from the bus stop just to the left as you leave the bus station. To get to Búzios, catch a bus from the stop across the road. Local buses cost US$0.90.

BÚZIOS

☎ 0xx24 • postcode 28925-000 • pop 8,600
Búzios, a lovely beach resort, is on a penin-sula scalloped by 17 beaches that juts into the Atlantic. A simple fishing village until the early sixties when it was 'discovered' by Brigitte Bardot and her Brazilian boyfriend, Búzios is now littered with boutiques, fine restaurants, fancy villas, bars and posh pou-sadas. During the holiday season (when the population explodes to 100,000!) prices here are twice what you'll find in the rest of Brazil.

Orientation

Búzios is not a single town but rather three settlements on the peninsula – Ossos, Man-guinhos and Armação de Búzios – and one on the mainland called Rasa. Ossos (Bones), at the northernmost tip of the peninsula, is the oldest and most attractive. It has a pretty harbor and yacht club, a few hotels and bars, and a tourist stand. Manguinhos, on the isthmus, is the most commercial; it even has a 24-hour medical clinic. Armação, in between, has the best restaurants, along with city necessities such as international telephones, a bank, gas station, post office and a pharmacy. Northwest along the coast is Rasa and Ilha Rasa (the island of Rasa), where the political dignitaries and rich of Brazil relax.

Information

The Secretaria de Turismo (☎ 2623-2099) has an information booth on Praça Santos Dumont in Armação, which is open daily from 9 am to 9 pm. The main office (☎ 0800-249999), at the entrance to Búzios, is open 24 hours a day. Also check out the Web site at www.buziosturismo.com. From any newsstand, pick up a copy of *Guia Verão Búzios* (US$3). It has information in English as well as Portuguese, including a list of places to stay (but no prices).

Malízia Tour (☎ 2623-1226) will change money at its offices: Shopping Praia do Canto, loja 16; Rua das Pedras; and Praia dos Ossos. There is an ATM at Praça Santos Dumont. Banco do Brasil is at Rua Manoel de Carvalho 70 in Armação.

Beaches

In general, the southern beaches are trickier to get to, but they're prettier and have better surf. The northern beaches are more sheltered and closer to the towns.

Going counterclockwise from south of Manguinhos, the first beaches are **Geribá** and **Ferradurinha** (Little Horseshoe). These are beautiful beaches with good surf, but the Búzios Beach Club has built condos here. Next on the coast is **Ferradura**, which is large enough for windsurfing, and **Lagoinha**, a rocky beach with rough water. **Praia da Foca** and **Praia do Forno** have colder water than the other beaches. **Praia Olho de Boi** (Bull's Eye) was named after Brazil's first postage stamp. It's a pocket-size beach reached by a little trail from the long, clean beach of **Praia Brava**.

João Fernandinho and **João Fernandes** are both good for snorkeling, as are the topless beaches of **Azedinha** and **Azeda**.

Praia dos Ossos, **Praia da Armação**, **Praia do Caboclo** and **Praia dos Amores** are pretty to look at, but a bit public and not so nice for lounging around on. **Praia da Tartaruga** is quiet and pretty. **Praia do Gaucho** and **Manguinhos** are town beaches farther along.

Places to Stay

Lodging is somewhat on the expensive side, especially in summer, so consider accommodations in Arraial do Cabo or Cabo Frio, or rent a house and stay a while. In the low season, however, you should be able to find rooms as cheap as those in Cabo Frio or Arraial. Most places charge the same price for singles as they do for doubles. Búzios is a romantic place, and solo travelers are unusual. In general, rooms to rent are cheaper than pousadas. All accommodations listed have showers, and prices include a light breakfast. Rates quoted here are for the low season. The high season is December to March and again in July.

Budget If you want to camp, *Country Camping Club* (☎ 2629-1122, *Rua Maria Joaquina 895)*, Praia Rasa, is a good spot but it's a bit out of the way. An alternative for solo travelers is the *Albergue da Juventude Praia dos Amores* (☎ 2623-2422, *Avenida Bento Riberio 92)*, about 20 minutes walking distance to Praia da Tartaruga. It fronts the busy road and has fairly simple facilities. Nevertheless, it offers OK accommodations in beautiful Búzios for US$13 per person including breakfast.

Mid-Range & Top End The *Pousada Mediterrânea* (☎ 2623-2353, *Rua João Fernandes 58)* is a whitewashed and tiled little hotel. Low season doubles with a lovely inland view are US$50. *Zen-Do* (☎ 2623-1542)*, across the road, is a private home with rooms to rent. Yesha Vanicore, a friendly lady who speaks English, runs a progressive household and has doubles for US$27 in the low season.

Pousadinha em Búzios (☎ 2623-1448, *Rua Turíbio de Farias 202)* is a small cutie of a place to stay in the town center, charging US$43. Not far away, right on the beach, the colonial-style *Pousada do Corsário* (☎ 2623-6443, fax 2623-6403, corsariobuz@visualnet.com.br, Rua Agripino de Souza 50) is quite pleasant. Its double rooms with sea views are a good value for US$58. The *Pousada la Chimere* (☎ 2623-1460, fax 2623 1108, Praça Eugênio Harold 36), in Ossos, is an excellent place of a splurge: It has a lovely courtyard, and large, well-appointed rooms with a view over the square. Doubles are US$95.

There are a couple of top-end places in Alto do Humaitá in Armação with stunning views. The *Byblos* (☎ 2623-1162, fax 2623-2828, byblos@byblos.com.br) doesn't have as many facilities, but is a charming place with nice gardens. Rooms here cost US$64/78 with sea view/sea view. Next door, the stylish *El Cazar* (☎/fax 623-1620, elcazar@uol.com.br, Rua A No 6) is the better of the two, and its facilities include a rooftop pool, sauna, Jacuzzis, tennis court, gym, and a games room. It charges US$133 for spacious double rooms.

Places to Eat

For good, cheap food, eat grilled fish right on the beaches. Brava, Ferradura and João Fernandes beaches have little thatched-roof fish and beer restaurants. Most of the better restaurants are in or near Armação.

The *Botequim do Baiano* (☎ 9214-0317, Rua Luis Joaquim Pereira 265), near Praça Santos Dumont, has the best prato feito in town, which usually includes fish or meat with rice, beans and salad for US$3. *Restaurante Boom* (☎ 2623-6254, Rua Turíbio de Farias 110) has an excellent and varied buffet for US$10/kg. *Restaurante Nautilus* (Avenida José Bento Ribeiro 1229), up the small hill on the way to Praia dos Ossos, has fish or meat dishes big enough for two for US$10.

For fancier and more expensive fare, go for a stroll on Rua das Pedras: *As Bruxas* (☎ 9953-0246), at No 21, has great pasta and northern Italian dishes; *Guapo Loco* (☎ 2623-657), at No 233, has colorful, fun

ambiance and Mexican food. Get sushi and sashimi at *Shiro uma Shushi* (☎ 2623-7445), at No 181, and French cuisine next door at *Au Cheval Blank* (☎ 2623-1445). *Chez Michou Crêperie* (☎ 2623-2169), at No 90, is a popular hangout because of its incredible crepes – any kind you want. The outdoor bar has delicious pinha coladas (US$2).

Entertainment

The center of action in Búzios is the Rua das Pedras in Armação. And it all starts late – don't even think of getting here before midnight. There are some good bars, restaurants and nightclubs (on weekends and in season), but mostly it seems that everybody just likes walking up and down the street looking at everybody else.

One of the most happening bars in town is the colorful Mexican *Guapo Loco*, number one with games, concerts and interesting drinks. The barman at the *Taka Taka Ta* is also a bit of a showman, and his fiery concoctions are legendary.

Getting There & Around

From Cabo Frio to Búzios (Ossos), take the municipal bus (a 50-minute, 20km trip). There are seven direct buses daily from Rio, the first at 6:30 am and the last at 7:15 pm. The three-hour trip costs US$9. There are air-con buses three times daily (9:30 am, 1:30 and 3:30 pm) for US$11 a ticket. The bus station in Búzios (☎ 2623-2050) is on Estrada da Usina Velha 444.

The schooner *Queen Lory* makes daily trips out to Ilha Feia, and to Tartaruga and João Fernandinho beaches. There is a 2½-hour trip for US$15 per person, and a five-hour trip for US$20. These trips are a good value, especially since caipirinhas, soft drinks, fruit salad and snorkeling gear are included in the price. To make a reservation, ask at your pousada or visit Queen Lory Tours (☎ 2623-1179), Rua Angela Diniz 35, in Ossos.

Bike Tour (☎ 2623-6365), has two locations, on Rua das Pedras 266 in Armação, and on Pousada Amendoeiras in Ossos. Both rent bicycles for around US$10 a day.

Espírito Santo

Travelers usually see the state of Espírito Santo only through bus windows as they ride between Rio de Janeiro and Bahia. But although parts of the state are heavily industrialized, its beaches offer the chance to really get off the beaten tourist path and experience beach life as the Brazilians do – your fellow beachgoers will likely be from Minas Gerais, southern Bahia or northern Rio state.

Inland, the lush and mountainous coffee- and strawberry-producing regions have interesting towns populated by Italian and German immigrants, along with ecological reserves and the splendid Parque Estadual da Pedra Azul.

The coastline ranges from calm blue inlets to surfing beaches where turbulent water creates a brownish hue. Some of the fishing villages and beaches on the southern coast are very attractive, and to the north, the sand dunes and beach at the Parque Estadual de Itaúnas are the state's highlight.

Excellent seafood is available in Espírito Santo; especially noteworthy is the *moqueca capixaba* (see Food in the Facts for the Visitor chapter).

Colonized in the 16th century, Espírito Santo became an armed region to prevent gold from being smuggled out of Minas. Coffee plantations, the prime source of income up until the 1960s, have been superseded by mining and shipping. Vitória is also home to Garoto, Brazil's famous (and delicious) chocolate.

VITÓRIA

☎ 0xx27 • postcode 29000-000
• pop 292,000

Vitória, the capital, is 521km northeast of Rio de Janeiro and 602km south of Porto Seguro, making it a convenient place to break the journey between Rio and Bahia. Founded in 1551, Vitória has little to show of its colonial past. It's a port city; export coffee and timber pass through here, and the port at nearby Tubarão is the outlet for millions of tons of iron ore.

Orientation

The bus station (☎ 222-3666) is on Ilha do Principe a kilometer west of town. There are two strips of beach: Praia do Camburí, a 10-minute bus ride northeast of Vitória's city center, and Praia da Costa, south of town, at Vila Velha.

Information

SETUR (☎/fax 222-1078), the state tourism authority, is at Rua Raimundo Nonato 116, Forte São João. It is open Monday to Friday from 9 am to 6 pm. At the bus station there's an information booth that is open only erratically; there is also a booth at the airport.

The best cash exchange rate can be found at the Miami souvenir shop (☎ 222-5973) off Avenida Marechal Mascarenhas. It is open Monday to Friday from 9 am to 5 pm. You can change traveler's checks at the Banco do Brasil on Avenida Governador Bley.

The main post office is in the center of town on Avenida Jerônimo Monteiro, and there's a branch at the bus station. There are three telephone posts: two in the center, on Rua do Rosário and at Praça Costa Pereira, and a third at the airport.

City Center

The yellow **Anchieta Palace**, on Praça João Climaco, is a 16th-century former Jesuit college and church. It's now the seat of state government, and the only part you can enter is the **tomb of Padre José de Anchieta** (1534-97), the co-founder of São Paulo and an early missionary who was hailed as the 'Apostle of Brazil.'

Close by is the **Catedral Metropolitana**, with its neogothic exterior and interesting stained-glass windows. **Teatro Carlos Gomes** on Praça Costa Pereira is a replica of La Scala in Milan. Capixabas (as local residents are called) like to walk and relax in the **Parque Moscoso**, just west of the city center along Avenida Cleto Nunes.

Vila Velha

Across the river, south of Vitória, this area was the first place in Espírito Santo to be colonized. The most interesting thing to do here is climb to the **Convento da Penha**, atop the 154m granite Morro da Penha. Even if you don't usually visit convents, the view over the islands and bay makes the trip well worth it. In the week after Easter, thousands of devotees come to this major pilgrimage center to pay homage to the image of NS de Penha, some even making the climb on their knees.

Beaches

Praia do Camburí, a 5km stretch of beach, is punctuated by kiosks, restaurants, nightspots and mid-range hotels. Don't swim near the bridge – it's polluted here. **Praia da Costa**, the main Vila Velha beach, has fewer hotels and restaurants than Camburí, but you can swim and bodysurf.

Places to Stay

In the center there are lots of cheap hotels. If you're really hard up, head for the marginally acceptable *Hotel Restaurante Imperial* (☎ 323-0108, Rua 7 de Setembro 44, 2nd floor) next to Praça Costa Pereira. Basic rundown quartos are US$10 a head, and doubles apartamentos go for US$14. The food in the hotel restaurant is cheap. The other cheapie, *Hotel Cidade Alta* (☎ 233-3346, Rua Pedro Palácios 213), is cleaner and is a better value, with quartos for US$8/12 singles/doubles and apartamentos for US$13/16.

The ***Cannes Palace Hotel*** (*☎ 222-1522, fax 222-8061, Avenida Jerônimo Monteiro 111*) is much better but more expensive – US$30/36 for singles/doubles. If you're going to spend that sort of money, you may as well be on the beach.

Out at Camburí, the cheapest beachfront place is the ***Hotel Praia*** (*☎ 227-8777, Avenida Dante Michelini 207*) with singles/doubles for US$34/44.

Praia da Costa in Vila Velha, although more expensive, is the best beach near Vitória. The three-star ***Hostess*** (*☎ 329-2111, Avenida Antônio Gil Veloso 412*) has singles/

doubles for US$44/53. Farther along the same street, ***Hotel Costa Mar*** (*☎ 200-4688*) is better positioned and has rooms with balconies for US$49/56. The ***Parthenon Pasárgada*** (*☎ 399-6500, pasargada@ebr.com.br, Avenida Antônio Gil Veloso 1856*), also on Praia da Costa, is a top-end place in Vila Velha with nice, comfortable rooms for US$80/90.

Places to Eat

In the center, the ***Sabor Natura Restaurante*** (*Rua 13 de Maio 90*) has a veggie-friendly self-serve lunch for US$4 per kilo.

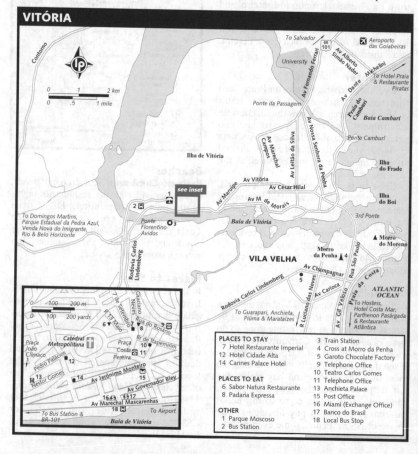

VITÓRIA

PLACES TO STAY
7 Hotel Restaurante Imperial
12 Hotel Cidade Alta
14 Cannes Palace Hotel

PLACES TO EAT
6 Sabor Natura Restaurante
8 Padaria Expressa

OTHER
1 Parque Moscoso
2 Bus Station

3 Train Station
4 Cross at Morro da Penha
5 Garoto Chocolate Factory
9 Telephone Office
10 Teatro Carlos Gomes
11 Telephone Office
13 Anchieta Palace
15 Post Office
16 Miami (Exchange Office)
17 Banco do Brasil
18 Local Bus Stop

Padaria Expressa (Rua Graciano Neves 22), just off Praça Costa Pereira, is excellent for stocking up on bread, cheese and snacks. It also has a good per-kilo buffet lunch.

Restaurante Atlântica (☎ 329-2341, Avenida Antônio Gil Veloso 80) in Vila Velha has excellent *moqueca capixaba* at US$18 for two and local seafood dishes from US$10. For self-catering travelers, there's a 24-hour deli around the corner from the Hostess Hotel Costa do Sol (not to be confused with the three-star Hostess hotel described earlier).

The *Restaurante Piratas (☎ 235-1622, Avenida Dante Michelini 747, Praia do Camburí)* has air-con and good seafood from US$10. If you are in the mood for meat, try *Churrascaria Gramado (☎ 225-1311, Avendia Rosendo Serapião Souza Filho 43)*.

Shopping

The Garoto chocolate factory (☎ 320-1200) makes the best chocolate in Brazil. Visit the factory store, where the stuff is really fresh, located at Praça Meyerfreund Glória, off Rodovia Carlos Lindenberg in Vila Velha – you can take bus No 500 from the city center.

Getting There & Away

Vitória's bus station (☎ 222-3366) is 1km west of the center of town on Ilha do Príncipe near the bridge. There are nine buses a day to Belo Horizonte (US$22, eight hours). To Ouro Prêto (US$20, eight hours), there's a direct bus at 10:45 pm. To Porto Seguro (US$25, nine hours), there's one daily bus at 9 am. Eleven buses a day make the eight-hour journey to Rio de Janeiro (US$22).

There is also a daily train to Belo Horizonte; see the Belo Horizonte section in the Minas Gerais state chapter, later in this book, for more information.

Getting Around

The airport is 10km northeast of the city center. Take the local bus marked 'aeroporto/rodoviária' to and from the center.

All local buses (US$0.55) run from the various stops outside the bus station; the route is written on the side of each bus. For the center, catch any bus that goes along Avenida Vitória. When you pass the yellow palace on the left-hand side, get out and you will be at the Anchieta Palace.

For Praia do Camburí, catch any bus that goes along Avenida Dante Michelini. To Vila Velha and Praia da Costa catch an all-yellow Transcol bus (US$0.80).

The Coast

CONCEIÇÃO DA BARRA

☎ 0xx27 • postcode 29960-000 • pop 19,000

Conceição da Barra lies 254km north of Vitória, between the mouths of the Itaúnas and Cricaré Rivers. There are some quiet beaches here – **Praia da Barra**, **Bugia** and **Guaxindiba** – except during the summer when they are swarmed by visitors from Minas and São Paulo states. From Conceição da Barra you can go on day trips to the main attraction in the region: the Parque Estadual de Itaúnas 23km north of Conceição.

Places to Stay & Eat

Piramide Hostel (☎ 762-1983, Rua 26 de Maio 89) next to the bus station, has basic rooms with bunk beds for US$5 per person without fans or breakfast. *Rustico's Hotel (☎ 762-1193, Rua Muniz Freire 299)* has air-con rooms around a courtyard and small pool for US$20 – you may be able to bargain the price down if you're alone.

The best places to eat are the kiosks on the beaches, which serve the local specialty *puã de caranguejo*, a tasty crab stew. These shacks also serve coconut milk, fried fish and killer *batidas*.

Getting There & Away

Buses leave Vitória for Conceição da Barra daily at 6:40 and 11:40 am and 4 pm. Returning to Vitória, buses depart daily from the bus station (☎ 762-1159) on Rua 26 de Maio at 6 am, 2 pm and 6 pm. The trip takes four hours and costs US$12.

ITAÚNAS
☎ 0xx27 • postcode 29965-000 • pop 2500

This pleasant fishing village is the gateway to the state reserve **Parque Estadual de Itaúnas** with its fantastic sand dunes. The fine sands engulfed the original village of Itaúnas – you can even walk on the remains of the top of the old church tower. From atop the dunes you have a great view of the Atlantic Ocean and the neighboring reserve, with its sand dunes and mangrove forest.

Until just a few years ago, the rebuilt Itaúnas was just a small fishing village with only a couple of places to stay. Now it has about 50 pousadas, and during summer is very popular with the young and beautiful crowd from Espírito Santo and the neighboring states of Minas and São Paulo. Visitors come for the lively *forró* dance parties and nightlife as much as for the beautiful surroundings.

Parque Estadual de Itaúnas
This 3674-hectare state reserve extends for 25km along the coast and has impressive 20m- to 30m-high sand dunes. The wilderness here is home to monkeys, sloths and

Sloths

jaguatiricas (wild cats). The park is also a base for the Projeto TAMAR (see the TAMAR Project boxed text in the Bahia chapter). From September to March you can view sea turtles hatching. It happens two to three times per week at about 5:30 pm.

The Itaúnas park office (☎ 762-1447, peitaunas@escelsa.com.br) is in the village next to the bridge over the Rio Itaúnas. It has a souvenir shop, as well as informative displays about the local flora, fauna and culture.

Places to Stay & Eat
The **Pousada Albergue Sol das Dunas** (☎ 359108-9654) at the end of Rua Honório Pinheiro da Silva, is recommended. It offers clean rooms with bunk beds and shared facilities for US$6 or private double rooms for US$20; a good breakfast is included. It has a cute lounge for TV and video, and the friendly owner is fluent in English and German. **Camping da Vila** (☎ 964-2462) at the back of Pousada Albergue Sol das Dunas, has good camping facilities and charges US$3 per person.

Pousada Ponta de Areia (☎ 762-1644, Rua Honório Pinheiro da Silva), is super cozy. The owner, an artist and a great cook, pays attention to the small details. It has four nice apartamentos for a maximum of two couples for US$26 per couple. If Ponta de Areia is full, try **Pousada das Araras** (☎ 969-0282) next door. It is similarly priced with apartments around a courtyard garden. The rooms downstairs also have a nice little garden at the back. **Pousada Arco Íris** (☎ 988-8282), on nearby Rua Teófilo Cabral, has a friendly atmosphere and simple singles/doubles with balconies for US$13/20.

Pousada A Nave (☎ 762-1644, Rua Ítalo Vasconcelos), has rustic-style rooms with wooden doors carved by the sculptor/owner, who is a real character. The round, open-sided thatched bar is a great place for a few late-night drinks. The place overlooks a mangrove forest and sand dunes. The rate is US$25 for doubles; negotiate a discount if it's not busy.

Another nice, rustic place is **Pousada do Coelho** (☎ 9988-0253, pousadadocoelho@zipmail.com.br) on Rua Projetada near the football field. It has good singles/doubles with mezzanines and balconies with nice views for US$23/30.

If you are suffering from the heat, try **Pousada Gajirú** (☎ 9918-5292, Rua Dercílio Ferreora da Fonseca), which offers air-con rooms and shaded gardens for US$33/40; prices are negotiable for longer stays.

There are plenty of inexpensive options for eating around Itaúnas. Both **Restaurante do Cizinho**, on Rua Adolfo Pereira Duarte just off the praça, and *Pargos*, on the praça. have great per-kilo buffets. The refeições at the simpler restaurants *Dona Pedrolina* and *Dona Teresa*, both just a block away from the plaza, are an excellent value.

Getting There & Away

From the bus stop in the plaza, there are five buses daily between Conceição da Barra bus station and Itaúnas. Tickets cost US$1.50.

GUARAPARI
☎ 0xx27 • postcode 29200-000

Thirty minutes south of Vitória by bus, Guarapari is Espírito Santo's most prominent resort. There are 23 beaches in the municipality, each with a lovely mountain backdrop and each swarming with Brazilian holidaymakers in the high seasons – it's certainly off the gringo tourist route. The best beach is **Praia do Morro**, north of the city. However, you should be aware that its so-called healing black monazitic sand is, in fact, said to be radioactive!

Orientation & Information

The center is 500m south of the bus station, across the bridge; the beach is 200m farther on. The tourist office (☎ 361-2322) at Praça Jerônimo Monteiro has city maps and information in Portuguese. The telephone post is on Avenida Des Lourival de Almeida, the main drag on the waterfront.

Places to Stay

Guaracamping (☎ 261-0475, *Avenida Antonio Guimarães, QD 40*) has tent sites (US$4 per person) on large, walled grounds within walking distance to the beach. It also has reasonable single/double apartamentos for US$26/40 and rundown rooms with bunk beds and shared facilities for US$15. It's a two-minute walk west of the bus station – cross the main road, take the next left and it's one block down on the right-hand corner. This area is known as *Muquiçaba* (mosquito nest), so bring repellent!

Hotel do Ângelo (☎/fax 261-0230, *Rua Pedro Caetano 254*) is a good deal, with friendly staff and singles/doubles costing

US$20/33. In the vicinity and with similar prices is the very friendly one-star hotel *Solar da Ruth* (☎ 261-1836, *Rua Dr Silva Melo 215*). *Coronado* (☎ 361-0144, *Avenida Lourival de Almeida 312*) is a three-star hotel right on the beach for US$60 a double – make sure you get one with views.

The *Mariner* (☎ 361-1100, fax 261-2929, *Avenida Beira Mar 1*), by Praia do Morro, is an architectural beauty from the 1970s, well positioned on the top of a big boulder on a point. It has spacious grounds, a swimming pool and nice views throughout. Rooms with sea views here are a good deal at US$42/53 for single/doubles during low season, but prices double at the peak season (in January and during Carnaval).

Places to Eat

The *Hotel Maryland* has a good self-serve restaurant (US$7/kg). A better deal is the US$3 buffet at *Delícia Mineira* on Rua Joaquim da Silva Lima. *Pizzaria do Ângelo* at the Hotel do Ângelo is good and cheap at lunch and but more expensive at dinner. *Peixada do Irmão* (☎ 261-0636, Rua Jacinto de Almeida 72) is a recommended spot for seafood. The rooftop restaurant at the *Coronado* hotel has great views and meals for US$10 per person.

Getting There & Away

Buses run between Vitória and Guarapari's bus station (☎ 261-1308, Rua Araxa 50) every hour from 6 am to 9 pm (US$1.50, 1¼ hours). Frequent buses make the 28km trip to Anchieta.

ANCHIETA

☎ 0xx27 • postcode 29230-000 • pop 13,200

Eighty-eight km south of Vitória, Anchieta's attractions are the 16th-century church of NS de Assunção and, alongside, the Museu Padre Anchieta (US$0.50, open daily). The church walls, built by local Indians and Padre José de Anchieta, are original. The interesting museum contains relics uncovered during restoration.

Places to Stay & Eat

The colonial *Hotel Anchieta* (☎ 536-1258), 100m south of the bus stop on Avenida Carlos Lindenberg, is a bit rundown but still retains some charm. Singles/doubles cost US$10/23. The *Hotel Porto Velho* (☎ 536-1181), right above the bus stop, has rooms with air-conditioning, TV and refrigerator for US$30/40. Accommodations at this hotel are overpriced and only worth it if you get one of the front rooms with balconies to the beach.

Restaurante Doce Prazer about 1km north of the bus stop on the main road, has US$4/kg lunch buffet and dinner for US$3. There are a couple of lanchonetes, with sandwiches and cheap burgers, near the bus stop.

Getting There & Away

To Guarapari, buses (US$1) run every 20 to 30 minutes from 6 am to 6:50 pm. To Vitória (US$3) they run five times daily. The bus stop (☎ 536-1150) is at Avenida Carlos Lindenberg 183, the main road through town.

AROUND ANCHIETA

Iriri

☎ 0xx27

A great, secluded, tree-lined beach with gentle surf is the attraction in Iriri, 7km south of Anchieta. Frequent buses connect it with Anchieta and Piúma, 5km south.

The best budget option in Iriri is the *Hotel Morubixaba* (☎ 534-1180, fax 534-1476, Rua Joffre Ferrari 100) about 100m from the beach. It has good fan-cooled singles/doubles from US$10/25; add about 20 to 30% for air-con rooms. More expensive but an excellent value is the *Hotel Pontal das Rochas* (☎/fax 534-1369) on Avenida Beira Mar on the rocky point overlooking the beach. It offers nice rooms with balconies offering gorgeous views for US$40/50 during low season. Expect to pay 40% more during peak season.

Ubu

☎ 0xx27

This small fishing village 9km north of Anchieta can be reached by catching one of the frequent Guarapari–Anchieta via Ubu buses. It has a nice little beach and a couple of seafood restaurants. There are also good accommodations at the Swiss-run *Pousada Aba Ubu* (☎ 536-5067, fax 536-5068, abaubu@terra.com.br), on Rua Manoel Miranda Garcia just uphill from the beach. It has a pool, tennis court and nice rooms around a courtyard garden for US$25/40 single/double.

There are a few good places on the beach to have seafood. *Peixada do Garcia* (☎ 536-5050), on Avenida Magno Ribeiro Muqui, is a 40-year-old seafood restaurant with an especially good reputation.

The Steps of Anchieta

José de Anchieta arrived in Brazil as a Jesuit missionary in 1553. Along with Manoel da Nóbrega he founded the village of Pira-tininga (today the megacity of São Paulo). On a trip down the São Paulo coast, he was captured by Tamoio Indians. While held hostage he began one of his most famous poems, the 'Poema da Virgem,' by tracing words on the beach sand. In addition to being a priest and poet, he was a teacher, nurse and church-builder, and he was re-garded as the 'Indian expert' of his time.

Anchieta walked along the coast of Es-pírito Santo in his mission to convert all the Indian tribes he came across. He ended up at Reritiba, today the town of Anchieta, where he chose to spend the last few years of his life. In 1980 he was beatified by the Pope and is now a candidate for sainthood.

The Associação Brasileiro dos Amigos dos Passos de Anchieta (☎ 315-5473, Rua Pe Antônio Ribeiro Pinto 195/1004, Vitória-ES) organizes an annual pilgrimage that retraces his 'steps.' The popular 100km walk along the beach from Vitória to Anchieta, held in June, takes three days.

PIÚMA
☎ 0xx27 • postcode 29285-000 • pop 15,000
The rarest shell in the world, the *oliva zelin-dea*, is occasionally found in Piúma, 100km south of Vitória. Nice beaches and some nearby offshore islands make this area worth a look.

The coastline is dominated by the 300m cone-shaped **Monte Aghá**, which is a good place for hang-gliding and climbing.

Islands & Beaches
Ilha do Gamba, an ecological reserve, is con-nected to the mainland by a thin isthmus. At low tide, you can walk from it to **Ilha do Meio**, which is a preserve for wild orchids and native trees. The next island is **Ilha dos**

Cabritos. In summer, boats (US$3) run from the first island to the latter two; otherwise, pay a fisherman to take you over.

There are beaches along the main road, within walking distance from the center. Praia Acaiaca to the north has calm water, while Praia Maria Nenen is a little more agitated. Avoid Praia da Boca da Barra – it's polluted.

Places to Stay & Eat
Be warned that hotel prices in Piúma double during summer. A nice place is the **Solar de Brasília** (☎ 520-1521, Avenida Eduardo Rodrigues 15). It has double rooms from US$15 during low season, the included breakfast is excellent, and there's a small swimming pool.

Next to the Solar de Brasília, **Dom Manuel Pousada e Camping** (☎ 520-1370) offers singles/doubles from US$10/16 and camping for US$3 per head. The **Coliseu Hotel** (☎ 520-1273) on Avenida Beiramar, is an OK deal at US$20/25 for rooms that have a sea view.

Most of Piúma's restaurants are located along the beachfront on Avenida Beiramar. **d'Angelus** has a very popular and inexpen-sive self-serve lunch. Farther south along the beach **Ancoradouro** has better quality, reasonably priced à la carte meals.

Getting There & Away
Four buses daily connect Piúma to Vitória (US$4). There are also frequent buses to Anchieta (US$0.50).

Inland

DOMINGOS MARTINS
☎ 0xx14 • postcode 29260-000 • pop 5800
• elevation 620m
Forty-one kilometers west of Vitória, Domingos Martins, also known as Camp-inho, is a small village settled by Germans in 1847. Dotted with *fachwerk* houses, it's a pleasant mountain retreat with cool fresh air, and it makes a good base for exploring the streams and forests of the mountains.

Kautsky Reserve

Roberto Kautsky is a dedicated botanist who has cultivated more than 100 species of orchids at his home (☎ 268-1209) at the south end of town (ask anyone) and on his mountainside reserve. He'll drive you, free for the asking, to the reserve in his ancient jeep and talk your ear off in German, 'bad English' or Portuguese – people come from miles around and it's a great experience. Show up before noon or from 2 to 6 pm.

Other Attractions

In the center, the **museum** on the first floor of the Casa da Cultura (☎ 268-1471, Avenida Presidente Vargas 513) has exhibits of the belongings and tools from the early settlers. Farther up Avenida Presidente Vargas, near the main praça and Lutheran church, the **Recanto dos Colibris** is a pretty gathering spot.

Places to Stay & Eat

Hotel e Restaurante Imperador (☎ 268-1115, Rua Duque de Caxias 275) is an old-ish hotel with traditional-style German architecture. It has a pool and sauna and is opposite a cute plaza and the Lutheran church; rooms cost US$23/30 single/double. A little more upmarket is the *Solar da Serra* (☎ 268-1691, Rua Pedro Gerhard 191). It has modern and comfortable double rooms with views from US$45.

Try some German food at *Bigosch* on Rua Francisco dos Santos Silva opposite the Casa da Cultura; expect to spend around US$6 per person. For a delicious and inexpensive per-kilo buffet go to *Restaurante dos Imigrantes* in the pedestrian mall in the center. Huge pizzas (US$10) come with free samples of local wines at *Adega Alemã Schwambach* (☎ 268-1423) just inside the city limits. Their Jubuticaba wine is simultaneously sweet and bitter. A liter costs US$4.

Getting There & Away

Ten buses Monday through Friday and six on Saturday and Sunday make the 41km trip (US$2, one hour) from Vitória bus station on Ilha do Príncipe to Domingos Martins bus station (☎ 268 1243), at Avenida Presidente Vargas 380. Any bus between Vitória bus station and Belo Horizonte will stop here on request, too.

AROUND DOMINGOS MARTINS
Parque Estadual da Pedra Azul

Vitória–Belo Horizonte buses also stop at the best reason to come inland: the 500m Pedra Azul, 50km west of Domingos Martins down Hwy BR-262. The rock, tinted by a bluish moss, is at the center of Parque Estadual da Pedra Azul (☎ 248-1156). Rangers escort hikers to the rock's nine **natural pools**, a moderately difficult hike from the base trail that takes about 1½ hours. It's free, but you must book a week in advance (US$3 per person).

Places to Stay & Eat

Serious climbers are permitted to camp in the park free, but you'll need to prove to the rangers that you know what's what. In winter, it is near freezing during the day and below freezing at night, so pack wisely.

The area is dotted by fancier resort hotels that all have horses for rent. The best is right near the park headquarters off Hwy BR-262 at Km 90 – the spectacular, amenity-packed *Aroso Paço Hotel* (☎ 248-1147, fax 248-1180). It has beautifully detailed, immaculate singles/doubles, from US$73/90 during weekdays or from US$160/200 for a two–night weekend; three meals a day are included in the prices. Ask for a room with a view of the rock.

At the park trail entrance the *Pousada Peterle* (☎ 248-1243) has nice rustic log cabins with fireplaces and balconies for US$45/60.

Just past the park trail entrance, 1.5km south of Hwy BR-262, the *Café Colonial* (☎ 248-1124) serves up tea and coffee along with dozens of types of cakes, cookies and salads. It's open weekends and holidays only, from 2 to 8 pm.

SANTA TERESA

☎ 0xx27 • postcode 29650-000 • pop 9700
• elevation 655m

Santa Teresa, 76 km northwest of Vitória, is a small town settled by Italian immigrants. It has a cheerful flowered plaza, a cool mountain climate and nearby vineyards. Worthwhile excursions include the valley of Canaã and the Reserva Biológica Nova Lombardia.

Museu Biológico de Professor Melo Leitão

Santa Teresa's main attraction, this biological museum represents the life's work of Augusto Ruschi, a staunch environmentalist and world-renowned hummingbird expert, who died in 1986 after being poisoned by a frog. The museum has a good collection of stuffed animals and also has a small zoo, a butterfly garden, a snake farm, and a large number of orchids and other flora. It's open only on Saturday and Sunday from noon to 5 pm. Time your visit to Santa Teresa accordingly, as the museum is very interesting.

Places to Stay & Eat

The *Hotel Pierazzo* (☎ 259-1233, *Avenida Getúlio Vargas 115*) has very nice singles/doubles for US$30/40. Cheaper than this is the *Globo* (*Rua Jerônimo Vervloet 190*), with rooms for US$10 per person.

Restaurante Zitu's, a few doors down from the Pierazzo above a lanchonete, does good pasta.

Getting There & Away

Seven buses a day make the journey from Vitória bus station on Ilha do Príncipe to Santa Teresa's bus station (☎ 259-1300), on Rua Ricardo Pasoline (US$4, two hours). There are, however, no roads directly linking Santa Teresa with Domingos Martins, which means the only way of getting there is to backtrack through Vitória.

Minas Gerais

Minas Gerais presents a welcome contrast to the rest of Brazil. While the name means simply General Mines, the state is packed with exquisite colonial towns, seemingly

Highlights

- Marveling at the modernist architecture of Niemeyer in Belo Horizonte
- Wandering among Brazilian baroque churches in the colonial towns
- Admiring the sacred sculptures of Aleijadinho
- Learning the fascinating history of Ouro Prêto and Diamantina
- Riding the steam train from São João del Rei to Tiradentes
- Trekking or riding along the Estrada Real
- Shopping for crafts from the Vale de Jequitinhonha in Diamantina
- Hiking in the Parque Nacional de Caparaó

frozen in another epoch. The baroque churches and sacred art, mostly sculptures by one of the world's great artists, Aleijadinho, represent more than half of Brazil's national monuments.

Minas is as large as France, part of a vast plateau that crosses Brazil's interior. Rising along the state's southern border with Rio and São Paulo is the Serra da Mantiqueira with some of Brazil's highest peaks.

The *cidades históricas,* historic colonial cities that grew up with the great gold boom, are clustered in three spots along the Serra do Espinhaço. São João del Rei, with Tiradentes nearby, is 200km south of Belo Horizonte; Ouro Prêto and Mariana are 100km southeast of it; and Diamantina is 290km north of it. The foothills and streams of the Serra do Espinhaço were scoured for gold throughout the 18th century.

Ouro Prêto has more of everything – baroque architecture, churches, Aleijadinho, museums and fame – than any other city in Brazil. It also has more tourists, traffic, boutiques and expensive hotels and restaurants.

Minas also has several hydro-mineral spa towns in the mountainous southwest corner, and a number of prehistoric caves close to the capital, Belo Horizonte.

The roads are good here, but travel is usually a sinuous affair. Terrain here is largely hilly, with deep valleys and plateaus running off the large mountain ranges.

The best time to visit Minas is between March and August (see the Climate section later in this chapter).

History

Around 1695, *bandeirantes* (groups of explorers from São Paulo in search of Indian slaves and precious metals) found gold along the banks and in the beds of rivers flowing from Brazil's oldest mountains.

The deposits were called *faisqueiras* (sparkles) because the larger pieces were actually visible – all the miners had to do was pick them up.

MINAS GERAIS

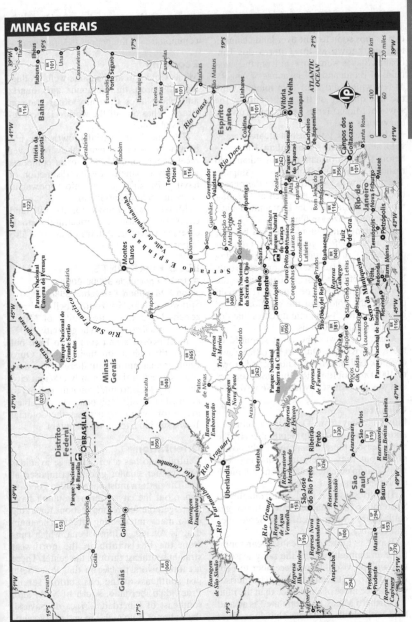

Word got out. Brazilians flocked to Minas, and Portuguese emigrated to Brazil. These two groups soon fought over land claims in the war known as the Guerra dos Emboabas. Slaves were brought from the sugar fields of Bahia and the savannas of Angola, as few whites did their own mining. Until the last quarter of the 18th century, the slaves of Minas Gerais were digging up half the world's gold.

Minas set the gold-rush standard – crazy, wild and violent – more than 100 years before the Californian and Australian gold rushes. Disease and famine were rampant. The mine towns were known for their licentiousness, and prostitutes such as the infamous Chica da Silva in Diamantina have been immortalized in film.

Merchants and colonial officials became rich, as did a few gold miners. Gold siphoned off to Portugal ended up feeding England's Industrial Revolution, so the only lasting benefits to come to Brazil were the development of Rio de Janeiro (the main port for the gold) and the creation of the beautiful, church-clad mining cities that dot the hills of Minas Gerais.

Ouro Prêto was the most splendid of these. Vila Rica de Ouro Prêto (Rich Town of Black Gold), as it was known, had grown to 100,000 people by the mid-18th century and was the richest city in the New World.

Climate

Minas is rainy from October to February and dry from March to September. In the rainy season there are almost daily downpours, but they rarely last for long. The rainy-season climate is warm, but still much cooler than the heat of Rio.

The dry season is cool, and from July to September the weather can actually get cold. There's often fog during September and October.

Travel is quite practicable year-round (take an umbrella during the rainy season), with one proviso – from December to February, Ouro Prêto can be deluged by tourists, who can be more of a nuisance than the rain.

Northern Minas, less populated, is an arid land with shrub-like trees that look dead during the dry season but quickly regain their foliage when it rains. The most common tree is the pepper tree (aroeira).

Economy

Minas Gerais wears its name well, producing more iron, tin, diamonds, zinc, quartz and phosphates than any other state in Brazil. It has one of the world's largest reserves of iron.

The state's industrial growth rate has been well above the national average over recent years, and Minas Gerais competes with Rio de Janeiro for the distinction of having Brazil's second most powerful economy, behind São Paulo.

Minas is also known for its milk and cheese production. The agricultural sector is diverse and strong, with fruit and cattle also important.

BELO HORIZONTE

☎ 0xx31 • postcode 30000-000
• pop 2.23 million • elevation 858m

Sprawling Belo Horizonte ('bell-ow-hree-zonch-eh') is the state capital of Minas Gerais, and Brazil's third largest city.

Most people aren't coming to Belo but rather through it, on their way to Ouro Prêto or Diamantina. But there's more than you'd expect in this vibrantly efficient city, and, if you look around, you'll find plenty to keep you busy. The colonial town of Sabará makes for a good day trip (see the Colonial Towns section later in this chapter).

Orientation

Central Belo has a grid of large avenidas and another smaller grid superimposed at 45°. The pattern must have looked good on paper, but the city planners couldn't have envisaged the future implications for traffic of so many intersecting streets. The main drag is Avenida Afonso Pena, which runs from the bus station in the northwest straight southeast through the center. There are three pivotal praças: bustling Praça Sete, just southeast of the bus station; serene Praça da Liberdade, south of Sete; and, southeast of Liberdade, Praça da Savassi, the center of Belo nightlife and café society.

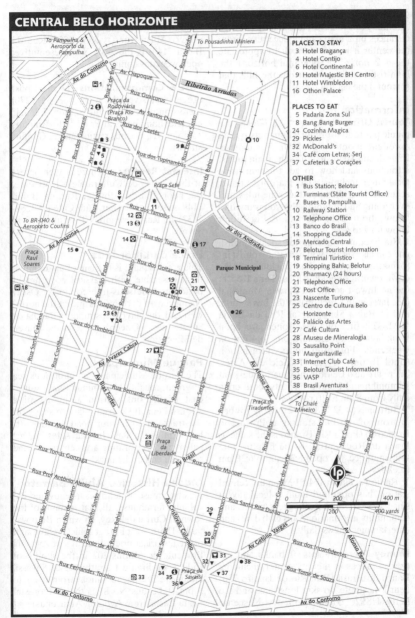

CENTRAL BELO HORIZONTE

PLACES TO STAY
3 Hotel Bragança
4 Hotel Contijo
6 Hotel Continental
9 Hotel Majestic BH Centro
11 Hotel Wimbledon
16 Othon Palace

PLACES TO EAT
5 Padaria Zona Sul
8 Bang Bang Burger
24 Cozinha Magica
29 Pickles
32 McDonald's
34 Café com Letras; Serj
37 Cafeteria 3 Corações

OTHER
1 Bus Station; Belotur
2 Turminas (State Tourist Office)
7 Buses to Pampulha
10 Railway Station
12 Telephone Office
13 Banco do Brasil
14 Shopping Cidade
15 Mercado Central
17 Belotur Tourist Information
18 Terminal Turistico
19 Shopping Bahia; Belotur
20 Pharmacy (24 hours)
21 Telephone Office
22 Post Office
23 Nascente Turismo
25 Centro de Cultura Belo
  Horizonte
26 Palácio das Artes
27 Café Cultura
28 Museu de Mineralogia
30 Sausalito Point
31 Margaritaville
33 Internet Club Café
35 Belotur Tourist Information
36 VASP
38 Brasil Aventuras

The train station is at the eastern end of Avenida Amazonas. Belo is a hilly town, so distances on a map can be deceptive. From the center it is now difficult to appreciate the *belo horizonte* (beautiful horizon); the high-rise buildings block out the hills that surround the capital.

Information

Tourist Offices Belotur (☎ 3277-7666), the municipal tourist organization, puts out an excellent monthly guide in Portuguese, English and Spanish. It lists the main tourist attractions and how to get to them using local buses, includes a city map, flight times, accurate long-distance bus schedules and everything and anything else you wanted to know about Belo Horizonte, but didn't know how to ask.

Staffmembers at Belotur speak English and can also supply you with state tourist information. Belotur has various booths downtown: at Avenida Afonso Pena 1055, at the northwest corner of Parque Municipal (see later in this section); at the bus station; and at Bahia Shopping at Rua da Bahia 1022. The first two mentioned are open weekdays from 8 am to 8 pm, to 4 pm on weekends. For after-hours information (until 10 pm), try the Palácio das Artes. There are also Belotur information desks at Pampulha and Confins airports (both open daily from 8 am to 10 pm).

Turminas (☎ 3272-8567, setur@mg.gov.br), in front of the bus station at Praça Rio Branco 56 (Praça Rio Branco is the same as Praça da Rodoviária), is the helpful state tourism office. It's open 8:30 am to 6:30 pm weekdays.

Radio Favela on 104.5 FM, an unlicensed station, has operated from a local favela since 1982. It broadcasts great music and community information, plus club dates and entertainment news daily.

Money There are lots of banks and exchange offices in the city center, including Banco do Brasil (Rua Rio de Janeiro 750) near Praça Sete. To skip long lines and the hefty US$20 commission, try Nascente Turismo, at Rua Rio de Janeiro 1314 (open 9 am to 6 pm weekdays, until noon on Saturday). Mastertur (☎ 3330-3655, Rua da Bahia 2140) is the AMEX representative; open weekdays only.

Post & Communications The main post office is at Avenida Afonso Pena 1270; there's another at the bus station. Telemar has telephone posts at Praça Sete, Rua dos Tamoios 311, the bus station and at Confins airport.

Internet Resources There is Web access at the Centro de Cultura Belo Horizonte, the neogothic building at Rua da Bahia 1149. Also try Internet Club Café (☎ 3282-3132) at Rua Fernandes Tourinho 385 in Savassi.

Praça da Liberdade

This green square is the site of an architectural ensemble with classical government buildings, a Jetsons-like condo by Oscar Niemeyer, art deco offices and, at the northwest end, the playful postmodern **Rainha da Sucata** (Scrap Queen), home to the Museu de Mineralogia.

Parque Municipal

The Parque Municipal is an enormous sea of green, roughly a 10-minute walk southeast of the bus station along Avenida Afonso Pena. It's a great place to shake off the traffic and get your head together. Its highlight is the **Palácio das Artes**, an art gallery and performing arts center near the southern end of the park.

Museu Histórico Abílio Barreto

This free museum features a renovated old colonial farmhouse, all that remains of the town of Curral del Rey, on which Belo was built. There's a photographic archive and other historical bric-a-brac. It's at Avenida Prudente de Morais 202 in the suburb of Cidade Jardim, just southwest of Savassi. Hours are Tuesday to Sunday from 10 am to 5 pm (take bus No 8103 'Nova Floresta/ Santa Lucia' from Avenida Amazonas).

Pampulha District

Fans of modernist architect Oscar Niemeyer won't want to miss his creations dotted around a huge artificial lake in the Pampulha district, in the north part of the city. Juscelino Kubitschek, mayor of Belo at the time, commissioned the recent architectural school graduate in the early 1940s.

The **Igreja de São Francisco de Assis** is an architectural gem, and the paintings by Portinari are beautiful. The **Museu de Arte de Belo Horizonte**, with its cute garden designed by landscape architect Roberto Burle Marx, is also worth a look. It was designed as a casino and shows the obvious influence of the modernist work of Le Corbusier. The **Casa do Baile** and **Iate Tênis Clube** also form part of the complex.

From the center of Belo (on Avenida Afonso Pena between Avenida Amazonas and Rua dos Tupinambás), take bus No 2004 'Bandeirantes/Olhos/d'Agua.'

Tilework, the Igreja de São Francisco de Assis

ROBYN JONES

Organized Tours

Brasil Aventuras (☎ 3013-0919, info@ brasilaventuras.com.br, Rua Paraíba 1317, shop 20), organizes trekking, caving, canyoning, rafting and biking expeditions.

If you're of an equestrian bent, Tropa Serrana (☎/fax 3344-8986, ☎ 9983-2356) offers horseback-riding treks through the countryside southeast of Belo that are a spectacular value. Trips, including meals and lodging, cost US$27/53/270 for one/two/five days. Túlio Marques Lopes, who's held more jobs than most LP writers, runs the tours. He speaks a bit of English and a smattering of Spanish. Túlio will pick you up at your hotel if it's central. The food served on the treks is excellent, consisting of surprisingly elaborate, authentic Mineiro specialties. Groups of four or more can ride along part of the Estrada Real (see the Colonial Towns section later in this chapter) or from Belo to Ouro Prêto (five days).

Places to Stay

Budget *Chalé Mineiro* (☎ 3467-1576, Rua Santa Luzia 288) has good dorm rooms for US$10, with discounts for HI members. It is about 2km east of the Parque Municipal. To get there from the bus station take bus No 9801 'Saudade/Santa Cruz' from Rua dos Caetés. Alternatively, take the metro to Santa Teresa station and cross the pedestrian bridge to Rua Santa Luzia.

The *Pousadinha Mineira* (☎ 3446-2911, fax 3442-4448, Rua Araxá 514) has dormitory rooms for US$7, and it's open 7 am to midnight. From the bus station, follow Avenida Santos Dumont to Rua Rio de Janeiro, then turn left and go up a couple of blocks to Avenida do Contorno. Cross it and follow Rua Varginha move up a few blocks to Rua Araxá.

There's a cluster of budget hotels in the sleazy red-light district just south of the bus station. By day the footpaths are crowded with *camelots* (street stalls). *Hotel Contijo* (☎ 3272-1177, Rua dos Tupinambás 731) has single/double quartos (ask for a clean one until you get it) from US$12/20, apartamentos for US$16/23. The slightly nicer *Hotel*

THE SOUTHEAST

Bragança (☎ *3212-6688, Avenida Paraná 109)* has decent rooms for US$20/27. The *Hotel Majestic BH Centro* (☎ *3222-3390, fax 3222-3146, Rua Espírito Santo 284)* belies its name – its a pretty ordinary place with quartos for US$10/20 and apartamentos for US$16/25.

Closer to the city center, a couple of blocks west of Avenida Afonso Pena, the *Hotel Continental* (☎ *3201-7944, Avenida Paraná 241)* is clean, friendly and not too noisy. Fifties-style apartamentos are a good deal at US$20/30.

Mid-Range & Top End The *Evora Palace* (☎ *3227-6220, fax 3227-6120, Rua Sergipe 1415),* in Savassi, has apartamentos for US$50/56, a reasonable value.

The central *Hotel Wimbledon* (☎ *3222-6160, fax 3222-6510, Avenida Afonso Pena 772)* is a good deal, with a rooftop pool and large rooms from US$80/100 (on weekends, discounts are for the asking).

The four-star *Othon Palace* (☎ *3273-3844, fax 3212-2318, belohorizonte@othon.com.br, Avenida Afonso Pena 1050)* is well positioned, opposite the park. It has singles/ doubles from US$140/160, with a 50% discount for two or more nights.

Places to Eat

Lots of lanchonetes and fast-food places are clustered around Praça Sete, including *Bang Bang Burger* (*Avenida Amazonas 322). Padaria Zona Sul* (*Avenida Paraná 163)* has super roast chickens at US$2 each. *Cozinha Magica,* on Rua Rio de Janeiro in the same block as Nascente Turismo, is a low-key place with a wood-fired oven and a per-kilo lunch. Shopping Cidade on Rua Rio de Janeiro and Shopping Bahia on Rua da Bahia both have *food courts.*

The better restaurants are in Savassi. On the eastern side of Praça da Savassi is the popular *Cafeteria 3 Corações,* good for coffee and cakes. *Pickles* (*Avenida Cristóvão Colombo 480)* serves a good quality lunch for US$6/kg.

The coolest place to hang out, write postcards, get great sandwiches, have wine by the glass, and meet travelers and expatriate English speakers is *Cafe com Letras* (☎ *3225-9973, Rua Antônio de Albuquerque 785),* near Praça da Savassi. Along with delectable sandwiches, crêpes and chocolates, the place has a bookshop that sells Lonely Planet guides and other English books. It's one-stop conversation, literary fix and culinary decadence.

If you are in the mood for a particular type of food, Belo can probably provide it – consult the *BH Guia Turístico,* available at the tourist office.

Entertainment

Belo is a cosmopolitan town with a vibrant art scene and plenty of nightlife. The *Palácio das Artes* (☎ *3237-7234),* in the Parque Municipal on Avenida Afonso Pena, regularly holds concerts, dance presentations and other shows. Check the papers or with the tourist office.

Downtown, *Café Cultura* (☎ *3222-1347, Rua da Bahia 1416)* has a bar and live music on Friday and Saturday night. *Estrella* (☎ *3222-6252, Rua Curitiba 1275)* has forró on Saturday night.

Praça da Savassi, just down Avenida Cristóvão Colombo from Praça da Liberdade (bus No 2003 from the center) is the best place for nightlife close to the center. Chic, flirty hordes descend on the corner of Rua Pernambuco and Rua Tomé de Souza to patronize *Sausalito Point* and *Margaritaville* (*Rua Tomé de Souza 851);* the crowd fills the streets and everyone joins in.

Shopping

The Sunday **Feira de Arte e Artesanato** is open, officially, from 6 am to 1 pm (but it often lasts to about 3 pm) along Avenida Afonso Pena between Rua da Bahia and Rua dos Guajajaras. If you wade through the crowds and stalls selling all sorts of imported rubbish, you'll find the odd one with some good local crafts. The food stalls are worthwhile.

The **Centro de Artesanato Mineiro** (☎ *3272-8572),* Avenida Afonso Pena 1537, in the Palácio das Artes at the edge of the Parque Municipal, is a government store with a varied assortment of Mineiro crafts:

ceramics, jewelry, tapestries, rugs, quilts and soapstone sculptures. It's probably worth holding off from buying, though, if you are heading to the colonial towns. The Centro is open daily, Saturday from 9 am to 1 pm and Sunday from 10 am to 2 pm.

Serj (Rua Antônio de Albuquerque 749) sells quality crafts. **Cachaças do Brasil** (Bahia Shopping, Rua da Bahia 1022) is a good place for tasting the local liquor. You can buy just about anything at the **Mercado Central**, downtown on the corner of Rua Curitiba and Rua dos Goitacazes. It is a good place for wandering, sampling the delicious local produce or socializing with the locals at one of the bars.

Getting There & Away

Air Belo Horizonte has two airports. Most planes use the international Aeroporto Confins, 40km north of the city. The Aeroporto da Pampulha is much more conveniently located, about 7km north of the center.

There are flights from the two airports to just about anywhere in Brazil. Flights to/from Rio, Brasília, Vitória and São Paulo by VASP, Varig or TransBrasil are frequent. City air offices include the following:

TransBrasil (☎ 0800-151151), Rua dos Tamóios 86
Varig (☎ 0800-992004), Avenida Getúlio Vargas 840
VASP (☎ 0800-998277), Avenida Getúlio Vargas 1492

Offices at Confins airport include these three:

TransBrasil (☎ 3689-2475)
Varig (☎ 3689-2350)
VASP (☎ 3689-2266)

Bus The bus station (☎ 3271-3000) is at the northern end of the city center on Praça da Rodoviária (also known as Praça Rio Branco), near the end of Avenida Afonso Pena. Buses take seven hours to get to Rio (US$13/27 for regular/executivo), 9½ hours to São Paulo's Bresser bus station (US$16/37 for regular/executivo), 12 hours to Brasília (US$30) and around 22 hours to

Salvador (US$56). There are 16 buses daily to Rio (between 9:30 am and midnight), about 30 daily to São Paulo (between 7:30 am and 11:30 pm) and twice daily to Salvador (at 6 pm and 7 pm). Buses take eight hours to Vitória (US$20/30 for regular/executivo), but the train's cheaper and nicer.

There are 17 buses a day to Ouro Prêto, the first at 6 am and the last at 11 pm. The trip takes about three hours and costs US$5.

There are 21 buses a day to Mariana (US$6, two hours), running from 5:30 am to midnight. Six buses go daily to Diamantina (US$17, 5½ hours), the first at 5:30 am and the last at midnight. Seven run daily to São João del Rei (US$7, 3½ hours), the first at 6:15 am and the last at 7 pm. Buses to Sabará (30 minutes) run every 15 minutes from 5 am to 11 pm; catch them at the local bus section of the bus station.

For the mineral spring resorts, buses run to Caxambú (US$20, five hours) at 7:30 am and 9:45 pm daily and to São Lourenço (US$20, 5½ hours) at 12:30 pm and 11 pm.

Train Trains run to Vitória (US$12/16 regular/executivo class; 14 hours) from Belo's main train station (☎ 3218-2255) at Praça da Estação just north of the Parque Municipal. They leave at 5:30 am daily, 3:30 pm Monday to Saturday and noon on Sunday. It is a beautiful trip. This train also stops in Santa Bárbara (US$3; three hours; see the Parks section later in this chapter) and Sabará.

Getting Around

Belo Horizonte has a good bus network (newspaper stands sell *Peg Bus* for about US$2, which has all of the timetables). There's a conventional bus (US$1.50, one hour) from the bus station to Confins airport, leaving every half hour to an hour between 4:45 am and 10:45 pm. An executivo bus (US$5) to Confins leaves from the Terminal Turístico (☎ 3271-4522) on Rua dos Guajajaras just southwest of Praça Raoul Soares every 45 minutes to an hour between 6 am and 9:45 pm.

Belo Horizonte also has a metro system, with two lines from the main railway station.

From Praça da Estação, one extends north to Minas Shopping (via Santa Teresa), and the other to the western suburbs via Estação Lagoinha (near the bus station).

CAVES

Three interesting and popular day trips from Belo Horizonte are to caves within two hours of the city.

Gruta de Maquiné

Gruta de Maquiné (☎ 3715-1078) is the most famous, and crowded, of the caves. Its seven huge chambers are well lit to allow guided tours to pass through. Admission is US$2, free for kids under five, and it's open 8 am to 5 pm. There are cafés at the cave.

Buses (US$6, 2¼ hours) to the caves departs from the bus station in Belo Horizonte three times daily, the first at 8:15 am and the last returning at 4:20 pm, which gives you ample viewing time.

Gruta da Lapinha

The highlight here (☎ 3681-1958) is the Véu da Noiva, a crystal formation in the shape of a bride's veil. Admission is US$2, US$0.50 for kids under five. The caves are open 9 am to 4:30 pm.

Buses (US$3, 45 minutes) leave Belo's bus station four times daily from 6:50 am, the last returning at 5 pm.

Gruta Rei do Mato

The Cave of the Forest King (☎ 3773-0888), near Sete Lagoas north of Belo, has prehistoric paintings and petroglyphs. Admission is US$1, free for kids, and it's open 8 am to 7 pm.

A bus (US$3, 1½ hours) leaves Belo's bus station every half hour starting at 6:30 am, and return buses run until 11 pm.

Colonial Towns

The colonial towns of Minas Gerais were linked by the **Estrada Real**, the old gold route built by slaves. For 150 years the gold and precious stones of Minas Gerais were carted along this path, south to the Rio

coast, from where boats ferried it off to Europe. From Diamantina in the north, it passed through Ouro Prêto, with a route down to Parati and another to Rio de Janeiro. You can take horseback-riding treks along part of the Estrada with Tropa Serrana – see Organized Tours in the Belo Horizonte section earlier in this chapter.

While the distances are large, it's quite easy to travel between the colonial towns. There are regular buses between them.

By car you can avoid the busy highways, as many of the back roads are paved. It is possible to give Belo Horizonte a miss, and head north from Ouro Prêto through to Diamantina via Mariana and Santa Bárbara, Guanhães and Serro.

SABARÁ

☎ 0xx31 • postcode 34500-000
• pop 112,000 • elevation 713m

Sabará stands on the muddy banks of the Rio das Velhas (Old Ladies' River), 25km southeast of Belo. It was the first major gold-mining center in the state, and at its peak, in the early 18th century, was one of the world's wealthiest towns. This prosperity is reflected in the houses, mansions, churches, statues, fountains and sacred art found here.

But Sabará is now a poor town dominated by a Belgian metalworks. In the boom years, when the Rio das Velhas was 15 times wider, slave boats would sail all the way up the Rio São Francisco from Bahia. Sabará produced more gold in one week than the rest of Brazil produced in a year. You can still pan the riverbed for gold flakes, but the nuggets are long gone.

Since it's only half an hour by bus from Belo, Sabará makes an easy and interesting day trip. Don't bother visiting here on a Monday – all the sites are closed.

There's an information booth at the entrance to town, but major attractions are easy to find, since there are signposts at the Praça Santa Rita telling where everything is.

Churches

Most of the churches have small entry fees, payable as you come through the door.

Matriz de NS de Conceição The Jesuits, cultural ambassadors of the far-flung Portuguese Empire, were among the first Westerners to make contact with the Far East. A tangible result is the Matriz de NS de Conceição (1720), on Praça Getúlio Vargas at the eastern end of town. It is a fascinating blend of Asian arts and Portuguese baroque – overwhelming with its gold leaf and red Chinese scrolls.

There are even pagodas on some of the church door panels by the sanctuary and several other interesting little details in the church. Floorboards cover the graves of the early parishioners; the gold and silver nuggets nailed on these tablets indicate whether the deceased was rich or poor.

On the ceiling of the church is the patron saint of confessors, John Nepomuceno of 14th-century Czechoslovakia, depicted holding his severed tongue. King Wenceslau ordered St Nepomuceno's tongue cut out because the saint refused to reveal whether or not the Moldavian queen was faithful. Nepomuceno died of his terrible wound, but became very popular posthumously in Czechoslovakian cult circles and, inexplicably, in Minas Gerais during the gold era. Look for the little angel at his side who gently shushes churchgoers with a finger to his lips.

The church is open 9 am to noon and 1:30 to 5 pm; closed Monday.

Igreja de NS do Ó After surviving an attack by his own troops in 1720, Captain Lucas Ribeiro de Almeida built a chapel in thanks to the Virgin Mary. Like NS de Conceição, the chapel has Oriental details and an ornate golden interior. It's popular with pregnant women and those who pray for fertility. It is at the eastern end of town on Largo Nossa Senhora do Ó; open Tuesday to Sunday 9 to 11:30 am and 2 to 5 pm.

Igreja de NS do Rosário dos Pretos This half-built church on Praça Melo Viana was started and financed by slaves but never finished. It now stands as a memorial to the abolition of slavery in 1888. It's open Tuesday to Sunday, 8 to 11 am and 1 to 5 pm.

Igreja NS do Carmo Aleijadinho had a lot to do with the decoration of this church on Rua de Carmo. His touch is everywhere, especially in the faces of the statues of São Simão and São João da Cruz. It's open 9 to 11:30 am and 1 to 6 pm (Sunday afternoons only); closed Monday.

Other Attractions
A testament to the wealth of bygone days is the elegant opera house of Sabará, **O Teatro Imperial** (1770), on Rua Dom Pedro II. It has crystal lamps and three tiers of seats made of carved wood and bamboo. It is open Tuesday to Sunday from 8 am to noon and 1 to 6 pm.

Housed in an old gold foundry (1730), the **Museu do Ouro** (Gold Museum), on Rua da Intendência, contains art and artifacts of the glory years of Sabará. It's open Tuesday to Sunday from noon to 5:30 pm.

Getting There & Away
From Belo, buses leave every 15 minutes from the local section behind the bus station. Return buses leave the bus stop on Avenida Victor Fantini in Sabará; you can also catch one on the road out of town.

CONGONHAS
☎ 0xx31 • postcode 36415-000
• pop 39,000 • elevation 871m
Little is left of the colonial past of Congonhas except the extraordinary *Prophets* of Aleijadinho at the Basílica do Bom Jesus de Matosinhos. While the town is dirty, industrial and commonplace, these dramatic statues are exceptional. Together, they are Aleijadinho's masterpiece and Brazil's most famed work of art. It's worth taking the trouble to get to Congonhas just to see them.

Congonhas is 72km south of Belo Horizonte, 3km off Hwy BR-040. The city grew up with the search for gold in the nearby Rio Maranhão, and the economy today is dominated by iron mining in the surrounding countryside.

The Prophets & the Chapels
Already an old man, sick and crippled, Aleijadinho sculpted the *Prophets* between 1800

and 1805. Symmetrically placed in front of the **Basílica do Bom Jesus de Matosinhos**, each of the prophets from the Old Testament was carved out of one or two blocks of soapstone. Each carries a Latin message: Some of them are hopeful prophecies, others warn of the end of the world.

Much has been written about these sculptures – their dynamic quality, the sense of movement (much like a Hindu dance or a ballet), how they complement each other and how their arrangement prevents them from being seen in isolation. The poet Carlos Drummond de Andrade wrote that the dramatic faces and gestures are 'magnificent, terrible, grave and tender' and commented on 'the way the statues, of human size, appear to be larger than life as they look down upon the viewer with the sky behind them.'

Before working on the *Prophets*, Aleijadinho carved (or supervised his assistants in carving) the wooden statues that were placed in the six little **chapels**, also designed by Aleijadinho. The chapels and their placement on the sloping site are superb in themselves and just as impressive as the prophets. The way the light falls on the pale sculpted domes against the dark mountain backdrop is truly beautiful. The sets in the chapels represent the Passion of Christ: The Last Supper, Calvary, Imprisonment, Flagellation and Coronation, the Carrying of the Cross and the Crucifixion. Some of the figures, such as the Roman soldiers, are very crude and clearly done by assistants, while others are finely chiseled. The statues were restored in 1957 by the painter Edson Mota, and the gardens were designed by landscape architect Roberto Burle Marx.

Romaria

From the prophets, wander downhill for about 200m to the Romaria, an unusual building where a long loop of rooms surrounds a huge oval courtyard. Originally designed as a pousada for pilgrims, it's now used as a cultural space. Among other things it has museums and souvenir shop.

Special Events

Held September 7 to 14, the **Jubileu do Senhor Bom Jesus do Matosinhos** is one of the great religious festivals in Minas Gerais. Every year approximately 600,000 pilgrims arrive at the church to make promises, do penance, receive blessings and give and receive alms. The **Holy Week** processions in Congonhas are also famous, especially the dramatizations on Good Friday.

Aleijadinho

The *Prophets* in Congonhas, and the Igreja de São Francisco de Assis and the façade of the Igreja de NS do Carmo, both in Ouro Prêto, were all carved by Aleijadinho (Antônio Francisco Lisboa), as were innumerable relics in Mariana, Sabará, Tiradentes and São João del Rei.

The Michelangelo of Brazil lost the use of his hands and legs at the age of 30, but, with a hammer and chisel strapped to his arms, he advanced art in his country from the excesses of the baroque to a finer, more graceful rococo. The Mineiros have reason to be proud of Aleijadinho – he is a figure of international prominence in the history of art. Aleijadinho's angels have his stylistic signature: wavy hair, wide-open eyes and big, round cheeks.

The son of a Portuguese architect and a black slave, Aleijadinho lived from 1730 to 1814 and was buried in the Matriz NS da Conceição, within 50 paces of his birth site. He was named patron of Brazilian arts by federal decree in 1973. For many years Manuel da Costa Ataíde, from nearby Mariana, successfully collaborated with Aleijadinho on many churches. Aleijadinho would sculpt the exterior and a few interior pieces, and Ataíde would paint the interior panels. With his secretly concocted vegetable dyes, Ataíde fleshed out much of Aleijadinho's work.

The best places to see Aleijadinho's work are Congonhas, Ouro Prêto, Sabará and São João del Rei.

Places to Stay & Eat
If you start early, you can avoid spending a night here – although it's a great spot to wake up if you get a room with a view at the *Colonial Hotel* (☎ 3731-1834, *Praça da Basílica 76*). The hotel is basic but the staff is friendly, and it's right across the street from the *Prophets*. Clean quartos cost US$10 per person, single/double apartamentos are US$13/27.

In the basement of the hotel is the *Cova do Daniel* restaurant. *Casa da Ladeira* (*Rua Dr Paulo Mendes 649*) just across the road is a better option.

Getting There & Away
There are six daily buses from Belo Horizonte to Congonhas (US$3, 1¾ hours). The last return bus to Belo Horizonte leaves Congonhas at 8:20 pm.

Buses leave every 45 minutes from 5:30 am to 10:30 pm for the Conselheiro Lafaiete bus station (☎ 3763-1271), costing US$1 for the 30-minute trip. From there, you can catch buses to Ouro Prêto (US$4, 2½ hours) which leave Monday to Saturday at 7:05 and 9 am, noon, and 3 and 6 pm; and Sunday at 6 am and 3 and 6 pm. Try to get to Lafaiete a bit early to make sure you get a bus; if you do miss the last bus, there are a couple of hotels across from the bus station.

From Ouro Prêto to Lafaiete, buses leave Monday to Saturday at 5 am and 9 am (no 5am bus Saturday), noon, and 2:50 and 6 pm; on Sunday they leave at 6 am, noon, and 2:40 and 6 pm.

There is a bus from Congonhas to Rio at 6:45 pm and another at 12:30 am (US$13).

From Congonhas to São João del Rei, catch one of the Belo Horizonte to São João del Rei buses that stop off at Congonhas. There are seven a day, the first at 7:30 am and the last at 8:20 pm (US$4).

Getting Around
The bus station is on Avenida Júlia Kubitschek, across town from the sites of interest. From here the Basílica buses leave every half hour to 40 minutes and costs US$0.50. It's a 15-minute ride up the hill to the basilica and the *Prophets*. Get off just after the bus passes the church (as it heads downhill) for the best approach and first view of the statues. The same bus returns you to the bus station, or you can have the Colonial Hotel staff call you a taxi (US$4).

OURO PRÊTO
☎ 0xx31 • postcode 35400-000
• pop 56,000 • elevation 1179m
Ouro Prêto, in the remote Serra do Espinhaço range, is truly the jewel in the Mineiro crown. The odd-shaped peak of Itacolomy (1752m), 18km from town, which the first bandeirantes to penetrate the region used as a reference point, is the first sign you're approaching the city.

The town is very hilly and the rain-slicked, cobblestone streets are extremely steep. Bring comfortable walking shoes with good tread.

If you plan to spend only one day in Ouro Prêto, make sure it's not a Monday, as almost all the museums and churches are closed then.

History
According to the Jesuit Antonil, a mulatto servant in the Antônio Rodrigues Arzão expedition went to the rivulet Tripui to quench his thirst and pocketed a few grains of an odd black metal he found in the stream bed. It turned out to be gold, of course, but the exact location of the river was forgotten during the long expedition; only the strange shape of the peak of Itacolomy was remembered.

In 1698, Antônio Dias de Oliveira rediscovered the area, and was convinced he had found the fabled El Dorado. The mines were the largest deposits of gold in the Western Hemisphere, and the news and gold fever spread fast. Stories abound of men who acquired fabulous wealth from one day to the next, and others who died of hunger with their pockets full of gold.

Portuguese King Dom João V was quick to claim a royal fifth in tax, and a chain of posts was established to ensure that the crown got its cut. In theory, all gold was brought to these *casas de intendências* to be weighed and turned into bars, and the royal

OURO PRÊTO

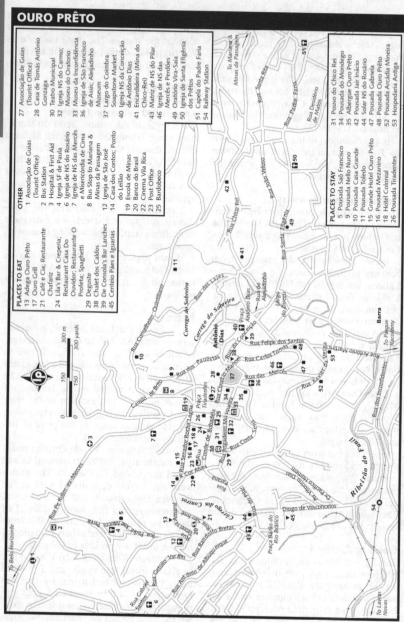

PLACES TO EAT
13 Adega Ouro Prêto
17 Ouro Grill
21 Café e Cia; Restaurante Chafariz
24 Lila's Bar & Creperia; Restaurant Casa Do Ouvidor; Restaurante O Profeta; Spaghetti
29 Deguste
38 Chalet dos Caldos
39 De Consola's Bar Lanches
45 Centeio Pães e Iguarias

OTHER
1   Associação de Guias (Tourist Office)
2   Bus Station
3   Hospital & First Aid
4   Igreja SF de Paula
6   Igreja de NS do Rosário
7   Igreja de NS das Mercês e Misericórdia de Cima
8   Bus Stop to Mariana & Minas da Passagem
12 Igreja de São José
14 Casa dos Contos; Ponto do Leilão
19 Escola de Minas
20 Banco do Brasil
22 Cinema Vila Rica
23 Post Office
25 Bardobeco
27 Associação de Guias (Tourist Office)
28 Casa de Tomás Antônio Gonzaga
30 Teatro Municipal
32 Igreja NS do Carmo; Museu do Oratório
33 Museu da Inconfidência
36 Igreja de São Francisco de Assis; Aleijadinho Museum
37 Largo do Coimbra Soapstone Market
40 Igreja NS da Conceição de Antônio Dias
41 Encardideira (Mina do Chico-Rei)
43 Matriz de NS do Pilar
46 Igreja de NS das Mercês e Perdões
49 Igreja de Santa Efigênia dos Prêtos
50 Oratório Vira-Saia
51 Capela do Padre Faria
54 Railway Station

PLACES TO STAY
5   Pousada Saô Francisco
9   Pousada Nello Nuno
10 Pousada Casa Grande
11 Pousada Toledo
15 Grande Hotel Ouro Prêto
16 Pousada Mezanino
18 Hotel Colonial
26 Pousada Tiradentes
31 Pouso do Chico Rei
34 Pousada do Mondego
35 Albergue Ouro Prêto
42 Pousada Jair Inácio
44 Solar NS do Rosário
47 Pousada Gabriela
48 Pousada Ouro Prêto
52 Pousada Arcádia Mineira
53 Hospedaria Antiga

fifth was set aside. Tax shirkers were cast into dungeons or exiled to Africa. One common technique used to avoid the tax was to hide gold powder in hollow images of the saints.

Bitter about the tax, the Paulista miners rebelled unsuccessfully against the Portuguese. Two years later, in 1711, Vila Rica de Ouro Prêto, the predecessor of the present town, was founded.

The finest goods from India and England were made available to the simple mining town. The gold bought the services of baroque artisans, who turned the city into an architectural gem. At the height of the gold boom in the mid-18th century, there were 110,000 people (mainly slaves) in Ouro Prêto, as contrasted to 50,000 in New York and about 20,000 in Rio de Janeiro.

The royal fifth, estimated at 100 tonnes of gold in the 18th century, quickly passed through the hands of the Portuguese court, built up Lisbon and then financed the British Industrial Revolution.

The greed of the Portuguese led to sedition by the inhabitants of Vila Rica (1720). As the boom tapered off, the miners found it increasingly difficult to pay ever-larger gold taxes. In 1789, poets Claudio da Costa and Tomás Antônio Gonzaga, Joaquim José da Silva Xavier (nicknamed Tiradentes, 'Tooth-Puller,' for his dentistry skills) and others, full of French revolutionary philosophies, hatched the Inconfidência Mineira.

The rebellion was crushed in its early stages by agents of the crown. Gonzaga was exiled to Mozambique, and Costa did time in prison. Tiradentes, the only man not to deny his role in the conspiracy, was abandoned by his friends, jailed for three years without defense, then drawn and quartered.

By decree of Emperor Dom Pedro I, Vila Rica, capital of Minas Gerais since 1721, became the Imperial City of Ouro Prêto. In 1897 the state capital was shifted from Ouro Prêto to Belo Horizonte. This was the decisive move that preserved the colonial flavor of Ouro Prêto.

The former capital assumes the symbolic role of state capital once a year, on June 24. The city was declared a Brazilian national monument in 1933, and in 1981 UNESCO proclaimed the town of Ouro Prêto a World Heritage Site.

Climate

The city is 1km above sea level, and temperatures vary from 2° to 28°C. Winters are pretty cold. It can be rainy and foggy all year round, but you can definitely expect daily showers in December and January.

Orientation

Praça Tiradentes is the town center. Ouro Prêto is divided into two parishes. If you stand in Praça Tiradentes facing the Museu da Inconfidência, the parish of Pilar is to the right, the parish of Antônio Dias to the left.

All of Ouro Prêto's streets have at least two names: the official one and the one used by the locals because the official one is too much of a mouthful. Rua Conde Bobadella, the street leading off to the right from Praça Tiradentes as you're facing the Museu da Inconfidência, is commonly known as Rua Direita. Rua Conselheiro Quintiliano is known as Rua das Lajes and Rua Senador Rocha Lagoa as Rua das Flores. To add to the confusion, the names are rarely posted.

Information

The Associação de Guias has two information offices, one on the main road from Belo Horizonte (☎ 3551-2504, fax 3551-2655) and the other at Praça Tiradentes 41 (☎ 3559-3269). Both are open 8 am to 6 pm Monday through Friday and 8 am to 5 pm on weekends. English and French are spoken, and staffers give out a leaflet indicating the opening times of the museums and churches. The association also arranges tours (see Organized Tours later in this section) and sell maps (US$2) and interesting books including *Visitando Ouro Prêto, Mariana e Congonhas*, by Ouro Prêto Turismo, in English and Portuguese (US$16).

It isn't possible to change traveler's checks here. The Banco do Brasil is at Rua São José 195, and most of the jewelry stores in town will change cash dollars. The Itaú bank is near the Casa dos Contos.

There is a post office on the corner of Rua Direita and Rua Coronel Alves.

Things to See

No 20th-century buildings defile this stunningly beautiful colonial town. Even Niemeyer has been uncharacteristically restrained in his design of the **Grande Hotel Ouro Prêto**, which is respectfully camouflaged under a sloping terracotta roof. Spend a day or days exploring the winding, narrow, roller coaster-like roads, wandering along the cobblestones and between the stone and whitewashed walls, past the colorful doors and windows and the sculpted fountains and statues. Through the early morning mist, against a backdrop of green and blue hills, is a brilliant vista of vibrant terracotta-tiled roofs and baroque church facades.

If you hustle it's possible to see most of the sights in the Antônio Dias parish in the morning, have lunch on or near Praça Tiradentes, and spend the afternoon visiting the Pilar parish, the mineral museum and the Museu da Inconfidência. But you need at the least two days to see the town and its surroundings properly.

Most churches charge admission of around US$2, so pick and choose if you're on a tight budget. Author favorites are, roughly in order of preference, Igreja de São Francisco de Assis (if you only visit one, make sure it's this one), Igreja de Santa Efigênia dos Pretos, Matriz de NS do Pilar and Capela do Padre Faria.

Ideally, start out at about 7:30 am from Praça Tiradentes and walk along Rua Conselheiro Quintiliano (Rua das Lajes), the road to Mariana, for a panoramic view of town.

Those after something strenuous can hike to the peak of Itacolomy; it's 18km from Praça Tiradentes. **Parque Itacolomy** is a pleasant excursion, with good walking trails, waterfalls and orchids (the easiest approach is from Mariana). See Organized Tours for guided treks.

Capela do Padre Faria Work your way downhill off the road to this chapel. Padre Faria was one of the original bandeirantes,

and the chapel (built between 1701 and 1704) is Ouro Prêto's oldest. The chapel is set behind a triple-branched papal cross (1756), the three branches representing the temporal, spiritual and material powers of the Pope. It's the richest chapel in terms of gold and artwork but, due to poor documentation, the artists are anonymous. In 1750 the church bell rang for Tiradentes (when his body was taken to Rio); later, it rang again for the inauguration of Brasília. Note that the angel on the right-hand side of the high altar has butterfly wings. The church is open 8 am to noon; closed Monday.

Santa Efigênia dos Pretos Descending the Ladeira do Padre Faria back toward town, you'll come to the Igreja de Santa Efigênia dos Pretos, built between 1742 and 1749 by and for the black slave community. Santa Efigênia, patron saint of the church, was the Queen of Nubia, and the featured saints – Santo Antônio do Nolo and São Benedito – are black. The slaves prayed to these images that they wouldn't be crushed in the mines.

The church is Ouro Prêto's poorest in terms of gold and its richest in terms of artwork. The altar is by Aleijadinho's master, Francisco Javier do Briton. Many of the interior panels are by Manuel Rabelo de Souza (see if you can find the painting of Robinson Crusoe), and the exterior image of NS do Rosário is by Aleijadinho himself. The church was financed by gold extracted from Chico-Rei's mine, Encardadeira (see the boxed text 'Chico-Rei'). Slaves contributed to the church coffers by washing their gold-flaked hair in baptismal fonts. Others managed to smuggle gold powder under fingernails and inside tooth cavities. The church is open 8 am to noon.

Oratório Vira-Saia At the beginning of the 18th century there was a rash of ghost incidents in the city. Phantoms sprang from the walls near Santa Efigênia church and winged through town, spooking the townspeople. These townsfolk, badly frightened, would drop their bags of gold powder, which the bandit-like ghosts would snatch. To keep evil

Religious icons, São Paulo

Chapel in Conhongas

Festival angel

Holy Week in Ouro Prêto

Bikes along the beach, Rio

With piranhas, it's eat or be eaten.

The confluence of the waters, Manaus

spirits at bay, the terrorized people obtained the bishop's permission to build oratories (glass-encased niches containing images of saints). Oratories were built on many street corners around the town.

Not many of them remain, but there's one on Rua dos Paulistas (also called Bernardo Vasconcelos) and another on Rua Antônio Dias; the most famous one of all is the Oratório Vira-Saia. Nowadays, these few remaining oratories are used to scare off evil spirits during Holy Week. See also the information about Museu do Oratório later in this section.

The small oratory of Vira-Saia is at the bottom of the Ladeira de Santa Efigênia (also known as Vira-Saia), on the corner with Rua Barão do Ouro Branco. 'Vira-Saia' has a double meaning: It originates from the Portuguese *virar* (turn) and *sair* (depart), and is also the word for turncoat or traitor.

In the latter part of the 18th century, gold caravans destined for the Portuguese crown were robbed on a regular basis, despite measures to conceal shipments by altering dates and routes. It didn't take long to surmise that the rash of robberies was an inside job and that someone working in the Casa de Fundição (gold smelter) was leaking information.

No one suspected that Antônio Francisco Alves – pillar of the community, upstanding citizen, mild-mannered businessman and gentle father – was the brains behind the Vira-Saia bandits who were looting the government's gold caravans. After a caravan's route was planned, Alves would steal out to the oratory and turn the image in the sanctuary of NS das Almas to face the direction of the gold traffic.

A reward was posted for the identity of the criminal. Finally a member of Alves' own band, Luis Gibut, turned him in. Gibut was a French Jesuit who fell in love with a beautiful woman, abandoned the order, became a highway bandit and, eventually, the turncoat's turncoat. This same Luis Gibut was responsible for teaching Aleijadinho the misspelled Latin phrases that the artist incorporated into many of his works.

Alves, his wife and his daughters were dragged off into the jungle to meet their fate. Sra Duruta, a good neighbor, came to the rescue and saved Alves, but it was too late for his wife and children. Alves was one step ahead of the long arm of the law, but he didn't get off scot-free. Shortly afterward, he was plugged by another unnamed vira-saia. The criminal gang continued to do successful robberies without its first chief. Luis Gibut, ex-Jesuit, traitor and poor speller, is probably still doing time in purgatory.

Largo do Dirceu Largo do Dirceu is next, just before you get to the Igreja Matriz NS da Conceição de Antônio Dias. This used to be a popular hangout of the poet Tomás Antônio Gonzaga and his girlfriend and muse, Marília. It figures prominently in *Marília de Dirceu,* the most celebrated poem in the Portuguese language.

Conceição de Antônio Dias The parish church of the Antônio Dias parish, Matriz NS da Conceição de Antônio Dias, was designed by Aleijadinho's father, Manuel Francisco Lisboa, and built between the years 1727 and 1770. Note the painting of the eagle; its head points downward, symbolizing the domination of the Moors by the Christians. Aleijadinho is buried by the altar of Boa Morte. The cathedral is open 8:30 am to 11:45 am and 1:30 to 4:45 pm; Sunday from noon to 4:45 pm only; closed Monday.

The **Museu do Aleijadinho** is opposite the church on Rua do Aleijadinho and has the same hours.

Nearby is the abandoned mine Encardideira or **Mina do Chico-Rei**, on Rua Dom Silvério 108 (ask around for directions). It can be visited from 8 am to 5 pm daily. Entry is US$2. It's fantastic but dangerous, full of crumbling secret passageways and rumored to be haunted.

Casa de Tomás Antônio Gonzaga Rua do Ouvidor 9 is the address of Tomás Antônio Gonzaga's house, now the seat of the municipal government. This is where Gonzaga, his poet friend Claudio da Costa

Chico-Rei

Brazil's first abolitionist was Chico-Rei, an African tribal king. In the early 1700s, amid the frenzy of the gold rush, an entire tribe, king and all, was captured in Africa, sent to Brazil and sold to a mine owner in Ouro Prêto.

Chico-Rei worked as the foreman of the slave miners. Working Sundays and holidays, he finally bought his freedom from the slave master, then freed his son Osmar. Together, father and son liberated the entire tribe.

This collective then bought the fabulously wealthy Encardadeira gold mine, and Chico-Rei assumed his royal functions once again, holding court in Vila Rica and celebrating African holidays in traditional costume.

News of this reached the Portuguese king, who immediately prohibited slaves from purchasing their freedom.

Chico-Rei is now a folk hero among Brazilian blacks.

(author of 'Vila Rica'), Tiradentes and others conspired unsuccessfully to put an end to Portuguese rule in Brazil. The sad little event came to be known as the Inconfidência Mineira.

Igreja de São Francisco de Assis Across the street from Gonzaga's house is the Igreja de São Francisco de Assis. After the *Prophets* in Congonhas, Aleijadinho's masterpiece, this is the single most important piece of Brazilian colonial art. It was lovingly restored in 1992. The entire exterior, a radical departure from military baroque style, was carved by Aleijadinho himself, from the soapstone medallion to the cannon waterspouts and the military two-bar cross. The interior was painted by Aleijadinho's long-term partner, Manuel da Costa Ataíde.

The sacristy is said to be haunted by the spirit of an 18th-century woman. In the dead of night, her head reportedly dissolves into a skull and she screams, 'I'm dying, call Father Carlos.' The annex of the church

holds some works from the Museu do Aleijadinho. The church and the annex are open Tuesday to Sunday from 8:30 to 11:45 am and 1:30 to 4:45 pm.

Praça Tiradentes Praça Tiradentes is the center of town. It's a good place to have lunch, catch your breath by the statue of Tiradentes, or take in some museums before the churches of the Pilar parish open in the afternoon.

The **Museu da Inconfidência**, formerly the old municipal headquarters and jail, is an attractive building that was built between 1784 and 1854. Used as a prison from 1907 until 1937, the museum contains the tomb of Tiradentes, documents of the Inconfidência Mineira, torture instruments and important works by Ataíde and Aleijadinho. The museum is open Tuesday to Sunday from noon to 5:30 pm.

Igreja NS do Carmo From Praça Tiradentes, head down Rua Brigadeiro Musqueira to the Igreja NS do Carmo. This church, begun in 1766 and completed in 1772, was a group effort by the most important artists of the area. The church features a facade by Aleijadinho. It's open Tuesday to Sunday from 1 to 4:45 pm

Museu do Oratório This new museum (www.oratorio.com.br) is in a triple-level colonial house next to the Igreja NS do Carmo. It has a fabulous collection of oratories (niches containing images of saints to ward off evil spirits). The display is well organized and multilingual. It's open daily from 9 am to noon and 1 to 5 pm. Entry is US$2. See Oratório Vira-Saia earlier in this section.

Casa de Tiradentes The home of Joaquim José da Silva Xavier (Tiradentes) was also near the Igreja NS do Carmo. After the failed rebellion against the Portuguese, Tiradentes was executed in Rio and his head was paraded around his hometown. His house was demolished, and its grounds were salted to ensure that nothing would grow there.

Escola de Minas The Escola de Minas in the old governor's palace in Praça Tiradentes has a very fine museum of metals and mineralogy. It's open noon to 5 pm Monday to Friday; 9 am to 1 pm weekends.

Casa dos Contos From Praça Tiradentes head west down Rua Senador Rocha Lagoa to Praça Reynaldo Alves de Brito at the bottom of the hill. Here you'll find the Casa dos Contos (Counting House; US$1), now a public library and art gallery. Claudio da Costa was imprisoned here after participating in the Inconfidência Mineira. It is open Tuesday to Saturday 12:30 to 5:30 pm, and Sunday 8:30 am to 1:30 pm. Next door is the **Ponto do Leilão**, where slaves were taken to be tortured.

Matriz de NS do Pilar Head west across the bridge, round along Rua São José and south along Rua Randolfo Bretas to the Matriz de NS do Pilar. This is the second most opulent church in Brazil (after Salvador's São Francisco) in terms of gold. It has 434kg of gold and silver and is one of Brazil's finest showcases of artwork. Note the wild-bird chandelier holders, the laminated beaten gold, the scrolled church doors, 15 panels of Old and New Testament scenes by Pedro Gomes Chaes, and the hair on Jesus (the real stuff, donated by a penitent worshipper).

Legend has it that the Pilar and Antônio Dias parishes vied for the image of NS dos Passos. In order to settle the argument, the image was loaded onto a horse standing in Praça Tiradentes and rockets were fired to scare the horse; the idea was that the image would belong to the parish to which the horse bolted. Since the horse knew only one path, it galloped straight to the Matriz do Pilar. The church is open Tuesday to Sunday from 9 to 10:45 am and noon to 4:45 pm.

Teatro Municipal Built in 1769 by João de Souza Lisboa, the Teatro Municipal, on Rua Brigadeiro Musqueira, is the oldest theater in Minas Gerais and perhaps in Brazil. It is open daily 1 to 5:30 pm, although at the time of writing it was closed for renovations.

Organized Tours
Official guides (US$20 for four-hour tours, US$40 for four to eight hours for up to 10 people) and interpreters (US$30) can be booked at the tourist office. Beware of unofficial guides, as there are some nasty characters hanging around.

The tourist office also organizes treks into the surrounding hills and horseback rides to Itacolomy. The cost is around US$40 for the day. Speak to João, Alexandre or Renaldo a day before you go, to give them enough time to get the horses ready. Take care and make sure you have an official guide: At the time of writing there were problems with robberies on some of the trails.

For five-day horseback treks from Belo Horizonte to Ouro Prêto, see the information given under Organized Tours in the Belo Horizonte section.

Special Events
Semana Santa (Holy Week) processions in Ouro Prêto, held on the Thursday before Palm Sunday and sporadically until Easter Sunday, are quite a spectacle.

The Congado is to Minas what Candomblé is to Bahia and Macumba is to Rio: the local expression of Afro-Christian syncretism. The major **Congado celebrations** are for NS do Rosário (October 23 to 25, at the Capela do Padre Faria), for the New Year and for May 13 (the anniversary of abolition).

You'd also be wise to reserve a pousada in late July, when a weeklong annual **winter festival** is held. This involves two universities and the town floods with students participating in 24-hour classes, exhibitions and parties.

Carnaval in Ouro Prêto is also popular. A special feature is the *janela erótica* (erotic window) on Rua Direita, where people dance naked behind a thin curtain.

The **Cavalhada**, held in Amarantina (near Ouro Prêto) during the Festa de São Gonçalo from September 17 to 23, isn't as grand as the one in Pirenópolis, but is impressive nonetheless. The Cavalhada is a re-enactment of the battles between Christians and Muslims in Iberia.

Places to Stay

Budget Ouro Prêto is a university town, with schools of pharmacy, biochemistry, mineralogy, geology and engineering. Student lodging, known as *repúblicas*, makes up 20% of the housing here. They are not recommended, although they are the cheapest places to stay in town; they're closed from Christmas to Carnaval, they're loud, and they stack as many people as possible into rooms with mattresses on the floor.

The best deal in town is the **Pousada São Francisco** (☎ 3551-3456, Rua Padre José Marcos Penna 202), next to the Igreja de São Francisco de Paula (not São Francisco de Assis). It has absolutely spectacular views and seriously friendly multilingual staff. Spotless dormitory beds are US$10 per person; apartamentos with view are US$20/27 for singles/doubles downstairs and an extra US$6 per person upstairs. Breakfast is included. From the bus station, walk 100m down the hill to the church; facing downhill, look for the break in the fence on the left and follow the path down to the pousada. If you pass the church you've missed the turn.

The **Pousada Jair Inácio** (☎ 3551-2582, Rua Conselheiro Quintiliano 722), northeast of the center, charges US$13/16 per person in quartos/apartamentos. It is a small-scale place with a great view of the town from the veranda.

The wonky-floored **Albergue Ouro Prêto** (☎ 3551-6705, albergue@feop.com.br, Rua Costa Sena 30, Largo de Coimbra) has a large dorm room facing the lovely Igreja São Francisco de Assis (US$10 per person) and simple apartments for US$27 a double. Discounts apply for HI cardholders.

Hospedaria Antiga (☎/fax 3551-2203, hantiga@barroco.com.br, Rua Xavier da Veiga 01), is a good value for US$13/27, including the TV, phone and fridge in a grand old house.

The **Pousada Nello Nuno** (☎ 551-3375, anamelia@feop.com.br, Rua Camilo de Brito 59), in a quiet location just northeast of Praça Tiradentes, is recommended. It has clean and airy apartamentos for US$23/33. It has lots of artwork and a cute courtyard.

Another fine bet is the **Pousada Ouro Prêto** (☎ 3551-3081, pousadaopreto@feop .com.br, Largo Musicista José dos Anjos Costa 72). You'll find it at the end of a narrow little street with the large name (also called das Mercês), right behind the Igreja NS das Mercês Perdões. It's a friendly place, and Gerson, who runs it, speaks English. It has a fantastic view too, and all the comforts that delight the traveler. It's US$20/33/47 for single/double/triple apartamentos; add another US$6 per person during high season.

The **Pousada Gabriela** (☎/fax 551-4734, pousadagabriela@feop.com.br), in the same street at No 58, is also very nice. Rooms here are similarly priced; 20% extra in high season.

There are lots of other hotels in this price range. **Pousada Mezanino** (☎ 3551-1289, Rua das Flores 131) is a friendly, family-run place. Quartos are US$20/33 in low season. **Pousada Arcádia Mineira** (☎ 3551-2227, Rua Xavier da Veiga 125) is an OK value for US$20/40, although views from the pousada are not of the colonial part of town.

Mid-Range There are a number of mid-range hotels close to the center of town. **Pousada Tiradentes** (☎/fax 3551-2619, Praça Tiradentes 70) is right in the noisy hub, opposite the tourist office. Double apartamentos are a good value at US$33/50 in low season, US$50/75 in high. Here you'll find Caribbean paintwork, huge rooms and friendly staff.

The **Hotel Colonial** (☎ 3551-3133, fax 3551-3361, colonial@feop.com.br, Travessa Camilo Veloso 26) is well positioned but lacks character. Low season single/double/triple apartamentos are US$30/40/47.

The charming **Pouso do Chico Rei** (☎ 3551-1274, Rua Brigadeiro Mosqueira 90) is a small quiet place with wonderful doubles, great views, and completely furnished in antiques. It is an exceptionally good value for the reasonable price of US$30/44 without/with bathroom.

There are two mid-range hotels on Rua Conselheiro Quintiliano. *Casa Grande* (☎/fax 3551-4314), at No 96, has rooms that offer panoramic views from the balcony from US$44/50. Farther along, at No 395, *Pousada Toledo* (☎ 3551-3366, fax 3551-5915) has rooms furnished with antiques for US$37/50.

Top End *Pousada do Mondego* (☎ 3551-2040, fax 3551-3094, Largo do Coimbra 38) is close to Igreja São Francisco de Assis. It is in an 18th-century colonial mansion with art and antiques. Singles/doubles start at US$80/110, more if you want the view. This is an excellent top-end choice.

The five-star *Solar NS do Rosário* (☎ 3551-5200, fax 3551-4288, sigestpes@ hotelsolardorosario.com.br, Rua Getúlio Vargas 270) has a pool and even boasts its own mine. Swank singles/doubles start at US$100/116.

Niemeyer's *Grande Hotel Ouro Prêto* (☎ 3551-1488, fax 3551-5028, Rua Senador Rocha Lagoa 164), with its subdued exterior but strictly modern interior, is in a great position with a pool and bar area overlooking the town. Ordinary rooms without view are US$53/66; much better accommodations with a stunning view and a mezzanine level are US$66/86.

Places to Eat

Most of the restaurants are clustered along two streets: the lively Rua Conde de Bobadela (popularly known as Rua Direita) and Rua São José. Ouro Prêto is a good place to try regional dishes. One typical Minas dish is *tutu a mineira*, a black-bean feijoada with *couve* (a type of kale). *Restaurant Casa Do Ouvidor* (☎ 3551-2141, Rua Direita 42) is the place to try it. While a bit on the expensive side, the food here is excellent. Also try down the road at No 65, *Restaurante O Profeta* (☎ 3551-4556), which has dishes from US$10 per person.

Also on Rua Direita are the more low-key *Lila's Bar & Creperia*, and opposite, below ground at No 138A, *Spaghetti*

(☎ 3551-3902), which features Italian-style pancakes and pizza and live music nightly.

Deguste (☎ 3551-6363, Rua Coronel Alves 15), opposite the theater, has good food and live music on weekends. Those in a carnivorous mood should head for *Ouro Grill* (☎ 3551-3139, Rua Senador Rocha Lagoa 61).

Down on Rua São José there are a few good options. *Café e Cia* (☎ 3551-4154), at No 187, is an old favorite for lunch and dinner (US$6 per kilo). It has a great view of the town. *Restaurante Sabor Minas* (☎ 3551-15390), at No 202A, has large pizza for US$6, and charges US$7 for various regional dishes that are big enough to share. *Restaurante Chafariz* (☎ 3551-2828), at No 167, has self-service Mineira cuisine for US$9 per person.

Another good bet nearby at is *Adega Ouro Prêto* (☎ 3551-4171, Rua Teixeira Amaral 24), on the steep street off Rua São José, on the way to pousada São Francisco. It has a set price lunch for US$5.

On the other side of town, on Rua Antônio Diaz, is *De Consola's Bar Lanches* (☎ 3551-4175, Rua da Conceição 18), a cozy informal place with a good wine selection. *Chalet dos Caldos* (☎ 3551-1614, Rua Carlos Tomaz 33) has excellent soup (under US$3) and pratos típicos to share for US$6. It's open for dinner only and is closed on Monday.

If you are after a late-night or early-morning snack, try the bakery *Centeio Pães e Iguarias* on Praça Barão do Rio Branco, at the southeastern end of the center; open 6 am to 10 pm.

Entertainment

The young crowd hangs out in Praça Tiradentes before thronging to *Club Ouro Prêto* (Praça de Sportes, Barra), just southeast of the center, for some slow and steamy dancing. It's open Saturday and Sunday nights from 8 to 11 pm. The rest of the week, especially on Friday and Saturday after 11 pm, there's a lot of spontaneous music in the bars and from buskers along Rua Direita. *Bardobeco* (Travessa do Arieira 15) is a very popular bar just up the lane off Rua Direita.

Acaso 85 in Largo do Rosário, opposite the Hotel Rosário, is a very chic place for drinks as well as lunch or dinner, set in a two-level limestone cellar with a fireplace.

The *Cinema Vila Rica* on Travessa Farm. Antônio de Brito, has first-run films in English and kids' films during the day.

Shopping

A soapstone quarry in Santa Rita de Ouro Prêto, 28km away, provides endless supplies for attractive carvings and imitations of Aleijadinho.

Wood carvings, basketwork and unglazed ceramics are sold in the souvenir shops of Praça Tiradentes. Largo do Coimbra, a block east, has a very good soapstone art market (open daily).

Imperial topaz is found only in this area of Brazil, and there are lots of gem shops around Praça Tiradentes. Make sure you obtain a certificate of guarantee.

Getting There & Around

There are frequent buses between Belo Horizonte and the Ouro Prêto bus station (☎ 3559-3252); see the earlier Belo section for more information (US$4, 2¾ hours). During peak periods, buy your tickets a day in advance – they sell out fast. One bus a day goes to Rio, at 11 pm (US$16, seven hours). There are buses to São Paulo at 6:45 am and 5 pm daily, and an extra one on Sunday at 5:25 pm. To Santa Bárbara (US$6) there are buses at 7:30 am and 5:45 pm.

From Ouro Prêto to Conselheiro Lafaiete, there are buses five times daily between 5 am and 6 pm from Monday to Friday, four between 9 am and 6 pm on Saturday, and four daily between 6 am and 6 pm on Sunday. From here you can catch buses to Congonhas.

The bus station, at Rua Padre Rolim 661, is at the northwest end of town. To get to Mariana or Minas de Passagem you can catch a local bus from the bus stop just northeast of Praça Tiradentes. The town is hilly but you can go everywhere on foot. A small bus (US$0.30) circulates between the

bus station and Capela do Padre Faria on the eastern side of town, making various stops along the way.

AROUND OURO PRÊTO
Minas de Passagem

You will get a kick out of this place, probably the best gold mine to visit in the Ouro Prêto region. There's an immense system of tunnels that goes down very deep and then spreads horizontally. Only a fraction of the mine is open to the public, but for most terrestrials, it's enough.

The descent into the mine is made in a rickety antique cable car (the guide is quick to assure you that the cable itself is new), giving you a first-hand idea of just how dangerous mining can be.

The mine opened in 1719. Until the abolition of slavery it was worked by black slaves, many of whom died dynamiting into the rock. Even after abolition, the life of the 'free' miner was little improved.

The mandatory guided tour, led by former miners and given in English where possible, is short and quite informative. It covers the history of the mine and details the methods used to extract the gold, quartz and other metals. There's a **shrine** to dead miners at the bottom.

The mine (☎ 3557-5000, fax 3557-5001, minadapassagem@bol.com.br) is open daily from 9 am to 5:30 pm, and the entry fee is US$10 per person. This is mitigated by the shallow, sparkling-clear 2km-wide **subterranean lake** in the mine, in which you are free to swim. The water's cold, averaging 16° to 18°C, but blue and pure. It's great fun, so bring a bathing suit.

The mine is between Ouro Prêto and Mariana. Take any local bus that runs between the two (US$0.50 from either town) and ask the driver to let you off at Minas de Passagem.

MARIANA
☎ 0xx31 • postcode 35420-000
• pop 39,000 • elevation 712m

Founded in 1696, Mariana is a pleasant old mining town with a character unlike its busy neighbor, Ouro Prêto, only 12km away by paved road. Mariana is visited by tourists but not overrun, retaining the high-altitude tranquility of many of the mining towns.

Information

The tourist terminal on Rua Antônio Olinto, near the river and where the bus from Ouro Prêto stops, contains the state information office (☎ 3557-9044). Next door is the more useful Associação dos Guias (☎ 3557-1158), which gives away excellent free maps.

Things to See & Do

The 18th-century churches are all worthwhile visiting. The **Catedral Basílica da Sé** (Praça Cláudio Manuel), with its fantastic German organ dating from 1701, holds **organ concerts** every Friday at 11 am and Sunday at 12:15 pm (US$6.50). It's open Tuesday to Sunday from 7 am to 6 pm. The **Museu Arquidiocesano de Arte Sacra** (Rua Frei Durão 49), behind the cathedral, is also worth a look. It has sculptures by Aleijadinho, paintings by Ataíde, and other religious objects. It is open Tuesday to Sunday from 9 am to noon and 1 to 5 pm.

There are two lovely churches on the Praça Minas Gerais. **Igreja NS do Carmo**, damaged by fire in 1999, was under renovation at the time of writing. **Igreja São Francisco de Assis**, where the painter Ataíde, Aleijadinho's partner, is buried along with 94 others, is open 8:30 am to 5 pm.

Farther up the hill on Rua Dom Silvério is the **Basílica de São Pedro dos Clérigos**, which was never completed. There is a great view from the elevated site. The town gallows, long since gone, used to be beside the church. It is open 9 am to 5 pm.

While walking through the old part of town, you'll come across painters and wood sculptors at work in their studios.

Places to Stay

The **Hotel Providência** (☎/fax 3557-1449, Rua Dom Silveiro 233) is an interesting cheapie. Originally living quarters for the nuns who still run a school next door, it has a chapel (for pious tightwads), and an excellent swimming pool. You have to go through the school to get to the pool, but don't walk

around in your swimming gear or the nuns might have heart attacks. Single/double quartos are US$15/27 and apartamentos cost US$23/33.

Just around the corner, the **Pousada do Chafariz** (☎/fax 3557-1492, chafariz@barroco.com.br, Rua Côn Rego 149) has modern rooms with TV and minibar (but obdurate staff) for US$23/37/50 singles/doubles/triples.

On the Praça Gomes Freire, the **Hotel Central** (☎ 3557-1630, Rua Frei Durão 8) is a cheapie, with quartos for US$7/13 a single/double and apartamentos for US$13/20. The best hotel in town is nearby – **Pouso da Typographia** (☎ 3557-1577, fax 3557-1311, Praça Gomes Freire 220). It's worth going in just to see the antique printing presses in the foyer. Singles/doubles cost US$37/53, but you can bargain during the week.

Places to Eat

Lua Cheia (☎ 3557-3232, Rua Dom Viçoso 23) has good per-kilo lunch. **Restaurante Tambaú**, on Travessa São Francisco near the town square, also has good regional food at reasonable prices, as does **Tempero de Minas**, which is two doors down from the Pousada do Chafariz on Rua Côn Rego.

Getting There & Around

There are regular buses between Ouro Prêto and Mariana (US$0.50, 35 minutes). During the day one leaves every half hour. In Ouro Prêto, the bus stop for Mariana is near the Escola de Minas, just northeast of Praça Tiradentes. In Mariana, the bus stop is next to the tourist information office on Rua Antônio Olinto. Mariana's bus station, Rodovia dos Inconfidêntes, located at Km 72 on the edge of town, services more distant destinations.

LAVRAS NOVAS

☎ 0xx31 • postcode 35140-000
• pop less than 1000

The very off-the-beaten-track village of Lavras Novas is 22km south of Ouro Prêto. The surrounding area is stunningly beautiful mountain country, and there are two waterfalls within easy hiking distance.

The town was founded as a *quilombo,* a refuge of runaway slaves – see the History section in the introductory Facts About the Country chapter for an explanation. Today it's a peaceful little place, which is invaded during weekends and holidays by Mineiro ecotourists and fun-seekers on their way through for climbing, hiking and swimming. The focal point is the Igreja Cristo Redentor.

Things to See & Do

You can ride or trek to the two closest waterfalls: **Chapada**, 9km west, with natural swimming pools, and **Moinho**, 2km north, which is peaceful and less frequented. Ask at Casa Antiga Taberna about hiring horses (US$13 to US$20 a half day). There are buses to Chapada from Ouro Prêto but none from Lavras Novas.

Places to Stay & Eat

There are lots of pousadas that are likely to be empty during the week and crowded on weekends. During the week you will have to make reservations for meals. At the east end of town, opposite the church, is *Pensão Dona Maria*. It has double quartos for US$13, and though Maria is nice, you get what you pay for. She's got a restaurant, charging US$2.50 for the plate of the day; *lingua de boi* (ox tongue) is a weekday specialty.

At the east end of town, behind the church, you'll find the excellent *Casa Antiga Taberna*, a cozy bar and restaurant with a fireplace, live music and food – the plate of the day is US$4. Follow the main road 200m to the end, where you will find *Villa Kokopelli Pousada Restaurante* (☎ 9961-1331, *Rua Nossa Senhora dos Prazeres 110*). Rooms here are US$40 for a double. The restaurant has a good atmosphere, with meat and pasta dishes and music on weekends. Nearby *Serra do Luar* (☎ 9961-2474, *Rua Nossa Senhora dos Prazeres 119*) has a restaurant with views; it's US$4 for a prato feito. Simple apartamentos here in a rustic cabin are US$20 to US$30 a double.

At the western end of town, *Pousada da Pedra* (☎ 9965-1133, *Rua da Fonte 102*) is a good option. The three different hippie-style cottages (US$50 per couple, including breakfast and nighttime soup) face a majestically serene landscape. As you enter the town, turn right as you pass the cross.

Getting There & Away

Local bus services are such that you'll have to spend at least a night here – a bus leaves Praça Tiradentes in Ouro Prêto daily at 5:15 pm and returns the following day at 6:45 am. Hitching is possible, but difficult and not necessarily safe; the road is well signed. If driving, from the suburb of Barra (southeast of the center of Ouro Prêto), take the road up along the southern ridge past the university, the town's newer residential suburbs and the aluminum factory. At the intersection with the main road, ignore signs to turn left or right, and go straight across. Of the 17km to Lavras Novas, 9km is unpaved. While the way is sometimes bumpy and precipitous, the trip is scenic.

SÃO JOÃO DEL REI

☎ 0xx32 • postcode 36300-000
• pop 74,000 • elevation 910m

São João del Rei is one of the original gold towns of Minas Gerais. The old city center, which is protected by Brazil's Landmarks Commission, features several of the country's finest churches and some fine colonial mansions – one of which belonged to the late and still-popular never-quite-president Tancredo Neves. It also has a good museum and a variety of other sites and activities, and is the gateway for excursions to the stunningly beautiful village of Tiradentes. While Tiradentes is busy on weekends and generally quiet during the week, São João is pretty empty on Sunday.

Floodlights illuminate the churches each night and give them a fantastic appearance. Opening times are unpredictable, but most will at least be open in the late afternoon. Monday is not a good day to visit São João – all the churches are closed, whereas in Tiradentes the attractions are closed on Tuesday.

Orientation

São João sits between the Serra de São José and the Serra do Lenheiro, near the south

THE SOUTHEAST

SÃO JOÃO DEL REI

PLACES TO STAY
1 Aparecida Hotel
2 Hotel Brasil
5 Hotel Lenheiro Palace
10 Hotel Província de Orense
24 Hotel Ponte Real
34 Pousada Beco do Bispo
36 Pousada Casarão

PLACES TO EAT
7 Restaurante Pelourinho
11 Restaurante Rex
12 Pizzeria Primus
17 Restaurante Portal del-Rey
21 Quinto do Ouro
30 Sandwicheria Big Burger
31 Café com Arte

OTHER
3 Igreja de NS do Carmo
4 Igreja de NS das Mercês
6 Museu Ferroviário; Railway Station
8 Banco do Brasil
9 Catedral de NS do Pilar
13 Pharmacy (24 hours)
14 Teatro Municipal
15 Cine Gloria
16 Igreja de NS do Rosário
18 Museu de Arte Sacra
19 Acaso 85
20 Capela de NS da Piedade
22 Cambitur
23 Museu Regional do SPHAN
25 City Hall
26 Post Office
27 Capela de NS das Dores
28 Capela de Santo Antonio
29 Igreja de São Gonçalo e Monumento ao Expedicionário
32 Museu Municipal
33 Tourist Office
35 Igreja de São Francisco de Assis

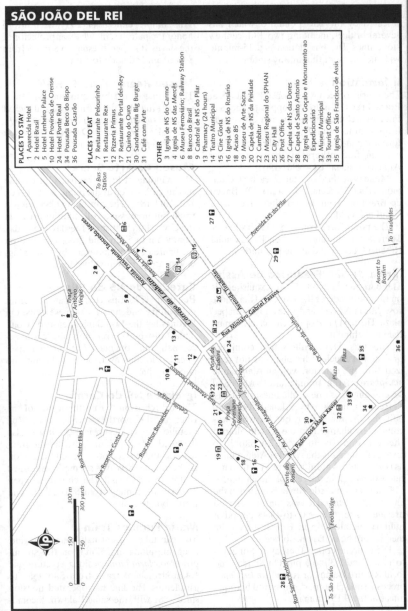

end of the Serra do Espinhaço. The town is bisected by the Rio Lenheiro, which has several bridges, including two 18th-century stone ones. The bus station is a 15-minute walk northeast of the railway station.

Information

The tourist office (☎ 3379-2952), upstairs at Praça Frei Orlando 90, opposite the São Francisco church, is useful and open daily from 8 am to 5 pm. There is also tourist information at the bus station. French speakers can find others of their ilk at the Alliance Française (☎ 9981-1904).

Monday to Friday, change cash at Cambitur (Rua Marechal Deodoro 40). Banco do Brasil on Avenida Hermílio Alves has a Visa/Plus ATM.

The post office is on Avenida Tiradentes. There are telephone posts on Rua Amelia Ribeiro Guedes and at the bus station.

Igreja de São Francisco de Assis

This baroque church (1774) is exquisite. It is on the south side of the river, on Rua Padre José Maria Xavier, and faces a lyre-shaped plaza. The best view of the church is from up the hill, behind it.

This was Aleijadinho's first complete project, but much of his plan was not realized. Still, the exterior, with an **Aleijadinho sculpture** of the Immaculate Virgin and several angels, is one of the finest in Minas.

Records are sketchy; Aleijadinho probably did the main altar, but his work was completely changed. In the second altar to the left, there is an image of São João Evangelista that is the work of Aleijadinho, as is the Santo Antônio. There's particularly fine woodwork in the rear of the church.

Politician Tancredo Neves is buried in the church graveyard. He was the first elected president after the 1960s-to-1980s period of military dictatorship in Brazil, though he died before he could take office.

The church is open Tuesday to Sunday 9 to 11 am and 2:30 to 5 pm. On Sunday, the local Ribeiro Bastos, or Rapadura (mulata), orchestra and choir perform sacred baroque music at the 9:15 am mass.

Igreja de NS do Rosário

This simple church (1719) was built to honor the patron saint who was protector of the slaves. It's open Tuesday to Sunday from 8 to 10 am and noon to 5 pm.

Museu Regional do SPHAN

This is one of the best museums in Minas Gerais – full of antique furniture and sacred art and housed in a colonial mansion (1859). It's at Rua Marechal Deodoro 12; open noon to 6 pm, closed Monday.

Museu de Arte Sacra

This building, at Praça Embaixador Gastão da Cunha 8, served as the public jail between 1737 and 1850. The museum (US$1) has a small but impressive collection of art from the city's churches; open Tuesday to Sunday from 9 am to 5 pm. The drops of blood on the figure of Christ mourned by Mary Magdalene are represented by rubies.

Catedral de NS do Pilar

Begun in 1721, this church has exuberant gold altars and fine Portuguese tiles. On Wednesday the Lira Sanjoanense, or Coalhada (all-white), orchestra and choir accompany the 7 pm mass. The church is open Tuesday to Sunday from 8 to 11 am and noon to 5 pm.

Igreja de NS do Carmo

This church is on the northern end of the river at the northeastern end of Rua Getúlio Vargas. Begun in 1732, it was also designed by Aleijadinho, who did the frontispiece and the sculpture around the door. In the second sacristy is a famous unfinished sculpture of Christ. The church is open Tuesday to Sunday from 8 to 11 am and from noon to 5 pm.

Maria Fumaça Train

You can take a great half-hour train ride, chugging along at 25km/h on the steam-powered Maria Fumaça along a picturesque 13km stretch of track from São João to Tiradentes. The line has operated nonstop since 1881 with the same Baldwin locomotives and, since being restored, the 76cm-gauge track is in perfect condition.

The train, which you catch at the train station on Avenida Hermilio Alves, runs only on Friday, Saturday, Sunday and holidays, leaving São João at 1 and 2:15 pm and returning from Tiradentes at 1:20 and 5 pm. Tickets are US$4/7 for single/return trip (including admission to the interesting Museu Ferroviário). It gets crowded, so be there early. Going to Tiradentes, sit on the left side for a better view.

If you're only going to Tiradentes for the day and need more time than the return train allows, you can easily take a later bus back to São João.

Museu Ferroviário

The expertly renovated railway museum (US$1 or free with a train ticket), at the train station, contains a wealth of artifacts and information about the steam train era of the late 19th century. Walk down the track to the large rotunda that looks like a coliseum – this is where the trains are kept and it's the best part of the museum, which is open Tuesday to Sunday 9:30 to 11:30 am and 1:30 to 5 pm.

Special Events

Someone's always celebrating something in São João. The list of festivals just goes on and on – 15 religious and 10 secular on one calendar – so stop by the tourist office for a schedule of events.

Locals boast, credibly, that their **Carnaval** is the best in Minas Gerais. The **Semana da Inconfidência**, from April 15 to 21, celebrates Brazil's first independence movement and the hometown boys who led it.

Another important festival is the **Inverno Cultural**, during July, with lots of theater, concerts, dances and short courses on offer. Contact FUNREI (☎ 3379-2500) to find out what's on.

Organized Tours

Vertentes Ecoturismo (☎ 3371-8235) has mountaineering and caving trips to Serra do Lenheiro. Lazer & Aventura Turismo Ecológico (☎/fax 3371-7956, Rua Antônio Josino de Andrade Reis 232) can organize 4WD trips around the region.

Places to Stay

There is a good stock of inexpensive hotels in the old section of the city, right where you want to be. Book ahead in December when the town is filled with students sitting for exams. The once-grand *Hotel Brasil (☎ 3371-2804, Avenida Presidente Tancredo Neves 395)*, facing the river, is OK for US$7 per person, US$10 in apartamentos; no breakfast, though.

Another cheapie option is the *Aparecida Hotel (☎ 3371-2540, Praça Dr Antônio Viegas 13)*, with quartos for US$7 per person and apartamentos for US$13/23 a single/double. Breakfast is small.

The *Hotel Provincia de Orense (☎/fax 3371-7960, Rua Marechal Deodoro 131)*, offers clean and relatively spacious quartos for US$20/32 a single/double and much larger apartamentos for US$40 for a double. There are also simple single rooms, which are a good value at US$11.

Up on the hill behind the Igreja de São Francisco is the lovely *Pousada Casarão (☎ 3371-7447, fax 3371-1224, Rua Ribeiro Bastos 94)*. Like many of the elegant mansions of Minas turned pousadas, this place is exquisite, and it has a small swimming pool. The fan-cooled rooms are US$33/43 for singles/doubles. A huge air-conditioned suite is US$35/50.

Pousada Beco do Bispo (☎ 3371-8844, bispo@mgconecta.com.br, Beco do Bispo 93), is a spotless new place with a great pool and air-con rooms for US$40/53.

The *Hotel Lenheiro Palace (☎/fax 3371-8155, Avenida Presidente Tancredo Neves 257)* is a multistory hotel facing the river. It has comfortable rooms for US$43/56/74 singles/doubles/triples; 20% less in low season.

The *Hotel Ponte Real (☎ 3371-7000, Avenida Eduardo Magalhães 254)* is São João's modern, four-star place. It has a nice pool and bar area friendly staff and singles/doubles for US$47/60.

Places to Eat

Café com Arte (☎ 3372-1034, Rua da Prata 132) (also known as Rua Padre José Maria Xavier), near the Tourist Office, has a varied menu, books (Portuguese) and a pleasant outdoor courtyard. It is closed on Monday. Across the road, on the corner of Avenida Tiradentes, *Sandwicheria Big Burger* also has good snacks. *Pizzeria Primus (Rua Arthur Bernardes 97)* has good pizza – try the Primus special, US$3.

Of the town's self-serve places, three stand out: *Restaurante Portal del-Rey, (Praça Severiano Resende),* is good if you get there around noon – before the wood-burning warmer overcooks all the food (US$4 per person) and it has great desserts. *Restaurante Pelourinho*, on Avenida Hermilio Alves opposite the Museu Ferroviário, and *Restaurante Rex (Rua Marechal Deodoro 124)* both have per-kilo meals.

For regional cooking, try *Quinto do Ouro (☎ 3371-7577, Praça Severiano de Resende 4).*

Entertainment

The music of Minas is extremely good and probably different from anything you've ever heard. The *Teatro Municipal*, on Avenida Hermilio Alves, usually has weekend concerts, but was being renovated at the time of writing. There is always something happening at the *Conservatório de Música* on Rua Padre José Maria Xavier, near the Museu Municipal, and at various other venues on weekends: Ask at the tourist office for advice.

Cine Glória on Avenida Tiradentes screens first-ish run movies nightly.

There is a concentration of bars on Rua Ministro Gabriel Passos and on Avenida Tiradentes near the tourist office.

Getting There & Away

The São João bus station (☎ 3371-5617) is at Rua Cristóvão Colombo, 1.5km northeast of town.

Direct buses for São João leave Rio (US$13 5½ hours) daily at 9 am, 4 pm and 11 pm. There is also a 7 am daily air-con bus from Rio to São João for US$14. The return

bus leaves at 8:30 am, noon, 4 pm and midnight Monday to Saturday, and at 4, 10 and 11:30 pm on Sunday. There are also frequent buses to Juiz de Fora (US$8), where you can transfer to a São João or Rio bus. For more bus information, see the Tiradentes section later in this chapter.

From São João to Belo Horizonte (US$9, 3½ hours), there are seven buses a day. From Monday to Friday, the first bus leaves at 6 am and the last at 6:30 pm. There are extra buses on Sunday night, until 10 pm. These buses stop at Congonhas (US$6, two hours).

To get to Ouro Prêto, catch the São Paulo-Mariana bus that goes via Ouro Prêto, departing São João at 5:30 pm and 3:30 am daily (US$13, four hours). To get the 3:30 am you need to buy tickets the day before.

It is also possible to take a picturesque train ride to Tiradentes; for details see the section on the Maria Fumaça train earlier in this chapter.

Getting Around

There are local buses (yellow) between the bus station (US$0.30, 10 minutes) and the center. The local bus stop in the center is in front of the train station.

The local bus stop at the bus station is to your left as you walk out of the station (in front of the butcher), not from the one directly in front of the door.

From the main bus station, you have two taxi options – traditional taxis (US$4) or the cool and totally cheap motorbike taxi (☎ 3371-5278). The information booth at the bus station will call one if you ask. The price to the center is only US$1. Drivers are safe and carry a helmet for the passenger. Use it!

TIRADENTES
☎ 00xx32 • postcode 36325-000
• pop 4160 • elevation 927m

They don't make towns any prettier than Tiradentes, São João del Rei's gold-era rival, 14km down the valley. Tiradentes is a picturesque town, with the blue mountains of Serra de São José as a backdrop. With few signs of change over the last two centuries, the town has that magic quality of another age – and for some odd reason, that's a very good feeling.

Originally called Arrail da Ponta do Morro (Hamlet on a Hilltop), Tiradentes was renamed to honor the martyred hero of the Inconfidência (see History in the Ouro Prêto section earlier in this chapter), who was born at a nearby farm.

The town's colonial buildings run up a hillside, where they culminate in the beautiful **Igreja Matriz de Santo Antônio**.

If you stand between the church's Aleijadinho facade and the famous sundial,

there is a colorful view of the terracotta-tiled colonial houses, the green valley, and the towering wall of stone formed by the Serra de São José.

Information

The Secretária de Turismo (☎ 3355-1212) is at Rua Resende Costa 71, the only three-story building in town. The staff has maps and other useful information. It is open 10 am to 5 pm. The post office is in the same building.

For English-language information about excellent hiking and horeseback-riding

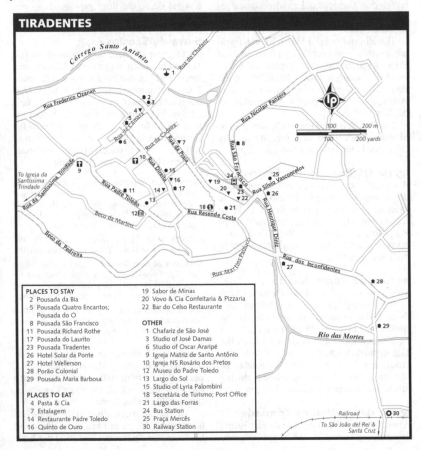

TIRADENTES

PLACES TO STAY
2 Pousada da Bia
5 Pousada Quatro Encantos;
   Pousada do O
8 Pousada São Francisco
11 Pousada Richard Rothe
17 Pousada do Laurito
23 Pousada Tiradentes
26 Hotel Solar da Ponte
27 Hotel Wellerson
28 Porão Colonial
29 Pousada Maria Barbosa

PLACES TO EAT
4 Pasta & Cia
7 Estalagem
14 Restaurante Padre Toledo
16 Quinto de Ouro

19 Sabor de Minas
20 Vovo & Cia Confeitaria & Pizzaria
22 Bar do Celso Restaurante

OTHER
1 Chafariz de São José
3 Studio of José Damas
6 Studio of Oscar Araripé
9 Igreja Matriz de Santo Antônio
10 Igreja NS Rosário dos Pretos
12 Museu do Padre Toledo
13 Largo do Sol
15 Studio of Lyria Palombini
18 Secretária de Turismo; Post Office
21 Largo das Forras
24 Bus Station
25 Praça Mercês
30 Railway Station

opportunities, try John Parsons, the owner of the Hotel Solar da Ponte (see Places to Stay later in this section for the location of the hotel).

Note that all of the churches are closed on Tuesday.

Igreja Matriz de Santo Antônio

Named for the town's patron saint, this church is on the hill at the southwest end of Rua da Câmara. Commenced in 1710 and restored in 1983, it is one of Brazil's most beautiful. There are two bell towers and a frontispiece by Aleijadinho. It is one of the last that he completed. Leandro Gonçalves Chaves made the sundial in front of the church in 1785.

The all-gold interior is rich in Old Testament symbolism. There is a painting by João Batista illustrating the miracle of Santo Antônio making a donkey kneel before the Pope. The polychrome organ was built in Portugal and brought to Tiradentes by donkey in 1798.

The church is usually open Wednesday to Monday from 9 am to 5 pm, but usually closes for lunch between noon and 2 pm.

Igreja NS Rosário dos Pretos

A beautiful stone church with paintings on the ceiling and images of black saints, the existing structure was built in 1708 to replace the original chapel on this site. It's at Praça Padre Lourival on Rua Direita. It is open Wednesday to Monday from 9 am to noon and 2 to 5 pm.

Museu do Padre Toledo

This museum is dedicated to another hero of the Inconfidência, Padre Toledo, who lived in this 18-room house where the Inconfidêntes first met. The museum features regional antiques and documents from the 18th century. It's at Rua Padre Toledo 190. Hours are 9 am to 5 pm Wednesday to Monday, but it usually closes during lunchtime between noon and 1:30 pm

Igreja da Santissima Trindade

After a short walk along Rua da Santissima Trindade, you arrive at this simple pilgrim-age church. Dating from 1810, it was built on the site of a small chapel where Tiradentes officials chose the triangle (representing the holy trinity) as the symbol for the flag of the new nation. The church is open Wednesday to Monday from 8 am to 5 pm.

Chafariz de São José

Constructed in 1749 by the town council, this beautiful fountain has three sections: one for drinking, one for washing clothes and one for watering horses. It's on Rua da Chafariz, just north of the Córrego Santo Antônio. The water comes from Mãe d'Agua via an old stone pipeline. It is open Wednesday to Monday 7 am to 4 pm.

Serra de São José

At the foot of these mountains there is a 1km-wide stretch of protected Atlantic rainforest, and you can hike along several trails. The most popular and simple is to **Mãe d'Agua**, the source of the spring at Chafariz de São José. From the Chafariz, follow the trail north for about 25 minutes into the Bosque da Mãe d'Agua. It is lush with moss and plants and the waters are clear and fresh. Other walks include the following:

Caminho do Mangue This walk heads up the Serra from the west side of town to Aguas Santas, and takes about two hours. There you'll find a mineral-water swimming pool and a very good Portuguese-owned churrascaria.

A Calçada This hike covers a stretch of the old road that linked Ouro Prêto with Rio de Janeiro.

Cachoeira do Bom Despacho This is a waterfall on the Tiradentes-Santa Cruz road, which can be reached by car and is therefore far more visited and littered than the other walking destinations.

Round Robin A fine six-hour walk would be up to A Calçada, then west across the top of the serra and down from Caminho do Mangue.

Locals advise against carrying valuables or trekking alone. For guides (US$6 to US$20 per walk) and information about walks into the mountains, ask at the tourist office or the Hotel Solar da Ponte.

All the above trails can be done on horseback. Horses are readily available in the town and cost from US$4 to $7 per hour with a guide. John Parsons at the Solar da Ponte offers a five-day ride from Tiradentes to Ouro Prêto and two-day rides to an 18th-century farmhouse; prices are on request and depend upon the size of your group.

Places to Stay

Budget Tiradentes has lots of good but expensive pousadas and only a few cheap places. If you can't find anything within your budget, ask around for homes to stay in, or commute from São João del Rei. Try to avoid staying here on the weekend, as it gets crowded and the prices quoted here can double.

The **Pousada do Laurito** on Rua Direita is the best cheapie in town, with a good central location and singles/doubles for US$12/17. Next to the bus station, the **Pousada Tiradentes** (☎ 3355-1232) has a certain amount of charm for the price of US$12/23. Across town, the **Hotel Wellerson** (☎ 3355-1226, Rua Fogo Simbólico 218) has little appeal; nevertheless, doubles are only US$22.

Pousada São Francisco (☎ 3355-1607) up on the hill on Rua Nicolau Panzera, has various rooms ranging in price from US$37 to $60 a double.

Near the train station, the **Porão Colonial** (☎/fax 3355-1251, Rua dos Inconfidêntes 447) has a pool and charges US$14/30 for singles/doubles.

There are a couple of pousadas down the hill from the Santo Antônio church. **Pousada da Bia** (☎ 3355-1173, gaedebg@mgconecta.com.br, Rua Frederico Ozanan 330) is like a home. Simple rooms go for US$23/30 on weekends, US$20/23 during the week. Around the corner on Rua da Camara (also known as Rua do Chafariz) is the **Pousada Quatro Encantos** (☎ 3355-1609). It has a few rooms with little courtyard gardens and charges US$23/46 for a single/double. Reserve the larger room. Next door, at No 25, **Pousada do Ó** (☎ 3355-1438) has a nice front garden and reasonable rooms for US$47 a double.

Mid-Range & Top End Right near the train station, the **Pousada Villa Real** (☎/fax 3355-1292, Rua Antônio de Carvalho 127) is a very warm and nice place owned by the same family that runs the Pousada Casarão in São João del Rei. Rates are US$50/65 for singles/doubles. Nearby is the overpriced **Pousada Maria Barbosa** (☎/fax 355-1227, Rua Antônio Teixeira de Carvalho 134), which offers rooms for US$47/65.

Pousada Richard Rothe (☎/fax 3355-1333, Rua Padre Toledo 124), is an excellent option (the street it is on is also called Rua do Sol). Stylish singles/doubles cost US$60/95 including pool, sauna and soup at night. Children under 12 are not accepted here, nor at the **Hotel Solar da Ponte** (☎ 3355-1255, fax 3355-1201, solar@prover.com.br, Praça dos Mercês). This is a magnificent re-creation of a colonial mansion on the site of a former one, and is one of the country's best hotels. It's the first building on the south side of the little stone bridge. The rooms are simple and beautifully decorated. There's a salon, pool and sauna, and afternoon tea is included in the US$90/140 price; there's a 20% discount in low season and a four-day minimum during Carnaval.

Places to Eat

Pasta & Cia (☎ 3355-1478, Rua Frederico Ozanan 327) has good Italian-style cooking. The **Restaurante Padre Toledo** (☎ 3355-1222, Rua Direita 250) has excellent bife acebolado (beef with onions). **Estalagem** (☎ 3355-1144, Rua Ministro Gabriel Passos 280) does a mean feijão com lombo (beans with pork).

On the street popularly known as Rua da Praia, **Sabor de Minas** (☎ 3355-1546, Rua Ministro Gabriel Passos 62) and **Bar do Celso Restaurante** (☎ 3355-1193) on the main square (Largo das Forras) both have good regional food at reasonable prices. A reader recommends **Restaurante Croustadas** (Rua dos Inconfidêntes 120) as a good place for lunch. **Quinto do Ouro** (☎ 3355-1197, Rua Direita 15) is one of the town's most upmarket restaurants, with both regional and international dishes.

For dessert and coffee, stroll up to **Vovó & Cia Confeitaria & Pizzaria** (Largo das

Forras 78). Also, you might try the teahouse *Maria Luiza (Largo do Ó 13),* next to Rua da Praia, as the best place for traditional sweets and relaxing. Try some cachaça at *Confidências Mineiras (Rua Ministro Gabriel Passos 210A).*

Shopping

Tiradentes has good crafts, antiques, wood-work and jewelry. The antique stores sell furniture, clocks, china and even chande-liers. There are interesting shops around town, especially along and around Rua Direita. Rustic timber sculptures are a good buy if you can take the weight – they are made near the neighboring town of Prados.

Many artists have studios in the town. The studio of Oscar Araripé (☎ 3355-1148, oscarararipepintor@usa.net) is at Ladeira da Matriz 92 (also known as Rua da Camara). He has beautiful prints and postcards of the town, and, if you are in the market, originals. He speaks English and enjoys a chat. Also visit the painter José Damas (Rua do Chafariz 130), and, in Rua Direita, the sacred art sculptor Jango at No 32, and Lyria Palombini (engravings) at No 183.

Getting There & Around

Tiradentes is 20 minutes (US$1) by bus from São João del Rei. The best approach is the wonderful train trip mentioned in the São João del Rei section of this chapter, but buses come and go between São João and Tiradentes every 40 minutes. The bus

ROBYN JONES
Local artisans sell their work.

station is just north of the main square, across the stream. The train station is about 700m southeast of the main square.

From the São João bus station, the first bus leaves for Tiradentes at 5:50 am on weekdays, at 7 am on Saturday, and 8:15 am on Sunday. The last buses leaves for Tiradentes at 5:45 pm on weekdays, at 5:45 pm on Saturday, and at 10 pm on Sunday.

From Tiradentes, the last bus back to São João del Rei leaves at 6:20 pm from Monday to Saturday and at 8:30 pm on Sunday.

Everything in Tiradentes is within easy walking distance, but you can hire a horse and buggy if you prefer.

DIAMANTINA

☎ 0xx38 • postcode 39100-000
• pop 37,000 • elevation 1113m

One of Brazil's prettiest and least visited colonial gems, Diamantina boomed when diamonds were discovered in the 1720s, after the gold finds in Minas. The diamonds petered out, but because of its isolation, Diamantina is a well-preserved colonial city, with fine mansions and excellent hiking in the surrounding mountains.

The center of the city, apart from the rel-atively new cathedral and a couple of in-congruous traffic lights, hasn't changed for hundreds of years. Because Diamantina re-ceived a UNESCO World Heritage listing in 1999, many of the churches and historical houses have been restored or are undergo-ing restoration.

Diamantina is 5½ hours north of Belo Horizonte. After you pass the town of Curvelo (the geographical center of Minas), the stark landscape of northern Minas, with its rocky outcrops and barren highlands, poses a sharp contrast to the lush hills in the south. Diamantina is the birthplace of Juscelino Kubitschek, former Brazilian president and the founder of Brasília.

Information

Staff at the municipal tourist office (☎/fax 3531-1857, pmdiamantina@dnet.br, Praça Monsenhor Neves 44) will give you a guide in Portuguese that includes a map.

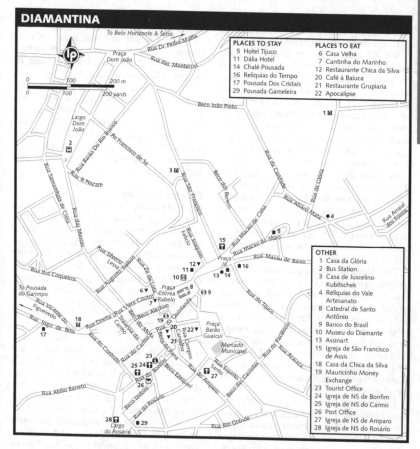

DIAMANTINA

PLACES TO STAY
5 Hotel Tijuco
11 Dália Hotel
14 Chalé Pousada
16 Reliquias do Tempo
17 Pousada Dos Cristais
29 Pousada Gameleira

PLACES TO EAT
6 Casa Velha
7 Cantinha do Marinho
12 Restaurante Chica da Silva
20 Café à Baiuca
21 Restaurante Grupiaria
22 Apocalipse

OTHER
1 Casa da Glória
2 Bus Station
3 Casa de Juscelino Kubitschek
4 Reliquias do Vale Artesanato
8 Catedral de Santo Antônio
9 Banco do Brasil
10 Museu do Diamante
13 Assinart
15 Igreja de São Francisco de Assis
18 Casa da Chica da Silva
19 Mauricinho Money Exchange
23 Tourist Office
24 Igreja de NS do Bonfim
25 Igreja de NS do Carmo
26 Post Office
27 Igreja de NS de Amparo
28 Igreja de NS do Rosário

Banco do Brasil on Praça Correa Rabelo has a Visa/Plus ATM. Head to Mauricinho's Money Exchange, a little shop on Beco do Motta near the southwest corner of Praça Correa Rabelo, for parallel rates on US dollars in cash.

There is a post office opposite the tourist office. The telephone office is on Rua Vieira Couto.

Things to See & Do

Most of the churches charge a US$0.50 entry fee and are open 2 to 5:30 pm Tuesday to Saturday and 9 am to noon Sunday; closed for lunch. Almost everything closes on Monday.

From Praça Correa Rabelo, head down to Rua do Carmo to see the **Igreja de NS do Carmo**. It's the most opulent church in Diamantina, and it's worth having a look inside. Constructed between 1760 and 1765, this church had its tower built at the rear – lest the bells should awaken Chica da Silva. The organ was made in Diamantina and wrought in gold; it is adorned with rich, golden carvings.

The oldest church in town is the **Igreja de NS do Rosário dos Pretos**, which dates from 1731. It's downhill on Largo do Rosário.

The **Casa da Chica da Silva**, a colonial mansion on Praça Lobo de Mesquita, was the home of diamond contractor João Fernandes de Oliveira and his mistress and former slave, Chica da Silva. Here it is possible to get an idea of the lifestyle of the extravagant *mulata*. The huge colonial door leads to her private chapel. Hours are Tuesday to Saturday from noon to 5:30 pm; 9 am to noon on Sunday.

Between Praça JK and the cathedral is the house of Padre Rolim, one of the Inconfidêntes. It's now the **Museu do Diamante**, exhibiting furniture, coins, instruments of torture and other relics of the diamond days. It's open Tuesday to Saturday from noon to 5:30 pm; 9 am to noon on Sunday. Admission is US$0.50.

The **Mercado Municipal** (market), built by the army in 1835, is in Praça Barão Guaicuí. The building's wooden arches inspired Niemeyer's design for the presidential palace in Brasília. On Saturday it has a food and craft market and live music. People from the Vale do Jequitinhonha still arrive on horseback with their wares. There is a small museum here, the Centro Cultural David Ribeiro, which has some fascinating old photos.

Consisting of two houses on opposite sides of Rua da Glória connected by an enclosed, vivid blue 2nd story passageway, **Casa da Glória** was originally the residence of the diamond supervisors and also the official palace of the first bishop of Diamantina. Today, appropriately, the building houses the Institute of Geology. It is open on the weekend from 9 am to 5 pm.

Casa de Juscelino Kubitschek, a small house at Rua São Francisco 241, reflects the simple upbringing of the former president, whose grandparents were poor Czech immigrants. Kubitschek himself believed that his early life in Diamantina influenced him greatly. There are some good photos of JK along the staircase in the Hotel Tijuco (see Places to Stay, below). The casa is open

Tuesday to Thursday from noon to 5:30 pm; Friday to Sunday from 9 am to 6 pm.

While you are in Diamantina, walk a couple of kilometers down the **Estrada Real** or **Caminho dos Escravos** to the **Serra da Jacuba**. This paved road, built by slaves, linked Diamantina with Parati on the Rio de Janeiro coast. From Praça JK, head along Rua Macau do Meio and Rua Arraial dos Forros. There are **waterfalls** at Toca, 5km south of town along Hwy BR-259. Paulo Santos (☎ 3531-2462), a local guide, leads city tours (US$10 per person; 3½ hours) and can organize regional tours.

Places to Stay

Chalé Pousada (☎ *3531-1246, Rua Macau de Baixo 52*) is a cute old house in a great location, with friendly staff and simple quartos (US$10 per person) and apartamentos (US$16 per person). *Pousada Gameleira* (☎ *3531-1900, Rua do Rosário 209*), a little budget place down opposite the Igreja NS do Rosário, is also an excellent value at US$13 per person.

The quaintly eclectic *Dália Hotel* (☎ *3531-1477, fax 3531-3526, Praça JK 25*) is another good deal, a nice old building next door to the Museu do Diamante. It has single/double quartos that cost US$16/27 and apartamentos that go for US$23/40, including a buffet breakfast. There are also rooms with four beds for US$40, or with better atmosphere and views for US$60.

Take a trip in time at *Reliquías do Tempo* (☎/*fax 3351-1627, Rua Macau de Baixo 104*). The gorgeous historical house has lots of character, great views and local artwork. It is an excellent value for US$20/33/47 singles/doubles/triples in immaculate rooms. Another romantic option is the *Pousada Dos Cristais* (*Rua Jogo de Bola 53*). Clean apartamentos here go for US$23/33 singles/doubles in the big old house, or US$20 per person in the new section. The new rooms have a veranda and some have a mezzanine. You can cook, and there is a 24-hour bar.

The modernist *Hotel Tijuco* (☎/*fax 3581-1022, Rua Macau do Meio 211*), a fine Niemeyer creation with spacious, airy rooms, costs US$30/43 for singles/doubles in the rear units. Pay the extra US$6 per person for a veranda and great view. The other top-end option is the *Pousada do Garimpo* (☎ 3531-2523, fax 3531-2316, pgarimpo@dnet.br, Avenida da Saudade 265). While a bit out of the historical center, at the west end of town, it's a tasteful place with a pool, sauna and excellent restaurant. The rooms are comfortable but nothing special. They cost US$50/60 for singles/doubles without a view or US$54/65 with a view.

Places to Eat

Café à Baiuca, just off the main square on Rua Campos Carvalho, is a favorite local place for coffee and cakes. A bit farther down the road, *Restaurante Grupiaria (Rua Campos Carvalho 12)* is a popular place, with Mineiro dishes, which (as in most restaurants in town) will cost you from US$7 to US$10.

Apocalipse, opposite the Mercado Municipal on Praça Barão Guaicuí, has excellent per-kilo meals served in a pleasant room upstairs. *Cantinha do Marinho*, upstairs at Rua Direita 113, on the main square, has a buffet lunch for US$3 per plate including a drink. At dinner try the *lombo com feijão tropeiro* (pork with beans) for US$5.

If you're on a date, head for the *restaurant* at Pousada do Garimpo. It's out of the way and a bit pricey, but Vandeca the chef is famous for his delicious regional dishes. More moderately priced, but still good, is the *Restaurante Chica da Silva* (☎ 3531-3059, Praça JK 27), behind the Dália Hotel. And very nice indeed is *Casa Velha* (☎ 3531-3538, Rua Direita 106), upstairs and opposite Cantinha do Marinho, with a terrific per-kilo lunch and very good Mineiro food at dinner.

Entertainment

Check with the tourist office to see if there is live music happening while you are in town. *Bar Vagalume* on Beco do Mota is recommended. Diamantina is a great place to spend Carnaval and Easter.

Shopping

Diamantina is one of the best spots in Minas for crafts. The ceramic figures from the Vale de Jequitinhonha are superb – a bit hard to stuff into a backpack though. Assinart (☎ 3531-1025), an artists cooperative at Praça JK 40, has good quality work at reasonable prices. Also try Reliquías do Vale (☎ 3531-1353, Rua Macau do Meio 401). There's also the interesting Saturday morning market (at Diamantina's Mercado Municipal at Praça Barão Guaicuí), where people from around the region arrive on horseback, bringing their produce and handicrafts.

Getting There & Around

Buses leave Belo Horizonte for Diamantina (US$15, five hours) daily at 5:30, 9 and 11:30 am, 3:30 and 6:30 pm and midnight. Buses return to Belo Horizonte Monday to Saturday at 1, 6 and 10:45 am, noon, and 3:30 and 6 pm; and on Sunday at 1 and 6 am, noon, and 3:30 and 6 pm and midnight. The buses take the Hwy BR-040 (the road to Brasília) and then head to Diamantina via Curvelo. The road surface is sealed, but at the time of writing, some sections had atrocious potholes. If driving, another option is to take the road up past the Parque Nacional da Serra do Cipó, via Guanhães and Serro.

There are also daily buses to the neighboring historical town of Serro (US$4).

The Diamantina bus station (☎ 3222-6666) is up on the hill on Avenida Juscelino Kubitschek 1455, about 500m uphill from the main square. The town's sites are easily reached on foot.

Mineral Spa Towns

The southern spa towns of Minas are well-developed health resorts, with excellent mineral springs that have various therapeutic applications. Been traveling hard and fast? Recovering from a tropical disease? Sick of beaches? Overdosing on baroque? If the answer to any of these questions is yes, the spa towns await you.

CAXAMBU
☎ 0xx35 • postcode 37440-000
• pop 22,000 • elevation 895m

Caxambu is a tranquil resort for the middle class and the elderly, who come here to escape the heat of Rio and the madness of Carnaval. Some couples have been coming every summer for 30 years or more.

The springs were first tapped in 1870. Realizing the curative properties of the waters, medical practitioners flocked to the town. In 1886, Dr Policarpo Viotti founded the Caxambu water company, which was nationalized in 1905.

Long before Perrier hit Manhattan singles bars, Caxambu water was being celebrated on the international water circuit, winning gold medals. It took the gold in the 1903 Victor Emmanuel III Exposition in Rome, and again in the St Louis International Fair of 1904. It was also awarded the Diploma of Honor in the University of Brussels Exposition of 1910.

These water Olympics were discontinued during WWI, and Caxambu's history was uneventful until 1981, when the private firms Supergasbras (no relation to lingerie manufacturer WonderBra) and Superagua took over the government concession. Caxambu water is sold throughout Brazil.

Information
Obtain maps and other information from the helpful tourist office in Praça Cônego José de Castilho Moreira (☎ 3341-9055; caxambu@netzoom.psi.br), next to the bus station, open weekdays from 1 to 6 pm.

The Banco do Brasil, on Rua Oliveira Mafra, will do cash advances – try the larger hotels for changing cash dollars. Forget traveler's checks.

The post office is on Avenida Camilo Soares, next to the Hotel Glória. The telephone office is at Rua Major Penha 265.

Things to See & Do
The Parque das Aguas is a rheumatic's Disneyland; people come to take the waters, smell the sulfur, compare liver spots, watch the geyser spout, rest in the shade by the canal and walk in the lovely gardens. There is an outdoor swimming pool where you can do laps in the spring water, and the Balneário Hidroterápico, a bath house where you can soak a hot bath, shower or relax in a sauna. The ornate building dates from 1912.

It has 12 founts, each housed in it's own architectural folly, and each with different properties. Liver problems? Drink from the Dona Leopoldina magnesium fountain. Skin disorders? Take the sulfur baths of Tereza Cristina. Itchy trigger finger? Hit the rifle range. VD? The Duque de Saxe fountain helps calm the bacteria that cause syphilis. And there's much more, from kidney stone cures to stomach ailment alleviators, and from eyebaths to anemia fixers.

The park is open daily from 8 am to 6 pm, and admission to the grounds is US$1. Separate fees are required for most activities, including the pools (US$3, US$1.50 for kids), and for the chairlift (US$3) to the top of Morro Cristo.

There is an image of Jesus on top of the Morro Cristo hill, 800m above sea level. The town gained notoriety after Princesa Isabela (daughter of Brazil's last emperor, Dom Pedro II) visited in 1868. After trying various treatments for infertility, she finally managed to conceive after taking the miraculous waters of Caxambu. In thanks she built the Igreja de Santa Isabel da Hungria on Rua Princesa Isabela. Jaunts around the town and into the countryside by horse and buggy depart from the park entrance. Prices range from US$13 to US$30 for up to four people.

The Fábrica de Doce, just outside of town on Hwy BR-354, Km 92, sells locally-produced honey (US$4), homemade fruit liqueurs (US$2), including jaboticaba and tangerine, and preserves (US$3). All of the produce is also available in town.

Many of the hotels have spas and offer massages.

Places to Stay
Caxambu is geared to prosperous travelers, but if you're here outside peak holiday times you can get some good deals. Most hotel prices include all meals.

The *Apart-Hotel São José* (☎ 3341-3133, *Rua Major Penha 264*) is an apartment

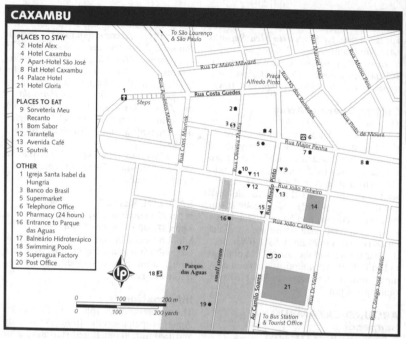

CAXAMBU

PLACES TO STAY
2   Hotel Alex
4   Hotel Caxambu
7   Apart-Hotel São José
8   Flat Hotel Caxambu
14 Palace Hotel
21 Hotel Gloria

PLACES TO EAT
9   Sorvetería Meu
    Recanto
11 Bom Sabor
12 Tarantella
13 Avenida Café
15 Sputnik

OTHER
1   Igreja Santa Isabel da
    Hungria
3   Banco do Brasil
5   Supermarket
6   Telephone Office
10 Pharmacy (24 hours)
16 Entrance to Parque
    das Aguas
17 Balneário Hidroterápico
18 Swimming Pools
19 Superagua Factory
20 Post Office

To São Lourenço
& São Paulo

Rua Dr Mano Millward

Rua Manoel João

Rua Afonso Pena

Rua Costa Guedes

Praça
Alfredo Pinto

Rua NS dos Remédios

Rua Pinto de Moura

Steps

Rua Américo Macedo

Rua Cons Mavrink

Rua Oliveira Mafra

Rua Alfredo Pinto

Rua Major Penha

Rua João Pinheiro

Rua João Carlos

Parque
das Aguas

small stream

Av Camilo Soares

Rua Dr Viotti

Rua Conego José Silverio

0   100   200 m
0   100   200 yards

To Bus Station
& Tourist Office

hotel with TVs, hot showers, a pool and a sauna. Single/double apartamentos are US$16/33 (with breakfast only).

Rooms at the **Hotel Alex** (☎ 3341-1331, Rua Oliveira Mafra 233) are simple and a good value for US$23/47, including meals. Try to get one of the front rooms with balconies on the street.

The **Hotel Caxambu** (☎/fax 3341-3300, hcaxambu@estancias.com.br, Rua Major Penha 145) is another lovely place; it has a pool, playground and a good restaurant, and is right in the center of town. Standard rooms are US$53/66 (US$27/37 breakfast only), and luxury rooms start at US$66/86.

The same owners have the **Flat Hotel Caxambu** (☎ 3341-1244, fax 3341-3368), on the same street at No 386. It has plain but good, large rooms with lots of beds for US$20/27/50/65 for singles/doubles/triples/quads. Registered guests of both places are allowed the use of a leisure complex located 3km away.

The **Palace Hotel** (☎ 3341-3341, Rua Dr Viotti 567) is a good top-end deal. With full board, singles/doubles are US$60/74. There's a huge pool out back with great slides.

Absolute top of the line is the magnificent **Hotel Glória** (☎/fax 3341-3000, Avenida Camilo Soares 590), a posh resort complex with a range of activities for the leisure set. Rooms, complete with TV, bath, bar, telephone and three meals a day, are US$80/100 Facilities include a large gym with indoor basketball court, a physical rehabilitation center and a sauna. Tennis is played on clay courts in the park opposite the hotel.

Places to Eat
Superb pastries, pies and juices are at **Avenida Café** (☎ 3341-4363, Avenida Camilo Soares 648), near the park entrance.

Bom Sabor (Rua João Pinheiro 329), hidden in a courtyard off the street, has a per-kilo lunch which is an excellent value.

Sputnik, on Avenida Camilo Soares, close to the park, is a good lanchonete for a snack. For ice cream, try *Sorvetería Meu Recanto* (*Avenida Camilo Soares 756*).

Tarantella (pronounced like the spider), at Rua João Pinheiro 326 near the park entrance, has the best pasta and pizza in town.

Getting There & Away

The bus station (☎ 3341-9048) is about 1km south of the center on Praça Cônego José de Castilho Moreira. A horse and buggy from there to your hotel costs US$5. There are two daily buses (8:25 am and 11 pm) from Belo Horizonte (see the Belo Horizonte section earlier in this chapter for details). Ten daily buses (US$2) make the 49km trip between Caxambu and São Lourenço on a winding, wooded road. There are six direct buses a day to São Paulo (US$12, 6½ hours), the first at 8 am and the last at 11:15 pm; two to Rio (US$10, 5½ hours), at 8 am and midnight; and, on Sunday, one Rio bus only, running at 4 pm.

AROUND CAXAMBU
Baependi
☎ 0xx35 • postcode 37443-000
• pop 12,000 • elevation 893m

Baependi is a small village on the river of the same name about 6km northeast of Caxambu. Its treasure is the baroque **Catedral Santa Maria** (1752), but the real attraction is the river and the peaceful waterfall 13km south of town. Rent horses in Caxambu (about US$7 per hour; check with the tourist office for a list of horse owners) and set out. Skip the first, more developed falls in favor of the second, **Caixão Branco (Gamarra)**. The ride is easy and takes about 1½ hours each way. Bring a picnic.

Alternatively, a horse and buggy tour from Caxambu to Baependi will cost US$27 (up to four people).

Aiuruoca
☎ 0xx35 • postcode 37450-000
• pop 3000 • elevation 979m

The small town of Aiuruoca is 45km east of Caxambu. The main attraction is the Vale do Matutu on the way from Aiuruoca to

Pedra Pico do Papagaio; in the dry season it is a great region for trekking, with lots of waterfalls. Accommodations include *Pousada Dois Irmãos* (☎/fax 3344-1373, *Rua Coronel Oswaldo 204*), in the town of Aiuruoca, with singles/doubles for US$13/27, and, at 1260m altitude within the Parque do Pico do Papagaio, *Pousada Pé da Mata* (☎ 3344-1421, *Vale do Matutu, Km 14*), which charges US$23/47 for singles/ doubles. Staff at the pousadas can arrange guides.

The bus station (☎ 3341-3839) is in Praça Côn José Castilho. There are regular buses to/from Caxambu.

SÃO LOURENÇO
☎ 0xx35 • postcode 37470-000
• pop 37,000 • elevation 874m

São Lourenço, a short distance south of Caxambu, is another city of mineral waters, though a bit more developed, smoggy and traffic-clogged.

Information

The tourist office, in front of the Parque das Aguas, is open every day from 8:30 to 11 am and 1:30 to 5:30 pm. Bored staff have a list of hotels and a map of the attractions.

Local banks don't exchange money, but surprisingly good rates can be had from the cashier at the Hotel Brasil (see Places to Stay & Eat later in this section).

The post office is on Rua Dr Olavo Gomes Pinto. The telephone office is at Rua Coronel José Justino 647.

Things to See & Do

The **Parque das Aguas** boasts healing waters, a lake with paddleboats, and a large amphitheater enclosed by giant living bamboo. It's open daily from 8 am to 5:20 pm (US$1.50 entry). A ride around the town by horse and buggy will set you back US$6 for up to four people

Members of the Brazilian Society of Euboise believe that a new civilization will arise in the seven magic cities of the region: São Tomé das Letras, Aiuruoca, Conceição do Rio Verde, Itanhandu, Pouso Alto, Carmo de Minas and Maria da Fe. You can visit the edifice erected by this society, the **Templo da Euboise**, which is north of the parque on Rua Rui Barbosa. It's open Saturday and Sunday 2 to 4 pm. You won't be allowed inside if you're wearing shorts or sandals.

Places to Stay

The ***Hotel Colombo*** (☎ *331-1577, 611 Avenida Dom Pedro II*) has the best price in town. Clean, carpeted rooms are US$10 per person. ***Hotel Metropóle*** (☎ *3332-6000, fax 3332-7475, info@hotelmetropole.com.br, Rua Wenceslau Brás 70*) is spotless, with lots of facilities including a pool and a sauna. Fan-cooled apartamentos go for US$27/40/56 for singles/doubles/triples; there are also air-conditioned rooms.

The ***Hotel Miranda*** (☎ *3332-3111, Avenida Dom Pedro II 545*) isn't bad, with not-so-clean quartos at US$27/37 a single/double with full board. Prices rise to US$43/56 in high season. Down the street at No 587, the ***Hotel Imperial*** (☎/fax *3332-1144*) has apartamentos for US$16 per person (breakfast only).

The four-star ***Hotel Brasil*** (☎ *3331-1313, fax 3331-1536, info@hotelbrasil.com.br, Rua*

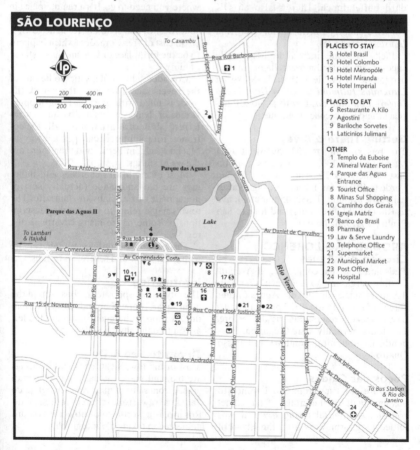

SÃO LOURENÇO

To Caxambu

Rua Rui Barbosa

0   200   400 m
0   200   400 yards

Rua Euripedes Prazeres

Rua Prof Henrique

Rua Antônio Carlos

Parque das Aguas I

Rua Saturnino da Veiga

Junqueira J de Souza

Parque das Aguas II

Lake

Av Daniel de Carvalho

To Lambari & Itajubá

Rua João Lage

Av Comendador Costa

Av Comendador Costa

Rio Verde

Rua Barão do Rio Branco

Rua Batista Luzardo

Av Getúlio Vargas

Rua Wenceslau Brás

Rua Coronel Ferraz

Av Dom Pedro II

Rua Ribeiro da Luz

Rua 15 de Novembro

Rua Coronel José Justino

Antônio Junqueira de Souza

Rua Melo Viana

Rua Santos Dumont

Rua dos Andradas

Rua Dr Olavo Gomes Pinto

Rua Coronel José Costa Soares

Rua Ipiranga

Av Damião Junqueira de Souza

Rua Jaime Sotto Maior

Rua Ida Lage

To Bus Station & Rio de Janeiro

PLACES TO STAY
3   Hotel Brasil
12 Hotel Colombo
13 Hotel Metropóle
14 Hotel Miranda
15 Hotel Imperial

PLACES TO EAT
6   Restaurante A Kilo
7   Agostini
9   Bariloche Sorvetes
11 Laticinios Julimani

OTHER
1   Templo da Euboise
2   Mineral Water Font
4   Parque das Aguas Entrance
5   Tourist Office
8   Minas Sul Shopping
10 Caminho dos Gerais
16 Igreja Matriz
17 Banco do Brasil
18 Pharmacy
19 Lav & Serve Laundry
20 Telephone Office
21 Supermarket
22 Municipal Market
23 Post Office
24 Hospital

João Lage 87), facing the park, is the top-of-the-line hotel in São Lourenço. Doubles with full board start at US$74, or at US$53 with breakfast only.

Places to Eat

Most of the restaurants in town can't compete with the food in the hotels. *Agostini (☎ 3331-1818)*, on Avenida Comendador Costa opposite the park, has pizza (US$7 for a large), pasta, trout and wood-fired oven dishes. *Restaurante A Kilo*, directly opposite the park entrance on Avenida Comendador Costa, has the standard buffet lunch. There's also an OK restaurant for lunch inside the park itself. For ice cream try *Bariloche Sorvetes (Rua Batista Luzardo 78)*.

Pick up some incredible homemade cheeses – marinated mozzarella or smoked provolone – for less than US$4/kg at *Laticinios Julimani (Avenida Dom Pedro II 696)*. *Caminho dos Gerais* at No 710 has snacks and is a cachaça boutique.

Getting There & Away

The bus station (☎ 3332-5966) at Rua Manuel Carlos 130, is about 2.5km southeast of the Park Entrance, across the Rio Verde (US$3 by taxi). There are eight buses daily to Caxambu (US$2, 45 minutes), five to Rio (US$12, five hours) and four to São Paulo (US$13, six hours).

AROUND SÃO LORENÇO
Circuito das Aguas

Taxis and vans that congregate at Avenida Getúlio Vargas in São Lourenço offer half-day tours of the Circuito das Aguas (Water Circuit) for US$16 to US$27 per person; it's best to make a reservation the day before. The tours normally visit Caxambu, Baependi, Cambuquira, Lambari and Passo Quatro.

Poços das Caldas

There are day trips from São Lorenço to this city, built on the crater of an extinct volcano. A mineral-spring town, it was settled by glassblowers from the island of Murano, near Venice. There are full-day tours to Poços das Caldas from São Lourenço (US$30 per person), which leave from in front of the Parque das Aguas at 7 am. Check with the tourist office to see if the day trips are still running.

SÃO TOMÉ DAS LETRAS

☎ 0xx35 • postcode 37418-000
• pop 3170 • elevation 1291m

If you're into mysticism or superstition, or just looking for a cheap, fun and idyllic place to rest up for a few days, the quaint village of São Tomé das Letras may be where you need to go. It's a remote place in the hills, north of the mineral spa towns and southwest of São João del Rei. The town is 38km east of Três Corações (which happens to be the birthplace of Pelé and has a statue of him).

Considered by local mystics to be one of the seven sacred cities of the world, the town is filled with grass-carrying hippies, stories of flying saucers and visiting extra-terrestrials or of a cave that is really the entrance to a subterranean passageway to Machu Picchu in Peru…and then there are the *weird* stories.

Most of the town's churches and buildings are old and made (actually sort of homemade) from slabs of quartzite. The town's name refers to the puzzling inscriptions on some of the many caverns in the region.

This is also a beautiful mountain region, with great walks and several waterfalls.

Information

The city hall is opposite the bus stop in the main square, but will provide little information. A shop in the main square, to the left as you face the church, sells maps.

Things to See & Do

Most of the town's churches and buildings are old, and made (actually sort of home-made) from slabs of quartzite. The **Igreja de Pedra**, a raw stone church in Praça do Rosário, is a worthwhile subject if you are interested in taking a photograph.

Up on the hill on the main square, Praça da Matriz, is one building without a stone face – the **Igreja Matriz de São Tomé** (1785). It contains some excellent **frescoes** by Joaquim José da Natividade. Next to the church is the **Gruta de São Tomé**, a small cave that has a shrine to São Tomé, as well as some strange inscriptions.

The lookout, only 500m from town, provides great views at sunset or sunrise, and it's the place to go for viewing flying saucers.

The caves **Carimbado** (3km away) and **Chico Taquara** (3.5km) both contain additional puzzling inscriptions. The popular waterfalls to walk to are **Euboise** (3km), **Prefeitura** (7km) and **Véu de Noiva** (12km). The army boys have been playing at Pico do Papagaio and have left unexploded mines there, so don't stroll off in that direction!

In August, the **Festas de Agosto** attract lots of pilgrims. The **Mystic Festival**, from late December to early January, attracts students and teachers of mysticism – it's a scene. Contact the town council for more information.

Places to Stay & Eat

Camping at *Gruta do Leão*, a cave that is supposedly stocked with enchanted water, is US$3 per person.

All pousadas charge between US$10 and $16, but not all provide breakfast. The spotless *Pousada Reino dos Magos* (☎ 3237-1300, Rua Gabriel Luiz Alvarez 47) provides fan-cooled rooms for US$11 per person. Its neighbor, the *Hospedaria dos Sonhos I* (☎/fax 3237-1235, Rua Gabriel Luiz Alvarez 28), has private rooms for US$11 per person with breakfast. *Hospedaria dos Sonhos II* (☎/fax 3237-1235), under the same management and with similar prices, is right near the stone church.

Pousada Arco Iris (☎/fax 3237-1212, Rua João Batista Neves 19) is popular with travelers and is a good value for US$16 per person, less during the week. Up the road, the *Pousada e Restaurante Serra Branca* (☎/fax 3237-1200, Rua Capitão João de Deus 7) has apartamentos for US$12 per person. Both have saunas and pools.

Ximana (☎ 3236-1345, Rua Camilo Rios 12) has good hot foods and salads for US$6/kg. On the main praça is *Mona Lisa Lanches*, as well as places for coffee and cakes and, at No 31, even a Japanese bar.

Getting There & Away

From Três Corações, São Tomé das Letras is 38km to the east (6km of which was by unpaved road at the time of writing). Três Corações is 10km east of Hwy BR-381, the main highway between Belo Horizonte and São Paulo.

There are three buses daily on weekdays and four on weekends (US$3) to São Tomé das Letras from Três Corações bus station (☎ 5232-1311, Praça dos Ferroviários).

From Caxambu to Três Corações bus station (☎ 5232-1311) on Praça dos Ferroviários, buses leave six times a day 6:30 am to 8:45 pm (US$3, 1½ hours).

There are several buses a day from São João del Rei to Três Corações (US$4, 2¼ hours).

Outbound buses depart from Praça Barão de Alfenas in São Tomé das Letras.

Parks

PARQUE NATURAL DO CARAÇA
☎ 0xx31

The Santa Bárbara region, 105km east of Belo Horizonte, is one of the most beautiful mountain retreats around. The Caraça Natural Park occupies a transition area between Mata Atlântica and wild mountain vegetation. The 110 sq km park (admission US$7) includes several mountains, including **Pico do Sol** (2070m), **Alto da Inficcionada** (2068m), **Morro do Piçarrão** (1839m), **Pico da Conceição** (1803m) and **Pico da Trindade** (1908m). The hillsides are lined with easily accessible hiking trails and creeks that form waterfalls and natural swimming pools.

The town of Santa Bárbara itself (pop 21,300) has a collection of lovely baroque colonial churches, including the **Igreja Matriz do Santo Antônio** and the **Igreja de Nossa Senhora das Mercês**.

The area's main attraction, 26km southwest of the town and inside the natural park, is a former monastery and boarding school which has been converted to a highly recommended pousada, the **Hospedaria do Colégio Caraça** (see Places to Stay & Eat for details about accommodations). It is still owned and run by the Catholic congregation who use the neogothic-style church for services. The *padres* offer very friendly advice on hikes and treks into the surrounding countryside, and prayers are not required! A highlight is when staff feed a couple of relatively tame wolves, which appear most nights for the feeding.

Places to Stay & Eat

Accommodations at the **Hospedaria do Colégio Caraça** (*☎/fax 3837-2698, pbcm@ acesso.com.br*) run from bare-boned quartos (US$23 for singles) off the courtyard down near the catacombs, to swank private doubles with bathroom from US$33 to US$40. Rates include three meals. The kitchen serves awesome Mineira cuisine – all ingredients are grown locally. You can fry your own eggs on the wood-fired stove. You need to make reservations if you're going for the weekend, as the place gets packed with escapees from Belo taking in the air. During the week, schoolkids come to visit the museum.

Another option is **Pousada Pico do Sol** (*☎/fax 3832-1836, bhnet.com.br/picodosol*), 14km southwest of Santa Bárbara, which is just outside the park gates. It is clean, has a gorgeous pool, and Antonio speaks excellent English. Single/double apartamentos here cost US$23/33; doubles in the chalé are US$50. From here you can catch a free ride 12km up to the monastery with the 6 am workers' bus, and back at about 4:30 pm.

In Santa Bárbara itself, accommodations are available at the **Hotel Karaíba** (*☎ 3832-1501, Praça Pio XII 281*), with quartos from US$6/12 and apartamentos from US$12/16.

Getting There & Away

The Belo-Vitória train stops in Santa Bárbara and there are five to 10 buses a day

from Belo Horizonte (US$4, 2½ hours). From Santa Bárbara, a taxi to the Hospedaria do Colégio Caraça will cost US$16 to $20 plus the US$6 admission for the car to the natural park (open 7 am to 5 pm, or to 9 pm for guests of the hospedaria).

PARQUE NACIONAL DE CAPARAÓ
☎ 0xx32

This 250 sq km national park is popular with climbers and hikers from all over Brazil. The panoramic views are superb, taking in the Caparaó valley that divides Minas Gerais and Espírito Santo. Caparaó contains the highest mountains in southern Brazil, including **Cristal** (2798m) and **Calçado** (2766m), as well as the third highest peak in the country, **Pico da Bandeira** (2890m). All three can be reached via the park's good network of trails. Climbing gear isn't necessary.

Despite being ravaged by fire in 1988 and by human interference for the last 300 years, the park has a few lush remnants of Mata Atlântica, mostly in Vale Verde, a small valley split by the Rio Caparaó.

Wildlife in the park is not exactly plentiful, but there are still some opossums, agoutis and spider monkeys to be seen. Bird life includes various eagles, parrots and hummingbirds.

Between November and January there's lots of rain and it's too cloudy for good views. The best time to visit the park is between June and August – although these are the coldest months, the days are clear. Bring warm clothes!

The park is open daily from 7 am to 10 pm and costs US$2 to enter. The entrance is 4km from Alto Caparaó. Make sure you pick up a map.

Places to Stay

It's possible to camp inside the park. There are two official campsites: **Tronqueira**, 8km from the park entrance, and **Terreirão**, another 4.5km away, halfway to the summit of Pico da Bandeira. Camping costs US$3 a night, and it's a good idea to reserve a site about a week before you arrive by calling IBAMA (☎ 3747-2555).

If you don't have a tent, the nearest place to stay to the park is the *Caparaó Parque Hotel* (☎ 3747-2559), on Rua Vale das Hortências, a short walk from the entrance. It's a pleasant place, but on the expensive side, with doubles from US$85. You'll pay less if it is not peak season.

In Alto Caparaó, the town closest to the park, the *Pousada do Bezerra* (☎ 3747-2628, fax 3747-2538), on Avenida Pico da Bandeira, has rooms from US$50 a double, meals included. Otherwise, ask around for a room to rent.

Getting There & Away

Caparaó can be reached via Belo Horizonte (370km), or from Vitória, in Espírito Santo. You'll need to catch a bus to the town of Manhumirim, and then another local bus to Alto Caparaó, an additional 25km away and 4km from the park.

Unfortunately, the bus timetables work against the budget traveler. There are two buses a day to Manhumirim from both Belo Horizonte and Vitória. From Belo, they leave at 10 am and 5 pm, from Vitória at 9:30 am and 3:30 pm. The trip from either direction takes around five hours. The problem is that there are only two local buses a day from Manhumirim to Alto Caparaó, at 8 am and noon. To avoid staying in Manhumirim, catch one of the many buses going to Presidente Soares and ask to be dropped off at the Caparaó turnoff – then you will have to hitch the rest of the way.

Alternatively, if you can afford it, take a taxi from Manhumirim to Alto Caparaó (US$20 to US$30, depending on the mood of the driver and your bargaining ability).

PARQUE NACIONAL DA SERRA DO CIPÓ

☎ 0xx31

Formed by mountains, rivers, waterfalls and open grasslands, the Parque Nacional da Serra do Cipó, about 100km northeast of Belo Horizonte, is one of the most beautiful parks in Minas. Its highlands, together with

an arm of the Serra do Espinhaço, divide the water basins of the São Francisco and Doce rivers.

Most of the park's vegetation is cerrado and grassy highlands, but the small river valleys are lush and ferny and contain a number of unique orchids. Fauna includes the maned wolf, tamarin monkey, banded anteater, tree hedgehog, otter, jaguar and large numbers of bats. Birdlife includes woodpeckers, blackbirds and hummingbirds. The park is also home to a small, brightly colored frog that secretes deadly toxins from its skin. Brazilians call it *sapo-de-pijama* (the pajama frog).

Other attractions of the park include a 70m waterfall called **Cachoeira da Farofa**, and the **Cânion das Bandeirantes**, named after the early adventurers from São Paulo who used the area as a natural road to the north in their search for riches.

The park is open daily from 8 am to 5 pm (US$2 entry fee).

Places to Stay

Camping e Chalés Véu da Noiva (☎ 3201-1166, Rod MG-010, Km 101, Santana do Riacho) has spaces for trailers and tents, plus hot showers, two restaurants and two natural swimming pools. Also try the nearby *Camping e Chalés Serra Morena* (☎ 3985-6871, Rod MG-010, Km 101, Santana do Riacho). If you wish to camp inside the park, contact IBAMA (☎ 3683-5117). Expect to pay around US$16 per person (including breakfast) in one of these chalés.

Getting There & Away

From Belo's bus station, take a Saritur (☎ 3201-6064) bus for Conceição do Mato Dentro. For the camping grounds, ask the driver to drop you off at Véu da Noiva. The road to Conceição do Mato Dentro passes through Cardeal Mota, the nearest town to the park entrance, which is 3km north of the bridge over the Rio Cipó.

Various Belo Horizonte trekking companies also take excursions to the park, including Brasil Aventuras (☎ 3261-9423) and Serras de Minas (☎ 3227-8397).

São Paulo State

São Paulo is South America's richest state – the industrial engine that powers the Brazilian economy. Thirty of Brazil's 50 largest companies are in São Paulo, as is 50% of the nation's industry. The state contains South America's largest city, São Paulo, a vast megalopolis with 17 million inhabitants in the city and its environs. One in every nine Brazilians lives in the city of São Paulo or one of its satellite cities.

The state's beaches are good and make a nice break if you're meandering your way up to Rio. And charming Campos do Jordão is a great weekend getaway any time of year.

São Paulo City

☎ 0xx11 • postcode 01000-000
• pop 10,500,000 • elev 760m

Brazil's most cosmopolitan and modern city, São Paulo is home to immigrants and ethnic neighborhoods. Millions of Italians came here at the end of the 19th century, millions of Japanese arrived in the 20th century, and millions of Brazilians from the countryside and from the Northeast are still pouring in.

This diversity and industrial development has produced Brazil's largest, most cultured and best-educated middle class. Paulistanos (inhabitants of the city; inhabitants of the state are called 'Paulistas') call their city 'Sampa,' and, despite constantly complaining about street violence, traffic problems and pollution, they wouldn't dream of living anywhere else.

São Paulo is on a high plateau; it's cold in the Brazilian winter and smoggy-hot in the summer. It can be an intimidating place, but if you know someone who can show you around or if you just like big cities it's worth a visit. At its best it offers the excitement and nightlife that you would expect from one of the world's great cities.

History

Founded in 1554 when a group of Jesuit priests led by Manoel da Nóbrega and José de Anchieta arrived at the Piratininga plateau, São Paulo remained a backwater for many years.

By the early 17th century, the area had a few churches and a small village. The growing Indian slave trade saw the town become a

SÃO PAULO STATE

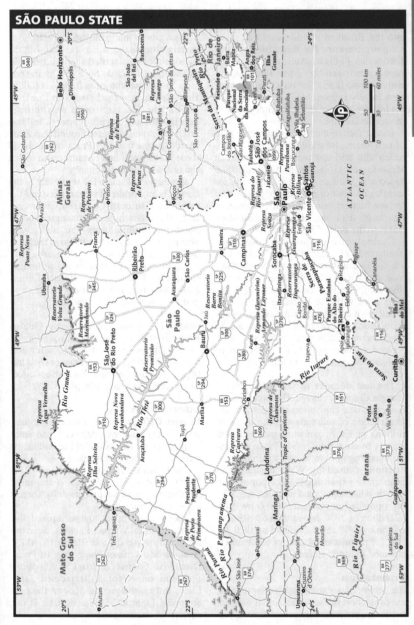

headquarters for groups of *bandeirantes* – the slave-trading pioneers who, in their treks into the Brazilian interior, explored much unknown territory. For them, the Treaty of Tordesillas (1494), which divided South America between Spain and Portugal, was nothing more than a line on a map, and they were largely responsible for expanding the boundaries of Portuguese territory west of the Tordesillas line.

By the 18th century the bandeirantes had turned their attention to mineral exploration and had discovered gold mines in Minas Gerais, Goiás and Mato Grosso. São Paulo was used as a stopover by the increasing number of pioneers, explorers and fortune hunters heading for the interior, as well as by sugar dealers taking their shipments to the port of Santos.

During the early 19th century, two events significantly changed São Paulo. The first was the declaration of Brazilian independence, which led to the city's becoming a provincial capital. The second occurred a few years later with the founding of the Law Faculty, which attracted a new, transient population of students and intellectuals. As a political and intellectual center, São Paulo became a leader both in the campaign to abolish slavery and in the founding of the republic.

The last decades of the 19th century brought dramatic change. The rapid expansion of coffee cultivation in the state, the construction of railroads and the influx of millions of European immigrants caused the city to grow rapidly. São Paulo's industrial base began to form, and the import restrictions caused by WWI meant rapid industrial expansion and population growth, which continued after the war. The city's population reached 580,000 by 1920, 1.2 million by 1940, two million by 1950, 3.1 million by 1960 and 5.2 million by 1970. By 2005 the population of greater São Paulo is expected to top 25 million.

Orientation

The *metrô*, São Paulo's subway system, is one of the best in the world. And it's cheap, too. Parks, museums, art galleries, zoos, you

name it – are spread throughout the metropolitan area.

As a city of immigrants, São Paulo hosts certain districts that are associated with the nationalities that settled there. Liberdade, just south of Praça da Sé, is the Asian area. Bela Vista (also known as Bixiga) is Italian. Bom Retiro, near the Estação da Luz train station (the Luz metrô also runs through here), is the old Jewish quarter. The large Arab community is based around Rua 25 de Março, to the north of Praça da Sé. In all these areas you'll find restaurants to match the tastes of their inhabitants.

Avenida Paulista, to the southwest of the center, is an avenue of skyscrapers, and the adjoining district of Cerqueira César contains the city's highest concentration of good restaurants, cafés and nightclubs. When people refer to São Paulo as the 'New York of the Tropics,' this is the area they have in mind. Farther west, adjoining Cerqueira César, is the stylish Jardins Paulista district, home to many of the city's middle- and upper-class residents.

Maps The *Guia São Paulo* by Quatro Rodas is probably the best all-round guide to the city, with street maps, hotel and restaurant listings and bus lines. *O Guia* has the clearest presentation of any street directory, and it also lists tourist points.

Information

Tourist Offices The city's tourist information booths have excellent city and state maps. They are also good for bus and metrô information. English is spoken.

The booth at Praça da República (☎ 231-2922), on Avenida Ipiranga, is the most helpful; it's open 9 am to 6 pm daily. There's a post office here also.

Locations of other tourist information booths include Avenida Paulista, near the Museu de Arte de São Paulo (MASP); Avenida São Luís, on the corner of Praça Dom José Gaspar; in front of Shopping Iguatemi on Avenida Brigadeiro Faria Lima; and on the ground floor of the new Shopping Light at Viaduto do Cha in the city center.

SÃO PAULO

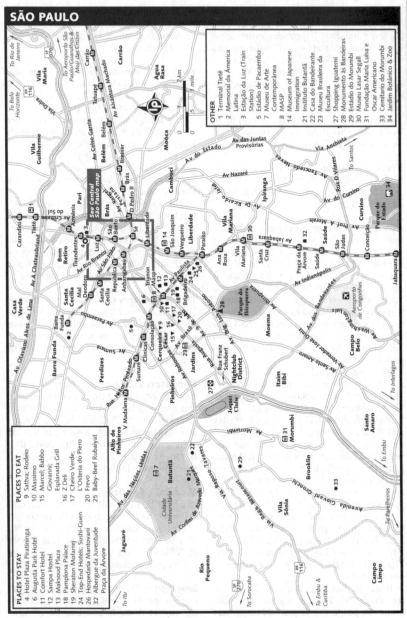

OTHER
1 Terminal Tietê
2 Memorial da América Latina
3 Estação da Luz (Train Station)
5 Estádio de Pacaembu
7 Museu de Arte Contemporânea
8 MASP
14 Museum of Japanese Immigration
21 Instituto Butantã
22 Casa do Bandeirante
23 Museu Brasileira da Escultura
27 Shopping Iguatemi
28 Monumento às Bandeiras
29 Estádio do Morumbi
30 Museu Lasar Segall
31 Fundação Maria Luísa e Oscar Americano
33 Cemitério do Morumbi
34 Jardim Botânico & Zoo

PLACES TO STAY
4 Hotel Plaza Piratininga
6 Augusta Park Hotel
11 Comfort Hotel
12 Sampa Hostel
13 Maksoud Plaza
18 Pamplona Palace
19 Sheraton Mofarej
24 Top-End Hotels; Sushi-Guen
26 Hospedaria Montovani
32 Albergue da Juventude Praça da Árvore

PLACES TO EAT
9 Sattva; Rodeio
10 Massimo
15 Marcel; Babbo Giovanni; Esplanada Grill
16 Z Deli
17 Cheiro Verde; L'Osteria do Piero
20 Frevo
25 Baby-Beef Rubaiyat

The state tourist office (☎ 239-5822) is at Praça Antônio Prado 9 in the art deco Banespa building. It provides information about São Paulo state as well as the city, and is open 9 am to 6 pm Monday to Friday.

São Paulo This Month is a monthly entertainment guide in English and Portuguese (free at large hotels). It includes prices and tells you where English is spoken. Pick up *Veja* magazine (from any newsstand) or go to a tourism booth for a comprehensive list of attractions and what's on.

Visas For visa and entry/exit card extensions, the Polícia Federal office is on the 1st floor at Avenida Prestes Maia 700, and is open 10 am to 4 pm.

Money Except on weekends, changing money is easy in São Paulo and you'll get top rates. Action Cambio (☎ 3237-0828), in the Shopping Light mall, loja 130A, is conveniently located in the city center, and is open 10 am to 7 pm Monday to Friday and 10 am to 4 pm Saturday. There are several travel agencies and exchange offices opposite the airline offices on Avenida São Luís close to Praça da República; they are a good bet. Most banks in this area have foreign-exchange counters.

The central branch of American Express (☎ 251-3383) is at the Sheraton Mofarrej Hotel, Rua Alameda Santos 1437, near the Trianon-Masp metrô. It is open Monday to Friday 9:30 am to 5:30 pm, closed Saturday and Sunday. It changes American Express checks without charging commission and sells US-dollar traveler's checks to American Express cardholders. American Express also has offices at the airport (☎ 6412-3515) and at Centro Empresarial (☎ 3741-8478), Avenida Maria Coelho Aguiar 215, 8th floor.

Thomas Cook and other checks can be changed (only by paying commission) at the Banco do Brasil branch at 1202-5 Rua 7 de Abril, one block from Praça da República. The bank charges US$20 per transaction – not per check.

Banespa has a branch at Praça da República 295. The Itaú Caixa Eletrônico branch opposite the Teatro Municipal has ATMs that accept MasterCard and Cirrus bank cards. Citibank machines, like the ones at Avenida Paulista 1111, accept Visa and Visa Plus cards.

Post & Communications The main post office is at Rua Líbero Badaró near the São Bento metrô station. The poste restante service will hold mail for 30 days.

The main long-distance telephone office is at Rua 7 de Abril, 200m from Praça da República. São Paulo telephone numbers can have seven or eight digits and were in a state of flux at the time of writing.

Fax services are available to the public at the post office.

The Kiosknet (☎ 3151-3645) on the 4th level of Shopping Light in the city center is a great spot for quick and efficient Internet access. The Cyber Café (☎ 881-9670), Rua Artur Azevedo 1339 (near MASP), is open until midnight, and the Internet Café, Avenida Paulista 1919, is open until 10 pm.

Travel Agencies Kangaroo Tours (☎ 3064-3055), Alameda Ministro Rocha Azevedo 456, conjunto 92, in the suburb of Jardins near Avenida Paulista, is a good source for deals on domestic and international flights and air passes.

Bookstores There's an OK selection of English books at the Book Centre, Avenida Ibirapuera 1789. Both Livraria Cultura, Avenida Paulista 2073, and Saraiva Megastore, Praça da Sé 423, have quite a wide variety of titles. Livraria Francesa, Rua Barão de Itapetininga 275, carries exclusively books in French.

Medical Services Einstein Hospital (☎ 3747-1233), Avenida Albert Einstein 627, in the southwestern corner of the city is one of the best in Latin America. (Catch bus No 7241 to Jardim Colombo from Rua Xavier de Toledo to reach it.)

City pharmacies are open seven days.

Emergency Deatur, the tourist police, has English-speaking staff. It has two offices in the city: at Avenida São Luís 95 (☎ 214-

Vendor, São Paulo

At the São Paulo market

Market day, Ouro Prêto

Copacabana soccer game, Rio

Calm waters, Ilha Grande

0209), open 8 am to 7 pm; and at Rua São Bento 380, 5th floor (☎ 3107-5642 or ☎ 3107-8332). Both offices are closed Saturday and Sunday. After hours you may be able to reach Senhor João Marco Queiroz, a Deatur officer, at ☎ 251-5738.

Dangers & Annoyances Reports of crime in the city have increased, and São Paulo is now said to be less safe than Rio, so travelers should exercise caution. Be especially careful in the center at night, and around the cheap hotels on Rua Santa Efigênia. Watch out for pickpockets on buses and at Praça da Sé.

Walking Tour

The triangle formed by Praça da Sé, the Estação da Luz metrô station and Praça da República contains the old center of São Paulo, and it's certainly worth having a look around this area.

A good place to start is the **Mercado Municipal**, Rua da Cantareira 306. Dating from 1933, this lively area used to be the city's wholesale market, until the CEAGESP (a huge new market) was built. Check out the German-made stained-glass windows with agricultural themes.

Not far from the market is Praça da Sé, the geographical center of the city, with the **Catedral Metropolitana**, which was completed in 1954. There are a lot of buskers here, but don't bring any valuables, because there are also lots of pickpockets and bag snatchers. Close by is the **Pátio do Colégio**, where the city was founded in 1554 by Jesuits José de Anchieta and Manoel da Nóbrega. The church and college have been reconstructed in colonial style.

A couple of blocks from Praça da Sé, in the Largo São Francisco, is the **Law Faculty** of the University of São Paulo. The nearby bars are local student hangouts, especially **Bar & Restaurante Itamaraty**.

Up Rua Libero Badaró and across the **Viaduto do Chá** (the bridge over the Vale do Anhangabaú) is the **Teatro Municipal**. The building, with its baroque and occasional art nouveau features, is the pride of the city. The area between here and Avenida Ipi-

ranga is for pedestrians only and is busy during the day. There are plenty of clothing, shoe, book and music shops, travel agencies, photo places and lunch counters.

On the corner of Avenida São Luís and Avenida Ipiranga is what's still one of the tallest buildings in town – the 41-story **Edifício Itália**. There's a restaurant and piano bar at the top, as well as a viewing terrace. Strictly speaking, you're supposed to be a customer to go there; if you're not, act like one. The best time to go up is right at sunset. This is the only time you'll ever get to see the horizon, and as the sun goes down over the nearby hills and the city lights start to sparkle, you could almost convince yourself that São Paulo is beautiful.

Next to the Itália is another one of the city's landmarks, **Edifício Copan**, with its famous curve – another architectural project by Oscar Niemeyer.

Along Avenida Ipiranga, just past Praça da República, is the intersection with Avenida São João. When people get nostalgic about the city (yes, some do), this is the place they write songs about. **Bar Brahma**, on the corner, is a classic bar where you may want to go and try to compose yourself.

The area between here and the Estação da Luz gradually deteriorates. Rua Santa Efigênia is where Paulistanos go for cheap electronic goods, and the area between here and the station is known as the **boca do lixo** (garbage mouth) – a red-light area with striptease shows, as well as desperate characters after dark.

Museu de Arte de São Paulo

The São Paulo Museum of Art (MASP; ☎ 251-5644), Avenida Paulista 1578 (metrô Paraíso, then change for Trianon-Masp), has Latin America's best collection of Western art in, some would say, its ugliest building. Some, though, will find the startlingly simple, confident design by architect Lina Bo Bardi a great example of modern architecture. As well as the work of many French impressionists, there are a few great Brazilian paintings; Cândido Portinari's work alone is worth the trip. There are also temporary exhibits, as well as a pleasant cafeteria on the

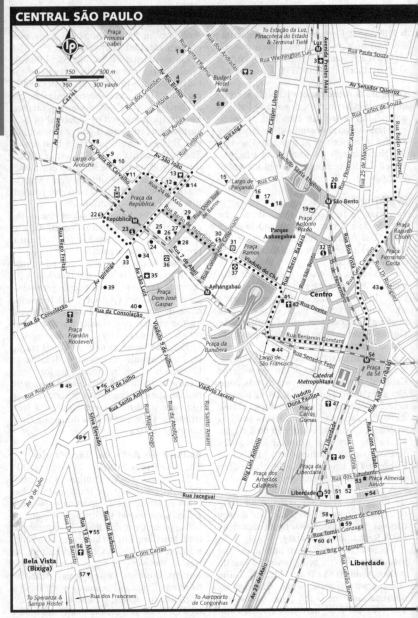

CENTRAL SÃO PAULO

PLACES TO STAY
1   Galeão Hotel
6   Paulicéia Hotel
7   Best Western São Paulo Centre
10 Hotel Itamarati
12 Plaza Marabá Hotel
14 Excelsior
16 Hotel Municipal Palace
17 Britannia Hotel
18 Hotel Central
25 Hotel São Sebastião
28 Hotel Rivoli
29 Hotel Joamar
41 Othon Palace
45 Grand Hotel Ca' d'Oro
51 Osaka Plaza
52 Hotel Isei
53 Ikeda Hotel
59 Banri

PLACES TO EAT
4   Lanches Aliados
5   Pão de Açucar
8   Arroz de Ouro
9   Carlino
11 Casa Ricardo
15 Ponto Chic
27 Rei do Mate
46 Famiglia Mancini
48 Il Cacciatore
50 Sunday Street Fair Food Stalls
54 Diego
55 Cantina e Pizzeria Lazzarella
57 Roperto
58 Kaburá
60 Gombe
61 Sushi-Yassu

OTHER
2   Bar Leo
3   Polícia Federal
13 Bar Brahma
19 Post Office
20 Mosteiro São Bento
21 Buses to Airports
22 Banespa
23 Tourist Information Booth; Post Office
24 Book Centre
26 Banco do Brasil
30 Itaú ATMs
31 Teatro Municipal
32 State Tourist Information
33 Edifício Itália
34 VASP
35 Deatur Tourist Police
36 Telephone Office
37 Shopping Light
38 Igreja NS de Consolação
39 Edifício Copan
40 Transbrasil
42 Igreja de Santo Antônio
43 Pátio do Colégio
44 Law Faculty
47 Igreja São Gonçalo
49 Igreja das Almas
56 Igreja NS Achiropita

— Ⓜ — Metro
         Ped Mall
• • • • • Walking Tour

1st floor. Admission is US$6 for adults, US$3 for students, free for those under 10 or over 60. It's open Tuesday to Sunday 11 am to 6 pm. Go early, as the light can be very bad late in the day.

On Sunday from 9 am to 5 pm, the **Feira de Antiguidades do MASP** (a market full of old odds and ends, big and small) is held below the massive underbelly of the building.

For a bit of relaxation after the museum, visit the Trianon park across Avenida Paulista – a small tropical oasis amid the mountains of concrete.

Pinacoteca do Estado
The neoclassical building housing the Pinacoteca do Estado (☎ 229-9844), Praça da Luz, has undergone an interesting renovation and was opened to the public in 1998. It has a good collection of modern art on display, including a few paintings by some of Brazil's big names such as Portinari and Di Cavalcanti.

One of the highlights here is the collection of French sculpture, with works on display by Auguste Rodin, Aristide Maillol and Camille Claudel. It is open Tuesday to Sunday 10 am to 6 pm; admission is U$3.

Parque do Ibirapuera
There's lots to do in this park, and many people doing it on weekends. Take the metrô to Santa Cruz and then bus No 775-C 'Jardim Maria Sampião,' or bus No 5121 'Santo Amaro' from Praça da República. The large edifice across the street from the park is the São Paulo state legislature. Just outside the park, at the end of Avenida Brasil, is Victor Brecheret's huge **Monumento Bandeiras**, built in memory of the pioneers of the city.

Inside the park is the **Museu de Arte Moderna** (☎ 5549-9688), the oldest museum of modern art in the country, with a huge collection of works from the 1930s to the 1970s. It is open Tuesday to Thursday noon to 6 pm, Friday to Sunday 10 am to 6 pm. Admission is US$3. There's also a **planetarium** (☎ 5575-5206), which has daily sessions (US$3), and other assorted monuments including a Japanese pavilion and, in the

Bienal building, several museums and a couple of enormous exhibition halls.

The **Museu de Arte Contemporânea** (☎ 3818-3039) is housed in Ibirapuera's Bienal building located at Rua da Reitoria 160, Cidade Universitária. This art museum has works by many of the big international names in modern art as well as possessing a good collection of modern Brazilian artists. However, at the time of writing it was temporarily closed for renovation.

The Bienal international art exhibition is also worth a mention. It's the largest in Brazil, and if you happen to be in town when it's on, don't miss it. It takes place every even-numbered year.

Museum de Arte Sacra & Jardim da Luz

The best of Brazil's many museums of sacred art (☎ 227 7694) is at Avenida Tiradentes 676 (metrô Tiradentes). The museum is open Tuesday to Friday 11 am to 6 pm, Saturday and Sunday 10 am to 7 pm; admission is US$2. Two blocks farther down Avenida Tiradentes are the Jardim da Luz and an old British-built metrô station, the Estação da Luz.

Museu da Imigração Japonesa

This fascinating museum (☎ 279-5465), Rua São Joaquim 381, is three blocks east of the São Joaquim metrô station. It has exhibitions on the exploits of the Japanese community, from the arrival in Santos of the first 781 settlers aboard the *Kasato-Maru* in 1908 through to today. It's open Tuesday to Sunday 1:30 to 5:30 pm. Entry is US$2.

Museu Lasar Segall

Lasar Segall was a great Lithuanian expressionist artist (1891–1957) who made Brazil his home and in the 1920s became the leader of its modern movement. In addition to displaying his work, the museum (☎ 5574-7322) gets some very good temporary exhibitions. It's a fair way from the city center, at Afonso Celso 362, Vila Mariana (metrô Santa Cruz), and it's open Tuesday to Sunday 2:30 to 6:30 pm. Admission is free.

Fundação Maria Luisa e Oscar Americano

This modern Brazilian home (☎ 842-0077), set in beautifully landscaped surroundings, is also a long way from the city center, at Avenida Morumbi 3700 in posh Morumbi. Take bus No 7241 Jardim Colombo from Praça da República. It contains imperial antiques and eight oils painted in Olinda by Dutch artist Frans Post. It's open Tuesday to Friday 11 am to 5 pm (Saturday and Sunday from 10 am) and is a great place for afternoon tea. Admission is US$3.

Instituto Butantã

The Butantã snake farm (☎ 813-7222) is one of the most popular tourist sights in town. It keeps over 1000 serpents, from which it milks venom for the production of antivenin to treat snake and spider bites, as well as for vaccines against a number of diseases, including typhoid fever, typhus and diphtheria. Its two museums are both open Tuesday to Sunday 9 am to 4:30 pm. The US$1 admission will get you into both museums. The farm is in a very nice park (good for picnics) at the edge of the Cidade Universitária. Take bus No 702-U 'Butantã-USP' from Praça da República.

Casa do Bandeirante

Not far from the snake farm, this typical pioneer's abode, with a sugar mill, oxcart and farm implements, is interesting if you're in the area. It's in Praça Monteiro Lobato, and is open Tuesday to Sunday 9 am to 5 pm.

Don't miss the snake.

Memorial da América Latina

Near the Barra Funda metrô station at Rua Mario de Andrade 664, this group of buildings is another Niemeyer creation. Outside is a 7m-high cement hand slashed with red. Inside are the **Centro de Estudos Latino Americano** (☎ 3823-9611), an auditorium that stages free concerts, and various interesting handicraft exhibits from regional Brazil and other Latin American countries. Portinari's painting *Tiradentes* hangs in the Salão de Atos, and huge panels by Carybé and Poty represent the people of South America. The memorial is open Tuesday to Sunday 9 am to 6 pm; admission is free.

Museu da Casa Brasileira

This former coffee baron's house has furniture from the 17th to 20th centuries. There is also a good restaurant on site. The museum is at Avenida Brigadeiro Faria Lima 2705, in Jardim Paulistano. It is open Tuesday to Sunday 1 to 6 pm; admission is US$3.

Museu Brasileiro da Escultura

Mube (☎ 881-8611), as this museum is popularly known, at Rua Alemanha 221 in Jardim Europa, is worth a look. The modern building was designed by architect Paulo Mendes da Rocha, the gardens by landscape architect Roberto Burle Marx. Mube features temporary exhibitions by contemporary artists. Hours are Tuesday to Sunday 10 am to 7 pm.

Parque do Estado

The Parque do Estado is a vast park south of the center in the suburb of Agua Funda. It includes three interesting sections: the **Jardim Botânico** (☎ 5584-6300), a lovely 100-year-old park with a promenade of imperial palms (open Wednesday to Sunday); the **Parque Burle Marx** (☎ 3746-7631); and the **Jardim Zoológico** (☎ 276-0811). The zoo is open Tuesday to Sunday (US$4 admission). The closest metrô station is Jabaquara.

Organized Tours

On Sunday there are three four-hour guided city tours, each costing only US$3. They provide an easy and cheap way to get your

---

A Dead King

Ayrton Senna da Silva, 34, was the third-highest-paid athlete in the world in 1993, earning US$18.5 million. To Brazilians he was a living legend, their triple champion and living proof that Brazilians could take on the world and win. Then, on May 1, 1994, during the Italian Grand Prix at the Imola circuit in San Marino, tragedy struck.

The race itself began badly: Pedro Lamy in a Lotus and JJ Lehto of Benetton collided at the start, and two of Lamy's tires hit four spectators. At one point, one of the tires from the Minardi driven by Michele Alboreto flew off and injured six people in the pits.

Then, at 9:13 am Brazilian time, Senna's Williams left the track at the Tamburello curve at 300km/h and smashed against the wall. It was transmitted live on TV, and the scene traumatized all of Brazil. The champion was dead.

Senna was awarded a state funeral with full honors. His Brazilian fans turned out in huge numbers to pay their respects. When the plane carrying his body arrived in São Paulo, 250,000 fans waited in sorrow. The service was attended by 110,000 mourners, and 250,000 followed their idol to the Morumbi cemetery.

In Brazil, Ayrton Senna is now worshiped as a sporting god. To visit his grave at Morumbi, southwest of the city center, take bus No 6291, 'Brooklin,' from Terminal Bandeiras.

---

bearings and visit some interesting sites. The 'Verde' (9:30 am to 1:30 pm) hits parks and gardens, the 'Cultural' (2 to 6 pm) visits museums, and the 'Histórico' (2 to 6 pm) tours old houses and monuments. Tours depart from near the information booth at Praça da República. Turn up at least 20 minutes before departure. For more information about the tours call ☎ 6971-5000.

Places to Stay

São Paulo has plenty of hotels, and they come in clusters, which makes it easy to find one that suits your style. Prices tend to be reasonable. Many give weekend discounts of 20%. Rooms are hardest to find midweek, and for the mid-range and top-end hotels, it's best to reserve a week in advance.

Places to Stay – Budget

Down and out in São Paulo is done in an area between the Estação da Luz and the Praça da República. There are dozens of budget and below-budget hotels on Rua dos Andradas and Rua Santa Efigênia and the streets that intersect them from Avenida Ipiranga to Avenida Duque de Caxias. The area is safe during the day but seedy at night. There's a lot of prostitution in this district, and some of the hotels here cater specifically to this high-turnover clientele. These are often the sleaziest places, and the management will usually let you know that you're not welcome. Alternatively, if you don't mind staying outside of the city center, there are a couple of hostels.

Hostels The best hostel is the *Albergue da Juventude Praça da Árvore* (☎ 5071-5148, info@spalbergue.com.br, Rua Pageú 266), in Chácara Inglesa, a quiet residential area south of the city center. It is in a large, modern house that's been converted into a hostel. It has excellent rooms upstairs with bunk beds, and balconies as well. It also offers a well-equipped kitchen and pleasant lounge downstairs, Internet access, cable TV and an area out back for barbecues. It charges US$12 per person for members, US$16 for nonmembers. To get there take the North (Tucuruvi)-South (Jabaquara) metrô line and get off at the Praça da Árvore station. Walk north for a block and turn right at Rua Orissanga and left at Rua Caramurú. Continue north until you get to No 260 and turn onto Rua Pageú.

The other hostel is very well positioned – within walking distance of Avenida Paulista, where you can find several good restaurants, cafés and nightclubs. *Sampa Hostel* (☎ 288 1592, Rua dos Franceses 100) isn't an HI hostel, and its rooms are pretty basic and in need of renovation. Nevertheless, it offers reasonable lodgings, security and cooking

facilities in a very good location for US$10 per person. To get there, take the North (Tucuruvi)-South (Jabaquara) metrô line to Paraiso station, change lines and get off at the next station of Brigadeiro. Walk northwest along Avenida Paulista (toward MASP for two blocks) and turn right down Rua Joaquim Eugênio de Lima, until Rua dos Franceses, the third street on your left.

Hotels In the pedestrian streets close to Praça da República are a few places worth a mention. A stone's throw from the tourist booth, *Hotel São Sebastião* (☎ 257-4988, Rua 7 de Abril 364) has musty single/double quartos for US$13/16 and apartamentos for US$19/22. Around the corner at *Hotel Rivoli* (☎ 231-5633, hotelrivoli@uol.com.br, Rua Dom José de Barros 28), you'll pay a little more but get better-value quartos and apartamentos. A nice little place a bit farther down the street at No 187 is *Hotel Joamar* (☎ 221-3611), with single/double/ triple apartamentos for US$20/25/32.

There are cheap places on Rua Santa Efigênia, however most are dives. *Paulicéia Hotel* (☎ 220-9733, Rua Timbiras 216), on the corner of Rua Santa Efigênia, is an OK deal though, and it's clean and relatively safe. Single quartos go for US$10 and doubles for US$16. Apartamentos cost US$20 for a single or double.

A step up in style and price are the hotels on the pedestrian strip on Avenida São João near Largo de Paissandu. There are three relatively cheap places – *Hotel Municipal Palace* (☎ 228-7833), at No 354; *Britannia Hotel* (☎ 222-9244), at No 300; and *Hotel Central* (☎ 222-3044), at No 288. The first has fine and clean quartos from US$20 per person (but you can bargain) and single/ double apartamentos from US$25/30. The second and third have single quartos for US$13 and apartamentos for US$16/23.

Liberdade An alternative to staying in the central district is to head over to Liberdade, the Japanese, Chinese and Korean area. The metrô stops very close to the hotels, and it's quieter, safer and more interesting at night. You can also pig out on cheap Japanese food. There are several less expensive hotels as you walk downhill from the metrô station at Praça da Liberdade (there's an information booth here that can give directions).

The really friendly **Ikeda Hotel** (☎ 278-3844, Rua dos Estudantes 134), has single/double quartos from US$14/25 and apartamentos (in a separate building) with singles/doubles/triples for US$29/40/50. The inconspicuous **Hotel Isei** (☎ 278-6677, Rua dos Aflitos 23) has single/double apartamentos from US$24/32.

Places to Stay – Mid-Range

There are loads of mid-range hotels on the streets around Praça da República. They come in clusters, by price, along certain streets.

The friendly **Galeão Hotel** (☎ 220-8211, Rua dos Gusmões 394) is a good value. Apartamentos start at US$40 a double, and it has cheapish single/double quartos for US$20/30. Discounts are possible and credit cards are accepted.

Northwest of Praça da República is Avenida Vieira de Carvalho, a dignified, quiet street. Along with some very expensive hotels is a mid-range favorite, the **Hotel Itamarati** (☎ 222-4133, fax 222-1878, info@ hotelitamarati.com.br), at No 150, close to the bus stop. It is a well-kept old place with clean rooms and helpful management. Single/double quartos are US$21/31, and apartamentos are US$29/39.

There are two bigger hotels on the 700 block of Avenida Ipiranga: **Plaza Marabá Hotel** (☎ 220-7811, fax 220 7227), with singles/ doubles for US$37/49; and the better, more expensive **Excelsior** (☎ 222-0377, 221 6653, vendas@hotelexcelsiorsp.com.br), with singles/doubles for US$65/79.

Across from the Estação da Luz, **Hotel Plaza Piratininga** (☎ 220-2811) is a good place in a crummy location, with singles/doubles for US$46/64.

Around Avenida Paulista There are no real bargains here; the two-star **Pamplona Palace** (☎ 285-5301, Rua Pamplona 851) is the closest you'll get. Singles/doubles go for US$25/40. The seriously friendly **Hospedaria**

Mantovani (☎ 3889-8624, Rua Eliseu Guilherme 269) is a large house that's been converted into a small hotel. It's clean and well kept, with double apartamentos for US$50.

Liberdade The more expensive places in Liberdade include **Banri** (☎ 270-8877, fax 278-9225, Rua Galvão Bueno 209), where air-con singles/doubles start at US$40/53, and **Osaka Plaza** (☎ 270-1311, fax 270-1788). The latter, right across the street from the Liberdade metrô, has all the modern amenities; doubles start at US$70 and a three-person suite for US$89.

Places to Stay – Top End

As in Rio, the residential hotels all offer excellent deals. **Augusta Park Hotel** (☎ 255-5722, fax 256-2381, Rua Augusta 922), in Consolação, is a fine option, with singles/doubles from US$57/73.

The well-located **Comfort Hotel** (☎ 283-0066, fax 283-0181, Alameda Casa Branca 363), near Avenida Paulista, has rooms from US$126/140. In the center the Soviet-looking **Othon Palace** (☎ 232-6000, Rua Líbero Badaró 190) has decent doubles starting at US$80.

Best Western São Paulo Centre (☎ 228-6033, fax 229-0959, Largo Santa Efigênia 40) is an old beauty; singles/doubles start at US$50/67.

São Paulo's luxury hotels include **Maksoud Plaza** (☎ 253-4411, fax 253-3145 8001, Alameda Campinas 150), in Bela Vista, with rooms for US$326; the magnificent **Grand Hotel Ca'd'Oro** (☎ 236-4300, fax 236-4311, Rua Augusta 129), with spacious rooms for US$200; and **Sheraton Mofarrej** (☎ 284-5544, fax 289-8670, Alameda Santos 1437), one of the most expensive places in town at US$350 for doubles.

Places to Eat

The best reason to visit São Paulo is to eat. Because of the city's ethnic diversity, you can find every kind of cuisine at reasonable prices. There are also a million cheap lanchonetes (snack places), pizzerias and great churrascarias and some of the best Italian and Japanese food that you'll find.

Paulistanos love to dine out, and they leave late. Although restaurants open earlier, most don't fill up until 9 or 10 pm on weekdays, and later on weekends, when many stay open until 2 or 3 am.

The places mentioned in this section are the more traditional ones. That they've been around for a long time is a recommendation in itself, since Paulistanos are very particular diners. The selection is limited to areas easily reached by public transportation. If you have a car, or don't mind grabbing a taxi, you can choose from hundreds of other great eateries. The best listing of good restaurants is in the São Paulo pullout section of the weekly *Veja* magazine.

City Center There are a few inexpensive places several notches above the rest. *Ponto Chic (Largo Paissandu 27)* is a friendly, informal restaurant only a few blocks from Praça da República, open until 2 am. The main reason to go there is for the famous Brazilian sandwich, the *bauru,* which Ponto Chic invented many moons ago. The bauru (US$4) consists of beef, tomato, pickle and a mix of melted cheeses, served on French bread. Not only is it popular in urban and backland Brazil, it is also served in Paris.

Another winner is *Lanches Aliados,* on the corner of Avenida Rio Branco and Rua Vitória. It's a cheap and cheerful lunch spot with excellent food and friendly service. *Casa Ricardo (Avenida Vieira de Carvalho 48)* features 20 different sandwiches and is reasonably priced. It is open until 7 pm.

Praça de Alimentação, a food court on the 5th floor of the Shopping Light on Viaduto do Cha, is an inexpensive and convenient option, with the popular *buffet á kilo* restaurants. Around the city are several small lanchonetes called *Rei do Mate* (there is one near Praça da República on Rua São José opposite the Hotel Rivoli). This local chain has delicious fruit juices mixed with *mate* (a kind of Brazilian tea), and good *salgados* (snacks).

If it's lean meat you seek, *Baby-Beef Rubaiyat* (☎ 289-6366, *Alameda Santos 86),* in Paraiso (near the Brigadeiro metrô station), offers the best meat you can get in

town. *Carlino* (☎ 223-1603, *Avenida Vieira de Carvalho 154)* is a reasonably cheap Italian restaurant that's been there for over a century. Farther up on Largo do Arouche is the *Arroz de Ouro* vegetarian restaurant and natural-products shop; it also serves nonvegetarian food.

Ca'd'Oro (☎ 236-4300), in the Grand Hotel Ca'd'Oro (see the Places to Stay – Top End section), is considered one of Sampa's best. It's very expensive; a jacket and reservations are recommended.

Bela Vista This district, also known as 'Bixiga,' is loaded with Italian restaurants and bars, and has some of the city's best nightspots. *Il Cacciatore* (☎ 256-1390, *Rua Santo Antônio 855)* and *Famiglia Mancini* (☎ 256-4320, *Rua Avanhandava 81)* are both very good and very Italian, with large selections of pasta and wine; they stay crowded until quite late with the after-theater crowd. They are moderately priced – US$16 buys a large plate of pasta.

Rua 13 de Maio has stacks of Italian restaurants. *Cantina e Pizzeria Lazzarella* (☎ 288-1995), No 589, is full of Brazilian kitsch. It's festive, the food is good, and large plates of pasta cost about US$5. *Roperto* (☎ 288-2573), No 634, is another good Italian place, and *Speranza* (☎ 288-8502), No 1004, is one of the best pizzerias around.

Cerqueira César There are lots of restaurants and bars in the area bounded by Avenida Paulista, Rua da Consolação, Rua Estados Unidas and Alameda Ministro Rocha Azevedo. Most are fairly expensive, but there are also quite a few reasonable ones. A good, very traditional sandwich place is *Frevo (Rua Oscar Freire 603).* If you want to be really Paulistano (local resident of São Paulo city), order one of the *beirute á moda* along with a *chopp* (draft beer). Servers calling for a chopp yell for a *rabo de peixe* (fish tail).

The churrascarias *Rodeio* (☎ 3083-2322, *Rua Haddock Lobo 1498)* and *Esplanada Grill* (☎ 3081-3199, *Rua Haddock Lobo 1682)* are excellent but expensive.

Sushi Guen (☎ 289-5566, *Avenida Brigadeiro Luis Antonio 2367*) is a reasonably priced Japanese place.

There are a few French restaurants in the area, but nothing cheap. If bucks aren't a worry, try the famous soufflés at *Marcel* (☎ 3064-3089, *Rua da Consolação 3555*).

The area has several fine and reasonably priced Italian restaurants. *L'Osteria do Piero* (☎ 3085-1082, *Alameda Franca 1509*) is a local favorite, with rotating specials; it's closed Monday. *Babbo Giovanni* (☎ 3867-4489, *Rua Bela Cintra 2305*) has good, cheap pizza. For a big splurge, many think *Massimo* (☎ 284-0311, *Alameda Santos 1826*) is the city's best Italian restaurant.

Z Deli (*Alameda Lorena 1689*) is a hugely popular Jewish deli. Vegetarians won't feel left out in this area: There's a healthy fixed menu at *Cheiro Verde* (☎ 289-6853, *Rua Peixoto Gomide 1413*), and *Sattva* (*Rua da Consolação 3140*) has some imaginative vegetarian dishes.

Liberdade Liberdade has lots of inexpensive Asian restaurants and spectacular food at the Sunday street fair, when stalls at the southern side of Praça da Liberdade have *gyoza* (dumplings) (US$1), sukiyaki (US$3) and much more.

There are several good Japanese restaurants on Rua Tomás Gonzaga. *Gombe* (☎ 279-8499), No 22, is always full. It has great sushi and sashimi, and excellent sukiyaki (US$24 for two). Other favorites include *Kaburá* (☎ 277-2918, *Rua Galvão Bueno 346*) and *Diego* (*Praça Almeda Junior 25*), with its strong Okinawan dishes. *Sushi-Yassu* (☎ 279-6622, *Rua Tomás Gonzaga 98*) is the most famous – and the most expensive, at about US$15 a meal; it's closed Monday.

Self-Catering The *Pão de Açúcar* is a well-stocked supermarket, right in the center of the city on Avenida Rio Branco, that accepts Visa, MasterCard and American Express credit cards. The Asian markets you can go to in Liberdade are open Sunday, when most other city supermarkets are closed.

Entertainment

São Paulo's nightlife approaches the excitement, diversity and intensity of New York's. Everyone is out playing until the wee hours, and you can get stuck in traffic snarls at 3 am! To enjoy it, all you need is money (plenty) and transportation. The best list of events is found in the weekly *Veja* magazine (US$2), which also lists restaurants, bars, museums, fairs etc. Another good source is the *Guia da Folha,* a section that comes with the Friday edition of the *Folha de São Paulo*.

Bars The *Bar Brahma*, on the corner of Rua São João and Avenida Ipiranga, in the heart of the central hotel district, is the city's oldest drinking establishment. From 7 pm to midnight, the antique surroundings host equally dated live music. The best tables are upstairs. It's friendly and relaxing and a popular after-work hangout for many Paulistano professionals. *Bar Leo* (*Rua Aurora 100),* another traditional bar, has the reputation for having the best chopp in São Paulo city.

Riviera Restaurant & Bar, on the corner of Rua Consolacão and Avenida Paulista, takes you right back to the seedy 1940s. It's inexpensive and unassuming – a good place to go with a friend. If you want to speak some English, try *Finnegan's Pub* (☎ 852-3232, *Rua Cristiano Viana 358),* in Pinheiros. Paulistanos know it as a gringo bar, and it gets lively.

Nightclubs Cover charges for clubs range from US$7 to US$15. The best street for clubs and such is Rua Franz Schubert, southwest of the center; from Terminal Bandeiras (see Getting Around later in this section) take bus No 6291 'Brooklin' to the corner of Avenida Cidade Jardim and Rua Franz Schubert. The biggest venue here is *Kremlin* (☎ 816-3747, *Rua Franz Schubert 193),* with techno, oldies and an older crowd. *Arccadia* and *Limelight* (☎ 816-3411) have a younger crowd and play plenty of techno.

The bars and restaurants along Rua 13 de Maio in Bela Vista also hum at night. They attract a young crowd, so prices are reasonable, and you can go there and plan out a full evening in one neighborhood. The biggest bar is *Café Piu-Piu (Rua 13 de Maio 134)*, which has music every night except Monday, including jazz, rock, and even American country music.

Spazio Pirandello (Rua Augusta 311) is always lively – the crowd includes both gay and straight clientele. There's art on the walls and a bookstore downstairs.

Live Music The classic spot is *Bourbon Street Music Club (☎ 5561-1643, Rua dos Chanés 127)*, in Moema, with jazz and Dixieland. *Santana Samba (Avenida Cruzeiro do Sul 3454)*, in Santana, features rap and other funky music, and there's samba nightly at *Mistura Brasileira (Rua Alfreres de Magalhães 103)*, also in Santana.

Classical Music There's a steady stream of opera and classical concerts in the Teatro Municipal; check there or at the tourist office to get tickets. Free classical concerts are held every Sunday at 11 am in the Parque do Ibirapuera.

Gay & Lesbian Venues São Paulo has a lively gay scene, and the straight/gay mix in gay places is pretty good. A popular club is *Corintho (Alameda dos Imarés 64)*, with live shows starting at 11 pm Wednesday to Sunday. *Restaurante Spot (☎ 283-0946, Alameda Maestro Rocha Azevedo 72)*, near the Consolação metrô, is a good meeting place with great food, especially the salads.

In Jardim Paulista, *Clube Massivo (☎ 883-7505, Alameda Itu 1548)*, has a good mix of straight, gay and lesbian, as does techno-heavy *Samantha Santa (Frei Caneca 916)*, in Cerqueira César.

Shopping

Shopping is almost as important to Paulistanos as eating out. Those who can afford it like to shop in one of the many large malls that dot the city. For the traveler, these malls don't hold much interest – prices tend to be higher than those in the center of town. However, if you're a big fan of malls, look for a list of addresses in the *São Paulo This Month* guide.

More interesting are the many **markets** and fairs that take place around town, especially on weekends. The most popular is at Praça da República, from 8 am to 2 pm Sunday. It's a great place for people watching (and getting pickpocketed). Offerings include Brazilian precious stones, leather gear, wood carvings, handmade lace and paintings. Some of the local painters are excellent.

Liberdade, the Asian district, has a big street fair all day Sunday and is only five minutes from the center by metro. The fair takes place in the area surrounding the Liberdade metro station.

Markets worth a look are the Mercado Municipal (see Walking Tour earlier) and the CEAGESP market (on Avenida Doutor Gastão Vidigal, in the district of Jaguaré). The huge CEAGESP market is the center of food distribution for the whole city, and it's quite a sight. The best time to go is Tuesday to Friday 7 am to noon, when there's a flower market as well. On other days, it just has lots and lots of fresh produce.

An excellent **market** takes place every weekend in Embu, 28km west of São Paulo, just off Hwy BR-116 toward Curitiba. It's renowned for its rustic furniture, ceramics, paintings and leather items, and you'll find things here from all over Brazil. If you can't make it to the fair on the weekend, it's still worth coming during the week, as most of the artists have permanent shops and there are stacks of handicrafts stores. While there, have a look at the **Igreja Jesuítico NS do Rosário** on Largo dos Jesuitas, the main square; it contains a small sacred-art museum, as well as the first organ even made in Brazil.

Getting There & Away

Air From São Paulo's airports (for details see Getting Around later) there are flights to everywhere in Brazil and to many of the world's major cities. São Paulo is the Brazilian hub for many international airlines and thus the first stop for many travelers.

Before buying a domestic ticket, be sure to check which airport the flight departs from and how many stops it makes (flights to coastal cities often make several stops along the way).

There are flights between São Paulo and Rio every half hour (or less) from the Aeroporto de Congonhas into Santos Dumont, in central Rio. The flight takes less than an hour, and you can usually go to the airport, buy a ticket and be on a plane within the hour. Most of the major airlines have offices on Avenida São Luís, near the Praça da República. They include the following:

TAM
(☎ 315-6700) Rua da Consolação 247, 3rd floor

Varig
(☎ 231-9400) Rua da Consolação 362

TransBrasil
(☎ 228-2022) Avenida São Luís 250

VASP
(☎ 220-3622, 0800-998277) Avenida São Luís 123

Bus São Paulo has four different bus stations, all accessible by metrô. If you need to check which terminal services your destination consult www.socicam.com.br.

The Terminal Tietê bus station (☎ 235-0322) is easy to reach – just get off at the Tietê metrô station, which is adjacent to and connected with it. It's an enormous building but quite easily navigated. There is an information desk in the middle of the main concourse.

Buses leave for destinations throughout Brazil and for international destinations. Bus tickets are sold on the 1st floor, and international ticket booths are at the southern end of the terminal – turn left from the metrô. There are buses to Montevideo in Uruguay (US$100, 30 hours), Buenos Aires in Argentina (US$125, 36 hours), Santiago in Chile (US$120, 56 hours) and to Asunción in Paraguay (US$50, 20 hours).

All the following buses leave from the Terminal Tietê. Frequent buses travel the 429km Via Dutra highway to Rio, taking six hours. The cost is US$15 for the regular bus and US$23 for the *leito*. There are also buses traveling to Brasília (US$37, 14 hours),

Belém (US$114, 46 hours), Belo Horizonte (US$21, eight hours), Foz do Iguaçu (US$40, 15 hours), Cuiabá (US$40, 13 hours), Porto Velho (US$109, 46 hours), Salvador (US$68, 32 hours), Curitiba (US$15, six hours) and Florianópolis (US$30, 12 hours).

Buses to Santos, Guarujá and São Vicente leave every half-hour from a separate bus station – the Terminal Intermunicipal do Jabaquara, which is at the end of the southern metrô line (metrô Jabaquara). The trip to Santos takes about one hour and costs US$5.

If you're staying outside the city center, find out whether there's a local bus station nearby at which buses stop on their way out of town. For example, several southbound buses on their way to Florianópolis, Curitiba etc stop at Itapemirim Turismo (☎ 3722-1222), Avenida Francisco Morato 2300, near the Cidade Universitária. If you catch the bus here, it saves an hour's drive into the city and an hour's ride back. For Foz do Iguaçu, there are also buses from Barra Funda bus terminal (☎ 664-4682).

Getting Around

To/From the Airport Aeroporto de Congonhas (☎ 5090-9000) serves Rio and other local destinations. It is the city's closest airport – 14km south of the city center. Taxis at the front of the terminal charge about US$17 to the center. For buses to the center, walk out of the terminal and then to your right, where you'll see a busy street with a pedestrian overpass. Head to the overpass but don't cross; you should see a crowd of people waiting for the buses along the street. Alternatively, ask for the bus to Terminal Bandeiras. The trip takes about an hour and the last bus leaves at around 1 am.

Aeroporto São Paulo/Guarulhos (☎ 6445-2945), São Paulo's international airport, is 30km east of the city. There are 'Airport Service' buses to Praça da República, the Terminal Tietê bus station and Congonhas airport every 30 to 40 minutes. All cost US$8 and leave from the stop just in front of the arrivals terminal. Another bus service from São Paulo's international airport (about US$8), does a circuit of 11 four- and five-star hotels in the center and the Jardins Paulista area. From the international airport to the center, a taxi will cost about US$30.

To get to the Guarulhos airport, you can catch 'Airport Services' buses from Praça da República, the Terminal Tietê bus station and Aeroporto de Congonhas. Alternatively, take the metrô to Bresser and grab a shuttle bus (US$1.50, 40 minutes) from the small bus terminal (☎ 6692-5191) on Rua do Hipódromo.

Bus Buses are slow, crowded during rush hours and not too safe. The tourist information booths are excellent sources of information about buses. Bus transfer points are at Praça da República and bustling Terminal Bandeiras, where you can catch buses to far-flung destinations within the city.

Metrô A combination of metrô and walking is the best way to see the city. The metrô is cheap, clean, safe and fast. It's open 5 am to midnight. The most useful ticket is the *multiplo 10*, which provides 10 rides for US$7. A single ride costs US$0.80; two rides run US$1.50.

There are currently three metrô lines, two of which intersect at Praça da Sé. The third runs along Avenida Paulista from the Paraiso station. See the main São Paulo map for more information.

Taxi Usually taxi services are metered; flag fall is US$3 and it's about US$0.80 per kilometer. Radio taxis (☎ 251-1733) will pick you up from anywhere in the city.

Paulista Coast

UBATUBA
☎ 0xx12 • postcode 11680-000 • pop 65,000
Ubatuba is a stunning stretch of shoreline on the northern São Paulo coast. The pre-eminent beach resort for well-to-do Paulistanos, it has elegant beach homes and hotels, especially south of the town of Ubatuba. To the north, all the way to Parati, the beaches are wilder and cleaner – and often deserted. There are few hotels, but plenty of campsites.

Most travelers don't go to Ubatuba unless they want to escape São Paulo for the weekend or are driving along the Rio-Santos coastal road.

While the beaches are top-notch, they're rather expensive, get crowded in summer and retain little of the fishing culture that animates so many Brazilian coastal towns.

Information
There's a tourist office shack (☎ 432-4255) where Rua Professor Thomaz Galhardo hits the bay. It's open 8 am to 6 pm, with helpful staff and a useful map.

Banco do Brasil has a branch on the corner of Rua Dona Maria Alves and Rua Carvalho. The post office is on Rua Dona Maria Alves, and the telephone post is at Rua Professor Thomaz Galhardo 81.

Beaches
Within the district of Ubatuba, there are some 74 beaches and 15 islands. Even if you don't have wheels, there's a fine beach (Praia Vermelha) a couple of kilometers southeast of town, with *barracas* (kiosks) and some surfing.

Regular buses run along the coastal road. Other recommended beaches south of Ubatuba include **Enseada** (8km), **Flamengo** (12km, on the Ponta do Flamengo), and **do Lázaro** (16km) and **Domingos Dias** (18km) both just off the highway. The big, loud party scene is 6km south of Ubatuba at **Praia Grande**.

North of town, the beaches are hidden away down the steep hillside. They're harder to find, but good for boogie-boarding and surfing and well worth the effort. The best are **Vermelha do Norte** (9km); **Itamambuca** (15km), where the river meets the sea, **Promirim** (23km), and **Ubatu-mirim** (33km).

Port
The port is at Praia de Saco da Ribeira, 12km south of Ubatuba. You can book daily cruises (US$16, 4 hours) into the Baía da Enseada and out to the Ilha Anchieta.

Festa de São Pedro Pescador

On June 29, Ubatuba celebrates the Festa de São Pedro Pescador with a big maritime procession.

Places to Stay

If you don't have a car the center is the most convenient place to stay. From here you can catch local buses to some of the beaches. **Pousada Columbus** (☎ 423-2136, col@iconet.com.br, Rua Gurany 536), in Itaguá, is about 15 minutes by foot or US$4 by taxi from the town center. It is clean and organized, and rooms are a good value at US$15/25/35 for singles/doubles/triples.

Pricier hotels near the bus station include **Hotel Xareu** (☎ 432-1525, Rua Jordão Homem da Costa 413), **Hotel São Nicolau** (☎/fax 432-3310, Rua Conceição 213) and **Parque Atlântico** (☎ 432-1336, Rua Conceição 185). All of these charge around US$25/45 for singles/doubles in low season, US$35/60 at peak times. **Ubatuba Palace** (☎/fax 432-1500, Coronel Domiciano 500) is the town's finest hotel; singles/doubles here cost US$50/90, including breakfast and dinner.

Praia do Lázaro (16km south of town) is recommended for those after a quiet time. It has good beaches for swimming, and there are a few options for accommodations and places to eat. **Camping Guarani** (☎ 442-0076) has good and secure facilities for campers (US$5 per person). It also has cabins for five to eight people for US$6 per person; bring mosquito repellent. Nearby **Pousada Ana Doce** (☎/fax 442-0102, panadoce@iconet.com.br, Travessa JK 54) is a small and very pleasant pousada just a couple of blocks from the beach. It offers spotlessly clean and comfortable doubles for US$45; try to get one with a little deck where you can dangle your feet in the pool. Another great place at Praia do Lázaro is **Hotel Solar das Águas Cantantes** (☎ 442-0178). This hotel has stylish rooms (US$48 double in low season), a lovely courtyard garden, a large lounge and game room upstairs, and a good swimming pool. The highlight here is the hotel's restaurant; see Places to Eat.

Places to Eat

Buchneiros (Rua Conceição 61) is a pizzeria with a huge wood-burning oven. On the waterfront near the center, **Cantina Perequim** (☎ 432-1354, Rua Guarani 385) is an Italian restaurant that's popular with locals. **Kilo & Cia** (Rua Dona Maria Alves 393), in the center, has a good self-serve buffet lunch. The best per-kilo buffet for lunch and dinner is at **Refúgio da Louca** (☎ 432-3509, Rua Guarani 737), about 15 minutes' walk south of the center in the suburb of Itaguá. The best seafood is at **Peixe com Banana** (☎ 432-1712, Avenida Guarani 255), opposite the airport entrance.

Hotel Solar das Águas Cantantes (see Places to Stay) has an excellent restaurant. It serves superb seafood – the moqueca de badejo is delicious!

Getting There & Away

There are two bus stations in Ubatuba, less than two blocks apart. The main bus station (☎ 432-6912) is on Rua Professor Thomaz Galhardo 513, between Rua Hans Staden and Rua Cunhambebe. The other bus station, on Rua Conceição between Rua Hans Staden and Rua Ap Santos Velloso, serves local destinations.

To São Paulo (US$14, four hours), there are eight buses daily, the first leaving at 12:30 pm and the last at 6:30 pm. Buses to Parati (US$2.50, 1½ hours) leave at 9:40 am and 4:45 and 8:40 pm. There are frequent buses to Rio (US$14, five hours). All of these services leave from the town's main bus station.

For São Sebastião, get a local bus to Caraguátatuba (US$1.20, 40 minutes), then change in front of the main bus station in Caraguátatuba to a São Sebastião bus.

Ubatuba is 72km southwest of Parati on the paved coastal road – a 1½ hour drive at a reasonable speed. Rio is 310km (five hours) away to the northeast of Ubatuba. Heading southwest along the coast from Ubatuba, you reach Caraguátatuba (54km), São Sebastião and Ilhabela (75km) and Santos (205km). After Caraguátatuba the road begins to deteriorate and an unending procession of speed bumps rears its ugly head.

São Paulo is 240km west of Ubatuba. By far the fastest route to São Paulo is to turn off the coastal road onto Hwy SP-099 at Caraguátatuba, then climb the escarpment until you meet the Rio–São Paulo highway, Hwy BR-116, at São José dos Campos. This is a beautiful, rapid ascent, and the road is in good condition.

SÃO SEBASTIÃO
☎ 0xx12 • postcode 11600-000 • pop 58,000

The coastal town of São Sebastião faces the Ilha de São Sebastião (popularly known as 'Ilhabela'), a 15-minute ferry trip away. Huge oil tankers anchor in the calm channel between the island and mainland, waiting to unload at São Sebastião. Most visitors who stay here do so either because they can't find lodging at Ilhabela or in order to enjoy the channel's excellent windsurfing conditions.

Information
The tourist office (☎ 452-1808), Avenida Doutor Altino Arantes 174, on the waterfront, is open weekdays 8 am to 6 pm and weekends 10 am to 6 pm. The Banco do Brasil at Rua Duque de Caxias 20 has a Visa Plus ATM.

Places to Stay & Eat
The *Hotel Roma* (☎ 452-1016, Praça Major João Fernandes 174) has simple air-conditioned singles/doubles for US$18/30. *Pousada da Sesmaria* (☎ 452-2347, Rua São Gonçalo 190), near the center, has singles/doubles from US$40/50.

The best place in town is the lovely and spotless *Pousada da Ana Doce* (☎ 452-1615, Rua Expedicionários Brasileiros 196), with good-value rooms from US$27/40.

Along the waterfront you'll find several good fish restaurants, including *Super Flipper* and, next door, *El Greco*; both have main courses from about US$10 that are usually big enough for two.

Getting There & Away
The bus station at Praça da Amizade 10 has regular service to São Paulo (US$14), to Rio (US$20), to Santos (US$7) and to Boiçucanga (US$5).

It's All Nicot's Fault

In 1542, in the early colonial days, a few tobacco plants were taken from Brazil as specimens for the botanical gardens in Lisbon. However, it wasn't until 20 years later that the habit of smoking took off in Europe. Jean Nicot, then French ambassador to Portugal, pinched a few of the plants from the gardens and gave them to Queen Catherine de Medici of France. After hearing stories of how the indigenous Brazilians smoked tobacco for pleasure as well as for medicinal and spiritual purposes, she was curious to try it. The queen, along with members of the French court, ended up taking up the habit.

For a period, smoking was strongly repressed in Europe. Until the end of the 16th century in England, its use could even lead to the death sentence.

Jean Nicot, while neither a smoker nor even an advocate of the habit, had his surname used for tobacco's active ingredient – nicotine.

The Rio-Santos highway is slow going between São Sebastião and Santos as there are a zillion speed bumps along the coastal road. The quickest route to São Paulo (200km) is to head north from Caraguátatuba on Hwy SP-099.

ILHABELA
☎ 0xx12 • postcode 11630-000 • pop 21,000 (winter), 100,000 (summer)

With an area of 340 sq km, Ilhabela is the biggest island along the Brazilian coast. The island's volcanic origins are evident from its steeply rising peaks, which are covered by dense tropical jungle. There are 360 waterfalls, and the flatlands are filled with sugarcane plantations. The island is known for its excellent jungle hiking and its fine *cachaça*.

Although Ilhabela is a beautiful place, visiting it can be a drag. During summer the island is besieged by Paulistas. Besides the threat to the environment, the crowds create all sorts of logistical difficulties: Hotels fill up, waits of two to three hours for the car ferry are common, and prices soar. The bugs are murder, especially the little bloodsuckers known as *borrachudos*. Use plenty of insect repellent at all times.

The time to go to Ilhabela is on weekdays in the low season. Once you arrive, the name of the game is to get away from the west coast, which faces the mainland and where almost all human activity is concentrated (see Getting There & Around later in this section).

Information
The Secretária de Turismo de Ilhabela (☎ 472-1091) is at the old airstrip, Campo de Aviação. It has a complete list of hotels, pousadas, chalets and campgrounds and is open daily 9 am to 6 pm. The post office and the ticket office for buses to São Paulo are in the same street.

There's also a tourist information post (☎ 472-7102) at the traffic circle 200m from the ferry dock, in the district of Barra Velha. It's open 9 am to 6 pm daily.

Colonial Buildings
Vila Ilhabela, on the northwestern part of the island, has quite a few well-preserved colonial buildings, including the slave-built **Igreja NS da Ajuda** (dating from 1532); the **Fazenda Engenho d'Agua** (1582), in Itaquanduba; and **Fazenda Santa Carmen**, at Feiticeira beach.

Beaches
There are more than 50 beaches on the island, but most of them are accessible only by boat or on foot. See Getting There & Around later in this section.

Of the sheltered beaches on the north side of the island, **Praia Jabaquara** is recommended; it's accessed by a 5km-long walking trail. On the east side, where the surf is stronger, try **Praia dos Castelhanos** (good camping and surf), **Praia do Gato** and **Praia da Figueira**. From Borrifos you can take a four-hour walk to **Bonete**, a windy surf beach lying on the southern side of the island.

Waterfalls
Two kilometers inland from Perequê beach (near the ferry terminal), **Cachoeira das Tocas** is made up of various small waterfalls with accompanying deep pools and water slides. It costs US$3 to get in; the price includes insect repellent. It's a great place to go if you're sick of the beach. **Cachoeira de Água Branca**, in the middle of the jungle at the southern end of the island, is another waterfall to check out. Access is from Veloso beach.

Pico São Sebastião
The 1379m peak of São Sebastião, in the district of Barra Velha, provides a great view – definitely worth it if you're feeling energetic.

Activities
Paulistas on holiday like their toys. As a consequence you can rent almost anything here: Motorboats, yachts, kayaks, sailboards, motorcycles, dune buggies, bicycles, tennis courts, helicopters and diving gear are just some of the options. Maremar (☎/fax 472-1488, maremar@iconet.com.br, Avenida Princesa Isabel 90), in Perequê, can organize just about anything.

Places to Stay & Eat
Reservations are a good idea, especially on weekends. Many choose to stay in São Sebastião, where hotels are cheaper.

Near the ferry terminal is the lovely *Pousada Caravela* (☎ 472-8295, Rua Carlos Rizzini 70), which has two-room suites with cooking facilities for US$33 per double in low season; it's best to book in advance.

Near the beach, *Pousada dos Hibiscos* (☎ 472-1375, Avenida Pedro Paula de Morais 714) has singles/doubles for US$44/66. It's 800m from town, just south of the yacht club. Similarly priced and just north of town is *Hotel Costa Azul* (☎ 472-1365, Rua Francisco Gomes da Silva Prado 71). There are lots of campgrounds near Barra Velha, where the ferry stops, and just a bit farther south, at Praia do Curral.

There is certainly no lack of expensive hotels on the island; the tourist office has a comprehensive list.

At the traffic circle near the tourist office is a good self-serve *ice cream place*. For self-catering, hit the *Ilha da Princesa* supermarket *(Avenida Princesa Isabel 2467)* in Barra Velha. In Vila Ilhabela itself there are a few good, cheap lanchonetes: two in the pedestrian mall, and a couple on Rua da Padroeira. *Cheiro Verde (Rua da Padroeira 109)* has a good *prato feito* (plate of the day) for US$5, while *Convés (Rua da Padroeira 139)* has tasty sandwiches. Right on the pier at *Pier Pizza* you can have a tasty chopp and watch the fishermen pull in the swordfish.

A bit farther from Vila Ilhabela is *Deck* (☎ 472-1489, Avenida Almirante Tamandaré 805), a popular seafood restaurant. *Recanto da Samba*, on the waterfront, is a great place to have a beer and stare at the mainland.

Getting There & Around

The five-minute ferry between São Sebastião and Ilhabela runs every half-hour from 5:30 am to midnight (often until much later in summer). Cars cost US$4.50, motorcycles US$2.50 and it's free for pedestrians. There are direct buses to São Paulo; the ticket office (☎ 472-1869) is on the same street as the tourist office near the old airstrip, Campo de Aviação.

A road runs the length of the western coast. Another unsealed road (22km) crosses the island. To get to the other side of the island requires either a 4WD, taxi (☎ 974-1046), a boat trip or a good strong pair of hiking legs.

BOIÇUCANGA & AROUND
☎ 0xx12 • pop 5000
A laid-back surfer town, charming Boiçucanga is well served by simple hotels and decent restaurants. There's good surf at nearby Maresias and Camburi, plus friendly people and some good walks into the Mata Atlântica (Atlantic rainforest).

Information

A good source of information here is José Mauro B Pinto e Silva, who runs a tourist information service called Amart (☎ 465-1453, zemauro@boicucanga.com.br), at Avenida Walkir Vergani 319. An English-speaking

budget traveler, José is a friendly guy who can help you out with just about anything, including cheap places to stay, Internet access, surfing and windsurfing information and details on treks into the forest.

Beaches

Some great beaches are strung along this stretch of coastline, all accessible by bus. Both **Maresias** (7km east), and **Camburi** (5km west) are great surf beaches. A creek and a small island divide Camburi – the western end is bigger, rougher and good for surfing, and the eastern end is calmer and good for swimming. **Barra do Sahy** (10km west) also has calmer water.

Islands

There are many nearby offshore islands you can visit (one called Alcatraz). José Benedito dos Santos (☎ 9715-1879) or Lili (☎ 9714-3732) can arrange to drop you off in the morning and pick you up at night. You can't camp. Trips average US$20 round-trip per person or US$13 per person for three or more people.

Places to Stay

There are campgrounds at all the beaches. In Boiçucanga, *Camping do Vovô Kido* (☎ 465-1157) has campsites for US$6 per person and very simple bed-in-a-box quartos for US$10 per person.

One of the cheaper hotels in Boiçucanga is *Pousada Boiçucanga* (☎ 465-1910, Avenida Walkir Vergani 522), just opposite the Casa Pedra restaurant, with dorm beds for US$13 or doubles for US$23, an OK value. *Dani Hotel* (☎ 465-1299, Avenida Walkir Vergani 455) charges US$24/30 for singles/doubles.

If you are willing to spend a bit more money, consider staying at picturesque **Camburi**. There are several places to stay, but off-season weekdays can be very quiet and some places close; call in advance. An enjoyable top-end place here is *Pousada das Praias* (☎ 465-1474, Rua Piau 70), just off the main road near the eastern end of the beach. It has good rustic-style doubles from US$40 on weekdays; US$100 on weekends.

Maresias also tends to be more expensive than Boiçucanga, but it may be well worth spending the extra money to have access to the beautiful beach, especially if you intend to surf. *Tubes Maresias (☎ 465-6107, Rua Silvina Auta Sales 44)* is a budget option, though. It has spacious chalets with cooking facilities for US$10 per person on weekdays, US$25 on weekends. To get there, ask to get off the coastal bus at the bridge on the eastern end of the beach. Walk along Rua Nova Iguaçu, just east of the bridge and keep going until you get to Rua Silvina Auta. There are two hotels, both also near the eastern end of the beach, that are worth a look. *Pousada Azul Banana (☎ 465-7167, Rua da Barra 15)* has spotless doubles for US$53 during low season. Another excellent option is *Hotel Villa del Mare (☎ 465-6744, Rua Nova Iguaçu 349)*, which has pleasant apartamentos, a pool, spa and sauna at US$50/70 for singles/doubles, higher at peak times.

Places to Eat

In Boiçucanga the *Big Pão* bakery, on the bend in the main road opposite the Dani Hotel, has good snacks and is open late. Across the road, *Casa Pedra (☎ 465-1675)* is a pleasant little restaurant backing on to the beach. *Restaurante Cheiro Verde*, up the road, is also good. *Cantina & Pizzeria Ibarape (☎ 465-1211)* has good pizza, chicken and drinks.

Maresias has lots of restaurants on the beachfront.

Getting There & Around

Buses run along the coast every 30 to 40 minutes from about 6 am to about 8 pm. There are a few bus stops along the main road, one right in front of the Big Pão bakery and another one opposite Amart tourist information.

GUARUJÁ

☎ 0xx13 • postcode 11400-000
• pop 265,000
Guarujá, 87km southeast of São Paulo, is the biggest beach resort in the state. The beaches are urban and often get crowded

because the town happens to be the closest resort to São Paulo. The condo-crammed beachfront has plenty of hotels, restaurants and boutiques. There's surf along **Praia do Tombo**.

Information

The tourist information office (☎ 3387-7199) is at Rua Quintino Bocaiúva 183; it's open weekdays 7 am to 6 pm. There are also information booths at the bus station and also at Shopping Enseada on Praia das Pitangueiras.

Places to Stay & Eat

The best budget bet is *Pensão Europa (☎ 3386-6879, Rua Rio de Janeiro 193)*, one block from Praia das Pitangueiras. It has simple singles/doubles for US$10/20 during low season; double at peak time.

Farther along the same street is *Hotel Rio (☎ 3386-6081, Rua Rio de Janeiro 131)*, a small and popular place with singles/doubles for US$30/50. *Pousada MiraMar (☎ 3354-1453, Rua Antônio Marques 328)* is in nice house couple of blocks from Praia do Tombo where you will find rooms with balconies for US$30/40 (at least twice as much during high season). There are many more expensive places.

Restaurants and bars line the waterfront. *Nutris (Avenida Leomil 538)* is a good self-serve place. *Restaurante do Joca (3391-1918, Avenida Miguel Stéfano 3035, Praia da Enseada)* has great seafood dishes large enough for two to share.

Getting There & Around

Guarujá is on a large island separated from the mainland by the Canal de Bertioga. The bus station (☎ 3386-2325) is on the edge of town on Via Santos Dumont. From there, catch local bus No 1 or 15 (US$1) to the beach. Buses 52 and 25 are good for getting around the town.

Buses leave every half-hour for São Paulo – the US$6 trip takes just over an hour. You'll pass through Cubatão, one of the most polluted places in the world. Depressed? Just think – it used to look even worse than it does now.

There is a car ferry across to Santos from 4km west of town. If driving toward Rio along the coast you can take a detour to Guarujá and avoid the busy highway for a while. Drive 28km to the northeastern tip of the island and take the ferry across to Bertioga on the mainland.

SANTOS
☎ 0xx13 • postcode 11000-000
• pop 416,000

On the island of São Vicente, Santos was founded in 1535 by Brás Cubas and is now the largest and busiest port in Latin America. The city has seen better days and, as a destination for travelers, it is of limited interest. Only the facades remain of many of the grand 19th-century houses built by wealthy coffee merchants, and some of the local beaches are polluted. But Santos is a vibrant city with a beautiful landscape, and recent years have seen the development of the foreshore and the restoration some of the grand old buildings, such as the Casa do Café in the city center.

Information

The tourist information tram (☎ 3222-4166, 0800-173887), on the beachfront at Praia do Gonzaga at the end of Avenida Dona Ana Costa, has helpful English-speaking staff and maps. There is also a tourist information booth at the bus station. If you need to change money, try Casa Branco, in the center at Praça da República 29, or on Rua Goitacazes 13 in Gonzaga.

Places to Stay & Eat

The waterfront, along Avenida Presidente Wilson, has a few cheaper accommodations and lots of restaurants. *Maracanã Santos* (☎ 3237-4030), at No 172, is acceptable, with singles/doubles from US$20/33. *Hotel Natal* (☎ 3284-2732, hotelnatal@hotelnatal.com.br, Avenida Floriano Peixoto 104) is well positioned. It offers simple rooms for US$12 per person or better apartamentos for US$20/33 single/double. Businesspeople cram the very nice *Mendez Plaza Hotel* (☎ 3289-4243, Avenida Floriano Peixoto 42), which has posh singles/doubles from US$97/115.

For something a bit special, try *Ilha Porchat Hotel* (☎ 468-3437, fax 468-3735, Alameda Paulo Gonçalves 264). It is up on the hill on picturesque Ilha Porchat, at the western end of the Santos beachfront. It's a great spot with bay views toward São Vicente. Standard rooms cost US$43/90 single/double, but the executive rooms with views are better values for US$50/73. Prices go up about 30% during summer holidays. A taxi to Ilha Porchat is US$4 from the bus station at São Vicente, US$11 from the bus station in Santos.

In the city, *Prato Restaurante*, behind the Prefeitura on Praça Visconde de Mauá, has a good-quality per-kilo buffet and a coffee shop. Avenida Ana Costa has lots of places to eat. There's good pizza at *Zi Tereza* (☎ 284-4832, Avenida Ana Costa 449). *Casa das Vitaminas*, a couple of blocks up from the information tram at Gonzaga on Avenida Ana Costa, has excellent-value juices and snacks.

Getting There & Away

The bus station (☎ 3219-2194) is right in the town center at Praça dos Andradas 45. Frequent buses go to São Paulo, 72km away. It is about a one-hour trip and costs US$6. The terminal for the ferry to Guarujá is at the eastern end of the island, at the end of Alameida Saldanha da Gama.

IGUAPE
☎ 0xx13 • postcode 11920-000
• pop 22,000

Iguape was founded in 1538, making it one of the oldest towns in Brazil. While the town itself is of limited interest to travelers, it can serve as a base for visiting the Estacão Ecologica Juréia-Itatins.

Information

Tourist information is available from the Prefeitura, Rua 15 de Novembro 272. It's open weekdays 8 to 11 am and 1 to 5 pm.

Things to See & Do

The town attractions are the **Museu de Arte Sacra**, in the Igreja do Rosário, and the **Mirante do Morro do Espia**, a lookout with a good view of the port and surrounding area. Iguape's **Museo Histórico e Arqueológico**, Rua das Neves 45, has samples of bones, ceramics and other objects from 5000-year-old civilizations.

There are also several beaches. **Ilha Comprida**, a 74km stretch of beach, is now linked to Iguape by a bridge, and its wild, barren character is being usurped by the rate of holiday-house development. To see a more beautiful beach you should head to **Praia da Juréia**, 40km northeast of Iguape toward the ecological reserve of Juréia. For information on organized tours to Juréia contact the park officer (☎ 0xx13-6849-1293), Avenida São Pedro 189, in Barra do Ribeira.

Places to Stay & Eat

The **Pensão Familiar** (☎ 6841-1694, Rua 15 de Novembro 130) is a well-positioned cheapie with basic rooms for US$6 per person. **Pousada Solar Colonial** (☎ 6841-1591), in a colonial building right on Largo da Basílica (the main church and plaza) offers good, clean singles/doubles for US$23/33. **Silvi Hotel** (☎ 6841-1421, Rua Candida Trigo 515) is another good option near the main plaza, starting at US$14/23.

Eating in Iguape means seafood, seafood and more seafood. **Panela Velha** (☎ 841-1869, Rua 15 de Novembro 190) has the best seafood in town, with main courses from US$8 to $13. On Ilha Comprida try **Gaivota** or **Arrastão**, both on the beachfront.

Getting There & Around

Four buses a day, the first at 6 am and the last at 8 pm, make the trip to São Paulo (US$15, four hours). For Cananéia, take a bus to Pariquero and switch there. Regular buses cross the bridge to Ilha Comprida. If you have a 4WD it is possible to drive along the long flat beach on Ilha Comprida and take the ferry across to Cananéia (US$4). There is a daily bus to Barra do Ribeira leaving at 6:30 am.

CANANÉIA

☎ 0xx13 • postcode 11990-000 • pop 10,000

Founded in 1531, Cananéia is considered the oldest city in Brazil, and it was the first

---

The Bachelor of Cananéia

One of the more notorious characters of Brazil's past was a man who was known only as the 'Bacharel de Cananéia' (Bachelor of Cananéia). As the story goes, he lived among Brazilian Indians like a white king, with six wives, 200 slaves and more than a thousand Indian warriors ready to defend him. All the coastal indigenous tribes, from São Paulo to Santa Catarina, feared and respected him – he was virtually the ruler of Brazil's southern coast.

No one knows for sure, but historians believe the Bacharel arrived as a convict on one of the first exploratory voyages of Amerigo Vespucci, in 1501. He remained in Brazil for at least 30 years, profiting fabulously from the slave trade. The Bacharel de Cananéia is thought to have been the first European resident in South America.

---

port of call for Martim Afonso de Sousa's fleet of Portuguese settlers.

Beaches

The beaches of **Ilha Comprida** are only 10 minutes away by boat. To the south are the popular **Prainha** and **Ipanema** beaches, along with a waterfall.

But the highlight of the area is a two-hour boat ride away: **Ilha do Cardoso**, an ecological reserve with some nice deserted beaches and walking tracks. Lagamar Boat (☎ 6851-1613), Rua Pedro Correia 47, runs organized boat trips (US$13 round-trip per person) to the Ilha do Cardoso beaches.

Other Attractions

There's not a lot to do in Cananéia itself; however some colonial buildings have been restored and the foreshore sea breeze on a late afternoon can be enjoyable. There's a simple **museum**, Rua Professor Bernard 133. You can walk 1km up **Morro de São João**, where you'll have a good view of the surrounding islands.

Places to Stay & Eat

Cananéia gets busy and hotels are often booked up during peak holiday season (January and February) and on weekends all summer long. **Recanto do Sol** (☎ 6851-1162, Rua Pedro Lobo 271) has reasonable singles/doubles for US$12/23. **Beira-Mar** (☎ 6851-1115, Avenida Beira-Mar 219) is a bit better value for the same price. **Hotel Pousada da Néia** (☎/fax 6851-1580, Avenida Independencia 150) is nice with clean, spacious rooms for US$20/25.

An excellent-value place to stay is **Pousada Caropá** (☎ 6851-1601, Avenida Beira-Mar 13). The renovated historic building is on the plaza and overlooks the ferry crossing to Ilha Comprida. It offers comfortable air-conditioned rooms for US$30/36.

There are simple accommodations on Ilha do Cardoso for US$20 per person. See Beaches earlier for transfers to the island.

Cananéia is renowned for its oysters. The town also has a couple of excellent Japanese restaurants; **Naguissa** (☎ 851-1382, Rua Teotônio Vilela 38) does fish specialties from March to November. For inexpensive per-kilo buffet try **Restaurant Tia Ines** (Rua Bandeirantes 48). **Bom Abrigo**, on Avenida Luís Wilson Barbosa, is open for dinner only and is closed Tuesday.

Getting There & Around

A direct bus leaves Cananéia for São Paulo twice daily (US$17, five hours).

The ferry terminal to Ilha Comprida is down from the main plaza. The ferry is free and leaves every one to 1½ hours (10 minutes). To get to Ilha do Cardoso, time your transfers with the Lagamar boat excursions (see Beaches earlier) or hire a *voadeira* (speedboat) for US$50 each way for up to four people.

Inland

IPORANGA

☎ 0xx15 • postcode 18330-000 • pop 2100

This small town is in the Vale do Ribeira in the hills near the São Paulo-Paraná border. Founded in 1576 after gold was discovered in the region, the area has one of the least disturbed areas of Brazilian Atlantic Forest and is of international importance for its biodiversity. Iporanga is a good base for visiting the Parque Estadual do Alto do Ribeira (Petar). This 360-sq-km state park, with its 280 cataloged caves, is known as Brazil's *Capital das Grutas* (Cave Capital).

Information

Iporanga has no tourist information office. Try contacting Janaina, the manager of Albergue da Juventude Capitão Caverna (see Places to Stay) or Nilton Rosa Pinto at the Prefeitura (☎ 556-1203). For information on the park call Petar, the state park administration in Iporanga (☎ 552-1528).

Caves

The Núcleos de Visitação (☎ 552-1875) are well-set-up visitors' centers with information on cave trips, guides (all in Portuguese) and campsites.

There are four Núcleos. Núcleo Santana (17km northwest of town) has good facilities for visitors and campers, four caves and a 3.5km-long trek to a beautiful waterfall; Núcleo Ouro Grosso (16km northwest of town) has basic accommodations for groups and offers cooking facilities, two caves and a walking trail; Núcleo Casa de Pedra (9km by road plus 3km by walking trail) is the base for visiting the caves. Casa de Pedra, famous for its 215m-high entrance and pristine Atlantic Forest; and Núcleo Caboclos (centrally located in the park 86km by road from town) has good camping facilities, basic visitors' lodgings and several caves.

Places to Stay & Eat

The **Pousada Iporanga** (☎ 556-1132, Rua Cel. Déscio 7) has good, clean apartamentos at US$12/23 for singles/doubles. **Albergue da Juventude Capitão Caverna** (☎ 556-1125, fax 556-1217, ajcapitaocaverna@ ig.com.br, Rua João Evilásio Nunes 160) is recommended. It's in Alto do Coqueiro, a short walk uphill from the center – the view from up here is great. Spotless rooms with bunk beds are US$9 for HI members,

US$11 for nonmembers, including home-made breakfast. It has caving equipment for rental and will help to organize guided cave tours.

Pousada Casa de Pedra(☎ 556-1157) is near the river just west of town. It has rustic dormitory accommodations for US$10 per person or US$25 for a double room. The restaurant at the pousada has tasty home-made meals, but you need to place your order for food a day in advance. *Churras-caria do Abel (Rua Barão de Jundiaí 88),* near the football field, serves large, inexpensive meals.

In Bairro da Serra, about 13km west of Iporanga toward Núcleo Santana, is *Pousada das Cavernas (☎ 543-3082, info@ pousadadascavernas.com.br).* It has a few cottages on a hilly site. Each has a couple of rooms with balconies overlooking the river and forested mountains. It has a great restaurant/lounge area and costs US$22 per person with breakfast and dinner.

Getting There & Away
There is one Intersul bus daily at 6:30 am from São Paulo's Barra Funda bus station to Eldorado (five hours). From Eldorado you can get the bus to Iporanga, departing at 2:30 pm.

CAMPOS DO JORDÃO
☎ 0xx12 • postcode 12460-000
• pop 44,000 • elev 1628m

Nestled in the Serra da Mantiqueira, three hours northeast by bus from São Paulo, is Campos do Jordão. It's a highly popular weekend mountain getaway for wealthier Paulistas who like to feel the cold and show off their leather outerwear. Campos looks very much like a southern German town – hills, wood smoke, *fachwerk* houses and picture-postcard views.

Restaurants and hotels keep up their end of this illusion by serving *glühwein* (spiced wine, served hot), holding an Oktoberfest, maintaining exorbitant prices, serving bland, heavy food and being pikers with the soap – *Bayern ist hier*!

But Campos' popularity is based on its undeniable prettiness – which, depending on your views, is either utterly sweet or indescribably twee.

At almost 1700m, Campos is a good place from which to check out some of the last remaining virgin *araucária* (Paraná pine) forests, and to hike to the top of some high peaks with spectacular views of the Paraíba valley and of the coastal mountain range, the Serra do Mar. The railway line that connects Campos with Santo Antônio do Pinhal (US$10 round-trip per person) is the highest in Brazil.

Information
Campos is made up of three main districts: Abernéssia (the oldest), Jaguaribe (where the bus station is located) and Capivari, the center. The three districts are connected by a *suburbio* (tram) that is an attraction in itself.

The tourist office (☎ 262-2799, setur@ ig.com.br) is at the gateway to the valley, on the main road into town about 2km before Abernéssia. It is open daily 8 am to 8 pm. Pick up a copy of *Nosso Guia-Turístico*- it lists just about everything and has a useful map. The Web site www.camposdojordao .com.br has a list of places to stay, restaurants and events.

There's a Banco do Brasil at Avenida Frei Orestes Girardi 837 in Abernéssia, and you should be able to change cash dollars at some of the boutiques in Capivari.

A telephone office is in Abernéssia, in front of the tram stop, and another is in Capivari near the church. The post office is also in Abernéssia, on Avenida Dr Januário Miraglia.

Things to See & Do
The Horto Florestal state park (US$2) is 14km east from Capivari. It contains the largest araucária reserve in the state, and there are some fine walks. The reception desk (☎ 263-3762), near the trout farm, can supply you with maps.

Another spot that deserves a visit is the **Pico do Itapeva**, 15km away. From 2030m it's possible to see almost the whole Paraíba valley, including its industrial cities and the Rio Paraíba.

Close to Capivari is a *miniférico* (chairlift; US$3) to the top of the **Morro do Elefante**, which has a good view of the town.

The **Palácio Boa Vista** (☎ 262-2966), 3.5km north of Abernéssia, is the state governor's summer residence; it contains many antiques. It's open Wednesday, Thursday and weekends and holidays 10 am to noon and 2 to 5 pm; entry is US$3.

The 19km **electric train ride** (US$10, 2½ hours round-trip) from Campos do Jordão to Santo Antônio do Pinhal is one of the country's best. It allows a 20-minute stopover in Santo Antônio – bring your own snack or you will be at the mercy of vendors. The train leaves Campos (from the Capivari terminal at the end of Avenida Emílio Ribas) Tuesday to Friday at 2 pm and Saturday, Sunday and holidays at 9:30 and 10 am and 1:30 and 2 pm. For the best views, sit on the right-hand side when leaving Campos.

Places to Stay

July is peak tourist period in Campos, when the town receives up to a million tourists. It is also in July that Campos hosts the winter music festival. Prices double or even triple during this period.

Camping The *Camping Clube do Brasil* (☎ 263-1130) has a campground 10km east of Capivari on the road to the Horto Florestal. It costs US$13 per person for nonmembers, US$6 for members.

Pousadas & Hotels The *Pousada Brasil* (☎ 262-2341, pousadabrasil@iconet.com.br, Rua Pereira Barreto 22), in Abernéssia near the tram stop, offers good hostel-type accommodations. It has clean and secure rooms with bunk beds for US$12 per person and double rooms for US$25. Another OK budget option is *Pousada Recanto do Sossego* (☎ 262-4224, Rua Professor Raul Pedroza de Moraes 74). On the way up to the Palácio Boa Vista, it is the street on the left, opposite the convent. It has rooms for US$20/33 singles/doubles, with breakfast.

Pousada do Conde (☎ 263-3635, Avenida Victor Godlinho 440), in Jaguaribe, has simple apartmentos for up to four people and charges US$33 a double, US$8 for each extra person. *Nevada Hotel* (☎ 263-1611, Praça Maria de Lourdes Gonçalves 27) is a good spot right on the hub of Capivari. It is clean and organized, but lacks style. Doubles here cost US$50 for breakfast only, US$75 for full board. Up at a beautiful spot and within walking distance from a forest reserve is *Pousada Alto da Boa Vista* (☎/fax 262-4900, pousada@altodaboavista.com.br, Rua das Hortencias 605), in Alto da Boa Vista, about 8km north of town (US$6 by taxi). It has very good chalets, a nice little outdoor spa, barbecue facilities and bar services. Singles/doubles cost US$16/32 during the week and US$30/60 on weekends.

The oldest and most stylish place to stay is *Hotel Toriba* (☎ 262-1566, fax 262-4211, Avenida Ernesto Diedericksen 2962), in the hills 4km south of Abernéssia. Rooms go for US$97/155.

Places to Eat

Campos has a good number and variety of eateries. The local specialty is *pinhãou* (pine nuts) fried in butter or served with rice, but it is seasonal – available only in July and August.

For a quick snack, try *Esquina do Pastel* (Avenida Macedo Soares 203), in Capivari. *Sergio's Restaurante* (Avenida Brigadeiro Jordão 688), in Abernéssia, has a good-value per-kilo buffet. Upstairs in the Aspen Mall, *Pizzeria Bremen* serves inexpensive sandwiches, pizzas and prato feito.

Bia Kaffe (Rua Isola Orsi 33), in Capivari, serves quality coffee, cakes and other sweets. Mushroom lovers must try *Restaurante Champignon* (☎ 263-1575, Rua Gilia 20), near the Tennis Club in Capivari; a meal for two costs about US$15. It is open Friday to Sunday for lunch and dinner. *Keller Haus* (Avenida Emilio Ribas 478), in Capivari, is a fairly good and reasonably priced German place; *Baden-Baden* (☎ 263-3610, Rua Djalma Forjaz 93) also does German food, but it's pricier. Nearby, in the Boulevard Geneve mall, there's a mock English pub, *Royal Flag*, upstairs in the watchtower, with live music or videos in high season at 9:30 pm nightly.

Shopping

Natureza Maluca, loja 10, Shopping Geneve Plaza, Rua Djalma Forjaz 100, in Capivari, is a great place for presents, especially for kids. It sells T-shirts with nice prints.

Getting There & Away

The bus station (☎ 262-1996) is on Avenida Dr Januário Miraglia (near Supermercado Roma) between Jaguaribe and Capivari. There are seven buses daily (each way) between São Paulo and Campos, between 6 am and 7 pm. The trip costs US$9.

To get to Ubatuba, take a bus to Taubaté (US$3, every two hours 6 am to 8 pm). From here catch a bus to Ubatuba (US$5).

Rio de Janeiro to Campos is a five-hour trip, and there are two buses daily (US$13).

For details of the train ride to Santo Antônio do Pinhal, see Things to See & Do earlier in this section.

Getting Around

The tram (US$0.40) runs about every half-hour between 7:15 am and 6:05 pm, and it gets very crowded. Local buses run out to the state park and to the campground. Take the Horto Florestal bus to its final stop.

Mountain bikes can be rented from the Zero Grau shop, around the corner from Hotel Nevada in Capivari, for US$3 per hour. Horses are available (for about US$5 per hour) at Centro Hipico Tarundu – check with the tourist office.

AROUND CAMPOS DO JORDÃO

Gruta dos Crioulos & Pedra do Baú

The Gruta dos Crioulos (Creoles' Cave) was used as a hideout by slaves escaping from the surrounding farms. It's 7km from Jaguaribé on the road to Pedra do Baú, which is a huge, 1950m rectangular granite block. To get to the top you have to walk 2km north and climb 600 steps carved into the rock. It's about 25km from Campos do Jordão.

Altus Turismo Ecologico (☎ 263-4122, contato@altus.tu.br), Avenida Brasil 108, in Capivari, organizes day trips to climb Pedra do Baú, mountain-bike tours and guided hikes to waterfalls around Pedra do Baú. Manager and guide Udo Wagner speaks German and English.

Krsna Shakti Ashram

There's a beautiful ashram (☎ 263-3168, ksa@siteon.com.br) 30km north of Campos that offers access to lovely mountainside waterfalls, a river and natural mineral-water pools, plus all meals, yoga classes and meditation, for US$100 per person per day (negotiable). You don't have to meditate to stay there!

It is also possible for you to come up just to enjoy a dinner in the vegetarian dining room, by prior arrangement. Most people at the ashram speak both English and German.

The South

The Southern region, known in Brazil as Região Sul, includes the states of Paraná, Santa Catarina and Rio Grande do Sul. It covers almost 7% of the country's land area and contains 25 million inhabitants – just under 15% of Brazil's population. Most of these people are descendants of German, Italian, Swiss and Eastern European immigrants who settled the region in the latter half of the 19th century. In many places, these immigrant groups have kept their Old World customs, language and architecture alive, so you'll see and onion-spired churches and painted wooden houses with steep roofs, and find small towns where Portuguese is still the second language.

Geographically, Paraná, Santa Catarina and the northern part of Rio Grande do Sul are dominated by *planaltos* (tablelands). The Planalto Atlântico, near the coast, is formed of granite, while the Planalto Meridional, in the interior, is formed of volcanic basalt and a rich red soil known as *terra roxa*. The Foz do Iguaçu waterfalls in the southwest corner of Paraná are Brazil's most spectacular natural wonder. In the southern interior of Rio Grande do Sul are the *pampas* (grassy plains). Along this state's coast are three large saltwater lagoons: Patos, Mirim and Mangueira.

With the exception of the north of Paraná, the climate is subtropical, and the vegetation varies from Mata Atlântica (Atlantic Forest) remnants on the Paraná and Santa Catarina coast to the almost-extinct Mata Araucária (Araucària Forest) and pine forests of the Planalto Meridional. Snow is not uncommon on the Planalto Meridional during winter.

The region's economy has changed dramatically in the last 40 years. Where huge herds of cattle were once driven across the

pampas by *gaúchos* (cowboys), there are now endless fields of soybeans, with much of the crop going to feed European cattle. Industrial development encouraged by cheap electricity from the Itaipu dam in Paraná, along with progressive educational and social policies, has transformed the South into Brazil's second-most-developed region.

Sulistas (southerners) – especially the gaúchos from Rio Grande do Sul – are proud of their differences from other Brazilians and periodically entertain the idea of separatism. Sulistas are willing partners in Mercosul, the free-trade grouping of Brazil, Argentina, Bolivia, Chile, Paraguay and Uruguay, and the regional economy is particularly tied to economic trends in Uruguay and Argentina.

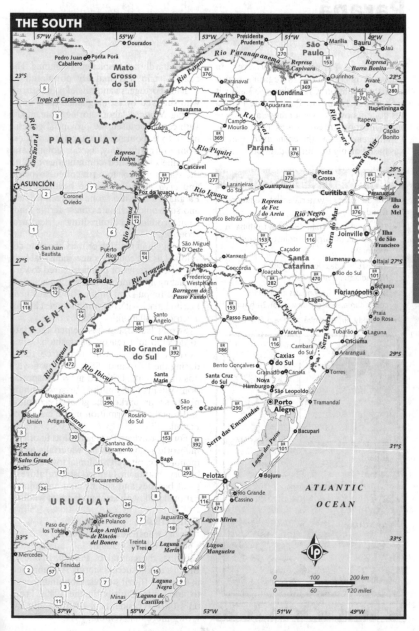

Paraná

The state of Paraná ('mighty river' in Guarani) is the southern region's major tourist destination. Created in 1853 after it broke away from São Paulo state, Paraná has gone its own way ever since and is one of the most progressive states in Brazil.

In the early years, the economy of Paraná was based on pig farming and timber extrac-tion – hardly an auspicious beginning. The coastal strip was sparsely populated by Indians, Portuguese and *caboclos* (mestizos), who survived by farming small plots or by fishing. When a labor shortage late in the 19th century caused the provincial govern-ment to encourage immigration, settlers from Germany, Italy, Japan, Poland and Ukraine established communities around the state's interior to farm coffee, soybeans and *erva mate* (a tea-like beverage). As Paraná is a transition zone between tropical and subtropical climates, these fertile lands soon produced a flourishing agricultural economy.

Throughout the 20th century, the state de-veloped as the country's new industrial hub, thanks to a series of policies geared toward attracting investments. One resulting project was the Itaipu Dam on the Rio Paraná near Foz do Iguaçu – it's the world's largest hydro-electric installation.

Strong leadership has helped the state to develop in a reasonable fashion. Jaime Lerner, mayor of Curitiba three times during the 1970s and 1980s and now gover-nor of the state, initiated mass transporta-tion systems and multiple urban planning projects that sparked the greatest economic and social transformation in the history of Paraná.

For the traveler, Paraná has lots to offer – the world's most awesome waterfalls, a cos-mopolitan capital city, colonial towns rich in history, hiking in lush coastal rainforest, great beaches and surfing, and an isolated national park with an abundance of wildlife.

Highlights

- Foz do Iguaçu – waterfalls that are natural wonders
- The spectacular train ride from Curitiba to Paranaguá through rainforest-covered mountains
- Inner-tube rides down the Rio Nhundiaquara near Morretes
- Barreado, delicious meats and spices cooked in a sealed clay pot for 24 hours
- Saturday night samba on Ilha do Mel

CURITIBA

☎ 0xx41 • postcode 80000-000
• pop 1.6 million • 900m

Curitiba, the capital of Paraná, is one of Brazil's urban success stories. As happened in many of Brazil's cities, thousands began to flood into Curitiba in the 1940s. From only 140,000 residents in 1940, the city has grown more than tenfold.

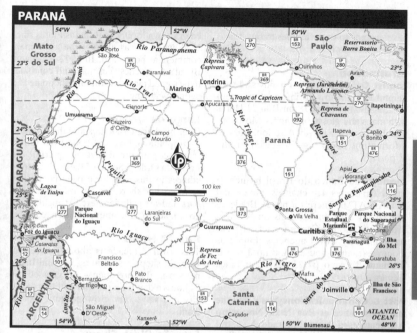

PARANÁ

Yet, with the help of a vibrant local and state economy, Curitiba has managed to modernize in a relatively sane manner – historic buildings have been preserved, a handful of streets have been closed to cars and there are many parks, gardens and wide boulevards.

When Paraná's current governor, Jaime Lerner, was mayor of Curitiba in the 1970s and 1980s, he instituted several progressive incentives, including a drive to get people out of their cars by lowering bus prices. The strategy worked: Traffic congestion was reduced, and today it's easier to get around in Curitiba than in most cities in Brazil. Drivers actually stop at red lights, and pedestrians can cross streets without fearing for their lives. The city has also taken innovative approaches to urban ills such as homelessness, pollution and poverty.

The local government has embraced new technology and provides free Internet access at 26 locations around the city. Both the state and city governments have developed excellent Web sites offering a wealth of information.

At 900m above sea level, Curitiba is on top of the great escarpment along the route from Rio Grande do Sul to São Paulo. Due to this location, it flourished briefly in the 19th century as a pit stop for *gaúchos* and their cattle until a better road was built on an alternative route. Curitiba quickly went back to sleep. It wasn't until the tremendous growth of the coffee plantations in northern Paraná, at the beginning of the 20th century, that the modern city of Curitiba began to take shape.

Today's Curitibanos are mostly the descendants of Italian, German and Polish immigrants. There is a large university population, which gives the city a young feel and a good music scene. Though there's not much in Curitiba for the visitor, it's possible to pass a pleasant day walking through the cobbled pedestrian streets or in waiting in a park for your bus or train to leave. It's a fairly easy city to walk around, so if you have errands to do or clothes to buy, this is a good place for it.

Information

Tourist Offices There's a handy and very helpful Paraná Turismo information booth (☎ 232-3692) at Shop 18 on Rua 24 Horas with maps and glossy brochures. Most staff members speak English. Also look for the information booth (☎ 381-1153) at the airport.

Money The Banco do Brasil branch at Praça Tiradentes 410 changes money and has Visa ATMs. There's a handy Bradesco branch for Visa withdrawals on Avenida Presidente Afonso Camargo, near the bus station. Many travel agencies double as money exchange houses. A central one is Triangulo Turismo (☎ 233-0311), at Praça General Osório 213.

Post & Communications You'll find the main post office at Rua 15 de Novembro 700, near Praça Santos Andrade. A central telephone office for collect and card calls is at Rua Visconde de Nacar 1388.

Curitiba is the best bargain for travelers looking to get online in southern Brazil – you'll get free access 24 hours a day. The local government runs a central Internet kiosk, Digitando o Futuro (☎ 350-6366), on Rua 24 Horas, Shop 16, with eight terminals available for residents and tourists alike. It's best to book ahead, especially at peak times (evenings and weekends).

Internet Resources It's not surprising that Curitiba and Paraná state have excellent Web sites – www.curitiba.pr.gov.br and www.pr.gov.br. Both sites have some information in English and Spanish.

Passeio Público

Take a stroll along the Passeio Público on Avenida Presidente Carlos Cavalcânti, where Curitibanos have relaxed since 1886. You'll see a lake and a small zoo. The park complex is closed Monday.

Rua das Flores

This section of Rua 15 de Novembro has been known locally as Rua das Flores since 1720, when it was already the city's main commercial boulevard. In 1972 it became Brazil's first pedestrian mall and continues to be a good place for walking, shopping and people-watching.

Largo da Ordem

Over by Praça Tiradentes and the Catedral Metropolitana, take the pedestrian tunnel to the cobblestoned historic quarter, the Largo da Ordem. Some of the city's historic edifices in this area have been beautifully restored, and there are several restaurants, bars and art galleries here. At night, it's a good place to eat dinner and listen to music.

Rua 24 Horas

This covered arcade is about 100m long, with gift shops, restaurants, bars and Internet kiosks that are open – you guessed it – 24 hours a day. It's a popular addition to the city, and stays very crowded until around 3 am.

Estação Plaza Show

This complex on Avenida 7 de Setembro has bars, restaurants, a dance club, a venue for live music and cinemas. The complex also houses the Museu Ferroviária, the old train station that has been restored.

Museu Paranaense

The Museu Paranaense on Praça Generoso Marquês is in an art nouveau building that once housed the municipal government. The museum has a hodgepodge of objects as well as a collection of artifacts from the Guarani and Caigangues Indians. It's open Monday 1:30 to 5:30 pm, Tuesday to Friday 9:30 am to 5:30 pm and weekends 10 am to 4 pm. Entry is free.

Museu de Arte Sacra

The Sacred Art Museum in the Igreja da Ordem (in the Largo da Ordem) is worth a look. It's open Tuesday to Friday 10 am to noon and 1:30 to 5:30 pm, and on the weekend 10 am to 2 pm.

THE SOUTH

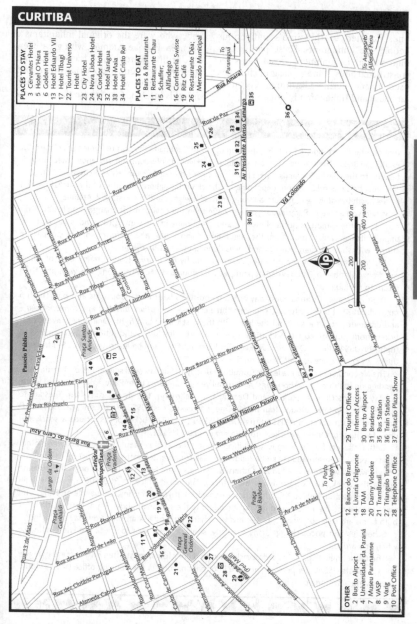

CURITIBA

PLACES TO STAY
3 Cervantes Hotel
5 Hotel O'Hara
6 Golden Hotel
13 Hotel Eduardo VII
17 Hotel Tibagi
22 Tourist Universo
   Hotel
23 City Hotel
24 Nova Lisboa Hotel
25 Condor Hotel
32 Hotel Jaragua
33 Hotel Maia
34 Hotel Cristo Rei

PLACES TO EAT
1 Bars & Restaurants
11 Restaurante Chau
15 Schaffer;
   Alfândego
16 Confeiteria Swisse
19 Ritz Café
26 Restaurante Déa;
   Mercado Municipal

OTHER
2 Bus to Airport
4 Universade da Paraná
7 Museu Paranaense
8 VASP
9 Varig
10 Post Office
12 Banco do Brasil
14 Livraria Ghignone
18 TAM
20 Danny Videoke
21 TransBrasil
27 Triangulo Turismo
28 Telephone Office
29 Tourist Office &
   Internet Access
30 Bus to Airport
31 Bradesco
35 Bus Station
36 Train Station
37 Estacio Plaza Show

Parks

Parks are a Curitiba specialty, especially ones devoted to the area's indigenous people and immigrants. These parks combine parkland, monuments, restaurants, reconstructed houses and replicas of churches used by pioneering Ukrainian, German, Japanese and Italian immigrants.

Some of the more interesting parks are Parque Tingui, dedicated to the Guarani tribe who were the original inhabitants of the area; Bosque Alemão, with great views of Curitiba; Parque São Laurenço, which contains the Centro do Criatividade; and Parque Barigui, where the Museu do Automóvel is located. All of these the parks and

Train Ride to Paranaguá

Run on a rail line completed in 1880, the train trip from Curitiba to the port of Paranaguá is the most exciting in Brazil. The train leaves from Curitiba at an altitude of 900m and descends a steep mountainside to the coastal lowlands. The 110km track goes through 13 tunnels and crosses 67 bridges. The view below is sublime and, depending on the cloud formations and tone of the sunlight, often surreal, with threatening mountain canyons, tropical lowlands and the vast, blue Atlantic.

When you arrive in Paranaguá, you will have seen the environment change rapidly and radically. Here, the climate is hot and muggy, and often rainy in the winter; the land is flat and low until it hits the wall of mountain; the vegetation is short, lush and uniform; and the people are sturdy, with strong Indian features and faces defined by years by the sea.

The line is traveled by the *trem* (regular train) and by the *litorina* (tourist train), both of which run from Curitiba to Paranaguá, stopping at Marumbi and Morretes along the way, and then return to Curitiba.

The trem leaves Curitiba every day at 9 am and starts back from Paranaguá at 3 pm. The trip takes about 3½ hours each way. There are three classes – *executivo, turístico* and *convencional* – and different prices for seats on the left (with the best views) and right. One-way convencional tickets from Curitiba cost US$11 (right side) or US$13 (left side), and return tickets are US$16 (right) or US$18 (left). One-way tickets from Paranaguá to Curitiba are cheaper (US$7) because the views aren't quite as spectacular on the way up.

The air-conditioned litorina leaves Curitiba Thursday to Sunday (and sometimes on Tuesday, depending on the number of bookings) at 8 am all year and returns from Paranaguá at 4 pm. During holiday periods (June to August and December to February), the litorina runs from Tuesday to Sunday. The trip takes around four hours. One-way tickets cost US$36 (right side) or US$46 (left side) and return tickets are US$60 (right) or US$66 (left). The ticket prices include a snack and drink for the trip. One-way tickets from Paranaguá cost US$22.

Getting tickets for the trem is not difficult during the week, except during January and other holiday periods. Reservations can be made by email (serraverde@softone.com.br) or via the Web site www.serraverdeexpress.com.br. Otherwise, you can buy tickets at the station in the morning during the week, but weekends are more tricky. The ticket office (☎ 323-4007) is at the train station *(ferroviária)* behind the bus station *(rodoviária)*. If you arrive in Curitiba late on Friday and want to take the train the next day, you should go to the station at about 6 am. Even if tickets for both trains are sold out, don't take the bus yet – hang out and ask around, you may get lucky.

Schedules and prices change fairly regularly, so it's a good idea to check the latest schedule when you arrive.

The Obra Prima Express is used occasionally for dinner tours, most often on Wednesday night. The tour costs US$50 per person. For more information, contact the booking office (☎ 323-4007, bestwaytrips@softone.com.br).

monuments are out of the city center, but the Linha Turismo bus from Rua das Flores (see the Getting Around section later in this chapter) stops at all of them.

Places to Stay

Budget The HI youth hostel *Albergue da Juventude da Curitiba* (☎ 233-2746, Rua Padre Agostinho 645) is in the suburb of Mercês. To get there, catch the Campo Comprido–Campina do Siqueirae bus from outside the bus station.

If you're leaving town the next day, there are cheap hotels on Avenida Presidente Afonso Camargo, just across from the *rodoferroviária* (bus and train station). The clean, well-run *Hotel Maia* (☎ 264-1684, Avenida Presidente Afonso Camargo 355) has single/double quartos for US$10/20, with breakfast included. *Hotel Cristo Rei* (☎ 264-9093, Avenida Presidente Afonso Camargo 381) is cheap, with basic quartos for US$7/14, but you don't get breakfast. One block away, *City Hotel* (☎ 264-3366, Rua Francisco Torres 816) is a cheapie that offers better value. Clean quartos cost US$7/12, but breakfast isn't included here either.

If you're staying a few days or want to be close to the bars and restaurants around Largo da Ordem, the central *Golden Hotel* (☎ 323-3603, Rua Tobias de Macado 26) is an excellent value. Apartamentos with fan and fridge cost US$12/16, which includes a good breakfast that can be eaten while overlooking Praça Tiradentes.

Mid-Range Just a block from the bus station, the *Hotel Nova Lisboa* (☎ 264-1944, Avenida 7 de Setembro 1948) is a clean, bright place with single/double/triple apartamentos for US$20/30/34. A few doors away, *Condor Hotel* (☎ 262-0322, Avenida 7 de Setembro 1866) is fairly plush, with a restaurant and pool. Air-conditioned singles/doubles with fridge and TV cost US$35/48.

In the center of town, *Cervantes Hotel* (☎ 222-9593, Travessa Alfredo Bufren 35) has some fading Old World charm, and smallish apartamentos with TV and fridge for US$18/34. *Hotel O'Hara* (☎ 232-6044, Rua 15 de Novembro 770), in a colonial building opposite Praça Santos Andrade, has singles/doubles for US$26/36.

Top End A comfortable top-end hotel across from the bus station is the *Hotel Jaragua* (☎ 362-2022, jaragua@bbs2.sul.com.br, Avenida Presidente Afonso Camargo 279), which charges US$45/60 for singles/doubles. It's worth asking for a discount here.

In the center of town, close to Praça Tiradentes, the *Hotel Eduardo VII* (☎ 322-6767, Rua Cândido de Leão 15) is the Old-Worldish choice. Singles/doubles go for US$38/44. Postmodernists prefer *Tourist Universo Hotel* (☎ 322-0099, Praça General Osório 63), where singles/doubles start at US$42/54. A stylish new joint in the center of town is the *Hotel Tibagi* (☎ 223-3141, info@hoteltibagi.com.br, Rua Cândido Lopes 318). Smallish rooms cost US$40/46.

Places to Eat

Rua das Flores has some classic *confeitarias* (pastry and confectionery shops). *Schaffer*, in the Galeria Schaffer at No 424, was founded in 1918 and is famous for its coffee, cakes and pastries. It's a bit of sting though so check prices before you order up. On the second floor, *Alfândego* is a good spot for a cheap (US$1.50) buffet lunch eaten overlooking the pedestrian mall.

The historic Largo da Ordem area has reasonably priced outdoor restaurants along its cobbled streets – walk around, look at menus and see what looks best. *Saccy Restaurante* (Rua São Francisco 350) is a good value for meals and has some live music at night. Large steak, chicken or fish dishes for two people cost around US$8. Nearby *Schwarzwald* is known for its roast duck and is a popular student hangout.

Other recommended restaurants, clustered around Praça Garibaldi at the top of the hill, are *Restaurante Vegetariano* (for lunch only), *Estrela da Terra* (an upmarket restaurant for regional food) and *The Farm* (for cheap pizza and soups).

Near the bus station, the *Mercado Municipal* has a great range of food in its basement. You can buy local produce; sniff around the delis, Asian food groceries and health-food shops; or eat a good meat and salad lunch at *Restaurante Déa* for US$2.50. The market is open until 6 pm.

You can get a cheap (US$2) Chinese lunch or dinner in the center at *Restaurante Chau (Rua Carlos de Carvalho 50)*. For a complete contrast, check out *Ritz Café* nearby at Rua Ébano Pereira, where the city's movers and shakers get their caffeine fix. *Confeiteria Swisse Restaurante (Rua Voluntários da Pátria 475)* is a Swiss restaurant/café with an executivo lunch plate for US$2.50. For the best (and most expensive) Italian food in town, head over to *Famiglia Calicetti Bologna (Rua Carlos de Carvalho 1367)*, in the suburb of Batel, about 2km east of the city center.

Entertainment
Curitiba has an active live-music and club scene. Around Praça Garibaldi in Largo do Ordem there are several bars and venues including *Schwardwald*, *Sal Grosso* and *Memorial Restaurante*.

In the center, *Danny Videoke*, on Rua Ébano Pereira near the corner of Rua das Flores, is a video/karaoke bar. For live music, head to *Bird's Bar (Rua Presidente Taunay 458)* for pop rock or *Jack's Blues (Rua Petit Carneiro 80)*, in the suburb of Agua Verde (about 2.5km south of the city center), for blues.

Shopping
The Feira de Arte e Artesanato, held in Praça Garibaldi on Sunday 9 am to 2 pm, offers an excellent variety of arts and crafts for sale.

Getting There & Away
There are flights from Curitiba to all major cities in Brazil. Most flights to the north and west stop in São Paulo or Rio.

From the bus station, there are many daily buses to São Paulo (US$20, 6½ hours) and Rio (US$32, 12 hours) and to all major cities to the south. Frequent buses go to Foz do Iguaçu: Semidirect buses cost US$30 and take 10 hours, the *leito* (overnight sleeper) costs US$62 and takes around nine hours.

There are regular buses to Joinville (US$6, two hours) and Florianópolis (US$12, four hours).

From Curitiba you can also get direct buses to South American capitals Asunción (US$40, 18 hours), Buenos Aires (US$66, 28 hours) and Santiago (US$120, 52 hours).

If you miss the train, there are plenty of buses to Morretes, Antonina and Paranaguá. The trip isn't as stunning as the train ride but it's still pretty.

For information on the spectacular passenger-train route between Curitiba and Paranaguá, see the boxed text 'Train Ride to Paranaguá.'

Getting Around
To/From the Airport Alfonso Pena airport (☎ 381-1515) is 18km from the city (US$22 by taxi). An Aeroporto-Centro bus (US$0.70, 35 minutes) leaves every 20 minutes from opposite Hotel Lizon, on the corner of Avenida Presidente Afonso Camargo near the bus station. From the airport, the bus, which leaves from a nifty tube-shaped station outside the airport, can drop you near the bus station (the fourth stop) or in the center along Rua Conselheiro Launindo (the fifth stop).

Bus A great way to see many sights you wouldn't see just walking around is the Linha Turismo bus, which does a two-hour tour of the city's main attractions. It departs from Praça Tiradentes every half-hour from Tuesday to Sunday – the first bus is at 9 am and the last leaves at 5:30 pm. You can get off the bus at any of the attractions and hop on the next white Linha Turismo bus that passes. There is a timetable posted at each stop. It costs US$4 for four tickets.

AROUND CURITIBA
Parque Estadual Marumbi
The park offers some great hikes. It is very popular with Curitibanos, who get off the train to Paranaguá and hike down the old pioneer trails that were the only connections between the coast and the Paranaense highland in the 17th and 18th centuries. The

two best walks are the Graciosa trail, which passes close to the Estrada da Graciosa, and the Itupava trail. Views from both are fantastic.

The trails are well signposted from the train station and within the park so a guide isn't necessary. For more information, contact the park information center (☎ 432-2072). You can camp in the park for free. Don't forget to take some insect repellent!

To get to the park, take the train from Curitiba and get off at Marumbi station.

Vila Velha

An interesting day trip is a visit to the 'stone city' of Vila Velha, 93km from Curitiba on the road to Foz do Iguaçu. Here you'll find a collection of sandstone pillars created by millions of years of erosion. There are also places to swim and a 54-meter-long elevator ride into a crater lake.

You can pick up a map of the trails and sights at the park center (☎ 228-1138), open daily 8 am to 6 pm. There's also a restaurant and kiosks for lunch.

To get there, catch a *semi-direto* (semi-direct) bus to Ponta Grossa from the bus station and ask to be let out at Vila Velha. There's nowhere to stay in the park, so make sure you get the last bus back, which you can flag down along the road at around 3:45 pm.

MORRETES

☎ 0xx41 • postcode 83350-000 • pop 7200

Founded in 1721 on the banks of the Rio Nhundiaquara, Morretes is a tranquil little colonial town in the midst of the lush coastal vegetation zone. It's a great place to relax, swim in the river and take some walks in the nearby Parque Estadual Marumbi during the week, but it gets busy on the weekend.

Several buses and the train stop at Morretes on the route from Curitiba to Antonina and Paranaguá. If you like the feel of the place, just hop off – the spectacular part of the train ride is over anyway. The town itself is very small and easy to get around in. To get to the Marumbi park from Morretes, catch a bus to São João de Graciosa. It's a

couple of kilometers from there to the park entrance.

Information

The Secretaria de Turismo is along the riverfront at Largo Dr Jose Pereira – it's the white colonial-style house with blue window frames. The Banco do Brasil on Rua 15 de Novembro in the center has a Visa ATM.

Rio Nhundiaquara

This river served as the first connection between the coast and the highlands. Now one of the best things to do on it is rent a large inner tube and float downriver (known as *boia cross*). To rent a *boia* (US$2 per day), contact Ibrahim at the Pousada Itupava (☎ 0xx41-462-1925, pousada@itupava.com.br) in the village of Porto de Cima, about 5km from Morretes.

Places to Stay & Eat

The *Hotel Nhundiaquara* (☎ 462-1228, Rua General Carreiro 13) is the best place to stay. The hotel hugs the river and has a breezy restaurant attached. Quartos cost US$7 per person and apartamentos US$10, with breakfast included. Book well ahead if you plan to arrive on a weekend.

The *Hotel Bom Jesus* (☎ 462-1282, Rua 15 de Novembro) charges the same rates but isn't nearly as pleasant. The most expensive hotel in town is the *Porto Real Palace* (☎ 462-1344, Rua Visconde de Branco 85), with singles/doubles for US$24/34. The red carpet is blindingly bright, but everything else is fading.

The specialty of the region is a filling dish called *barreado*, which is a delicious mixture of meats and spices cooked in a sealed clay pot for 24 hours. Originally it was cooked during Carnaval, to give the revelers a huge protein fix, and today it's considered the state dish. Quite a few new restaurants have sprung up along the riverfront in the last few years serving barreado and seafood (unfortunately, the trend is toward bigger places, with parking). Most are open for lunch only, so don't plan on doing anything strenuous in the afternoon!

THE SOUTH

Most of the restaurants are along Largo Dr Jose Pereira on the riverfront. *Restaurante Casarão*, an upmarket place with a balcony on the river, serves barreado for US$8. Just across the bridge, *Restaurante Madalozo* has a seafood barreado (lunch only) for the same price.

The *restaurant* at the Hotel Nhundiaquara is the original and probably the best – it has been serving barreado for more than 50 years. Cost is US$5 per person.

ANTONINA

☎ 0xx41 • postcode 83370-000 • pop 15,800

Antonina is 14km east of Morretes and 75km east of Curitiba, on the Baía de Paranaguá. Like Morretes, Antonina is old and peaceful. Its first settlers panned for gold in the river. The fine church in the center, the Igreja de NS do Pilar, dates from 1715, and was rebuilt in 1927. The town festival is held on August 15.

The beaches along the bay are muddy, but there are good views of the Baía de Paranaguá.

Frequent direct buses link Antonina to Curitiba and Paranaguá, but trains no longer stop here.

Places to Stay & Eat

The value for the price is the *Hotel Monte Castelo* (☎ 432-1163, *Praça Coronel Macedo 46*), located on the main square. It has double quartos for US$16 and double apartamentos for US$20. The *Regency Capela Antonina* (☎ 432-1357, *Praça Coronel Macedo 208*) could be worth a splurge. Comfortable apartamentos start at US$26/34 a single/double – the rooms at the front have breezy balconies with views of the bay. There's a bar and *seafood restaurant* attached.

Seafood is the order of the day in Antonino. *Refúgio Pousada das Montanhas* (☎ 432-2266), along the waterfront on the road to Bairro Alto, is highly recommended and reasonably priced. It's only open for lunch. *Restaurante Albatroz* (*Travessa Marquês do Herval 14*), just below the church, has seafood dishes for about US$12 for two. There's a great view of the bay from the upstairs room.

PARANAGUÁ

☎ 0xx41 • postcode 83200-000
• pop 122,000

The train ride from Curitiba isn't the only reason to go to Paranaguá. It's a colorful city, with an old section near the waterfront that has a feeling of tropical decadence. There are several churches, a good museum and other colonial buildings that are worth a look. Paranaguá is also the jumping off spot for Ilha do Mel.

One of Brazil's major ports, Paranaguá is 30km from the open sea, on the Baía de Paranaguá. Goods from a vast inland area are shipped through here. The primary exports used to be gold, yerba mate, wood and coffee, and are now corn, soy, cotton and vegetable oils.

Paranaguá's old section is being restored, with bars, restaurants and hotels popping up along the waterfront. The historic area is small enough to wander around without a set itinerary – without much effort, you can see the waterfront and most of the colonial buildings, churches and markets in a couple of hours.

Information

The main tourist information office (☎ 422-6882) is along the waterfront on Rua General Carneiro. It's open every day from 8 am to 6 pm. There's another office inside the train station; it's open every day from noon to 4 pm.

If you need to change money, try Tassi Turismo on Rua Faria Sobrinho. For Visa cash withdrawals, the Banco do Brasil is at Largo Conselheiro Alcindino 103, just off Avenida Gabriel de Lara.

Museu de Arqueologia e Etnologia

Many Brazilian museums are disappointing; this one isn't. Housed in a restored Jesuit school that was built between 1736 and 1755 (the Jesuits didn't get to use the school for long, as they were expelled from Brazil in 1759), the museum has many indigenous artifacts, primitive and folk art, and some interesting old tools and wooden machines. The museum is along the waterfront, at Rua

PARANAGUÁ

PLACES TO STAY
3 Sultan Palace Hotel
4 Hotel Litoral
12 Hotel Karibe
15 Dantas Palace
22 Hotel Ponderosa
27 Pousada Itiberê

PLACES TO EAT
11 Café Vitória
17 Mercado Municipal do Café
18 Dirienzo Cucina
19 Tia Bela
23 Divina Gula
25 Restaurante Danúbio Azul
28 Gáto Nerô

OTHER
1 Post Office
2 Local Bus Station
5 Telephone Office
6 Train Station
7 Tourist Office
8 Igreja de São Benedito
9 Igreja NS do Rosário
10 Banco do Brasil
13 Tassi Turismo
14 Igreja São Francisco das Chagas
16 Museu de Arqueologia e Etnologia
20 Boats to Ilha do Mel & Guaraqueçaba
21 Tourist Office
24 Boats to Rio Itiberê
26 IBAMA
29 Bus Station
30 Handicraft Market
31 Bars

15 de Novembro 567. It's open Tuesday to Sunday from noon to 5 pm. Admission costs US$1.50.

Churches

The city's churches are simple but beautiful. Unfortunately, many are in a perilous state of disrepair. The Igreja de NS do Rosário is the city's oldest. Also worth visiting are the Igreja São Francisco das Chagas (1741), **Igreja de São Benedito** (1784) and Igreja de NS do Rocio (1813).

Waterfront

Down by the waterfront, you'll find the new and old **municipal markets**. The old market now houses five small cafes (see Places to Eat, later in this section) while the new market is the place to go for handicrafts and local produce. Depending on the time and day, both can be lively.

Three tourist boats explore the Rio Itiberê from Praça Manoel Ricardo, just below the Restaurante Danúbio Azul. There are five departure times between 10 am and 5 pm, but the 1½-hour tour (US$3.50) won't go ahead until 10 people show up.

Places to Stay

There are cheap places near the waterfront and bus station; the area has character and is being gradually restored, but it can be a bit seedy at night.

Pousada Itiberê (☎ 423-2485, Rua Princesa Isabel 24) is a good, secure cheapie right on the waterfront. Basic but clean single/double quartos cost around US$10/16. Housed in a colonial building, ***Hotel Karibe*** (☎ 423-4377, Rua Fernando Simas 86) has a wide range of rooms, starting with quartos for US$9/16.

Hotel Ponderosa (☎ 423-2464, Rua Prescilinio Corrêa 68) is also in a restored colonial building, this one a block back from the waterfront. It's a bargain – light, clean, tastefully furnished double rooms cost US$18.

Closer to the train station, a good cheapie is the **Hotel Litoral** (☎ 423-1734, Rua Correia de Freitas 65), which is run by a group of lovely older women. Large, clean quartos cost US$7 per person. You can get a double apartamento for US$12, but you might need to show wedding rings! In the same area, the **Sultan Palace Hotel** (☎ 423-1044, Rua Julia da Costa 230) has some character. Clean single/double/triple quartos cost US$12/20/28.

The best hotel in town is the very comfortable **Dantas Palace** (☎ 423-1555, Rua Visconde de Nácar 740). Singles/doubles/triples start at US$56/70/80, but a 30% discount applies on weekends.

Places to Eat

The **Café Vitoria**, on the main plaza, is a good place for coffee and people-watching.

Divina Gula, on the corner of Rua Benjamin Constant and Rua Santa Isabel, is a per-kilo joint that's popular with locals for lunch. The **Mercado Municipal do Café** is also a good spot for lunch. It's been restored, and contains five small cafés serving cheap seafood and snacks. **Tia Bela**, at Rua General Carneiro 394 along the waterfront, is a friendly place which serves a barreado lunch for US$5.50 per person.

At night, **Gáto Nerô**, on Rua Benjamin Constant along the waterfront, has cheap pizza, chopp and empadãoes (a tasty meat, vegetable, egg and olive pie). **Restaurante Danúbio Azul** (Rua 15 de Novembro 95) has views and seafood (US$12 for two) upstairs, beer and pizza downstairs. The **bars** on the waterfront between the bus station and the craft market offer drinks and light meals.

A fairly new and very stylish Italian restaurant with outdoor tables along the waterfront is **Dirienzo Cucina** at Praça Leoncio Correia 16. Tasty pasta dishes start at US$8; seafood dishes start at US$15.

Getting There & Away

Bus All out-of-town buses leave from the bus station on the waterfront. There are regular buses to Curitiba (US$5.50, 1½ hours), Antonina and Morretes. There's a daily bus to Ciudad del Este (for Foz do Iguaçu) at 7:30 pm. The trip costs US$30 and takes 13 hours.

Two buses a day go to Guaraqueçaba (for access to Parque Nacional do Superaguí), at 9 am and 2 pm. The trip costs US$8 and takes five hours, but the boat is quicker.

If you're going south, hourly buses go to Guaratuba, where you can get a connecting bus to Joinville. Direct buses to Joinville (US$5.50, three hours) leave Paranaguá at 7:40 am and 3:45 pm. There are hourly buses to Pontal do Sul (US$0.80, 1½ hours) for boats to Praia das Encantadas on Ilha do Mel.

Train The train returns to Curitiba daily at 3 pm. From Thursday to Sunday, the litorina returns at 4 pm (see the Train Ride to Paranaguá boxed text earlier this chapter).

Boat Boats to both Nova Brasília (US$3.50, two hours) and Praia das Encantadas (US$3.50, 1½ hours) on Ilha do Mel leave from the jetty opposite the tourist office Monday through Friday at 3 pm. Boats also depart at 9:30 am and 1 pm on Saturday and at 9:30 am on Sunday.

Boats to Guaraqueçaba (for access to Parque Nacional do Superaguí) leave Paranaguá at 1 pm Monday to Friday, at 9:30 am and 1 pm on Saturday and at 9:30 am on Sunday. The trip takes about three hours and costs US$3.50, but it's easier to get to the national park from Ilha do Mel.

ILHA DO MEL

☎ 0xx41 • postcode 83251-000 • pop 1100

Ilha do Mel, an odd-shaped island at the mouth of the Baía de Paranaguá, wasn't visited by the Portuguese until the 18th century. In 1767, King Dom José I ordered a fort built to secure the bay and its safe harbors from French and Spanish incursions. Since then, not much has happened. The few people on the island were ordered out during WWII, in the name of national defense.

The island is a favorite in the summer because of its excellent beaches, scenic walks and relative isolation – there are no roads or cars on the island. Its undoing might be its increasing popularity. However, it's administered by the Instituto Ambiental do Paraná (IAP), which intends to preserve the island more or less as it is. A recent move introduced a small environmental tax on visitors and capped the number of daily tourists on the island at 5000. Unfortunately, the limit on visitors is almost impossible to enforce.

Human intervention also can't stop the sea from making changes. Erosion has almost opened a channel at Nova Brasília, which eventually may cut the island in two. As you walk from Nova Brasília to the fort,

you'll see the remains of houses that have crumbled into the sea.

From January to Carnaval and during Easter, the island is very popular with a young party crowd. If you're traveling up or down the coast, it's crazy not to visit the island at least for a day. Many people end up staying much longer.

Orientation

The island has two parts, connected by the beach at Nova Brasília, where most of the locals live. The bigger part is an ecological station, thick with vegetation and little

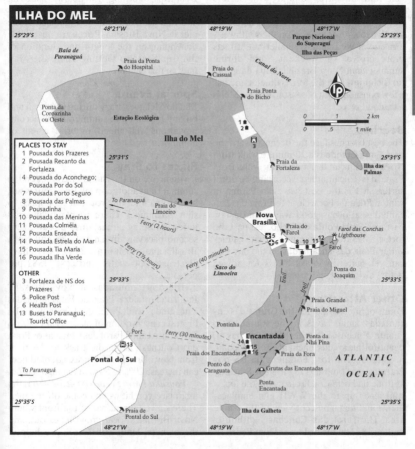

ILHA DO MEL

PLACES TO STAY
1 Pousada dos Prazeres
2 Pousada Recanto da Fortaleza
4 Pousada do Aconchego; Pousada Por do Sol
7 Pousada Porto Seguro
8 Pousada das Palmas
9 Pousadinha
10 Pousada das Meninas
11 Pousada Colméia
12 Pousada Enseada
14 Pousada Estrela do Mar
15 Pousada Tia Maria
16 Pousada Ilha Verde

OTHER
3 Fortaleza de NS dos Prazeres
5 Police Post
6 Health Post
13 Buses to Paranaguá; Tourist Office

Baía de Paranaguá
Parque Nacional do Superaguí
Ilha das Peças
Canal do Norte
Praia da Ponta do Hospital
Praia do Cassual
Praia Ponta do Bicho
Ponta da Coroazinha ou Oeste
Estação Ecológica
Ilha do Mel
Praia da Fortaleza
Ilha das Palmas
To Paranaguá
Praia do Limoeiro
Ferry (2 hours)
Nova Brasília
Praia do Farol
Farol das Conchas Lighthouse
Ferry (1½ hours)
Ferry (40 minutes)
Saco do Limoeira
Farol
Ponta do Joaquim
Praia Grande
Praia do Miguel
Pontinha
Encantadas
Ponta da Nhá Pina
Port
Ferry (30 minutes)
Praia da Fora
ATLANTIC OCEAN
Pontal do Sul
Praia dos Encantadas
Ponto do Caraguata
Grutas das Encantadas
Ponta Encantada
To Paranaguá
Praia de Pontal do Sul
Ilha da Galheta

25°29'S 48°21'W 48°19'W 48°17'W
25°31'S
25°33'S
25°35'S

0 1 2 km
0 .5 1 mile

visited except for Praia da Fortaleza. On the ocean side are the best beaches – Praia da Fora, Praia do Miguel and Praia Ponta do Bicho. Praia do Miguel and Praia da Fora are reached by a trail that traverses the beaches and coves and the steep hills that divide them. To get to Praia Ponta do Bicho, walk north along the beach toward the fort and keep going. The island's bay side is muddy and covered with vegetation.

Boats from Paranaguá and Pontal do Sul arrive at either Nova Brasília or Praia das Encantadas. Nova Brasília and nearby Praia do Farol are the most laid-back places you can find, and are popular with surfers because they're near Praia Grande. They're also closer to the fort, which is definitely worth a look. Encantadas, on the southwestern side of the island, is smaller but attracts more crowds on weekends and during summer than Nova Brasília. Praia da Ponta do Bicho, just past the fort, is quieter and has a few pousadas. Out of season, Ilha do Mel is a tranquil place.

Beaches
The best beaches face the ocean, toward the east. **Praia Grande** is a 20-minute walk from Nova Brasília and a two-hour walk from Praia das Encantadas. According to local surfers, it has the best waves in Paraná in winter. **Praia da Fora**, close to Praia das Encantadas, also has good waves and a few barracas. **Praia Ponta do Bicho**, just past the fort, is a beautiful sweeping bay with calmer water. **Praia das Encantadas** on the bay side can get quite dirty; ask locals for advice before swimming.

Other Attractions
Points of interest include the **Grutas das Encantadas**, small caves at the southern tip (Ponta Encantada) where, legend has it, beautiful mermaids enchant all who come near them. The fort, **Fortaleza de NS dos Prazeres**, was built in 1769 to guard the bay at Praia da Fortaleza. From inside the fort, a trail leads up to the WWII gun emplacements and a magnificent view of the whole area. The **Farol das Conchas** lighthouse, built in 1872 on the orders of Dom Pedro II,

stands at the island's easterly point, on Praia do Farol.

Walking
You can walk around the entire island in eight hours, but the best walking by far is along the ocean side (east), from the southern tip of the island up to the fort. A warning: When the surf is big, the stretch from Praia Grande to Praia da Fora should only be attempted at low tide. Take some strong footwear for rock-hopping or cliff-scaling.

Boating
Boat trips for fishing or to nearby islands including Ilha do Superaguí, Ilha das Palmas and Ilha das Peças can be organized at the pier in Nova Brasília. Prices are negotiable depending on the length and duration of the trip. See also Getting There & Away, later in this chapter.

Special Events
Ilha do Mel goes crazy during Carnaval and on any full moon in summer. Book accommodations well ahead, or bring a tent or hammock.

Places to Stay
If you arrive on the island on a weekend in summer or at another peak time, rooms will be hard to find, but you can rent space to sling a hammock. There are plenty of designated camping areas: just about every second backyard in Encantadas and Nova Brasília and two at Praia do Farol. All have electricity and water and cost US$2 per person.

There are pousadas at Nova Brasília, Praia da Fortaleza, Praia do Farol, Praia das Encantadas and Praia do Limoeiro. The biggest concentration of places is at Praia do Farol (also called Farol das Conchas or Praia das Conchas), along the track to the right from Nova Brasília. The prices quoted here can increase 20% to 50% in the high season.

Pousada Porto Seguro (☎ 455-2300) is the first place you hit as you come off the pier. There's a restaurant/bar at the front where Nova Brasília's local crew hangs out, and the owners, Jamil and Carol, are helpful with information. Apartamentos cost US$10 per person.

A good cheapie close to the pier is **Pousada das Palmas** (☎ 335-6028), with quartos for US$10 per person – do ask for a discount for longer stays. **Pousadinha** (☎ 978-3662) was one of the original places at Nova Brasília – it's getting a tad over-priced but is still a pleasant place to stay. Low-season prices are US$17 per person for basic apartamentos. **Pousada das Meninas** (☎ 426-8023) is a relaxed little place. Rustic quartos cost US$14 per person and apartamentos with fan and fridge go for US$20 per person. Check the place out at www.pousadadasmeninas.com.br.

Farther out toward the lighthouse in a quieter location are two good options: **Pousada Colméia** (☎ 426-8029), with a shady balcony and quartos for US$16 per person, and the more upmarket **Pousada Enseada** (9978-4200), with comfortable double apartamentos for US$36.

Right on the beach at Praia do Limoeiro, **Pousada do Aconchego** (☎ 978-3648) and **Pousada Por do Sol** (☎ 426-8009) have bed-and-breakfast deals for US$20 per person.

During summer, Praia da Fortaleza is a good option if you want to escape the crowds. There are three pousadas and two restaurants close together on the fine beach just past the fort. **Pousada dos Prazeres** (☎ 978-3221) is last along the beach but not the least – it's a friendly place with a seafood café and rooms for US$16 per person. The pousada can organize boat trips to Ilha do Superaguí. Closer to the fort, **Pousada Recanto da Fortaleza** (☎ 978-1367) offers room and full board for US$24 per person.

At Praia das Encantadas, there are several beachfront pousadas. Straight ahead as you come off the pier, **Pousada Tia Maria** (☎ 9978-3352) is a good value. Clean, comfortable apartamentos cost US$14/28. To the left of the pier, **Pousada Estrela do Mar** (☎ 9978-2010) is a similar standard and the same price. At the end of the beach to the right of the pier, **Pousada Ilha Verde** (☎ 978-2829) has quartos for US$10 per person and double apartamentos for US$28 in a pleasant garden setting.

Places to Eat

There are barracas with food and drinks at Nova Brasília, Praia das Encantadas and Praia da Fora. At Nova Brasília, **Toca do Abutre** is a surf bar, seafood restaurant and music venue rolled into one, with views across the water. You can get a fresh *peixe completo* (fish) with rice, salad and fries for US$4.50, or a tasty *stroganoff de camarão* (shrimp stew) for US$5. Close by, **Restaurante Porto Seguro** serves a *peixe grehaldo* (grilled fish) for US$4, and strong caipirinhas. Along the path toward the lighthouse, **Pousada Tropical** has a per-kilo restaurant attached.

At Praia das Encantadas, there are barracas lining the small bay. **Zorro** and **Éphira** are the best of the bunch, but they all serve much the same thing – seafood. You'd have to be crazy to eat any other kind of meal on Ilha do Mel.

Entertainment

On Friday and Saturday night, you'll find samba and other live music and probably a beach *festa*. At Nova Brasília, **Toca do Abutre** has a video bar and live music on weekends (in summer at least). **Toca da Coelho**, on the bay side toward Praia do Limoeiro, is a beach bar, live venue and dance club on the weekend.

Getting There & Around

See the Paranaguá section for boats from there. In high season, there are hourly boats from Pontal do Sul between 8 am and 7 pm Monday to Friday to Praia das Encantadas. On weekends, boats leave every half hour. The trip takes about 40 minutes and costs US$3 one way, including the US$1.50 environmental tax. There is an information booth (☎ 455-1144) at the port in Pontal do Sul where you can check the latest schedules.

From Nova Brasília boats leave for Paranaguá at 8 am on weekdays and at 3:30 pm on Sunday. There are no boats from Nova Brasília on Saturday, but you can get a water taxi for four people back to the mainland at Pontal do Sul (US$15) or one over to Encantadas (US$10), from where regular boats return to Pontal do Sul.

THE SOUTH

No regular boats go to Ilha do Superaguí (in the Parque Nacional do Superaguí), but water taxis from Nova Brasília will take you there in 40 minutes for around US\$35 one way for up to four people. A half-day return trip to Ilha do Superaguí costs around US\$60 for up to four. Ask around at the pier.

Water taxis for up to four can ferry you from Nova Brasília to Encantadas (US\$10) or Praia da Fortaleza and the fort (US\$10 to US\$12).

PARQUE NACIONAL DO SUPERAGUÍ
☎ 0xx41

Comprised of the Superaguí and Peças islands in the Baía de Paranaguá, this park was created in 1989. It is renowned for mangroves and salt marshes and contains a great variety of orchids, dolphins, jaguars and parrots, many which are threatened by the shrinking of the Mata Atlântica (Atlantic rainforest). The national park was among the 4700 sq km of Atlantic forest reserves in Paraná and São Paulo states that were given Unesco World Heritage listing in 1999.

The park's principal island, Ilha do Superaguí, is the most visited. It's an isolated place with good hiking and long stretches of deserted, open beaches. Boats disembark at Vila Superaguí, a fishing settlement with a population of about 350.

To help maintain the environment, all visitors should call at the IBAMA checkpoint. It's about 2km from the village.

Beaches away from Vila are deserted. The longest is Praia a Deserta, an 18km-long strip of fine, white sand. The water is generally calm, but swimmers need to be on the lookout for the stinging jellyfish that appear when the water gets warm in November.

Information
For more information about the park, contact IBAMA in Vila do Superaguí (☎ 455-1564), Paranaguá (on the corner of Rua Benjamin Constant and Rua Manoel Bonifaço) or in Guaraqueçaba (☎ 482-1262).

Places to Stay
There are six basic pousadas in Vila do Superaguí and all charge US\$10/20 for singles/doubles. The best is *Pousada Superaguí* (☎ 9978-9522, pousadasuperagui@lol.com.br). If you call ahead, staff here can organize a boat to pick you up from Ilha do Mel or Paranaguá for around US\$50 for up to four people. Other recommended pousadas are *Pousada Costa Azul* (☎ 9978-6013) and *Pousada Bela Ilha* (☎ 455-1564).

If you get stuck in Guaraqueçaba, there are a couple of hotels. *Hotel Gaurakessaba* (☎ 482-1273, Rua 15 de Novembro 16) has air-conditioned rooms for US\$18/36.

Getting There & Away
There are no regular boats to Ilha do Superaguí. The closest town is Guaraqueçaba, which is accessible by bus from Curitiba and by bus and boat from Paranaguá (see the Paranaguá section earlier in this chapter for details). The boat trip is interesting, passing through mangroves and providing a great view of one of the world's best-preserved saltwater lagoons.

In Guaraqueçaba, boats anchor in front of the old municipal market, and it's possible to negotiate a ride to the island. Boats from the island have 'S.AGUI' painted on the bow or stern.

Boats return from Guaraqueçaba to Paranaguá at 5 pm Monday to Friday and at 3:30 pm on weekends.

A more reliable way to get to Ilha do Superaguí is from Ilha do Mel – see the Ilha do Mel section earlier in this chapter.

FOZ DO IGUAÇU & AROUND
☎ 0xx45 • postcode 85850-000
• pop 256,000

Rising in the coastal mountains of Paraná and Santa Catarina (the Serra do Mar), at the modest elevation of 1300m, the Rio Iguaçu snakes west for 600km, pausing behind the Foz do Areia Cruz Machado and Salto Santiago dams and picking up a few dozen tributaries along the way. It widens majestically and sweeps around a magnificent forest stage before plunging and crashing in tiered falls. The 275 falls occupy an

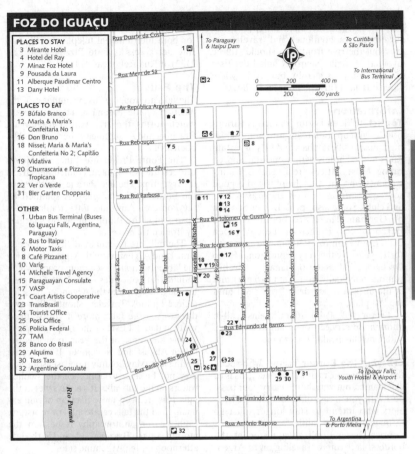

FOZ DO IGUAÇU

PLACES TO STAY
3 Mirante Hotel
4 Hotel del Ray
7 Minaz Foz Hotel
9 Pousada da Laura
11 Alberque Paudimar Centro
13 Dany Hotel

PLACES TO EAT
5 Búfalo Branco
12 Maria & Maria's Confeitaria No 1
16 Don Bruno
18 Nissei; Maria & Maria's Confeiteria No 2; Capitão
19 Vidativa
20 Churrascaria e Pizzaria Tropicana
22 Ver o Verde
31 Bier Garten Chopparia

OTHER
1 Urban Bus Terminal (Buses to Iguaçu Falls, Argentina, Paraguay)
2 Bus to Itaipu
6 Motor Taxis
8 Café Pizzanet
10 Varig
14 Michelle Travel Agency
15 Paraguayan Consulate
17 VASP
21 Coart Artists Cooperative
23 TransBrasil
24 Tourist Office
25 Post Office
26 Policia Federal
27 TAM
28 Banco do Brasil
29 Alquima
30 Tass Tass
32 Argentine Consulate

THE SOUTH

area more than 3km wide and 80m high, which makes them wider than Victoria, higher than Niagara and more beautiful than either. Neither words nor photographs do them justice – they must be seen and heard. They are the sort of thing the Romantic poets had in mind when they spoke of the awesome and the sublime.

Thousands of years before they were 'discovered' by whites, the falls were a holy burial place for the Tupi-Guarani and Paraguas tribes. Spaniard Don Alvar Nuñes, also known as Cabeza de Vaca (Cow's Head – so-called presumably because of his

stubbornness), happened upon the falls in 1541 in the course of his journey from Santa Catarina, on the coast, to Asunción. He named the falls the Saltos de Santa María, but this name fell into disuse and the Tupi-Guarani name, Iguaçu (Great Waters), was re-adopted. In 1986 Unesco declared the region a World Heritage Site.

Foz do Iguaçu went through a frenzied period during the 18 years the Itaipu dam was under construction. The population increased from 35,000 in 1973 to 190,000 in 1991. It was an edgy place then, but it's settled down in the years since then and shows signs of becoming an affluent town. Avenida Brasil, the main drag, is full of jewelry stores, boutiques and travel agencies, but the riverfront area should still be avoided at night. Nearby Ciudad del Este (in Paraguay) is shabby but lively, while Puerto Iguazú (in Argentina) is mellow.

Information

Tourist Offices Foztur maintains various booths with up-to-date information, including maps, bus timetables and lists of restaurants and of hotels with a one-star and up rating. Most staffers are English-speaking students who are very helpful and a good source of information on cheap eats, bars and clubs. Some also speak Italian, Spanish or German. There are booths on Rua Barão do Rio Branco in the city (open daily from 7 am to 11:30 pm and managed for 12 years by the very professional Fabio Oranges D'Alessandro Viana); at the bus station (open daily from 6 am to 6 pm); and at the airport (open daily from 8 am until the last plane).

Teletur (☎ 0800-451516) maintains a call-in information service from 7 am to 11:30 pm, with English-speaking operators.

Crossing the Border Visitors who spend the day outside Brazil will not need visas or exit stamps, but you should carry your passport with you in case of border checks. Travelers who intend to stay longer must go through all the formalities.

Local buses don't always stop at the borders, so if you're traveling on to Argentina or Paraguay, make sure you ask the bus driver to stop so you can get your exit/entry stamp at the border. See the introductory Facts for the Visitor chapter for information on consulates on either side of the borders.

Money Banco do Brasil on Avenida Brasil changes cash and has Visa ATMs. Caribe Turismo (☎ 523-8584) at the airport changes Visa and American Express traveler's checks without commission. There are dozens of money-exchange houses all over town and most give a better rate for cash than the banks.

Post & Communications The post office is on Praça Getúlio Vargas. The best place for both international telephone calls and Internet access is Café Pizzanet (☎ 523-2122) at Rua Rebouças 950.

The Falls

The falls are roughly 20km southeast of the junction of the Paraná and Iguaçu rivers, which forms the tripartite Paraguayan, Brazilian and Argentine border (marked by obelisks).

The Ponte Presidente Tancredo Neves bridges the Rio Iguaçu, connecting Brazil to Argentina. The Rio Paraná, which forms the border with Paraguay, is spanned by the Ponte da Amizade. Fifteen kilometers upstream is the Itaipu, the world's largest hydroelectric project.

The falls are unequally divided between Brazil and Argentina, with Argentina taking the larger portion. To see them properly you should visit both sides – the Brazilian park for the overview and the Argentine park for a close-up look. Travelers should allow two days to see the falls; more if you want to visit Ciudad del Este or the Itaipu dam.

The best time of the year to visit is between August and November. If you come during the May to July flood season, you may not be able to approach the swollen waters on the catwalks. It's always wet at the falls. This area gets more than 2m of rain annually, and the falls create a lot of moisture. Lighting for photography is best in the morning on the Brazilian side and in the late afternoon on the Argentine side.

Brazilian Side Although the Brazilian side has a smaller chunk of the falls, it offers a grand view across the churning lower Rio Iguaçu to the raging falls. The Brazilian national park is larger, with 1550 sq km of rainforest, but the Argentine forest is in better shape. The Brazilian side of the park is closed on Monday.

Walk to the observation tower by the Floriano falls, then over to Santa Maria falls. The walkway gives you an even better view of the Garganta do Diablo (Devil's Throat) and an invigorating cold shower.

IGUAÇU FALLS

If you have the cash, you can treat yourself to a helicopter ride over the waterfalls. For US$60, you get ten minutes in the air. The choppers will take up to three passengers, and it's best to sit by the edge of the bubble. Helisul Taxi Aereo (☎ 523-1190, helisul@foz.net) operates from just outside the park entrance. Travelers flying into Foz or Puerto Iguazú with accommodating weather and pilots can see the falls from the air.

You can catch a boat (US$35 per person) to the Garganta do Diablo from the boat ramp 3km back along the road to Foz. The bus can drop you there on the way in or out. Contact Macuco Safari de Barco (☎ 527-3010, ilhadosolmacuco@foznet.com.br).

Both the Brazilian and Argentine parks are undergoing major infrastructure remodeling in what cynics might see as an attempt to drain every last dollar from this natural wonder. Judging from the project plans, the Brazilian falls are in danger of becoming a glassed-in theater. Plans include a huge new visitors' center with parking lot, elevators and mobile walkways, food court, souvenir shops, heliport and 'VIP' rooms, along with a center for environmental education and research. It's due to be completed by the end of 2001.

Argentine Side The Argentine side is noted for its close-up views of the falls and the forest. The entrance to the Argentine park is 18km from Puerto Iguazú. There are three separate walks on the Argentine side: the Passeios Inferiores, the Passeios Superiores and the Garganta do Diablo, which should be saved until last for dramatic effect.

The Passeios Inferiores is a 1.5km circuit offering a view of the falls from below. Take the boat to Isla San Martín (the service operates from 9 am to 4:30 pm) to get a more close-up view of the falls. The boat ride is included in the park entrance fee.

The Passeios Superiores' concrete catwalks behind the waterfalls used to go as far as the Garganta do Diablo, until floods swept them over the edge. A new trail and walkway to Garganta do Diablo should be in operation by the time this book is published, as part of a major infrastructure project. The path will start from the new visitors' center due to be completed in late 2001. There will also be a tourist train running from the center to Porto Canoas.

There's a shuttle bus (US$0.50) from the visitors' center to Puerto Canoas, a few kilometers along a dirt road. From here you can take a hair-raising boat ride (US$4) out to Garganta do Diablo, where 13,000 cubic meters of water per second plunge 90m in 14 falls arranged around a tight little pocket.

The view at the precipice is hypnotizing. Visitors will be treated to a multisensory experience, with roaring falls, huge rainbow

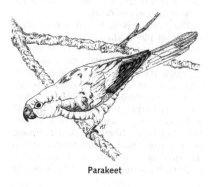

Parakeet

THE SOUTH

arcs, drenching mist and, in the distance, parrots and hawks cruising over deep, green forest. Watch for the swifts, which drop like rocks into the misty abyss, catch insects in midair, shoot back up and dart behind the falls to perch on the cliffs.

Exploring the Park

There's more to the 550-sq-km Argentine park than just waterfalls. If you want to do a forest walk, do it on the Argentine side; the parkland has been better protected than the Brazilian side. There are guides at the visitors' center (☎ 3757-420-180) in the park, but the staff seems more interested in nudging you toward one of the expensive tours (see Organized Tours later in this section). They will give you a free map and point you in the direction of the (only) road to Porto Macuco behind the visitors' center. The trail for the jungle walk (known as Sendero Macuco) runs off to the right, about 2.5km from the visitors' center. There's a small shelter near the entrance. About 3km along the trail, there is another short trail to some falls at Salto Arrechea. There is a bridge across the falls – don't cross it, as it's in a poor state of repair. Instead, double back and continue on down to the Rio Iguazu Inferior. The walk is about 6.5km each way. It's a good idea to bring repellent, sunscreen, a hat, water and some lunch on the hike.

If you can convince one of the guides to come along, the standard rate is US$50 for a half-day for up to 10 people. Special bird-watching tours can also be arranged at the same rate. Contact José Luis, Ingrid or Patricia at the visitors' center.

The foliage is lush and lovely: 2000 species of plants stacked in six different layers, from forest-floor grasses, ferns and bushes, to low, middle and high tree canopies. Try to pick up a wildlife list to study, and arrive early in the morning, before it gets too hot and when birds and wildlife are easier to spot. If possible, go in a small group and bring binoculars. You'll see fantastic butterflies (they congregate around pools of urine and on sweaty handrails to sip the salty fluid), parrots, parakeets, woodpeckers, hummingbirds, lizards, 3cm-long ants, beautifully colored spiders and all sorts of orchids, lianas and vines.

There are four species of toucan in the park. Their long beaks are deceptive; they're actually so light and spongy that the birds are back-heavy and therefore clumsy fliers.

Other creatures in the park include monkeys (there's a large colony of the mono caí variety), deer, sloths, anteaters, raccoons, jaguars, tapirs, caimans and armadillos, but, as in other tropical rainforests, large animals are not very abundant and tend to be nocturnal. It's wise to be cautious though; in 1997, the forest tour to Macuco was suspended after a ranger's son was killed by a jaguar. The park administration provides a leaflet with some safety hints for encounters with big cats. Among other things, you're advised to stay calm, try to appear bigger and to not get close to the cats (especially if they are feeding cubs).

Organized Tours

From within the Argentine park near the visitors' center, Iguazu Jungle Explorer (☎ 3757-421-600, iguazujunglexplorer@foz.net) runs a range of adventure tours.

Small operators in Foz offer tours to both sides of the falls through all the budget hotels. Discovery Turismo (☎ 523-6419, Rua Marechal Floriano 1851), in the city center, runs half-day trips to the Argentine falls for US$20 per person, including transportation and the park's entrance fee. A half-day tour to the Brazilian falls costs US$7, not including the entrance fee.

Itaipu Dam

How did Brazil manage to run up such a huge foreign debt? Part of the answer can be found in mammoth projects like Itaipu, the world's largest hydroelectric works. The US$18 billion joint Brazilian-Paraguayan venture has the capacity to generate 18 million kilowatts – enough electricity to supply the energy needs of Paraguay and 25% of Brazil's total energy. The concrete used in this dam could pave a two-lane highway from Moscow to Lisbon.

Fortunately, the dam does not affect the flow of water in Iguaçu, but it has destroyed

Sete Quedas (which was the world's most voluminous waterfall, with 30 times the water spilled by Iguaçu) and created a 1400 sq km lake. The complete environmental repercussions of these changes will not be felt for decades.

The Itaipu dam is 19km from Foz. A one-hour guided tour of the dam is given six times a day (between 8 am and 4 pm) from Monday to Saturday. From Monday to Friday, the tourist office in Foz can arrange tours inside the dam and technical tours for small groups. All the tours are free. For information, visit the Itaipu dam Web site at www.itaipu.gov.br.

Parque das Aves
Bird Park (☎ 523-1007) is a five-hectare aviary where you can see many of the birds native to the region. It's a good place to identify birds you will hopefully see in their natural habitat on a forest walk at the falls.

The park is close to the entrance to the Brazilian falls – get there on a Cataratas or Parque Nacional bus. It's open daily from 8:30 am to 6:30 pm and entrance costs US$8.

Ciudad del Este (Paraguay)
Across the Ponte da Amizade, at Ciudad del Este, you can play roulette or baccarat at the Casino de Leste, or purchase up to US$150 of duty-free imported goods (no great deals), or some nifty Paraguayan lacework and leather goods.

Places to Stay – Budget
The budget accommodations scene is very competitive in Foz, which is a boon for travelers. You'll get more bang for your buck here than in most other tourist areas in southern Brazil.

Camping The closest camping ground to the falls is *Camping Clube do Brasil* (☎ 523-8599). Just before the entrance to the park, there's a dirt road to the left. The camping ground is 600m along this track.

Hostels The two HI youth hostels in Foz have an information desk at the bus station open daily from 5 am to 6 pm. Either hostel will pay half your taxi fare. *Albergue Paudimar Campestre* (☎ 572-2430) is 12km from town on the way to the falls along Avenida das Cataratas. It's more like a miniresort, with a swimming pool, bar, cheap meals and Internet access – all for US$9 per person. In the center, *Albergue Paudimar Centro* (☎ 574-5503, paudimarcentro@paudimar .com.br, Rua Rui Barbosa 634) is clean and safe. For reservations or more information on the hostels, go to www.paudimar.com.br.

Hotels One of the best places for budget travelers is the *Pousada Evelina* (☎ 574-3817, pousada.evalina@foznet.com.br, Rua Irlan Kalichewski 171), 3.5km from Foz on the way to the falls. Spotless apartamentos cost US$11 per person, including a good breakfast. English, French and Spanish are spoken. To get there from the bus station, take either a J das Flores, Argentina or Parque Nacional bus and ask to get off at the Supermercado Chemin. Walk down the hill toward the city and it's the third street on the left.

Another recommended budget option is *Pousada das Flôres* (☎ 574-4533, flowers@ foznet.com.br), in a quiet location 2.5km from town at Avenida Imigrantes 344. Rooms cost US$10 per person and the friendly management will pick you up from the bus station or airport if you book ahead. English and French are spoken.

There is a cluster of cheap hotels around Rua Rebouças in the center, but the area can be seedy at night. The *Minas Foz Hotel* (☎ 574-5208, Rua Rebouças 809) has basic apartamentos for US$7 per person, not including breakfast. The rooms facing the street are the best.

Pousada da Laura (☎ 574-3628, Rua Naipi 629) is centrally located. English, French and Spanish are spoken. Basic apartamentos cost US$8 per person; better rooms inside the house cost US$10 per person.

Places to Stay – Mid-Range & Top End
You can negotiate discounts at all of these hotels outside the high season. *Hotel Del Rey* (☎ 523-2027, Rua Tarobá 1020) has

large, clean rooms with air-con and fridge for US$16/24. The hotel has a pool and is close to the local bus terminal. Make reservations at www.hoteldelreyfoz.com.br. *Dany Hotel* (☎ 523-1530, danyhotel@danyhotel.com.br, Avenida Brasil 509) is a smart new place right in the heart of town. It has a range of rooms with fridge, TV and air-con for US$24/48.

In the center, *Mirante Hotel* (☎ 523-2311, Avenida República Argentina 672) is a four-star joint with a hint of faded glamour. Singles/doubles cost US$54/78.

If you're traveling on someone else's money or you really want to splash out, you'll be staying at the *Hotel Tropical das Cataratas* (☎ 574-1688) right next to the Brazilian falls. Singles/doubles cost US$198/226 (30% less in the low season), but hey, at least you'll save on park entrance fees and bus fares!

Places to Eat

For lunch in town, *Maria & Maria's Confeitaria* is good for empadoês, sandwiches and pastries. There are two locations: Avenida Brasil 505 and Avenida Brasil 1285. *Ver o Verde* (Rua Edmundo de Barros 111) has a vegetarian buffet for US$3.50 per person, or you can pick up supplies at *Vidativa*, (Travessa Júlio Pasa 105a), a good food store. *Churrascaria e Pizzaria Tropicana* (Avenida Juscelino Kubitschek 198) is a popular student hangout with something for everyone – food per kilo, meat rodízio (US$3), a buffet with salads and meat (US$2.50) or a rodízio de pizza (US$3). It also has special discounts early in the week.

Next door, *Nissei* is a cross-cultural eatery with a Brazilian buffet lunch for US$2 and à la carte Japanese food at night. Sashimi for two will set you back US$12. *Don Bruno*, on Rua Almirante Barroso, has an airy terrace above the street and good Italian dishes for around US$5 per person. *Zaragoza* (Rua Quintino Bocaiuva 882) is an upmarket Spanish-style seafood restaurant.

The longest-established churrascaria in town is *Búfalo Branco* (Rua Rebouças 530), which charges US$12 per person. Avenida Jorge Schimmelpfeng is the place for drinks and fast food in barn-sized restaurants. *Bier Garten Choppparia*, at the corner of Rua Marechal Deodoro da Fonseca, serves up steaks, pizza and chopp.

Entertainment

There are some big dance clubs in Foz, but most have a minimum drink charge of US$10. The main strip for bars and clubs is Avenida Jorge Schimmelpfeng. Try *Tass Tass* on the corner with Avenida Marechal Floriano Peixoto for dance music, or *Alquimia* next door for techno. *Capitão* is a big video bar on the corner with Rua Almirante Barroso. *Kremlin* is a popular gay bar in town at Rua Marechal Floriano 1056.

Getting There & Away

Air There are frequent flights from Foz do Iguaçu to Asunción, Buenos Aires, Rio, São Paulo and Curitiba. On Avenida Brasil, TAM (☎ 523-6246) is at No 640, VASP (☎ 523-8331) is at No 821 and TransBrasil (☎ 523-5205) is at No 1225. Varig (☎ 523-2111) is at Avenida Juscelino Kubitscheck 463.

In Puerto Iguazú, Aerolineas Argentinas (☎ 3757-420-194) at Aguirre 295 offers daily services to Buenos Aires Aeroparque for US$145.

Bus All long-distance buses arrive at and depart from the international bus station, 6km from the center of town.

The trip from Foz do Iguaçu to Curitiba (US$20) takes 9½ hours; there are 14 buses a day. Six buses a day make the 16-hour trip to São Paulo (US$40). To Rio, there are four buses a day (US$50, 22 hours). Two buses a day run to Campo Grande (US$24, 16 hours).

There are regular buses from Ciudad del Este to Asunción (US$10, 5 hours), and two daily to Pedro Juan Caballero. Frequent buses go from Puerto Iguazú to Buenos Aires (US$35, 20 hours).

Getting Around

To/From the Airport The airport is 16km from the center. To go there, catch a bus marked P Nacional (US$2, 30 minutes) from any stop along Avenida Juscelino Kubitschek. Buses run every 22 minutes from 5:30 am to 7 pm and then every hour until 12:40 am. A taxi from the center costs around US$14.

To/From the Bus Station From outside the bus station, catch any Centro bus to town (US$0.60). A taxi costs US$5.50.

To/From the Falls Take a green Cataratas bus (US$1) to the Brazilian side of the falls. Buses run on the hour every day (except Monday morning, when the park is closed) from the local bus terminal on Avenida Juscelino Kubitschek, the first at 7 am and the last at 6 pm. Buses also return to the city on the hour; the last bus leaves the falls at 7 pm.

If you want to see both sides of the falls and do it in one day, get off the bus back to Foz where the road turns off to Puerto Iguazú (ask the conductor to let you know). Follow the road sign to Argentina – there's a bus stop about 100m along the road where you can pick up a bus that will take you right to Puerto Iguazú.

In Foz, catch a Puerto Iguazú bus from the local bus terminal or any stop along Avenida Juscelino Kubitschek. Buses start running at 6:30 am and leave every 13 minutes (on Sunday, every 50 minutes) until 7:30 pm. The fare is US$1.50. You'll have to show your passport at the border; if you're traveling on into Argentina, you'll have to get exit and entry stamps.

At the bus station in Puerto Iguazú, transfer to an El Pratico bus to the falls. You can pay in Argentine pesos or Brazilian reais: The bus costs US$6 and park entry costs US$5.

Buses return to Puerto Iguazú from the visitors' center at the falls on the hour. The bus back to Foz leaves Puerto Iguazú every hour on the half-hour from 6:30 am to 7:30 pm.

Itaipu Dam Catch a Conjunto C bus from any stop along Rua Almirante Barroso in the center to Itaipu. There's one every 13 minutes from 5:27 am until midnight, but Itaipu closes for visits after 4 pm. The last bus stop is at the Ecomuseu (worth a look), about 400m from the Itaipu visitors center.

Ciudad del Este (Paraguay) From the local bus terminal in Foz, buses run to Ciudad del Este every 10 minutes (every 30 minutes on Sunday) from 6:15 to 8:30 pm.

THE SOUTH

Santa Catarina

Unlike most immigrants to Brazil, who worked on large plantations, the Germans and Italians who settled in Santa Catarina in the 19th century owned their small family-run farms. This European model of land use has produced a far more egalitarian distribution of wealth than in most of Brazil, and many of the state's 5.3 million people still own their own rich farmland. Combined with some healthy small-scale industry, this has created one of Brazil's most prosperous states.

The state's relative affluence and its efficient services give Santa Catarina the feel of Europe rather than of Brazil – at least in the highlands, which are green and pastoral. But if Santa Catarina is reminiscent of Switzerland, it's less because of geography than because of middle-class consumerism.

Most travelers don't come to Santa Catarina for the culture – they come for the beaches. There's no doubt that the beaches are beautiful: There are wide beaches offering some of Brazil's best surfing, as well as Caribbean-like bays with clear, clean turquoise water. While there are plenty of calm beaches for swimming, the rip currents can be dangerous at surfing beaches, so be careful.

Many of Santa Catarina's beaches have become fashionable vacation spots for well-to-do Paulistas, Curitibanos and Argentines; during the January to February holiday season and on summer weekends, the beaches and hotels are jammed.

Santa Catarina is consistently hot during the summer. In winter, the wind along the coast picks up considerably, although it never gets too cold. Unless you like crowds, the best months to go are March, April, November and December.

Compared with other parts of Brazil, this is a polite and proper place. You may be excluded from a bar if you're not wearing a shirt, and shorts are the briefest attire acceptable on intercity buses – no swimsuits.

Highlights

- Surfing and hanging out at the beach on Ilha da Santa Catarina
- Snorkeling around the islands of the Reserva Biológica do Avoredo in Bombinhas
- Celebrating Oktoberfest in Blumenau
- Sand-surfing at Praia Joaquina on Ilha da Santa Catarina
- Whale-watching at Praia da Rosa

São Paulo

Tropic of Capricorn

Paraná

Joinville page 371
ARGENTINA
Blumenau page 374
Florianópolis page 377
Rio Grande do Sul
Ilha de Santa Catarina page 380

Santa Catarina page 369

JOINVILLE
☎ 0xx47 • postcode 89200-000
• pop 414,000

Imagine a city where blonds stroll and cycle through clean, well-lit streets, perusing Bavarian-facaded shops full of modern appliances, amidst parks and houses with well-

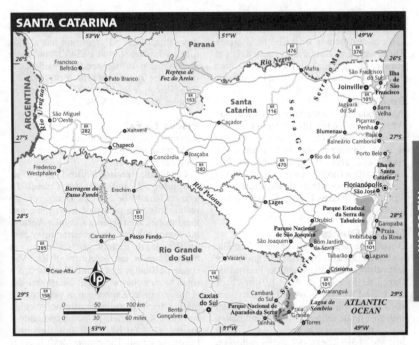

SANTA CATARINA

THE SOUTH

manicured lawns; a city that is polite and efficient. Now here's the hard part: Imagine this city is in Brazil.

Joinville (pronounced 'jovial') is Santa Catarina's largest city but not the capital. It is described as an 'industrial city' though Joinvilleans prefer to call it 'the city of flowers.' The industrial activity is tucked away outside the pleasant inner city, which seems like the kind of place to raise a family. For the traveler, Joinville is relaxed, if unexciting.

Information

The tourist office (☎ 423-2633) is in the convention center at Avenida José Vieira 315 on the riverfront, around 1.5km from the center.

Bradesco, on Rua 15 de Novembro behind the local bus terminal, has Visa ATMs. Casa Roweder Câmbio e Turismo, Rua do Principe 158, changes traveler's

checks. The post office is on Rua Princesa Isabel and the telephone office is on Praça Nereu Ramos.

The city's official Web site (www.promotur .com.br) is good for general information. Check out www.tudojoinville.com.br for listings of clubs and bars.

Museu Nacional da Imigração

Housed in the old palace (built in 1870) at Rua Rio Branco 229, this museum dedicated to immigration is full of objects used by the pioneers of the state. It's open 9 to 11:30 am and 2 to 5:30 pm Tuesday to Friday.

Museu da Bicicleta

Housed in the old train station at Avenida Getúlio Vargas 1614, the bicycle museum has over 15,000 bikes dating back to 1906. It's open Tuesday to Sunday from 9 am to noon and from 2 to 6 pm.

Museu de Arte de Joinville

This interesting museum is set in lovely gardens and houses works by local artists. There's a small restaurant attached. It's at Rua 15 de Novembro 1400 and is open Tuesday to Sunday from 10 am to 8 pm.

Boat Trips

A day-boat trip to the historic town of São Francisco do Sul (on Ilha de São Francisco) aboard the *Barco Príncipe* sails through the Baía de Babitonga and its 14 islands. The boat leaves from the main dock (☎ 455-0824), on the Rio Cachoeira around 1.5km east of the city center, at 10 am, returning at 5 pm. The trip costs US$12 per person and includes lunch.

Special Events

During the second half of July, Joinville hosts one of Latin America's largest **dance festivals**. Contact the Instituto Festival de Dança de Joinville (☎ 423-1010) or check the festival Web site at www.festivaldedanca .com.br. Joinville is the only city in Brazil with an affiliate school of the **Bolshoi Ballet**. It's in the convention center on Avenida José Vieira 315. The school allows visitors on Saturdays from 8 am to noon and 2 to 5 pm.

The **Festival of Flowers** (☎ 422-5585, promotur@promotur.com.br) is in mid-November.

Places to Stay

The central *Hotel Ideal* (☎ 422-3660, Rua Jerônimo Coelho 98), has single/double quartos for US$14/17 and apartamentos for US$17/24. A bit farther out, *Hotel Mattes* (☎ 433-2447, Rua 15 de Novembro 801) has comfortable apartamentos for US$17/24. Next door, *Hotel Mendes* (☎ 433-9368) is rock-bottom option, with basic rooms for US$6/12.

The *Hotel Príncipe* (☎ 433-4555, Rua Jerônimo Coelho 27) is centrally located, clean, and has a friendly staff and a very good breakfast. Singles/doubles start at US$18/30. Another mid-range option is the *Hotel Trocadero* (☎ 422-1469, Rua Visconde de Taunay 185), in a colonial building. Singles/doubles cost US$16/24.

The *Colón Palace Hotel* (☎ 433-6188, colon.joi@zaz.com.br, Rua São Joaquim 80) faces Praça Nereu Ramos and has a pool. Singles/doubles start at US$40/50, but there are discounts on weekends. Joinville's top hotel is the *Tannenhof Othon* (☎ 433-8011, Rua Visconde de Taunay 340). Singles/doubles start at US$70/94.

Places to Eat

Italian and German food are staple restaurant fare in Joinville. The city is also a major chocolate producer.

For lunch, *Recanto Natural (Rua 15 de Novembro 78)* and *Tempeiro Crioulo II*, also on Rua 15 de Novembro, are per-kilo restaurants with plenty of fresh salad and meat dishes. *Restaurante Cozinha Natural* is a reasonably priced vegetarian restaurant on Rua Jacob Richlín. For cheap eats at night, *Chaplin*, on the corner of Rua Visconde de Taunay and Rua Pedro Lobo, is a small student bar with light meals and live acoustic music. *Expresso* is a popular up-market bar/restaurant nearby on Avenida Juscelino Kubitschek. Its house speciality is 'beirutes,' a fairly bland imitation of a Lebanese kebab. The *chopp* (draft beer) is good, though.

The *Bierkeller (Rua 15 de Novembro 497)* has the city's best values for German food. Dinner costs around US$10 to US$15 for two people, but the restaurant serves a cheap lunch buffet for US$2 from Monday to Friday. *Fatirella* on Rua Pedro Lobo has a cheap rodízio de pizza and a breezy terrace to munch it in. *La Finestra (Rua Rio Branco 193)* has good pasta dishes for two people from US$6 to US$10 – ask for a half-portion (US$4 to US$6) if you're dining solo. Farther down the street, *Pinheiro (Rua Rio Branco 299)* has the city's best fish, but it's expensive.

Getting There & Around

Air The airport is 12km from the city; Aeorporto buses leave from the local bus terminal on Praça da Bandeira. There are regular flights from Joinville to Curitiba, Florianópolis, Brasília, Rio and São Paulo. Trans-Brasil (☎ 422-6060) is at Rua São Joaquim

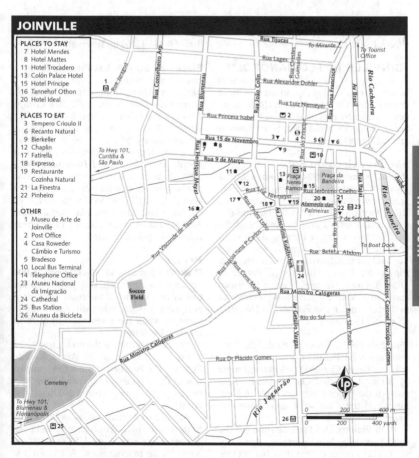

JOINVILLE

PLACES TO STAY
7 Hotel Mendes
8 Hotel Mattes
11 Hotel Trocadero
13 Colón Palace Hotel
15 Hotel Príncipe
16 Tannehof Othon
20 Hotel Ideal

PLACES TO EAT
3 Tempero Crioulo II
6 Recanto Natural
9 Bierkeller
12 Chaplin
17 Fatirella
18 Expresso
19 Restaurante
    Cozinha Natural
21 La Finestra
22 Pinheiro

OTHER
1 Museu de Arte de
   Joinville
2 Post Office
4 Casa Roweder
   Câmbio e Turismo
5 Bradesco
10 Local Bus Terminal
14 Telephone Office
23 Museu Nacional
   da Imigração
24 Cathedral
25 Bus Station
26 Museu da Bicicleta

THE SOUTH

70, next to the Colón Palace Hotel; Varig
(☎ 433-2800) is at Rua Alexandre Dohler
277 and TAM (☎ 433-2023) is at Rua 9 de
Março 737.

Bus The bus station is 2km from the city
center. Local buses to the city center leave
regularly from outside the bus station.

Interstate buses make the trip from
Joinville to Curitiba (US$5, 2½ hours)
every hour, and there are two buses a day to
São Paulo (US$22, nine hours). Daily buses
head north to Paranaguá (US$6.50, 3½
hours) at 7 am and 3:45 pm. Alternatively,

you can catch one of five buses a day to
Guaratuba (US$3.50, 1½ hours), where you
can get a connection to Paranaguá.

If you're going south, Hwy BR-101 runs
close to the coast, and many intercity buses
stop at beach towns such as Itajaí, Piçarras
and Barra Velha. To Florianópolis (US$11,
2½ hours), there are 18 buses a day – three
of them are express. The *semi-direitos* (semi-
direct) run via Itajaí and Balneário Camboriú. Six buses a day run to Blumenau
(US$7, 2½ hours), one goes to Porto Alegre
(US$24, nine hours) and one to Foz do
Iguaçu (US$26, 16 hours).

The closest beaches are on Ilha de São Francisco. Plenty of local buses run there, especially on weekends.

JOINVILLE TO FLORIANÓPOLIS

This stretch of coast has many beautiful beaches, but it's being developed rapidly. In general, the more famous a beach, the more developed and ugly it is. Balneário Camboriú, the area's best-known beach town, is an excellent example.

São Francisco do Sul
☎ 0xx47 • postcode 89240-000 • pop 30,000
This historic city's island setting was 'discovered' way back in 1504 by the Frenchman Binot Paulmier de Goneville, but the city itself wasn't settled until the middle of the next century. Later, it became the port of entry for German immigrants who settled the land around Joinville. Several streets in the center – Ruas Babitonga, Fernando Dias, Reinoldo Tavares, Floriano Peixoto and Lauro Muller – have now been given protection under the Patrimônio Histórico (National Heritage list).

Beaches The beaches on Ilha de São Francisco are good, but their proximity to Joinville (and even Curitiba) makes them some of the most crowded. On the positive side, most of the beaches are accessible by local buses and there are some good point and beach breaks for surfing.

Both **Prainha** and **Praia Grande** (to the south) are ocean beaches exposed to a lot of swell. They are good for surfing, but not safe for swimming. Closer to the city, **Praia da Ubatuba** and **Praia de Enseada** are pretty bays and safe for swimming, but they're developed and get very crowded on weekends. Some of the more secluded beaches are **Praia Itaguaçu** and **Praia do Forte** on the island's northern tip. You can get to them by local bus from São Francisco do Sul or Praia de Enseada.

Boat Tours In town, boats leave the port for tours of the Baía de São Francisco do Sul, stopping for lunch at the historic town of Vila da Glória on the mainland. The tour

costs US$10, including lunch. Contact Scuna São Francisco (☎ 444-1680) or Marakie Tour (☎ 444-1260) for reservations.

Places to Stay & Eat Praia de Enseada has several hotels, and you can catch a direct bus there from Joinville. *Pousada Estrela do Mar (☎ 442-3104, Rua Corupá 180)* is a good cheap option 100m from the beach at Praia de Enseada. Double apartamentos cost US$20, or there are small chalets with cooking facilities for up to six people for US$40. *Hotel Turismar (☎ 422-2060, Avenida Atlântica 1923)* is in a good position on the beachfront. Singles/doubles start at US$55/65. Seafood is the way to go on the island. In Enseada, *Restaurante Parorámico (Avenida Atlântica 1288)* serves reasonably priced seafood.

Penha
☎ 0xx47 • postcode 88385-000 • pop 16,000
Penha is a fishing town, and the nicest place to stay on this part of the coast. Even so, it gets seriously crowded on weekends in summer, when the main beachfront turns into one big festa.

The ocean is calm at the pretty, tree-lined town beaches, Praia da Armação and Prainha. The beaches to the south – in particular Praia Grande (5km) and Praia Vermelha (9km) – are beautiful and much less crowded.

At Praia da Armação, you can rent a boat to the nearby islands of Itacolomi and Feia. The going rate is about US$30 for three hours for up to five people. Ask around at the pier, or contact Alexandre (☎ 9997-3568), captain of the *Capitão Gato*.

Places to Stay & Eat There are campgrounds and some good hotels and seafood restaurants on Praia da Armação. The friendly *Hotel Itapocoroí (☎ 345-5015, Rua Maria da Costa 62)* is close to the beach and charges US$20 for a double apartamento during the week (a little more on weekends). Nearby on the beachfront, *Costamar Praia Hotel (☎ 345-6861, Avenida Elizabeth Kondor Reis 556)* charges US$24 for double apartamentos with air-con.

Immigrants from the Portuguese Azores Islands have created a unique regional cuisine that blends indigenous and Azorean flavors. The best place to try it (washed down with a dizzying variety of cachaças) is *Pirão d'Agua* on the beachfront at Avenida São João. Close by, *Restaurante do Alírio (Avenida Elizabeth Kondor Reis 26)* has excellent, cheap seafood meals.

Getting There & Away Intercity buses don't stop in Penha. There is a bus terminal at Piçarras (6km north) where you can take a local Circular or Navagantes bus to Penha.

Balneário Camboriú
☎ 0xx47 • postcode 88330-000 • pop 58,000
This little Copacabana, with its sharp hills dropping into the sea, nightclubs with 'professional companions,' and an ocean boulevard named Avenida Atlântica, is out of control. In summertime, the population increases tenfold.

Balneário Camboriú is Santa Catarina's most expensive town. Here you can meet well-heeled Argentines, Paraguayans and Paulistas who spend their summers in beach-hugging high-rise buildings.

Porto Belo
☎ 0xx47 • postcode 88210-000 • pop 9950
The small peninsula that fans out from Porto Belo boasts the last good mainland beaches before Ilha de Santa Catarina. **Praia Bombinhas** (9km from town) and **Praia Bombas** (3km) are the best beaches around with accommodations. Both have several condominium developments under construction. There are boat trips and diving opportunities from both Porto Belo and Bombinhas.

Information G8 Turismo (☎ 369-2526) on Rua Parati in Bombinhas changes cash US dollars and German marks.

Activities Dive operators in Bombinhas offer half-day diving tours to the Reserva Biológica do Avoredo, a marine park consisting of three islands – Avoredo, Galés and Deserta. The coral reefs surrounding the islands are home to a variety of exotic fish, dolphins, stingrays and turtles. Half-day tours leave from the pier at Praia Bombinhas Thursday through Sunday and cost around US$50 per person. For reservations contact Submarine (☎ 369-2223, submarin@melim.com.br) on Rua Manoel Dos Santos in Bombinhas.

Places to Stay & Eat You can camp at Bombinhas at *Camping Bombinhas* (☎ 369-2322) at the end of the beach on Avenida Manoel José dos Santos. *Pousada do Holandês* (☎ 369-1281, Rua José Esteven 553) in Bombas has chalets with cooking facilities for up to five people for US$50. Right next to the bus stop at Bombinhas, *Pousada Bombinhas* (☎ 369-1448, Avenida Manoel José dos Santos 872) has singles/doubles for US$14/20. *Refúgio do Corsário* (☎ 369-2126, Rua Tilápia 74) has cabanas with cooking facilities for US$60 for up to five people. In Bombinhas, *Restaurante Comandante Dória, (Rua Tainha 129)*, in the hotel of the same name, is a reasonably priced seafood restaurant. *Portofino (Avenida Manoel José dos Santos 120)* has cheap parrillada to cater to homesick Argentine tourists.

Getting There & Away There are 12 buses a day from Balneário Camboriú to Bombinhas (US$3.50, 1½ hours) that stop in Porto Belo and Bombas. Semi-direito buses from Florianópolis and Joinville stop at Camboriú.

BLUMENAU
☎ 0xx47 • postcode 89000-000
• pop 242,000
Blumenau is 60km inland from Itajaí. Nestled in the Vale do Itajaí on the Rio Itajaí, Blumenau and its environs were settled largely by German immigrants in the second half of the 19th century. The area is serene, but the city is busy and promotes its German culture with the commercial flair of Walt Disney.

Information
There's an information booth in the center on the corner of Rua 15 de Novembro and Rua Nereu Ramos. Staff speak German, and

THE SOUTH

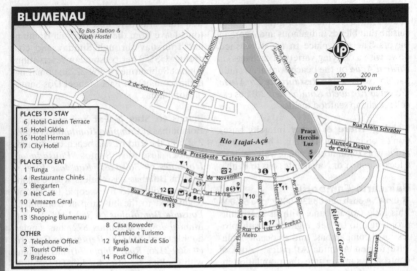

BLUMENAU

To Bus Station & Youth Hostel

2 de Setembro

Rua República Argentina

Rua Gertrude Sirtoli

Rua Itajaí

0   100   200 m
0   100   200 yards

Rio Itajaí-Açú

Praça Hercilio Luz 5

Rua Alwin Schrader

Alameda Duque de Caxias

Avenida Presidente Castelo Branco

Rua 15 de Novembro

Rua 7 de Setembro

Dr Curt Hering

Rua Angelo Dias

Rua Nereu Ramos

Av Rio Branco

Rua Floriano Peixoto

Rua Dr Luiz de Freitas Melro

Riberão Garcia

Rua Amazonas

PLACES TO STAY
6   Hotel Garden Terrace
15 Hotel Glória
16 Hotel Herman
17 City Hotel

PLACES TO EAT
1   Tunga
4   Restaurante Chinês
5   Biergarten
9   Net Café
10 Armazen Geral
11 Pop's
13 Shopping Blumenau

OTHER
2   Telephone Office
3   Tourist Office
7   Bradesco

8   Casa Roweder
    Cambio e Turismo
12 Igreja Matriz de São
    Paulo
14 Post Office

THE SOUTH

have useful maps and information about other towns in the Itajaí region.

The Bradesco branch at Rua 15 de Novembro 849 has Visa ATMs. Casa Roweder Cambio e Turismo at Rua Curt Hering 20 changes cash and traveler's checks at a good rate.

The post office is on Rua Padre Jacobs. The telephone office is at Rua 15 de Novembro 710 – it's just a small doorway off the street, so keep your eyes peeled.

Oktoberfest

Blumenau hosts an increasingly popular Oktoberfest during the middle two weeks of October. Call (☎ 326-6968) or check the Web site www.oktober.com.br for a full program of events.

Places to Stay

Pousada Grun Garten Albergue da Juventude (☎ 323-4332, Rua São Paulo 2437) in the suburb of Itoupava Seca is the city's HI youth hostel. It has a restaurant attached. *Hotel Herman* (☎ 322-4370, Rua Floriano Peixoto 213) has single/double apartamentos for US$14/24, but the beds are about as comfortable as an ironing board. Close by,

City Hotel (☎ 322-2205, Rua Ângelo Dias 263) has quartos for US$10/16 and apartamentos for US$15/26.

Moving up the price scale, the rather grand *Hotel Glória* (☎ 326-1988, Rua 7 de Setembro 954) has apartamentos for US$30/50. Nearby *Hotel Garden Terrace* (☎ 326-3544, Rua Padre Jacobs 45) is one of Blumenau's fanciest sleeperies. Rooms start at US$74/100.

Places to Eat

Some of the cheaper hotels don't provide breakfast, so head to the grand dining room at *Cafehaus Glória* in the Hotel Glória for *café matinal* (US$5) or to a cute hole-in-the-wall café, *Net Café* on Rua Curt Hering, for coffee and snacks.

For a cheap lunch, *Pop's* on Rua Nereu Ramos is a per-kilo restaurant. *Shopping Blumenau* on Rua 7 de Setembro offers plenty of variety in its food hall – pizza, Italian, Chinese and Lebanese. For à la carte Chinese food, head to *Restaurante Chinês* on the corner of Rua 15 de Novembro and Avenida Rio Branco.

At night, the chopperias near the Rua República Argentina bridge such as *Tunga* have cheap pizza, chopp and some live music. *Biergarten* on Praça Hercílio Luz is another good spot for a beer and snack overlooking the river. *Armazen Geral (Rua Floriano Peixoto 55)* is where members of Blumenau's young and blond set meet and graze.

Getting There & Around

There are more than 20 buses a day to Florianópolis. The direct buses (US$10, 2½ hours) leave at 8 am, noon, and 3 and 6:30 pm. Semi-direitos stop at Itajaí, Balneário Camboriú and Itapema, and take three hours. There are 17 buses a day to Joinville (US$7, 2½ hours), and ten to Curitiba (US$13, 4½ hours).

From inside the bus station, hourly buses go to the city. Otherwise, walk out of the bus

---

The Beat of a Different Drum

The people of Blumenau are largely descended from German immigrants who settled in the south of Brazil in the second half of the 19th century. Locals are proud of their differences from other Brazilians and have kept their customs, language and architecture alive.

Tourists from all over Brazil come to experience this outpost of German culture, which reaches a peak during the first week of October when the town hosts Brazil's biggest Oktoberfest. The party starts off in traditional fashion, with lively folk-dancing displays by lederhosen-clad locals, folk songs, bratwurst and beer. But as the night wears on and the normally sedate southerners get a few *cervejas* under their belts, the party undergoes a change of direction.

Although musicians have been flown over from Germany specifically for the festival, the brass and accordions are put away and the sounds of samba and *frevo* take over. The good old German knees-up is abandoned, and the bump-and-grind of the Northeast fires the party on until the early hours of the morning.

---

station to the far side of Avenida 2 de Setembro and take a Fortaleza or Troncal bus (US$0.60) to Rua 7 de Setembro in the center. A taxi costs US$7.

FLORIANÓPOLIS
☎ 0xx48 • postcode 88000-000
• pop 322,000

Florianópolis, the state capital, has two distinct sides to its character – in fact, half of the city is on Ilha de Santa Catarina and the other half is on the mainland. The mainland side is industrial and modern, while the downtown area on the island side faces the Baía Sul and has cobbled pedestrian streets and colonial buildings around a shady central square. The island side, where you'll probably spend your time, has a relaxed, small-city feel and there are regular public buses to the island's beautiful beaches. The two sides of the city are joined by two bridges, including Brazil's longest steel suspension bridge.

Information

There are handy information booths at the bus station (☎ 224-2777) and next to the old customs house (☎ 222-4906). They provide good maps and information about transport and accommodations. Staff can make reservations for island lodging and tours. Spanish is spoken.

Lots of touts wait at the bus station. They have information on accommodations (they get a commission of course) and transport, and can be useful.

There's an active black market for cash dollars in the pedestrian mall on Rua Felipe Schmidt – even the tourist office will direct you there! Otherwise, change your cash at a money-exchange house. To change traveler's checks and make Visa withdrawals, go to the Banco do Brasil at Praça 15 de Novembro 20.

The post office faces Praça 15 de Novembro. The telephone office is on the corner of Rua Dumont and Rua Visconde de Ouro Prêto.

Moncho, at Rua Tiradentes 181, is a combined telephone office and Internet café. Internet access costs US$4 for the first hour

Guga Serves for Sports-Mad Brazilians

Gustavo Kuerten – 'Guga' to his millions of Brazilian fans – was anointed the country's new sporting hero in 2000 when he became the world's number-one-ranked tennis player. Guga, who lives in Florianópolis, unleashed a wave of national pride when he claimed the top spot in the last match of the season by defeating North American Andre Agassi at the Tennis Masters Cup.

Guga burst onto the world tennis scene in 1997 by winning his first French Open as a 21-year-old. But even in a country that places its sporting heroes on the highest pedestal, Guga has stayed refreshingly laid-back. He is a scrupulously good sport on the court, is active in several charities and is every Brazilian mother's dream son.

When in Florianópolis, Guga hangs out at night with friends (he's a famously slow starter in early matches), surfs on Ilha da Santa Catarina and goes to watch his favorite soccer team, Avaí.

and US$2 every hour after that. The bookstore Livraria Catarinense at Rua Felipe Schmidt 60 also offers Internet access.

Around Praça 15 de Novembro

While you'll probably want to get out to the beaches as soon as possible, it's worth wandering around the city and taking a little time to look at some of the well-preserved colonial buildings.

From Praça 15 de Novembro and its 100-year-old **fig tree**, cross Rua Arcipestre to the pink **Palácio Cruz e Souza**. It's the state museum, but the most interesting things to see are the ornate parquetry floors and the outrageous 19th-century ceilings. Entry is US$1. It's open Tuesday to Friday from 10 am to 7 pm, and on weekends from 1:30 to 7 pm.

On the high point of the plaza is the **Catedral Metropolitana**, the cathedral was remodeled in the 20th century, so not much from the colonial era remains. The least remodeled colonial church is the **Igreja de NS do Rosário**, farther up from the cathedral on Rua Guilherme.

Waterfront

Back down on the old waterfront are the **Alfândega** (customs house) and the **Mercado Municipal** (municipal market), both colonial buildings that have been well preserved. The market is a good place to drink chopp, snack and people-watch in the late afternoon.

Organized Tours

Veleiro Tur (☎ 225-9939), at Rua Silva Jardim 1050 in the suburb of Prainha, offers half-day (US$14) and full-day tours (US$17) to the main beaches and attractions on the island. Scuna Sul (☎ 224-1806) and Scuna Central (☎ 232-3062) run boat tours from the city to islands in the Baía Norte. The tour lasts about six hours and costs US$14 per person. The tourist office or your hotel can make reservations for all these tours.

Places to Stay

Hotels in Florianópolis are fairly expensive and fill up during the summer. Most of the budget places are in the center of town. There are few budget hotels out on the island's beaches, though it is possible to economize by renting an apartment with a group of people. There are also many places to camp.

The good HI hostel *Albergue da Juventude Ilha de Catarina* (☎ 222-3781, *Rua Duarte Schutel 227*) is a 10-minute walk from the bus station.

The *Hotel Cruzeiro* (☎ 222-0675, *Rua Conselheiro Mafra 324*) is seedy but OK. Basic quartos cost US$8 per person – this includes cable TV! On the next parallel street you'll find the *Hotel Central Sumaré* (☎ 222-5359, *Rua Felipe Schmidt 423*). It's a friendly place and has large, clean rooms, but the beds are pretty bad. Single/double quartos cost US$14/24 and apartamentos go for US$24/32. Breakfast is not included.

Another reasonable place is the *Felippe Hotel* (☎ 222-4122, Rua João Pinto 26). It charges US$14 per person (breakfast included) for pretty grungy quartos – the walls stop about halfway to the ceiling so they are noisy as well.

The city has finally got a couple of decent, central, mid-range hotels, but they are often full. The *Hotel Baía Sul* (☎ 224-0810, Rua Tiradentes 167) is a good option if you can get in. Singles/doubles cost US$26/36. A bit more expensive, but worth a splurge, is the elegant *Centro Sul Hotel* (☎ 222-9110, csh@ centrosulhotel.com.br, Avenida Hercílio Luz 652). Apartamentos go for US$35/46. Otherwise, *Hotel Valerim Center* (☎ 222-1100, Rua Felipe Schmidt 554) has standard apartamentos for US$30/42.

Many of the top-end hotels are out on the beaches, but in town, *Florianópolis Palace* (☎ 224-9633, Rua Artista Bittencourt 14) is a five-star hotel with the works, including thermal spa and massage. Singles/doubles cost US$96/105.

Places to Eat

In the center of town, *Restaurante Villa* (Rua Trajano 91) is a great per-kilo lunch

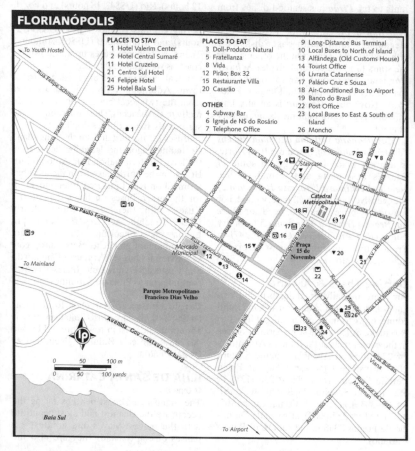

FLORIANÓPOLIS

PLACES TO STAY
1 Hotel Valerim Center
2 Hotel Central Sumaré
11 Hotel Cruzeiro
21 Centro Sul Hotel
24 Felippe Hotel
25 Hotel Baía Sul

PLACES TO EAT
3 Doll-Produtos Natural
5 Fratellanza
8 Vida
12 Pirão; Box 32
15 Restaurante Villa
20 Casarão

OTHER
4 Subway Bar
6 Igreja de NS do Rosário
7 Telephone Office
9 Long-Distance Bus Terminal
10 Local Buses to North of Island
13 Alfândega (Old Customs House)
14 Tourist Office
16 Livraria Catarinense
17 Palácio Cruz e Souza
18 Air-Conditioned Bus to Airport
19 Banco do Brasil
22 Post Office
23 Local Buses to East & South of Island
26 Moncho

THE SOUTH

spot with good salads housed in a breezy colonial building. There are plenty of cheap *lanchonetes* in town, many of which are health-food oriented – try **Doll-Produtos Natural** on Rua Vidal Ramos for veggie burgers or a breakfast of muesli and fruit salad. Vegetarians can also lunch at **Vida**, on Rua dos Ilheus, next door to the Alliance Française building. **Café das Artes** *(Rua Esteves Junior 734)*, about 1.5km from the waterfront, is a cool café for coffee, snacks and drinks at night.

The old market is full of character and there are some interesting seafood restaurants to try. **Pirão** has seafood dishes from US$5, and **Box 32** has great seafood snacks. **Fratellanza**, on Estrada do Rosario, is an elegant restaurant with pasta dishes for around US$12 for two. On the other side of the stairs (and the cultural divide), **Subway Bar** is an alternative bar for drinks and snacks. Set in a colonial building on Praça 15 de Novembro, **Casarão** is an airy bar/café that is good for light meals and a drink at night.

Macarronada Italiana *(Avenida Rubens de Arruda Ramos 2458)*, on the Baía Norte, is a great place to splurge on some of Brazil's best pasta and formal service. Nearby, **Sushimasa** *(Travessa Harmonia 2)* is expensive, but the sushi is very good. For reasonably-priced seafood, head for **Peixe na Brasa** *(Travessa Harmonia 50)*, or try **Gugu** *(Rua Antôio Dias Carneiro 147)* in Praia Sambaqui for excellent Azorean-influenced seafood.

Getting There & Around

Air There are daily direct flights from Florianópolis to São Paulo and Porto Alegre, and connections to most other cities. Flights to Rio make at least one stop. Airlines offices in the center include Aerolineas Argentinas (☎ 224-7835), at Avenida Tenente Silveira 200; TransBrasil (☎ 236-1380), at Praça Pereira Oliveira 16; Varig (☎ 236-1121), at Rua Tenente Silveira 225, Room 710; VASP (☎ 236-3033), at Avenida Osmar Cunha 105; and TAM (☎ 236-0003), at Avenida Diomício de Freitas 3348 in the suburb of Bairro Carianos.

The airport is 12km south of the city (US$16 by taxi). Red local buses marked Correador Sudoeste run to the airport (US$0.60, 45 minutes) every 15 minutes until midnight. They leave from the local bus terminal on Rua Antônio Luz. An air-conditioned Correador Sudoeste bus to the airport (US$1.50, 30 minutes) leaves every 20 minutes from the bus stop next to the cathedral on Praça 15 de Novembro.

Bus Long-distance buses link Florianópolis with Porto Alegre (US$20, 6½ hours), Curitiba (US$17, 4½ hours), São Paulo (US$28, 12 hours), Rio (US$42, 18 hours) and Foz do Iguaçu (US$32, 15 hours), as well as to neighboring capitals Buenos Aires (US$88, 24 hours) and Montevideo (US$62, 20 hours). There are frequent buses up and down the coast, as well as inland to Blumenau.

Local buses serve all of the island's beach towns. Additional yellow microbuses leave from the two local bus stations and go directly to the beaches. These microbuses take surfboards; regular buses don't.

Buses for the east and south of the island (including Lagoa and Joaquina) leave from the local bus terminal on Rua Antônio Luz. Buses for the north leave from the local bus terminal on Rua Francisco Tolentino. Look for the green buses on the last platform. Buses, with their destinations clearly marked, include services for Sambaqui, Lagoa da Conceição, Rio Vermelho, Moçambique, Campeche, Barra da Lagoa, Canasvieiras (Jurerê), Armação, Pântano do Sul, Costa de Dentro, and Ingleses (which continues on to Praia do Santinho).

Car To rent a car, Barcellos Rent a Car (☎ 9982-0173, barcellos@linhalivre.net) is about the cheapest in town (around US$40 per day), or call Baía Sul Rent a Car (☎ 225-7666).

ILHA DE SANTA CATARINA
☎ 0xx48

The island's east coast beaches, facing the ocean, are the cleanest and most beautiful, with the biggest waves and greatest expanses of empty sand. They are also the most popular for day trips and, as a result, many do not have hotels. The north coast beaches have calm, bay-like waters (not always particularly clean) and resorts with many apartment-hotels and restaurants. The west coast, facing the mainland, has a Mediterranean feel and small, unspectacular beaches.

East Coast

The following beaches are listed from north to south and prices quoted are for low season. Prices can double between December and February.

Praia dos Ingleses, 34km from Florianópolis, is a nice beach but is quite developed. Most hotels and restaurants here cater to Brazilian, Argentine and Uruguayan tourists. *Pousada Sol & Mar (☎ 269-1271)* on Rua Dom João Backer has the best values for accommodations in town. It's right on the beach, and has singles/doubles for US$16/28.

Praia do Santinho is one of the island's most beautiful beaches and has one excellent pousada. The coast road ends here, which keeps the traffic and crowds down, although there is a new resort at the southern end of the beach and a couple of new barracas along the beach. *Pousada do Santinho (☎ 269-2836, pousadasantinho@ig.com.br)* is highly recommended. Large, comfortable apartamentos (some with views) start at US$24/34 for singles/doubles, with a big breakfast included. There are also chalets available that work out cheaper for bigger groups. The hotel's restaurant serves good seafood meals, and the owner's granddaughter Raia is our vote for the best host in Brazil. The Ingleses bus from Florianópolis stops right at the door. You can rent houses for longer stays (ask at the little yellow hut on the roadside) and learn to surf from the nice people at the Escola de Surf (☎ 983-1586, escolasurfcostasantinho@bol.com.br).

The island's longest beach, **Praia do Moçambique** (also called Praia Grande) is 14km long and undeveloped. A pine forest hides it from the road (Hwy SC-406) that runs a couple of kilometers inland from it. The camping here is good. The closest ac-commodations are at **São João do Rio Vermelho**, close to the lake on Hwy SC-406. There are a couple of pousadas along the main road, including *Pousada Ilha Náutica (☎ 269-7060, ilhanautica@brasilnet.net)*, which offers spacious three-room cabanas with cooking facilities for US$27 a double, or US$46 for four people. Breakfast is included. It's about a 20-minute walk from the beach and the pousada has a pool as well. In a quiet bush setting 400m off Hwy SC-406, *Pousada Ryo Vermelho (☎ 269-1337)* is also an excellent value. It's a comfortable place with a pool and beautifully decorated rooms. Breezy apartamentos with air-con and fridge cost US$35 a double (US$70 in high season).

Barra da Lagoa, a big, curved beach at the end of Praia do Moçambique, is a short bus trip from Florianópolis. It's still home to fisherfolk descended from the original Azorean colonists. Although there are more hotels and restaurants here than anywhere else on the east coast (except Praia dos Ingleses), they aren't modern eyesores. There are plenty of houses for rent. Two blocks from the beach, *Hotel Cabanas (☎ 232-7032, Rua Altomire Barcellos 1504)* is a rustic place with a bar and grill out front and small cabanas out back for US$10 per person. There's a communal kitchen and English and German are spoken. Along the bay, *Pousada 32 (☎ 232-3665, Rua Angelina Joaquim dos Santos 300)* has two-room flats for US$28 a double, and US$7 per person for extra people.

Praia Mole is a beautiful stretch of beach, with a single hotel, the four-star *Praia Mole Resort Hotel (☎ 232-5231, cabanas@iaccess.com.br)*. Singles/doubles start at US$106/130. The beach is very cool in summer with a young crowd – there's plenty of opportunity for people-watching and noshing at the beach barracas.

Praia da Joaquina hosts the Brazilian surfing championship in January and is the busiest beach on the island. The surf pumps, but the beachfront is pretty barren. There are a few restaurants overlooking the beach. You might want to try dune-surfing on the Joaquina dunes – you can hire a

THE SOUTH

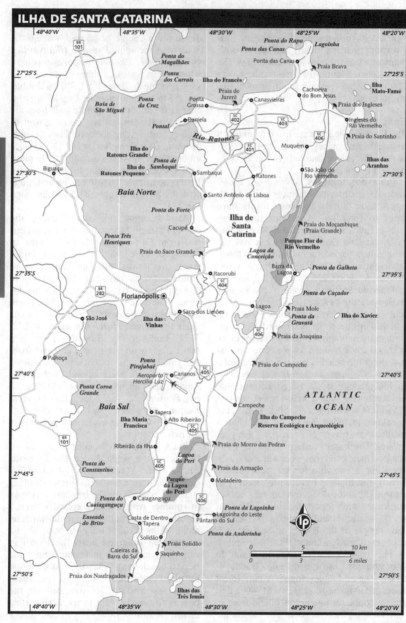

ILHA DE SANTA CATARINA

board there. The *Joaquina Beach Hotel* (☎ 232-5059) has doubles for US$54. About a kilometer back along the approach road, *Pousada Felicidade da Ilha* has basic double apartamentos with cooking facilities for US$20. Close by, the more upmarket *Pousada Bizkaia* (☎ 232-5273) has doubles for US$30.

The three main beaches to the south are more remote, and quite spectacular. **Praia do Campeche** has a few barracas, and the beach is long enough for everyone to find a private patch of sand. A great place to stay is the friendly *Pousada Vila Tamarindo* (☎ 237-3464, tamarindo@fastlane.com.br), about 3km from the main beach along the road heading north to Lagoa da Conceição. The pousada has large gardens with a pool and it's a short walk over sand dunes to the beach. Double apartamentos cost US$40.

Another interesting option is a **boat tour** from Campeche to the Reserva Ecológica e Arqueológica on **Ilha do Campeche**. It's a beautiful, undeveloped island with some ancient inscriptions, and you can snorkel in some pretty lagoons. The tours cost around US$15. Call Scuna Sul (☎ 224-1806) or Scuna Central (☎ 225-9939) for reservations.

Praia da Armação is similarly undeveloped and, as at Campeche, the current is often strong. At the HI youth hostel *Albergue Armação* (☎ 9973-1339, Rua Canoinhas 60), rooms cost US$7 per person, or US$8 with breakfast included. The hostel is open all year. Otherwise, there is camping at the main beach or houses to rent – look for the 'Aluga-se' signs.

Pântano do Sul is a small fishing village with a couple of restaurants. The mountains close in on the sea, which is calm and protected. The *Pousada Sol da Costa* (☎ 237-7116) is a tranquil place on the beach at Costa de Dentro, about 4km past Pântano do Sul. Double apartamentos with cooking facilities start at US$35, and the owner, Valdir, speaks English. To get there, take the Costa de Dentro bus from Florianópolis.

The area is one of the best places on the island for observing birds and other wildlife. There are some great walks along the hilly

trails from either Armação or Pântano do Sul. Around 3km south of Costa de Dentro, **Praia Solidão** has been recommended by readers.

North Coast

The north coast is the most developed coast on the island, and the beaches are narrow; however, the sea here is calm and warm.

Canasvieiras has many (mostly expensive) apartments and vacation homes. During summer it turns into one of the busiest beach towns on the island and attracts a party crowd.

The HI youth hostel *Albergue da Juventude Canasvieiras* (☎ 266-2036, Rua Dr João de Oliveira 100) is open from December to February. There are a few apartmenthotels that are affordable for groups of three or four. *Hotel Residêncial Lacabana* (☎ 266-0400, Avenida das Nações 525) ain't exactly pretty, but it's five minutes from the beach. Two-room apartments with cooking facilities cost US$16/24/30 for singles/doubles/triples. *Canasbeach Hotel* (☎ 266-1227, Avenida Madre Maria Villac 1150), one block from the beach, has double apartamentos for US$35.

A few kilometers west, **Jurerê** is similar, but a bit quieter. Out at **Praia do Forte** are the ruins of the **Fortaleza de São José da Ponta Grossa**, built in 1750.

Lagoa da Conceição

It's not just the beaches: The whole island is beautiful. **Lagoa da Conceição** is the most famous region in the interior, but it gets very busy on weekends. The views of the lagoon, surrounding peaks and sand dunes make for some great walks or boat rides. Boats can be rented right next to the bridge at Lagoa, the main settlement on the shores of the lagoon. A typical price is US$15 for two hours, but the boats can take up to 10 people.

One of the cheaper places to stay in this area is *Hotel Cabanas Ilha da Magia* (☎ 232-5468), right next to the spot where you rent the boats. Cozy (or poky, depending on how claustrophobic you are) cabanas for up to four people cost US$50.

THE SOUTH

SOUTH OF FLORIANÓPOLIS
Garopaba
☎ 0xx48 • postcode 88495-000 • pop 10,700
The first beach town south of Florianópolis, Garopaba is 95km away, including a 15km drive from Hwy BR-101. The beaches are good, it's not too crowded (other than December to February) and you can still see fishing communities at work. Praia do Silveira, 3km away, has good surf, and Siriú (11km) has large dunes for sand-surfing and is close to Laga do Siriú, which is good for swimming.

Regular buses go to Garopaba from Florianópolis (US$5, two hours). Heading south, more regular intercity buses leave from Imbituba on Hwy BR-101.

Places to Stay & Eat For a cheap sleep, there are lots of campgrounds on Praia Garopaba. Or ask around for rooms in houses. One block back from the beach, *Lobo Hotel* (☎ 254-3129, *Rua Marques Guimarães 81*) has clean single/double apartamentos for US$10/15, including breakfast. *Pousada da Praia* (☎ 254-3334, *pousadadapraia@terra.com.br, Avenida dos Pescadores 121*), is pretty bland, but it's family-run and well situated on the beach front. Apartamentos here cost US$26/30.

On the beachfront, *Champagne* (*Avenida dos Pescadores 51*) has a buffet lunch for US$3.50 and basic seafood dishes for dinner from US$5. On the same street, *Embarcação* is a slightly more upmarket seafood restaurant. Try the *camarão a milenesa* (US$10) – it's enough for two people.

Praia da Rosa
☎ 0xx48 • postcode 88780-000 • pop 800
Recently voted the best beach in Brazil by a glossy magazine, Praia da Rosa is the latest hip beach on the Santa Catarina coastline. The beach is beautiful – a sweeping bay with pumping surf framed by thickly forested hills – but its real claim to fame is whale-watching.

The bay is a breeding ground for southern right whales from June to October, when mothers and calves can be seen from the beach. Projeto Baleia Franca, a conservation group created to protect and study these unique mammals, is based here (see the boxed text 'Saving the Whales').

There is no village to speak of at Praia da Rosa, just a few red dirt roads and a handful of upmarket pousadas and restaurants.

Places to Stay & Eat Most of the accommodations are set back about 1km from the main beach on cliffs overlooking the bay. All the pousadas are well sign-posted. For longer stays, look around for houses to rent (with 'Aluga-se' signs).

The cheaper places are surfers' hangouts and can be pretty grungy. *Pousada Uluwatu* (☎ 335-6089) has basic apartamentos for US$16/32. *Pousada Watu Kerere* (☎ 335-6055) and *Pousada Rosa e Canela* both charge US$20/40 and are a bit more comfortable. *Pousada Rosa Sul* (☎ 355-6088) is the only place right on the beachfront. It's a

---

Saving the Whales

In September 2000, President Fernando Henrique Cardoso approved the creation of Brazil's first whale sanctuary, in Santa Catarina. The sanctuary encompasses a 130km stretch of ocean from the southern tip of Ilha da Santa Catarina to Imbituba, just south of Praia da Rosa.

The sanctuary is the result of years of lobbying by the Projeto Baleia Franca to protect the endangered southern right whales who give birth and nurse their young in these waters between June and November every year. Projeto Baleia Franca (☎ 234-0021) is now based at Praia da Rosa.

Whaling stations operated for more than 300 years in Santa Catarina until the last one, in Imbituba, was closed down in 1973 after the local whale population had been all but wiped out.

The Imbituba station is about to be rebuilt and turned into a museum about whale conservation, and the towns of Garopaba, Praia da Rosa and Imbituba are set to experience a boom in whale-watching tourism.

reasonable value with double apartamentos going for US$50.

The well-located *Fazenda Verde (☎ 355-6060, info@fazendaverdedorosa.com.br)* is a small resort overlooking the beach. It has a pool, jacuzzi, bar and horseback riding. Rooms cost US$75 a double.

Shanti is a rarity in Brazil: an Indian restaurant. It's on Estrada Geral do Ouvidor about 1km inland and is one of the cheaper places to eat, but is only open in summer. *Margherita Grill* is a good place for reasonably priced meat, chicken and salad dishes. For the seafood splurge, head to *Pedra da Vigia Bistrô* in the Hotel Regina Guest House.

Getting There & Away There are two buses a day from Florianópolis to Praia da Rosa (US$5, two hours). The bus drops you off on Hwy BR-101 at the turnoff to Praia da Rosa, around 7km from the beach. Local buses run from here into Praia da Rosa about every hour.

Laguna
☎ 0xx48 • postcode 88790-000 • pop 37,200
Laguna has an active fishing industry and is the tourism center for the southern coast of Santa Catarina. This is a historic city situated on the line that, in the 1494 Treaty of Tordesillas, served as the division between the Spanish and the Portuguese Americas. It was settled by Paulistas in the 1670s. Laguna was occupied by the Farrapos soldiers and declared part of the southern republic of Piratiny in 1839 during the Guerra dos Farrapos, which was fought between rebels (chiefly from Rio Grande do Sul) and monarchists.

For your cash needs, Banco do Brasil and Bradesco, both on Rua Cons Jerônimo Coelho, have Visa ATMs.

If it's raining, have a look at **Museu Anita Garibaldi** on Praça República Juliana. It honors the Brazilian wife of the Italian leader and is open from 9 am to noon and 2 to 5:30 pm. Entry is US$1. The **Casa de Anita Garibaldi**, on Praça Vidal Ramos, contains some of her personal possessions and is open the same hours.

The best beaches are out at **Farol de Santa Marta**, 18km south of town on a dirt road plus a 10-minute ferry ride. It's a quiet, isolated place with beautiful dunes. **Mar Grosso**, the city beach, is lined with concrete high-rise hotels and restaurants, but the beach itself is OK.

Places to Stay & Eat Many hotels in Laguna are only open on weekends from March to November. Your best bet in town is the *Hotel Recanto (☎ 644-0902)*, on the waterfront at Rua Engenho Colombo Salles 108. Basic single/double apartamentos cost US$7/14. In Mar Grosso, there's a *youth hostel (☎ 644-0015, Avenida João Pinho 530)*; it's only open during summer. *Laguna Palace Hotel (☎ 647-0548, Avenida Senador Galotti 635)* is a reasonable mid-range option. Double apartamentos go for US$26.

At Farol de Santa Marta, you can camp or ask about rooms to rent in *Pousada Farol de Santa Marta (☎ 9986-1257)*, close to the lighthouse with great views. Singles/doubles cost US$26/46.

Seafood is the order of the day. In Mar Grosso, you can get a cheapish seafood meal on Avenida Senador Galotti at *Arrastão* (No 629) or *Spettus* (No 418).

Getting There & Around Plenty of buses go north to Florianópolis. If you're traveling south to beach towns in Rio Grande do Sul, take a bus to Vila São João (US$5.50, four hours), where you can pick up a connecting bus to Torres.

Buses run to Farol de Santa Marta every day except Sunday from the bus station – or meet it where the *balsa* (ferry) crosses the lagoon en route, about 3km from town. Pick up a timetable from the Zannattur agency at the bus station.

São Joaquim
☎ 0xx49 • postcode 88600-000 • pop 16,100
São Joaquim, 240km southwest of Florianópolis, is Brazil's highest city, at 1355m. Not many foreign travelers come to Brazil for snow, but plenty of Brazilians are fascinated by the idea of snow in their country. The mountains are scenic in winter.

One of the cheaper places to stay in São Joaquim is the **Nevada Hotel** (☎ 233-0259, *Rua Manoel Joaquim Pinto 190*). Single/double quartos cost US$10/20.

There are daily buses from Florianópolis to São Joaquim.

Bom Jardim da Serra

In the middle of the Serra do Rio do Rastro, Bom Jardim da Serra is a hair-raising but beautiful 45km drive from São Joaquim. **Parque Nacional de São Joaquim**, known for its araucaria forests, is a few kilometers north of the town. It's undeveloped, so if you want to explore, contact the park administration (☎ 0xx49-278-4002) on Rua Felicíssimo Rodrigues Sobrinho in the town of Urubici, 56km from São Joaquim, or IBAMA (☎ 0xx48-222-8299) at Rua Felipe Schmidt 485 in Florianópolis.

Rio Grande do Sul

Rio Grande do Sul, Brazil's southernmost state, shares borders with Uruguay to the south and Argentina to the west. The vast *pampas* (plains) of the southern province attracted Portuguese *gaúchos* (cowboys), who explored the territory from the early 18th century. Resisting central authority over their lands, they fought a civil war with the Brazilian army, declaring Rio Grande do Sul a republic (the Republic of Piratiny) during the Guerra dos Farrapos against Brazilian imperial forces from 1835 to 1845.

The wave of German, Italian, Swiss and Eastern European immigrants that arrived in the latter half of the 19th century added to the cultural makeup of the region. The result is an independent and liberal-minded people who are proud of their differences from other Brazilians. Periodically, the populace still half-seriously entertains the idea of separatism.

The state has strong trade unions and the Partido dos Trabalhadores (PT; Workers' Party) has been in office for more than 12 years. Porto Alegrenses proudly claim their city as the most livable in Brazil. In February 2001 it hosted the first World Social Forum, a forum opposing globalization, held at the same time as the World Economic Forum in Switzerland.

When visiting, don't forget that Rio Grande do Sul has distinct seasonal weather changes: It gets very hot in summer (30° to 40°C), and you'll need a good jacket in winter.

PORTO ALEGRE

☎ 0xx51 • postcode 90000-000
• pop 1.32 million

Porto Alegre, Brazil's seventh-largest city, lies on the eastern bank of the Rio Guaíba at the point where its waters empty into the huge Lagoa dos Patos. This lively modern city makes a living from its freshwater port and commerce. Porto Alegre was settled in 1742 by immigrants from the Portuguese Azores to keep the Spanish out. The city was never a center of colonial Brazil; it's mainly a product of 20th-century German and Italian immigration.

Although many travelers just pass right through Porto Alegre, it's an easy place in which to spend a few days. There are some interesting museums and impressive neoclassical buildings, as well as some good

Highlights

- The sound and light show at the ruins of São Miguel das Missões
- Awe-inspiring Cânion do Itaimbezinho in the Parque Nacional de Aparados da Serra
- Friendly gaúcho hospitality and know-how
- Hiking in the Serra Gaúcha
- Chairlift ride to Cascata do Caracol in the Parque Estadual do Caracol
- The region's primeval araucaria tree

Tropic of Capricorn

Paraná

Santa Catarina

ARGENTINA

Canela page 392
Gramado page 390
Porto Alegre page 388

URUGUAY

Rio Grande do Sul page 386

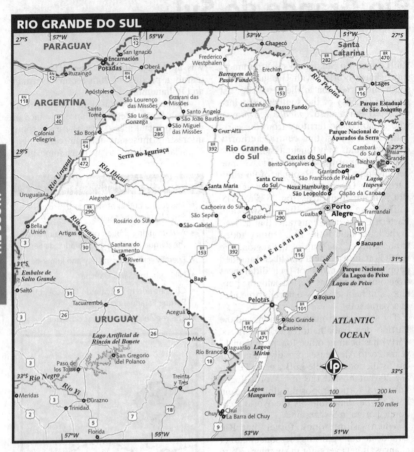

RIO GRANDE DO SUL

restaurants and nightlife, and the friendly gaúcho hospitality. City beaches are too polluted for swimming, but the once-popular Ipanema beach has some good bars and cafés.

Information

Tourist Offices Porto Alegre Turismo (☎ 214-1734, turismo@smic.prefpoa.com.br) offers extensive tourist information services; the handiest offices are at the long-distance bus station (☎ 225-0677), open daily from 8 am to 9 pm; the Mercado Público on Praça 15 de Novembro, open daily from 9 am to 6 pm; and at the airport (☎ 371-4441), open daily from 9 am to 11 pm. Staffers can provide good maps, entertainment and cultural guides, and advice on trips to national parks.

Porto Alegre Turismo organizes free walking tours of the city's historical areas on Saturday and Sunday. The tours leave from the tourist information desk at the Mercado Público at 3 pm and last for about two hours. For reservations, call ☎ 311-5289.

Money There are lots of money-exchange houses in Porto Alegre. Try Prontur in the center at Avenida Borges de Medeiros 445, or Victoria Câmbio at the long-distance bus station. The Banco do Brasil at Avenida Uruguai 195 exchanges money and has Visa ATMs.

Post & Communications The post office is at Rua Siqueira Campos 1100. For international collect and card calls, the telephone office can be found on the corner of Rua Gen Andrade Neves and Avenida Borges de Madeiros.

Espaço@ is a good Internet café at Rua Praça 15 de Novembro 16, in the Edifício Phenix. It's on the 12th floor and has a bar. Otherwise, check out .com Cyber Café at Rua dos Andradas 1001.

Internet Resources The state government tourism department, Setur, has an excellent Web site with information (in Portuguese) about attractions throughout Rio Grande do Sul. It's at www.turismo.rs.gov.br.

Bookstores Livraria do Globo at Rua dos Andradas 426 was established in 1883 and is a great place to browse. English-language books, including Lonely Planet guidebooks, are available.

Things to See & Do

The interesting **Museu Histórico Júlio de Castilhos**, near the cathedral at Rua Duque de Caixas 1231, contains diverse objects concerning the history of the state, such as special moustache cups, a pair of giant's shoes and a very intricate wooden chair. It's open from 10 am to 7 pm Tuesday to Friday, and from 2 to 6 pm on weekends. Entry costs US$1.50.

In the Praça da Alfândega, the **Museu de Arte do Rio Grande do Sul** has a good collection of works by gaúcho artists. It is open from 10 am to 7 pm Tuesday to Sunday.

The **Mercado Público** (public market), constructed in 1869, and the adjacent Praça 15 de Novembro are the heart of the city center. The market houses cafés, produce stalls and shops selling the unique tea-drinking equipment of the gaúchos, the *cuia* (gourd) and *bomba* (silver straw).

Parque Farroupilha, the big central park (also known as Parque da Redenção), can be a good place to see gaúchos at play. On Sunday morning, the Brique da Redenção (a market/fair) fills up a corner of the park with a craft market, food stalls and music.

If you're really interested in gaúcho traditions, check out the Museu de Tradições Gaúchas (☎ 223-5194) at Rua Guilherme Schell 60 in the suburb of Santo Antônio. It doesn't have regular opening hours, but the tourist office can call ahead to organize a time for you to visit.

The Centro de Tradições Gaúchas (CTG) (☎ 336-0035) is a gaúcho cultural center at Rua Ipiranga 5200 in the suburb of Santa Cecília. It has a *churrascaria* (a restaurant featuring barbecued meat) attached.

River Cruises

Cisne Branco (☎ 224-5222) runs tourist cruises on the river, passing many of the uninhabited islands in the river delta. Trips range from 'happy hour' cruises (US$7) to three-hour dinner cruises (US$18). The boat leaves from the waterfront at the end of Rua Caldas Júnior, in the city center. Timetables change frequently so ask for a schedule at the tourist office.

Places to Stay

Budget The *Hotel Ritz* (☎ 225-3423, Avenida André da Rocha 225) is Porto Alegre's non-HI youth hostel. English and Spanish are spoken.

The *Hotel Uruguai* (☎ 228-7864, Rua Dr Flores 371) is secure and cheap. Small single/double quartos cost US$8/14, and apartamentos go for US$14/20. Breakfast is not included. Nearby, the friendly *Hotel Palácio* (☎ 225-3467, Avenida Vigarió José Inácio 644) is popular with travelers. Large quartos cost US$14/20 a single/double, and apartamentos go for US$18/24.

Over on Rua Gen Andrade Neves there are a few hotels (and some good bars and places to eat). At No 123, the *Hotel Marechal* (☎ 228-3076) is a bit tough on the nose, but the manager is friendly. Single/double/triple quartos cost US$7/12/16 (without breakfast).

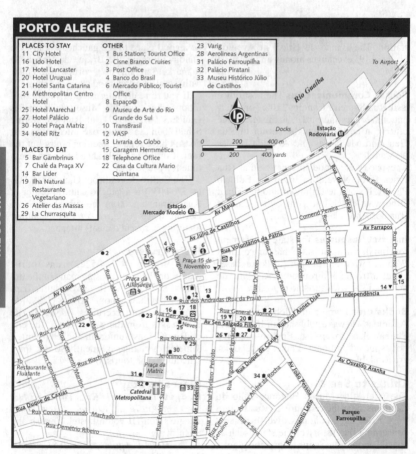

PORTO ALEGRE

PLACES TO STAY
11 City Hotel
16 Lido Hotel
17 Hotel Lancaster
20 Hotel Uruguai
21 Hotel Santa Catarina
24 Methropolitan Centro
     Hotel
25 Hotel Marechal
27 Hotel Palácio
30 Hotel Praça Matriz
34 Hotel Ritz

PLACES TO EAT
5   Bar Gambrinus
7   Chalé da Praça XV
14 Bar Lider
19 Ilha Natural
     Restaurante
     Vegetariano
26 Atelier das Massas
29 La Churrasquita

OTHER
1   Bus Station; Tourist Office
2   Cisne Branco Cruises
3   Post Office
4   Banco do Brasil
6   Mercado Público; Tourist
     Office
8   Espaço@
9   Museu de Arte do Rio
     Grande do Sul
10 TransBrasil
12 VASP
13 Livraria do Globo
15 Garagem Hermmética
18 Telephone Office
22 Casa da Cultura Mario
     Quintana

23 Varig
28 Aerolineas Argentinas
31 Palácio Farroupilha
32 Palácio Piratani
33 Museu Histórico Júlio
     de Castilhos

An interesting place to stay that is also a good value is the **Hotel Praça Matriz** (☎ 225-5772, Largo João Amorim de Albequerque 72), an ornate old building on Praça da Matriz. Comfortable single/double apartamentos with television and fridge cost US$17/27.

Mid-Range & Top End There are two good mid-range options on Rua Gen Andrade Neves. The **Methropolitan Centro Hotel** (☎ 212-7599, Rua Gen Andrade Neves 59), has bright but smallish apartamentos

for US$27/40. The two-star **Hotel Lancaster** (☎ 224-4737, Travessa Eng Acelino de Cavalho 67) has single/double apartamentos for US$30/37. **Hotel Santa Catarina** (☎ 224-9044, Rua General Vitorino 240) has standard apartamentos for US$24/34.

The **City Hotel** (☎ 224-2988, cityhotel@ emrede.com.br, Rua Dr José Montaury 20) is a grand place with rooms starting at US$54/64. The **Lido Hotel** (☎ 226-8233, Rua Gen Andrade Neves 150) is another elegant top-end alternative. Singles/doubles cost US$58/70.

Places to Eat

The city is filled with churrascarias and the steaks here are very tender, so it's a good place to get your iron level up. On the flip side, there's enough natural food around to keep vegetarians happy.

La Churrasquita (Rua Riachuelo 1331) is a vegetarian's nightmare, with more meat than you can poke a barbecue fork at. A plate-sized filet for two costs around US$12. *Bar Lider (Avenida Independência 408)* is a casual bar/restaurant serving delicious *filé* for US$10 (enough for two). *Bar do Beto (Rua Venâncio Aires 876)*, in Cidade Baixa near the southern corner of Parque Farroupilha, is a buzzy place for juicy steaks and salads.

Another classic chopp and churrasco restaurant that is always busy is *Barranco (Avenida Potásio Alves 1578)* in the suburb of Petrópolis. Try the house specialty *lombo ao queijo* (spicy loin sausage filled with cheese; US$9) with a side salad – it's a delicious meal.

The Mercado Público has a central food hall and a bunch of cafés on its perimeter for lunch; *Bar Gambrinus* is a rustic little place that's been around for 130 years. It's famous for its tainha fish filled with shrimp. *Ilha Natural Restaurante Vegetariano (Rua General Vitorino 35)* also packs the locals in for a vegetarian buffet lunch.

Atelier das Massas (Rua Riachuelo 1482) is an ambient Italian restaurant with original art on the walls and good pasta dishes from US$14 (enough for two). For vegetarian food with an Indian flavor, try *Ocidente*, on the corner of Avenida Osvaldo Aranha and Rua General João Telles, near the northeastern corner of Parque Farroupilha.

One real Alegre tradition is to have a late afternoon chopp at the *Chalé da Praça XV* on Praça 15 de Novembro, in front of the market. Constructed in 1885, it's a landmark bar/restaurant and a great place to people-watch.

Locals rave about the sunsets and seafood snacks at *Restaurante Flutuante*, on the waterfront at the end of Rua Riachuelo, behind the impressive building housing the Espaço Cultural do Trabalho Usina do Gasômetro (a cultural center).

Entertainment

From the tourist office, newsstand or large hotel, pick up a copy of *Programa*, a monthly guide to what's happening in the city and state.

Casa da Cultura Mario Quintana (Rua dos Andradas 736) is the place to go for local theater and art movies. On the 7th floor, Café Concerto Majestic has an outdoor terrace where you can have a drink and watch the sunset over Lago Guaíba. There's free live music between 7 and 9 pm – a US$2 cover charge applies after 9 pm.

Bars and clubs are concentrated around two streets – Avenida Goethe and Rua Fernando Gomes. Some good bars are the perennially popular *Dado Bier (Avenida Nilo Peçanha 3228)*, *Cult Bar (Rua Lima e Silva 806)* with live acoustic music and *Ossip (Rua da República 677)*. *Bar do Goethe (Rua 24 de Outobro 112)*, in Moinhas de Vento, holds an international student cultural exchange night on Tuesday.

For live music, head to *Dr Jekyll (Travessa do Carmo 76)* for pop-rock, or *Opinão (Rua José do Patricínio 834)* in Cidade Baixo and *Garagem Hermmética* on Rua Dr Barros Cassal near Bar Lider for indie music.

Liquid (Rua João Telles 54) is a big dance club and for techno and an eclectic crew, check out *Fim de Século Club (Rua Plínio Brasil Milano 427)*.

Shopping

Apart from the Mercado Público, a good place to hunt for gaúcho crafts and souvenirs is Cooparigs, a local artisans' cooperative at Rua 24 de Outobro 1385.

Getting There & Away

Air There are direct flights from Porto Alegre to São Paulo (with connections to Rio), Brasília, Salvador, Curitiba and Florianópolis. Both Aerolineas Argentinas and Varig fly from Porto Alegre to Montevideo and Buenos Aires.

Bus The busy long-distance bus station on Largo Vespasiano Julio Veppo is open 24 hours a day. It has one terminal for international and interstate buses and another for intercity buses within Rio Grande do Sul. International buses run to Montevideo (US$58, 12 hours), Buenos Aires (US$64, 20 hours) and Santiago (US$116, 36 hours). Other long-distance buses service Foz do Iguaçu (US$41, 15 hours), Florianópolis (US$17, seven hours), Curitiba (US$30, 11 hours) and Rio de Janeiro (US$70, 24 hours).

Regular buses run to Torres (US$10, three hours) and Gramado (US$7.50, two hours). For access to the Parque Nacional de Aparados da Serra, there's a daily bus to Cambará do Sul (US$8, 5½ hours) at 6:15 am. There are frequent buses to Pelotas and Rio Grande. To Santo Angelo (for São Miguel das Missões; US$28, six hours) there are six buses a day.

Getting Around
Porto Alegre has a very clean and efficient one-line metro with 15 stations. The most useful ones for visitors are Estação Mercado Modelo (the central station by the port), Estação Rodoviária (the next stop, for the bus station) and the airport (three stops farther on). A ride costs US$0.40.

SERRA GAÚCHA
As you travel north of Porto Alegre, you quickly begin to climb into the Serra Gaúcha. The bus ride is beautiful, as are the mountain towns of Gramado and Canela. Settled first by Germans (in 1824) and later by Italians (in the 1870s), the region is as close to the Alps as Brazil gets. It's known as the Região das Hortênsias (Hydrangea Region). Both Gramado and Canela are popular resorts and are often crowded with Porto Alegrenses, particularly when it's hot in the big city. There are plenty of hotels and restaurants, especially in Gramado, and many have a German influence. The accommodations in Canela are less expensive than Gramado's.

Hikers abound in the mountains here. In winter there are occasional snowfalls and in

spring the hills are blanketed with flowers. The best spot is the Parque Estadual do Caracol, reached by local bus from Canela.

Gramado
☎ 0xx54 • postcode 95670-000 • pop 23,300
This popular mountain resort promotes itself as 'naturally European' and is a favorite with well-to-do Argentines, Uruguayans, Paulistas and gaúchos. It has lots of cozy restaurants, manicured gardens and expensive Swiss-style chalet/hotels.

Gramado hosts the Festival de Gramado Cinema Brasileiro e Latino during the first two weeks of August. It's the most prestigious film festival in Brazil and attracts the international jet set.

Information There's a useful Centro de Informações in the center of town on Praça Major Nicoletti. It's open daily from 9 am to 7 pm. The Banco do Brasil on Rua Garibaldi exchanges money and has Visa ATMs. The telephone office in the mall between Avenida Borges de Medeiros and Rua Garibaldi offers Internet access, but it might be the most expensive email you

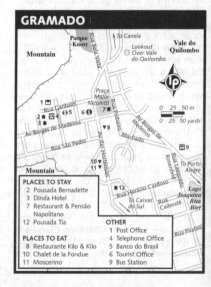

GRAMADO

PLACES TO STAY
2 Pousada Bernadette
3 Dinda Hotel
7 Restaurant & Pensão Napolitano
12 Pousada Tia

PLACES TO EAT
8 Restaurante Kilo & Kilo
10 Chalet de la Fondue
11 Moscerino

OTHER
1 Post Office
4 Telephone Office
5 Banco do Brasil
6 Tourist Office
9 Bus Station

ever read. Access costs US$0.20 per minute, or US$12 per hour.

Parks Well-kept parks close to the town center include the Lago Negro, at Rua 25 de Julho 175 to the southeast, and the Parque Knorr, at the end of Rua Bela Vista. The Lago Negro park has a small lake, while the Parque Knorr has good views of the spectacular Vale do Quilombo.

Places to Stay & Eat There are no cheap accommodations in Gramado. *Pousada Tia* (☎ 286-1146, Avenida das Hortênsias 1020) is a simple, friendly place. Clean rooms cost US$20 per person. The *Dinda Hotel* (☎ 286-2810, Rua Augusto Zatti 160) has single/double/triple apartamentos for US$28/46/60. *Pousada Bernardette* (☎ 286-1569, Rua Augusto Zatti 200) is a bed-and-brekky with double apartamentos for US$46. On the main drag, the *Restaurante & Pensão Napolitano* (☎ 286-1847, Avenida Borges de Medeiros 2512) is a cheaper option – basic singles/doubles go for US$17/34.

There's no shortage of top-end places. The best ones are out on the road between Gramado and Canela. The *Villa Bella Gramado* (☎ 286-2688, Rua Villa Bella 125) has an attractive park setting, a pool and kids' playground. Rooms cost US$60/90.

Gramado has lots of German, Italian and cheesy (sorry) fondue restaurants. *Moscerino* (Avenida das Hortênsias 1095) has excellent pasta for about US$15 for two, or head to *Tio Muller* (Avenida Borges de Medeiros 4029) for a relatively inexpensive rodízio of German food.

Fondue lovers should wear bellbottoms to the cutesy *Chalet de la Fondue* (Avenida das Hortênsias 1297). For a straight-up per-kilo feed, *Restaurante Kilo & Kilo* on Avenida das Hortênsias is the serious place to fill up.

Getting There & Around The bus station is a short walk east of the center. There are frequent buses to Porto Alegre (US$7.50, two hours). Frequent local buses make the 15-minute trip to Canela – pick them up at the bus station.

Canela
☎ 0xx54 • postcode 95680-000 • pop 31,000
Canela is the best jumping-off point for some great hikes and bicycle rides in the area. There are cheaper hotels here than in Gramado, so budget travelers should make this their base.

Information The tourist office (☎ 282-2200, centraldeinformacoes@canela.com.br) is right in the center of town at Lago da Fama 227. It has maps and a list of recommended agencies for half-day tours of the main attractions (US$30 per person), and for rafting trips and mountain-bike adventures. For more information, see the town's comprehensive Web site www.canela.com.br.

Parks The major attraction of the **Parque Estadual do Caracol**, 9km from Canela, is the spectacular Cascata do Caracol, a 130m free-falling waterfall. It's incredibly beautiful in the morning sun – the water sparkles as it cascades down. If you're feeling fit, you can walk to the base of the waterfall down (and back up) 927 stairs. Along the road to the park, 2km from the center of Canela, is the Pinheiro Grosso, a 700-year-old 42m-tall araucaria pine.

The park is open daily from 8:30 am to 5:30 pm. Entry is US$2.50. The Linha Turística bus runs to the park from the outside the tourist office every two hours from 9:30 am to 5:30 pm (except Monday).

In the **Parque Floresta Encantada de Canela**, which is a 45-minute hike or short bus ride from Parque do Caracol, is a gorgeous chairlift ride along a canyon that provides a front view of the Cascata do Caracol. Entry to the park (including the chairlift ride) is US$4. The Linha Turístico bus runs to the park.

A 6km hike along Estrada Ferradura from the Parque do Caracol entrance brings you to the **Parque da Ferradura**, a stunning 420m horseshoe-shaped canyon formed by the Rio Santa Cruz. There are three lookouts that you can hike to along well-marked trails – the longest takes around two hours. The park (☎ 282-2299) is open daily from 9 am to 5:30 pm. Entry is US$2.50.

THE SOUTH

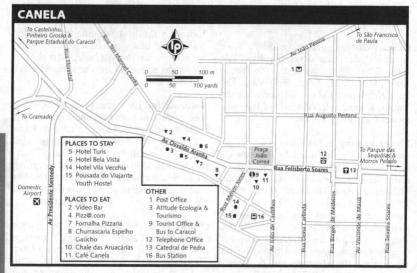

CANELA

PLACES TO STAY
5 Hotel Turis
6 Hotel Bela Vista
14 Hotel Vila Vecchia
15 Pousada do Viajante
    Youth Hostel

PLACES TO EAT
2 Video Bar
4 Pizz@.com
7 Fornalha Pizzaria
8 Churrascaria Espelho
    Gaúcho
10 Chale das Aruacárias
11 Café Canela

OTHER
1 Post Office
3 Atltude Ecologia &
    Tourismo
9 Tourist Office &
    Bus to Caracol
12 Telephone Office
13 Catedral de Pedra
16 Bus Station

One of the oldest houses in the area, **Castelinho**, is on the road to the park. Now a pioneer museum containing a German restaurant and a chocolate shop, Castelinho was built without using metal nails.

Just 2.5km from town, the **Parque das Sequóias** was created in the 1940s by Curt Menz, a botanist who cultivated more than 70 different tree species with seeds from around the world. The plantation occupies 10 hectares, and the rest of the park (25 hectares) is native forest. Entry is US$1.50. To get there, walk behind the Catedral da Pedra in town and follow the signs or take the Linha Turística bus. It's open 10 am to 5 pm daily.

Morros Pelado, Queimado & Dedão
These hills provide stunning views of the Vale do Quilombo, and on clear days you can see the coast. They're 5, 5.5 and 6.5km from Canela respectively and can be hiked to via the road to Parque das Sequóias. The Linha Turística bus can drop you at the base of the each of the Morros.

Activities Adventure tourism is the latest thing in Canela, but it's fairly gentle adventure on the whole. There are opportunities for rock climbing, rappelling (abseiling), rafting, mountain biking and bungee jumping in the Ferradura, Sequóias and Corredeiras parks. A 2½-hour rafting trip along the Rio Paranhana costs around US$30 and rappelling and rock climbing at Ferradura costs around US$20, including transport and equipment.

A couple of agencies in town specialize in adventure tourism. At!tude (☎ 282-6305, atitude@serragaucha.com.br) is at Avenida Osvaldo Aranha 391, Shop 16, and JM Rafting (☎ 282-1542, jmrafting@via-rs.net) is at No 1038, Shop 4 on the same street.

Special Events In the last week of May, some 80,000 pilgrims arrive in town to celebrate the **Festa de NS de Caravaggio**. A highlight of the festival is a 6km procession from the Igreja Matriz to the Parque do Saiqui. In mid-October, Canela hosts an international **theater festival**.

Both Canela and Gramado go Christmas crazy. The towns compete to see which can create the most extravagant Christmas decorations. Canela's **Sonho de Natal festival** starts in the middle of November!

Places to Stay Camping is available at *Camping Sesi* (☎ 282-1311, Rua Francisco Bertolucci 504), 2.5km from town. The HI youth hostel, *Pousada do Viajante* (☎ 282-2017, Rua Ernesto Urban 132), is next to the bus station and charges US$10 per person.

The central *Hotel Turis* (☎ 282-2774, Avenida Osvaldo Aranha 223) has had a facelift and offers basic quartos for US$14 per person. The *Hotel Bela Vista* (☎ 282-1327, Rua Osvaldo Aranha 160) has a few quartos for US$10 per person or apartamentos for US$32/40. The *Vila Vecchia* (☎ 282-1051, Rua Melvin Jones 137) has comfortable apartamentos with TV and fridge for US$40 a double.

The *Pousada das Sequóias* (☎ 282-1373) in the park of the same name is 2km from the center. It has cute chalets in picturesque surroundings for US$34/40 a single/double.

The best top-end place to stay is the *Laje de Pedra* (☎ 282-4300), 3km from the center on Avenida Presidente Kennedy. It has great views of the Vale do Quilombo. Rooms start at US$80/140.

Places to Eat It's not quite a one-street town, but all the restaurants are around the main drag, Avenida Osvaldo Aranha. Big meat-eaters will enjoy the barn-sized *Churrascaria Espelho Gaúcho*, just off Avenida Osvaldo Aranha, where you can chow down on juicy steak (US$14 for two).

Fornalha Pizzaria is a flexible joint – it has a per-kilo lunch or 32 different pizzas for dinner. It's hard to get away from pizza anywhere in Canela – *pizz@.com* has a cheap pizza rodízio as well. *Chalé das Aruacárias*, near the tourist office, has a US$2.50 buffet lunch in a pretty garden setting. For music and snacks at night, check out *Video Bar* or *Café Canela*, both on Avenida Osvaldo Aranha.

Getting There & Around There are frequent buses from Canela to Porto Alegre via Gramado. There are also buses to São Francisco de Paula (US$1.50, one hour), where you can connect to Cambará do Sul for access to the Parque Nacional de Aparados da Serra.

The Linha Turística buses make it easy (and cheap) to get to most of the nearby attractions. Pick up a full schedule from the tourist office.

PARQUE NACIONAL DE APARADOS DA SERRA

One of Brazil's natural wonders, this magnificent national park has portions in two states: The majority is in Rio Grande do Sul, while a small part lies in Santa Catarina. The park is 70km north of São Francisco de Paula and 18km from the town of Cambará do Sul, which serves as the base for visitors.

The park preserves one of the country's last araucaria forests, but the main attraction is the **Cânion do Itaimbezinho**, a narrow canyon with sheer 600 to 720m parallel escarpments. Two waterfalls drop into this incision in the earth, which was formed by the Rio Perdiz's rush to the sea.

There are three hiking trails through the park. **Trilha do Vértice** runs for 2km to an observation point for the canyon and the Cascata do Andorinhas. **Trilha Cotovelo** is a 3km trail (2½-hours round-trip) passing by the Véu de Noiva waterfall with wonderful vistas of the canyon. **Trilha do Rio do Boi** is best approached from the town of Praia Grande in Santa Catarina. From the Posto Rio do Boi entrance to the park, the trail follows the base of the canyon for 7km, much of it over loose rocks. It's for experienced hikers and a guide is highly recommended. During rainy season the trail is closed because of the danger of flooding.

Parque Nacional da Serra Geral was created in 1992 as an extension of the northern and southern borders of the Parque Nacional de Aparados da Serra. The larger northern section contains this second park's most stunning attraction – **Cânion da Fortaleza**, an 8km stretch of escarpment with 900m drops. On clear days you can see the coast from here. Nearby, on one side of the canyon, is the **Pedra do Segredo**, a 5m monolith with a very small base.

Cânion da Fortaleza and the Pedra do Segredo are 23km from Cambará, but unfortunately in a different direction from Cânion do Itaimbezinho.

Information

Parque Nacional de Aparados da Serra is open from 9 am to 4 pm Wednesday to Sunday. Entry is US$4. The new visitor's center (☎ 0xx54-251-1262) has maps, guides for hire (US$2 per person for the Trilha Cotovelo) and a café for lunch. Guides can also be hired through Acontur, the local guide association in Cambará do Sul (☎ 0xx54-251-1265) and Praia Grande (☎ 0xx48-532-0330).

There is no infrastructure in Parque Nacional da Serra Geral. Entry is free and camping is allowed, but there are no facilities. Contact Acontur (see above) to hire a guide.

Places to Stay

Cambará do Sul has small pousadas and many families rent rooms in their houses. Close to the bus station on Rua Dona Ursula, **Pousada Itaimbeleza** *(☎ 0xx54-251-1367)* is the best setup for travelers. Rooms cost US$10 per person. **Hotel e Churrascaria Sabrina** *(☎ 0xx54-251-1147)*, on Avenida Getúlio Vargas, charges the same prices. Two kilometers from town on the road to Ouro Verde, **Pousada Corucacas** *(☎ 0xx54-251-1128)* is a working farm, with horseback riding and fishing. Rooms cost US$16/32 with breakfast and dinner included. Reservations are necessary.

Inside the Parque Nacional da Serra Geral, there are good spots to camp near the old Paradouro Hotel and near the Cânion da Fortaleza.

Getting There & Around

There's one daily bus from Porto Alegre to Cambará do Sul (US$8, five hours) at 6:15 am via São Francisco de Paula. Buy your tickets the night before. If you're coming from the north, there's a daily bus from Torres on the north coast of Rio Grande do Sul to Cambará do Sul at 4 pm. The trip takes around three hours on a spectacular road from the coast. There are also buses from Torres to Praia Grande (in Santa Catarina state) for access to the park's Trilha do Rio do Boi.

No public buses go to the parks. The dirt roads are rough and driving is very slow. Sr Rezende at Pousada Itaimbeleza (in Cambará do Sul) can organize a mini-van to either park (US$30 for up to six people), or contact the town's two taxi drivers, Sr Borges and Sr Nureu, at the bus station. A taxi costs around US$22 for up to four people; the driver will wait and drive you back to town.

LITORAL GAÚCHO

The Litoral Gaúcho is a 500km strip along the state of Rio Grande do Sul – from Torres, on the border with Santa Catarina, to Barra do Chuí at the Uruguayan border. Of all Brazil's coastline, this stretch is the least distinguished. The beaches are really one long beach uninterrupted by geographical variations – wide open, with little vegetation and occasional dunes. The sea here is choppier and the water less translucent than in Santa Catarina.

In winter, currents from the Antarctic bring cold, hard winds to the coast. Bathing suits disappear, as do most people. Most hotels shut down in March, and the summer beach season doesn't return until November, with the arrival of the northern winds.

The resort towns on the northern part of the litoral fill up in summer with Porto Alegrenses, Uruguayans and Argentines: This is not a place to get away from it all.

Torres

☎ 0xx51 • postcode 95560-000 • pop 27,500

Torres, 205km from Porto Alegre, is the exception to the state's uninviting coastline. The town is well known for its fine beaches and the beautiful basalt-rock formations along the coast. This is good country in which to walk and explore, and is especially worthwhile if you can get here early or late in the season, when the crowds have thinned out.

Information There's a good tourist office (☎ 664-1219) on the corner of Avenida Barão do Rio Branco and Rua General Osório. It publishes a list of hotels, including the cheapest ones, and a good city map.

There are a few money-exchange offices in town and for Visa withdrawals, Banco do

Brasil is standing by at Avenida Barão do Rio Branco 236.

Boat Trips Boats to the ecological reserve on Ilha dos Lobos leave from Ponte Pênsil on the Rio Mampituba. To get to the jetty, walk to the end of Rua Benjamin Constant and turn left. The trip lasts about 45 minutes and costs US$5 per person.

Places to Stay & Eat Torres has plenty of campgrounds and a surprising number of reasonably priced hotels. If you're staying here in the low season, make sure you get a discount.

The HI *Albergue da Juventude São Domingos* (☎ 664-1865, Rua Júlio de Castilhos 875) functions during summer. Bookings are necessary. The cheapest hotel in Torres is the *Hotel Medusa* (☎ 664-2378, Rua Benjamin Constant 828). Small but clean singles/doubles cost US$10/14. *Hotel Costa Azul* (☎ 664-3291, Avenida José Bonifácio 382) is a friendly family-run place one block from the bus station. Comfortable apartamentos go for US$14/20 with breakfast included. Close to the beach, *Pousada Brisa do Mar* (☎ 664-2019, Rua Borges de Medeiros 51) is a good mid-range option. Well-appointed apartamentos cost US$25/46.

For seafood, *Mariskão* (Avenida Beira Mar 145) is recommended. For churrasco, *Bom Gosto* (Avenida Barão do Rio Branco 242) is an excellent place to eat.

Getting There & Away There are hourly buses to Porto Alegre (US$10, three hours) and one daily bus to Cambará do Sul, which goes at 4 pm.

Pelotas
☎ 0xx53 • postcode 96000-000
• pop 301,000
Pelotas was a major port in the 19th century for the export of dried beef, and home to a sizable British community. The wealth generated is still reflected in some grand neoclassical mansions around the main square, Praça General Osório. Today the town is an important industrial center,

and many of its canned vegetables, fruits and sweets are exported.

There's really no reason to stay in Pelotas, but if you're waiting for a bus connection and have time to spare, it's worth checking out.

Places to Stay & Eat The *Palace Hotel* (☎ 222-2223, Rua 7 de Setembro 354) is the best value in town. It's a bright place with quartos for US$10/15 a single/double, and apartamentos for US$14/21. There's a good *churrascaria* in the hotel as well.

Getting There & Away Pelotas is a transport hub for the area. There are regular buses to Uruguay and buses to Porto Alegre and Rio Grande every half-hour.

Rio Grande
☎ 0xx53 • postcode 96200-000
• pop 179,000
This interesting but little visited port city is a relaxing place to break your journey in this area. Once an important cattle center, Rio Grande is the oldest town in the state. It lies near the mouth of the Lagoa dos Patos, Brazil's biggest lagoon.

To the north, the coast along the lagoon is sparsely inhabited. There's a dirt road along this stretch, which is connected to Rio Grande by a small ferry. Estação Ecológica do Taim is a protected area for 230 species of migratory birds, 80km south of Rio Grande. It's not open to the public.

Information For Visa withdrawals, Bradesco is at Rua Floriano Peixoto 196. International telephone calls can be made from the phone booths on Praça Dr Pio, next to the post office.

Catedral de São Pedro The oldest church in the state, this cathedral was erected by the Portuguese colonists. Baroque in style, it's classified as part of the Patrimônio Histórico (National Heritage registry). It's on Praça Dr Pio, in the center. Homesick Australians might want to sniff around the massive *Eucalyptus globulus* tree in the middle of the square, which was planted in 1877.

THE SOUTH

Museums The **Museu Oceanográfico** (☎ 232-9107), 2km from the center on Rua Capitão Heitor Perdigão, is one of the most complete of its type in Latin America. It has a large shell collection, and skeletons of whales and dolphins. It's open daily from 9 to 11 am and 1:30 to 5:30 pm.

The **Museu da Cidade** is in the old customs house that Dom Pedro II ordered built on Rua Richuelo along the waterfront. It's open on weekdays only from 9 to 11:30 am and 2 to 5 pm.

Boat Trips Boats leave the terminal on the waterfront every 30 minutes for the trip across the Lagoa dos Patos to the fishing village of São José do Norte. This is a nice trip to do around sunset. The roundtrip costs US$2.

Places to Stay & Eat There are a few cheap hotels in Rio Grande, but the one to head for is the *Paris Hotel* (☎ 231-3866, Rua Marechal Floriano 112). The 19th-century building has seen better days, but its court-yard is an excellent place in which to sit and contemplate the glory days of the city. Single/double quartos cost US$9/14, and apartamentos US$12/17.

Moving up in price, the *Hotel Europa* (☎ 231-3933, Rua General Netto 165) opposite Praça Tamandaré costs US$35/40. Ask for a discount. The top hotel in town is the *Atlântico Rio Grande* (☎ 231-3833, Rua Duque de Caixas 53), opposite Praça Xavier Ferreira. Singles/doubles cost US$38/76.

Restaurante Marco's (Avenida Silva Paes 400) has lots of seafood and meat dishes for US$12 to US$15 for two people. For lunch, *Armazem Macrobiotica* (Rua General Bacelar 218) has a vegetarian buffet, or you can get a per-kilo lunch at *Buffet D'Italia* (Rua Marechal Floriano Peixoto 385), opposite Praça Xavier Ferreira. For coffee and a sandwich or a late-afternoon beer, *Plaza Café* is on Rua General Netto, opposite Praça Dr Pio.

Getting There & Away Buses connect Rio Grande with all major cities in southern Brazil, but they run more regularly from

Pelotas. There are two buses a day to Chuí (US$11, 3½ hours) on the Uruguayan border.

Chuí

☎ 0xx53 • postcode 96235-000 • pop 5000
The small border town of Chuí is about 245km south of Rio Grande on a good sealed road. One side of the main street, Avenida Brasil, is in Brazil; the other side is in the Uruguayan town of Chuy. The Uruguayan side is a good place to eat, change money and buy cheap duty-free Scotch whisky.

Should you need a Uruguayan visa, it's better to get it in Porto Alegre than in Chuí. It can be done here, but you might have to wait overnight. See the introductory Facts for the Visitor chapter for details of the Uruguayan consulate in Chuí.

Places to Stay & Eat If you're stuck in Chuí, the best cheapie is *Rivero Hotel* (☎ 265-1271, Calle Colombia 163) on the Brazilian side. Bright apartamentos cost US$10 per person. On the same street at No 191, the *Hotel e Restaurante São Francisco* (☎ 265-1096) charges the same prices.

There are some good restaurants on the Uruguayan side of Avenida Brasil. Try the *Jesus* for good, inexpensive parrillada. On the Brazilian side, the restaurant in the Hotel São Francisco is as good as it gets.

Getting There & Away The bus station is about three blocks from Avenida Brasil. There are regular buses to Pelotas for connections to Porto Alegre, and two daily buses to Rio Grande (US$11, 3½ hours). You can buy tickets to Montevideo from the bus agencies on the Uruguayan side of Avenida Brasil.

All buses crossing into Uruguay stop at the Brazilian Polícia Federal post on Avenida Argentina, a couple of kilometers north of town. You must get off the bus here to get your Brazilian exit stamp. In Uruguay, the bus will stop again for the Uruguayan officials to check your Brazilian exit stamp and Uruguayan visa (if you need one).

JESUIT MISSIONS

Soon after the discovery of the New World, the Portuguese and Spanish kings authorized Catholic orders to create missions to convert the natives into Catholic subjects of the crown and the state. The most successful of these orders were the Jesuits, who established a series of missions in a region that spanned parts of Paraguay, Brazil and Argentina. In effect, it was a nation within the colonies, a nation which, at its height in the 1720s, claimed 30 mission villages inhabited by more than 150,000 Guarani Indians. Buenos Aires was merely a village at this time.

Unlike those established elsewhere, these missions succeeded in introducing European culture largely without destroying the Indian people, their culture or the Tupi-Guarani language.

The first mission was founded in 1609 following the 1608 order from Hernandarias, governor of the Spanish province of Paraguay, to the local Jesuit leader, Fray Diego de Torres, to send missionaries to convert the infidels. Preferring indoctrination by the Jesuits to serfdom on Spanish estates or slavery at the hands of the Portuguese, the Indians were rapidly recruited into a chain of missions. The missions covered a vast region that encompassed much of the present-day Brazilian states of Paraná, Santa Catarina and Rio Grande do Sul as well as portions of Paraguay and northern Argentina.

The Jesuit territory was too large to defend, and the Portuguese *bandeirantes* (bands of Paulistas who explored the Brazilian interior while searching for gold and Indians to enslave) found the missionary settlements easy pickings for slave raids. Thousands of Indians were captured, reducing the 13 missions of Guayra (a province roughly encompassing the present-day state of Paraná) to two. Fear of the bandeirante slavers caused these two missions to be abandoned, and the Indians and Jesuits marched westward and founded San Ignacio Miní (1632) in Argentina, having lost many people in the rapids of the Paraná. The remaining missions north of

Iguaçu were decimated by attacks from hostile Indian tribes and were forced to relocate south.

Between 1631 and 1638, activity was concentrated in the 30 sites that the mission Indians were able to defend. In one of the bloodiest fights, the battle of Mbororé, the Indians beat back the slavers and secured their lands north of San Javier, a mission close to the Argentine border with Rio Grande do Sul.

The missions were miniature cities built around a central church, and included baptisteries, libraries, dormitories for the Indian converts and the priests, and cemeteries. They became centers of culture and intellect as well as of religion. An odd mix of European Baroque and native Guarani arts, music and painting developed. Indian scholars created a written form of Tupi-Guarani and, from 1704, published several works in Tupi-Guarani, using one of the earliest printing presses in South America.

As the missions grew, the Jesuit nation became more independent of Rome and relations with the Vatican became strained. The missions became an embarrassment to the Iberian kings, and finally, in 1777, the Portuguese minister Marquês de Pombal convinced Spanish King Carlos III to expel the Jesuits from Spanish lands. Thus ended, in the opinion of many historians, a grand 160-year experiment in socialism, where wealth was equally divided and religion, intellect and the arts flourished – a utopian island of progress in an age of monarchies and institutionalized slavery. Administration of the mission villages passed into the hands

of the colonial government. The communities continued until the early 1800s, when they were destroyed by revolutionary wars of independence, then abandoned.

Today, the 30 Jesuit missions are in ruins. Seven lie in Brazil (in the northwestern part of Rio Grande do Sul), eight are in the Itapuá region of southern Paraguay, and the remaining 15 are in northeastern Argentina. Of these 15 Argentine missions, 11 lie in the province of Missiones.

Brazilian Missions

The city of Santo Ângelo is the jumping-off point for exploring the Brazilian missions. The municipal tourist office (☎ 0xx55-313-1600) is on Praça Pinheiro Machado and there's a 24-hour Visa ATM at Bradesco on Avenida Brasil. In São Miguel, the tourist office (☎ 0xx55-381-1294, saomiguel.turismo@san.psi.br) is at Rua 29 de Abril 129. For information on visiting all the missions (in Portuguese), check out www.rotamissoes.com.br.

São Miguel das Missões, 53km from Santo Ângelo, is the most interesting and intact of the Brazilian missions. It was given Unesco World Heritage listing in 1984. Every evening there's a spectacular sound and light show. Entry to the mission is US$2; the sound and light show costs US$1.50.

Also nearby are the missions of **São João Batista** (on the road to São Miguel) and **São Lourenço das Missões** (18km past the turnoff to São Miguel).

Organized Tours In Santo Ângelo, Missiotur (☎ 0xx55-312-4055, missiotur@terra.com.br) in the Hotel Santo Ângelo Turis at Rua Antônio Manoel 726, organizes tours of the Brazilian, Paraguayan and Argentine missions. A three-night package to the Brazilian missions costs US$190 for two, with transfers, accommodations, transport and entry fees included.

Places to Stay & Eat In Brazil, Santo Ângelo has a range of hotels, but it's great to stay out at São Miguel to see the sound and light show. *Pousada das Missões* (☎ 0xx55-381-1202, turjovem@zaz.com.br) is a new HI youth hostel right next to the

São Miguel mission. Dorm rooms cost US$9 per person; the hostel also has a range of single/double apartamentos starting at US$16/25. It fills up with school groups, so it's best to book ahead via email or the hostel's excellent Web site at www.albergues.com.br/saomiguel. If it's booked up, the other option is *Hotel Barichello* (☎ 0xx55-381-1327, Avenida Borges do Canto 1559). Rooms cost US$15/22 and it has a good *churrascaria* attached.

Getting There & Around There are daily flights from São Paulo and Porto Alegre to Santo Ângelo with RioSul (☎ 0800-992004). Also, there are six buses a day from Porto Alegre to Santo Ângelo (US$28, 6½ hours).

From Santo Ângelo, local buses run four times a day to São João Batista and São Miguel das Missões. It's possible to rent a car in Santo Ângelo (as well as from Encarnación or Posadas), but driving a rental car over borders is difficult. In Santo Ângelo, call Sulmive (☎ 0xx55-312-1000).

Paraguayan Missions

The most important mission to see in Paraguay is **Trinidad**, 25km northeast of Encarnación. The red-stone ruins are fascinating. Use Encarnación as a base for visiting the missions of Paraguay – it has some cheap, modest hotels and restaurants. If you're looking for something a bit more upscale, you can stay in Posadas, just across the border from Encarnación.

From the Paraguayan border town of Ciudad del Este, opposite Foz do Iguaçu, there are daily buses to Encarnación, which is 320km south.

Argentine Missions

In Argentina, don't miss **San Ignacio Miní**, 60km northeast of Posadas on Hwy 12, where there's a sound and light show every night. Of lesser stature is **Santa María la Mayor**, 111km southeast of Posadas on Hwy 110. There's an excellent information office (☎ 01-4322-0686) for the Argentine missions in Buenos Aires at Avenida Santa Fé 989. In Posadas, there is an information office (☎ 3752-447-540) at Avenida Colon 1985.

In Argentina, Posadas is the best bet as a base for exploring the Argentine missions. It's just across the Rio Paraná from the Paraguayan town of Encarnación. The food and lodgings are better on the Argentine side (there are 25 hotels to choose from), but budget travelers may find the Paraguayan town easier on the wallet.

To access the Argentine missions, there are seven daily buses from Puerto Iguazu (just across the border from Foz do Iguaçu) to San Ignacio (US$20, five hours). These buses continue on to Posadas.

The most direct route from Santo Angelo to Argentina is via Hwy BR-285 to the border town of São Borja, 195km to the southeast. From here it's possible to cross the Rio Uruguai by barge to the Argentine town of São Tomé, where there are buses to Posadas. Another option is to cross the border at Puerto Xavier (Brazil) to San Javier (Argentina).

Uruguaiana, 180km south of São Borja, is the most commonly used border crossing from Rio Grande do Sul to Argentina. Buses operate from Uruguaiana to Buenos Aires, Santiago do Chile and Montevideo. See the introductory Facts for the Visitor chapter for details of the Argentine and Uruguayan consulates in Uruguaiana.

THE SOUTH

The Central West

Known to Brazilians as the Centro-Oeste, this region comprises almost 19% of the country's land area but is the most sparsely populated in Brazil, with only 7% of the total population. It is made up of the states of Mato Grosso, Mato Grosso do Sul and Goiás, as well as the Distrito Federal, which includes Brasília, the country's capital.

This massive terrain was, until the 1940s, one of the last great unexplored areas on earth. It still offers enormous scope for adventure travelers and is growing in popularity as an ecotourism destination both for Brazilians and for foreigners. Huge distances and a limited road network make travel slow, but the major routes are well serviced by buses.

In the southwest of Mato Grosso and the west of Mato Grosso do Sul is the wildlife paradise called the Pantanal Matogrossense. It's a unique geographical depression that was a huge inland sea before it dried up millions of years ago. Large portions are covered by water during the rainy season.

In addition to the Pantanal, which is the major drawing card of the region, the Central West boasts many other natural attractions. The Planalto Brasileiro has been greatly eroded to form the Guimarães, Parecis and Veadeiros *chapadões* (tablelands) between the river basins. There are spectacular mountainous national parks, Chapada dos Veadeiros and Chapada dos Guimarães, the remote Parque Nacional

das Emas, home to Brazil's largest bird, the rhea; and the river beaches of the Rio Araguaia, which extends into the northern state of Tocantins. The Bonito area has become popular in recent years for its crystal-clear rivers and natural springs surrounded by lush forest.

There are also interesting colonial towns (Pirenópolis and Goiás Velho) and large, planned cities (Goiânia and Brasília) that are worth a look.

THE CENTRAL WEST

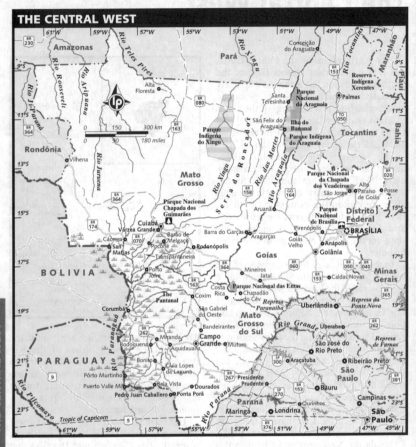

Distrito Federal

The Distrito Federal is the result of long-held Brazilian dreams to harness the vast resources of its inland territories. Central to this dream, first mooted in 1823 by Brazilian statesman José Bonifácio, was the establishment of an inland capital that would catalyze the economic development of the interior.

Brasília's location was also influenced by John Bosco (known to Brazilians as Dom João Bosco), a Salesian priest living in Turin, Italy. In 1883 he dreamed that a new civilization would emerge in the center of Brazil, somewhere between the 15th and 20th parallels. Bosco's dream became well known to Brazilians, and in the 1891 Constitution, land in the region was set aside for the construction of the new capital. Finally, in 1955, after almost 150 years of debate, President Juscelino Kubitschek proposed that the Distrito Federal be carved out of the state of Goiás to house the new capital, Brasília.

BRASÍLIA
☎ 0xx61 • postcode 70000-000
• pop 2.04 million

I sought the curved and sensual line. The curve that I see in the Brazilian hills, in the body of a loved one, in the clouds in the sky and in the ocean waves.

– Oscar Niemeyer, Brasília architect

Brasília is a utopian horror. It should be a symbol of power, but instead it's a museum of architectural ideas.

– Robert Hughes, art critic

The impression I have is that I'm arriving on a different planet.

– Yuri Gagarin, cosmonaut

Brasília must have looked good on paper, and it still does in photos. In 1987 it was added to the Unesco list of World Heritage Sites, being considered one of the major examples of the

Highlights

- Cruising Brasília, looking at its town plan and unique architecture
- Experiencing the weird and wonderful religious sects and rituals around Brasília

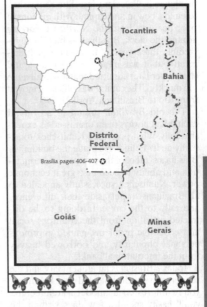

Tocantins

Bahia

Distrito Federal

Brasília pages 406-407 ○

Goiás

Minas Gerais

20th century's modern movement in architecture and urban planning.

But the world's great planned city of the 20th century is built for cars and air conditioners. Distances are enormous and no one walks. The sun blazes, but there are few trees for shelter. It's also a difficult city to get hold of. The planned city's division into sectors – each with its specific purpose (hotels, banks etc) – means you never sense you're in the heart of it.

Bureaucrats and politicians were lured to Brasília by 100% salary hikes and big apartments in the 1960s. Even today, as soon as the weekend comes, they get out of the city – to Rio, to São Paulo, to their private clubs in the country. Brasília is also one of the most expensive cities in Brazil. The poor live in satellite cities as far as 30km from the center.

All this is the doing of three famous Brazilians: an urban planner (Lúcio Costa), an architect (Oscar Niemeyer) and a landscape architect (Burle Marx), who were commissioned by President Juscelino Kubitschek to build a new inland capital. With millions of poor peasants from the Northeast working around the clock, Brasília was built in an incredible three years – it wasn't exactly finished but it was ready to be the capital (Niemeyer later admitted that it was all done too quickly). The capital was officially moved from Rio to Brasília on April 21, 1960.

The old Brazilian dream of an inland capital had always been dismissed as expensive folly. What possessed Kubitschek to actually do it? Politics. He made the building of Brasília a symbol of the country's determination and ability to become a great economic power. Kubitschek successfully appealed to all Brazilians to put aside their differences and rally to the cause. In doing so, he distracted attention from the country's social and economic problems, gained enormous personal popularity and borrowed heavily from the international banks.

Today's Brasília is an affluent city and the residents are well educated and helpful. If you're interested in modern architecture, you'll easily spend a few days visiting the city's impressive buildings and monuments. Otherwise, come here if you must see the capital or as a stopover en route to the Pantanal, Parque Nacional da Chapada dos Veadeiros (Goiás) or Ilha do Bananal (Tocantins).

Orientation

Seen from above, Brasília looks like an airplane, or a bow and arrow. The *plano piloto* (pilot plan) specified that the city would face the giant artificial Lago do Paranoá. In the fuselage (or the arrow) are all the government buildings and monuments. The plaza of three powers – with the Palácio do Planalto, the Palácio do Congresso and the Palácio da Justiça – is in the cockpit. Out on the *asas* (wings) are block after numbered block of apartment buildings (known as Superquadras or Quadras) but little else.

To get the full effect, you can take a 10-minute helicopter flight over the city from the heliport at the base of the TV Tower. The flight costs US$36 per person and bookings can be made by calling ☎ 323-8777.

Otherwise, you can do a bus tour, rent a car or combine a ride on local buses from the city bus station (No 104 or 108 are the best) with some long walks to see the bulk of Brasília's edifices. Remember that many buildings are closed on weekends and at night.

Information

Tourist Offices The best place for information is the tourist office (☎ 364-9135) at the airport, open daily from 7 am to 11 pm. Staff speak English and can make bookings and organize discounts at city hotels. They can also give you a coupon for a discount taxi ride to the city.

The head office of Adetur (☎ 321-3318), the government tourist agency, is about 2km from the center at the Centro de Convenções (3rd floor) on the Via SI Oeste. It's more administrative office than tourist information service, but staff do their best to help and have some glossy brochures. To get there, take bus No 131, which runs between the *rodoferroviária* (train and long-distance bus station) and the city bus station. It's open Monday to Friday from 9 am to 5 pm.

If all you need is a map or a list of attractions, simply pick up a brochure from the front desk of any large hotel or travel agency.

Foreign Embassies This being the national capital you would expect them all to be here. Most are located along Avenida das Nações between Quadras 801 and 809 in the Setor de Embaixadas Sul (Embassy Sector South). See the introductory Facts for the Visitor chapter for details.

Money There are banks with money changing facilities in the Setor Bancário Sul

(SBS; Banking Sector South) and Setor Bancário Norte (SBN; Banking Sector North). Both sectors are close to the city bus station. Banco do Brasil in the Setor Comercial Sul (Commercial Sector South) has a Visa ATM and its handy branch at the airport changes money, has a Visa ATM and is open on Saturday. Travel agencies will change cash dollars.

Post & Communications The post office is in the Setor Hoteleiro Sul (SHS; Hotel Sector South) just off the Via S-1 Oeste. There is no telephone office, but you can make international calls from most public phones. For international collect calls, dial ☎ 101.

Internet cafés are few and far between. The most lively one is akky.cyber.c@fe.br (☎ 327-9640), at Setor Comercial Local Norte 303, Bloco E, Loja 32. Access costs US$4 per hour, more on weekends. Other Internet cafés are clustered around 505 Sul and 303 Norte.

Memorial JK
Along with the tomb of JK (President Juscelino Kubitschek) on Praça do Cruzeiro, the memorial (☎ 321-3318) features several exhibits relating to the construction of the city. It's open Tuesday to Sunday from 9 am to 5 pm. Entry is US$2.

TV Tower
The 75m-high observation deck of the TV tower (☎ 325-5735), on the Eixo Monumental, is open Tuesday to Sunday from 8 am to 8 pm and Monday from 2 to 8 pm. There's a handicrafts fair at the base of the tower on weekends.

Catedral Metropolitana
With its 16 curved columns and its stained-glass interior, the cathedral (☎ 224-4073) is worth seeing. At the entrance are the haunting **Four Disciples** statues carved by Ceschiatti, who also made the aluminum angels hanging inside. The cathedral is on the Eixo Monumental and is open daily from 8 am to 6 pm. To get there, take a No 108 bus from the city bus station.

Government Buildings
Down by the tip of the arrow you'll find the most interesting government buildings. The **Palácio do Itamaraty**, home to the Foreign Ministry, is one of the best – a series of arches surrounded by a reflecting pool and landscaped by Burle Marx. It is open Monday to Friday from 3 to 5 pm and on weekends from 10 am to 2 pm.

There's also the **Palácio da Justiça** (Supreme Court building), which has water cascading between its arches. It's open Monday to Friday from 10 am to noon and 3 to 5 pm.

The **Palácio do Congresso** (Parliament) features 'dishes' and twin towers; it's open Monday to Friday from 10 am to noon and 2:30 to 4:30 pm and weekends from 9 am to 1 pm.

The **Palácio do Planalto** (which houses the President's office) is closed to the public, but you can watch the changing of the guard outside the gates, usually at 8:30 am and 5:30 pm every day.

Santuário Dom Bosco
As impressive as the cathedral, the Santuário Dom Bosco (Dom Bosco's Shrine; ☎ 223-6542) is made of concrete columns and has blue stained-glass windows. Located near the budget hotels at Quadra 702 along Via W3 Sul, it's open daily from 8 am to 6 pm.

Parks
In the northern reaches of the city limits, the **Parque Nacional de Brasília** is a good place to relax if you're stuck in the city. This ecological reserve is open daily from 8 am to 4 pm and is very popular on weekends. It has natural swimming pools and is home to a number of endangered animals, including deer, banded anteaters, giant armadillos and maned wolves. Bus No 128.1 from the city bus station goes past the front gate. There's a visitors center (☎ 233-5322) where you can get information about the park and walking trails.

A good park not far from the city center is the **Parque da Cidade**, where you'll find a swimming pool with artificial waves and kiosks where you can grab a snack.

THE CENTRAL WEST

THE CENTRAL WEST

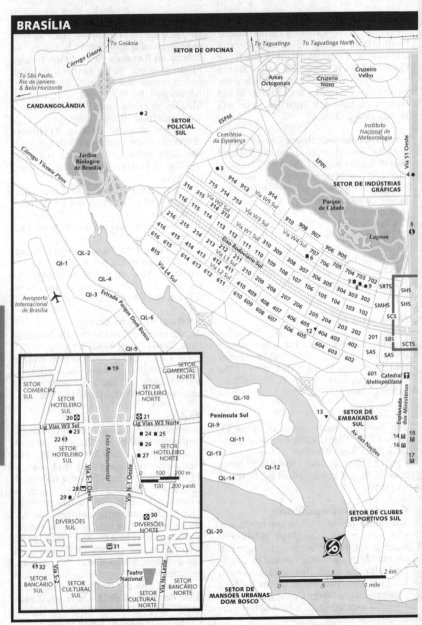

BRASÍLIA

To Goiânia

SETOR DE OFICINAS

To Taguatinga　To Taguatinga North

Córrego Guará

To São Paulo,
Rio de Janeiro
& Belo Horizonte

Áreas
Octogonais

Cruzeiro
Novo

Cruzeiro
Velho

CANDANGOLÂNDIA

●2

SETOR
POLICIAL
SUL

ESPM

Cemitério
da Esperança

Instituto
Nacional de
Meteorologia

Via 51 Oeste

Córrego Vicente Pires

Jardim
Biológico
de Brasília

●3

EPIN

SETOR DE INDÚSTRIAS
GRÁFICAS

4●

715 714 713
316 315 Via W2 Sul
314 313
116 115 114
216 215 214 113 112
416 415 414 413 213 212 211
616 615 614 613 472 471
815 210 209 208
Via L4 Sul

914 913
Via W5 Sul
914
Via W3 Sul
910 908 907
Via W1 Sul 310 309 Via W4 Sul
Eixo Rodoviário Sul 308
111 110 109 307 306 305
Via L1 Sul 107 106 105 304 303 302
Via L2 Sul 207 206 205 204 103 102
610 609 608 607 606 605 404 403 402
604 603 602

Parque
de Cidade

Lagoon

●6 707 706 705 704 703 702
7● 8● ●9
SRTS
SMHS SHS SHS
SCS
201 SBS
SAS SCTS
SAS

QL-2
QI-1
QL-4
QI-3 Estrada Parque Dom Bosco
QL-6
QI-5

Aeroporto
Internacional
de Brasília

●5

12

601 Catedral
Metropolitana

SETOR
COMERCIAL
NORTE

●19

SETOR
HOTELEIRO
NORTE

SETOR
COMERCIAL
SUL

SETOR
HOTELEIRO
SUL

20

21

Lig Vias W3 Sul ●23
22

24 ■25

●26

SETOR
HOTELEIRO
SUL

27

SETOR
HOTELEIRO
NORTE

Lig Vias W3 Norte

QL-10

Península Sul
QI-9

QI-11

QI-13

QI-12

QL-14

SETOR DE
EMBAIXADAS
SUL

Esplanada dos Ministérios

13

14　15
16　17

Av das Nações

Eixo Monumental

Via S-1 Oeste

Via N-1 Oeste

0　100　200 m
0　100　200 yards

28

29

DIVERSÕES
SUL

30

DIVERSÕES
NORTE

31

32

SETOR
BANCÁRIO
SUL

Via S-Leste

SETOR
CULTURAL
SUL

Teatro
Nacional

Via Ns-Leste

SETOR
CULTURAL
NORTE

SETOR
BANCÁRIO
NORTE

QL-20

SETOR DE CLUBES
ESPORTIVOS SUL

SETOR DE
MANSÕES URBANAS
DOM BOSCO

0　1　2 km
0　.5　1 mile

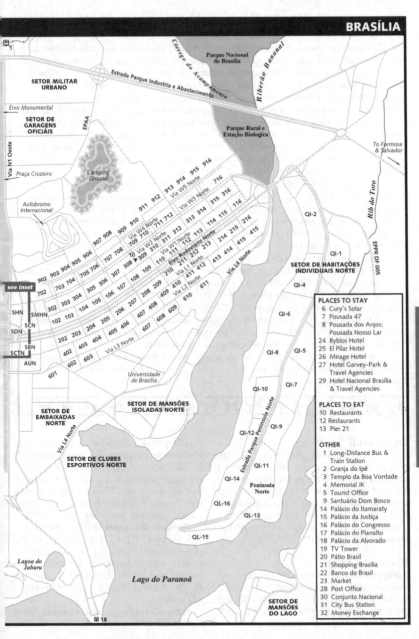

BRASÍLIA

THE CENTRAL WEST

PLACES TO STAY
6 Cury's Solar
7 Pousada 47
8 Pousada dos Anjos;
 Pousada Nosso Lar
24 Byblos Hotel
25 El Pilar Hotel
26 Mirage Hotel
27 Hotel Garvey-Park &
 Travel Agencies
29 Hotel Nacional Brasília
 & Travel Agencies

PLACES TO EAT
10 Restaurants
12 Restaurants
13 Pier 21

OTHER
1 Long-Distance Bus &
 Train Station
2 Granja do Ipê
3 Templo da Boa Vontade
4 Memorial JK
5 Tourist Office
9 Santuário Dom Bosco
14 Palácio do Itamaraty
15 Palácio da Justiça
16 Palácio do Congresso
17 Palácio do Planalto
18 Palácio da Alvorado
19 TV Tower
20 Pátio Brasil
21 Shopping Brasília
22 Banco do Brasil
23 Market
28 Post Office
30 Conjunto Nacional
31 City Bus Station
32 Money Exchange

Brasília – Capital of the Third Millennium

In 1883 an Italian priest, John Bosco, prophesied that a new civilization would arise between parallels 15 and 20, and that its capital would be built between parallels 15 and 16, on the edge of an artificial lake. Many consider Brasília to be that city, and a number of cults have sprung up in the area.

About 45km east of Brasília, near the satellite city of Planeltina, you'll find the Vale do Amanhecer (Valley of the Dawn), founded in 1959 by a clairvoyant, Tia Neiva. The valley is actually a small town where you can see (or take part in) Egyptian, Greek, Aztec, Indian, Gypsy, Inca, Trojan and Afro-Brazilian rituals. The mediums in the town believe that a new civilization will come during the third millennium. The town's main temple was inspired by spiritual advice received by Tia Neiva. In the center is an enormous Star of David, which forms a lake, pierced by an arrow. The valley is only open to visitors daily from 10 pm to midnight. Get there by Bus No 617 from the center of Brasília. For more information, call ☎ 389-1258.

About 100km west of Brasília, near the town of Santo Antônio do Descoberto (Goiás), is the Cidade Eclética (Eclectic City). Founded in 1956 by Yokanam, an ex-airline pilot, the group's aim is the unification of all religions on the planet through fraternity and equality. Its ceremonies take place Wednesday to Friday from 8 to 10 pm, and Sunday from 3 to 6 pm. There are strict dress regulations, but if you're not dressed suitably, they will give you a special tunic to wear. For more information, call ☎ 626-1391.

In Brasília itself, the Granja do Ipê (Ipê Estate; ☎ 380-1825, paz@tba.com.br) at the city's southern exit is the site of the City of Peace and Holistic University. This institution aims to form a new generation with a mentality suited to the needs of the third millennium.

The Templo da Boa Vontade (Temple of Goodwill) at No 75/76, 915 Sul, was created by the Legion of Goodwill in 1989 as a symbol of universal solidarity. It incorporates seven pyramids, joined to form a cone that is topped with the biggest raw crystal you will ever see. Inside there's a meditative space. It's open 24 hours a day, every day of the week. Get there on bus No 105 or 107 from the city bus station. For more information, call ☎ 245-1070.

Some people also believe that in certain regions around Brasília extraterrestrial contacts are more likely – at Km 69 on Hwy BR-351, for instance, or on the plateau in the smaller city of Brasilândia. Believe it, or not!

Organized Tours

If you want to save your feet, half-day guided tours of the city start at around US$20. The Hotel Nacional Brasília and the Hotel Garvey-Park both house several travel agencies offering sightseeing tours. You can also book bus tours through the tourist office at the airport, or contact the guide Eliane directly (☎ 223-5730).

Places to Stay

Budget Camping is possible between the long-distance bus/train station and the city in the Setor de Garagens Oficiais. To get there, take a No 109 or 143 bus from the city bus station. Campsites cost US$6.

There are no cheap hotels in Brasília. The cheapest accommodations are at pensions in W3 Sul. Some of these pensions are used by people getting treatment at nearby hospitals, and the rooms aren't much more than cubicles. To get there from the long-distance bus station, catch any bus going along W3 Sul.

Pousada dos Anjos (☎ 223-0549, *Quadra 703, Bloco C, Casa 55*) is a clean, well-run place just off Via W3 Sul. Walk up from the corner where Santuário Dom Bosco is located and it's the first street on the left. Rooms start at US$20 per person, breakfast not included.

Almost directly opposite, *Pousada Nosso Lar* (☎ 225-1901, *Quadra 703, Bloco B, Casa*

48) is another reasonable option. Single/ double quartos with TV cost US$35/50 with breakfast included; apartamentos go for US$40/60.

Nearby, **Pousada 47** *(☎/fax 223-5718, Quadra 703, Bloco A, Casa 41/47)* is a friendly place that charges US$20/30/45 for singles/doubles/triples with breakfast, but it's right on noisy Via W3 Sul.

Cury's Solar *(☎ 244-1899, Quadra 707, Bloco I, Casa 15)*, run by Neusa Batista Ribeiro, is another friendly place, in which guests are encouraged to make themselves at home. French and German are spoken. Prices vary according to room size, starting at US$20 (with breakfast) or US$18 (without breakfast) per person. Get off at the stop between Quadras 707 and 708. Walk up through the park and turn right at the third row of houses.

If you need a bed near the airport, **Ilhabela Park Hotel** *(☎ 486-1286, Praça Central, Lote 4B, 3a Avenida, Nucleo Bandeirante)* is about 5km southwest of the airport. Large, modern, single/double apartamentos with air con cost US$26/34.

Mid-Range The cheapest hotels fall into the mid-range category. The best place to head is Setor Hoteleiro Norte (SHN) where three hotels are clustered together. The best is the **Mirage Hotel** *(☎/fax 328-7150, SHN, Quadra 2, Bloco N)*, but it's often full during the week. Book ahead if you can. It charges US$50/82/105 for singles/doubles/triples with breakfast included. There's also a restaurant in the hotel.

Next best is the two-star **El Pilar Hotel** *(328-5915, SHN, Quadra 3, Bloco C)* with rooms starting at the same prices as the Mirage, while the inexplicable three-star rating for the **Byblos Hotel** *(☎ 326-1570, SHN, Quadra 3, Bloco E)* means overpriced rooms at US$82/108/138.

The tourist office at the airport can organize discounts at these hotels, but it's always worth asking yourself, especially on weekends when you can negotiate discounts of up to 40%.

Top End The **Hotel Nacional Brasília** *(☎ 321-7575, SHS, Quadra 1, Bloco A,* *hotelnacional@tba.com.br)* is a popular five-star joint with an adjoining shopping mall full of travel agents. Singles/doubles start at US$158/176 during the week, or US$100/120 on weekends. There are lots of three- and four-star hotels, and a few other five-star ones, in the hotel sectors. The tourist office at the airport has a complete list, with photos and prices.

Places to Eat
Shopping-mall culture is taking hold in Brasília and while it might not be the traveler's cup of tea, there are two important things to be said for it – air-conditioning and concentration.

With buildings so spread out and few street stalls, finding somewhere to eat and drink out of the heat during the day can require endurance. Not surprisingly, the locals flock to three centrally located oases – Shopping Brasília, Pátio Brasil and Conjunto Nacional – to chow down. All have small cafés and food courts with enough variety to cater to most tastes.

There are also a couple of good per-kilo lunch places behind the daily market, which is the closest thing to the heart of the city.

A good selection of restaurants and bars is clustered in two strips between Quadras 405 and 404 Sul and between Quadras 308 and 309 Norte. The Norte strip has more pubs and bars and is generally the cheaper of the two. To get there, take a W3 Norte bus from the center.

There are good restaurants scattered around the city. In the following addresses, SCL means Setor Comércio Local, which is the space provided in the quadras for shops, restaurants etc. The letter N or S immediately after SCL means *Norte* (North) or *Sul* (South), and is followed by the quadra number, the block number and the shop number.

Bar Beirute *(☎ 244-1717, SCLS 109, Bloco A, Loja 2/4)* is an institution in Brasília. It has some Middle Eastern-themed dishes, and you can sit at outdoor tables under trees. Meals cost around US$15 for two.

For very good *nordestino* (Northeastern) cuisine, the **Xique-Xique** *(☎ 244-5797, SCLS*

THE CENTRAL WEST

107, Bloco E, Loja 1) has *carne de sol* and *feijão verde* with *manteiga da terra* for US$15 (two people).

Vegetarians needn't feel left out. For good natural food, **Planeta Saúde** (☎ 349-4415, 707 Norte, Bloco G) is open Monday to Friday from 9 am to 11 pm and weekends from 10 am to 3 pm. Or for a per-kilo veggie lunch, try **Naturama** *(SCLS 102, Bloco B, Loja 9).*

Pier 21 is a new restaurant and shopping development near Setor de Embaixadas Sul. It's in a pleasant location overlooking the Lago do Paranoá – it's a pity the parking lot took precedence over the food hall for prime waterfront position. You'll find seafood, pizza, Chinese and other fast-food outlets along with barn-sized pub/restaurants with a distinctly country 'n' western flavor.

Entertainment

Claiming to be the longest-established bar in the city, the **Gate's Pub** *(☎ 225-4576, SCLS 403, Bloco B, Loja 34)* is still going strong. Most nights there's live music with a rock, reggae and funk flavor, followed by dance music until 3 am. A US$5 cover charge applies.

For dance music, try **Hyppo's** *(☎ 248-6569, SHIS, Quadra I05 Bloco D, Loja 24),* in the Centro Comercial Gilberto Salomão, for garage and techno. It's open Tuesday to Sunday from 10 pm and there are a couple of other clubs in the complex. **Café Cancun** *(☎ 327-1566, SCN, Shopping Liberty Mall, 1st floor)* is a popular dance club with a Caribbean theme, but has a hefty minimum charge of US$15.

Getting There & Away

Air With so many domestic flights making stopovers in Brasília, it's easy to catch a plane to almost anywhere in Brazil. Flying time to Rio is 1½ hours; to São Paulo, it's 80 minutes. Major domestic airlines with offices in Brasília include TAM (☎ 365-1560), TransBrasil (☎ 363-9300), Varig (☎ 365-1550) and VASP (☎ 329-0300), but the easiest way to book a flight is through the travel agencies in the Hotel Nacional complex.

International airlines with offices at the Hotel Nacional complex include Air France (☎ 223-4152), KLM (☎ 321-5266), Swissair (☎ 223-4382) and Lufthansa (☎ 223-8202). British Airways (☎ 327-2333) is in the Liberty Mall at SCN, Quadra 2, Tower B, Room 1019 and American Airlines (☎ 321-3322) is in the Edifício Mineiro at SCS, Quadra 4, Bloco A, Room 401/402.

Bus From the giant train and long-distance bus station *(rodoferroviária,* ☎ 233-7200), due west of the city center, there are buses to places you've never heard of, but no trains. Bus destinations include Goiânia (US$10, three hours), Rio (US$78, 17 hours), São Paulo (US$55, 14 hours) and Salvador (US$85, 24 hours). There are also buses to Cuiabá (US$69, 18 hours) and Porto Velho (US$98, 42 hours).

A daily bus runs north via Hwy BR-153 to Belém (US$113, 34 hours), but the road around the Tocantins border can be impassable during rainy season.

Six buses a day go to Pirenópolis (US$7, three hours) and three to Alto Paraíso (US$13, four hours) for access to the Parque Nacional da Chapada dos Veadeiros.

Getting Around

The international airport (☎ 365-1941) is 12km south of the center. To get to the airport from the city center, take a No 102 bus (US$1.30, 40 minutes) or a No 30 minibus (US$1.80, 25 minutes) from the city bus station. A taxi between the airport and the city center costs US$18 if you book through the tourist office, or around US$23 otherwise.

To get from the city bus station to the long-distance bus and train station, take local bus No 131.

There are car rental agencies at Brasília's airport, at the Hotel Nacional and at the Hotel Garvey-Park.

The long-awaited Metro DF, which first began construction in 1992, is finally due to begin operation in late 2001. Initially, the metro will run from the city bus station along the southern 'wing' of the city to the outer suburbs of Taguatinga and Samambaia.

AROUND BRASÍLIA
Salto de Itiquira

Itiquira is a Tupi-Guarani Indian word meaning 'water that falls.' From the viewpoint at this 170m-high free-fall waterfall, you can see the valley of the Paranãs to the south. There's forest, several crystal-clear streams with natural pools for a swim and the requisite restaurants and bars.

Itiquira is 110km northeast of Brasília; you need a car to get there or you can take a bus from the long-distance bus station to the city of Formosa and try your luck organizing a lift from there. If you're driving, leave Brasília via Hwy BR-020, which takes you through the satellite cities of Sobradinho and Planaltina to Formosa. The falls are 35km from Formosa at the end of the dirt road.

Cachoeira Saia Velha

This is a pleasant swimming hangout not too far from the city. Take Hwy BR-040 in the direction of Belo Horizonte for about 20km. When you reach the **Monumento do Candango** – a ridiculous statue made by a Frenchman to honor the people who built Brasília – there's a sign to the waterfall. The road is to the left of the monument. There are also several natural swimming pools, restaurants and camping areas but no hotel.

Goiás

On the heels of the gold discoveries in Minas Gerais, bandeirantes (bands of Paulistas who explored the interior) pushed farther inland in search of more precious metals and, as always, Indian slaves. In 1682, a bandeira headed by the old Paulista Bartolomeu Bueno da Silva visited the region. The Goyaz Indians gave him the nickname anhanguera (old devil) when, after burning some cachaça (sugarcane rum) – which the Indians believed to be water – on a plate, he threatened to set fire to all the rivers if they didn't show him where their gold mines were. Three years later, having been given up for dead, the old devil returned to São Paulo with a few survivors, and with gold and Indian slaves from Goiás.

In 1722, da Silva's son, who had been on the first trip, organized another bandeira. The gold rush was on. It followed a pattern similar to that in Minas Gerais: First came the Paulistas, then the Portuguese Emboadas (immigrants who had arrived for the earlier gold rush in Minas Gerais) and soon the black slaves. With everything imported from so far away, prices in Goiás were high. Many suffered and died, particularly the slaves. The gold rush ended quickly.

In recent years, Goiás has become the center of a campaign aimed at protecting the cerrado, the savanna-like landscape that sprawls across Brazil's central high plains. The cerrado, the country's second largest ecoregion after Amazonia, is only now being recognized for its incredible diversity of flora. Of the 10,000 species of plants found in the cerrado, 44% are found nowhere else in the world.

The cerrado is a mosaic of grassland, palm stands (known as veredas) and dry gallery forests. While there is more unique flora than animals, the cerrado does boast some of Brazil's most rare and endangered species – including the maned wolf, giant otter, giant armadillo, tapir, pampas deer and giant anteater.

Highlights

- Pirenópolis and Goiás Velho, the historic colonial towns of Goiás
- The *empadão,* a tasty savory pie filled with meat, vegetables, olives and egg
- Hot springs at Caldas Novas
- Unique high-cerrado flora in Parque Nacional da Chapada dos Veadeiros
- The Vale da Lua (Valley of the Moon), near Parque Nacional da Chapada dos Veadeiros
- River beaches of the Rio Araguaia
- Wildlife sightings in Parque Nacional das Emas

Since the 1970s, increased use of agricultural chemicals has converted vast tracts of cerrado to soybean, rice, corn, wheat and cattle production. The rate of habitat loss is

THE CENTRAL WEST

greater than in any of Brazil's other eco-regions, including Amazonia.

A saving grace for the cerrado could be Goiás' growing popularity as an ecotourism destination. Tourism infrastructure has improved in recent years, and national parks such as Parque Nacional da Chapada dos Veadeiros and Parque Nacional das Emas are more accessible than before. Goiás is also a gateway to the river beaches of the mighty Rio Araguaia, which forms the border with Mato Grosso state, and to the Ilha do Bananal in Tocantins state, the world's largest river island.

GOIÂNIA
☎ 0xx62 • postcode 74000-000
• pop 1.1 million

The capital of the state of Goiás, Goiânia is 200km southwest of Brasília and 900km from both Cuiabá and São Paulo. Planned by urbanist Armando de Godói and founded in 1933, it's a reasonably pleasant place, with lots of open spaces laid out around circular streets. There are three main zones – housing is in the south, administration is in the center, and industry and commerce are in the north. Goiânia's economy is based on the commercialization of the règion's cattle.

Information
The information desk (☎ 217-1100) at the Centro de Convenções on the corner of Rua 30 and Rua 4 in the center opens on weekdays; there's more likely to be someone attending when a convention is being held.

Turisplan Turismo (☎ 224-1941) is at Rua 8, No 388. This central travel agency sells airline and bus tickets and can be helpful with information.

The main branch of the Banco do Brasil at Avenida Goiás 980 changes money. There's a handy Bradesco ATM at the bus station. If you're traveling on to the national parks, get money in Goiânia.

The post office is right in the center of town, at Praça Cívica 11. International collect and phone-card calls can be made from the telephone center on Rua 7, No 333.

Internet access is available at Ponto Com Saber on the first floor of Shopping Center Bougainville, Rua 9, No 1855, Setor Oeste.

Things to See & Do
There's not much for the visitor in Goiânia. Our advice is to get out to one of the national parks or nearby colonial towns as quickly as you can. If you have some time to kill, try the **Parque Educativo**, on Avenida Anhanguera in Setor Oeste. It has a zoo, a zoological museum and an anthropology museum.

The weekend markets – **Feira da Lua** a few blocks west of the Centro Cívico at Praça Tamandaré on Saturday afternoon and **Feira do Doce, do Mel e da Natureza** at Praça do Sol on Sunday afternoon – are worth a look if you're in town.

Excursions within 200km of Goiânia include the **Caldas Novas** hot springs, **Lagoa de Pirapitinga** and the interesting rock formations of **Paraúna**.

Places to Stay
Ask for discounts at all city hotels on weekends. The mid-range and top-end hotels in particular drop as much as 50% off their prices on weekends.

The *Hotel Del Rey* (☎ 213-7595, Rua 8, No 321) on the pedestrian mall has the cheapest rooms in town, but it's often full. Shabby single/double apartamentos cost US$10/15. the comfortable *Lord Hotel* (☎ 224-0385, Avenida Anhanguera 4999) has single/double/triple apartamentos with fan and fridge for US$29/40/52. Rooms at the front with balconies are light and airy, but the downside is noise from the street. A good cheapie nearby on Avenida Anhanguera is the *Goiânia Palace* (☎ 224-4874), which charges US$15/22/29 for clean quartos and US$29/36/43 for apartamentos with air-con and fridge. The *Príncipe Hotel* (☎ 224-0085, Avenida Anhanguera 2936) has a homier feel than many of the city hotels. Single/double quartos cost US$23/40.

In the mid-range, the *Vila Rica Hotel* (☎ 223-2733, Avenida Anhanguera 3456) has standard apartamentos for US$49/60. *Hotel Bandeirantes* (☎ 212-0066, Avenida Anhanguera 5106) is a bit more expensive

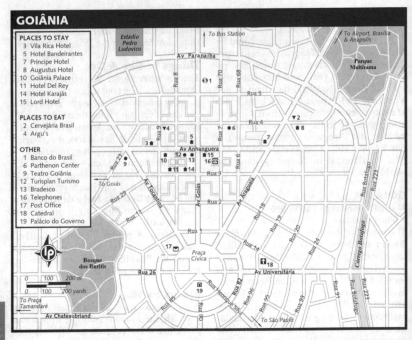

GOIÂNIA

PLACES TO STAY
3 Vila Rica Hotel
5 Hotel Bandeirantes
7 Principe Hotel
8 Augustus Hotel
10 Goiânia Palace
11 Hotel Del Rey
14 Hotel Karajás
15 Lord Hotel

PLACES TO EAT
2 Cervejária Brasil
4 Argu's

OTHER
1 Banco do Brasil
6 Parthenon Center
7 Teatro Goiânia
12 Turisplan Turismo
13 Bradesco
16 Telephones
17 Post Office
18 Catedral
19 Palácio do Governo

but has groovy brown shagpile carpet in the foyer. Rooms start at US$55/86.

There are plenty of top-end alternatives. In the center, *Hotel Karajás* (☎/fax 224-9666, karajas@cultura.com.br, Rua 3, No 860) has double rooms for US$100, while the *Augustus Hotel* (☎ 224-1022, augustus@augustus-hotel.com.br, Avenida Araguaia 702) charges US$96/116 for singles/doubles.

Places to Eat

Since they are surrounded by cattle, locals eat lots of meat. They also like to munch on pamonha, a very tasty green-corn snack sold at stands around town.

If you want to taste some typical Goiânian dishes, such as arroz com pequi, arroz com guariroba or peixe na telha, the best places to head are *Tacho de Cobre* (☎ 242-1241, Rua 72, No 550) in the Serra Dourada stadium in the suburb of Jardim Goiás, or *Aroeira* (☎ 241-5975, Rua 146, No 570, Setor Marista). A meal will cost around $US10 per

person. One favorite dish is the empadão de Goiás, a tasty meat, vegetable, olive and egg pie.

For the best per-kilo lunch in the center, check out *Argu's* (Rua 4, No 811). The center is almost deserted at night, but one of the livelier spots for a drink and snack is *Cervejaria Brasil* on the corner of Rua 4 and Rua Araguaia.

Praça Tamandaré, a short ride on the Eixo T-7 or Vila União bus or a long walk from the center, is a better bet at night. It's the pizza capital of Goiânia: *Ze Colmeia* and *Modiglianni* are a couple of good places, or just wander around and see what takes your fancy.

Getting There & Around

Major airlines include Varig (☎ 224-5049), VASP (☎ 224-6389) and TransBrasil (☎ 225-0033). Aeroporto Santo Genoveva (☎ 265-1500) is 6km from the city center – US$8 by taxi.

From the huge bus station, hourly buses leave for Brasília (US$8, three hours), Cuiabá (US$28, 13 hours) and Goiás Velho (US$9, three hours). Two of the buses to Goiás Velho (at 8 am and 2 pm) continue on to Aruanã (US$12, six hours), for access to the Rio Araguaia.

Eight buses a day run to Caldas Novas (US$8, three hours) and two go to Pirenópolis (US$7, two hours), at 7 am and 5 pm. There's a daily bus to Foz do Iguaçu (US$40, 19 hours) at 10 am.

You can walk from the bus station into town – it takes 15 minutes to get to the corner of Avenida Anhanguera and Avenida Goiás, but you might melt along the way. From outside the bus station, take a Rodoviária-Centro bus to town, or grab a cab (US$6).

GOIÁS VELHO
☎ 0xx62 • postcode 76600-000 • pop 20,000
The historic gold town of Goiás Velho had its heyday in the late 18th century and has slowly faded ever since. The former state capital is slow-paced and stuck in a time warp: Its narrow, cobbled streets aren't very well suited to cars, but its baroque churches

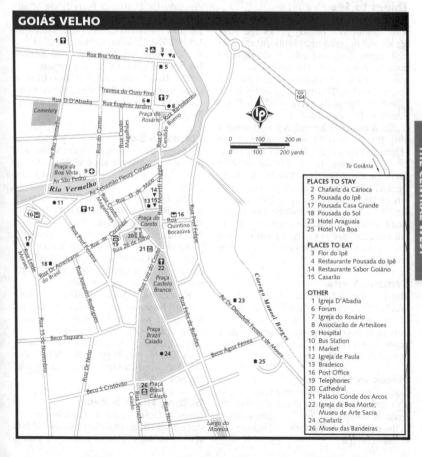

GOIÁS VELHO

PLACES TO STAY
2 Chafariz da Carioca
5 Pousada do Ipê
17 Pousada Casa Grande
18 Pousada do Sol
23 Hotel Araguaia
25 Hotel Vila Boa

PLACES TO EAT
3 Flor do Ipê
4 Restaurante Pousada do Ipê
14 Restaurante Sabor Goiáno
15 Casarão

OTHER
1 Igreja D'Abadia
6 Forum
7 Igreja do Rosário
8 Associação de Artesãoes
9 Hospital
10 Bus Station
11 Market
12 Igreja de Paula
13 Bradesco
16 Post Office
19 Telephones
20 Cathedral
21 Palácio Conde dos Arcos
22 Igreja da Boa Morte;
   Museu de Arte Sacra
24 Chafariz
26 Museu das Bandeiras

THE CENTRAL WEST

still shine during Semana Santa (Holy Week). Some restoration work is underway in the town, in particular the magnificent colonial-era hospital on the banks of the Rio Vermelho.

Goiás Velho is 144km from Goiânia and is en route to both Cuiabá in Mato Grosso and Aruanã (for access to the Rio Araguaia).

Information

There is no tourist office in Goiás Velho. Visa withdrawals can be made from Bradesco on Praça do Coreto.

Things to See

Walking through Goiás Velho, the former state capital, you quickly notice the main legacies of the gold rush: 18th-century colonial architecture, and a large mulatto and mestizo population. The streets are very narrow, with low houses, and there are seven churches. The most impressive is the oldest, the **Igreja da Paula** (1761), at Praça Zaqueu Alves de Castro.

The **Museu das Bandeiras** is well worth a visit. It's in the old town council building (1766), at Praça Brasil Caiado. Other interesting museums are the **Museu de Arte Sacra,** (in the old **Igreja da Boa Morte** dating from 1779, on Praça Castelo Branco), with lots of 19th-century works by local Goiânian Viega Vale, and the **Palácio Conde dos Arcos**, which is the old governor's residence. All museums are open from 8 am to 5 pm Tuesday to Saturday and from 8 am to noon on Sunday.

Semana Santa

The big occasion in Goiás Velho is Holy Week. The main streets are lit by hundreds of torches carried by the townsfolk, and dozens of hooded figures participate in a procession reenacting the removal of Christ from the cross and his burial.

Places to Stay

Goiás is a popular getaway from Goiânia, so it's a good idea to book ahead if you're arriving on a weekend. You can camp in town at the *Chafariz da Carioca*, just behind the Pousada do Ipê.

The most pleasant place to stay is *Pousada do Ipê* (☎ 371-2065, Rua do Forum 22) with rooms set around a shady courtyard. It's moving upmarket with a new swimming pool and bar/restaurant, but prices are still reasonable. It's often full. Apartamentos start at US$20/26 for singles/doubles, with a healthy breakfast included.

Another good option is the *Pousada do Sol* (☎ 371-1717, Rua Dr Americano do Brasil 17), in a lovely colonial building with apartamentos at US$17/24/30 for singles/doubles/triples. Cheaper, but not as pleasant, is the *Hotel Araguaia* (☎ 371-1462, Avenida Dr Deusdeth Ferreira de Moura 8). It's a hike from the bus station – about 15 minutes – but has clean apartamentos for US$9/17/20. Close to the bus station on Rua 15 de Novembro, *Pousada Casa Grande* has basic rooms for US$7 per person.

The *Hotel Vila Boa* (☎ 371-1000) is up on Morro Chapéu do Padre, offering views and a swimming pool. Singles/doubles go for US$52/68.

Places to Eat

The empadão reigns in Goiás Velho and the tasty savory pie filled with meat, vegetables, olives and egg is served just about everywhere.

The Ipês are taking over the restaurant scene. *Restaurante Pousada do Ipê* and *Restaurant Flor do Ipê*, close together on Praça da Boa Vista, both serve good regional food. Both have shady garden settings and buffets for around US$5 per person, so it's a tough choice. And both fill up on weekends, so get in early.

Restaurante Sabor Goiáno on Rua Moretti Foggia offers a per-kilo dinner and is popular with locals. *Casarão*, a simple place upstairs on Praça do Coreto, serves great empadões for US$2.50. The entrance is on Rua Moretti Foggia. This plaza is also the place to go for music, drinks and snacks at night.

Getting There & Away

Buses to Goiás Velho stop at the new bus station first, then continue on to the old bus station in the center of town (see map).

Christy the Redeemer, Rio

Rocinha, the largest favela in Rio

ROBYN JONES

Edge of Mata Atlantica, Iporanga

ANDREW DRAFFEN

Barra de Lagao, Santa Catarina

JUDY BELLAH

Iguaçu Falls, Paraná

There are frequent buses running between Goiás Velho and Goiânia (US$8, three hours). Direct buses leave for Goiânia at 6 am and 4 pm and are much quicker. There are two buses a day to Aruanã (US$7, three hours), at 11 am and 5 pm, for access to the Rio Araguaia, and a bus to Barra do Garças (US$16, six hours) at 8:40 am, where there are frequent connections to Cuiabá (Mato Grosso).

PIRENÓPOLIS
☎ 0xx62 • postcode 72980-000 • pop 12,500

Pirenópolis, another historic colonial gold city, is 128km from Goiânia and 165km from Brasília, on the Rio das Almas. It's a laid-back, picturesque town that's a popular weekend retreat for Goiânians and a good base for exploring the unique terrain of the cerrado.

Founded in 1727 by a bandeira of Paulistas in search of gold, Pirenópolis was originally called Minas da NS do Rosário da Meia Ponte. In 1989 it was placed on the Patrimonio Nacional (National Heritage) register. The city's colonial buildings sit on striking red earth under big skies.

Information
The tourist office (☎ 331-1299) on Rua do Bonfim has maps and can organize transport and guides for local sights.

Visa cash withdrawals can be made from Banco do Brasil and Bradesco, alongside each other on Rua Sizenando Jayme, the main commercial strip.

Churches
The **Igreja NS do Rosário Matriz** (1732) is the oldest sacred monument in the state. The **Igreja NS do Bonfim** (1750), with its beautiful altars, contains an image of the Senhor de Bonfim brought here from Portugal in 1755. The **Igreja NS do Carmo** (1750) was built by the Portuguese and today houses the **Museu de Arte Sacra**.

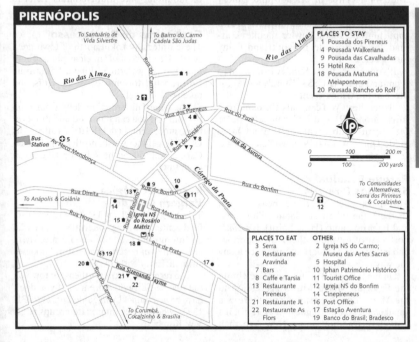

PIRENÓPOLIS

To Santuário de Vida Silvestre
To Bairro do Carmo Cadela São Judas
Rio das Almas
Rio das Almas
Rua do Carmo
Rua dos Pireneus
Rua do Fuzil
Rua do Rosário
Rua da Aurora
Bus Station
Av Neco Mendonça
Córrego da Prata
Rua do Bonfim
To Comunidades Alternativas, Serra dos Pirineus & Cocalzinho
Rua Direita
Rua do Bonfim
To Anápolis & Goiânia
Rua Nova
Igreja NS do Rosário Matriz
Rua Matutina
Rua da Prata
Rua Sizenando Jayme
Rua do Carmo
To Corumbá, Cocalzinho & Brasília

0   100   200 m
0   100   200 yards

THE CENTRAL WEST

PLACES TO STAY
1 Pousada dos Pireneus
4 Pousada Walkeriana
9 Pousada das Cavalhadas
15 Hotel Rex
18 Pousada Matutina Meiapontense
20 Pousada Rancho do Rolf

PLACES TO EAT
3 Serra
6 Restaurante Aravinda
7 Bars
8 Caffe e Tarsia
13 Restaurante Pireneus
21 Restaurante JL
22 Restaurante As Flors

OTHER
2 Igreja NS do Carmo; Museu das Artes Sacras
5 Hospital
10 Iphan Patrimónío Histórico
11 Tourist Office
12 Igreja NS do Bonfim
14 Cinepireneus
16 Post Office
17 Estação Aventura
19 Banco do Brasil; Bradesco

Festa do Divino Espírito Santo

Pirenópolis is famous for performing the story of Festa do Divino Espírito Santo, a tradition begun in 1819 that is more popularly known as Cavalhadas.

For three days, starting 45 days after Easter, the town looks like a scene from the Middle Ages. *Cavalhadas, congadas, mascarados, tapirios* and *pastorinhos* perform a series of medieval tournaments, dances and festivities, including a mock battle between the Moors and Christians in distant Iberia. Riding richly decorated horses, the combatants wear bright costumes and bull-headed masks. The Moors are defeated on the battlefield and convert to Christianity, proving that heresy doesn't pay in the end.

The festival is a happy one, and more folkloric than religious. The town's population swells severalfold during the festival. If you're in the neighborhood, make a point of seeing this stunning and curious spectacle, one of the most fascinating in Brazil.

Santuário de Vida Silvestre – Fazenda Vagafogo

Six kilometers northwest of town, the Vagafogo Farm Wildlife Sanctuary (☎ 9969-3090) is well worth a visit. Landowners Evandro Engel Ayer and Catarina Schiffer have set aside 44 hectares of cerrado and gallery forests on the margins of the Rio Vagafogo as a nature reserve. Fauna includes brown capuchin and black howler monkeys, armadillos, pampas deer, agouti and many bird species.

It's open Tuesday to Sunday from 8 am to 5 pm and entry is US$3. There's a café for lunch at the visitor's center.

To get there, you can walk the 6km from town along Rua do Carmo if you're feeling fit, grab a cab or contact local guide Diniz (☎ 331-1392), who can organize transport.

Parque Estadual da Serra dos Pirineus

This park contains three peaks – Pai (Father), the tallest at 1385m, Filho (Son) and Espírito Santo (Holy Spirit). It's 18km northeast of town and there are waterfalls and interesting rock formations to see along the way.

On the full moon in July, locals celebrate the Festa do Morro with a procession to the Morro dos Pireneus, where there is a small chapel on the highest peak (Pai). It's a modern tradition, more New Age than religious, and is accompanied by some serious partying.

Excursions to the park can be organized with local guides Diniz (☎ 331-1392) or with Renata Oliveira (☎ 331-1059, renata@arrobatur.com.br). For more ambitious treks or mountain bike tours, contact Estação Aventura (☎ 331-1069) at Rua da Prata 9.

Cachoeiras de Bonsucesso

These waterfalls 4.5km north of town are a good place to cool off in clear pools. There are six small waterfalls along a 1.5km trail. Be prepared to jump off some cliffs, and take your snorkel.

The waterfalls are open daily from 7 am to 5 pm and you can buy food and drinks at the visitor's center (☎ 331-1057). Entry costs US$3. To get there, walk north along Rua do Carmo and follow the signs or take a cab from town.

Reserva Ecológica Vargem Grande

This 3.6 sq km park (☎ 331-1171) on private land contains two big waterfalls – Caldeirão do Inferno and Caldeirão do Lázaro. There are small river beaches and natural pools to swim in. Entry costs US$3.

The reserve is 11km northeast of town on the road to Serra dos Pireneus. If you don't have a car, contact local guide Diniz (☎ 331-1392), who can accommodate groups in his VW Kombi.

THE CENTRAL WEST

Places to Stay & Eat

Pirenópolis is busy on weekends, during the Cavalhadas festival and for Carnaval, when prices can double those quoted here. When the pousadas fill up, most visitors camp out near the Rio das Almas or rent a room from a local.

There is a good range of pousadas in town, starting with the basic but clean *Hotel Rex* (☎ 331-1121, Praça Emmanoel Lopes 15), with quartos for US$7 per person. The *Pousada das Cavalhadas* (☎ 331-1261, Praça da Matriz 1) is centrally located and has single/double apartamentos with air conditioning for US$17/30. Housed in a pink and white colonial building, the *Pousada Matutina Meiapontense* (☎ 331-1101, Praça Emmanoel Jaime Lopes 2) is a friendly, comfortable place with a swimming pool. Apartamentos with fan go for US$17/24.

Pousada Rancho do Ralf (☎ 331-1162, Rua Benjamin Constant 17) is kitschy but comfortable and an OK value at US$50 for a double bungalow – there's a swimming pool and even a mini chapel in the shady gardens. *Pousada Walkeriana* (☎ 331-1260, Rua do Rosário 37), in an immaculately restored colonial building with a pool and gardens, has singles/doubles for US$60/66.

A couple of expensive top-end places have sprung up in the last few years, including the *Pousada dos Pireneus* (☎ 331-1345, Rua do Carmo 80). Cross the bridge and follow the signs – this place has got the works, including donkey rides for the kids! Prices start at US$80/92 for a single/double.

On the corner of Rua do Rosário and Rua do Bonfim, *Restaurante Pireneus* has a per-kilo lunch that's very popular with locals. Two places close together on Avenida Sizenando Jayme – *Restaurante As Flor* and *Restaurante JL* – both serve good caseira (home-cooked regional cuisine) for around US$5 per person, as does *Serra* on Rua dos Pireneus. The *Restaurante Aravinda* on Rua do Rosário has an extensive menu with some vegetarian dishes. *Caffe & Tarsia* (☎ 331-1274, Rua do Rosário 34) is a more upmarket Italian restaurant.

Shopping

Pirenópolis is considered the national silver capital, with more than 100 silversmithing studios scattered around town.

At Piretur, on Avenida Comandante Joaquim Alves, and the Centro de Cultura e Tourismo on Rua do Bonfim, you'll find a good selection of other local craft products made from ceramic, leather, wood, straw and soapstone.

Getting There & Away

There are six buses a day to Brasília (US$5, three hours), and two to Goiânia (US$7, two hours) at 6 am and 5 pm. There are more frequent local buses to Anápolis, where you can catch a connection to Goiânia.

CALDAS NOVAS

☎ 0xx62 • postcode 75690-000 • pop 47,000
Caldas Novas, 187km from Goiânia and 393km from Brasília, has more than 30 hot springs, with average temperatures of 42°C (107°F). Studies have shown that the waters are beneficial for people suffering from high blood pressure, poor digestion, weak endocrine glands or impotence.

Now an upmarket, high-rise resort, the town's population swells to around 200,000 during holiday periods.

Information

The tourist information booth (☎ 453-1868) in the center of town on Praça Mestre Orlando is open daily from 9 am to 9 pm. The Banco do Brasil at Rua Capitan João Crisostomo 325 has a 24-hour Visa ATM.

Places to Stay & Eat

Six kilometers from the city, on the road to Pires do Rio, *Camping Lagoa Quente* (☎ 453-1250, lquente@ih.com.br) has two thermal swimming pools. The cost is US$8 a head.

A couple of relatively cheap places are *Hotel Diadema* (☎ 453-1327, Rua Joaquim Rodrigues de Rezende 65), with single/double apartamentos for US$20/27, and *Pousada Paraíso* (☎ 453-5913, Avenida Martinho Palmerston 880), 2km from town. The pousada has a pool and charges US$17/34 for singles/doubles.

Wet & Wild Goes Hot & Healthy

It might not be everyone's bag, but a visit to a watery wonderland is a must-do for some travelers. It's active, it's fun, it's a great way to cool off…or is it?

The natural hot springs in the Caldas Novas area have given rise to a new type of aquatic playground – one that's hot, and good for you. Many hotels in the city have thermal pools, but the most over-the-top example of a health spa gone mad is Pousada do Rio Quente, 30km from Caldas Novas. This full-blown resort complex includes two five-star hotels and a service town of 2000 people to house its workers.

You don't have to stay at the hotels to get a slice of the action, though. The resort includes Hot Park – a massive complex of landscaped swimming pools with slides (reaching speeds of 25 to 30km), toboggans, 'rivers' and bars in more than 4,000 square meters of water heated to 40°C (104°F). Entry costs US$15.

The waters are made up of mineral components including calcium, potassium, sodium, magnesium and traces of iron – a potent mix that is claimed to be beneficial for poor digestion, rheumatism, allergies, high blood pressure and sexual vitality. For more information, check the Web site (in Portuguese) at www.rioquenteresorts.com.br.

In the mid-range, *Hotel Aguas Claras Thermas* (☎ 453-1738, Rua Cirilo Lopes de Morais 21) has a thermal pool and a sauna. Singles/doubles go for US$36/48.

There is no shortage of top-end places in town and a handful of ultra-luxurious resort complexes in the surrounding areas (see the boxed text on Pousada do Rio Quente).

For lunch, *Ki Kilo Restaurante e Pamonharia* (☎ 453-2562), on Avenida Orcalino Santos in the center, has a per-kilo buffet. *Papas Restaurante e Pizzaria*, right in the heart of town at Praça Mestre Orlando 12, has regional food and pizza for around US$20 for two people.

Getting There & Away

The bus station is at the end of Rua Antônio Coelho de Godoy. Regular buses run to Brasília (US$26, six hours) and Goiânia (US$10, three hours), as well as to Rio de Janeiro and São Paulo.

CHAPADA DOS VEADEIROS

☎ 0xx61

Just over 220km north of Brasília and 420km from Goiânia, this spectacular national park in the highest area of the Central West showcases the unique landscape and flora of high-altitude cerrado.

With high waterfalls, natural swimming pools and oasis-like stands of wine palms, the park is a popular destination for ecotourists. In fact, the whole area is beautiful, with its big skies, exotic flora and dramatic hills rising up like waves breaking across the plains.

The sublime landscape, much of it based on quartz crystal, has also attracted New Agers who have established alternative communities and a burgeoning 'esoturismo' industry in the area.

The town of Alto Paraíso (38km from the park) is the center of these communities, but most travelers will use the former crystal mining hamlet of São Jorge (2km from the national park entrance) as a base. You'll need two or three days to see the main attractions within the park, but it won't be difficult to spend longer soaking up the atmosphere of the area.

Mammals in the area include maned wolves, banded anteaters, giant armadillos, deer, capybaras and tapirs. Birds include rheas, toucans, macaws, hawks and vultures. The best time to visit the park is between April and October, before the rivers flood during the rainy season and access is difficult. The World Wildlife Fund for Nature uses its base in the nearby town of Alto

Paraíso to develop ongoing projects for conservation of the surrounding cerrado. For more information, call ☎ 646-1117.

Information
There's an excellent tourist office (☎ 646-1159) in Alto Paraíso. It's 200m from the bus station on Avenida Ari Valadão and is open weekdays from 8 am to 5 pm, Saturday from 8 am to 8 pm and Sunday from 9 am to noon. Say hi to Helvia and pick up a copy of Chapada dos Veadeiros: Guia do Paraíso.

Visiting the Park
All visitors to the park must be accompanied by an accredited guide. Guides can be organized at the park entrance (☎ 646-1570), through local guide associations ACVCV (☎ 646-1690) or Servitur (☎ 646-1235), or at most hotels in São Jorge. The park is open daily from 8 am to 5 pm and entry is US$2 per person.

The guides run separate six-hour tours to each of the park's three main attractions – the canions (canyons), cachoeiras (waterfalls) and cariocas (rocks). The tours cost US$20 for up to 10 people.

The canions tour weaves along the Rio Preto, which runs through the middle of the park. The river has cut two large canyons (imaginatively named Canion I and Canion II) through rock with sheer 20m-high walls on either side. There are natural platforms for diving into the cold water.

The cachoeiras tour takes in Salto do Rio Preto I and II, two beautiful waterfalls (80m and 120m respectively) that cascade to the ground just 30m apart. The falls are set in a picturesque valley at the end of a trail that weaves through classic cerrado landscape of meadows and gallery forests.

The cariocas tour runs through a river valley with interesting rock formations. There's also a small white-sand river beach for cooling off and cascading waters for a natural spa massage.

There are several sights adjacent to the road between Alto Paraíso and São Jorge. Because they are inside the park, you're obliged to hire a guide to access them, but there are no regular tours. **Morro da Baleia** (Whale's Hill), with its humpback rising from the plain, is ideal for hiking and there's a spot for a swim on the first plateau. There's a 2.5km hiking trail to the top – it takes about two hours each way.

The imposing **Morro do Buracão**, made up of craggy outcrops of quartz rock, lies close to the road but is difficult to access.

Vale da Lua
A unique sight in the Chapada dos Veadeiros area is the Vale da Lua (Valley of the Moon). Over millions of years, the rushing waters of the Rio São Miguel have sculpted rock formations and craters with a striking resemblance to a lunar landscape. Shades of silver, gray and white reflect from rocks and the chilly emerald waters add to the otherworldly atmosphere.

Vale da Lua is outside the national park, so you don't need a guide, but the area is subject to flash flooding during the rainy season, so check with locals before you head off. It's around 5km from São Jorge on a well-marked walking trail that follows the Rio São Miguel. Take sunscreen and water with you. Entry costs US$2.

Other Attractions
Some of the alternative communities in the Alto Paraíso area receive guests. **Fazenda Lua** (☎ 646-1613) runs workshops for healing, meditation and permaculture. It's 18km back along Hwy GO-118 from Alto Paraíso towards Brasília and 42km along a dirt road – plus a 4km walk and a canoe ride!

Thirty-five kilometers along a horse trail from Alto Paraíso, the Rainbow Tribe is based at **Fazenda Macaco** (no phone). The Tribe offers accommodations with vegetarian meals and trekking included. To get there, it's 35km on foot or by horse, or around 50km by car or mountain bike.

The best offbeat attraction is **Aeroporto de UFO**, 4km from Alto Paraíso. Local myth has it that a wealthy believer built the runway to receive UFOs. It's a popular spot for mystic rituals, meditations and concerts.

Organized Tours

Trans Chapada Tourismo (☎ 646-1345, info@transchapada.com.br) is directly opposite the bus station in Alto Paraíso at Rua dos Cristais 7. The agency can organize transport and guides for a variety of tours and activities, including trekking, mountain biking and canyoning. They also rent cars for US$40 per day.

Other agencies in Alto Paraíso offering similar deals include Alpatur (☎ 646-1821, alpatur@altoparaiso.com) at Rua das Nascentes 129 and Travessia (☎ 646-1595, travessia@tba.com.br) at Avenida Ary Valadão Filho 979.

Places to Stay & Eat

Alto Paraíso has a wide range of accommodations, including upmarket options, but most travelers stay in the village of São Jorge. Prices quoted below are for weekdays; they rise by up to 30% on weekends.

There are plenty of campgrounds (mostly in backyards) in São Jorge costing US$5 per person.

There are three good pousadas close together two blocks from São Jorge's main street. *Pousada Trilha Violeta* (☎ 985-6544) is a friendly place with single/double apartamentos for US$18/27. A good breakfast is included and Heneta, the manager, can organize guides and transport. *Pousada Aguas de Marco* (☎ 347-2082) is a rustic, ambient little place with rooms starting at US$12/24. You enter the comfort zone at *Pousada Mundo dha Lua* (☎ 234-7493), where rooms go for US$40/46. The most expensive accommodations in São Jorge are at the *Pousada Casa das Flores* (☎ 234-7493), one block farther down the hill. It's a mini New Age resort with a pool and small chalet-style apartments for US$45/58.

Villa São Jorge is a laid-back outdoor restaurant and bar with a great atmosphere. Their natural pizzas (US$7) are wood-fired and served on impressive wood plates. *Restaurante da Nenzinha*, run by Dona Nenzinha, offers a hearty, home-cooked buffet of regional food for US$4 per person. There's not much open in town during the afternoon siesta, so stock up for afternoon munchies.

Getting There & Away

From Goiânia, there's a daily bus to Alto Paraíso at 9 pm (US$18, six hours). There are three buses a day from Brasília to Alto Paraíso (US$9, 3½ hours), at 10 am, 3 pm and 10:30 pm. From Palmas (in Tocantins), Expresso União runs a bus at 9:30 pm daily (US$16, seven hours) via Natividade.

There is one daily bus from Alto Paraíso to São Jorge (US$2, one hour) at 4 pm for access to the park. The bus returns from São Jorge to Alto Paraíso daily at 8 am.

PARQUE NACIONAL DAS EMAS

Parque Nacional das Emas is a relatively small (1300 sq km) park in the remote southwest corner of Goiás, where it meets the states of Mato Grosso and Mato Grosso do Sul.

Surrounded by farmland, the park is on a high plateau and is considered the best-preserved cerrado in the country. There's little foliage to obstruct the sighting of wildlife, which includes tapirs, anteaters, deer, capybaras, foxes, peccaries, armadillos, blue and yellow macaws and the emas (South American rheas) that give the park its name. The flightless ema is Brazil's biggest bird, growing to a height of 1.4m and weighing around 30kg. The park is also the exclusive sanctuary of the jacamari (a species of wolf) and other endangered wolves.

An interesting spectacle is the 2m-high termite mounds that 'glow' in the dark (most often at the start of rainy season in October) – the result of bioluminescence produced by the termite larvae.

The park is a long way from any major city – 480km from Goiânia and 375km from Campo Grande, the capital of Mato Grosso do Sul. There are two entry points: Portão Jacuba (80km from Mineiros in Goiás) and Portão Guarda da Bandeira (25km from Chapadão do Céu in Goiás and 40km from Costa Rica in Mato Grosso do Sul).

The area gets seriously hot, and there are few trees for shade within the park. It's recommended that you visit in the early morning or late afternoon – take sunscreen, a hat, water and food as there is no infrastructure within the park.

The park lies along the Brazilian great divide, between the Amazon and Paraná river basins, at the headwaters of the Araguaia, Formoso and Taquari Rivers. Despite all the surrounding rivers, during dry season (July to October) the area is dry enough for fires to ignite spontaneously. Be careful with sparks!

Information & Organized Tours

No public transport goes to the park, so your options for getting there are to hire a car or to arrange a guided tour. You aren't obliged to enter the park with a guide, but guides aren't expensive, and they can organize transport.

In Goiânia, you can contact IBAMA (☎ 0xx62-224-2441) and the Fundação Emas (☎ 0xx62-661-4407) for information about the park and guides. In Mineiros, staff at the prefeitura (town hall; ☎ 0xx62-661-2411) can contact IBAMA-accredited guides for trips to the park. The tourist office in Chapadão do Céu (☎ 0xx62-634-1228) on Praça do Sol can do the same.

In Chapadão do Céu, recommended guides include 'Seu' Rubens (☎ 0xx62-634-1228) and Elaine Peixoto (☎ 0xx62-634-1309). There are two accredited guides at Fazenda Santa Amelia (see Places to Stay) – Nadir (who is the owner) and João Pereira (☎ 0xx62-634-1215). Rates start at around US$25 per day for groups of up to 6 people, not including transport.

Places to Stay

In Mineiros, the cheapest places to stay are **Boi na Brasa** (☎ 0xx62-661-1532, Rua 11, No 11), which was singles/doubles for US$10/20 per night, and **Hotel Pinheiros** (☎ 0xx62-661-1942, Rua 8, No 90), which charges US$7/14. The best hotel in the area is the **Pilões Palace** (☎ 0xx62-661-1547) on Praça Jose Alves de Assis. It has air conditioning and a bar/restaurant. Rooms cost US$40/60.

In Chapadão do Céu, the best place to stay for organizing park visits is **Fazenda Santa Amelia** (☎ 0xx62-634-1380) on Hwy G0-302, 12km from town. The owner is an accredited guide. Quartos cost US$22/44 and newer chalets go for US$34/68.

In Costa Rica (Mato Grosso do Sul), you'll find reasonably priced accommodations at **Hotel Beira Rio** (☎ 0xx67-247-1091, Rua José Narciso Sobrinho 703) and **Hotel Irapuru** (☎ 0xx67-247-1347, Avenida José Ferreira da Cost 1289). Both charge around US$16/32 for singles/doubles.

Getting There & Away

Access to the park is tough: Even though it's surrounded by farmland, there are no paved roads or regular bus routes. Buses go from Goiânia to Mineiros (US$20, 7 hours) via Hwy BR-364, passing through Jataí (110km before Mineiros), where you can transfer to a bus for Chapadão do Céu.

From Campo Grande (the capital of Mato Grosso do Sul), you can take a bus to Chapadão do Céu via Cassilândia.

RIO ARAGUAIA

For information on places along this large river, which forms a long stretch of the Goiás-Mato Grosso state border, refer to the Rio Araguaia section in the Pará, Amapá & Tocantins chapter.

THE CENTRAL WEST

Mato Grosso & Mato Grosso do Sul

Today, Mato Grosso and Mato Grosso do Sul are separate states, although until the late 1970s this region was all Mato Grosso state. This chapter contains a separate section on the Pantanal, the vast wetlands that extend across parts of both states.

Mato Grosso

There's a well-known story about a naturalist in the Mato Grosso. Disoriented by the sameness of the forest, the naturalist asked his Indian guide – who had killed a bird, put it in a tree and, incredibly, knew where to return for it at the end of the day – how he knew where the tree was. 'It was in the same place,' the Indian replied.

To begin to appreciate the Mato Grosso's inaccessibility and vastness, read Peter Fleming's classic *Brazilian Adventure,* which also happens to be one of the funniest travel books ever written. Fleming tells the story of his quest to find the famous British explorer Colonel Fawcett, who disappeared in the Mato Grosso in 1925 while searching for the hidden city of gold.

Mato Grosso means bundu, savanna, bush, outback; an undeveloped thick scrub. Part of the highland plain that runs through Brazil's interior, the Mato Grosso is a dusty land of rolling hills and some of the best fishing rivers in the world, such as the Araguaia.

This is also the land where many of Brazil's remaining Indians live. They are being threatened by rapid agricultural development (which is bringing in the poor from the South and Northeast who are desperate for land) and by a government that is less than fully committed to guaranteeing them their rights.

There's a saying in Brazil that 'progress is roads.' Key routes such as the roads from Belém to Brasília, Cuiabá to Porto Velho, and Cuiabá to Santarém have catalyzed the

Highlights

- Wildlife sightings and piranha fishing in the Pantanal
- The vistas of Parque Nacional da Chapada dos Guimarães
- Safaris in Alta Floresta, in the southern Amazon rainforest
- Swims with exotic fish in Bonito's crystal-clear rivers

opening of vast stretches of the Mato Grosso to cattle, rice, cotton, soya bean, corn and manioc, as well as to mining.

Mato Grosso is now the biggest producer of soybeans in Brazil and accounts for 12% of the country's total agricultural output. The imminent arrival of a gas pipeline from Bolivia will fuel the region's development for years to come.

This is Brazil's Wild West, where the struggle for land between the poor, Indians, miners, rich landowners and hired guns leads to violence and illegal land expropriation.

CUIABÁ

☎ 0xx65 • postcode 78000-000
• pop 476,000

Cuiabá is a frontier boom town. In 1719, a Paulista, Pascoal Moreira Cabral, was hunting Indians along the Rio Cuiabá when he found gold. A gold rush followed, but many of those seeking gold never reached the new settlement at Cuiabá. Traveling more than 3000km from São Paulo by river took five months; along the way, gold-seekers found little food, many mosquitoes, dangerous rapids, lengthy portages, disease and incredible heat.

With the end of the gold boom and the decay of the mines, Cuiabá would have disappeared, except that the soil along the Rio Cuiabá allowed subsistence agriculture, while the river itself provided fish.

As in many mining towns, there was tension here between Paulistas and recent Portuguese immigrants. In 1834, following Brazilian independence, the small town was torn apart by the Rusga (Brawl), in which a nativist movement of Paulistas slaughtered many of the Portuguese.

During the 1970s and 1980s, Cuiabá's population grew at 14% annually (a national record) as vast tracts of land were opened up for agriculture. The population explosion has tailed off in recent years, but Cuiabá is still one of Brazil's fastest-growing cities. It has been named the *boca de sertão* (mouth of the backlands).

Cuiabá has few historic or cultural attractions to interest travelers. However, it's a lively place and a good starting point for excursions to the Pantanal and Chapada dos Guimarães, as well as a useful rest stop on the way to the Amazon or Bolivia.

The city is actually two sister cities separated by the Rio Cuiabá: old Cuiabá and Várzea Grande (where the airport is located, by the Rio Cuiabá).

Information

Sedtur (☎ 624-9060, secdetur@zaz.com.br), the Mato Grosso tourist authority, is in the city center on the Praça da República. The office is open Monday to Friday from 8:30 to 6 pm.

The Banco do Brasil on the corner of Avenida Getúlio Vargas and Rua Barão de Melgaço changes money and has Visa and Mastercard ATMs. There are ATMs at the airport for Visa cash withdrawals.

The post office is on Praça da República, next to the tourist office. The telephone office is on Rua Barão de Melgaço, near the corner of Avenida Isaac Póvoas.

The tourist office has free Internet access for 30 minutes to check your email, but there's only one machine, so you might have to book a time. Otherwise, the Copy Center (☎ 322-2554) at Avenida Mato Grosso 432 has several terminals, but it's pricey at US$6 per hour.

The state government and Sedtur have developed an excellent Web site with information in both Portuguese and English – www.turismo.mt.gov.br.

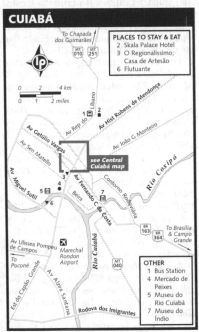

CUIABÁ

To Chapada dos Guimarães

MT 010   MT 251

0   2   4 km
0   1   2 miles

Av Rep do Libano
Av Hist Rubens de Mendonça
Av Getúlio Vargas
Av Sen Matello
Av João G Monteiro
Av Miguel Sutil
see Central Cuiabá map
Av Fernando C da Costa
Rio Coxipó
Beira
Contorno Rodoviária

Av Ulissea Pompeu de Campos
Marechal Rondon Airport
To Poconé
Est do Capão Grande
Av Alzira Santana
Rio Cuiabá
Rodova dos Imigrantes

BR 163   BR 364   To Brasília & Campo Grande
MT 040

PLACES TO STAY & EAT
2 Skala Palace Hotel
3 O Regionalissimo; Casa de Artesão
6 Flutuante

OTHER
1 Bus Station
4 Mercado de Peixes
5 Museu do Rio Cuiabá
7 Museu do Índio

Museu do Índio

The Indian museum (☎ 615-8489) has exhibits of the Xavante, Bororo and Karajá tribes and is worth a visit. It is at the university, on Avenida Fernando Correia da Costa, and is open Monday to Friday from 8 to 11 am and 2 to 5 pm, and weekends from 8 to 11 am. To get there, catch a No 406 Jd Universitário bus, on Avenida Tenente Coronel Duarte.

Museu do Rio Cuiabá

The old fish market (☎ 623-1440, museudorio@ cuiaba.mt.gov.br) on Avenida Beira Rio along the riverfront has been restored and now houses a museum and art gallery. It's about 2.5km from the center and is open Tuesday to Friday from 9 to 11 am and 2 to 5 pm, and weekends from 2 to 5 pm. To get there from the center, you can walk along Rua 13 de Junho.

Mercado de Peixes

Close to the Museu do Rio Cuiabá, the fish market by the bridge is worth a visit, at least before the heat of the day. It's interesting not so much as a place to shop but as a venue to look at the people and their products.

Santo Antônio de Leverger

Cuiabános go to enjoy the river beaches from June to October at Santo Antônio de Leverger, also the site of Mato Grosso's best Carnaval. It's on the Rio Cuiabá, 28km south of Cuiabá in the direction of Barão de Melgaço. To get there, take a 'Santo Antônio' bus from Avenida Isaac Póvoas in the center.

Organized Tours

Travel agencies and small operators in town can arrange day trips to the Parque Nacional Chapada dos Guimarães. Anaconda (☎ 624-4142, anaconda@zaz.com.br) at Avenida Isaac Póvoes 606, Natureco (☎ 624-5116, natureco@zaz.com.br) at Rua Barão do Rio Branco 2015, Faunatour (☎ 682-0101, faunatour@zaz.com.br) and Shalom Tour (☎ 322-6352, shalomtr@terra.com.br) at Rua Commandante Costa 649 all run day trips to Chapada for around US$40 per person, including lunch.

For details about excursions from Cuiabá into the Pantanal, see Organized Tours in the Pantanal section.

Festa de São Benedito

This festival takes place during the first week of July at the Igreja NS do Rosário and the Capela de São Benedito. The holiday has a more Umbanda than Catholic flavor; it's celebrated with traditional foods such as *bolos de queijo* (cheese balls) and *bolos de arroz* (rice balls), and regional dances such as O Cururu, O Siriri, Danças do Congo and dos Mascarados.

Places to Stay

There's a shortage of budget accommodations in Cuiabá. *Pousada Ecoverde (☎ 624-1386, pousadaecoverde@terra.com.br, Rua Pedro Celestino 391)*, run by local guide Joel Souza and his family, is a very good value. It's a small oasis in the middle of the city, with a shady courtyard and garden, a library and laundry facilities. It's centrally located two blocks from Praça Alencastro in the old part of town. Rooms cost US$7 per person with breakfast included. There are only four rooms, so book ahead if you can.

One of the better cheapies is the central *Hotel Samara (☎ 322-6001, Rua Joaquim Murtinho 270)*, which offers basic quartos for US$9 per person and boxy apartamentos at US$11/17 for singles/doubles. *Hotel Panorama (☎ 322-0072, Praça Moreira Cabral 286)* has more airy apartamentos with fan at US$15/22/26/30 for singles/doubles/triples/quads – overpriced if you're solo but reasonable value for groups. *Hotel Plaza (☎ 323-2018, Rua Antônio Maria 428)* has clean but basic single/double quartos at US$7/14 and apartamentos for US$14/20.

Of the mid-range options, the central *Hotel Mato Grosso (☎ 614-7777, Rua Comandante Costa 2522)* is a good choice. Small apartamentos with fan cost US$26/32 or US$32/44 with air-con. *Hotel Real (☎ 321-5375, Praça Ipiranga 102)* is not as grand, but it has large apartamentos with air-con and fridge for US$16/27. The *Jaguar Palace Hotel (☎ 624-4404, Avenida Getúlio Vargas 600)* is a three-star hotel with a pool. Singles/

The Indians of Mato Grosso

To reach Cuiabá in the 18th century, goldseekers had to cross the lands of several groups of Indians, many of whom were formidable warriors. They included the Caiapó (who even attacked the settlement at Goiás), the Bororo of the Pantanal, the Parecis (who were enslaved to mine gold), the Paiaguá (who defeated several large Portuguese flotillas and caused periodic panic in Cuiabá) and the Guaicuru (skilled riders and warriors who gained many years of experience fighting the Europeans).

Despite some important victories, many Indians had been killed or enslaved by the time the gold boom began to fade in the mid-18th century. Today, however, several tribes remain in northern Mato Grosso, living as they have for centuries. The Erikbatsa, noted for their fine featherwork, live near Fontanilles and Juina; the Nhambikuraa are near Padroal; and the Cayabi live near Juara. The only tribe left in the Pantanal still subsisting by hunting and fishing is the Bororo. There are also the Cinta Larga Indians of Parque Indígena Aripuanã and, of course, the tribes under the care of FUNAI in the Parque Indígena do Xingu, which was set up in the 1950s as a safe haven for several groups of Indians, including some dispossessed groups from outside the park. In an important victory in late 2000, the Panara, who were forcibly moved to Xingu in 1975, were handed back their traditional lands 400km north of Cuiabá. In a landmark settlement, the tribe was also awarded compensation from the government for suffering caused by its dispossession.

You probably won't be able to overcome the many obstacles to visiting Indian reserves, but if you should want to try, contact FUNAI (☎ 0xx65-644-1850) in Cuiabá, or visit the Web site www.funai.gov.br for more information. See also the Visiting Indigenous Lands section in the introductory Facts about Brazil chapter.

---

doubles go for US$40/50, but you can negotiate discounts of up to 30% for cash.

If you're overnighting or arrive late on the bus, **Skala Palace Hotel** (☎ 621-3067, *Avenida Jules Rimet 26*) is directly opposite the bus station. Comfortable apartamentos with air-con, fridge and TV are good value at US$16/27/40 for singles/doubles/triples. It's worth asking about discounts.

At the top end, the Best Western **Mato Grosso Palace** (☎ 614-7000, *Rua Joaquim Murtinho 170*) is a four-star job offering singles/doubles starting at US$80/90.

Places to Eat

Cuiabá offers some great fish dishes, including *pacu assado com farofa de couve*, *piraputanga assado* and *pirão de bagre* – try one at the floating restaurant **Flutuante**, near Rua Sarita Baracat next to Ponte Nova bridge in Varzea Grande. It's complicated to reach by public bus, but it's a 20-minute walk from the Mercado de Peixes.

On Rua 13 de Junho next to the Casa do Artesão is **O Regionalissimo**, which serves excellent regional food per kilo – lots of fish and the sweetest of sweets. It's open daily except Monday for lunch.

In the center, there are wholesome per-kilo lunch spots close together on Rua Commandante Costa – **Miranda's** and **En Casa**. Up toward the old town, **Restaurant Casarão** (*Rua Pedro Celestino 119*) also offers a per-kilo lunch in a quieter location. Walk through the handicrafts shop at the front – the dining room is out the back.

The center is almost deserted at night, but there are good restaurants nearby on Avenida Getúlio Vargas. Close to the Jaguar Palace Hotel, **Restaurante Hong Kong** (*Avenida Getúlio Vargas 647*) offers a tasty all-you-can-eat Chinese buffet for US$6 per person. Around five minutes farther on, **Getúlio** (*Avenida Getúlio Vargas 1147*) is an upmarket bar/restaurant popular with young Cuiabános. There's a sushi bar, too, if you're craving raw fish. Last on the Getúlio

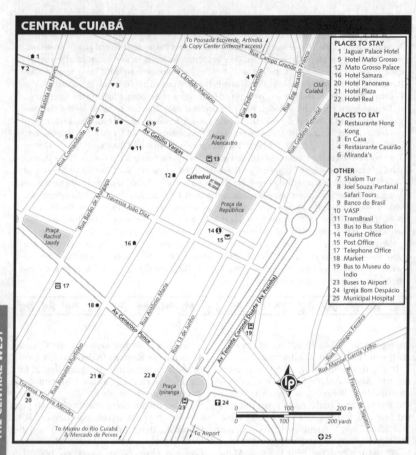

CENTRAL CUIABÁ

PLACES TO STAY
1 Jaguar Palace Hotel
5 Hotel Mato Grosso
12 Mato Grosso Palace
16 Hotel Samara
20 Hotel Panorama
21 Hotel Plaza
22 Hotel Real

PLACES TO EAT
2 Restaurante Hong Kong
3 En Casa
4 Restaurante Casarão
6 Miranda's

OTHER
7 Shalom Tur
8 Joel Souza Pantanal Safari Tours
9 Banco do Brasil
10 VASP
11 TransBrasil
13 Bus to Bus Station
14 Tourist Office
15 Post Office
17 Telephone Office
18 Market
19 Bus to Museu do Índio
23 Buses to Airport
24 Igreja Bom Despácio
25 Municipal Hospital

Vargas strip, but certainly not least, ***Choppão*** on Praça 8 de Abril is a classic Cuiabá eatery. Obscenely large meals of meat or fish with salad cost US$11 for two people, and you can drink the coldest *chopp* (draft beer) in town in specially iced tankards.

Entertainment

There are two main nightlife clusters in town, along Avenida Getúlio Vargas and around Avenida Mato Grosso.

Apoteose *(Avenida Mato Grosso 442)* is a popular dance club, as is **Deck Avenida** *(Avenida Rúbens de Mendonça 635)*. ***Maito Bier*** at Avenida Mato Grosso 422 is a lively joint for a beer and has live music. For a taste of cool Brazilian country music – sertaneja – head for ***Estrebaria*** *(Rua Floriano Peixoto 401)*.

Shopping

The FUNAI Artíndia shop (Rua Pedro Celestino 317) has a good range of Indian baskets, bows and arrows, jewelry and headdresses for sale. The Casa do Artesão on Praça João Bueno along Rua 13 de Junho has local handicrafts, including ceramics, woodcarvings, straw baskets, paintings and woven hammocks.

Getting There & Away

There are flights between Cuiabá and many airports in Brazil (with the notable omission of Corumbá in Mato Grosso do Sul) by TAM (☎ 682-1702), Varig (☎ 682-1140), TransBrasil (☎ 682-3597) or VASP (☎ 682-3737).

Six buses a day make the two-hour trip to Poconé (US$6, 2½ hours); the first leaves at 6 am. To Barão de Melgaço (US$8, 4½ hours), there are two daily buses at 7:30 am and 3 pm. For Chapada dos Guimarães (US$9, two hours) there are buses every hour, but take an early bus if you're doing a day trip.

Six buses a day go to Cáceres (US$12, 3½ hours) with connections to Santa Cruz in Bolivia. Porto Velho is a hard 24-hour (US$50) ride away. There are frequent buses to Goiânia (US$27, 13 hours) and Brasília (US$35, 16 hours) – most of them stop in Barra do Garças (US$14, 7 hours), where you have access to the Rio Araguaia. Most of the eight buses a day to Campo Grande (US$26, 10 hours) stop at Coxim (US$16, seven hours). To Alta Floresta (US$35, 13 hours), there are four buses a day.

Getting Around

Marechal Rondon airport (☎ 682-2213) is in Varzea Grande, 7km from Cuiabá. To catch the local bus to town, turn left as you leave the airport and walk to the Las Velas Hotel. Opposite the hotel entrance, catch a Jardim Marajoara, 24 de Dezembro or Pireneus bus. A taxi costs US$10.

Cuiabá's bus station (☎ 621-3629) is 3km north of the center on the highway towards Chapada dos Guimarães. From inside the bus station, you can get a Centro bus to Praça Alencastro. More frequent buses marked 'Centro' leave from outside the bus station and can drop you along Avenida Isaac Póvoas. A ticket taxi from inside the bus station costs US$6 – or if you're traveling light, grab a motor taxi outside for around US$2.

All the car-rental places have branches in the center and in or near the airport. There

are often promotional rates, so shop around. Locadora (☎ 627-3500) and Localiza (☎ 624-7979) are a couple of reliable companies. The best car for the Pantanal is the Volkswagen Gol.

On average, a rental car with unlimited kilometers will cost around US$60 a day.

CHAPADA DOS GUIMARÃES
☎ 0xx65

After the Pantanal, the Parque Nacional da Chapada dos Guimarães is Mato Grosso's leading attraction. The park is located on a rocky plateau 64km northeast of Cuiabá and 800m higher, offering a cool change from the state capital. The region is reminiscent of the American Southwest and surprisingly different from the typical Mato Grosso terrain. The town of the same name is a convenient base for exploring the park and surrounding areas.

The area surrounding the park has numerous attractions. About 41km northeast of Chapada town is the 1100m-long **Aroe Jari** cavern and, in another cave close by, the **Lagoa Azul** (Blue Lake). On the way from Cuiabá to Chapada town, you pass **Rio dos Peixes**, **Rio Mutaca** and **Rio Claro**, which are popular weekend bathing spots for Cuiabános. The sheer 80m drop called **Portão do Inferno** (Hell's Gate) is also unforgettable. Take a waterfall shower at **Cachoeirinha** and peek into the chapel of **NS de Santãna**, a strange mixture of Portuguese and French baroque.

Parque Nacional da Chapada dos Guimarães

The two exceptional sights inside the park are the 60m **Véu de Noiva** (Bridal Veil) falls and the **Cidade de Pedra** (Stone City). The major attraction is the impressive Véu de Noiva, a 86m free-falling waterfall. Véu de Noiva is around 15km west of the town of Chapada dos Guimarães. There is a visitor's center (☎ 791-1133) open daily from 8 am to 6 pm.

You can get off the bus from Cuiabá and walk to Véu de Noiva from the road, spend a couple of hours there, then flag down the next bus coming through to the town of Chapada dos Guimarães. Start walking downhill over the bluff, slightly to your right. A small trail leads to a magical lookout, perched on top of rocks with the canyon below. This is Chapada's most dazzling place.

The Cidade de Pedra has wonderful vistas and rock formations reminiscent of stone temples. It's 20km north of Chapada town along the road to Água Fria. The turnoff to Água Fria is 6km west of Chapada town on Hwy MT-251.

Mirante

The Mirante (Lookout) is the unofficial geographic center of South America. It's outside the national park, 8km from the town of Chapada dos Guimarães. Take the last road in Chapada on your right and go 8km; you'll see a dirt road. The rim of the canyon is a couple of hundred meters away. The view is stupendous; off to your right you can see the Cuiabá skyline.

Organized Tours

If you don't have a car, your best bet is to take an excursion with Jorge Mattos, who runs Eco Turismo Cultural (☎ 301-1393; ecoturismo@chapadadosguimaraes.com) at Praça Dom Wunibaldo 57 in Chapada town. Jorge runs four excursions: to the national park (which contains the most spectacular waterfalls); to the Lagoa Azul and the Aroe Jari cavern; to the Cidade de Pedra; and to Água Fria, a diamond-mining town 40km from Chapada. All tours cost US$100 for up to five people (US$20 per person), except Aroe Jari cavern, which is US$115 (US$23 per person) for up to five people. Prices don't include lunch or park entrance fees.

Places to Stay & Eat

There is free camping with facilities at Salgadeira, just before the climb into the Chapada park.

Lodging in the town of Chapada ranges from the basic **Hotel São José** (☎ 301-1563, Rua Vereador José de Souza 50), where rooms start at US$5 per person, to the new **Pousada Penhasco** (☎ 301-1555), 2km from town on Avenida Penhasco, which charges US$100 a double.

In between are a couple of good alternatives. The **Rios Hotel** (☎ 301-1126) on Rua Tiradentes has a range of rooms, starting with quartos for US$10/16. **Turismo Hotel** (☎ 301-1176, Rua Fernando Correo Costa 1065) is run by a German family. Single/double apartamentos cost US$30/40.

Restaurants and bars in Chapada town are clustered around Praça Dom Wunibaldo. **Nivio's Tour** (Praça Dom Wunibaldo 631) has excellent regional food – all you can eat for US$9. Unfortunately, it's only open for lunch. Also popular for regional food at lunchtime (and a bit cheaper) is **O Mestrinho** (Rua Quinco Caldas 119). **Nutriquilo** (Rua Cipriano Curvo 729) is a decent per-kilo joint. **Trapiche** (Rua Cipriano Curvo 580), just off the main square, is good for a drink and music at night.

If you need inspiration while you eat, **Restaurante Morro dos Ventos** could be worth a splurge. It's 4km east of town along Hwy MT-251 in the direction of Campo Verde, and has spectacular views across the Morro dos Ventos.

Getting There & Around

Buses leave Cuiabá's bus station for Chapada town (US$9, two hours) hourly from 7 am to 7 pm. In the other direction, the first bus leaves Chapada town at 6 am and the last at 6 pm.

Because it can be difficult to access the park and other attractions from the town, you may wish to rent a car and explore the area on your own, stopping at different rock formations, waterfalls and bathing pools at your leisure. If you do have the use of a car, drop by the Secretária de Turismo (☎ 301-1690) on Rua Quinco Caldas (on the left-hand side as you drive into Chapada town, just before the square). A useful map is available – you'll need it!

BARRA DO GARÇAS

☎ 0xx65 • postcode 78600-000 • pop 48,000

Situated almost halfway between Brasília and Cuiabá, Barra do Garças is appealing as a place to break a long journey, but it's also a pleasant river town and a launching pad for travel along the Rio Araguaia.

Barra do Garças and its twin town Aragarças lie on the banks of the Rio das Garças, a major tributary of the Rio Araguaia. Close to the center of town, Praia de Aragarças and other sandy river beaches are uncovered between May to October when the waters recede.

You'll need written permission to visit the nearby reserves of the Bororo and Xavante Indians. For information about visiting Indian reserves, contact FUNAI (☎ 401-2018) at Rua Pires de Campos 681. In town, there's an excellent range of indigenous artifacts at Berô Can, Avenida Min João Alberto 437.

Information
The Fundatur tourist office (☎ 861-2227) on Praça Tiradentes can help with information about tours along the Rio Araguaia. The Banco do Brasil on Praça Tiradentes has a Visa ATM.

Organized Tours
Aventur (☎ 401-1709, aventur@continet .psi.br) is a central travel agency that can organize boat tours along the Rio Araguaia and to local attractions such as Parque Estadual da Serra Azul.

Places to Stay
There is a campsite close to the center at Porto Bae – access is from Avenida Marechal Rondon. If you're passing through, look for some cheap hotels opposite the bus station on Rua Bororós – *Hotel Santa Rosa* (☎ 401-1482) is the best of a pretty awful bunch. *Pousada Tropical* (☎ 401-4213, Rua Valdir Rabelo 1520) is a reasonable mid-range hotel. It's new and clean and has air-conditioned singles/doubles for US$15/30. *Hotel Toriuá Parque* (☎ 638-1472), on Avenida Min João Alberto is along the riverfront in Aragarças. The hotel has a restaurant and pool. Singles/doubles cost US$36/50.

Getting There & Away
There are two buses a day to Cuiabá (US$14, seven hours), at 4:30 and 11:30 pm, and a daily bus to Goiás Velho (US$16, six

hours). Two buses a day, at 5:30 am and 9 pm, make the 14-hour, 565km trip to São Felix do Araguaia on the Rio Araguaia, where you may be able to arrange boat trips to the Ilha do Bananal. The road turns to dirt about halfway to São Felix, at Dona Rosa.

ALTA FLORESTA
☎ 0xx65 • postcode 78580-000 • pop 37,000
Alta Floresta, 873km north of Cuiabá, is situated in the extreme north of Mato Grosso, at the edge of pristine southern Amazon rainforest. The area is considered one of the best in the Brazilian Amazon for spotting rare birds and mammals, including the endangered white-nosed bearded saki monkey, brown titi monkey, tapir, giant river otter, three-toed sloth and five species of macaws.

Alta Floresta is the end of the road: Beyond it to the north is the vast expanse of the jungle. The town itself has no attractions and has grown rapidly as an agricultural and logging center since its foundation in the early 1970s.

Places to Stay
Many visitors to the area are naturalists on expensive package tours to isolated jungle lodges, but independent travelers will find a few good accommodations options in town.

Floresta Amazônica (☎ 521-3601, cristalino@brazilnature.com, Avenida Perimetral Oeste 2001) is located in a nice park location and has single/double apartamentos with air-con for US$34/40. One of the cheaper places is *Lisboa Palace* (☎ 521-2876, Avenida do Aeroporto 252, Setor C). Singles/doubles cost US$24/30.

The top place in the area is *Cristalino Jungle Lodge* (☎ 521-3601) on the banks of the Rio Cristalino around 38km north of Alta Floresta (one hour by boat or two hours by road). The lodge employs bilingual guides for boat and hiking expeditions. Single/double quartos cost US$82/164 and apartamentos cost US$120/185 – prices include all meals. Packages can be booked through Focus Tours, who have worked in the area for 10 years (see Organized Tours in the Natural Brazil special section earlier in the book).

THE CENTRAL WEST

The Harpy Eagle's Fight for Survival

The harpy eagle is the world's largest eagle and the most powerful predatory bird in South America. It's threatened by deforestation, destruction of nesting sites and poaching, and since 1992 just nine nests have been confirmed in Guyana, 10 in Venezuela, eight in Panama – and one in Brazil, in northern Mato Grosso. Harpy eagles are about 85cm long and have a wingspan of almost two meters. Females are one-third larger than males and weigh from 7 to 9kg. The female's powerful talons are up to 12cm long – as long as the claws of a grizzly bear – all the better to hunt their prey, which includes sloths, monkeys, deer and reptiles. Harpy eagles mate for life and build large nests very high (40m and above) in the forest canopy. Females lay one or two eggs in a clutch, but only one survives. Both parents care for the young. Sure, they're hunters, but they love their kids!

If you're serious about your birds, you'll want to see the harpy eagle nest, which is close to Pousada Currupira das Araras (currupira@inter-fox.com.br), near the town of Barra do Bugres in the Serra das Araras, 130km northwest of Cuiabá.

Getting There & Away

From Cuiabá, there are four buses a day to Alta Floresta (US$35, 13 hours). Trip Airlines (☎ 682-2549) at the airport in Cuiabá flies to Alta Floresta Monday to Friday at 11:50 am. Round-trip tickets cost about US$360.

CÁCERES

☎ 0xx65 • postcode 78200-000 • pop 66,000

The city of Cáceres, founded in 1778 on the left bank of the Rio Paraguai, is an access point for a number of Pantanal lodges and for Bolivia. It's a relaxed town that has kept the charm of a small river settlement – except during September, when it hosts the world's biggest river fishing competition. Located 215km from Cuiabá on Hwy BR-070, it's close to the Ilha de Taiamã ecological reserve.

In the past, a steady stream of travelers arrived in Cáceres to take cement barges along the Rio Paraguai to Corumbá. These days, you'll need a lot of luck and plenty of time to hang around: There are no regular itineraries and passenger travel on cargo boats is officially not allowed. Your best bet is to ask around the port; if you do find someone willing to take you downstream to Corumbá, the trip takes three to six days.

If you're traveling on to Bolivia, get a Brazilian exit stamp from the Polícia Federal, 4km from town on Avenida Getúlio Vargas, next to the *prefeitura* (city hall). Taxis want US$8 to take you there and back.

Organized Tours

Pantanal Tours (☎ 223-1200) at Rua Coronel Faria 180, one block back from the riverfront, can organize tours into the Pantanal, and boat and fishing trips along the Rio Paraguai.

Places to Stay & Eat

The best place near the bus station is the ***Capri Hotel*** (*☎ 223-1771, Rua Getúlio Vargas 99*). Spacious, air-conditioned singles/doubles cost US$14/17. Basic but clean apartamentos cost US$6/12. Closer to the river and the center, the ***Rio Hotel*** (*☎ 223-3084*) on Praça Major João Carlos is a good option. Its quartos with fan cost US$9/16 and apartamentos are US$12/20.

Pantanal Explorer (☎ 682-2800), at Avenida Governador Ponce de Arruda 670 in Várzea Grande, Cuiabá, organizes accommodations at a number of isolated (and mostly expensive) fishing lodges on the Rio Paraguai around Cáceres.

All the action centers around the riverfront and nearby Praça Barão do Rio Branco, where there are several restaurants and bars. *Restaurante Kaskata Flutuante* on Rua Coronel José Dulce is a floating restaurant with an extensive menu of regional fish dishes for around US$10 per person. Nearby along the riverfront, *Corimba (Rua 6 de Outubro 27)* is an upmarket pizzeria and chopperia with tables set up outside overlooking the river. *Restaurant Hispano*, in the center on Praça Barão do Rio Branco, is a per-kilo restaurant with river views.

Getting There & Away

Six daily buses make the journey between Cuiabá and Cáceres (US$12, 3½ hours). There are also bus services to Porto Velho. For information on buses to Bolivia, see the Land section of the Getting There & Away chapter.

BARÃO DE MELGAÇO

☎ 0xx65 • postcode 78190-000 • pop 3600

Like Cáceres and Poconé, the small town of Barão de Melgaço 135km southeast of Cuiabá, is a northern entrance into the Pantanal. The town hugs the banks of the Rio Cuiabá. Nearby are two huge bays full of fish – Chacororé (15km in diameter) and Sia Mariana – and ruined fortresses left from the Paraguayan wars.

A reasonably priced hotel along the riverbank in town is the *Barão Tur Hotel (☎ 713-1166)*, which charges US$60 a double. The best-known hotel in the area though is the *Pousada Mutum (☎ 323-1223, reservations ☎ 623-7022)* set on the Rio Mutum between the two bays around 40km southeast of town. It has a restaurant, swimming pool and offers horse and boat tours. Singles/doubles cost US$60/120. Check its Web site at www.pousadamutum.com.br for more details.

Two buses a day make the four-hour trip from Cuiabá, leaving at 7:30 am and again at 3 pm. You can buy a one-way ticket for US$8.

POCONÉ

☎ 0xx65 • postcode 78175-000 • pop 22,000

The main entry point to the Pantanal for travelers heading south from Cuiabá, Poconé marks the beginning of the Transpantaneira 'highway.' Many of the local residents are descendants of Indians, and the original tribe in the area, the Beripoconeses, gave the town its name. Some of the older men hunted the *onça* (jaguar) and have amazing stories to tell.

In May, Poconé celebrates the week-long Semana do Fazendeiro e do Cavalo Pantaneiro with a cattle fair and rodeos.

Orientation

When you arrive at the bus station, you are 2km from the start of the dirt road that becomes the Transpantaneira; the center of town is about halfway. To get there, turn left as you leave the bus station, walk two blocks down Avenida Anibol de Toledo to Rua Antônio João, then turn right. Walk up seven blocks – you'll be in the large town square (more like a rectangle). The Hotel Skala is 100m to your right. On your left, behind the church, is the road that leads to the beginning of the Transpantaneira. There are a few pousadas here.

Organized Tours

Local boat captain Gonçalo de Arruda (☎ 345-1460, Rua 13 de Junho 50) offers boat trips from Poconé along the Rio Cuiabá and Rio Paraguai as far as Corumbá in Mato Grosso do Sul. The *Laura Vicuña* sleeps around 20 people and trips cost US$45 per day per person (not including food and drinks). Drop a line over the side and you might end up with a big *pintado* (catfish) on your plate.

The boat is smallish and caters mostly to fishing tours. A trip to Corumbá takes around four days. Take plenty of insect repellent, a mosquito net and water.

Places to Stay & Eat

If you just need a bed for the night, *Dormitório Poconé (Avenida Anibol de Toledo 1510)* near the bus station has basic rooms with fan for US$6 per person. Nearby on the same street, *Foi na Brasa* does a hearty buffet lunch for US$4. In the middle of town, the *Hotel Skala* (☎ 345-1407, Praça Bem Rondon 64) is a more comfortable option, with single/double apartamentos at US$26/34.

The best places to stay, especially if you're trying to organize a lift down the Transpantaneira, are a couple of kilometers out of town near the beginning of the road. The first one you'll pass is the *Pousada Pantaneira* (☎ 345-1630), which charges US$8 per person. Accommodations are pretty grim, but the hotel restaurant serves a good rodízio for US$6. Just up the road, on the same side, the *Hotel Santa Cruz* (☎ 345-1439) is an attractively rustic place with basic apartamentos for US$18/28.

Getting There & Away
There are six buses a day from Cuiabá to Poconé (US$5, 2½ hours), from 6 am to 7 pm, and six in the opposite direction, from 6 am to 7:30 pm. Get a window seat if you want to appreciate the vegetation typical of the Pantanal's outskirts: pequís, piúvas, babaçus, ipês and buritis.

The Pantanal

The Amazon may attract more fame and glory, but the Pantanal is a better place to see wildlife. In the Amazon, the animals hide in the dense foliage, but in the open spaces of the Pantanal, wildlife is visible to the most casual observer. If you like to see animals in their natural environment, the Pantanal – with the greatest concentration of fauna in the New World – should not be missed.

A vast wetlands in the center of South America, the Pantanal is about half the size of France – some 230,000 sq km. Something less than 100,000 sq km of this is in Bolivia and Paraguay; the rest is in Brazil, split between the states of Mato Grosso and Mato Grosso do Sul.

The Pantanal (also called Terra de Ninguem, Nobody's Land) has few people and no towns. Distances are so great and ground transport so poor that people get around in small airplanes and motorboats;

4WD travel is restricted by the seasons. The only road that runs deep into the Pantanal is the Transpantaneira. This raised dirt road sectioned by 118 small wooden bridges ends 145km south of Poconé, at Porto Jofre. Two-thirds of the intended route from Poconé to Corumbá (at the border with Bolivia) has been left incomplete for lack of funds and ecological concerns.

The Parque Nacional do Pantanal Mato-grossense occupies 1350 sq km in the south-west of Mato Grosso state, but most of the Pantanal is privately owned. The national park and three smaller private nature reserves nearby were given Unesco World Heritage listing in 2000.

Geography & Climate
Although *pantano* means 'swamp' in both Spanish and Portuguese, the Pantanal is not a swamp but, rather, a vast alluvial plain. In geological terms, it is a sedimentary basin of quaternary origin, the drying remains of an ancient inland sea called the Xaraés, which began to dry out, along with the Amazon Sea, 65 million years ago.

First sea, then immense lake and now a periodically flooded plain, the Pantanal – 2000km upstream from the Atlantic Ocean yet just 100 to 200m above sea level – is bounded by higher lands: the mountains of the Serra de Maracaju to the east, the Serra da Bodoquena to the south, the Paraguayan and Bolivian Chaco to the west and the Serra dos Parecis and Serra do São Geronimo to the north. From these highlands, the rains flow into the Pantanal, forming the Rio Paraguai and its tributaries (which flow south and then east, draining into the Atlantic Ocean between Argentina and Uruguay).

During the rainy season (October to March), the rivers flood their banks, inundating much of the low-lying Pantanal and creating *cordilheiras* (patches of dry land where the animals cluster together). The waters reach their high mark – up to 3m – in January or February, then start to recede in March. This seasonal flooding has made systematic farming impossible and has severely limited human incursions into the area.

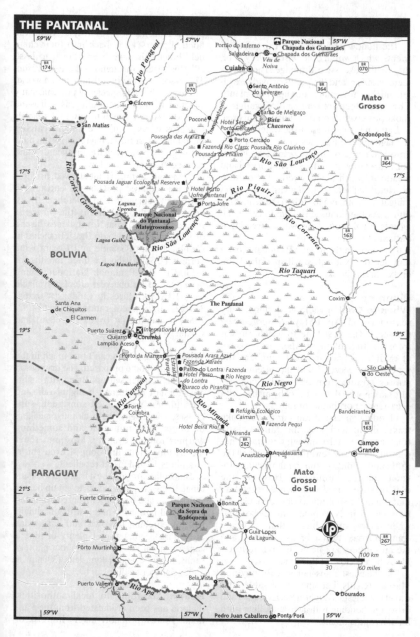

THE PANTANAL

However, it does provide an enormously rich feeding ground for wildlife.

The floodwaters replenish the soil's nutrients, which would otherwise be very poor, due to the excessive drainage. The waters teem with fish, and the ponds provide excellent niches for many animals and plants. Enormous flocks of wading birds gather in rookeries several square kilometers in area.

Later in the dry season, the water recedes, the lagoons and marshes dry out, and fresh grasses emerge on the savanna (the Pantanal's vegetation includes savanna, forest and meadows, which blend together, often with no clear divisions). The hawks and *jacarés* (alligators) compete for fish in the remaining ponds. As the ponds shrink and dry up, the jacarés crawl around for water, sweating it out until the rains return.

For more on the unique Pantanal ecosystem, see the Natural Brazil special section earlier in this book.

Planning

When to Go If possible, go during the dry season (from April/May to September/October). The best time to watch birds is from July to September, when the birds are at their rookeries in great numbers, the waters have receded and the bright-green grasses pop up from the muck. Temperatures are hot by day and cool by night – with occasional short bursts of rain.

Flooding, incessant rains and heat make travel difficult during the rainy season (October to March), though this time is not without its special rewards – this is when the cattle and wildlife of the Pantanal clump together on the cordilheiras. However, the islands are covered with dense vegetation that can make spotting wildlife difficult. The heat peaks in November and December, when temperatures higher than 40°C are common, roads turn to breakfast cereal, and the mosquitoes are fierce and out in force. Many hotels close at this time.

The heaviest rains fall in February and March. Roads become impassable and travel is a logistical nightmare. Every decade or so, the flooding is disastrous, killing both humans and animals.

Fishing is best during the first part of the dry season (April to May), when the flooded rivers settle back into their channels, but locals have been known to lasso 80kg fish right throughout the dry season. This is some of the best fishing in the world. There are about 20 species of piranha, many vegetarian and all good eating, as well as the tasty dourado, a feisty fellow that reaches upwards of 9kg. Other excellent catches include pacu, suribim, bagre, giripoca, piraputanga, piapara, cachara, pirancajuva and pintado, to name but a few.

Although hunting is not allowed, fishing – with the required permits – is encouraged between February and October. It is, however, prohibited during the *piracema* (breeding season) from November to the end of January. The Banco do Brasil branches in Cuiabá, Campo Grande and Coxim issue permits (US$9) valid for three months for fishing in the Pantanal. National fishing permits valid for one year are also available from IBAMA offices in Cuiabá (☎ 0xx65-313-2212), Campo Grande (☎ 0xx67-782-2966), Corumbá (☎ 0xx67-231-6096) and Coxim (☎ 0xx67-291-2310).

What to Bring You can't buy much in the Pantanal, so come prepared. The dry season is also the cooler season. Bring attire suitable for hot days, coolish nights, rain and mosquitoes. You'll need sunscreen, sunglasses, a hat, lightweight clothes, sneakers or boots, light rain gear and something warmer for the evening. Mosquito relief means long pants and long-sleeved shirts, vitamin B-12 and insect repellent.

Binoculars are your best friend in the Pantanal. Bring an alarm clock (to get up before sunrise), an audio recorder (for recording the wonderful bird calls) and a strong flashlight (to go searching for owls and anacondas after dark). Don't forget plenty of film, a camera, and if you're serious about photography, a tripod and a long lens (300mm is about right for wildlife).

Health According to local authorities, malaria has been eradicated from the Pantanal. There's probably a very low risk of contracting malaria, but it's best to consult with a travel health expert for the latest information before you leave home. For more on malaria and other traveler's health concerns, see the Health section of the Facts for the Visitor chapter of this book, or check out Lonely Planet's *Healthy Travel – Central & South America*, by Isabelle Young.

In Cuiabá, the municipal hospital (☎ 0xx65-624-4222) is at Praça do Seminário 141. In Campo Grande, the public hospital (☎ 0xx67-523-1355) is at Rua São Paulo 1597. The best place for medical treatment in Corumbá is at Clínic Samec (☎ 0xx67-231-3308) at Rua Colombo 1249.

Organized Tours

There are three main approach routes to the Pantanal: via Cuiabá in Mato Grosso and via Corumbá or Campo Grande in Mato Grosso do Sul. You can arrange guided tours (or head off on your own) from any of these three towns.

A good guide can enhance your Pantanal experience by spotting and identifying animal and bird species, explaining the diverse ecology and taking care of any hassles along the way. That said, you don't necessarily need a guide. The Transpantaneira is the only road to follow and you'll see plenty of wildlife – many species of birds, jacarés, capybaras and the occasional deer – close to the road. But if you're hoping to catch a glimpse of rarer animals such as anteaters, anacondas, otters, iguanas and jaguars, a guide is indispensable. Animals that spend most of their time in trees will also be hard to spot from the road. A guide who is familiar with the area will also know the location of nests of rare birds.

Mato Grosso From Cuiabá, the capital of Mato Grosso, small tour operators arrange safaris into the Pantanal that include transportation, accommodations on farms, and guides.

In addition to their skills in the wild, the guides are also expert at spotting another large mammal – the tourist – wandering the streets of Cuiabá. You'll probably be approached by a tour operator not long after arriving, which can save you time slogging around town in the heat.

Fortunately, while there is healthy competition between tour operators in Cuiabá, it's not as intense as in Mato Grosso do Sul. Tours from Cuiabá are generally well organized trips.

Joel Souza's Pantanal Safari Tours (☎ 0xx65-624-13860, joelsouza@terra.com.br) offers bird-watching and nature tours for US$50 per day including accommodation on farms, meals, hikes and boat rides. Joel's office is next to the Hotel Presidente at Avenida Getúlio Vargas 155A (2nd floor), or you can contact him at Pousada Ecoverde (see Places to Stay in the Cuiabá section). He speaks English, German and Spanish. Joel doesn't often work as a guide these days but is passing on his enthusiasm for and knowledge of the Pantanal to his son Lauro.

Faunatour (☎ 0xx65-682-0101, faunatur@zaz.com.br) is run by Laércio Sá, who has worked as a guide in the Pantanal for 14 years. He offers a range of tours from one to four days with accommodations on farms for US$50 per day. An interesting alternative is a four-day bike tour along the Transpantaneira. You'll need your own bike and at least three people to make the tour. You can contact Laércio through the Hotel Real (see Places to Stay).

Munir Nasr from Natureco (☎ 0xx65-321-1001, natureco@natureco.com.br) is another recommended guide who organizes tours into the Pantanal. His office is at Rua Barão de Melgaço 2015, in the suburb of Porto. Other tour operators offering similar deals include Shalom Tour (☎ 0xx65-322-2522, shalomtr@terra.com.br) at Rua Commandante Costa 649, Centro and Anaconda Turismo (☎ 0xx65-624-4142, anaconda@zaz.com.br) at Avenida Isaac Póvoas 606, Centro.

Mato Grosso do Sul Many budget travelers are choosing to go on cheap three- to four-day tours into the southern Pantanal from Corumbá or Campo Grande. Most trips are better organized than in the past, but they are still rough-and-ready affairs. Accommodations are at bush camps in

THE CENTRAL WEST

Tripping Through the Southern Pantanal

The Southern Pantanal is incredibly beautiful – a peaceful haven of brilliant green meadows broken up by pockets of dense jungle, mighty rivers and picturesque lagoons that are home to a rich variety of vegetation and wildlife.

Unfortunately, at times it is also a battleground for rival budget tour operators trying to monopolize a growing trade in foreign travelers. Much worse, there has been a spate of allegations against Pantanal guides that include sexual assault and abandonment in the Pantanal. Some of these incidents are still being investigated by the authorities amid an ongoing battle of words among tour operators.

The good news is that local tourism authorities are acting to regulate the industry, with particular emphasis on budget tour operators and guides. Corumbá's city tourist authority, Sematur, is working with local guides to form a guide association. At the time of writing, 26 guides had completed an accreditation course and been issued licenses – these guides have Monitor Ambiental badges. The tourist office in Corumbá has a complete list of the licensed guides and details about how to get in touch with them.

In early 2001, a permanent guard post was set up at the entrance to Estrada Parque, where most of the budget tour operators have their camps. In the future, only licensed guides will be allowed to work in the area.

These are all positive steps. The real remaining concern is that the good old boys' network – politicians, public servants and businesspeople – might create a monopoly of their own and squeeze out some good operators.

Choosing a Tour You don't have to find a guide, they find you. If you arrive at the bus station or airport in either Corumbá or Campo Grande, you're almost guaranteed to be greeted by a friendly tour company representative. The sell job is fairly standard: albums with photos of the camp and close encounters between travelers and the star inhabitants of the Pantanal – anacondas, jacarés, anteaters and capybaras.

The first general rule is this: If the guide spends more time running down the opposition than winning you over with genuine enthusiasm for the Pantanal, give that person the flick. Although it can involve a bit of legwork, you need to make sure you shop around and compare at least two or three companies.

Your experience in the Pantanal depends most on the motivation of guides at your camp. Guides tend to freelance and swap companies regularly, so ask other travelers for recommendations and make sure you establish before you leave which guides will be at your camp.

The Tours Most of the operators offer similar packages at camps along Estrada Parque, a 117km stretch of dirt road through the region known as Nhecolândia. All the camps consist of either a mosquito-netted communal hut with hammocks, or a communal dining hut and tents. The 'bathroom' is a hole in the ground, or behind a faraway tree (hopefully upwind) and the 'bath' is the nearest river or lake. While some travelers are understandably reluctant to swim in waters crawling with critters great and small, there have been no reported tourist casualties. You can trust the guides on this one – you won't be sent to swim with piranhas! Food is basic – breakfast is bread and fruit, and dinner is usually plain rice or pasta with veggies.

You'll go on long hikes at sunrise and sunset when the animals are feeding and at night to search for anacondas and owls. Wildlife spotting by canoe, and fishing and horseback riding, are available at some of the camps.

netted communal huts with hammocks or in tents. Food is generally OK, though you should take some extra snack food and water. Some of the guides are ex-hunters and their attitude towards animals can be less than sensitive, but the drift is toward minimal-impact ecotourism. You'll see lots of birds, capybaras and jacarés, but larger mammals are harder to spot.

All the budget tour operators operating in the area offer similar packages at camps along Estrada Parque, a 117km stretch of dirt road through the region known as Nhecolândia. Estrada Parque runs off the main Campo Grande to Corumbá road (Hwy BR-262) at Buraco da Piranha, 72km from Corumbá and 324km from Campo Grande. The first stretch of Estrada Parque penetrates 47km into the Pantanal, before it doglegs back toward Corumbá. At Porto da Manga, a barge ferries vehicles over the Rio Paraguai before Estrada Parque rejoins Hwy BR-262 at Lampião Aceso, about 12km from Corumbá.

Estrada Parque is much closer to Corumbá than to Campo Grande. And even though Corumbá is a more pleasant place to hang out than Campo Grande, unless you're traveling to or from Bolivia, there's no real need to travel all the way to Corumbá to join a tour. Campo Grande is a travel hub and more convenient for onward travel to other parts of Brazil.

In Campo Grande, Pantanal Discovery (formerly Gil Tours) (☎ 0xx67-725-0457; gilstour@starbox.com.br), is based on the ground floor of the bus station. A recent move to Campo Grande from Corumbá and the growing numbers of travelers have stretched the operation logistically – their camp is still on Estrada Parque, around six hours' travel away. Recommended guides are Alex (who speaks English), Pedro and Marcelo.

Packages start at US$125 for three days and two nights; extra days are US$30 per day, and you can negotiate discounts for longer stays. The price includes bus fare to the pick-up point (Buraco da Piranha) at the entrance to Estrada Parque, meals, accommodations in hammocks or tents, and

boat and horse rides. There's a netted communal hut, but it's worth taking a mosquito net and plenty of repellent. Take extra bottled water and some snack food for between meals. The camp has running water and a toilet.

Ecological Expeditions (☎ 0xx67-782-3504, ecoexpeditionsbr@hotmail.com), at Rua Joaquim Nabuco 185, is a relatively new organization with an office just opposite the bus station in Campo Grande. In a short time they have established a good reputation, and recommended guides are Israel, Gabriel and Elcio. Tour prices are the same as for Pantanal Discovery.

In Corumbá, four companies operate budget tours to camps in Nhecolândia around Estrada Parque. Pantanal Saldanha Tour (☎ 0xx67-231-4405, saldanha_v@hotmail.com), at Rua Porto Carreiro 896, is run by Eliane, who has trained as a Monitor Ambiental guide. She doesn't work as a guide now but organizes the tours from Corumbá, contracting guides as she needs them. Some recommended guides are Johnny Indiano, who has 15 years of experience in the Pantanal, and Marcia. Tours start at US$90 for two nights and three days – negotiate prices for longer stays and for groups. Eliane can also be contacted at the Hotel Angola.

Green Track (☎ 0xx67-231-2258, greentk@pantanalnet.com.br), at Rua Delamare 576, run out of the pousada of the same name, is the biggest budget tour operator in Corumbá and employs about 10 local guides. They specialize in hiking and offer a range of itineraries from two-night/three-day camping tours to five-day hiking tours to several campsites. Costs are US$30 per day. Several readers have recommended Leonel (or Nene) as an excellent guide.

Look for Anacondas in the Panatal.

Pantanal Safari (☎ 0xx67-232-4775, safari@pantanalnet.com.br), at Rua Colombo 1114, is a small operator offering similar tours from Corumbá at US$30 per day. Flavio or Indi are recommended guides.

Before signing on for a trip, there are a few things you should check out. Ask for a detailed itinerary, in writing if possible. Check out the truck. Does it look OK? Does it have a radio or carry a first-aid kit in case of emergency?

Expect to spend at least half a day traveling into the Pantanal. Finding wildlife depends less on how far you travel than on your guide's knowledge of the Pantanal. Allow at least two days if you hope to see wildlife close up. Definitely insist on doing this on foot – vehicles should be used only for access, *not* for pursuit. Your chances of enjoying the Pantanal and its wildlife are greatly increased if you go with a reputable guide who forsakes the 'mechanical chase' approach, leads small groups (preferably no more than ten people) and takes you on walks at the optimum times to observe wildlife (before sunrise, at dusk and during the night). A trip along these lines will require at least three days, preferably four.

Insist on meeting your guide before you leave (or make it clear in writing that you will go only with a designated guide). A smooth-talking frontperson might sign you on, but they usually won't be your guide on the trip. How many years has your guide been in the Pantanal? Speaking English well is less important than local knowledge. Someone who has spent his or her life in the Pantanal won't speak much English.

Prior to departure, be sure to read What to Bring earlier in this section.

If you want something more comfortable, and riding around in the back of a pickup truck doesn't grab you, pay a bit more and stay at a hotel-fazenda for a few days.

If time is a problem and money isn't, or if you'd just like one of the best guides around, write or call Doug Trent at Focus Tours in the USA. Focus Tours specializes in nature tours and is active in trying to preserve the Pantanal (for its contact details, see the Organized Tours section in the Getting There & Away chapter).

Places to Stay

Pantanal accommodations are divided into four general categories: fazendas, pousadas, *pesqueiros* and *boteis*. Fazendas are ranch-style hotels that usually have horses and often boats for rent. Pousadas range from simple to top-end. Pesqueiros are hangouts for fishermen, and you can usually rent boats and fishing gear from them. A botel (a contraction of boat and hotel) is a floating lodge.

Nearly all accommodations are on the expensive side, but the devaluation of the *real* has made prices more reasonable. If you have doubts about roughing it on the budget tours, it's probably better to spend a bit more money for basic comforts – a bed, running water and some hope of avoiding a million mosquito bites for example!

Rates will usually include transport by 4WD, boat or plane from Corumbá or Cuiabá, good food and modest lodging. Reservations are often handled by a travel agent, but in many cases you can make reservations directly via email.

Reservations are needed for all accommodations in July, when lots of Brazilians vacation here.

Mato Grosso Accommodations along the Transpantaneira are plentiful. At Km 30, the

Pousada das Araras (☎ 0xx65-682-2800) has a pool, as well as boats and horses. A very informative wildlife and bird list is available. Full board is US$54/108 for singles/doubles. The lodge also organizes package tours along the Transpantaneira, with stays at several different lodges. For more information (in English) and reservations, check out the Web site at www.araraslodge.com.br.

Moving on down the road to the Rio Claro at Km 42, you'll find two places: Our advice is to check both before deciding where to stay, as their prices and facilities are similar. *Fazenda Rio Claro* (☎ 0xx65-9982-0796, 0xx65-626-1285 for reservations) and *Pousada Rio Clarinho* (☎ 0xx65-9977-8966, 0xx65-345-1860 for reservations) both offer full board for US$35/70 and boat and horse rides.

At the Rio Pixaim at Km 65, the *Pousada do Pixaim* (☎ 0xx65-345-2091, 0xx65-9973-1801 for reservations) is a rustic place – a classic wooden Pantanal building on stilts. It has air-conditioning, tasty meals (included in the accommodations price), and the last gas pump until you return to Poconé – so fill up! Prices are US$40/80 for singles/doubles.

Forty kilometers farther down the road the *Pousada Jaguar Ecological Reserve* (☎ 0xx65-345-1545) was formerly the Pousada O Pantaneiro. It's situated on the Jaguar Ecological Reserve and charges US$35 per person for room and board.

Porto Jofre is where the Transpantaneira meets its end, at the Rio Cuiabá. It's a one-hotel town – in fact, it's not even a town, just a few buildings strung out along the river and a small port. The only hotel is the expensive *Hotel Porto Jofre Pantanal* (☎ 0xx65-623-0236, prtjofre@dinet.com.br) costing US$100/170/240 for singles/doubles/triples. Alternatively, you can camp on the grounds for US$5 per person and buy meals at the hotel restaurant (US$7 to US$10). The hotel has a swimming pool and boats for hire. It's closed from November to February. For more information on the hotel, go to http://www.portojofre.com.br.

There are also several fazendas off the Transpantaneira. Accessible by car along the road to Porto Cercado is the *Hotel Sesc Porto Cercado* (☎ 0xx65-391-1255), in a beautiful setting along the Rio Cuiabá, 42km from Poconé. The hotel is within the 90,000-hectare Reserva Particular Patrimônio Natural (RPPN) do Sesc, which is an ecological station dedicated to preserving the natural flora and fauna of the area. Comfortable singles/doubles cost US$75/114 including meals. You can book reservations online at the excellent Web site www.sescpantanal.com.br.

About 2km away, *Hotel Cabanas do Pantanal* (☎ 0xx65-345-1887, 0xx65-9972-6755 for reservations) is geared toward fishing tours. The hotel offers full board, a pool and horse rides for US$60/68.

Mato Grosso do Sul Southern gateways to the Pantanal are the cities of Corumbá, Campo Grande, Aquidauana and Miranda. Most travelers head to Campo Grande or Corumbá, while Aquidauana and Miranda are popular with Brazilian anglers.

Around Aquidauana are a number of mid-range to expensive hotel-fazendas. *Pousada Aguapé* (☎ 0xx67-686-1036), 60km north of Aquidauana, has double rooms for US$68, but you can camp for US$5 a day and buy meals at the restaurant. A cheaper option along the Rio Aquidauana is *Fazenda Pequi* (☎ 0xx67-686-1042), 48km from Aquidauana, where double apartamentos cost US$55 and large chalets cost US$68/80 for singles/doubles. Both these places can be reached via a dirt road at Km 467.5 on Hwy BR-262 (the main road between Campo Grande and Corumbá).

The *Fazenda Rio Negro* (☎ 0xx67-751-5191, r.lourival@conservation.org.br) is on the banks of the Rio Negro 40 minutes by plane from Aquidauana (one hour from Campo Grande). Accommodations here cost US$120/150 a day. For more information, go to the tourist office in Campo Grande or the Panbratour (☎ 0xx67-241-3494) office on Rua Estevao Alves Correa in Aquidauana.

One of the cheaper places to stay in the Miranda area is the *Hotel Beira Rio* (☎ 0xx67-726-2055, dionross@enersulnet.com.br), right on the banks of the Rio Miranda 7km from town. The hotel is rigged out like a fishing lodge – accommodations are simple but clean, and full board costs US$32 per person. The hotel also has a 'floating headquarters' at the delta of the Rio Miranda and Rio Aquidauana (six hours by boat from Miranda), where you can sleep on houseboats. For more info, check the Web site at www.brart.com/br.html or go to the Ecoaventuras office on Rua Barão do Rio Branco in Miranda.

The top-end place in the southern Pantanal is the *Refúgio Ecológico Caiman* (☎ 0xx67-687-2102, caiman@attglobal.net; reservations ☎ 0xx11-3079-6622 in São Paulo, sales@caiman.com.br), on a working ranch 36km north of Miranda. Caiman was a pioneering ecotourism destination in the southern Pantanal and is the base for Project Blue Macaw, which focuses on the preservation of this magnificent, endangered bird. There are five lodges in different areas of the 530 sq km fazenda. Caiman offers a wide variety of hiking, horseback and boat tours – see the full range on its Web site at www.caiman.com.br. All tours are led by multilingual guides who live on the fazenda. It isn't cheap, but if you book direct, it's a good value at US$150 a double.

Farther into the Pantanal along Estrada Parque, there are several farm hotels. At Passo do Lontra, 7km along the road, *Pousada Passo do Lontra* (☎ 0xx67-231-6136) is an excellent classic Pantanal wood-on-stilt structure, with lots of wildlife around. It charges US$45 per person, including full board, but is willing to bargain out of season. It's highly recommended.

Another 20km along the road is the turnoff for *Hotel Fazenda Xaraés* (☎ 0xx67-231-4094). The hotel is set along the Rio Abobral and costs US$54/106 for singles/doubles, with meals included.

Pousada Arara Azul (☎ 0xx67-9987-1530, hfagropecuaria@uol.com.br) is 10km farther along Estrada Parque at the Rio Negro. The pousada caters to groups and conventions, but it's in a good location overlooking the river and has a pool. Full board costs US$66/126.

Driving down the Transpantaneira

Why the Transpantaneira? First, it's one of the best places in South America to see wildlife, which is drawn to the roadway at all times of the year. Second, renting a car in Cuiabá to drive into the Pantanal gives you flexibility and is comparable pricewise with other Pantanal excursions, especially if there are three or four of you in the car. (Most Pantanal tours require flying, boating or hiring a guide with a 4WD vehicle.) If you're on a tight budget, you can take a bus to Poconé and hitch from there, if necessary returning to Poconé for cheap lodging.

During the wet season, the Transpataneira is an island for wildlife driven from the floodwaters, and during the dry season, the ditches on either side of the road serve as artificial ponds, drawing birds and game toward the tourist. Thousands of birds appear to rush out from all sides; ocelots and capybaras seem frozen by the headlights; and roadside pools are filled with hundreds of dark silhouettes and gleaming, red jacaré eyes.

If you are driving from Cuiabá, head out early. Leave at 4 am to reach the Transpantaneira by sunrise, when the animals come to life. The Transpantaneira highway officially starts 17km south of Poconé. There's a sign and a guard station, where you pay a small entrance fee.

Stopping to see wildlife and slowing down for 118 little wooden bridges and meter-wide potholes, it's possible to pass the whole day driving the Transpantaneira. Weekdays are better for driving, as there's less traffic kicking up dust. The best time to hitch is on the weekend, when locals drive down the Transpantaneira for a day's fishing.

To get to Estrada Parque you can take the Campo Grande-Corumbá bus and arrange for your lodge to pick you up from the intersection, where there's a Posto Florestal guard station.

Serious fishing enthusiasts should consider the **Pesqueiro Tarumá** (☎ 0xx67-231-4197, pescapantanal@pescapantanal.com.br) on the Rio Paraguai 70km from Corumbá. It's well equipped, with fridge, air conditioning, hot showers and boats, and costs US$60 per person a day, including meals.

Boteis defy any permanent address. Most of them operate out of Corumbá and are used for fishing trips. Arara Pantaneira (☎ 0xx67-231-4851) and Pantanal Tours (☎ 0xx67-231-4683) both organize trips that cost around US$170 per person a day, all inclusive.

Getting There & Away
From Cuiabá, the capital of Mato Grosso, there are three gateways to the Pantanal – Cáceres, Barão de Melgaço and Poconé.

Campo Grande, the capital of Mato Grosso do Sul, is a transport hub, while Corumbá is best accessed by or bus from Campo Grande (unless you're traveling overland from Bolivia). The route to Corumbá from Campo Grande runs via Aquidauana and Miranda. For transportation details, see the relevant city and town sections.

Coxim, a small town on Hwy BR-163, east of the Pantanal and accessible by bus from either Campo Grande or Cuiabá, is yet another possible point of entry to the Pantanal.

There are direct flights to Cuiabá and Campo Grande from Brasília and connecting flights from Rio and São Paulo. TAM is the only major Brazilian airline connecting other capitals, including Campo Grande, and São Paulo to Corumbá.

Getting Around
Since the lodges are the only places to sleep, drink and eat, and public transport is very limited, independent travel is difficult in the Pantanal. Driving is not easy. Only a few roads reach into the periphery of the Panta-nal; they are frequently closed by rains, and reconstructed yearly. Only the Transpantaneira in Mato Grosso and Estrada Parque in Mato Grosso do Sul go deep into the region. See the boxed texts 'Driving Down the Transpantaneira' and 'Tripping Through the Southern Pantanal.'

In Cuiabá, there are car rental agencies just outside the airport grounds, and they're often cheaper than the agencies inside the airport. No matter what anyone tells you, you don't need a 4WD vehicle to drive the Transpantaneira. The best car is a VW Gol or a Fiat Uno. Don't forget to fill up your fuel tank in Poconé and at the Pousada do Pixaim.

From the airport in Campo Grande, Pantanal Rent a Car (☎ 0xx67-724-7788) or Localiza (☎ 0xx67-763-1401) rent cars from around US$60 per day.

Hitching may be the cheapest way to go, but it doesn't allow you to stop whenever you want along the road to observe wildlife. There's quite a bit of traffic going up and down the Transpantaneira, during the dry season at least, and if you make your way to one of the pousadas, you can then do walks, or rent a horse or boat.

Mato Grosso do Sul

CAMPO GRANDE
☎ 0xx67 • postcode 79000-000
• pop 655,000
The capital of Mato Grosso do Sul, Campo Grande is developing as a major gateway to the Pantanal and with good reason: It's a transport hub and has an excellent tourist office that tries hard to give independent advice. There's not much to see in the city itself, but it's a lively place with a young population.

Founded around 1875 as the village of Santo Antônio de Campo Grande, Campo Grande really began to grow when the railway came through in 1914. By decree of military president Ernesto Giesel, the city became the capital of Mato Grosso do Sul in 1977 when the new state splintered off from Mato Grosso. It is known as the

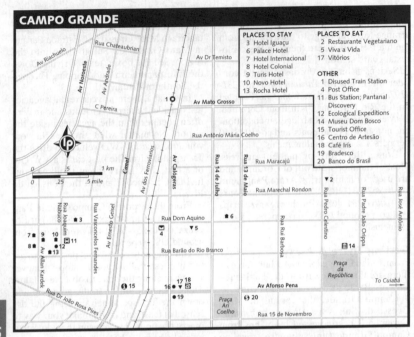

CAMPO GRANDE

PLACES TO STAY
3 Hotel Iguaçu
6 Palace Hotel
7 Hotel Internacional
8 Hotel Colonial
9 Turis Hotel
10 Novo Hotel
13 Rocha Hotel

PLACES TO EAT
2 Restaurante Vegetariano
5 Viva a Vida
17 Vitórios

OTHER
1 Disused Train Station
4 Post Office
11 Bus Station; Pantanal Discovery
12 Ecological Expeditions
14 Museu Dom Bosco
15 Tourist Office
16 Centro de Artesão
18 Café Irís
19 Bradesco
20 Banco do Brasil

Cidade Morena because of its red earth. Manganese, rice, soy and cattle are the traditional sources of its wealth, while education (there are four universities in the city), commerce and tourism are growing industries. Campo Grande lies 716km south of Cuiabá and 403km southeast of Corumbá.

Information

Campo Grande has the best tourist office (☎ 724-5830) in the region. It's on the corner of Avenida Afonso Pena and Avenida Noroeste, has friendly staff (most are tourism students), an excellent city map and an extensive database with information about hotels and attractions throughout the state. Take all recommendations and complaints in their guest book with a grain of salt: This may be the front line in the war of words between Pantanal tour operators. The office is open from 8 am to 7 pm Tuesday to Saturday, and from 9 am to noon Sunday.

The Banco do Brasil exchanges money at Avenida Afonso Pena 2202.

The post office is on the corner of Rua Dom Aquino and Avenida Calógeras. To make an international collect call from a public telephone, dial ☎ 000-108. Café Iris (☎ 784-6002), at Avenida Afonso Pena 1975, is a newsstand, bar, acoustic venue and Internet café rolled into one small, friendly space. Internet access costs US$3 per hour.

Museu Dom Bosco

The Museu Dom Bosco, at Rua Barão do Rio Branco 1843, is the only museum in town that's worth a look. It has an excellent collection of over 10,000 insects, including 7000 butterflies. There are lots of stuffed animals, and interesting exhibits about the Bororo, Moro, Karajá and Xavante Indians. Reasonably priced handicrafts are also available. The museum is open daily from 8 to 11 am and 1 to 5 pm.

THE CENTRAL WEST

Organized Tours
If you don't want to rough it on a camping tour of the Pantanal, travel agencies in Campo Grande sell packages at farm hotels. A couple of central agencies are N & T Japan Tour (☎ 784-2820) and NPQ Tourismo (☎ 725-6414), both located in a small shopping arcade at Avenida Afonso Pena 2081.

Places to Stay
Most budget accommodations are clustered around the bus station. Some of the dives have got their act together recently, but the area is still a bit seedy at night.

Popular with local students and travelers is the *Hotel Iguaçu (☎ 784-4621, Rua Dom Aquino 761)*, opposite the bus station. It's not the cheapest, but apartamentos with fan and phone are a good value at US$14/20 for singles/doubles. *Novo Hotel (☎ 721-0505, Rua Joaquim Nabuco 185)* is also clean and friendly, with apartamentos for US$10/15. Close by, the *Rocha Hotel (☎ 725-6874, Rua Barão do Rio Branco 343)* has the same management and price.

One block west of the bus station on Avenida Alan Kardek is a cluster of three hotels: The *Turis Hotel (☎ 782-7688)* has basic apartamentos at US$10/14; *Hotel Colonial (☎ 724-6061)* has a range of apartamentos starting at US$15/22/29; and the more upmarket *Hotel Internacional (☎ 724-6061)* has apartamentos starting at US$19/30. The better rooms are on the outside of the building.

In the center, *Hotel Americano (☎ 721-1454, Rua 14 de Julho 2311)* has the cheapest rooms around at US$8 per person, but it's pretty grotty. More comfortable is the *Palace Hotel (☎ 784-4741, Rua Dom Aquino 1501)*, with singles/ doubles for US$24/30. It's often full.

Places to Eat
In the city center, *Vitórios* on Avenida Afonso Pena has hearty meat, fish and chicken dishes for US$5. The bars nearby have standard menus and chopp.

For a por-kilo vegetarian lunch, *Restaurante Vegetariano (Rua Pedro Celestino 1696)* is open from 11 am to 2:30 pm every day except Saturday. *Viva a Vida (Rua Dom Aquino 1354)*, next to the Bolivian consulate, is another good natural-food place for lunch. For excellent regional food, head to *Fogo Caipira (Rua José Antônio 145)*.

If you feel like a stroll before dinner, there are a couple of upmarket restaurants in the suburb of Jardim dos Estados, 2km east of the city center along Avenida Afonso Pena. *Casa Colonial* at No 3997 is a stylish place with a good rodízio for US$7 per person or à la carte regional and Italian food. It has a breezy courtyard out the back. Nearby at No 4329, *Barroarte* is a gallery and bar with live music at night and small meals. Heading downhill and downmarket, *Shopping Campo Grande* is a shopping mall with the usual fast food outlets.

Entertainment
Campo Grande has a few live music venues and some good bars that cater for students. The city can get pretty wild on the weekends when the gaúchos come to town. In the center, both *Acustic Bar (Rua 13 de Junho 945)* and *Aldeia Bar (Rua Jose Antônio 954)* have live bands. *Park's Burguer (☎ 782-6829)* at Rua Itacuru in Itanhanga has live *música popular*, or try *Stones Blues (☎ 726-4957)* on Avenida Ceará for the blues and jazz. For alternative music and metal, check out *Barfly*, which is on the corner of Avenida Mato Grosso and Avenida Bahia.

Shopping
Centro do Artesão, on the corner of Avenida Afonso Pena and Avenida Calógeras, and Barroarte, at Avenida Afonso Pena 4329, both stock a good range of indigenous ceramics, woodcarvings and local artwork.

Getting There & Around
Air There are daily connections to São Paulo, Cuiabá, Corumbá, Rio, Brasília and Porto Velho, and three flights a week to Vilhena and Curitiba. For additional details call TAM (☎ 763-4100), Varig (☎ 763-0000) or VASP (☎ 763-2389).

There are several air-taxi companies at the airport for trips into remote areas of the Pantanal, including Globo (☎ 763-1322) and Mato Grosso do Sul (☎ 763-1131).

Aeroporto Internacional de Campo Grande (☎ 763-2444) is 7km from town; to get there, take the Indubrasil bus from the bus station. To get a bus to the center from the airport, walk out of the airport to the bus stop on the main road. A taxi costs US$9.

Bus The bus station is huge, with lots of bars, barbers and travel agencies. There are ten buses a day to Corumbá (US$24); four are direct and do the trip in around six hours, including a relaxing 45-minute barge trip across the Rio Paraguai. However, a new bridge under construction will cut the trip time and put a few hardworking souvenir salesmen out of business. Non-direct buses to Corumbá stop in Miranda and Aquidauana, and can drop you at the intersection with Estrada Parque.

Regular buses make the 10-hour trip to Cuiabá (US$28) and there are three buses a day, at 6 and 11 am and 3 pm, to Bonito (US$14, 5½ hours). The route to Bonito via Aquidauana is paved all the way. There are 12 buses a day to Ponta Porã (US$16, seven hours) on the Paraguayan frontier. There are also daily buses to São Paulo (US$54, 14 hours) and Foz do Iguaçu (US$24, 16 hours).

CORUMBÁ

☎ 0xx67 • postcode 79300-000 • pop 86,000
This port city close to the Bolivian border is a southern gateway to the Pantanal. The city sits atop a steep hill overlooking the Rio Paraguai; on the far side of the river, the huge expanse of the Pantanal stretches to the horizon.

Corumbá is 403km northwest of Campo Grande by road. Due to its strategic location near the Paraguayan and Bolivian borders (Puerto Suárez, Bolivia, is only 19km away), it has a reputation for poaching and drug smuggling, but travelers are generally left alone. (See the introductory Facts for the Visitor chapter for details of the Bolivian consulate.) There are signs that the city is returning to prosperity on the back of the tourist trade: Banks are popping up everywhere and an effort is being made to restore some of the town's historic buildings.

Corumbá, also known as Cidade Branca (White City), was founded and named in 1776 by Captain Luis de Albuquerque. By 1840 it was the biggest river port in the world, boasting a dozen foreign consulates. Ships would enter the Rio de la Plata in the South Atlantic; sail up the Rio Paraná to its confluence with the Rio Paraguai; and then continue up to Corumbá. The impressive buildings along the waterfront reflect the wealth that passed through the town during the 19th century. With the coming of the railway, Corumbá lost its importance as a port and went into decline.

Information

Immigration While the situation changed five times during one recent year, at present all Brazilian border formalities (including entry and exit stamps) must be completed in Corumbá at the Polícia Federal office on Praça de República, next to the Museu do Pantanal – not at the border itself. Bolivian entry/exit formalities can all be completed at the border post. If you're just crossing over to Bolivia for a few hours to buy train tickets, you don't need to get a Brazilian exit stamp.

Moneychangers at the border accept cash only and will change both *reais* and dollars.

You won't be allowed to enter Brazil without a current yellow-fever vaccination certificate, so do yourself a favor and organize one well in advance. If you need a vaccination, Sucum at Rua Ladário 788 in Corumbá is the best place to go; head there before you get an entry stamp at the Polícia Federal. (See the Health section in the Facts for the Visitor chapter for more information about vaccinations).

See the Facts for the Visitor chapter for details of Paraguayan and Brazilian consulates at this border.

Tourist Office The Sematur tourist office (☎ 231-6899) is at Rua Manoel Cavassa 275 as you begin the descent to the port. It's not well marked and the building looks derelict from the street. Staff can provide a list of Pantanal guides and tour companies, hotels, and boat trips. The office is open Monday to Friday from 8:30 am to noon and 1:30 to 6 pm.

Money The Banco do Brasil at Rua 13 de Junho 914 has Visa ATMs. The bank won't change traveler's checks and gives very bad rates for cash. It's open from 10 am to 3 pm Monday to Friday. Check the cash rates at Casa de Câmbio at Rua Frei Mariano 361, and for MasterCard cash advances, go to HSBC on Rua Delamare.

Post & Communications The post office is on Rua Delamare, across from the Praça da República. International calls can be made from the telephone office on Rua Dom Aquino.

Corumbá is well connected – Pantanal Net, the local service provider, has an office at Rua América 403. It's the fastest connection in town but is closed on weekends. Café.com is a central Internet café at Rua Frei Mariano 635. Access costs US$4 per hour.

Things to See & Do
Corumbá's star attraction is the Pantanal; you can get a preview of it from the highest point in the area, **Morro Urucum** (1100m), 20km south of Corumbá.

Tourists looking for something different might consider a two-day excursion to **Forte Coimbra**, which is a seven-hour boat trip south on the Rio Paraguai. In days gone by, the fort was a key to the defense of the Brazilian west. You need permission from the Brigada Mista (Avenida General Rondon 1735) to go there, because it's still used occasionally for military training.

Organized Tours
Pantanal tours and boat and fishing tours of the Corumbá environs are available from all travel agencies. Some good ones are Mutum (☎ 231-1818), at Rua Frei Mariano 17, and Pantur (☎ 231-2000), at Rua Frei Mariano 1013.

An all-day boat trip along the Rio Paraguai will cost US$24, including lunch.

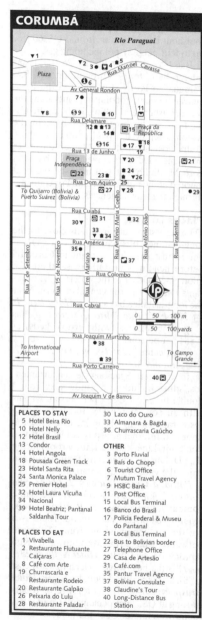

PLACES TO STAY
5 Hotel Beira Rio
10 Hotel Nelly
12 Hotel Brasil
13 Condor
14 Hotel Angola
18 Pousada Green Track
23 Santa Rita
24 Santa Monica Palace
25 Premier Hotel
32 Hotel Laura Vicuña
34 Nacional
39 Hotel Beatriz; Pantanal Saldanha Tour

PLACES TO EAT
1 Vivabella
2 Restaurante Flutuante Caiçaras
8 Café com Arte
19 Churrascaria e Restaurante Rodeio
20 Restaurante Galpão
26 Peixaria do Lulu
28 Restaurante Paladar

30 Laco do Ouro
33 Almanara & Bagda
36 Churrascaria Gaúcho

OTHER
3 Porto Fluvial
4 Baís do Chopp
6 Tourist Office
7 Mutum Travel Agency
9 HSBC Bank
11 Post Office
15 Local Bus Terminal
16 Banco do Brasil
17 Policia Federal & Museu do Pantanal
21 Local Bus Terminal
22 Bus to Bolivian border
27 Telephone Office
29 Casa de Artesão
31 Café.com
35 Pantur Travel Agency
37 Bolivian Consulate
38 Claudine's Tour
40 Long-Distance Bus Station

THE CENTRAL WEST

Along Rua Manoel Cavassa on the waterfront, Urçabar is a small operator offering four-hour boat trips for around US$60 (for up to four people), not including gas.

Baís Navegacão (☎ 0xx67-726-1033) runs longer boat tours south along the Rio Paraguai to Porto Murtinho (on the Paraguayan border), stopping at points along the way for fishing and hiking. Its boat, the *Comodoro*, is the biggest tour boat in the region, sleeping up to 24 people in cabins. Tours cost around US$80 per day with meals included. Baís Navegacão is based in Poro Murtinho, but you may see the boat moored at the port in Corumbá or contact it through the travel agencies.

Places to Stay

There are some cheap hotels close to the long-distance bus station that are OK if you're just spending a night in Corumbá before heading out. Otherwise, there are good places closer to the waterfront, restaurants and bars in the center of town. Near the long-distance bus station, *Hotel Beatriz* (☎ 231-4665, *Rua Porto Carrero 896*) has very basic quartos (with terrible beds) at US$4 per person.

In the center, *Hotel Angola* (☎ 231-7727, *Rua Antônio Maria Coelho 124*) is well set up for travelers. Spacious, clean apartamentos, some including a kinda sexy round double bed, cost US$7 per person. Rooms with air-con go for US$10/14. There's a restaurant serving cheap meals on the top floor and Internet access is available. If you don't mind the stairs, ask for a room facing Rua Delamare on the third floor so you can enjoy the view of the Pantanal.

Pousada Green Track (☎ 232-6627, *Rua Antônio João 21*) is run by the same company that organizes Pantanal tours. Rooms cost US$6 per person. There is a cluster of cheapies on Rua Delamare between Rua Frei Mariano and Rua Antônio Maria Coelho. *Hotel Nelly* (☎ 231-6001) is the best value – clean quartos cost US$7/11/15 for singles/doubles/triples. *Hotel Brasil* (☎ 231-6940) has a range of rooms starting at US$7 per person and *Condor* has rooms with fan for US$5 per person.

There are some good deals in the mid-range. *Hotel Santa Rita* (☎ 231-5453, *Rua Dom Aquino 860*) is run by a friendly family and has big apartamentos starting at US$14/20. More expensive rooms at the front have small balconies: Don't lean on the railings, though, as they're very flimsy.

Just around the corner, *Premier Hotel* (☎ 231-4937, *Rua Antônio Maria Coelho 389*) is a good value; rooms with air-con and TV go for US$10 per person. The *Hotel Laura Vicuña* (☎ 231-2663, *Rua Cuiabá 775*) is in a quiet spot. Single/double apartamentos with air conditioning cost US$19/30.

An interesting place to stay on the waterfront is the *Hotel Beira Rio* (☎ 231-2554, *Rua Manoel Cavassa 109*). It is popular with anglers, and costs US$14 per person.

The favorite for group tours is the two-star *Santa Monica Palace* (☎ 231-3001, *stmonica@pantanalnet.com.br, Rua Antônio Maria Coelho 345*). It charges US$40/58/70 for singles/doubles/triples. The *Nacional* (☎ 231-6868, *hnacion@brasinet.com.br, Rua América 936*) is the plushest hotel in town. Singles/doubles go for US$50/64.

Places to Eat

The snazziest per-kilo restaurant in town (if not the whole state) for lunch is *Churrascaria e Restaurante Rodeio* (*Rua 13 de Junho 760*). It has 43 different salad dishes (go on, count 'em) to choose from and plenty of tasty meat as well. Another joint popular with locals for dinner is *Churrascaria Gaúcho* on Rua Frei Mariano. It has an all-you-can-eat buffet for US$4 (get there at 8 pm when the food is fresh), good people-watching on the sidewalk tables and a bit of live music as well.

Peixaria do Lulu (*Rua Dom Aquino 700*) is the best fish restaurant in town. It serves regional fish dishes such as *pacu frito com pirão e arroz* (fried pacu with tapioca pudding and rice) for US$10 per person.

The eatery with the best views over the Pantanal (and good Italian food) is *Vivabella*, a small bar/restaurant tucked away behind the park at the bottom of Rua 7 de Setembro. Pizza, pasta and salad dishes for US$12 are enough for two. If you're *sozinho*

Transportation, the Pantanal

Pousada Caiman Refuge, the Pantanal

A Cebu cow, the Pantanal

Wildlife habitat in the Pousada Caiman Refuge

Igreja NS do Carmo, Olinda

Igreja e Convento de NS do Carmo, Salvador

(alone) ask for half a portion. *Café com Arte* on Rua Delamare is a cool little bar/restaurant for light meals, drinks and live music at night. *Restaurante Paladar* on Rua Antônio Maria Coelho is a travelers' favorite for pizza and pasta dishes at US$6 to US$8. There are two Lebanese restaurants – *Almanara* and *Bagda* next to each other on Rua América.

For as much fish, churrascaria and pizza as you can eat for around US$6, try *Laço do Ouro*, on Rua Frei Mariano, or *Restaurante Galpão* on the corner of Rua 13 de Junho and Rua Antônio Maria Coelho. *Restaurante Flutuante Caiçaras* is a floating restaurant on the waterfront along Rua Manoel Cavassa that serves big fish dishes for around US$10 per person.

Entertainment
In the evening, Avenida General Rondon and Rua Frei Mariano is where young Corumbáns hang out to see and be seen. Bars around the waterfront plaza serve chopp and snacks. Across the road, *1054* is a dance club that gets packed on weekends. For a quieter drink on the waterfront, *Baís do Chopp (Rua Manoel Cavassa 275)* is a stylish bar with a restaurant attached.

Shopping
The Casa de Artesão, in the old prison at Rua Dom Aquino 405, has an excellent selection of indigenous and local art and artifacts. Each cell is a small gallery for an individual artist and, despite its bleak past, the old prison is a peaceful haven in the town.

Getting There & Away
Corumbá is a transit point for travel to/from Bolivia and Paraguay.

Air Corumbá airport (☎ 231-3322) is 3km east of the town center. TAM (☎ 231-7177 at the airport) is the only major Brazilian airline flying into and out of Corumbá. There are direct flights to and from Campo Grande and connecting flights to and from São Paulo.

Flights from Corumbá to Bolivian airports have been discontinued, but there are several weekly flights from Puerto Suárez,

just over the Bolivian border: TAM-Bolivia flies to Santa Cruz (US$54), La Paz (US$68) and Cochabamba (US$92) on Tuesday and Saturday at 1 pm, and LAB and Aerosur have joined forces for flights to Santa Cruz (US$83), Cochabamba (US$92) and La Paz (US$142) departing on Monday and Friday at 5:30 pm. These schedules change often and delays are common, so check the latest information in Corumbá at Pantur (see Organized Tours earlier in the Corumbá section), which acts as an agent for both LAB and TAM-Bolivia.

Bus From the long-distance bus station, buses run to Campo Grande (US$24) nine times a day from 8:30 am to 11:30 pm. Direct buses do the trip in around six hours. To Aquidauana (US$14, five hours) there are five buses a day. There's a daily bus to Bonito (US$22, seven hours) at 5:30 am. If you miss it, take a bus to Anastácio (US$14, five hours) and pick up a bus there for Bonito at 5 pm.

Train Once across the Bolivian border (see the To/From Bolivia later in this section), most people will be heading toward Santa Cruz. From Quijarro (the Bolivian border town opposite Corumbá) to Santa Cruz, the Rápido Tren service runs daily at 3 pm and takes about 18 to 20 hours. Tickets cost US$21/18/8 for bracha/pullman/first class.

This train service is known as the Death Train – in days gone by the journey was less than safe, with deaths from derailments, heat exhaustion and dehydration. These days, however the journey is a beautiful one, passing through the steamy, sticky Pantanal area to lush jungle and chaco scrub. Be sure to have plenty of insect repellent on hand, since there are often unexplained stops in swampy areas and the zillions of mosquitoes get voraciously hungry in those parts. Take plenty of drinking water as well.

The passenger train service between Corumbá and Campo Grande has been discontinued.

Ferrobus The luxury trip between Quijarro and Santa Cruz is on the ferrobus, a bus on

THE CENTRAL WEST

bogies (wheels). It is considerably faster than the train and has air conditioning. It leaves from Quijarro for Santa Cruz on Monday, Wednesday and Friday at 7 pm. Tickets cost US$40 and the trip takes at least 12 hours.

Boat Passenger boat services between Corumbá and Asunción (Paraguay) have been discontinued. Boat transport up through the Pantanal is infrequent – inquire at the port.

To/From Bolivia The Bolivian border town of Quijarro is not much more than a muddy little collection of shacks. Taxis operate between the border and Quijarro station, a distance of about 4km – the going rate is around US$2.50.

For US$0.60, the Fronteira-Corumbá bus will take you from the border to Corumbá, dropping you on Rua Frei Mariano in the center or at the local bus terminal near the corner of Rua 13 de Junho and Rua Tiradentes. If you're heading from the city to the border, catch the bus on Praça Independência on Rua Dom Aquino. It runs every 30 minutes and costs US$0.60. If you're in a hurry, grab a motor taxi for US$2. Taxis want US$6.

Getting Around

The cost of a taxi from Corumbá's long-distance bus station on Rua Porto Carrero to the center is down from US$7 to US$3.50 – they must have heard we were onto them!

From the bus stop outside the long-distance bus station, the Cristo Redentur bus (US$0.60) runs to the local bus terminal on Rua 13 de Junho. Going to the long-distance bus station, you can take a motor taxi (US$1) from the local bus station on Rua Antônio Maria Coelho (near the Hotel Angola), if you're light on luggage.

From the local bus terminal on Rua 13 do Junho, the Aeroporto bus runs (spookily) to the airport. The taxi drivers that formerly tried to rip people off at the long-distance bus station have moved to the airport. They want US$8 for the 3km trip to town – make

sure the taxi has a meter or establish a price before you get in.

AQUIDAUANA

☎ 0xx67 • postcode 79200-000 • pop 34,000
Aquidauana and Anastácio are twin towns situated on the Rio Aquidauana, 138km from Campo Grande. These towns represent an entry point to the southern Pantanal, and there are a number of excellent hotel-fazendas in the area. In Aquidauana there's not much to interest the traveler, but it's a friendly and relaxed place. The local government is actively promoting it as a base for Pantanal excursions.

Information

The Fundetur office on Praça do Estudantes near the old train station has videos and information about the Pantanal. Banco do Brasil, at Rua Manoel Antônio Paes de Barros 535, has a Visa ATM. International calls can be made from the telephone office next door.

Panbratour (☎ 241-3494), at Rua Estevão Alves Correa 586, specializes in the Pantanal. Staff can give you the latest information on hotel-fazendas. Buriti Turismo (☎ 241-2718), at Rua Manoel Antônio Paes de Barros 720, is another helpful agency.

Places to Stay & Eat

A good cheapie right in the center is *Hotel Lord* (☎ 241-1857, Rua Manoel Antônio Paes de Barros 239). Quartos cost US$6/11 for singles/doubles, and apartamentos cost US$10/19. On the same street, *Aquidauana Palace* (☎ 241-3596, aquidauanapalace@zoonet.com.br, Rua Manoel Antônio Paes de Barros 904) is a newish place that offers double apartamentos with air-con for US$20. In the mid-range, *Portal Pantaneiro Hotel* (☎ 241-4328, Rua Pandía Calógeras 1067) is an excellent value, with singles/doubles starting at US$28/48.

O Casarão (Rua Manoel Antônio Paes Barros 533) is still the top restaurant in town. It has a varied menu with dishes for around US$8 to US$10 per person. The best place for lunch and snacks is *Elias Lanchonete* (Rua 7 de Setembro 590).

Getting There & Around

There are frequent buses between Campo Grande and Aquidauana. There's a daily bus to Bonito at 5 pm. The road turns to dirt around 30km from Aquidauana.

Motorcycle taxis can ferry you around town – from the bus station to the center costs US$1.50.

COXIM

☎ 0xx67 • postcode 79400-000 • pop 27,000
Coxim is a small town about halfway between Cuiabá and Campo Grande, on the eastern border of the Pantanal. The town's main draw is the Piracema, when fish migrate up the Taquari and Coxim Rivers, leaping through rapids to spawn. The Piracema takes place from November to January; fishing is not allowed during this period, but if you're traveling through it's worth stopping off to have a look.

The fishing – for pacu, pintado, curimbatá, dourado and jaú – is best from August to October. A fishing permit is required – you can pick one up at IBAMA (☎ 291-2310) at Rua Floriano Peixoto 304 or at the Banco do Brasil at Rua Antônio de Alberqueque 248. A permit valid for three months costs US$9. In the center, Isca Viva is the place to rent fishing rods and buy bait – it's open 24 hours a day.

Coxim is also an entry point to the Pantanal, but it has limited infrastructure for wildlife-spotting tours, with most operators catering exclusively to fishing tours.

Places to Stay

There are a number of cheap hotels in town. If you arrive late at night, the *Hotel Neves* (☎ 291-1273, Avenida Gaspar Ries Coelho 1931) is next to the bus station. Clean quartos with fan cost US$8 per person. The town is 3km away, on the banks of the river.

Coxim Hotel (☎ 726-2055, dionross@ enersulnet.com.br), 4km from town on the road to Campo Grande, is well set up for fishing tours. Apartamentos with air-con start at US$14/25/31. Check its Web site at www.brart.com/coxim/Coxim01.htm.

A reasonable hotel with a river frontage closer to town is the *Rio* (☎ 291-1295, Rua

Filinto Muller 651). Singles/doubles with fan go for US$14/28.

Getting There & Around

There are plenty of buses from both Cuiabá (US$16, 6½ hours) and Campo Grande (US$12, 3½ hours) to Coxim.

All the hotels along the river have small outboard boats for hire; daily rates start at about US$60.

BONITO

☎ 0xx67 • postcode 79290-000 • pop 13,000
Bonito is an ecotourism boom town. This small town in the southwestern corner of Mato Grosso do Sul has no attractions itself, but the natural resources of the area are spectacular. There are subterranean caves with lakes and amazing stalactite formations, beautiful waterfalls and incredibly clear rivers surrounded by lush forest, where it's possible for divers to swim eyeball to eyeball with hundreds of fish. Since Bonito was put on the ecotourism map in the early 1990s, the number of visitors has risen dramatically every year. Despite its popularity, it's still a great place to kick back outside peak holiday periods (December to February and July).

Information

Bradesco, at Rua Coronel Pilad Rebua 1942, has Visa ATMs, as does Banco do Brasil, just off the main plaza at Rua Luiz da Costa Leite 2279. The post office is at Rua Coronel Pilad Rebua 1759. At No 1499 on the same street, Bla-bla-bla.com.b@r is the town's new Internet café.

For descriptions of the area's key attractions, see the Organized Tours section below.

Organized Tours

The local government has strict regulations in place for visiting the area's natural attractions, partly because many are on private land, and partly to minimize the impact on some pristine areas. Most attractions have a daily limit on the number of visitors they will accept, and visitors at all sites must be accompanied by a guide.

It's Clear to See: Bonito Is Beautiful

Bonito's incredibly clear rivers were produced by a happy accident of nature. The river waters spring from subterranean sources in a limestone base, which releases calcium carbonate into the water. The calcium carbonate calcifies all impurities in the water, which then sink to the riverbed (this is the reason you're asked to stay afloat and not touch the bottom during river tours). The result is an area filled with natural aquariums surrounded by lush forest, a beautiful environment in which to study the abundant numbers of fascinating fish in the rivers. The robust *dourado* (gold) fish is known as the 'shark of the river' – a sinister-looking creature, it cruises the river eating its fellow fish. Meter-long catfish lurk in grottos, while the huge, black *pacu* move with surprising quickness along the river in large schools.

The river tours are a unique experience and not to be missed – the only drawback is that the area's popularity brings its own challenges. While there are limits on the number of daily visitors to most of the area's natural attractions, those limits are being reached most days. At some attractions, 'rest periods' of two to three months each year are being introduced to allow for the fragile vegetation to regenerate.

Only guides from local travel agencies are authorized, so you're obliged to book tours through them. There are about 25 travel agencies in Bonito offering about 30 different tours. Unfortunately, few tours are cheap and they don't include transport, which you have to arrange yourself. (See the Getting Around section for more information.) For this reason, you might find it easier to tack onto a group that has already organized transport through the more popular agencies.

The main street, Rua Coronel Pilad Rebua, is lined with travel agencies. Some of the better ones are Iberê Tour (☎ 255-1166, iberetur@bonitonline.com.br) at No 1890; Muito Bonito Tourismo (☎ 255-1645, muitobonito@uol.com.br) at No 1448; and Ygarapé Tour (☎ 255-1733, ygarape@bonitonline.com.br) at No 1853.

There are about 30 attractions in the area now, but only seven or eight are exceptional. There have been exciting recent developments in more radical adventure tours (including rappelling down to and diving in underground lakes), but these are also the most expensive. Prices quoted here are for low season – they rise by around 25% in high season (December to February, July and other holiday periods). In the high season, many of these tours are booked up

months ahead. If you're traveling during these times, it's a good idea to book well in advance.

Seven kilometers southeast of Bonito, **Aquário Natural Baía Bonita** is a beautiful natural spring where you can swim among 30 different varieties of fish and then float gently downstream to small waterfalls. The three-hour tour costs US$28, including wetsuits and snorkels. A wetsuit will take the edge off the cold water and also protect you from the sun – you aren't allowed to wear sunscreen in any of the river tours because it taints the water. The Aquário is managed by a Frenchman, Laurent. **Rio Sucuri**, 20km southwest of Bonito, is similar to Aquário Natural – with springs and a crystal-clear river full of fish and subaquatic gardens, surrounded by lush forest – but it's farther out in the wild. The cost is US$24 for three hours.

Within a fazenda 50km south of Bonito, the **Rio da Prata** tour includes a short trek through rainforest and a 2km swim downstream along the river. The five-hour tour costs US$24. A buffet lunch is offered for US$5.50 per person.

The bargain attractions are **Gruta do Lago Azul** (US$7 entry), a large cave with a luminous underground lake and stalactite formations 20km west of Bonito, and the **Balneário Municipal** (US$6 entry), a natural swimming pool with clear water and lots of fish on the Rio Formoso, 7km southeast of town. You don't need a guide for the Balneário Municipal – you can spend the whole day there and have lunch at the kiosk.

Abismo de Anhumas, 22km west of Bonito, is a 72m abyss that descends to an underground lake. It has incredible stalactite formations including *Os Dedos* (The Fingers), *O Vigilante* (The Vigilant) and *Cascatas* (Cascades). The tour involves rappelling (abseiling) down to the bottom and snorkeling in the lake (or you can opt for scuba diving if you have a basic certificate). The rappelling part of the tour costs US$100; scuba diving costs an extra US$70.

Lagoa Misteriosa, 42km south of Bonito, is a small 'bottomless' lake (its depth is estimated at 180 to 200m) with submerged rock and stalactite formations. Snorkeling or diving to a depth of 25 to 30m is allowed on tours. A 35-minute scuba dive costs US$56.

Places to Stay

Accommodations in Bonito are tight and more expensive during the high season and on weekends throughout the year.

You can camp next to the *Balneário Municipal* for US$3 per person, and buy meals at the kiosks there.

The HI hostel *Albergue da Juventude do Ecoturismo* (☎ 255-1462, *booking@ajbonito .com.br*, *Rua Lúcio Borralho 716*) is approximately 1.5km from the center, but staff meet buses and bikes are available for trips to town. Rooms start at US$11 per person, and you can buy meals there for around US$4 or cook in the kitchen. The hostel can also book tours and arrange transport. Visit the Web site at www.ajbonito.com.br.

A bit closer to the center, *Pousada Muito Bonito* (☎ 255-1645, *muitobonito@uol.com.br, Rua Coronel Pilad Rebua 1448*) is a good option. Comfortable apartamentos with fan cost US$11 per person with a good breakfast included. The owner, Mario Doblack, speaks English, French, German, Spanish and Italian and is helpful with information. He also has houses for rent for longer stays.

A good cheapie in town is the friendly *Pousada São Jorge* (☎ 255-1956, *saojorge@*

bonitonline.com.br, Rua Coronel Pilad Rebua 1605). Basic but clean apartamentos with air-con cost US$8 per person. Internet access is available.

Pousada Caramachão (☎ 255-1674, *caramanchao@caramanchao.com.br, Rua das Flores 1203*) is a more upmarket place in a quiet spot off the main drag. Apartamentos with air-con cost US$14/19.

Places to Eat

Just off the main street, *Restaurante da Vovó* on Rua Felinto Muller is an excellent per-kilo joint serving regional food. Leave some room for the *mousse maracujá* (US$0.70) for dessert – it's special. Another popular per-kilo restaurant specializing in fish is *O Casarão (Rua Coronel Pilad Rebua 1843)*. It's a good place to try some of the local fish you swam with during the day!

A reasonably priced à la carte fish restaurant is *Aquário* on the corner of Rua Coronel Pilad Rebua and Rua Felinto Muller. The *pintado* plate for two costs US$14. *Tapera (Rua Coronel Pilad Rebua 480)* has meat, chicken and fish dishes for two people for around US$10. For a cheap lunch of fresh pastries, pies and juices, go to *Lanchonete Tutti Frutti* on Rua Coronel Pilad Rebua. You can pig out for less than US$2.

Entertainment

In Bonito's short history as a tourist town, *Taboa Bar (Rua Coronel Pilad Rebua 1841)* has become an institution. Located in the heart of the main street, it's the place where locals and travelers converge for drinks and live music on weekends.

Shopping

Berô-Can, at Rua Felinto Muller 568, has an excellent range of indigenous artifacts from tribes in Mato Grosso and farther afield.

Getting There & Away

There are three daily buses to Bonito from Campo Grande (US$14), at 6 and 11 am and 3 pm. Buses return to Campo Grande from Bonito via Aquidauana and Anastacio at 5:30 am, noon and 4 pm. There are daily buses (except for Sunday) to Ponta Porã (US$16, six hours) at 12:10 pm, and to Corumbá (US$22, seven hours) at 12:30 pm. If you're in a hurry or can't hack overcrowded buses, private Kombi vans based in town do runs to Campo Grande, Corumbá, Foz do Iguaçu and Anastácio. Contact Gauchinho through the youth hostel for more information.

Getting Around

Unfortunately, many of Bonito's attractions are a fair hike from town, and there's no public transport apart from a shuttle bus that runs on weekends to the Balneário Municipal (US$1). Tours booked with travel agencies in Bonito don't include transport. If you book a tour with a busy travel agency, you might be able to scrounge a ride with Brazilian tourists, most of whom are traveling by car or minibus.

Otherwise, your options are to rent a car (from US$25 per day, plus US$0.20 per km) from Yes Rent-a-Car (☎ 255-1702, yes@yes-rentacar.com.br), at Rua Felinto Muller 656, or grab a motor taxi. Motor taxi prices are negotiable: To the Rio Sucuri (40km round-trip) and Gruta do Lago Azul (40km round-trip) and back to town costs US$7 to US$10 per person; to the Aquário Natural (14km round-trip) costs US$3. The drivers wait around for the duration of the tour. To Balneário Natural (7km) is US$1.50 (one-way).

During high season, Mario Doblack at Muito Bonito Tourismo runs a daily bus to Rio da Prata (108km round-trip) for US$7.

PONTA PORÃ

☎ 0xx67 • postcode 79900-000 • pop 54,000
Ponta Porã is a border town divided from the Paraguayan town of Pedro Juan Caballero by Avenida Internacional. It was a center for the yerba maté trade in the late 1800s, long before it started attracting Brazilians who like to play in the Paraguayan casinos and shop for perfumes, electronics and musical condoms.

Information

Immigration Getting exit/entry stamps involves a bit of legwork, so if you're in a hurry, grab a cab. For Brazilian entry/exit

stamps, go to the Polícia Federal (☎ 431-1428) on Avenida Presidente Vargas in Ponta Porã, near the Paraguayan consulate. It's open daily from 8 am to 5 pm. For Paraguayan entry/exit stamps, the new Paraguayan immigration office is on Avenida Dr Francis (no number), about 2km east of the local bus terminal. It's a large, brown building and is open Monday to Friday from 7 am to noon and 2 to 5 pm, and on Saturday from 7 am to noon.

See the Facts for the Visitor chapter for details of Paraguayan and Brazilian consulates at this border.

Money The Banco do Brasil on the corner of Avenida Brasil and Rua Guia Lopes in Ponta Porã has a Visa ATM.

In Pedro Juan Caballero, Los Angeles Câmbio on the corner of Calle Mariscal López and Calle Curupayty changes cash at a reasonable rate.

Places to Stay & Eat

There are plenty of cheap places to spend the night in both countries. The accomodations on the Paraguayan side of the border don't include breakfast.

In Ponta Porã, the *Hotel Alvorada* (☎ 431-5786, Avenida Brasil 2977) is a good value. Quartos go for US$6/10/12 a single/double/triple and apartamentos cost US$8/14/16. The *Hotel Internacional* (☎ 431-1243, Avenida Internacional 2604) is another good option. Quartos with fan cost US$6/12/16, and apartamentos with air-con are US$14/24. The *Hotel Guarujá* (☎ 431-1619, Rua Guia Lopes 63) is a good mid-range option. Large apartamentos with air-conditioning go for US$13/24. Across the road at No 57, *Hotel Barcelona* (☎ 431-3061) has gone upmarket; comfortable apartamentos cost US$27/42.

Over the border in Pedro Juan Caballero, there are a few cheap hotels on Calle Mariscal López. The best is the friendly *Hotel Peralta*, at No 1257, which charges US$3/6 for single/doubles.

On the Brazilian side, *Choppão (Rua Marechal Floriano 1877)* is a popular spot with an extensive menu of meat, fish and

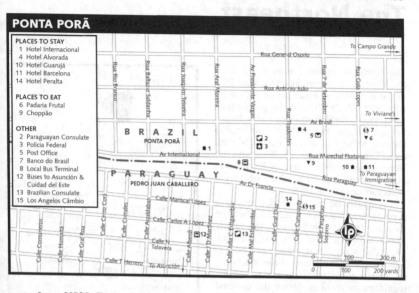

PONTA PORÃ

PLACES TO STAY
1 Hotel Internacional
4 Hotel Alvorada
10 Hotel Guarujá
11 Hotel Barcelona
14 Hotel Peralta

PLACES TO EAT
6 Padaria Frutal
9 Choppão

OTHER
2 Paraguayan Consulate
3 Polícia Federal
5 Post Office
7 Banco do Brasil
8 Local Bus Terminal
12 Buses to Asunción & Cuidad del Este
13 Brazilian Consulate
15 Los Angelos Câmbio

pasta from US$5. For a cheap lunch or dinner, *Padaria Frutal* on Rua Guia Lópes near the corner of Avenida Brasil has pies, pastries and snacks. The best (and most expensive) meal in town is at *Viviane's (Avenida Brasil 4128)*.

Getting There & Around

From the long-distance bus station in Ponta Porã (about 4km east of the center), there are 14 buses a day to Campo Grande (US$14, 5½ hours). There's a daily bus to Corumbá, via Bonito, at 6 am.

For Foz do Iguaçu, take a bus from the bus station on Calle Alberdi in Pedro Juan Caballero (on the Paraguayan side) to Ciudad del Este. Cuidad del Este (Paraguay) is just across the border from the Brazilian town of Foz do Iguaçu. There are two overnight buses to Ciudad del Este – a leito (US$10, eight hours) at 9:30 pm and a directo at 10:30 pm. You don't need a Paraguayan visa to transit through Paraguay on your way to Foz do Iguaçu. From the same bus station in Pedro Juan Caballero, there are also frequent buses to Asunción, the capital of Paraguay (US$18, seven hours).

The local bus terminal (just a few tin shelters, so keep your eye out) is on Avenida Internacional, near the hotels. If you're coming into town from the Brazilian side, the bus can drop you here on the way in.

THE CENTRAL WEST

The Northeast

The Northeast region, known in Brazil as the Nordeste, accounts for more than 18% of the country's area and has 48 million inhabitants, nearly 30% of the population. The region is divided into nine states: Bahia, Sergipe, Alagoas, Pernambuco, Paraíba, Rio Grande do Norte, Ceará, Piauí and Maranhão. The archipelago of Fernando de Noronha, over 500km east of Recife, was placed under the political administration of Pernambuco state in 1988.

The Northeast can be divided into four geographic and economic regions. The *zona da mata* (forest zone) covers the fertile coastal area, extending up to 200km inland. The Atlantic rainforest, known as the Mata Atlântica, now exists only in tiny pockets – the rest was destroyed to make way for sugarcane cultivation during the colonial period. With the exception of Teresina in Piauí state, all the major cities of the Northeast were established in this zone. The economy of the zona da mata depends on crops such as sugar and cacao, and on the petroleum industry, which is based on the coast.

Farther west, the *agreste* forms a transitional strip of semifertile lands that merges into the *sertão* (backlands). Its inhabitants live from subsistence farming, small-scale agriculture (vegetables, fruit, cotton and coffee) and cattle ranching (beef and dairy).

The sertão is characterized by a dry and temperate climate. Droughts, sometimes lasting many years, have been the bane of this area for centuries. The land is commonly referred to as *caatingas* because the landscape is dominated by vast tracts of caatinga (a scrubby shrub). The largest towns of the sertão are dotted along the Rio São Francisco, which provides irrigation. The sertão's economy is based on cattle ranching, cotton cultivation and subsistence farming that puts the carnaubeira, a type of palm, to a multitude of uses. The bleak and brutal life of the Sertanejos (inhabitants of the sertão) has re-

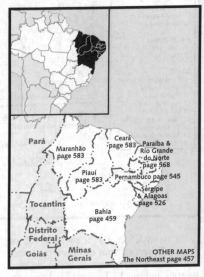

Pará
Maranhão page 583
Ceará page 583
Paraíba & Rio Grande do Norte page 568
Piauí page 583
Pernambuco page 545
Tocantins
Sergipe & Alagoas page 526
Bahia page 459
Distrito Federal
Goiás
Minas Gerais
OTHER MAPS
The Northeast page 457

ceived literary coverage in *Os Sertões* (published in English as *Rebellion in the Backlands*) by Euclides da Cunha, and the novel *Vidas Secas (Dry Lives)* by Graciliano Ramos. The Cinema Novo films of Glauber Rocha depict violence, religious fanaticism, official corruption and hunger in the sertão.

The state of Maranhão and the western margin of Piauí state form the *meio norte,* a transitional zone between the arid sertão and the humid Amazon region. The meio norte is economically reliant on babaçu, another type of palm, which provides nuts and oil. The latter is converted into lubricating oil, soap, margarine and cosmetics.

For the traveler, the region is one of the most fascinating and diverse in Brazil. The beautiful coastline stretches for more than 2000km. From Bahia to Paraíba the beaches are tropical paradises of palm trees, white sand and blue sea. From Rio Grande do Norte to Maranhão the beaches are drier, with huge sand dunes built up by the strong

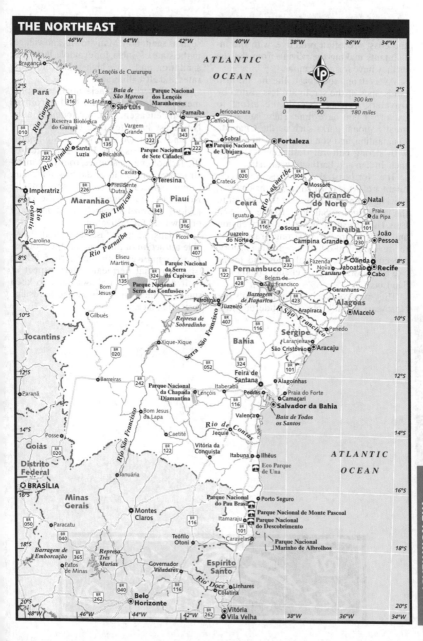

winds that sweep in from the Atlantic Ocean. The small fishing villages that dot the coast are often primitive, with the inhabitants making their living from the sea as they have for generations.

Away from the coast, the harsh, arid landscapes of the sertão are less visited by travelers, but well worth the effort to explore if you have time. There are some great national parks such as the Chapada Diamantina, and you'll find friendly people with strong cultural traditions based on their Indian and Portuguese ancestry.

The Northeast also contains the largest number of African-Brazilians in the country, most of whom live on or near the coast or in the large cities of Salvador, Recife and São Luís. The African influence in music, religion and cuisine here is very strong. Travelers to the region will also find it steeped in history, especially in the colonial cities and towns like Salvador, Lençóis, Penedo, Olinda and São Luís.

The massive social problems of the Northeast include poverty, underemployment, housing shortages, a decaying education system and an absence of basic services such as sanitation. Many towns and villages in the state of Bahia, for example, lack basic sanitation and have high infant mortality rates and 50% illiteracy.

The Superintendência do Desenvolvimento do Nordeste (SUDENE), the official government agency for development in the Northeast, has attempted to attract industry and boost the economy of the region, but these efforts have been hampered by the lack of energy sources, transport infrastructure, skilled labor and raw materials. Many Nordestinos (inhabitants of the Northeast) have emigrated to the other regions in Brazil in search of a living wage or new land for cultivation.

Perhaps the most fascinating and enjoyable attraction of this region is the Nordestinos themselves, with their rich, folkloric traditions that permeate every aspect of their daily lives and allows them to keep smiles on their faces despite the hardships they often face.

Bahia

Bahia is Brazil's most historic state, and has retained strong links with the African heritage of many of its inhabitants. The state capital, Salvador da Bahia, was the capital of colonial Brazil from 1549 to 1763, and was the center of the sugar industry, which sustained the prosperity of the country until the decline in international sugar prices in the 1820s.

The state of Bahia can be divided into three distinct regions: the *recôncavo*, the *sertão* and the *litoral*.

The recôncavo is a band of hot and humid lands that surrounds the Baía de Todos os Santos. The principal cities are Cachoeira, Santo Amaro, Maragojipe and Nazaré, which were once sugar and tobacco centers and the source of wealth for Salvador.

The sertão is a vast and parched land on which a suffering people eke out a meager existence raising cattle and tilling the earth. Periodically, tremendous droughts, such as the great drought of 1877–79, sweep the land. Thousands of Sertanejos pile their belongings on their backs and migrate south or anywhere they can find jobs. But with the first hint of rain in the sertão, the Sertanejos return to renew their strong bond with this land.

South of Salvador, the coast has beautiful endless beaches. This is a cacao-producing region and encompasses important cities like Valença, Ilhéus and Itabuna. North of Salvador the coast is only sparsely populated with a few fishing villages. The southern beaches are calm, while the northern beaches are often windy, with rough surf.

Salvador is a fascinating city loaded with colonial relics, including many richly decorated churches – one for every day of the year, according to popular belief. But be sure to take the time to explore outside Salvador and visit Bahia's smaller cities, towns and villages, where life is unaffected by tourism and even less affected by the 20th century.

If beaches are what you want, the only difficulty is choosing. You can go to Porto

Highlights

- Lasting African heritage and culture – music, dance, religion, cuisine and annual festivals
- Fascinating candomblé ceremonies and festivals in Salvador and Cachoeira
- Lively Tuesday-night music shows in Salvador's Pelourinho
- *Roda da capoeira*: semicircles of musicians and dancer/fighters on the streets of Bahian towns
- The Igreja São Francisco in Salvador, with baroque artwork by African-slave artisans
- Great diving and whale-watching in the Parque Nacional Marinho dos Abrolhos
- Magnificent beaches south of Porto Seguro
- Great hikes and water slides in the Parque Nacional da Chapada Diamantina

Parque Nacional da Chapada Diamantina page 522
Lençóis page 518
Baía de Todos os Santos & Recôncavo page 481
Ilhéus page 500
North of Salvador page 488
Cachoeira page 484
Salvador page 462
Central Salvador pages 464–465
Porto Seguro page 505
Bahia page 460

Ceará

Rio Grande do Norte

Paraíba

Pernambuco

Piauí

Alagoas

Sergipe

Minas Gerais

THE NORTHEAST

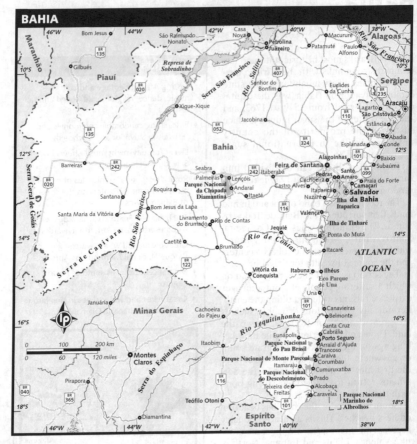

BAHIA

Seguro for beaches with fancy hotels and restaurants or cross the river to Arraial d'Ajuda, Trancoso and Caraiva for a hipper, less developed beach scene. To really escape civilization, you can go to the beaches up north around Mangue Seco, or along the Peninsula do Maraú south of Valença.

The inland regions of Bahia are less well known, but definitely worth a visit. Cachoeira and Lençóis are both interesting colonial towns and Lençóis provides a handy base for hiking trips in the Parque Nacional da Chapada Diamantina. Travelers might also like to explore the bizarre moonscapes of the sertão, where the Sertanejos have maintained a rich culture despite the poor environment.

Salvador

☎ 0xx71 • postcode 40000-000
• pop 2.4 million

Salvador da Bahia, often abbreviated to Bahia by Brazilians, is the capital of Bahia state and one of Brazil's cultural highlights. This city retains its African soul, with a unique, vibrant culture. Ornate churches still stand on cobblestone streets, while Candomblé services illuminate the hillsides. Festivals are spontaneous, wild, popular and frequent. Capoeira and *axé* (groups playing this Bahian music, which has a strong African beat) dance through the streets.

The restoration of the historic center of Salvador has revitalized areas that were previously considered dangerous and largely off-limits to tourists. However, despite the current boom in tourism, Salvador also suffers from social and economic problems, and has a great number of citizens who are jobless, homeless, hungry, abandoned and sick.

HISTORY

According to tradition, on November 1, 1501, All Saints' Day, the Italian navigator Amerigo Vespucci sailed into the bay, which was accordingly named Baía de Todos os Santos. In 1549, Tomé de Sousa came from Portugal under royal orders to found Brazil's first capital, bringing city plans, a statue, 400 soldiers and 400 settlers, including priests and prostitutes. He founded the city in a defensive location: on a cliff top facing the sea. After the first year, a city of mud and straw had been erected, and by 1550 the surrounding walls were in place to protect against attacks from hostile Indians. Salvador da Bahia remained Brazil's most important city for the next three centuries.

During its first century of existence, the city depended upon the export of sugarcane, but tobacco cultivation was later introduced and cattle ranching proved profitable in the sertão. The export of gold and diamonds mined in the Bahian interior (Chapada Diamantina) provided Salvador with immense wealth. The opulent baroque architecture is a testament to the prosperity of this period.

Overlooking the mouth of Baía de Todos os Santos, which is surrounded by the recôncavo, Brazil's richest sugar and tobacco lands, Bahia was colonial Brazil's economic heartland. Sugar, tobacco, sugarcane brandy and, later, gold were shipped out, while slaves and European luxury goods were shipped in.

After Lisbon, Salvador was the second city in the Portuguese Empire and the glory of colonial Brazil, famed for its many gold-filled churches, beautiful mansions and numerous festivals. It was also renowned as early as the 17th century for its bawdy public life, sensuality and decadence – so much so that it became known as the Bay of All Saints and of nearly all sins!

Salvador remained Brazil's seat of colonial government until 1763 when, with the decline of the sugarcane industry, the capital was moved to Rio.

The first black slaves were brought from Guinea in 1538, and in 1587 historian Gabriel Soares estimated that Salvador had 12,000 whites, 8000 converted Indians and 4000 black slaves. A black man was worth six times as much as a black woman in the slave market. The number of blacks eventually increased to constitute half of the population and the traditions of Africa took root so successfully that today Salvador is called the African soul of Brazil.

Blacks in Salvador preserved their African culture more than anywhere else in the New World. They maintained their religion and spirituality, within Catholicism. African food and music enriched the homes of both blacks and whites, while capoeira developed among the slaves. *Quilombos* (communities of runaway slaves) terrified the landed aristocracy, and uprisings of blacks threatened the city several times.

In 1798, the city was the stage for the Conjuração dos Alfaiates (Conspiracy of the Tailors), which intended to proclaim a Bahian republic. Although this uprising was quickly quelled, the battles between those who longed for independence and those loyal to Portugal continued in the streets of Salvador for many years. It was only on July 2, 1823, with the defeat in Cabrito and Pirajá of the Portuguese troops commanded by Madeira de Melo, that the city found peace. At that time, Salvador numbered 45,000 inhabitants and was the commercial center of a vast territory.

For most of the 19th and 20th centuries the city stagnated as the agricultural economy,

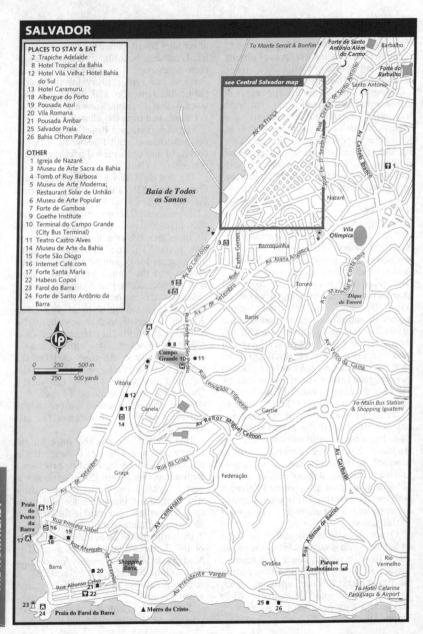

SALVADOR

PLACES TO STAY & EAT
2 Trapiche Adelaide
8 Hotel Tropical da Bahia
12 Hotel Vila Velha; Hotel Bahia do Sul
13 Hotel Caramuru
18 Albergue do Porto
19 Pousada Azul
20 Vila Romana
21 Pousada Âmbar
25 Salvador Praia
26 Bahia Othon Palace

OTHER
1 Igreja de Nazaré
3 Museu de Arte Sacra da Bahia
4 Tomb of Ruy Barbosa
5 Museu de Arte Moderna; Restaurant Solar de Unhão
6 Museu de Arte Popular
7 Forte de Gamboa
9 Goethe Institute
10 Terminal do Campo Grande (City Bus Terminal)
11 Teatro Castro Alves
14 Museu de Arte da Bahia
15 Forte São Diogo
16 Internet Café.com
17 Forte Santa Maria
22 Habeus Copos
23 Farol do Barra
24 Forte de Santo Antônio da Barra

see Central Salvador map

To Monte Serrat & Bonfim

Forte de Santo Antônio Além do Carmo

Barbalho

Forte do Barbalho

Santo Antônio

Av da França

Av Castelo Branco

Nazaré

Baía de Todos os Santos

Vila Olímpica

Barroquinha

Av Joana Angélica

Av do Contorno

Rua Carlos Gomes

Tororó

Av Marechal Costa Silva

Dique do Tororó

Rua 7 de Setembro

Barris

Av 7 de Setembro

Campo Grande

Vitória

Rua Forte de São Diogo

Rua Leovigildo Filgueiras

Av Vasco da Gama

To Main Bus Station & Shopping Iguatemi

Canela

Av Reitor Miguel Calmon

Garcia

Graça

Rua da Graça

Federação

Av 7 de Setembro

Av Cardeal

Praia do Porto da Barra

Rua Princesa Isabel

Rua Marquês de Caravelas

Barra

Shopping Barra

Rua Alfonso Celso

Av Centenário

Av Ademar de Barros

Ondina

Parque Zoobotânico

Rio Vermelho

To Hotel Catarina Paraguaçu & Airport

Praia do Farol da Barra

Morro do Cristo

Av Presidente Vargas

0   250   500 m
0   250   500 yards

THE NORTHEAST

based on archaic arrangements for land distribution, organization of labor and production, went into uninterrupted decline. Only recently has Salvador begun to move forward economically. New industries such as petroleum, chemicals and tourism are producing changes in the urban landscape, but the rapidly increasing population is still faced with major social problems.

ORIENTATION

Salvador sits at the southern tip of a V-shaped peninsula at the mouth of the Baía de Todos os Santos. The left branch of the 'V' is on Baía de Todos os Santos; the right branch faces the Atlantic Ocean; and the junction is the Barra district, which is south of the city center.

A steep bluff divides central Salvador into two parts: Cidade Alta (Upper City) and Cidade Baixa (Lower City). These are linked by the Plano Inclinado Gonçalves (a funicular railway), the Elevador Lacerda and some *ladeiras* (very steep roads).

Cidade Alta

This is the historic section of Salvador. Built on hilly, uneven ground, the site of the original settlement was chosen to protect the new capital from Indian attacks. The most important buildings – churches, convents, government offices and houses of merchants and landowners – were constructed on the hilltops. Rational long-term planning was not a high priority.

The colonial neighborhoods of Terreiro de Jesus, Pelourinho, and Anchieta are filled with 17th-century churches and houses. The area has been undergoing major restoration work since 1993, and this continues today. The result is that Pelourinho has been transformed into a tourist mecca, packed with restaurants, bars, art galleries and boutiques. Although it's lost some of its character in the process, the area is now much safer and tourist police are posted on just about every other corner. Approximately 200m southwest of Praça da Sé is Praça Tomé de Souza and the large, cream-colored birthday-cake building called Palácio Rio Branco. Close by is the Lacerda Elevator. A few blocks

farther south is Praça Castro Alves, a major hub for Carnaval festivities.

From here, Avenida 7 de Setembro runs southwards (parallel to the bay) until it reaches the Barra district, which has many of the city's top-end and mid-range hotels and bars, and the Atlantic Ocean.

Heading east from the Barra district is the main road along the Atlantic coast, sometimes called Avenida Presidente Vargas (at least on the maps). It snakes along the shore all the way to Itapoã. Along the way it passes the middle-class Atlantic suburbs and a chain of tropical beaches.

Cidade Baixa

This is Bahia's commercial and financial center and its port. Busy during workdays and filled with lunch places, the lower city is deserted and unsafe at night and on weekends. Heading north, away from the ocean and along the bay, you pass the port and the ferry terminal for Ilha de Itaparica, and continue to the bay beaches of Boa Viagem and Ribeira (very lively on weekends). The suburbs along the bay are poor, and the farther you go from the center the greater the poverty. Watch for the incredible architecture of the *lagados,* which are similar to favelas but built on the bay.

Navigating the City

Finding your way around Salvador can be difficult. On addition to the complications of upper city and lower city, there are too many one-way, no-left-turn streets that wind through Salvador's valleys and lack any coherent pattern or relationship to the rest of the existing paved world. Traffic laws are left to the discretion of drivers. Gridlock is common at rush hour.

Perhaps most difficult for the visitor is the fact that street names are not regularly used by locals, and when they are, there are often so many different names for each street that the one you have in mind probably doesn't mean anything to the person you're asking to assist you. The road along the Atlantic coast, for instance, sometimes known as Avenida Presidente Vargas, has at least four aliases.

Street-name variations include:

Terreiro de Jesus – called Praça 15 de Novembro on many maps

Rua Dr JJ Seabra – popularly known as Bairro do Sapateiro (Shoemaker's Neighborhood). In early colonial days, this street was the site of a moat, the first line of defense against the Indians.

Rua Francisco Muniz Barreto – also called Rua das Laranjeiras (Street of Orange Trees)

Rua Inácio Accioli – also known as Boca do Lixo (Garbage Mouth)

Rua Leovigildo de Caravalho – known as Beco do Mota

Rua Padre Nobrega – commonly referred to as Brega. The street was originally named after a priest. It developed into the main drag of the red-light district, and with time, Nobrega was shortened to Brega, which in Brazilian usage is now synonymous with brothel.

Maps

Most newsstands have maps for sale, but they lack detail and only give an overview of city layout. Bahiatursa (see Tourist Offices) sells the useful *Mapa Turístico de Salvador* for US$1.

INFORMATION
Tourist Offices

Bahiatursa is the useful state government tourist body. Their most convenient office is at Rua Francisco Muniz Barreto 12, Pelourinho (☎ 321-2463). It's open daily from 8:30 am to 10 pm. The staff are helpful and provide advice (in English, German, French and Spanish) on accommodations, restaurants, events, and where and when to see capoeira and Candomblé. The notice board inside the office has messages that may help you to find friends, rent houses and boats, buy guidebooks and even purchase international airline tickets.

There are also Bahiatursa offices at: Mercado Modelo (☎ 241-0242), open Monday to Saturday 9 am to 6 pm; the main bus station (☎ 450-4500), open daily 7:30 am to 9:30 pm; the airport (☎ 204-1244), open daily 8:30 am to 10:45 pm; the Centro de Convençoes da Bahia (☎ 370-8494), open Monday to Friday 8 am to 6 pm; and Shopping Iguatemi (☎ 350-5050) near the main

PLACES TO STAY
1 Pousada Villa Carmo
6 Albergue da Juventude Solar
7 Albergue da Juventude do Pelô
8 Albergue Pousada do Passo
11 Hotel Solara
15 Hotel Pelourinho
25 Albergue Vagaus
52 Albergue de Juventude das Laranjeiras
58 Hotel Arthemis
70 Hotel Chile
71 Palace Hotel
72 Hotel Pousada da Praça
75 Hotel Maridina

PLACES TO EAT
10 Kilinho
14 Senac
22 Uauá
23 Casa da Gamboa
24 Don Rafaello
26 Mamabahia
35 Cantinho da Lua
38 Sorriso da Dadá
40 Senzala
44 Maria Mata Mouro

OTHER
2 Igreja e Convento de NS do Carmo; Museu do Carmo
3 Igreja da Ordem Terceira do Carmo
4 Banco do Brasil
5 Igreja do Santíssimo Sacramento do Passo
9 Internet Café.com
12 Igreja NS do Rosário dos Pretos
13 Praça do Reggae & Bar do Reggae
16 Fundação Casa de Jorge Amado
17 Museu da Cidade
18 Filhos de Ghandi
19 Fundação Mestre Bimba
20 Teatro Miguel Santana
21 Post Office
28 Habeus Copos
29 Didá
30 Casa Olodum
31 Post Office
32 VASP
33 Plano Inclinado Gonçalves (Funicular Railway)
34 Antiga Faculdade de Medicina (Old Medical School); Museu Afro-Brasileiro; Museu de Arqueolgia e Etnologia
36 Igreja São Pedro dos Clérigos
37 Internet Café.com
39 Largo de Tereza Batista
41 Bradesco ATM
42 Bahiatursa Tourist Office
43 Largo do Pedro Arcanjo
45 Teatro XVIII
46 Grupo Gay da Bahia
47 Catedral Basílica
48 Igreja da Ordem Terceira de São Domingus
49 Toursbahia
50 Praça dos Artistas
51 DELTUR Tourist Police
53 Terminal Turístico Marítimo
54 Small Boats to Ilha de Itaparica
55 Mercado Modelo
56 Casa dos Azulejos
57 Igreja da Misericórdia
59 Banco do Brasil
60 Banco do Brasil
61 Igreja da Terceira Ordem do São Francisco
62 Igreja São Francisco
63 Bunda Statue
64 Avenida da França Bus Station (Buses to Mercado São Joaquim, Ferry & Igreja NS do Bonfim)
65 Palácio Rio Branco
66 Câmara Municipal
67 Buses to Airport
68 Casa de Ruy Barbosa
69 Igreja NS da Conceição
73 Livraria Brandão
74 Varig

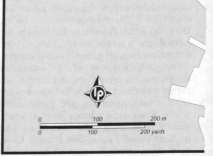

0   100   200 m
0   100   200 yards

CENTRAL SALVADOR

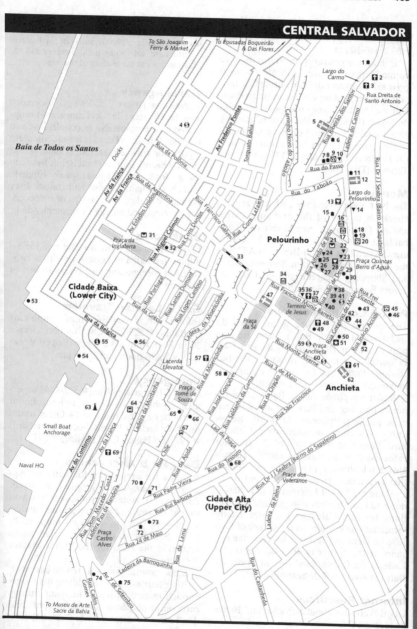

To São Joaquim Ferry & Market

To Pousadas Boqueirão & Das Flores

Largo do Carmo

Rua Dreita de Santo Antonio

Baía de Todos os Santos

Docks

Rua Ribeirão dos Santos

Rua da Polônia

Caminho Novo do Taboão

Ladeira do Carmo

Rua Dr J J Seabra (Bairro do Sapateiro)

Av Frederico Pontes

Torquato Bahia

Rua do Passo

Rua do Taboão

Largo do Pelourinho

Av da França
Av da França

Rua da Argentina

Rua Francisco Galves

Rua Cons Lafaiete

Pelourinho

Av Estados Unidos

Rua Miguel Calmon

Rua Cons Dantas

Praça da Inglaterra

Rua Alfredo de Brito

Rua João de Deus

Praça Quincas Berro d'Agua

Rua Frei Vicente

**Cidade Baixa
(Lower City)**

Rua Portugal

Rua Santos Dumont

Rua Lopes Cardoso

Rua da Grécia

Rua da Misericórdia

Rua Francisco Muniz Barreto

Rua João Tolás

Terreiro de Jesus

Rua Gregório de Matos

Rua Inácio Accioli

Rua da Bélgica

Praça da Sé

Ladeira da Montanha

Praça Anchieta

Anchieta

Lacerda Elevator

Rua Monte Alverne

Rua 3 de Maio

Small Boat Anchorage

Praça Tomé de Souza

Rua José Gonçalves

Rua Saldanha da Gama

Rua da Oração

Rua São Francisco

Naval HQ

Av do Contorno

Av da França

Rua Chile

Laed da Praça

Rua da Ajuda

Rua do Tesouro

Rua Dr J J Seabra (Bairro do Sapateiro)

Praça dos Veteranos

Ladeira da Palma

Rua Padre Vieira

**Cidade Alta
(Upper City)**

Rua Rui Barbosa

Rua 24 de Maio

Rua da Lama

Rua do Castanheda

Rua Dom Dom Macedo Costa

Ladeira Baú da Bandeira

Praça Castro Alves

Ladeira da Barroquinha

Rua Carlos Gomes

Av 7 de Setembro

To Museu de Arte Sacre da Bahia

bus station and Shopping Barra (☎ 339-8222), both open Monday to Saturday 8:30 am to 10 pm.

Bahiatursa operates an alternative accommodations service to locate rooms in private houses and the like during Carnaval and summer holidays. This can be an excellent way to find cheap rooms. Information on travel throughout the state of Bahia is also available, but don't expect much detail.

For general tourist information or help (in English), try dialing ☎ 131 for Disque Turismo (Dial Tourism).

Money

The best place to change cash or traveler's checks is in one of the exchange places around Cruzeiro de São Francisco. Toursbahia at No 4 gives a good rate. Visa withdrawals can be made at Bradesco ATMs at the airport, the bus station, Shopping Barra and Shopping Iguatemi and on Largo de Teresa Batista in Pelourinho.

Post & Communications

The central post office is on Praça da Inglaterra in Cidade Baixa. There are also post offices at Rua Alfredo de Brito 43, Pelourinho; at the airport; and at the bus station. Watch out for overcharging and make sure that items are stamped.

Making a phone call in Bahia often requires patience and luck. For international calls, public telephones are pretty useless unless you have an international phone card. Your best bet is one of the Internet cafés listed in the next paragraph. There's also a telephone office at the bus station that's open daily from 7 am to 11 pm.

There are lots of Internet cafés in Salvador and most hostels also provide connections. Internet Café.com has three handy locations: one upstairs on the corner of Rua João de Deus and Terreiro de Jesus; one upstairs at the corner of Rua do Passo and Ladeira do Carmo; and one in Porto da Barra at Avenida 7 de Setembro 507.

Internet Resources

Good Web sites about Salvador and Bahia include the following:

www.bahiatursa.ba.gov.br – Bahiatursa's Web page

www.vivabrazil.com/bahia.htm – in English and Portuguese, with some good pictures and excellent links at the bottom of the page

Travel Agency

Toursbahia (☎/fax 322-3676, tbi@compos .com.br, Cruzeiro de São Francisco 4) is operated by a Brazilian/Swiss couple, José and Regula Iglesias. They offer a complete service for travelers, including natural and cultural history tours around Bahia. Between them, José and Regula speak English, French, German, Spanish and Italian. They are happy to deal with groups or independent travelers, and are highly recommended.

Bookstores

Livraria Brandão (Rua Rui Barbosa 15B) is a huge secondhand bookstore with a large range of foreign-language books to buy or exchange.

Gay & Lesbian Travelers

Information is available from Grupo Gay da Bahia (☎ 322-2552), at Rua Frei Vicente 24 in Pelourinho. The office is open weekdays 9 am to noon and 2 to 6 pm.

Emergency

DELTUR tourist police (☎ 322-7155) operates 24 hours a day in Pelourinho at Cruzeiro de São Francisco 14. Other useful numbers include Pronto Socorro (first aid) ☎ 192, and Polícia Civil (police) ☎ 197.

Dangers & Annoyances

Salvador has a reputation for theft and muggings, and tourists clearly make easy targets. Paranoia is counterproductive, but you should be aware of the dangers and understand what you can do to minimize problems. See the Dangers & Annoyances section in the Facts for the Visitor chapter for more tips.

Some general points to remember when visiting Salvador: Dress down; take only enough money with you for your outing; carry only a photocopy of your passport; and don't carry a camera outside Pelourinho.

Look at a map for basic orientation before you set out to see the sights. Although tourist police maintain a highly visible presence in the center of Salvador, particularly in Pelourinho, this does not apply in other areas. It's also difficult to see how the police in Pelourinho can control pickpockets and bag-snatchers on crowded Sunday and Tuesday nights, so don't carry any valuables then. The Elevador Lacerda is renowned for crime, especially at night around the bottom, and pickpocketing is common on buses and in crowded places. Don't hesitate to use taxis during the day and especially after dusk.

On the beaches, keep a close eye on juvenile thieves, often referred to as *capitões d'areia* (captains of the sand), who are quick to make off with unguarded possessions.

During Carnaval, tourist authorities highly recommend that tourists form small groups and avoid deserted places, especially narrow alleyways.

CIDADE ALTA

Historic Salvador is easy to see on foot, and you should plan on spending a couple of days wandering among the splendid 16th- and 17th-century churches, homes and museums. One good approach is to ramble through the old city in the morning, head out to the beaches in the afternoon, and then devote the evening to music, dance or Candomblé.

The most important sections of the colonial quarter extend from Praça Castro Alves along Ruas Chile and da Misericórdia to Praça da Sé and Terreiro de Jesus, and then continue down through Largo do Pelourinho and up the hill to Largo do Carmo.

Catedral Basílica

On the Terreiro de Jesus (Praça 15 de Novembro on many maps) you'll find the Cathedral of Bahia. It's the biggest church on the plaza and served as a Jesuit center until the order was expelled in 1759. The cathedral was built between 1657 and 1672, and its walls are covered with marble – used as ballast for returning merchant ships. Many consider this to be the city's most beautiful church. The interior has many seg-

mented areas and the emphasis is on verticality – raise your eyes to admire the superb ceiling. The cathedral is open pm Monday to Saturday 8 to 11:30 am and 2 to 5:30 and Sunday 8 am to noon.

Museu Afro-Brasileiro

The Antiga Faculdade de Medicina (Old Medical School) houses the Afro-Brazilian Museum, with its small but excellent collection of *orixás* (gods; see Candomblé in the Religion section of the Facts about Brazil chapter for more information) from both Africa and Bahia. There is a surprising amount of African art, ranging from pottery to woodwork, as well as superb ceremonial Candomblé apparel.

Other highlights include wooden panels representing Oxum (an orixá revered as the goddess of beauty) that were carved by Carybé, a famous Argentine artist who has lived in Salvador for many years. Entry is US$0.50 and the museum is open Monday to Saturday 9 am to 5 pm.

In the basement of the same building is the **Museu de Arqueologia e Etnologia** (Archaeology and Ethnology Museum), open Monday to Friday 9 am to 5 pm.

Igreja São Francisco

Defying the teachings and vows of poverty of the saint to which it is dedicated, this baroque church on Praça Anchieta is crammed with displays of wealth and splendor. Gold leaf is used like wallpaper. There is an 80kg silver chandelier and imported *azulejos* (Portuguese ceramic tiles).

Forced to build their masters' church and yet prohibited from practicing their own religion – Candomblé *terreiros* (venues) were hidden and kept far from town – the African slave artisans responded through their work: The faces of the cherubs are distorted, some angels are endowed with huge sex organs, others appear to be pregnant. Most of these creative acts were chastely covered by 20th-century sacristans. Traditionally, blacks were seated in far corners of the church without a view of the altar.

Notice the polychrome figure of São Pedro da Alcântara by Manoel Inácio da

Costa. The artist, like his subject, was suffering from tuberculosis. He made one side of the saint's face more ashen than the other, so that São Pedro appears to become more ill as you walk past him. José Joaquim da Rocha painted the hallway ceiling using perspective technique, which was considered a novelty during the baroque period.

The poor come to Igreja São Francisco on Tuesday to venerate Santo Antônio and receive bread. The Candomblistas respect this church's saints and come to pray both here and in Igreja NS do Bonfim.

Depending on restoration work, the church is open Monday to Saturday 7:30 to 11:30 am and 2 to 6 pm, and Sunday 7 am to noon.

Igreja da Ordem Terceira de São Francisco

Close to the Igreja São Francisco is the 17th-century Church of the Third Order of St Francis. The beautiful baroque facade was actually covered in the late 18th century and remained hidden until it was accidentally discovered in the 1930s when a workman hammered off some plaster to install wiring. It is open Monday to Friday 8am to noon and 1 to 5 pm.

Igreja São Pedro dos Clérigos

The Igreja São Pedro dos Clérigos is on Terreiro de Jesus, next to Cantinho da Lua (see Places to Eat). This rococo church, like many others built in the 18th century, was left with one of its towers missing in order to avoid a tax on finished churches. It is open Monday to Friday 1 to 5 pm.

Pelourinho

To see the city's oldest architecture, turn down Rua Alfredo de Brito, the small street that descends from Terreiro de Jesus into the Pelourinho district.

Pelourinho means 'whipping post,' and this is where the slaves were tortured and sold (whipping of slaves was legal in Brazil until 1835). The old slave-auction site on Largo do Pelourinho (also known as Praça José de Alencar) has recently been renovated and converted into the **Fundação**

Casa de Jorge Amado (Jorge Amado Museum). The exhibition is disappointing, but you can watch a free video of *Dona Flor* or one of the other films based on Amado's books. The museum is open 9 am to 9 pm daily except for Tuesday when it closes at 6 pm and Sunday when it's closed all day. According to a brass plaque, Amado lived across the street in the Hotel Pelourinho when it was a student house.

Next door to the Amado museum is the **Museu da Cidade**. The exhibitions on display include costumes of the orixás of Candomblé, and the personal effects of the Romantic poet Castro Alves, author of *Navio Negreiro,* and one of the first public figures to protest against slavery. Hours are 9:30 am to 6:30 pm on Monday, Wednesday, Thursday and Friday, 1 to 5 pm on Saturday and 9 am to 1 pm on Sunday. It's closed on Tuesday. Entry costs US$0.50 (free on Thursday).

Igreja NS do Rosário dos Pretos

This church, across the Largo do Pelourinho, was built by and for the slaves. The 18th century church has some lovely azulejos and is beautifully lit up at night. The church is open Monday to Friday 7:30 am to 6 pm, and Saturday and Sunday 7:30 am to noon.

Igreja do Santíssimo Sacramento do Passo

From Pelourinho, go down the hill and then continue uphill along Ladeira do Carmo. You will reach a set of steps on the left that lead up to this church in an approach that is reminiscent of the Spanish Steps of Rome. *O Pagador de Promessas,* the first Brazilian film to win an award at the Cannes film festival, was filmed here.

Igreja e Convento de NS do Carmo

This church, at the top of the hill on Ladeira do Carmo, was founded in 1636 and contains a baroque altar and an organ that dates from 1889.

The convent next door is moderately interesting. Among the sacred and religious articles on display is a famous sculpture of Christ created by Francisco Chagas (also known as O Cabra). For a glimpse of old Salvador, continue walking for a few blocks past dilapidated buildings that teem with life. Also notice an odd-looking public oratory, **Oratório da Cruz do Pascoal**, plunked in the middle of Rua Joaquim Távora, a continuation of Largo do Carmo.

Praça Tomé de Souza

While not officially recognized or protected by the Brazilian historical architecture society SPHAN, this plaza in the center has some beautiful and important sites. The imposing **Palácio Rio Branco** was built in 1549 to house the offices of Tomé de Sousa, the first governor general of Brazil. Facing the plaza is the **Câmara Municipal**, the 17th-century city hall, which features several impressive arches.

Elevador Lacerda

The Lacerda Elevator, inaugurated in 1868, was an iron structure with clanking steam elevators until these were replaced with a new system in 1928. Today, electric elevators truck up and down a set of 85m vertical cement shafts in less than 15 seconds, and carry more than 50,000 passengers daily.

Things weren't always so easy. At first, the Portuguese used slaves and mules to transport goods from the port in Cidade Baixa to Cidade Alta. By 1610, the Jesuits had installed the first elevator to negotiate the drop. A clever system of ropes and pulleys was manually operated to carry freight and a few brave souls.

You should watch out for petty crime around the elevator, particularly after dusk (see the earlier Dangers & Annoyances section).

CIDADE BAIXA

Descending into the lower city you'll be confronted by the **Mercado Modelo**. Filled with souvenir stalls and restaurants, it's Salvador's worst concession to tourism. If you've missed capoeira, there are displays for tourists outside the building – anyone contemplating taking photos is well advised to negotiate a sensible price beforehand or risk being suckered for an absurd fee. The modernist sculpture across the street is referred to as *bunda* (ass) by the locals – which gives it a much more appealing aspect. There are many cheap, stand-up snack bars in Cidade Baixa and the area is worth exploring.

NORTH OF THE CENTER
Mercado São Joaquim

To see a typical market, take either the Ribeira or the Bonfim bus heading north from the bus stop near the bottom of the Elevador Lacerda (US$0.70). Get off after about 3km (you'll be able to spot the market). Mercado São Joaquim is a small city of waterfront bars open all day, every day except Sunday. It's not exactly clean – watch out for the green slime puddles – and the meat neighborhood can turn the unprepared into devout vegetarians. You are bound to come across spontaneous singing and dancing at bars where *cachaça* (sugarcane rum) is served.

Igreja NS do Bonfim

Take the Bonfim bus across the road from the Mercado São Joaquim to the Igreja NS do Bonfim, farther along the Itapagipe Peninsula. Built in 1745, the shrine is famous for its miraculous power to effect cures. In the Sala dos Milagres you will see votive offerings: replicas of feet, arms, heads and hearts, representing parts of the body devotees claim were cured.

For Candomblistas, Bonfim is the church of Oxalá and thus their most important church. In January, the Lavagem do Bonfim, one of Bahia's most important festivals, takes place here and *mães de santo* (Candomblé priestesses) lead the festivities together with Catholic priests. See the Special Events section later in this chapter for more details. There are also huge services held at Bonfim on the first and last Friday of each month.

When you approach the church you'll undoubtedly be offered a *fita* (ribbon) to tie around your wrist for a small donation. With the fita you can make three wishes that will come true by the time it falls off. This usually

THE NORTHEAST

takes over two months and you must allow it to fall off from natural wear and tear. Cutting it off is said to bring bad luck.

The church is open Tuesday to Sunday 6:30 am to noon and 2 to 6 pm.

The Bay

From the Igreja NS do Bonfim there is a very interesting half-hour walk to the bay, where you'll find the old **Monte Serrat lighthouse** and **church**. Nearby is **Praia da Boa Viagem**, where one of Bahia's most popular and magnificent festivals, the Procissão do Senhor Bom Jesus dos Navegantes, takes place on New Year's Day. See Special Events later in this section for more details.

The beach is lined with bars and is animated on weekends. It's a poorer part of town and quite interesting. From Boa Viagem, there are buses back to the bus stop beside the bottom of Elevador Lacerda.

SOUTH OF THE CENTER
Museu de Arte Sacra da Bahia

This museum, south of the city center at Rua do Sodré 276, is housed in a beautifully restored 17th-century convent. The sacred art on display includes excellent and varied sculptures and images in wood, clay and soapstone; many were shipped to Salvador from Portugal. Hours are Monday to Friday 11:30 am to 5:30 pm. Entry costs US$3.

Museu de Arte Moderna

On the bay, farther south from the center towards Campo Grande on Avenida do Contorno, is the **Solar do Unhão**, an old sugar estate mansion that now houses the small Museu de Arte Moderna, a restaurant and a ceramic workshop. Legend has it that the place is haunted by the ghosts of tortured slaves. One look at the ancient *pelourinho* (whipping post) and torture devices on display makes the idea credible. However, it's a lovely spot; the art exhibits are often good and the restaurant has a tranquil atmosphere and a great view (see Places to Eat).

This area has a reputation for crime (especially mugging of tourists), and buses don't pass close to it, so it's better to take a taxi to and from the Solar do Unhão. Hours are Tuesday to Friday 1 to 9 pm, Saturday 3 to 9 pm and Sunday 2 to 7 pm. Entry is free.

BEACHES

The ocean beaches of **Pituba**, **Armação**, **Piatã**, **Placaford** and **Itapoã** may not be as famous as Ipanema and Copacabana, but they are just as beautiful. Although these beaches are all within 45 minutes (or more depending on traffic) of the center by bus, Pituba, Armação and Piatã are becoming increasingly polluted and are now not recommended for swimming. Head for Placaford, Itapoã or farther north. For information on beaches north of Itapoã, see the North of Salvador section later in this chapter.

If you just want to experience Salvador's beach scene, **Barra** is the closest and the liveliest – but swimming is not advisable on the Atlantic Ocean side, due to heavy pollution. Surprisingly, the water on the bay side at Barra certainly *looks* clear and inviting – locals love it, so you can make up your own mind. There are plenty of restaurants and bars along the waterfront, although it can get a bit sleazy at night. You can see Bahia's oldest fort here, the polygonal **Forte de Santo Antônio da Barra**, which was built in 1598 and fell to the Dutch in 1624. The view of Ilha de Itaparica from the fort is splendid.

See Getting Around for details of transportation to these beaches.

CANDOMBLÉ

Before doing anything in Salvador, find out the schedule for Candomblé ceremonies so you don't miss a night in a terreiro. Bahiatursa has many Candomblistas on its staff who can provide the addresses of terreiros – the *Bahia Cultural* guide available at Bahiatursa offices lists a monthly schedule with transport details. Activities usually start around 8 or 9 pm and may be held any day of the week. For details about Candomblé, refer to the Religion section in the Facts about Brazil chapter; see the boxed text 'An Evening of Candomblé' for a description of a service.)

An Evening of Candomblé

A long evening of Candomblé in Casa Branca, Salvador's oldest *terreiro,* is quite an experience. The women dress in lace and hooped skirts, dance slowly, and chant in Yoruba. The men drum complex and powerful African rhythms. The terreiro is dominated by the women: only women dance, and only they enter a trance, the principal goal of the ceremony. Men play a supporting role.

The dance is very African, with graceful hand motions, swaying hips and light steps. When a dancer enters the trance, she shakes and writhes while assistants embrace and support her. Sometimes, even spectators go into trances, although this is discouraged.

The *mãe de santo* or *pai de santo* runs the service. The *mãe pequena* is entrusted with the training of priestesses; in this case, two *filhas de santo:* one girl over seven years of age, the other a girl under seven. The initiates are called *abian.*

On a festival morning, the celebration commences with an animal sacrifice. Only initiates may attend this service. Later in the afternoon the *padê* ceremony is held to attract the attention of Exú, and this is followed by chanting for the *orixás,* which is accompanied by *alabés* (drummers).

The festival we attended was for Omolú, the feared and respected orixá of plague and disease. He is worshipped only on Monday, and his Christian syncretic counterpart is either St Lazarus or St Roque. His costume consists of a straw belt encrusted with seashells, a straw mask and a cape and dress to cover his face and body, which have been disfigured by smallpox.

When the dancers have received the spirit of Omolú in their trance, some leave the floor. They then return with a person dressed from head to toe in a costume of long strawlike strands to represent Omolú. The dancing resumes.

Although the congregants of Casa Branca are friendly and hospitable, they don't orient their practice to outsiders. Westerners may attend, and many white Brazilians are members. After the ceremony, guests are invited to the far end of the house for sweets and giant cakes – one cake decorated like the Brazilian flag.

CAPOEIRA SCHOOLS

To visit a capoeira school, it's best to get the up-to-date schedule from Bahiatursa, which has a complete listing of schools and some class schedules in its monthly *Bahia Cultural* guide. The Associação de Capoeira Mestre Bimba has an excellent school, **Fundação Mestre Bimba**, at Rua Francisco Muniz Barreto 1, 2nd floor, Terreiro de Jesus, and has lessons Monday to Friday, 9 am to noon and Saturday 3 to 9 pm. Its *roda da capoeira* is on Tuesday to Friday at 8 pm and Saturday at 6 pm. See the boxed text 'Capoeira' for the history of this unique combination of martial art and dance.

SPECIAL EVENTS

Salvador's Carnaval receives the greatest emphasis, but it is by no means the only festival worth attending. There are many others, particularly in January and February, that attract huge crowds. Since the 17th century, religious processions have been an integral part of the city's cultural life. Combining elements of the sacred and profane, Candomblé and Catholicism, many of these festivals are as wild as Carnaval and possibly more colorful.

Note that many of these festivals don't have fixed dates each year. Check with Bahiatursa for the current dates.

Carnaval

Carnaval in Salvador is justly world famous. For four nights and three days, the masses go to the streets and stay until they fall. There's nothing to buy, so all you have to do is follow your heart – or the nearest *trio elétrico* (electrified music played on the top of trucks) – and play.

Carnaval, usually held in February or March, always starts on a Thursday night

THE NORTHEAST

and continues until the following Monday. Everything, but everything, goes during these four days. In recent years, Carnaval has revolved around the trios elétricos. The trios play a distinctively upbeat music from the tops of trucks that slowly wind their way through the main Carnaval areas (Praça Castro Alves, Campo Grande and Barra). Surrounding the trios is a sea of dancing, drinking revelers.

Carnaval brings so many tourists and so much money to Salvador that there's been an inevitable tendency towards commer-cialization, although the trend here is still light years behind that in Rio. Fortunately, local residents have been very critical of this trend, and arts and community groups have now been given a greater say in the arrange-ments of Salvador's Carnaval. A more au-thentic festival has resulted from this: Events have been decentralized, and freer and more impromptu expression is encour-aged. Let's hope the spontaneity continues.

Take a look at the newspaper or go to Bahiatursa for a list of events. Don't miss the *afoxés* (Carnaval groups), such as

Capoeira

Capoeira originated as an African martial art developed by slaves to fight their masters. The art was prohibited by the slave owners and banished from the *senzalas* (slave barracks). The slaves were forced to practice clandestinely in the forest. Later, in an attempt to disguise this act of defi-ance from the authorities, capoeira was developed into a kind of acrobatic dance. The clapping of hands and plucking of the *berimbau*, a stringed musical instrument that looks like a fishing rod, originally served to alert fighters to the approach of the boss and subsequently became incorpo-rated into the dance to maintain the rhythm.

As recently as the 1920s, capoeira was still prohibited and Salvador's police chief organized a police cavalry squad to ban it from the streets. In the 1930s, Mestre Bimba established his academy and changed the emphasis of capoeira from its original function as a tool of insurrection to a form of artistic expression that has become an institution in Bahia.

Today, there are two schools of capoeira: the Capoeira de Angola, led by Mestre Pastinha, and the more aggressive Capoeira Regional, initiated by Mestre Bimba. The former school believes capoeira came from Angola; the latter maintains it was born in the plantations of Cachoeira and other cities of the recôncavo region.

Capoeira combines the forms of the fight, the game and the dance. The movements are always fluid and circular, the fighters always playful and respectful. It has become very popular in recent years, and throughout Bahia and the rest of Brazil you will see the *roda da capoeira* (semicircles of spectator-musicians who sing the initial *chula* before the fight and provide the percussion during the fight). In addition to the musical accompaniment from the berimbau, blows are exchanged between fighters/dancers to the beat of other instruments, such as the *caxixi, pandeiro, reco-reco, agogô* and *atabaque*.

Badauê, Ilê-Aiyê, Grupo Olodum, Ara Ketu, Timbalada, Muzenza and the most famous, Filhos de Gandhi (Sons of Gandhi). The best place to see them is in Liberdade, Salvador's largest black district, a couple of suburbs north of Pelourinho.

Also, explore Carnaval Caramuru in the southern suburb of Rio Vermelho and the smaller happenings in Itapoã, the old fishing and whaling village that has a fascinating ocean procession on the last day of Carnaval, when a whale is delivered to the sea. The traditional gay parade is held on Monday at Praça Castro Alves.

Many of Brazil's best musicians return to Salvador for Carnaval, and the frequent rumors that so-and-so will be playing on the street are often true (for example, Gilberto Gil and Baby Consuelo have both taken part).

Many clubs have balls just before and during Carnaval. If you're in the city before the festivities start, you can also see some of the *blocos* (percussion groups) practicing. Just ask Bahiatursa.

It's most convenient to stay near the center or in Barra. Violence can be a problem during Carnaval, and some women travelers have reported violent approaches from locals. A common problem you may encounter at Carnaval is being sucked into the crowd right behind a trio elétrico and having to dodge all the dancers with their flying elbows! See the Dangers & Annoyances section earlier in this chapter for more details on avoiding crime.

Other Celebrations

The **Procissão do Senhor Bom Jesus dos Navegantes**, which originated in Portugal in 1750, is one of Bahia's most popular celebrations. On New Year's Eve, the image of the Senhor dos Navegantes is taken to Igreja NS da Conceição, close to Mercado Modelo in Cidade Baixa. On the morning of New Year's Day, a maritime procession consisting of dozens of boats transports the image along the bay and returns it to the beach at Boa Viagem, which is packed with onlookers eager to celebrate with music, food and drink. Also of Portuguese origin,

the **Festas de Reis** is held in Igreja da Lapinha on January 5 and 6.

Another of Salvador's popular events, the **Lavagem do Bonfim** is held on the second Thursday in January, and is attended by huge crowds. It culminates with the ritual *lavagem* (washing) of the Igreja NS do Bonfim (see the earlier section on this church) by mães and filhas de santo. Abundant flowers and lights provide impressive decoration, and the party atmosphere continues with the Filhos de Gandhi and trios elétricos providing musical accompaniment for dancers. If you want to do the 9km walk to the church from the Mercado Modelo, it's best to leave early with the mães, before the trio elétricos blast into action. On the last Sunday in January, the **Festa de São Lázaro** is dedicated to the Candomblé orixá, Omolú, and culminates with a mass, procession, festival and another ritual cleansing of the church.

A grand maritime procession takes flowers and presents to Iemanjá, the Mãe e Rainha das Águas (Mother and Queen of the Waters) for the **Festa de Iemanjá**. One of Candomblé's most important festivals, it's celebrated on February 2 in Rio Vermelho and is accompanied by trios elétricos, afoxés and plenty of food and drink. Next is the warm-up for Carnaval, the **Lavagem da Igreja de Itapoã**. Celebrated in Itapoã 15 days before Carnaval, this is all music and dance, with blocos and afoxés.

After Carnaval comes the **Festa São João**. This festival is celebrated all over town on June 23 and 24 with pyrotechnics and many parties on the street where *genipapo* (a local liqueur) is consumed in very liberal quantities. Next is the **Festa Santa Bárbara**, held from December 4 to 6. This is the Candomblé festa of the markets; probably the best spot to watch the festivities is in Rio Vermelho at the Mercado do Peixe. Two days later, the **Festa de NS da Conceição** takes place on December 8 and features a procession in Cidade Baixa followed by Candomblé ceremonies in honor of Iemanjá. To round out the year, **Passagem do Ano Novo** (New Year's Eve) is celebrated with all the zest of Carnaval – especially on the beaches.

PLACES TO STAY

Salvador has many hotels, but they can all fill up during the Carnaval season, so reservations are a good idea. Bahiatursa can help you find lodging – just provide the staff with a general idea of your preferred price range and type of lodging. Bahiatursa also has lists of houses that take in tourists and these can be a source of excellent, cheap lodgings when hotels are full, especially during summer holidays and Carnaval. But beware: The tourist office makes selective referrals and it helps if you don't look too burnt-out or broke.

Budget

Keep in mind that hostels and cheap hotels in the Pelourinho can get very noisy in the evenings, with lots of live music.

Camping On the outskirts of Itapoã is *Camping Ecológico* (☎ 374-0201, *Alameda da Praia s/n*) at Praia do Flamengo. Sites cost US$4 per person.

Hostels There aren't a lot of hostels throughout Brazil, but in Salvador you're spoiled for choice. There are some excellent hostels close to the city center, mostly clustered around Pelourinho. *Albergue da Juventude das Laranjeiras* (☎/fax 321-1366, *alaranj@zaz.com.br, Rua Inácio Accioli 13*) is a very well-run HI hostel that's popular with backpackers. Another favorite is *Albergue Pousada do Passo* (☎ 326-1951, fax 351-3285, *passoyouthhostel@yahoo.com, Rua do Passo 3*). The friendly owner, Fernando, speaks English, French and Spanish. He has very clean dormitories for singles and couples starting at US$7 per person. Double apartamentos cost US$24.

Next door, the HI *Albergue da Juventude do Pelô* (☎/fax 242-8061, *Rua do Passo 5*) is also popular and conveniently located. (The official name of this street is Rua Ribeiro dos Santos but locals and most maps call it Rua do Passo.) Close by is the *Albergue de Juventude Solar* (☎ 241-0055, *Ladeira do Paço 45*), which charges US$8 per person. *Albergue Vagaus* (☎/fax 322-1179, *vagaus@elitenet.com.br, Rua Alfredo Brito 25*) has basic dorm rooms for US$8 per person, and the very friendly owners Zuleide and Clarice make you feel right at home.

The HI *Albergue do Porto* (☎ 264-6600, fax 264-3131, *Rua Barão de Serigy 192*), in an old house at Porto da Barra, is a comfortable hostel only a block from the beach. Dorm bunks cost US$10 and doubles with air-conditioning go for US$30.

Hotels The cheaper hotels in the old part of town are around Praça da Sé, Terreiro de Jesus, Praça Anchieta and Pelourinho. Prices have risen since the restoration of the area, and outside the hostels, cheap accommodations are hard to find close to the historic center.

The *Hotel Caramuru* (☎ 336-9951, fax 336-4553, *Avenida 7 de Setembro 2125*) is away from the center in a quiet location, but is a very good value. It's in a large colonial mansion with a breezy, elevated eating area. Spacious and spotless single/double quartos cost US$15/20; apartamentos cost US$20/25. The hotel also organizes Candomblé excursions, and trips to Itaparica and other destinations.

The *Hotel Pelourinho* (☎/fax 243-2324, *Rua Alfredo de Brito 20*), right in the heart of Pelourinho, has long been a favorite with travelers but is getting pricey. It's an older, converted mansion (reputedly the setting for Jorge Amado's novel *Suor*), and the management is reasonably security-conscious (there's a guard posted at the entrance to the building). Small apartamentos with fan cost US$30/40/60 for singles/doubles/triples. In the hotel courtyard there are handicraft shops and, right at the end, a restaurant/bar with views and regular live music, so it gets noisy. Avoid their overpriced tours.

About 20m downhill from Largo do Pelourinho is the *Hotel Solara* (☎ 326-4583, *Praça José de Alencar 25*), which has apartamentos starting at US$13/20/30 for singles/doubles/triples. Rooms are also used by locals for stays as short as two hours.

The *Hotel Arthemis* (☎/fax 322-0724, *Praça da Sé 398, Edifício Themis, 7th floor*) offers great views. There's a bar and a restaurant. Apartamentos without a view cost US$17/24/31; with view US$20/28/36. The *Hotel Pousada da Praça* (☎/fax 321-0642, Rua Rui Barbosa 5), close to Praça Castro Alves, offers basic, but clean, quartos at US$13/18. Apartamentos cost US$15/20.

Just a short walk from Praça Tomé de Souza is the *Hotel Chile* (☎ 321-0245, fax 321-8421, Rua Chile 7, 1st floor). Dark and beat-up quartos start at US$12/17. Apartamentos cost US$30 for a double with air-conditioning, and US$20/25 with fan. The *Palace Hotel* (☎ 322-1155, fax 243-1109, Palace@e-net.com.br, Rua Chile 20) is a good value and right in the center of the city. It's the best place for its price in the area. Comfortable apartamentos with air-conditioning start at US$35/40, while quartos with fan are cheaper. Close by is the *Hotel Maridina* (☎ 242-7176, fax 452-5269, Ladeira de São Bento 6, 2nd floor), just off Avenida 7 de Setembro where Ladeira da Barroquinha changes its name. This is a friendly family-run hotel that offers good value for money. Quartos are US$15/25. Apartamentos with fan cost US$20/30, those with air-conditioning are US$25/35.

In Barra, *Pousada Azul* (☎ 264-9798, fax 245-9798, pousada@provider.com.br, Rua Praguer Fróis 102) is a friendly, comfortable, highly recommended pousada. Beatriz and her helpful, all-female staff speak Spanish, English, German and Italian. It's popular with solo women travelers. There are dorm rooms and some rooms for singles and couples. At US$15 per person with a good breakfast, it's a good value and only a couple of blocks from the beach as well.

Also located in Barra, *Pousada Âmbar* (☎ 264-6956, fax 264-3791, ambarpousada@ambarpousada.com.br, Rua Afonso Celso 485) is a lovely family-run pousada with a relaxed atmosphere. Christine and her daughters are excellent hosts. Christine is French and speaks English and German. They charge US$13 for the dorm room and US$27/34 for single/double apartamentos.

Just past Itapoã at Praia do Flamengo is *Pousada Garten* (☎/fax 374-3080, Rua Dalmo Pontal Quadra 28, Lot 9A). There's

no sign but you can read the address on the gate. It's a few minutes walk from clean beaches and has a nice garden area. It has large, spotless six-bed, four-bed and two-bed quartos for US$15 per person with breakfast. It's highly recommended by readers.

Mid-Range

If you want to stay in a pousada with charm and character, we highly recommend these four. *Pousada Vila Carmo* (☎/fax 241-3924, Rua do Carmo 58) is excellent. Friendly hosts Ana and Luca have tastefully renovated this old house and the views of the bay are wonderful. Single rooms start at US$30 and a double room with sea view goes for US$60. A bit farther from Pelourinho, you'll find Fernanda's *Pousada do Boqueirão* (☎ 241-2262, fax 241-8064, boqueirao@bahianet.com.br, Rua Direita de Santo Antônio 48) is beautifully furnished and very comfortable. The cheapest rooms start at US$25 a single and go up to US$60 a double with sea view. There are also some larger rooms for groups. A bit farther along the same street, *Pousada das Flores* (☎/fax 243-1836, Rua Direita de Santo Antônio 442) has lovely rooms ranging from US$50 a double to ones with a veranda for US$80. In Barra, the *Villa Romana Hotel* (☎/fax 264-6748, villaromana@allways.com.br, Rua Prof Lemos de Brito 14) is full of antiques and polished floors. It's a short walk to the beach and they have a pool and restaurant. Apartamentos cost US$35/52/70 for singles/doubles/triples.

Close to the Hotel Caramaru in Vitória are two more modern mid-range options. *Hotel Vila Velha* (☎ 336-8722, fax 336-5663, Avenida 7 de Setembro 1971) is a three-star Embratur hotel with rooms for US$55/65. Almost next door, *Hotel Bahia do Sol* (☎ 336-7211, fax 337-7776, Avenida 7 de Setembro 2009) is a bit better and has apartamentos for US$65/70.

At Rio Vermelho, the *Hotel Catarina Paraguaçu* (☎/fax 334-0089, Rua João Gomes 128) is set in an old colonial building and offers comfortable apartamentos for $US75/90. The ones in the older building are larger.

Top End

At Praia Ondina are two top-class hotels: the **Bahia Othon Palace** (☎ 203-2000, fax 245-4877, Avenida Oceânica 2456), with rooms for around US$180/220; and the **Salvador Praia** (☎ 245-5033, fax 245-5003, Avenida Oceânica 2338), which has a private stretch of beach and charges US$120/160. Both are popular with package tourists and service is quite impersonal.

The **Hotel Tropical da Bahia** (☎ 255-2000, fax 255-2075, Praça 2 de Julho 2) is a five-star hotel between the city center and Barra. Room prices start at US$150/200, with a 20% discount for cash or credit card payment. It also has a business center.

PLACES TO EAT

Bahian cuisine is an intriguing blend of African and Brazilian based on characteristic ingredients such as coconut cream, ginger, hot peppers, coriander, shrimp and dendê oil. Dendê, an African palm oil with a terrific flavor, is used in many regional dishes (you'll also smell it everywhere). Since dendê has a reputation for stirring up trouble in travelers' bellies, you are advised to consume it in small quantities until you've become accustomed to it. For names and short descriptions of typical Bahian dishes, refer to the Food section in the Facts for the Visitor chapter.

Pelourinho

The Pelourinho area is packed with restaurants, though many of them cater to tourists and are expensive. The best values for lunches are found at the popular self-serve restaurants. **Senzala** (Rua João de Deus 9, 1st floor) and **Kilinho**, close to the Pousada do Passo, are a couple of the best places.

A long-time favorite on Terreiro de Jesus is **Cantinho da Lua** (☎ 241-7383, Praça 15 de Novembro 2), which is a popular hangout and offers affordable meals. Nearby, **Mamabahia** (☎ 322-4397, Rua Alfredo Brito 21) is a popular churrascaria (barbecued meat house). A picanha (plateful of meat) is US$20 and feeds three. **Don Rafaello** (☎ 323-0078, Rua Alfredo de Brito 31) is the place to head for excellent pizza or calzone.

Sorriso da Dadá (☎ 321-9642, Rua Frei Vicente 5) is a lively, casual restaurant with tasty seafood – the moqueca de caranguejo and moqueca de peixe are good. Three people can eat well for around US$35. **Dona Chika Ka** (☎ 321-1712, Rua João Castro Rabelo 10) continues to get rave reviews for its bobó de camarão (US$15 for two).

Casa da Gamboa (☎ 321-3393, Rua João de Deus 32) is highly recommended for its great ambience and moqueca de camarão (US$20 for two).

On Largo do Pelourinho is **Senac** (☎ 321-5502, Praça José de Alencar 13), a cooking school that offers a huge spread of 40 regional dishes in the form of a self-service buffet. It's not the best Bahian cooking, but for US$15 you can discover which Bahian dishes you like and eat...till you explode! Senac is open Monday to Saturday from 11:30 am to 3:30 pm and 6:30 to 10:30 pm. It's only open for lunch on Sundays. Folklore shows are presented on Thursday and Saturday from 8 to 9 pm – tickets cost US$5 per person.

A terrific restaurant for regional cuisine is the colorful **Uauá** (☎ 321-3089, Rua Gregório de Matos 36, 1st floor). They also have live forró on Friday and Saturday nights. **Maria Mata Mouro** (☎ 321-3929, Rua Inácio Accioli 8), next to the Igreja São Francisco, is beautifully decorated with rustic furniture and a cozy garden area. The pernil de carneiro ao molho de tamarindo (lamb in tamarind sauce) is recommended. The desserts are great, too.

Cidade Baixa

Solar do Unhão (☎ 329-5551, Avenida Contorno s/n), which houses the Museu de Arte Moderna, has a restaurant in its lower level in the old senzala (slave quarters). Ironically, the view from the restaurant is one of the best in the city and during happy hour it's as good a reason as any for a visit. The buffet dinner is usually accompanied by live music and a folklore show at 9 pm – expect to pay a cover charge. Crime is a problem in this area, so you should take a taxi.

Also in the lower city is arguably the best international restaurant in Salvador, the **Trapiche Adelaide** (☎ 326-2211, Praça Tip-

inambás 2). The kitchen is coordinated by famous French chef Claude Troisgras from Rio de Janeiro. Try the grilled lobster with banana for US$30. They have an extensive wine list and the attached *Bar da Ponta* on the pier is a top spot for a sunset drink.

ENTERTAINMENT

Salvador is justly renowned for its music. The blending of African and Brazilian traditions produces popular styles such as trio elétrico (which dominates Carnaval), *tropicalismo,* afoxé, *caribé, axé* and reggae.

Bars and clubs tend to come and go quickly in Salvador, so ask around and check the newspaper to confirm the following suggestions. *Bahia Cultural,* available from Bahiatursa, gives a comprehensive rundown of music events, theater and dance performances, and art exhibitions. The Friday editions of local newspapers *A Tarde* and *Correio da Bahia* contain listings of what's on during the weekend.

Pelourinho

Pelourinho is the nightlife capital of Salvador; its cobblestone streets are lined with bars, and blocos practice almost every night. Make sure you get a copy of Bahiatursa's *Pelourinho Dia & Noite* program. Grupo Olodum plays on Sunday nights in the Largo do Pelourinho and draw crowds of dancers into the streets. The famous *Filhos de Gandhi* have their center close by, at Rua Gregório de Matos 53, and rehearse on Tuesday and Sunday night. *Didá,* a music and dance school at Rua João de Deus 19, has a street practice on Thursday night. One of the highlights is the 18-piece, all-female drum outfit.

During summer, the city sponsors free live music at several outdoor venues, including *Largo de Tereza Batista, Largo do Pedro Arcanjo* and *Praça Quincas Berro d'Agua.*

You'll also find several hip bars at Praça Quincas Berro d'Agua – *Habeus Copos* (☎ 321-1798) is the most popular spot (there's another location in Barra). *Bar do Reggae* (☎ 327-0063), right on the Pelourinho, tends to have dancers spilling out onto the street just about every night. Music varies from reggae to axé, pagode and hip-hop. They serve drinks, but no food. Cover charge is around US$2.

Tuesday night is probably the biggest night in Pelourinho. Traditionally, important religious services known as *Terça da Bencão* (Tuesday's Blessing) have been held every Tuesday at the Igreja São Francisco. The services have always drawn locals to Pelourinho, and since the restoration of the area, the weekly celebrations have turned into a mini-festival.

Grupo Olodum play at *Largo de Tereza Batista* (US$15 entry or US$8 for students) on Rua Gregório de Matos, and other bands set up on Terreiro de Jesus, Largo do Pelourinho and anywhere else they can find space. Crowds pour into Pelourinho to eat, drink and dance, and the party lasts until the early hours of the morning.

The best folklore show is the *Balé Folclórico da Bahia* (☎ 321-1155, Rua Gregório de Mattos 47) in the Teatro Miguel Santana, with performances Monday, Wednesday and Saturday at 8 pm. Tickets cost US$15 and are well worth it. Other folklore shows, usually consisting of mini-displays of Candomblé, capoeira, samba, lambada etc, are presented in the evening at *Senac* in Pelourinho (see Places to Eat) and *Solar do Unhão,* south of the city center (see Places to Eat).

Elsewhere in Salvador

Ilê-Aiyê, one of the most exciting Carnaval groups, gives free concerts for the public from 9 pm every Saturday (at least during summer) at Rua Curuzu 197 in Liberdade, north of Pelourinho. African culture is kept alive in Liberdade, which is a good place to see afoxé.

Teatro Castro Alves (☎ 532-2323), on Campo Grande (Praça Dois de Julho) south of the city center, is the biggest music theater in Salvador. The big acts play here, and they're often Brazil's best.

Farther south, Barra is full of bars, discos and music. Some places are quite good, but it's more touristy and is starting to get a sleazy reputation. *Habeus Copos* (☎ 267-4996, Rua Marquês de Leão 172) is an old favorite (and attracts an older crowd). From Thursday to Saturday it has live bossa, samba and chorinho.

Of the other beaches, Rio Vermelho has some good nightspots. A couple of the happening bars are **Póstudo** (☎ *334-0484, Rua João Gomes 87)*, with live jazz on Tuesday and live blues on Thursday nights, and **Extudo** (☎ *334-0671, Rua Lidio Mesquita 4)*, an arty place where the food names are inspired by cinema and world literature. In the wee hours, everyone seems to gravitate to the **Mercado do Peixe** on Largo da Mariquita in Rio Vermelho. There are 16 bars with great food and cold beer, open 24 hours a day.

Most of the young and hip now head for the **Aeroclube Plaza Show**, a conglomeration of bars, restaurants and boutiques that includes the **Rock in Rio** (☎ *461-0300)*, a live music and dance venue that gets very crowded on weekends. The Carnaval group **Ara Ketu** (☎ *247-6784)* performs in the 'hangar' of the Aeroclube every Tuesday and Wednesday night. It's a large space but gets crowded.

Folk Art

Bahia has some of Brazil's best artisans, who usually have small shops or sell in the local market. You can buy their folk art in Salvador, but the best place to see or purchase the real stuff is in the town of origin, because so much of the production is regional and specialized.

The main materials used in Bahian folk art are leather, wood, earth, metal and fiber. The city of Feira de Santana is known for its leatherwork. Maragojipinho, Rio Real and Cachoeira produce earthenware. Caldas do Jorro, Caldas de Cipo and Itaparica specialize in straw crafts. Rio de Contas and Muritiba have metalwork. Ilha de Maré is famous for lacework. Jequié, Valença and Feira de Santana are woodworking centers. Santo Antônio de Jesus, Rio de Contas and Monte Santo manufacture goods made of leather and silver.

SHOPPING

If you're after handicrafts, browse through Mercado Modelo, Praça da Sé, Terreiro de Jesus and the numerous shops and galleries in Pelourinho – all places where articles and prices are geared to tourists. For a large local market, try Mercado São Joaquim (see the earlier section on this market, which is also known as Feira São Joaquim), which is just north of the city center next to the ferry terminal for the Itaparica Fast Cat. Dedicated shoppers should head for Shopping Iguatemi (Salvador's largest shopping center), opposite the bus station, and Shopping Barra, both gigantic complexes with dozens of shops. It's easy to get lost in them.

GETTING THERE & AWAY
Air

The big domestic airlines all fly to Salvador, as does Nordeste, which also goes to smaller cities in the region like Ilhéus and Porto Seguro. You can fly to most cities in Brazil from Salvador, but make sure you find out how many stops the plane makes: Many flights in the Northeast operate as 'milk runs,' stopping at every city along the Atlantic seaboard, which makes for a long ride.

The only regular direct scheduled international flight is between Salvador and Lisbon with TAP every Wednesday and Saturday. Flights to and from other international destinations go via São Paulo or Rio.

Following is a list of Brazilian and foreign airlines with offices in Salvador:

TAM (☎ 0800-123100), airport

TAP Air Portugal (☎ 243-6122, fax 243-6968), Avenida Estados Unidos 137, sala 401, Comércio

TransBrasil (☎ 0800-155511), airport

Varig/Nordeste/Rio Sul (☎ 0800-997000), Rua Carlos Gomes 103, Centro

VASP (☎ 0800-121191), Avenida Antônio Carlos Magalhães 2487, Itaigara

Bus

Daily executivo buses to Rio leave at 7 am and 3 pm (US$82, 26 hours). A standard bus leaves for São Paulo daily at 7:50 pm (US$73, 32 hours). There is also an executivo bus leaving daily at 8:30 pm (US$79) and *leitos* (super-comfortable overnight express buses) leaving at 8 pm (US$87). To Belo Horizonte there is a daily executivo bus leaving at 6 pm (US$58, 23 hours).

There are six standard buses (US$13) and five executivo buses (US$18) departing daily to Aracaju (Sergipe) – buses traveling via the Linha Verde road take around five hours. All stop at the bus station in Estância. For the 13-hour trip to Recife, a standard bus (US$28) departs daily at 3:30 pm, and an executivo (US$37) leaves daily at 9 pm. There is one daily departure to Fortaleza at 9 pm (US$55, 20 hours).

There are two daily departures to Lençóis, at 7 am and 11:30 pm (US$15, six hours) – the night bus is quicker because there's less traffic. There are two departures daily to Valença (US$11, four hours), at 7:50 and 11:50 am. Four buses depart daily for Ilhéus (US$24, seven hours), and there is an evening departure to Porto Seguro at 9 pm (US$37, 10 hours). There are frequent departures for Cachoeira (US$4, two hours) between 5:30 am and 9:30 pm. Take the bus marked São Felix and get off in Cachoeira.

For access to beaches along the north coast, six buses run daily to Praia do Forte (US$3.50, 1½ hours) and 10 buses daily run to Conde (US$6, three hours). These buses usually continue on to Sítio de Conde, but ask to make sure.

Boat

Boats to points on Baía de Todos os Santos leave from the Terminal Turístico Marítimo (☎ 326-6603), on Avenida da França, one block towards the water from the Mercado Modelo. There are also tours of the bay featuring Ilha de Itaparica and Ilha dos Frades, and irregular boats to Maragojipe. The small dock beside the Mercado Modelo has irregular motorboats to Mar Grande and Itaparica. See the Around Salvador and Recôncavo sections for further detail on boats to all these destinations.

During summer (December to March), there are two daily boats to Morro de São Paulo from the Terminal Turístico Marítimo. The noon boat is a large launch that makes the trip in about 1½ hours. A smaller, cheaper motorboat leaves at 2 pm and takes four hours.

GETTING AROUND

Venice has its canals and gondolas; Salvador has its bluff, elevators, hills, valleys and one-way streets. The Elevador Lacerda runs daily from 5 am to midnight, linking the low and high cities. The Plano Inclinado Gonçalves, behind the cathedral near the Praça da Sé, makes the same link and is more fun (and less claustrophobic), but only operates Monday to Saturday from 5 am to 10 pm.

To/From the Airport

Aeroporto Deputado Luís Eduardo do Magalhães (☎ 204-1010) is more than 30km east of the city center, inland from Itapoã. The two taxi companies represented at the airport share a *bilheteria* (ticket office) and have the same prices. The table displayed in the office shows prices to several destinations in the city (US$25 to Praça da Sé). The best way to reach the city center is to take the green and white Ondina executivo bus marked Praça da Sé/Aeroporto. The bus actually stops just off Rua Chile, close to the Praça. The fare is US$2.

There are supposed to be Ondina buses leaving for the airport from Rua Chile (the stop is signposted) every half-hour between 6 am and 7 pm, but the schedule is rather flexible, so leave yourself plenty of time. The bus goes down Avenida 7 de Setembro to Barra, and continues all the way along the coast before heading inland to the airport. You can flag it down along the way. In light traffic, the ride takes about an hour; with traffic allow 1¾ hours.

A municipal Aeroporto bus (fare US$0.70) follows the same route to the airport, but it gets very crowded, and isn't recommended if you're carrying a bag.

Bus

The two most useful municipal bus stops in the city center are the one off Rua Chile and the one on Avenida da França.

Buses from Rua Chile go to Campo Grande, Vitória and all the Atlantic coast beaches as far as Praia Flamengo, just past Praia Itapoã.

The Avenida da França stop is in Cidade Baixa beside the Elevador Lacerda. From here, take either the Ribeira or the Bonfim bus to get to the Itaparica ferry (get off after a couple of kilometers) or the Mercado São Joaquim (get off at the stop after the ferry terminal) or continue to Igreja NS do Bonfim and Ribeira.

To/From the Bus Station
Salvador's modern bus station (☎ 900-1555 for information between 6 am and 10 pm) is 8km east of the city center, but it can be a bit messy taking a bus there. Many buses marked 'Rodoviária' drive all over the city – and can take up to an hour during rush hour. For a quicker trip, it's advisable to take a taxi, which costs US$9 from Praça da Sé.

The most convenient way to go by bus to the main bus station is to take the Iguatemi bus from the bus stop on Rua Chile. From Shopping Iguatemi (Salvador's largest shopping complex), use the long footbridge to cross the highway to the bus station. The bus goes via Barra and Ondina and takes about 45 minutes. The fare is US$0.70.

The bus station is a self-contained complex with a Bahiatursa office, a telephone office, a supermarket, a luggage storage service, and a couple of inexpensive eateries. For more complex requirements, you can cross the footbridge and visit Shopping Iguatemi.

Baía de Todos os Santos

ILHA DE ITAPARICA
☎ 0xx71 • postcode 44600-000
• pop 18,000

Many Bahians love Itaparica, the largest island in Baía de Todos os Santos. They prefer to swim in the calm waters of the bay than in the rough and tumble of the ocean, and it's quite a pretty island. However, this is not really a must-see destination. Weekends here are crowded (especially in summer),

transportation can be slow without a car, and the beaches aren't as pretty as the more accessible beaches north of the city.

The island is built up with many weekend homes, and has few budget hotels. Many of the beaches are dirty and the best part of the island is owned by Club Med. Yet there are still a few clean beaches where you can just lie on the sand beneath windswept palms and gaze across the bay at the city (try Barra Grande or Aratuba).

Information
There is a tourist information office near the Bom Despacho ferry terminal. It's supposed to be open daily from 8:30 am to noon and 1:30 to 6 pm, but it's not particularly useful.

Things to See & Do
Itaparica City At the northern tip of the island are the city of **Itaparica** and the **São Lourenço Fort**. Built by the Dutch invaders in the 17th century, the fortress figured prominently in Bahia's battle for independence in 1823. The **Solar Tenente Botas** (Mansion of Lieutenant Botas), on the square of the same name; the **Igreja Matriz do Santíssimo Sacramento**, on Rua Luís Gama; and the **Fonte da Bica** (mineral-water fountain) complete the city sights.

Along the Coast Southeast along the coast, between Itaparica City and Bom Despacho, is **Ponta de Areia**, a thin strip of sand with beach bars. The water is clear and shallow, and the sandy floor slopes gently into the bay.

Mar Grande is perhaps the most likeable town on the island, with lots of bars and restaurants and a relaxed atmosphere. The beaches to the south, **Barra do Gil**, **Barra do Pote** and **Coroa**, all have excellent views of Salvador, while on the other side of Club Med is **Barra Grande**, which is Itaparica's finest open-to-the-public beach. The beaches farther to the south up to and including **Cacha Pregos** are dirtier and generally less beautiful, although many Bahians consider Cacha Pregos the best beach on the island.

BAÍA DE TODOS OS SANTOS & RECÔNCAVO

Places to Stay

There's a campground on the beach at *Praia de Berlinque* (☎ 638-3746). It's 4km north of Cacha Pregos; sites are US$5 per person. In Aratuba is *Zimbo Tropical* (☎ 638-1148), a pleasant place owned by Philippe and Suely Kemlin. Philippe is the classic case of the French traveler who came to visit and never left. The bungalows are in a beautiful garden setting with small monkeys in the trees. They cost US$12/25 single/double. From Bom Despacho, take the bus or VW kombi to Aratuba and ask the driver to let you off at the blue and white telephone exchange on the right-hand side just before you enter Aratuba. The pousada is 200m down Rua Iemenjá towards the beach, which is a further 200m away. (You can pick up a Kombi ride at the ferry terminal for about US$3).

In Mar Grande, a good cheap option is the *Pousada Koisa Nossa* (☎ 633-1028, Rua da Rodagam 173). As you exit the dock, walk across the square and follow the road for about 200m. It's a relaxed place, with a restaurant serving fresh, tasty seafood meals. Double quartos cost around US$20 with breakfast. If you want something more comfortable, have a look at the *Pousada Arco Iris* (☎/fax 633-1130, Estrada da Gamboa 102). This pousada is in the restored mansion of an old *fazenda* (ranch) set in spacious, shady gardens with a swimming pool and restaurant. Double quartos cost US$30; double apartamentos start at US$50. You can usually get a good discount from April to November.

On the beach at Praia Conceição is *Club Méditerranée* (☎ 680-7141 or ☎ 0800-213782, fax 880-7165). Singles/doubles cost US$90/175, all-inclusive.

Places to Eat

The best eating on the island is the seafood at the beach bars. Another option, the *Manga Rosa* restaurant in the Pousada Arco Iris, is good but expensive, with main dishes starting around US$15. In Aratuba, pay a visit to the **Wunderbar** on the point, run by German expat Limo. It's a party on the weekends, with much drinking and craziness.

Getting There & Away
Bus Frequent buses leave from the bus/ferry terminal at Bom Despacho south for Valença (US$4, two hours).

Boat There are three boats from Salvador to Itaparica. The first is a small boat that leaves from the Terminal Turístico Marítimo behind the Mercado Modelo and goes directly to Mar Grande. The trip costs US$1.20 (US$1.50 on weekends) and takes around 50 minutes. Boats depart daily every hour between 5:30 am and 10 pm. The last boat returns from Mar Grande at 5 pm. This schedule often changes. Other boats leave occasionally for Mar Grande from the small dock beside the Mercado Modelo.

The second boat is a giant car-and-passenger ferry that operates between São Joaquim and Bom Despacho. The fare is US$1.45 and the ride takes 35 minutes. Ferries operate every half-hour from 6 am to 7:30 pm (later in summer). Expect a long wait to get on the ferry on weekends, especially in summer.

The third and fastest way to do the trip is in one of the 'Fast Cat' catamarans with airplane-like interiors, attendants and air-conditioning. These take 20 minutes and cost US$4. They begin at 5:30 am and run every half-hour between São Joaquim and Mar Grande until 7 pm (later in summer).

To reach São Joaquim from the Salvador city center take either the Ribeira or Bonfim bus from the Avenida da França bus stop (beside the Elevador Lacerda) for a couple of kilometers.

Getting Around
Bom Despacho is the island's transportation hub. Buses, minibuses, VW Kombis and taxis meet the boats and will take you to any of the beaches for around US$2. Bicycles are widely available to rent for around US$10 per day and are a useful option if you want to explore under your own steam. Although the São Joaquim-Bom Despacho ferry operates until midnight during summer, island transport becomes scarce after 8 pm.

OTHER ISLANDS
The easiest way to cruise the lesser Baía de Todos os Santos islands and the bay itself is to get one of the tourist boats that leave from the Terminal Turístico Marítimo (☎ 0xx71-326-6603), close to Mercado Modelo in Salvador. There are various tours; most take half a day, stopping at Ilha dos Frades, Ilha da Maré and Itaparica. The cost is about US$15.

Alternatively, hire a cheap, small boat from the small port next to the Mercado Modelo. Bahiatursa's notice board often has advertisements for boat trips.

Popular islands include **Ilha Bom Jesus dos Passos**, which has traditional fishing boats and artisans; **Ilha dos Frades** (named after two monks who were killed and cannibalized there by local Indians), which has attractive waterfalls and palm trees; and **Ilha da Maré**.

Ilha da Maré has the **Igreja de NS das Neves**, the quiet beaches of **Itamoabo** and **Bacia das Neves**.

Apart from the tours, boats to Ilha da Maré (US$1 or a bit more on weekends) leave from São Tomé, about one hour by a Base Naval/São Tomé bus from the Avenida da França bus stop – get off at the end of the line. To get to Ilha dos Frades, take an Oxalá bus from the main bus station in Salvador to Madre de Deus (70km northwest of the city) and catch a boat for Praia de Paramara for around US$0.50.

Recôncavo

The recôncavo is the region of fertile lands spread around the Baía de Todos os Santos. Some of the earliest Brazilian encounters between Portuguese, Indian and African peoples occurred here, and the lands proved to be among Brazil's best for growing sugar and tobacco.

The region prospered not only because of the excellent growing conditions but also from its relative proximity to Portuguese sugar markets, the favorable winds for sailing to Europe and the excellent harbors afforded by the Baía de Todos os Santos. By 1570 there were already 18 *engenhos* (sugar mills), and by 1584 there were 40. The sugar-plantation system was firmly entrenched by the end of the 16th century and continued to grow from the sweat of African slaves for another 250 years.

Tobacco came a bit later to the recôncavo. Traded to African slave-hunters and kings, it was the key commodity in the triangle of the slave trade. Tobacco was a more sensitive crop to grow than sugar and the estates were much smaller. The big fortunes were made growing sugar, not tobacco. On the other hand, tobacco required fewer slaves – about four per farm – so many poorer Portuguese settlers went into tobacco and a less rigid social hierarchy developed. Many settlers even did some of the work!

A second, subsidiary industry in the recôncavo area was cattle ranching, which provided food for the plantation hands and transport for the wood that fueled the sugar mills and for delivery of the processed cane to market. Cattle breeding started in the recôncavo and spread inland, radiating west into the sertão and Minas Gerais, then northwest into Piauí.

If you have time for only one side trip from Salvador, visit Cachoeira and perhaps squeeze in Santo Amaro. A suggested itinerary is to take a boat to Maragojipe and then the bus along the banks of the Rio Paraguaçu to Cachoeira. If you're in Cachoeira on Friday or Saturday night, you may be able to attend a terreiro de Candomblé. You can then take one of the frequent buses from Cachoeira back to Salvador, visiting Santo Amaro on the way. (Boats from Salvador to Maragojipe are infrequent, so you'll need to plan ahead to do this trip. See the Maragojipe section later for details.)

CACHOEIRA

☎ 0xx75 • postcode 44300-000
• pop 16,000

Cachoeira, 121km northwest of Salvador and 40km west of Santo Amaro, is below a series of hills beside the Rio Paraguaçu. The river is spanned by Ponte Dom Pedro II, built by the British in 1885 as a link with Cachoiera's twin town, São Felix. Affectionately known as the jewel of the recôncavo, Cachoeira is at the center of Brazil's best tobacco-growing regions. Apart from tobacco, the main crops in the area are cashews and oranges.

The town is a relaxed place, full of beautiful colonial architecture uncompromised by the presence of modern buildings and tourist hordes. As a result, it was pronounced a national monument in 1971 and the state of Bahia started paying for the restoration and preservation of historic buildings. However, these funds appear to have dried up of late and the municipal authorities of Cachoeira are attempting to continue the work on their own dwindling budget.

Cachoeira is also a renowned center of Candomblé and the home of many traditional artists and artisans. If you get an early start, Cachoeira can be visited in a day from Salvador, but it's less hectic if you stay overnight.

History

Diego Álvares, the father of Cachoeira's founders, was the sole survivor of a ship bound for the West Indies that was wrecked in 1510 on a reef near Salvador. This Portuguese Robinson Crusoe was saved by the Tupinambá Indians of Rio Vermelho, who dubbed the strange white sea creature Caramuru, or 'Fish-Man.' Álvares lived 20 years with the Indians and married Catarina do Paraguaçu, the daughter of the most powerful Tupinambá chief. Their sons João Gaspar Aderno Álvares and Rodrigues Martins Álvares killed off the local Indians, set up the first sugarcane fazendas and founded Cachoeira.

By the 18th century, tobacco from Cachoeira was considered the world's finest, sought by rulers in China and Africa. Tobacco also became popular in Brazil. The holy herb, as it was called, was taken as snuff, smoked in a pipe or chewed.

Early in the 19th century, Cachoeira achieved fame as a center for military

CACHOEIRA

Igreja de NS do Conceição do Monte

Rua Rodrigo Brandão

Igreja de NS dos Remédios

Mercado

Rua Comendador Albino

1

Rua Lauro de Freitas

Praça Maciel

2 Praça Manoel Vitorino

3

Rua Cons Virgílio Damasio

4

Praça Dr Milton

Ponte Dom Pedro II to São Felix

Rio Paraguaçu

5

6 7 Largo da Ajuda

8 ●9

10 ●12

11 ●13

14

Praça 13 de Maio

Rua Ana Nery

Igreja de NS do Rosário do Porto do Cachoeira

To Salvador

15

Praça Teixeira de Freitas

16

17 18

19

20

21

Praça da Aclamação

Rua Benjamin Constant

Rua 25 de Junho

Rua 7 de Setembro

22

23

Av Paraguaçu

Rua 13 de Maio

Rua Vera Lopes

Rua Dr João

0   25   50 m
0   25   50 yards

PLACES TO STAY
13 Pousada do Guerreiro
15 Pensão Tia Rosa
16 Pousada & Restaurant do Pai Tomáz
23 Pousada do Convento do Cachoeira

PLACES TO EAT
3 Gruta Azul
10 Pizzaria Vick
11 Nair (Rian)
19 Cabana do Pai Tomáz

OTHER
1 Bus Station
2 Railway Station
4 Santa Casa de Misericórdia
5 Post Office
6 Museu da Boa Morte

7 Prefeitura
8 Igreja de NS da Ajuda
9 Atelier do Doidão
12 Atelier do Louco
14 Museu Hansen Bahia
17 Tourist Office
18 Telephone Office
20 Museu do SPHAN
21 Casa da Câmara e Cadeia
22 Igreja da Ordem Terceira do Carmo

operations in Bahia to oust the Portuguese rulers. On June 25, 1822, the town became the first to recognize Dom Pedro I as the independent ruler of Brazil.

Orientation & Information

Cachoeira and São Felix are best seen on foot. There's nothing that you really *have* to see, so it's best to just take it easy and explore.

The tourist office (☎ 425-1123) on Praça da Aclamação should be able to help with accommodations and general details about the town's sights. It's usually open week-

days during working hours – a somewhat ambiguous term in Cachoeira. Other good sources of information are the helpful staff at the Museu Hansen Bahia. At some of the sights, especially churches, theft has been a problem, so you may have to phone the tourist office to arrange a visit.

Things to See & Do

Casa da Câmara e Cadeia On the same square as the tourist office is the yellow-with-white-trim Casa da Câmara e Cadeia, the old prefecture and prison. Organized criminals ran the show upstairs and disorganized criminals were kept behind bars downstairs. The building dates back to 1698 and served as the seat of the Bahian government in 1822. The old marble pillory in the square was removed after abolition.

Museu do SPHAN Across the square, a colonial mansion houses the humble SPHAN museum (☎ 425-1123), with squeaky bats flapping over colonial furnishings. The museum is open daily 9 am to noon and 2 to 5 pm (closed Monday).

Igreja da Ordem Terceira do Carmo The Church of the Third Order of Carmelites, just south of Praça da Aclamação and alongside the Pousada do Convento do Cachoeira (see Places to Stay), features a gallery of suffering polychrome Christs imported from the Portuguese colony in Macao and paneled ceilings. Christ's blood is made from bovine blood mixed with Chinese herbs and sparkling rubies. The church is now being promoted by the adjacent pousada as a convention center. It's certainly a novel idea to seat delegates where there were once pews.

Hours are Tuesday to Saturday 1 to 5 pm, except for Friday when it's open 2 to 6:30 pm.

Museu Hansen Bahia This museum occupies the birthplace and former home of Brazilian heroine Ana Neri, who organized the nursing corps during the Paraguay War. Today the work of German (naturalized Brazilian) artist Hansen Bahia is displayed here. Among his powerful lithographs of human suffering is a series of illustrations of Castro Alves' poem *Návio Negreiro* (Slave Ship). The museum, on Rua 13 de Maio, is open Tuesday to Friday 9 am to 5 pm and on weekends 9 am to 2 pm. Prints and T-shirts are also on sale here.

NS do Rosário The blue church with yellow trim, just down the street from the Hansen Bahia museum, on the corner of Rua Ana Neri and Rua Lions Club, is the NS do Rosário do Porto do Cachoeira. The church has beautiful Portuguese tiles and a ceiling painted by Teófilo de Jesus. Opening hours are erratic (although it's usually open

in the mornings) so if it's closed, try knocking. If the custodian is there, he may also take you round the Museu das Alfaias, on the second floor. This museum contains remnants from the abandoned 17th-century Convento de São Francisco do Paraguaçu.

Igreja de NS da Ajuda On Largo da Ajuda is Cachoeira's oldest church, the tiny NS da Ajuda, built in 1595 when Cachoeira was known as Arraial d'Ajuda. Adjacent to the church is the **Museu da Boa Morte**, with interesting displays of photos and ceremonial apparel used by the exclusively female Boa Morte cult (see Special Events).

Santa Casa de Misericórdia A few blocks north across Praça Dr Milton is the municipality's oldest hospital. The complex contains a pretty chapel (founded in 1734) with a painted ceiling, gardens and an ossuary. It's usually open on weekdays 2 to 5 pm.

NS do Conceição do Monte At the far end of town, near the bridge and the railway station, is the Igreja de NS do Conceição do Monte. The climb to this 18th-century church is rewarded by a good view of Cachoeira and São Felix.

Praça Manoel Vitorino Across from the ruined grand facade of the railway station, the wide cobblestone Praça Manoel Vitorino feels like an Italian movie set, except for the Texaco station plonked in the middle. Try your Italian on the ice-cream seller or the pigeons, then cross the river to São Felix.

São Felix When you cross the old Ponte Dom Pedro II, a narrow and dilapidated bridge where trains and cars must wait their turn, be careful where you step: Loose planks have claimed the life of at least one person in recent years. When vehicles pass over the bridge it emits a wild cacophony of sounds – a bit like one of those urban/industrial/primitive percussion acts!

Apart from the view towards Cachoeira, São Felix has two other attractions. The **Casa da Cultura Américo Simas** is on Rua

Celestino João Severino da Luz Neto (open Tuesday to Sunday 8 am to 5 pm). Its temporary exhibitions are worth a visit. Exhibits of a different sort can be found at the **Centro Cultural Dannemann** (☎ 425-2208), along the riverfront at Avenida Salvador Pinto 29 (open daily 8 am to noon and 1 to 5 pm).

The Dannemann center has displays of old machinery and the techniques used for making *charutos* (cigars). The rich tobacco smells, the beautiful wooden working tables, and the sight of workers handrolling monster cigars will take you back in time. The art space in the front of the building has exhibitions of sculpture, painting and photography. The handmade cigars sold here make good souvenirs or presents. Admission is free.

Candomblé Try to see Candomblé in Cachoeira, one of its strongest and perhaps purest spiritual and religious centers. Long and mysterious Candomblé ceremonies are held in small homes and shacks that are up in the hills, usually on Friday and Saturday nights at 8 pm.

Visitors are not common here and the tourist office is sometimes reluctant to give out this sort of information, but if you show an interest in Candomblé and respect for its traditions, you may inspire confidence.

Special Events
The **Festa da NS da Boa Morte** falls on the Friday closest to August 15 and lasts three days. This is one of the most fascinating Candomblé festivals and it's worth a special trip to see it. Organized by the Irmandade da Boa Morte (Sisterhood of the Good Death) – a secret religious society – the festival is celebrated by the descendants of slaves, who praise their liberation with dance and prayer and a mix of themes from Candomblé and Catholicism.

The **Festa de São João**, celebrated from June 22 to 24, is the big popular festival of Bahia's interior. It's a great celebration of folklore, with music, dancing and a generous amount of food and drink. Don't miss it if you're in Bahia.

Other festivals include: **NS do Rosário** (second half of October), which includes games, music and food; **NS da Ajuda** (first half of November), which features ritual cleansing of the church and a street festival; and **Santa Bárbara** or **Iansã** (December 4), a Candomblé ceremony held in São Felix at the Fonte de Santa Bárbara (Santa Bárbara Fountain).

Places to Stay
Expect prices quoted here to almost double during the main festivals in Cachoeira.

A clean and comfortable budget option is *Pousada do Pai Tomáz* (☎ 425-1288, Rua 25 de Junho 12), which has apartamentos for US$10 per person. Across the river in São Felix, the *Pousada do Paraguaçu* (☎ 425-2550, Avenida Salvador Pinto 1) is a relaxed place along the riverfront, with a veranda overlooking the water. Apartamentos with fan cost US$13/23, or US$20/30 with air-conditioning. There's a good restaurant attached.

The *Pensão Tia Rosa* (☎ 425-1792, Rua Ana Neri 12) has basic quartos for US$12 per person and a double apartamento for US$17, with a good breakfast included. The *Pousada do Guerreiro* (☎ 425-1104, Rua 13 de Maio 14), opposite Museu Hansen Bahia, has ragged but clean quartos for US$7 per person and apartamentos for US$10. Ask for an upstairs room.

The best place in town is the *Pousada do Convento de Cachoeira* (☎/fax 425-1716, Praça da Aclamação), a lovely old hotel with a courtyard and swimming pool. The dark-wood rooms of the former convent now have air-conditioning, minibar and hot showers, and cost US$35/40 single/double – including a major spread for breakfast. An extra bed costs US$15, or you can splurge on the suite for US$60.

Places to Eat
The *Gruta Azul* (☎ 425-1295, Praça Manoel Vitorino 2) is Cachoeira's best restaurant for lunch. The place has character: special recipes for seafood and batidas and a delightful shaded courtyard. Try the shrimp dishes for US$14 or *maniçoba*, the spicy

local dish composed of manioc and various meats for US$5. If you're adventurous ask for the *boa morte* (good death) drink. Hours are Monday to Friday 11 am to 5 pm, Saturday and Sunday 11 am to 2 pm.

On Rua 25 de Junho, there's more good food at *Cabana do Pai Tomáz* (the restaurant is across the road from the pousada). Check out the sensational scrap-yard roof decorations and the carved wooden panels and furniture. *Pizzaria Vick (Rua 13 de Maio 28)* is open daily in the evenings and serves a decent pizza.

Just up from the Museu Hansen Bahia (also on Rua 13 de Maio) is the *Nair* restaurant. It's named after the owner, but locals delight in turning things around and calling it Rian. The menu includes moqueca dishes and local specialties.

In São Felix, be sure to try the restaurant in the Pousada do Paraguaçu, which is open from 11 am to 11 pm.

Entertainment
Cruise the riverfront for beer drinking and *forró* dancing (dancing to the traditional music of the Northeast) at the riverside bars. Praça Teixeira de Freitas, which has a few bars, is the Times Square of Cachoeira – if you sit around a while, most of the locals will pass by.

Shopping
On Wednesday, Friday and Saturday, there's an open market on Praça Maciel – a good place to pick up handicrafts and observe local life.

Cachoeira has a wealth of wood sculptors, some of whom do very fine work, and you will see plenty of studios as you walk through town. This is some of the best traditional art still available in Brazil. Two of the best sculptors are Doidão and Louco, who carve beautiful, heavy pieces.

Getting There & Around
There are hourly buses to Salvador and Feira de Santana between 4:20 am and 6:30 pm (US$2.50, two hours). The bus station (☎ 425-1214) is tiny and easy to miss – it's a small yellow and blue building

on Rua Rodrigo Brandão (see map). Buses to Maragojipe leave from São Felix nine times a day between 7:10 am and 8:30 pm (US$1, half an hour). The station is at Praça Antônio Carlos Lobo Maia.

For Valença, take either the 7:40 am or 12:20 pm bus from São Felix to Santo Antônio and catch a connection from there to Valença.

Cachoeira is just the right size to cover on foot. If you want to cross the river to São Felix by canoe, rather than crossing the bridge on foot, you can hire one for a couple of dollars at the waterfront.

SANTO AMARO
☎ 0xx75 • postcode 44200-000
• pop 45,000

Santo Amaro is an old run-down sugar town that sees very few tourists and has an unpretentious charm. If you're passing through on your way from Cachoeira, think about stopping for a few hours, especially if it's a market Saturday, when the town comes to life. If you decide to stay the night, there's often very good local music. *Pousada Amaro's (☎ 241-1202, Rua Conselhor Saraiva 27)* is a good accommodation option, with apartamentos for US$8/10 single/double and a decent restaurant out back

In colonial days, Santo Amaro made its fortune from sugar. Today, the major industry is paper production; the paper mill is on the road to Cachoeira. The mill has spoiled the Rio Subaé and bamboo has replaced sugarcane on the hillsides.

Reminders of Santo Amaro's sugar legacy are the decrepit pastel mansions of the sugar barons and the many churches. The plantation owners lived on Rua General Câmara, the old commercial street, and an effort is being made to restore some of these buildings.

Many of the churches have been closed since a gang of thieves stole most of the holy images and exported them to France. The largest church, **Santo Amaro da Purificação**, is still open.

The Festa de Santo Amaro (January 24 to February 2) is celebrated by the ritual *lavagem* (washing) of the church steps.

Santo Amaro is the birthplace of two of Brazil's most popular singers: Caetano Veloso and his sister Maria Betânia. During Carnaval, they've been known to put in an appearance between trios elétricos.

Getting There & Away

The bus station (☎ 241-1119) is on Rua Wanderlei Pinto. There is frequent bus service between Salvador and Santo Amaro (US$2, 70 minutes), and you'll find that most buses continue the 32km west to Cachoeira/São Felix.

MARAGOJIPE
☎ 0xx75 • pop 21,000

Surrounded by Baía de Todos os Santos and rich green fields patched with crops, Maragojipe is a pleasantly decaying tobacco-exporting port, 32km north of Nazaré and 24km south of Cachoeira. The port is surrounded by mangrove swamps, and locals push off from the pier in *saveiros* (homemade fishing boats) and dugout canoes.

For information, try the Fundação Suerdieck Casa da Cultura on Praça da Matriz.

Things to See & Do

The Suerdieck & Company Cigar Factory (established in 1920) is open for tours Monday to Friday 8 am to 5 pm, and on Saturday morning. This is also a good place to get information about other local sights.

On weekend nights, head down to the dockside bars for local music. Swimming off the cement pier is popular.

Strolling through town, look out for the striking wrought-iron grille and sculpted facade of the pale-blue building on Rua D Macedo Costa.

Places to Stay & Eat

The *Oxumaré Hotel* (☎ 726-1104, *Rua Heretiano Jorge de Souza 3*) has cramped single/double quartos that cost US$10/15.

Jumbo shrimp is the local delicacy here. Otherwise, go to the port for some pizza at *Pizzaria Recreio do Porto* or to *City Bar* on Praça da Matriz for juices and snacks.

Getting There & Away

Buses from Salvador to Maragojipe go frequently via Santo Amaro and Cachoeira. The trip takes three hours and costs US$5. There are no buses via Itaparica. Go by boat if possible.

Boats from Salvador to Maragojipe are infrequent, so you'll need to call the Terminal Turístico Marítimo in Salvador (☎ 0xx71-326-6603) or get Bahiatursa to do it for you. Stops are made at São Roque, Barra do Paraguaçu and Enseada. There are no boats from Maragojipe to Cachoeira since the Rio Paraguaçu silted up, but there are frequent buses.

North of Salvador

The coastal road north from Salvador is called the Rodovia do Côco (Coconut Highway). The excellent paved road runs a few kilometers inland as far as the entrance to Praia do Forte, 80km north of Salvador. From Praia do Forte, the Linha Verde (Green Line) road spans 142km to Itanhi, on the border with Sergipe. The Linha Verde, constructed in 1993 and hailed as Brazil's first

'ecologically planned' road, runs between 3 and 12km from the coast. The 'ecological planning' runs to a restriction on the construction of gas stations and roadside restaurants, and to the fact that the road doesn't hug the coast, as was originally planned.

There are access roads off the Linha Verde to several small towns and fishing villages, many of which are now developing into popular weekend destinations for Salvadorans. Regular buses run from Salvador's main bus station to Praia do Forte and along the Linha Verde to Conde and Sitio, entering a few coastal towns on the way. There's also a huge new resort complex at Costa do Sauípe. See the separate sections for each town for details.

AREMBEPE
☎ 0xx71 • postcode 42800-000

Arembepe was one of Brazil's first hip beaches in the 1960s. Mick Jagger and Janis Joplin got the joint rolling and many local and foreign hippies followed. It is no longer a particularly attractive or popular retreat. Exclusive private homes and pollution from the giant chemical plant to the south have tainted the rocky coast.

If you want to head to the sea for a day from Salvador, there are prettier beaches than Arembepe, and if you're getting out of Salvador, there are less spoiled fishing villages along the Bahian coast.

Places to Stay
If you do end up in Arembepe, you can head for the campground near the Aldeia Hippie (hippie village), or try the *Pousada da Fazenda* (☎ 624-1030), which looks like one of the few leftovers from the hippie days. Singles/doubles cost US$17/27. The *Praias de Arembepe Hotel* (☎ 624-1415), across from the praça, has single/double apartamentos for around US$10/20 without breakfast. The rooms are beat-up but clean, and rooms 101 and 201 have sea views.

PRAIA DO FORTE
☎ 0xx71 • postcode 48280-000

Up the coast, Praia do Forte, 3km south of the meeting point of the Rodovia do Côco

and the Linha Verde, has fantastic beaches, a beautiful castle fortress and a sea-turtle reserve. Formerly a small, rustic fishing village, Praia do Forte has been developed as an ecologically sensitive upmarket beach resort. The development has so far been held in check, but the palm-lined beaches get very crowded on weekends and in summer. If you can, time your visit for the full moon and walk along the beach past the resort at sunset, when the sun turns the waters of the Rio Timeantube red as the moon rises over the sea. It's an unforgettable sight.

Praia do Forte was the seat of one of the original 15 captaincies established by the Portuguese. The huge estate extended inland all the way to the state of Maranhão.

TAMAR Turtle Reserve
The reserve is on the beach right next to the lighthouse. It's open from 9 am to 6:30 pm daily. Entry is US$1.30, or free after 6 pm. See the boxed text, later in this chapter, for details on TAMAR's efforts to protect endangered sea turtles.

Castelo do Garcia d'Ávila
Desperate to colonize as a way to control his new territory, the king of Portugal set about granting lands to merchants, soldiers and aristocrats. For no apparent reason Garcia d'Ávila, a poor 12-cow farmer, was endowed with this huge tract of land.

For the site of his home, Garcia chose a prime piece of real estate – an aquamarine ocean-view plot studded with palm trees on Morro Tatuapaçu – now a 3km walk from town. The Castelo do Garcia d'Ávila, dating from 1552, was the first great Portuguese edifice in Brazil. Today it's an impressive ruin that's slowly being restored. The Castelo is open daily 8 am to 6 pm. Admission is US$1.50.

Places to Stay
Budget travelers should visit during the week, out of season, when there are heavy discounts on accommodation. One cheap place to stay is at the campground, which is just 10 minutes on foot from the beach, has cold-water showers, shady, sandy sites, and

basins for washing clothes. There's also a very good HI youth hostel, *Albergue Praia do Forte* (*☎/fax 676-1094, albpraia@zaz.com.br, Rua da Aurora 3)*, not far from the beach. Bunks in a six-bed dorm cost US$9 for members and US$11 for non-members. They also have double rooms for US$22 (US$26 nonmembers).

Montreaux Pousada (*☎/fax 676-1494, Rua da Aurora 22)* offers spotless doubles with verandas for US$20, with discounts for longer stays and off-season. A more exotic option is the *Pousada dos Artistas* (*☎ 676-1147, fax 379-2082, Praça dos Artis-*

tas), with friendly management, and double apartamentos with fridge and hot water for US$60. It's in a tropical garden setting wth lots of artwork to enjoy. Also recommended is the friendly *Pousada Ogum Marinho* (*☎/fax 676-1165, Alameda do Sol)*, which has lovely double apartamentos with fan for US$40 and US$50 with air-conditioning.

The top place to stay is the renowned *Praia do Forte Resort* (*☎ 676-1111, fax 676-1112)*, an excellent beachfront resort hotel with fabulous food. Room rates start at US$250 for doubles, all-inclusive.

The TAMAR Project to Save Sea Turtles

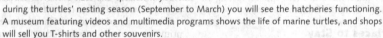

TAMAR is an abbreviation of the Portuguese name for sea turtles, TArtaruga MARinha. The highly successful TAMAR project was created in 1980 by IBAMA (the Brazilian Environment Agency) and as it quickly expanded, a nonprofit foundation (Fundação Pró TAMAR) was created to support, raise money and co-administer TAMAR with the government. Its goal is to reverse the process of extinction of the five species of sea turtles in Brazil: loggerhead, hawksbill, olive ridley, green and leatherback.

At the Praia do Forte station you can see several small exhibiting pools with marine turtles of various sizes and species. If you visit during the turtles' nesting season (September to March) you will see the hatcheries functioning. A museum featuring videos and multimedia programs shows the life of marine turtles, and shops will sell you T-shirts and other souvenirs.

TAMAR researchers protect around 550 nests a year along 50km of coast close to Praia do Forte. The eggs – moist, leathery, ping-pong size balls – are buried in the sand when laid and either left on the beach or brought to the hatcheries for incubation. When they hatch, the baby turtles are immediately released into the sea.

TAMAR has another 18 stations along the coast and two stations on oceanic islands. The Comboios station (Espírito Santo state, north of Vitória and near Linhares) protects the loggerhead and leatherback turtles. The Fernando de Noronha station protects green and hawksbill turtles. Praia do Forte station protects loggerhead, hawksbill, olive ridley and green turtles. Of the 60km of beach under the jurisdiction of the TAMAR project in Bahia, 13km are patrolled by the scientists alone; the remainder is protected by a cooperative effort in which fishermen – the very same who used to collect the eggs for food – are contracted to collect eggs for the scientists.

Nowadays, commerce in endangered turtle species is illegal, but shells are still sold in Salvador's Mercado Modelo, and in Sergipe turtle eggs are still popular hors d'oeuvres.

Places to Eat

The beach bars serve local seafood and snack food. For some great Bahian home cooking, try *Sabor da Vila* (☎ 676-1156) on Alameda do Sol. *Bom Bordo* (☎ 676-1320) on Rua da Aurora is a more expensive place for good seafood.

Getting There & Away

Frequent buses to Praia do Forte run daily from the bus station in Salvador. It takes 1½ hours and costs US$3.50. The last bus back to Salvador leaves at 5:45 pm.

PRAIA DO FORTE TO CONDE

With the opening of the Linha Verde, access to the small towns and fishing communities along the Bahian north coast is easier, at least as far as the Conde area. All through this region there are fenced-off tracts of land and small real-estate offices selling beachfront property.

Imbassaí is a fine beach with choppy, rough surf. The small Rio Barroso runs parallel to the beach and is good for swimming. It's 1km off the Linha Verde. The beach towns of **Porto de Sauípe**, **Subaúma** and **Baixio** are 4km, 9km and 8km respectively off the Linha Verde, with paved-road access to all of them. Porto de Sauípe is the site of the huge Costa do Sauípe tourist resort (see boxed text), but there are some nice beaches to the south with calm water for swimming. Subaúma is already quite developed, with lots of weekend beach homes and land being bought up to construct more. There's a decent beach with strong surf, and a couple of hotels. Baixio is a pretty, clean town, but the beach is rocky and not great for swimming.

CONDE

☎ 0xx75 • postcode 48300-000 • pop 11,000
On the Rio Itapicuru, Conde is 3km off the Linha Verde and about 6km from the sea. It's the little 'big town' of the area, and is also the logical jumping-off point for several beaches, the closest being Sítio. On Saturday, Conde hosts a large market where fisherfolk and artisans come to peddle their goods. In October, a series of rodeos takes place, when cowboys from the inland regions hit town to strut their stuff.

Getting There & Away

The bus station (☎ 429-1275) is on Rua Juracy Magalhães. The town has regular bus service to Esplanada, Alagoinhas, Feira de Santana and Salvador, and local shuttle services to Sítio. There's plenty of river traffic on market days, which makes it easy to get a ride down the river to the ocean. During summer, however, the river is often too low for boats to make the passage.

North of Conde, there are only direct buses along the Linha Verde to Aracaju in Sergipe, with some making a stop in Estância (for access to Mangue Seco). You should be able to get off the bus at other points along the road, but local transport is scarce and you'll need to hitch or walk to get to beaches.

SÍTIO

☎ 0xx75 • postcode 47610-000
From Conde it's a pleasant 6km drive to Sítio (also known as Sítio do Conde), passing wet lowlands full of cattle. The town has a decent beach, and is popular with surfers. From Sítio you can walk north or south along the coast to some beautiful, isolated beaches. **Seribinha** is a quiet fishing community about 14km north of Sítio along a dirt road (no buses) that passes through picturesque coconut-palm forest. The village is set on a thin strip of land between the Rio Itapicuru and the Atlantic Ocean, close to where the river meets the sea. Small boats will take you across the river; from here it's about a half-hour walk to **Cavalho Russo**, a red-water lake.

Places to Stay & Eat

Close to the beach, the *Pousada Beira Mar*, which has no phone, has single/double apartamentos for US$15 per person. The *Laia Restaurante e Pousada* (☎ 449-1254), also close to the beach, is a reasonably good value, with apartamentos for US$10/15. Ask for discounts during the low season (April to November) at all the pousadas.

There are a couple of good restaurants in town. *Zecas & Zecos*, on the main plaza, is

The Cancun of Brazil

The latest resort in Bahia is the immense, US$230 million Costa do Sauípe complex. When it's complete, it will consist of five luxury hotels and six high-quality pousadas, totaling almost 1500 apartments. Facilities include an 18-hole golf course, an equestrian center, a lake for windsurfing, and 15 tennis courts. The only thing it lacks is a good natural beach. There's even an imitation colonial-style village with colorful bars, restaurants and boutiques. Walking around here makes you feel like you're on a movie set.

It's bound to be popular with rich Brazilian family groups and foreign visitors who go for this type of thing.

At the time of research, the hotels and pousadas were yet to be inaugurated, but their debut was not far off. Information about them should be readily available from Bahiatursa in Salvador or through your local travel agent.

the best place for seafood. The **Restaurant Panela de Barro**, on the left as you come into town, serves tasty home-style cooking and has charmingly off-hand service.

Getting There & Away

Most buses from Salvador to Conde go on to Sítio and Barra do Itariri. If you get stuck in Conde, there are buses to Sítio at 8:10, 9 and 10 am and 4, 4:30 and 6 pm.

BARRA DO ITARIRI
☎ 0xx75

Barra is a 14km drive along a dirt road south from Sítio. The road is never more than a few hundred meters from the sea, which is hidden behind a running dune spotted with coconut palms. Barra has become more popular since the construction of the Linha Verde, but it is still a charming spot, set along the banks of the Rio Itariri. The river can be waded or swum across, and the southern bank leads to an endless stretch of deserted

beach. To the north are more deserted beaches; this stretch is known as *Corre Nu* (Run Naked). South of the river is the laid-back **Hotel Resort Itariri** (☎ 449-1142, fax 449-1212, hotelitariri@nworld.com.br). It's a quiet, comfortable resort with horses, boats and bicycles. Double rooms start at US$85 in low season and US$115 in high. Barra also has a couple of restaurants.

There are regular buses from Barra to Sítio. Buses from Salvador run to Barra via Conde and Sítio. Buses stop in the main street in town.

MANGUE SECO
☎ 0xx79 • postcode 48325-000 • pop 1000

Mangue Seco is a remote and tiny town on the northern border of Bahia and Sergipe, at the tip of a peninsula formed by the Rio Real. The town was the setting for the Jorge Amado novel *Tieta do Agreste*, and also for a soap opera based on the novel, filmed in the village, which captured the imagination of millions of Brazilians. Access to the town is still limited, but it is receiving more tourists since the opening of the Linha Verde. The lovely setting by the river is topped off by fine, white-sand ocean beaches 1.5km away.

Places to Stay & Eat

There is a rough campground by the river close to town. Cheap pousadas in town include the new **Pousada Suruby** (☎ 9121-0803) at Praia do Rio Real, with single/double quartos for around US$10/25. The backpackers' favorite is **Pousada O Forte** (☎ 9985-1217), 500m north of town. It's a friendly place with a good bar/restaurant attached. It has comfortable apartamentos for US$15/25 during the low season. The **Village Mangue Seco** (☎ 9985-1678) is the most upmarket place, with a swimming pool, around 1km from town along the road to the beaches. Double apartamentos cost US$30 in the low season.

There are some good seafood restaurants in town with great riverfront locations – try **Asa Branca** (☎ 9985-3886), **Restaurant Frutas do Mar** (☎ 9985-1021) or **Suruby** in the pousada of the same name.

Getting There & Away

The easiest access to Mangue Seco is from Pontal in Sergipe. From Pontal there are frequent boats during summer across the Rio Real to Mangue Seco (US$1 per person, 20 minutes) until around 6:30 pm. A daily bus runs to Pontal from Estância at 4 pm. The bus runs via Indiaroba, near the border with Bahia, then doubles back to Pontal. If you are coming from Salvador, you can pick up the bus in Indiaroba at around 4:30 pm. The last 10km or so to Pontal over a rollercoaster dirt road is entertaining, with locals egging on the driver to get airborne over the bumps! If the bus doesn't make the last boat, or you arrive outside of summer, you'll have to bargain for a ride across – most boats want US$15 to make the crossing. They'll take up to four passengers for this price. The bus returns from Pontal to Estância via Indiaroba daily at 5:30 pm.

South of Salvador

VALENÇA

☎ 0xx75 • postcode 45400-000 • pop 56,000

For most travelers, Valença is simply a stepping stone to the beaches of Morro de São Paulo, but it's also a small, friendly city worth a visit en route.

After routing the local Tupiniquin Indians, the Portuguese settled here along the Rio Una in the 1560s but were in turn expelled by the Aimores tribes. In 1799 the Portuguese returned to resettle and founded Vila de Nova Valença do Santíssimo Coração de Jesus.

Today, everything happens around the busy port and large market beside the Rio Una, where there are boats, historic buildings, and food and lodging facilities. The town is populated by a varied and interesting assortment of shipbuilders, *vaqueiros* (cowboys), artisans, fisherfolk and peasants.

Information

To obtain maps and information about Valença, boat schedules and pousadas, visit the helpful tourist office (☎ 741-3311) on Rua Comandante Madureira close to the port. It's open daily from 8 am to 6 pm. If you need money, there is a Banco do Brasil branch on Rua Governador Gonçalves and a Bradesco ATM at Rua Governador Gonçalves 178. You can check your email at Internauta (Praça da República 34). It's open daily from 8 am to 7 pm.

Things to See & Do

In the center of town, wander around the port, the central plaza and the market. At the far end of the port, the timbered ribbing of boat hulls resembles dinosaur skeletons. The saveiros are used by the local fisherfolk, who pull out of port early in the morning and return by mid-afternoon with the catch of the day. The smell of sap and sawdust, old fish and sea salt mingles with the wonderful smell of nutmeg. Picked from nearby groves, the nutmeg is set on a cloth and left to dry in the sun.

For a good trek, follow the left bank of the Rio Una upstream towards the Igreja NS de Amparo on the hill. At the base of the hill there's a trail straight up to the church that commands a beautiful view.

Special Events

In addition to the traditional festivals of Bahia, Valença also celebrates Sagrado Coração de Jesus in June and a weeklong festival in honor of the patron saint of workers, NS do Amparo, which climaxes on November 8.

Boi Estrela is a folklore event that happens during Christmas and Carnaval. Men and women dressed as cowhands accompany Catarina the Baiana through the city streets while they play tambourines and chant. Zambiapumba, another folklore festival, features musical groups playing weird instruments and running through the city streets on New Year's Eve.

There's also a good Carnaval with trios elétricos, and the Carnaval-like Micareta festival held 15 days after the end of Lent.

Places to Stay & Eat

The following prices are for the low season – prices rise by around 20% in the high season (Christmas to Carnaval). The

Hotel Valença (*☎/fax 741-3807, Rua Dr Heitor Guedes De Mello 15*) has clean, basic single quartos for US$8 and double aparta-mentos for US$15. Across the road, the *Pousada Universal* (*☎ 741-2391, Rua Marquês do Herval 98*) is cheaper, with single/double quartos for US$5/9, including breakfast. The *Hotel Guaibim* (*☎ 741-1114, fax 741-5108, Praça da Independência 74*) is one block in from the port. Single/double/triple apartamentos cost US$15/21/37.

A good mid-range option is *Hotel Rio Mar* (*☎ 741-3408, fax 741-2714*) on Avenida Dendezeiros. It has a pool, and comfortable apartamentos for US$20/35.

The *Hotel Portal Rio Una* (*☎/fax 741-5050*), on Rua Maestro Barrinhão by the riverside, has more comforts and is accord-ingly more expensive – double apartamen-tos with air-conditioning, fridge and TV start at around US$60.

There's a good self-serve restaurant, *Res-taurante Ponto Chic* (*☎ 741-4704, Avenida Maçonica 11*) just across the bridge from the center of town. The Hotel Guaibim also has a decent self-serve lunch buffet. *Restaurant Capixaba* (*Rua Comandante Madureira 88*), along the riverfront, has a wide range of seafood dishes for around US$8 and is popular with locals. At night, all the action takes place at the kiosks along the river-bank. There's often live music.

Getting There & Away

The airport is 15km from the center, and there are daily flights to Salvador.

The bus station (*☎ 741-4805*) is on Rua da Água, about 1.5km from the port. There's frequent bus service daily to Salva-dor. The shortest route is via Ilha de Ita-parica (104km, US$4, two hours), where the bus drops you off at Bom Despacho for the 45-minute ferry ride to Salvador; other buses go all the way around Baía de Todos os Santos (248km, US$6, four hours) into Salvador. There are also regular buses south to Camamu (US$2.50, 1½ hours).

There are daily boat trips to Morro de São Paulo, Gamboa and Boipeba. Although Salvador is only 110km away by sea, the boat service is irregular.

AROUND VALENÇA

The best mainland beach in the vicinity is 16km north of town at **Guaibim**, which is a popular local resort. There are frequent buses, and the beach gets packed at week-ends. If you need anything on the beach, check out the beach bar Cabana Nativa. The owner, Horácio, speaks good English and is happy to give you information about local attractions and activities.

VALENÇA TO ILHÉUS
Morro de São Paulo
☎ 0xx75 • postcode 45410-000

Morro de São Paulo, at the northern tip of Ilha de Tinharé, was an isolated fishing village that was 'discovered' by Brazilian and international tourists 20 years ago. Morro has regularly made it on to the best-beach lists of several Brazilian magazines. The beaches are wonderful, but unfortu-nately the constant noise of tractors rolling up and down the beaches disturbs the peace considerably (tractors are the only vehicles rugged enough for this area). The village is loaded with pousadas, restaurants and bars. Outside summer, it's much less crowded.

Information There's a small information booth as you come off the pier – hours are very erratic. A better source of information is Batuke (*☎ 483-1280, fax 483-1248, batuke@neth.com.br*) on Caminho de Praia, Morro's main street. This well-organized travel agency is also the place to go if you want to find a house for rent. They also provide Internet access.

Change money before you get to Morro. Once there, you'll be able to change cash dollars, but not traveler's checks. There are no ATMs. Many pousadas and restaurants accept Visa and MasterCard.

Things to See & Do Morro de São Paulo has sandy streets where only beach bums, mules and horses tread – there are no roads and no cars. Unfortunately, there are lots of noisy tractors! The clear waters around the island are ideal for scuba diving and for lobster, squid and fish. The settlement com-prises three hills – Morro de Mangaba,

Morro de Galeão and Morro de Farol. Climb from the harbor through the 17th-century **fortress gate** and up to the **lighthouse** (1835). From the top you can survey the island and its beaches. The western side of the island – the river or Gamboa side – is mostly bordered by mangroves, while the eastern side is sandy.

There are four beaches in Morro de São Paulo: **Primeiro Praia**, the rather dirty village beach; **Segunda Praia**, the 'action' beach with nightclubs, beach bars and 24-hour snack huts; **Terceira Praia** with some good pousadas and less development; and **Quarta Praia**. This fourth beach is by far the best – a long, lovely stretch of sand graced by tall, swaying palms bordering the eastern half of the island, and only one bar in sight!

There are daily sailboat trips (☎ 483-1144) to Boipeba, where you can enjoy the sun, drink and swim. Boats leave at around 8 am and return by 6 pm; the trip takes around two hours each way and costs US$15.

Places to Stay Without a doubt, the best deal for longer stays is to rent a house. Outside summer, it's possible to get large, comfortable houses with cooking facilities and beds for seven or eight people for around US$100 to $150 a month. Contact the Batuke travel agency if you want to make arrangements.

Accommodation touts jump on the boat at Gamboa, the stop before Morro, and swarm the tourists; many try to take first-timers to the pousadas along the second beach. It gets very noisy at night here because of the discos, so avoid it if you are looking for peace and quiet. The accommodation scene changes quickly and can be tight during the summer. There are now more than 100 pousadas in Morro de São Paulo, so it's definitely worth hunting around before you commit yourself.

Pousada Ilha do Sol (☎ 483-1118), next to the steep concrete ramp at the beach end of Caminho da Praia, has spacious apartamentos with hammocks, and beach views from the top rooms. It charges US$10/20 single/double in the low season and US$18/28 in during the high.

Pousada O Casarão (☎ 483-1049, fax 483-1022, Praça Aureliano Lima 90), offers great views from the pool and apartamentos for US$35/40 in the low season and US$70/80 in the high. Close to the huge *amendoeira* (almond) tree up the hill from the dock, ***Pousada Natureza*** (☎/fax 483-1044, natureza@neth.com.br, Praça da Amendoeira 46) is a comfortable, colonial-style pousada with swimming pool and sea view. Double apartamentos start at US$40 in low season and US$65 in high season.

If you want something a bit quieter in the wooded hills behind the village, head up Rua da Fonte, the street off Praça Aureliano Lima. The street splits three ways when you come to Fonte Grande, a lovely spot where locals do their washing. Off to the left you'll find the ***Pousada Cairu*** (☎ 483-1074), which has clean quartos for US$10 per person, or US$13 with breakfast. The street running straight ahead (Rua da Lagoa) leads to the ***Pousada Bougainville*** (☎ 483-1158, Rua da Lagoa 195), a breezy, quiet place with double apartamentos with fan for US$20. If you take the right fork, along Rua Porto de Cima, and go to the top of the hill you reach the ***Pousada Colibri*** (☎/fax 483-1056, pousada.colibri@neth.com.br), run by a friendly German family. Bungalows for two to four people all have private bathrooms and verandas. The views are sensational, the location is quiet and the breakfast is excellent. Low-season rates are US$25 for a double, while high season costs US$45. They also have suites for US$30 for a double (US$55 high season). The pousada rents horses and organizes horse safaris on the island. They also offer free baggage transport on their mules from the dock, but you need to call them in advance to arrange it.

The ***Pousada Govinda*** (☎ 483-1244, simonepousadadagovinda@bol.com.br), along Terceira Praia, is a simple, comfortable pousada. Apartamentos cost US$20 per person in the low season. They also provide Internet access. Near the far end of the beach, the ***Pousada Fazenda Caeira*** (☎/fax 483-1042) has spacious grounds and a resort look, but offers reasonable deals on a variety of accommodations. Prices start at US$60/90 single/double.

Places to Eat The main street of Morro, Caminho da Praia, is a regular restaurant strip. New places spring up every summer but the good ones tend to remain. *Ponte de Encontro* offers a wide range of excellent, tasty per-kilo vegetarian food. *Canto do Mar* and *Sabor da Terra* both have good seafood dishes for around US$5. *Espaguetaria Strega* (☎ 483-1033) is a tiny restaurant with excellent pasta – just inside the door is a small bar tended by Messias, a rasta who makes excellent espresso and offers about 40 different sorts of cachaça with native herbs. On Praça Aureliano Lima, *Restaurante Gueto* (☎ 483-1072) seems more like a museum full of antiques. The food is good and it's nice to sit on the veranda and watch the nightly artisan market. If you're renting a house behind town, buy your daily bread and yogurt at *Padaria Seu Bonzinho* in front of the fountain. It's run by Daniel, a friendly Argentine who's lived in Morro for many years. There's a notice board with housing options for rent and other useful information.

Getting There & Away There are several daily flights to Morro from Salvador airport. It's a beautiful 20-minute flight in a small plane and costs US$50. Call Aerostar (☎ 0xx71-377-4406 in Salvador, ☎ 483-1112 in Morro) or Adey Taxi (☎ 0xx71-377-1993 in Salvador, ☎ 483-1280 in Morro).

Boats leave almost every hour from Valença to Morro de São Paulo between 7:30 am and 5:30 pm – later in summer (US$15). If you arrive at Valença later, you should still be able to find someone at the port in Valença to take you, but expect to pay double the price. Nine boats depart daily from Morro for Valença between 6:15 am and 5 pm. It's a relaxing 1½-hour boat ride (US$2). You'll pass mangroves, yachts, doublemasted square-rigged Brazilian 'junks,' and palm-lined beaches that rival the Caribbean and South Pacific in tropical beauty.

If you're in a hurry (don't be!), there are fast boats called *lanchas rapidas,* which do the trip in 25 minutes for US$5.

The ever-increasing popularity of Morro de São Paulo will undoubtedly cause frequent schedule changes – if you're in Salvador you can confirm departure times at Bahiatursa first.

There are also daily direct boats to and from Salvador. The catamaran *Gamboa do Morro* (☎ 0xx75-9147-1677) leaves Morro for Salvador at 9:30 am and arrives at 11:30 am. It leaves from behind the Mercado Modelo in Salvador at 2 pm and arrives in Morro at 4 pm. Cost one-way is US$20.

Boipeba
☎ 0xx75

The island directly south of Ilha da Tinharé is Ilha de Boipeba. The name comes from the Tupi *mboy-peba,* meaning troublesome snake. The village of Velha Boipeba, on the northeastern tip of the island, is much quieter than Morro and more rustic. The coastline is primitive, with more than 20km of beautiful, deserted beaches. Close to the dock where the boat from Valença arrives are the **Primeira Praia** and **Boca da Mata** beaches. Other ocean beaches, from north to south, are **Tassimirim**, **Cueira**, **Moreré**, **Bainema** and **Ponta de Castelhanos**, this last an excellent spot for diving.

Places to Stay & Eat Boipeba gets crowded in summer, and the pousadas fill up quickly. The prices quoted here are for low season.

There are a couple of excellent places to stay in Pontal da Barra, at the southern tip of Ilha de Tinharé where the Rio do Inferno meets the sea. The best is *Pousada Marina de Boipeba* (☎ 9981-1302) on the riverfront, which has apartamentos for US$15 per person. Close by is *Pousada Tassimirim* (☎/fax 9981-2378). It's a bit more expensive, with comfortable apartamentos for US$35.

More rustic accommodation can be found in the center of Velha Boipeba and Vila de Moreré, a smaller settlement close to the beach of the same name. In Velha Boipeba, try *Pousada 7* (☎/fax 9981-5427,

Praça Santo Antônio), which has apartamentos for US$13 per person.

The beach bars serve great seafood snacks. Other good options in Velha Boipeba include **Belladonna** (☎ 783-1039, *Rua da Prainha 5)* for pasta dishes, and **Tinharé** (☎ 783-1161) also on Rua da Prainha, for seafood. Both are simple and cheap.

Getting There & Away There is a boat leaving Valença daily at noon for the 3½- to four-hour trip to Boipeba. In summer there's also a boat at 4 pm. The journey is an initiation into local nature and culture, as the boat weaves through the mangroves and crosses the small rivers that separate these islands. There's a short stopover in the historical town of Cairu, where you can soak up the atmosphere of an old Bahian village, before the boat arrives in Boipeba. The fare is US$3.

If you're in Morro, there's a tractor that leaves for Boipeba every morning. It goes along the beach and drops you off on the northern riverbank. Check times and costs at Batuke in Morro.

Camamu
☎ 0xx73 • postcode 45445-000 • pop 12,000
On the mainland, farther down the coast towards Ilhéus, Camamu is a quiet, picturesque town that sits on a hill above a maze of mangrove-filled islets and narrow channels (no beaches). The town is the port of call for the many tiny fishing villages in the region, and has access by boat to stunning beaches along the Peninsula de Maraú. There's a lively dockside morning market with fish, fruit and drying nutmeg.

Saveiro fishing boats are built and repaired right outside the port. The **Açaraí Waterfalls** are 5km away by local bus or taxi (US$15 roundtrip) and are worth a visit.

Places to Stay & Eat The *Pousada Green House* (☎ 255-2178, *Rua Djalma Dutra 61),* near the port opposite the bus station, is friendly and family-run, and is a great value, with spotless quartos for US$7 per person and larger single/double apartamentos for US$15/20. The downstairs restaurant serves good seafood prato feito for US$3 as well as per-kilo food. *Hotel Rio Açaraí* (☎ 255-2315) is on Praça Dr Francisco Xavier Borges, in the Cidade Alta. However, after a tough walk up the very steep road from the port, what you find is a garish modern hotel with apartamentos from US$25/35.

Getting There & Away The bus station (☎ 255-2222) is near the port in the lower part of town. Buses depart for Valença and Salvador almost hourly, and five buses run daily to Ubaitaba (US$2, 1½ hours) on Hwy BR-101 via Travessão. If you are coming from the south, buses run to Camamu via Ubaitaba and Travessão.

Peninsula de Maraú
☎ 0xx73
If you want to get off the beaten path, this is the place. But you better hurry, because the place is developing into a popular 'hip' holiday destination for Brazilians. The peninsula that goes out to Ponta do Mutá and the village of Barra Grande has one long, dirt road (often impassable after rain), infrequent buses and a handful of very small fishing villages (you won't find many of them on most maps). It's an unspoiled area with some breathtaking beaches, but they are hard to get to without a car.

Barra Grande is a tranquil, slow-paced fishing village at the tip of the peninsula – a great place to stop for a while. The village is bordered by the calm beaches of Camamu Bay on one side and the surf beaches of the Atlantic Ocean on the other. It's the most easily accessible village on the peninsula, and has a wide variety of pousadas and restaurants.

Places to Stay & Eat There are accommodations choices and eateries in Barra Grande and at the beaches. Lots of new pousadas are being built in Barra Grande. The usual price in summer for a double apartamento is around US$35 a night. A couple of good, cheaper options are *Pousada da Dejanira*, with doubles for US$20, and *Pousada do Dendê*, a charming little place with apartamentos for US$33 a

THE NORTHEAST

double. A really fine place is *Pousada Tubarão*, with nice apartamentos for US$40 for a double. There's also a good restaurant attached that serves tasty, fresh seafood dishes. Another good seafood restaurant is the *Restaurante da Naiá*. Lots of restaurants only open during summer.

If you prefer a beach, Praia de Saquaria has the most upmarket pousadas with facilities and prices to match. Try the *Pousada Bahia Boa* (☎ 258-2129, fax 258-2185) or the *Pousada Maraú* (☎ 258-2113, fax 258-2214). Expect to pay around US$60 for a double apartamento.

Getting There & Around During summer, there is a motorboat making two trips daily from Camamu to Barra Grande and back. This is a delightful two-hour voyage (US$3) weaving through several small, isolated islands, including Ilha Pedra Furada, Ilha Grande and Ilha de Campinhas. During summer the boat leaves the port at Camamu at 9 am and 6 pm, and returns from Barra Grande at 7 am and 3 pm. During the rest of the year, it runs only at the earlier time, but there are often boats taking locals to market at Camamu – you should be able to organize a ride by asking around at the pier in Camamu.

Leaving from Itacaré, there are regular jeep services to Barra Grande.

A variety of vehicles serve as 'taxis' in Barra Grande and can ferry you to beaches along the peninsula nearby – prices are always negotiable but average around US$3. You can find them anywhere in town.

Itacaré
☎ 0xx73 • postcode 45530-000 • pop 8000
Itacaré is a quiet colonial fishing town at the mouth of the Rio de Contas, and has some of the best surf south of Salvador. In the past, distance and bad roads shielded Itacaré from a rapid growth in tourism, but with the new coastal road cutting the trip from Ilhéus from four to 1½ hours, the tourist boom has only just begun. **Ribeira, Concha, Tiririca** and **Resende** beaches, to the south of town, are recommended for a swim and surf.

To get to the deserted beaches north of Itacaré, cross the river by long dugout canoe or take the ferry at the waterfront next to the river. The first ferry leaves around 9 am; tickets are US$2 per person. If you feel energetic and are traveling light, you might consider walking 40km north to Barra Grande along stretches of coconut-palm-lined beaches.

Information Itacaré Ecoturismo (☎/fax 251-2224, Rua Lodônio Almeida 209), organizes treks, horse rides and rafting trips in the area, as well as jeeps to Barra Grande. They also rent bikes for US$7 per day. You can rent surfboards for around US$10 a day from Thor Surf Design, on Rua Pedro Longo.

Places to Stay Camping *Estrela do Mar* (☎ 251-2119) has a good location and facilities, right on Praia da Concha near the lighthouse. It gets a bit damp, so don't forget the insect repellent. Sites cost US$5 (US$7 in summer). They also have some chalets for rent for US$35 a double. The best place to stay, especially if you surf, is *Sage Point* (☎/fax 251-2030), 1km from town on Praia Tiririca. It's run by Ana, a friendly Cuban-American who serves a huge, healthy breakfast. Her beautiful wooden chalets get booked up quickly during the summer, but if you can get one, you'll be tempted to stay a while. Low-season prices are US$20/30 single/double; in the high season prices double. Closer to town, a cheaper option is *Pousada do Costinha* (☎ 251-2005, Rua Pituba 2), on a street running parallel to the main road. This pousada has clean apartamentos with balconies and hammock for US$8/15 in the low season and US$40 a double in the high season. *Pousada Estrela* (☎ 251-2006) on Rua Pedro Longo is a clean, friendly place with apartamentos starting at US$10/20, including a big breakfast.

If you're after more comfort, try *Papa Terra Pousada and Restaurante* (☎/fax 251-2137) at Praia da Concha. It has well-appointed apartamentos for US$40/55 during the low season; prices double in summer. The top-end place in Itacaré is the Swiss-developed *Itacaré Eco Resort* (☎/fax

251-2233, reservas@ier.com.br) on Praia São José. It's a sophisticated five-star resort, and tasteful apartments start at US$150 for a double.

Places to Eat Itacaré's restaurant strip is on Rua Lodônia Almeida. *Boca do Forno* (☎ *251-2174)*, on Beco das Flores, serves excellent pizzas in a beautiful floral outdoor setting. The pizzas cost between US$8 and $13, but they're worth it. *Berimbau Restaurante*, on Rua Lodônia Almeida, is a friendly restaurant run by João and Barbara. Their bobó de camarão is a specialty and serves two for US$15. *O Restaurante* (☎ *251-2012, Rua Pedro Longo 150)*, out toward the beaches, serves a good seafood and salad prato feito for US$6. *Mistura Fina*, across the road, is also a good feed. For health foods, stop in at the *Almazen Alimentos Integral (Rua João Coutinho 188)*. Look for the surf mural on the wall outside.

Getting There & Around The bus trip along the scenic coastal road south from Itacaré to Ilhéus takes about 1½ hours and costs US$3. From Ilheús, there are frequent buses, the first leaving at 7 am and the last departing at 7:40 pm.

If you need help with your luggage, boys with wheelbarrows meet every bus arriving in Itacaré. The town center is only a few minutes walk away, but the beaches are a bit of a hike.

ILHÉUS
☎ 0xx73 • postcode 45600-000
• pop 162,000

Ilhéus, the town that Jorge Amado (Brazil's best-known novelist, who died in August 2001) lived in and described in his novel *Gabriela, Cravo e Canela* (Gabriela, Clove and Cinnamon), retains some of the charm and lunacy that Amado fans know well. The colonial center is small and distinctive, with its strange layout and odd buildings; the people are affable; the city beaches are broad and beautiful; and a short walk beyond these, there are even better beaches.

The best thing to do in Ilhéus is just wander. The center is lively, with several old,

gargoyled buildings such as the Prefeitura. If you walk up the hill to the Convento NS da Piedade, there's a good view of the city and coastline. Wherever you end up, it won't be more than a stone's throw from the beach. The Praia da Avenida, close to the city center, is always active.

History
Ilhéus was a sleepy place until cacao was introduced into the region from Belém, in 1881. At the time, Brazil's many sugar estates, which had not followed the lead of other countries and introduced new production techniques to increase sugar output, were reeling from a drop in world sugar prices. Simultaneously, the slave system was finally coming to an end, with many slaves escaping and others being freed. With the sugar plantations in the doldrums, impoverished agricultural workers in the Northeast – black and white – flocked to the hills surrounding Ilhéus to farm the new boom crop: cacao, known as the *ouro branco* (white gold) of Brazil.

Sudden, lawless and violent, the scramble to plant the white cacao fruit displayed all the characteristics of a gold rush. When the dust settled, the land and power belonged to a few ruthless *coroneis* (rural landowners) and their hired guns. The landless were left to work, and usually live, on the fazendas, where they were subjected to a harsh and paternalistic labor system. This history is graphically told by Amado, who grew up on a cacao plantation, in his book *Terras do Sem Fim* (published in English as *The Violent Land)*.

The dreaded *vassoura de bruxa* (witch's broom) disease hurt the area's economy dramatically in the early 1990s. The lush tropical hills are now covered with skinny, shriveled cacao trees unable to bear fruit. If you take a drive you will still see cacao fazendas and rural workers like those Amado wrote about. You can also visit the small Museu Regional do Cacau, the port and a fazenda.

Orientation
The city is sandwiched between hills, beach and a small harbor at the mouth of the Rio

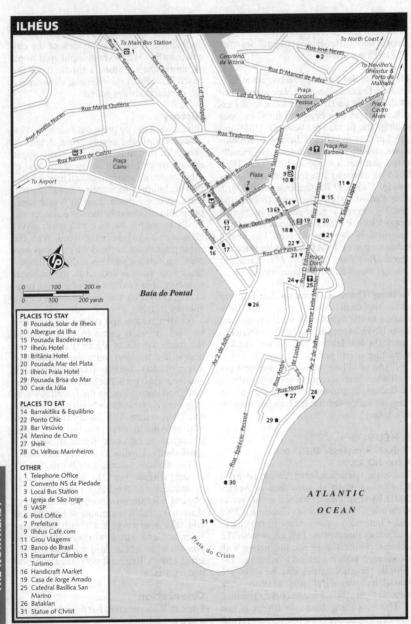

ILHÉUS

Baía do Pontal

ATLANTIC OCEAN

Praia do Cristo

0	100	200 m
0	100	200 yards

To Main Bus Station
To North Coast
To Novilho's, Ilheústur & Porto do Malhado
To Airport

Rua 7a de Setembro
Rua Carneiro da Rocha
Ld Teresópolis
Rua José Neves
Rua D. Manoel de Paiva
Cemitério da Vitória
Ladº da Vitória
Praça Coronel Pessoa
Rua Bento Bento
Rua General Câmara
Praça Castro Alves
Rua Maria Quitéria
Prof. Amélia Nunes
Rua Tiradentes
Rua Araújo Pinto
Praça Rui Barbosa
Rua Ramiro de Castro
Praça Cairu
Rua Marquês de Paranaguá
Rua Eustáquio Bastos
Rua Santos Dumont
Rua Alm. Barroso
Plaza
Rua P. Valladares
Rua Alm. Lemos
Rua Alm. Aurélio
Ave Dom Pedro II
Rua Cel Paiva
Rua D. Eduardo
Praça Dom Eduardo
Traverse Leite Mendes
Av. Soares Lopes
Av. 2 de Julho
Rua Nossa
Rua Angel
Rua Lurdes
Rua Eustácio Pessoa

PLACES TO STAY
8 Pousada Solar de Ilhéus
10 Albergue da Ilha
15 Pousada Bandeirantes
17 Ilhéus Hotel
18 Britânia Hotel
20 Pousada Mar del Plata
21 Ilhéus Praia Hotel
29 Pousada Brisa do Mar
30 Casa da Júlia

PLACES TO EAT
14 Barrakitika & Equilíbrio
22 Ponto Chic
23 Bar Vesúvio
24 Menino de Ouro
27 Sheik
28 Os Velhos Marinheiros

OTHER
1 Telephone Office
2 Convento NS da Piedade
3 Local Bus Station
4 Igreja de São Jorge
5 VASP
6 Post Office
7 Prefeitura
9 Ilhéus Café.com
11 Grou Viagems
12 Banco do Brasil
13 Emcamtur Câmbio e Turismo
16 Handicraft Market
19 Casa de Jorge Amado
25 Catedral Basílica San Marino
26 Bataklan
31 Statue of Christ

THE NORTHEAST

Cachoeira. The airport and the road to the Olivença beaches are in the southern part of town, beyond the circular harbor.

Information

Tourist Office Ilhéustur (☎ 634-3510, Avenida Soares Lopes 1741), opposite the convention center, has limited information, and is open daily from 9 am to noon and 2 to 6 pm. They have a good Web site in Portuguese at www.ilheus.com.br. The information booth at the bus station is only open December to February. Travel agencies (see below) are more useful and can set up excursions easily at reasonable prices.

Money Emcamtur Câmbio e Turismo (☎ 634-3900, Avenida Dom Pedro II 116) changes cash and traveler's checks. It's open weekdays 9 am to 5 pm and Saturday from 9 am to noon. Banco do Brasil is at Rua Marquês de Paranagua 112. There are Banco do Brasil and Bradesco ATMs close to the cathedral.

Post & Communications The post office is on Rua Marquês de Paranagua 200. There's Internet access and good espresso available at Ilhéus Café.Com (Rua General Câmara 38).

Travel Agencies Emcamtur Câmbio e Turismo (☎ 634-3900) can book bus and airline tickets. Grou Viagems (☎ 634-8741, fax 634-8426, Avenida Soares Lopes 528) has reasonable prices and a flexible attitude to planning trips. Trips to Rio do Engenho, Lagoa Encantada and the Eco Parque da Una are worthwhile. Another recommended trip is to Primavera Fazenda, where you'll be taken through the process of cacao production.

Casa de Jorge Amado

The house at Rua Jorge Amado 21, where the great writer lived with his parents while working on his first novel, *O País do Carnaval*, has been restored and turned into a Casa de Cultura, with an interesting display about the man himself. Not many writers can boast this sort of recognition while still

alive, but Amado became a national treasure well before his death in 2001 (see the boxed text for more on his work). It's open daily 9 am to noon and 2 to 4 pm. Cost of admission is US$0.50.

Churches

The **Igreja de São Jorge** on Praça Rui Barbosa is the city's oldest church, dating from 1534, and houses a small sacred-art museum. It's open Tuesday to Sunday from 8 to 11 am and 2 to 5:30 pm. The **Catedral Basílica San Marino** on Praça Dom Eduardo is a unique, eclectic mix of architectural styles.

Museu Regional do Cacao

This museum displays cacao artifacts and modern painting by local artists. It's at Rua AL Lemos 126, and is open Tuesday to Friday 2 to 6 pm, and Saturday and Sunday from 3 to 6 pm. During the holiday season, from December to March, it's also open 9 am to noon.

Special Events

As any knowledgeable Jorge Amado fan would guess, Ilhéus has highly spirited

---

Eco Parque de Una

Forty-five kilometers south of Olivença is the Eco Parque de Una. Here a 2km trail leads through a reserve of lush Atlantic rainforest, where you can spot rare species like the golden-headed lion tamarin.

These unusual monkeys (*Leontopithecus chrysomelas*) have the look and proud gaze of miniature lions: a blazing yellow, orange and brown striped coat, a golden mane and a long, scruffy tail. If you're lucky you'll also see *tatus* (armadillos), *pacas* (agoutis), capybaras and *veados* (deer), which are also native to the area.

Guides will take you on the trail, which includes four suspended bridges, for two hours. There's a nice pool at the end of the trail for a dip. Grou Viagems in Ilhéus runs trips to the park for US$20.

THE NORTHEAST

festivals. The best are the **Gincana da Pesca** in early January; **Festa de São Sebastião** (much samba and capoeira) from January 11 to 20; **Festa de São Jorge** (featuring Candomblé) on April 23; **Festa das Águas** (Candomblé) in December; and, of course, the festivities of **Carnaval**, with its full complement of trios elétricos.

Bahia's Favorite Son

Nobody is more responsible for bringing Bahia to the rest of the world than Jorge Amado. Brazil's most famous romanticist author, Amado's tales have been translated into 49 languages and read the world over.

Born in 1912, Jorge spent his youth in Ilhéus, the scene of many of his later novels. After secondary studies in Salvador, Amado studied law in Rio, but instead of going into practice he decided to become a writer. He surprised critics and the public by publishing his first novel, *O País do Carnaval*, when he was only 19 years old.

An avowed communist, Amado participated in the rebel literary movement of the time, launching two romances set in the cacao zone around Ilhéus: *Cacau* and *Suor*. The first novel was banned by the fascist-leaning Vargas government, an act that only served to increase his popularity. Sent to prison several times for his beliefs, Amado was elected a federal deputy for the Brazilian communist party (PCB) in 1945, but he lost his seat after a disagreement with the party several years later. He left Brazil and lived for more than five years in Europe and Asia, finally breaking ties with the communist party after the crimes of Stalin were revealed to the world.

With *Gabriela, Cravo e Canela* (Gabriela, Clove and Cinnamon), published in 1958, he entered a new writing phase, marked by a picturesque style that intimately described the colorful escapades of his Bahian heroes and heroines.

Amado died of heart failure in Salvador in August 2001, just short of his 89th birthday.

Places to Stay

The accommodations scene in Ilhéus has improved – there's now more of it, and some good budget options. In summer, the prices quoted here rise by about 25%. For camping, see the Olivença section later.

The **Albergue da Ilha** (☎ 231-8938, *Rua General Câmara 31*), is a clean, friendly place with good security. The owner, Murilo, speaks good English and loves his city. It has a dorm for US$5 per person without breakfast. It also has quartos for US$10 per person. Close by, **Pousada Solar de Ilhéus** (☎ 231-5125, *Rua General Camârca 50*) has spotless single/double/triple quartos with fan that cost US$15/22/30, with a good breakfast included. Some of the rooms are better than others – try to get one with windows. Another good deal is **Pousada Mar del Plata** (☎ 231-8009, *Rua AL Lemos 3*). It's well located, clean, and serves breakfast. Single/double quartos go for US$10/15 and apartamentos for US$15/25. **Pousada Bandeirantes** (☎ 231-5760, *Rua AL Lemos 69*) has basic quartos for US$5/10 in the low season and US$10/15 in the high season.

The **Britânia Hotel** (☎ 634-1722, fax 634-1772, *Rua Jorge Amado 16*) is a pleasant old-style hotel with quartos for US$10/20 and apartamentos for US$20/25. **Ilhéus Hotel** (☎ 634-4242, *Rua Eustáquio Bastos 44*), in the center, has a fading grandeur about it. Apartamentos with air-conditioning cost US$15/20/25 for singles/doubles/triples.

The **Pousada Brisa do Mar** (☎ 231-2644), on the beachfront at Avenida 2 de Julho 136, is an art deco building with large, comfortable apartamentos for US$15/20 with fan or US$25 with air-con. The rather dark **Ilhéus Praia Hotel** (☎ 634-2533, fax 634-2550, *Praça Dom Eduardo*) has single/double apartamentos starting at US$90/100, with discounts of 50% out of season.

A special B&B is the **Casa da Júlia** (☎ 231-2756, juliaher_99@yahoo, *Rua Epitácio Pessoa 333*). Her beautiful house, high above the statue of Christ, has a panoramic view to the south of the city. Júlia rents just one double room for US$150, so book well in advance. Murilo of the Albergue da Ilha also rents rooms in his antique-laden house

(☎ 231-3163, *Rua Jorge Amado 89*). The suite has a double bed and two singles and costs US$100, and the quarto with two single beds is US$80. All prices quoted include breakfast and lunch.

If you're feeling like a total splurge, there is the resort hotel *Transamérica Ilha de Comandatuba* (☎ 686-1122, fax 686-1457), which is on its own island (Ilha de Comandatuba) opposite the town of Una, 80km south of Ilhéus. For around US$200 per person per day, you have all meals included, the run of immense grounds, a private beach and every imaginable (well almost) recreational facility.

Places to Eat

Behind the Catedral, along the beach, there are several reasonably priced *seafood stands* with outdoor tables. The center is filled with cheap *restaurants* offering self-serve lunches for a few dollars. *Barrakítika* (☎ 231-8300, *Praça Antônio Muniz 39*) is a popular hangout with outdoor tables, seafood and pizza. There's good live music here on Thursday, Friday and Saturday.

For seafood and great views of the beach, try *Os Velhos Marinheiros* (☎ 231-6671) on Avenida 2 de Julho, with dishes for around US$10 to $25 for two. The recently renovated *Bar Vesúvio* (☎ 634-4724) on Praça Dom Eduardo, has been described in Amado's books and is consequently a popular spot for tourists. It (naturally) serves Arab dishes. Nearby is *Menino de Ouro* (☎ 634-4902, *Rua Luiz Viana 15*), which serves good, cheap dishes, including half-serves. Near the tourist office, *Novilho's* (☎ 9961-2640, *Avenida Lomanto Jr 1808*) is popular with locals and is also a late-night hangout. For fine Arab food and great views of the city, don't miss *Sheik* (☎ 634-1799). Locals consider it to be on Alto do Oiteiro (literally on the heights above the Oiteiro church), although its official address is on Rua NS de Lurdes. It's also crowded late in the evening.

For a great ice cream, try the local fruit flavors at *Ponto Chic*, next door to the Teatro Municipal. There's also good espresso from the kiosk in the plaza out front.

Getting There & Away

Air There is a small airport serviced by Nordeste/Rio Sul/Varig (☎ 0800-710737), VASP (☎ 0800-998277) and TAM (☎ 0800-123100). All have offices at the airport; VASP is also near the post office.

You can fly to several major cities including Rio, Salvador, Recife and Belo Horizonte. If you're returning to Rio, the flights stop at Salvador but are still cheaper than flying directly from Salvador.

Bus Ilhéus is 460km south of Salvador and 315km north of Porto Seguro. From Hwy BR-101 at Itabuna, it's a beautiful 30km descent through cacao plantations to Ilhéus and the sea. For most major destinations, buses leave more frequently from Itabuna than Ilhéus, so it's usually quicker to go to Itabuna first, shuttling to or from Ilhéus. To get to Itabuna from Ilhéus, take the local bus that leaves from the front of the Ilhéus bus station every 30 minutes and costs about US$1.

Buses to Salvador use two different routes. The regular route follows the long sweep around the recôncavo, and is recommended if you want to stop at Cachoeira on the way to Salvador. The other route runs via Nazaré and Ilha de Itaparica, where you change to the ferry for a stunning 45-minute ferry ride into Salvador.

From Ilhéus there are seven buses a day north to Salvador (US$20, seven hours) and two a day south to Porto Seguro (US$11, five hours). To get to Valença, you'll need to go to Itabuna.

Getting Around

To/From the Airport The airport (☎ 231-7629) is at Praia do Pontal, 3.5km from the center. Taxis cost US$5.

Bus The long-distance bus station (☎ 634-4121) in Ilhéus is a 15-minute bus ride from the center. Take any local bus that has Centro as its destination or written on the side near the front door. Local bus rides cost US$0.30. The city bus station is close to Praça Cairu, on the edge of the center. From the station, there is bus service to

Canaveiras, Itabuna, Olivença, the main bus station and the airport.

AROUND ILHÉUS
Olivença
☎ 0xx73

There are good clean beaches, many with beach bars, all the way from Ilhéus to Olivença, a spa town 16km south. You can continue south of Olivença to more remote beaches. The beaches in Olivença are busy on weekends and there's some good surfing at **Batuba** and **Backdoor**, both not far from town. Before you reach Porto Seguro is Eco Parque de Una (see the boxed text earlier).

Places to Stay A good campground en route to Olivença is *Camping Estância das Fontes* (☎ 269-1480) 15km from Ilhéus. It's close to the beach and charges US$5 per person for a campsite.

In Olivença, the excellent HI *Albergue da Juventude Fazenda Tororomba* (☎ 269-1139), on Rua Eduardo Magalhães, is set on a large property with a swimming pool, bar and restaurant. Rates are US$10 per person.

Getting There & Around To get to Olivença take one of the frequent Olivença buses from the city bus station in Ilhéus. The bus travels close to the beaches, so you can pick one to your liking and quickly hop off.

PORTO SEGURO
☎ 0xx73 • postcode 45810-000 • pop 80,000

Porto Seguro, once a settlement of pioneers, is now a refuge for swarms of Brazilian and international tourists who come to party and take in some mesmerizing beaches. The town itself has no beaches, but it has an international airport and well-developed tourist facilities, and there are plenty of beaches nearby. Porto Seguro's coastline is protected by reefs; the ocean is clear, shallow, and calm. Swimming is safe.

Tourism is the number-one industry here – at last count there were more than 800 hotels and pousadas in Porto Seguro, Arraial d'Ajuda and Trancoso! Mercifully, local building regulations limit construction to two stories, so there are no multistory eyesores to spoil the landscape. Other regional industries are lumber, fishing, beans, sugarcane, manioc and livestock.

History

After sighting Monte Pascoal in April 1500, early explorer Pedro Cabral sailed for three days up the coast to find a safe port. The landing, officially considered the first Portuguese landfall in Brazil, was not at Porto Seguro (literally Safe Port), but 16km farther north, at Coroa Vermelha. The sailors celebrated their first mass in the New Land, stocked up on supplies, and set sail after only 10 days on shore. Three years later the Gonçalvo Coelho expedition arrived and planted a marker in what is now Porto Seguro's Cidade Alta (Upper Town). Jesuits on the same expedition built a church, now in ruins, in Outeiro da Glória. In 1526, a naval outpost, convent and chapel (Igreja NS da Misericórdia) were built in Cidade Alta.

In 1534, when Portugal divided its slice of South America into hereditary captaincies, Porto Seguro was given to Pero de Campos Tourinhos. He founded Porto Seguro and seven other villages. Although each village boasted a church, Tourinhos was denounced to the Holy Inquisition as an atheist – apparently the captain didn't keep the holidays and, worse, forced the colonists to work on Sunday. He was shipped off to Portugal, leaving his son to inherit the captaincy.

The Tupininquin, not the Pataxó, were the indigenous tribe around the site of Porto Seguro when the Portuguese landed. They were rapidly conquered and enslaved by the colonists, but the Aimoré, Pataxó, Cataxó and other inland tribes resisted Portuguese colonization and constantly threatened Porto Seguro. Military outposts were built along the coast in Belmonte, Vila Viçosa, Prado and Alcobaça to defend the Portuguese from European attacks by sea and Indian attacks by land.

The Indians still managed to take Porto Seguro on two occasions and, according to colonial documents, reduced Porto Seguro to rubble in 1612 (thus undermining the city's claims to have 16th-century buildings).

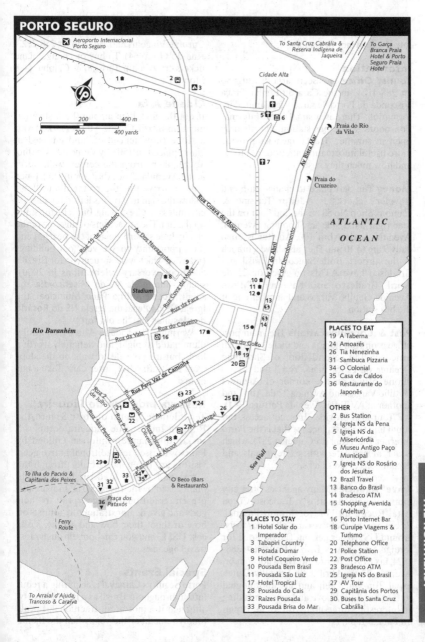

PORTO SEGURO

ATLANTIC OCEAN

Rio Buranhém

Stadium

To Ilha do Pacvio &
Capitania dos Peixes

To Arraial d'Ajuda,
Trancoso & Caraíva

Ferry Route

Cidade Alta

To Santa Cruz Cabrália &
Reserva Indígena de
Jaqueira

To Garça
Branca Praia
Hotel & Porto
Seguro Praia
Hotel

Aeroporto Internacional
Porto Seguro

Praia do Rio
da Vila

Praia do
Cruzeiro

O Beco (Bars
& Restaurants)

Praça dos
Pataxós

Sea Wall

PLACES TO EAT
19 A Taberna
24 Amoarés
26 Tia Nenezinha
31 Sambuca Pizzaria
34 O Colonial
35 Casa de Caldos
36 Restaurante do
   Japonês

OTHER
2 Bus Station
4 Igreja NS da Pena
5 Igreja NS da
   Misericórdia
6 Museu Antigo Paço
   Municipal
7 Igreja NS do Rosário
   dos Jesuitas
12 Brazil Travel
13 Banco do Brasil
14 Bradesco ATM
15 Shopping Avenida
   (Adeltur)
16 Porto Internet Bar
18 Curuípe Viagens &
   Turismo
20 Telephone Office
21 Police Station
22 Post Office
23 Bradesco ATM
25 Igreja NS do Brasil
27 AV Tour
29 Capitânia dos Portos
30 Buses to Santa Cruz
   Cabrália

PLACES TO STAY
1 Hotel Solar do
   Imperador
3 Tabapiri Country
8 Posada Dumar
9 Hotel Coqueiro Verde
10 Pousada Bem Brasil
11 Pousada São Luíz
17 Hotel Tropical
28 Pousada do Cais
32 Raízes Pousada
33 Pousada Brisa do Mar

0   200   400 m
0   200   400 yards

THE NORTHEAST

In 1759, the captaincy of Porto Seguro passed to the Crown and was incorporated into the province of Bahia.

Information

Tourist Office The Secretaria de Turismo (☎ 288-4124) in the Casa da Lenha, Praça Visconde de Porto Seguro, offers limited information. There is a small hotel information booth at the bus station, but it's only open in summer. Travel agencies provide more useful information about things to do and how much they cost.

Money The best place to change cash and traveler's checks is Adeltur Turismo & Câmbio, Shop No 53 on the 2nd floor on the rear right-hand side in Shopping Avenida, Avenida 22 de Abril 100. Adeltur is open daily 9 am to 10 pm. They also have a branch at the airport. Both Banco do Brasil and Bradesco have ATMs on Avenida 22 de Abril. Bradesco also has an ATM on Avenida Getúlio Vargas and another one at the bus station.

Post & Communications The main post office is on Rua Itagibá and there's a branch office on the second floor of Shopping Oceania on Praça Inaiá. You'll find a telephone office on the corner of Avenida Getúlio Vargas and Avenida 22 de Abril and another at AV Tour (Avenida Portugal 344). AV Tour also provides Internet access, but you'll find the best place for that is the Porto Internet Bar (Rua do Cajueiro 237), which is a real net café with six terminals and decent coffee and snacks.

Travel Agencies Many agencies offer city tours and schooner trips to Trancoso, Coroa Alta, Recife da Fora or Monte Pascoal. Prices are competitive, and all seem to be around US$10 per person. The best one for foreign travelers is Brazil Travel (☎ 288-1824, fax 879-1276, braziltravel@uol.com.br, Avenida 22 de Abril 200). Friendly Dutch expat Ton van Creij and his multilingual staff offer all the above and more, including an interesting three-hour visit to the Jaqueira Pataxó Indians.

To buy bus tickets without having to go up to the bus station, go to the helpful Curuípe Viagems and Turismo (☎ 288-2223, Rua do Golfo 64). To buy or change plane tickets, try Adeltur Turismo & Câmbio (see Money).

Cidade Alta

If not the first, then among the first settlements in Brazil, Cidade Alta is marked with a stone (now fenced off and encased in glass) placed in 1503 by Gonçalvo Coelho. To get there from the center, walk north along Avenida 22 de Abril about 1km. Once you've arrived at the roundabout, don't follow the sign that points left to the historic city, unless you're driving, but take the stairs up the hill. The attractions of this part of the city include superb views of the beaches and the opportunity to see very old buildings (many of which were spruced up for Brazil's 500th-anniversary celebrations in 2000), such as the **Igreja NS da Misericórdia**, the small **Museu Antigo Paço Municipal**, the **Igreja NS da Pena**, the **Igreja NS do Rosário dos Jesuitas** and the **old fort**.

Warning: The Cidade Alta is beautifully illuminated at night, and definitely worth a look, but it's not safe to walk up the steps from the traffic circle after dark. Take a bus or taxi.

Reserva Indígena de Jaqueira

Ten kilometers north of Porto Seguro, the Reserva Indígena de Jaqueira occupies 8 sq km of Atlantic rainforest. Guided by Pataxós dressed in traditional native gear, visitors are taken along trails through the forest and shown medicinal and edible plants used by the Indians. The Indians also present traditional dances, pray to their gods and give demonstrations to tourists on how to shoot their bow and arrows. Visits cost US$17 and you can book through most travel agencies.

Special Events

Porto Seguro's **Carnaval** is acquiring a reputation throughout Brazil as a hell of a party, although it is not at all traditional. Locals fondly remember the year when the theme was the Adam and Eve story. Costumes were pretty skimpy to start with, then everyone stripped off as if on cue. The police were called in the following year.

Many of Brazil's favorite musicians have beach homes nearby, and often perform during Carnaval.

Municipal holidays celebrated are listed below.

Terno de Reis January 5–6 – celebrated in the streets and at the churches. Women and children carrying lanterns and *pandeiros* (tambourines) sing *O Reis* and praise the Reis Magos (Three Wise Men).

Puxada de Mastro January 20 – features a group of men who parade a *mastro* (symbolic figure) to the door of Igreja NS da Pena. Decorated with flowers, the mastro is hung in front of the church with the flag and image of São Sebastião, and women then sing to the saint.

Discovery of Brazil April 19–22 – commemorated with an outdoor mass and Indian celebrations. This seems a rather baffling celebration since the Indians were here first and later fared badly at the hands of their 'discoverers.'

Festa de NS d'Ajuda August 15 – the culmination of a pilgrimage starting on April 9. A mass procession, organized in homage to the miraculous saint, is followed by food, drink and live music.

Festa de NS da Pena September 8 – the same as Festa de NS d'Ajuda. This version features the additional enlivenment of fireworks.

Festa de São Benedito December 25–27 – celebrated at the door of the church of NS do Rosário. Boys and girls from Cidade Alta blacken their faces and perform African dances, such as *congo da alma*, *ole* or *lalá*, to the percussion of drums, *cuica atabaque* and *xeque-xeque*.

New Year's Eve December 31 – traditional celebration. This is when everyone rushes around shouting *'Feliz ano novo Baiano/a!'* (Happy New Year, Bahian!), strangers kiss and serious partying ensues.

Places to Stay

Accommodations in Porto Seguro are generally more expensive and abundant than farther south at Arraial d'Ajuda. During the low season there must be at least 20 vacant rooms for every tourist and prices go down by as much as 50%. On the other hand, during the high season rooms can be hard to find. Prices quoted here are for low season.

Places to Stay – Budget

If you intend to camp, try *Mundaí Praia* (☎ 679-2287), opposite the beach 4km north of town on the road to Santa Cruz da Cabrália, or *Tabapiri Country* (☎ 288-2269), just across from the bus station. Both charge around US$5 per person for a tent site.

The *Pousada do Cais* (☎ 288-2112, fax 288-2540, Avenida Portugal 382) is an arty, rustic place with individually decorated single/double rooms for US$10 per person. It's a friendly, family-run place and Neide speaks a bit of English and is very helpful.

Other cheapies close to the action and the ferry south include *Raízes Pousada* (☎ 288-4717, Praça dos Pataxós 196), which has clean, basic apartamentos for US$8 per person without breakfast, and *Pousada Brisa do Mar* (☎ 288-2943, Praça Dr Manoel Ribeiro Coelho 188), which charges US$10 per person with breakfast.

Places to Stay – Mid-Range

The *Pousada Dumar* (☎ 288-1477, estelita@portonet.com.br, Avenida Travessa do Navegantes 11) is a lovely pousada in a quiet location. The owners are friendly and rent good size rooms for US$20 per person. The *Hotel Coqueiro Verde* (☎ 288-2621, coqueiro@coqueiroverde.com.br, Rua Oscar da Rosa Teixeira 1) is an arty place, with lots of interesting sculptures and paintings. It's also a good place for kids, with a small play area and pool. Prices start at US$25 a double. *Pousada Bem Brasil* (☎/fax 288-2532, Avenida 22 de Abril 343) is a well-located pousada, with a pool, parking area and car and buggy rental. Spotless apartamentos are US$23/26. A few doors down, *Pousada São Luíz* (☎ 288-2238, fax 288-2508, pousadasaoluiz@uol.com.br, Avenida 22 de Abril 329) is an excellent mid-range option, with apartamentos for US$24/33. A bit closer to the center of town is *Hotel Tropical* (☎/fax 288-2502, Rua do Cajueiro s/n), a modern hotel with double apartamentos with fridge and fan for US$35.

Opposite the beach at Taperapuan, 6km north of the center, the *Garça Branca Praia Hotel* (☎ 879-2514, fax 879-2574, Avenida Beira Mar Km 67) is another good spot for families, with a large pool and games room. Double apartamentos go for US$60, but they may discount more in low season.

Places to Stay – Top End

The poshest hotel in the area, the *Porto Seguro Praia* (☎ 288-9319, fax 288-2069), about 4km north of town, is set back from the coastal road on Praia de Curuípe. There's a large shady garden and a good recreation set-up for families. Apartamentos start at US$90 a double. Opposite the airport, the *Hotel Solar do Imperador* (☎ 288-1581, fax 288-2647, Estrada do Aeroporto 317) has a pool and great views of Porto Seguro for US$80 a double.

Places to Eat

Restaurants in Porto Seguro are becoming expensive – at least in summer, when many places have a minimum charge per table. Seafood is the obvious specialty here – it's cheap and fresh.

For good sushi, sashimi and hot shrimp dishes (US$5 to $15), try the popular *Restaurante do Japonês* (☎ 288-2592) on Praça dos Pataxós. *Bahiaitalia* on O Beco is a good place for pasta. Also on O Beco, *Bistrô do Helô* (☎ 288-2637) has excellent Bahian seafood – try the spicy moqueca. For the best pizza in town, head for *Sambuca Pizzaria* (☎ 288-2366), on the corner next to Praça dos Pataxós.

Highly recommended is *Casa de Caldos* (Praça Dr Manoel Ribeiro Coelho 7), which serves tasty traditional soups like the seafood *mariscada*, and the beef *vaca atolada*. The soups come with bread and paté, and are cheap at US$3. Next door you'll find Porto Seguro's most chic restaurant, *O Colonial* (☎ 288-1469). It serves expensive seafood dishes but their crepes are reasonably priced and it has a good ambience. *Amoarés* (Avenida Getúlio Vargas 245) serves a good, cheap per-kilo lunch. *Tia Nenezinha* (Avenida Portugal 170) has excellent Bahian cuisine.

Entertainment

Even during the low season, Porto Seguro has lots of budget-package tourists taking advantage of the low prices, and most party very late.

For live music and booze go to Passarela de Álcool ('Booze Alley'), otherwise known as Avenida Portugal. The street is lined with bars and restaurants and the beautiful fruit displays of stalls selling killer *capetas* (a mixture of pineapple, nutmeg, guaraná, condensed milk and vodka).

There's usually live music on O Beco from early on, but after midnight is when the action really starts. If you want to party there's a different hotspot for every night of the week, usually one of the clubs along the northern beaches close to town. They're easy to find, because everyone else is going there too! Clubs charge between US$5 and $10 admission and you can buy tickets in town. Free buses run to and from the shows all night, leaving from Avenida do Descobrimento (walk to the right when you reach the traffic circle and you'll see the buses below).

A couple of the strangest clubs are *Transylvania* (☎ 288-1136), a theme bar complete with cemetery, bats, spiders and monsters, on the beach at Taperapuan, and *Capitania dos Peixes* (☎ 288-3912), on the small island (Ilha do Pacuio) in the middle of the river close to town. It's a surreal place in the evenings, and combines large fishtanks and loud music.

Shopping

Porto Seguro is loaded with shops that sell '5 for $10' T-shirts and '6 for $10' baseball caps. Despite this, there are some talented artisans in town. Check out the galleries on O Beco for some high-quality stuff. There's also a daily hippie market close to Avenida Portugal (Passarela de Álcool). Porto Seguro also has souvenir shops that sell Pataxó jewelry, basketware and earthenware.

Getting There & Away

Air Varig/Nordeste (☎ 288-3327), VASP (☎ 288-1205) and TAM (☎ 288-4926) all have regular flights to Porto Seguro. There is daily service to/from Rio, Brasília and Salvador, and flights on Saturday and Sunday to/from Belo Horizonte.

Bus The turnoff for Porto Seguro from Hwy BR-101 is at Eunápolis, a little over 660km south of Salvador. The bus station is 1.5km outside town on the road to Eunápolis. Schedules change in high season, so there may be more buses than those we list here. The São Geraldo company starts the 24-hour trip to São Paulo at 10 am and 2:40 pm. The first is an executivo bus for US$50 and the later one a leito for US$80. They also run an executivo bus to Rio at 2:40 pm (US$40, 18 hours). Aguia Branca has two daily buses making the 11-hour trip to Salvador. The first leaves at 7:10 pm and costs US$35. The second is a leito costing US$50. There are four daily buses to Ilhéus (US$11, five hours) and 10 to Itabuna (US$9, 4½ hours).

Between 5:30 am and 9:30 pm, buses depart almost hourly to Eunápolis (US$2, one hour) – some are direct buses, others make several stops along the way. Eunápolis is a large transport hub with more frequent departures than Porto Seguro.

Buses to Santa Cruz Cabrália (40 minutes north) run about every hour between 6:20 am and 7 pm. You can also pick them up on Avenida Getúlio Vargas in the center. Four daily buses run north to Belmonte, the first at 8:10 am and the last at 4 pm.

Getting Around
Taxis to the airport or bus station usually cost US$5.

The ferries across the Rio Buranhém provide access to the road towards Arraial d'Ajuda, Trancoso and Caraíva. The pedestrian ferry charges US$0.50 and seems to operate every 15 minutes from dawn until late in the evening, but the car ferry charges US$3 per car (plus US$0.50 per passenger) and operates every half an hour between 7 am and 9 pm. The crossing takes about 10 minutes.

Most local buses running northwards along Avenida Getúlio Vargas pass the bus station, with the exception of the Taperapuan and Santa Cruz Cabrália buses, which run to the northern beaches.

NORTH OF PORTO SEGURO
North of Porto Seguro, next to the sealed coastal road, are several attractive beaches easily accessible by bus and, consequently, not as pristine as those to the south. The nicest are **Mundaí**, 5km north of town, and **Coroa Vermelha**, which has Pataxó craft stands as well as a monument to the discovery of Brazil.

At Km 25, the town of **Santa Cruz Cabrália**, with its terracotta roofs and palm trees, is pleasant enough, but not worth staying overnight. Climb up to the bluff for the view overlooking the town and to visit Igreja NS da Imaculada Conceição, the lonely white church built by the Jesuits in 1630. The elderly caretaker will be happy to tell you the history of the region, as well as the inside story on Cabral's expedition. Fried shrimp and a batida de côco, available at the bars by the church, enhance the view of the offshore reef, the boats and the palm trees that grow in and about the bay of Cabrália.

If you continue north and cross the Rio João de Tiba, you'll come to **Vila de Santo André**, a pretty fishing village that is just starting to feel the effects of tourism. It's a lovely spot.

Places to Stay
Highly recommended is *Victor Hugo* (☎ 0xx73-282-1366), a relaxing pousada on the beach at Vila de Santo André, with very comfortable doubles for US$60.

SOUTH OF PORTO SEGURO
The road south from the ferry across the Rio Buranhém follows a long stretch of dreamlike beaches, with a bluff backdrop. Up on the bluff, a short walk from the beach, are the villages of Arraial d'Ajuda (also known as NS da Ajuda) and Trancoso, which are 4.5km and 26km, respectively, from the ferry crossing. The rush to develop the region south of Porto Seguro continues in full swing. The roads in Arraial d'Ajuda are now paved and there's a sealed road to Trancoso. South of Trancoso, a good unsealed road continues for 42km to the small village of Caraíva.

Arraial d'Ajuda

☎ 0xx73 • postcode 45820-000

Twenty-five years ago, before the arrival of electricity or the road from Porto Seguro, Arraial was a poor fishing village removed from the world. Since then, the international tourist set has discovered Arraial and its desolate beaches, and a time-honored way of life has all but vanished. The village has become chic, and slick shopping galleries sit awkwardly alongside rustic reggae cafés. The increasingly littered main beach is lined with bars and the beach-lounge set, while farther south, the beaches at **Pitinga**, **Lagoa do Sul** and **Taípe** are slightly less developed.

Yet, for some, Arraial d'Ajuda is the place to be. Younger and wilder than Porto Seguro, it's a wonderful place to tan and slough off excess brain cells. Newcomers soon fall into the routine: going crazy every evening, recovering the following morning and crawling back onto the beach for more surf, sun and axé music.

Orientation From the Rio Buranhém ferry, the 4.5km road to Arraial d'Ajuda runs about 100m inland of Praia do Arraial and passes many pousadas. Arraial d'Ajuda itself is built on a little hilltop by the sea, while most pousadas are tucked away on the ocean side of this hilltop. The village's main street, running from the church to the cemetery, is called Broadway. Many of the cheaper restaurants and bars are here. Mucugê is the name of the beach that lies below the maze.

Heading south from Arraial d'Ajuda towards Trancoso, the road passes a series of beaches – Pitinga, Taipe and Rio da Barra – before reaching Trancoso.

Information Arraial now has a post office, telephone office, Internet connections and money exchanges. All are on or close to Broadway.

Travel Agency Arco-Iris Turismo (☎ 575-1672) on Broadway organizes schooner trips to Trancoso and Caraíva. Three-day catamaran trips to the Parque Nacional Marinho de Abrolhos can be arranged for US$150 per person (minimum four people), including food and lodging (bunks on board).

Warning There's now a police post in Arraial d'Ajuda and the attitude of the police toward drug-taking is less tolerant than in the past. Locals also enjoy ripping off gringos on drug deals, so be wary.

Beaches & Paradise Water Park The **Praia Mucugê** is good until 3 or 4 pm when the sun hides behind the hill. Many of the beach bars are venues for do-it-yourself samba and guitar music. They also have good fried shrimp for a few dollars.

Praia Pitinga, the beach closest to Arraial d'Ajuda, has red and green striped sandstone cliffs, sparkling water and large-grained sand.

It's acceptable for women to go topless anywhere on the beaches. Nude sunbathing is OK for both men and women on Pitinga beach and points farther south.

Billed as the largest water park in Latin America, **Paradise Water Park** is a magnet for Brazilian and Argentine tourists, who just love its large pools and water slides. It's next to the beach on Praia Mucugê, with an entry fee of US$20 (half-price for children), a bit cheaper if you buy a ticket at its office in Porto Seguro. It's open daily 10 am to 5 pm in high season.

Places to Stay Out of season, pousadas discount heavily, making some of the midrange options quite good deals. Make sure your room has a properly fitting mosquito net over the bed or, preferably, a fan.

A good cheapie is *Pousada Alto Mar* (☎ 575-1935) at the end of Rua Bela Vista, the dead-end road heading right from behind the church. Comfortable, basic apartamentos with fan go for US$15 per person. It's a quiet place with a great view. For more cheap deals check out Rua Jotobá, which runs parallel to Broadway one block closer to the beach. At the end of the street, the *Pousada Mir a Mar (no phone)* has clean apartamentos with hammocks slung outside for US$5 per person.

Off Caminho do Mar (the street running to the beach, also known as Estrada do Mucugê), you can follow the signs to the *Pousada Erva Doce* (☎ 575-1113, fax 575-1071, ervadoce@portonet.com.br, Caminho da Praia 200). Large, comfortable apartamentos in a beautiful garden setting cost US$15/30 in the low season.

Tucked away on Rua das Amendoeiras, the *Pousada Céu Azul* (☎ 575-1312, Rua das Amendoeiras 61) has a pool, and small, clean apartamentos that go for US$10 per person in the low season and US$20/30 in high season.

A recommended upmarket place is *Pousada Caminho do Mar* (☎/fax 575-1099, Estrada do Mucugê 246), with comfortable apartamentos for US$60 for a double.

Places to Eat If you prefer quantity to quality, *Churrascaria Boi no Quilo*, close to the cemetery, has an 'eat as much as you can' deal for US$3. If you like to eat by the kilogram, *Águia D'Ajuda* (☎ 575-1440, Estrada do Mucugê 130) is the local favorite. It also provides Internet access.

Behind the church on the edge of the bluff, *Mão na Massa* (☎ 575-1257, Rua Bela Vista 125) serves tasty pasta and fish dishes. There's a great view as you eat. *Manguti* (☎ 575-1565) on Rua Caminho do Mar is recommended. Try its filé manguti for US$5. *Rosa das Ventas* (☎ 575-1271, Alameda das Flamboyants 225) is not cheap (mains are about US$20) but its creative mix of Austrian/Bahian cuisine is definitely worth a try. Marcelo's *Sushi Bar* (☎ 575-1679) in Beco das Cores has excellent fresh sushi.

The bars down at the beach have good fried shrimp and other seafood. *Barraca do Faría* at Pitinga is recommended.

Entertainment Arraial d'Ajuda is pretty lively in the evenings. Every summer new bars compete to become the happening place for the season. Cruise Broadway for drinking and lambada or forró dancing – *Raizes do Arraial* is a popular bar. The small shopping lanes off Caminho do Mar – A Galeria d'Ajuda, Beco das Cores and Galería Girassol – have some slick bars for more cashed-up travelers. *Gringo Louco* on Caminho do Mar near Beco das Cores, gets very busy late in the evening. People also gather on Praia de Mucugê to sing, dance and howl at the full moon.

Getting There & Around For ferry details, see the Getting Around section for Porto Seguro. From the ferry landing there are four approaches to Arraial d'Ajuda: a lovely 4km hike along the beach, a taxi to town, a VW Kombi to Mucugê beach or a bus to town. VW Kombis also congregate in front of the church on Broadway to ferry passengers to the beaches. Bicycles can be hired at several shops on Broadway.

Trancoso
☎ 0xx73 • postcode 45820-000

Trancoso lies on a grassy bluff overlooking the ocean and fantastic beaches. The central praça, known as Quadrado, is lined with small, colorful colonial buildings and casual bars and restaurants nestling under shady trees. Horseback riding is quite popular around the area, and there are some lovely walks along the beaches. Double hanggliding is also popular at Rio da Barra, 3km north of town.

Places to Stay Trancoso is busy in the summer, but you should be able to negotiate sizeable reductions (around 50%) during the low season. For New Years and January, on the other hand, it's almost impossible to find a bed without reservations. Your best bet if you are planning a long stay is to rent a house in the village, as places on the beach are expensive. Generally, you should be able to rent a house for around US$10 a day in low season. Look for signs reading casa de aluguel or aluga casa as you wander around. The young touts who congregate at the entrance to the Quadrado can also be helpful in finding a place, but if you go with them you're unlikely to get as good a discount as if you went alone. Prices quoted here are for low season.

The colorful *Pousada Sol da Manhã* (☎/fax 668-1003, aart@uol.com.br), on the Quadrado, is a rustic place with clean group rooms for US$10. A short walk from the Quadrado, *Pousada Mundo Verde*(☎ 668-1279, mundoverde@portonet.com.br) is a lovely place set on the bluff leading down to the Rio Trancoso. Large apartamentos with verandas and sea views are US$30 for a double. Next to the school with the water tower on Rua Itabela is the friendly *Pousada Quarto Cresente* (☎/fax 668-1014). The pousada has comfortable apartamentos, a well-stocked library, a swimming pool and superb breakfast. Double quartos with fan start at US$20, double apartamentos at around US$25 (US$45 in the high season). They also have a few houses for rent.

The *Pousada Puerto Bananas* (☎/fax 668-1017) on the Quadrado, is probably the prettiest in town. It's a bit more expensive, with double apartamentos for US$45 and some fully equipped chalets for up to four people for US$55.

Places to Eat The *Maré Cheia*, on the Quadrado, has a good self-serve per-kilo for US$3 and prato feito for US$2. *Sorvetería Trancoso*, close by, serves tasty homemade ice cream.

Away from the Quadrado, food is cheaper. *Jonas* and *Amendoeira*, both on the asphalt road (turn left if you're walking away from the Quadrado), serve good, cheap seafood. On the beach, head for beach bar *Raios do Sol*, where they prepare peixe amendoeira – fish that are wrapped and them cooked in the leaves of the large almond tree behind the bar. *É uma delícia.*

Entertainment The scene changes from summer to low season, when many places close. If you want out-of-season nightlife, make sure you're here from Thursday to Saturday. *Para-Raio* is an ambient restaurant and dancing bar with outdoor tables under massive trees. One of the owners is famous singer Elba Ramalho. They have live concerts in summer but close in low season. Next to the telephone office, *Loucas Lanches* serves sandwiches during the day, but at night it's a real gathering point for locals and visitors. *Geração 2000* is a large dance club open on weekends. Occasionally,

raves are organized at secluded locations along the beach out of town, complete with bars, sophisticated sound and lighting systems and all-night dancing. Trancoso's three-day New Year's techno raves on the beach are legendary.

Getting There & Away From Porto Seguro, there are two ways to get to Trancoso. The first is via Hwy BR-367, but the 82km-long paved road is much farther than if you cross from Porto Seguro to Arraial d'Ajuda. From Arraial, you have several options: a beautiful 13km walk along the beach, the dirt road that begins 2km south of town, or the paved road. Buses will take the sealed road, but the dirt road has more charm. The bus from Arraial to Trancoso leaves every two hours from 7 am to 7 pm and costs US$3. Buses from Trancoso to Porto Seguro leave almost every hour from 7 am to 7 pm. Schedules change with the seasons, so check times, which are posted on the window of the bus ticket office in Trancoso (near the square).

Another way to get to Trancoso is by schooner from Porto Seguro – they leave daily at 9 am and cost around $10 per person.

Caraiva
☎ 0xx73 • postcode 45824-000

Without electricity, cars or throngs of tourists, the hamlet of Caraiva is primitive and beautiful. The village is strung up along the eastern bank of the mangrove-lined Rio Caraiva. The bus stops on the far side of the river (which is becoming rapidly developed), where small dugout canoes ferry passengers across to the village for US$0.50. The beaches are long and deserted and dashed by churning surf. A warning: The black-sand streets of the village get incredibly hot – take footwear with you at all times.

Boat trips up the Rio Caraiva and to the Parque Nacional de Monte Pascoal, and horseback riding to a Pataxó Indian village are easily organized in the village.

Places to Stay & Eat The *Pousada da Terra* (☎ 9985-4417) is a rustic establishment right on the beach, with a natural-food restaurant attached. Simple quartos cost US$15 per person, with breakfast included. The *Pousada da Lagoa* (*☎/fax 9985-6862, lagoa@caraiva.com.br*) is more comfortable and has a generator and a bar/restaurant. Single/double apartamentos cost US$20/40 in the low season. Another good option is the *Pousada Casinhas da Bahia* (*☎ 9985-6826*), with apartamentos for US$15/30. There are a few even simpler and cheaper places to stay. Try the well-kept *Cantinho da Duca* (*☎ 288-2329*) on the beach for US$12/20. Duca also makes great vegetarian food.

Brilho do Mar is a simple restaurant serving typical Bahian food – the *bobó de camarão* and seafood moquecas (US$10 for two) are recommended. It's run by a fisherman who brings the fish in his own boat. Another good place is the *Restaurante do Pacha* on the beach.

Curuípe, a tiny fishing village, 9km north of Caraiva, now has accommodations. Most are very expensive, but one cheaper place is *Pousada Paradiso Curuípe*, which charges US$20 per person in low season. It's also possible to stay with villagers – speak to Baiano at his restaurant on the beach.

Getting There & Away Buses leave Trancoso daily at 9:20 am and 12:30 pm for the 42km trip (US$2, two hours) along a reasonable dirt road to Caraiva. Buses return to Trancoso twice daily. There is a daily bus from Caraiva at 7 am to Itabela, on Hwy BR-101, for connections north and south.

There is no road south along the coast from Caraiva – the options are to hire a boat or walk. It's a beautiful 40km walk along the beach to the small town of Cumuruxatiba, passing through the Parque Nacional de Monte Pascoal and the village of Corumbau (12km from Caraiva), where there are accommodations. Cumuruxatiba also has several accommodation options and daily buses to/from Itamaraju on Hwy BR-101. The walk is best done over two days, and it's only necessary to cut inland once.

Corumbau
☎ 0xx73 • postcode 45980-000

Corumbau, on the southern side of the national park, is not as primitive as Caraiva, but it's a beautiful spot, with lots of things to do. You can go canoeing through the mangroves or on the Rio Corumbau, snorkel on offshore reefs, visit the Pataxó Indian village, or just wander along trails through the rainforest.

Places to Stay The *Jocotoka Eco Resort* (*☎ 288-2291, fax 288-2540, jocotoka@uol.com.br*) is not your usual Brazilian resort hotel – there's not a TV in sight. Run by German expat Jochen Heckhausen, the resort is geared toward taking maximum advantage of the natural beauty of the area, and has all the equipment for you to enjoy it, like kayaks and diving gear. Bungalows go for US$30/45 single/double in the low season (US$60/80 in high season). Prices include breakfast. If you're in Porto Seguro, drop in and ask for Jochen at the Pousada do Cais for more details. It's definitely worthwhile, especially if you're trying to get away from the tourist hordes in summer. If you're looking for something a bit less expensive, there are a couple of simple pousadas in the village.

Getting There & Away One bus leaves the large town of Itamaraju on Hwy BR-101 for Corumbau daily at 2:30 pm. The trip takes about three hours and costs US$3. It's is also possible to be picked up by a Jocotoka boat in Caraiva (US$60 for up to 4 passengers).

PARQUE NACIONAL DE MONTE PASCOAL

On April 22, 1500 the Portuguese, sailing under the command of Pedro Álvares Cabral, sighted the broad, 536m-high hump of Monte Pascoal (Mt Easter), their first glimpse of the New World. The sailors called the land Terra da Vera Cruz (Land of the True Cross).

The 225 sq km national park, 690km from Salvador and 479km from Vitória, contains a variety of ecosystems: Atlantic rainforest, secondary forests, swamplands and shallows, mangroves, beaches and reefs. The variety of the landscape is matched by the diversity in flora and fauna. There are several monkey species, including the endangered spider monkey, two types of sloth, anteaters, rare porcupines, capybaras, deer, jaguars and numerous species of bird.

The visitors' center is 14km from the western (Hwy BR-101) end of the park. It's open daily 8 am to 4 pm, and you can pick up a guide there who can accompany you on the trails or a climb of the mountain itself. The coastal side is accessible by boat or on foot from Caraiva to the north and Corumbau to the south. The northeastern corner of the park, below Caraiva, is home to a small number of Pataxó Indians, who took over control of the park in 2000.

There are no direct buses to the park. The closest town to the park is Itamaraju – a taxi from there to the visitors' center will cost approximately US$15.

CARAVELAS
☎ 0xx73 • postcode 45900-000 • pop 10,000
Caravelas, 74km east of Teixeira de Freitas (which is on Hwy BR-101), is not only a gateway to Parque Nacional Marinho de Abrolhos (see that section, following, for access information) but also an interesting town in its own right, with a large fishing community and good beaches nearby.

Information
The Instituto Baleia Jubarte (Humpback Whale Institute), at Rua 7 de Setembro 214, operates a visitors' center 8 am to 6 pm weekdays. It also shows videos about whales and has useful information about the Parque Nacional Marinho de Abrolhos. Abrolhos Turismo (☎ 297-1149, fax 297-1109), on the Praça Dr Imbassahi, is a commercial travel agency, but it also acts as a kind of unofficial tourist office. Staffers speak English, French, German and Spanish. There is also a small tourist information

office at Sectur (☎ 297-1113, Rua Barão do Rio Branco 65).

Visa card cash withdrawals can be made at the Banco do Brasil on Praça Dr Imbassahi.

Things to See & Do
To get a feel for the town's thriving fishing industry, check out the **Cooperativa Mista dos Pescadores**, on Rua da Cooperativa opposite the hospital, or wander along the riverfront to **Praça dos Pescadores**, where the fishermen hang out after coming in with the day's catch. For beaches, head for **Praia Grauçá** (8km north of town on a dirt track) and **Pontal do Sul** (across Rio Caravelas). In addition, there are the island beaches of **Coroa da Barra** (half an hour by boat) and **Coroa Vermelha** (1½ hours by boat).

It's possible to go by boat along the mangrove-lined Rio Caravelas to the next beach town to the south, **Nova Viçosa**. Ask at the tourist office, Abrolhos Turismo (see Information earlier in this section) or Abrolhos Embarcações (see the Parque Nacional Marinho de Abrolhos section). A snorkeling day trip to the island of Coroa Vermelha costs US$30 per person with lunch.

Places to Stay & Eat
All prices in Caravelas rise at least 20% during its Carnaval, considered by locals to be the third best in the state after those of Salvador and Porto Seguro. Similar price increases can also be expected during summer.

There's a basic campground, *Camping Ubaitá*, at the entrance to Caravelas, but it's a long walk from the center. In town, *Pousada Shangri-Lá* (☎ 297-1059, Rua Barão do Rio Branco 219) is a friendly, cheap place to stay. Quartos cost US$5/10 single/double and apartamentos go for US$7/15. The *Pousada Caravalense* (☎/fax 297-1182) is across the road from the bus station. This pousada has apartamentos that are US$10/15.

Across the river on Ilha da Caçumba, the *Pousada & Spa da Ilha* (*☎/fax 297-1109*) is a real retreat, with a bar and a vegetarian restaurant. You can also get a massage here. Rooms cost around US$15 per person. To get there, call the pousada and they will send someone across in a boat to pick you up.

At Praia Grauçá, the budget option is the *Pousada do Juquita* (*☎ 674-1038*), close to the final bus stop. Clean apartamentos cost US$10 per person. Also on Praia Grauçá is Caravelas' top-end option, the four-star *Hotel Marina Porto Abrolhos* (*☎ 674-1082, fax 674-1060, Rua da Baleia 333*) with chalets starting at US$70.

The best places to eat are out along the beach at Praia Grauçá. Seafood enthusiasts should head for *Museu da Baleia* for a seafood plate. In town try *Gaiola Aberta* (*Rua 7 de Setembro 178*) for home cooking, or *Encontro dos Amigos* (*☎ 297-1600, Rua das Palmeiras 370*) for seafood specials.

Getting There & Away

Air The Aeroporto das Conchas (*☎ 297-1183*) is 14km from town. Pantanal Linhas Aéreas flies to Caravelas from São Paulo.

Bus The bus station (*☎ 297-1151*) is in the center of town on Praça Teófilo Otfoni. The Expresso Brasileiro bus company runs five buses daily from Teixeira de Freitas on Hwy BR-101 to Caravelas via Alcobaça, the first at 6:50 am and the last at 6:20 pm. The trip takes about two hours and costs US$3.

Regular local buses to Barra (for Praia Grauçá) leave hourly from 7:30 am until 10 pm. The fare is US$0.50.

PARQUE NACIONAL MARINHO DE ABROLHOS

Abrolhos, Brazil's first marine park, covers an archipelago 80km offshore from Caravelas and nearby reefs and expanses of ocean. In 1832, Charles Darwin visited here while voyaging on HMS *Beagle*. The archipelago consists of five islands, but the only inhabited one is Santa Bárbara, which has a lighthouse, built in 1861, and a

handful of buildings. Abrolhos is being preserved because of its coral reefs and crystal-clear waters. Underwater fishing within the park is prohibited. The only approach is by boat, and staying on the islands is prohibited. The Brazilian navy considers the area strategic, so only underwater photography is permitted.

From June to October the 913 sq km park is home to a large number of humpback whales, which come to give birth in the warm waters. Whale-watching is becoming very popular.

Getting There & Around

Caravelas is the most popular gateway to the park, with several operators offering a wide range of options, from day trips to five-day cruises. From Caravelas, Abrolhos Turismo (see the Caravelas Information section) runs a popular two-day schooner trip, with an overnight stay on board, for US$140 per person. The price includes park entrance fees, all meals, soft drinks and water. Snorkel rental costs an extra US$10. They also offer day trips for US$80. Abrolhos Embarcações (*☎ 0xx73-297-1172*), at Avenida das Palmeiras 2 in Caravelas, offers a similar two-day trip, or day trips by launch for US$75, including snacks and drinks.

From Arraial d'Ajuda, Arco Iris Turismo (*☎ 0xx73-9985-6606*) on Broadway organizes three-day catamaran trips that cruise south along the Bahian coast, then on to Abrolhos. The fare of US$150 per person includes food, lodging (bunks on the boat), transport and visitor's license from the Capitânia of Porto Seguro. A minimum of four passengers is needed.

West of Salvador

FEIRA DE SANTANA
☎ 0xx75 • postcode 44000-000
• pop 430,000

At the crossroads of Hwys BR-116 and BR-324, Feira de Santana is the main city of Bahia's interior, and a great cattle center. There's not much to do or see here except the **Feira do Couro**, the big Monday cattle market – which is great fun, with lots of leather bargains – and the **Mercado de Arte Popular** (open daily except Sunday).

Special Events

Two months after Carnaval, in April or early May, Feira de Santana is the scene of the **Micareta** – a 65-year-old local version of Carnaval that brings together the best trios elétricos of Salvador, with local blocos, samba schools and folklore groups. It also attracts around 150,000 spectators.

The main action of the Micareta takes place on Avenida Getúlio Vargas, the city's main street, where 20 trios bop along for five days. The festivities begin on Thursday with a boisterous dance and opening ceremony. For those who missed out on Carnaval in Salvador, the Micareta could be the next best thing.

Places to Stay & Eat

There are several cheap hotels near the bus station, such as the **Hotel Samburá** (☎ 221-8511, Praça Dr Jackson do Amauri 132), which charges US$10/20 for singles/doubles. In the top price range, there's the **Feira Palace** (☎ 221-5011, fax 221-5409, Avenida Maria Quitéria 1572). It's a four-star affair with double apartamentos starting at US$60. For good regional food, try **O Picuí** (☎ 221-1018, Avenida Maria Quitéria 2463).

Getting There & Away

Frequent buses make the two-hour journey from Salvador for US$3. The bus station on Avenida Presidente Dutra features an eye-catching mural that was painted by Lénio Braga in 1967.

LENÇÓIS

☎ 0xx75 • postcode 46960-000 • pop 6400

Lençóis (pronounced leng-**sow**-iss) lies in a gorgeous, wooded mountain region – the Chapada Diamantina, an oasis of green in the dusty sertão. You'll find solitude, small towns steeped in the history and superstitions of the garimpeiros (prospectors), and great hiking to peaks, waterfalls and rivers. If you want to see something different in Brazil, and have time for only one excursion

into the Northeastern interior, this is the place to go.

The natural beauty of the region and the tranquility of the small, colonial towns have attracted a steady trickle of travelers for several years; some have never left. These new residents spearheaded an active environmental movement that successfully lobbied the government to declare much of the surrounding region a national park.

History

The history of Lençóis epitomizes the story of the diamond boom and subsequent bust. After earlier expeditions by bandeirantes (bands of Paulistas who explored the Brazilian interior while searching for gold and Indians to enslave) proved fruitless, the first diamonds were found in Chapada Velha in 1822. After large strikes in the Rio Mucujê in 1844, a motley collection of prospectors, roughnecks and adventurers arrived from all over Brazil to seek their fortunes.

Miners began searching for diamonds in alluvial deposits. They settled in makeshift tents which, from the hills above, looked like sheets of laundry drying in the wind – hence the name of Lençóis (sheets). The tents of these diamond prospectors grew into cities: Vila Velha de Palmeiras, Andaraí, Piatã, Igatú and the most attractive of them all, the stone city of Lençóis. Exaggerated stories of endless riches in the Diamantina mines precipitated mass migrations, but the area was rich in dirty industrial stones, not display-quality gems.

At the height of the diamond boom, the French – who purchased diamonds and used them to drill the Panama Canal (1881–1889), St Gothard Tunnel, and London Underground – built a vice-consulate in Lençóis. French fashions and bons mots made their way into town, but with the depletion of diamonds, the fall-off in French demand (and subsequently the fall in diamond prices on the international market), the abolition of slavery, and the newly discovered South African mines, the boom went bust at the beginning of the 20th century.

The town's economy has long since turned to coffee and manioc cultivation and to tourism. But diamonds are what the locals still dream of. Powerful and destructive water pumps were banned in 1995, so the last few miners have returned to traditional methods to extract diamonds from the riverbeds.

Geology

According to geologists, the diamonds in Chapada Diamantina were formed millions of years ago near present-day Namibia (Bahia was contiguous with Africa before the continental drift). The diamonds were mixed with pebbles, swept into the depths of the sea that covered what is now inland Brazil, and imprisoned when the seabed turned to stone. Ultimately this layer of conglomerate stone was elevated, and the forces of erosion released the trapped diamonds, which then came to rest in the riverbeds.

Information

The Secretária de Turismo Lençóis (☎ 334-1327) has a tourist office on Avenida Senhor dos Passos. They display photographs of the main attractions in the Chapada Diamantina and sell copies of Roy Funch's excellent *A Visitor's Guide to the Chapada Diamantina Mountains*. Hours are 8 am to 6 pm daily.

Money Banco do Brasil on Praça Horacio de Mattos charges a US$10 fee to change cash and US$20 for traveler's checks (any amount). It doesn't charge for Visa withdrawals. It's always possible to change dollars around town with no fee – ask at your pousada or one of the travel agencies.

Travel Agencies For information about tours in Lençóis or the Chapada Diamantina, seek out Olivia Taylor, a very helpful young Englishwoman who has made Lençóis her home. Olivia speaks English, Spanish, some French, and Portuguese with a Lençóis accent. She can be contacted at her agency H2O in the Pousada dos Duendes (see Places to Stay – Budget). Olivia can arrange all of the trips available in Lençóis, either with her own car or through the other agencies.

Lentur (☎/fax 334-1271), on Avenida 7 de Setembro, runs day trips by car to several

destinations within the national park for US$15 per person (a guide, admission fees and flashlights are included in the price). Cirtur (☎ 334-1133, Rua da Baderna 41) offers similar deals.

Things to See & Do

The city is pretty and easily seen on foot, although, unfortunately, most of the buildings are closed to the public. See the 19th-century **French vice-consulate**, a beige building where diamond commerce was negotiated, and **Casa de Afrânio Peixoto** (House & Museum of Afrânio Peixoto), with the personal effects and works of the writer. The **Prefeitura Municipal**, at Praça Otaviano Alves 8, is a pretty building with interesting black-and-white photos of old Lençóis. Also worth a visit is **Museu do Garimpo & Lanchonete Zacáo**, a small museum run by local historian Mestre Oswaldo, which displays various mining relics and artifacts.

If you've been doing a lot of walking and need a massage, visit Deiter (☎ 334-1200), a German artist who has a gallery in town. He has magic hands, and charges US$20 for an hour – it's well worth it!

Special Events

The principal holidays take place in January and September. **Festa de Senhor dos Passos** starts on January 24, and culminates on February 2 with the *Noite dos Garimpeiros* (Prospectors' Night). **Semana de Afrânio Peixoto**, a week dedicated to the author, is held from December 11 to 18 and coincides with the municipality's emancipation from slavery. **Lamentação das Almas** is a mystical festival held during Lent. (Lençóis is also noted for Jarê, the regional variation of Candomblé.)

Another important celebration is the **Festa da São João**, from June 23 to 25. There's a huge street party, bonfires outside every house, and traditional dancing.

Places to Stay

Lençóis has plenty of places to stay, but you should still try to reserve at weekends – and definitely book in advance during the high seasons: January/February and June/July.

THE NORTHEAST

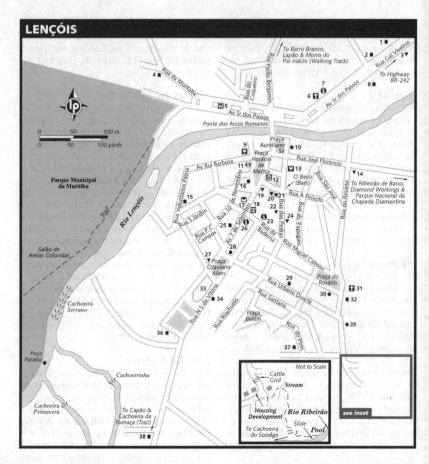

LENÇÓIS

To Barro Branco,
Lapão & Morro do
Pai Inácio (Walking Track)

Rua Cel Viveiros

To Highway
BR-242

Rua da Muritiba

Rua do Coqueiro

Av Sr dos Passos
Ponte dos Arcos Romanos

Parque Municipal
da Muritiba

Praça
Aureliano
Sé

Praça
Horácio
de
Mattos

Av Rui Barbosa

Rua José Florencio

O Beco
(Bars)

Rua São José

To Ribeirão de Baixo,
Diamond Workings &
Parque Nacional da
Chapada Diamantina

Rio Lençóis

Rua Voluntários Pátria

Rua 10 de Novembro

Rua das Pedras

Rua do Rosário

Rua do Papagaio

Salão de
Areias Coloridas

Rua S Jardim

Rua 7 de Setembro

Rua P C
Campos

Rua da
Baderna

Rua A Peixoto

Rua Miguel Calmon

Praça
Otaviano
Alves

Praça do
Rosário

Cachoeira
Serrano

Rua N S da Vitória

Rua Urbano Duarte

Rua Santana

Rua Riachuelo

Praça
Belém

Rua
do Pires

Poço
Paraíso

Cachoeirinha

Cachoeira
Primavera

To Capão &
Cachoeira da
Fumaça (Trail)

Not to Scale

Cattle
Grid
Stream

Housing
Development

Rio Ribeirão

Slide

Pool

see inset

To Cachoeira
do Sossego

Most of the cheaper places have collective rooms and charge on a per-person basis. For longer stays, contact a travel agency about renting a house.

Places to Stay – Budget

Pousada & Camping Lumiar (☎ 334-1241) on Praça do Rosário has shady campsites, new bathrooms, a bar and an excellent but pricey French restaurant. The cost for a site is US$4 per person. There's also a pousada with rooms with shared bathrooms in an old, very beautiful colonial house for US$10 per person without breakfast.

The ***Pousalegre*** (☎/fax 334-1124) on Rua Urbano Duarte is a favorite with travelers. The rooms are certainly basic (there's a lack of windows and furniture), but the friendly staff and good breakfast (and other meals) more than compensate. Quartos cost US$5 per person without breakfast or US$8 per person with it included.

The ***Pousada dos Duendes*** (☎/fax 334-1229, oliviadosduendes@zaz.com, Rua do Pires s/n) is a small pousada with a relaxed atmosphere. It's a short walk from the center in a quiet location. Collective rooms cost US$5 per person, or US$8 with breakfast.

LENÇÓIS

PLACES TO STAY
1 Casa da Geléia
2 Estalagem Alcino
4 Pousada Casa da Hélia
8 Pousada Canto das Águas
15 Pousada Diangela
25 Pousada Nossa Casa
29 Pousalegre
32 Pousada & Camping Lumiar
34 Hotel Colonial
36 Pousada de Lençóis
37 Pousada dos Duendes
38 Portal Lençóis

PLACES TO EAT
3 Pizza na Pedra
14 Beco da Coruja
19 Beija Flor
20 Acaraje e Cia
21 Trattoria Bell'Italia
22 Salon Mistura Fina
24 Dona Joaninha
27 Picanha na Praça

OTHER
5 Bus Station
6 Igreja Senhor dos Passos
7 Tourist Office
9 Venedo Bar
10 Mercado Municipal
11 Banco do Brasil
12 Museu Zacáo
13 Club 7
16 Old French Vice Consulate
17 Post Office
18 Telephone Office
23 Cirtur
26 Lentur
28 Prefeitura Municipal
30 Casa de Afrânio Peixoto
31 Igreja Rósario
33 Open-Air Theater
35 Sr Dazim Horse Rental

They also have new apartamentos, some with verandas, for US$10 including breakfast. The pousada also has Internet facilities, but it's quite expensive as there's no local service provider and you must call long-distance to Salvador to connect. They also serve dinner every evening, with tasty vegetarian options and vegan meals on request.

The *Pousada Diangela* (☎ 334-1192) on Rua Voluntárias da Patria, is a large, bright building with a pleasant eating area and

quartos for US$8 per person (US$10 with breakfast). Apartamentos cost US$15 per person with breakfast.

Pousada Nossa Casa (☎ 334-1258), in the center of town on Avenida 7 de Setembro, is a friendly place run by Ana and Ze Henrique. An excellent budget option, quartos are US$10 per person with breakfast, a bit less in the low season. They also have new apartamentos for US$15 per person.

The *Pousada Casa da Hélia* (☎ 334-1143) on Rua da Muritiba is in a quiet area a short walk from the bus station. It's another traveler's favorite, with quartos for US$10 per person with the pousada's famous breakfast included.

Places to Stay – Mid-Range

The *Estalagem Alcino* (☎/fax 334-1171, Rua Tomba Surrão 139) is in a beautifully converted colonial building. Quartos cost US$15 per person and apartamentos US$30, including a highly recommended breakfast. Local artist Alcino speaks a bit of English and French.

The *Hotel Colonial* (☎/fax 334-1114, Praça Otaviano Alves 750) has pleasant single/double/triple apartamentos for US$15/30/45. Discounts of up to 20% apply in the low season. Highly recommended for solo, mature travelers, *Casa da Geléia* (☎/fax 334-1151, Rua Gal Viveiros 36) has several apartamentos for rent, including some new ones with great views of the surrounding countryside. Hosts Zé Carlos and Lia are very friendly. Zé Carlos, a lawyer in town, speaks good English and is also a keen birder. The cost for a double is US$25 in the low season and US$35 in the high. The range of homemade jams here is unbelievable, and even if you don't choose to stay here, come along and have a taste! You won't be able to resist taking some trekking with you.

Places to Stay – Top End

Discounts of up to 30% apply at all these hotels in the low season. The *Pousada Canto das Águas* (☎/fax 334-1154, cantodasaguas@gd.com.br) on Avenida Senhor dos Passos has a great position in a landscaped garden

THE NORTHEAST

beside the river. Facilities include a restaurant, bar and swimming pool. The apartamentos overlook the small cascades that provide the pousada's background music and name ('Song of the Waters'). Prices start at US$40/50/60 for singles/doubles/triples, including an enormous breakfast. Book well in advance during summer. At night, dinner-plate-sized toads guard the front gate!

At the top end of town is the attractive **Pousada de Lençóis** (☎ 334-1102, fax 334-1201, Rua Altina Alves 747), with gardens, swimming pool, restaurant and bar. Single/double apartamentos with air-conditioning start at US$40/60. Books about the region are sold at the reception desk.

The luxury five-star hotel in town is the **Portal Lençóis** (☎/fax 334-1233, portal@svn.com.br), on Rua Chacára Grota. Suites start at US$90 a double. There are great views of Lençóis from the poolside, but it's a long, uphill walk from the center.

Places to Eat

If you like breakfast, you'll never want to leave Lençóis, where it's included in the room price of numerous lodgings, which seem to be competing for the coveted 'BBB' (Best Breakfast in Brazil) title. A local breakfast staple is *baje* (a warm, buttered manioc pancake with the consistency of a very chewy Styrofoam polymer). After breakfast, you've only got a few hours until you're faced with equally magnificent culinary options for the other meals of the day.

If you're camping or not eating breakfast at a pousada, check out **Dona Joaninha** on Rua das Pedras, which serves an excellent spread. **Beija Flor** on Praça Horacio de Mattos, the town's main square, offers yummy potato bread sandwiches, crepes, juices, yogurt and fruit salads.

Starfruit for your salad

The vegetarian restaurant **Beco da Coruja**, on Rua do Rosário, offers tasty soups, pizza and other specialties. Carnivores should head for **Picanha na Praça** (☎ 334-1248, Praça Otáviano Alves 62) for a highly recommended barbecue. Over the river on Rua Gal Viveiros, the rustic **Pizza na Pedra** (☎ 334-1272) makes the best pizza in town and is open only at night.

Acaraje e Cia serves great juices and amazing *bolinho de queijo* (hot fried balls of dough filled with melted cheese), a must in cold weather. It's on a small square on the Rua das Pedras as is **Trattoria Bell'Italia** (☎ 334-1146, Rua das Pedras 68), a good Italian restaurant with friendly hosts/cooks/waiters Claudia and Dario. For a real taste of Europe, visit **Salon Mistura Fina**, also on the square just off Rua das Pedras. They serve good, cheap food, with vegetarian options. It's owned by Dalvinha, who likes to chat while cooking.

The **Pousalegre** (see Places to Stay earlier in this section) serves inexpensive meals – Rosa's moqueca is justly famous.

Entertainment

Veneno Café Bar on Praça Horacio de Mattos is the only bar that stays open late. It has good music and ambience. On weekends, it all heats up at **Club 7** on Rua das Pedras. Locals refer to it fondly as Inferninho (Little Hell).

Shopping

Night stalls on Praça Horácio de Mattos sell crochet, lacework, trinkets and bottles of colored sand collected at nearby Salão de Areias Coloridas. Many craft stores on Rua das Pedras and Rua Miguel Calmon sell similar stuff. For jams, you can't go past the Casa da Geléia (see Places to Stay earlier in this section).

Getting There & Away

Air The airport is 25km east of Lençóis. There are flights Monday, Wednesday and Friday to and from Salvador and Brasília with Varig/Nordeste (☎ 334-1394), and a chartered flight from São Paulo every Saturday, for which you can get tickets from

Venturas e Aventuras Turismo (☎ 0xx11-3872-0362) in São Paulo.

Bus The bus station is on the edge of town, beside the river. Buses to Salvador leave daily at 11:30 pm and Monday, Wednesday and Friday at 7:30 am. Buses to Lençóis leave Salvador at 7 am and 11:30 pm. The six-hour trip costs US$15. If you arrive in Lençóis in the early hours, there will always be tour reps and pousada owners waiting to greet you. Most allow you to stay in their pousada the rest of the night and will only charge for breakfast. If you want to change pousadas next day, there's usually no problem. Tour company reps are also happy to drop you off at the pousada of your choice if you've already organized one.

Car Lençóis is 13km off Hwy BR-242, the main Salvador-Brasília route. There's a fuel station some 22km east of Lençóis on Hwy BR-242, in Tanquinho. The nearest station to the west is around 30km away. It's not a good idea to rely on the improvised fuel station in Lençóis, which may or may not be open, have fuel or want to sell it.

Getting Around
A taxi to or from the airport will cost around US$20. Once there, the town is easily covered on foot. For transport farther afield, see the following section on Parque Nacional da Chapada Diamantina.

PARQUE NACIONAL DA CHAPADA DIAMANTINA
Many of the foreigners and Brazilians who came to visit have settled permanently in Lençóis. They have been the backbone of a strong ecological movement, in direct opposition to the extractive mentality of the diamond miners and many of the locals. Riverbeds have been dug up, waters poisoned and game hunted for food and sport. Much of the land is continually ravaged by forest fires, while the hunting and depletion of habitat has thinned the wild animal population severely.

After six years of bureaucratic battles, biologist Roy Funch helped convince the government to create the Parque Nacional da Chapada Diamantina to protect the natural beauty of the area. Signed into law in 1985, the park very roughly spans the quadrangle between the towns of Lençóis and Mucujê, Palmeiras and Andaraí. The park, 1520 sq km of the Sincora Range of the Diamantina Plateau, has several species of monkey, beautiful views, clean waterfalls, rivers and streams, and an endless network of trails. Although bromeliads, velosiaceas, philodendrons and strawflowers are protected by law, these plants have been uprooted nearly to extinction for the ornamental plant market.

The park is particularly interesting for rock hounds, who will appreciate the curious geomorphology of the region.

For information regarding minimizing the impact of camping on fragile ecosystems, see the Minimum Impact Camping section under Accommodations in the Facts for the Visitor chapter.

Information
The park has little, if any, infrastructure for visitors. However, camping in the park is free and you don't need a permit; you can either stay in tents or small caves. For one-day trips you need a daypack, walking shoes, hat, sunscreen and insect repellent. For overnight trips you also need a sleeping bag, a big backpack and reasonably warm clothes. You can easily rent gear in town.

The Parque Nacional da Chapada Diamantina map included in this book should give you a good idea of the great hiking opportunities in the park. If you can, get hold of a copy of Roy Funch's book *A Visitor's Guide to the Chapada Diamantina Mountains*, which has a lot of information in English on the flora, fauna, history and geology of the area.

There are three types of guides to be found in Lençóis: those who simply show the way, those who go to the same place that you're going, setting a cracking pace so you need to keep up with them, and guides who have made the effort to learn and pass on information about the local flora and fauna. We highly recommend you choose one of the latter.

THE NORTHEAST

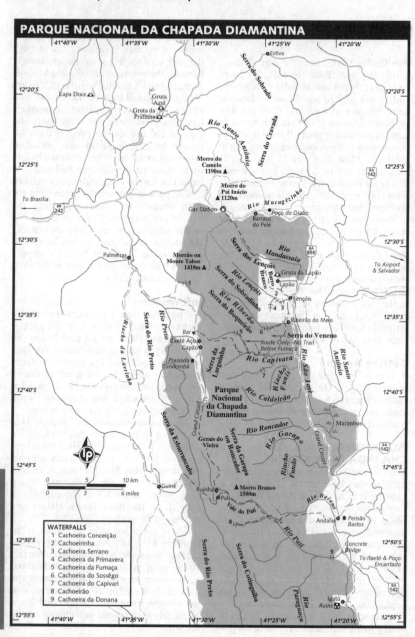

PARQUE NACIONAL DA CHAPADA DIAMANTINA

WATERFALLS
1 Cachoeira Conceição
2 Cachoeirinha
3 Cachoeira Serrano
4 Cachoeira da Primavera
5 Cachoeira da Fumaça
6 Cachoeira do Sossêgo
7 Cachoeira do Capivari
8 Cachoeirão
9 Cachoeira da Donana

Knowledgeable guides, such as Roy Funch and Olivia Taylor, can greatly enhance enjoyment of any trip into the park, and we recommend you take one. Whether you do or not, you should definitely not go alone. In the descriptions of park hikes that follow, we've indicated those trips that would be dangerous without a guide.

Funch, an ex-American from Arizona and now a naturalized Brazilian citizen, came to Brazil 20 years ago with the Peace Corps. He has very detailed knowledge of the region. Contact him through the Fundação Chapada Diamantina (☎ 0xx75-334-1305), at Rua Pé de Ladeira 212 in Lençóis.

Taylor (see Travel Agencies in the Lençóis section) is an excellent guide who knows the history, geography and biology of the area, as well as the trails. For the three-day walk to Cachoeira da Fumaça, she charges US$20 per day, including food. In the village of Capão, Claude Samuel runs trips into the park from the Pousada Candombá (☎ 0xx75-332-2176). Claude speaks English and French, and his treks have been recommended by readers.

Recommended local guides are Rao (☎ 0xx75-334-1544), João (☎ 0xx75-334-1221), Trajano (☎ 0xx75-334-1143), Zoi (ask for him in town or at the hotels), Luiz Krug (☎ 0xx75-334-1102 or ask for him at the Pousada de Lençóis), Henrique Gironha (☎ 0xx75-334-1326), Virginia (☎ 0xx75-334-1331) and Rosa from the Pousalegre. All are based in Lençóis and most speak English.

Andrenalina (☎ 0x75-334-1261) and Nativos da Chapada (☎ 0xx75-334-1314) will take you rappelling at the Lapão cave and elsewhere in the park.

For horse rental, contact Senhor Dazim (marked on the Lençóis map as 'Sr Dazim Horse Rental'), who has horses available. There's no sign on his house, so you may have to ask around – everyone in the neighborhood knows him. You can choose from his list of horse rides and treks, which are all accompanied. Sample prices per person are one hour for US$3, half a day for US$20, full day for US$26, and three days for US$60. Negotiate discounts for groups of three or more. Taurino on Rua das Pedras

also organizes horse trips. You can also watch him making his colored sand creations, which is very interesting.

Bus service is infrequent and scarce, particularly to the remote parts of the park.

Day Trips

These trips all begin in Lençóis. Some can be done on foot or horseback, while others are best by car or in a tour arranged by local agencies. Several should be done only with an accompanying guide.

Rio Lençóis You can start a pleasant hike along the Rio Lençóis by following a trail southwest from the bus station (see the Lençóis map) and continuing through the Parque Municipal da Muritiba, upstream to Cachoeira Serrano (a series of rapids) and Salão de Areias Coloridas (literally 'Room of Colored Sands'), where artisans gather their matéria prima for bottled sand paintings. If you continue up the river, you'll see Cachoeirinha waterfall on a tributary to your left, and after passing Poço Paraíso water hole, you'll see the Cachoeira da Primavera waterfall on another tributary on your left. The walk from the bus station to Cachoeira da Primavera should take around 1½ hours on foot.

Ribeirão do Meio The relaxing hike from Lençóis to Ribeirão do Meio takes about 45 minutes. Take the road up from Camping Lumiar, ignoring the left turn you'll see after 100m, and continue until the road comes to an end at an upmarket housing development. After continuing for a short distance, take a left fork onto a trail that descends and crosses a stream. Keep following the track until you reach a ridge overlooking Rio Ribeirão, a tributary of Rio São José.

At the foot of the ridge, you'll find Ribeirão do Meio, a series of swimming holes with a natural waterslide (bring old clothes or borrow a burlap sack). It is *very* important not to walk up the slide: Several bathers who have done so have met with nasty accidents. Instead, swim across to the far side of the pool and climb the dry rocks at the side of the slide before launching off.

THE NORTHEAST

Upstream from Ribeirão do Meio, a trail leads to the lovely **Cachoeira do Sossêgo** waterfall, with a deep pool at its base and rock ledges for diving. The hike involves a great deal of stone-hopping along the riverbed. Don't attempt this hike without a guide, as there have been several fatal accidents recently. On *no* account should you attempt this trail during high water or rain: The river stones are covered with lichen, which becomes impossibly slippery. To walk from Lençóis to Cachoeira do Sossêgo and back takes around five hours.

Gruta do Lapão This is probably the largest sandstone cave in South America. Access is tricky and it's necessary to take a guide. The walk takes around four hours one way.

Other Caves These three sights are best visited by car – the guided day trips offered by travel agencies and pousadas in Lençóis usually take in all of them. **Lapa Doce** (70km northwest of Lençóis, then a 25-minute hike to the entrance) is a huge cave formed by a subterranean river. Access to the cave is via an immense sinkhole. Inside there's an impressive assortment of stalagmites and stalactites that prompt erotic comparisons. Entry is US$1.

About 12km from this cave are **Gruta da Pratinha** and **Gruta Azul**, two more interesting caves that you can visit for US$1.

Rio Mucugêzinho This river, 25km from Lençóis, is a super day trip. Take the 7 am Lençóis to Salvador bus and ask the driver to let you off at Mucugêzinho Bar – the bus passes this place again at around 4 pm on its return trip to Lençóis. Pick your way about 2km downstream to **Poço do Diabo** (Devil's Well), a swimming hole with a 30m waterfall. About 200m upstream from where the bus drops you off you'll find Rita and Marco, who have set up house in a cave, and run a snack bar outside.

Morro do Pai Inácio Morro do Pai Inácio (1120m) is the most prominent peak in the immediate area. It's 27km northwest of Lençóis and easily accessible from the highway. An easy but steep trail takes you to the summit (200m above the highway) for a beautiful view.

Hikers may want to take the trail along Barro Branco between Lençóis and Morro do Pai Inácio – allow four or five hours one way for the hike.

Palmeiras & Capão Palmeiras, 56km west of Lençóis by car, is a drowsy little town with a slow, slow pace and a scenic riverside position. The streets are lined with colorful houses. There is one pousada in the town and a couple of cheap places to stay.

The hamlet of Capão is 20km southeast of Palmeiras by road (see the later Grand Circuit section for a description of the hiking trail connecting Capão with Lençóis). From here, there's a 6km trail (two hours on foot) to the top of **Cachoeira da Fumaça**, also known as the Glass Waterfall after missionary George Glass, which plummets 420m – the longest waterfall in Brazil. The route to the bottom of the waterfall is very difficult, and isn't recommended without a guide.

The Three-Day Walk

To go to the bottom of Cachoeira da Fumaça is a tiring three-day walk, but much easier than the Inca Trail. The walk itself is extremely beautiful, passing other waterfalls on the way and enabling you to sleep in caves. You leave Lençóis in the morning of the first day and arrive in Capão on the third day, taking detours along the way to see the many waterfalls. An extra day can be added walking back to Lençóis or you can continue with the Grand Circuit.

The Grand Circuit

The grand circuit of the park covers around 100km and is best done on foot in a counterclockwise direction. It takes about five days, but you should allow eight days to include side trips such as Igatú and Cachoeira da Fumaça. We strongly recommend that you undertake this circuit with a guide. Recently, a man who has been living in Lençóis for nearly two years got lost for five days here with no food and only just survived.

Lençóis to Capão You'll need a full day to hike this section. From Lençóis, follow the main trail south and then west, crossing Rio Capivara several times. When you reach the 'bar,' take the track to the left. When you reach Caeté Açu, follow the road to Capão.

The tiny settlement of Capão serves as a base for the highly recommended hike to Cachoeira da Fumaça (see the description in earlier Day Trips section). In Capão, you can camp or stay at the *Pousada Candombá* (*☎/fax 0xx75-332-2176*) for US$15 per person. It's a rustic place in a beautiful natural setting.

Capão to Vale do Patí This section, which crosses the beautiful plains region of Gerais do Vieira, is best covered in two comfortable days, although it's possible to do it in one very long day. You can camp overnight on the plains or sleep in a cave called Toca do Gaucho.

Vale do Patí & Ruinha to Andaraí This section takes a day, but you should also allow a day to putter around the Vale do Patí before leaving: for example, doing a side trip to Cachoeirão (a delightful waterfall) or enjoying the atmosphere in the tiny ghost settlement of Ruinha.

Poço Encantado & Igatú Once you reach Andaraí, these side trips are highly recommended. Poço Encantado, 56km from Andaraí, is an underground lake that is clear blue and stunningly beautiful. You'll need a car to get there; hitching is difficult because there is very little traffic. (Your guide can arrange for a car here, or you can arrange for a car to be brought down from Lençóis that can then take you back to Lençóis after the side trips.)

Igatú, 12km from Andaraí, is a small community with an intriguing set of ruins from the diamond era and earlier (highly recommended). Either walk or drive to Igatú. You can stay overnight here at either *Pedras de Igatú* (US$20 per person and highly recommended) or the cheaper *Pousada Diamantina*. If you need to stay in Andaraí, either camp or try *Pousada Ecológica* (*☎ 0xx75-335-2176*) a comfortable pousada with a pool and bar that runs about US$15 per night per person.

Andaraí to Lençóis This is not a very interesting walk. It's along a dirt road, not a trail, and the scenery is the destruction caused by machine mining. Many choose to bus this section, but if you decide to walk, allow two days. Buses run irregularly; if you are doing a trek your guide should arrange transport ahead of time. On the first night, camp at a site near Rio Roncador. After the Rio Roncador, you pass Marimbus, a microregion with characteristics similar to the Pantanal. Olivia Taylor (see the Lençóis Travel Agencies section) organizes excellent canoe trips that pass the Cachoeira do Roncador and continue to the Rio Paraguaçu – the biggest river that starts and finishes in Bahia. The two-day camping/canoeing trip costs US$100 including transport, equipment, guides and food.

Sergipe & Alagoas

Sergipe

Sergipe is Brazil's smallest state. It has the four zones typical of the Northeast: *litoral, agreste, zona da mata* and *sertão*. The coastal zone is wide and is sectioned with valleys, and many towns are dotted along the rivers.

What is there to see? There are a couple of interesting historical towns – Laranjeiras in particular is well worth a visit – and the towns along the Rio São Francisco, principally Propriá and Neópolis, have a unique and captivating culture. The beaches, with their shallow, muddy waters, are not up to snuff, and you may find that the capital, Aracaju, is about as memorable as last Monday's newspaper.

ARACAJU
☎ 0xx79 • postcode 49000-000
• pop 430,000

Aracaju just may be the Cleveland of the Northeast. The city has little to offer the visitor – there is no colonial inheritance – and it is visually quite ordinary. Even the beaches are below the prevailing high standard of the Brazilian Northeast. That said, it has a friendly and relaxed environment and is a pleasant enough place to spend a couple of days if you have plenty of time on your hands. If you're coming from the south, it's the first city with a real 'Northeastern' feel about it.

Aracaju, 367km north of Salvador and 307km south of Maceió, was Brazil's first planned city. The modest requirements of the original plan called for a grid-pattern intersected by two perpendicular roads less than 2km long. The city outgrew the plan in no time, and the Brazilian norm of sprawl and chaotic development returned to the fore. In recent years, the center of the city has been revitalized, with many impressive old buildings being restored and pedestrian malls created.

History

Aracaju was not the most important city in Sergipe during the colonial era. In fact, when it was chosen as the new capital in 1855, Santo Antônio de Aracaju was a small settlement with nothing but a good deep harbor – badly needed at the time to handle the ships transporting sugar to Europe.

With residents of the old capital of São Cristóvão on the verge of armed revolt, the new capital was placed on a hill 5km from

Highlights

- Day trips to historic sugar towns of Laranjeiras and São Cristóvão in Sergipe

- Propriá, Neópolis, Penedo and other colonial river towns along the Rio São Francisco

- Magnificent palm-lined beaches north of Maceió

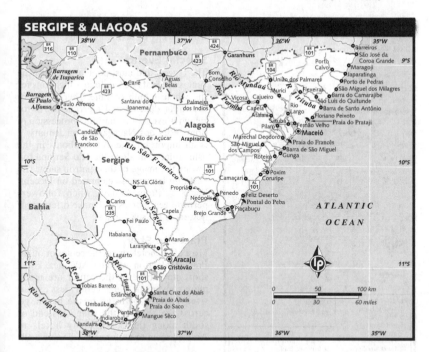

SERGIPE & ALAGOAS

the mouth of the Rio Sergipe. Within a year an epidemic broke out that decimated the population of the city, which the residents of São Cristóvão naturally saw as an omen telling them that Aracaju was destined to be a poor capital.

Information

Tourist Office Emsetur, the state tourist organization in Sergipe, is trying hard to grab a slice of the rich tourist cake that its adjacent states, Bahia and Alagoas, have been enjoying in recent years. The Centro do Turismo on Rua Propriá houses the Bureau de Informações Turísticas (☎ 214-6446), which sells useful maps of Aracaju and São Cristóvão for US$0.10 each. It's open daily 8 am to 8 pm. The complex also backs onto an arts and crafts market, the Rua 24 Horas shopping arcade, bars and cafés. For tourist information in Portuguese, there's an information hotline you can reach at (☎ 1516).

Money There is a branch of Banco do Brasil at Praça General Valadão 341 in the center. Bradesco has an ATM at Praça Fausto Cardoso for Visa withdrawals.

Post & Communications The central post office is at Rua Laranjeiras 229. The telephone office is on the other side of the road at No 296, opposite Rua 24 Horas, and is open daily from 7:30 am to 9 pm. Aracaju has no Internet cafés.

Internet Resources Some useful sites about Aracaju and the rest of the state include:

www.aracaju.com.br – in Portuguese, but with some great links

www.guiasergipano.com.br – in Portuguese, but easy to surf around, with some good links and photos

www.vivabrazil.com/sergipe.htm – in English and Portuguese, with photos and useful links at the bottom of the page

THE NORTHEAST

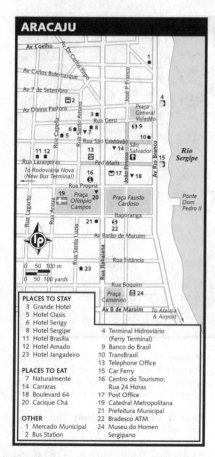

ARACAJU

PLACES TO STAY
3 Grande Hotel
5 Hotel Oasis
6 Hotel Serigy
8 Hotel Sergipe
11 Hotel Brasília
12 Hotel Amado
23 Hotel Jangadeiro

PLACES TO EAT
7 Naturalmente
14 Carraras
18 Boulevard 64
20 Cacique Chá

OTHER
1 Mercado Municipal
2 Bus Station

4 Terminal Hidroviário
    (Ferry Terminal)
9 Banco do Brasil
10 TransBrasil
13 Telephone Office
15 Car Ferry
16 Centro do Tourismo;
    Rua 24 Horas
17 Post Office
19 Catedral Metropolitana
21 Prefeitura Municipal
22 Bradesco ATM
24 Museu do Homen
    Sergipano

Beaches

On the sandy barrier island of Santa Luzia, at the mouth of the Rio Sergipe, **Praia Atalaia Nova** (*atalaia* is Portuguese for watchtower) is a popular weekend beach.

Praia das Artistas, **Praia Atalaia** and **Praia Aruana** are the closest beaches to the city. They are crowded (watch out for traffic jams on weekends) and heavily developed with hotels and motels, restaurants and beach bars, the latter a source of inexpensive seafood.

Farther south on the road to Mosqueiro, **Praia Refúgio** is the prettiest and most se-

cluded beach close to Aracaju. It's 15km from the city by taxi or local bus.

Special Events

The biggest and most popular event of the year is the **Festa de São João**, which runs for the whole month of June. There's lots of fireworks, dancing and merriment. As for religious events, the maritime procession of **Bom Jesus dos Navegantes**, on January 1, is an important one. All the boats in the fishing fleet sail along the Rio Sergipe following the image of their patron saint. The **Festa de Iemanjá** is celebrated on December 8 at Praia Atalaia, when followers perform ceremonies and make offerings of flowers to the sea goddess.

Places to Stay

Most of the hotels are in the center or out at Praia Atalaia on Avenida Atlântica. For a short stay, those in the center are much more convenient and generally less expensive. If you want to go to the beach, go across the river to the island instead of south along the coast. Many hotels in Aracaju seem to prefer cash – don't we all!

Budget The best budget option in town is the *Hotel Amado* (☎/*fax 211-9937, Rua Laranjeiras 5320*). It has clean quartos for US$8/14 single/double. Apartamentos cost US$10/18 with fan or US$15/23 with air-conditioning. A rock-bottom choice in the center of town is the *Hotel Sergipe* (☎ *214-2898, Rua Geru 250*), where quartos are US$6 per person and apartamentos US$10. Be aware that this hotel is favored by local clientele as a short-time joint, and the area at night is a transvestite hangout.

For much better value, try the *Hotel Oasis* (☎ *214-2125, fax 222-5288, Rua São Cristóvão 422*), which has bright apartamentos starting at US$18/27. The *Hotel Brasília* (☎ *224-8020, fax 224-8023, Rua Laranjeiras 580*) has apartamentos with cable TV for US$22/32, with a 10% discount for cash payment.

Mid-Range & Top End A boxy but popular mid-range hotel is the *Hotel Jangadeiro*

(☎/fax 211-1350, Rua Santa Luzia 269) in the city center. It provides clean apartamentos at US$30/40. The *Hotel Serigy* (☎ 211-1088, fax 214-5928, Rua Santo Amaro 269) has well-worn but comfortable apartamentos costing US$35/45. It offers a 20% discount for cash payment.

A bit fancier is the three-star *Grande Hotel* (☎/fax 211-1383, Rua Itabaiana 371), which provides a good value: apartamentos with air-conditioning and fridge for US$30/40/51 for singles/doubles/triples, with a 15% discount for cash.

If you want a five-star hotel in Aracaju, the modern *Del Mar Hotel* (☎ 255-1000, fax 255-2324, Avenida Santos Dumont 1500) is the place. Doubles cost US$90, with a 30% discount for cash payment.

Places to Eat

Cacique Chá (☎ 214-3739) is a garden restaurant on Praça Olímpio Campos and a popular meeting place for the 'in' crowd. *Naturalmente* (Rua Santo Amaro 282) is a well-stocked health-food store that serves vegetarian lunches. The cafés at Rua 24 Horas are good for snacks and drinks. A couple of good self-serve lunch places in the center are *Carraras* (☎ 224-6866, Rua São Cristóvão 165) and *Boulevard 64* (☎ 213-7086, Rua João Pessoa 64).

There are lots of restaurants serving Northeastern specialties like *carne do sol*. A really good one is *O Miguel* (☎ 243-1444, Avenida Antônio Alves 340). Popular with locals is *Boigordo Caju-Ieba* (☎ 243-1101), on Rua do Boigordo in the beach town of Aruana. In addition to regional favorites they have good seafood. Praia Atalaia has a lot of bars and restaurants and is a good spot to wander if you're looking for cheap eats at night, when the center is pretty dead.

Getting There & Away

Air The major Brazilian airlines fly from Aracaju to Rio, São Paulo, Salvador, Recife, Maceió, Brasília, Goiânia and Curitiba.

You'll find a Varig office (☎ 224-4477) at Rua Itabaiana 390, VASP (☎ 224-1792) at Avenida Barão de Maruim 67 and Trans-Brasil (☎ 211-1233) at Rua São Cristóvão 14.

Bus Long-distance buses leave from the Rodoviária Nova (New Bus Station), 4km east of the center. There are eight buses a day to Salvador. Fares on standard buses are US$8, on executivos US$20 and on *leitos* (super-comfortable overnight expresses) US$33. Four of these buses take the Linha Verde route south along the coast (4½ hours), and the rest go inland via Entre Rios (six hours). There are four departures a day for the trip north to Maceió (US$12, five hours); some sections of the road are heavily potholed, so it can be slow going. Two departures a day to Recife take nearly nine hours and cost US$21. There's one direct bus a day to Penedo (US$5, three hours), and seven buses a day to Neópolis, where there is access to Penedo by a short ferry ride across the Rio São Francisco.

For details on transport to São Cristóvão and Laranjeiras, see those town sections. Note that bus services for these two towns operate mostly from the Rodoviária Velha (Old Bus Terminal, in the center on Avenida Divina Pastora).

Getting Around

To/From the Airport The airport (☎ 212-8500) is 11km east of town, just past Praia Atalaia. From the Rodoviária Velha, take the Aeroporto bus (US$0.50). A taxi from the center will cost about US$8.

Bus The Rodoviária Nova is connected to the Rodoviária Velha by a frequent shuttle service (US$0.50, 15 minutes). It departs from a large shelter with a series of triangular roofs about 100m to your right as you exit the Rodoviária Nova. A taxi to the center from here costs US$3.

The Rodoviária Velha is the terminal for local runs, including trips to São Cristóvão and Laranjeiras. To reach Praia Atalaia, take a bus marked Caroa Domeio/Santa Tereza from the Rodoviária Velha.

Boat From the Terminal Hidroviário (Ferry Terminal), there are frequent ferries to Barra dos Coqueiros (US$0.40) and Praia Atalaia Nova (US$0.55, or US$0.80 on weekends) on Ilha de Santa Luzia until 11 pm. The ferry terminal at Praia Atalaia Nova is sinking into the river, so the ferry now docks a short bus ride away from the main beach.

LARANJEIRAS

☎ 0xx79 • postcode 49170-000 • pop 22,000

Nestled between three lush, green, church-topped hills, Laranjeiras is the colonial gem of Sergipe, and an easy day trip from Aracaju. Filled with ruins of old sugar mills, terracotta roofs, colorful colonial facades and stone roads, the town is relatively unblemished by modern development. There are several churches and museums worth visiting and the surrounding hills offer picturesque walks with good views. It's a charming little town, easy to get to and well worth a few hours sightseeing or a day or two exploring the town, the nearby sugar mill and the countryside.

History

Laranjeiras was first settled in 1605. During the 18th and 19th centuries it became the commercial center for the rich sugar and cotton region west of Aracaju. At one point there were more than 60 sugar mills in and around Laranjeiras. The sugar was sent on the Rio Cotinguiba about 20km downstream to Aracaju and on to the ports of Europe. The large number of churches is a reminder of past prosperity.

Information

There is a city tourism office inside the Trapiche building in the Centro de Tradições on Praça Samuel de Oliveira where you can obtain brochures and information about guides for hire. It's open Tuesday to Sunday open 8 am to 5 pm (usually).

Churches

Out at the Engenho Boa Sorte, 4km upriver from town, is the baroque **Igreja de Comandaroba**, constructed by the Jesuits back in 1734. Its altar is currently undergoing restoration. There's also a 1km tunnel leading to the Gruta da Pedra Furada (a large cave built by the Jesuits to escape their persecutors and used for masses in the early days). The tunnel has been closed due to cave-ins.

At the top of the hill called Alto do Bonfim, the 19th-century **Igreja do Bonfim** has been restored, although the main reason for going up there is the fine view. If the door is closed, go around to the back and ask to be let in.

Museums

Laranjeiras is considered to be the stronghold of African culture in Sergipe. The small **Museu Afro-Brasileiro** is at Rua José do Prado Franco; it's open Tuesday to Friday 8 am to 5 pm and on weekends 1 to 4 pm. Entry costs US$0.50.

Also recommended is the **Museu de Arte Sacra** (Sacred Art Museum) in Igreja NS da Conceição on Rua Dr Francisco Bragança.

Trapiche

The Trapiche is a large, impressive structure that was built in the 19th century to hold cargo waiting to be shipped down river. It now houses the tourism office on Praça Samuel de Oliveira.

Engenho

This old, partly restored sugar mill a few kilometers from town is in a lovely setting. It's now privately owned and not generally open to the public, but it may be possible to arrange a visit from the tourist office. If you go, you can walk or hire a guide and a car.

Encontro Cultural

This folklore festival is held during the first week of January. There's a lot of traditional dancing and music; if you're in the area, don't miss it.

Places to Stay

The only pousada in town is the *Pousada Vale dos Outeiros* (☎ 281-1617, Rua José do Prado Franco 124). There are good views of the surrounding hills from the back rooms. Single quartos with fan cost US$10 or US$15 with air-conditioning. Double apartamentos with air-conditioning cost US$20.

Getting There & Away

Laranjeiras is 21km northwest of Aracaju and 4km off Hwy BR-101. Buses and minivans leave from and return to the Rodoviária Velha in Aracaju about every hour. It's a 35-minute ride (US$0.50) – the first bus leaves for Laranjeiras at 6 am and the last one returns at 9 pm. There are also lots of collective taxis from Laranjeiras to Aracaju that cost the same as the bus.

Any bus traveling on Hwy BR-101 can let you off at the turnoff for Laranjeiras. There's a small bar at the turnoff, so you can play pool, have a drink and snack while you wait to flag down a bus from Aracaju. Otherwise, you can walk or hitch to town.

SÃO CRISTÓVÃO
☎ 0xx79 • postcode 49100-000 • pop 58,000

Founded in 1590, São Cristóvão is reputedly Brazil's fourth oldest town and was the capital of Sergipe until 1855. With the decline of the sugar industry, the town has long been in the economic doldrums and is currently trying to become a tourist attraction to bring in some cash.

Things to See
The old part of town, up a steep hill from the bus station, has a surprising number of 17th- and 18th-century colonial buildings along its narrow stone roads. Of particular distinction are the Igreja e Convento de São Francisco, on Praça São Francisco, which has a good sacred-art museum; the Igreja de Senhor dos Passos, on Praça Senhor dos Passos; the Antiga Assembléia Legislativa; and the Antigo Palácio do Governo.

Festival de Arte de São Cristóvão
Every year the town comes alive for this weekend festival. There are both fine and popular arts, with lots of music and dance. The festival is held during the last 15 days of October.

Places to Stay & Eat
There are no real accommodations in São Cristóvão, but it's an easy day trip from Aracaju.

If you've got a sweet tooth, São Cristóvão is renowned for its sweet-makers, who produce a wide variety of *doces caseiros* (tempting homemade confectionery and cakes). The Benedictine nuns at the Convento do Carmo make and sell *bricelete*, a crunchy lemon-flavored cookie. Make sure you try some.

Getting There & Away
São Cristóvão is 25km southwest of Aracaju by a good sealed road, and 7km off Hwy BR-101. The bus station is down the hill below the historic district on Praça Dr Lauro de Freitas. Frequent buses to São Cristóvão (US$0.50, 45 minutes) leave from the Rodoviária Velha in Aracaju. If you are traveling south to Estância, note that buses do not run there from São Cristóvão. You can take a bus back to the junction of Hwy BR-101 and try to flag down a bus to Estância, or return to the Rodoviária Nova in Aracaju and take one from there.

ESTÂNCIA
☎ 0xx79 • postcode 49200-000 • pop 51,000

Estância, 68km south of Aracaju, is one of the oldest towns in the state. The city has a certain amount of character, and a few historic buildings in the center, but there's little reason to stop in Estância unless you want to head to the nearby beaches (see the Mangue Seco section in the Bahia chapter) or want to avoid spending the night in Aracaju.

Information
Estância has all basic services, including a large supermarket. The São João festivals in June are major events, attracting big crowds all month.

Places to Stay & Eat
The town has a couple of hotels facing the main square, Praça Barão do Rio Branco. The *Hotel Turismo Estanciano* (☎/fax 522-1404, Praça Barão do Rio Branco 176) is spotless and comfortable, and has lots of character. Single/double apartamentos go for US$20/30, but you can usually negotiate a discount. Some of the rooms have high ceilings – so high that the walls don't actually reach them! Try to get a room away from the restaurant.

Close by, the **Hotel Dom Bosco** (*☎/fax 522-1887, Rua Exp João Ferreira Silva 218*) has apartamentos starting at US$10/15 – going up to US$30 if you want the TV, minibar and air-conditioning.

The **Hotel Continenti**, tucked behind the bus station, has beat-up quartos for the truly desperate at US$3 without breakfast.

Getting There & Away

The town is actually a bit off Hwy BR-101, but most long-distance buses still stop at Estância's bus station (☎ 522-1466). There are buses directly from Salvador, Aracaju, Propriá and Maceió to the north.

If you are traveling south from Estância along the Linha Verde and want to visit the beach towns north of Salvador, the Bonfim bus company, which runs the Aracaju-Salvador route, makes you pay the full fare from Estância to Salvador (US$12) no matter where you get off along the way. There are 12 buses a day from Estância to Salvador.

For access to Mangue Seco in Bahia, a bus leaves Estância daily at 4 pm for Pontal, where there are boats across the river to Mangue Seco. The 42km trip to Pontal via Indiaroba takes about two hours. For more details see the Mangue Seco section.

PROPRIÁ

☎ 0xx79 • postcode 49900-000 • pop 24,000

Propriá is 81km north of Aracaju, where Hwy BR-101 crosses the mighty Rio São Francisco. While the town is less interesting than the cities of Penedo and Neópolis farther downstream (see the Penedo section later in this chapter), it has the same combination of colonial charm and river culture. Thursday and Friday are the weekly market days in Propriá, when goods are traded from communities up and down the São Francisco.

Boat Trips

In recent years there has been a steady decline in long-distance boat travel along the Rio São Francisco. That said, you should still be able to find boats going upriver from Propriá as far as Pão de Açúcar, about a seven-hour ride by motorboat, with stops at all the towns along the way.

One scheduled boat departure leaves Propriá at 7 am on Tuesday and returns from Pão de Açúcar on Monday. There's also a regular boat at 5 am that travels downriver to Penedo and that takes about three hours. It leaves daily except for Sunday. A word of advice for the tender and claustrophobic – the wooden seats get pretty hard after you sit for a few hours, and the boat is too small to get up and wander around. Fares are US$4.

There are also smaller boats that leave irregularly for other destinations. You can bargain for a ride on any of them, including the beautiful sailing boats with their long, curved masts and striking yellow or red sails. The best sources of information about boats are the older women who tend the riverfront bars.

Bom Jesus dos Navegantes

Held on the last Sunday in January, this festival is a colorful affair involving a maritime procession and *reisado* – a dramatic dance that celebrates the epiphany. It is highly recommended.

Places to Stay & Eat

Facing the main church, the **Hotel Imperial** (*☎ 322-1294, Praça Antônio Cabral 95*) has nice apartamentos (with fan) costing US$10/15 single/double. It's a very clean and friendly place with a pool table.

Also recommended is **Pousada Gramame** (*☎ 322-1219, Rua Getúlio Vargas 100*), with large quartos for US$5 per person and the added attraction of a friendly host. The **Hotel Pan Americano** is a rock-bottom option along the riverfront in town charging US$3 per person for basic quartos. At the other end of the scale, the **Hotel do Velho Chico** (*☎/fax 322-1941*) has a fine riverside position at the southern end of the bridge over the river. Its comfortable double apartamentos range in price from US$30 to US$40.

For a pleasant place to eat with a view of the river, you may wish to try **O Veleiro**, on Avenida Nelson Melo.

Velho Chico: The River of National Unity

For the Brazilian, particularly the Nordestino, it's impossible to speak about the Rio São Francisco without a swelling of pride and emotion. There is no river like the São Francisco, which is the third most important river in Brazil, after the Amazonas and the Paragua. Those who live along its banks speak of it as a friend – hence the affectionate nickname *Velho Chico* or *Chicão* (Chico is a nickname for Francisco).

The geographical situation of the São Francisco gave it a prominence in the colonial history of Brazil that surpassed the Amazon. Born in the Serra da Canastra, 1500m high in Minas Gerais, the Rio São Francisco flows north across the greater part of the Northeast sertão, and completes its 3160km journey at the Atlantic Ocean after slicing through the states of Minas Gerais and Bahia, and delineating the Bahia/Pernambuco and Sergipe/Alagoas state borders.

For three centuries the São Francisco, also referred to as the 'river of national unity,' represented the only connection between the small towns at the extremes of the sertão and the coast. 'Discovered' in the 17th century, the river was the best of the few routes available to penetrate the semi-arid Northeastern interior. Thus, the frontier grew along the margins of the river. The economy of these settlements was based on cattle, which provided desperately needed food for the gold miners in Minas Gerais in the 18th century and later fed workers in the cacao plantations throughout southern Bahia.

Although the inhabitants of the region were often separated by enormous distances, cattle ranching proved a common bond and produced a culture that can be seen today in the region's folklore, music and art.

The history of this area is legendary in Brazil: the tough *vaqueiros* (cowboys of the Northeast) who drove the cattle; the commerce in salt (to fatten the cows); the cultivation of rice; the rise in banditry; the battles between the big landowners; and the religious fanaticism of Canudos. For more information, see the History section in the Facts about Brazil chapter.

The slow waters of the São Francisco have been so vital to Brazil because, in a region with devastating periodic droughts, the river provides one of the only guaranteed sources of water. The people who live here know this, and thus, over the centuries, they have created hundreds of stories, fairy tales and myths about the river.

One example is the *bicho da água* (beast of the water). This creature, part animal and part human, walks on the bottom of the river and snores. The crews on the riverboats throw tobacco to the bicho da água for protection.

The river's width varies from two hand-spans at its source in the Serra da Canastra, an empty, uninhabitable region where little grows, to 40km at Bahia's Lagoa do Sobradinho, the biggest artificial lake in the world. Nordestinos believe that São Francisco is a gift of God to the people of the sertão to recompense all their suffering in the drought-plagued land.

Getting There & Away

Propriá is 1km off Hwy BR-101. There's no real bus station, only a café/ticket agency where all the buses stop. Its on Rua Graço Cardoso near the intersection with Avenida Tavares de Lyra. There are seven daily buses to Aracaju, the first at 6:30 am and the last at 5:15 pm. There is a daily bus connection with Neópolis at 12:30 pm.

Alagoas

You will find the small state of Alagoas to be one of the most pleasant surprises of the Northeast. The capital, Maceió, is a relaxed, modern city, and its beaches are enchanting, with calm, emerald waters. The city of Penedo is the colonial masterpiece of the state, with a fascinating river culture on the Rio São Francisco.

Along the coast are many fishing villages with fabulous beaches shaded by rows of coconut trees. Buses run along the coastal roads to the north and south of Maceió connecting the villages that are beginning to be discovered by tourists and property developers.

History

The mighty republic of runaway slaves – Palmares – was in present-day Alagoas and Pernambuco. During the invasion by the Dutch in 1630, many slaves escaped to the forest in the mountains behind the coasts of northern Alagoas and southern Pernambuco. Where the towns of Viçosa, Capela, Atalaia, Porto Calvo and União dos Palmares stand today, there were once virgin forests with thick growth and plenty of animals to support the escaped slaves. (For more on Palmares, see History in the Facts about Brazil chapter.)

Alagoas today has the highest population density in the Northeast.

MACEIÓ

☎ 082 • postcode 57000-000 • pop 795,000

Maceió, the capital of Alagoas, is 292km north of Aracaju and 259km south of Recife. A manageable place for the visitor, the city has a modern feeling, apart from a small historical area in the commercial center, and offers endless sun and sea. Maceió has experienced a tourist boom over recent years, and the city beaches are good, but quite developed, particularly between Ponta Verde and Praia de Jatiúca north of the center.

Orientation

The bus station is 4km north of the city center, which has inexpensive hotels and the bustle of commerce. On the eastern side of the city are Praia de Pajuçara and Praia dos Sete Coqueiros, which are 2km and 3km, respectively, from the center.

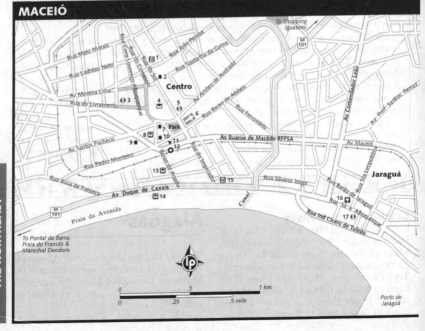

MACEIÓ

Information

On the beach at Pajuçara, there's a useful tourist information booth (☎ 216-1503, Avenida Dr Antônio Gouveia 1143) with loads of information on hotels, restaurants and transport tucked away in folders – including where to have your tarot cards read or your dog washed! There are also information booths at the airport and bus station.

There are branches of Banco do Brasil in the center at Rua do Livramento 120 and on the corner of Rua do Sol and Avenida Aristeu de Andrade. Aero Turismo changes money at the same rate as the banks. It has a branch at Rua Barão do Penedo 61, in the center, and one in the Iguatemi shopping center. Bradesco has an ATM on Avenida Senador Robert Kennedy at Praia dos Sete Coqueiros and another handy one near the nightclubs in Jaraguá.

There is a post office on Rua do Sol in the city center. Telemar, the phone company, has offices along the beachfront at Praia Pajuçara, Ponta Verde and Praia Jatiúca, and at the airport and bus station. Leo's Net & Café (Rua Jangadeiros Alagoanos 1292) is a small Internet café in the arcade at the Pajuçara Othon Hotel.

The following are useful sites about Maceió and Alagoas:

www.vivabrazil.com/alagoas.htm – in Portuguese and English, with some good links at the bottom of the page

www.geocities.com/TheTropics/5141/ – a great photo gallery of Alagoan beauty spots

www.dialnet.com.br/maceio/maceio/htm – in Portuguese but easy to get around, with an online booking service for some hotels and a good review of nightlife

Museums

In the center on Rua do Sol, the **Museu do Instituto Histórico & Geográfico de Alagoas** has exhibits about regional history. It's open Monday to Friday 8:30 to 11:30 am and 2 to 5 pm. Entry costs US$0.50.

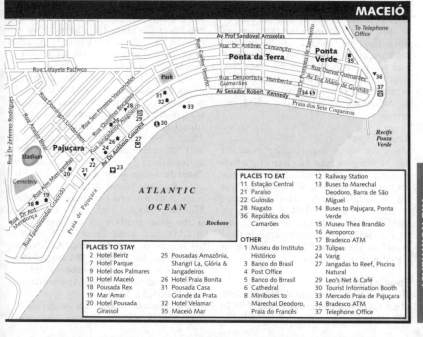

MACEIÓ

ATLANTIC OCEAN

PLACES TO STAY
2 Hotel Beiriz
7 Hotel Parque
9 Hotel dos Palmares
10 Hotel Maceió
18 Pousada Rex
19 Mar Amar
20 Hotel Pousada Girassol
25 Pousadas Amazônia, Shangri La, Glória & Jangadeiros
26 Hotel Praia Bonita
31 Pousada Casa Grande da Prata
32 Hotel Velamar
35 Maceió Mar

PLACES TO EAT
11 Estação Central
21 Paraíso
22 Gulosão
28 Nagato
36 República dos Camarões

OTHER
1 Museu do Instituto Histórico
3 Banco do Brasil
4 Post Office
5 Banco do Brrasil
6 Cathedral
8 Minibuses to Marechal Deodoro, Praia do Francês
12 Railway Station
13 Buses to Marechal Deodoro, Barra de São Miguel
14 Buses to Pajuçara, Ponta Verde
15 Museu Thea Brandão
16 Aeroporco
17 Bradesco ATM
23 Tulipas
24 Varig
27 Jangadas to Reef, Piscina Natural
29 Leo's Net & Café
30 Tourist Information Booth
33 Mercado Praia de Pajuçara
34 Bradesco ATM
37 Telephone Office

Museu Theo Brandão in an attractive colonial building on the seafront, has some interesting folkloric exhibitions. It's open Monday to Friday from 8 am to noon and from 2 to 5 pm.

Beaches

The beaches of Praia do Sobral and Avenida, just a short walk from the center, are polluted. **Praia de Pajuçara** and **Praia dos Sete Coqueiros** sometimes suffer from pollution as well. Your best bet is to head farther north for some of the best beaches in the Northeast. Protected by a coral reef, the ocean at Maceió is calm and a deep emerald color. On shore there are loads of bars, *jangadas* (local sailing boats) and plenty of beach action.

The beaches to the north are **Ponta Verde** (5km from the city center), **Jatiúca** (6km), **Jacarecica** (9km), **Guaxuma** (12km), **Garça Torta** (14km), **Riacho Doce** (16km) and **Pratagi** (17km). See Getting Around for details on getting to these beaches.

You won't go wrong with any of these tropical paradises, but they do get busy on weekends and throughout the summer, when many local buses cruise the beaches. On Pajuçara, you'll find jangadas that will take you out about 1km to the reef, where you can swim in the *piscina natural* (natural swimming pool) and observe the marine life (best done at low tide). The cost is US$3 per person.

Boat Trips

Many schooners depart daily from the nearby village of Pontal da Barra for a five-hour cruise to islands and beaches. The price per person is usually US$15 with lunch, or US$10 without lunch. Atlântico Turismo (☎ 231-1008) charges US$25 for its trips. Small motorboats such as the *Turis Gomes* (☎ 221-0458) make similar cruises from Pontal da Barra for US$7 per person, or US$15 with lunch included.

Special Events

The big event in Maceió is **Maceió Fest**, which takes place from December 7 to 10 and features active samba clubs and *trios*

elétricos. Locals reckon Barra de São Miguel, 35km south, has the best **Carnaval** in the area.

Places to Stay – Budget

City Center The *Hotel dos Palmares* (☎ 223-7024, Praça dos Palmares 253) has basic quartos at US$6 per person (breakfast not included), or US$9 per person for apartamentos with breakfast. There's a nice, elevated eating area that catches the breeze. Nearby, the *Hotel Maceió* (☎ 336-0954, Rua Dr Pontas de Miranda 146) offers clean, cell-like apartamentos for US$7 per person. It's secure and friendly.

Although conveniently central and cheap, the *Hotel Parque* (☎/fax 223-4247, Rua Dom Pedro Segundo 73) is rather institutional and drab, and doesn't merit its two stars. Single/double apartamentos rent for about US$13/20.

Beaches Praia de Pajuçara is the best place to base yourself, as it's midway between the city center and the better beaches, and has more budget accommodations than the beaches farther north. There are two clusters of cheapies – all one block from the beach. Prices quoted here are for the low season – expect hikes of 20 to 30% in summer.

On Rua Dr Antônio Pedro de Mendonça, *Pousada Rex* (☎ 231-4358) at No 311 is a family-run place with apartamentos starting at US$8/12. It can also arrange boat trips. Close by is *Mar Amar* (☎/fax 231-1551) at No 343, with bright apartamentos for US$8 per person with fan or US$10 with air-conditioning. Just up the road, the *Hotel Pousada Girassol* (☎ 231-4000, fax 231-0651, Rua Jangadeiros Alagoanos 535) is a colorful maze of well-worn but clean rooms. Most have double beds and a couple of singles, so it's good for groups. Singles start at US$15 and doubles cost US$25. It also has private parking. The *Pousada Saveiro* (☎ 231-9831, fax 327-5060, Rua Jangadeiros Alagoanos 905), a bit farther along, is friendly and better value. Apartamentos start at US$15 a double.

The *Pousada Shangri La* (☎ 231-3773, fax 327-5229, Rua Jangadeiros Alagoanos

1089) is bright and clean – apartamentos with fan are US$10/20 and US$15 per person with air-conditioning. This is another good place for groups. Next door, the *Pousada Amazônia* (☎ 237-4534) is a bit dingy and cheaper – apartamentos cost US$7 without breakfast. Across the road, above the *padaria* (bakery) is *Pousada Glória* (☎ 231-3261), with reasonable apartamentos for US$15 a double. Opposite is the newer *Pousada Jangadeiros* (☎ 327-7538, Rua Quintino Bocaiúva 292), which charges US$20 a double with breakfast and US$15 without.

The *Hotel Casa Grande da Praia* (☎ 231-3332, fax 231-9881, hcgpraia@matrix.com.br, Rua Jangadeiros Alagoanos 1528) is a friendly, quiet place a block from the beachfront. Apartamentos with air-conditioning and fridge cost US$15/20.

Places to Stay – Mid-Range

City Center If you want a good hotel in the center, try the *Hotel Beiriz* (☎ 336-6200, fax 336-6282), on Rua João Pessoa (Rua do Sol). It's a large three-star hotel with a pool and restaurant. Discount rooms with air-conditioning, fridge and TV cost US$20/25.

Beaches The older hotels along Praia de Pajuçara are more reasonably priced than the newer hotels farther north on Ponta Verde and Praia Jatiúca. There are some very good out-of-season prices at the mid-range beach hotels, as you can see from the low-season prices quoted below.

The beachfront *Hotel Praia Bonita* (☎/fax 231-2565, Avenida Dr Antônio Gouveia 943) has clean single/double apartamentos with air-conditioning for US$20/25. Its jangada reception desk is a nice touch. The *Hotel Velamar* (☎ 327-5488, fax 231-6849, atendimento@hotelvelamar.com.br, Rua Dr Antônio Gouveia 1359) is a cute little place dwarfed by the square-block hotel next door. Apartamentos cost US$25/30 in the low season, US$30/40 in summer.

The *Pousada Cavalo Marinho* (☎ 355-1247, fax 355-1265, cavalomarinho@dialnet.com.br, Rua da Praia 55), 17km northeast

of the center at Praia Riacho Doce, has been recommended by readers. Double rooms start at around US$20, with use of canoes, bicycles and body boards. The owner speaks English and German. To get there, take a São Domingos 'Riacho Doce' bus and follow the many signs.

Places to Stay – Top End

The *Jatiúca Resort* (☎ 355-2020, fax 355-2121, Lagoa da Anta 220) has good recreation facilities and offers direct beach access. It's 7km northeast of the center and costs from US$160 for a double.

Closer to town , the *Maceió Mar* (☎ 231-8000, fax 327-7026, Avenida Álvaro Otacílio 2991) is opposite the beach at Ponta Verde. All rooms have a sea view, and the area is a busy one. Double rooms start at US$90.

Places to Eat

A very cheap, decent lunch place in the center is *Estação Centro*, opposite the railway station. It has an all-you-can-eat buffet for US$2.

The best places to eat are at the beaches. Most offer a wide choice of food, with bars serving seafood and local dishes along the beachfront. Probably the two best spots are Lagoa Mundaú to the south of the city and Praia de Pajuçara.

Local seafood specialties worth trying are *sururu* (a small mussel) and *maçunim* (shellfish) cooked in coconut sauce, served as dishes on their own, or in a *caldinho* (cup of sauce) that can be eaten or drunk. Other tasty local seafood dishes include *peixe agulha* (deep-fried needlefish) and *siri na casca com coral* (crab in the shell with roe). Beachside food stalls also serve some delicious snacks which should be tried: *acarajé* (a bean paste deep-fried in dendê oil and filled with shrimp and potato) and tapioca pancakes filled with grated coconut or *queijo coalhado* (compressed bean curd).

On Praia de Pajuçara, *Paraíso* (Avenida Álvaro Otaglio 877) is a casual little café with a great range of juices and snack foods. *Gulosão* (Rua Domingos Lordesleen 848) is a friendly place with reasonably priced seafood, meat and chicken meals. *Nagato*

THE NORTHEAST

(Rua Jangadeiros Alagoanos 1163) is a good, reasonably priced Japanese restaurant.

At Praia de Ponta Verde, **República dos Camarões** (☎ 231-8262, *Avenida Prof Sandoval Arroxelas 670)* is a popular seafood *barraca* on the beach.

Two very good but more expensive restaurants are out in Jatiúca. **Bar das Ostras** (☎ 325-8551, *Rua Paulina Mendonça 153)* is a traditional oyster bar where you can snack or dine on all types of seafood, raw or cooked. The lobster with shrimp sauce is delicious. **Divina Gula** (☎ 235-1016, *Rua Eng Paulo Brandão Nogueira 85)* is a rustic place with regional food that gets packed on weekends. During the week it remains quite busy, except for Monday when it's closed.

Entertainment

The two main nightlife areas are Jatiúca and Jaraguá. Jatiúca is more of a beach bar scene, but there's also **Lampião** (☎ 325-4376, *Avenida Álvaro Otacílio s/n)*, a big place with a dance floor and lots of forró and axé music.

In Jaraguá, Rua Sá e Albuquerque is a semi-restored street with lots of trendy bars, restaurants, discos and the beautifully restored Associação Commercial building. It's where the young, restless and cashed-up locals hang out. The main nightclub, **Aeroporco** (☎ 326-4762, *Rua Sá e Albuquerque 588)*, has DJs and live music Thursday to Saturday. The cover charge is around US$10.

Many of the seafront bars have live music, especially on weekends. **Tulipas**, on Praia de Pajuçara, is one of the hotspots.

For reviews and listings of the latest bars, dance spots and cultural events in Maceió, check out the daily entertainment section of *O Jornal*, the local newspaper.

Shopping

There is a nightly craft market on Praia de Pajuçara with dozens of stalls selling figurines, lacework, hammocks and jewelry.

The fishing village of Pontal da Barra, around 8km southwest of Maceió, is also a crafts center. The streets are lined with shops selling fine lacework and embroidery, and prices are generally lower there than in the city. You can often see women weaving outside the shops. The Mercado do Artesanato, next to the food market in the city center, is also a good place to shop for hammocks – a decent double hammock goes for around US$15.

Getting There & Away

Air Maceió is connected by air with Rio, São Paulo, Brasília and all the major centers of the Northeast. For reservations, call the following toll-free numbers: Varig (☎ 0800-997000), VASP (☎ 0800-998277), TAM (☎ 0800-123100). All airlines have offices at the airport; Varig also has an office on Avenida Dr Antônio Gouveia.

Bus There are numerous daily bus services to Recife (US$8, four hours) and Aracaju (US$12, five hours).

Buses run six times a day to Salvador (US$23, 10 hours). Some of these take the inland route while others go via the Linha Verde along the coast. If you want to make a 2256km bus trip to Rio (US$78, 36 hours), there's a daily departure at 4 pm.

Buses leave for Penedo four times a day. The route via Hwy AL-101 along the coast is much quicker if you take an executivo – 2½ hours compared to 4½ in a normal bus (see the later Penedo section and boxed text 'Dripping Along the Coast' for details of the slow bus route). The fare is US$3.50. The São Domingos bus company serves the coastal towns north of Maceió with regular buses to Barra de Santo Antônio, Barra do Camarajibe, Porto de Pedras and Japaratinga.

Getting Around

To/From the Airport Aeroporto dos Palmares is 20km north of the center. Rio Largo buses to the airport can be picked up at the railway station. Fare is US$1.50. A taxi to the airport costs around US$13. There are buses and taxis from the airport into the center.

To/From the Bus Station To reach the center, take the bus marked Ouro Prêto. A taxi to the center costs US$3.50, and US$2 more to Pajuçara. Take a taxi from the center to the bus station; buses take indirect routes.

To/From the Beaches Buses marked Santuário, Jardim Vaticano or Ponta Verde run from the center to Pajuçara. The Jatiúca bus runs from the center to Praia Jatiúca. If you want to travel farther from the center, the bus marked 'Riacho Doce' runs along the beaches north of town as far as Riacho Doce, 17km away (recommended).

Buses run south to Pontal da Barra from the bus stop on Rua Pedro Montero, near Praça dos Palmares. Catch the Santuário Pontal or the Pontal Iguatemi bus.

SOUTH OF MACEIÓ
Praia do Francês
☎ 0xx82

Only 22km south of Maceió, this is a popular weekend beach that is being rapidly developed and beginning to suffer from the ravages of tourism. The beach is lined with bars and the ocean is lined with reefs. At one end, the water is calm and better for wading than swimming while at the other end there's usually surf. It's a very social beach on weekends, with plenty of drinking, seafood, soccer and music.

Life's a beach!

Places to Stay & Eat There are a few cheap options very close to the beach in Praia do Francês. The *Pousada João* (☎ 260-1220) and *Pousada Nataly* are pretty

grungy crash pads, with single/double quartos for US$8/12. The best-value cheapie is the *Pousada Tortuga* (☎ 260-7876, Avenida dos Arrecifes), which has clean double apartamentos for US$15. The owner is a surfer and speaks perfect English. *Pousada Kanamary* (☎/fax 260-1213, Rua Estrela do Mar 49) is a good deal with singles/doubles for US$25/30.

Numerous bars along the beach are a good source of seafood. It's not always cheap, despite the surroundings, so make sure you ask the price. *Restaurant Aboriginé*, near the cheap pousadas, has large portions and is reasonably priced. More upmarket is *Oficina de Sabores* (☎ 260-1316, Rua Vermelha 20).

Getting There & Away From Maceió, either take the bus from the stop outside the railway station (hourly departure) or use the more frequent VW minibus service that leaves from about 50m down the street (US$4 for either). The same minibuses also run between Praia do Francês and Marechal Deodoro.

Marechal Deodoro
☎ 0xx82 • pop 30,000

Beside Lagoa Manguaba, a lagoon 21km southwest of Maceió, is the city of Marechal Deodoro, which was the capital of Alagoas between 1823 and 1839. Small and quiet, the town is worth a visit, perhaps combined with Praia do Francês as a day trip from Maceió.

Things to See Marechal Deodoro has several churches, the most famous of which are the Igreja e Convento São Francisco, constructed in the 17th century, and the Igreja de NS da Conceição.

Inside the Igreja e Convento São Francisco is the Museu de Arte Sacra (Museum of Sacred Art). It's open 9 am to 1 pm daily except on Sunday when it's closed.

Brazilian history buffs may want to see the old governor's palace and the house where Marechal Deodoro was born. The latter has been turned into the Museu Deodoro, which is open 9 am to 5 pm daily except on Sunday when it's closed. The

THE NORTHEAST

exhibits give a 'deodorized' view of Manuel Deodoro da Fonseca, emphasizing his role as a military hero and the first president of Brazil, but omitting to mention that he achieved this position with a military putsch in 1889 and later proved to be a poor politician. The shop next door sells the lace and homemade sweets for which the town is renowned.

The weekend market, which is held along the waterfront, is a lively, colorful event.

Places to Stay & Eat The *Hospedaria Deodorense*, just off Praça Pedro Paulinho, is a clean, very basic place to stay – usually booked solid on weekends. Single/double quartos with fan cost US$3/5. Breakfast is US$3. For other meals, speak to Dona Terezinho, in the house two doors up towards Praça Paulino. There are lots of breezy bars along the lagoon.

Getting There & Away Buses to Marechal Deodoro (US$1) depart hourly from the bus stop outside the railway station in Maceió. It's quicker to go by one of the minibuses that leave every 15 minutes or so from the stop 50m away from the railway station (US$2, half-hour). Yes, the minibus is definitely quicker; the demon drivers keep their accelerator foot down to the board, and your heart pressed to the roof of your mouth!

Barra de São Miguel
☎ 0xx82 • pop 5200
Barra is situated 35km south of Maceió at the mouth of the Rio São Miguel. The fine beach is protected by a huge reef and there are kayaks for rent. Barra is not too crowded midweek, but it is being built up with summer homes for Maceió's wealthy. **Praia do Gunga** is a popular beach across the river with some expensive bars. You can just relax here or go parasailing.

Places to Stay & Eat The *Pousada Mar e Sol* (☎ 272-1159, fax 272-1440) on Rua Salvador Aprato near the beach, has apartamentos at US$22/30 for singles/doubles. It's overpriced but in an attractive position. If

you have a group, the chalets (with cooking facilities) for up to six people are a better value. The *Pousada Rio Mar* (☎ 272-1432, fax 272-2064) near the beach charges US$35 for a six-person chalet.

Bar do Tio (☎ 272-2015) on Praça São Pedro has good shrimp and fish dishes for US$5 to US$15. Try the super mussels.

Getting There & Away Buses run four times a day from Maceió to Barra, at 7:20 and 11:30 am and 3:20 and 7:20 pm. They leave from the bus stop at the railway station. The last bus leaves Barra for the return trip to Maceió at 5:30 pm from the bus station on Praça Miriel Cavalcanti.

South of Barra de São Miguel
The upgrading of Hwy AL-101 along the south coast has made access to the beaches and villages south of Barra de São Miguel much easier. The road runs about 1km from the coast, and regular buses travel along it from Maceió to Penedo on the Rio São Francisco. See Getting There & Away for Maceió and Penedo for details.

PENEDO
☎ 0xx82 • postcode 57200-000 • pop 41,000
Penedo is best known as the *capital do baixo São Francisco* (capital of the lower São Francisco). On the shore of the often-anthropomorphized river, this important historic town rises imposingly on its rock platform.

Among the attractions of the city, 42km off Hwy BR-101, are its many baroque churches and colonial buildings, and the opportunity to travel on the Rio São Francisco. Penedo bustles with people from villages up and down the river who come to buy and sell goods.

History
Penedo was founded in either 1535 or 1560 (opinions differ) by Duarte Coelho Pereira, who descended the Rio São Francisco in pursuit of Caeté Indians responsible for killing a bishop. Penedo is claimed to be the river's first colonial settlement. It was also the scene of a fierce battle between the

Dutch and Portuguese for control of the Northeast in the 17th century.

Information

There's a helpful tourist information office (open 8 am to 6 pm daily) in the Casa da Aposentadoria (☎ 551-2728) on Praça Barão de Penedo. They have good maps showing all the main tourist attractions. Portuguese-speaking guides are available for a one-hour walking tour of the town.

Market

The street market is held daily in Penedo, but Friday and Saturday are the big days when the city is transformed into a busy port of call for farmers, fisherfolk and artisans. The waterfront becomes a pageant as families disembark – old people with finely carved features topped by strange hats, many grasping chickens by the neck with one hand and boisterous children by the neck with the other. On the riverbank, traditional musicians play accordions. The market is filled with ceramics, baskets and shrimp traps made of reeds.

Churches

Penedo has a rich collection of 17th- and 18th-century colonial buildings, including many churches. The **Convento de São Francisco e Igreja NS dos Anjos**, on Praça Rui Barbosa, is considered the finest church in the state. Even Dom Pedro II (Brazil's second and last emperor) paid a visit. Construction began in 1660 and was completed in 1759. Note especially the rococo altar made of gold and the saint on the left by Aleijadinho. The church is open Tuesday to Sunday 7:30 to 11 am and 2 to 5 pm.

The **Igreja da Senhora das Correntes** was completed in 1764. It has some fine work done with *azulejos* (glazed blue tiles), and a rococo altar. The church is open 8 to 11 am and 2 to 5 pm, Tuesday to Sunday. You'll find it at Praça 12 de Abril.

The **Igreja NS do Rosário dos Pretos**, also known as the Catedral do Penedo, was built by slaves. It's on Praça Marechal Deodoro and is open every day 8 am to 6 pm. The recently restored **Igreja de São Gonçalo Garcia**

was built at the end of the 18th century and has some of the city's finest sacred-art pieces in a small museum. It's on Avenida Floriano Peixoto, and is open 8 am to noon and 2 to 6 pm daily. The small **oratório** on Praça Barão de Penedo is where the condemned spent their last night praying before being hanged.

Casa do Penedo

This small museum has relics and photographs from Penedo's rich history at Rua João Pessoa 156. It's open 8 am to 6 pm, Tuesday to Sunday, and admission is free. It sells excellent postcards.

Boat Trips

Saturday (the major market day) is the easiest day to find a boat up or down the São Francisco, but it's difficult now to find boats going upriver as far as Propriá.

The ferry between Penedo and Passagem, on the opposite side of the river, crosses every half-hour, but is only of interest if you're driving. From Passagem there's a road to **Neópolis**, which is linked by another road to Hwy BR-101. A better excursion is one of the motorboat crossings direct to Neópolis, a few kilometers downriver. The 15-minute trip costs US$0.50 and boats usually depart every half-hour between 5:30 am and 10 pm. Neópolis is an old colonial town on a hill overlooking the river, with some interesting buildings and good crafts for sale. For another short boat excursion, take one of the frequent boats (operating between 6 am and 6 pm) to **Carrapicho**, a small town 4km upriver noted for its ceramics.

River Cruises A large motorboat for up to 30 people cruises to Carrapicho, Neópolis and river islands, with stops for swimming. The cost is US$10 per hour per boatload. A sailing boat makes a similar trip, depending on the wind and tides, for US$7 per hour. Ask at the tourist office for departure times.

Festa do Senhor Bom Jesus dos Navegantes

This festival, held over four days from the second Sunday of January, features an elaborate procession of boats and an exciting sailboat race.

Places to Stay

Penedo has some interesting hotels. Most are down by the waterfront, on or near Avenida Floriano Peixoto.

On the riverfront, you'll spot a couple of cheap-looking places. The best is *Pousada Estylos* (☎ 551-2691, Avenida Floriano Peixoto 51), with friendly management and clean, collective quartos for US$4 per person. Private rooms cost US$10 per person.

For another budget option, try the *Pousada Familiar* (☎ 551-3194, Rua Siqueira 77) with quartos for US$5 with a basic breakfast (coffee, bread and an egg) or US$7 with a better breakfast. If you prefer a place where the walls reach the ceiling, walk a bit farther up the same street to the *Hotel Turista* (☎ 551-2237) at No 143 which offers clean, basic single/double apartamentos with ceiling fans for US$10/15 with breakfast.

The *Pousada Colonial* (☎ 551-2355, Praça 12 de Abril) is a beautiful converted colonial home on the waterfront with spacious apartamentos featuring stained-wood floors and antique furniture. Make sure you get one with a view of the river. Prices start at US$20/30.

The *Hotel São Francisco* (☎ 551-2273, fax 551-2274, hotelsaofrancisco@bol.com.br), on Avenida Floriano Peixoto, is a 1960s-style hotel that's been in the time warp for the last 40 years. It's clean, quiet and has comfortable apartamentos with balconies and great hot showers starting at US$35/50. It usually gives a 30% discount for paying with cash.

Places to Eat

There are plenty of bars and food stalls where locals eat. Try *Forte da Rocheira* (☎ 551-3273, Rua da Rocheira 2), which serves abundant portions of seafood and meat for US$8 to $20. The restaurant is in an old replica fort overlooking the river. Just follow the signs to get there. The restaurant in the Pousada Colonial also serves good fish and meat dishes.

Getting There & Away

The bus station (☎ 551-2602) is on Avenida Duque de Caxias. There are 10 buses a day to Maceió (US$3.50). Expesess executivo buses leave daily at 5:30 and 9:30 am, and at 1 and 4:30 pm, taking 2½ hours. The standard bus – known as the *pinga litoral* (literally, 'dripping along the coast') – leaves at 5:30 am and 2:30 pm, taking 4½ hours. These six buses take the coastal route along Hwy AL-101, which is much quicker and more interesting than the inland route via São Miguel taken by the other four daily buses. See the boxed text 'Dripping Along the Coast' for more on the pinga litoral.

There's one bus, at 6 am, from Penedo to Propriá (US$3, 1½ hours), continuing to Aracaju (US$6, three hours). A quicker and more convenient way to Aracaju is to take the ferry across the river to Neópolis, where there are frequent buses to Aracaju (US$5, 2½ hours).

If you are driving to Penedo, you'll take a 41km paved road from Hwy BR-101 in Sergipe to Neópolis, on the Sergipe side of the river, and then a short drive from Neópolis to Passagem, where a ferry makes the 10-minute river crossing to Penedo every half-hour (US$4 for a car).

NORTH OF MACEIÓ

The Alagoas coast north of Maceió is ideal for independent travelers. Many places along here have very little infrastructure for tourists. The beaches are mostly undisturbed and tropically perfect, and the sea is calm and warm. There are several fishing villages with little tourism apart from a simple hotel or two – although the state government's Costa Dourada (Golden Coast) development plans have brought about rapid changes, and they aren't pretty.

The coastal road, Hwy AL-101, which is mostly paved, runs within a few hundred meters of the ocean, a rare occurrence along the Brazilian coast. The stretch from Barra de Santo Antônio to Barra do Camarajibe is often in disarray and you have to cross some small rivers on local ferries, so check road conditions before departing. Alternatively, from Barra de Santo Antônio the main road and most through traffic detours inland along Hwy AL-413. It's a stunning drive (try to stop at Porto Calvo) through rolling hills covered in sugarcane and past the odd hill topped with virgin forest that escaped land clearing. You'll also see a large sugarcane plant processing sugarcane alcohol that fuels some of Brazil's cars. The Empresa de Santo Antônio employs about 800 workers in the factory and 4000 in the fields.

From AL-413 you have the option of returning to the coast at Barra do Camarajibe by a good road from the town of São Luis do Quitunde. From Barra do Camarajibe, the coast road is sealed as far as Porto de Pedras, about 16km before Japaratinga.

Barra de Santo Antônio
☎ 0xx82 • postcode 57925-000 • pop 9500
Barra is built along the mouth of the Rio Jirituba, below a small bluff. It is a relaxed fishing village only 40km from Maceió and attracts tourists and people with beach houses. Consequently, it gets busy on weekends and in summer.

The best beaches are out on the Ilha da Croa (a narrow peninsula on the other side of Rio Jirituba). You can catch a small boat across the river (US$0.30) and walk some 2km across the peninsula to the beaches, or take a motorboat all the way (US$1). *Balsas* (ferries) take cars across the river for US$3. You can catch the ferry from beside the Banco do Brasil.

Tabuba beach is a quiet, pretty beach with a few bars and a couple of pousadas, just 3km south of Barra de Santo Antônio. There is a piscina natural off the beach – ask at the bars about a ride there by jangada.

Places to Stay & Eat In Barra, the *Pousada Brisa E Sonhos* (☎ 998-5843) is a friendly place on the river with single/double quartos for US$10/15 with a good breakfast included. The pousada also serves good meals for nonguests. At Tabuba beach, the *Pousada Arco Iris* (☎ 291-1250, fax 291-1326, arcoiris@gmx.net, Rua 10, 6) is an excellent pousada only 30m from the beach. Heinz, the very friendly Swiss owner, speaks German, English, French and Spanish.

Dripping along the Coast

The *pinga litoral* – which literally translates to 'dripping along the coast' – is the best bus to take from Penedo to Maceió if you want to see the coast and the people who live there. The extra two hours are worth it if you don't mind buses that stop for anyone who wants to get on or off at any time.

From Penedo, the bus travels along the river toward the coast, passing the thatched huts of the fishermen who live in **Piaçabuçu**, then swings in from the river and north to **Pontal do Peba**, where it does a U-turn on the beach. From there it passes through **Feliz Deserto**, which has lots of cowboys and coconuts, one pousada and lots of seafood.

The bus turns off Hwy AL-101 a bit farther north at **Miaí de Cima**, where there are no pousadas, but many locals on the beach on weekends. The next time the bus turns off the main road is into **Barreiras**, also with good beaches but no pousadas. It then comes to **Coruripe** before continuing to **Pontal do Coruripe**, its lighthouse and fine beaches. Pontal just may become a backpackers' stopover. It has a couple of pousadas, English is spoken at *Pousada da Ada* (☎ 0xx82-273-7209).

Next stop is **Lagoa da Pau**, with lots of shrimp and a few weekend houses. Then it's on to **Poxim**, past cane fields and coconut palms. Approaching Maceió, the bus doesn't enter either **Barra de São Miguel** or **Praia do Francês** but only stops at the turnoffs. Passing the huge estuaries of the **Mundaú** and **Manguaba** lagoons, it's not long before the bus reaches the capital.

If you plan to stay at Pajuçara or beaches farther north, get off the bus after it turns off the coast road into the center of Maceió. This will save you going to the bus station. Just cross back over the coast road and catch a local bus going along the beaches. (Destinations are on signs near the back door.) As the local bus travels through Pajuçara, it doesn't follow the beach, but goes along the first road parallel. For the cheap pousadas, get out at the first gas station and walk across the road.

THE NORTHEAST

Comfortable apartamentos are US$15/25 in low season and double in high season. At Paripueira beach, 7km south of Barra de Santo Antônio, *House of Leia* (☎ 293-1362, *Rua Eugênio Costa 1162*) has apartamentos on the beachfront for US$15/25.

The *Peixada da Rita* (☎ 291-1110, *Rua Antônio Baltazar 36*) beside the river in Barra de Santo Antônio, serves sensational seafood.

Getting There & Away Direct buses and minibuses to Maceió (US$2, one hour) operate from 4:30 am to 10:30 pm from Largo Dr Pio in Barra de Santo Antônio. You can also walk (20 minutes) or hire a local cab to the main road, where you can flag down the buses that bypass the town.

Barra do Camarajibe
☎ 0xx82

This idyllic fishing village, 33km farther north up the coast from Barra de Santo Antônio, offers fish, beer, a couple of pousadas and a beautiful beach. The *Pousada & Restaurante Barra Mar* (☎ 258-5141) and the *Pousada & Restaurante Foz do Camaragibe* (☎ 258-5140) are almost next door to each another on Rua São José at the entrance to the town. Both charge US$10/20 for basic but comfortable singles/doubles. The seafood is great, but not super cheap. Buses run to Barra do Camarajibe from Maceió via São Luis do Quitunde. See the Porto de Pedras section earlier for further bus information.

São Miguel dos Milagres
☎ 0xx82 • pop 1750

A bit bigger than its neighbors, São Miguel has soft beaches with warm, shallow seas protected by offshore reefs. There's one pousada, the *Restaurante & Pouzada do Gordo* (☎ 295-1181), which charges US$7/15 for simple rooms with fan. It's a five-minute walk to the beach. See the following Porto de Pedras section for bus information.

Porto de Pedras
☎ 0xx82 • pop 5200

Continuing north, you've got to catch the local ferry to cross the river here. (It runs 6 am to 8 pm and costs US$3 for cars and US$0.50 for foot passengers.) Porto de Pedras is a lively little fishing village with a road that connects with Hwy AL-413 at Porto Calvo. In the village there are bars, restaurants and, on the main street, the cheap and basic *Pousada São Geraldo* (☎ 298-1119).

The São Domingos bus to Porto de Pedras runs via the abovementioned beach towns of Barra do Camarajibe and São Miguel dos Milagres from the bus station in Maceió. There are eight buses a day between 5 am and 6 pm. The trip to Porto de Pedras takes three hours and costs US$4 if you go all the way.

Japaratinga
☎ 0xx82 • pop 2500

Ten kilometers south of the town of Maragoji, Japaratinga's shallow waters are protected by coral reefs and the beaches are backed by coconut trees and fishing huts. Under the moonlight you can walk a couple of kilometers into the sea. The town has a gas station, a few pousadas and a telephone office. If you decide to stay, the *Hotel e Restaurante Solmar* (☎ 297-1140) is a good option. A single/double with fan costs US$15/20, including breakfast.

Maragoji
☎ 0xx82 • pop 13,000

Slightly more developed, Maragoji has some weekend homes for Pernambucanos and a couple of cheap hotels – try the *Pousada Olho D'Agua* on the beachfront (☎/fax 296-1263, olhodagua@interway.com.br). Singles/doubles with verandas and views go for US$25/30, while those without views cost US$20/25. The sea is protected by reefs and is ideal for swimming.

To get to Maragoji or Japaratinga by bus, take the frequent São Domingos bus to Maragoji from the bus station in Maceió. From Recife, the Real Alagoas 'Comum Litoral' buses travel along the coast and take five to six hours to reach Maceió because they stop for anyone who wants to get on or off. They leave the bus station in Recife at 9:30 am and 12:30 pm.

Pernambuco

One of Brazil's major tourist destinations, Pernambuco has a lot to offer the visitor. There's the colonial architecture of Olinda (a UNESCO World Heritage Site), interesting architectural remnants of the Dutch administration in Recife, good beaches and the beautiful Parque Nacional Marinho de Fernando de Noronha. The Pernambucanos preserve a rich cultural tradition, from the lively Carnaval in Olinda to the marketplace of Caruaru. The passion play in Nova Jerusalem is the largest in the world, drawing crowds of 80,000. Sugarcane still dominates the economy, and Recife is the second largest industrial center in the Northeast after Salvador.

The Coast

RECIFE
☎ 0xx81 • postcode 50000-000
• pop 1.4 million

Recife ('hess-**eef**-ay') is the Northeast's third biggest city and the capital of Pernambuco. This 'Venice of Brazil' (a rather hopeful comparison) is a city of water and bridges with *arrecifes* (reefs) offshore. Its sister city Olinda is a beautiful enclave of colonial buildings filled with artists, students and bohemians.

Amid all the recent development, Recife retains a rich traditional side, with some of Brazil's best folk art, including painting and sculpture, dance, music and festivals. It takes time to discover this side of the city, but it's well worth the effort. However, unless you want to be right on the beach, stay in Olinda, which has more cheap accommodations and is a more interesting place to stay.

History
Recife developed in the 17th century as the port for the rich sugar plantations around Olinda. With several rivers and offshore reefs, Recife proved to be an excellent port and began to outgrow Olinda. By the 17th century, Recife and Olinda combined were the most prosperous cities in Brazil, with the possible exception of Salvador da Bahia. The neighboring Indians had been subdued after brutal warfare, and the colonial aristocracy living in Olinda was raking in profits with its many sugar *engenhos* (mills). Naturally, all the work was done by slave labor.

Highlights

- Frenetic Carnaval in Olinda
- The golden Capela Dourada in Recife
- Excellent beaches around Porto de Galinhas
- Bizarre sculptures at Olaria de Brennand in Recife
- Fascinating market and artist workshops at Caruaru and Alto de Moura
- Natural wonders of the Parque Nacional Marinho de Fernando de Noronha

Fernando de Noronha page 563 →

Rio Grande do Norte

Ceará

Piauí

Pernambuco pages 546-547

Paraíba

Olinda page 558
Central Recife page 548

Alagoas

Sergipe

Bahia

No other European country had managed to grab a part of Brazil from the Portuguese until 1621, when the Dutch, who were active in the sugar trade and knew the lands of Brazil well, set up the Dutch West India Company to sink its teeth into the Brazilian cake. A large fleet sailed in 1624 and captured Salvador, but a huge Spanish-Portuguese militia of 12,000 men recaptured the city the following year. Five years later the Dutch tried again, this time in Pernambuco. Recife was abandoned, the Dutch took the city and by 1640 they controlled a great chunk of the Northeast, from Maranhão to the Rio São Francisco.

The Dutch had hoped the sugar planters wouldn't resist their rule, but many Brazilian planters took up arms against the non-Catholic Dutch. In 1654, after a series of battles around Recife, the Dutch finally surrendered. This was the last European challenge to Portuguese Brazil.

Recife prospered after the Dutch were expelled, but in spite of the city's growing economic power, which had eclipsed that of Olinda, political power remained with the sugar planters in Olinda, and they refused to share it. In 1710 fighting began between the *filhos da terra* (the sugar planters of Olinda) and the *mascates* (the Portuguese merchants of Recife and more recent immigrants). The Guerra dos Mascates (War of the Mascates), as it came to be known, was a bloody regional feud between different sections of the ruling class. In the end, with the help of the Portuguese Crown and their superior economic resources, the mascates of Recife gained considerable political clout at the expense of Olinda, which began its long, slow decline.

More dependent on sugar than Rio or São Paulo, Recife was eclipsed by these two centers as the sugar economy floundered throughout the 19th century. Recife is now the port of entry for many charter flights

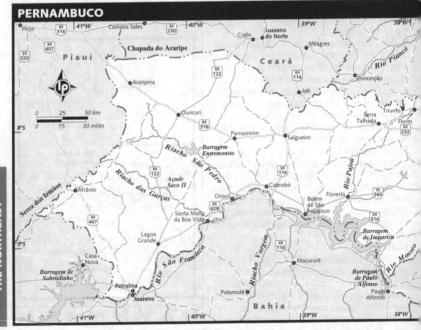

from Europe and has recently been trying to broaden its tourist appeal.

Orientation

Recife is large, modern and more difficult to negotiate than most cities in the Northeast. The city center is a confusing mixture of high-rise offices, colonial churches and popular markets. During the day, traffic and tourists get lost in the maze of winding one-way streets.

The heart of Recife, containing the old section of town, ranges along the riverfront in the Boa Vista district, across the Rio Capibaribe to the Santo Antônio district and then across to Ilha do Recife and the Recife Antigo district. All are connected by bridges. Olinda is 6km to the north over swamps and rivers, while Boa Viagem is 6km to the south.

Information

Tourist Offices The headquarters of Empetur (☎ 3427-8183), the state tourism

bureau, is inconveniently located in the monolithic Centro de Convenções between the city center and Olinda. There are more accessible information booths at Rua Bom Jesus 197, the Casa da Cultura, and the Terminal Integrado de Passageiros (TIP), the combined metro and bus station. The information desk at the airport has English-speaking attendants, sells maps and can book hotels. Disque Turismo (☎ 3425-8409) is the local tourist hotline.

Useful publications available from tourist offices include the *Recife & Olinda Tourism Map – Rota do Sol*, with a map of the beaches around Recife, and *Informativo Pro Lazer*, a bimonthly mini-guide to Recife. All are in Portuguese. *Jornal do Commércio*, one of the local newspapers, has cultural listings (museums, art galleries, movie theaters) in its daily Caderno C section.

Money In Boa Viagem, Norte Câmbio Turismo has a branch at Avenida Boa Viagem

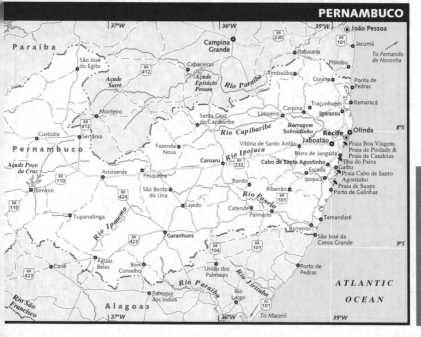

PERNAMBUCO

THE NORTHEAST

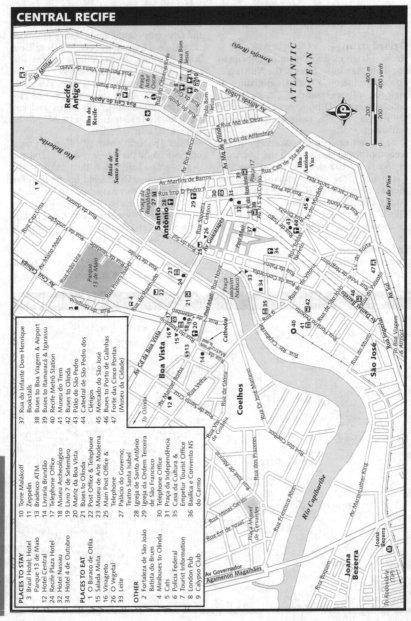

CENTRAL RECIFE

PLACES TO STAY
3 Brasil Hotel; Hotel
   Parque 13 de Maio
12 Hotel Central
24 Recife Plaza Hotel
32 Hotel Nassau
34 Hotel 4 de Outubro

PLACES TO EAT
1 O Buraco de Otília
15 Salada Mista
16 Vinagreto
26 O Vegetal
33 Leite

OTHER
2 Fortaleza de São João
   Batista do Brum
4 Minibuses to Olinda
5 Cats
6 Polícia Federal
7 Tourist Information
8 London Pub
9 Calypso Club
10 Torre Malakoff
11 Zeppelin
13 Bradesco ATM
14 Livraria Brandão
17 Telephone Office
18 Museu Archeológico
19 Livro 7 de Setembro
20 Matriz da Boa Vista
21 Buses to Olinda
22 Post Office & Telephone
23 Museu de Arte Moderna
25 Main Post Office &
   Telephone
27 Palácio do Governo;
   Teatro Santa Isabel
28 Igreja de Santo Antônio
29 Igreja da Ordem Terceira
   de São Francisco
30 Telephone Office
31 Praça da Independência
35 Casa de Cultura &
   Empetur Tourist Office
36 Basílica e Convento NS
   do Carmo
37 Rua do Infante Dom Henrique
   Bookstalls
38 Buses to Boa Viagem & Airport
39 Buses to Itamaracá & Igarassu
40 Recife Metrô Station
41 Museu do Trem
42 Buses to Olinda
43 Pátio de São Pedro
44 Catedral de São Pedro dos
   Clérigos
45 Mercado do São José
46 Buses to Porto de Galinhas
47 Forte das Cinco Pontas
   (Museu da Cidade)

500, Shop B. There are branches of Banco do Brasil at the airport, in the center at Avenida Dantas Barreto 541 (Santo Antônio), and in Boa Viagem at Avenida Conselheiro Aguiar 3600. Bradesco has lots of ATMs in the center of the city and Boa Viagem.

Post & Communications The main post office is at Avenida Guararapes 250 in Santo Antônio. The posta restante (postcode 50001-970) counter is in the basement. There are also post offices at the airport and the TIP.

Telemar has telephone stations with international service at the TIP, at the airport, and in Boa Vista at Rua do Hospício 148. In the old part of Recife, there's an Internet café in the Torre Malakoff at Praça do Arsenal do Marinha. There is also one in Boa Viagem at the Shopping Iguatemi mall.

Internet Resources Some useful Web sites about Recife and Pernambuco include:

www.recife.com – in English, with information about nightlife and restaurants, as well as online accommodations booking

www.vivabrazil.com/pernambuco – in English and Portuguese, with some nice photos and good links at the bottom of the page

darkwing.uregon.edu/~sergiok/brasil/recife.html – in English, with some good links to other relevant sites and a brief overview of the city and state

Travel Agencies Andratur (☎ 3465-8588, andratur@hotmail.com), Avenida Conselheiro Aguiar 3150, Shop 5, in Boa Viagem, provides national and international tickets at discounted prices. It also sells package trips to the Fernando de Noronha marine park.

Bookstores There are several bookstalls along Rua do Infante Dom Henrique. The airport bookstore and the Livro 7 de Setembro are the best bets if you're looking for foreign-language books. For lots of used books in French and English, try Livraria Brandão (Rua da Matriz 22).

Dangers & Annoyances Something to be careful of in Boa Viagem, aside from the prostitution scene, is sharks. Many hotels post shark warnings advising visitors to swim inside the reefs. Don't panic! The only attacks in recent years have been on surfers outside the reefs.

Museums & Galleries

With such a long and important history, it's not surprising that Recife is loaded with churches and museums, but few of them are must-sees.

The best museum, the **Museu do Homem do Nordeste**, is west of the city center along Avenida 17 de Agosto. Catch the Dois Irmãos bus from Parque 13 de Maio (north of Boa Vista) and ask the driver to let you off at the right spot (about 30 minutes). The museum is divided into three sections: an anthropology section about the people of the Northeast; a popular-art section with some superb ceramic figurines, including many from Caruaru; and a pharmaceutical exhibit about the region's indigenous herbal medicine. It's open Tuesday, Wednesday and Friday 11 am to 5 pm, Thursday 8 am to 5 pm, and weekends 1 to 5 pm. Entry is US$2.

The **Horto Zoobotânico**, a zoo and botanical garden combined (both renovated in 1990), is in the same neighborhood as the Museu do Homem do Nordeste. Hours are 8 am to 5 pm Tuesday to Sunday.

Train enthusiasts might like to visit the **Museu do Trem** (Train Museum) adjacent to Recife metro station. It's open Tuesday to Saturday 9 am to noon and 2 to 5 pm, and Sunday 2 to 5 pm.

For a look at some paintings by renowned artists of Pernambuco, including an impressive mural by Francisco Brennand, you can visit the **Museu de Arte Moderna** at Rua da Aurora 265. It's open from Tuesday to Sunday from noon to 6 pm.

Archaeology buffs will want to find time to browse in the **Museu Arqueológico** at Rua do Hospício 130. It's open Tuesday and Wednesday 2 to 4 pm.

These museums each have token admission charges of US$1 to US$2.

Historic Recife

To see the old city, start at Praça da República on the tip of Santo Antônio, where you'll see the **Teatro Santa Isabel** (1850) and the **Palácio do Governo** (1841). Close by is the **Igreja da Ordem Terceira de São Francisco** (1697). If you go into only one church in Recife, make sure this is it. It contains the beautiful **Capela Dourada** (Golden Chapel), one of the finest examples of Brazilian baroque you'll ever see. Also take a look at **Igreja de Santo Antônio** (1753) near Praça da Independência, and then visit **Catedral de São Pedro dos Clérigos** on Pátio de São Pedro, an artists' hangout. There are many intimate restaurants, shops and bars here, all with interesting local characters. On weekends there's often good music.

Walk from here down Rua Vidal de Negreiros to the **Forte das Cinco Pontas**, which was built by the Dutch in 1630, then rebuilt in 1677. Inside there's the **Museu da Cidade**, which displays maps and photos of the city. Hours are 9 am to 6 pm Monday to Friday, and 1 to 5 pm Saturday and Sunday.

Nearby at Praça Dom Vital is the daily **Mercado do São José** and the **Basílica e Convento NS do Carmo**. The market used to be a major center for food and crafts from throughout Pernambuco, but now you'll find mostly manufactured goods here.

Another interesting area is the **Recife Antigo** (Old Recife) neighborhood where the city was founded. There are lots of beautiful old buildings here, many of which have been restored as bars, restaurants and cultural centers. Wander around Rua Bom Jesus, Rua do Apolo and the Praça do Arsenal da Marinha, which contains the **Torre Malakoff**, a former observatory that now houses temporary exhibitions and an Internet café.

Casa da Cultura de Recife

The Casa da Cultura de Recife, across the street from the metro station, once served as a huge, colonial-style prison, but was decommissioned and renovated in 1975. It's now home to many craft and souvenir shops. Good traditional music and dance shows are often performed outside the building. It's open Monday to Saturday 9 am to 7 pm and Sunday 10 am to 5 pm.

Boa Viagem

Site of nightclubs and restaurants for the well-to-do, and most of the mid-range to expensive hotels, Boa Viagem has wide beaches that are essential for escaping Recife's muggy heat. The water is not always very clean and, apart from the beach, the area is ugly and boring.

Olaria de Brennand

The Olaria, a ceramics factory and exhibition hall, is set in thickly forested surroundings, a rare landscape for suburban Recife and an even rarer chance for travelers to see what the Atlantic rainforest looked like several centuries ago. The buildings and exhibits in the Olaria de Brennand are perhaps the most bizarre highlight of the Northeast – highly recommended.

The Irish forebears of the present owner, Francisco Brennand, arrived in Brazil in 1823 to work as peasant farmers. The unmarried daughter of a sugar magnate took a liking to Brennand's father, who was employed by her father. She later inherited her father's property and, when she died, willed her entire estate and immense wealth to the elder Brennand.

Brennand's father founded a brickworks in 1917 and continued this business until 1945. The house in which Francisco Brennand was born, in 1927, was imported from England in prefabricated form. Francisco studied art in France and was influenced by Picasso, Miró, Léger and Gaudí. The property in Recife remained abandoned from 1945 until 1971, when Brennand returned from Europe and set about restoring the dilapidated buildings.

Wander around sculptured collages of cubes, spheres and rectangles absorbed into animal shapes: worms with balaclava hats; blunt-headed lizards bursting out of parapets; cuboid geckos straddling paths; geese with flying helmets; birds of prey hatching from half-shells lodged in the walls; pigs formed from giant nails; and vistas of busts, buttocks, breasts, and phalluses. Meanwhile, black swans glide over schools of goldfish in ponds dotted with vulvas shaped like tortoises. Kooky, but fun.

THE NORTHEAST

The gallery/museum is open from 8 am to 6 pm Monday to Friday (US$3). For information, contact Oficina Ceramica Francisco Brennand (☎ 3271-2466).

To get to the Olaria from the center of Recife costs around US$10 in a taxi. Alternatively, take the bus marked 'CDU-Várzea' from outside the post office for the 11km ride to the bus terminus. From there continue by walking about 100m away from the city and over the bridge. Then take the first road on the left – easily recognized by the roadside statue of Padre Cicero. Walk about 2km, past a couple of stray hotels, until you reach a gaudy housing development. Take the road that goes to the left at the T-junction and continue for about 3km through dense forest to the office. Shady characters hang out in the area, so it's best if you are in a group. The walk will take about 1¼ hours.

You can also take a taxi from the bus terminal or the bridge to the Olaria and walk back after your visit. Tour companies and taxi companies will also do the trip from the center of Recife or Olinda, but it's expensive unless you can form a small group to share the costs. For a recommended taxi company, see Getting There & Around in the later Olinda section.

Carnaval

The Recife-Olinda combination may be the best Carnaval in Brazil, but even if you decide to do Carnaval in Rio or Salvador, Recife starts celebrating so early that you can enjoy festivities there and then go somewhere else for Carnaval proper. Two months before the start of Carnaval, there are *bailes* (dances) in the clubs and Carnaval *blocos* (percussion groups) practicing on the streets, with dancing to *frevo* (fast-paced music that originated in Pernambuco) everywhere. Galo da Madrugada, Recife's largest bloco, has been known to bring 20,000 people in costume onto the beaches at Boa Viagem to dance.

There are supposedly 500 different Carnaval blocos in the Recife area, and they come in all 'shakes' and colors. There are the traditional and well organized, and the

modern and anarchic. There are samba schools, *afoxés* (music of Bahia), Indian tribes and *maracatus* (African processions accompanied by percussion musicians), but the main dance of Carnaval in Pernambuco is the frenetic frevo. The Fundação da Cultura do Recife, which runs Carnaval, has on occasion organized public frevo lessons held at the Pátio de São Pedro for the uninitiated.

Along Praia Boa Viagem, Carnaval groups practice on weekends, and as Carnaval approaches they add *trios elétricos* (electrified frevo played on top of trucks) to the tomfoolery. The week before Carnaval Sunday, the unofficial Carnaval really starts. Several groups march through the city center each day and at least one ball kicks off each evening – time to practice that frevo.

Big-time Carnaval takes place from Saturday to Tuesday, nonstop. The big Carnaval groups parade in wonderful costumes, singing and dancing. (For the parade route and schedule, check the local papers or the tourism office.) Along Avenida Guararapes there's a popular frevo dance that starts on Friday night and goes on and on.

Places to Stay – Budget

Although details are included here for accommodations in Recife, most budget travelers prefer staying in Olinda: It's cheap and beautiful, there's lots happening and you can walk everywhere. If you want the beach, head to Boa Viagem, where there is a hostel and a few reasonably priced hotels.

City Center There are a couple of cheap places in central Recife near Parque 13 de Maio, but you should only consider them if you're on the tightest budget. The *Brasil Hotel* (☎ 3222-3534, *Rua do Hospício 687*) has grungy quartos at US$5/8 for singles/doubles and apartamentos with fan for US$7/10. Almost next door, the *Hotel Parque 13 de Maio* (☎ 3231-7627, *Rua do Hospício 671*) is a little more expensive, with basic apartamentos for US$12/15. Closer to the nightlife in Recife Antigo, *Hotel Nassau* (☎ 3224-3977, *Rua Largo do*

Rosário 253) has large, well-worn but clean rooms with good-sized bathrooms. Located in a pedestrian mall, it's a good value, with apartamentos for US$15/25. The *Hotel Central* (☎ 3423-6411, *info@hotelcentral .com.br, Rua Manoel Borba 209)* is a 1930s hotel with a pleasant, rambling design and a classic antique elevator. Quartos are reasonable at US$14/20, while apartamentos start at US$20/25. You can negotiate a discount for longer stays.

Boa Viagem The *Albergue de Juventude Maracatus do Recife* (☎ 3326-1221, *ajmr@ elogica.com.br, Rua Dona Maria Carolina 185)* is clean and well located, and has a swimming pool. Four-bed dormitory rooms cost US$9 per person with breakfast. Sheet and towel rental is US$3.

Places to Stay – Mid-Range
City Center The *Hotel 4 de Outubro* (☎/fax 3224-4900, *4deoutubro@uol.com.br, Rua Floriano Peixoto 141)* is a modern, functional hotel near the metro station. Apartamentos start at around US$35/40, with a 20% discount given for cash. The *Recife Plaza Hotel* (☎/fax 3231-1200, *atendimento@recifeplazahotel.com.br, Rua da Aurora 225)* overlooks the Rio Capibaribe in the center of town. Its apartamentos start at US$50/60, but it also gives a 20% discount outside of summer.

Boa Viagem The moderately priced hotels here fill up during summer. Prices are quoted for the low season – expect an increase of around 30% during summer.

The *Navegantes Praia Hotel* (☎/fax 3326-9609, *Rua dos Navegantes 1997)* is a small, well-located two-star hotel one block from the beach. Apartamentos start at US$25/30. *Hotel Portal de Arrecifes* (☎/fax 3326-5921, *Rua Boa Viagem 864)* is a small beachfront place. Apartamentos here start at US$20/28.

Three blocks from the beach, the *Hotel Pousada Aconchego* (☎ 3326-2989, fax 3326-8059, *aconchego@novaera.com.br, Rua Felix de Brito Melo 382)* features a swimming pool, a 24-hour-a-day restaurant and

some interesting original art in the foyer and halls. It also changes cash and traveler's checks at a decent rate. Apartamentos go for US$40/50.

Places to Stay – Top End
On the beachfront are the well-appointed five-star *Recife Palace Lucsim* (☎ 3465-6688, fax 3465-6767, *Recifepalace@lucsimhoteis .com.br, Avenida Boa Viagem 4070)*, with double rooms starting at US$150, and the *Internacional Palace* (☎ 3465-5022, fax 3326-7661, *Internacionalpalace@lucsimhoteis.com .br, Avenida Boa Viagem 3722)*, where room prices start at US$120.

Places to Eat
After a trip to Europe, the mayor of Recife decided that the restaurants and nightclubs of the city were too scattered, and successfully created two major leisure areas. One is in Recife Antigo and is called **Polo Bom Jesus**; the other is at the northern end of Boa Viagem and is known as **Polo Pina**. At night in the center it should be easy to find something to your liking around the lively Pátio de São Pedro or at the Polo Bom Jesus. Both areas offer a surprising variety of prices and styles.

Leite (☎ 3224-7977, *Praça Joaquim Nabuco 147)* is a famous traditional lunch place near the Casa da Cultura. For vegetarians, *O Vegetal (Avenida Guararapes 210)* on the second floor, is open Monday to Friday for lunch. For great regional cuisine, go to *O Buraco de Otília* (☎ 3231-1528, *Rua da Aurora 1232)*. Their *pouco de tudo* (a little of everything) special is self-explanatory and worthwhile. Find a hammock afterwards! The city center is also loaded with self-serve lunch places – try *Vinagreto (Rua do Hospício 203)* or the nearby *Salada Mista (Rua do Hospício 50)*.

In Polo Pina in Boa Viagem, *Prá Voces* (☎ 3465-1379, *Avenida Herculano Bandeira 115)* serves traditional seafood dishes; it's not cheap, but the fish stew is very good. The restaurants in Boa Viagem outside of Polo Pina are widely scattered. *Sabor de Beijo (Avenida Conselheiro Aguiar 2994)* is a classy self-serve lunch place that's very popular with locals. *Caxinguelê (Rua Mamanguape 157)* is a self-serve place with stacks of different salads and cold cuts. The *Flore de Cheiro (☎ 3325-0028, Avenida Domingos Ferreira 2840)* is a well-patronized pizza restaurant. Try the Pizza Flore de Cheiro.

Entertainment

Nightlife is concentrated in Polo Bom Jesus and Polo Pina; Polo Bom Jesus is the more interesting area. Every night of the week it is crowded with well-to-do locals (no riff-raff!), and it's a trip just hanging about watching them party.

In Polo Bom Jesus, popular nightclub options include *Calypso Club (☎ 3224-4855,*

Mangue Beat

'Os pés em Pernambuco, a cabeça no infinito' (Feet in Pernambuco, head in the infinite)
– mangue beat motto

Recife is the center of an influential music genre known as 'mangue beat' – a mixture of international and local rhythms. 'Brazilian music has a new address: Recife in Pernambuco,' wrote Jon Pareles in the *New York Times* when mangue emerged in the mid-1990s.

Internationally known exponents of mangue beat are Chico Science e Nação Zumbi (tragically, Chico Science was killed in an auto accident in 1997), Mestre Ambrósio and Mundo Livre S/A. Mestre Ambrósio is a group that combines guitar with *rabeca* (a type of rustic violin) and electric bass with *zabumba* (a big drum). Their choreography is based on regional folkloric dances. O Faces do Subúrbio combine American hip-hop with traditional Northeastern music.

If you want to see one of the mangue beat bands, check newspapers and cultural magazines to find out where the shows are. If you're in Recife in April, don't miss Abril Pro Rock – a large rock festival that features all the mangue beat bands, as well as other Brazilian groups.

Rua Bom Jesus 147); *Cats (☎ 3307-5646, Rua do Brum 85)*; *Zeppelin (☎ 3424-4334, Rua Bom Jesus 206)*; and *London Pub (☎ 4224-0750, Rua Bom Jesus 207)*. All have cover charges of a few dollars.

In the Torre district of town you'll find the best entertainment venue, the *Fun House (☎ 3227-4466, Rua Real da Torre 1013)*. It has nine different settings, ranging from the *caliente* Mexican Bar to the sophisticated Japan Club. The mix of rhythms changes from the *Espaço Brasil* (Brazilian space) and the nostalgic Woodstock to the reggae of the African Bar. It's open Wednesday to Saturday 10 pm to 5 am. Cover charge varies depending on the performers.

Hot venues change rapidly in Recife, so it's worth having a look at the Cultura page of the site www.recife.pe.gov.br, or you can go to www.guiametropole.com.br.

Shopping

Recife is a good place to look for Pernambuco's traditional handicrafts, such as clay figurines, wood sculptures, carpets, leather goods and articles made from woven straw. Check out the shops and stalls in the Casa da Cultura de Recife, the recently renovated Pátio de São Pedro, and markets such as Mercado do São José or the Feirinha de Arte e Artesanato, which is held in Boa Viagem Wednesday to Sunday, during the late afternoon and evening. On Sundays there's an interesting food and handicraft market on Rua Bom Jesus.

The Shopping Center Recife, at Rua Padre Carapuceiro 777 in Boa Viagem, bills itself as the largest mall in Brazil. It's a maze of stores, movie theaters, recreation and event complexes. Many locals even take their daily exercise walking around here.

Getting There & Away

Air From Recife, there are flights to most major Brazilian cities, and also direct flights to Lisbon.

The following airlines all have offices in Recife:

TAM (☎ 3462-4185), Aeroporto Guararapes

THE NORTHEAST

TAP (☎ 3465-8800), Avenida Conselheiro Aguiar 1472, Boa Viagem

TransBrasil (☎ 3423-2566), Avenida Conde da Boa Vista 1546, Boa Vista

Varig/Nordeste (☎ 3464-4440), Avenida Cons Aguiar 456, Boa Viagem

VASP (☎ 3421-3611), Avenida Manoel Borba 488, Boa Vista

Bus The Terminal Integrado de Passageiros (TIP; ☎ 3452-1103) is a combined metro terminal and bus station 14km southwest of the center. The TIP handles all interstate buses as well as many connections for plenty of local destinations.

There are frequent departures to Maceió (US$9, four hours), two a day for Salvador (US$38, 12 to 14 hours) and two daily to Rio (US$84, about 36 hours).

Heading north, it is two hours to João Pessoa (US$4), five hours to Natal (US$14), 12 hours to Fortaleza (US$35), 24 hours to São Luís (US$56) and 32 hours to Belém (US$65). There is frequent service to Caruaru (US$6, two hours), Garanhuns (US$10, 3½ hours), and Triunfo (US$20, eight hours).

Buses to Igarassu and Itamaracá leave from the center of Recife.

Getting Around

To/From the Airport Guararapes airport (☎ 3464-4188) is 10km south of the city center. Taxis cost about US$10 to the center – catch a regular taxi, not a special airport taxi, which is almost twice as expensive.

From the airport there are also regular buses and microbuses. The Aeroporto bus runs to Avenida Dantas Barreto in the center of Recife, stopping in Boa Viagem on the way. To Olinda, take the Aeroporto bus to Avenida Nossa Senhora do Carmo in Recife and pick up a Casa Caiada bus from there. Another option is to get off in Boa Viagem and take a Piedade/Rio Doce bus from there to Olinda.

To/From the Metro/Bus Station The shiny metro system is very useful for the 25-minute trip (US$0.40) between the TIP and the metro terminus at the Recife metro station, in the center. Travelers who want to

go straight to Boa Viagem from the TIP should get off at metro stop Joana Bezerra and catch a bus from there to Boa Viagem. To Olinda, you can catch the metro into the center, then take a Rio Doce/Princesa Isabel bus from the stop outside the metro station.

To/From Olinda From the city center to Olinda, catch any bus marked 'Rio Doce.' From outside the central metro station, catch a Rio Doce/Princesa Isabel bus. The main bus stop in Olinda is Praça do Carmo. Ask the conductor to let you know when you get there, as it's easy to miss. The Rio Doce/ Piedade and Barra de Jangada/Casa Caiada buses run between Olinda and Boa Viagem. Taxis from the center of Recife to Olinda cost US$6 and take 20 minutes. A taxi from the airport to Olinda will cost US$15.

To/From Boa Viagem From the center to Boa Viagem, take any bus from Avenida NS do Carmo marked 'Aeroporto,' 'Shopping Center,' 'Candeias' or 'Piedade.' To return to the center, take any bus marked 'Dantas Barreto'. Buses run along Avenida Engenheiro Domingos Ferreira in Boa Viagem, three blocks from the beach. A taxi from the center to Boa Viagem costs around US$5; VW Kombis cost the same as buses (US$0.60).

Bus & Taxi Buses generally have signs that show the origin of the bus followed by its destination. Local bus fare is US$0.60. To telephone a taxi, dial Teletaxi (☎ 3421-4242). Taxis are a good option in Recife. They are plentiful, distances are short, and the drivers are usually quite friendly.

BEACHES SOUTH OF RECIFE

This is excellent beach territory protected by coral reefs. The sea is calm, the waters are crystal clear and the beaches are lined with coconut palms and white sand dunes. The coastal Hwy PE-060 doesn't hug the ocean like the road in northern Alagoas, so you have to drive a dozen or so kilometers on an access road to see what each beach is like. There is frequent bus service to all these beach towns from Recife. Many of the towns have one or two simple hotels and, being away from Recife, all have excellent camping.

Gaibu & Cabo de Santo Agostinho

Although Gaibu is the larger town, beach bums need head only as far as Cabo de Santo Agostinho. There are facilities for snorkeling and spearfishing. Take a walk to the ruins of the **Forte Castelo do Mar**, next to the church.

On a hill between Gaibu and Calhetas (you have to ask around for directions) there's a small freshwater stream that's used for nude bathing.

Suape & Ilha do Paiva

Ilha do Paiva, nicknamed the island of lovers, is popular for its nude beaches. Take a boat from Barra de Jangada – it's worth a visit. You'll see boats along on the beach (US$5, 15 minutes).

The mainland beaches here – **Candeias**, **Venda Grande**, **Piedade** – are semi-urban with many beach bars, hotels, and crowds on weekends. But they are still good beaches, with clean water and sometimes strong surf. Suape has been developed as an industrial port and is worth avoiding.

Porto de Galinhas
☎ 0xx81

Sixty kilometers south of Recife is Porto de Galinhas (Port of Chickens). The name came as a result of the slave trade, which secretly continued after abolition. Upon hearing that the chickens from Angola had arrived, the masters of Recife knew to expect another load of slaves.

Porto de Galinhas has one of Pernambuco's most famous beaches, which curves along a pretty bay lined with coconut palms, mangroves and cashew trees. Unfortunately, there are some new housing developments creeping towards the town of Porto de Galinhas and it gets very crowded on weekends, even in the off season. Most of the beach, 3km from town, is sheltered by a reef. The water is warm and clear – you can see the colorful fish playing around your

feet. There are plenty of *jangadas* (local sailing boats) for rent (US$4 per person per hour). Other boats can take you out to Ilha de Santo Alexio for US$13 per person.

Should you tire of Praia de Porto de Galinhas, head for Praia de Maracaípe, a more secluded beach 3km away, which also has accommodations and some excellent waves for surfers.

Places to Stay & Eat Many of the visitors here either own homes (the celebrities and politicos of Pernambuco), rent for the season or camp (there's a campground at Praia de Maracaípe). There are several cheap pousadas along Rua da Esperança, all within 100m of the beach, including *Pousada da Benedita* (☎/fax 3552-1343) at No 425 and *Pousada Litoral* (☎/fax 3552-1046) across the road at No 410.

During the low season, competition is keen and apartamentos go for around US$10/15 for singles/doubles, but expect to pay nearly double these prices in the high season. Chalets sleeping up to six people, with cooking facilities, are a good cheap option for groups – try *Pousada Som das Ondas* (☎/fax 3552-1339, somdasondas@ somdasondas.com.br), which rents comfortable chalets for US$40 in the low season. The *Pousada Beira Mar* (☎/fax 3552-1052, beiramar@elogica.com.br, Avenida Beira Mar 16) is a great option on the beachfront. It has doubles for US$45 in the low season.

Famed for its seafood, Porto de Galinhas has several eateries. The most renowned is *Beijupirá* (☎ 3552-1271) on the road to Praia Maracaípe. Don't miss the *camarulu* – shrimp in sugarcane syrup with passionfruit sauce. Other fine restaurants in town include *Peixe na Telha* (☎ 3552-1323) on the beachfront, and *Itaoca* (☎ 3552-1309, Rua da Esperança 10). All these restaurants serve lobster, squid, shrimp and local fish cooked with coconut milk, pepper and cumin sauces. Try the beach bars along the beach for fresh crabs. The locally made *genipapo* liqueur is worth tasting, too.

Getting There & Around Eight buses a day travel to Porto de Galinhas (US$3, 1½ hours) from the intersection of Avenida Dantas Barreto and Rua do Peixoto (on the right-hand side of Dantas Barreto facing north) in Recife. VW Kombi vans and minibuses make the trip for US$6.

Minibuses and VW Kombis serve local destinations. A beach buggy to Praia do Maracaípe should cost around US$5.

Tamandaré
☎ 0xx81

South of Porto de Galinhas, the best place to turn into the coast again before Maceió is Tamandaré, 10km from the main highway on a good road. This is a small fishing village with a few restaurants and a couple of cheap hotels. Try the friendly and funky *Pousada Pega Leve* (☎ 3676-1577, *Rua São José 204*) on the beachfront. Apartamentos go for US$15/20. It's busy on weekends, but during the week the beach is idyllic and you can see the 17th-century Forte Santo Inácio.

São José da Coroa Grande
The first beach town you reach after crossing into Pernambuco from Alagoas is São José da Coroa Grande. It's 120km from Recife on coastal Hwy PE-060. This former fishing town now has many weekend homes and some irresponsible idiot was allowed to build a multi-story hotel that is totally out of place. Avoid it and continue your journey.

OLINDA
☎ 0xx81 • postcode 53000-000
• pop 360,000

Beautiful Olinda, placed on a hill overlooking Recife and the Atlantic, is one of the largest and best-preserved colonial cities in Brazil. Although many buildings were originally constructed in the 16th century, the Dutch burnt virtually everything in 1631. Consequently, most of what you now see was reconstructed at a later date. For information on Olinda's history, refer to History in the introduction to the Recife section.

While Recife plays the role of an administrative and economic center, Olinda is recognized as its cultural counterpart: a living city with bohemian quarters, art galleries, museums, music in the streets and always some kind of celebration in the works.

Orientation
Olinda is 6km north of Recife. The historical district, which constitutes about 10% of the city, is concentrated around the upper streets of the hill and is easily visited on foot. The beaches immediately adjacent to the city, Milagres for example, suffer from pollution and swimming is not recommended.

Information
Whatever services you don't find in Olinda you can secure in Recife. Sepactur, the main tourist office (☎ 429-1927), Rua Bernardo Vieira de Melo in the Mercado da Ribeira, has maps, walking-tour brochures and information about art exhibitions and music performances. The office is open Monday to Friday 8 am to 1:30 pm.

Throughout Olinda you'll no doubt hear the cry *'Guia!'* (guide). If you're carrying this book, they'll be of little use, although using one guide means the others won't be hassling you all the time. Yellow-shirted young apprentice guides *(guias mirins)* are available free from the tourist office. Freelance guides who cluster near the bus stop on Praça do Carmo charge between US$5 and $10 for a three-hour tour (fix the price before starting) and are a bit more informative.

Banco do Brasil is on Avenida Getúlio Vargas. Take a bus marked 'Ouro Prêto' from Praça do Carmo to the Bank Itau stop, then walk about 100m farther north.

The main post office, near Praça do Carmo, offers a posta restante service (postcode 53001-970). The telephone office is on Praça do Carmo. Cheap international telephone calls and email connections can be made at the Internet café across the road.

Police are fairly scarce in Olinda, so take the precaution of not carrying valuables in the street at night. Robberies are common during Carnaval.

Walking Tour
Starting at Praça do Carmo, visit the restored **Igreja NS do Carmo** (1580). Then follow Rua de São Francisco to **Convento**

São Francisco (1585), which is a large structure containing three elements: the convent, the Capela de São Roque (chapel) and the Igreja de NS das Neves (church). Approximate hours for these are Monday to Friday 7 to 11:30 am, and Saturday 2 to 5 pm and 7 am to noon.

At the end of the street, turn left onto Rua Frei Afonso Maria and you'll see the Seminário de Olinda and Igreja NS da Graça (1549) on the hill above (open 8 to 11:30 am and 3 to 5 pm).

Continue up the street and then onto Rua Bispo Coutinho. Climb up to Alto da Sé (Cathedral Heights), a good spot to enjoy the superb views of Olinda and Recife. There are outdoor restaurants here, and a small craft market with woodcarvings, figurines and jewelry. The imposing Igreja da Sé (1537) is open 8 am to noon and 2 to 5 pm daily.

Continue a short distance along Rua Bispo Coutinho until you see the Museu de Arte Sacra de Pernambuco (MASPE) on your right. MASPE is housed in a building constructed in 1696 that once functioned as Olinda's Episcopal Palace & Câmara (Government Council). The museum contains a good collection of sacred art and a photographic homage to the city. It's open Monday to Friday 8 am to 12:45 pm.

About 75m farther, turn right into a patio to visit the Igreja NS da Conceição (1585). Then retrace your steps and continue down the street, now named Ladeira da Misericórdia, to Igreja da Misericórdia (1540), which has fine azulejos (Portuguese ceramic tiles) and gilded carvings inside. It's open daily 8 am to noon and 2 to 5 pm.

From here, turn right onto Rua Saldanha Marinho to see the recently restored Igreja NS do Amparo (1613). It's open daily from 8 to 11:30 am.

Farther along this street is the Casa dos Bonecos, which houses the Bonecos Gigantes de Olinda, giant papier-mâché puppets used in Carnaval. Go in and have a look (it's usually open 8 am to noon, but if the doors are open you can usually pop in for a look).

Go back along Rua do Amparo to join Rua 13 de Maio to see the Museu de Arte Contemporânea (MAC), a museum of contemporary art recommended for its permanent and temporary exhibits. The museum is housed in an 18th-century ajube (a jail used by the Catholic Church during the Inquisition). It's open Tuesday to Friday 9 am to noon and 2 to 5 pm, and weekends 2 to 5 pm.

Rua 13 de Maio continues in a tight curve to a junction with Rua Bernardo Veira de Melo and Rua São Bento. If you turn left here up Rua Bernardo de Melo, you'll come to Mercado da Ribeira, an 18th-century structure that is now home to art galleries and souvenir shops. If you retrace your steps down to Rua São Bento, you'll reach the huge Mosteiro de São Bento (1582), which has some exceptional woodcarving in the chapel. Brazil's first law school was housed here for 24 years (it's difficult to say what lawyers actually did in colonial Brazil, but it had little to do with justice). The monastery is open daily 8 to 11 am and 2 to 5 pm, and celebrates mass on Sunday morning at 10:30 am, complete with Gregorian chants. Delicious homemade liqueurs are sold here too.

Beaches

The city beaches are polluted, and not recommended for swimming. However, there are many excellent beaches north of Olinda, which are described later in this chapter.

Special Events

Olinda's Carnaval has been very popular with Brazilians and travelers for several years. The historic setting combined with the fact that so many residents know each other provides an intimacy and security that you don't get in a big-city Carnaval. It's a participatory festival – costumed blocos parade through the city dancing to frevo music and everyone else follows. Everyone dresses for the Carnaval, too, so you'll want some sort of costume.

In recent years, there have been complaints of commercialization creeping into Olinda's Carnaval. On the other hand, Recife's Carnaval has been getting better reviews lately. Since the two cities are so close, you could try out both of them. Publications with full information on Carnaval

OLINDA

ATLANTIC
OCEAN

Mercado
Popular
(Market)

Rio Beberibe

To Recife

To Olinda

Praça
Dantas
Barreto

To
Beaches

Ladeira da
Misericórdia

Biordas 4 Cantos

Praça do
Carmo

Praça
João
Alfredo

0   50   100 m
0   50   100 yards

••• Walking Tour

schedules and events are supplied by the tourist office in Olinda.

Carnaval in Olinda lasts a full 11 days. There are organized Carnaval events, including balls (of course), a night of samba and a night of afoxé, but everything else happens in impromptu fashion on the streets. The official opening events – with the pomp and ceremony of the Olympic Games – commence with a bloco of more than 400 'virgins' (men in drag), and awards for the most beautiful, the most risqué and the biggest prude.

The Carnaval groups of thousands dance the frevo through the narrow streets. It's playful and very lewd. Five separate areas have orchestras (as the bands call themselves) playing nonstop from 8 pm to 6 am every night.

Apart from Carnaval, the festival known as **Folclore Nordestino,** held at the end of August, features dance, music and folklore from many parts of the Northeast. It's highly recommended.

Places to Stay

If you want to stay in Olinda during Carnaval, book several months in advance and be prepared for massive price hikes. During

OLINDA

PLACES TO STAY
6 Pousada Peter
7 Pousada do Amparo
16 Sete Colinas
20 Pousada dos Quatro Cantos
24 Albergue de Olinda
27 Pousada Saude
28 Pousada Olinda

PLACES TO EAT
5 Oficina do Sabor
8 Goya
12 Manoá
29 Creperie
30 Maison do Bonfim
33 Sabor da Terra
39 Etnia Sushi
40 Taberna Amsterdam

OTHER
1 Casa dos Bonecos
2 Igreja NS do Amparo
3 Igreja NS da Conceição
4 Farol de Olinda
9 Igreja da Misericórdia
10 Observatorio Astronômico
11 Museu de Arte Sacra de Pernambuco
13 Igreja da Sé
14 Igreja NS da Graça; Seminário de Olinda
15 Convento São Francisco
17 Museu do Mamulenco
18 Igreja NS do Bonfim
19 Viagems Sob O Sol
21 Senado Ruins
22 Mercado da Ribeira
23 Maria Maria
25 Igreja da Boa Hora
26 Museu de Arte Comtemporânea
31 Igreja NS do Carmo
32 Buses to Recife
34 Telephone Office
35 Internet Access
36 Post Office
37 Atlântico
38 Igreja São Pedro
41 Palácio dos Governadores
42 Mosteiro de São Bento

summer, prices are up to 30% higher as well. At the budget end there are several pousadas and hostels. Lots of quasi-official pousadas crop up before Carnaval, which can be good deals.

An excellent budget option is the *Albergue de Olinda* (☎ 3429-1592, albergueolinda@ hotmail.com, Rua do Sol 233), with clean rooms that sleep two to six people for US$9

per person (US$7 for members), including sheet rental and breakfast. Apartamentos are also available at US$15/25 for singles/ doubles. There's a pleasant hammock and pool area here. The *Pousada Saude (Rua 7 de Setembro 8)* is not exactly plush, but it's run by a large, chirpy family and has quartos at US$9 per person.

The *Pousada d'Olinda* (☎ 3439-1163, *Praça João Alfredo 178)* is a friendly place with a swimming pool and garden. It has a variety of options: dorm rooms for US$10 per person, quartos with fan for US$20/25, apartamentos with fan for US$25/35 and apartamentos with air-conditioning for US$40/45. English, French and German are spoken.

The popular *Pousada do Amparo* (☎ 3439-1749, fax 3429-6889, klebber@ elogica.com.br, Rua do Amparo 191) is a charming place with a lovely garden, pool and views. Very tasteful air-conditioned suites range from US$30/35 single/double to US$40 double (20% more in the high season). English, German and Spanish are spoken. Another tasteful place with a pool close by is *Pousada Peter* (☎ 3439-2171, *Rua do Amparo 215)*. Quartos go for US$25/30 and prices for apartamentos start at US$35/40.

Moving up in cost, the *Pousada dos Quatro Cantos* (☎ 3429-0220, fax 3429- 1845, Rua Prudente de Morais 441) is housed in a fine colonial building with a leafy courtyard. Quartos in the old mansion and apartamentos outside cost around US$40/50 for singles/doubles, though they will discount the quartos for longer stays or outside the high season. The splurge option is the suite (with two rooms plus a veranda), which costs US$75/85. English is spoken.

A new top-end option is *Hotel 7 Colinas* (☎/fax 3439-6055, Ladeira de São Francisco 307). Set on spacious grounds in the heart of Olinda, the pousada offers modern apartamentos for US$50/60.

Places to Eat

The old city has a variety of restaurants tucked away among its cobblestone streets.

THE NORTHEAST

Some are pricey, but there are usually a few reasonably priced dishes on the menu.

Down on Praça do Carmo, **Sabor da Terra** is a cheap self-serve lunch place crowded with locals. **Manoá** *(Alto da Sé 645)* is a rustically decorated bar/restaurant with a great view and live music nightly.

Facing Praça João Alfredo, **Taberna Amsterdam** *(Rua 27 de Janeiro 65)* is a trendy bar/restaurant with a large dance area out the back. Next door is **Etnia Sushi**, a stylish Japanese restaurant. For the flavors of France, there's the cute **Creperie** on Rua Prudente de Morais and the **Maison do Bonfim** *(☎ 3429-1674, Rua do Bonfim 115)*.

Oficina do Sabor *(☎ 3429-3331, Rua do Amparo 335)* is an elegant place with views – it's worth a splurge. Another interesting restaurant is **Goya** *(☎ 3439-4875, Rua do Amparo 157)*, where the owners are artists who display their work in the restaurant. The food is creative too.

Entertainment

There are several bars with music and a live-music venue in the old town near Pousada dos Quatro Cantos that are busy on the weekends. Alto da Sé has bars/restaurants that are open late with live music – but remember to ask the price of drinks before you indulge.

Closer to the beach, **Atlântico** is a concrete cavern on Praça do Carmo with live frevo, samba and dancing until daylight over the weekend, or there's the **Maria Maria** *(Rua do Sol 225)*, which is open to gay and straight alike.

Getting There & Around

Viagens Sob O Sol (☎ 3429-3303, ☎ 9971-8102, fax 3327-2175), opposite Pousada dos Quatro Cantos, has a variety of vehicles for rent, with or without a guide or driver. This is an interesting option if you can form a group of four or more. Trips can be arranged to Porto de Galinhas, Itamaracá, Fazenda Nova (Nova Jerusalém), Caruaru, Olaria de Brennand and various art and handicraft showrooms. There is a Web site at www.megon.com.br/viagem.

To/From Recife The main bus stop in Olinda is on Praça do Carmo. Buses marked 'Rio Doce/Conde da Boa Vista' and 'Casa Caiada' go to the center of Recife. The Rio Doce/Princesa Isabel bus stops outside the central metro station in Recife. Taxis cost about US$6 and take about 20 minutes. From Recife, take any Rio Doce, Casa Caiada or Jardim Atlântico bus to Olinda.

Buses marked 'Rio Doce/Piedade' or 'Barra de Jangada/Casa Caiada' run between Olinda and Boa Viagem (US$0.80).

BEACHES NORTH OF OLINDA

You've got to get out of town for a fine, clean beach. Head north at least as far as **Rio Doce** (6km), past that to **Janga** beach (8km) or beyond to **Praia do Ó** (12km), **Praia do Pau Amarelo** (14km), **Praia da Conceição** (17km) and **Praia da Maria Farinha** (23km). The road goes along close to the beach, but don't be deterred by the ugly development beside the road; the beaches are generally undisturbed except for beach bars and crowds on weekends. Enjoy the local *siri* (small crab) and *caranguejo* (big crab) at the beach bars. There are local buses to these beaches from Praça do Carmo about every half-hour during the day.

ITAMARACÁ

☎ 0xx81 • postcode 53900-000
• pop 13,000

Only 50km north of Recife, the island of Itamaracá is a pleasant and popular weekend beach scene. During the week it's usually empty. There is a regular bus service to the island, but getting to its many beaches takes time if you don't have a car.

There are 12 buses a day to the center of Recife from Itamaracá town.

Beaches

Itamaracá has a long history and a lot of beach. The better beaches are north and south of **Pilar**, Itamaracá's built-up town beach. Two kilometers north of town is **Jaguaribe**, a white-sand beach with beach bars and reclining chairs for weekend sun worshippers. For more isolated beaches, hike

5km farther north along the coast to **Praia Lance dos Cações** and **Fortinho**. Immediately south of town is **Praia Baixa Verde**, and every 3km south are more beaches: **Praia Rio Ambo, Praia Forno de Cal, Praia de São Paulo** and finally **Praia de Vila Velha**, which also is an historic old port near Forte Orange. All these beaches are on the ocean side of the island.

Forte Orange

This fort was built on the south end of the island by the Dutch in 1630 and served as a base in a series of battles against the Portuguese colonies in Recife and Olinda. It's an impressive bastion, right on the water. There's now a four-star hotel nearby and souvenir shops rearing their ugly little heads, but during the week it's still very quiet. The fort is open to visitors daily 9 am to 4:30 pm.

Centro Peixe-Boi

Close to the fort, this IBAMA-run center for studying the endangered *peixe-boi* (manatee or sea cow) is open Tuesday to Sunday 10 am to 4 pm. There is a tank containing some live specimens, but keep your voice down or they'll dive down to the bottom where they're hard to see. They also customarily nap after lunch, and you're asked not to wake them.

Coroa do Avião

Straight across from the fort is the small island of Coroa do Avião. Boat tours to the island (US$5) depart from the Itapissuma bridge, which connects Itamaracá with the mainland to the west. From the bridge you can catch a speedboat or raft to the fort, or head to the natural reef pools for a swim. They are approximately 20 minutes away from the fort by boat.

Vila Velha

Farther south from town is **Vila Velha** (1526), the first port in the Northeast, and its church, **NS da Conceição** (1526), the second oldest in Brazil. Take a VW Kombi to get to these and other distant points from the town of Itamaracá.

Places to Stay & Eat

The good news is that there are some inexpensive accommodations on the island. At Pilar, *Albergue Ciranda da Itamaracá* (☎ 3544-1810) has dorm rooms for US$8 per person. The *Pousada de Itamaracá* (☎/fax 3544-1152, Rua Fernando Lopes 205), near the center of Itamaracá town, is a modern hotel with a swimming pool and apartamentos at US$40 for a double.

In Rio Âmbar, 4km south of Itamaracá town, the *Itamaracá Parque Hotel* (☎ 3544-1255, Estrada do Forte, Km 1) is a reasonable option, with apartamentos costing US$45 a double.

There are lots of seafood restaurants around. *Peixada Forte Orange* (☎ 3544-1220, Estrada do Forte Orange 3400) and *A Petitosa* (☎ 3544-1081, Estrada do Forte Orange 700) are both recommended. There are lots of bars at the Pátio do Forte Orange.

Fernando de Noronha

☎ 0xx81 • postcode 53990-000 • pop 2050

The archipelago of Fernando de Noronha lies 145km from Atol das Rocas, 525km from Recife and 350km from Natal. The 21 islands of the archipelago cover a total area of only 26 sq km.

With its crystal-clear water (average temperature 24°C) and rich marine life, the archipelago here is a heavenly retreat for underwater pleasures. The main island (Ilha de Fernando de Noronha) is sparsely populated and tourism has become the main source of income for locals. It's now easier for independent travelers to visit, but it is possible that organized tours will be made compulsory again if numbers of visitors prove detrimental to the environment. Even though Fernando de Noronha is now protected as a national marine park, the effects of tourism on its fragile ecosystem need to be monitored carefully (see the following History section).

THE NORTHEAST

History
The archipelago was discovered by the Spanish adventurer and cartographer Juan de la Cosa, who had been Columbus' pilot in 1492, and first appeared on the maps by the name of Quaresma (Lent). A Portuguese aristocrat, Fernão de Noronha, was awarded the islands by his friend King Dom Manoel in 1504. He never set foot on the islands and forgot about them. They were taken back by the Crown years later.

The islands, with their strategic position between Europe and the New World, were occupied by the French and the Dutch, but in 1737 the Portuguese managed to reclaim Fernando de Noronha. They built 10 forts: All that remains today are the ruins of the fortresses of NS dos Remédios and São Pedro do Boldró, along with a few sunken shipwrecks.

Over the years, the islands have been used as a military base by the US (during WWII), a prison, a weather station, an air base and, most recently, a tourist resort.

There has already been some misguided tampering with the island ecology. The teju, a black-and-white lizard, was introduced to eat the island rats that had come ashore with the Europeans in colonial days. Unfortunately, the teju prefers small birds and crabs to rat.

A struggle between developers and environmentalists over the future of the islands was resolved in 1988 when most of the archipelago was declared a Parque Nacional Marinho (marine national park) in order to protect its natural treasures. These treasures include 24 different species of marine bird; two species of marine tortoise, one of which – the *tartaruga-de-pente (Eretmochelys imbricata)* – is in danger of extinction; sharks; stingrays; dolphins; whales; and a vast number of fish species.

Tourism has proved a blessing for the economy and a bane for the ecosystem of the archipelago.

Visitors are limited to 480 at any one time, and IBAMA keeps tight control of access to some beaches. It has 12 guards on the islands, and plenty of signs.

Planning
The rainy season is from February to July and the time zone in the islands is one hour ahead of Brazilian Standard Time. Bring everything you'll need for your stay (eg sunscreen, insect repellent, magazines and snorkeling gear) as prices are high due to the cost of transporting goods from the mainland. Take sufficient Brazilian money with you. Don't count on changing money on Fernando de Noronha, where the exchange facilities are virtually nil and the exchange rates are low.

Orientation
On the largest and only inhabited island, the population is concentrated in the small village of Vila dos Remédios. Morro do Pico, the highest point on the island, is 321m above sea level – and more than 4300m above the ocean floor, as the island is an extinct volcanic cone.

Information
Information is available from the Divisão de Turismo (☎ 3619-1352) in the Palácio São Miguel in Vila dos Remédios. Its hours vary daily. There are great views from here. The Visitor Center at the Projeto TAMAR (☎ 3619-1171) on Alameda do Boldró, the main road in town, is also a good source of information.

The island's one and only bank is Banco Real in Vila dos Remédios. Visa withdrawals are possible.

The post office is also in Vila dos Remédios. The telephone office is in the Hotel Esmeralda do Atlântico, on Alameda do Boldró.

Two of the island's better travel agencies are Dolphin Travel (☎ 3619-1129) and Mubatur (☎ 3619-1266), both on Alameda do Boldró.

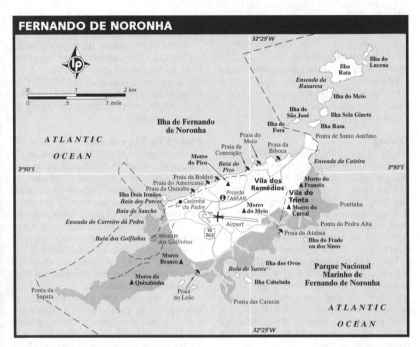

FERNANDO DE NORONHA

The Hospital São Lucas (☎ 3619-1377) in Vila dos Remédios looks after medical emergencies. The Polícia Civil (☎ 3619-1179) has its headquarters at Vila do Trinta.

Visitors Tax The state government imposes a daily environment preservation tax on visitors to the island. For the first week, it's US$14 a day. After that, it increases: Two weeks costs US$235 and a month is US$1200. A week is long enough to see the sights. For current fees and lots of other information about the island, check out an excellent Web site, which is in English, at www.noronha.com.br/english.

Beaches
Inside the boundaries of the park, IBAMA allows bathing at certain beaches, but restricts access to others in the interest protecting marine life.

The 26 island beaches are clean, beautiful and almost deserted. The beaches facing the mainland – **Conceição**, **Boldró**, **do Americano**, **Quixaba** and **Cacimba do Padre** – are the surfers' favorites. Cacimba do Padre is the only one with fresh water. Facing the Atlantic are the beaches of **Atalaia**, **Caiera** and **do Leão**, considered by many to be the most beautiful on the island. **Baía do Sueste** is the site of the TAMAR station, where it's possible to swim with the turtles.

Baía dos Golfinhos (Dolphin Bay) is strictly off-limits to swimmers, but access is permitted to **Mirante dos Golfinhos**, a viewpoint where you can watch hundreds of dolphins cavorting in the water early every morning. It's a real spectacle.

You can get to **Baía do Sancho** either by boat or by following a trail from Mirante dos Golfinhos that leads through bramble and bush, past almond trees and over sharp rocks to a beautiful beach.

Tourism has already affected the ecosystem of the archipelago. As a result IBAMA requires visitors to obey the following rules:

THE NORTHEAST

- Don't dump trash or food on the ground, in the sea or on the beach.
- Don't remove coral, shells or marine creatures.
- Don't use spearguns or traps.
- Don't take any plants or animals to or from the archipelago.
- Respect ecological protection areas.
- Don't swim with the dolphins.
- Don't hunt underwater.

Diving

Diving is the island's major attraction. Its transparent waters have a 40m visibility, 230 fish species, 15 coral varieties and five types of (harmless) shark. Snorkeling is best at Baía dos Porcos, Ponta das Caracas, Baía do Sueste and Atalaia, where there is a large pool at low tide. Scuba divers prefer Ilha Rata, Ilha de Morro de Fora, Enseada da Rasureta and Ponta da Sapata.

Both Águas Claras (☎ 3619-1225) and Noronha Divers (☎ 3619-1112) organize scuba-diving excursions with instructors and rent diving equipment. Cost is between US$50 and $70. Ask if diving is still permitted in Baía de Santo Antônio, the site of the wreck of the Greek ship *Asturia,* sunk in 1940.

Surfing

The best time for waves is between December and March. The best beaches for surfing are **Praia do Meio, Conceição, do Americano, Quixaba, Boldró** and **Cacimba do Padre.**

Organized Tours

Organized tours sold by travel agencies in Recife usually include your airfare to and from Fernando de Noronha, lodging (apartamento, including full board) and guided tours of the island by land and sea. Higher prices apply during the high season and for apartamentos with air-conditioning (which isn't really necessary).

Independent travelers can buy airline tickets directly from Nordeste or Trip, and should have little difficulty negotiating lower prices for lodging and board on the island. This independent approach also allows you to pick and choose your accom- modations and avoid the overpriced lodg- ings of most package tours.

In Recife, Fernando de Noronha tours are packaged by Andratur (☎ 0xx81-465-8588, andratur@elogoca.com.br) with four-day/three-night packages for US$420. In Natal, Manary Ecotours (☎ 0xx84-219-2900, manary@digi.com.br) has a Fernando de Noronha package.

Places to Stay & Eat

The only classified hotel, the *Esmeralda do Atlântico* (☎/fax 3619-1255, Alameda do Boldró) is very expensive (US$100 per person) and usually fully booked with package tours. There are over 70 pousadas and *pensões* (pensions), and many of the is- landers rent out quartos in their private homes. Recommended pousadas include the very friendly *Pousada Tia Zéte* (☎ 3619-1242, fax 3619-1459, Rua Nice Cordeiro 8), 500m from Vila dos Remédios in the Flo- resta Velha neighborhood.

Many travelers now choose to stay in Vila do Trinta, around five minutes walk from Vila dos Remédios. It's a bit quieter and there's a small supermarket for daily needs. A clean and friendly pousada in Vila da Trinta is the *Pousada Barcelar* (☎ 3619-1249, fax 3619-1461, Avenida Major Costa 128), which charges US$30 per person in an apartamento with air-conditioning and a minibar (useful for keeping drinks and food). A bit more upmarket is the *Pousada Monsieur Rocha* (☎ 3619-1252, fax 3619-1138, Rua D Juquinha 139) in Vila da Trinta. Rates for apartamentos start at around US$40 per person and include breakfast, lunch and dinner. Quartos are about US$5 less per person.

Many accommodation prices include full board but this is starting to change and some now offer only breakfast. Good restaurants in Vila dos Remédios include *Ekologicus* (☎ 3619-1404, Estrada do Sueste), with seafood platters for US$25, or *Nascimento* (☎ 3619-1456, Avenida Major Costa 115) which serves a great seafood *caldeirada* (stew). The self-serves at the *Restaurante do Biu* (☎ 3619-1235) in the Floresta Nova neighborhood and *Pousada*

Atalaia (☎/fax 3619-1300, Rua D Juquinha 126) are cheap and recommended. On Saturday night, everyone goes to the **Bar do Cachorro** in Vila dos Remédios. The rest of the week is fairly calm.

Getting There & Away
Nordeste and Trip each fly twice daily between Recife and Fernando de Noronha. The flight takes 1½ hours and a round-trip ticket costs around US$280. Trip also flies twice a day to and from Natal for around US$230 round-trip.

Nordeste (☎ 3619-1144) is on Alameda do Boldró. Trip (☎ 3619-1379) is on Avenida Major Costa in Vila dos Remédios. The airport (☎ 3619-1182) is a couple of kilometers from the center of Vila dos Remédios.

From Natal, José Martino (☎/fax 0xx84-221-4732) charters his four-berth yacht *Delícia* for US$400 a day. The trip out takes around 48 hours, while the return trip takes 38 hours.

Getting Around
Buggies, cars, small motorcycles and bicycles are available from several operators, including Eduardo Galvão de Brito Lira (☎ 3619-1355) at the Esmeralda do Atlântico Hotel. The average cost of buggies and cars is US$70 per day with a driver. Motorcycles are US$30 a day and a good idea if you want to go to see the dolphins arriving at the Baía dos Golfinhos at 5:30 am. Bicycles are US$10 a day. Boats are available at Vila Porto de Santo Antônio near the point. Hitching is possible and taxis may even take you for free if you're heading in their direction.

Inland

CARUARU
☎ 0xx81 • postcode 55000-000
• pop 217,000

If you like folk art and you wake up in Recife on a Tuesday or Saturday feeling like a day trip, you're in luck. Caruaru, South America's capital for ceramic-figurine art, is only a couple of hours west.

Feira Livre
The Feira Livre (Grand Open Fair), held in the center of Caruaru on Tuesday and Saturday, is a hot, noisy crush of Nordestinos: vendors, poets, singers, rural and town folk, tourists, artisans and musicians. *Zabumba* (drum) bands are accompanied by the music of *pífanos* (flutes), and *sulanqueiros* (rag merchants) hawk their scraps of clothing.

The fair has become a popular tourist attraction, and many items on sale are produced for tourists. Alongside pots, leather bags and straw baskets are representations of strange beasts and mythical monsters crafted by artists almost as famous as Caruaru's original master, Mestre Vitalino. To see the artists at work, visit Alto de Moura (described later in this section). If you want to buy some figurines, wait until you see what is offered in Alto de Moura before buying at the fair.

In addition to ceramics, you can hear singers and poets perform *literatura de cordel* (literally 'string literature'), poetry by and for the people, sold in little brochures that hang from the fair stands by string (hence the name). The poems tell of political events, national figures, miracles and festivals, as well as traditional comedies and tragedies (for example, one is about a woman who lost her honor to Satan). Although its role in diffusing popular culture is threatened by TV, literatura de cordel is still written, sold and performed in public by Caruaru's poets.

In a separate section of the main fair, there's the *feira do troca-troca* (barter fair), where junk and treasure are traded.

Other Fairs
The **Feira de Artesanato**, a handicraft fair, is open daily 6 am to 5 pm on Parque 18 de Maio. **Feira da Sulanca** is the largest textile and clothing fair in the Northeast. It is also set up on Parque 18 de Maio and runs non-stop from 2pm on Monday until 2 pm Tuesday.

Museums
The **Museu do Forró** contains personal effects, documents and photos of the father of forró, Luis Gonzaga. The interesting

exhibit also includes records and musical instruments. The museum, on Praça José Vasconcelos, is open Tuesday to Saturday 8 am to 5 pm, and Sunday 9 am to 1 pm. Visit **Museu do Barro** to see displays of pottery produced by famous local artists, including works by Mestre Vitalino. The museum is inside the Espaço Cultural Tancredo Neves, at Praça José Vasconcelos 100. It's open Tuesday to Saturday 8 am to 5 pm and Sunday 9 am to 1 pm.

Alto de Moura

Alto de Moura, 6km west of Caruaru, is a small community of potters that specializes in producing *figurinhas* (figurines). Many of the potters are descendants of Mestre Vitalino, who brought fame to Alto de Moura. Other noted artists are Zé Caboclo, Manuel Eudocio and Cunhado de Zé Caboclo. The **Museu Casa do Mestre Vitalino** (Master Vitalino House Museum), housed in the simple home of the master, contains his tools and personal effects. It's open Monday to Saturday 8 am to noon and 2 to 6 pm, and Sunday 8 am to noon.

Take a taxi or bus here, then wander the streets and browse through the dozens of workshops and galleries. If you want to purchase figurines, you're better off buying them here than in Caruaru.

Places to Stay & Eat

Caruaru is a long day trip from Recife, but there's no real need to stay here overnight. If you do decide to stay, the **Hotel Central** (*☎/fax 3721-5880, Rua Vigario Freire 71*) is a good budget place, with clean and basic apartamentos for US$15 a double with a good breakfast.

Fortunately, there's plenty of cachaça (sugarcane rum) and sugarcane broth to quench your thirst, and local foods like *dobradinhas* (tripe stew) and *sarapatel* (a bloody goulash of pork guts) to appease your appetite. Spartan, inexpensive places for this type of food are **Bar do Biu** (*Rua Sanharó 8*) and **Bar da Linguiça** (*Rua Nunes Machado 278*).

If the appeal of these local foods fades, try **Barrilândia** (*Rua Silva Jardim 71*), a good

pizzeria with the feel of a Wild West saloon. On the flip side, for excellent regional cuisine in a tasteful setting, pull into the highly recommended **Do Korôca** (*☎ 3721-8207, Rua Floriano Peixoto 160*).

Getting There & Around

Caruaru is linked by shuttle buses from the TIP in Recife every half-hour. The trip takes two hours and costs US$6. There is daily bus service (US$2, one hour) from Caruaru to Fazenda Nova. The bus station (*☎ 3721-3869*) is at Km 68 on Hwy BR-104, 3km from the center, from which it's very easy to get a taxi, Kombi or local bus into town.

FAZENDA NOVA & NOVA JERUSALÉM

☎ 0xx81 • postcode 55175-000 • pop 4000

The small town of Fazenda Nova, 50km northwest of Caruaru, is famous for its theater-city reconstruction of Jerusalem, known as Nova Jerusalém. Surrounded by a 3m-high wall with seven gateways, 70 towers and 12 granite stages, the reconstruction occupies an area equivalent to one-third of the walled city of Jerusalem as it stood in the time of Jesus.

The time to visit is during *Semana Santa* (Holy Week, which is the week before Easter and falls in March or April; dates vary), when several hundred of the inhabitants of Fazenda Nova perform the *Paixão de Cristo* (Passion Play).

Places to Stay

There's a campground, **Camping Fazenda Nova**, at Nova Jerusalém. In the center of Fazenda Nova, you can stay at the **Grande Hotel** (*☎ 3732-1137*) on Avenida Poeta Carlos Pena Filho, which has apartamentos costing US$14 per person.

Getting There & Around

During Holy Week, there are frequent bus services direct from Recife, and travel agencies sell package tours to see the spectacle. During the rest of the year, there are daily bus connections between Fazenda Nova and Caruaru.

GARANHUNS
☎ 0xx81 • postcode 55290-000
• pop 103,000 • elevation 842m

Garanhuns, 104km southwest of Caruaru and 222km southwest of Recife, is popular as a holiday resort because of its relatively high altitude. It's not exactly the 'Suiça Pernambucana' (Switzerland of Pernambuco) that's touted in the tourist brochures, but it does have pleasant parks and gardens and cool air – all of which are a respite from the oppressive heat of the interior of the state.

Places to Stay & Eat
The *Hotel Permanente* (☎/fax 3762-9080, Avenida Santo Antônio 179) has reasonable apartamentos at US$20/25 for singles/doubles. On the same street *Hotel Village* (☎ 3761-3624, fax 3761-0365, Avenida Santo Antônio 149) has apartamentos for US$20/29.

Fondue-lovers prepared to pay a bit extra should visit *Chez Pascal* (☎ 3761-2643, Avenida Rui Barbosa 891). The local food specialty is called *buchada de bode* (goat stomach). It's a classic Northeastern dish and you should try it at *Buchada do Gago* (☎ 3761-3894, Rua Mariana), a rustic place 5km from town in Vila do Quartell.

Getting There & Away
The bus station (☎ 3761-1554) is on Avenida Caruaru in Heliópolis, 3km from town. There are taxis and local buses from there. There are several bus departures a day to Recife (3½ hours, US$8).

TRIUNFO
☎ 0xx81 • postcode 56870-000
• pop 6600 • elevation 1004m

This small town 448km west of Recife is an important sugarcane center, and it remains the major producer of *rapadura* (a popular Northeastern sweet) in Brazil. The cool climate and abundant vegetation have earned it the nickname Cidade Jardim (Garden City).

Things to See & Do
The **Museu do Cangaço** displays a collection of weaponry and assorted personal items used by *cangaçeiros*, turn-of-the-20th-century brigands whose most famous and fearsome leader was Lampião (described under History in the Facts about Brazil chapter). The museum is open Monday to Friday 7 am to noon and 1 to 5 pm, and weekends 8 am to noon.

The town also has some fine architecture. The **Cine Teatro Guarany** (1922), on Praça Carolina Campos, is a stunning neoclassical piece. Unfortunately it's not open to visitors but you can admire it from the outside.

For excursions in the region around the town, you could visit **Pico do Papagaio**, the state's highest peak (1260m) with a great view, 10km from town; **Cachoeira do Grito**, with a waterfall and swimming hole, 6km from town along the Flores road, then 2km on foot; or the pictographs at **Sítio Santo Antônio**, 3km from town.

Places to Stay & Eat
The *Pousada Recanto* (☎ 3846-1140, Avenida Manuel Paiva dos Santos 20) is a small modern guesthouse charging US$15 per person. A bit better is *Pousada Baixa Verde* (☎ 3846-1103, fax 3846-1410, Rua Manoel Paiva dos Santos 114) with single/double apartamentos for US$30/35 – and guests are allowed free into the water park 150m from the pousada. It's also possible to order meals here, or try *Serra Linda* (☎ 3846-1365, Praça 15 de Novembro 174).

Getting There & Away
The bus station (☎ 3846-1356) is on Avenida Laurindo Diniz. There are daily bus departures for Recife (US$20, eight hours).

Paraíba & Rio Grande do Norte

Paraíba

Sandwiched between Pernambuco and Rio Grande do Norte, the small, sunny state of Paraíba contains the easternmost point of the continent, Ponta de Seixas. The coastal strip is this small state's most important economic region, fueled by tourism, sugarcane and pineapples. The interior is severely affected by drought, and those Paraíbanos who haven't already left it live in poverty and misery.

For most travelers, Paraíba means colored coastal cliffs, coconut palms and the most famous nude beach in Brazil – Praia de Tambaba.

JOÃO PESSOA
☎ 0xx83 • postcode 58000-000
• pop 595,000

The coastal city of João Pessoa is the capital of Paraíba and the third oldest city in Brazil. It lies 120km north of Recife, 185km south of Natal and 688km southeast of Fortaleza. The city center has a few interesting churches and other buildings, and Praia de Tambaú, 7km east, is a pleasant place to hang out for a few days.

Founded in 1585, the city was originally known as Vila de Felipéia de Nossa Senhora das Neves. It was later renamed for João Pessoa, the governor of Paraíba who formed an alliance with Getúlio Vargas to run for the presidency of Brazil in 1929. In response to advances from other political parties attempting to gain his support, João Pessoa uttered a pithy 'nego' ('I refuse'), which is now given prominence in all Brazilian history books, and is emblazoned in bold letters on the state flag of Paraíba.

João Pessoa's aspirations to the vice-presidency were short-lived: In July 1930 he was assassinated by João Dantas, an event that sparked a revolutionary backlash that eventually swept Getúlio Vargas to power (with considerable help from the military) in October 1930.

Orientation

The bus station is on the western edge of the city. The main hotel and shopping district, known as Praça, is farther east, and close by is Parque Solon de Lucena, a park containing a large lake circled by trees, which locals simply call Lagoa. There are numerous bus

Highlights

- Hair-raising buggy rides in the dunes at Genipabu
- João Pessoa's beautiful Igreja da São Francisco
- Wonderful beaches around Tibaú do Sul
- The tangled mass of the world's largest cashew tree in Pirangi
- Tambaba's famous nude beach
- Bizarre dinosaur footprints at Sousa
- Lively out-of-season Carnaval in Natal

Paraíba & Rio Grande do Norte page 569

Ceará

Rio Grande do Norte

North of Natal page 582

Natal page 575

South of Natal page 580

João Pessoa page 570

Paraíba

Pernambuco

stops here, which are convenient for local transport to, for example, the beach district of Tambaú or farther along the coast to Cabo Branco (see the Getting Around section).

Information

Tourist Offices PBTUR (☎ 226-7078), at Avenida Almirante Tamandaré 100 in Tambaú, is a good source of maps and leaflets. You'll find it inside the Centro Turístico, diagonally across from the Tropical Hotel Tambaú. English is spoken. It's open daily 8 am to 7 pm (until 8 pm in summer). There are also helpful tourist information stands at the bus station (open 8 am to 6 pm) and the airport (open 10 am to 4 pm). PBTUR also operates an English-speaking tourist telephone hotline called Disque Turismo (☎ 1516).

Money Banco do Brasil is on Praça João Pessoa, a couple of doors down from Hotel Aurora. It's open Monday to Friday 10 am

to 4 pm. In Tambaú, the branch in the Centro Turístico is open the same hours. There are Bradesco ATMs in the center on Rua Duque de Caxias and on the beachfront in Tambaú. Câmbio Turismo also changes cash and traveler's checks. It has branches at Rua Visconde de Pelotas 54 and inside the shopping center at Tambaú.

Post & Communications The main post office in the center of town is on Avenida Guedes Pereira. The main telephone office is on Rua Visconde de Pelotas 259. Both have branches in the bus station. There's a good Internet café, Gameleira Internet (☎ 247-8642), in the arcade at Avenida João Maurício 157. The owner David, from San Diego, is also a good source of unofficial tourist information.

Travel Agencies Cliotur Viagens e Turismo (☎/fax 247-4460, cliotur@cliotur.com.br), Avenida Almirante Tamandaré 310, shop 2

PARAÍBA & RIO GRANDE DO NORTE

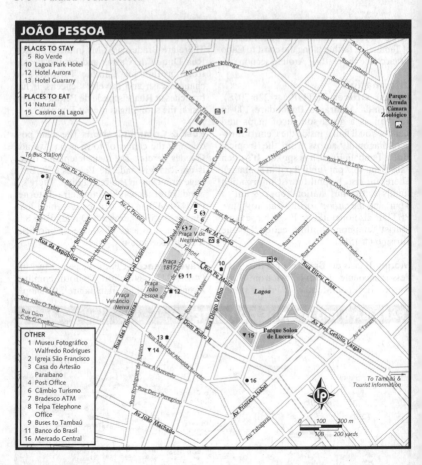

JOÃO PESSOA

PLACES TO STAY
5 Rio Verde
10 Lagoa Park Hotel
12 Hotel Aurora
13 Hotel Guarany

PLACES TO EAT
14 Natural
15 Cassino da Lagoa

OTHER
1 Museu Fotográfico
   Walfredo Rodrigues
2 Igreja São Francisco
3 Casa do Artesão
   Paraibano
4 Post Office
6 Câmbio Turismo
7 Bradesco ATM
8 Telpa Telephone
   Office
9 Buses to Tambaú
11 Banco do Brasil
16 Mercado Central

in Tambaú, offers a wide range of tours in and around the city. They include a three-hour city tour for US$10 and an eight-hour tour of the south coast including Tambaba for US$16.

Igreja São Francisco

The principal tourist attraction in the center is the Igreja São Francisco on Praça São Francisco, considered one of Brazil's finest churches. Construction was interrupted by successive battles with the Dutch and French, resulting in a beautiful but architecturally confused complex that was built over three centuries. The facade, church towers and monastery (of Santo Antônio) display a hodgepodge of styles. Portuguese tiled walls lead up to the church's carved jacaranda-wood doors. The church is open 9 am to noon and 2 to 5 pm daily. The complex also contains a cultural center and an exhibition hall with temporary art exhibits.

Museu Fotográfico Walfredo Rodrigues

This museum in the old Casa da Pólvora (Powder House), Ladeira de São Francisco, has an interesting collection of pictures of the old city. It's open Monday to Friday 8 am to noon and 1:30 to 5:30 pm.

Beaches

Aside from the rusty remains of battles against the French and Dutch, the beaches are clean. **Praia de Tambaú**, 7km directly east of the center, is rather built-up, but nice. There are bars, restaurants, coconut palms and fig trees along Avenida João Maurício (north) and Avenida Almirante Tamandaré (south).

South of Tambaú is **Praia Cabo Branco**. From here it's a glorious 15km walk along **Praia da Penha** – a beautiful stretch of sand, surf, palm groves and creeks – to **Ponta de Seixas**, the easternmost tip of South America. Clear water and coral make this a good spot for diving.

Immediately north of Tambaú there are good urban beaches: **Manaíra**, **Praia do Bessa**, **Praia do Macaco** (a surfing beach) and **Praia do Poço**.

Twenty-five kilometers north of Tambaú, **Praia Cabedelo** has a couple of pousadas, restaurants and bars. Boats to **Ilha de Areia Vermelha**, an island of red sand that emerges from the Atlantic at low tide, also leave from here. In summer, dozens of boats park around the island and the party lasts until the tide comes in.

Places to Stay

João Pessoa's main attraction is Praia de Tambaú, and that's where many of the hotels are. Although there are cheaper hotels in the center, it's worth spending a bit extra to stay near the beach.

Camping If you fancy camping at the easternmost tip of Brazil, the Camping Club of Brazil runs an excellent campground *CCB-PB-01* (☎ 251-1034) on the beach at Praia da Ponta de Seixas, 17km south of the city center. To get there, take one of the infrequent (about every two hours) Penha buses from the local bus station. Campsites cost US$7 per person. It fills up in summer, so it's advisable to book in advance then.

City Center The *Hotel Aurora* (☎ 241-3238, *Praça João Pessoa 51)* has adequate quartos at US$8 per person. Single/double apartamentos with fan cost US$12/19. Avoid the rooms overlooking the street, which can be noisy. The *Rio Verde* (☎ 222-5899, *Rua Duque de Caxias 111)* has clean, basic, windowless apartamentos for US$8/10 with fan or US$10/15 with air-conditioning. The price includes a surprisingly decent breakfast.

The *Hotel Guarany* (☎ 241-2308, *Rua Marechal Almeida Barreto 181)* is a clean, functional business hotel. Single/double apartamentos with fan start at US$25/40, while those with air-conditioning start at US$30/45.

The *Lagoa Park Hotel* (☎ 241-1414, fax 241-1404, *Parque Solon de Lucena 19)* next to the Lagoa is a modern hotel with well-appointed rooms at US$40/45 in the high season. In the low season, it gives a 40% discount.

Tambaú The best place to stay at Tambaú is the friendly *Pousada do Caju* (☎ 247-8231, fax 247-6871, *pousadadocaju@terra.com.br, Rua Helena Meira Lima 269)*. This sprawling, comfortable guesthouse is two blocks from the beach and contains two swimming pools and a large games area. There are dorm rooms for US$14 per person and apartamentos ranging in price from US$23/40/58 for singles/doubles/triples.

Hotel Pousada Mar Azul (☎ 226-2660, *Avenida João Maurício 315)* is a good deal, with huge apartamentos including a kitchen and refrigerator for US$15 (US$20 in the high season), single or double. Breakfast is not included. The *Hotel Pousada Gameleira* (☎/fax 226-1576, *Avenida João Maurício 157)* has standard apartamentos with air-conditioning for US$20/25. Both these hotels are opposite the beach.

The *Hotel dos Navegantes* (☎ 226-4018, fax 226-4592, *Avenida NS dos Navegantes 602)* has apartamentos costing US$50/65 in the high season. It's two blocks from the beach and has a swimming pool. The *Aruanda Praia* (☎ 226-1864, aruanda@ hotmail.com, *Avenida Almirante Tamandaré 440)* is a small hotel with comfortable apartamentos for US$25/35. A bit more expensive is the **Rhema** (☎ 247-1900, Avenida Antônio Lira 127), a clean, modern hotel with apartamentos for US$40/50. Highly recommended is the **Pousada dos Estrangeiros** (☎/fax 226-4667, annacat@zaz .com.br, Rua Alberto Falcão 67) in the suburb of Miramar, a bit closer to the center. Apartamentos cost US$30/40 and facilities include a pool and bike rental.

The five-star resort **Tropical Hotel Tambaú** (☎ 247-3660, fax 247-1070, rectht@ tropicalhotel.com.br, Avenida Almirante Tamandaré 229) is the city's entry into the world of modern architecture. From a distance this immense edifice on Praia de Tambaú bears a close resemblance to a rocket launching pad. The hotel (part of the Varig hotel group) has standard rooms for US$102/118, and luxury ones with a sea view for US$145/164.

Places to Eat

City Center *Cassino da Lagoa* (☎ 221-4275) has an open patio and a fine position beside the Lagoa. The food is ordinary but the view is great. Seafood and chicken dishes are recommended. The self-serve restaurants in the Hotel Guarany and Lagoa Park Hotel are good values and they're both air-conditioned. Vegetarians can head for *Natural* (Rua Rodrigues de Aquino 177), but it only serves lunch.

Tambaú Rua Coração de Jesus, one block from the beach and close to the Tropical Hotel Tambaú, is a compact restaurant strip with a variety of styles. *Adega do Alfredo* (☎ 226-4346) at No 22 specializes in Portuguese dishes, but it's a bit of a tourist trap. For cheap seafood, there's *Peixada do Duda* (☎ 247-2498) at No 147. The *ensopado de caranguejo* (crab stew) here is superb.

For excellent regional food, try the buffet at *Mangai* (☎ 226-1615, Avenida General Édson Ramalho 696). They're closed on Monday and don't serve alcohol.

Entertainment

Nightlife in Tambaú centers around the beachfront along Rua João Maurício and Avenida Olinda, which run off the beachfront near the Tropical Hotel Tambaú.

Bahamas Chopp (☎ 226-3767), on Rua João Maurício next to the pier, is a popular meeting place and has live music on the weekend. Along Avenida Olinda there's usually some live music on weekends. *Miralha* (☎ 226-1299, Avenida Epitácio Pessoa 4468) is a barbecue house during the day, but on Monday nights they have Forró com Turista, with authentic *pé de serra* (foot of the hills) forró. The dancing is spectacular.

For details of current events, ask at the tourist office, or check *Caderna 2* in the daily newspaper *Correio da Paraiba*.

Shopping

The craft market on Avenida Rui Carneiro, Praia de Tambaú, has ceramic, wicker, straw and leather goods for sale. On weekends, craft stalls set up in front of Tropical Hotel Tambaú. In the city center, Casa do Artesão Paraibano, Rua Maciel Pinheiro 670, also has crafts for sale.

Getting There & Away

Air Presidente Castro Pinto airport (☎ 232-1200) is 11km west of the city center. Flights operate to Rio, São Paulo and the major cities of the Northeast and the North.

The addresses for Brazilian airlines are:

TransBrasil, Avenida Epitácio Pessoa 2055 (☎ 244-5900)

Varig, Avenida Epitácio Pessoa 1251 (☎ 244-8300)

VASP, Rua Corálio Soares de Oliveira 497 (☎ 241-7114).

Bus The bus station (☎ 221-9611) is on Avenida Francisco Londres west of the city center. There is frequent service to Recife (US$5, two hours), Natal (US$7, 2½ hours) and Fortaleza (US$26, 10 hours), and 11 departures a day direct to (or via) Sousa (US$19, seven hours).

Getting Around

The platforms for local buses are directly in front of the main bus station. Walk straight ahead as you leave the bus station and pass through the many stalls. You'll find three parallel platforms. Buses to Tambaú leave from the first platform you reach, and buses to Jacumã leave from the third platform. Bus Nos 510 and 511 run frequently to Tambaú (US$0.50, 25 minutes). If you catch them from the Lagoa they will loop back through the city, pass the bus station and continue to Tambaú. Bus No 507 runs to Cabo Branco. Most local buses pass the Lagoa.

A taxi to the airport from Tambaú costs around US$13; from the bus station to Tambaú costs around US$7. To telephone a taxi, call Rádio Taxi (☎ 0800-1234).

SOUTH OF JOÃO PESSOA
Jacumã
☎ 0xx83

Thirty-five kilometers south of João Pessoa is Praia Jacumã, a long, thin strip of beach featuring colored sandbars, natural pools, mineral water springs and bars. It's a relaxing place to spend a few days, and the forró in the evenings gets very lively.

Jacumã makes a good base to explore the area's many fine beaches, including **Praia de Carapibus**, **Praia da Tabatinga** and the nude beach at **Tambaba**.

Places to Stay & Eat The best bet for budget backpackers is *Pousada das Flores* (☎ 9332-9495), next to the beach at Carapibus, just south of Jacumã. Scattered in a lovely garden setting, bungalows with bathroom and fan are available for US$10/15 single/double. There's also a pleasant veranda and eating area.

The *Hotel Viking* (☎ 290-1015, fax 290-1400, hotel_viking@hotmail.com) is perched on a hill overlooking the ocean a short walk south from Jacumã. Run by Leif, who has traveled widely in Brazil, the hotel has comfortable apartamentos for US$20/23, with a huge Swedish/Brazilian breakfast included. There's a large pool area and the attached bar/restaurant serves excellent local dishes with a Swedish touch. In summer there's always live music. *Pousada do Inglês* (☎ 290-1168, pousadadoingles@uol.com.br) is right next to the beach in the center of Jacumã. Well-appointed rooms start at US$20/28 and there's a pool and mini-golf. A more upmarket option is the excellent *Pousada das Conchas* (☎ 9301-3053, fax 222-2005) right on the beach at Tabatinga, 5km south of Jacumã. It's a new place built in a rustic style, and all apartamentos have verandas and hammocks. There's also a pool, craft shop and ice-creamery. Rooms cost US$25/35 with a large breakfast.

Seafood is fresh and plentiful. Try it at *Peixada de Jacumã* (☎ 290-1397) on Avenida Beira Mar in the center of town. *Zekas* (☎ 290-1185) has good food with a great view. The traditional meat and bean soups are very tasty. It's close to the main road leading to Praia de Carapibus. There's a big sign out the front.

Getting There & Away There's a new coast road south from João Pessoa. Driving from Tambaú to Jacumã now takes about 15 to 20 minutes by car and by the time you read this, there should be regular buses on the route. Ask for details at the tourist information booth at the bus station. Traveling north from Pernambuco state on Hwy BR-101, ask to be dropped off at the Conde/Jacumã turnoff, and take a local bus from there to Jacumã.

Tambaba
☎ 0xx83

About 10km south of Jacumã is Praia de Tambaba, the only official nudist beach in the Northeast. The beach, rated by Brazilians as among the top 10 in Brazil, is divided into two parts: one section is reserved exclusively for nudists, and the other is clothing-optional. To prevent problems, the nude section has public relations officers who explain the rules to bathers. Men are not allowed in the nude section unless accompanied by a woman. Interestingly, lesbian couples are permitted but gay male couples are not (unless accompanied by women).

Dom Quinzote (☎ 290-1185) is a rustic pousada right on the beach. It may well be Brazil's only nudist hotel, although the staff wear clothes. Basic but comfortable rooms cost US$30 for a double with breakfast.

The road is now paved all the way to Tambaba from Jacumã. You should be able to arrange transport easily at your pousada; otherwise it's a 1½-hour walk along the beach from Jacumã.

Pitimbu

Praia Pitimbu, 75km south of João Pessoa, has a long, broad beach, a coconut grove, some thatched-roof houses, and a couple of bars frequented by sugarcane farmers, fisherfolk and sailmakers for *jangadas* (the beautiful sailing boats of the Northeast). There are no hotels, but if you look friendly and bring a hammock, someone will put you up for a nominal fee.

Traveling north on Hwy BR-101 from Pernambuco state into Paraíba state, there's a turnoff just after the border that leads 35km down to Praia Pitimbu.

BAÍA DA TRAIÇÃO
☎ 0xx83 • pop 2900

Despite its peaceful, reef-sheltered waters, coconut palms and gentle breezes, Baía da Traição has a bloody past. In 1501, the first Portuguese exploratory expedition was slaughtered here by the Tabajara Indians. In 1625 the Portuguese had it out with the Dutch. They claimed victory and left some rusty cannons and the ruins of a fortress in their wake.

This fishing village, 85km north of João Pessoa, is more pleasant than the built-up beaches at **Cabedelo** and **Lucena** farther south.

Pousada Ponto do Sol Nascente (☎ 296-1050, Rua Dom Pedro 537) is a friendly place with double apartamentos starting at US$20. Ask for a room upstairs to catch the sea breeze. They also serve local dishes. A more upmarket place is the *Hotel Pousada Tropical* (☎ 296-1223) on Rua Osvaldo Trigueiro, with apartamentos for US$40 a double. It has a decent self-serve restaurant and convenience store.

There's a turnoff to the beach from Hwy BR-101 at Mamanguape. The Rio Tinto bus company operates buses twice daily, at 5:30 am and 3 pm, from João Pessoa's bus station (US$2.50, two hours).

SOUSA
☎ 0xx83 • postcode 58800-000 • pop 46,000

Sousa, 451km west of João Pessoa, is known for an offbeat tourist attraction: dinosaur tracks. The tracks were discovered in 1920 by a geologist who was researching drought – a major preoccupation in the *sertão* (the drought-stricken interior of the Northeast). Later discoveries of tracks at over 13 different sites along the Rio do Peixe showed that the whole region had once been a *vale dos dinossauros* (valley of dinosaurs). There are at least three sites in the vicinity of Sousa. The best is 4km from town, at **Sítio Ilha**, on the banks of the Rio do Peixe, where at least 50 prints have been left by dinosaurs that, judging by the depth and size of the imprints, weighed between three and four tonnes each.

This site is subject to flooding during the rainy season and is best visited with a guide. Transport options are limited to either hiring a taxi at the bus station in Sousa or asking the staff at the Hotel Gadelha Palace to arrange for transport and a guide.

Travelers interested in handicrafts should make a side trip to the town of **Aparecida**, 14km east of Sousa, which is famed as a center for the production of superb hammocks, textiles and goods made from leather and straw.

Places to Stay & Eat

The *Hotel Gadelha Palace* (☎ 521-1880, Rua Presidente João Pessoa 2) has single/ double apartamentos for US$20/25. There's a restaurant in the hotel, or if you hanker for pizza, try *Tropical* (☎ 521-2500, Rua José Vicente 2) on the pedestrian mall in the center of town.

Getting There & Around

The bus station (☎ 521-1458) is on Rua José Facundo de Lira. There are six bus departures a day that run via Patos and Campina Grande to João Pessoa (US$18, seven hours). Buses also depart four times a day to Juazeiro do Norte (described in the Ceará chapter). Taxis from the bus station to Sítio Ilha charge around US$12.

Rio Grande do Norte

Pure air, sun, fine beaches and sand dunes symbolize this small state in the extreme northeast of Brazil. This is where the coast changes direction from north/south to northwest/southeast, and the strong, dry ocean winds pile sand in huge dunes – the most famous being the 50m-tall dunes at Genipabu. The Potiguenses, as locals are known, are a friendly bunch and delight in their favorite dish, *carne do sol*. As in

Paraíba, the interior of the state is drought-stricken, and many former inhabitants have already migrated to other parts of Brazil.

NATAL
☎ 0xx84 • postcode 59000-000
• pop 710,000

Natal, the capital of Rio Grande do Norte, is a clean, bright city that is being developed at top speed into the beach capital of the Northeast. With the introduction of cheap charter flights from Europe, the city (along with Fortaleza) has seen a dramatic increase in foreign visitors. There is very little to see

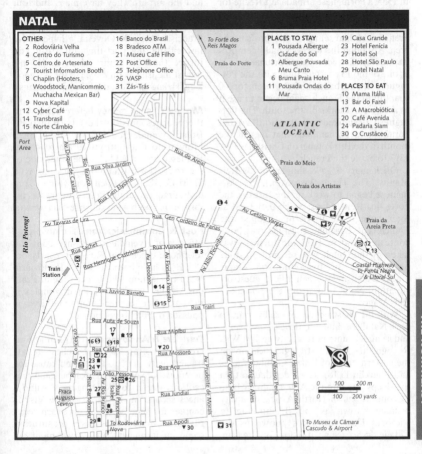

NATAL

OTHER
2 Rodoviária Velha
4 Centro do Turismo
5 Centro de Artesenato
7 Tourist Information Booth
8 Chaplin (Hooters,
   Woodstock, Manicommio,
   Muchacha Mexican Bar)
9 Nova Kapital
12 Cyber Café
14 Transbrasil
15 Norte Câmbio
16 Banco do Brasil
18 Bradesco ATM
21 Museu Café Filho
22 Post Office
25 Telephone Office
26 VASP
31 Zás-Trás

PLACES TO STAY
1 Pousada Albergue
   Cidade do Sol
3 Albergue Pousada
   Meu Canto
6 Bruma Praia Hotel
11 Pousada Ondas do
   Mar
19 Casa Grande
23 Hotel Fenícia
27 Hotel Sol
28 Hotel São Paulo
29 Hotel Natal

PLACES TO EAT
10 Mama Itália
13 Bar do Farol
17 A Macrobiótica
20 Café Avenida
24 Padaria Siam
30 O Crustáceo

To Forte dos
Reis Magos

Praia do Forte

ATLANTIC
OCEAN

Praia do Meio

Praia dos Artistas

Praia da
Areia Preta

Coastal Highway
to Ponta Negra
& Litoral Sul

Port
Area

Rua Simões

Av Duque de Caxias

Rio Branco

Rua Silva Jardim

Rua do Areial

Av Presidente Café Filho

Rua Gen Elycerio

Av Tavaras de Lira

Rua Gen Cordeiro de Farias

Av Getúlio Vargas

Rio Potengi

Rua Sachet

Rua Henrique Castriciano

Rua Manoel Dantas

Av Deodoro

Av Floriano Peixoto

Av Nilo Peçanha

Train
Station

Rua Juvino Barreto

Rua Traíri

Rua Auta de Souza

Rua Mipibu

Rua Caldas

Rua Mossoró

Rua Açu

Av Prudente de Morais

Av Campos Sales

Av Rodrigues Alves

Av Alfonso Pena

Av Hermes da Fonseca

Rua João Pessoa

Rua Princesa Isabel

Rua Jundiaí

Praça
Augusto
Severo

Rua Bartolomeu

Rua Branco

To Rodoviária
Nova

Rua Apodi

To Museu da Câmara
Cascudo & Airport

0   100   200 m
0   100   200 yards

of cultural or historical interest in Natal: The main attractions are beaches, buggy rides and nightlife.

Natal's **Carnatal** (out-of-season Carnaval), in the first week of December, draws huge crowds from all over Brazil. It's basically an excuse to party, and if you can't make it to Carnaval, this is the next best thing. (Some locals think it's even better.) Carnatal features the same kind of music and dance as the real Carnaval – lots of forró til you drop.

History

In 1535, a Portuguese armada left Recife for the mouth of the Rio Ceará-Mirim (12km north of present-day Natal) to drive out the French, who had set up trading posts in the area. Although the territory had been proclaimed by King João III of Portugal in 1534 as one of the 15 coastal captaincies, the Portuguese then abandoned the area for 60 years, until the French again began to use it as a base for attacks on the south. The Portuguese organized a huge flotilla from Paraíba and Pernambuco that met at the mouth of the Rio Potengi on Christmas Day 1597 to battle the French.

On January 6, 1598, the day of Os Reis Magos (The Three Wise Men), the Portuguese began to work on the fortress, the Forte dos Reis Magos, which they used as their base in their victory against the French. The Brazilian coastline was hotly contested, and in 1633 the fortress was taken by the Dutch, who rebuilt it in stone but retained the five-point star shape. Under Dutch and thereafter Portuguese occupation, Natal grew from the Forte dos Reis Magos.

With the construction of a railway and a port, Natal continued to develop as a small and relatively unimportant city until WWII. Recognizing Natal's strategic location on the eastern bulge of Brazil, Getúlio Vargas and Franklin D Roosevelt decided to turn the sleepy city into the Allied military base for operations in North Africa. The city became known as the 'Trampoline to Victory.' These days, it's known as the Cidade do Sol (Sun City), for good reason.

Orientation

Natal is on a peninsula flanked to the northwest by the Rio Potengi and the east by Atlantic reefs and beaches. The peninsula tapers, ending at the Forte dos Reis Magos, the oldest part of the city. The city center, Cidade Alta, was developed around the river port, which was built in 1892.

Information

Tourist Offices Setur's headquarters in the Centro Convenções de Natal is a bit out of the way. More convenient and useful are the information booths at Praia dos Artistas and the airport. They have maps and tour pamphlets. The best time to go to the booth at Praia dos Artistas is in the evenings, when Francisco Assis de Oliveira, a hyperactive lawyer fighting part-time for truth and justice (and his commission) in Natal's tourist industry, is on duty. He speaks good English and can help out with most things.

Money Change money before heading to the beaches outside the city. Banco do Brasil, Avenida Rio Branco 510, is open Monday to Friday from 10 am to 4 pm. Bradesco has an ATM on the other side of the road. Norte Câmbio & Turismo, Rua Trairi 433, shop 2, is open from 8 am to 8 pm daily. Francisco at the Praia dos Artistas information booth will exchange cash dollars.

Post & Communications The main post office is at Avenida Rio Branco 538. The telephone office is at Rua Princesa Isabel 687. Both have branches at the Rodoviária Nova bus station. The Cyber Café at Praia dos Artistas, close to the Chaplin complex, is the best place to check your email if your pousada or hotel is not online.

Dangers & Annoyances The dramatic increase in visitors to the beaches has attracted petty thieves. There's no cause for paranoia, but you should take the usual precautions – refer to the Dangers & Annoyances section in the Facts for the Visitor chapter for general advice on beach security. Praia dos Artistas has a prostitution scene and it can get a bit sleazy at night.

Things to See

The principal non-beach attractions of Natal are the pentagonal **Forte dos Reis Magos** (open Tuesday to Sunday 8 am to 4:30 pm) at the tip of the peninsula, and the **Museu da Câmara Cascudo** (☎ 212-2795), at Avenida Hermes da Fonseca 1398. This museum of folklore and anthropology features a collection of Amazon Indian artifacts. It's open from 8 to 10:30 am and from 2 to 4:30 pm Tuesday to Friday.

The **Museu Café Filho**, Rua da Conceição 601, will probably only appeal to history buffs. This museum is housed in the splendid mansion that once belonged to João Café Filho, and now displays his personal effects. Café Filho was the Brazilian vice president who assumed the presidency in 1954 after President Getúlio Vargas, presented with a military ultimatum to resign, had left a patriotic note and shot himself through the heart. Café Filho muddled through political crises until he suffered a major heart attack in 1955 and gave way to Carlos Luz. Café Filho recovered quickly and tried hard to be reinstated, but he'd lost his place on the political carousel and had to be content with his one brief moment of fame as the first person from Rio Grande do Norte to become president. The museum is open Monday to Friday 8 am to 5 pm and Saturday 8 am to 2 pm.

Beaches

Natal's city beaches – **Praia do Meio**, **Praia dos Artistas**, **Praia da Areia Preta**, **Praia do Pinto** and **Praia Mãe Luiza** – stretch well over 9km south from the fort to the Farol de Mãe Luiza lighthouse. These are mostly urban beaches, with bars, nightlife and big surf. The ones closest to the fort are rocky and closed in by an offshore reef.

Buggy Rides

Beach-buggy excursions are offered by a host of *bugeiros* (buggy drivers), mostly in Brazilian-built vehicles with brand names such as Bird, Baby, Praya or Malibuggy. An excursion lasting from 8 am to 4 pm costs around US$70 with four passengers in the buggy (a tight squeeze). The price includes transport and driver/guide, but excludes food and ferry fees (minimal). Take sunscreen, a tight-fitting hat and swimwear; and keep all photo gear in a bag as protection from sand.

Bugeiros seem to be a crazy bunch of wannabe racing drivers (check out the drag-strip traffic lights in the center) intent on demonstrating a variety of buggy tricks and spins on the dunes. They will ask you if you want the trip *com emoção* (with emotion). If you agree, you may be treated to some or all of the following: Wall-of-Death, Devil's Cauldron, Vertical Descent, Roller-Coaster,

Natal to Fortaleza by Buggy

Many adventurous travelers – those who don't mind sand in their faces or wind in their hair – choose to travel the 760km between Natal and Fortaleza along the shore. The trip takes five days, and during that time you'll pass approximately 92 beaches. You can travel in either direction, but whichever you take, it's an adventure.

Beach buggies average 40 km/h, and it takes a skilled driver to negotiate the uneven tracks, soft sand and small rivers that empty into the sea. You also have to drive at low tide. Locals will ferry you on their jangadas over the wide river mouths.

This stretch of coastline is one of the most beautiful in Brazil. There are cliffs of colored sands, rolling dunes, salt flats, reefs, palm-lined beaches and beaches with freshwater lagoons. It's fascinating to pass through or stay the night in the small fishing villages where the pace of life is slow.

Anyone can hire a buggy in Fortaleza or Natal and drive on the beaches, but a trip of this kind requires an experienced driver, like Cládio Chueiri (☎ 0xx84-641-2019) or Marcelo Cossi (☎ 0xx84-236-4217), both from Natal. Top Buggy (☎ 0xx84-219-2820) in Natal and HM (☎ 0xx85-242-7799) in Fortaleza are both recommended agencies that can organize this trip. Average cost is around US$100 a day, including the drivers.

and something best described as Racing the Incoming Tide – if you lose, the surf claims the buggy and the passengers scramble for high ground.

There are pirate bugeiros and accredited bugeiros, and the latter are represented by the Associação de Bugeiros (☎ 225-2077). You can usually arrange a deal through your hotel, and hostels may be able to negotiate a discount. A recommended driver is Celio Barreto, who works for Top Buggy (☎ 235-1430, ☎ 981-0190 mobile).

Places to Stay

Natal's hotel districts are around Cidade Alta (in the city center) and along the city beaches. Ponta Negra, 14km south of the city, also has a wide variety of hotels and pousadas, including some low-budget options. See the Places to Stay section in Ponta Negra.

City Center *Albergue Pousada Meu Canto* (☎ 212-2811, Rua Manoel Dantas 424), in a beautiful garden setting, offers basic quartos for US$8 per person (US$7 for HI members) with a good breakfast. Tia Helena is a delightful host who will treat you as a member of her family. It's highly recommended. There's another good central hostel, the *Pousada Albergue Cidade do Sol* (☎ 211-3233, Avenida Duque de Caxias 190), near the Rodoviária Velha. It has quartos for US$9 per person. Double apartamentos are US$20 with air-conditioning.

The *Hotel Natal* (☎ 222-2792, fax 222-0232, Avenida Rio Branco 740) has standard apartamentos at US$10/14, but a better value are the apartamentos with air-conditioning at US$12/16. Another popular budget option is the *Hotel Fenícia* (☎ 211-4378, Avenida Rio Branco 586), although it's looking a bit the worse for wear. Apartamentos here cost US$10/15 without breakfast. The recently renovated *Hotel São Paulo* (☎ 211-4485, Avenida Rio Branco 697) has apartamentos with fan for US$8 per person without breakfast.

The *Casa Grande* (☎ 211-4895, fax 211-0555, Rua Princesa Isabel 159) is comfortable as well as moderately priced, with

apartamentos with fan costing US$15/25 for singles/doubles.

The two-star *Hotel Sol* (☎ 221-1154, fax 221-1157, Rua Heitor Carrilo 107) has nice double apartamentos for US$30 but often offers discounts. There's also a good self-serve lunch place inside.

City Beaches At Praia dos Artistas, *Pousada Ondas do Mar* (☎ 202-3480), on Rua Valentim de Almeida, has adequate apartamentos with fan for US$8/14. The *Bruma Praia Hotel* (☎ 202-4303, Avenida Presidente Café Filho 1176) is a stylish hotel with doubles that are a good value for US$30 (US$50 in summer).

Places to Eat

For natural food, you can head for *A Macrobiótica* (☎ 222-6765, Rua Princesa Isabel 528), where the healthy atmosphere is accentuated by staff running around in white coats! For a cheap self-serve lunch in the center, try *Padaria Siam* (Avenida Rio Branco 596).

O Crustáceo (☎ 222-1122, Rua Apodi 414) specializes in seafood. The ambience is enhanced by a large tree poking through the roof in the center of the restaurant. Coffee enthusiasts should get their caffeine fix at *Café Avenida*, on the corner of Rua Mossoró and Avenida Deodoro. It also serves a delicious selection of pastries and cakes. The *Casa Grande* is a stylish place with regional food. It's in front of the pousada of the same name.

Mama Itália (☎ 202-1622, Rua Silvio Pedrosa 43) in Praia dos Artistas has a wide range of excellent pastas and pizzas. The spaghetti *fruta do mar* is chock-full of seafood and delicious. For seafood with a view, *Bar do Farol* (☎ 202-2005, Rua Silvio Pedrosa 105) is a local favorite. Their large servings feed two easily.

Rio Grande do Norte boasts a few good brands of cachaça (sugarcane rum). Try a shot of Ohlo d'Água, Murim or Caranguejo with a bite of cashew fruit.

Entertainment

Chaplin (☎ 211-7457, Avenida Presidente Café Filho 27) is a huge entertainment complex on Praia dos Artistas. It contains various bars – Manicommio, Woodstock and Hooters – each with a different ambience. Across the road, *Nova Kapital* (☎ 202-7111) has good live music most nights and a lively dance floor.

For folkloric shows and dancing, try *Zás-Trás (Rua Apodi 500)*. It has a restaurant section and the shows start at around 8 pm. After the show, the dancers will teach guests dances such as forró, *ciranda de roda* (round dancing) and something called *aeroreggae*. From 11 pm onwards, the dance floor gets crowded and the action heats up. Forró com Turista, on Thursday nights from 10 pm in the *Centro do Turismo (☎ 211-6149, Rua Aderbal Figueiredo 980)*, sounds corny but it's a lot of fun and the live music is great.

Shopping

The Centro de Turismo has lots of stalls selling bottles of colored sand, ceramics and other local handicrafts. On Praia dos Artistas, the Centro de Artesanato is a good spot to look for that perfect gift.

Getting There & Away

Air There are flights to all major cities in the Northeast and the North, and to Rio and São Paulo. Airline offices in the Cidade Alta are as follows:

VASP, Rua João Pessoa 220 (☎ 643-1137)

Varig/Cruzeiro, Rua Mossoró 598 (☎ 643-1100)

TransBrasil, Avenida Deodoro 363 (☎ 643-1135)

Trip, Rua Prudente Morais 4283 (☎ 0800-558747)

Bus There are nine buses a day to Recife (US$14, 4½ hours), frequent service to João Pessoa (US$6, 2½ hours) and a daily departure to Salvador at noon (US$50, 18 hours). Six regular buses (US$18, eight hours) and one *leito* (US$33) depart daily for Fortaleza. Two buses a day depart for Rio (US$95, 44 hours), at 12:30 and 1:45 pm. There is one bus a day for Juazeiro do Norte, Ceará (US$23, 11 hours), which leaves at 7 pm.

Getting Around

To/From the Airport Natal's Augusto Severo airport (☎ 643-1811) is 15km south of town on Hwy BR-101. Bus A-Aeroporto runs between the airport and the Rodoviária Velha (Old Bus Station) in the city center. The taxi fare to the city center is about US$17.

Bus The Rodoviária Nova (☎ 205-4377), the new bus station for long-distance buses, is 6km south of the city center at Avenida Capitão Mor Gouveia 1237. Bus Nos 38 and 20 connect the Rodoviária Nova with the Rodoviária Velha (Old Bus Station) on Praça Augusto Severo in the city center.

The Rodoviária Velha is the hub for bus service to the airport (Bus A), the Rodoviária Nova, city beaches such as Praia dos Artistas (Nos 21 and 38), beaches farther south such as Ponta Negra (Nos 46 and 54) and Pirangi, and beaches as far to the north as Genipabu.

Local bus fare is US$0.50.

Taxi The taxi fare to the center from the Rodoviária Nova is US$5. A taxi from the center to Praia dos Artistas costs around US$3, while to Ponta Negra it's US$8.

SOUTH OF NATAL
Ponta Negra
☎ 0xx84

Ponta Negra is 14km south of Natal. The beach is nearly 3km long and full of hotels, pousadas, restaurants, beach bars and sailing boats – on weekends the place really jumps. The water is calm towards the end of the bay and safe for weak swimmers. At the far end of the beach is **Morro da Careca**, a monstrous sand dune. Its face is inclined at 50 degrees and drops straight into the sea. The slope is now closed off to save the dune from ending up in the sea, but the locals still dune surf in the morning before the guards arrive.

Evening activities consist of beer drinking and snacking at the beach bars, and gazing for shooting stars and straying rockets (from the nearby air force base).

Places to Stay There's an excellent HI youth hostel, the *Albergue de Juventude Lua Cheia (☎ 236-3696, fax 236-4747,*

THE NORTHEAST

SOUTH OF NATAL

Coringa Lemos 333), a beautiful hotel with a sea view, swimming pool and very comfortable apartamentos for US$35/40. The manager, Rogério, speaks fluent English and is very helpful.

Pirangi do Sul & Pirangi do Norte
☎ 0xx84

The pretty twin beach towns of Pirangi do Sul and Pirangi do Norte, 14km south of Ponta Negra, are split by a river that weaves through palm-crested dunes on its way to the ocean. It's a quiet area where wealthy folk from Natal have put up their beach bungalows. There are a few pousadas in the palm grove where the road crosses the river. The town is home to the **world's largest cashew tree**: Its rambling sprawl of branches is over half a kilometer in circumference, and it's still growing!

The *Pousada Esquina do Sol (☎ 238-2078, fax 211-5637, Avenida Marcío Marinho 2210)* is a friendly place right on the main street, offering single/double apartamentos at US$25/30 with air-conditioning and US$15/20 with fan.

Búzios to Senador Georgino Avelino
☎ 0xx84

This stretch of coast has some of the best beaches in Rio Grande do Norte, a state with so many great beaches it's difficult to find one that's not worth raving about.

Búzios is a beach town 40km south of Natal. The beach is nice, but the area is a bit dry and barren. A couple of hotels here cater to weekenders. The *Varandas de Búzios (☎ 239-2121)* has large chalets on the beach at US$40/45 singles/doubles.

But resist the temptation to get off the bus at Búzios. After Búzios, the road crosses a stream and follows the coast – there's nothing here but small waves crashing against the beach, white dunes, coconut palms, uncut jungle and pretty little farms. The place is idyllic.

Getting There & Away From Natal five buses a day go directly to Senador Georgino

luacheia@digi.com.br, Rua Dr Manoel Augusto Bezerra de Araújo 500) in Ponta Negra. From the outside, it looks like a castle and the theme is 'witchy.' Facilities are good and staffers are helpful. HI members pay US$11 a night and nonmembers pay US$14.

There are dozens of pousadas and hotels. Prices quoted here rise by approximately 30% in summer. The cheaper ones along the beachfront include *Pousada Bella Napoli Praia (☎ 219-2667, fax 211-2821, Avenida Erivan Franca 3188),* with apartamentos for US$23/33 single/double, and *Pousada Sol (☎ 236-2107, Avenida Erivan Franca 11),* with quartos with a sea view for US$15 per person and apartamentos for US$20 per person.

Readers have recommended *Pousada Free Willy (☎/fax 236-2825, Rua Francisco Gurgel 9292)* for its friendly owners and good location on the beach. Low season rates are US$33/36 single double.

An excellent mid-range option is *Hotel Tubarão (☎/fax 641-1029, Rua Manoel*

Avelino, but it's more fun to take a bus along the winding, cobblestone coastal road. From Natal take one of the frequent Tabatinga buses as far as Búzios (US$2, one hour).

Tibaú do Sul

The small and rocky beaches just south of Tibaú do Sul – **Praia da Madeira**, **Praia da Cancela** and Praia da Pipa (see the following section) are said to be among the finest in Rio Grande do Norte. From Goaininha, 75km south of Natal on Hwy BR-101, there's a 20km paved road to the coast.

Praia da Pipa

☎ 0xx84 • postcode 59173-000

Pipa is the main attraction of Tibaú do Sul. It has developed into a small, laid-back resort with lots of pousadas, boutiques, restaurants and bars, many of which are run by foreigners. There is an excellent Web site with more information on the area, which you can peruse in either Portuguese or English at www.pipa.com.br.

The main beach is lovely, but it can get crowded on the weekend and during the summer. North and south of town, there are plenty of isolated beaches. Apart from beaches, there's the **Santuário Ecológico** 1km north of town, a flora and fauna reserve on 14 hectares in which an attempt is being made to re-create the natural environment of the area.

Places to Stay *Espaço Verde* (☎ 969-5180) on Avenida Baía dos Golfinhos (Pipa's main street) offers basic campsites for US$2 (US$4 in the high season), but the ground isn't very flat.

Pousada do Golfinho (no phone) on Avenida Baía dos Golfinhos, is run by a friendly Italian family. Some rooms have a sea view. The family also serves good, cheap Italian food. Apartamentos cost US$10/15 single/double (US$25/35 in the high season). The *Pousada Aconchego* (☎/fax 246-2439, aconchego@bluemail.com), just up from the main street opposite Pousada do Golfinho, has comfortable, spacious chalets in a nice garden setting. They have individual verandas and hammocks and go for US$15/20

(US$20/30 in the high season). Other good options include *Oásis* (☎ 502-2340, oasis@ digi.com.br), also on Avenida Baía dos Golfinhos, with apartamentos for US$35 (US$50 in the high season), and *Pousada da Pipa* (☎ 246-2271, pousadadapipa@uol.com .br) on Rua do Cruzeiro, a small cul-de-sac off the main road opposite the Oásis. Apartamentos are US$15 (US$20 in the high season).

Highly recommended is the *Pousada da Mata* (☎ 502-2304, pousadadamata@uol.com .br), set in the forest about 2km north of the center of Pipa. It has luxurious quartos for US$20/40, apartamentos for US$30/60 and lovely private chalets for US$30/60. Prices vary a bit depending on the rooms, which vary in size.

Places to Eat There are some very good restaurants in Pipa. *A Vivenda* (☎ 246-2294), on Avenida Baía dos Golfinhos, serves pasta, grilled meat and seafood in a pleasant setting. *Creperia da Pipa*, also on Avenida Baía dos Golfinhos, is a good option if you're sick of prato feito and pizza. *Cruzeiro do Pescador* (☎ 246-2262), near Pousada da Pipa, has great seafood. Two French restaurants in town are *La Provence*, run by Jean Louis, and *Chez Liz*, run by Patrick. Both offer excellent food. Patrick's soups are just sensational. *Cocobongo* is recommended for its large servings, and *Espaço Verde* has the cheapest self-serve lunch in Pipa. Good bars in town are *Garagem* and *Lampião*, which has forró.

Getting There & Around From the Rodoviária Nova in Natal, there are six buses a day to Pipa (US$3, two hours) between 7:15 am and 6:45 pm. If you come from the south, get out at Goaininha (1½ hours from João Pessoa). Taxi drivers will take you to Pipa for around US$8. From Pipa, frequent buses and minibuses leave for Natal daily.

NORTH OF NATAL

The beaches immediately north of Natal, where sand dunes plunge into the surf, are beautiful, but not quite as spectacular as the southern beaches.

Praia Redinha

Praia Redinha, 25km north of Natal by road, features 40m-high dunes, a good view of Natal, lots of bars and *capongas* (freshwater lagoons). Catch a ferry from the waterfront close to the Rodoviária Velha in Natal for the 20 minute trip to Redinha. It's more relaxing than the bus.

Genipabu
☎ 0xx84

About 5km farther north is Genipabu, where golden sand dunes, palm trees and dune buggies converge on a beach lined with numerous beach bars, pousadas and restaurants. It's a popular, crowded place,

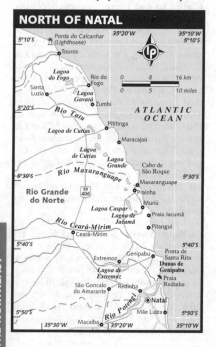

NORTH OF NATAL

where you can swim, toboggan down the dunes, or take a half-hour boat trip. The beach has lots of buggy traffic, so it's not a good place to lie around.

Among the cheapest of the area's pousadas is the *Casa de Genipabu* (☎ 225-2141, Avenida Beira Mar 55), which charges US$30/40 for single/double apartamentos with a sea view. The *Pousada Villa do Sol* (☎ 225-2132, fax 225-2037), 3km northwest of town next to the river is a more upmarket place with a swimming pool. Apartamentos start at US$40 a double but it will discount heavily during the week. Lon, the American owner, has lived here for many years and is a good source of local knowledge.

For great seafood, try Italian Lúcio's *Restaurante 21* (☎ 224-2484). The *peixada* for US$15 will feed two easily.

Buses to Genipabu and Redinha leave Natal regularly from the Rodoviária Velha. If you haven't come here via dune buggy from Natal, you can rent one with a driver at the **Parque de Dunas Moveis** for around US$40 a day.

Touros
☎ 0xx84

Ninety-one kilometers north of Natal is Touros, a fishing village that has several beaches, bars and a couple of cheap pousadas. It's a convenient base from which to explore isolated beaches to the north, such as **São Miguel do Gostoso** and **Praia do Cajueiro**.

The *Pousada do Atlântico* (☎ 263-2218, Avenida Atlântica 4), on the waterfront, has friendly management and apartamentos at US$20 a double. The *Pousada Rio do Fogo* (☎ 221-5872), on Praia Rio do Fogo, offers similar accommodations. *O Castelo* (☎ 263-2325, Avenida Atlântica 427) serves tasty local seafood.

Seven buses a day leave the Rodoviária Nova in Natal for Touros from 6:15 am to 6:15 pm (US$3, 1½ hours).

Ceará, Piauí & Maranhão

Ceará

The pride of Ceará is its coastline – nearly 600km of glorious beaches. The beach in this part of the Northeast engenders a special way of life. In nearly all of the small beach towns, the people of Ceará continue to live out their unique folklore every day of the year. They make old-fashioned lacework and handicrafts, cook according to traditional recipes, sleep in hammocks, sail out on *jangadas* (the beautiful traditional sailing boats of the Northeast) to catch fish, and live in thatch-roofed homes.

Should you stray inland into the sertão, you will see a rugged, drought-plagued land, a landscape of dust and caatinga, peopled by *vaqueiros* (cowboys) who still rely on their cattle for almost everything. The dried meat serves as food, tools are fashioned from the bones, and the hides make clothing – no part is wasted.

For a complete contrast in landscape, visit the Serra de Baturité, a small chain of hills southwest of Fortaleza, which features an agreeable climate and coffee and banana plantations.

For all its size and rich culture, much of Ceará is poor. Almost half of its seven million people live in absolute poverty.

FORTALEZA
☎ 0xx85 • postcode 60000-000
• pop 2.1 million
Fortaleza is one of the Northeast's major fishing ports and commercial centers. Its tourist attractions include a small historic section, a large selection of regional handicrafts, and an active nightlife scene along Praia de Iracema and Praia do Meireles. There are some super beaches beyond the city limits in either direction.

History
According to some revisionist Cearense historians, the Spanish navigator Vicente Yañez Pinzón supposedly landed on Praia Mucuripe on February 2, 1500, two months before Pedro Álvares Cabral first sighted Monte Pascoal, in Bahia. Despite this claim of an early landing, it wasn't until 1612 that the first colonists sailed from the Azores to

Highlights

- Vast stretches of deserted coastline
- Lively beach towns such as Canoa Quebrada and Jericoacoara
- The beautiful Parnaíba river delta
- Interesting national parks at Ubajara and Sete Cidades
- The colonial center of São Luís
- The journey along the coast from Parnaíba to Barreirinhas
- Magnificent dunes in the Parque Nacional dos Lençóis Maranhenses

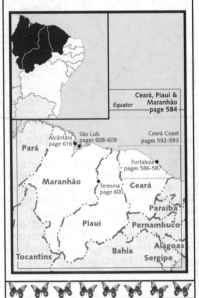

Ceará, Piauí & Maranhão
page 584

Equator

Pará

Alcântara page 616
São Luís pages 608-609

Maranhão

Teresina page 600

Ceará

Ceará Coast pages 592-593

Fortaleza pages 586-587

Paraíba

Piauí

Pernambuco

Tocantins

Bahia

Alagoas

Sergipe

THE NORTHEAST

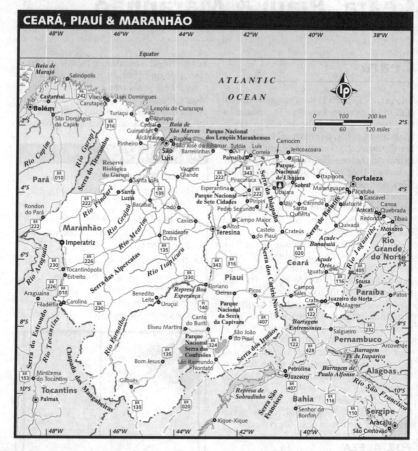

CEARÁ, PIAUÍ & MARANHÃO

actually settle on the banks of the Rio Ceará.

This settlement at present-day Fortaleza was hotly contested: It was taken over by the Dutch in 1635, then, in turn, lost to the Tabajara Indians. In 1639, the Dutch under the command of Matias Beck, landed once again, fought off the Indians and constructed a fortress. In 1654 the Portuguese captured the fortress and reclaimed the site. A town grew around the fortress, which was given the name of Fortaleza de Nossa Senhora da Assunção (Fortress of Our Lady of Assumption). Fierce battles with the local Indians continued to delay colonization for many years.

Orientation

The city is laid out in a convenient grid pattern. The center lies above the old historic section and includes the new Mercado Central (Central Market), the Catedral da Sé and major shopping streets and government buildings.

East of the center are the beaches of Praia de Iracema and Praia do Ideal; then farther eastward, Avenida Presidente Kennedy (also known as Avenida Beira Mar) links Praia do Diário and Praia do Meireles, which are lined with high-rise hotels and restaurants. Beyond here are Porto do Mucuripe (the port) and the Farol Velha (Old Lighthouse). Praia do Futuro begins at the lighthouse and extends 5km southward along Avenida Dioguinho to the Clube Caça e Pesca (Hunting and Fishing Club).

Information

Tourist Offices Setur, the state tourism organization, has a convenient branch office in the Centro de Turismo (☎ 231-3566, Rua Senador Pompeu 350), inside a renovated prison. It has English-speaking attendants and stacks of information and can help with booking accommodations, tours to the beaches and details on bus transportation. The Centro de Turismo is open 7 am to 6 pm every day except Sunday, when it's open 7 am to noon.

There is also a Setur booth at the airport, open 24 hours a day, and another at the bus station, open daily from 6 am to 9 pm.

Funcet, the municipal tourism organization, has an information booth in the center on Praça da Ferreira (open daily from 9 am to 5 pm), one on Praia do Meireles (open daily from 8 am to 10 pm), and one in the Mercado Central (open daily from 9 am to 5 pm). They give away good maps.

A tourist information telephone service, Disque Turismo (English spoken), is also available – just dial ☎ 1516.

Money Banco do Brasil has a branch in the city center on Rua Floriano Peixoto open Monday to Friday from 10 am to 3 pm. In Meireles, there's a branch on Avenida Abolição, open the same hours. Bradesco has ATMs in the center and in Iracema. There are lots of *casas de câmbio* (money-exchange houses) in Meireles, and large hotels there will also change cash at a lower rate.

Post & Communications The main post office in the center is on Rua Floriano Peixoto. Telemar has useful phone stations at the airport (open 24 hours a day), the bus station and Praia Iracema. Internet access is available at Cyber Café.com at Avenida Abolição 2030 and the Cyber Room at Avenida Monsenhor Tabosa 1001, shop 6.

Internet Resources Interesting sites about Fortaleza and Ceará include the following:

http://ceara.tur.br – in Portuguese, but fairly easy to get around

www.cearalink.com.br – in Portuguese; click on the Turismo bar for some good links

www.vivabrazil.com/ceara – in English and Portuguese, with some nice photos and links at the bottom of the page

Travel Agencies Libratur (☎ 248-3355) on Avenida Abolição has friendly bilingual staff and competitive prices for national and international ticketing. They also run a money-exchange service. Other helpful travel agencies include Lafluente Turismo (☎ 242-1010) at Avenida Senador Virgílio Tavora, Ernanitur (☎ 244-9363) at Avenida Barão de Studart 1165 and Maretur (☎ 242-8283) at Avenida Beira Mar 2982 next to the Clube Náutico.

Dangers & Annoyances Travelers have reported pickpocketing in the city center and petty theft on the beaches. We've also heard reports about solicitous females on the city beaches who cuddle up to travelers, drug them (in their drinks) and relieve them of their valuables.

Museums

The **Centro de Turismo** contains a folk museum, tourist information office and shops. It's open Monday to Friday 8 am to 6 pm and Saturday from 8 am to noon. Inside, the **Museu de Arte e Cultura Popular** houses a variety of interesting displays of local handicrafts, art and sculpture. Its hours are the same. Entry is US$0.50.

The **Museu do Ceará**, a museum devoted to the history and anthropology of Ceará, is in the old provincial assembly building at

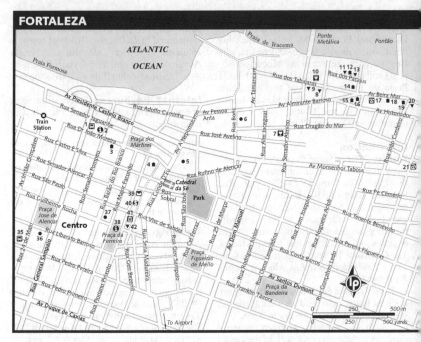

FORTALEZA

Rua São Paulo 51 in the center. It is open 8:30 am to 5:30 pm Tuesday to Friday, and Saturday 8:30 am to 2 pm.

Car enthusiasts will want to visit the **Museu do Automóvel**, Avenida Desembargador Manoel Sales de Andrade 70, in the Água Fria district on the southern edge of the city. The museum displays a variety of veteran cars including Buicks, Pontiacs, Cadillacs and Citroens. It's open Tuesday to Saturday 9 am to noon and 2 to 5 pm and Sunday from 9 am to 1 pm. Admission is US$0.50.

Teatro José de Alencar

On the Praça José de Alencar, the José Alencar theater (☎ 252-2324), dating from 1910, is an impressive building – a pastel-colored hybrid of classical and art nouveau architecture, which was constructed with cast-iron sections imported from Scotland. It is now used for cultural events and is worth a visit in the evenings, especially Friday and Saturday nights.

Centro Dragão do Mar de Arte e Cultura

A wonderful new addition to the city, this cultural center at Rua Dragão do Mar 81 includes a planetarium, cinemas, theaters and art galleries in a modern complex that blends well with the old surrounding buildings, many of which have been restored and now house bars and restaurants. It's a popular place with locals and a good alternative to the Iracema bar/restaurant scene, especially on weekends.

Parque Ecológico do Côco

This park, opposite Shopping Center Iguatemi, is the city's main recreational park. It was set up in 1991 after local ecological groups pressed for protection of the mangrove swamps from encroaching highways and the industrial zone. Entrances to the park, which is 7km southeast of the center, are on Avenida Engenheiro Santana and Rua Vicente Leite. From the center,

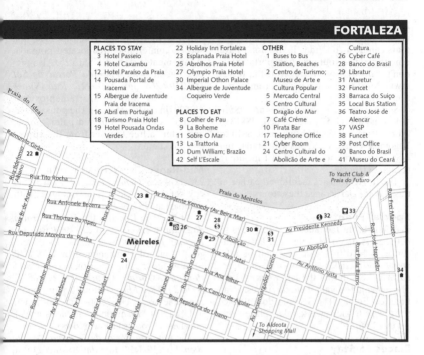

FORTALEZA

PLACES TO STAY
3 Hotel Passeio
4 Hotel Caxambu
12 Hotel Paraíso da Praia
14 Pousada Portal de
   Iracema
15 Albergue de Juventude
   Praia de Iracema
16 Abril em Portugal
18 Turismo Praia Hotel
19 Hotel Pousada Ondas
   Verdes

22 Holiday Inn Fortaleza
23 Esplanada Praia Hotel
25 Abrolhos Praia Hotel
27 Olympio Praia Hotel
30 Imperial Othon Palace
34 Albergue de Juventude
   Coqueiro Verde

PLACES TO EAT
8 Colher de Pau
9 La Boheme
11 Sobre O Mar
13 La Trattoria
20 Dum William; Brazão
42 Self L'Escale

OTHER
1 Buses to Bus
   Station, Beaches
2 Centro de Turismo;
   Museu de Arte e
   Cultura Popular
5 Mercado Central
6 Centro Cultural
   Dragão do Mar
7 Café Créme
10 Pirata Bar
17 Telephone Office
21 Cyber Room
24 Centro Cultural do
   Abolição de Arte e

Cultura
26 Cyber Café
28 Banco do Brasil
29 Libratur
31 Maretur
32 Funcet
33 Barraca do Suiço
35 Local Bus Station
36 Teatro José de
   Alencar
37 VASP
38 Funcet
39 Post Office
40 Banco do Brasil
41 Museu do Ceará

take the bus marked 'Edison Quieroz' to Shopping Center Iguatemi.

Beaches

The city beaches of Fortaleza are generally less than clean, with the exception of Praia do Futuro, but the locals don't seem to worry about it, so you can make up your own mind. The best beaches all lie farther away from Fortaleza.

Near the Ponte Metálica, the old port, **Praia de Iracema** was a source of inspiration to Luís Assunção and Milton Dias, Ceará's bohemian poets of the 1950s, and some of this atmosphere lives on in a few bars and restaurants around Rua dos Tabajaras. The Ponte Metálica has been restored and includes a space for cultural exhibitions and an outdoor music stage that has occasional free concerts. There's a lovely promenade along the waterfront, and a capoeira school often practices here in the evenings.

The **Praia do Meireles** fronts Avenida Presidente Kennedy and is the upmarket hotel and restaurant strip. Its beach bars are popular places to hang out during the day.

Praia do Futuro is a clean length of sand that stretches 5km toward the south along Avenida Dioguinho to the Clube Caça e Pesca. It is the best city beach. Like Barra de Tijuca in Rio de Janeiro, it's being built up at an alarming rate. There are bars here that serve fried fish and shrimp.

The beaches immediately northwest of Fortaleza, **Cumbuco** and **Iparana**, are both pleasantly tranquil. Harried travelers can relax, string up a hammock in the shade of a palm tree, sip coconut milk and rock themselves to sleep.

Organized Tours

There are several tours available from Fortaleza, mostly to beach destinations such as Beach Park, Cumbuco, Lagoinha, Jericoacoara, Canoa Quebrada, Morro Branco,

THE NORTHEAST

Iguape and Prainha. Although there are regular bus services to all these places, the tours can be a good idea if you don't have time to arrange your own transportation or don't want to stay overnight at the beach towns. Most tour prices include transportation only.

Some sample per-person prices are US$10 to Beach Park, US$7 to Cumbuco, US$13 to Morro Branco, US$10 to Iguape, US$10 to Lagoinha, US$20 to Canoa Quebrada, and US $50 to Jericoacoara (the last including accommodations).

The travel agencies mentioned earlier in this chapter can arrange these tours.

Special Events
The **Regata de Jangadas**, a sailing regatta between Praia do Meireles and Praia Mucuripe, is held in the second half of July. **Fortal**, Fortaleza's lively out-of-season Carnaval, is held during the last week of July. The **Iemanjá festival** is held on August 15 at Praia do Futuro. The **Semana do Folclore**, the town's folklore week, takes place from August 22 to 29.

Places to Stay
Budget There are lots of dives in the center – shop around for cleanliness rather than price, and check that you're not paying by the hour. The *Hotel Passeio* (☎ 226-9640, fax 253-6165, Rua Dr João Moreira 221) has reasonable apartamentos with fan at US$13/19 for singles/doubles.

The best places to stay are close to the beach. Praia de Iracema is generally less expensive than Praia do Meireles, and a more interesting area to explore. The *Albergue de Juventude Praia de Iracema* (☎ 219-3267, Avenida Almeida Barroso 998), on Praia de Iracema, is a convenient distance from the center. The *Albergue de Juventude Coqueiro Verde* (☎ 267-1998, Rua Frei Mansueto 531) is a friendly, comfortable hostel close to the glitz of Praia do Meireles. Both charge US$10 for HI members.

The friendly *Abril em Portugal* (☎ 219-9509, Avenida Almirante Barroso 1006) has the cheapest apartamentos in Iracema, at US$8/13 for singles/doubles. The *Chalé*

Suiço (☎/fax 248-3752, reugg@fortalnet .com.br, Rua Antônio Augusto 141) is a secure, comfortable, well-located pousada. Apartamentos start at US$15/25. Also recommended is the *Pousada Portal do Sol* (☎ 219-6265, fax 231-5221, Rua Nunes Valente 275). Massive apartamentos cost US$20 (in the low season). The pousada has a large swimming pool and palm garden, and offers a free transfer from the airport and bus station.

Mid-Range The *Hotel Caxambu* (☎/fax 231-0339, Rua General Bezerril 22), near the city center, has clean apartamentos (with minibar) at US$25/30.

At Praia de Iracema, the *Hotel Paraíso da Praia* (☎ 219-3387, fax 226-1964, Rua dos Pacajus 109), has a swimming pool and good standard apartamentos at US$30/40 (double in the high season). The *Hotel Pousada Ondas Verdes* (☎ 219-0871, Avenida Beira Mar 934) has bright double apartamentos at US$23/30 (with sea view), or US$17/24 with minibar and fan (some of the cheaper rooms lack windows).

The *Pousada Portal de Iracema* (☎ 219-0066, fax 219-3411, Rua das Ararius 2) is a renovated pousada in a great location. The rooms are a bit small, but position makes up for it. Quartos are US$15/20 and air-conditioned apartamentos are US$30/35. The *Turismo Praia Hotel* (☎ 219-6133, fax 219-1638, Avenida Beira Mar 894) has apartamentos at US$30/35 (US$40/55 in the high season). It's also well located and has a small pool.

The *Abrolhos Praia Hotel* (☎/fax 248-1217, Avenida Abolição 2030) is a bright little mid-range place in Meireles, 100m from the beach. There's an Internet café out front. Standard apartamentos are good value at US$25/35, and comfortable suites are US$40/50.

Top End Most of the top-end hotels are on Praia do Meireles, which has been heavily developed with competing hotels, many of which resemble multistory parking garages. The *Esplanada Praia Hotel* (☎ 248-1000, fax 248-8555, Avenida Beira Mar 2000) has been renovated, and all rooms have a sea view. Room prices start at around US$90 a double in low season. The *Imperial Othon Palace* (☎ 242-9177, fax 242-7777, Avenida Beira Mar 2500) has double rooms from US$140, with discounts in the low season.

The *Olympio Praia Hotel* (☎ 266-7200, fax 248-2793, Avenida Beira Mar 2380) is a very slick four-star hotel with a swimming pool and all the modern amenities. Rates start at US$100/130, and the hotel offers a 30% to 40% low-season discount.

The new *Holiday Inn Fortaleza* (☎ 455-5000, holidayinn@fortalnet.com.br, Avenida Historiador Raimundo Girão 800) is opposite the beach in Iracema, but it's not a particularly nice stretch. The hotel, however, is excellent. Rooms start at US$130/145, and you'll receive a 20% discount for advance bookings.

Places to Eat

You can eat well in Fortaleza. There's delicious crab, lobster, shrimp and fish, and a fantastic variety of tropical fruit and nuts, including, among others, cashews, coconuts, mangos, guavas, sapotis, graviolas, passion fruit, murici and cajá.

There are several local dishes worth tasting. *Peixe a delícia* (fish with melted cheese and assorted herbs and spices) is a highly recommended favorite. Try *paçoca*, a typical Cearense dish made of sun-dried meat ground with a mortar and pestle, mixed with manioc and then roasted. The tortured meat is usually accompanied by *baião de dois*, which is a mixture of rice, cheese, beans and butter.

The city center has lots of eateries that offer self-serve per-kilo lunches. A good one is *Self L'Escale*, just off Praça da Ferreira. The Mercado Central also has lots of food stalls. In the evening, you have a much wider choice at the city beaches.

At the beaches, there are some excellent restaurants along Rua Tabajaras and Praia de Iracema, near the Ponte Metálica. For Italian food, try *La Trattoria* (Rua dos Pacajus 125), where the owner proudly claims, 'Cutting spaghetti is a crime, ketchup is forbidden, and no one will be served

beans and rice!' *La Boheme* (☎ 219-3311, Rua dos Tabajaras 380) is a sophisticated, arty restaurant with a gallery attached – even the chairs are individually painted works of art. If you are feeling like a major splurge, try the seafood dishes.

Sobre O Mar (☎ 219-7999, Rua dos Tremembés 2) is a beautiful restaurant, with great but expensive seafood dishes. *Colher de Pau* (☎ 219-4097, Rua dos Tabajaras 412) serves great regional food and is always packed. The original *Colher de Pau* (☎ 267-3373, Rua Frederico Borges 204) is in the Varjota district, and is popular with locals. A couple of cheap eateries in Iracema are *Dum William* on the corner of Rua João Cordeiro and Avenida Beira Mar, which has a decent self-serve lunch daily, and *Brazão*, a 24-hour place next door.

Meireles is packed with restaurants, including some very good ones. *Cemoara* (☎ 263-5001, Avenida Abolição 3340A) is a chic seafood place where no shorts are allowed. The grilled lobster is delicious. *Al Mare* (☎ 263-3888, Avenida Beira Mar 3821) is a good, breezy seafood restaurant on the beach. The Japanese restaurant *Mariko* (☎ 466-5000, Avenida Beira Mar 3980), in the Caesar Park Hotel, is also recommended for some fine dining.

Entertainment

Pirata Bar (Rua dos Tabajaras 325), at Praia de Iracema, is clearly the place to go, at least on Monday when it proclaims *a segunda-feira mais louca do planeta* (the craziest Monday on the planet). The action includes live music for avid fans of forró or lambada, who can dance until they drop. Admission is around US$10. The surrounding bars also get very lively.

On Tuesday the hotspots are *Oásis* (☎ 234-4970, Avenida Santos Dumont 6061), a gigantic dance hall with room for several thousand people and *Alô Brasil* (☎ 263-3309, Rua do Mirante 21), billed as the biggest singles night in town. All the tables have phones so you can talk to people at other tables. On Thursday, *Chico de Caranguejo* (☎ 234-6808, Avenida Zezé Diogo 4930), on Praia do Futuro, hosts a big music night with plenty of forró, pagode and axé. There are a couple of comedy acts as well. On Saturday check out the *Clube de Vaqueiro* on Anel Contôrno, between Hwys BR-116 and CE-04. It's a huge forró club a long way from the center that is best reached by taxi. During the holiday season, the bars along the beaches are a constant source of entertainment in the evenings.

A good alternative to the Iracema beach-bar scene are the bars and cafés surrounding the Centro Cultural Dragão do Mar. From Thursday to Sunday night there are usually a few places with live music. Try *Café Créme (Rua Dragão do Mar 322),* a lively place where there's lots of street action.

Shopping

Fortaleza is one of the most important centers in the Northeast for crafts. Artisans work with carnaúba palm fronds, bamboo, vines, leather and lace. Much of the production is geared to the tourist, but there are also goods for urban and sertanejo customers. The markets and fairs are the places to look for clothing, hammocks, carvings, saddles, bridles, harnesses and images of saints. Markets are held about town (usually starting at around 4 pm) from Tuesday to Sunday. Setur has a complete listing.

There is a craft fair every night on Praia Meireles, where you can purchase sand paintings, watch the artists work and have them customize your design.

Lacework, embroidery, leather goods, ceramics, and articles made of straw are also available from the Central de Artesanato Luiza Távora (Handicrafts Center), at Avenida Santos Dumont 1589, in Aldeota district; the Centro do Turismo, at Rua Senador Pompeu 350; the Mercado Central, which has cheaper prices; and tourist boutiques along Avenida Monsenhor Tabosa (for clothing, jewelry, fashion). Cashew nuts are also an excellent value in Fortaleza.

Getting There & Away

Air Pinto Martins airport (☎ 272-6166) is 6km south of the city center. Flights operate to Rio, São Paulo and major cities in the Northeast and the North. Fortaleza is also a point of entry for charter flights from Europe. Following are the addresses for Brazilian airlines:

TransBrasil (☎ 0800-151151), Rua Barão do Rio Branco 1261

Varig/Nordeste (☎ 0800-9970000), Avenida Santos Dumont 2727, Aldeota

VASP (☎ 0800-998277), Rua Barão do Rio Branco 959

Bus The bus station (☎ 186 for information or ☎ 256-4080) is 6km south of the center.

Buses run daily to Salvador (US$55, 22 hours), Rio de Janeiro (US$112, 48 hours), Natal (US$18, eight hours), Teresina (US$22, 10 hours), São Luís (US$36, 16 hours), Recife (US$30, 12 hours) and Belém (US$55, 22 hours).

The Redencão bus company runs buses at 9 am each day to Jericoacoara (US$12, 6½ hours) and 13 times a day to Quixada (US$6, 3½ hours). Empresa São Benedito runs four buses a day to Canoa Quebrada (US$6, 3½ hours). Empresa Redentora runs 10 a day to Baturité (US$4, 2½ hours). Ipu Brasileira runs services to Ubajara six times a day (US$11, six hours) and four times a day to Camocim via Sobral (US$10, 7½ hours). Six buses a day run to Juazeiro de Norte (US$18, nine hours).

Getting Around

Pinto Martins airport is just a couple of kilometers from the bus station. Highly recommended if you're traveling to or from the airport or bus station is the air-conditioned Guanabara Top Bus, which loops from the airport and bus station through the center and on to Praias Iracema and Meireles. The fare is US$2. From the airport there are also Aeroporto/Benfica buses to Praça José Alencar in the center costing US$0.50. A fixed-price taxi to the center costs around US$15, a normal one US$10.

The air-conditioned Guanabara Top Bus passes the local bus stop outside the bus station every 30 minutes from 7 am to 10:15 pm daily. To reach the city center, you can also take any bus marked '13 de Maio' or

'Aguanambi' (passes the Centro de Turismo). A taxi to the center costs around US$6.

From Rua Dr João Moreira outside the Centro de Turismo, take the bus marked 'Circular' along the beachfront to Praia de Iracema and Praia do Meireles. Meireles buses also go to Praia do Meireles. A taxi from the center to Praia de Iracema costs US$4.

From Avenida Castro E Silva (close to the Centro de Turismo), Praia do Futuro and Serviluz buses run to Praia do Futuro.

For beaches west of the city, such as Icaraí and Cumbuco, you can take a Cumbuco bus from Praça Capistrano Abreu, on Avenida Tristão Gonçalves. You can also get to Cumbuco if you pick up the Vitória minibus that runs frequently along Avenida Presidente Kennedy.

BEACHES SOUTHEAST OF FORTALEZA

The coastal road from Fortaleza southeast to Aracati, Hwy CE-040, runs about 10km inland. It's mostly a flat, dry landscape of shrubs, stunted trees and some lakes. The towns are small, with good beaches, jangadas and dunescapes.

Beach Park

This full-blown aquatic park, 22km from Fortaleza, is one of the most modern in Brazil, complete with surfboards, dune buggies and ultralight planes. It also features a huge swimming pool complex with the highest water slide in Brazil – the adrenaline-inducing Insano (Insane) – 41m high, with speeds up to 110km/h. The park is quite expensive and would probably appeal most to tourists in search of structured fun. Admission is US$30, but children under a meter tall get in free. From Praça Tristão Gonçalves in Fortaleza, take a Beach Park bus to Beach Park. This bus also runs along Avenida Presidente Kennedy. Tours to Beach Park cost US$8.

Iguape
☎ 0xx85

Iguape, 46km southeast of Fortaleza, has a long stretch of white-sand beach with jangadas, a few lonely palm trees and sand dunes breaking the clean line of the horizon. The kids from town ski down the dunes on planks of wood.

In Iguape, women and children make wonderful lacework. Four or more wooden bobs are held in each hand and clicked rapidly and rhythmically, laying string around metal pins that are stuck in burlap cushions. Using this process, beautiful and intricate lace flowers are crafted.

Save your buying for Centro das Rendeiras, 6km inland, where the lacework is just as fine and cheaper. Also on sale are sweet cakes made from raw sugarcane broth that is boiled into a thick mass, pressed and reboiled in vats.

There are hotels in town, but you can also easily rent rooms or houses. A comfortable option is **Hotel Sol Leste** (☎ 361-6233), on Rua São Pedro, which has a pool and charges US$30 a double. Recommended seafood restaurants are **Peixado do José Almir** (☎ 361-6033), on Avenida da Praia, and **João do Camarão** (Rua Luis Eduardo Studart 8).

São Benedito buses from Fortaleza to Iguape leave every hour until 8 pm from Fortaleza's Terminal Domingos Olympio, on the corner of Avenida Domingos Olympio and Avenida Aguanambi.

ARACATI
☎ 0xx88 • postcode 62800-000
• pop 39,000

Aracati is a large town by the Rio Jaguaribe, which in the 18th century provided transport for sugarcane, and thus, for wealth.

Things to See & Do

Although Aracati is not in the best of shape architecturally, some of its historical buildings are worth visiting. The **Igreja Matriz de NS do Rosário**, on Rua Dragão do Mar, dates from the late 18th century and is a fine example of colonial architecture. The attractive **Sobrado do Barão de Aracati** houses the **Museu Jaguaribano**, which contains sacred art and local handicrafts. For a look at more colonial houses, some of which have retained their *azulejo* (ceramic tile) facades, wander down Rua do Comércio (Rua Grande).

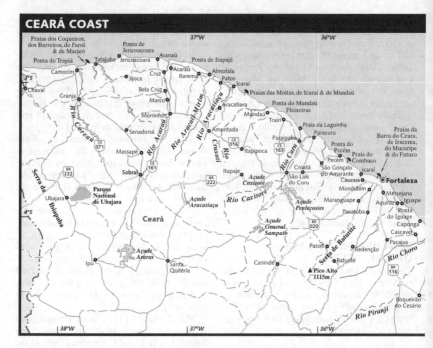

CEARÁ COAST

The town is also known for its handi-crafts, and the best time to see them is at the **Feira do Artesão** (Artisan Market) held on Saturday. Aracati's street Carnaval is the liveliest in the state.

Places to Stay & Eat

There are a few inexpensive hotels near the bus station, but it's worth going direct to Canoa Quebrada (see the next section). If you do choose to stay over in Aracati, the ***Pousada Litorânea*** (☎ *421-1001, Rua Cel Alexandrino 1251*) is best, with single/double apartamentos at US$8/12. There's a restaurant downstairs. The ***Brisa Rio*** (☎ *421-1881, Rua Cel Alexandrino 1179*) is similarly priced. ***Churrascaria Raimundo do Caranguejo*** (*Rua Hilton Gondim Bandeira 505*) serves good crab dishes.

Getting There & Away

From the bus station in Fortaleza, take one of the frequent daily buses to Aracati. The 2½- to four-hour trip (depending on stops) costs US$4. There are frequent services to Fortaleza and Natal from Aracati.

There are sharks waiting at Aracati's bus station to whisk you off to Canoa Quebrada in taxis for US$10 – ignore them and walk 800m down to Rua Dragão do Mar and take a bus, passenger truck, minibus, motor-cycle taxi or VW Kombi from the stop across from the Igreja Matriz. The fare is US$1. There are also regular buses from Aracati to the nearby resort of Majorlândia.

CANOA QUEBRADA
☎ 0xx88

Once a tiny fishing village cut off from the world by its huge, pink sand dunes, Canoa Quebrada, 13km southeast of Aracati, is still small and pretty, but it is no longer the Shangri-la it was in the past. The road to town is paved, and there is electricity and nightlife. There are lots of gringos running about, and on weekends it's a party town,

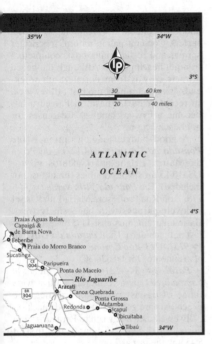

secrel.com.br), on Rua Nascer do Sol, which has a pool with a great view on the roof. The pousada also provides a good breakfast at any time of the day. Doubles go for around US$30 – cheaper if you stay awhile.

Pousada Oásis do Rei *(☎/fax 421-7081, oasisdorei@secrel.com.br, Rua Nascer do Sol 112)* is very nice, with a pool and lots of greenery. Doubles are US$20 and it has a good restaurant. Other good options include ***Pousada Califórnia*** *(california@ secrel.com, Rua Nascer do Sol 136)*, with clean, modern rooms and a pool and bar, starting at US$30 a double; ***Pousada Por do Sol*** *(☎ 421-7064, pordosol@yahoo.com.br)*, a colorful place with doubles for US$25.

Cinema fans will want to stay at ***La Dolce Vita*** *(☎ 9964-3834)*, where all the rooms are named after Fellini films. It has a pool and Italian restaurant; doubles go for US$30. Groups should find the large chalets at ***Pousada Chataletta*** *(☎ 9964-8968, chataletta@yahoo.com.br)* a good deal at US$25 a double, plus US$8 per extra person. ***Pousada Lua Morena*** *(☎ 416-1030, neike@secrel.com.br)*, at the end of the main street toward the beach, has great sea views from the front rooms, which are larger than the ones at the rear. Apartamentos start at US$25 a double.

Apartamentos are US$40 a double at ***Tranquilandia*** *(☎ 421-7012, tranquilandia@ secrel.com)*, which has a grassy courtyard (a rare sight among the sandy streets of the village) and a pool.

Places to Eat

The main street of Canoa Quebrada, officially known as Rua Principal but locally called Broadway, is the restaurant and bar strip. Recommended eateries you'll find along here include ***Casa Verde*** for cheap pratos feitos, and ***Restaurant Dali*** with good pizzas and other Italian dishes. For creative dishes, try ***Feitiço da Lua***. Broadway also hosts a few lively bars, including the stylish ***Todo Mundo***, run by Toby from Denmark. ***Bar Meia***, opposite Todo Mundo, is the town dancetaria.

On the beach the best bar is ***Barraca do Paulinho***.

with tourist buses rolling in to dwarf the village. Other than the beach, the main attractions are watching the sunset from the dunes, tearing around in buggies and dancing forró or reggae. If you still have energy remaining after a night of dancing, the beautiful 70km stretch of coastline south to Tibaú is well worth exploring – take a hammock!

Places to Stay

There are lots of foreign-owned pousadas in Canoa Quebrada, and the standards are high. In summer, it's better to make a reservation. Outside summer this shouldn't be necessary. Prices quoted here are for the low season; expect a stiff price hike in summer.

The ***Pousada Holandes*** *(☎ 9964-3504, Rua Nascer do Sol 128)* is a friendly place and a good value at US$6 per person without breakfast. Highly recommended is ***Pousada do Toby*** *(☎ 421-7094, pousadadotoby@*

Getting There & Around

There are four buses daily to Canoa Quebrada from Fortaleza's bus station, at 8:30 and 11 am, and 1:40 and 3:40 pm (US$6, 3½ hours).

Buggies with drivers to hire all congregate in Canoa Quebrada at the corner of Rua Principal and the Aracati road. Buggy rental for a day trip is around US$80 a day for four people. Destinations include Ponta Grossa, Redonda and Cumbe.

SOUTHEAST TO RIO GRANDE DO NORTE

Access by road to this stretch of coast is limited, so there are some great deserted beaches and small fishing villages. Buggies zoom along, but the rest of the time it's pretty quiet. The first town after Canoa Quebrada is **Majorlândia**, 7km southeast, a popular resort which gets crowded on weekends. There are places to stay, but they're not as nice as others you can find, so it's best to keep moving. Four kilometers southeast of Majorlândia on a sandy track are the distinctive, chalky-white sandstone bluffs of **Quixaba**. From the bluffs, cut by gullies between cacti and palms, you can see the pink hills of Canoa Quebrada, where you can rent a jangada and visit the neighboring beaches.

The 60km southeast from Quixaba to the border with Rio Grande do Norte is just a series of primitive little beaches and towns that are mostly off the maps and definitely out of the guidebooks: **Lagoa do Mato**, **Fontainha**, **Retirinho** and **Retiro Grande Mutamba**, **Ponta Grossa**, **Redonda** and **Retiro** (a waterfall), **Peroba**, **Picos**, **Barreiras** and **Barrinha** and, finally, **Icapuí**.

A dirt road from Icapuí continues to **Ibicuitaba** and **Barra do Ceará** beach. It's possible to drive from there to Tibaú, in Rio Grande do Norte.

BEACHES NORTHWEST OF FORTALEZA
Paracuru

☎ 0xx85 • postcode 62680-000 • pop 17,000

About 100km northwest of Fortaleza, Paracuru is a Cearense version of Búzios in Rio de Janeiro state. It's a clean, relaxed and fairly affluent town, popular with local surfers. Coconut palms, natural freshwater springs and rustic fishing boats complete a tranquil beach picture. Although the beach attracts crowds from Fortaleza on weekends, it's quiet during the rest of the week. In recent years, Carnaval in Paracuru has become a byword amongst Cearenses for hot beach action.

A good budget lodging option is the **Pousada da Praça** (☎ 344-1271), on Praça da Matriz. Bright apartamentos go for US$10/15 for singles/doubles (breakfast not included). The **Pousada Villa Verde** (☎ 344-1181), on Rua Professora Maria Luiza, is set in lovely gardens with huge, shady trees. Basic apartamentos cost US$20/25 (breakfast not included). The **Pousada da Gaviota** (☎ 9151-0213, Rua Coroneu Meireles 97) has apartamentos for US$20/30.

Paiol (☎ 344-1216, Rua Ormezinda Sampaio 811) is a restaurant with a wide range of pastas and seafood dishes. The beach bars are good for a seafood snack.

Twelve buses a day run to Paracuru from Fortaleza (US$2, 2½ hours), the first at 5:45 am, the last at 7 pm.

Praia da Lagoinha

☎ 0xx85

Praia da Lagoinha, a short distance up the coast from Paracuru, has coconut palms and a small deep lagoon near the sand dunes. The beach is considered, to be in the top three in the state, and its relative isolation has so far kept crowds down.

Don't expect hot-water showers here. The **Pousada O Milton** (☎ 363-1232, ext 102) is right on the beachfront and has a popular restaurant – try the delicious fish stew. Double apartamentos are US$20.

On top of the cliff is **Pousada Mar á Vista** (☎ 362-1232, ext 142), with small, well-equipped rooms and a great view for US$40 a double. A more expensive place is the **Lagoinha Praia Hotel** (☎ 363-1232, ext 122), which has singles/doubles for US$30/50.

Five buses a day run to Lagoinha from Fortaleza, the first at 7:15 am and the last at 3:30 pm (US$4, three hours).

Mundaú, Guajira & Fleixeiras

☎ 0xx85

The beaches of Mundaú, Guajira and Flei-xeiras, 155km from Fortaleza via Hwys BR-222 and CE-163, are traditional fishing areas with wide, unspoiled stretches of sand.

For decent budget accommodations in Fleixeiras, head to the ***Pousada do Edmar*** *(☎ 351-1134, ext 115)*, on Rua da Praia. Single/double apartamentos are US$15/20. On the beach, the mid-range ***Solar das Fleixeiras*** *(☎ 351-1184, ext 60)* has a restaurant and swimming pool. On Praia Mundaú, there's the ***Mundaú Dunas Hotel*** *(☎ 350-1011)*, on Rua do Grupo. It has a restaurant attached.

Buses run from the bus station at Fortaleza to Mundaú and Fleixeiras daily at 6:15 am and 4 pm (US$6, around four hours).

JERICOACOARA

☎ 0xx88 • postcode 62598-000 • pop 1500

The small fishing village of Jericoacoara is another remote 'in' beach, popular among backpackers, hip Brazilians and wind-surfers. It's a long haul to get there, so you might as well stay a while – in fact, it may be harder to leave. It's a beautiful spot where dozens of palms drowning in sand dunes face jangadas stuck on a broad gray beach. Goats, horses, cows, bulls and dogs roam the sandy streets at will.

Bichos de pé (unpleasant bugs that burrow into human feet) are less prevalent since IBAMA, the government environ-mental agency, started fining pig-owners for letting their swine wander. If you stay bicho-free, you can practice your steps at the forró gathering held in an outdoor courtyard every Wednesday and Saturday – just follow the music. You can also climb the sand dunes (watching the sunset from the top is mandatory, but dune-surfing down is only for crazies), go for a ride on a fishing boat, or walk to **Pedra Furada**, a rock 3km east along the beach. At low tide the beach route is easier than the hill route. You can also rent horses and gallop along the beach. The strong afternoon cross-shore winds means there are always a few windsurfers out.

Organized Tours

Fortaleza tour operators and also upmarket pousadas in Jericoacoara offer tour pack-ages for Jericoacoara. Two-day trips cost around US$50, including accommodations. Extra days cost around US$20 each.

Places to Stay

There is plenty of cheap lodging in Jerico-acoara and also several upmarket options. For longer stays, ask around about renting a local house – you should be able to get something for about US$5 per night outside summer. Words to the wise: Bring a large cotton hammock or bedroll with sleeping sack. During summer (December to Febru-ary), expect prices quoted here to be almost double.

Reservations for hotels and pousadas can be made by calling the village telephone office (☎ 621-1144), although some places do have private lines.

An excellent inexpensive option is the ***Pousada Calandra*** *(☎/fax 9961-4149)*, close to the last bus stop beside the Duna Por do Sol (Sunset Dune) on Rua das Dunas. It's quiet, and has a nice bar/restaurant. Staff speak English, Spanish and German, and charge US$15 per person for comfortable apartamentos.

Opposite is ***Pousada Casa do Turismo*** *(☎/fax 621-0211)*, which has well-equipped single/double apartamentos with fan for US$20/30. The pousada also serves as the agent for the Fortaleza bus. Another good budget option is the ***Pousada Isalana***, on Rua Principal, which offers apartamentos for US$10 per person.

Places to Eat & Drink

The best place in town to eat is ***Isabel***, on the beach at the end of Rua do Forró. In a large, seafront patio setting, Dona Isabel prepares fantastic seafood dishes; try her peixada. At the beach end of Rua Principal, ***Mama na Égua*** also serves good-value seafood; ***Pizzaria Dellacasa***, close to the telephone office, is the best pizzeria in town, while ***Alexandre Bar*** is the prime location along the beach for afternoon drinks, sunset-gazing and seafood dishes.

Later in the evening, everyone goes to **Bar do Forró** or **Mama Africa**. Just follow the music.

Getting There & Away

Three buses a day leave Fortaleza's bus station for Jericoacoara (US$15, about seven hours), at 9 and 10:30 am and 6:30 pm. The 10:30 am bus goes along the beach via Preá for the last stretch. The other buses go to Jijoca, where you are transferred to a passenger truck (included in the ticket price) for the 24km rodeo ride to Jericoacoara. The night bus is quicker and cooler, but you arrive in Jericoacoara at around 3:30 am. Someone from one of the pousadas will meet the bus, and you can always move to another pousada later in the day.

If you have come by car, leave it parked in Jijoca, where some of the pousada owners can keep an eye on it. The ride to Jericoacoara – over and around sweeping dunes, lagoons, bogs and flat scrub terrain – is beautiful, but very hard on people and machines. Transport leaves Jericoacoara for Fortaleza at 6 am and 2, 2:45 and 10:30 pm.

A Boa Esperança bus runs from Sobral at 11:15 am over an abysmal road to Jijoca (US$7, three hours), and should connect with the Fortaleza bus there. To get from Jericoacoara to Sobral, you will have to catch a minibus leaving Jijoca at 2 am – take the 10:30 pm truck out of Jericoacoara and think up new and interesting ways to amuse yourself in Jijoca for three hours.

If you want to travel from Jericoacoara along the coast to Piauí, you'll need to hire a beach buggy (around US$25) to take you to the river at Camocim. After crossing the river by boat you can then catch the daily bus to Parnaíba.

For details about transport from Camocim to Jericoacoara, see Getting There & Away in the Camocim section later in this chapter.

TATAJUBA
☎ 0xx88

Tatajuba, about 30km west of Jericoacoara, is a tiny, isolated fishing village at the mouth of a tidal river. The beach is broad and lonely, and there's a lagoon surrounded by extensive dunes about 2km from the village. **Pousada Brisa do Mar** (☎ 621-1543) lives up to its name (which means sea breeze) and offers simple quartos for US$8 per person.

There is no regular transport to Tatajuba. The walk along the beach from Jericoacoara takes about five hours; leave early in the morning and take water. At Guriú, a little less than halfway, there's a river to cross – canoes will take you over for about US$2. The river at Tatajuba can be waded at low tide. Don't try to cross it if the water is high, as the current is very strong.

Alternatively, you should be able to rent a boat or buggy in Jericoacoara to take you there; ask around at the beach.

CAMOCIM
☎ 0xx88 • postcode 62400-000 • pop 41,000

Camocim is a lively fishing port and market town at the mouth of the Rio Coreaú, in northwestern Ceará, near the Piauí border. The town's economy revolves around the saltworks, lobster fishing and a busy daily market.

Just a short distance from town, you can sip coconut milk while tanning at **Praia dos Barreiros**, **Praia do Farol**, **Praia dos Coqueiros** or Praia de Maceió.

Places to Stay & Eat

The **Pousada Ponta Pora** (☎ 621-0505), the colorful **Pousada Beira Mar** (☎ 621-0048), and the **Municipal Hotel** (☎/fax 621-0165), are all along the riverfront, on Avenida Beira Mar. All have cheap quartos and apartamentos. Riverbank restaurants serve local seafood and typical Cearense dishes.

Getting There & Away

Camocim's bus station (☎ 621-0028) is in Praça Sinhá Trévia. Four buses a day run to Camocim via Sobral from Fortaleza's bus station (US$12, 7½ hours), the first at 7:30 am and the last at 6:30 pm.

A jeep leaves the central market in Camocim for Jijoca at around 10:30 am daily, and if there are enough people, it will carry on to Jericoacoara. An alternative is to hire a beach buggy in Camocim for the ride to Jericoacoara. Prices are very negotiable.

During the high season there are boats sailing from Camocim to Jericoacoara – the trip takes four hours. Half the adventure is getting there.

SOBRAL
☎ 0xx88 • postcode 62000-000
• pop 135,000

Sobral has two minor sights – faded glories from a time before everything was changed by the construction of Hwy BR-222. The **Museu Diocesano Dom José** (a museum of sacred art), on Avenida Dom José, houses an eclectic collection of images of saints. It's open 8 to 11 am and 2 to 5 pm on weekdays and 8 am to noon on weekends. The **Teatro Municipal São João**, on Praça Dr Antônio Ibiapina, is an impressive neoclassical theater, built in 1880.

Very close to the bus station, the *Hotel Beira Rio* (*☎/fax 611-5775, Rua Dep João Aldeodato 400*) has apartamentos costing US$30/45 a single/double. You can eat breakfast there for US$4, even if you're not staying.

There are six buses a day to Camocim from Sobral. The earliest bus to make the 2½-hour trip leaves at 5:30 am, the last at 7 pm. One bus leaves Sobral daily at 11:15 am for Jijoca, where you can connect with a truck that will take you to Jericoacoara.

SERRA DE BATURITÉ

The interior of Ceará is not limited to the harsh landscapes of the sertão. There are also ranges of hills, which break up the monotony of the sun-scorched land. The Serra de Baturité is the range closest to Fortaleza. A natural watershed, it is an oasis of green where coffee and bananas are cultivated around the cliffs and jagged spines of the hills. The climate is tempered by rain, the evenings are cool and morning fog obscures Pico Alto (1115m), the highest point in the state.

Baturité
☎ 0xx85 • postcode 62760-000 • pop 21,000

Founded in 1745, the town of Baturité (95km west of Fortaleza) was once at the forefront of the fight against slavery, and is now the economic and commercial center of the region. Most of points of interest in the town are grouped around the **Praça Matriz** and include the **pelourinho** (whipping post), the baroque church of **Matriz NS de Palma** (1764), the **Palácio Entre-Rios** mansion, and the **Museu Comendador Ananias Arruda**, which contains exhibits from the town's past (though surprisingly little on the struggle to abolish slavery). There are also a few *termas* (resorts with mineral pools) clustered around the town. Local handicrafts on sale in Baturité include embroidery, tapestry and straw goods.

You can stay in the nearby villages of Guaramiranga and Pacoti (see the next section), or in Baturité at the *Hotel Canuto* (*☎ 347-0100, Praça Santa Luiza 703*) or the *Balneário Itamaracá Club* (no phone) at Sítio Itamaracá. You can get a double at either hotel for approximately US$25.

Ten buses leave Fortaleza's bus station daily for Baturité (US$3, 2½ hours).

Guaramiranga & Pacoti
☎ 0xx85

The two prettiest villages on the heights of Serra de Baturité are Guaramiranga and Pacoti, 19km and 26km respectively from Baturité.

The hills are a popular weekend retreat from Fortaleza, so prices rise about 20% on weekends. The *Hotel Escola de Guaramiranga* (*☎/fax 321-1106*), a training center for hotel staff in Guaramiranga, has well-worn but spotless apartamentos, a bar, a swimming pool and ping-pong tables. The single/double rooms cost US$32/38. The hotel is tricky to find (no sign), but it's a good deal.

Close to Pacoti is the *Estância Vale das Flores* (*☎ 325-1233, fax 494-3297*), at Sítio São Francisco (a *sítio* is like a ranch). It's set in a park with a swimming pool, sports facilities, horse rental and mini-zoo. Chalets cost US$40 a double including breakfast and lunch.

The Empresa Redentora bus company runs daily buses direct to Guaramiranga from Fortaleza's bus station, at 7:30 am and 3 pm (US$3.50, three hours). From Baturité, there's a bus at 10 am to Guaramiranga and

Pacoti, and another at 5:30 pm to Guarami-ranga only.

PARQUE NACIONAL DE UBAJARA
☎ 0xx88

The Parque Nacional de Ubajara is just a few kilometers from the small town of Ubajara, 350km west of Fortaleza by Hwy BR-222. The main attractions are the cable-car rides down to the caves and the caves themselves.

The park, with its beautiful vistas, forest, waterfalls and 3km trail to caves, is well worth a visit. At 850m above sea level, temperatures in the surrounding area are cool and provide a welcome respite from the searing heat of the sertão.

Information

The IBAMA office (☎ 634-1388), 5km from Ubajara proper, at the entrance to the park, provides guides for caves tour daily between 8 am and 5 pm. Entry costs US$0.50. If you fancy a strenuous hike take the 3km trail down to the caves. Allow at least half a day for the roundtrip. Start in the cool of the early morning, wear sturdy footwear and take enough to drink. Alternatively, you can walk down to the caves and take the cable car back up.

Cable Car & Caves

In 1987 the lower station of the *teleférico* (cable car) was wiped out by boulders that fell after winter rains. The cable-car system has been replaced, and now operates every day from 10 am to 3:30 pm. The ride costs US$3. Guides accompany you on the one-hour tour through the caves.

Nine chambers with strange limestone formations extend more than half a kilometer into the side of a mountain. The main formations seen inside the caves are **Pedra do Sino** (Bell Stone), **Salas da Rosa** (Rose Rooms), **Sala do Cavalo** (Horse Room) and **Sala dos Retratos** (Portrait Room).

Places to Stay & Eat

The *Sítio do Alemão* (☎ 9961-4645), set in a shady coffee plantation about 1.5km

from the entrance to the park, is run by a German-Brazilian couple who can provide walking maps for the park and loads of information about local attractions. There are wonderful vistas over the sertão from the property. Day trips to Parque Nacional de Sete Cidades (140km away on a good road) can also be arranged. Spotless chalets cost US$10 per person, with a generous breakfast.

There are two pousadas near the park entrance: the *Pousada da Neblina* (☎/fax 634-1270), which has single/double apartamentos at US$20/30 and a swimming pool; and the *Pousada Gruta de Ubajara* (☎ 634-1375), with apartamentos for US$10/20. Both of these pousadas have restaurants.

The *Churrascaria Hotel Ubajara* (☎ 634-1261, Rua Juvêncio Luís Pereira 370) in Ubajara has quartos for US$10/15.

Getting There & Around

Empresa Ipu-Brasília has four buses a day from Fortaleza to Ubajara (US$11, six hours). The first bus leaves at 6:30 am, the last one at 9 pm. There are also bus connections to Teresina (US$11, six hours), the capital of Piauí state.

To reach the park entrance from the town of Ubajara, either walk the 3km or take a taxi (US$5).

JUAZEIRO DO NORTE
☎ 0xx88 • postcode 63000-000
• pop 200,000

Juazeiro do Norte, 528km to the south of Fortaleza, is a magnet for believers in Padre Cícero, who lived in this town in the early 20th century and became a controversial figure of the sertão. Not only was he a curate with several miracles to his credit, he also exercised a strong political influence. His astonishing rise to fame started when an elderly woman received the host from him at mass and claimed that it had miraculously turned to blood. Soon he was being credited with all kinds of miracles, and later became drawn into a leading role in the social and political upheavals in the Northeast. Padre Cícero died in 1934, and, despite the Catholic Church's unwillingness to beatify him, the claims and adoration of his followers seem to be as strong as ever.

The best time to witness Padre Cícero's magnetic attraction and the devotion he inspires is during the festivals and pilgrimages. On March 24, the Aniversário do Padre Cícero celebrates Padre Cícero in legend and song. The commemoration of his death takes place on July 20. The *romaria* (pilgrimage) to Juazeiro do Norte in honor of Padre Cícero takes place on November 1 and 2 and is known as the Dia do Romeiro e Festa do Padre Cícero.

The city of Padre Cícero is rich in wood and ceramic sculpture. Look for the work of Expedito Batista, Nino, Cizinho, José Celestino, Luís Quirino, Maria de Lourdes, Maria Cândida, Francisca, Daniel, José Ferreira and Maria das Dores.

Logradouro do Horto

On the hill above the town, accessible either by road or via a path laid out with the stations of the cross, is the colossal statue of **Padre Cícero** (25m), which was built in 1969 and ranks as the fourth tallest statue in the record books – beaten by Cristo Rey (Cochabamba, Bolivia), Cristo Redentor on Corcovado (Rio) and the Statue of Liberty (New York). Nearby are a small chapel and a building filled with votive offerings that represent the diseases, afflictions and problems from which worshippers have been freed – wooden or wax replicas of every conceivable body part, and graphic representations of survival from accidents.

Padre Cícero's tomb is beside the Capela NS do Perpétua Socorro, on Praça do Socorro.

Gráfica de Literatura de Cordel

If you are interested in *literatura de cordel* (literally, 'string literature'), cheaply produced pamphlets for the masses with topics such as biographies of famous figures, love stories, opinions and views, visit this workshop on Rua Santa Luzia, where you can see the pamphlets being produced for sale on the premises. It's open 7 to 11 am and 1 to 5 pm Monday to Friday. It's closed on Saturday afternoon.

Places to Stay & Eat

Since this town is a pilgrimage center, there is no lack of accommodations, except during the main festivals. Try the **Pousada Portal do Cariri** (☎/fax 571-2399, Avenida Leão Sampaio 2120), with good-value apartamentos at US$16/30 a single/double, or the more expensive but superior **Panorama** (☎ 512-3100, fax 512-3110, Rua Santo Agostinho 58), which offers comfortable apartamentos for US$35/40.

The restaurant **O Capote** (☎ 511-4219, Rua José Barbosa dos Santos 83) is recommended for good regional food.

Getting There & Away

The bus station (☎ 571-2868) is on Rua Delmiro Gouvéia. There are four departures a day for Fortaleza (US$18, nine hours), and regular buses to all the major cities in the Northeast.

Piauí

Piauí, one of the largest states in the Northeast, is also one of the poorest in Brazil, due to regular debilitating droughts brought on by the oppressively hot and arid climate in the eastern and southern regions. The odd shape of the state – broad in the south, tapered at the coast – is due to a unique pattern of settlement, which started from the sertão in the south and gradually moved toward the coast.

The climate on the Piauí coast is kept cool(er) by sea breezes. If you're heading into the interior, the best time for festivals and cool breezes is during July and August. The worst time, unless you want to be sunbaked to a frazzle, is between September and December.

Although Piauí is usually bypassed by travelers, it has several attractions worth stopping for – superb beaches along its short coast, the Delta do Parnaíba, interesting rock formations and hikes in the Parque Nacional de Sete Cidades, prehistoric sites and rock paintings in the Parque Nacional da Serra da Capivara (one of the top prehistoric sites in South America) and, for rock hounds, the chance to visit Pedro Segundo, the only place in South America where opals are mined.

TERESINA

☎ 0xx86 • postcode 64000-000
• pop 675,000

Teresina, the capital of Piauí, is famed as the hottest city in Brazil. Promotional literature stresses heat, heat and yet more heat, with blurb bites such as 'Even the wind here isn't cool' and 'Teresina – as hot as its people.'

It's an interesting, quirky place, which seems addicted to giving a Middle Eastern slant to the names of its streets, hotels and sights. The city itself is a Mesopotamia of sorts, sandwiched between the Rio Poty and Rio Parnaíba. Teresina is unpretentious, and tourists are still reasonably rare. Like the British, residents of Teresina instantly warm to discussion of the weather, and especially of their favorite topic: *o calor* (the heat).

We recommend a visit if you yearn for attention or would like to feel famous for a day or so. And there's got to be something good going for a city that hosts an annual festival of humor!

Information

Piemtur (☎ 221-7100), the state tourism organization, has its head office at the Centro do Convenções, close to the Rio Poty. The helpful staff happily doles out literature and advice. More convenient is the booth inside the Centro de Artesanato on Praça Dom Pedro II. Both are open 8 am to 6 pm Monday to Friday and 9 am to 1 pm on Saturday.

For tours to sights in Piauí, contact Aldatur (☎ 221-3932), Rua Lizandro Nogueira 1384.

Museu do Piauí

This state museum is divided into a series of exhibition rooms devoted to the history of the state; religious art; popular art; archaeology; fauna, flora and minerals; and an eclectic assortment of antique radios, projectors and other ancient wonders. Hidden in the corner of one room is a pathetic cabinet containing a flag, kerchief and some scribbled notes from *comunistas,* a flexible

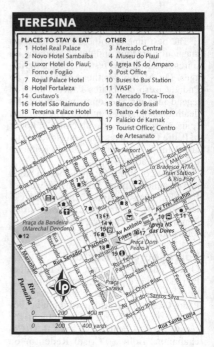

TERESINA

PLACES TO STAY & EAT	OTHER
1 Hotel Real Palace	3 Mercado Central
2 Novo Hotel Sambaiba	4 Museu do Piauí
5 Luxor Hotel do Piauí;	6 Igreja NS do Amparo
Forno e Fogão	9 Post Office
7 Royal Palace Hotel	10 Buses to Bus Station
8 Hotel Fortaleza	11 VASP
14 Gustavo's	12 Mercado Troca-Troca
16 Hotel São Raimundo	13 Banco do Brasil
18 Teresina Palace Hotel	15 Teatro 4 de Setembro
	17 Palácio de Karnak
	19 Tourist Office; Centro
	de Artesanato

term used here to describe a group of independent thinkers who were wiped out by the government in 1937.

The museum is on Praça da Bandeira (also called Marechal Deodoro), and is open 8 am to 5 pm on weekdays and from 8 am to noon on weekends. Admission is US$1.

Palácio de Karnak

This neo-classical structure on Avenida Antônio Freire was once the governor's residence and contained valuable works of art and antiques. In the late 1980s, the outgoing governor made a quick exit along with much of the valuable contents. The gardens were planned by Burle Marx, Brazil's most famous landscape designer.

Parque Ambiental Encontro dos Rios

This park at the confluence of the Parnaíba and Poty rivers is 7km northwest of the center. There's a restaurant and small leisure area here, as well as an interesting statue of Cabeça de Cuia deflowering virgins (see the boxed text). The best time to come here is at sunset, and the easiest way to get here is to hop on a motorcycle taxi for US$3.

Centro de Artesanato

This is a center for crafts from all over Piauí. It is pleasant to browse among the shops that sell leather articles, furniture, extremely intricate lacework, colorful hammocks, opals and soapstone (from Pedro Segundo), and liqueurs and confectionery made from such native plants as genipapo, caju, buriti and maracujá.

Mercado Troca-Troca

In an attempt to perpetuate the old traditions of *troca troca* (barter), the government has made a permanent structure out of what was once an impromptu barter market. Unless you are curious to see the river, it's not worth a visit.

Potycabana

If you hanker after aquatic frolics and games as a respite from the searing heat, visit the Potycabana, an aquatic entertainment center with water tobogganing and a surf pool, close to the Rio Poty.

Special Events

The main festivals, with dancing, music and cuisine typical of the Northeast, are held between June and August. Exact dates vary from year to year. The Salão Internacional de Humor do Piauí (Piauí International Festival of Humor) is held during October or November and features comedy shows, exhibitions of cartoons, comedy routines and lots of live music.

Places to Stay

Camping Club do Nordeste (☎ 222-6202) is 12km out of the city on Estrada da Socopo, the road running east toward União.

The best cheapie is *Hotel São Raimundo* (☎ 221-3397, Rua Senador Teodoro Pachêco 1199), a friendly place with quartos for US$8/12 for singles/doubles, and apartamen-

tos at US$20/25. The *Hotel Fortaleza* (☎ 221-2984, Rua Coelho Rodrigues 1476) is another option, with quartos (with fan) at US$10/20. Apartamentos with air-conditioning cost US$20/30.

The two-star *Teresina Palace Hotel* (☎ 221-2770, fax 221-4476, Rua Paissandu 1219) is a good value and worth considering. It has a swimming pool, and its apartamentos (with air-conditioning) start at US$25/35. The *Novo Hotel Sambaíba* (☎ 222-6711, Rua Gabriel Ferreira 230) has decent apartamentos at US$30/40, but no pool.

The *Royal Palace Hotel* (☎/fax 221-7707, Rua 13 de Maio 233) has apartamentos

---

Watch Out for Bowl-Head!

Any virgins named Mary need to be very careful when traveling in Teresina. Locals tell the story of Crispim, a young man who lived with his old, sick mother and fished along the banks of the Rio Parnaíba, close to its junction with the Rio Poty.

One day, after fishing without success, he returned home angry and frustrated. When he asked his mother what there was to eat, she could only offer a thin bone soup. Irritated, Crispim screamed that it was only fit for a dog, grabbed the bone out of the soup and started beating his mother with it.

Revolted by what he had done, Crispim ran out and threw himself into the river. As his mother died in agony, she laid a curse on Crispim that turned him into a terrible monster – Cabeça-de-Cuia (Bowl-Head). The only way he can break the curse is to deflower seven virgins named Mary.

So far, this hasn't happened, so Cabeça-de-Cuia rises from the depths to scare women washing clothes on the riverbank and threaten those who take more fish from the river than they need. During nights of the full moon, Cabeça-de-Cuia transforms himself into an old man and wanders the streets of Teresina. There's an impressive statue of Cabeça-de-Cuia at the Parque Encontro dos Rios in Teresina.

(with air-conditioning) starting at US$43/48, but it usually offers a discount. The *Hotel Real Palace* (☎ 221-2768, fax 221-7740, reserva@realpalacehotel.com.br, Rua Areolino de Abreu 1217) is a flash mid-range option with a pool. Apartamentos are US$40/50.

Shaped like a pyramid, the five-star *Rio Poty Hotel* (☎ 223-1500, fax 222-6671, Avenida Marechal Castelo Branco 555) is the poshest place in town. Double rooms start at US$140.

Another luxury pad with very smooth service is the *Luxor Hotel do Piauí* (☎ 221-4911, fax 221-5171, Praça da Bandeira 310), which has rooms from US$55/65.

Places to Eat
Gustavo's, on the corner of Rua David Caldas and Rua Álvaro Mendes, is an excellent per-kilo lunch place, with a great variety of salads and an air-conditioned dining room upstairs.

If you feel like seafood, try *Camarão do Elias* (☎ 232-5025, Avenida Pedro Almeida 457). The house specialty is moqueca á moda do Elías, a delicious seafood stew with lemon sauce, garlic and vegetables. *O Pesqueirinho* (☎ 225-2268, Avenida Jorge Velho 6889) is a popular spot, several kilometers outside town on the riverside. It serves crab and shrimp stew. For a splurge, visit the *Forno e Fogão*, inside the Hotel Luxor Palace, which charges US$8 per person for a gigantic buffet lunch.

Getting There & Away
Air The airport is on Avenida Centenário, 6km north of the center. There are flights between Teresina and Brasília, Rio, São Paulo, and the major cities in the Northeast and North.

Varig (☎ 223-4940) has an office at Rua Frei Serafim 1932, and VASP (☎ 223-3222) is at No 1826. TAM (☎ 221-1912) is at Rua Félix Pacheco 2008.

Bus Teresina has regular bus connections with Sobral (US$13, six hours), Fortaleza (US$22, or US$42 for leito, 10 hours), São Luís (US$15 for numerous daily services,

seven hours) and Belém (US$25, 15 hours, four times daily).

To Parnaíba there are two executivo buses (US$15, five hours) and several standard buses (US$13, six hours) every day. Buses run twice a day (2:45 and 8:30 pm) to São Raimundo Nonato (US$20, nine hours). Buses run hourly between 5:45 am and 7 pm for Piripiri (US$4, three hours), and there are several buses a day to Pedro Segundo (US$8, four hours).

Teresina's main bus station is 6km from the center on BR-343. From the center, you can catch a local bus to the bus station from the bus stop on Avenida Frei Serafim.

Getting Around
A taxi to the airport from the center is US$5.

The cheapest option from the bus station is to take the bus from the stop across the road – it's OK if you arrive at night, when it's cooler, but during the day it's a frying pan on wheels. Taxis into the center will cost around US$5.

PARNAÍBA
☎ 0xx86 • postcode 64200-000
• pop 125,000

Parnaíba, a major port at the mouth of the Rio Parnaíba until the river silted up, is now a peaceful, charming town. It's well worth a trip from Teresina, and onward travel to Maranhão state is possible for adventurous travelers.

Information
The Piemtur office (☎ 321-1532) is at Rua Dr Oscar Clark 575. It is supposed to be open Monday to Friday 8 am to 1 pm and 2:30 to 6 pm, although these hours are not always strictly adhered to. Staff can provide limited information about boat trips around the Delta do Parnaíba and buses to local destinations.

Ana at Portal Viagens e Turismo (☎/fax 321-1029) speaks English, Italian and Spanish (as well as Portuguese) and is a good source of information.

The Banco do Brasil on Praça da Graça changes money. Bradesco has an ATM opposite the telephone office on Avenida Presidente Vargas.

The main post office is on Praça da Graça, next to the Banco do Brasil. The telephone office is at Avenida Presidente Vargas 390. You can use the Internet facilities at Morais Brito Viagens Turismo to check your email.

Several operators run boat trips into the delta. Two recommended ones with easy-to-find offices in Porto das Barcas are Igaratur (☎ 322-2141) and Morais Brito Viagens Turismo (☎ 321-1969). Both operators run delta trips for US$20, including lunch. Outside summer they only go on weekends, leaving at 8 am and returning at 4 pm. Morais Brito also offers a variety of tours around the state, as well as to Jericoacoara and Lençois Maranhenses.

Porto das Barcas

Porto das Barcas, the old warehouse section along the riverfront, has been restored and contains a maritime museum, an art center, art galleries, bars and restaurants. Check out the old pharmacy.

Delta do Parnaíba

The Delta do Parnaíba, the only delta in the Americas facing the open sea, is a 2700 sq km expanse of islands, beaches, lagoons, sand dunes and mangrove forest straddling the Piauí/Maranhão state border, which teems with abundant wildlife. Some 65% of its area is in Maranhão, but the easiest access is from Parnaíba. Day trips by boat around the delta run from Porto das Barcas on weekends, with a stop on Ilha do Caju; the cost is around US$20 (see Information earlier in this section). Ilha do Caju has been owned for several generations by an English family, who has established an ecological reserve there.

Beaches & Lagoons

The 66km coastline of Piauí is the result of a land swap with Ceará in the late 1800s. There are some fine beaches, many of which are fast being developed. **Praia Pedra do Sal**, 15km northeast of the center, on Ilha Grande Santa Isabel, is a good beach, divided by rocks into a calm section suitable

for swimming and a rough section preferred by surfers. **Lagoa do Portinho** is a lagoon surrounded by dunes about 14km east of Parnaíba on the road to the small town of Luís Correia. It's a popular spot for swimming, boating, sailing and fishing.

The prime beaches east of Luís Correia are **Praia do Coqueiro** and **Praia de Atalaia**. The latter is very popular on weekends and has plenty of bars selling drinks and seafood. The nearby lagoon, **Lagoa do Sobradinho**, is renowned for its shifting sands that bury surrounding trees. **Macapá**, a small fishing village 43km east of Luís Correia, which only recently received electricity, is a good base for exploring the deserted beaches farther east – **Barra Grande**, (considered by many to be the pick of the bunch), **Barrinha**, **Sardi**, **Morro Branco** and **Cajueiro da Praia**. Adventurous travelers should bring their hammocks if they want to stay at these beaches. In Macapá, there's a good pousada (see Places to Stay later in this section).

Places to Stay

The *Pousada Porto das Barcas* (☎ 321-1856, Avenida Getúlio Vargas 53) is a friendly hostel in a restored warehouse right in Porto das Barcas. Dormitory rooms cost US$8 per person with breakfast. Ricarte, the owner, also has an interesting gemstone workshop on the premises. The *Hotel Cívico* (☎ 322-2470, fax 322-2028, Avenida Governor Chagas Rodrigues 474), in the center of town, has a swimming pool and single/double apartamentos starting at US$20/30, with a huge buffet breakfast.

At Luís Correia, the *Amarracão Hotel* (☎/fax 367-1300, amarracao@secrel.com.br, Avenida José de Freitas 3650) is a bright, modern hotel a short walk from the beach, with apartamentos for US$28/33. The stylish *Aimberê Resort Hotel* (☎ 366-1144, fax 366-1204, guilherme@aimbereresorthotel.com .br), on Praia do Coqueiro, is the best top-end choice in the area. It's an architect-designed former beach mansion that's been transformed into a resort. The cheapest rooms start at US$45 a double and go up to US$100 for the luxury suite in high season.

In Macapá, stay at the *Pousada Macapá* (☎ 983-1635). The restaurant there features a great fish dish called *peixada macapense*. Simple, comfortable rooms are US$15/20 a single/double.

There is one pousada on Ilha do Caju, the *Pousada Ecológica Ilha do Caju*. For more details, contact the pousada office (☎/fax 321-1308, ilhadocaju@ilhadocaju.com.br) at Avenida Presidente Vargas 235 in Parnaíba. Three-day/two-night packages cost around US$300.

Places to Eat

Zé Grosso (☎ 983-1530), on the riverbank on Ilha Grande, is a very friendly place with great, cheap regional dishes. It's 3km from town, over the bridge, but well worth the effort it takes to get there. *Feito a Mão* (☎ 321-1241) is the best place on the Beira Rio restaurant strip.

Sabor e Arte (☎ 323-3616, *Avenida Getúlio Vargas 37*) in Porto das Barcas is a relaxed little place with interesting original art on the walls. The dishes themselves are works of art – beautifully presented, delicious fruit and meat combinations. Also in Porto das Barcas, the chic *Rio's Restaurante & American Bar* (☎ 322-1362) has a great riverfront patio, and local seafood dishes at reasonable prices. They have live music most nights.

Getting There & Away

There are frequent bus services between Parnaíba and Teresina. The six-hour trip costs US$13.

For the short trip to Luís Correia, buses leave every hour from the local bus station next to Praça Santo Antônio. Agencia Empresa São Francisco runs two buses daily from Praça Santa Cruz to Tutóia (Maranhão state), at noon and 5 pm. The trip takes about 2½ hours over a good dirt road. From Tutóia there are trucks running via Rio Novo to Barreirinhas, for access to the Parque Nacional dos Lençóis Maranhenses (see Tutóia in the Maranhão section later in this chapter).

A small wooden boat plies daily through the Delta do Parnaíba to Tutóia (US$5,

about six hours). This is a good way to check out some of the delta – if you have a hammock (cheap ones at the market cost US$8), you can sling it on the top deck, relax and enjoy the voyage. The boat leaves from Porto Salgado, on the riverfront close to Porto das Barcas, between 10 am and noon – check at the port in the morning for departure times. Take some food and water along.

There's a bus to Camocim, Ceará every morning at 6:45 am. The trip takes two hours and costs US$4.

PARQUE NACIONAL DE SETE CIDADES
☎ 0xx86

Sete Cidades is a small national park with interesting rock formations that resemble *sete cidades* (seven cities). Some researchers who have analyzed nearby rock inscriptions have deduced that the formations are indeed ruined cities at least 190 million years old.

The Austrian historian Ludwig Schwennhagen visited the area in 1928 and thought he'd found the ruins of a Phoenician city. The French researcher Jacques de Mabieu considered Sete Cidades to be proof that the Vikings had found a more agreeable in South America than in their homeland. And Erich van Daniken, the Swiss UFOlogist, theorized that extraterrestrials were responsible for the cities, which were ruined by a great fire some 15,000 years ago. There's clearly a lot of scope here for imaginative theories. See what you think!

The road around the park's geological monuments starts 1km before the Centro de Visitantes (Visitors Center) on the road in from the park entrance. The visitors center includes the IBAMA office and a hostel. The loop is a leisurely couple of hours' stroll – more if you go to the swimming pool at Primeira Cidade. It's best to start your hike early in the morning. Bring drinking water because it gets hot, and watch out for the *cascavelas* – poisonous black-and-yellow rattlesnakes.

The park is open 8 am to 5 pm. Entry costs US$2 for 24 hours. The IBAMA office

(☎ 343-1342) can supply a useful map; guides are available at a small cost. **Sexta Cidade** (Sixth City) and **Pedra do Elefante** (Elephant Rock), the first sites on the loop, are lumps of rock with strange scaly surfaces. The **Pedra do Inscrição** (Rock of Inscription) at **Quinta Cidade** (Fifth City) has red markings, which some say are cryptic Indian runes. The highlight of **Quarta Cidade** (Fourth City) is the **Mapa do Brasil** (Map of Brazil), a natural hole in the rock shaped almost exactly like a backward-facing Brazil. The **Biblioteca** (Library), **Arco de Triunfo** (Triumphal Arch) and **Cabeça do Cachorro** (Dog's Head) are promontories with good views.

Places to Stay & Eat

Six kilometers from the park entrance, the **Centro de Visitantes** (☎ 343-1342) includes a hostel that is good value – apartamentos with fan cost US$15 and can sleep up to four people. There's a restaurant attached to the hostel. Designated campsites are also available here for US$4.

The **Hotel Fazenda Sete Cidades** (☎/fax 276-2222), a two-star resort hotel just outside the park entrance, has attractive apartamentos at US$30/42 for singles/doubles. Even if you don't stay overnight, it's good for lunch and a quick dip in the pool. The **Hotel Martins** (☎ 276-1273), at the intersection of Hwy BR-222 and the road into Piripiri (2km from the center), has clean, simple apartamentos with fan for US$8/12 or US$15/25 with air-conditioning. It also has a quarto with two beds for US$5.

Getting There & Around

The park is 180km from Teresina and 141km from Ubajara (Ceará state). Buses leave Teresina hourly between 5:45 am and 6 pm for Piripiri (US$4.50, three hours). There are several daily buses from Piripiri to Fortaleza (US$11, nine hours) and Parnaíba (US$4, three hours).

The small IBAMA courtesy bus for the 26km trip to the park leaves from Praça da Bandeira, in the center of Piripiri, daily at 7 am. There is usually some transportation returning from the Abrigo do IBAMA to

Piripiri in the morning between 9 and 10 am, and the bus returns at 5 pm. A taxi from Piripiri costs around US$15. A moto-taxi (motorcycle) is US$5. Hitchhiking is also effective, and reported to be less dangerous here than in some areas. In the park itself, you can drive on the roads or follow the trails on foot – they're well marked.

PEDRO SEGUNDO
☎ 0xx86 • pop 21,000

The town of Pedro Segundo (also written Pedro II) lies in the hills of the Serra dos Matões, around 50km southeast of Piripiri. Close to the town are several mines that are the only source of opals in South America.

The only place to stay in town is the **Hotel Rimo Pedro Segundo** (☎ 271-1543), on Avenida Itamaraty.

For bus services between Pedro Segundo and Teresina, see Getting There & Away in the Teresina section.

PARQUE NACIONAL DA SERRA DA CAPIVARA

The Parque Nacional da Serra da Capivara, in the south of the state, was established in 1979 to protect the many prehistoric sites and examples of rock paintings in the region. It is the only national park set entirely in caatinga country.

The park was declared a UNESCO World Heritage Site in 1991. Archaeological research in the park has dated the human presence here as far back as 50,000 years – much earlier than used to be believed for anywhere in the Americas.

There are more than 300 excavated sites that are opened to the public depending on the research schedule. If the staff have time, you may be lucky enough to be given a lift and be shown around. For details about guides, access and archaeological sites, contact the Fundação Museu do Homem Americano (FUMDHAM; ☎ 0xx86-582-1612), at Rua Abdias Neves 551, in São Raimundo Nonato. Paved roads have been made to some of the 260 rock-painting sites (with 30,000 paintings), and 30 sites are open to visitors. Entry to the park costs US$2 for three days.

THE NORTHEAST

The closest hotel to the park is the *Serra da Capivara* (☎/fax 0xx86-582-1389), 2km north of São Raimundo Nonato on Hwy PI-140. It has a restaurant, pool and comfortable single/double apartamentos for US$33/38. It can also provide information about park visits.

For bus services between São Raimundo Nonato and Teresina, see Getting There & Away in the Teresina section earlier in this chapter.

Maranhão

Maranhão, with an area of 333,367 sq km and a population of more than five million, is the second largest state in the Northeast, after Bahia.

For many years after they first came to Brazil, the Portuguese showed little interest in the area that now forms the state of Maranhão. It was the French who arrived in 1612 to construct a fort at São Luís, which later became the capital of the state. See the São Luís section below for more on the history of Maranhão.

Although the southern and eastern areas of Maranhão are characterized by vast expanses of babaçu palms and typical sertão landscapes, the western and northwestern regions of the state merge into humid Amazon rainforests.

The rural economy of Maranhão is dependent on the babaçu, a plant which serves an amazing multitude of purposes: The nuts can be eaten straight out of the fruit or crushed to produce vegetable oil (for margarine) or industrial lubricating oils; the tips of the young palms can be eaten as 'hearts of palm'; and the older trunks are used for the construction of huts, with roofing material supplied by the leaves – which can also be used for the production of cellulose and paper. The residue from the crushed nuts provides excellent fertilizer and cattle feed, and the hulls of the fruit are used in the production of acetates, tar and methyl alcohol. Finally, the hulls are turned to charcoal for use in smelting. Things go better with babaçu!

SÃO LUÍS
☎ 0xx98 • postcode 65000-000
• pop 835,000

São Luís, the capital of Maranhão, is a city with unpretentious colonial charm and a rich folkloric tradition – definitely a highlight for travelers in the Northeast. It was declared a World Heritage Site by UNESCO a few years ago. The population is a diverse mixture of Europeans, blacks and Indians. Apart from the attractions of the restored colonial architecture in the historical center, São Luís offers passable beaches only 10 minutes by bus from the center (with better ones farther afield), as well as an opportunity to cross Baía de São Marcos to visit Alcântara, an impressive historic town slipping regally into decay.

History

São Luís is the only city in Brazil that was founded and settled by the French. In 1612 three French ships sailed for Maranhão to try to cut off a chunk of Brazil. They were embraced by the local Indian population, the Tupinambá, who hated the Portuguese. Once settled in São Luís, which was named after King Louis XIII, the French enlisted the help of the Tupinambá to expand their precarious foothold by attacking tribes around the mouth of the Rio Amazonas.

But French support for the new colony was weak, and in 1614 ships from Portugal set sail for Maranhão. A year later the French fled, and the Tupinambá were 'pacified' by the Portuguese.

Except for a brief Dutch occupation between 1641 and 1644, when the city was important and busy, São Luís developed slowly as a port for the export of sugar, and later cotton. As elsewhere, the plantation system was established with slaves and Indian labor, despite the relatively poor lands. When demand for these crops slackened in the 19th century, São Luís went into a long and slow decline.

In recent years the economy of São Luís has been stimulated by several megaprojects. A modern port complex has been built to export the mineral riches of the Serra dos Carajás in the southeast of neighboring Pará state, a range of hills with the world's largest deposits of iron ore. In the 1980s, Alcoa built an enormous factory for aluminum processing – you'll see it along the highway south of the city. The US$1.5 billion price tag for this project was the largest private investment in Brazil's history. A missile station has been built near Alcântara, and oil has been found in the bay.

Orientation

Perched on a hill overlooking the Baía de São Marcos, São Luís is actually on the island from which it takes its name. The historic core of São Luís, now known as Projeto Reviver (Project Renovation), lies below the hill. Going north from the old town, the Ponte José Sarney bridge will take you across to São Francisco, a new and affluent district with several hotels, restaurants and trendy nightspots.

It's easy to get around on foot – despite the hills and confusing street layout – because everything is so close together. In fact, as long as you're in the old part of town, a bus is rarely needed.

The most confusing thing about getting around São Luís is the existence of several different names for the same streets. There are the new official names that are on street signs and the historical names or nicknames that the locals use. No two city maps seem to be the same.

The following is a short list of streets, with their official names in parentheses:

Rua do Giz (Rua 28 de Julho)
Rua da Estrêla (Rua Candido Mendes)
Rua Formosa (Rua Afonso Pena)
Rua do Sol (Rua Nina Rodrigues)
Rua do Egito (Rua Tarquinho Lopes)
Rua do Veado (Rua Celso Magalhães)
Rua dos Afogados (Rua José Bonifácio)
Rua de Nazaré (Rua de Nazaré e Odilo)
Rua das Barrocas (Beco dos Barracas; Rua Isaacs Martins)
Rua da Cascata (Rua Jacinto Maia)
Rua Portugal (Rua Trapiche)
Rua da Alfândega (Rua Marcelino de Almeida)
Praça Dom Pedro II (Avenida Dom Pedro II)
Rua da Cruz (Rua 7 de Setembro)

Information

Tourist Office São Luís operates well-developed tourist-information facilities. The most useful office is run by Fumtur (☎ 231-9086), on Praça Dom Pedro II. It provides brochures and maps in English and French, as well as helpful English-speaking attendants. The office hours are weekdays 8 am to 7 pm and Saturday 9 am to 5 pm.

Money Banco do Brasil acts as a *casa de câmbio* (money-exchange house) at Avenida Gomes de Castro 46. Banco da Amazonia, at Avenida Pedro Segundo II 140, also changes money. Bradesco has an ATM near the Mercado Central. There are also moneychangers hanging about outside Fumtur, who change cash and traveler's checks at good rates.

Post & Communications The main post office is on Praça João Lisboa. There's a handy Telemar telephone office on the corner of Rua da Palma and Rua de Nazaré. Some hostels and hotels in the old part of the city have Internet access. If you want an Internet café, there's one on the first floor of the Monumental shopping mall. It's open 9 am to 9 pm every day except Sunday.

Internet Resources Some good Web sites about São Luis and Maranhão include:

www.vivabrazil.com/maranhao/htm – in English and Portuguese, with some good photos and interesting links at the bottom of the page
www.wojner.de/slz – in English; a German traveler gives his impressions of the city and provides some useful travel tips

Travel Agencies Highly recommended is Giltur (☎ 231-7065, fax 232-6041, giltur@ farolweb.com.br), at Rua Montanha Russa 22. It offers organized tours of the historic center, Alcântara, Parque Nacional dos Lençóis Maranhenses and other destinations

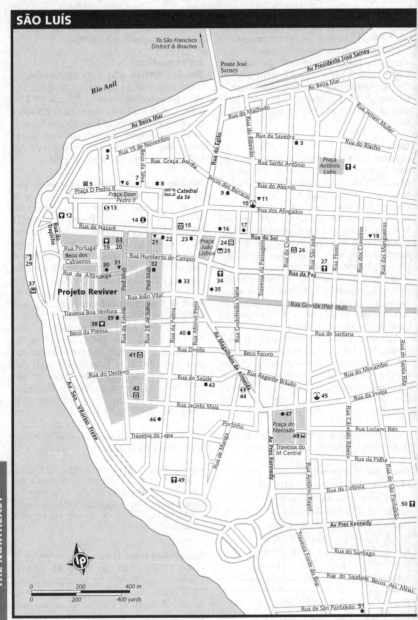

SÃO LUÍS

To São Francisco
District & Beaches

Ponte José
Sarney

Av Presidente José Sarney

Rio Anil

Av Beira Mar

Rua do Machado

Rua Jansen Müller

Rua da Savedra

Rua do Riacho

Av Beira Mar

Rua do Ribeirão

Rua 15 de Novembro

2

Rua Santo António

Praça
António
Lobo

4

Rua Graça Aranha

7

8

5

Praça D Pedro II

Catedral
da Sé

Becos dos Barracas

Rua do Alecrim

Praça Dom
Pedro II

9

Rua dos Afogados

10

11

13

14

15

Rua de Nazaré

Rua do Sol

16

17

12

Rua do Egito

18

Rua de Trapiche

19 20

21 22

23

Praça
João
Lisboa

24

25

26

27

Rua Portugal
Beco dos
Catraeiros

Rua Humberto de Campos

32

Rua da Paz

29

30 31

Rua da Alfândega

33

34

35

37

Projeto Reviver

Rua João Vital

Rua Grande (Ped Mall)

Travessa Boa Ventura

38 39

Beco da Prensa

40

Rua de Santana

41

Rua do Desterro

Rua Direita

Beco Escuro

42

Rua do Saúde

43

Rua do Mocambo

Rua Jacinto Maia

44

45

Rua da Inveja

46

Portinho

47

Praça do
Mercado

48

Rua Luciano Reis

Travessa da Lapa

Travessa do
M Central

Rua da Palha

49

Rua da Cotovia

50

Av Pres Kennedy

Rua do Santiago

Rua do Saudade Becos das Minas

Rua de São Pantaleão

51

0   200   400 m
0   200   400 yards

THE NORTHEAST

in the state at very reasonable prices. In the shopping gallery at Rua do Sol 141, there are several travel agencies offering package tours, and they also sell bus tickets at the same price as at the bus station. An efficient one is Taguatur (☎ 232-0906, fax 232-1814) at Shop 15.

Bookstore Poem-se, a second-hand bookstore on Rua Humberto de Campos, has many books in English, French and German. It also has a large collection of used CDs and magazines.

Catedral da Sé

Constructed by the Jesuits in 1629 as the Igreja NS da Boa Morte, this building on Praça Dom Pedro II became the official cathedral in 1762. Inside are ceiling frescoes decorated with babaçu motifs and a fine baroque altar.

Palácio dos Leões

Originally a French fortress, this is now the Palácio do Governo, the state governor's residence and office. Built in 1612 by Daniel de la Touche, during the reign of Louis XIII, the palace interior reflects the pomp of Versailles and French architectural tastes. At the time of writing it was being restored for use as a cultural center. It's at the western end of Avenida Dom Pedro II.

Teatro Artur Azvedo

Dating from 1815, this is one of the most beautiful theaters in Brazil and has been lovingly restored. If you can, go to a show here. Guided tours are available (US$1) at 3 pm from Wednesday to Sunday. The entrance is at Rua do Sol 180.

Projeto Reviver

During the late 1980s state authorities finally agreed to restore the historical district, which had been neglected and decaying for many decades. The initial restoration project was completed in 1990, and the city's UNESCO status should ensure funds for ongoing work.

More than 200 buildings have already been restored, and the district has been

THE NORTHEAST

turned into one of the architectural highlights of Brazil. To appreciate the superb colonial mansions and the many designs and colors of their tiled facades, just wander around the district. *Azulejos* (decorative ceramic tiles, often blue or blue-and-white) were first produced in Portugal and later became a popular product in France, Belgium and Germany. Since tiles provide a durable means of protecting outside walls from the humidity and heat in São Luís, their use became standard practice during colonial times.

Museu de Artes Visuais

This museum, at Rua Portugal 273, has a fine collection of old azulejos, engravings, prints and paintings. It's open from 9 am to 7 pm Tuesday to Saturday.

Opposite the museum is the old round market, where you can shop with the locals for dried salted shrimp (eaten with shell and all), cachaça, dried goods and basketwork, or visit the lunch counters for cheap local cooking.

Cafua das Mercês & Museu do Negro

In Cafua das Mercês, the building that held the old slave market, you'll find the Museu do Negro. This is where slaves were kept after their arrival from Africa and until they were sold – notice the absence of windows. A small and striking series of exhibits documents the history of slavery in Maranhão. The museum is at Rua Jacinto Maia 43 and is open 9 am to 6 pm, Tuesday to Saturday.

The slaves brought to Maranhão were Bantus from Africa. They toiled primarily on the sugar plantations, and to a lesser extent worked on the cultivation of rice and cotton. They brought their own type of Candomblé, which is called Tambor de Mina in this part of Brazil. The museum director, Jorge Babalaou, is an expert on Candomblé and Bantu/Maranhense folklore. He may be able to indicate where you can visit a ceremony, but the major local houses – the Casa das Minas, Casa de Nagô and Casa Fanti-Ashanti-Nagô – do not welcome visitors.

Museu do Centro de Cultura Popular

Just a few minutes on foot from the Cafua das Mercês, at Rua do Giz 221, this popular culture museum displays a good collection of handicrafts from the state of Maranhão, and Bumba Meu Boi costumes and masks (see the boxed text 'Bumba Meu Boi' in this chapter). It's open 9 am to 7 pm daily except Sunday and Monday, when it is closed.

Museu Histórico e Artístico do Estado de Maranhão

Housed in a restored mansion built in 1836, this museum provides an insight into daily life in the 18th century, with an attractive display of artifacts from wealthy Maranhão families. You will see furnishings, family photographs, religious articles, coins, sacred art – not to mention President José Sarney's bassinet. It's at Rua do Sol 302 and is open 9 am to 6 pm Tuesday to Friday and on weekends 2 to 6 pm.

Centro do Criatividade

The exhibition and performance space at Rua da Alfândega 200, in the heart of Projeto Reviver, is for culture vultures interested in the local art scene. There's a theater for local plays and dance productions, an art gallery, and a cinema showing arthouse films. It's open 8 am to 10 pm Tuesday to Friday.

Igreja do Desterro

This church on Largo do Desterro, notable for its facade, was built between 1618 and 1641 and is the only Byzantine church in Brazil. There's a small adjoining museum, the Museu de Paramentos Eclesiásticos, containing a display of ecclesiastical apparel.

Fountains

The **Fonte das Pedras**, at Rua Antônio Rayol 363, was built by the Dutch during their brief occupation of São Luís. It marks the spot where, on October 31, 1615, Jerônimo de Albuquerque and his troops camped before expelling the French. The fountain is inside a small, shady park.

The **Fonte do Ribeirão**, a delightful fountain on Largo Do Ribeirão, was built in 1796 and has spouting gargoyles. The three metal gates once provided access to subterranean tunnels that were reportedly linked to churches as a means to escape danger.

Beaches

The beaches are beyond the São Francisco district, and they are all busy on sunny weekends. You should beware of rough surf and tremendous tides in the area: Ask for local advice about safe times and places to swim before you head for the beaches.

Ponta d'Areia is the closest beach to the city, only 3.5km away, but the pollution has put a stop to swimming. It's a popular beach for those who want to make a quick exit from the city and visit the bars and restaurants for beach food.

The best local beach, **Calhau**, is broad and beautiful and only 7.5km from the city. The locals like to drive their cars onto Calhau (as well as the next beach, Olho d'Água), park and lay out their towels alongside their machines. On weekends this causes congestion that can spoil the enjoyment of these good city beaches.

Olho d'Água, 11.5km from São Luís, has more beach bars and soccer games than the other beaches. It's active and fun on weekends.

Praia do Araçagi, 4km farther, is the quietest and most peaceful of these beaches. There are only simple bars and a few weekend beach houses here.

Organized Tours

The tour agencies described under Travel Agencies earlier in this section offer city tours of São Luís and day trips to São José do Ribamar and Alcântara. Prices average US$25 per person per day and include transport and guide services only – you pay for admission fees and meals.

Special Events

São Luís has one of Brazil's richest folkloric traditions, evident in its many festivals. There are active samba clubs and distinctive local dances and music. During Carnaval most activity is out on the streets and the tourist influence is minimal. **Marafolia**, the out-of-season Carnaval, is held in mid-October, and is reputed to be more lively than the main one.

The **Tambor de Mina** festivals, held in July, are important events for followers of the Afro-Brazilian religions in São Luís. They city's famous **Bumba Meu Boi** festival commences in the second half of June, and its special events continue until the second week of August. The **Festa do Divino**,

---

Bumba Meu Boi

São Luís is famous for its Bumba Meu Boi – a fascinating, wild folkloric festival. Derived from African, Indian and Portuguese influences, it's a rich mixture of music, dance and theater. There's a Carnavalesque atmosphere in which participants dance, sing and tell the story of the death and resurrection of the bull – with plenty of room for improvisation. Parade groups spend the year in preparation, costumes are lavish and new songs and poetry are invented.

The story and its portrayal differ throughout the Northeast, but the general plot is as follows:

Catrina, goddaughter of the local farm owner, is pregnant and feels a craving to eat the tongue of the best *boi* (bull) on the farm. She cajoles her husband, Chico, into killing the beast. When the dead bull is discovered, several characters (caricatures drawn from all levels of society) do some detective work and finally track down the perpetrator of the crime. Chico is brought to trial, but the bull is resuscitated by various magic incantations and tunes. A pardon is granted, and the story reaches its happy ending when Chico is reunited with Catrina.

The festival starts in the second half of June and continues into the second week of August. Give the São Luís Fumtur tourist office (☎ 231-9086) a call to get the exact dates of all the events.

THE NORTHEAST

celebrated 40 days after Lent, is especially spectacular in Alcântara.

Places to Stay

Budget Two hostels have sprung up fairly recently in the old part of town, the *Albergue Juventude Solar das Pedras* (☎/fax 232-6694, Rua da Palma 127) and the *Albergue Dois Continentes* (☎/fax 222-6286, Rua do Giz 129). In renovated colonial houses, both offer clean dorm rooms for US$8 per person and double rooms for US$25.

Another good budget option is the *Hotel Casa Grande* (☎ 232-2432, Beco dos Barracas 98). Large, basic apartamentos cost US$10/12/15 for singles/doubles/triples, with a bread and coffee breakfast included. Some of the rooms on the third floor have views over the river.

There are several very cheap places right in the heart of town, but the area is not too safe at night – be aware of muggers. The *Hotel Estrêla* (☎/fax 232-7172, Rua da Estrêla 370) is a popular cheapie in the heart of the historic district. Quartos (with fan) cost US$8/13. Don't leave valuables in your room – there's a safe at reception. The *Pousada Central* (☎ 221-1649, Rua de Nazaré 340) offers clean quartos for US$8 a single and apartamentos for US$12/17.

The *Hotel São Marcos* (☎/fax 232-3768, Rua do Saúde 178) has friendly hosts and a relaxed atmosphere. Smallish apartamentos cost US$19/25. There's a swimming pool and restaurant; the hotel also provides off-street parking.

A good deal is the *Hotel Lord* (☎ 221-4655, Rua de Nazaré 258). It's a large, time-worn place that's seen grander days. Even though the red carpet is a bit frayed, it still provides comfortable quartos at US$15/20, and apartamentos at US$23/28.

Mid-Range The *Pousada do Francês* (☎ 231-4844, fax 232-0879, Rua 7 de Setembro 121) is housed in a beautifully restored colonial building. Apartamentos with air-conditioning, fridge and TV cost US$40/55 (with a 15% discount for cash), and some of the higher rooms have views. There's also a swish bar/restaurant in the hotel. It's an ex-

cellent value. The *Pousada Colonial* (☎/fax 232-2834, Rua Afonso Pena 112), in a restored colonial mansion, also offers a good value. Comfortable apartamentos cost US$30/35, but there's often a 20% discount.

At Praia do Araçagi, a good, medium-priced hotel is the *Chalé da Lagoa* (☎ 226-4916) on Rua da Lagoa. It's a relaxing place surrounded by gardens. Doubles are US$28 with fan and US$35 with air-conditioning. *Pousada Tia Maria* (☎ 227-1534, Quadra 1, lot 12), at Praia da Ponta d'Areia, is recommended for those who want to spend time sitting around the beach bars. Singles/doubles are US$25/32.

Top End The five-star *Vila Rica* (☎ 232-3535, fax 232-7245, vilaricabc@elo.com.br, Praça Dom Pedro II 299) is very central, with a view overlooking the bay. Apartamentos cost US$70/78. The presidential suite is US$190.

The five-star *Sofitel Quatro Rodas* (☎ 235-4545, fax 235-4921) is a beach resort hotel surrounded by spacious gardens, on Avenida Avicênia at Praia do Calhau, a 15-minute drive from town. It has rooms for US$110/130.

Places to Eat

The best Maranhense food comes from the sea. In São Luís you'll find many of the familiar dishes of the Northeast, and regional specialties such as *torta de sururu* (mussel pie), *casquinha de caranguejo* (stuffed crab), *caldeirada de camarão* (shrimp stew) and the city's special rice dish – *arroz de cuxá* (rice with vinegar, local vegetables and shrimp).

City Center There are plenty of *lanchonetes* (stand-up snack bars) serving cheap food. Across from the Fonte do Ribeirão, you'll find a couple of decent self-serve lunch spots. *Fonte de Sabor* is a good one of this lot.

The *Base da Lenoca* (☎ 231-0599, Praça Dom Pedro II 181) is a popular seafood restaurant, with a great position overlooking the Rio Anil – order a beer and a snack and enjoy the breeze. In the heart of the historic district, there's the **Restaurante Antiga-mente** (☎ 221-2020), which has seafood and meat dishes, and tables on the street. There's live music here in the evening on weekends. **Senac** (☎ 232-6336, Rua de Nazaré 452) offers fine dining in a lovely colonial building. **Naturista Alimentos** (☎ 222-4526, Rua do Sol 517) has the best vegetarian food in the city.

Beaches At Ponte d'Areia, **Tia Maria** (☎ 227-1535) has good seafood, and it's also a fine place to watch the sunset while enjoying a cool drink. This is also the closest beach to the city with bars serving food.

Entertainment

São Luís is currently the reggae center of the Northeast, and many bars and clubs here have regular reggae nights. The tourist office has a list of places to check out – some of them can be a bit dangerous, although this seems to be a prerequisite for a happening place! It's worth asking locals for recommendations. The daily newspaper *Estado do Maranhão* has an entertainment listing. Reggae fans should tune their FM radios to 94.3 weekdays from 8 am to 10 pm for the local music show. For information about reggae parties, call Pinto da Itamarati (☎ 9971-8376).

Reggae bars include **Bar do Nelson** on Avenida Litorânea at Praia do Calhau, with live music Fridays and Saturdays after 11 pm and **Creôle** at Ponta d'Areia near the Number One Flat, a landmark in the area.

For dancing to something other than reggae, try **Extravagance** (☎ 235-9090, Rua Búzios, Quadra 33, 20) at Calhau, or **Exótico** (☎ 221-3855, Rua da Estrêla 210).

Good music bars in the old city are **Taberna Cantaría**, on Beco da Prensa, **Bar do Porto** (Rua do Trapiche 49) and **Canto do Tônico** on Rua Portugal.

The beaches at Ponta d'Areia and Calhau are very active on weekends, with lots of live music and revelry. A couple of popular music places to check are **Zanzibar** (☎ 248-4067), on Avenida Litorânea in Calhau, and **Kaya na Rede**, at Ponta d'Areia next to the Praia Mar Hotel.

Shopping

São Luís is the place for the traditional handicrafts of Maranhão, such as woodcarving, basketry, lacework, ceramics, leatherwork, and woven goods made from linen. Also on sale are featherwork and items made from straw or plant fibers (from baskets to bracelets) by the Urubus-Caapor and Guajajara Indians, both from the interior of Maranhão state.

The Centro de Artesanato, at Rua de São Pantaleão 1232, is housed in a renovated factory and functions as an exhibition hall and sales outlet for handicrafts. It's open Monday to Saturday 9 am to 7 pm. On Sunday it closes at 1 pm. Also worth visiting are the Mercado Central on the Praça do Mercado and the many craft stores in the surrounding streets.

Getting There & Away

Air Domestic air services connect São Luís with Rio, São Paulo and the major cities in the Northeast and the North.

These are the addresses for Brazilian airlines:

TAM (☎ 231-3623), Rua dos Afogados 16
TransBrasil (☎ 232-1414), Praça João Lisboa 432
Varig/Nordeste (☎ 231-5066), Avenida Dom Pedro Segundo 221
VASP (☎ 231-4433), Rua do Sol 43

Bus The bus station (☎ 243-2320) is 8km southeast of the city center on Avenida dos Franceses. Tickets can be purchased in the city center at travel agencies listed under Information earlier in this section.

There are four daily buses to Teresina (US$15, seven hours); two to Belém (US$35, 12 hours); one via Imperatriz to Carolina (US$27, 12 hours); two to Guimarães (US$18, 10 hours); four to Fortaleza (US$37, 18 hours); and two to Recife (US$57, 24 hours).

Boat The *hidroviária* (boat terminal) is on the quayside, just beyond the western end of Rua Portugal. From here, it's possible to take passage on boats sailing along the coast. Sailing times are approximate and depend on the tides. The regular daily service to Alcântara is described in Getting There & Away in the Alcântara section in this chapter.

There are also departures at least once a week to Guimarães, a major center for boat-building and fishing, and infrequent departures from there to destinations farther along the western coast such as Turiaçu, Luís Domingues and Carutapera (on the Pará border).

Getting Around

Aeroporto do Tirirical (☎ 245-1515) is 15km southeast of the city. The bus marked 'São Cristóvão' runs from the bus stop opposite Banco do Brasil on Praça Deodoro to the airport in 35 minutes. There's a ticket booth for taxis at the airport – a taxi to the center costs around US$12.

Several buses go to the bus station from Praça Deodoro, and you can also pick one up at the Praia Grande bus terminal on Avenida Beira Mar. From the bus station to the city center costs US$7 by taxi.

Buses run to Ponta d'Areia and Calhau from the Praia Grande bus terminal – take buses marked 'Ponta d'Areia,' 'Calhau' or 'Cal Litorâneo.' For buses to Araçagi, Raposa and São José do Ribamar, there's a bus stop beside the Mercado Central. To get

to Olho d'Água, take a bus marked 'Olho d'Água' from Praça Deodoro.

ILHA DE SÃO LUÍS
Raposa

Out at the tip of the Ilha de São Luís, 30km from the city, is the interesting and very dirty fishing center of Raposa, which is chiefly worth visiting for its well-known lacework. It's a poor town, built on stilts above mangrove swamps, which gives it an unusual appearance. The bulk of the population is descended from Cearense immigrants. There are no tourist facilities, but the ocean here is pretty and very shallow. There are lots of small fishing boats and it's not too hard to negotiate a ride. Bathing at the beach is dangerous due to extreme tidal variations. The water recedes by as much as a kilometer at low tide.

There are frequent buses from São Luís – a convenient bus stop there is the one beside the Mercado Central. The trip takes 45 minutes.

São José do Ribamar

This fishing town is on the east coast of the island, 30km from the city. There's a busy little waterfront where you can catch one of the boats leaving for small towns along the coast – a good way to explore some of the

---

The São José do Ribamar Miracle

The origins of the town date back to the early 18th century, when a Portuguese sailing ship went astray and started to flounder on the sandbanks of the Baía de São José. The desperate crew begged for mercy from São José das Botas and promised to procure the finest statue of the saint and construct a chapel for it if they were spared.

The ship and its crew were miraculously saved, and several years later the promise was kept – a fine statue of the saint was installed in a chapel at the tip of the cape where the disaster was narrowly avoided. The settlement on this site later received the name São José do Ribamar, a fusion of the saint's name and the local Indian name for the rock formation at the cape.

According to local legend, the statue was moved away from its site beside the shore, but it miraculously reappeared in its original position the next day, without any signs of human intervention. This miracle was repeated a few more times, until the locals decided the statue should be left in the place it seemed to prefer. During its trek, the statue left deep footprints along the rocky coastline, rock formations that are now venerated by the townsfolk, who hold the annual Festa do Pedroeiro in September in honor of the saint.

more out-of-the-way villages on the island. On Sunday buses go from São José to nearby Ponta de Panaquatira, a popular weekend beach.

Frequent buses and minibuses leave from the convenient bus stop beside the Mercado Central in São Luís for the 45-minute trip to São José do Ribamar. The last bus back to São Luís leaves at 10:30 pm.

ALCÂNTARA
☎ 0xx98 • postcode 65250-000 • pop 5700
Across the Baía de São Marcos from São Luís is the colonial town of Alcântara. Built in the early 1600s with extensive slave labor, the town was the hub of the region's sugar and cotton economy. The people who benefited from this wealth, Maranhão's rich landowners, preferred living in Alcântara to São Luís.

While the town has been in decline since the latter half of the 19th century, it is still considered an architectural treasure, and some experts claim that it is the most homogeneous group of colonial buildings and ruins from the 17th and 18th centuries in Brazil.

In the early 1990s the construction of the Centro do Lançamento de Alcântara (CLA), a nearby rocket-launching facility, caused mutterings among residents, who disagreed with the forceful resettlement policy undertaken to clear the construction site. There couldn't be a greater contrast with this slumbering colonial town than a space-age launching pad!

Information
Fumtur, the tourist office in São Luís, has brochures and information about Alcântara.

Things to See & Do
The town is very poor and decaying, but don't miss the following: the beautiful row of two-story houses on **Rua Grande**; the **Igreja de NS do Carmo** (1665) on Largo do Carmo; and the best-preserved **pelourinho** (whipping post) in Brazil, on Praça da Matriz.

The **Museu Histórico**, on the Praça da Matriz, displays a collection of sacred art, festival regalia and colonial furniture. Each room has its own guardian – a source of employment for the locals. Open hours for the museum are Tuesday to Sunday from 9 am to 5 pm.

Once you've seen the main sights, you can walk to the beaches or take a boat trip out to nearby islands.

Special Events
The Festa do Divino is held on the first Sunday after Ascension Day. Check the date for the festival (usually held in May) with Fumtur in São Luís.

This is considered one of the most colorful annual festivals in Maranhão. It represents a fusion of African and Catholic elements and features two children dressed as the emperor and empress, who are paraded through the town accompanied by musicians.

Places to Stay & Eat
Alcântara has simple campsites close to Praça da Matriz and near the lighthouse. There are also several inexpensive pousadas. The *Pousada Pelourinho* (☎ 337-1150), on Praça da Matriz, has spacious single/double quartos for US$10/15 – check out the Egyptian-style dance space out the back. *Pousada do Mordomo Régio* (☎ 337-1197, Rua Grande 134) has quartos for US$12/20 and apartamentos for US$30.

The *Pousada dos Guarás* (☎ 337-1339) is located right on the beachfront at Praia da Baronesa. It's a quiet, relaxing place to stay – simple chalets cost US$15 per person and there's a good restaurant/bar as well. Keep an eye out for red ibis (*guará* in Portuguese), beautiful red birds that are plentiful here but threatened with extinction in other parts of Brazil.

All the hotels mentioned here have restaurants, and there are also two acceptable, inexpensive restaurants close together on Rua Direita – *Restaurante Copos e Bocas* and *Restaurante da Josefa* (☎ 337-1109).

Getting There & Away
Boats from São Luís to Alcântara depart from the hidroviária (boat terminal) on the

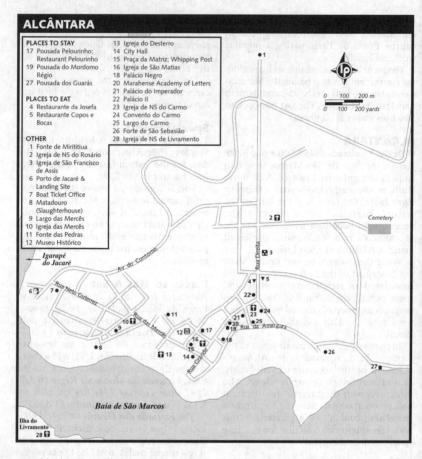

ALCÂNTARA

PLACES TO STAY
17 Pousada Pelourinho;
   Restaurant Pelourinho
19 Pousada do Mordomo
   Régio
27 Pousada dos Guarás

PLACES TO EAT
4 Restaurante da Josefa
5 Restaurante Copos e
   Bocas

OTHER
1 Fonte de Miritituia
2 Igreja de NS do Rosário
3 Igreja de São Francisco
   de Assis
6 Porto de Jacaré &
   Landing Site
7 Boat Ticket Office
8 Matadouro
   (Slaughterhouse)
9 Largo das Mercês
10 Igreja das Mercês
11 Fonte das Pedras
12 Museu Histórico

13 Igreja do Desterro
14 City Hall
15 Praça da Matriz; Whipping Post
16 Igreja de São Matias
18 Palácio Negro
20 Marahense Academy of Letters
21 Palácio do Imperador
22 Palácio II
23 Igreja de NS do Carmo
24 Convento do Carmo
25 Largo do Carmo
26 Forte de São Sebastião
28 Igreja de NS de Livramento

Igarapé do Jacaré

Av. do Contorno

Rua Neto Guterrez

Rua das Mercês

Rua Direita

Rua da Amargura

Rua Grande

Cemetery

Baía de São Marcos

Ilha do Livramento

quayside, just beyond the western end of Rua Portugal. It's a good idea to book your ticket the day before departure, and check the departure times, which vary according to the tide.

Three types of boats make the trip to Alcântara. The *Diamantina* is a large motorboat that leaves twice a day, at 7 and 9:30 am. Its crossing takes about one hour and costs US$3.50

For the more adventurous, there are two sailing boats straight out of pirate tales – the *Newton Belle* and the *Mensageiro da Fé*. Both leave from the São

Luís boat terminal twice a day, at around 6:30 am and 4 pm. Pandemonium reigns as the last passengers and cargo get stuffed below at sailing time. Try to avoid the crush by sitting outside at the front of the boat. The trip takes about 1½ hours and costs US$3.

The third option is to go by catamaran. These double-hulled boats are probably more suited to travelers able to cope with rough seas. Make sure you protect cameras etc with plastic. The boats don't run on any particular schedule, so ask at the port for departure times

PARQUE NACIONAL DOS LENÇÓIS MARANHENSES

The attractions of this 1550 sq km national park halfway between São Luís and the Piauí border include beaches, mangroves, lagoons, dunes and some interesting fauna, especially turtles and migratory birds. The park's name refers to the immense dunes, which look like *lençóis* (bedsheets) strewn across the landscape. The area's designation as a national park in 1981 staved off ecologically ruinous land speculation. The best time to visit is between March and September, when rain that has filtered through the sand forms crystal-clear pools between the dunes.

Information

The park has minimal tourist infrastructure, but it's possible to arrange a visit from the town of Barreirinhas, two hours by boat from the dunes. You can get a ride on a boat going downriver to the beginning of the park for a few dollars. Get to the Barreirinhas riverfront early and ask around.

Organized Tours

Pousada Lins (see Places to Stay & Eat in the Barreirinhas section) organizes tours of the park – a day trip by boat down the Rio Preguiça costs US$80 for up to five people.

Giltur (☎ 0xx98-231-6041) in São Luis also runs tours to the park. A three-day tour costs around US$190, including accommodations in Barreirinhas, bus and boat transport. A three-day package where you fly instead of taking a bus, costs US$315 per person. The aerial view of the park is spectacular.

Places to Stay

As you go downriver from Barreirinhas, the boat passes the tiny fishing villages of **Mandacaru**, with its lighthouse, and **Caburé**, where the very basic *Pousada e Restaurante Lençoes de Areia* charges US$8 per person for a quarto or US$5 to sling a hammock.

Farther downriver, close to the park, is the small village of **Atins**, where you should stay at *Filhos do Vento* (☎ *0xx98-9966-7100, filhosdovento@yahoo.com.br*).

Barreirinhas

☎ 0xx98 • postcode 65590-000 • pop 13,000

Barreirinhas, the jumping-off point for the national park, is also a pretty little town on the banks of the Rio Preguiça. There is a river beach with sand dunes near the center of town, and some good pousadas and restaurants.

The *Pousada Lins* (☎ *349-1203, Avenida Joaquim Sueiro de Cavalho 550*) is the nicest place to stay. Quartos with fan cost US$11 per person, and spotless single/double apartamentos with air-conditioning go for US$12/24. *Pousada Giltur* (☎ *349-1177, Avenida Brasília 259*) has comfortable apartamentos for US$15 per person.

Restaurant Brisa do Mar (*Avenida Joaquim Soeiro de Cavalho 583*) is a friendly place serving local seafood and chicken dishes. *Restaurant Lins*, under the same management as Pousada Lins, offers a similar menu.

There are two bus services a day to Barreirinhas from the bus station in São Luís, leaving at 9:30 am and 9:45 pm (US$15, around eight hours). By the time you read this, the paving of the road should be complete, and the journey should be much faster. The return service from Barreirinhas departs daily at 6 am (10 am on Sunday). The bus fills up quickly, so while you're in Barreirinhas you should book tickets in advance at Taguatur on Rua Inaçio Lins.

To get to Tutóia, there are a couple of ruts through the sand passable only by 4WD vehicles. You'll need to go via Rio Novo, about halfway to Tutóia, where there is one pousada. The 'road' passes by (and over) some superb dunescapes and very isolated, traditional fishing communities of straw huts. From Rio Novo, there are regular (though not that frequent) jeeps to Tutóia.

Rio Novo

☎ 0xx98

A small fishing and farming community between Barreirinhas and Tutóia, Rio Novo is a tranquil little place with one main attraction. Its coastal dunes are almost an extension of those in the park to the west, and

THE NORTHEAST

they're much more easily accessible – a short walk from the village itself.

The only pousada in town is *Pousada Oásis dos Lençóis* (☎ 9966-1351). It's very comfortable and has the river running past the back gate. Dona Mazé oozes tranquility and cooks a fabulous moqueca. She charges US$8 per person for quartos and US$10 for apartamentos with breakfast. The only entertainment in Rio Novo is at the bar next to the bridge, where you may be able to persuade the proprietor, Seu Zézico, to pull out his mandolin.

There are 4WD Toyotas leaving for Tutóia (US$4, 1½ hours) and Barreirinhas (US$5, two hours) each morning. For the rest of the day, there's usually someone coming or going, but there's no set timetable.

Tutóia
☎ 0xx98 • postcode 65580-000 • pop 11,600
Tutóia is a fishing port and beach town on the edge of the Delta do Parnaíba, the 2700 sq km expanse of rivers, dunes, beaches and mangrove forest that straddles the border of Maranhão and Piauí.

The best budget option is *Pousada Tremembes* (☎ 479-1109), Praça Tremembes 49. The owner, Cacau, is a very helpful gentle giant. He can arrange for the 4WD to Rio Novo to pick you up in the morning. Simple quartos are US$6 per person with breakfast. The restaurant in the pousada serves a good, cheap plate of the day.

On the beachfront, the *Pousada Embarcação* (☎ 479-1309) is a beach shack with a bar decorated with shark's jaws and snakeskins. It's on Rua Magalhães de Almeida. Apartamentos will cost you US$8/12 a single/double. The most upmarket place in town is the *Tutóia Palace Hotel* (☎ 479-1115, fax 479-1247, Avenida Paulino Neves 1100), near the waterfront, to the left as you get off the boat. Apartamentos cost US$15/30.

Two buses a day run over a good road to Parnaíba (Piauí). The trip takes about 2½ hours. A small motorboat cruises through the delta daily to Parnaíba (US$5, about seven hours). To Rio Novo, there's a 4WD truck leaving daily at around 10 am from Praça Getúlio Vargas. You can pick up another truck or jeep there to Barreirinhas, but you should be prepared to stay overnight.

THE NORTH COAST
The town of Guimarães is a center for boat building and fishing. Farther north is Cururupu, a small town that is the gateway to the Lençóis de Cururupu – a huge expanse of coastal dunes similar to, but not to be confused with, those in the Parque Nacional dos Lençóis Maranhenses.

About 80km offshore is Parcel de Manoel Luís, a coral reef named after the *Manoel Luís,* the first ship to be lost there. According to the experts, this reef, extending over 288 sq km, is the largest in South America; there are plans to turn it into a marine park. There are also plans to develop and exploit it as one of the world's top attractions for divers, especially those with nice fat wallets tucked into their wetsuits.

IMPERATRIZ
☎ 0xx9865900-000 • pop 220,000
Imperatriz is a rapidly expanding city 636km southwest of São Luís, on the border with Pará. The expansion is due to the rabid logging and mining of the surrounding region, which is turning the forests into an ecological nightmare. The only possible reason to visit would be to change buses – otherwise, just keep going.

CAROLINA
☎ 0xx98 • postcode 65980-000 • pop 14,500
The town of Carolina, 242km south of Imperatriz, lies beside the Rio Tocantins and is a handy base for visiting nearby natural attractions. **Pedra Caída**, 35km north of town (toward Estreito), is a dramatic combination of canyons and waterfalls. Some of the other spectacular waterfalls in the region are **Cachoeira do Itapecuruzinho**, 27km from town on the BR-230 road that goes east toward Riachão; **Cachoeira de São Simão**, at Fazenda São Jorge, about 10km from Carolina; and **Cachoeira da Barra da Cabeceira**. There are rock paintings and inscriptions at **Morro das Figuras**. Bat enthusiasts will want to visit the colony of bats in **Passagem Funda**, a large cave 70km from Carolina.

Places to Stay

The ***Pousada do Lajes*** (☎ 731-1499), 3km outside town toward Riachão, has chalets for US$30. The ***Recanto Pedra Caída*** (☎ 731-1318) is a tourist complex, with chalets and sports facilities, at the Pedra Caída waterfalls. Apartamentos are US$20/25.

Getting There & Around

There's a daily bus service from São Luís (US$27, 12 hours), and four services daily from Imperatriz (four hours).

A frequent ferry service (a 15-minute ride) operates across the Rio Tocantins to the town of Filadélfia in the state of Tocantins.

The North

The North of Brazil is made up of seven states: Pará, Amapá, Tocantins, Amazonas, Roraima, Rondônia and Acre.

In 1541 a Spanish expedition from Quito, led by Gonzalo Pizarro, ran short of supplies while exploring east of the Andes in what is today Peru. Pizarro's cousin Francisco de Orellana offered to take 60 men along with the boats from the expedition and forage for supplies.

Orellana floated down the Rio Napo all the way to its confluence with the Amazon, near Iquitos (Peru), and thence to the mouth of the Amazon. Along the way his expedition suffered attacks by some of the estimated several million Indians who inhabited Amazonia at the time. Some of the Indian warriors, they reported, were female, like the Amazons of Greek mythology – and thus the world's greatest river got its name.

No one made a serious effort to claim this sweaty territory, however, until the Portuguese built a fort near the mouth of the river at Belém in 1616, and sent Pedro Teixeira up the river to Quito and back in 1637–39. On his journey Teixeira claimed lands up to the Rio Napo for Portugal.

The Amazon basin, 6 million sq km of river and jungle (of which 3.6 million sq km are in Brazil), contains 17% of the world's fresh water. It has 80,000km of navigable rivers, and oceangoing vessels can sail 3500km inland up the Amazon mainstream to Iquitos, Peru. The main river's flow at its mouth is 12 billion liters a minute – 12 times that of the Mississippi!

Many of the Amazon's tributaries are also enormous: Rio Madeira-Mamoré flows for 3200km and the Rio Tocantins for 2750km. The Rio Negro is a mere 1550km. Upstream from its confluence with the Negro (a few kilometers from Manaus) to the end of Brazilian territory at Tabatinga, the Amazon is known locally as the Rio Solimões. Below and above that stretch it's called the Amazonas. The Amazon rises in

the Andes in Peru, and only half its total length is in Brazil.

Most of the rivers are so wide you won't see much flora and fauna from the boats. To see the wildlife of Amazonia (alligators, monkeys, pink and gray river dolphins, anacondas, toucans, macaws, eagles), you must explore the *igarapés* (channels cutting through the jungle, so narrow that the forest may brush your face). If you make a jungle trip, try to make sure that it includes visiting igarapés by motorless canoe or small boat, since noisy motorboats scare the wildlife away. A good time for jungle trips is when the water level is high – March to July in most of Amazonia but about three months earlier along most of the southern tributaries. At high water, canoes can slide through the flooded forests almost at jungle canopy level, bringing you closer to the wildlife. (See the Natural Brazil special section for more information on Amazonia's amazing fauna, flora and ecosystems and on how you can experience them.)

THE NORTH

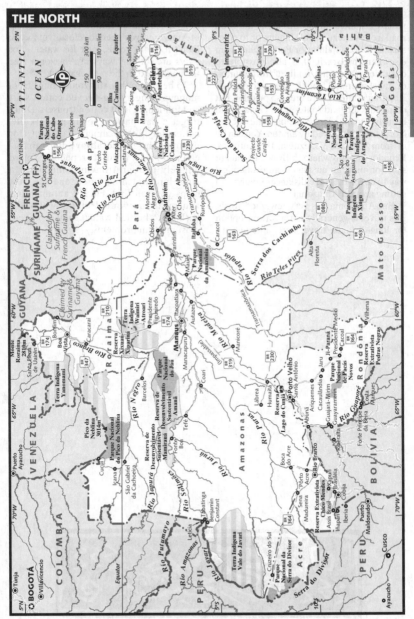

There are many routes into Brazilian Amazonia, including by bus along the good road from Venezuela to Manaus, or to cities such as Belém, Palmas or Porto Velho from elsewhere in Brazil. It is also possible to come down the Amazon itself from Iquitos, or travel overland from Bolivia into Acre or Rondônia states. There are also possible, but more difficult, land routes from Guyana and French Guiana. The principal cities of the North are well served by air, too. You can fly in from the US, Venezuela, the Guianas, Ecuador and anywhere in Brazil. If you are short on time, an air pass is an economical way to cover the huge distances involved in getting around Amazonia.

But Amazonia has very few good roads. Bus travel is generally not a serious option for long-distance travel here, although it's more feasible around the peripheries. When looking for transportation routes on a map of Amazonia, you need to refocus your eyes: Don't look for roads, look for water – for rivers are the highways of Amazonia (see the boxed text in the next chapter).

To help stop the Amazonian bugs from nipping, bring a long-sleeved cotton shirt and full-length light cotton trousers. Don't forget a day pack, a torch, pocketknife, hat, water bottle, camera, fast film (for photography in the always-dim rainforest) and plenty of insect repellent. You're unlikely to regret having binoculars, a good bird-watching guide, and the best maps you can find. Finally, antimalarials and purifying your drinking water (or sticking to bottled water) should prevent most medical problems.

Pará, Amapá & Tocantins

Brazil's territory in eastern Amazonia is comprised of the states of Pará, Amapá and Tocantins.

Pará covers 1.25 million sq km and includes a major stretch of the Rio Amazonas and all or part of such huge tributaries as the Rio Tocantins, Rio Xingu, Rio Tapajós and Rio Trombetas. Its attractions include the cities of Belém and Santarém, Ilha de Marajó, a huge river island, and some fine Atlantic beaches.

The small state of Amapá, with an enlightened, environmentalist administration since 1995, straddles the equator in the northeastern corner of Brazil, on a challenging route to or from French Guiana.

Tocantins, inland and south of Pará, has attractive natural destinations such as the Rio Araguaia, the Ilha do Bananal and the unique Jalapão region.

Pará

The Tupi tribe who lived beside the Rio Amazonas estuary prior to colonization used the term *pa'ra* (vast ocean) to describe its awesome size. In 1500 the Spanish navigator Vicente Yáñez Pinzón sailed past the estuary and, noting the huge volume of fresh water issuing into the ocean, turned back to investigate. Concluding that navigation to the source of such a gigantic 'ocean river' was too risky, he headed back to Spain to report his discovery. For information on the subsequent history of Pará state, see the Belém section later in this chapter.

Pará, especially the eastern part, has borne the brunt of Amazonian deforestation. The region to the south of the state capital, Belém, contains the world's biggest hydroelectric installation, at Tucuruí, and one of its biggest mining projects, the Provincia Mineral de Carajás. This is a Wild-West-like zone, infamous for human and ecological problems and for highway robberies and murdered land-rights campaigners.

Pará is divided into two time zones. East of the Rio Xingu, the state uses Brasília time; west of the Xingu, the time is one hour behind that.

Highlights

- Beautiful, wild Atlantic beaches at Algodoal and on Ilha de Marajó
- The village of Alter do Chão, with its river beaches and indigenous art center.
- Great birdwatching on Ilha do Bananal, the world's biggest river island
- The rubber boomtown of Belém, with a thriving port, excellent zoo of Amazonian fauna and colonial architecture
- Charming historic town of Natividade, deep in the backcountry of Tocantins
- Looking across the Rio Amazonas from the Ilha de Marajó in the middle of it – and not being able to see the shore

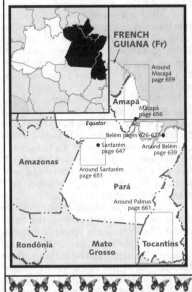

623

BELÉM

☎ 0xx91 • postcode 66000-000
• pop 1.27 million

Belém is the economic center of the North and the state capital of Pará. It's a lively and absorbing city, with a unique culture derived from the peoples and ways of the forest and river. It is animated by the biggest port on the Amazon (where 56% of all cargo carried is timber). From here you can set sail for any navigable port of the river or its tributaries. The city's central area is pleasant, with streets and parks shaded by mango trees, and some fascinating monuments and architecture.

History

The Portuguese, having expelled the French from Maranhão in 1615, landed at Belém in 1616, building a fort to deter French, English, Spanish and Dutch ships from sailing up the Rio Amazonas and claiming territory. Until 1774 the area encompassing present-day Pará and Maranhão was governed as a colony separate from the rest of Brazil, with its capital in São Luís, Maranhão.

Creating a separate administration for this territory made sense: The prevailing winds and currents made the voyage from Belém to Salvador much longer and more arduous than the six-week trip from Belém to Lisbon, and the inland route was long and perilous.

In 1637–39 Pedro Teixeira journeyed from Belém to Quito (Ecuador) and back, claiming lands as far as the Rio Napo (Peru) for Portugal. As elsewhere in Brazil, Jesuits came to Amazonia to 'save' the Indians and install them in *aldeias* (mission villages). It was through these missionaries and a scattering of forts that Portugal began to take control of the region.

The economy of colonial Belém relied on the *drogas do sertão* (spices of the backlands). The Portuguese settlers (predominantly poor farmers from the Azores islands) were dependent on the labor of the *filhos do mato* (sons of the forest), Indians who knew the ways of the Amazon and who could find cacao, vanilla, indigo, cinnamon, animal skins and turtle shells for export to Europe. These riches, and the enslavement of the Indians, made Belém a relatively prosperous settlement. It survived by striking farther and farther into Amazonia, destroying tribes of Indians in one slaving expedition after another. Epidemics killed many Indians, while Catholicism killed much of their culture. Some Indians escaped this fate by fleeing deeper along small tributaries into Amazonia.

With the depletion of the Indian labor force, Belém's economy began to decline, and the 1820s and 1830s saw a period of intense civil war (see the boxed text 'The Cabanagem Rebellion' later in this chapter).

Decades later, the regional economy was revitalized by the rubber boom. Vast numbers of poor peasants fled the drought-plagued Northeast, particularly Ceará, to tap Amazonia's rubber trees. Most of these *seringuieros* (rubber gatherers) arrived and then died in debt. By 1910 rubber constituted 39% of Brazil's total exports.

The population of Belém grew from 40,000 in 1875 to more than 100,000 in 1900. The city had electricity, telephones, streetcars and a distinctly European feel. Officials erected a few grand monuments such as the Teatro da Paz, earning the city the nickname 'the tropical Paris.' The docks and warehouses that still line the riverfront were built during this period.

Climate

Belém is one of the rainiest cities in the world. There's no dry season: October has the least rain and December to June have a greater abundance and frequency of rain. This is not as bad as it sounds: The rain is often a brief, welcome relief from the early afternoon heat. It is not unusual for the locals to arrange appointments according to daily rainfall time, saying 'I'll meet you tomorrow after the rain'! Humidity is very high, but, unlike Manaus, Belém gets refreshing breezes from the Atlantic Ocean.

Orientation

As it approaches the Atlantic, the Rio Amazonas splinters into countless branches and channels. Many of its tributaries do a similar thing on a smaller scale, and Belém stands 120km from the Atlantic at the point where one tributary, the Rio Guamá, enters a wider channel called the Baía de Guajará. The Baía de Guajará then empties into the widest of the estuaries of Amazonas, the Baía de Marajó.

Belém's main street is Avenida Presidente Vargas, leading up from the waterfront to the leafy central park, Praça da República. The largest concentration of hotels is on or near this axis.

Narrow shopping streets lead southwest off Avenida Presidente Vargas through the Comércio district where, on the waterfront, you'll find the renowned Mercado Ver-o-Peso. Beyond Comércio is the Cidade Velha (Old Town), with most of Belém's fine old architecture.

East of the center, toward the famous Basílica de NS de Nazaré, is a relatively prosperous area with wide streets lined with mango trees, some good restaurants and a few more hotels. Avenida Visconde de Souza Franco, running down toward the port, has many bars and restaurants that get busy at night.

Information

Tourist Offices Paratur (☎ 212-0669), the state tourism agency, has its main office at Praça Waldemar Henrique s/n, open 8 am to 6 pm Monday to Friday. Some of the staff here are positively knowledgeable and enthusiastic about helping you make the most of your stay. The office has free brochures and maps.

Belemtur (☎ 242-0900), the city tourism department, has an information office at Avenida Governador José Malcher 592, open 8 am to 6 pm from Monday to Friday. It has some brochures and maps and does its best to answer questions.

Both departments also have desks at the airport, where Belemtur offers a free hotel reservation service from 7 am to 11 pm daily. Belemtur also has an information booth on Praça do Operário, outside the bus station.

Money Banco do Brasil's exchange office at Rua Santo Antônio 432, off Avenida

Presidente Vargas, is open 10 am to 4 pm Monday to Friday, but it could take all six of those hours to change a traveler's check. Exchange offices with good rates and much quicker procedures for currency and traveler's checks are Banco da Amazônia (BASA) on Rua Carlos Gomes opposite Praça da República; Monopolio, Avenida Braz de Aguiar 202A; and Casa de Francia, Travessa Padre Prudencio 40.

HSBC at Avenida Presidente Vargas 670 has lots of ATMs; Bradesco, HSBC, Banco do Brasil and others have ATMs at the airport.

Post & Communications The central post office is at Avenida Presidente Vargas 498. Telemar has long-distance telephone offices on the corner of Avenida Presidente Vargas and Rua Riachuelo (open 6:45 am to 10:30 pm daily), and on Rua João Alfredo in Comércio (open 8:30 am to 6:30 pm Monday to Friday and 8:30 am and 3:30 pm Saturday).

The cheapest central email/internet place is Internet Point on the top floor of the Iguatemi Shopping center on Travessa Padre Eutiquio. It's open 10 am to 10 pm Monday to Saturday and 3 to 10 pm Sunday, charges US$2.50 an hour and is sometimes chock-full of people. There's also access at Telemar on Avenida Presidente Vargas, Estacão Amazonia (in the Boulevard das Artes at Estacão das Docas), and the Hilton Hotel Business Center.

Internet Resources Paratur's sites www.cdpara.pa.gov.br/turismo/turismo.html and www.paratur.pa.gov.br have quite a lot of information in Portuguese on the attractions of Pará state.

Travel Agencies Belém has a range of travel agencies offering city tours, river tours and trips to Ilha de Marajó and other places outside the city. See the Organized Tours section for more on what's offered. Well-established agencies include:

Amazon Star Turismo (☎ 241-8624, fax 212-6244, amazonstar@amazonstar.com.br, www.amazonstar.com.br), Rua Henrique Gurjão 236

BELÉM

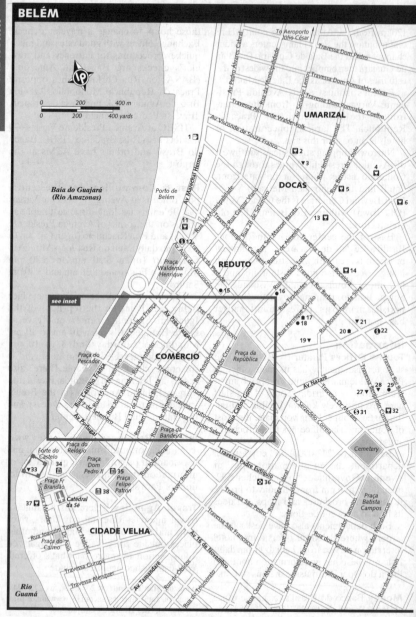

Baía do Guajará
(Rio Amazonas)

Rio Guamá

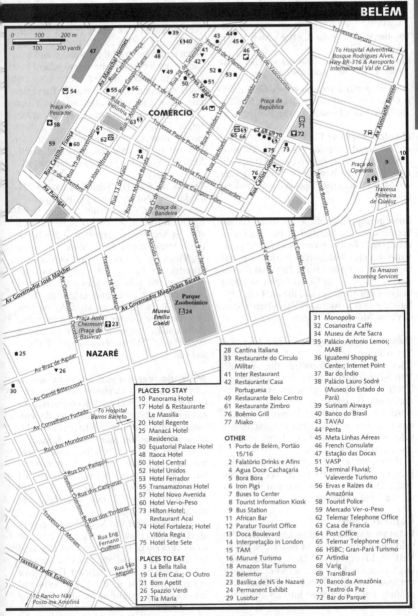

BELÉM

THE NORTH

PLACES TO STAY
10 Panorama Hotel
17 Hotel & Restaurante Le Massilia
20 Hotel Regente
25 Manacá Hotel Residencia
30 Equatorial Palace Hotel
48 Itaoca Hotel
50 Hotel Central
52 Hotel Unidos
53 Hotel Ferrador
55 Transamazonas Hotel
57 Hotel Novo Avenida
60 Hotel Ver-o-Peso
73 Hilton Hotel; Restaurant Acaí
74 Hotel Fortaleza; Hotel Vitória Regia
75 Hotel Sete Sete

PLACES TO EAT
3 La Bella Italia
19 Lá Em Casa; O Outro
21 Bom Apetit
26 Spazzio Verdi
27 Tia Maria
28 Cantina Italiana
33 Restaurante do Circulo Militar
41 Inter Restaurant
42 Restaurante Casa Portuguesa
49 Restaurante Belo Centro
61 Restaurante Zimbro
76 Boêmio Grill
77 Miako

OTHER
1 Porto de Belém, Portão 15/16
2 Falatório Drinks e Afins
4 Agua Doce Cachaçaria
5 Bora Bora
6 Iron Pigs
7 Buses to Center
8 Tourist Information Kiosk
9 Bus Station
11 African Bar
12 Paratur Tourist Office
13 Doca Boulevard
14 Interpretação in London
15 TAM
16 Mururé Turismo
18 Amazon Star Turismo
22 Belemtur
23 Basílica de NS de Nazaré
24 Permanent Exhibit
29 Lusotur
31 Monopolio
32 Cosanostra Caffé
34 Museu de Arte Sacra
35 Palácio Antonio Lemos; MABE
36 Iguatemi Shopping Center; Internet Point
37 Bar do Índio
38 Palácio Lauro Sodré (Museu do Estado do Pará)
39 Surinam Airways
40 Banco do Brasil
43 TAVAJ
44 Penta
45 Meta Linhas Aéreas
46 French Consulate
47 Estação das Docas
51 VASP
54 Terminal Fluvial; Valeverde Turismo
56 Ervas e Raízes da Amazônia
58 Tourist Police
59 Mercado Ver-o-Peso
62 Telemar Telephone Office
64 Post Office
65 Telemar Telephone Office
66 HSBC; Gran-Pará Turismo
67 Artíndia
68 Varig
69 TransBrasil
70 Banco da Amazônia
71 Teatro da Paz
72 Bar do Parque

Amazon Incoming Services (☎ 274-4904, amazon@ amazonservice.com.br), Avenida Gentil Bittencourt 3552

Lusotur (☎ 241-2000, fax 223-5054), Avenida Braz de Aguiar 471

Mururé Turismo (☎ 241-0904, guaras@interconect .com.br), Rua Aristides Lobo 906

A good agency if you just want a flight ticket is Gran-Pará Turismo (☎ 212-3233, fax 224-1687), Avenida Presidente Vargas 676.

Medical Services The Hospital Adventista (☎ 246-8686), Avenida Almirante Barroso 1758, is one of the better general hospitals. Hospital Barros Barreto (☎ 249-2323), Rua dos Mundurucus 4487, specializes in tropical diseases.

Emergency The Policia Turística (Tourist Police) can be contacted 24 hours daily at ☎ 212-0948. Tourist Police headquarters is at Paratur, Praça Waldemar Henrique s/n, but they also have posts at the Terminal Fluvial next to Estação das Docas (open 24 hours daily except Monday) and the old Cafe Chic building next to Mercado Ver-o-Peso (open daytime, Monday to Friday).

Dangers & Annoyances The Mercado Ver-o-Peso is notorious for harboring thieves and pickpockets (see the Mercado Ver-o-Peso section later in this chapter). Theft is also a danger when you stay at rock-bottom hotels.

Avoid walking around empty or near-empty streets or parks alone at night: Play it safe by taking a taxi to or from outlying restaurants or nightspots.

If you intend to travel by boat from Belém, watch your gear carefully (see Boats under Dangers & Annoyances in the Facts for the Visitor chapter).

Central Area
Estação das Docas
In an ambitious redevelopment reminiscent of Barcelona's Port Vell or Liverpool's Albert Dock, three large, down-at-heel port warehouses near the foot of Avenida Presidente Vargas have recently been converted into an attractive leisure zone.

Estação das Docas is painted in pastel shades and fronted by a 500m waterside walk and a line of yellow cranes, standing like sentinels of Belém's past. It houses clean and comfy restaurants, cafes and bars (and even a boutique brewery), where you can sit in air-conditioned coolness or out front watching the river traffic. There are also a few shops, a theater and exhibition spaces displaying interesting historical material. Estação das Docas is open daily except Monday – and couldn't be in greater contrast to the crowded, dirty and smelly Mercado Ver-o-Peso just to its southwest!

Teatro da Paz The Teatro da Paz (☎ 224-7355), overlooking Praça da República, is one of Belém's finest rubber-boom buildings. Constructed in 1868–74 in neoclassical style, it has hosted Brazilian and international stars ranging from Anna Pavlova to the Vienna Boys' Choir to the Cossacks. The architecture has all the sumptuous trappings of the rubber-boom era: columns, busts, crystal mirrors and an interior decorated in Italian theatrical style. At the time of writing the theater was closed for refurbishment, but normally it's open for guided visits (US$1.25) from 9 am to 6 pm, Tuesday to Friday.

Mercado Ver-o-Peso Spanning several blocks along the waterfront, this big market operates all day, every day. It originated as a checkpoint where, in colonial times, the Portuguese would *ver o peso* (check the weight) of merchandise in order to impose taxes. It comprises two main buildings and a large surrounding area with stalls, a harbor and so on. The four-turreted iron Mercado de Ferro housing the fish section was brought over in parts from Britain, assembled and inaugurated in 1901.

At and around the Ver-o-Peso, be very alert for pickpockets, who may operate alone or in gangs. One reader even reported being robbed at knifepoint as he stepped out of a taxi outside the market. Don't take anything of value to the Ver-o-Peso, and avoid hanging around there after 5 pm or on Sunday afternoon. Don't wander around dreamily with a camera – you risk being accosted by a big, dirty fish knife! If you feel insecure about visiting the market by yourself, ask the nearby Policia Turística (see the Emergency section earlier in this chapter) to accompany you.

Dangers (and smells of putrefaction) apart, the display of fruits, vegetables, plants, animals and fish, not to mention the people, is fascinating. It's best to get there early, when the fishing boats are unloading at the southwest end of the market. Look for the *mura,* a human-size fish.

The most intriguing section is filled with medicinal herbs and roots, snakeskins, alligator teeth, amulets with mysterious powers, and potions for every possible occasion. There are stalls selling weird and wonderful religious objects used for Macumba ceremonies, such as incense to counter *mau olho* (evil eye) and *guias* (necklaces that, when blessed, are used to provide a connection with the spirit world). There are also food stalls for cheap meals.

Cidade Velha

The oldest part of Belém, south of the Mercado Ver-o-Peso, is fairly run down. You should avoid walking around here after dark, but the area does contain most of the city's finest and most interesting buildings and some good museums, mostly grouped around two large *praças*.

Forte do Castelo A small rise on the riverbank a short distance southwest of the Mercado Ver-o-Peso has been the site of a fort since the first Portuguese settlers in Belém built a stockade here in 1616. Today the building is dilapidated, with a few old cannons and a lot of graffiti, but apparently in line for refurbishment. You can enter from 8 am to noon and 2 to 6 pm daily. Admission is free.

Palácio Antonio Lemos & MABE This rubber-boom palace on Praça Dom Pedro II was built to serve as the city hall between 1860 and 1883. By the early 1990s the palace was almost derelict and had animals roaming around inside, but it underwent renovation and now once again houses the municipal government headquarters as well as the Museo de Arte de Belém (MABE; ☎ 242-3344).

Constructed in the Brazilian imperial style, the building has a grand central staircase of Portuguese marble. The museum, upstairs, has a collection of Brazilian 20th-century paintings – a highlight is Cândido Portinari's 1957 oil *Seringal* – and a selection of opulent imported furniture, including a Louis XVI arrangement. The mayor's office, in a grandiose room upstairs at the rear, is not generally open to visitors.

The Palácio Antônio Lemos is open 10 am to 6 pm Tuesday to Friday, 9 am to 1 pm Saturday and Sunday. Admission is US$0.50.

Palácio Lauro Sodré

This former residence of Portugal's representatives in Belém, and later of various governors of Pará state, is also on Praça Dom Pedro II; it now houses the Pará State Museum ((Museo do Estado do Pará, ☎ 225-2414). It was built between 1762 and 1772 by architect Antônio Landi, and is an attractive Portuguese version of the neo-Palladian style. In 1835 the Cabanagem invaded the palace, killing the governor, Ernesto Lobo, on the staircase (see the boxed text 'The Cabanagem Rebellion').

In the early 20th century, in response to the French influence on Belém's bourgeois culture, the main rooms were redecorated, each in a different style. A small chapel, from which Belém's earliest Círio processions had started out, was built over during those reforms, but rediscovered and restored in the 1970s.

The state museum is open 10 am to 4 pm Tuesday to Saturday, 10 am to 2 pm Sunday and holidays. Admission is US$1.25 and an English-speaking guide is usually available.

Museu de Arte Sacra The excellent Sacred Art Museum (☎ 225-1125), on Praça Frei Brandão, consists of the Igreja do Santo Alexandre and the adjoining Palâcio Episcopal (Bishop's Palace), both recently restored. Santo Alexandre, the first church in Belém when founded by Jesuits in the early 17th century, was rebuilt in baroque style in the 18th century. It contains some brilliant sculpture, done by Indians in plaster and red cedar from that era. The building stood abandoned for 50 years before its recent restoration.

The Palâcio Episcopal houses a well-displayed collection of religious art from Belém: Highlights include the 18th-century saints sculpted by Indians in workshops attached to the church.

It's all open 10 am to 6 pm, Tuesday to Sunday (admission: US$2.50).

Catedral da Sé Belém's cathedral, on Praça Frei Brandão, is a 1750s colonial baroque-cum-neoclassical construction by Antônio Landi. The twin-towered main facade is handsome; the interior is unremarkable. It's normally open 7 am to noon and 2 to 7:30 pm daily.

East of the Center

The walk from the city center along Avenida Nazaré to the Basílica de NS de Nazaré and Museu Emílio Goeldi takes about 30 minutes. Alternatively, the 'Aero Club,' 'Cid Nova 6' and 'Pedreirinha P Vargas' buses all run from Avenida Presidente Vargas.

Basílica de NS de Nazaré The basilica, on Rua da Basílica facing Praça Justo Chermont, 1.25km east of Praça da República, is visited by more than a million worshippers during the annual Círio de Nazaré (see the Special Events section later in this chapter). It was built in 1909, inspired by the Basilica of St Paul in Rome. The artisans, as well as much of the material, were imported from Europe, and the colorful interior is lined with fine marble. An elaborate altarpiece frames the tiny but all-important statue of NS de Nazaré, while the top of the facade has a mural depicting the arrival of the Portuguese colonizers in Brazil. Included among Indians, soldiers and priests are a couple of men in suits and ties – the wealthy patrons who sponsored this church's construction. It's open 3 to 5:30 pm Monday, and 6:30 to 11:30 am and 2:30 to 6:30 pm other days (staying open till 9 pm Saturday and Sunday).

Downstairs is a sacred-art museum, the Museu do Círio, where you can buy traditional *briquedos de abaetetuba* (balsa wood toys that are sold in the streets during the Círio festival).

Museu Emílio Goeldi The best museum in Belém (☎ 249-1233), at Avenida Governador Magalhães Barata 376, a couple of blocks east of the Nazaré basilica, contains an excellent collection of Amazonian fauna in its lush, 52,000 sq m botanic garden (the Parque Zoobotánico), and a permanent exhibit with Amazonia's best archaeological displays.

The Cabanagem Rebellion

In the 1820s, a split between the white ruling classes of Belém led to civil war, which soon spread to the dominated Indians, mestiços, blacks and mulattos. After years of fighting, the war developed into a popular revolutionary movement that swept through Pará like wildfire. The Cabanagem rebellion was a guerrilla war fought by the wretched of the Amazon.

In 1835 the guerrilla fighters marched on Belém, taking the city after nine days of bloody fighting. They installed a popular government, which expropriated the wealth of the merchants, distributed food to all the people and declared Belém's independence. But the revolutionary experiment was immediately strangled by a British naval blockade, Britain being the principal beneficiary of trade with Brazil at the time.

A year later, a large Brazilian government force recaptured Belém. The vast majority of the city's population fled to the interior to resist again. Over the next four years, the military hunted down and slaughtered anyone they thought could be hostile. The Cabanagem massacre was one of the most savage of Brazil's many military campaigns against its own people. Altogether some 30,000 people out of Pará's population of 150,000 died in the conflict.

In the park you'll see many exotic and rare Amazonian animal species, from manatees, alligators and anacondas to jaguars, black panthers and giant otters. There's an aviary with several species of macaw and an aquarium with piranhas. It all adds up to one of the best zoos in South America.

The permanent exhibit, called 'Amazonia: Man and the Environment,' includes displays on Amazonia's mineral and botanical riches; the artifacts and lives of Amazonian Indian peoples; and a very interesting archaeological section with intricately decorated burial urns from the Santarém area and Ilha de Marajó (see the boxed text 'Prehistoric Amazonia' later in this chapter).

All this is part of a research institution for the study of the flora, fauna and peoples of Amazonia, founded in 1866 and reorganized in the 1890s by Dr Emílio Augusto Goeldi. The museum also has a research campus elsewhere in Belém, and a jungle research base, the Estação Científica Ferreira Penna, in the Floresta Nacional Caxiuanã, 350km west of Belém. Amazon Star (see Travel Agencies in the Information section) organizes ecotourism programs to the base for groups of at least five people (see the Web site www.amazonriver.com/E-caxiuana.htm for more information).

The park, aquarium and permanent exhibit (admission is US$0.70 for each) are all open 9 to 11:30 am Friday, 9 am to 5 pm Saturday, Sunday and holidays, and 9 to 11:30 am and 2 to 5 pm Tuesday to Thursday. The park contains a cafe and a good gift/crafts shop.

Bosque Rodrigues Alves This park is 160,000 sq m of preserve native forest at Avenida Almirante Barroso 2453 is the largest patch of greenery anywhere near central Belém. A pleasant place to relax, it has a lake, and a zoo with turtles and alligators, and is frequented by couples kissing in the grottoes. Avoid it on Sunday, though, when little brats torment the turtles and alligators by throwing plastic bags filled with water at their heads – one reader felt like feeding the perpetrators to the victims!

Hours are 7 am to 5 pm, Tuesday to Sunday. To get there take the 'Aero Club' bus from Avenida Presidente Vargas, the Nazaré basilica or the Museu Emílio Goeldi.

Organized Tours

The travel agencies mentioned earlier, in the Information section, offer various tours. City or river tours can be good if you are short on time.

Prices start around US$25 per person for a standard full-day (six or seven hours) river tour, which is not particularly exciting. You'll cruise the river, go down a channel, get out on an island, and walk down a path where many have walked before to see the local flora (rubber and mahogany trees, *açaí* palms, *sumauma*, mangoes and cacao trees). This voyage into the known is recommended only if you have no time to really see the jungle and rivers.

Amazon Star, a French-run agency with multilingual guides, is more enterprising than many of its competitors. Its day tour (US$40 to US$45 per person) explores *igarapés* (creeks) where other operators generally don't venture.

Trips to the Ilha dos Papagaios (Parrot Island) usually start before dawn so that you see lots of parrots and other birds leaving the island at daybreak to search for food. Amazon Star's 'Early Bird' version costs US$25 per person (US$35 each for two people).

For a quick trip on the river, the easiest option is an outing on the boat *Tribo dos Kayapós* from the Terminal Fluvial at Estação das Docas. Sunset and after-dark cruises of 1½ hours go daily except Monday for US$7. For more information visit Valeverde Turismo (☎ 212-3388) at the Terminal Fluvial.

Special Events

Every year on the morning of the second Sunday of October, Belém explodes with the sounds of hymns, bells and fireworks. Started in 1793, the Círio de Nazaré is Brazil's biggest religious festival (the name Círio comes from the Latin *cereus*, meaning large wax candle). People from all over the

Buses of the Waterways

If time is on your side, boats are a great way to experience the North. Rivers are roads in Amazonia, and river boats are the equivalent of buses. To join the locals, you just need to invest a few dollars in a hammock, buy a ticket and get on board. Distances along the rivers are great, and river travel is slow and can be dull. Gazing at long, thin, strips of forest between wider bands of river and sky starts to pall fairly soon – but it's certainly cheap.

Public Amazon river boats could not be called comfortable. The passenger-carrying public boats average about 20m long, have two or three decks and at a guess carry 300 to 500 people when full. Conditions are crowded, toilets are few and you have to watch your gear very carefully (see Dangers & Annoyances in the Facts for the Visitor chapter for more on security). Here are a few tips that apply to river travel throughout the region.

• Things can get very wet, so bring along a hooded poncho or windbreaker to keep yourself dry and a cloth or large plastic bag to wrap your backpack in. Plastic bags to compartmentalize things inside the backpack provide further protection.

• You'll also need a hammock (fabric is preferable to net), some rope to suspend your backpack above the deck, and a sheet, blanket or sleeping bag to place in your hammock.

• Boats often moor at the departure port for a couple of days before sailing, so you can check them out before buying your ticket.

• Fares from A to B vary little among boats.

• It's a good idea to buy your ticket a day or so in advance and, if you're going on a long trip, to get to your boat early on the morning of departure to secure a good hammock spot. It's more comfortable (if more expensive) on the cooler upper deck, toward the bow.

• Most passengers travel hammock (rede) class: You just sling your hammock wherever you can find the most convenient space. You can often take up position the night before departure for no extra charge. By departure time, the hammock areas will be pretty crowded with hammocks and their occupants and baggage. You might end up with other passengers swinging above you or underneath you. It's not hard to get to know people!

• Most boats have a few cabins (camarotes), for two or four people, costing about double the hammock fare per person. Sometimes you can just book one place in a cabin and share with whoever else turns up. Cabins are bare, basic, very hot and stuffy but provide a little privacy.

• Three simple meals a day – mainly rice, beans and meat – and drinks, are included in fares, but it's advisable to bring bottled water as well as supplemental snacks.

• Downstream travel is considerably faster than up, but boats heading upriver go closer to the shore, which makes for a more scenic trip.

country flock to Belém, and even camp in the streets, to participate in the grand event.

The image of NS de Nazaré is believed by the faithful to have been sculpted in Nazareth (Galilee) and to have performed miracles in medieval Portugal before getting lost in Brazil. After its disappearance, it was rediscovered in 1700 by a humble cattleman, Placido de Souza, on the site of the basilica, to which it later returned of its own accord after being moved away several times.

The day before the main annual event, the little statue, having previously been taken 23km north to Icoaraci, is carried in a river procession back to the cathedral in Belém. On the Sunday itself, around a million people fill the streets to accompany the image from the Catedral da Sé to the Basílica de NS de Nazaré.

The image is placed on a flower-bedecked carriage. While the faithful pray, sing hymns, give thanks or ask favors of the Virgin, the pious (often barefoot) bear heavy crosses and miniature wax houses, and thousands squirm and grope in an emotional frenzy to get a hand on the 300m rope pulling the carriage. Five hours and just 3.5km from the cathedral, the Virgin reaches the basilica, where she remains for the duration of the festivities.

After the parade, there is the traditional feast of *pato no tucupi* (duck cooked in manioc extract). Belém ducks dread the Círio just like US turkeys dread Thanksgiving. From the basilica, the multitudes head to the fairgrounds for mayhem of the more secular kind: food, drink, music and dancing. The party continues unabated for two weeks. On the Monday 15 days after the first procession, the crowd reassembles for the Recírio parade, in which the Virgin is returned to her niche in the basilica and the festivities are concluded.

Places to Stay

Budget There are rock-bottom cheap dives near the waterfront, on and off Avenida Castilho França, but you may have to compromise on security and cleanliness. Some of these places also rent by the hour for prostitutes and their clients.

The **Transamazonas Hotel** (☎ 212-1547, *Rua da Indústria 17*) charges US$7 for fan-cooled quartos with one bed (single or double) and US$10 for rooms with twin beds. It's fairly clean, and the street door is kept locked. If you like the atmosphere of the waterfront and market, a more upmarket option is **Hotel Ver-o-Peso** (☎/fax 241-2022, *Avenida Castilho França 208*). Air-con apartamentos cost from US$16.50 to US$25.50, single or double, and the rooftop restaurant has good views of the river and the market.

Hotel Fortaleza (☎ 212-1055, *Travessa Frutuoso Guimarães 276*), in the Comércio district, is the backpackers' favorite. It's an old house with wonky stairs and a cute TV area upstairs. The rooms are small and basic, with fan, and the shared bathroom is *very* basic. Singles/doubles/triples cost US$7/10/12 without breakfast, or US$8/12/16 with (eggs, fruit juice, bread and coffee). There's a discount for stays of three days or more.

Hotel Vitória Régia (☎/fax 212-2077, *Travessa Frutuoso Guimarães 260*) has less of a traveler's atmosphere but rooms are clean and more private, if mostly dilapidated, and have private bathrooms. Singles/doubles/triples/quads cost US$13.50/16.50/20/21 (with fan) to US$27/33/47/60 (air-con 'suites').

Hotel Sete Sete (☎ 222-7730, *Travessa Primeiro de Março 673*) is in an area where prostitutes hang out, near Praça da República. But it offers decent smallish singles/doubles with bathroom for US$16/20, or US$23 for doubles with a view. Breakfast is included.

Near the bus station, the **Panorama Hotel** (☎ 226-9724, *Travessa Primeira de Queluz 81*) offers simple, clean, fan-cooled singles/doubles for US$16/18.

Mid-Range Several mid-range places charge pretty reasonable rates, so even if you're on a tight budget you might consider a minor splurge. Most of these hotels are ideally located on or close to Avenida Presidente Vargas.

The **Hotel Central** (☎ 242-4800 or ☎ 241-8177, *Avenida Presidente Vargas 290*) is a large art deco hotel that is popular with foreign travelers. It charges US$14.50/19.50 for singles/doubles with fan and shared bath, and US$23.50/33.50 for air-conditioned apartamentos. The rooms are bare but high-ceilinged and relatively spacious (especially the apartamentos), and mostly in good shape. Those facing Avenida Presidente Vargas can be noisy. There's a nice top-floor breakfast room.

Hotel Novo Avenida (☎ 242-9953, fax 223-8893, Avenida Presidente Vargas 404) is just as convenient but has less character. Nevertheless, it offers clean apartamentos for US$17.50/20 with fan and TV, or US$25.50/29.50 with air-con and cable TV.

Hotel Unidos (☎ 224-0660, fax 252-1880, Rua Ó de Almeida 545), a few steps off Avenida Presidente Vargas, is an almost-new hotel (opened in 2001), with spotless and comfortable rooms for US$28.50/35.50 (less 10% for cash), good service and good breakfast. Nearby and under the same ownership, the nine-story **Hotel Ferrador** (☎ 241-5999, ferrador@amazon.com.br, Rua Aristides Lobo 485) provides clean, decent-sized but utterly plain rooms for US$36 single or double, with a 15% discount usually available.

The comfortable **Itaoca Hotel** (☎ 241-3434, itaoca@interconect.com.br, Avenida Presidente Vargas 132), down toward the waterfront, has apartamentos for US$48/55 plus 10% service charge.

The French-run **Hotel Le Massilia** (☎/fax 224-7147, le_massilia@yahoo.com, Rua Henrique Gurjão 236), close to the center, has a guesthouse atmosphere and a cute French restaurant at the front. Very clean, attractive and homey singles/doubles, with air-con, cost US$33/43. It's worth booking ahead, as there are only seven or eight rooms.

The **Manacá Hotel Residência** (☎/fax 222-6227, Travessa Quintino Bocaiúva 1645), in a stylishly renovated old house, is another good value. It's well located, secure, and has colored walls hung with art. Single/double/triple apartamentos with fan, TV and phone cost US$24/28/32.50. Breakfast is an extra US$4.50 per person, and air-conditioning is US$4.50 per room.

Top End The **Hotel Regente** (☎ 241-1222, fax 242-0343, Avenida Governador José Malcher 485) has neat rooms made cozier with the addition of colored bedspreads and art prints. Singles/doubles start at US$68/76 plus 10%. Discounts are available if you stay a few days.

The most upmarket option in Belém, with all the amenities you could hope for, is the high-rise **Hilton Hotel** (☎ 217-7000, belemhil@amazon.com.br, Avenida Presidente Vargas 882), overlooking Praça da República. Standard singles/doubles cost US$180/200 plus 5% tax, but there's 40% off if you book in advance.

The **Equatorial Palace Hotel** (☎ 224-4012, fax 223-5222, Avenida Braz de Aguiar 612) is another high-rise, with fairly good rooms for US$59/66 plus 10% service. The 15th-floor restaurant offers a good buffet lunch and dinner for US$10, and there's a coffee shop too.

Places to Eat

The cuisine of Belém features a bewildering variety of fish and fruit, and includes several delicious regional dishes. Pato no tucupi is a lean duck cooked in tucupi sauce (yellow and slightly bitter, made from the juice of manioc root). Maniçoba is a stew that takes a week to prepare: Shoots of maniva (a variety of manioc) are ground, cooked for at least four days, then combined with jerked beef, calves' hooves, bacon, pork and sausages. If you enjoy feijoada, Brazil's national dish, you'll appreciate maniçoba. Also try the local unhas de caranguejo (crab claws) and casquinha de caranguejo (stuffed crab).

Good local fish include filhote (a giant catfish), dourada (another catfish and probably the best tasting) and pescada amarela (yellowfish). Açaí, acerola, uxi, murici, bacuri and sapoti are just a few of the luscious Amazonian fruits which make fantastic juice and ice cream.

Estação das Docas (Rua Castilho Franca s/n) has about a dozen places to eat, mostly in its central building, the Boulevard da Gastronomia. The downstairs places here have table service; for self-serve go up to the mezzanine. Downstairs, **Restô das Docas** serves a quality lunch buffet for US$8 plus drinks and 10% service charge; upstairs, **Spazzio Verdi** has high-grade, US$10.50 per-kilo self-serve. All these places are open for lunch and dinner, daily except Monday.

For cheap eats, snack bars throughout the city serve sanduiches, burgers, juices and so on. Another moderately-priced way to eat is to self-serve. Get to self-serve restaurants early (some open as early as 11 am) for the best choice and the freshest food. **Inter Restaurant** (Rua 28 de Setembro 304) does decent self-serve for US$8 per kilo, or a 'quentinha' plate of fish/meat/chicken with rice, farofa and beans for just US$2.50.

Cheaper (US$6 per kilo) is **Restaurante Zimbro** (Rua 15 de Novembro 314). **Boêmio Grill**, on Rua Carlos Gomes, has per-kilo lunch including grilled meats for US$7.50/kg (closed Sunday). East of the center, the main branch of **Spazzio Verdi** (Avenida Braz de Aguiar 824) and **Bom Apetit** (Travessa Rui Barbosa 1059) have some of the best self-serve food in the city for around US$11 per kilo. Both are open for lunch daily.

The friendly **Restaurante Belo Centro** (Rua Santo Antônio 264), upstairs, cooks up quite tasty vegetarian self-serve for US$5.50 per kilo and serves a few options for carnivores, too. It is open for lunch, Monday to Friday.

The food court on the top floor of the **Iguatemi Shopping** center is another site for inexpensive eating, with Italian, burger, grill and sushi spots, another **Spazzio Verdi** and **Cairu** which may have the best ice cream in town.

There aren't many cheap dinner options close to downtown, but if your budget is not too tight, **Restaurante Casa Portuguesa** (☎ 242-4871, Rua Senador Manoel Barata 897) is a very reliable choice. Chicken and meat dishes cost US$4 to US$8, fish and seafood US$7 to US$14. The **Miako** (☎ 242-4485, Travessa Primeiro de Março 766), behind the Hilton Hotel, serves good Japanese and Chinese dishes for US$7 to US$14. The **Hilton Hotel** itself serves very good lunch and dinner buffets (US$16) in its lobby-floor **Restaurant Acaí**.

There are also some very good restaurants not far east of the center. Two restaurants on the same site are **Lá Em Casa** and **O Outro** (☎ 223-1212, Avenida Governador José Malcher 247). The latter is indoors, air-conditioned, and a bit smart, while Lá Em Casa is outdoors and a little more casual. Both restaurants serve a big range of fare, including all the best regional dishes, at prices between US$8 and US$20.

Cantina Italiana (☎ 225-2278, Travessa Benjamin Constant 1401) has quality pasta dishes and excellent self-serve antipasti, all between US$7.50 and US$12.50. Between noon and 8 pm Monday to Saturday, **Tia Maria** (Travessa Benjamin Constant 1366) is great to pop into for croissants, cakes and coffee. For French cuisine head for **Restaurante Le Massilia** (☎ 224-7147, Rua Henrique Gurjão 236). Dishes are between US$12 and US$20, and it's open 7 to 11 pm daily except Sunday.

Avenida Visconde de Souza Franco is primarily a drinking and music zone but it does have places to eat too. At least half of them are Italian, with **La Bella Italia** (Avenida Visconde de Souza Franco 567) among the best.

Restaurante do Circulo Militar (☎ 223-4374), in the Forte do Castelo in the Cidade Velha, has a great bay view, gray-tuxedoed servers and good regional cooking. Main dishes cost from US$7 to US$20.

Entertainment

It's nice to enjoy a drink or two at the outdoor tables overlooking the river at **Estação das Docas** (Avenida Castilho Franca s/n). You can hardly choose a better spot here than the boutique brewery **Cervejaria Amazonas**, open Tuesday to Sunday, which has 300ml beers for US$1.30 and good, if not cheap, German-inspired food.

Bar do Parque (Praça da República s/n) is a 24-hour outdoor bar and popular meeting place – male travelers may be approached by prostitutes here.

Cosanostra Caffé (☎ 241-1068, Travessa Benjamim Constant 1499), just east of downtown, is a wood-beamed, air-conditioned bar popular among intellectual and professional types. There's varied live instrumental music starting at 11 pm nightly (8pm on Sunday), and good food at middling prices.

Belém has a good live music scene, especially from Thursday to Saturday. Check the daily 'Agenda' page in *O Liberal* newspaper. The 'Docas' area along Avenida Visconde de Souza Franco has the busiest after-dark scene in Belém. Numerous bright bars, most at least partially open-air and some also serving food and/or live music, get packed with a buzzing 20s and 30s crowd. The *Doca Boulevard* building has several. Inside Doca Boulevard is *Usina*, a *boate* (music and dance space), where at the time of research the popular local rock/reggae band A Firma was playing on Thursday and Sunday, starting at about midnight (admission: US$2.50).

Bora Bora (☎ 241-5848, *Rua Bernal do Couto 38*), almost opposite Doca Boulevard, has several spaces and a varied program that includes a good Amazonian cultural show starting around 11 pm on Thursday (admission: US$3.50), where you can familiarize yourself with some of the great traditional music and dance forms of Pará. These include *carimbó*, an exciting, colorful dance named after the drum used in its performance, *lundúm*, whose origin goes back to Bantu slaves from Africa, and *siriá*, whose movements imitate a crab, as well as *brega*, the local country party dance music which is a bit tedious to listen to but fun for dancing. Most nights there'll be live bands and/or DJs at Bora Bora too.

Additional live music spots to check out in this area are *Falatório Drinks e Afins* on Avenida Visconde de Souza Franco, *Iron Pigs* (*Travessa Almirante Wandenkolk 593*) and *Agua Doce Cachaçaria* also on Travessa Almirante Wandenkolk. Their music (generally MPB or *pagode*) starts any time after 9 pm.

If any shows by Banda Wlad, Banda Xeiro Verde or Rossy War are advertised, they'll be worth checking out. They all play *zouk*, a bouncy and infectious Belém goodtime music.

The *African Bar* (☎ 241-1085), on Avenida Marechal Hermes, often stages samba groups from about 10 pm on Saturday. *Interpretação in London* (☎ 223-8699, *Travessa Quintino Bocaiúva 945*) is a trendy bar/restaurant with a London theme, and live music or DJs starting around 11 pm Thursday to Saturday.

Bar do Índio (☎ 222-8411, *Rua Siqueira Mendes 264*), in the Cidade Velha, has good river views and pulls in a fun 25-to-35 crowd for its Thursday rock nights, which start about midnight (admission: US$3).

The top samba club is *Rancho Não Posso me Amofiná* (☎ 225-0918, *Travessa Honório José dos Santos 764*), in the Jurunas district. It operates on weekends all year-round, but the best time to go is around Carnaval (in February).

Shopping

The Feira de Artesanato, a large crafts fair in Praça da República every Friday to Sunday, has the city's biggest range of attractive art work, and a lot of it is homemade. The fair is well worth a visit.

The Belém area has a strong ceramics tradition. It's possible to buy replicas of precolonial artifacts made by the Marajoara, as well as beautiful modern pieces. There are superb huge pots – unfortunately, a bit ungainly in your backpack! Souvenir shops along Avenida Presidente Vargas sell pottery, but if you want to buy it direct from the makers, visit the township of Icoaraci (see the Around Belém section later in this chapter).

A handful of interesting shops on Rua Gaspar Viana, including Ervas e Raízes da Amazônia, at No 196B, specialize in natural medicines from the Amazon region. Fantastic aromas waft among the leaves, roots, herbs, barks and powders. There are treatments for just about any illness, from diabetes to cancer. Try *casca de copaiba* for bronchitis or *cabeca de negro* for impotence. The Mercado Ver-o-Peso also has many stalls selling medicinal plants, perfumes, balms, trinkets and items made from the scented *pacholi* root. Rua João Alfredo is a good place for finding cheap clothes and hammocks.

The Artíndia shops in the arcade at Avenida Presidente Vargas 762 and in the large Iguatemi Shopping center on Travessa Padre Eutiquio all sell authentic Indian crafts.

Iguatemi Shopping is probably the best place to go for any single item you're in need of. It has several music stores, selling officially released CDs at double or triple the price of the bootleg versions on the streets. Look for recordings by local carimbó maestro Pinduca and other popular local performers such as Banda Wlad, Nilson Chaves and Banda Nova.

Getting There & Away

Air Varig, TAM, TransBrasil and VASP fly between Belém's Aeroporto Val de Cães (☎ 257-0522) and the major Brazilian cities. Regional carriers such as Meta, Penta and TAVAJ fly to/from smaller places around Amazonia. Penta also flies daily to/from Cayenne, French Guiana; Surinam Airways links Belém with Cayenne, Paramaribo (Suriname) and Georgetown (Guyana) and points in the Caribbean; and Varig flies weekly to/from Miami (USA). See the Getting There & Away chapter for some fares.

The following airlines have offices in Belém:

Meta Linhas Aéras (☎ 223-1082), Avenida Assis de Vasconcelos 448

Penta (☎ 222-6000), Avenida Assis de Vasconcelos 396

Surinam Airways (☎ 212-7144), Rua Gaspar Viana 488

TAM (☎ 212-2166), Avenida Assis de Vasconcelos 265

TAVAJ (☎ 212-1201), Rua Senador Manoel Barata 925

TransBrasil (☎ 212-6977), Avenida Presidente Vargas 780

Varig, Nordeste & Rio Sul (☎ 211-3344), Avenida Presidente Vargas 768

VASP (☎ 224-5588), Avenida Presidente Vargas 345

Air taxis fly from Aeroporto Júlio César (☎ 233-3986), at Avenida Senador Lemos 4700. Carriers include Kovacs (☎ 233-1600), Leopoldo (☎ 233-1707) and Dourado (☎ 222-7840).

Bus From Belém's long-distance bus station (☎ 246-7442), on Praça do Operário, buses run to São Luís (US$32, 12 hours, four daily), Fortaleza (US$50 to US$58, 25 hours, five daily), Recife (US$70, 34 hours, one daily), Salvador (US$83, 36 hours, one daily), Palmas (US$42, 19 hours, two daily), Brasília (US$82, 34 hours, two daily), Rio de Janeiro (US$124, 50 to 55 hours, two daily) and São Paulo (US$110, 46 hours, two daily).

Boat Boats to Macapá and up the Rio Amazonas leave from Galpão (Shed) 10 of Belém port, entered by Portão (Gate) 15/16 on Avenida Marechal Hermes. Boat companies have their ticket desks inside the entrance here, and it's advisable to buy your tickets a day or two before departure. You can often check out the boats before deciding which one to take.

For information on boats to islands near Belém, see the relevant island sections.

Most boats to Manaus call at seven or eight ports en route, including Monte Alegre and Santarém. The upstream voyage to Manaus takes five days (to Santarém, three days). Boats depart at 6 or 7 pm on Monday to Wednesday and Friday. Sometimes two or three boats will leave around the same time on the same day. On most boats the hammock fare including food is US$70 to Manaus and US$48 to Santarém; in a cabin it's US$140 and US$90 per person, respectively. The most comfortable accommodations are on Marques Pinto Navegação's *Santarém*, which leaves Belém every second Tuesday (and sets off back from Manaus on intervening Wednesdays). The *Santarém* has an air-conditioned hammock area (US$80), and its cabins are air-conditioned with private bathrooms. Amazon Star (see Travel Agencies under Information, earlier) offers an advance-booking service for the *Santarém*.

The national shipping company, ENASA, has a cheaper boat leaving for Manaus every second Wednesday (US$50 in hammock), but it's super-crowded, with poor food, and the danger of theft is high.

The Arapari company (☎ 241-4977) operates the fast *Lívia Marilia*, which makes the trip to Macapá in about 12 hours. This boat has airplane-style seating and the fare is US$40. Departures are at 7 am Monday, Wednesday and Friday. Navegaçao Bom Jesus (☎ 224-4121) has conventional boats leaving for Macapá every morning except Thursday and Sunday; the trip takes 20 to 24 hours and costs US$40 hammock class or US$60 per person in cabins.

Getting Around
Aeroporto Val de Cães, used by all scheduled flights, is 8km north of the center, on Avenida Júlio César. The 'Pratinha-P Vargas' bus runs between the airport and Avenida Presidente Vargas (US$0.60, 40 minutes). At the airport it stops by the traffic circle about 50m from the end of the airport terminal building. A taxi from airport to center or vice-versa is about US$10 by the meter.

The bus station (☎ 228-0500) is on the corner of Avenida Almirante Barroso and Avenida Ceará, 3km east of the city center. For a city bus to the center from the bus station, get across to the far side of Avenida Almirante Barroso and catch any bus saying 'Aero Club' or 'P Vargas' to Avenida Presidente Vargas. Going out to the bus station, take an 'Aeroclube,' 'Cid Nova 6' or 'Pratinha-P Vargas' bus from Avenida Presidente Vargas.

AROUND BELÉM
Icoaraci
The small town of Icoaraci, 23km north of Belém, is the source of nearly all the imitations of prehistoric Marajoara pottery that you see in Belém and elsewhere. The talented potters of Icoaraci's Paracuri district also produce some beautiful original designs and plenty of utilitarian ware too. Head along Travessa Soledade, the first main street to the right as you enter Icoaraci from the south, and you'll come upon a dozen workshops with products on display. You can observe the pottery-making process and, if you buy the products, you know your money is going directly to the craftspeople.

Frequent city buses marked 'Icoaraci' leave from Avenida Presidente Vargas in central Belém.

Ilha do Mosqueiro
☎ 0xx91 • postcode 66000-000 • pop 25,000
Thousands of *Belenenses* (Belém people) attempt to beat the heat by flocking to Mosqueiro's 18 freshwater beaches on the east side of the Baía de Marajó. Some well-to-do residents even commute from the island to the city. The island is particularly crowded between July and October. The beaches on Ilha de Marajó and the Atlantic coast are much nicer, but if you just want to get out of Belém for a day or so, Mosqueiro's aren't bad.

Beaches The best beaches are (from west to east) Praia do Farol, Praia Chapéu Virado and Praia do Murubira (these three form an almost continuous beach strip 4 or 5km long on the northwest coast), and Praia do Paraíso and the more remote Baía do Sol on the north coast. Watch out for stingrays on the sea floor (see the Fauna section in the Natural Brazil special section for how to avoid their stings).

Special Events Mosqueiro's traditional folklore festival, in June, features the dance and music of carimbó and *bois-bumbás*. The Círio de NS do Ó is celebrated on the second Sunday of December. Like Belém's Círio, this is a beautiful and joyous event, well worth seeing if you're in the area.

Places to Stay & Eat *Hotel Farol* (☎ 771-1219, Praça Princesa Isabel 3295, Praia do Farol), a pleasant old building on a little headland at the west end of Farol beach, offers quartos with shared bathroom for US$16 and apartamentos for US$30/35, with fan/air-conditioning. From Monday to Thursday, there's a discount of up to 20%, except during July and January. The *Ilha Bela* (☎ 771-1612, Avenida 16 de Novembro 409-463), 400m back from Praia do Farol, has air-conditioned apartamentos behind its restaurant for US$24 single or double.

Hotel Murubira (☎ 772-1256, Avenida Beira Mar s/n, Praia do Murubira) offers dull apartamentos for US$40. Three doors south, *Hotel Furacão* (Avenida Beira Mar 34) charges US$14 for small wooden

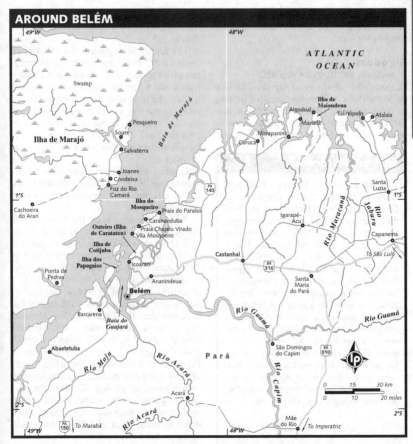

AROUND BELÉM

quartos. Toilets and showers, downstairs behind the hotel's restaurant, are included. *Hotel Fazenda Paraíso* (☎ 772-2444), at Praia do Paraíso, offers nice timber chalets at US$63 for up to four people, and single/ double apartamentos for US$50/53. Its restaurant serves seafood meals big enough for two at US$10 to US$15. Praia do Paraíso is one of the best beaches on the island, but gets really busy during the weekends.

There are lots of *barracas* (food stalls) serving inexpensive local fare on Praça Matriz, the main square in Vila Mosqueiro,

and also along Praia do Farol and Praia Chapéu Virado (try tapioca *com recheio de queijo*).

Getting There & Around Ilha do Mosqueiro is connected to the mainland by a road bridge, 55km from Belém by good, paved roads. From the bridge it is 25km farther to Vila Mosqueiro, at the western tip of the island. Buses from the Belém bus station (every half-hour, 6 am to 11 pm) go along Murubira, Chapéu Virado and Farol beaches on their way to Vila Mosqueiro (US$1.50, 1½ hours). Local island buses run from Vila Mosqueiro to Praia do Paraíso and Baía do Sol via Praia do Farol and Praia Chapéu Virado.

Algodoal

☎ postcode 68710-000 • pop 800

The small fishing village of Algodoal on Ilha de Maiandeua, 180km northeast of Belém, attracts younger Belenenses and a few foreign travelers. It's a beautiful, natural retreat with windswept, sandy beaches and

a sometimes turbulent sea. Algodoal is in the process of being 'discovered' – but very slowly....

The name 'Maiandeua' comes from an Indian word meaning 'uncountable riches beneath the sea.' The island has no motor traffic and no public electrical supply, and in 2001 the only telephone (except for cell phones) was one public pay phone. People on the mainland just call this phone (☎ 0xx91-497-2020), and anyone passing by will answer and pass on a message to an islander.

Unlike in Belém, it rains little in the second half of the year here. Wildlife found in the interior includes anteaters, ocelots and coatis.

Algodoal village is on the island's west coast. **Praia do Farol** (not to be confused with the beach of the same name on Ilha do Mosqueiro), divided from the village by an igarapé that is wadable at low tide, stretches north to the tip of the island. Beautiful **Praia da Princesa**, backed by dunes and palms and without any buildings, stretches the 20km length of the east coast. **Lagoa da Princesa** is a freshwater lake about an hour's walk inland from Algodoal village or 20 minutes from Praia da Princesa. You can climb the white dunes around it for fine panoramas. The tropical forest reserve of **Rio Centenário**, the largest igarapé on the island, has a forest of *miritizeiros* (Amazonian royal palms) and other native species, and lots of orchids in some seasons.

Places to Stay The village has several rustic places to stay. Some raise their prices during Carnaval, Semana Santa, the month of July and all holiday weekends.

Hotel Bela Mar (☎ 0xx91-222-7582 in Belém), on Avenida Beira Mar, is the accommodations closest to the boat pier. Double rooms with fan cost US$27 with shared bath and US$34 with shower; both rates include breakfast. A bit farther along the beach is *Caldeirão* (☎ 0xx91-227-0984 in Belém). It's less clean but a bit cheaper: US$16/24 for single/double apartamentos with mosquito net (no fan).

Yachts at Alcantara, Maranhão

At Praia de Genipabu, Natal

One of the faces of Lençóis

Cashew fruit, João Pessoa

Coastline south of Natal

Colonial architecture, Olinda

Pousada ABC and *Pousada Chalés do Atlântico* (☎ *0xx91-226-9855 in Belém)*, both a couple of blocks into the village, offer simple rooms with bath and breakfast for around US$25. The *Cabanas Hotel* (☎ *0xx91-223-1804 in Belém)*, on Rua Magalhães Barata at the far end of the village, has rustic, fan-cooled single/double apartamentos for US$10/15 including breakfast.

Eden (☎ *0xx91-265-1489 in Belém, jardimdoeden@hotmail.com)* is run by a friendly, English-speaking, Brazilian-and-French couple, Evandro and Veronique. It is near the northern tip of the island – a 20 to 30-minute walk from the boat pier (or less by a hired horse and cart). Accommodations are in two houses of original design (one stone, one brick) with solar energy, showers and small kitchens, at US$16 per person including breakfast. You can also camp for US$7 per person. Eden offers a variety of walking, canoeing, sailing, horse-cart and fishing trips, and have a Web site at www.chez.com/algodoal.

Places to Eat The *Cabanas Hotel* and *Hotel Bela Mar* serve meals for US$8 to US$10; the Bela Mar's are enough for two. *Eden* serves good US$10 lunches of salad, bread, a fish or chicken dish, fruit and coffee (for hotel locations see the Places to Stay section, above).

Restaurant Prato Cheio, on the town beach, has good views and a varied menu, with prices similar to the Cabanas and the Bela Mar.

Up near the tip of the island are the beach bars *Bar do Gil*, *Julia* and *Porquinho*, which all serve beers, fried fish and carangueijo *toc-toc* (whole crab).

Getting There & Away Access to Algodoal is via the mainland village of Marudá, which has several inexpensive hotels and an OK beach, so it's no problem if you're stuck there overnight. Cars cannot make the journey to Algodoal and must be left at Marudá. The roads from Belém to Marudá are fully sealed and the bus trip takes about 3½ hours. In Marudá, take a boat from the Maré Mansa port to Algodoal for US$2 (40

minutes). Arriving at Algodoal, you'll have to lug your gear along the sand to the village or take a donkey/horse-cart taxi for a couple of dollars.

Both Rápido Excelsior buses (US$5.50) and Alternativo vans and microbuses (US$6.50) leave the Belém bus station for Marudá four or five times daily; the first departure is at 6 am and the last at 4:30 pm (7 pm on Friday). To be sure of getting onto the island the same day, leave Belém by 12:30 pm. The last bus back leaves Marudá for Belém at 3 pm (5 pm on Sunday); the last van goes a bit later.

Salinópolis
☎ 0xx91 • postcode 68721-000
• pop 28,500

Salinópolis (also called Salinas), 220km northeast of Belém, is the major Atlantic resort of Pará, with good, long, sandy beaches. This is where the well-to-do of Belém have their summer homes, and during the July holiday month and over Christmas-New Year the town becomes very crowded. If you want beautiful, deserted strands, steer clear! The best beach is **Praia do Atalaia** at Atalaia, 14km east of the center, and it's quite a scene. Everyone drives to the beach, and the wide expanse of hard sand becomes the car park. If you haven't got wheels you'll feel left out. There are lots of outdoor bars and restaurants here and the water is great for swimming.

The action in Salinópolis itself centers on the recently face-lifted Orla do Maçarico area. Here restaurants and bars (and even phone booths in the shape of leaping fish) overlook the dunes. A short boardwalk through the mangroves leads to sandy Praia da Corvina, where there are a couple of spots to dance the night away.

Places to Stay Accommodations are on the expensive side, but rates are flexible. During Carnaval, Easter, July and Christmas-New Year, rates can triple; in the off-season good discounts are often available.

Pousada Ipanema (☎ *423-3799, Travessa Balduino Borges 184)* is not far from the bus station on the street heading uphill off of Avenida Miguel Santa Brigida (look for the Restaurante Bife de Ouro on the corner); it offers very basic singles/doubles with fan but no windows for US$10/13. The owner is friendly. *Pousada Dona Lindalva* (☎ 423-2764, Travessa Balduino Borges 1013), across the street, has better rooms with fan and bathroom for US$13 single or double, and an upstairs apartment at US$35 for up to six people.

On the Orla do Maçarico, *Hotel Flórida* (☎ 423-2155) offers OK small single/double apartamentos at US$20/27 and quartos with fan for US$13 single or double. Breakfast is included. An alternative here is *Hotel Mar e Onda* (☎ 423-3045), charging US$30 a double.

Hotel Salinópolis (☎ 423-1239, Avenida Beira Mar 26) is a good small hotel with a great seafront location southeast of Orla do Maçarico. Cozy, air-conditioned singles/doubles with bathroom are US$54/60 with breakfast, and you could get 40% off in low season. The hotel has a swimming pool.

There are also a few hotels at Praia do Atalaia. Here, the main access to the beach is a boardwalk through mangroves, and the hotels are near the entrance to the boardwalk. *Pousada Marisol* (☎ 464-1097, Estrada do Atalaia s/n), has clean rooms for US$33 for up to four people, including breakfast.

The *Atalaia Inn* (☎ 423-1122, Caminho das Dunas 1) opens right onto Praia Farol Velho, the westward extension of Praia Atalaia. Singles/doubles are US$44/50.

Places to Eat The *Restaurante do Nicolau* (Avenida Almirante Barroso 549), 1km west of the Orla do Maçarico, is one of the best restaurants. The deck overhanging the water has a great view and is very pleasant in the evenings. Try the delicious sopa de caranguejo (US$4.50) or some of the fish or prawn dishes (US$8 to $13).

For good-quality meat meals under US$7 go to *Restaurante Bife de Ouro* (Avenida Miguel Santa Brigida 376), on the main road into the center; it is a short walk from the bus station.

Options at Orla do Maçarico range from fast food at the *Praça de Alimentação*, pizza or pasta at *Restaurante Caiçara* or seafood at *Restaurante do Barra*; these are all moderately priced and on the inland side of the road. Good meat dishes are available at the more expensive *Marujo's Grill*, overlooking the dunes.

Getting There & Around The Boa Esperança company runs seven or more daily buses and 'micros' (small buses) from the Belém bus station to Salinópolis and back. The 3½-hour trip (one way) costs US$6.

Local buses shuttle between Orla do Maçarico, Praia do Atalaia and Salinópolis bus station (☎ 423-1148), 1km south of the lighthouse in the town center.

Ilha de Marajó
☎ 0xx91 • postcode 66053-000
• pop 250,000

The 50,000-sq-km Ilha de Marajó, slightly larger than Switzerland, lies at the mouths of the Amazonas and Tocantins Rivers. Its people live in a few towns and villages and on the many *fazendas* (ranches) spread across the island. This is a world apart, where bicycles and buffalo rule the grassy streets, and half the island is under water half the year, giving waterways much greater importance than roads.

The eastern half of Marajó, the *região dos campos*, is characterized by low-lying, savanna-type fields, sectioned by strips of remaining forest. Palms and dense mangrove forests line the coast. The island's western half, the *região da mata*, is primarily forest.

Marajó has two seasons: the very rainy, from January to June, and the less rainy, from July to December. In fact there's little rain between August and November. During the wet season the região dos campos becomes submerged under a meter or more of water, and the island's few roads are often impassable.

Fauna The herds of buffalo wandering the fields are well adapted to the swampy terrain and provide both food and income for Marajó. Legend has it they are descended from animals that swam ashore from a French ship that sank while en route from India to French Guiana.

The island also has many snakes, most notably large boas. There are hordes of birds, especially during the dry season, including the graceful scarlet ibis *(guará* in Portuguese), with its long, curved beak. The sight of a flock of these deep-pink birds flying against the green backdrop of Marajó is truly spectacular.

Warning: *Bichos de pé* (unpleasant bugs that burrow into human feet) are found in and around the towns, and the island has other nasty parasites. Keep your shoes on!

Getting There & Away Air taxis fly regularly from Belém to the island. A five-seater to Soure costs around US$350. It's a beautiful 25-minute flight over the immense river and thick forests. Aero Taxi Leopoldo is one firm specializing in Marajó trips; for further details see Getting There & Away in the Belém section of this chapter.

From Belém port (Galpão 10, Portão 15/16), Arapari Navegação runs passenger boats at 7 am and 1 pm, daily except Sunday, to the small port of Foz do Rio Camará (often just called Camará) on Marajó. The 1¾-hour crossing costs US$5.50. Returning to Belém, Arapari boats leave Camará at

Prehistoric Amazonia

Compared with all the attention given to the region's fauna and flora, the story of early *Homo sapiens* in Amazonia has been little studied. But the sequence of events that can be pieced together as you travel around the region is revealing.

Stone-age hunter-collectors, living in extended family groups, inhabited the Amazon basin starting from about 10,000 BC. The earliest known human creations, found near Monte Alegre, 100km northeast of Santarém, are rock paintings of handprints and human, animal and geometric figures.

More than 6000 years ago the Tapajoara culture left stone figures and fragments of some of the earliest known pottery in the Americas – burial urns and animal and human representations – in and near Santarém itself. Around this time people started fishing and collecting shellfish, and rudimentary agriculture began.

By the last few centuries BC, groups of maybe thousands of people, led by chiefs, were cultivating maize and manioc intensively and making good-quality pottery. The techniques of itinerant agriculture still practiced by some rainforest peoples today – planting and burning selectively and allowing soils to regenerate – may already have been developed.

On the Ilha de Marajó, in the mouth of the Rio Amazonas, people built earth platforms called *aterros* to escape the annual floods, and buried their dead in elaborate urns. The Marajó cultures reached their most advanced stage in the Marajoara phase (AD 400 to 1350), when hundreds of aterros up to 6m high and 250m long were built around Lago Arari. Marajoara ceramics – elaborate funerary and ceremonial vases and simpler domestic ones – are the most sophisticated artifacts known from pre-colonial Brazil, exhibiting exuberant decoration in red, black and white. Marajoara influence reached as far as Lago de Silves, 200km east of Manaus, and the Rio Cunani in northern Amapá.

When Europeans hit the Marajó area in the 17th century, the Aruãs people, successors to the Marajoara, traded with the Dutch and consequently got at cross-purposes with the Portuguese, from whom they eventually fled by migrating up the Rio Amazonas in the 18th century. No trace survives of what happened to them there.

9 am and 3 pm Monday to Friday, 9 am Saturday and 3 pm Sunday.

The state shipping company, ENASA, has a slightly cheaper boat to Foz from the same place in Belém, supposedly at 10:30 am Tuesday, Wednesday and Thursday (returning at 3 pm the same days) – but this boat's adherence to stated schedules is a bit erratic.

ENASA also runs a weekly boat to Soure from the same port in Belém at 8 pm Friday, returning from Soure at 4 pm Sunday.

Getting Around Buses and minivans (US$1 each) meet the boats arriving at Camará to carry passengers the 27km to Salvaterra or a few kilometers farther to the bank of the Rio Paracauari facing Soure. Small motorboats carry passengers across the Paracauari for US$0.70, or you can go free on the vehicle ferry *(balsa),* almost hourly from 6 am to 6 pm.

The buses and minivans from Camará may be willing to take you into Joanes; if not, get off at the Joanes junction *(trevo)* and walk or hitchhike the 5km.

Heading back to Camará, buses and vans run south from Salvaterra and from the riverbank opposite Soure to connect with the departing boats. Buses from Salvaterra to Joanes run till about 6 pm.

Local fishing boats sail the high seas, and it's possible to use them to get all the way around the island and to some of the fazendas. To hook up with one of these, just ask around where you see fishing boats, in places such as Soure or Salvaterra.

Joanes The first coastal village of any size that you can reach from the port at Foz do Rio Camará is Joanes, 5km off the main road. It's a very slow-moving spot with a fine, sandy beach and the scanty ruins of a 17th-century Jesuit church. It's thought that Spanish navigator Vicente Yáñez Pinzón landed on Joanes beach on February 26, 1500 – a couple of months before Pedro Cabral's 'discovery' of Brazil for Portugal.

A good reason to make your way to Joanes is *Pousada Ventania do Rio-Mar* (☎ 9992-5716, pousadas@hotmail.com), atop a breezy small headland at the south end of the beach. The Brazilian-Belgian owners created this good, small place with international budget travelers very much in mind. Individually decorated rooms, with nicely tiled bathrooms, cost US$20/27 a single/double, including a good breakfast. Inexpensive guided walks, fishing trips and horse, bike and canoe rental are all available. Room rates are lower if you stay a few days.

Pousada Paraíso de Joanes (☎ 276-7600, 9989-8664), a few meters back up the same grassy street, is also pleasant. Rooms range from US$16.50 to US$33, single or double.

The *Pousada Ventania do Rio-Mar* should have opened its restaurant by the time you read this. The *Peixaria* on the beach does straightforward cheap meals; stop by and order in advance if you want to have dinner.

Salvaterra About 18km north from Joanes, this town (pop 5800) is larger and a little livelier. It's set on the south bank of the mouth of the Rio Paracauari, with views across to Soure and also a 1km, east-facing ocean beach, Praia Grande.

The beach is popular on weekends, when the barracas open. Salvaterra is a good place to see the fish corrals that dot the coastline of Marajó; these corrals are pole fences that use the falling tide to capture fish, and, from the air, they appear as a string of heart shapes near the water's edge.

Pousada Bosque dos Aruãs (☎/fax 765-1115, jurandir@supridados.com.br), immediately above the ocean at the east end of Segunda Rua, just north of Praia Grande, is an excellent choice. Comfortable, very clean wooden cabins with bathrooms cost US$13/16 for singles/doubles with fan or US$16/20 with air-con, all including breakfast. The restaurant here is a very good value. The friendly owner, Jurandir da Conceição, is widely traveled and speaks respectable English, and he rents bicycles for US$4 a day.

A few minutes south along the beach, *Pousada Tropical* (☎ 765-1164) has small apartamentos with mosquito nets, bathroom and fan for US$16 single or double.

The more upmarket *Pousada dos Guarás* (☎/*fax 242-0904, guaras@interconect.com.br)*, farther south on the beach, has spacious rooms in garden bungalows costing US$50/57/62/70 for singles/doubles/triples/quads (20% discount usually available). A number of Belém travel agencies offer package trips here.

Praia Grande has several straightforward *beach restaurants* where you can eat quite well for around US$5.

Soure The principle town in Marajó, Soure (pop 17,000) is on the north bank of the mouth of the Rio Paracauari, and, like Salvaterra, it fronts the Baía de Marajó. Tides here can oscillate a remarkable 3m.

Like all the coastal towns of Marajó, Soure is primarily dependent on fishing, but it's also the commercial center for the island's buffalo business. These animals have undisputed right of way on this relaxed town's wide, shady, grassy streets!

Soure has a few car and motorcycle taxis, but a good way to get around is by bicycle. You can hire one for about US$10 a day at Bike Tur, on the corner of Rua 3 and Travessa 14.

Orientation & Information The streets parallel to the river are Ruas (with Rua 1 closest to the river). The perpendicular streets are Travessas, with Travessa 1 closest to the seashore.

Soure has no money-exchange service, but you can get Visa cash advances at Banco do Brasil on Rua 3 (open 10 am to 3 pm, Monday to Friday). The Telepará phone office is at Rua 4 No 835 (between other buildings numbered in the 1600s).

Beaches The bay beaches near Soure, fronting on water that is a mixture of salt and fresh, are excellent and often covered with fantastic seeds washed down from the Amazonian forests. You can easily bicycle or walk the 3km to **Praia Barra Velho**. Simply follow Travessa 14 out of town and across farmland till you see the path to this beach diverging to the right. If you continue past the Barra Velho turning you soon reach

a river where you will see the ruins of a footbridge. If a boat is on hand to take you over, you can reach **Praia de Araruna**, the most beautiful beach, just beyond the river. At low tide you can walk about 5km in either direction along the beach, which is practically deserted most of the time.

Praia do Pesqueiro, 9km from town (reached by heading inland along Rua 4), is another very nice beach, popular on weekends. Ask about buses at Soure. Barracas here serve great crab.

Fazenda Bom Jesus This fazenda 8km from Soure is open for visits (US$7) Monday to Saturday afternoons. There are lots of birds, and you can ride a buffalo or a horse. It's obligatory to make a reservation; call ☎ 741-1243. A taxi here and back from Soure is around US$20.

Special Events On the second Sunday in November, Soure has its own Círio de Nazaré. The festival features a beautiful procession, and the town bursts with communal spirit. Just about everyone in the region comes to Soure for the festival, so accommodations can be difficult to find.

Places to Stay & Eat The *Soure Hotel* (☎ *741-1202, Rua 3 No 1347)*, in the center of town, has simple single/double apartamentos for US$10/13 (with fan) or US$16/24 (with air-conditioning). It has little atmosphere, but lots of mosquitoes. *Hotel Araruna* (☎ *741-1347)*, on Travessa 14 next to the Cosampa water towers, is better. It has simple, private and clean rooms with air-con for US$20/30, including a simple breakfast.

Hotel Ilha do Marajó (☎ *741-1315)*, at the ocean end of Rua 8, is Soure's best. It's nicely arranged in a couple of double-story blocks linked by raised walkways and has disabled access and a good swimming pool. Spotlessly clean rooms cost US$44/52, with a US$10 discount usually available. In the good *open-air restaurant* you can eat a buffalo steak for US$5, or beef steak or fish for US$6.50 to US$9.

Restaurante Minha Deusa (*Travessa 14 No 1193)*, just outside town on the road to

Praia Barra Velho, has good food too. A big buffalo steak is US$6.50.

Other Destinations In the pretty, rustic town of **Cachoeira do Arari**, 50km southwest of Foz do Rio Camará by unpaved road, is the Museo do Marajó (☎ 758-1102). This interesting museum contains ancient Marajoara pottery and other Marajó memorabilia assembled by an Italian priest, Giovanni Gallo. It's open 8 am to 6 pm daily (admission: US$1.25). In the second half of the year a bus runs from Salvaterra to Cachoeira at about 10 am, returning early the next morning. A taxi day-trip from Salvaterra (possible in the dry season only) costs around US$65. There are primitive accommodations in Cachoeira do Arari at *Pousada do Manoel Filho* (☎ 758-1245).

Ilha Caviana, off the north coast of Ilha de Marajó, is an excellent base for observing the pororoca (the thunderous collision between the Atlantic tide and the Rio Amazonas). The best time to see this phenomenon is around the full moon in March. English-speaking pilot/guide Marcelo Morelio (☎ 0xx91-223-5794 in Belém, ☎ 9114-5794,

latzero@zaz.com.br) charges around US$600 for up to five people for an excursion from Belém to Ilha Caviana to see the pororoca. He also has accommodations at his fazenda on Caviana and is starting up a spot of eco/adventure tourism there – check the Web site www.armando.com.br.

Remote fazendas, where the buffalo roam, are enormous estates occupying most of the eastern half of Marajó. Some are centered on lovely old houses. The properties are beautiful, rustic refuges, filled with birds and monkeys. Several of them are set up to receive visitors.

Fazenda Carmo-Camará (☎ 0xx91-241-2202 in Belém) is a beautiful spot, accessible only by boat along the Rio Camará or (during the second half of the year) by plane. It's well organized for visits, with horseback and canoe outings available. Full board costs around US$55 per person but Amazon Star (see Travel Agencies in the Belém section earlier in this chapter) offers three-day/two-night packages that include transportation (boat-car-boat) from Belém, meals and activities, from US$180.

Fazenda Bom Jardim (☎ 0xx91-242-1380 in Belém) is beside an igarapé about 45km from Soure (2½ hours by river, one hour by road from September to December). Air taxis take half an hour from Belém. Full board is US$65 per person. There's lots of wildlife here, and guests can join in ranching activities, ride horses, fish for piranhas and go alligator-spotting at night.

SANTARÉM
☎ 0xx91 • postcode 68000-000
• pop 177,000

Santarém is a pleasant city, blessed with river breezes and a relatively mild climate (22 to 36°C). It is nearly impossible to reach overland, but is set at a junction of river transportation routes, at the confluence of the creamy-brown Rio Amazonas and the darker brown Rio Tapajós, about halfway between Belém and Manaus. The two rivers flow side by side for a few kilometers before their waters mingle; seen from the city's waterfront, their bands of different-colored water are clearly distinguishable.

Far from the Beaten Track

The **Tataquara Lodge**, which opened in 2000, is a low-impact ecolodge on an island in the Rio Xingu, 3½ hours by boat from the town of Altamira, which is on the Transamazônica highway, about 300km southeast of Santarém. It has been set up as part of an economic self-sufficiency program by eight Indian tribes in the Xingu region. Indian guides take visitors canoeing, fishing, walking, and animal and bird-watching. Four- and five-day programs are available for US$180 a day per person, including transfers from/to Altamira (which you can fly into) and one night in a hotel in the town. For information visit the Web site www.amazoncoop.org or contact Amazoncoop, Rua Tancredo Neves s/n, Altamira, Pará 68371-020, or you can email to coopamazon@aol.com.

Though the third largest city on the Rio Amazonas, Santarém is a sleepy backwater compared with Manaus and Belém. But it's well worth a stop. Outstanding among nearby destinations is the charming little river-beach resort Alter do Chão, about 35 km away.

The Santarém region has been a center of human settlement for many thousands of years (see the boxed text 'Prehistoric Amazonia' earlier in this chapter). In 1661, more than 20 years after Pedro Teixeira's expedition first contacted the local Tupaiu Indians, a Jesuit mission was established at the meeting of the Tapajós and Amazonas. In 1758 the village that grew around the mission was named Santarém, after the city of that name in Portugal.

The later history of Santarém was marked by the rubber boom and bust, and a series of gold rushes that started in the 1950s. In the 1970s the construction of the Transamazônica highway and the Cuiabá-Santarém highway attracted hordes of Northeastern immigrants to the backlands of this region.

The economy is based on rubber, hardwoods, Brazil nuts, black pepper, mangoes, soybeans, jute and fish. The discovery of gold and bauxite and the construction of the Curuá-Una hydroelectric dam, 60km southeast of Santarém, have brought some development in the last 25 years, but the road links opened in the 1970s are now virtually useless. The BR-163 to Cuiabá is paved for only 84km south from Santarém, and the following unpaved 700km can take a week to drive in the wet season. It's a similar story with the Transamazônica. There is a popular movement to try to reverse the effects of this isolation by forming a new state of Tapajós in the hope of winning more government funding for the area.

Orientation

The Docas do Pará, where most of the long-distance river boats dock, are toward the

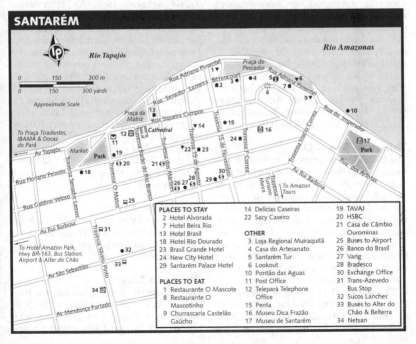

SANTARÉM

Rio Tapajós	Rio Amazonas

Approximate Scale

To Praça Tiradentes, IBAMA & Docas do Pará

To Hotel Amazon Park, Hwy BR-163, Bus Station, Airport & Alter do Chão

Cathedral

Market

Park

To Amazon Tours

PLACES TO STAY
2 Hotel Alvorada
7 Hotel Beira Rio
13 Hotel Brasil
18 Hotel Rio Dourado
23 Brasil Grande Hotel
24 New City Hotel
29 Santarém Palace Hotel

PLACES TO EAT
1 Restaurante O Mascote
8 Restaurante O Mascotinho
9 Churrascaria Castelão Gaúcho

14 Delícias Caseiras
22 Sacy Caseiro

OTHER
3 Loja Regional Muiraquitã
4 Casa do Artesanato
5 Santarém Tur
6 Lookout
10 Pontão das Aguas
11 Post Office
12 Telepará Telephone Office
15 Penta
16 Museu Dica Frazão
17 Museu de Santarém

19 TAVAJ
20 HSBC
21 Casa de Câmbio Ourominas
25 Buses to Airport
26 Banco do Brasil
27 Varig
28 Bradesco
30 Exchange Office
31 Trans-Azevedo Bus Stop
32 Sucos Lanches
33 Buses to Alter do Chão & Belterra
34 Netsan

west end of the city. The Centro district, with most of the accommodations, shops, travel agencies and places of interest, is 2.5km east of the Docas.

Information

Banco do Brasil and Bradesco, both on Avenida Rui Barbosa, have Visa ATMs. HSBC, Rua Floriano Peixoto 743, has Cirrus ATMs. You can change traveler's checks and cash US dollars at Banco do Brasil, Santarém Tur travel agency and the nameless and signless exchange office at Avenida Rui Barbosa 646. Casa de Câmbio Ouárominas, Travessa dos Mártires 198, changes cash US dollars.

The central post office and the Telepará telephone office (where you can make pay-per-minute international calls) are on Rua Siqueira Campos, facing Praça da Matriz. Internet and email are available for US$2 an hour at Netsan, Travessa Silvino Pinto 470.

The Web site of Amazon Tours, www.amazonriver.com, is informative about the Santarém area.

There is no tourist office, but you can get information and book tours and flights with the friendly staff at Santarém Tur (☎ 522-4847, santaremtur@tap.com.br), Rua Adriano Pimentel 44. Also a good person to speak to is Steve Alexander, an American who has lived here many years and runs Amazon Tours (☎ 522-1928, amazontours@amazonriver .com), Travessa Turiano Meira 1084.

Things to See & Do

The **Museu de Santarém**, also called Centro Cultural João Fona, is just east of the center, facing the waterfront. It's open 7:30 am to 5:30 pm Monday to Friday (you pay by donation) and features an interesting collection of stone pieces and pottery, such as animal and human figures and burial urns, from the Tapajoara culture that flourished locally more than 6000 years ago. The building dates from 1867 and has been a jail, city hall and courthouse.

The **Museu Dica Frazão**, Rua Floriano Peixoto 281, displays the amazing creations of Dona Dica Frazão (born 1920), who makes women's clothing and fabrics from natural fibers such as grasses and wood pulp. The work is unbelievably detailed, and some of it is very beautiful; items can take three months to make. Those on display include reproductions of a dress made for a Belgian queen, a tablecloth for Pope John Paul II and costumes for the Boi-Bumbá festival at Parintins. Dona Dica, a slight figure who has received many awards for her work, may well show you round herself. The museum is also her home and workshop and it's open during daylight hours whenever she is in.

The prettily blue-painted **Cathedral**, facing Praça da Matriz, dates from 1761. Its predecessor church, constructed of palm fronds in 1661, was Santarém's first building. From the cathedral you can take an interesting **waterfront walk** westward along Avenida Tapajós, passing colorful markets and innumerable boats.

Organized Tours

Travel agencies (see the Information section, earlier) offer a range of excursions from the city. Trips available with Santarém Tur include boat trips to the 'Meeting of the Waters,' where the Amazonas and Tapajós Rivers meet (US$25 per person for groups of two to four), or a full-day river and lake trip with a wildlife emphasis (US$55). Amazon Tours does half-day botanical excursions to the Bosque Santa Lucia, 18km south of town, where there are over 400 tree species (about US$20). If you're looking for an independent guide for a jungle trip, you could try Franklin Chaves (☎ 522-2435), Rua Galdino Veloso 200, who has been well recommended.

Special Events

The patron saint of fishermen, São Pedro, is honored on June 29, when boats decorated with flags and flowers sail in procession before the city.

Places to Stay

Hotel Brasil (☎ 523-5177, Travessa dos Mártires 30), in a large old building in the commercial area, doesn't look like much from outside, but has good-value, clean singles/

doubles with fan and big exterior windows for US$7/14, plus a couple of air-con rooms for US$16/20, all including breakfast. *Hotel Beira Rio* (☎ 522-2519, *Rua Adriano Pimentel 90*) has simple quartos with fan for US$7/14. *Hotel Alvorada* (☎ 522-5340, *Rua Senador Lameira Bittencourt 179*), opposite Restaurante O Mascote, has quartos with fan for US$8/14 and air-con apartamentos for US$16/24. The airy front rooms with river views are not bad.

The *New City Hotel* (☎ 522-4719, *Travessa Francisco Correa 200*) has friendly staff and decent air-conditioned apartamentos with TV and minibar for US$20/27. *Hotel Rio Dourado* (☎ 523-2174, *Rua Floriano Peixoto 799*), near the market, has comfy apartamentos with air-con, polished wood floors, TV, minibar and cold showers for US$24/30, if you pay in cash.

The *Brasil Grande Hotel* (☎ 522-5660, *Travessa 15 de Agosto 213*) has good, large, bright, air-con apartamentos for US$26/34. Rooms at the *Santarém Palace Hotel* (☎ 523-2820, *Avenida Rui Barbosa 726*) are of similar standard for US$30/36.

The *Hotel Amazon Park* (☎ 523-2800, *Avenida Mendonça Furtado 4120*), looking out to the Rio Tapajós in the west of town, is the only luxury hotel. The large, air-con rooms with TV, balcony and nice bathrooms cost US$55/60 plus 10% tax. The hotel has a good pool, and the pool bar stays open till 4 am.

Places to Eat

For reliably good food it's hard to beat *Sacy Caseiro* (*Rua Floriano Peixoto 521*), open daily for good-quality buffet lunch at US$8 per kilo. *Delícias Caseiras* (*Travessa 15 de Agosto 121*) does reasonable self-serve for US$6.50 per kilo.

Restaurante O Mascote (*Praça do Pescador 10*), with both an air-conditioned section and outdoor tables, has good-quality fish meals from US$8 (enough for two); try the tucunaré ao molho de camarão (peacock bass in shrimp sauce) for US$10.50. East along the waterfront, *Restaurante O Mascotinho* is a large open-air on a terrace overlooking the river where you can enjoy a

beer, burger, pizza or sanduich. *Churrascaria Castelão Gaúcho* (*Avenida Adriano Pimental 142*), just along the street to the east, does an evening rodizio where you can fill up for just US$5 on endless meat and lots of salads, rice, beans and fried bananas.

Restaurante Tapaiu, in the Hotel Amazon Park, has a pleasing menu with main dishes from US$8 to US$10. The *Brasil Grande Hotel* also has a decent restaurant.

Shopping

Loja Regional Muiraquitã and Casa do Artesanato, both on Rua Senador Lameira Bittencourt, sell local handicrafts.

Getting There & Away

Air Varig (☎ 522-2488), with an office at Avenida Rui Barbosa 790, flies to/from Belém (US$190) and Manaus (US$130) daily. Regional airlines fly these routes for up to 40% less, usually with stops en route, as well as flying to/from many lesser Amazonian cities. Penta has the most flights, including to Cuiabá for US$257, Macapá for US$83, Altamira for US$70 and Parintins for US$52 (all fares one-way). Its office (☎ 523-2220) is at Travessa 15 de Novembro 183. The phone number at the airport is ☎ 523-1021.

Bus The bus station (☎ 522-3392) is on the southwest edge of the city, 5km from the center. During the rainy season (roughly December to May) bus travel is not normally possible beyond Rurópolis (US$9.50, about six hours, once or twice daily), 220km south, where the Santarém-Cuiaba Hwy BR-163 meets the Transamazônica.

From about June to November buses run to Cuiabá (US$70, about three days, one daily) and to Itaituba, 170km west of Rurópolis on the Transamazônica (US$16, nine hours, two daily). Some of these buses sometimes start from Travessa Silvino Pinto in central Santarém. You can get information in the bar/restaurant almost opposite the Trans-Azevedo bus stop there. During the drier part of the year there may also be buses (which are not recommended) along the Transamazônica to Marabá (1177km) in southeast Pará, a rough frontier town in an area noted for highway robberies.

Boat Information about boats to and from Manaus, Belém and Macapá (each two days from Santarém) can be found at the Docas do Pará (☎ 522-1757), 2.5km west of the city center. Tickets are sold at booths outside the docks entrance. Boats usually leave for Manaus (US$30 in hammock) around 3 pm, daily except Sunday; for Belém (US$48), around noon from Wednesday to Sunday; and for Macapá (US$34) daily at 6 pm. You may have to ask for a 'desconto' in order to pay the above fares. Cabins are normally already taken in Manaus or Belém.

Most of these boats call at the main intermediate towns such as Monte Alegre, Alen-

quer and Parintins. For some of the closer destinations there are also smaller boats from various points along the riverfront. Fast boats to Monte Alegre (US$9, 3½ hours) go from the Pontão das Águas, a floating jetty-cum-restaurant just east of the center, at 2 pm Monday to Friday and noon on Saturday. Slower boats to Monte Alegre and boats to Itaituba (US$20/40 in hammock/cabin, 14 hours, 6 pm daily) go from the Praça Tiradentes port about 1km west of the center.

Getting Around

The airport is 14km west of the city center; buses (US$0.50) run to the city nine times between 6:15 am and 6:15 pm. Going out to the airport, the buses (marked 'Aeroporto') leave a stop on Avenida Rui Barbosa, west of Travessa Barão do Rio Branco, between 5:30 am and 5:30 pm. Avoid buses marked 'Aeroporto V…'; these go elsewhere.

The New City and Rio Dourado hotels offer clients free transportation from the airport in their shared van, and charge US$7 (open to anyone) to go back to the airport.

The taxi fare is about US$22.

The 'Orla Fluvial' bus shuttles travel between the city center and Docas do Pará about every half hour till about 7 pm. The 'Circular Esperança' bus (US$0.50) runs from the center to the Docas and then the bus station.

AROUND SANTARÉM
Alter do Chão
☎ 0xx91

There are plenty of river beaches in and around Santarém, but you shouldn't miss Alter do Chão, 33km west by paved road and easily reached by bus. This village stands beside the Rio Tapajós at the entrance to a picturesque lagoon, Lago Verde. With its white-sand beaches, relaxed atmosphere and beautiful location, it's a good place to chill out – many travelers find themselves postponing departure more than once. Alter do Chão also possesses a very interesting museum and some good craft shops, and serves as a weekend retreat for the people of Santarém.

The Transamazônica

The idea of the Transamazônica was born in 1970, during the military dictatorship, when President Garrastazu Médici decided that drought-stricken Northeasterners should colonize Amazonia. To facilitate this grand movement of people, a 5600km 'Highway of National Integration' was to be cut across the *caatinga* and rainforests from João Pessoa on the Atlantic coast to Boquerão da Esperança on the Peruvian border.

Only 2500km were actually constructed, from Aguiarnópolis in Tocantins to Lábrea in southern Amazonas. And only a few short stretches of this were paved. The Transamazônica today is full of potholes and rickety bridges and basically impassable in the wet season, from November to April. During the dry, buses struggle 34 hours to cover the 1000km from Marabá to Itaituba. The 400km from Itaituba to Jacareacanga was closed altogether from 1985 to 1997 and again from 1999 onward.

About a million people somehow continue to live along the Transamazônica and its side tracks, known as *vecinais*, and the cities of Altamira and Itaituba now have around 70,000 inhabitants each.

Centro de Preservação das Artes Indígenas This excellent exhibit of indigenous art and artifacts (☎/fax 527-1176, cpci@ netsan.com.br), at Rua Dom Macêdo Costa 500, far surpasses any such collections in Manaus or Belém. Set up in the early 1990s by an American artist and his Kaxinawá Indian wife, it was recently in the process of being transferred to the ownership of an organization of indigenous chiefs from around Brazil. The center possesses arguably Brazil's best collection of indigenous art, with useful information on the country's Indian peoples and their struggles to survive.

It also has a good library (open to visitors) and a shop with a fine range of indigenous art and artisanry. The organizers are trying to make the center into a focal point for Brazil's indigenous peoples and others interested in their culture and issues. Hours are 9 am to noon and 2 to 5 pm daily. Admission is US$2 (students: US$0.70).
Web site: www.pamiriwi.hpg.com.br

Beaches The long sandbar that almost separates Lago Verde from the Rio Tapajós is justly the subject of 1000 postcards – probably the best river beach in Amazonia.

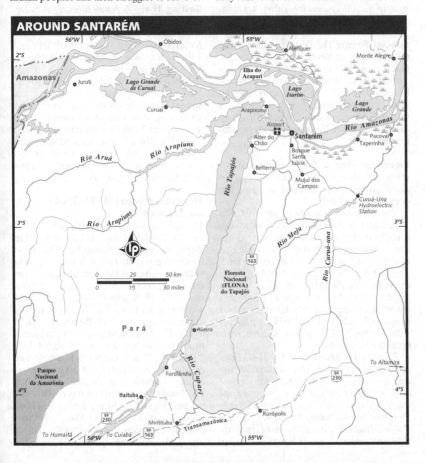

AROUND SANTARÉM

Rowboats take up to four people across from the village for US$0.70. A line of beach-shack restaurant/bars serves your consumption needs, and you can rent a kayak for US$1.25 an hour, or follow the clear path from the left (west) side of the beach to the top of the hill beyond for great views. It's not a difficult hike, but allow two hours to get there and back.

Another good sandy beach faces the Tapajós on the west side of the village.

Like others in the Santarém area, the beaches of Alter do Chão are usually under water in June and July, and when the water is at its lowest (November) they get a bit muddy at the water's edge.

Special Events The Festa do Çairé in the second week of September is the major folkloric event in western Pará. The Çairé is a standard that is held aloft to lead a flower-bedecked procession: its origins may go back to symbols used by early missionaries to help convert Indians. Look for many dances and other folkloric events happening during the Çairé.

Places to Stay & Eat Accommodations are provided by a number of low-key pousadas. Breakfast is included at all of the ones described here.

The friendly *Pousada Alter-do-Chão* (☎ 522-3411, Rua Lauro Sodré 74), which has a restaurant overlooking the beach, has simple apartamentos costing US$16 single or double with fan or US$20 air-conditioned. Those at the front are best. A block inland, *Pousada Vila da Praia* (☎ 527-1138, Rua Copacabana s/n) has quite good air-conditioned apartamentos for one or two people at US$20, and 'chalets' for up to five with TV for US$27 (plus US$2 for each breakfast beyond two).

Pousada Tia Marilda (☎ 527-1144, Travessa Antônio A Lobato s/n) has smallish aircon apartamentos at US$16/20 for singles/doubles, and a couple of breezier, bigger upstairs quartos with fan, for US$10/13. *Pousada Tupaiulândia* (☎ 527-1157, Rua Pedro Teixeira 300) offers the most comfortable accommodations. It has two circular blocks, each with four apartamentos with air-conditioning, TV and fridge for US$24/33, plus US$7 each for up to three more people.

The several restaurants on the central Praça 7 de Setembro and all the others in town offer pretty much the same range of beef, chicken and fish dishes. These cost US$9 to US$12 for two at the *Alter Nativo* on the *praça* and a little less at the beach places or the restaurant at the *Pousada Alter-do-Chão*, another of the best spots. The *Muiraquitã*, on the praças, does prato feito for US$2.50.

Getting There & Away Monday to Saturday, buses to Alter do Chão (US$1.20, one hour) leave Santarém from a stop on Avenida São Sebastião east of Travessa Silvino Pinto. At the time of writing departures were at 4:50, 5:50, 7:10, 9:10 and 10:20 am, and 12:50, 2:50, 4:35 and 5:50 pm, plus 11:50 am Monday and Friday. On Sunday and holidays buses go from Praça Tiradentes, 1km west of Santarém center, hourly from 7 am to 1 pm and at 3, 4 and 5 pm. The first and last buses back to Santarém leave Alter do Chão at 5:45 am and 7:20 pm Monday to Saturday, and 8 am and 6 pm Sunday and holidays.

Floresta Nacional (FLONA) do Tapajós

This 6500-sq-km reserve on the east side of the Rio Tapajós is the only accessible large virgin forest near Santarém. The most hassle-free way to visit it is on a day trip with Santarém Tur (see Travel Agencies in the Santarém section earlier in this chapter), which gives you a few hours' walking in the forest for US$75 per person in groups of two to four (US$50 in groups of five to 10). Otherwise you need authorization from Senhor Robson (☎ 0xx91-523-2964 or ☎ 523-2847) at the Santarém office of IBAMA, the government environmental agency, Avenida Tapajós 2267. There's a US$2 daily fee to visit the forest. IBAMA has buildings at Km 83 and Km 117 on Hwy BR-163 south of Santarém where you theoretically can sleep in a hammock (US$4 a night). You might be able to get a guide for around US$10 a day at Km 83; but at the time of writing the Km 83 post was occupied by research workers, and Km 117 was under repair.

You can reach the FLONA on a 'Km 115' city bus from Avenida Rui Barbosa in Santarém or a bus bound for Rurópolis or beyond (see Getting There & Away in the Santarém section).

Belterra
☎ pop 5100

A 50km trip southwest of Santarém, Belterra, founded in 1933, was the heart of the larger of two Amazonian rubber plantations established by Henry Ford in an effort to break the British monopoly of the rubber business. (The other was Fordlândia, founded in 1928 and still in existence, 170km southwest of Belterra.) Ford managed to create American-style townships, with wide, straight streets lined with cute little wooden houses. But he failed to cultivate rubber efficiently in the Amazon, and abandoned the project in 1946. Belterra is a curious spot, which a good guide can make fascinating (check with one of the travel agencies in Santarém). At the heart of Belterra is a large, grass-covered praça, with a green Catholic church on one side, a smaller Baptist church on the other, and a couple of very basic restaurants nearby.

Buses to Belterra (US$1.30) are run a few times daily, both by Trans-Azevedo from Travessa Silvino Pinto in Santarém and by Cidade de Belterra from a stop on Avenida São Sebastião (tickets for the latter are sold in the Sucos Lanches *lanchonete*, opposite).

Parque Nacional da Amazônia

This large (9940 sq km) Amazonian rainforest national park lies west of the town of Itaituba (population: 65,000), which is 250km southwest of Santarém. To visit, you must obtain prior permission from the IBAMA office (☎ 0xx91-518-1530) at Avenida Marechal Rondon s/n, Itaituba, and an IBAMA staff member must accompany you on your visit. It is possible to stay at rudimentary facilities at an IBAMA post

inside the park, but there's no real visitor infrastructure here.

See the Santarém section earlier in this chapter for details on boat and bus transport to Itaituba. You can also fly, for around US$45, with Penta, Meta or TAVAJ.

Monte Alegre
☎ 0xx91 • postcode 68220-000 • pop 21,000

This town, on the north bank of the Rio Amazonas and 120km downstream from Santarém, is the base from which to visit the oldest known human creations in Amazonia: the rock paintings of the Serra Paytuna and Serra Ererê, estimated to be 12,000 years old. To arrange a visit to these sites, about 30km from town, contact the local teacher and engineer who bears much of the credit for the paintings' conservation, Nelsí Sadeck (☎/fax 533-1430, nelsi@ netsan.com.br), Rua do Jaquara 320. In a 4WD trip of five to seven hours (US$80 for up to 10 people), Nelsí will take you not only to the paintings of human handprints and animal, human and geometric figures, but also to lookout points, strange rock formations and caves.

Nelsí can also provide other attractive outings in the area for US$20 to US$30 for four people, such as to the Serra do Itauajuri, which offers good walking and waterfall bathing; to the jungle waterfall Cachoeira do Açu das Pedras; or by boat through the area's flooded forests.

Monte Alegre stands on one of Amazonia's rare hills. The *Monte Alegre Palace* (☎ 533-1222), on Avenida Presidente Vargas in the Cidade Baixa (the lower part of town), has quartos with fan for US$6 per person including breakfast. Among the better places to stay is the *Pousada Panorâmica* (☎ 533-1282), on Praça da Matriz in the Cidade Alta (upper town). Here air-con apartamentos cost US$13 per person including breakfast, and there's a restaurant.

Restaurante Panorama (*Travessa Oriental 100*) is a reasonable fish restaurant with dishes averaging US$6.

See the Getting There & Away section under Santarém, earlier in this chapter, for details of boats from there. Most boats from

Piracy & Paranoia

Biopirataria (biopiracy) is a new term but an old occupation. In 1876 Henry Wickham took 70,000 rubber seeds from Amazonia to Britain and ruined the Brazilian rubber boom (see the boxed text 'Henry Wickham' in the Facts about Brazil chapter). He was committing biopiracy.

Nature is the basis of some of the most profitable formulations of the pharmaceutical and cosmetic industries, and tropical forests are a hothouse for new products when developed with the aid of indigenous knowledge. It's estimated that 40% of the world's medicaments derive from natural sources (30% from plants, 10% from animals or microorganisms). The incredible biodiversity of the Amazonian forest, with maybe 30 million different species, is a rich and formidable source of potential new products.

Modern biopirates take, for example, the age-old knowledge possessed by indigenous peoples of the medicinal properties of plants and make money from these plants and knowledge outside Brazil. And research and development agreements between Brazilian organizations and foreign companies have set the alarm bells ringing in the Brazilian media – so much so that the word *bioparanóia* has been coined. Brazilian companies do lag behind foreign companies in the commercial exploitation of Amazonia's biological potential. Blame is laid upon a lack of government support for research in Brazil, and the absence of an adequate legal framework establishing Brazilian rights. Senator Marina Ailva from Acre state tried to get a law on access to Brazilian biodiversity through the federal congress in 1995, and by 2001 she had still not succeeded.

An estimated 5000 Amazonian plants with medical and cosmetic properties have been catalogued thus far. Those already being put to use include the following:

- Muira puama *(Ptychopetalum olacoides Benth)* – This aphrodisiac plant from Amazonas and Pará states produces an extract that is already being commercialized outside Brazil.

- Pau rosa *(Aniba roseodora Ducke)* – This is used as a base ingredient for perfumes.

- Unha-de-gato *(Uncaria tomentosa)* – Some AIDS treatments have begun to use this antioxidant and anti-inflammatory that strengthens the immune system; it comes from plants found chiefly in Peru and the Brazilian state of Acre.

- Cunani *(Clibatium sylvestre)* – This plant gets made into a paste used by Indians, such as the Wapixana of Roraima, to poison fish in the water without damaging their nutritional value; Brazilian lawyers are suing for the revocation of patents on this plant taken out in Europe and the US.

Belém to Santarém also make a stop at Monte Alegre.

Amapá

Stretching from the Amazon delta to the borders of French Guiana and Suriname, Amapá has just 476,000 inhabitants, more than half of whom live in the capital, Macapá. The climate is equatorial and superhumid, though drier from September to November. Owing to the proximity of French Guiana, many *Amapaenses* speak some French.

The English, Dutch and French all tried to establish themselves on the north side of the Amazon before Portugal settled colonists at Macapá in 1738, building an imposing fort later. The Treaty of Vienna (1815) fixed the French/Portuguese border at the Rio Oiapoque. But most of Amapá remained a no-man's-land (and refuge for escaped slaves from Brazil) until the 1893 Rio Calçoene gold rush. This prompted French invasion attempts, but international arbitration definitively awarded Amapá to Brazil, upon which it was promptly annexed by Pará. This annexation greatly displeased the Amapaenses, who relentlessly pursued autonomy until it was finally granted in 1943. The left-wing environmentalist João Alberto Capiberibe, elected state governor in 1995, set Amapá firmly on a path of environmentally sustainable development.

MACAPÁ
☎ 0xx96 • postcode 68900-000
• pop 270,000

The state capital lies on the equator, in a strategic position on the north side of the Rio Amazonas estuary. It's an orderly, relatively prosperous and safe place, with delectable sea breezes and a couple of interesting sights.

Information
The Amapá tourism department, Detur (☎ 212-5335, detur@prodap.org.br), at Rua Independência 29, has detailed and genuinely useful information, such as transportation schedules, as well as material on other destinations in Amapá. It's open 9:30 am to noon and 2:30 to 6 pm Monday to Friday.

Banco do Brasil on Rua Independência will exchange US and French currencies in cash or traveler's checks, from 9 am to 3 pm Monday to Friday. If the ATMs here won't cooperate with your Visa card, try the ATMs at Bradesco, Rua Cândido Mendes 1316. The ATMs of HSBC, Avenida Presidente Vargas 50, give cash on MasterCard, Cirrus and American Express cards. Casa Francesa, Rua Independência 232, does cash exchanges for US or French currency.

The central post office is on Avenida Coriolano Jucá. You can make international phone calls, but only by card, at Telemar on Rua São José. Internet access costs US$1.35 an hour at TV Som, Avenida Mendonça Furtado 253 (open daily).

Fortaleza de São José de Macapá
The Portuguese built this large stone fort between 1764 and 1782 to defend the north

side of the Amazon against French incursions from the Guianas. It's an impressive construction, square in plan with pentagonal bastions at the corners, and still in good condition. Protected inside the massive stone walls are the buildings that served as soldiers' quarters, a hospital, jail cells, gunpowder and rations stores, a chapel and the commandant's house. More than 800 laborers were involved in the construction, mostly Indians, blacks and *caboclos* (people of mixed Indian and Portuguese parentage). Many died from accidents in the wet conditions on the riverbank. Many others died at the hands of the repressive and violent administration. The fort is open 9 am to 6 pm Tuesday to Friday, 10 am to 7 pm Saturday, Sunday and holidays. Entry is free; Portuguese-language guided tours are obligatory, but relaxed.

The long pier just north of the fortaleza, the Trapiche Eliezer Levy, dates from the 1930s. Reconstructed in 1998, it makes a pleasant stroll.

Museu Sacaca de Desenvolvimento Sustentável
The very interesting Sacaca Sustainable Development Museum (☎ 212-5342), about 700m from the city center at Avenida Feliciano Coelho 1509, focuses on projects related to Amapá's sustainable development program. Exhibits (all in Portuguese) cover medicinal uses of plants; the traditional curing practices of shamans; ecosystems of Amapá; and the many uses of plants such as the açaí palm and brazil-nut tree. There's also material on the pororoca, the thunderous collision of the incoming Atlantic tide with outflowing rivers. This phenomenon is particularly intense in Amapá, notably on the Rio Araguari, and at its strongest at full moon between January and May, when it can create waves several meters high moving upriver at 50km/h.

The museum is open 8:30 am to noon and 3 to 6 pm, Monday to Saturday (free).

Monumento do Marco Zero
The 'Zero Line Monument,' a large obelisk-cum-sundial, stands on the equator, about

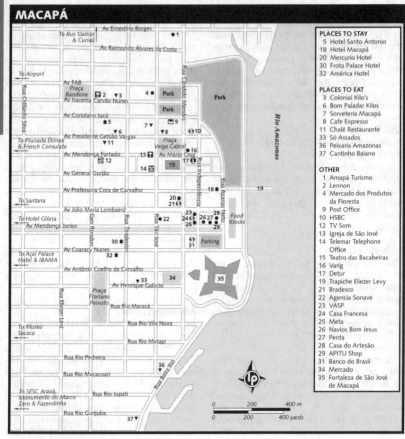

MACAPÁ

PLACES TO STAY
5 Hotel Santo Antonio
18 Hotel Macapá
20 Mercurio Hotel
30 Frota Palace Hotel
32 América Hotel

PLACES TO EAT
3 Colonial Kilo's
6 Bom Paladar Kilos
7 Sorveteria Macapá
8 Cafe Expresso
11 Chalé Restaurante
33 Só Assados
36 Peixaria Amazonas
37 Cantinho Baiano

OTHER
1 Amapá Turismo
2 Lennon
4 Mercado dos Produtos
   da Floresta
9 Post Office
10 HSBC
12 TV Som
13 Igreja de São José
14 Telemar Telephone
   Office
15 Teatro das Bacabeiras
16 Varig
17 Detur
19 Trapiche Eliezer Levy
21 Bradesco
22 Agencia Sonave
23 VASP
24 Casa Francesa
25 Meta
26 Navios Bom Jesus
27 Penta
28 Casa do Artesão
29 APITU Shop
31 Banco do Brasil
34 Mercado
35 Fortaleza de São José
   de Macapá

6km southwest of the city center A
hemisphere-straddling sports stadium and a
sambadrome are part of the same complex.
The 'Zerão' bus southbound on Rua
Tiradentes at Avenida Mendonça Furtado
will get you there.

Organized Tours

Amap\'a Turismo (☎ 222-2553), Avenida
Ernestino Borges 319, offers city tours
(US$25 to US$35), Rio Amazonas day trips
(US$40) and longer-range outings of two or
three days with forest walks, boat rides and
so on (around US$125). During full moons

from January to May, groups of five or more
can travel by plane or boat to witness the
pororoca on the Rio Araguari (US$100 to
US$160) or the nearer Canal do Itamarati
(US$70 to US$100).

Special Events

O Marabaixo is an Afro-Brazilian celebration, with music and dance, 40 days after
Semana Santa (Holy Week).

Places to Stay

*Hotel Santo Antonio (☎ 222-0026, Avenida
Coriolano Jucá 485)* is probably the best

budget option in Macapá. It has communal rooms for US$6 per person and single rooms with shared bath for US$6.50. Single/double apartamentos cost US$10/15.50 with fan and US$14/18 with air-conditioning.

The *América Hotel* (☎ 223-2819, Avenida Coaracy Nunes 333) has small quartos with fan for US$8.50/13.50. Those at the front are best. Apartamentos with TV cost US$13.50/16.50 with fan, US$15.50/23.50 with air-con, and US$16.50/25.50 with minibar. The *Açai Palace Hotel* (☎ 223-4899, Avenida Antônio Coelho de Carvalho 1399), 300m from the city center, offers OK single/double apartamentos for US$13.50/16.50 with fan and US$16.50/23.50 with air-con.

The *Mercurio Hotel* (☎ 223-5622, Rua Cândido Mendes 1300) has large, clean, slightly worn single/double/triple apartamentos with air-conditioning for US$19.50/26/30 (US$23.50/30.50/40 with TV and minibar), including breakfast. The *Hotel Glória* (☎ 222-0984, Rua Leopoldo Machado 2085), not far from the center, is a good value. Neat, air-conditioned singles/doubles with hot shower go for US$17/29.

The friendly *Frota Palace Hotel* (☎ 223-3999, fax 223-7011, Rua Tiradentes 1104) has bare but spacious apartamentos with hot shower, TV and air-con for US$37/45 (cash). The hotel also offers transportation to/from Varig, TAM and VASP flights for US$2.50 (see the hotel's airport desk on arrival).

The choicest accommodations can be found at *Pousada Ékinox* (☎ 223-0086, j-f@uol.com.br, Rua Jovino Dinoá 1693), run by the French honorary consul and his Brazilian wife, a hospitable couple. It has a fitness area, video and book library, courtyard and a restaurant with superb food. The 14 pleasant rooms with air-conditioning, hot shower, fridge, TV and VCR cost US$53/67 with breakfast or US$80/100 full board. Advance booking is essential.

Hotel Macapá (☎ 217-1350, mcphotel@zaz.com.br, Rua Azarias Neto 17), facing the waterfront, has a big pool, a restaurant and decent-sized bar rooms for US$64/76, or US$76/92 with verandah overlooking the river. The latter might be worth the money; the former aren't.

Places to Eat

Two of Macapá's best restaurants have beautifully breezy upstairs settings on the waterfront Avenida Beira Rio, south of the fort. *Peixaria Amazonas* serves good fish dishes at around US$10 for two and is open for lunch and dinner daily. *Cantinho Baiano* (Avenida Beira Rio 328) has tasty Bahian food at similar prices. They'll do one-person portions if you're alone.

For good per-kilo meals, try *Bom Paladar Kilos* (Avenida Presidente Getúlio Vargas 456), charging US$8/kg. *Colonial Kilo's* (Avenida Iracema Carvão Nunes 282) and *Só Assados* (Avenida Henrique Galúcio 290) are also OK and charge the same price.

The *Chalé Restaurant* (Avenida Presidente Getúlio Vargas 499) has a finer ambience, a large variety of dishes and wines, and good service. Seafood, chicken and pasta dishes for two people here cost between US$10 and US$20; one-person portions are also available in many cases.

Sorvetaria Macapá (Rua São José 1676) has the best ice cream in town. The *food kiosks* lining the waterfront north of the fort are popular for evening snacks.

At *Cafe Expresso* (Avenida Presidente Getúlio Vargas 184), you can get a jug of freshly squeezed juice, or two shots of strong coffee, for US$2.

Entertainment

Macapá's a fairly quiet town, but one place worth trying is *Lennon*, an open-air bar facing Praça Bandeira, with variable live music most nights. *SESC Araxá* (☎ 214-1314, Rua Jovino Dinoá 4311), about 3km south of the city center, stages musical performances on Tuesday night. A Peruvian folk group was one of the offerings at the time of research.

Shopping

The APITU shop, on Avenida Mendonça Junior, sells the excellent artisanry of the Tumucumaque indigenous people from the mountainous borders of Amapá, Pará and Suriname at bargain prices: seed and bead necklaces for US$1, large woven baskets around US$12, ceremonial costumes for

US$40. Next door, the Casa do Artesão sells non-indigenous crafts, with a few artisans working on site.

Another shop well worth a visit is the Mercado dos Produtos da Floresta, Rua São José 1500, which sells medicines, oils, shampoos, nuts, drinks, basketwork, cookies and other interesting and inexpensive forest products from Amapá's sustainable development program.

Getting There & Away

Air Varig (☎ 223-1759), Rua Cândido Mendes 1039, VASP, on Avenida Júlio Maria Lombaerd, and TAM will all fly you to other main Brazilian cities. Most flights from Macapá leave very early in the morning and you'll at least touch down in Belém, if not change planes there. The regional airlines Penta (☎ 223-5226, Avenida Mendonça Junior 12) and Meta, not far away on the same street, also fly to Belém (for around US$65) and to other destinations around Amazonia. Penta's destinations include Cayenne (French Guiana), and Oiapoque on the Amapá/French Guiana border (see the Getting There & Away chapter for more information).

Bus Macapá is linked by Hwy BR-156 to Oiapoque, the Brazilian town on the border with French Guiana, 532km north. Only about the first 140km of the road is paved. Buses to Oiapoque leave from Macapá's shiny new bus station (☎ 251-5045) on the BR-156 in Bairro São Lázaro, about 3km north of the center on the edge of the city. There are supposed to be at least two daily buses making the trip in each direction, but during the rainiest months (roughly January to June) buses may not be able to go every day. The trip costs US$30 and should take between 12 and 24 hours depending on the season. In the wet season, the going can be fairly rough.

Boat Trips to Belém, Santarém and Manaus go from the large port town of Santana, some 25km southwest of Macapá. You can buy boat tickets in Macapá at Agencia Sonave (☎ 223-9090), Rua São José 2145,

and Navios Bom Jesus at Avenida Mendonça Junior 12. You can catch a bus to Santana (US$0.70) from any northbound stop on Rua São José in central Macapá.

The quickest sailings to Belém are with Arapari Navegação (☎ 9972-5858), which has fast boats with airplane-style seating. The trip takes about 12 hours for US$40, departing at 7 am Tuesday, Thursday and Saturday. Conventional boats leave every morning except Wednesday and Sunday and take 20 to 24 hours for US$40 in hammock (US$46 with air-con) or US$50 to US$75 per person in cabins.

Boats to Santarém (US$40/100 in hammock/cabin, about 2½ days) and Manaus (US$80/200, five days) leave at 6 pm Monday and Friday.

Getting Around

The airport is about 3.5km northwest of the center; a taxi costs around US$6.

Buses 'Jardim I/Bairro' and 'Brasil Novo/Universidade' (US$0.70) run to the bus station from Praça Veiga Cabral.

AROUND MACAPÁ
Curiaú

This African village 8km northeast of Macapá was founded by escaped African slaves. They chose this area for its natural pastures, perfect for raising buffalo. The main street is lined with distinctive timber houses. You can hire a local to take you on a canoe trip on the lakes and rivers in the area, which are particularly picturesque in the late afternoon and feature plenty of bird life. The surrounding area is an Área de Protecão Ambiental (Environmental Protection Area; see the Natural Brazil chapter for more on such areas).

The Festa de São Joaquim in Curiaú, running from about August 11 to 18, is an Afro-Brazilian party with *ladainha* (praying), *folia* (dancing in colorful costumes) and most notably *batuque* (drumming).

Local buses run from Macapá to Curiaú.

Praia da Fazendinha

Buses run to Praia da Fazendinha, the local beach, 16km southwest of Macapá. The

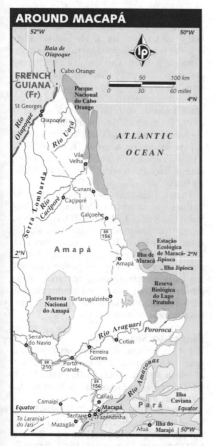

AROUND MACAPÁ

a key point on the overland route between the Guianas and northeastern Brazil.

The Brazilian Polícia Federal post here, where you must get your passport stamped and obtain or surrender your entry/exit card if crossing the border, is open daily except Sunday. Oiapoque has branches of Banco do Brasil and Bradesco, but you can't get any money out of them with cards, so you need to have some currency to exchange.

There are a few cheap places to stay; the **Hotel do Governo** (☎ 521-1809) and **Hotel Kayama** (☎ 521-1448) are probably the best options. The three hotels you'll find in St Georges are more expensive, around US$27 for a double room.

Getting There & Away

For details on buses to/from Macapá, see Getting There & Away in the Macapá section. For information on land travel between St Georges and Cayenne, see the Land section of the Getting There & Away chapter. You can also fly between Macapá and Oiapoque, or St Georges and Cayenne, or even Macapá and Cayenne – see the Air section of the Getting There & Away chapter.

Tocantins

The state of Tocantins was created in 1989 by hiving off what was previously the northern half of Goiás. Southern Goiás had mostly been colonized by people from southern Brazil, who mixed little with the local Indians or black slaves. Northern Goiás had mostly been colonized by people from Northeastern Brazil, with mixing between Indians, blacks and those of European descent creating a distinctive culture. Separatist campaigns in what's now Tocantins began in the early 19th century.

Tocantins has no big cities, but a lot of fazendas and small towns. The energy expended and the many projects undertaken in order to get the young state off the ground, especially the construction from nothing of the capital, Palmas, have made

beachside restaurants **Julião** and **Naira** are recommended for seafood.

Oiapoque
☎ 0xx96 • pop 7500

This is the remote town at the end of Hwy BR-156, 532km north of Macapá on the Brazil side of the Rio Oiapoque. On the other side of the river (a US$5, 20-minute motorboat ride) is the town of St Georges, French Guiana, the end point of a road that was due to be opened in 2001 from Cayenne, the French Guiana capital, about 200km farther northwest. Oiapoque is thus

Tocantins – in parts at least – a land of opportunity. In 2000 Tocantins, which covers 286,706 sq km, had 1.16 million inhabitants.

The climate is humid, with average temperatures between 25 and 36°C. Most rain falls between October and April. Ecologically, Tocantins is a transition zone between the Amazon rainforest that makes up its northern part and the *cerrado* (scrubland) in the southeast. This variety means there are considerable natural attractions for those with time and budget on their side. Most notable is the Rio Araguaia/Ilha do Bananal zone in the west, where Pantanal-like wetlands meet rainforest and cerrado.

PALMAS
☎ 0xx63 • postcode 77000-000
• pop 131,000

The state capital is a planned city, strategically placed in the center of Tocantins, 1000km from Brasília and 1600km from Belém. In 1989 this site was just a scattering of rural fazendas. Today it's a clean, organized, low-crime city, still growing fast and still possessed of a youthful energy – it's an obvious starting point for traveling to most Tocantins destinations.

A new hydroelectric dam was due to become operational in late 2001 at Lajeado, 50km north, flooding the Rio Tocantins valley all the way south to beyond Porto Nacional. The 630 sq km reservoir thus created will be crossed by the Palmas-Paraíso do Tocantins road on a bridge several kilometers long. An artificial river beach, backed by a park, is slated to be created on the western edge of Palmas.

Orientation & Information
At the heart of the city is Praça dos Girassóis, a 300 sq meter park with the Palácio Araguaia, the state government building, in its center. Most services you'll need are within a block of Praça dos Girassóis, either on the main east-west axis, Avenida Juscelino Kubitschek, known as 'Jota-Ka' (JK), or the main north-south axis Avenida Teotônio Segurado.

Most Palmas addresses are based on *quadra* (block) numbers. Blocks average 600 sq meters and are divided into *conjuntos,* which are separated by ruas and subdivided into *lotes*. The quadra numbering system was recently changed, and the new numbers are given here.

For tourist information you could try the state tourism secretariat, Setur (☎ 218-2310), in Quadra 104-S facing the southeast corner of Praça dos Girassóis. Banks with ATMs abound on Avenida JK in the block east of Praça dos Girassóis. You can change cash dollars and traveler's checks at Banco do Brasil here.

Bananal Ecotour (☎ 215-4333, travel@ bananalecotour.com.br, Quadra 103-S, Conjunto 03, Rua SO 11, Lote 28), is the best agency for trips to almost any of the attractions of Tocantins. It's the ecotourism arm of the dynamic Ecológica institute, which is also involved in a range of projects, including carbon sequestration research, plant nurseries, reforestation, and community environmental education. See the Web site: www.bananalecotour.com.br.

Places to Stay & Eat
There are no true budget hotels anywhere near the city center. The following four are all on or just off Avenida JK in the block west of Praça dos Girassóis and have rooms with bath. Prices include breakfast.

Hotel Brasília (☎ 215-2707, Avenida JK, Quadra 103-N, Conjunto 1, Lote 20) is plain but adequate. Singles/doubles with fan are US$12/18, with air-con US$16/24. Better is the *Alvorada Hotel (☎ 215-3401, Quadra 103-N, Conjunto 2, Rua NO 1, Lotes 20 & 21),* a block north of Avenida JK, charging US$14/20 with fan and US$20/26 with air-conditioning. The upstairs rooms are best. *Hotel Victória Plaza (☎ 215-2808, fax 215-2858, Avenida JK, Quadra 103-S, Conjunto 1, Lote 11A)* has good rooms for US$42/54, and its breakfast is substantial. *Hotel dos Buritis (☎ 215-1936, Avenida JK, Quadra 103-N, Conjunto 1, Lotes 4-6)* is of similar standard, charging US$36/48. Rooms upstairs are best, and there's a nice pool area.

An excellent choice at an in-between price, though 1km south of Praça dos Girassóis on Avenida Teotônio Segurado, is the friendly *Hotel Casa Grande (☎ 215-1713, hotelcg@terra.com.br, Quadra 201-S, Conjunto 1, Lote 1)*. Clean air-con rooms are US$30/36, and there's a decent pool.

The *Palmas Shopping* mall, immediately south of Praça dos Girassóis, has a food court with a dozen fairly economical eateries. *Saladas & Grelhados* will combine a grill and a salad for around US$7, and there are several per-kilo spots.

The open-air *Cabana do Sol (Quadra 103-S, Conjunto 2, Lote 40)*, just off Avenida NS-1, half a block from Praça dos Girassóis, does an excellent spread of carne do sol plus side dishes at US$10.50 for two people, or just US$13 for three or four. For lighter eats head to one of the *botecos*, beer bars with tasty tira-gostos such as frango a passarinho (fried bread-crumbed chicken chunks). One, with live music, is *Frutas da Terra*, facing the east side of Praça dos Girassóis; another is *Pirraca Bar* on Avenida JK, 150m west of Praça dos Girassóis.

Getting There & Around

A new airport was due to open in 2001, 14km south of the center. TAM (☎ 216-1969) and Nordeste (☎ 0800-992004) both fly daily to/from Brasília. TAM also serves Belém.

A new bus station, too, was opening in 2001, in Quadra 1212-S, an inconvenient 10km southeast of the center. Destinations include Alto Paraíso do Goiás (US$16.50, seven hours, one daily), Belém (US$49, 20 hours, one or more daily), Brasília (US$34, 14 hours, one daily), Goiânia (US$25, 13 hours, three daily), Gurupi (US$9, four hours, three or more daily), Natividade (US$7.50, three to four hours, three daily) and Paraíso do Tocantins (US$1.50, one to 1½ hours, 16 daily). There are also daily buses to Fortaleza, Rio de Janeiro, Salvador and São Luís. More frequent buses to Belém, Brasília, Gurupi and Goiânia go from Paraíso do Tocantins.

A taxi from the new airport to the center will be about US$20, and from the new bus

station about US$15. City buses will certainly link the bus station, at least, with the center.

AROUND PALMAS
Taquarussú

The green Serra do Carmo around this pleasant small valley town, 30km southeast of Palmas, is studded with beautiful waterfalls. A 1.5km unsignposted path to the 58m Roncador and 40m Macaco falls starts from a lookout point 2.5km from Taquarussú on the Buritirana road. A good guide to these falls, who can take you abseiling, is the friendly Andrey Luciano (☎ 0xx63-216-2234 in Palmas, or contact him through Bananal Ecotour there). Andrey has a cute house in Taquarussú, available for accommodations, and Bananal Ecotour is building a rural pousada nearby.

You can reach Taquarussú by Palmas city buses from stops near Praça dos Girassóis.

Paraíso do Tocantins
☎ 0xx63 • pop 34,000

This town 70km west of Palmas is on the Brasília-Belém Hwy BR-153 and is a bit of a transportation hub. If you need a room,

AROUND PALMAS

head for **Hotel Triangulo** (☎ 602-2330, Rua Alfredo Nascer 941), opposite the bus station, charging from US$5.50/8 to US$10.50/16.50 for singles/doubles. The better **Fernando's Hotel** (☎ 602-6100, Avenida Transbrasiliana 1416) is on the main highway and charges US$17/25.

Buses from the station in Paraíso (☎ 602-6644) on Rua Alfredo Nascer include at least 10 daily to Goiânia (US$24, 13 hours), eight to Brasília (US$32, 14 hours), four to Belém (US$43, 18 hours) and 16 to Palmas (US$1.50, one to 1½ hours).

Jalapão

Jalapão is a unique 34,000 sq km area in far eastern Tocantins, combining cerrado vegetation, hills, caves, crystalline rivers and springs, 40m-high sand dunes, waterfalls, freshwater bathing spots, odd rock formations, quite a range of wildlife – including anteaters, armadillos, macaws and rheas – and very few people indeed. The season to explore Jalapão is the dry season from June to September. You need three days from Palmas (preferably four) and a vehicle (4WD if at all possible), and a guide is highly advisable. Bananal Ecotour (see Information in the Palmas section earlier in this chapter) offers trips, usually led by Andrey Luciano (see the Taquarussú section, earlier), who is probably the most experienced and best equipped Jalapão guide. A four-day/three-night trip for up to four people costs around US$1000.

A trip with Andrey is great for your language skills, for he's adept at communicating with people who think they know hardly any Portuguese. Another activity option in Jalapão is rafting: Bananal Ecotour offers trips.

RIO ARAGUAIA & ILHA DO BANANAL

The Rio Araguaia rises in the southwest of Goiás state and flows 1600km northward along the western boundaries of Goiás and Tocantins before joining the Rio Tocantins near Marabá. About 650km from its source the Araguaia bifurcates, the lesser (eastern) branch being known as the Rio Javaés. The

Javaés rejoins the main river some 350km north, and the 19,000 sq km island thus formed, the Ilha do Bananal, is the world's biggest river island.

This section covers the middle stretch of the Araguaia, from just north of the Ilha do Bananal upstream to Aruanã in Goiás. You can also access the river farther south via Barra do Garças in Mato Grosso state (see the Mato Grosso & Mato Grosso do Sul chapter).

Things to See & Do

Ecotourism, marvelous fishing, river beaches and visits to Indian communities are among the reasons to make the effort of getting to the Araguaia. For the most part the river is not very easily accessible, but organized tours help.

The region attracts Brazilian holiday-makers during the dry season (June to September) when the receding waters uncover white riverbank beaches. Many camp on the banks of the river. Peter Fleming, in his excellent and hilarious book *Brazilian Adventure*, describes an excursion in this region undertaken in an attempt to discover what had happened to the disappeared explorer Colonel Fawcett.

The Araguaia around Ilha do Bananal and upstream to Aruanã offers some of the best freshwater fishing in the world. During the May to October fishing season, fish such as tucunaré (peacock bass), pintado, pirarucu and pacu are there for the taking. You can apply for a fishing license at any Banco do Brasil in the region.

If you're serious about fishing and have the money, there are boat-hotel tours from Aruanã on which you sail around the Ilha do Bananal. The boats carry freezers, and Brazilian participants take home huge quantities of fish. In Aruanã, contact the Associação dos Barqueiros de Aruanã (☎ 0xx62-376-1436), on Praça Couto Magalhes; in Barra do Garças, Aventur (☎ 0xx65-401-1709, aventur@continet.psi.br); in Goiânia, Turisplan Turismo (☎ 0xx62-224-1941), Rua 8 No 388; in Brasília, Ecoturismo Expedicões (☎ 0xx61-347-5274), SQN 116, Bloco H, Sala 309.

A cheaper option is to take a bus from Barra do Garças to São Felix do Araguaia, which is opposite the Ilha do Bananal itself, and hire a boat there or contact Bananal Tur (☎ 0xx65-522-1746) for tour options.

Ilha do Bananal

This island in the middle of a river is so big that it has its own 250km-long rivers within it! Three ecosystems – rainforest, cerrado and wetland – converge here, and it's a very good area indeed for birdwatching, with plenty of other wildlife too. About 82% of the island is cerrado, 18% rainforest, and 75% is flooded during the high-water season (which peaks about March).

Some 3500 indigenous people inhabit the island – chiefly the Karajás and Javaés tribes – some of whom produce skillfully painted pottery figurines and neatly carved wooden animals. Most of the island is *terra indígena* (indigenous territory). An area of 5623 sq km in the north and northeast forms the Parque Nacional do Araguaia, but the Indians occupied this too in 2000 after falling out with IBAMA, the government environmental agency.

Centro Canguçu (BIRC) The Centro de Pesquisas Canguçu (Canguçu Research Center), also known as Bananal Island Research Center (BIRC), is both one of Brazil's most beautiful and comfortable ecolodges and a research center for the Palmas-based Ecológica institute. A chief goal of Ecológica's many projects is to preserve 2000 sq km of virgin tropical rainforest on the Ilha do Bananal and in the Parque Estadual Cantão to its north.

Centro Canguçu, a marvelous, rambling, stilt-built wooden construction, stands on the east bank of the Rio Javaés facing the northeastern Ilha do Bananal. It's 220km from Palmas, of which about 100km is by dirt road (in good condition).

A standard three-day, two-night eco-touristic visit here includes forest walks, night-time alligator spotting, boat trips, visits to a freshwater turtle rescue program and an optional visit to the Javaé Indian village of Boto Velho (three hours up the

river). The birding is great, and mammals inhabiting the lodge area – many are nocturnal – include jaguars, pumas, margays, tapirs, brocket deer, crab-eating raccoons and crab-eating fox. Among the most regularly seen river animals are pink and gray dolphins, black caimans and giant river turtles. June to August is best for bird and animal observation and is also when the river beaches are uncovered.

Tapirs are found on this island.

The rooms in the lodge are comfortable (some are very large), and the food – as long as Rosana, the manager/chef with a degree in nutrition, is on hand – is undoubtedly the best you will taste in Brazil.

Visits can be organized through Bananal Ecotour (see Information in the Palmas section) or through Focus Tours in the US (see Organized Tours in the Natural Brazil special section). The cost through Bananal Ecotour is US$85 per person per day, plus transfer. An Ecológica vehicle goes from Palmas about three times a week and can normally carry a few visitors for US$10 to US$15 each.

Boto Velho Boto Velho is a Javaé Indian village on the eastern shore of the Ilha do Bananal that receives a trickle of visitors. It has an artisan center, and Ecológica institute is helping to start an ecotourism program with indigenous guides. Contact Ecológica (see Information in the Palmas section) to organize a visit. Unless you're going from the Centro Canguçu, access to Boto Velho is from Barreira da Cruz, the fazenda on the opposite bank of the Rio

Javaés. Barreira da Cruz is 60km by good dirt road from Lagoa da Confusão.

Lagoa da Confusão This small town (☎ 0xx63, population 3400), set beside a 15-sq-km lake in a rural area east of the Ilha do Bananal, is a popular regional tourist spot, with a year-round sandy beach. The lake has a protruding rock near the far shore: Some say the town's name ('Lake of Confusion') comes from disagreement over whether the rock moves around the lake!

The Secretaria Municipal de Turismo (☎ 364-1148) has an information office opposite the pier, open daily.

Hotel Da Pedra (Avenida Vitorino Panta s/n), on the main road opposite the gas station, has primitive quartos from US$7 to US$10. *Pousada Lady (☎ 364-1118, Avenida Raimundo F Sousa 208)*, on the waterfront, has clean apartamentos for US$16 with fan or US$26 with air-conditioning. Room prices may rise when Lagoa gets busy during Carnaval, Easter week and summer.

Hotel Lagoa da Ilha Praia Clube (☎ 364-1110, Rua Neuza Ribeiro s/n), on the west edge of town, has a large pool in grassy gardens and its own lake beach. Clean, sizable, air-conditioned doubles go for US$59 on Saturday or Sunday and US$36 other days.

Buses to Lagoa da Confusão leave from Paraíso do Tocantins (US$6, two hours) at 3:30 pm and from Gurupi, on Hwy BR-153 in southern Tocantins, at 2:30 and 6 pm (US$6 to US$8, three hours).

São Felix do Araguaia In Mato Grosso state, São Felix (☎ 0xx65, population 6000) is near the western shore of Ilha do Bananal. In July, the town may well be flooded with local tourists looking to catch some rays.

The cheap lodging option is *Hotel Xavantes (☎ 522-1305, Avenida Severiano Neves 391)*, where singles/doubles cost US$16/24. A couple of upmarket hotels along the river cater for fishing tours. *Pousada Recanto do Sossego (☎ 522-1655, Avenida Porto da Suiá, Lago dos Ingleses)* is a reasonable option 2km from town. Apartamentos cost US$30/60, with fishing

gear thrown in. *Pousada Kuryala (☎ 215-1313)* is a 30-minute boat trip along the river (also accessible by road from June to November). It's built on stilts, with apartamentos at US$100/200 for full board, again with fishing equipment included. The best restaurant in town is *Botu's*, alongside the river on Avenida Araguaia.

You can arrange boat trips along the river and to Ilha do Bananal with fishing boat owners and locals along the waterfront on Avenida Araguaia.

Sete (☎ 0800-627777) is an air-taxi service that also operates scheduled flights to São Felix from Palmas (US$200 one-way) and Gurupi (US$160). Air taxis fly from Goiânia, Brasília and Barra do Garças airports. From Barra do Garças there are also buses; but it's a hot, dusty, 14-hour ride (see the Mato Grosso & Mato Grosso do Sul chapter).

Aruanã

☎ 0xx62 • postcode 76710-000 • pop 3800

Aruanã, in Goiás state 318km northwest of Goiânia, has campgrounds and several mid-range hotels. *Acampamento do Sol (☎ 225-3727)*, a 15-minute boat ride from town, has small cabins for US$28 per person, with meals included. *Hotel Araguaia (☎ 376-1251, Praça Couto Magalhães 53)*, in front of the port, charges $US36/50 for singles/doubles. The best restaurant is *Estrada do Sol (Rua Sebastião Rosário 40)*.

In summer, boat excursions run along the river to Ilha Redonda, Ilha Cavalo and Lago Rico from the port. For information about more ambitious river trips, contact the Associaçao dos Barqueiros de Aruanã (☎ 376-1436) on Praça Couto Magalhães.

It's easiest to reach Aruanã from Goiás: Buses run both from Goiânia (310km) and Goiás Velho.

NATIVIDADE

☎ 0xx63 • postcode 77370-000 • pop 6200

The charming little town of Natividade is 230km from Palmas in southeast Tocantins, in a valley beneath the green and wooded Serra Geral. Natividade is Tocantins' oldest town, founded in 1734. Portuguese and their African slaves had come to the Serra Geral in a minor gold rush in the 1720s. When the gold gave out they moved down the hill and turned to cattle herding.

Things to See & Do

The cobbled streets and prettily painted, one-story, tile-roofed, 18th and 19th century houses of Natividade's historic center are protected as part of the national historic heritage. The most evocative building is the tall stone **Igreja NS do Rosário dos Pretos**, known as the Igreja dos Escravos (Slaves' Church). Built in 1828 by slaves (who were not allowed to use the whites' church), this church stands roofless. Some say its construction was never completed.

The **Museu Municipal**, in the old prison on Praça Leopoldo de Bulhões, includes a tree trunk to which slaves were tied for whipping. Half a kilometer down a side street from this praça – and reputedly connected to it by a tunnel – are the **Poções**, a series of small waterfalls and refreshing natural bathing pools. From the Poções a trail leads up the Serra Geral to the remains of **São Luiz**, the original settlement of the 1720s gold prospectors. Children from the town will lead you up there for a dollar or two; you should allow a few hours for the outing.

A famous local spiritual medium, **Dona Romana**, awaits the end of the world amid a garden of her own fantastic sculpture, 1.5km north along Hwy TO-280 toward Dianópolis from the Trevo Norte junction at the north end of town. Dona Romana will cleanse your spirit if you take along some *pinga (cachaça)* – she mixes it with herbal potions and prays for bad spirits to be released as you drink. Or take candles and she'll place them around you and pray for the evil to depart. Or you can just talk with her and she'll walk you through the garden and tell

you about the *ligações* (connections) she has experienced and about what's going to happen when the Earth's axis tilts....

About 4km from town in the same direction are the **Cachoeiras do Paraíso**, another series of natural bathing pools (dry from July to September).

Organized Tours

There are several trained guides in town. Try Felizberta at the Hotel Serra Geral. She charges US$33 per group for a full day's tour of all the sights and experiences mentioned above, or US$16.50 if you omit the walk to São Luiz.

Places to Stay & Eat

Small pousadas in the historic center, such as *Hotel Brazão* on Rua Deocleciano Nunes and *Hotel July* on Rua 7 de Setembro, charge around US$3/6 for plain single/ double quartos and US$11/15 for apartamentos. *Hotel Serra Geral* (☎/fax 372-1160), 1.7km north of the center and 300m before the Trevo Norte, has decent air-con apartamentos for US$15/22.50. You can eat next door at the *Churrascaria de Ouro*. There are a few self-service eateries in the center.

Getting There & Away

Natividade is on the best road between Palmas and Brasília (an eight-hour drive along much better surfaces than Hwy BR-153), a route which will also take you past Parque Nacional da Chapada dos Veadeiros in Goiás.

Three daily buses run to Natividade from Palmas (US$7.50, three to four hours) and two from Gurupi (6 and 11 am). There are also daily buses to/from Lençóis, Salvador, Brasília and Goiânia.

Amazonas & Roraima

The state of Amazonas covers most of the western Amazonian River basin, an area of 1.58 million sq km, and is Brazil's largest state. The Amazon flows eastward across approximately the middle of the state from the triple frontier where Brazil, Peru and Colombia all come together, meeting one of its major tributaries, the Rio Negro, a few kilometers from the state's largest city, Manaus. Pico da Neblina (3014m), Brazil's highest peak, stands on Amazonas' northern border with Venezuela. The small state of Roraima is tucked into northeastern Amazonas, bordering Venezuela and Guyana. The only long-distance road link out of Manaus is Hwy BR-174, which heads north into Roraima, crossing the equator, then heads on to Venezuela and the Caribbean Sea.

Highlights

- Observing the plentiful floodplain wildlife at the Mamirauá Reserve
- Exploring the little known Rio Javari, along the Peruvian border
- Taking riverboat trips on the Amazon
- Engaging in close encounters with the giant pirarucu in the Museu de Ciências Naturais in Manaus
- Staying in jungle lodges on the beautiful lakes outside Manaus

Amazonas

Half of Amazonas' 2.8 million inhabitants live in the metropolis of Manaus. The rest are scattered in small and medium-sized villages and towns along the state's myriad rivers. Remote and far from fully explored, this state harbors more of the great Amazon rainforest and more indigenous people than any other in Brazil. With a few exceptions – chiefly the Manaus area and close to the Solimões, Amazonas and Madeira Rivers – the forests are relatively intact, and opportunities for jungle experiences and wildlife spotting are at their most abundant here. Amazonas also has fewer kilometers of paved road than almost any other state, so travel here is chiefly a choice between airplane and boat. The Rio Madeira, on which you can reach Porto Velho, the capital of Rondônia state, by boat from Manaus, is the main river transportation route after the Solimões-Amazonas.

Most of Amazonas state is one hour behind Brasília time. The area west of a line drawn southeast from Tabatinga on the Colombian border to Porto Acre in eastern Acre state is two hours behind Brasília time.

MANAUS
☎ 0xx92 • postcode 78900-000
• pop 1.4 million

Manaus stands on the north bank of the Rio Negro, 10km upstream from the Negro's confluence with the Solimões, beyond which the mighty combined river is called the Rio Amazonas. The city is an international port some 1500km from the mouth of the Amazonas – and only 40m to 80m above sea level. Upstream, it's 1500km to Leticia, Colombia, and 1900km to Iquitos, Peru.

The city itself is sweaty and not very clean and has limited appeal, and the flora and fauna have been despoiled for some distance around it. Many travelers use Manaus only for a brief stopover before making excursions far beyond it, where it is still possible to experience the rainforest wonders that Manaus cannot deliver.

See the Around Manaus section for information on jungle trips that you can make from here and places to stay in the surrounding area.

History

In 1669 the fortress of São José da Barra was built here by Portuguese colonizers. In 1856 the village that had grown up around the fort was renamed Manaus, after the Manaos, a tribe of Indians who lived in the Ponta Negra area (on the northwest edge of the modern city). It remained little more than a minor trading outpost populated by traders, black slaves, Indians and soldiers until the rubber boom pumped up the town.

In 1842 the American Charles Goodyear developed the vulcanization process that made natural rubber durable, and in 1890 Ireland's John Dunlop patented pneumatic rubber tires. Soon there was an unquenchable demand for rubber in the recently industrialized US and Europe, and the price of rubber on international markets soared.

In the 1880s, as Manaus abolished slavery, a feudal production system was established that locked the *seringueiros* (rubber-tappers) into a cruel serfdom. Driven from the *sertão* (countryside) by drought, and lured into the Amazon with the false promise of prosperity, they signed away their freedom to the *seringalistas* (owners of rubber-bearing forests).

The seringalistas sold goods – fishing line, knives, manioc flour, hammocks – to the seringueiros on credit and purchased the seringueiros' balls of latex. The illiteracy of the seringueiros, the brutality of the *pistoleiros* (hired guns), deliberately rigged scales, and the monopoly of sales and purchases all combined to perpetuate the seringueiros' debt and misery. The seringueiros also had to contend with loneliness, jungle fevers, Indian attacks and all manner of deprivation.

The landowners, rubber traders and bankers prospered and built palaces with their wealth. Gentlemen sent their shirts to London to be laundered, and ladies sported the latest French fashions. Manaus was the second city in Brazil (after Rio de Janeiro) to get electricity, and an opera house was built in the heart of the jungle.

Despite Brazilian efforts to protect their world rubber monopoly, Henry Wickham managed to smuggle rubber seeds from the Amazon to London. (For the story of this episode, see the History section in the Facts about Brazil chapter.) Botanists in Kew Gardens, London, grew rubber-tree seedlings and exported them to the British colonies of Ceylon and Malay, where they were planted in neat and efficient groves. Brazil's rubber monopoly was punctured, and as more Asian rubber was produced, the price of latex on the world market plummeted. By the 1920s the boom was over, and Manaus declined in importance.

During WWII, when Malay was occupied by Japan, Allied demand created a second brief rubber boom. The seringueiros became known as the 'rubber soldiers,' and 150,000 nordestinos were recruited once again to gather rubber. Rubber prices sank again after WWII, however, and have never again reached anything like boom levels.

Brazil has always feared foreign domination of the Amazon region. One of the official slogans of the military government of the 1970s was *Integrar para não entregar* (Integrate or give it away). Governments have made a determined attempt to consolidate Brazilian control of Amazonia by cutting roads through the jungle and colonizing the interior.

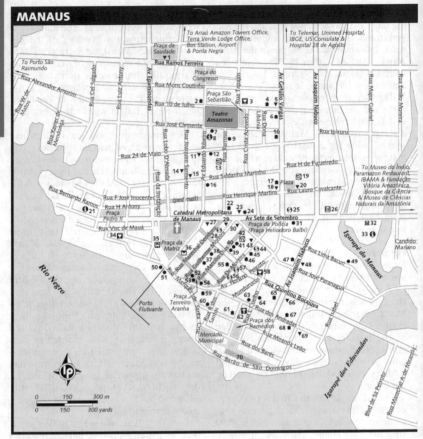

MANAUS

They have also made Manaus an industrial city. In 1967 Brazil established a *zona franca* (low-tax zone) in Manaus to encourage manufacturing, especially of electronic consumer goods. Multinational companies, drawn by tax and tariff benefits, set up manufacturing plants, and shoppers and traders flocked from all over Brazil to buy their products, which were relatively inexpensive. Many Brazilian TVs, videos, music systems, air-conditioners and even motorcycles are made in Manaus. The zona franca imports many of its parts and materials from abroad, so it hasn't benefited the rest of Brazilian industry much, but it has certainly invigorated Manaus, which grew into one of Brazil's biggest cities by the 1990s.

Climate

Manaus, three degrees south of the equator, is hot and humid. During the rainy season (December to May), count on a brief but hard shower nearly every day; the area gets over 2m of rainfall per year. The river level varies 10m to 14m between the high-water level (March to July) and the low-water period (August to February).

Orientation

Downtown Manaus stretches from the Rio Negro to the Teatro Amazonas area, about 1km back from the waterfront. The streets nearest the main passenger port, the Porto Flutuante (Floating Dock), are crowded and fairly grungy. A little inland is an area of shopping streets known as the Zona Franca (Free Trade Zone), lined with street vendors by day and heaped with piles of garbage in the evening. This ends at Avenida Sete de Setembro, the main east-west downtown artery. Praça da Polícia (officially Praça Heliodoro Balbi), on the south side of Sete de Setembro, is a focal point. From Avenida Sete de Setembro, Avenida Eduardo Ribeiro, a fancier shopping street, heads north to the Teatro Amazonas, which tops a small rise.

Budget lodgings mostly cluster a few streets southeast of the Zona Franca. Several of the better hotels are strung along Avenida Getúlio Vargas, which heads north from Praça da Polícia.

Suburbs and slums spread far to the north, west and east. The bus station and airport are respectively 6km and 13km north of the Teatro Amazonas.

Maps Local phone books contain maps covering Manaus' outer suburbs. There are two sources of detailed topographical maps of parts of Amazonas state. One, slightly harder to reach but with a better range of maps for sale, is the army geographical service (☎ 625-1585 or ☎ 625-1717): Exército Brasileiro, Diretoria de Serviço Geográfico, 4ª Divisão de Levantamento, Avenida Marechal Bittencourt 97, Compensa I. It's about a US$6 taxi ride northwest of the city center and is open 9 am to noon Monday to Friday. You should find some maps at scales as large as 1:50,000 here. They cost US$16.50 each. The other option is IBGE, the Instituto Brasileiro de Geografia e Estatística (☎ 633-2433), Rua Afonso Pena 38. Its maps are cheaper (US$6.50) but it stocks few at scales bigger than 1:250,000.

Information

Tourist Offices The Amazonas state tourism secretariat runs tourist information offices at the airport, open from 7 am to 11 pm daily (☎ 652-1120); in the Centro de Atendimento ao Turista (Tourist Assistance Center) on Avenida Eduardo Ribeiro, open 9 am to 6 pm Monday to Friday, 9 am to 2 pm Saturday and 8 am to 1 pm Sunday (☎ 231-1998); and at its head office behind the Palácio Rio Negro, Avenida Sete de Setembro 1546, open 8 am to 5 pm Monday to Friday (☎ 633-2850). A mobile information trailer also pops up here and there from time to time. The offices have information on jungle lodges and tour operators as well as

Manaus itself. At all of them there's usually someone who speaks English.

The Centro de Atendimento ao Turista also includes a police station, bookshop-café, Internet service and crafts shop.

The Manaus city tourist office, Manaustur (☎ 622-4948), Avenida Sete de Setembro 157, is open 8 am to 6 pm Monday to Friday.

Money Amazônia Turismo, at Rua Dr Moreira 88, gives good rates for US dollars cash and traveler's checks. It's open 9 am to 5:30 pm Monday to Friday, 9 am to noon Saturday. Training, Rua Dr Moreira 60, gives a good rate too but only exchanges cash (open 8:30 am to 6 pm Monday to Friday, 8:30 am to 2 pm Saturday). Cortez Câmbio e Turismo, Avenida Sete de Setembro 1199, is a convenient and easy place to change cash and (at a slightly lower rate) traveler's checks (open 9 am to 5:30 pm Monday to Friday, 9 am to 12:30 pm Saturday).

Banco do Brasil, at Rua Guilherme Moreira 315, exchanges cash and traveler's checks 9 am to 3 pm Monday to Friday; go up to the 3rd floor, where the Western Union international money transfer service is also available. This bank's ATMs will sometimes grant cash to foreign-issued Visa cards, as will HSBC, Rua Dr Moreira 226, for MasterCard, Maestro, Cirrus and American Express cards.

At the airport, you might have success with a Cirrus, MasterCard, Maestro or American Express card in the Banco 24 Horas ATM just outside the terminal building.

The American Express representative is Selvatur (☎ 622-2577) on Praça Tenreiro Aranha.

Post & Communications The main post office, Rua Marechal Deodoro 117, is open 9 am to 5 pm Monday to Friday and 8 am to noon on Saturday.

Discover Internet, Rua Marcílio Dias 304, offers phone calls via the Internet to many countries including the US, Australia and much of Europe for US$0.40 a minute. You can call to any phone by this method. It's open 9 am to 7 pm Monday to Friday, 9 am to 3:30 pm Saturday.

You can make international calls on ordinary card pay phones inside Telemar, Avenida Getúlio Vargas 950 (open 7 am to 8 pm daily), and at the phones inside the south end of the Mercado Municipal and inside the east end of the airport terminal.

Internet Cyber City, Avenida Getúlio Vargas 188/04, offers Internet access for US$2.25 an hour in comfortable surroundings 8:30 am to 10 pm Monday to Saturday. Discover Internet offers Internet access for US$2.75 an hour. Magicopia, Rua Barroso 279 near the Teatro Amazonas, charges US$2 an hour and is open 8 am to 8 pm Monday to Friday and 8 am to noon Saturday. There's also Internet access in the airport departures lounge for US$3.50 an hour.

Internet Resources The Web site of the Amazonas state culture and tourism secretariat, www.visitamazonas.com.br, is in English as well as Portuguese and is reasonably informative on Manaus and trips out from it. The site www.manausonline.com is in Portuguese only but can still be useful for tourist and what's-on information.

Useful Organizations The Manaus office of FUNAI (☎ 236-3681), the government Indian agency, is at Rua Recife 2305 in the suburb of Adrianópolis. COIAB (☎ 233-0548, coica-dh@buriti.com.br), an important coordinating body for independent Indian organizations, is at Avenida Ayrão 235, in the Presidente Vargas neighborhood, a couple of kilometers north of the center.

Medical Services Unimed (☎ 633-4431), Avenida Japurá 241, is one of the best private hospitals in the city. The Hospital 28 de Agosto (☎ 236-0326), Rua Recife 1581, in Adrianópolis 3km north of the center, is the main public general hospital and has an emergencies section. The Instituto de Medicina Tropical de Manaus (☎ 656-1441) is at Avenida Pedro Teixeira 25.

Emergency Call ☎ 190 for the police and ☎ 192 for an ambulance. There's a police station at the Centro de Atendimento ao

Turista (see Tourist Offices earlier in this section).

Dangers & Annoyances See the Jungle Trips section, later, for a warning on touts who approach new arrivals at the airport.

Theft is a risk at rock-bottom hotels. Duplicate keys have sometimes been used to gain access to rooms. After 11 pm steer clear of the port area and take care if you go through Praça da Matriz.

For more tips, see the Dangers & Annoyances section of the Facts for the Visitor chapter.

Teatro Amazonas

Manaus' famous opera house, the Teatro Amazonas (☎ 622-2420), was designed in eclectic neoclassical style by engineers from Lisbon and a team of interior designers at the height of the rubber boom, and opened in 1896. More than any other building associated with the administration of Mayor Eduardo Ribeiro, this beautiful theater symbolizes the opulence that once was Manaus. The artists and most of the materials (Italian marble and glass, Scottish cast iron) were imported from Europe. The wood is Brazilian but even some of that was sent to Europe to be carved. One truly homespun feature was the roadway outside the entrance; it is made of rubber, so that late-arriving carriages wouldn't create too much noise.

The Teatro Amazonas is open for interesting guided tours (available in English) from 9 am to 4 pm daily except Sunday (US$3.50). The theater has been restored four times (most recently in 1990) and stages concerts (classical and popular), opera, theater and dance events all year, with tickets rarely costing more than US$6.50.

Porto Flutuante & Alfândega

The Porto Flutuante (Floating Dock) is where you'll disembark if you come to Manaus by boat. Inaugurated in 1902 and designed by the British, it was considered a technical marvel because it rises and falls with seasonal water levels, which can vary as much as 14m (annual high-water points are marked on the wall beside the bridge leading to the dock). It's quite a scene and well worth a look even if you're not taking a boat; you can watch the river craft being loaded with produce and the swarms of people traveling on them.

The Alfândega (Customhouse) beside the Porto Flutuante's entrance dates from 1906. It was imported from the UK in prefabricated blocks. You can visit 9 am to noon and 2 to 5 pm Monday to Friday (free).

Mercado Municipal

This imposing cast-iron city market building opened in 1882, a copy in miniature of Paris' famed Les Halles market. Although the Art Nouveau ironwork was imported from Europe, the place has acquired Amazonian character. In and around the market, you can purchase some Indian crafts and provisions for jungle trips: strange fruits, odd vegetables, several varieties of cookies and crackers, sacks of beans and rice, lanterns, rope, hats of leather, palm or cloth, and exotic herbal and traditional medicines. Much more food however is now sold at the newer and smellier Feira do Produtor market a little farther east.

Palácio Rio Negro

This handsome mansion (☎ 232-4450) at Avenida Sete de Setembro 1546 was built in the early 20th century as a home for an eccentric German rubber baron, Waldemar Scholz. In 1918 Amazonas state bought it to serve as the state government seat, then in the 1990s it was converted into a cultural center, which is well worth visiting. The main house, with its period decor, hosts concerts and temporary art exhibits and has a good coffee shop. Outlying buildings contain the **Pinacoteca de Amazonas** (the state art gallery), a museum of coins, a sound-and-image library and a tourist office. A few typical traditional regional buildings and boats are displayed in the igarapé-side garden.

Except for the tourist office, it's all open 10 am to 5 pm Tuesday to Friday, and 4 to 9 pm Saturday and Sunday (free). Free guided tours (sometimes available in English) are given to some parts.

Museu do Homem do Norte

The Museum of Northern Man (☎ 232-5373), at Avenida Sete de Setembro 1385, is an ethnology and anthropology museum dedicated to the lifestyle of the people of northern Brazil, especially the riverbank-dwelling *caboclos* (people of mixed Indian and colonist ancestry). Most of the museum has been closed for renovations recently, but it was hoped to reopen in 2001. The collection includes an interesting array of Indian weapons, including the vicious *furador de olhos* (eye piercer). The museum is open 8 am to noon and 1 to 5 pm, Monday to Friday.

Museu do Índio

This interesting museum, run by Salesian nuns, displays ceramics, featherwork, artisanry, musical and hunting instruments, food preparation and fishing tools and traditional medicine objects of the Indian tribes of the northwest of the state, where the nuns operate as missionaries. Explanatory material is in Portuguese, English and German. There is also a shop selling Indian handicrafts. The museum (☎ 234-1422), Rua Duque de Caxias 356, is open 8 am to noon and 2 to 5 pm Monday to Friday, 8 am to noon Saturday (US$2.75). It's a bit of a walk east from the center along Avenida Sete de Setembro (about 1km), but there are a few interesting examples of rubber-boom architecture along the way, and views of precarious and resourceful stilt houses along the river inlets. Alternatively, bus No 606 from Avenida Floriano Peixoto opposite Praça da Policia stops almost outside the museum door (US$0.70).

Bosque da Ciência

The Bosque da Ciência (Forest of Science) is a 130,000 sq m plot of rainforest within the city, attached to the Instituto Nacional de Pesquisas da Amazônia (INPA; National Institute of Amazonia Research). The Bosque is intended to spread awareness of INPA's research, promote environmental education and provide a badly needed leisure area for Manaus. On view in fairly small enclosures are animals – such as giant otters, manatees and alligators – being studied by INPA scientists. (Avoid feeding time in the alligator zone if you don't want to see live mice sacrificed!) Sloths, agouti, tree-dwelling anteaters, monkeys and pied bareface tamarins supposedly roam free, but you'll probably be lucky to see any except the ground-dwelling agouti. An exhibit on bees points out that one effect of deforestation is destruction of bee habitats, which in turn reduces plant pollination. Without bees to pollinate them, many Amazonian plants would die out within a couple of generations.

Also within the Bosque is the Casa da Ciência, an exhibit about INPA's research in fields such as aquatic mammals, medicinal plants, entomology and its medicinal and agricultural applications, forest management and the negative effects of hydroelectric projects and gold prospecting.

The Bosque da Ciência is open 9 to 11 am and 2 to 5 pm Tuesday to Sunday; if you're in by 11 am, you can stay on during the lunch break. Admission is US$2.50. The entrance is on Rua Otávio Cabral in the Petrópolis district, 5km northeast of central Manaus. Bus No 519 from Praça da Matriz, or from Avenida Floriano Peixoto opposite Praça da Policia, takes about 20 minutes and stops just outside.

INPA itself (☎ 643-3300) is around the corner at Avenida André Araújo 2936. This federal institute, with more than 700 staff, manages biological reserves and experimental stations in the jungle and country around Manaus, and it carries out scientific and technological research for the environmental conservation and sustainable development of the Amazon region. INPA's Web site is at www.inpa.gov.br.

Museu de Ciências Naturais da Amazônia

The Amazonia Natural Sciences Museum (☎ 644-2799), at Estrada Belém s/n in Colônia Cachoeira Grande in the Aleixo district, has an extensive exhibit of stuffed

Street market, Manaus

Home on the Amazon River, Amazonas

AIDS awareness poster, Belém

A warm day on the Rio Amazonas

Serving up fried bananas in Manaus

fish, lovely butterflies and some unnervingly large beetles and spiders from the region, with descriptions in English, Portuguese and Japanese. A small aquarium contains several beautiful, 2m-long pirarucu fish. The museum shop sells some Indian crafts. Open 9 am to 5 pm Monday to Saturday, the museum is somewhat out of the way (8km from the center), but it's worth the trip. Admission is US$4.50 (US$2.25 with a student card).

You can get close by bus No 519 (the same bus that goes to the Bosque da Ciência, making it easy enough to combine the two visits). Tell the conductor you're going to the museum, and you should end up alighting opposite the Aços da Amazônia plant on Rua Raimundo A Borges in the Conjunto Petro housing development, about 10 minutes from the Bosque da Ciência. Walk on down Rua Raimundo A Borges and follow 'Museu' signs to the museum (about 15 minutes' walk).

Parque do Mindú

This park, which lies 6km north-northeast of the center, occupies 330,000 sq m of forest within the urban area of Manaus. It's one of the last refuges of the pied bareface tamarin, a small primate threatened with extinction. The park has trails, elevated walkways, an orchid house, a library and a cute amphitheater. It's open 8 am to 5 pm Tuesday to Sunday (free). The entrance is on Avenida Perimetral in the Parque Dez district. You can get there in about 30 minutes by taking bus No 423 or 433 from Praça Matriz.

Ponta Negra

Praia de Ponta Negra, a strip of river beach on the edge of Manaus 13km northwest of the center, is a popular weekend hangout. It has many restaurants and bars and a riverbank amphitheater. The best time to go to the beach is between September and December (sometimes as early as July), when the waters recede, and locals sunbathe and play soccer on the beach. After March the high waters flood the sand and cleanse the beach for the following season. While here you can pop into the luxury Hotel Tropical

(see Places to Stay). From Praça da Matriz or the corner of Avenida Floriano Peixoto and Rua Quintino Bocaiúva, take the No 120 'Ponta Negra Centro' bus (30 minutes). On the way you will see the contrast of *favelas* (slums) with fenced residential compounds, and the beginnings of high-rise, beachfront development.

Festival Folclórico do Amazonas

This June festival features a wide variety of regional folklore performances, including rehearsals of the Parintins *Boi-Bumbá* teams (see the Parintins section, later, in this chapter). The festival culminates on June 29 with the Procissão Fluvial de São Pedro (St Peter River Procession), when hundreds of riverboats parade on the Rio Negro before Manaus to honor the patron saint of fishers.

Places to Stay

For information on jungle lodge accommodations outside the city, see the Around Manaus section, later in the chapter.

Budget There's plenty of cheap lodging in Manaus, ranging from grungy to reasonable. The main cluster of respectable budget hotels is along and just off Rua dos Andradas. One of the better ones is *Hotel Ideal* (☎ 622-0038, Rua dos Andradas 491), where bright air-conditioned apartamentos, some with a little balcony, cost US$13/17 for singles/doubles. Dingier but clean apartamentos with fan are US$8.50/13, while *luxe* rooms are US$18.50/23, all including breakfast. *Hotel Rio Branco* (☎ 233-4019, Rua dos Andradas 484), across the street, is a bit less inviting but still respectable. Small, dark apartamentos with fan are US$8/12. Air-conditioned apartamentos cost US$11.50/16. There are also single quartos with fan for US$6.50, and triple quartos for US$18 (fan) and US$24 (air-con). Prices include a simple breakfast.

Pensão Sulista (☎ 234-5814, Avenida Joaquim Nabuco 347) is another decent choice. Small but clean single/double quartos with fan, downstairs, cost US$8.50/13, while apartamentos with air-conditioning and TV, upstairs, are US$20 single or double. Breakfast is included. **Hotel Doral** (☎ 232-4102, Avenida Joaquim Nabuco 687) has musty singles/doubles for US$6.50/10 with fan, or US$10/13 air-conditioned. There are other cheapies nearby on Rua José Paranaguá but most of them double as short-stay hotels.

The **Hotel Continental** (☎ 233-3342, Rua Coronel Sergio Pessoa 189), just off Rua dos Andradas, is a good value for Manaus, with amiable staff and reasonably sized air-conditioned apartamentos for US$17/22, including a not-bad breakfast.

The rambling **Hospedaria de Turismo 10 de Julho** (☎ 232-6280, htdj@internext.com.br, Rua 10 de Julho 679) is another good choice. It's in a better area, not far from the Teatro Amazonas, and has varied clean apartamentos with air-con, TV and breakfast for US$15/18. **Hotel Brasil** (☎ 233-6575, Avenida Getúlio Vargas 657), on a busy avenue, has large, bare, clean, air-conditioned apartamentos for US$20 single or double, or US$13 if you occupy them for less than 12 hours.

Mid-Range In this range, air-conditioning, TV and breakfast are standard.

Hotel Rei Salomão (☎ 234-7374, Rua Dr Moreira 119) has single/double apartamentos for US$28/33 if you pay in cash. **Hotel Central** (☎ 622-2600, fax 622-2609, Rua Dr Moreira 202) offers pleasant apartamentos for US$44/51 downstairs and US$48/59 upstairs. A couple of doors down, **Hotel Internacional** (☎ 633-7034, fax 231-2177, Rua Dr Moreira 168) has clean, sizable rooms in decent condition for US$45/56.

Well located opposite the library, **Hotel Krystal** (☎ 233-7535, krystalhotel@internext .com.br, Rua Barroso 54) is a good value, offering clean apartamentos for US$48/59, with a great breakfast and a 20% discount often available. The 10-story **Ana Cassia Palace Hotel** (☎ 622-3637, fax 622-4812, Rua dos Andradas 14) has nice apartamentos at US$59/71. The higher ones have spectacular views, as do the top-floor restaurant and pool.

Top End
The **Hotel Manaós** (☎ 633-5744, manaos@ argo.com.br, Avenida Eduardo Ribeiro

881), well located across from the Teatro Amazonas, has a bit of old-fashioned solidity and comfort, with excellent singles/ doubles sporting thick wood cupboards and even potted plants in the bathrooms, for US$65/80 (with a 10% discount for cash payments if you stay two nights).

The **Plaza Hotel** (☎ 232-7766, plazahot@ internext.com.br, Avenida Getúlio Vargas 215) is comfortable but unspectacular, charging US$77/93. It has a restaurant. **Holiday Inn Taj Mahal** (☎/fax 633-1010, tajmahal@ internext.com.br, Avenida Getúlio Vargas 741) offers high-rise apartamentos and a view of the opera house for US$95/106.

The 601-room **Hotel Tropical** (☎ 658-5000, fax 658-5026), Manaus' premier luxury hotel, is a self-contained resort 13km northwest of the center at Ponta Negra. Singles/doubles start at US$180/203, and suites at US$414, all plus 12% taxes (but you might get a cheaper deal through a travel agency). This huge complex boasts lush gardens, its own little shopping center, a mini-zoo, travel agencies, an orchidarium, a superb giant pool and numerous sports facilities.

Places to Eat
Before taking a long river trip or foray into the jungle, have a splurge on a couple of good meals in Manaus. The local fish specialties are tucunaré, tambaqui, pirarucu and the small, spiny but tasty jaraqui, served na brasa (grilled) or caldeirada (stewed). Many of the best restaurants are a few kilometers away in the suburbs: **Paramazon Restaurant** (☎ 233-7768, Rua Santa Isabel 1176, Cachoeirinha) is recommended for good fish and other regional dishes, mainly in the US$10 region. A cab should take you there and back for around US$7.

Also recommended for fish is the simpler and more central **Galo Carijó**, opposite the corner of Rua dos Andradas and Rua Pedro Botelho. It's open for lunch only Monday to Saturday, with fish dishes costing from just US$2 to US$8. Locals like to drop in for uma cerveja estupidamente gelada (an idiotically cold beer). **Restaurante Brazeiro** (☎ 658-4686, Estrada da Ponta Negra 6720), a couple of kilometers before Praia da Ponta Negra, is a good bet for a meal on your way to or way back from the beach. Expect to spend around US$10 or US$12. On Thursday evening and Sunday lunchtime there's a *rodízio* with as much fish, meat and salads as you can manage, and there's live music and dancing from Wednesday to Saturday nights.

Popular with locals and tourists alike, *Ristorante Fiorentina (Rua José Paranaguá 44)*, on Praça da Polícia, serves a good per-kilo buffet lunch for US$11/kg, and equally good a la carte fare in the evening, with pasta for US$8 to US$10 and fish around US$13. It's open daily. At the east end of Praça da Polícia, *Confeitaria Alemá (Rua José Paranaguá 126)* offers more low-key

dining, with a reasonable per-kilo lunch for US$8/kg, and a wide range of *refeições* (main platters, US$3.50 to US$5.25) and sanduiches (US$1 to US$4.50) all day. At the west end of Praça da Polícia, *Brunella's* on Avenida Sete de Setembro is a cheap fallback for sanduiches and its lunchtime self-service *prato feito* (just US$2.25).

Most of the hotels on Avenida Getúlio Vargas have reasonable restaurants. The calm, air-conditioned coffee shop at the *Holiday Inn Taj Mahal (Avenida Getúlio Vargas 741)* does quality sanduiches for US$3 to US$7. The same hotel's rooftop *Restaurante Giratório* is a revolving restaurant overlooking the Teatro Amazonas with an international menu where you'll spend

Guaraná: Fountain of Eternal Youth

Indigenous Amazonians have drunk guaraná for hundreds of years. The Sateré-Maûé Indians believe themselves to be descended from a guaraná tree, and *çapo* of guaraná, prepared from the tree's berries, is a ritual drink for them. The berries, which resemble eyeballs, are collected before the fruit opens, dried, washed, and cooked in earth ovens. Water is added, and the guaraná is molded into black sticks, which are then dried in a smokehouse. The Maûé shave guaraná flakes from the sticks, using either the raspy tongue of the pirarucu fish or a rough stone. The flakes are then mixed into water to make the çapo.

The Maûé drink çapo of guaraná on important occasions – to affirm the life force, to cure all illness, to bring strength in times of war, and enhance fertility in times of peace. Originally their lands encompassed the vast stretch of jungle between the Madeira and Tapajós Rivers. Today the Maûe live in a small tribal territory. In late November or early December, the Festa do Guaraná is celebrated in the town of Maués (about 200km east of Manaus), in the main guaraná-cultivating area.

Guaraná is drunk by other Brazilians both in carbonated 'champagne' form and in cocktails with other liquids such as milk, syrups, liquidized peanuts or cashews or even quail eggs. The drink has a higher caffeine content than coffee.

Guaraná can – if you'll just believe it – right almost any wrong. The following were among the powers claimed for it by one enthusiastic devotee we encountered:

- increases spontaneous activity
- improves blood circulation
- combats arteriosclerosis
- maintains sexual vigor
- corrects gastrointestinal disturbances
- overcomes mental tiredness
- regulates the intestines
- cures diarrhea in children
- relieves migraines
- eases alcoholic hangovers

- regulates the functioning of the uterus, ovaries and fallopian tubes
- reduces 'menstrual colic'
- moderates the appetite without interfering with daily meals, helping in weight reduction
- helps treatment of hemorrhoids
- recomposes facial skin cells
- acts as a diuretic
- invigorates and rejuvenates

around US$10 for lunch or US$15 for dinner. On the next corner up Getúlio Vargas, the open-air *Scarola Pizzaria (Rua 10 de Julho 739)* has an unbeatable combination of good pizzas (from US$6 small to US$14 family-size), good service and good chopp. It's open 4 pm to midnight daily.

Vegetarians should head for *Filosóphicus (Avenida Sete de Setembro 752)*. This upstairs restaurant, open 11 am to about 2 pm Monday to Friday, serves vegetarian buffet for US$6/kg. *Churrascaria Búfalo (Avenida Joaquim Nabuco 628)* is decidedly non-vegetarian: In addition to gigantic steaks, it has an interesting buffet lunch for US$7.50/kg. On the same street, *Você Decide*, opposite Pensão Sulista, is a budget option with prato feito for US$2 and good-value soup for under US$1. *Restaurante Mandarim (Rua Joaquim Sarmento 221)* serves decent Chinese-style dishes for around US$4 and a daily per-kilo lunch for US$7.50/kg.

Bold palates will venture to street stalls and sample tacacá, a gummy soup made from lethal-if-not-well-boiled manioc root, lip-numbing jambu leaves and relatively innocuous dried shrimp. Tip: tacacá sem goma (without the gooey stuff) is less off-putting. Praça da Saudade has several *barracas de tacáca* (tacáca stalls) with tables and chairs, open from about 4 pm. Some of them offer other homemade dishes too, including good desserts; you can just point at what you want, and it's an economical place for an evening meal.

For dessert, there's always strange fruit to taste, including pupunha, bacaba and buriti. *Glacial* is the most popular ice-cream chain in town. It has two branches opposite each other at Avenida Getúlio Vargas 161 and 188; No 161 sells per kilo – a good way to sample flavors. Since your body will be craving liquids, try *Skina dos Sucos* (Juice Corner), which has branches on Avenida Eduardo Ribeiro and Rua Joaquim Sarmento. It serves great juices of those exotic fruits (US$1.25 for a large glass). Try guaraná, maracujá, acerola, cupuaçu or graviola. Some juice bars specialize exclusively in that all-purpose life-

force guaraná, offering it in a dizzying array of combinations with other liquids. One such bar is *Guaraná Amazônia (Rua Guilherme Moreira 395)* with drinks from US$1 to US$2. (See the boxed text 'Guaraná: Fountain of Eternal Youth.')

Entertainment

Near the opera house, *Bar do Armando (Rua 10 de Julho 593)* is a traditional rendezvous for Manaus' intellectual types and it is known for its ice-cold beer; it's open noon to midnight. *Choparia São Marcos (Rua Quintino Bocaiúva 369)*, on the noisy corner of Avenida Floriano Peixoto, is another traditional bar recommended for the best chopp and bolinhos de bacahau (fish balls, US$0.75) in town. It's open 8 am to 8 pm daily except Sunday. *Você Decide* is an open-air bar, on Avenida Joaquim Nabuco opposite Pensão Sulista, which can get a bit sleazy late at night but is frequented by some travelers.

A hot spot on Friday nights is *Tukannu's Club (☎ 658-3335, Avenida do Turismo 3156)* in the Tarumã district between the airport and Ponta Negra, where DJs play house, techno and other electronic dance music for clubbers. It opens at 10 pm (admission US$3 for men, US$1.50 for women). *Coração Blue (☎ 658-4057, Estrada de Ponta Negra 3701)*, a bit over halfway from the center to Ponta Negra, has a night for just about every Brazilian musical genre you can think of; it is open from 9 pm daily except Sunday (admission: US$3). Next door is *Hype (Estrada de Jonasa 100)* with electronic dance sounds from 10 pm Thursday to Saturday.

Turbo Serven, on Rua Vivaldo Lima west of Praça Matriz, is a gay club offering transvestite shows, video room and dark room – open from 10 pm Saturday and 8 pm Sunday (admission US$5). *Enigma (☎ 234-7985, Rua Silva Ramos 1054)* is a GLS *boate* about 1km north of the center, with mixed rhythms to dance to (from 11 pm open Thursday to Saturday).

For current bar, music and boate listings, pick up the free monthly magazine *Guia madrugad'adentro*, from tourist offices, on the Internet at www.madrugadadentro.com.br, or the 'guia rápido' pages of *A Critica* newspaper. Quite a lot of restaurants have live music. Look to tourist offices and on the Web site www.visitamazonas.com.br for calendars of events, including the many at the Teatro Amazonas and Palácio Rio Negro.

Shopping

A good place to buy Indian crafts is Artíndia, in the Pavilhão Universal on Praça Tenreiro Aranha, a prefabricated English-built cast-iron building from the rubber-boom days. It's open 7:30 am to 5 pm Monday to Friday. The shop at the Museu do Índio sells Indian crafts including some good baskets and palm-fiber hammocks.

There are many souvenir and craft shops near the Teatro Amazonas, including Artesanato da Amazônia, Rua José Clemente 500. For cloth or artificial-fiber hammocks, try Casa das Redes, on Rua Rocha dos Santos, or the street vendors around Praça Tenreiro Aranha. Prices range from about US$10 for one-person hammocks to US$20 for large double ones.

The Mercado Municipal (see that section earlier) is good for inexpensive crafts and T-shirts, cheap stuffed piranhas (US$3 to US$6) and natural medicines. The shops in the Zona Franca are useful if you need athletic shoes or something electronic. Carrefour on Avenida Eduardo Ribeiro is the biggest and best downtown supermarket.

On Sunday morning, visit the stretch of Avenida Eduardo Ribeiro north of Avenida Sete de Setembro for a street market, open from about 6 am to 1 or 2 pm. It's a chance to browse some unusual homemade crafts, soak up a relaxed atmosphere and eat inexpensive home-cooked food. Often there's an entertainment stage too.

For photographic supplies (even 400 ISO slide film), head to Foto Nascimento, at Avenida Sete de Setembro 1194.

Getting There & Away

Air The Aeroporto Internacional Eduardo Gomes (☎ 652-1212) is at Avenida Santos Dumont 1350, 13km north of the city center.

Varig and Lloyd Aéreo Boliviano (LAB) both fly weekly to/from Miami. LAB also flies to/from Santa Cruz, Bolivia, twice weekly. Aéropostal flies to/from Caracas, Venezuela, twice weekly, with connections for Miami; and Ecuatoriana flies to/from Guayaquil and Quito, Ecuador, twice weekly.

Varig, VASP, TransBrasil and TAM between them offer direct flights to 17 destinations in Brazil, with connections to many others. Varig has easily the most flights, including to/from Brasília (US$261, four daily), Rio de Janeiro (US$336, two daily), Belém (US$205, two daily), Santarém (US$130, one daily) and Tabatinga (US$184, three weekly). Other destinations served direct daily by Varig are São Luís, Fortaleza, Recife, São Paulo, Rio Branco, Porto Velho and Boa Vista. You can reach nearly all these destinations cheaper with TransBrasil (which also flies to Salvador) or VASP (which also goes to Natal and Recife).

Smaller regional airlines use the airport's separate Terminal 2, called Eduardinho, about 600m east of the main one. The busiest of these is Rico, serving about 20 large and small destinations all over northern Brazil, among them Tabatinga (US$162) three times a week. Meta flies to/from Belém and Boa Vista weekdays. Airline offices in the city include:

Aéropostal (☎ 233-8547), Rua Marcílio Dias 292

Ecuatoriana (☎ 622-3470), Avenida Sete de Setembro 993

LAB (☎ 622-3470), Avenida Sete de Setembro 993

Meta Linhas Aéreas (☎ 232-9278), Rua Barroso 352

Rico Linhas Aéreas (☎ 633-5135), Rua 24 de Maio 60

TAM (☎ 232-5936), Avenida Joaquim Nabuco 1846

TransBrasil (☎ 622-3738), Rua Guilherme Moreira 170

Varig (☎ 622-4522), Rua Marcílio Dias 284

VASP (☎ 622-3470), Avenida Sete de Setembro 993

Bus The long-distance bus station (☎ 642-5805) is 6km north of the center at Rua Recife 2784. You may be asked to show a yellow-fever certificate before traveling: if necessary, you can get the jab and card at a vaccination post in the bus station.

União Cascavel (Eucatur, ☎ 235-2411) runs five daily air-conditioned buses along the paved Hwy BR-174 to/from Boa Vista (US$33, 12 hours). One continues all the way to Santa Elena de Uairén (Venezuela) and the Venezuelan coast at Puerto de la Cruz (US$80, 33 hours).

One daily bus goes to Silves, 270km east (US$12, seven hours by mostly paved road). Several a day head to Itacoatiara, 235km east by paved road (US$8.50, five hours), and to the towns of Manacapuru, 100km southwest, and Presidente Figueiredo, 120km north.

Road travel south to Porto Velho on Hwy BR-319 has been suspended since 1991.

Boat Nearly all passenger boats arrive and depart from the Porto Flutuante, opposite the bottom of Avenida Eduardo Ribeiro. Tickets are sold at the glass-windowed office of SERPE (Serviços Portuários Especializados, ☎ 231-1236), just inside the entrance. Little information is posted, so you have to elicit times and prices verbally from the staff. They're helpful enough, but don't count on anyone being able to speak anything except Portuguese. *A Crítica* newspaper publishes a daily list of boats, departure times and fares. For most destinations, the majority of boats set off on a few fixed days of the week, though there's a chance of a boat any day to almost anywhere. Departures are usually between 3 and 6 pm. See the North introduction chapter for general tips on Amazonian boat travel.

The main routes from Manaus are down the Rio Amazonas as far as Belém; up the Rio Solimões as far as Tabatinga on the 'triple frontier' (where Brazil meets Colombia and Peru); and up the Rio Madeira (a southern tributary of the Amazonas) to Porto Velho. Boats stop at different combinations of ports along the way. The major services to Belém make about four stops – maybe Itacoatiara, Parintins, Santarém and Monte Alegre. Main ports between Manaus and Tabatinga include Tefé and Benjamin Constant; and the main ports between Manaus and Porto Velho are Manicoré and Humaitá.

A few services from the Porto Flutuante go up the Rio Purus and Rio Japurá, tributaries of the Solimões upstream of Manaus. Boats going up the Rio Negro leave from Porto São Raimundo, in the Bairro São Raimundo, an unsavory district 1.5km northwest of the Porto Flutuante (bus No 112 from Praça da Matriz goes to Bairro São Raimundo). A few boats a week go as far as São Gabriel da Cachoeira, a voyage of five or six days costing about US$80 in a hammock.

Getting Around

City buses and downtown streets get fearfully busy around 1 to 2 pm and 5 to 7 pm; avoid trying to move too far across the city at these times. Buses cost US$0.70.

To/From the Airport Bus No 306 'Aeroporto Centro' runs about every half-hour between the airport and the city center bus terminus on Praça da Matriz (US$0.70, 30 minutes). To get it at the airport, walk to the right outside the terminal; the stop is about 200m along the road, around a left-hand

---

River-Boat Schedule

River Boats from Manaus (Porto Flutuante)

Destination	Days	Time	Upper Deck	Lower Deck	Cabin
Santarém	Mon–Sat	30–36 hrs	US$36	US$30	US$65–400
Belém	Mon, Wed, Fri	4 days	US$75	US$68	US$265–400
Tefé	Tues, Thurs	2 days	US$36	n/a	US$65–150
Tabatinga	Wed, Sat	5–6 days	US$85	n/a	US$165–330
Porto Velho	Tues, Fri	4 days	US$63	US$60	US$165–265

bend. The first bus leaves the airport at 5 or 5:30 am, but it's probably safer to wait till 6 am when there are more people about. The last bus from Praça da Matriz to the airport is supposed to leave at midnight, but it's best to catch one before 11 pm in case they pack up early. Outbound from the center, it also stops at the corner of Avenida Floriano Peixoto and Rua Quintino Bocaiúva, and opposite the Plaza Hotel on Avenida Getúlio Vargas.

The official flat rate for a taxi between the airport and center is US$23, and by meter it costs much the same, but if you walk out to the airport bus stop you'll often find one waiting there which will take you for US$7 or less. Going out from the city to the airport, you can try bargaining, and you may get a cab for US15 if you're lucky.

To/From the Bus Station

Coming from the center, Bus No 306 'Aeroporto Centro' (see the preceding section) stops on Avenida Constantino Nery, a one-minute walk from the long-distance bus station; tell the conductor you're going to the *rodoviária* (bus station) and get off at the second stop after the stadium on the left.

To get to the center from the bus station, cross Rua Recife by the pedestrian bridge to the gas station opposite, then turn left along the busy street on the far side of the gas station. The bus stop is 100m along, on the far side of the street; catch the No 306 'Aeroporto Centro.'

A taxi from the bus station to the center costs around US$8.

AROUND MANAUS

On the face of it a city of 1.4 million people is an odd place to head for if you want to experience the jungle. Virtually all the land within 70km of Manaus, except to the north-west, is severely deforested. Along the Amazonas and Solimões Rivers and Hwy BR-174 north of the city, the zone of serious degradation stretches some 200km or so. However Manaus offers Brazilian Amazonia's greatest concentration of agencies, guides and other facilities for taking either a short 'taster' trip or for setting up a longer, more adventurous and demanding one.

Encontro das Águas & Ecológico Janauary

The Encontro das Águas (Meeting of the Waters) is where the 'black' (actually dark brown) waters of the Rio Negro meet the 'white' (light brown) Rio Solimões, just a few kilometers downstream from Manaus. The two flow side by side without mingling for a few kilometers.

Agencies such as Amazon Explorers (☎ 232-3052) and Selvatur (☎ 622-2577), both on Praça Tenreiro Aranha in Manaus, run daily trips combining the Encontro das Águas and the Parque Ecológico Janauary (the park is centered on Lago Janauary, on the point of land between the Negro and Solimões). These outings include a motorized canoe trip along the Janauary waterways, notable for their huge Vitória-Régia water lilies, and a spot of lunch at a floating restaurant. There's a seriously packaged feel to these tours. Everyone bangs on the flying buttresses of the same sambaiaba tree, cuts the same rubber tree for latex sap, looks at the same monkey, sloth, snake and alligator tied up to amuse visitors and browses the same make-believe Indian craft stalls. They last from about 9 am to 4 pm, for US$30 to US$40 per person.

Alternatively you can visit these sites by motorized canoe for around US$50 for four people. Find an Associação dos Canoeiros member at the Porto Flutuante to organize this (see the Jungle Trip Agencies & Guides section, later, for information on the canoe guides).

Another way of seeing the Meeting of the Waters is from the *balsa* (ferry) that crosses between Ponta do Catalão, 12km east of downtown Manaus, and Careiro on the far shore of the Amazonas. You can reach the ferry by taxi or by bus No 713 from Praça da Matriz.

Amazon Ecopark & Amazon Monkey Jungle

These neighboring establishments up the Igarapé Tarumã Açu, a tributary of the Rio Negro, are half an hour by boat from Manaus and make for an interesting day trip. Amazon Ecopark is a private nature reserve and

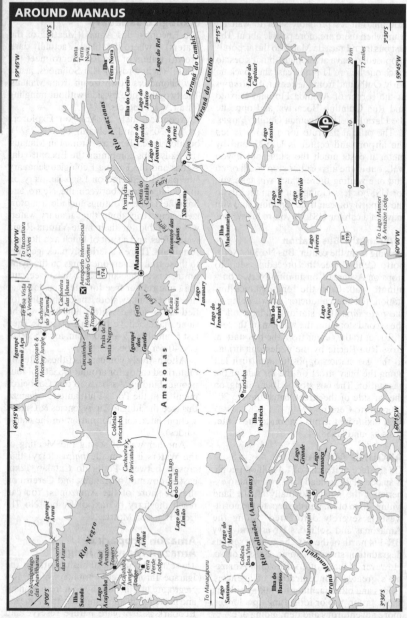

AROUND MANAUS

jungle lodge, while the Monkey Jungle is a project of the Fundação Floresta Viva (Living Rainforest Foundation) for rehabilitating and returning to the wild monkeys that have been illegally captured or are from areas scheduled to be flooded for dams. Twelve different monkey species were in residence at the time of writing. A one-day visit (US$40) normally includes travel there and back, a jungle walk, visits to an orchid garden, bird sanctuary and the monkey jungle, lunch, a canoe trip and a visit to a rubber tapper's home. A half-day trip is US$25. You can book by calling ☎ 234-0939 or ☎ 232-5223 or through Amazon Ecopark's office in Rio de Janeiro (☎ 0xx21-2275-5285, fax 0xx21-2275-6544, Rua Lauro Müller 36, Suite 510).

Amazon Ecopark also offers one-day rainforest survival courses for groups; the instructors are retired Brazilian army officers. See www.amazonecopark.com.

Jungle Trips

The top priority for most foreign visitors to Manaus is a jungle trip. It's possible to arrange anything from an excursion of a few hours or a short stay at a comfortable jungle lodge to trips of up to several weeks using more basic accommodations, camping in the jungle or sleeping aboard river boats.

Standard activities on trips with at least one overnight stay include piranha fishing, walking in the jungle, visiting a simple *caboclo* home (riverbank dwellers of mixed Indian and immigrant descent), and nighttime alligator-catching. You'll probably see dolphins along the way and witness abundant waterside bird life. Alligator-catching is common: Your guides dazzle the reptiles with a strong flashlight and try to grab one by hand from a canoe. If they succeed, the animal is passed around for all to have a hold of (by the neck) before being returned to the water.

On a trip of just a few days from Manaus you can't expect to meet remote Indian tribes or dozens of free-ranging beasts. If you have five or six days (although twice as long would be better), you can start to think about reaching areas of primary forest with chances of spotting more wildlife and/or visiting Indians who are still living a fairly traditional lifestyle.

Planning High-water season, roughly April to July with the main rivers rising by up to 14m, enables you to navigate at treetop level through *igapós* (flooded forests), and reach the upper reaches of *igarapés*, which are too narrow and shallow at low water. Monkeys come to eat fruit in the flooded forests then.

Dozens of agencies want your business. If you're short of leads, tourist offices and Amazon tourism-related Web sites can provide you with long lists of agencies. Once you've decided what kind of trip you want, take the time to compare offers closely, pinning down the operators on just how you'll be spending the time and details such as:

- Does the tour include extended travel in small boats (without use of motor) along igarapés?
- How much time is spent getting to and from your destination?
- Will you and your guide share a common language?
- What is the cost breakdown (food, drinks, lodging, fuel and guides)? You may want to buy at least some of your own food, or pay some of these expenses en route, thereby avoiding fanciful markups, and – unless the agency is very well established – you should insist on paying only part of the price at the beginning of the trip, settling the rest at the end.

Allow at least a day to agree upon a deal, change money and buy provisions. If you are traveling solo, you can try to join a group to make the trip more economical. Several of the agencies mentioned under Agencies & Guides can bring travelers together to reduce per-person costs.

Try to meet the actual guide prior to committing yourself to a trip, and remind that person to bring fishing gear, straps and cords (to suspend packs above the boat floor) – and of course cachaça, sugar and lemons for *caipirinhas* at the end of the day! Don't scrimp on water – carry at least four liters of bottled water per person per day. It's nice to have two styrofoam coolers on board, one to keep perishables from spoiling and the second to keep valuables dry when the weather becomes wet and wild. Not least, insist on life jackets.

There are more enthusiastic letters from readers who thoroughly enjoyed their tours than complaint letters from travelers who

Black & White

Once upon a time the Amazon flowed west into the Pacific Ocean, not east into the Atlantic. Then, maybe 15 million years ago, up rose the Andes. The Amazon turned north to the Caribbean, and the western Amazon basin became a huge wetland. Eventually the Amazon broke through the slightly raised terrain in the Manaus-Santarém area and flowed out to the Atlantic.

Today the multitudes of rivers snaking their way across the Amazon basin are classified into three types – black, white and clear. Though these terms are really euphemisms for different shades of brown, they point out some interesting differences.

The 'white-water' (actually more of a creamy brown) rivers, such as the Rio Solimões and Rio Madeira, are laden with sediments carried down from the geologically young and still-being-eroded Andes.

The 'black-water' Rio Negro, and others flowing from the north, originate in lowland forests with sandy soils in northern Amazonia. They're slower and warmer than the Solimões. The rotting vegetation that gives them their color also makes them more acidic, which in turn means that they are much less insect-ridden than white-water rivers, and insect-borne diseases such as malaria are rarer. Beaches along the Negro tend to be sandy while those on the Solimões are more often muddy. On the other hand, Solimões tributaries reputedly attract more wildlife than those of the Negro.

'Clear-water' rivers, such as the Rio Tapajós flowing down from the Brazilian shield to the south, come from an older geological formation now lacking in sediment and organic materials.

felt they were ripped off. What you get out of your trip depends on several factors: your expectations, experience, ability to cope with a few of the discomforts of Amazon life, and the competence and breadth of knowledge of tour operators and guides. There's also an element of luck: One group spent three whole days pondering which trip to take, then on their carefully chosen tour they spent a sleepless night in hammocks camped across an ant path, several ended up with mild food poisoning, and the inebriated guide became a little too flirtatious!

Warning In the past it has been common practice for tour touts to accost travelers arriving at Manaus airport offering 'information' on jungle trips and maybe even a free ride to a city hotel (from which they probably get a commission), in the hope of talking you into making a trip with them. Reports were that some purported 'representatives' didn't even have tours to sell and simply hustled people off to be robbed and occasionally beaten. Recently, Amazonas state tourism officials were handing out leaflets to travelers warning against 'tourist services offered by unauthorized people who may meet you in the airport lobby,' adding, 'We will not be held responsible for your personal safety.'

If you haven't made prior tour arrangements, you should make your own way to accommodations in the city and start your planning from there. Tourist offices in the city can confirm the credentials of any officially registered agency or guide.

Agencies & Guides Manaus has several budget agencies geared to foreign backpackers, and these are among the most flexible on price. They won't expect you to accept their initial asking price. For a basic trip, they'll ask about US$50 per person per day, and you'll probably end up paying between US$25 and US$40 depending on season, demand and your bargaining ability. This should include all meals, drinking water and transportation there and back.

Most agencies can set up almost anything you might want to do, but some have certain experience and expertise in particular kinds of trip.

Amazonas Indian Turismo (☎/fax 633-5578), Rua dos Andradas 311, is one of the most prominent budget agencies and receives generally satisfactory reports. It uses English-speaking Indian guides and a camp with rustic cabanas on the Rio Urubú, northeast of Manaus (200km by bus and motorized canoe). Trips can last from two to 10 days and there's a virgin rainforest area to investigate to the northeast.

Another popular budget agency is Green Planet Tours (☎ 232-1398, gplanet@usa.net), Rua Guilherme Moreira 116. Their typical trip is three days and two nights, based at a small floating lodge on the Rio Solimões, about 25 km southwest of Manaus. You'll travel there via the Encontro das Águas. A 'jungle survival' extension, camping overnight, is also possible.

Eco-Discovery Tours (☎ 232-6898), Rua Leovigildo Coelho 360, offers a basic trip like Green Planet's, using the same floating lodge but with the option of camping the second night. It can also do customized small-group motorized-canoe trips.

An attractive trip that Green Planet, Eco-Discovery and others can organize is to Lago Mamori, a lake with plentiful bird life about 60km south of Manaus (about a six-hour trip by road, ferry and motorized canoe). You'll sleep in cabanas or simple local homes.

Travelers have reported favorably about Geraldo 'Gero' Mesquita (☎ 9983-6273, ☎/fax 232-9416, geromesquita@hotmail.com), at the Hospedaria de Turismo 10 de Julho (see Manaus Places to Stay), who arranges guided trips to Lago Mamori and up the Negro and Solimões Rivers. Gero is a friendly, English-speaking guy who has gone out of his way to help many travelers. For Mamori he quoted daily prices of around US$200 for a group of up to four people.

A recommended outfit doing trips to Lago Juma is Jungle Experience (☎ 233-2000), run by experienced guide Gerry Hardy. A minimum of four people are needed but they'll put travelers together to make up the numbers. The quoted daily price is US$60 per person but Hardy's colleague Christopher Gomes can also set you up with other, more economical guides. Their office is in the Hotel Ideal and they run Amazon Lodge (see Jungle Lodges later).

Wildlife enthusiasts with the time and money for a longer trip should consider Jaguar Adventure Tours (☎/fax 663-2998, 9982-7285, jaguartours@objetivonet.com .br), Vila Operária N 23 A, Cachoeirinha. Trips, based on a 17m riverboat belonging to the multilingual guide Carlos Damasceno, are to relatively unfrequented areas such as the Rio Abacaxi (Pineapple River), where there are good chances of seeing jaguars. A 10-day-long trip costs around US$2000 each for two people or US$1500 each for six.

Web site: www.objetivonet.com.br/jaguar-tours

Swallows and Amazons (☎/fax 622-1246, swallows@internext.com.br), Rua Quintino Bocaiúva 189, run by an American and Brazilian couple, offers riverboat trips and lodge stays (separate or combined) mainly on the Rio Negro. Its rustic Over Look Lodge is on the Negro just before the first of the 400 islands of the Anavilhanas archipelago, about 60km from Manaus. (The Anavilhanas are known as a particularly good area for bird-watching, and during low water, many sandy beaches are uncovered.) Riverboat trips (up to 14 days) cost an average US$120 per person per day for small groups, including side trips by canoe and on foot. A four-day/three-night combined riverboat-and-lodge trip is US$450. The Web sites www.swallowsandamazonstours .com and www.amazonriver.com/E-manaus .htm can be helpful.

Other guides with reliable recommendations include Celio Spinola (☎ 92-9968-6200, celioguide@zipmail.com.br), Edvan Lima Regis (☎ 658-3216) and Mike Kartwright (mike_ariau@bol.com.br). The last two can also be contacted through the Ariaú Amazon Towers office (see Jungle Lodges later). All these guys speak good English and in some cases other languages too.

If you are setting up an independent trip, consider renting a boat. You can start by asking at the Porto Flutuante, your hotel or a tourist office. In general, a small river boat on which a small group can travel and sleep shouldn't cost more than US$100 a day including the services of the crew. If you want to set things up in advance, you'll find several boat operators listed under *operadores de cruzeiros* on the tourism secretariat Web site, www.visitamazonas.com.br.

A motorized canoe with shade is smaller but faster than a traditional riverboat. The canoe people have their own association, the Associação dos Canoeiros (☎ 238-8880), whose president, Antonio Franco, speaks English. Look for members of the association around the SERPE office at the Porto Flutuante, wearing green jackets with badges of the association. While a trip with these folk may be less predictable than an organized tour, it may be more authentic. Usually you stay with caboclo families from the surrounding river settlements. A four-day jungle trip should cost US$50 to US$60 a day, plus provisions and anything you pay for accommodations.

Jungle Lodges Within 250km of Manaus are at least a dozen jungle lodges – basically rustic but quite comfortable wooden hotels in the jungle, always with a waterside setting. Some are a little more luxurious than others. Tourist offices can give you leaflets on all of them. Visits are normally by packages of two, three or more days, which include transportation (usually by river boat) from and back to Manaus, all meals and a program of outings and activities (jungle walks, piranha fishing, alligator-catching, canoe trips and so on). Drinks are usually not included in the price. You can book most lodges through a variety of Manaus travel agencies. The city's tourist offices can suggest plenty of agencies if you're having trouble finding one.

The largest lodge, *Ariaú Amazon Towers*, is on a tongue of land dividing the Rio Negro from a narrow tributary, the Rio Ariaú, two hours up the Negro from Manaus. This complex for over 300 guests

stands on stilts, with towers linked by walkways through the treetops, a 50m-high observatory, a convention center and helipad. Two- and three-day travel packages cost US$280 and US$340 per person respectively. The Manaus office (☎ 234-7308, treetop@internext.com.br) is at Rua Leonardo Malcher 699. There's also a US office (☎ 305-371-7871, info@ariautowers.com) at 905 Brickell Bay Dr, Suite 1930, Miami, Florida 33131. Web sites are www.ariau.tur.br and www.ariautowers.com

In contrast, *Amazon Lodge*, a cute small-scale floating lodge on Lago Juma, 60km southeast of Manaus (about five hours by ferry, bus and speedboat), caters for 28 guests. A three-day package costs US$495 per person (minimum two people); four days starts at US$535 per person. Travelers report very favorably about the helpfulness and friendliness of the staff here. For further information or bookings visit the Web site www.naturesafaris.com, or contact Nature Safaris (☎ 656-6033, fax 656-6101, email marketing@naturesafaris.com), Rua Flavio Espírito Santo 1, Kissia II, Manaus.

Terra Verde Lodge is one of the more economical options, a small and friendly place about 50km west of Manaus (a three-hour river trip). It's located off Lago Acajatuba on the south side of the Rio Negro, on a 110 sq km private jungle reserve. Two/three-day packages cost US$170/220 per person. The Manaus office (☎ 622-7305, terraverde@internext.com.br) is at Room 304, Hotel Mônaco, Rua Silva Ramos 20. If you go there, you may meet the amiable owner, Polish-born film director Zygmunt Sulistrowski, who's quite a character. Web site: www.internext.com.br/terraverde

Two/three-day packages at *Acajatuba Jungle Lodge* on Lago Acajatuba itself start at US$230/310 per person. Reserve through Anaconda Turismo (☎ 233-7642, fax 622-5072), upstairs at Rua Lima Bacuri 345. Web site: www.acajatuba.com.br

Hotel Aldeia dos Lagos is on Silves island in the Rio Urubú, amid a lake-strewn area some 240km east of Manaus (4½ hours by road and river). The hotel is an ecotourism venture by a local community group, with outside financial aid, intended to provide income to help the local subsistence fishing community protect its fish stocks, which are threatened by larger-scale Manaus-based commercial operations. Money earned from the hotel helps pay for measures such as patrolling local lakes to stop illegal fishing. The hotel has 12 double rooms with bath, terrace, fan and mosquito screens, and it offers a variety of interesting outings. Contact it directly (☎/fax 528-2124, aldeiadoslagos@terra.com.br), or book through Viverde Turismo (☎/fax 248-9988, amazon@viverde.com.br), Rua dos Cardeiros 26, Conjunto Acariquara Coroado III, Manaus. A four-day package through Viverde is around US$370 per person.

Web site: www.viverde.com.br

Also on Silves island is the larger 68-room *Pousada dos Guanavenas*, where three-day packages are US$450/670 for singles/doubles. You can book through Guanavenas Turismo (☎ 656-3656, fax 238-1211, reservas@guanavenas.com.br), Rua Constantino Nery 2486, Flores, Manaus.

Web site: www.guanavenas.com.br

The *Amazon Ecopark* (see earlier section) also offers lodge accommodations close to Manaus. A two-day package is US$210 per person (in double rooms).

PARINTINS

☎ 0xx92 • postcode 69150-000 • pop 56,000

Parintins is 420km east of Manaus, on the island of Tupinambarana in the Rio Amazonas, near the border of Pará state. The Boi-Bumbá festival held here on June 28, 29 and 30 is the biggest annual shindig in Amazonas. It's an Amazonian version of *bumba-meu-boi*, a traditional Brazilian folkloric festivity of mixed African and European origins. Combining theater, drums, music, dancing and circus, it enacts the kidnapping, death and resurrection of an ox, a metaphor for agricultural cycles. In Parintins the event is turned into a competition between two Boi teams, each with several thousand members – Caprichoso, in blue, and Garantido, in red. The rivalry between the teams apparently grew out of a 'friendly' feud between two families.

Tens of thousands of people descend on Parintins to watch the dazzling Boi parades – which incorporate diverse Amazonian tales and legends – in the *bumbódromo,* a purpose-built, 35,000-capacity stadium. The event is increasingly professionalized, with well known singers participating. The teams are judged on their music, dance performance and costumes. The competition is intense, every citizen supports either red or blue, and the over-the-top spectacle rivals Rio's Carnaval.

Places to Stay

Parintins hotels are quickly booked during the festival, and many people take package tours that include nightly accommodations aboard a boat. A five-night boat trip from Manaus (transportation, hammock space and meals) costs around US$200.

The *Hotel Avenida* (☎ 533-1158, Avenida Amazonas 2416) and *Pousada Ilha Bela* (☎/fax 533-2737, Rua Agostinho Cunha 2052) both have apartamentos with air-conditioning, TV and minibar for around US$30 at normal times, but you should expect prices to rise during the festival. Other options are the *Hotel Uyrapurú*, *Hotel Palace*, *Hotel Cabocla*, *Hospedaria Siridó* and the *Hotel Torres de Melo*. Private houses also rent rooms during the festival.

Getting There & Away

The regional airlines Rico, Penta and TAVAJ fly to Parintins from Manaus and Santarém. Air taxis also make the trip, more often during the festival. Penta makes the one-way trip from Santarém for US$52.

Boats go daily from Manaus' Porto Flutuante (around US$20, 16 hours), and most upstream boats from Santarém call at Parintins too.

NORTHWEST OF MANAUS

The remote regions northwest of Manaus offer outstanding opportunities for jungle, river and nature lovers with a bit of cash. (For more on traveling in this region, see also Reserva Xixuaú-Xipariná in the Roraima section, later in this chapter.)

Parque Nacional do Jaú

This 22,720-sq-km park in the Rio Negro basin is Brazil's biggest national park and one of the world's largest pieces of protected tropical rainforest. Extremely rich in biodiversity, the park received UNESCO World Heritage listing in 2000. This remote area has only 1000 inhabitants and is far from fully explored. If you have a boat at your disposal you can enter the park with a permit from IBAMA in Manaus; it's about a 16-hour trip from the city to the confluence of the Rio Jaú and Rio Negro where the park begins, but visitor facilities are nonexistent.

For information on the park consult the Fundação Vitória Amazônica, an environmental non-governmental organization involved in the park's management (Web site: www.fva.org.br). Both IBAMA and Vitória Amazônica are at Avenida Ministro João Goncalves de Souza s/n, BR-319 Km 1, Distrito Industrial, Manaus (☎ 0xx92-613-3093).

King's Island Lodge

About 1000km up the Rio Negro from Manaus, this lodge stands on an island in the river in the far northwest of Amazonas near the town of São Gabriel da Cachoeira (population 11,500). This region has a mostly indigenous population. Three-day/two-night packages start at US$499 per person including flights from and back to Manaus. Various special-focus trips can be made including bird and wildlife spotting, trekking, river trips and even the ascent of 3014m Pico da Neblina, Brazil's highest mountain (US$1850 per person). Like the recommended Amazon Lodge (see the Jungle Lodges section in Around Manaus earlier), King's Island Lodge lodge is run by Nature Safaris, and contact details are the same. Web site: www.naturesafaris.com

TEFÉ

☎ 0xx92 • postcode 69470-000 • pop 48,000
Tefé is the largest town on the Rio Solimões between Manaus and the Colombian/Peruvian border. The main reason to come here is as a stepping stone to the Mamirauá reserve. The Mamirauá ecotourism people whisk most of their clients straight out from Tefé airport to the reserve, but if you should need or want to linger in this medium-sized Amazonian river town, there are some reasonable hotels in the center. Tefé's economy is based on fishing, logging and drugs. Tributaries entering the Solimões not far upstream from Tefé include the Rio Japurá, which flows down from one of Colombia's supposed coca- and cocaine-producing areas, and the Rio Juruá, which comes from Peru's coca-producing area.

Tefé's only exchange facilities are at Banco do Brasil, Rua Olavo Bilac 298, in the center, which gives over-the-counter cash advances on Visa cards for a charge of US$5 and will change some traveler's checks.

Places to Stay & Eat

A fairly clean cheap option is **Hotel Raydiene** (☎ 343-4871) on Rua Olavo Bilac. Fan-cooled quartos are US$7/10 a single/double, and there are air-conditioned doubles for US$12. Best is **Hotel Anilçe** (☎ 343-2416, *Praça Santa Tereza 294),* with single/double air-conditioned apartamentos for US$20/30. The best places to eat are **Stylos** *(Rua Floriano Peixoto 190),* with fish and meat dishes for two costing only US$3.50 to US$7, and **Petisco** *(Praça Santa Tereza 286)* charging US$2 for home-style beef kebabs with rice or US$3 for prato feito.

Getting There & Away

Varig flies to Tefé three days a week from Manaus (US$120 one way) and twice weekly from Tabatinga. Rico flies from both places daily (US$103 from Manaus). Plenty of riverboats go up and down the Solimões to/from Manaus and Tefé. The hammock fare to/from Manaus is around US$35, taking about two days, with departures in both directions most days.

MAMIRAUÁ RESERVE

The Reserva de Desenvolvimento Sustentável Mamirauá (Mamirauá Sustainable Development Reserve) covers 11,240 sq km between the Rio Solimões and Rio Japurá, a little over halfway between Manaus and the triple frontier. The reserve is the last large intact area of *várzea* (floodplain forest) in Brazilian Amazonia – a beautiful, pristine environment of jungle, rivers and lakes. It also has a very well-run ecotourism program that provides some of the best wildlife viewing in Amazonia. Declared an Amazonas state reserve in 1996, Mamirauá is a pioneer of the sustainable development reserve concept, which aims to combine nature conservation and scientific research with improved opportunities for the local population. In this case, such activities include ecotourism, forest management, commercialization of fishing and health and education programs.

On a three-day visit at the time of research, the following were seen: four species of monkey (including howlers and the rare white uakari with its unmistakable crimson face and shaggy white coat), dozens of pink dolphins and alligators, numerous gray dolphins, sloths, squirrels, piranhas, the leaping aruanã fish and quite a lot of the reserve's 400-odd recorded bird species including trogons, hoatzin, toucans, macaws, horned screamer, anhinga, kingfishers, hummingbirds, woodpeckers, herons, egrets and hawks. High water here is in May/June, and low water in October/November.

Ecotourism is restricted to the southeast tip of the reserve, about 25km up the Solimões from Tefé. Accommodations are provided here in comfortable floating bungalows with bathrooms and mosquito screens. Prices, for example, are US$240 per person in a triple room for a three-day/two-night package and include river trips, guided walks and boat transfers from/to Tefé. English-speaking staff, books and videos provide all the explanations and background information you could hope for, and you'll normally get the chance to meet and talk with some of the biologists working there as well as local *ribeirinhos*. Researchers are investigating pink dolphins, manatees, alligators and various botanical topics.

The Mamirauá reserve, together with the neighboring and even bigger Reserva de Desenvolvimento Sustentável Amanã (23,500 sq km, declared in 1997) and the Jaú national park, makes up a uniquely large 57,000-sq-km corridor of protected tropical rainforest.

To arrange a visit or find out more, visit the Mamirauá Web site (www.cnpq.br/mamiraua) or contact the Mamirauá office in Tefé (☎/fax 0xx92-343-4160, ecomami@pop-tefe.rnp.br), Avenida Brasil 173 & 197.

THE TRIPLE FRONTIER

The Brazilian town of Tabatinga and the Colombian town of Leticia, both on the east bank of the Amazon about 1100km west of Manaus, are separated by nothing except an international border line. The opposite bank of the river here, and the islands in the middle of it, are Peru. This 'triple frontier' provides travel routes linking all three countries and is also a good area for taking jungle trips. From this area there is relatively easy access to somewhat remote areas up the Rio Javari, which forms the Brazil-Peru border to the west, and up the Rio Amazonas in Colombia. The high-water period here is April to June, and the least rainy months are July to September.

Leticia is a more prosperous place than Tabatinga and overall a more pleasant place to hang out. The Peruvian border settlement here, Santa Rosa, is just a small village on an island.

See the Embassies & Consulates section in the Facts for the Visitor chapter for

Mamirauá has more than 400 bird species.

THE TRIPLE FRONTIER

details of the Colombian consulate in Tabatinga and the Brazilian consulate in Leticia (Colombia). There's also a Peruvian consulate in Leticia at Calle 13 No 11-48, open 9 am to 1 pm, Monday to Friday.

Tabatinga

☎ 0xx92 • postcode 69640-000 • pop 27,000
Most of the transportation connections in the 'twin towns' can be found in Tabatinga.

Orientation & Information The international border, where Leticia's Avenida Internacional becomes Tabatinga's Avenida da Amizade, is marked by nothing more than a money-exchange hut on the Brazil side and a police post on the Colombian side. You needn't break stride as you cross. From the border, Avenida da Amizade runs about 2km southward, parallel to the river and 600m east of it, to the Polícia Federal post (☎ 412-2180), Avenida da Amizade 650, where you must go when entering or

leaving Brazil. The airport is 1.5km farther south beyond the Polícia Federal.

The most important streets leading off Avenida da Amizade toward the river include (in north-south order): Rua Marechal Rondon (250m from the border), Rua Rui Barbosa (650m), Avenida Marechal Mallet (900m) and Rua Santos Dumont (1.2km). Rua Santos Dumont leads directly to the Porto da Feira, one of Tabatinga's two ports; you can also reach the Porto da Feira by going down Avenida Marechal Mallet, turning left at the end and passing the market.

Numbers along Avenida da Amizade go down as you go away from the international border: anything numbered higher than 2000 will be north of Rua Rui Barbosa. Tabatinga's other port, the Porto Fluvial, for bigger riverboats, is at the end of the street that leaves Avenida da Amizade beside the Hospital de Guarnicão de Tabatinga, 500m south of Rua Santos Dumont.

CNM Cambio e Turismo (☎ 412-3281), Avenida da Amizade 2017, will change cash and traveler's checks but usually pays less per dollar than you can get in Leticia. For Visa-card cash advances, try Banco do Brasil on Avenida da Amizade just north of Avenida Marechal Mallet (they say it depends on exactly which type of Visa card you have). It's open 8 am to noon Monday to Friday.

D'Joy Internet Café, on Rua da Pátria one block north off Avenida Marechal Mallet, offers Internet access.

Places to Stay & Eat The *Traveller's Jungle Home* (*amazonasdiscover@yahoo .com, Rua Marechal Rondon 86*) is the house of jungle guides Tony 'Mowgli' Vargas and Sophie Coyaud (see the Rio Javari section, later, for information on their trips). They offer accommodations for US$6 per person. The house is 600m from Avenida Amizade.

Tabatinga hotels are mostly grubby and smelly, but *Hotel Cristina* (*☎ 412-2558, Avenida Marechal Mallet 248*) has basic but clean quartos with fan for US$5/7 a single/ double, and apartamentos with TV for US$8/10 (fan) or US$14/16 (air-con).

Tabatinga also has an eatery that's one of the best values in the two towns: ***Restaurante Tres Fronteiras*** on Rua Rui Barbosa, 200m west of Avenida da Amizade. This is a nice palm-roofed, open-air place open daily for lunch and dinner, with caipirinhas and chicken/meat/fish selections starting at US$4.50. Churrasco and some fish specialties are more.

Restaurante Blue Moon, a beautifully breezy spot on stilts at the Porto da Feira, has similarly priced main dishes, and good guaraná-combination juices for US$1.25.

Getting There & Away Varig (☎ 412-2356) flies to/from Manaus (US$184) three days a week. At the time of writing the flights stopped at Tefé on the Manaus-Tabatinga leg on Wednesday and on the Tabatinga-Manaus leg on Monday and Friday. Rico (☎ 412-4000) flies to/from Tefé and Manaus (US$162) four days a week. CNM Cambio e Turismo (see Information) and Waymintur (☎ 412-2244), Avenida da Amizade 2271, sell plane tickets.

TANS (☎ 412-2045), also called Grupo Aereo No 42, operates a seaplane to/from Iquitos, Peru, on Monday, Wednesday and Saturday. The fare for the 1½-hour flight is US$55 from Tabatinga and US$50 from Iquitos. TANS' office is at Rua Pedro Teixeira 100 but it's also easy to contact them at the Restaurante Blue Moon (see Places to Stay & Eat). In Leticia you can buy tickets at Almacén Pacífico, Calle 8 No 11-35.

Boats to Tefé and Manaus leave on Wednesday and Saturday (and sometimes other days too) from the Porto Fluvial. They take about five days to Manaus for a hammock/cabin fare of around US$40/80 per person. You can usually sleep on board the night before departure.

To Iquitos, Peru, fast passenger boats make the trip in about 10 hours, leaving about 5 am. Transtar (☎ 412-3186), Avenida Marechal Mallet 308, and Expreso Loreto (☎ 412-2945), Avenida Marechal Mallet 248, go on alternate days, except Monday, for US$50. You go through Peruvian immigration in Santa Rosa. The downstream trip from Iquitos to Tabatinga, on the same days

and for the same price, takes about eight hours.

Deslizadores (small, fast, passenger launches) go whenever they have a boatload from the Porto da Feira across to Santa Rosa, Peru, for US$1.25 per person, and to Benjamin Constant, the Brazilian town at the mouth of the Rio Javari, for US$4 (US$7 after 5 pm).

Getting Around For a *coletivo* (minibus) from the airport to town (US$1), walk to the left outside the airport terminal and down the approach road to the corner of the main road. Some vehicles continue into Leticia from Tabatinga.

A taxi from the airport costs US$7 to central Tabatinga and US$10 to central Leticia.

Leticia (Colombia)
☎ 098 • pop 27,000

The far southern corner of Colombia in which Leticia lies had remained mercifully free from the troubles afflicting much of the country at the time of writing, and hopefully will stay that way. It attracts some Colombian tourists eager to see Indian tribes, buy their handicrafts, and get a taste of the Amazon jungle. See the Parque Nacional Amacayacu and Rio Javari sections, later in this chapter, for jungle trip possibilities from here.

Information The Departamento Administrativo de Seguridad (DAS, ☎ 592-7189), the security police office on Calle 9, is open 8 am to 12:30 pm and 2:30 to 6 pm daily. This is where you get your passport stamped (free) when leaving or entering Colombia. If you're staying in Leticia less than 24 hours then returning to Brazil, no one is likely to mind if you don't bother with these formalities.

The Amazonas Department tourist office (☎ 592-7505), Carrera 11 No 11-35, is open 7 am to noon and 2 to 5:45 pm Monday to Friday.

Several shops and offices on Calle 8, near Carrera 11, will exchange Colombian, Brazilian, Peruvian or US currency. Banco

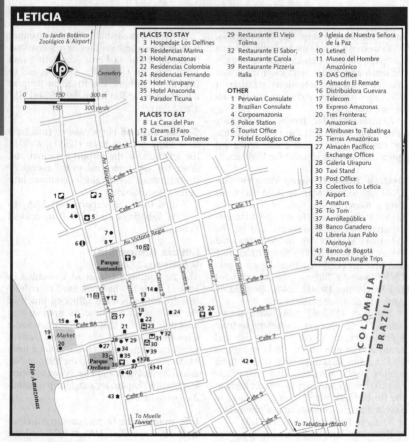

LETICIA

To Jardín Botánico Zoológico & Airport

Cemetery

0   150   300 m
0   150   300 yards

PLACES TO STAY
3 Hospedaje Los Delfines
14 Residencias Marina
21 Hotel Amazonas
22 Residencias Colombia
24 Residencias Fernando
26 Hotel Yurupany
35 Hotel Anaconda
43 Parador Ticuna

PLACES TO EAT
8 La Casa del Pan
12 Cream El Faro
18 La Casona Tolimense

29 Restaurante El Viejo
   Tolima
32 Restaurante El Sabor;
   Restaurante Carola
39 Restaurante Pizzería
   Italia

OTHER
1 Peruvian Consulate
2 Brazilian Consulate
4 Corpoamazonia
5 Police Station
6 Tourist Office
7 Hotel Ecológico Office

9 Iglesia de Nuestra Señora
   de la Paz
10 Letinet
11 Museo del Hombre
   Amazónico
13 DAS Office
15 Almacén El Remate
16 Distribuidora Guevara
17 Telecom
19 Expreso Amazonas
20 Tres Fronteras;
   Amazonica
23 Minibuses to Tabatinga
25 Tierras Amazónicas
27 Almacén Pacífico;
   Exchange Offices
28 Galería Uirapuru
30 Taxi Stand
31 Post Office
33 Colectivos to Leticia
   Airport
34 Amaturs
36 Tío Tom
37 AeroRepública
38 Banco Ganadero
40 Librería Juan Pablo
   Montoya
41 Banco de Bogotá
42 Amazon Jungle Trips

Calle 14

Av Vásquez Cobo

Calle 13

Calle 12

Calle 11

1 2

3

4 5

7

8   Av Victoria Regia

6

10

Parque Santander 9

Calle 10

Av Internacional

11 12

13

14

Calle 9

15 16
Calle 8A

19 Market

20

17

18

21

22
23

24

25 26

Calle 8

27

28 29

34
35
36 37

33

38

41

40

Parque Orellana

30
31
32

39

Calle 7

42

COLOMBIA
BRAZIL

Río Amazonas

43 Calle 6

Calle 5

Calle 4

To Muelle Fluvial

To Tabatinga (Brazil)

Ganadero on Calle 7 has an ATM giving cash on at least some foreign Visa cards and changes American Express traveler's checks, but not cash dollars. The ATMs at Banco de Bogotá across the corner may work with a Cirrus card, but not with Visa. Banco de Bogotá won't change dollars or traveler's checks.

The post office is on Calle 8 and the Telecom office, open daily for long-distance phone calls, is on Carrera 11 near Calle 9. When telephoning to Leticia from outside Colombia, use the Colombia country code 57 and drop the 09 of the area code.

Letinet, at Carrera 9 No 10-20, charges US$1/1.50 for 15/30 minutes of Internet access. It is open 8:30 am to noon and 2 to 7 pm Monday to Saturday.

Things to See The **Museo del Hombre Amazónico** on Carrera 11, has a small collection of Indian artifacts and implements; it's open 8 am to noon and 2 to 6 pm Monday to Friday. The **Jardín Botánico Zoológico**, near the airport, has a poor sample of the local flora and some monkeys, crocodiles, anteaters and anacondas; it's open 8 am to 5 pm daily.

Places to Stay Leticia has a good range of accommodations. Probably cheapest is the basic *Residencias Colombia* (☎ 592-7034, Carrera 10 No 8-56). It was recently closed for painting, but the singles/doubles with hard beds and shared bath are likely to cost US$6/7.50. *Residencias Marina* (☎ 592-6014, Carrera 9 No 9-29) has rooms of similar standard for US$7.50/12.50, and Sky TV in the hall.

At the pleasant *Residencias Fernando* (☎ 592-7362, Carrera 9 No 8-80), you'll pay US$9/13 with fan or US$15/20 for bigger, more modern air-conditioned rooms, all along a nice little strip of garden.

For all-round value it's hard to beat the peaceful, friendly *Hospedaje Los Delfines* (☎ 592-7488, Carrera 11 No 12-83). Nice, clean rooms along a tree-filled patio, with fan, hammock, bathroom and fridge, cost US$10/15. *Hotel Amazonas* (☎ 592-8026, Calle 8 No 10-32) is also a decent value: Good, clean rooms are US$10/15 with fan or US$12.50/20 with air-conditioning. It has a pool.

Hotel Yurupany (☎ 592-4743, Calle 8 No 7-26) is a bit more upmarket, with nice, spacious, almost new rooms sporting air-con, cable TV and fridge for US$22/35. It has a pleasant little restaurant too, and there'll probably be a discount if you stay more than one night. Prices at Leticia's top hostelry, *Hotel Anaconda* (☎ 592-7119, Carrera 11 No 7-36) are pretty negotiable, but you can expect to pay around US$45/60. Try for a room on the top floor with nice views over the Amazon to make it worth the money. The *Parador Ticuna* (☎ 592-7273, Carrera 11 No 6-11) has enormous rooms for US$20/27.50, plus US$7.50 for each extra person, around a nice tropical garden with a big pool, but has an oddly under-used atmosphere.

Places to Eat On Calle 8, *El Sabor* does a good *menú del día* (set meal) of soup, main course and juice for US$2, and its banana pancakes (US$1.25) are a treat. It's open 24 hours daily except Monday. Next door, *Restaurante Carola* serves filling plates of pirarucu, meat or chicken with trimmings for US$2. Even cheaper set lunches are to be had at *La Casona Tolimense* (Carrera 10 No 8-62), charging US$1.25, and *Restaurante El Viejo Tolima* on Calle 8, charging US$1.50. *Restaurante Pizzería Italia* on Carrera 10, run by a real Italian, is a new place that's shaping up to be a bit of a traveler's hangout, with an amiable atmosphere and good homemade pizza at US$1 a slice or pasta portions for US$2.

La Casa del Pan (Calle 11 No 10-20), facing Parque Santander, is an excellent spot for breakfast (eggs, French bread, coffee and juice for US$2) or for a coffee while watching the park's hordes of screeching parrots return to their nests at dusk.

The classiest restaurant is *Cream El Faro* (Carrera 11 No 9-42), with smooth waiter service and a choice between air-conditioned cool and open-air tables. Excellent meat and fish dishes cost US$4.50 or so. The name of the restaurant is not posted outside.

Entertainment There are several bars along Calle 8. *Tierras Amazónicas* next to the Hotel Yurupany is mellow one, popular with a 20s and 30s crowd. *Tío Tom* opposite Parque Orellana is fairly popular downtown bar with some outside tables.

Shopping You can buy hammocks for US$10 to US$25 at Almacén El Remate and Distribuidora Guevara, both on Calle 8A. Galería Uirapuru at Calle 8 No 10-35 has a good stock of crafts for sale.

Getting There & Away It can be difficult to get on flights out of Leticia unless you book in advance. AeroRepública, with its office at Calle 7 No 10-36, flies four times weekly to Bogotá for US$100. Avianca flies twice weekly for US$140: Tickets are sold at Amaturs (☎ 592-6126), Carrera 11 No 7-84. You may be able to get a place on a cargo flight with Aerosucre, which shuttles from Leticia to Bogotá almost daily and takes passengers for about US$50. Ask at the Aerosucre *bodega* (warehouse) at the airport, behind the passenger terminal, as early in the morning as you can manage.

Tickets for small, fast *deslizadores* up the Amazonas to the Parque Nacional Amacayacu visitor center are sold at small offices at the west end of Calle 8, just outside the market. There are three companies here, Expreso Amazonas, Tres Fronteras and Amazonica, and one or another leaves about 1 or 2 pm every day. The 1½-hour trip costs US$9. Most boats continue to Puerto Nariño (Colombia) and/or Caballococche (Peru). Boats return from the park to Leticia in the morning.

Small boats will carry you across to Santa Rosa, Peru, for US$1 per person from Leticia's Muelle Fluvial at the end of Calle 3 (250m west from the south end of Carrera 11, or 1km west from the international border).

Getting Around *Colectivos* (minibuses) to Leticia airport go from Parque Orellana. From central Leticia to Tabatinga airport, take a colectivo from the corner of Carrera 10 and Calle 8. Those marked 'Comara' will take you to Tabatinga airport. A taxi from central Leticia to Tabatinga airport is US$7.

Parque Nacional Amacayacu

Agencies in Leticia offer various excursions outside the town, but definitely the most worthwhile trip is one you can easily make yourself if you have a night or two available. This is to the Amacayacu national park, which covers 2935 sq km of jungle on the north side of the Amazonas, 75km upstream from Leticia. See Leticia's Getting There & Away section for information on boats to the park.

The park has a spacious visitor's center beside the river, where accommodations in a bunk/hammock cost US$8.50/6.50 per person, and three meals a day cost US$8; add US$3 for the park entry fee. From the center you can explore the park by marked paths or (especially during the May-July high-water period) by boat. A guide for up to five people costs around US$12 per day. You can book your accommodations and pay at Corpoamazonia (☎ 592-7124), at Carrera 11 No 12-45, open 8 am to 5 pm Monday to Friday.

Rio Javari

The Rio Javari forms the Brazil-Peru border for about 500km upstream from its confluence with the Rio Solimões at the town of Benjamin Constant (named for the 19th century Brazilian positivist thinker and politician), 20km southwest of Tabatinga. The jungle region it runs through is very remote, and the hinterlands even more so. The area known as the Vale do Javari (Javari Valley), south and east of the river on the Brazilian side, is little populated except for 3000 or 4000 Indians. Most of it is in the process of registration as the Terra Indígena Vale do Javari, an 85,000 sq km area that forms one of the largest Indian lands in Brazil.

There are believed to be several uncontacted Indian groups in the forests here; some of the known tribes have a reputation for aggressiveness to outsiders. You'll probably hear tales of the isolated Korubo tribe, which lives somewhere up the Rio Ituí. Its members have assassinated dozens of intruders such as loggers and rubber tappers (and at the same time have themselves been assassinated in even greater numbers). Anyone interested in this region should try to get hold of Petru Popescu's book *Amazon Beaming,* which relates photographer Loren McIntyre's extraordinary experiences among the Mayoruna (Matses) people.

Jungle Lodges Three good jungle lodges provide the chance to get close to nature and the riverbank caboclos along the lower reaches of the Javari. All offer typical jungle lodge activities such as forest walks, fishing, night-time alligator spotting, bird-watching, dolphin watching, village visits and the chance to camp out in the jungle. You can also plan a customized trip based on your interests and time available.

The nearest of the three jungle lodges to 'civilization' is **Zacambu Lodge,** about a 70km boat trip from Tabatinga (three hours by motorized canoe) in an area of lakes on the Peruvian side of the Javari. It's reportedly a good area for wildlife spotting. Prices for trips here for groups of four or more are US$50 to US$60 per person per day, including transportation there and back from

Tabatinga. Book through Amazon Jungle Trips (☎ 098-592-7377, fax 098-592-5583), Avenida Internacional 6-25, Leticia.

Reserva Natural Palmari is about 40km farther up the Javari and stands on the south bank of the river itself, overlooking a bend where pink and gray dolphins are often seen. It's a well run, pleasant lodge in a small private nature reserve, with good guides, good food and good prices, if you go independently. Prices run US$15 per person in a bed or US$10 in a hammock. Breakfast is US$5, lunch and dinner US$8 each. If you're seriously into wildlife observation it's best to go during the high-water season when canoes can get you in a couple of hours to more remote areas that would take several hours to reach on foot.

If there's a boat going to the lodge, it'll probably be able to take you for around US$20. Otherwise you can either hire a boat and pilot from Leticia's Muelle Fluvial or Tabatinga's Porto da Feira (US$80 to US$100 one way to Palmari, a trip of about four hours), or get to Benjamin Constant by 9 am to catch the *recreo* boat that leaves then for Atalaia do Norte (US$4, three hours), where you have to hire a local boat to Palmari for about US$10 (30 minutes to two hours depending on the boat). It's OK to turn up unannounced at the lodge. For further information or to organize a visit, check the Web site at www.palmari.org or contact the owner, Axel Antoine-Feill, in Bogotá (☎ 091-6234265 or ☎ 091-2363813, info@palmari.org), or his representative in Leticia, Marcela Torres (☎ 098-592-7344). Both speak several languages including English.

The third lodge is the *Hotel Ecológico*, in another fine location overlooking a lake off the Rio Itaquai, a southern tributary of the Javari. Prices per person for a three-day/two-night package including transportation are US$186 in a three- or four-person group, or US$219 if there are only two people. For information and bookings visit the hotel's office at Carrera 10 No 11-27, Leticia (☎ 098-592-7457).

It's also possible to set up an adventurous trip staying in Indian or caboclo villages. Brazilian Tony 'Mowgli' Vargas and his French wife Sophie Coyaud, based at Traveller's Jungle Home (see Places to Stay & Eat in the Tabatinga section), are experienced jungle guides who offer a range of trips in the Javari area. Sophie's jungle exploits have been written up in several French magazines. You can often get ahold of Mowgli at the Librería Juan Pablo Montoya newsstand on Carrera 11 in Leticia. They'll provide tents, hammocks, mosquito nets and even vegetarian food on request. Trips can range from staying with villagers in Zacambu village for about US$50 per person per day up to a 10-day expedition visiting the Marubo and other Javari valley Indian tribes (US$2500 for one person plus US$500 for each additional person). There are plenty of possibilities in between.

Roraima

The remote and beautiful mountain region straddling Roraima's frontier with Venezuela is perhaps the ultimate Amazon frontier. With just 324,000 inhabitants, Roraima is the least populated state in Brazil. Still, it has quite a lot more than the 19,700 people that were counted here in 1943. The equator passes through southern Roraima, and much of the state is still tropical rainforest, but the northeast is chiefly savanna. Roraima includes most of the Brazilian territories of the Yanomami, one of the country's largest surviving indigenous peoples (for more on this indigenous group, see the boxed text 'The Yanomami' in the Facts about Brazil chapter), and several other sizable Indian territories. Roraima state governments are not renowned, however, for favoring indigenous or nature reserves that hamper such activities as mining or logging.

Access to most places off the main north-south Hwy BR-174 is not easy, and although the capital, Boa Vista, has a few places of interest, for many travelers Roraima is just somewhere to pass through between Venezuela and Manaus.

BOA VISTA

☎ 0xx95 • postcode 69300-000
• pop 197,000

The state capital, a planned city on the banks of the Rio Branco, is home to more than half of Roraima's population. Many are public servants who were lured to the frontier by government incentives.

Although it's on a sealed road between Manaus and Venezuela, and many locals take vacations to the Caribbean, Boa Vista still feels quite isolated. Despite public investment in parks, sports facilities and so on, poverty is still very visible.

Orientation

The city is laid out in an arch shape, with the base on the Rio Branco and the arch itself formed by Avenida Major Williams along with Avenida Terencio Lima. The state government building at the center of the arch, and the crude Monumento ao Garimpeiro (Monument to the Gold Prospector) in the

---

The Road Through a Reserve

The Manaus–Boa Vista highway (BR-174) has a violent history. A 125km stretch of this road cuts across the 25,000 sq km Terra Indígena Waimiri Atroari.

The Waimiri fiercely defended their land against the construction of the road, combating the forces of the Brazilian army in the 1970s. During the confrontations more than 200 soldiers were killed by poison arrows. Casualties on the Indian side, however, were a lot higher. From a population of 1500 in 1974, their numbers were reduced to a mere 374 in 1986, when finally they agreed to negotiate with the government.

Today the population is increasing, with around 800 people living in 14 *aldeias* (villages). On the part of the road that crosses Indian land, drivers are not allowed to get out of their vehicles, and (with a few exceptions such as the Manaus–Boa Vista bus service) the road through the reserve is closed between 6 pm and 6 am.

---

park in front of it, marks the center of the street plan. Broad avenues radiate from the arch, dividing the outskirts into wedges. The city planners were clearly a race of giants: The scale of the place is totally unsuited to pedestrians who could quite easily spend a whole day trying to do a couple of errands.

Boa Vista's commercial district stretches between the central park, Praça do Centro Cívico, and the river.

Information

The office of Codetur (☎/fax 623-1230), the state tourism administration, is at Rua Coronel Pinto 241. The staff can answer questions but has little printed material for public consumption. It's open 7:30 am to 1:30 pm Monday to Friday. There is also an information desk at the airport, open when flights arrive in the evening, and another at the bus station, which was never found open at all in four visits (you may be luckier).

Banco do Brasil at Avenida Glaycon de Paiva 56, close to Praça do Centro Cívico, is open for exchange (including US dollar traveler's checks) 8 am to noon Monday to Friday. Other useful money changers, who exchange US, Venezuelan and Guyanese currencies, are Pedro José, Rua Araújo Filho 287, and Edson Ouro Safira Joyas, Avenida Benjamin Constant 64 W. Both are open 8 am to noon and 2 to 6 pm Monday to Friday, and 8 am to noon Saturday. Pedro José also exchanges US dollar traveler's checks.

The post office is on the northeast side of Praça do Centro Cívico. Long-distance phone calls can be made from the card phones outside the Telemar building at Avenida Capitan Ene Garcez 100.

The area at the bottom of Avenida Dr Silvio Botelho, toward the river, can get fairly seedy with drunks, so it's best to steer clear of this area.

Parque Anauá

This park on Avenida Brigadeiro Eduardo Gomes is about 2.5km northwest of the center. Within its vast grounds are gardens, a lake, a museum, an amphitheater and various sporting facilities. The museum,

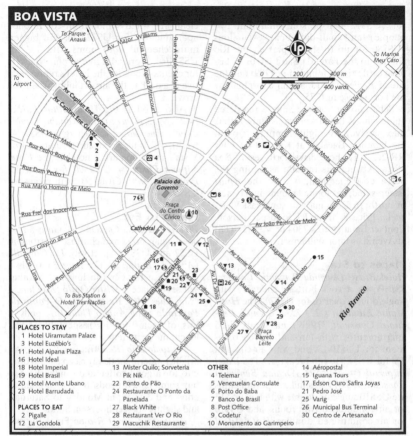

BOA VISTA

PLACES TO STAY
1 Hotel Uiramutam Palace
3 Hotel Euzébio's
11 Hotel Aipana Plaza
16 Hotel Ideal
18 Hotel Imperial
19 Hotel Brasil
20 Hotel Monte Libano
23 Hotel Barrudada

PLACES TO EAT
2 Pigalle
12 La Gondola

13 Mister Quilo; Sorveteria
   Pik Nik
22 Ponto do Pão
24 Restaurante O Ponto da
   Panelada
27 Black White
28 Restaurant Ver O Rio
29 Macuchik Restaurante

OTHER
4 Telemar
5 Venezuelan Consulate
6 Porto do Baba
7 Banco do Brasil
8 Post Office
9 Codetur
10 Monumento ao Garimpeiro

14 Aéropostal
15 Iguana Tours
17 Edson Ouro Safira Joyas
21 Pedro José
25 Varig
26 Municipal Bus Terminal
30 Centro de Artesanato

Museu Integrado de Roraima, is open 8 am to 6 pm every day. Its exhibits are limited in number but range over the state's archaeology, indigenous peoples, wildlife and history, and free guided tours (available in English most mornings) make this an interesting visit. The museum is 300m into the park from the entrance opposite the end of Rua General Penha Brasil.

Beaches

The main beach is **Praia Grande**, opposite Boa Vista on the Rio Branco, though it's only big enough to be worthwhile during the low-water season (about December to April). You can get there on small boats (US$2 roundtrip) from the Porto do Baba at the end of Avenida Major Williams. Baba is a local who organizes the Festa do Luau, a party held at low-water time on the beach under a *lua cheia* (full moon) with an open fire, and drinks and fruit provided.

Organized Tours

Iguana Tours (☎ 9971-7006, iguana@ technet.com.br), Rua Floriano Peixoto 505, is run by Eliezer Rufino de Souza, a local artist and tour operator who speaks

English. He offers two-hour riverboat tours for (US$12 per person, minimum two people) and half-day boat excursions (US$80 for up to six people) up the Rio Branco to the Fazenda São Marcos (a historic cattle ranch founded in 1799) and the site of the Forte São Joaquim, a fort built by the Portuguese in 1775.

Sebastião de Souza e Silva, a registered guide who is better known as Baba, offers inexpensive two-night camping trips to the Fazenda Bacabal at Km 140 on Hwy RR-203, a 1¾-hour drive northwest of Boa Vista. Attractions include ascending the Serra de Tepequém, one of the *tepuis* (steep-sided, flat-topped mountains) typical of northern Roraima and southeast Venezuela. Price is around US$30 per person. Contact Baba (☎ 623-7304 or ☎ 9971-7686) at Avenida Major Williams 1.

Places to Stay

Hotel Brasil (Avenida Benjamin Constant 331 W) is a rock-bottom cheapie, with single/double quartos for US$7/8. The *Hotel Monte Libano (☎ 224-7232, Avenida Benjamin Constant 319 W)* has drab, tired apartamentos with fan and shared bathroom for US$10/13, and with air-con and TV for US$13/16 (no breakfast). The *Hotel Imperial (☎ 224-5592, Avenida Benjamin Constant 433 W)* is similar: apartamentos are US$10 single or double with fan, US$13 for air-conditioned twin rooms and US$16 for air-conditioned doubles. *Hotel Ideal (☎ 224-6342, Rua Araújo Filho 533)* is a bit better looked after and has bare but clean single/double apartamentos that cost US$11/15 with fan and US$15/20 with air-con, all with breakfast. For US$3 more, you can have a TV or fridge. *Hotel Tres Nações (☎ 224-3439, Avenida Ville Roy 8534),* near the bus station, charges US$12/16 for its air-conditioned rooms.

Hotel Barrudada (☎ 623-9335, Rua Araújo Filho 228) is one of the newest hotels in town and one of the best values, so it's often fully booked (call ahead). Spotless apartamentos with air-conditioning, TV, fridge and phone cost US$33/40 including an excellent breakfast. *Hotel Euzébio's*

(☎ 623-0300, Rua Cecília Brasil 1107) has clean but small standard air-conditioned apartamentos for US$22/26, and bigger, more cheerful *lujo* rooms with TV for US$34/44. It provides free airport transfers for clients – look for the hotel's representative at a desk in the airport lobby when you arrive.

Also good is the *Uiramutam Palace (☎ 224-9912, palace@technet.com.br, Avenida Capitan Ene Garcez 427),* charging US$34/47 (cash), with a nice pool and restaurant. Boa Vista's most upmarket hotel is the *Hotel Aipana Plaza (☎ 224-4800, fax 224-4116, Praça do Centro Cívico 53)* with rooms for US$60/74.

Places to Eat

Pigalle (Avenida Capitan Ene Garcez 153) does cheap pizza and churrasco starting at US$2 and US$3 respectively. *La Gondola (Avenida Benjamin Constant 35 W)* is a good place for per-kilo lunches. Another self-serve place is *Mister Quilo (Rua Inácio Magalhães 346).* *Restaurante O Ponto da Panelada (Rua Araújo Filho 161)* pulls in lots of locals for its respectable US$2 lunchtime prato feito.

Ponto do Pão (Rua Araújo Filho 251) is a bright, modern, spotlessly clean café to drop into for a good coffee and sandwich or to buy some baked goods. It is open 6 am to noon and 3 to 9 pm Monday to Saturday, and slightly shorter hours on Sunday.

Restaurant Ver O Rio on Praça Barreto Leite has a fine spot just above the river (there's even a breeze sometimes) and serves good fish dishes at around US$6/12 for one/ two people. You can also just relax over a beer here if you like. Just behind the Ver O Rio and also overlooking the river is the *Macuchik Restaurante,* which serves a good-value lunch buffet for US$5, and a la carte fare from pizzas to fish for US$4 to US$20. *Black White* on the far side of the praça has good local fish dishes and pizza too.

The *Hotel Barrudada* (see Places to Stay) has a good restaurant with generous fish and meat main dishes for around US$6. The restaurants at the *Aipana Plaza* and *Uiramutam Palace* hotels are good too.

Marina Meu Caso is an enjoyable riverside spot at the end of Avenida Santos Dumont, about 1.5km upstream from the center, with big portions of good barbecued fish for US$4.

The *Sorveteria Pik Nik (Rua Inácio Magalhães 340)* is a good spot for ice cream.

Shopping
The small Centro de Artesanato, Rua Floriano Peixoto 158, has some handicrafts.

Getting There & Away
Varig (☎ 224-2226), Rua Araújo Filho 91, operates daily direct flights to/from Manaus (US$135 one-way), Brasília and Rio de Janeiro. Meta (☎ 224-7677), at the airport, flies to Manaus (US$104), Santarém, Belém and Macapá Monday to Friday. The Venezuelan airline Aéropostal (☎ 0800-998547), Rua Bento Brasil 44, flies to Barcelona, Margarita and Caracas (all in Venezuela) twice weekly. Meta flies to Puerto Ordaz, Venezuela, twice weekly. There are no longer any scheduled flights to Georgetown, Guyana.

Eucatur (☎ 623-2233) leaves for Manaus (US$33, 12 hours) six times daily (five are air-conditioned buses). It also has three departures to Santa Elena de Uairén, Venezuela (US$6, 3½ hours), one of which continues all the way to Puerto La Cruz on Venezuela's Caribbean coast (US$46, 20 hours). For information on buses to and from Bonfim, near the Guyana border, see the following Bonfim & Lethem section.

Getting Around
Taxis marked 'Lotação' go along roughly fixed routes for US$1 per passenger. Just ask if they're going where you want – they'll sometimes deviate a bit for you.

The airport (☎ 224-4143) is 3.5km northwest of the city center. To get there, you can take an 'Aeroporto' bus (US$0.70) from the municipal bus terminal on Avenida Dr Silvio Botelho. Most flights, however, arrive late at night. A regular taxi from the airport to the center is around US$7. Going out from the city to the airport, taxis may try to enforce a fixed rate of US$9.50.

The bus station (☎ 623-2233), on Avenida das Guianas, Bairro São Vicente, is 2.5km southwest of the center. Buses marked 'Jockei Clube' go there from the municipal bus terminal. A regular taxi from the center to the bus station costs about US$4.

AROUND BOA VISTA
Bonfim & Lethem (Guyana)
Bonfim: ☎ 0xx95 • pop 3000
Lethem: ☎ 072
The small town of Bonfim, 125km northeast of Boa Vista, is the stepping stone to Guyana. The Guyanese town of Lethem is about 5km west across the Rio Tacutu. Whichever direction you're crossing the border in, start early to get to your destination before nightfall.

You'll find the Polícia Federal (for Brazilian immigration procedures) between the Bonfim bus station and the river, so you have to walk or get taxis (about US$1.25 each time) to the police and onward from

AROUND BOA VISTA

there. You can either wade the river or get a canoe across for US$0.70. You should check in with the police at Lethem (about 1.5km from the river) immediately. You need to have your paperwork in order, as officials are wary about smuggling on this border.

Places to Stay The Kanuku mountains near Lethem are full of wildlife and there are several expensive ecotouristic ranches in the area; for information, try Don & Shirley's shop at the Lethem airstrip. *Takatu Guest House (☎ 2040)* is a good place to stay in Lethem itself, with rooms for about US$7 and inexpensive meals. The Guyana telephone country code is ☎ 592. Bonfim hotels are bad, but if you're stuck there try *Pousada Fronteira (☎ 552-1294, Rua Aluísio de Menezes 26)*, with doubles for about US$9.

Getting There & Away Buses of Amatur (☎ 0xx95-224-0009) travel three or four times daily each way between the Boa Vista bus station and Bonfim (US$6, two hours). In the dry season, trucks make the very rough 500km journey between Lethem and Georgetown for US$30 or so per passenger, taking at least 36 hours. There are planes all year, and you can try booking in advance by calling Weiting & Richter, a Georgetown travel agency (☎ 02-65121).

RESERVA XIXUAÚ-XIPARINÁ

This 1720 sq km ecological reserve, run by a joint Brazilian and international NGO, the Associação Amazônia, is on the west side of the Rio Jauaperí in southern Roraima. It is reached by a boat trip of 500km (1½ days) northwest from Manaus. The Associação Amazônia is involved in nature conservation and research and in health, employment and education projects with the sparse local population.

The reserve is a virtually untouched area of primary rainforest, and you can observe many species of Amazonian fauna, including the rare giant otter, relatively easily here. In the heart of the reserve is a group of palms where hundreds of macaws nest. Sport fishing, naturalist tours and ecotours – expeditions is perhaps a better word – are

available for groups of four to 10 people from eight to 15 days, starting from Manaus. The opportunities for wildlife photography are outstanding. Accommodations are in *malocas* (Indian-style dwellings). Prices per day per person, including travel from and back to Manaus, range from US$60, if there are 10 in the group, to US$100 in a four-person group. You can find out much more at the Associação Amazônia's Web site, www.amazonia.org. Officials include Plinio Leite da Encarnação (☎ 0xx92-232-1757, plinio@amazonia.org), in Manaus, and Christopher Clark (chris@amazonia.org), who is based in Italy.

SANTA ELENA DE UAIRÉN (VENEZUELA)
☎ 088 • pop 12,000
Santa Elena is a few kilometers north of the only land-border crossing between Brazil and Venezuela. It's a pleasant and relaxed border town, higher and cooler than Boa Vista, and it provides access to southeast Venezuela's vast, beautiful and silent Gran Sábana and to Mt Roraima, the spectacular mountain rising where Brazil, Venezuela and Guyana meet.

Brazilian and Venezuelan immigration procedures are all dealt with at the border

---

Venezuelan Entry Requirements

At the time of writing, travelers of many nationalities, including US and British passport-holders, needed to obtain a Venezuelan tourist card in advance in order to enter Venezuela by land (though not for entry by air). The card is free and can normally be issued in an hour or so by Venezuelan consulates in Brazil (see the Embassies & Consulates section in the Facts for the Visitor chapter). Normal requirements are your passport and a photocopy of its personal data and validity pages; one passport photo; a photocopy of your yellow-fever vaccination certificate; and a photocopy of your Brazilian immigration entry/exit card.

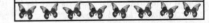

post itself. Entering Brazil, a yellow-fever certificate is required, and there is a Brazilian health-ministry vaccination post on the spot should you not have the certificate.

Orientation & Information

The central area is small and it's easy to find things. For several years the bus station has been on the verge of moving to a new location on the Ciudad Guayana road about 2km east of the center. Your guess is as good as ours as to whether or not it will still be at its old site on Avenida Mariscal Sucra in the north of town.

Banco Industrial de Venezuela on Calle Bolívar gives Visa card cash advances 8:30 am to 3:30 pm Monday to Friday. Money changers dealing in cash hang around the corner of Calle Bolívar and Calle Urdaneta.

You can make international phone calls at CANTV, on Calle Bolívar next to Hotel Augusta, and access the Internet at Interfaz Amazónica, on Calle Urdaneta, for US$0.90 per quarter-hour.

Organized Tours

Santa Elena has various tour operators offering standard two- or three-day jeep tours around La Gran Sábana. Two of the best established are Ruta Salvaje Tours (☎/fax 951134, rutasalvaje@cantv.net), on Avenida Mariscal Sucra beside the old bus station, and Tayukasen Tours (☎/fax 951505), on Calle Urdaneta in the center. Prices are negotiable up to a point: count on roughly US$25 to US$35 per person per day for a group of three or four, plus accommodations (usually in budget establishments) and food.

Many operators also offer five-night, six-day Mt Roraima expeditions for around US$250 to US$300 per person in a group of four to six (this includes transportation, camping equipment, food, porters and a guide). Some operators will drop off or pick up from Paraitepui (the starting point for the Roraima trek) for around US$100 each way per jeep for up to six or seven people. Ruta Salvaje also specializes in river rafting. A rafting or canoeing trip costs around US$35 per person per day; this price does not include accommodations.

Places to Stay & Eat

There is no shortage of possibilities. Decent cheap places to stay include *Hotel Gabriela* (☎ 951379) and *Hotel Panama* (☎ 951474), both on Calle Mariscal Sucre, with singles and doubles starting around US$10, and the central *Hotel Luz* (☎ 951505) at US$8.50 for bare rooms with private bathroom. *La Casa de Gladys* (☎ 951530, Calle Urdaneta 187) is a long-running budget place where basic singles/doubles/triples with shared bathrooms are US$6.50/10/13 and dormitory places are US$3. You can do your own cooking.

Posada La Aventura (☎ 951574, Avenida Perimetral 64) offers good, clean rooms with hot showers for US$10/12/18/20. A very nice recently opened place is *Hotel Augusta* (☎ 951654, fax 951440), centrally placed on Calle Bolívar. Spick-and-span singles and doubles in jolly colors with fan, hot shower and fridge are US$11.50; triples with television are US$17.

For a good value, go to *Pollo Asado La Dorada*, on Calle Zea, for roast chicken with potatoes, rice, salad and bread (US$2). *Cafe Colonial* (Calle Urdaneta 25) does bargain breakfasts (eggs, ham, bread, butter, jam, coffee and juice for US$2.50). *Pizzeria Texas* next door to Posada La Aventura does OK pizzas mostly for US$3.50.

Getting There & Away

Santa Elena's airport is 7km south of town. There is no public transport and taxis cost about US$6. You can fly to/from several places in Venezuela. Servivensa (☎ 951330), with an office in the town on Calle Icabarú, flies three times weekly to Canaima and Puerto Ordaz (US$106), with connections for Caracas (US$165). Avior and Rutaca, with offices at the airport, fly respectively to Puerto Ordaz (US$93) and Ciudad Bolívar (US$71).

A dozen daily buses by various companies head north. One goes to Puerto La Cruz on the coast (US$26, 16 hours) and two to Caracas (US$29 to US$32, 21 to 20 hours). All go through either Ciudad Guayana or Ciudad Bolívar (both US$10 to US$12, 10 to 12 hours).

Three head south to Boa Vista (US$6, 3½ hours), one continuing to Manaus (US$40, 16 hours).

MT RORAIMA & THE GRAN SÁBANA

Mt Roraima, straddling Brazil, Venezuela and Guyana, is one of the largest and highest of the tepuis that dot this border region. It's also one of Brazil's highest peaks, at 2810m. By far the easiest access to this spectacular and botanically unique mountain is from the Venezuelan side. This popular ascent involves no technical climbing and can be done by anyone who's fit. Agencies in Santa Elena de Uairén (see that section) offer organized trips that take some of the strain out of setting it up. If you want to do it independently, you must rent the necessary gear from any of several places in Santa Elena: For six days you'll pay approximately US$30 for a two/three-person tent, US$17 for a sleeping bag, US$5 for a foam mattress, and US$30 for a stove with cooking and eating equipment (not counting gasoline or gas fuel for the stove). You've got to take food too. Then you've got to get to San Francisco de Yuruaní, an indigenous village 69km north of Santa Elena on the main road (buses cost US$4.30). From San Francisco, it's 22km east to Paraitepui, another Indian village. A jeep will take a group of people from San Francisco to Paraitepui (and back when you come down) for around US$120. You must hire a guide in either San Francisco or Paraitepui. From Paraitepui, a guide costs US$30 a day and a porter US$22 a day.

Good water can be found in streams every 4 or 5km along the walk. The trail has spectacular waterfalls. At the top, Mt Roraima is a moonscape; it would be very easy to get lost, so don't wander far. You might consider spending an extra day on top of the mountain, but be prepared for cool drizzle and fog.

A straightforward roundtrip trek from Santa Elena takes five days, but some people allow up to two weeks in the area.

The Gran Sábana is dotted with many more tepuis and spectacular waterfalls. This rolling grassy highland is vast, wild, beautiful, empty and silent. It's best to visit the area in the dry season (December to April), but even then you will still be wet much of the time.

Rondônia & Acre

The states of Rondônia and Acre, previously undeveloped frontier regions, underwent rapid development and severe deforestation in the 1970s and 1980s, as a result of government colonization programs and the construction of Hwy BR-364 from Cuiabá in Mato Grosso. Vast tracts of land were left looking like the aftermath of a holocaust, and the hopes of many colonists were quickly dashed as their plots of cleared jungle soon turned infertile. The main beneficiaries of the environmental destruction were a small number of large-scale loggers and ranchers.

Many travelers simply pass through these states en route to or from neighboring Peru or Bolivia, but all should be aware that Acre and Rondônia are the conduits for most of the considerable amount of cocaine entering Brazil from these countries. Border towns such as Assis Brasil (Acre) and Guajará-Mirim and Costa Marques (Rondônia) are major entry points for the drug, and towns on Hwy BR-364 in Rondônia such as Ariquemes, Cacoal and Ji-Paraná are major distribution centers. The two state capitals, Porto Velho and Rio Branco, have a brash, edgy feel, but travelers are generally left alone if they mind their own business.

Rondônia

Rondônia is a transition zone between dense Amazonian forests and *cerrado*, and despite its sad environmental past, it still has some of the richest fauna and flora in Amazonia.

There's useful information about Rondônia in Portuguese at www.rondonia.ro.gov.br (the state government site), www.ronet .com.br and www.rondonia.com.

History

During the 17th and 18th centuries, Portuguese *bandeirantes* in pursuit of gold and Indian slaves crossed the line drawn by the Treaty of Tordesillas and entered what is now Rondônia to roam the Guaporé and Madeira River Valleys. Portugal secured its new possessions by building the Forte Príncipe da Beira, an imposing fortress on the Guaporé, between 1776 and 1783.

By the 1903 Treaty of Petrópolis, Bolivia ceded Acre to Brazil in return for UK£2 million and a promise to build a railway bypassing the waterfalls and rapids on the Rio Mamoré and upper Rio Madeira. This

Highlights

- Visiting Xapuri, hometown of Chico Mendes, Acre's environmental martyr
- Riding Rondônia's historic 'Death Railway,' the Estrada de Ferro Madeira-Mamoré
- Enjoying great meals at the Remanso do Tucunaré in Porto Velho and Anexo Espaço Gastronômico in Rio Branco

would give landlocked Bolivia access to world rubber markets via the Amazon. Since the railway never reached its ultimate intended goal (the Bolivian town of Riberalta, on the Rio Beni), and the price of rubber soon plummeted on the world market, the project turned out to be effectively useless. However, the towns of Porto Velho and Guajará-Mirim were founded at either end of the completed section in Brazil (see the boxed text 'Death Railway').

In 1943 President Getúlio Vargas created the Territory of Guaporé from chunks of Amazonas and Mato Grosso. In 1981 it became the state of Rondônia, named for Marechal Cândido Rondon, the enlightened and humane soldier who 'tamed' this region in the 1920s when he constructed a telegraph line linking it to the rest of Brazil. Rondon also founded the Serviço de Proteção ao Índio (SPI), predecessor of FUNAI. He exhorted SPI agents to *'morrer, se preciso for, matar nunca !'* ('Die, if necessary, but never kill!').

In 1981 the Polonoroeste program opened Rondônia to agricultural colonization by land-hungry settlers from all over the country. Rondônia's population leapt from 111,000 in 1970 to 1.13 million in 1991, while about one-fifth of the virgin jungle that covered almost the whole state was felled. The rate of deforestation in the 1980s was equivalent to more than a football field a minute, for a whole decade.

A major impetus of all this was the paving of Hwy BR-364 from Mato Grosso in 1983-84, with World Bank funding. This project was described by George Monbiot in *Amazon Watershed* (1991) as 'perhaps the single most destructive piece of engineering in the world.' Indian populations suffered severely from new diseases and deliberate killings. And since only about 10% of Rondônia is suitable for agriculture, many of the new farms failed, adding further social problems.

In the 1990s deforestation slowed, but timber remains Rondônia's biggest industry, with cocaine commerce a possible second. In 1997 the capital of Porto Velho was the site of the largest seizure of cocaine ever made by federal officials, and it is suspected that only a portion of the shipment was apprehended. Cattle ranching on cleared land is another huge activity: the cattle population in the state is over six million strong. Expulsions and attacks on some of the small number of surviving Indians (estimated at 6700 in 1998) have seemingly continued, albeit on a reduced scale.

PORTO VELHO
☎ 0xx69 • postcode 78900-000
• pop 262,000

The 1980s gold rush and the main influx of colonists are now history, and Porto Velho's central streets have been paved and sport ever glossier shops. But Rondônia's capital is still a frontier town. The outlying *bairros* are slums of straw-roofed shacks. The newspapers tell of shootouts between police and cocaine dealers, and of arrests at the airport of carriers attempting to move the drug to the Brazilian southeast.

Orientation
The main street is Avenida Sete de Setembro, running east from the Madeira-Mamoré train station just back from the Rio Madeira riverfront. A few blocks farther north, parallel to Sete de Setembro and dotted with the city's glossiest shops, is Avenida Carlos Gomes, which passes the bus station on Avenida Jorge Teixeira nearly 3km from the river.

Information
Porto Velho has no tourist information office. Travel agents can answer some questions, as can the small state tourism authority, Setur (☎ 229-1159, seturo@zipmail.com.br), at Esplanada das Secretarias, Rua Pio XII. Setur is a US$2.50 taxi ride from the center, and is open from 8 am to noon and from 2 to 6 pm Monday to Friday.

The state office of IBAMA (☎ 223-3597/8), Avenida Jorge Teixeira 3559, in Bairro Costa e Silva a couple of kilometers north of the center, can give information on protected natural areas in Rondônia, some of which have incipient ecotourism programs. Bus No 201 'Hospital de Base via Aeroporto' (see Getting Around) passes the IBAMA office (US$0.75).

Be aware that English-speakers are a rarity at all these places. The Web sites mentioned under Internet Resources earlier include some tourist information, although it is all in Portuguese only.

Casa de Câmbio Marco Aurélio (☎ 221-2551), Rua José de Alencar 3353, changes cash US dollars and all brands of traveler's checks 8:30 am to 3 pm Monday to Friday. Banco do Brasil, Rua Dom Pedro II 607, changes traveler's checks and cash US dollars 10 am to 2 pm Monday to Friday. The ATMs at HSBC, Avenida Jorge Teixeira 1350, next door to the bus station, will give cash to Cirrus cardholders.

The main post office is on Avenida Presidente Dutra. You can make international phone calls at the Posto Telefônico at Avenida Presidente Dutra 3034, open 24 hours daily. You can use the Internet for US$2.50 an hour at the store called Games & Videos, Avenida Sete de Setembro 1925, open till 10 pm daily.

Two useful travel agencies for booking your visits to other places in Rondônia are Princetur (☎ 224-8003, fax 224-2052), Avenida Carlos Gomes 1675, and Nossa Viagens e Turismo (☎ 224-4777), Rua Tenreiro Aranha 2125.

Shops and offices generally close here from noon to 2 pm.

Estrada de Ferro Madeira-Mamoré

The Madeira-Mamoré Railway (see the boxed text 'Death Railway') is Porto Velho's only real sight of interest. Its little station and several huge sheds stand around the

Death Railway

An American, Colonel George Earl Church, was the first to try to build a railway bypassing the 23 waterfalls and rapids that make navigation impossible on the Madeira and Mamoré Rivers between Porto Velho and Guajará-Mirim. The idea was to carry rubber from the Mamoré and Guaporé Valleys down to the navigable section of the Madeira and thus also to the Rio Amazonas, North America and Europe. In 1871 Church contracted Britain's Public Works Construction Company to build the line. The first construction materials reached Santo Antônio do Madeira, 7km southwest of Porto Velho, in 1872 by ship from the USA. But the project was abandoned a year later in the face of rampant disease among workers, attacks by Indians and mounting costs. The US firm of P & T Collins tried again for Church in 1878, managing to build 11km of embankments and nine bridges before it gave up in 1879 for the same reasons.

Following Brazil's commitment to build the railway in the 1903 Treaty of Petrópolis (see the Rondônia History section), another American, Percival Farquhar, contracted the US firm of May, Jeckyll and Randolph to build the line. Work started in 1907, and a 364km line to Guajará-Mirim was completed in five years by old Panama Canal hands and other workers from Brazil and elsewhere. The northern terminus was moved from Santo Antônio to a healthier spot 7km downstream, around which the town of Porto Velho grew up.

The line rapidly became known as the Railway of Death and with good reason. Building it is believed to have cost the lives of at least 5000 workers – some say 25,000 – from tropical diseases, Indian and animal attacks, accidents, gunfights, disappearances in the jungle and so on. 'One death for every railway sleeper' was the expression of the day.

And their sacrifice was pretty much wasted, because just as the railway was being completed, the new British rubber plantations in Malay killed demand for the more expensive Amazonian rubber. Percival Farquhar's Madeira Mamoré Railway Company had a 60-year contract to operate the line, but it ceased operations in 1931. Brazil's government took over the railway, finally closing it in 1972 when the Porto Velho-Guajará-Mirim road opened. The road largely follows the course of the railway, and still uses some of the line's ancient bridges on the stretch north of Guajará-Mirim.

PORTO VELHO

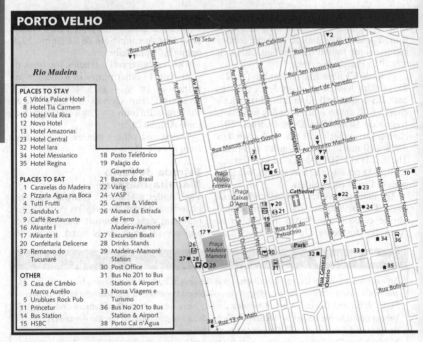

Rio Madeira

PLACES TO STAY
6 Vitória Palace Hotel
8 Hotel Tia Carmem
10 Hotel Vila Rica
12 Novo Hotel
13 Hotel Amazonas
23 Hotel Central
32 Hotel Iara
34 Hotel Messianico
35 Hotel Regina

PLACES TO EAT
1 Caravelas do Madeira
2 Pizzaria Agua na Boca
4 Tutti Frutti
7 Sanduba's
9 Caffé Restaurante
16 Mirante I
17 Mirante II
20 Confeitaria Delicerse
37 Remanso do
   Tucunaré

OTHER
3 Casa de Câmbio
   Marco Aurélio
5 Urublues Rock Pub
11 Princetur
14 Bus Station
15 HSBC

18 Posto Telefônico
19 Palácio do
   Governador
21 Banco do Brasil
22 Varig
24 VASP
25 Games & Videos
26 Museu da Estrada
   de Ferro
   Madeira-Mamoré
27 Excursion Boats
28 Drinks Stands
29 Madeira-Mamoré
   Station
30 Post Office
31 Bus No 201 to Bus
   Station & Airport
33 Nossa Viagens e
   Turismo
36 Bus No 201 to Bus
   Station & Airport
38 Porto Caí n'Água

parklike Praça Madeira Mamoré at the river end of Avenida Sete de Setembre.

In 1979 the state government restored part of the railroad to preserve a bit of history and serve as a tourist attraction. Currently the Maria Fumaça (Smoking Mary) steam locomotive chugs to and from Santo Antônio, beside the Cachoeira de Santo Antônio waterfalls on the Rio Madeira, 7km southwest of Porto Velho (Sunday only). This excursion costs US$2 roundtrip. Santo Antônio was the original northern terminus of the Madeira-Mamoré Railway. All that remains there today is a chapel, built in 1913, but it's a popular dry-season swimming spot.

One of the huge sheds by the Porto Velho station houses the **Museu da Estrada de Ferro Madeira-Mamoré**, displaying train relics, memorabilia, and photographs charting the railway's story. The locomotive 'Colonel Church,' built by the Baldwin Locomotive Works of Philadelphia, became the first locomotive to run in Amazonia when it inaugurated the Madeira-Mamoré Railway in 1878. At the time of research the museum opened 9 am to 5 pm Sunday only (free). A variety of other old US- and German-made locomotives and rolling stock can be seen any day, standing around nearby.

River Trips

The broad Rio Madeira forms the western boundary of Porto Velho. Measurements of the length of the mud-brown river usually include its main tributary the Rio Mamoré and *its* tributaries, which originate in the Bolivian Andes, making the Madeira 3200km long. With an average flow of 1.4 billion liters a minute, the Madeira has the sixth greatest volume of all the world's rivers. It enters the Rio Amazonas 150km downstream from Manaus.

From about 9 am to 6 pm daily, riverboats make 45-minute cruises along the Rio Madeira from the dock in front of the

and TV are US$13.50/20. Prices include a simple breakfast (except Sunday). Of a similar standard is the *Vitória Palace Hotel* (☎ 221-9232, *Rua Duque de Caxias 745*). Simple fan-cooled rooms cost US$13.50/17, and rooms with air-conditioning and TV are US$17/20, all including breakfast.

Near the bus station, *Hotel Amazonas* (☎ 221-7735, *Avenida Carlos Gomes 2838*) has clean single quartos for US$5 and apartamentos with TV for US$6.75/10 single/double.

Hotel Iara (☎ 221-2127, *Rua General Osório 255*) has fairly ordinary single/double apartamentos with air-conditioning starting at US$17/21. A little more comfortable is *Hotel Regina* (☎ 224-3411, *Rua Almirante Barroso 1127*). Clean apartamentos with air-con, fridge and TV cost US$19/29. Close to the bus station, *Novo Hotel* (☎ 224-6555, *Avenida Carlos Gomes 2776*) has average apartamentos with air-conditioning, TV and fridge for US$20/30.

Hotel Central (☎ 224-2099, fax 223-5114, *Rua Tenreiro Aranha 2472*) is a good value if you have more to spend. Good apartamentos are US$35/47, with an excellent breakfast.

Hotel Vila Rica (☎ 224-3433, *Avenida Carlos Gomes 1616*) is Porto Velho's finest hotel and one of the few tall buildings in the city. It has an impressive foyer, nice bar, swimming pool and small business center. Discounts usually bring the price down to around US$59/70.

Madeira-Mamoré train station. While not exactly thrilling, this is a reasonable way to idle away an hour or so. With luck you'll see a few pink dolphins. Cost is US$2, with drinks and disgusting food available on board.

Places to Stay

The *Hotel Messianico* (☎ 221-4084, *Avenida Sete de Setembro 1180*) has single/double quartos with fan for US$5/7. Apartamentos (with bath) cost US$10 single or double with fan, or US$13.50 with air-con and TV. The rooms are small but they open onto a courtyard and are kept reasonably clean. Breakfast isn't included.

Hotel Tia Carmem (☎ 221-7910, *Avenida Campos Sales 2895*), in a quieter and better location, offers a range of clean rooms, though they're musty till you get some air circulating. Basic quartos with fan are a reasonable value at US$7/10 single/double; apartamentos with fridge, air-conditioning

Places to Eat

Porto Velho is not widely celebrated for its haute cuisine, but it does have some decent restaurants. A very good place for fish is the *Remanso do Tucunaré* (☎ 221-2353, *Avenida Brasília 1506*). Soccer star Garrincha figures among the restaurant's eminent guests as evidenced by his picture hanging on the wall. Many of the excellent dishes cost around US$7 to US$10, and they'll feed two. Try a delicious *caldeirada* of *tucunaré* or *tambaqui* – big fish chunks boiled with onion and tomatoes in a soup-like sauce, accompanied by rice. The restaurant is open 10:30 am to 1:30 am daily (to 4 pm on Sunday). The

Caravelas do Madeira (☎ 221-6641, Rua José Camacho 104), overlooking the river, reportedly has good fish dishes too, typically between US$10 and US$20. It's open for lunch and dinner Tuesday to Saturday.

Caffé Restaurante (Avenida Carlos Gomes 1079) does a good daily lunch buffet in air-conditioned cool for US$7.50/kg, including six or eight types of salad and succulent desserts.

Pizzaria Agua na Boca (☎ 221-6488, Rua Tenreiro Aranha 201) has Porto Velho's best pizza and excellent service. It's a large but pleasant restaurant with outdoor and indoor tables and a large TV screen so you don't escape the Brazilian soaps. Pizzas cost from US$6 to US$15, and there are plenty of other options. It's open 6 pm to midnight daily except Monday. Another large, open-air restaurant is *Tutti Frutti (☎ 224-7650, Avenida Pinheiro Machado 1133).* Here you can get good sizable meat or fish dishes for US$10 or so; pasta or pizza start around US$5 or US$6.

The *Confeitaria Delicerse (Rua José de Alencar 3050)* has excellent *salgados* (savory snacks) and juices for US$1. At *Sanduba's (Avenida Campos Sales 2913),* a big multi-ingredient burger with all the trimmings costs US$3 or US$4.

The *Mirante I (☎ 221-8960, Rua Major Amarante 182)* has a great river view and both indoor and outdoor tables. Fish or meat dishes or pizzas cost between US$6 and $14. The *Mirante II,* a block away at the end of Rua Dom Pedro II, is a bit lower-key, with outdoor tables. It serves fish dishes for US$7 to $15 and sandwiches for US$1 to $2.50.

Entertainment

The riverbank by the Madeira-Mamoré train station has a dozen drink stands with tables, and a couple of floating docks that double as bars, with live music Saturday and Sunday nights. If you're looking for beer and sweaty dancing, this is the place to head for. It can get a bit seedy late at night – check to see if police security is around. The *Mirante* restaurants (see Places to Eat) also have live music most nights, from *pagode* or *forró* to MPB or rock. *Urublues Rock Pub*

(Rua José de Alencar 3292) might be worth a look on the weekend.

Getting There & Away

Air Varig (☎ 224-2262), Avenida Campos Sales 2666, and VASP (☎ 223-3755), Rua Tenreiro Aranha 2326, both fly daily to/from Manaus, Rio Branco, Brasília, Rio de Janeiro and São Paulo. Transbrasil (☎ 223-8702) and TAM (☎ 224-2118) operate farther long-distance flights, while Rico (☎ 225-1299) and TAVAJ (☎ 229-5908) provide regional flights to/from places in Amazonas and Acre States. One-way fares to Manaus/Brasília/Rio are US$150/270/335 with Varig from the Porto Velho airport (☎ 225-1675).

Bus Viação Rondônia (☎ 224-2344) runs four daily buses each to both Guajará-Mirim (US$13.50, 5½ hours) and Rio Branco (US$18, seven to eight hours). For Guajará-Mirim you have the alternative of a shared cab from the bus station (US$20 per person, three hours).

Eucatur/União Cascavel (☎ 222-2233) runs the best long-distance buses, including to Cuiabá (US$50, 21 hours, four daily), São Paulo (US$115, 48 hours, two daily) and Brasília (US$89, 38 hours, one daily). Andorinha (☎ 225-3025) runs twice daily to Brasília (US$68) and, with a change at Campo Grande, twice daily to Rio de Janeiro (US$143, 56 hours). Açailândia goes all the way to Belém (US$150, three days-plus, three times weekly).

Hwy BR-319 to Manaus has been impassable from not far beyond Humaitá, 205km north of Porto Velho, since 1991.

Boat Boats to Manaus via the Rio Madeira and Rio Amazonas usually leave around 6 pm on Tuesday and Friday from the Porto Cai n'Água, the dock at the end of Rua 13 de Maio. Barring delays, the trip takes three to 3½ days, costing US$40 in a hammock or US$135 for a two-person cabin, including meals. There are ticket offices on Rua 13 de Maio: you might need to bargain a bit. Check out the boat and fellow passengers for unsavory characters before committing yourself.

Getting Around

Aeroporto Belmont is about 6km north of the center. Bus No 201 'Hospital de Base via Aeroporto' (US$0.75) runs between the city center and airport via the bus station. Heading out from the center, it stops on Avenida Sete de Setembro near the corners of Avenida Presidente Dutra and Rua Marechal Deodoro. A taxi between the airport and center costs US$13.

Buses head west toward the city center from the stop opposite the north side of the bus station, but check with the driver or conductor that they're actually going *to* the centro.

AROUND PORTO VELHO
Reserva Extrativista do Lago do Cuniã

This 558 sq km reserve, created in 1999, lies 150km down the Rio Madeira from Porto Velho, accessible only by river. It's Rondônia's largest fish spawning ground (pirarucu and aruanã are among the species breeding here) and is renowned for its abundant bird

This reserve is renowned for its bird life.

life. Pink and gray dolphins, alligators and, with luck, manatee can also be seen. IBAMA has been working as an intermediary between the reserve's inhabitants and agencies such as Nossa Viagens e Turismo to set up an ecotourism program with basic lodging and walking trails. Visits were due to start up in 2001 and expected to cost around US$25 a day per person. (For contact information for the agencies listed here, see Information the Porto Velho section, earlier.)

GUAJARÁ-MIRIM
☎ 0xx69 • postcode 78957-000
• pop 32,000

This low-key town on the Rio Mamoré came into existence as the southern terminus of the Madeira-Mamoré Railway. Both Guajará-Mirim and its Bolivian neighbor across the river, Guayaramerín, are free trade zones attracting a steady stream of shopping tourists.

Information

See the Polícia Federal (☎ 541-2437) for exit/entry stamps if you are leaving/entering Brazil. The office is at the corner of Avenida Presidente Dutra and Avenida Quintino Bocaiúva.

Over-the-counter Visa-card cash withdrawals are available at Banco do Brasil, Avenida Mendonça Lima 388, open 9 am to 2 pm Monday to Friday (8 am to 1 pm from mid-October to mid-February). This bank will also exchange cash US dollars but not traveler's checks. A signless exchange house at Avenida Mendonça Lima 145 exchanges cash US and Bolivian currencies, 8 am to noon Monday to Friday. The door is immediately east of Drogaria Fialho.

Informática (☎ 541-4270), Avenida Presidente Dutra 331, offers Internet access for US$3.50 an hour.

The Bolivian consulate in Guajará-Mirim normally issues 30-day tourist visas (to nationalities that need them) within 20 minutes; take your passport. See the Embassies & Consulates section of Facts for the Visitor for the consulate's contact information.

Museu Histórico Municipal

This slightly interesting museum, in the old Madeira-Mamoré train station on Avenida 15 de Novembro, has two old steam locomotives parked outside. The exhibits focus on natural history, with a few stuffed examples of Rondônia fauna. A stuffed anaconda stretches the length of the main salon; a pair of Siamese-twin piglets are preserved in formaldehyde. Hours are 8 am to noon and 2:30 to 6 pm Monday to Friday, 9 am to noon and 3 to 6 pm Saturday, 9 am to 1 pm Sunday and holidays. Admission is free.

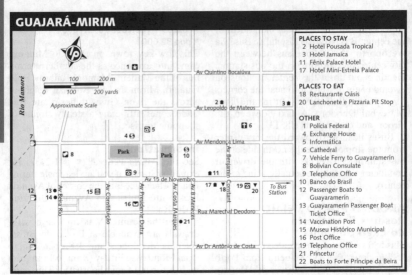

GUAJARÁ-MIRIM

PLACES TO STAY
2 Hotel Pousada Tropical
3 Hotel Jamaica
11 Fênix Palace Hotel
17 Hotel Mini-Estrela Palace

PLACES TO EAT
18 Restaurante Oásis
20 Lanchonete e Pizzaria Pit Stop

OTHER
1 Polícia Federal
4 Exchange House
5 Informática
6 Cathedral
7 Vehicle Ferry to Guayaramerín
8 Bolivian Consulate
9 Telephone Office
10 Banco do Brasil
12 Passenger Boats to Guayaramerín
13 Guayaramerín Passenger Boat Ticket Office
14 Vaccination Post
15 Museu Histórico Municipal
16 Post Office
19 Telephone Office
21 Princetur
22 Boats to Forte Príncipe da Beira

Places to Stay & Eat

It might be worth calling ahead to book a hotel if you're arriving on a weekend. Breakfast is included in all the following prices.

The friendly *Hotel Pousada Tropical* (☎ 541-3308, Avenida Benjamin Constant 376) offers small but clean single/double apartamentos with fan for US$8/13.50, or with air-conditioning for US$10/13.50.

Two hotels facing each other on Avenida 15 de Novembro are better than their drab exteriors look. At the *Fênix Palace Hotel* (☎ 541-2326, Avenida 15 de Novembro 459), varied quartos with fan are US$6.50/12 and good air-conditioned apartamentos are US$10/16.50. Across the road, the *Hotel Mini-Estrela Palace* (☎ 541-1140, Avenida 15 de Novembro 460) has basic air-conditioned apartamentos for US$9/12, and ones with TV and fridge for US$13.50/20. Those upstairs are better.

The best place in town is *Hotel Jamaica* (☎ 541-3721/2, Avenida Leopoldo de Mateos 755), with comfortable, air-conditioned apartamentos for US$27/32.

The recently opened *Pakaas Palafitas Lodge* (☎/fax 541-3058) is a superior jungle hotel 20 minutes by boat up the Rio Mamoré

from town. It offers 50 comfortable chalets, over 2.5km of walkways, restaurant, bar with dance floor, swimming pool, jungle walks, boat trips and alligator-spotting expeditions. Initial prices for singles/doubles when the hotel opened in 2000, including breakfast and transportation to/from Guajará-Mirim, started at US$84/144 Monday to Friday, and US$96/168 Saturday to Sunday and holidays. You can book through Princetur in Porto Velho (see Information in the Porto Velho section) or in Guajará-Mirim (☎ 541-2387, Avenida Costa Marques 807), through Cristours in Guayaramerín (see River Trips under Guayaramerín), or online at www.pakaas.com.br.

The *Restaurante Oásis* (*Avenida 15 de Novembro 460*) is Guajará-Mirim's best restaurant. It is open for lunch only (11 am to 3 pm) for a good buffet costing US$7.50/kg. The popular *Lanchonete e Pizzaria Pit Stop* (*Avenida 15 de Novembro 620*) has pretty good pizzas. The medium size costs US$4 to US$7.

Getting There & Around

Viação Rondônia runs four daily buses to/from Porto Velho (US$13.50, 5½ hours), and one (at noon) to/from Rio Branco (US$17, eight hours). The bus station is on ☎ 541-2448.

Passenger launches across the Rio Mamoré to/from Guayaramerín, Bolivia go about every 15 minutes in both directions from 7 am to 6 pm. From 6 pm to 7 am they leave when they have 10 passengers. Fare for the five-to-10-minute trip is US$1. The port in Guajará-Mirim is in front of the Museu Histórico Municipal.

A vehicle ferry to Guayaramerín goes from a dock 200m north of the passenger ferry point. Travelers entering Brazil at Guajará-Mirim may well be required to show a yellow-fever vaccination certificate. If you don't have one, you can get the jab at a vaccination post beside the passenger ferry ticket office. See the Getting There & Away chapter for more information on crossing the border.

Usually two or three passenger-carrying boats a week sail up the Mamoré and Guaporé Rivers from Guajará-Mirim to the Forte Príncipe da Beira. Ask at the moorings at the end of Avenida Dr Antônio da Costa. The trip takes two to three days going upstream, and about half that coming back. The hammock fare is around US$14. Fast launches known as *voladores* can do the trip in about eight hours for about US$50 a person, but they need eight passengers.

Occasional boats go up the Guaporé as far as Vila Bela da Santíssima Trindade in Mato Grosso.

A taxi between the town center and bus station (2km east along Avenida 15 de Novembro) costs US$4.50.

GUAYARAMERÍN (BOLIVIA)
☎ 0855 • pop 35,000
Guayaramerín, on the Rio Mamoré opposite Guajará-Mirim, is a frontier town, river port, trading center and the start of a road to La Paz, the Bolivian capital, via Riberalta (90km away) and Rurrenabaque. Accommodations here are cheaper than in Guajará-Mirim.

Information
For entry/exit stamps, go to Migración (Bolivian immigration) just east of the ferry building (open 8 am to 8 pm daily).

There's no tourist office but the small Policía Nacional office in the ferry building, the Migración office and Cristours (see River Trips) are worth trying for information.

You can interchange Bolivian, Brazilian and US currencies, in cash, at the money changers' desks in the ferry building, at the Hotel San Carlos reception, and at Milán Cambio on Plaza Principal. The hotel will also exchange American Express traveler's checks denominated in US dollars.

See Embassies & Consulates in the Facts for the Visitor chapter for information on the Brazilian consulate in Guayaramerín.

River Trips
Cristours/Green Adventure Tours (☎ 4050), on Avenida Federico Román one block from the ferry building, offers boat trips up the Rio Mamoré to Laguna La Merced. This area of virgin jungle offers many opportunities to spot wildlife. A three-day trip, with the two nights spent in the home of a villager, costs US$300 per person for four people or more.

Places to Stay & Eat
The mellow *Hotel Litoral* (☎ 3985), on Calle 25 de Mayo near the airport, has clean singles/doubles with private bathroom and fan for just US$4/8 (US$3.25/6.50 with shared bathrooms). Across the street, the quiet and shady *Hotel Santa Ana* (☎ 3900, Calle 25 de Mayo 611) offers similar amenities for the same prices.

Hotel Central (☎ 3911, Calle Mariscal Santa Cruz 235) has a courtyard with colorful flowers, lined by basic but spotless rooms costing only US$2.50/5. The shared baths are very clean too. *Hotel San Carlos* (☎ 3555, Calle 6 de Agosto 347) is the upmarket place in town, with a restaurant and billiards table. Air-conditioned rooms with TV and bath cost US$24/33 including breakfast.

Itauba Eco-Resort (☎ 3514), set among lakes about 3km from the river along Avenida Federico Román, offers comfy chalets for US$25/35 including breakfast. You can go canoeing or horseback riding here. You can book through Cristours.

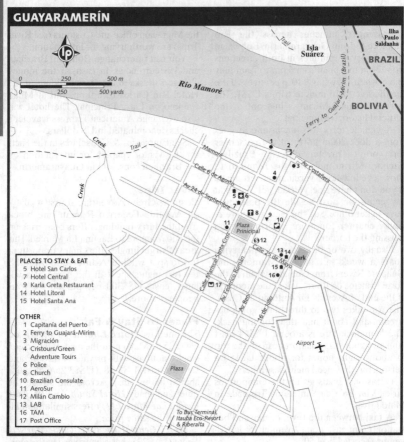

GUAYARAMERÍN

Río Mamoré

PLACES TO STAY & EAT
5 Hotel San Carlos
7 Hotel Central
9 Karla Greta Restaurant
14 Hotel Litoral
15 Hotel Santa Ana

OTHER
1 Capitanía del Puerto
2 Ferry to Guajará-Mirim
3 Migración
4 Cristours/Green
   Adventure Tours
6 Police
8 Church
10 Brazilian Consulate
11 AeroSur
12 Milán Cambio
13 LAB
16 TAM
17 Post Office

Karla Greta Restaurant on Avenida Federico Román near the Plaza Principal serves a functional set lunch for just US$1.25. A la carte, meat and fish dishes cost US$3 to US$4.50.

Getting There & Away

Air Guayaramerín's airport is on the eastern edge of town. You can fly to many Bolivian destinations. TAM (☎ 3924), the Bolivian military airline, flies to Trinidad (US$62) on Wednesday and Thursday, to Santa Cruz (US$95) Wednesday and Sunday, to Rurrenabaque and La Paz (US$95) Monday and

Friday, and to Cochabamba (US$82) on Tuesday. AeroSur (☎ 3594) and LAB (☎ 3788) both fly almost daily to Trinidad (US$79) and also twice weekly to Cobija (US$64); some flights have connections for Santa Cruz, La Paz, Cochabamba or Sucre. You can book these flights through the individual airline offices in town or through Cristours.

Bus & Car The bus terminal is 2.5km from the river along Avenida Federico Román. The Guayaramerín company (☎ 3528) runs six buses daily to Riberalta (US$3.25, two hours), one at 7 am daily except Wednesday and Saturday to Trinidad (US$27, 24 hours), and one at 6 am Tuesday, Thursday and Saturday to Cobija (US$16, 15 hours). Flota Yungueña (☎ 4514) has a daily 8 am departure for Riberalta, Santa Rosa, Reyes, Rurrenabaque and La Paz (US$27, 36 hours), and buses at 7 am Wednesday and Saturday to Riberalta and Trinidad (US$27, about 24 hours). Most of the roads the buses travel are gravel. In the wettest months (late December to late February), journey times beyond Riberalta can double (or more), and some services may be cancelled.

You can also reach Riberalta by shared car from the bus terminal (US$4.75 per person, US$19 for the whole vehicle).

Boat Boats usually leave the port every day or two for Trinidad, which is five to seven days up the Rio Mamoré (from US$30 to US$40 in a hammock, including meals). Some go as far upstream as Puerto Villarroel, on the Rio Ichilo (a tributary of the Mamoré). The office of the Capitanía del Puerto has a notice board listing all sailings.

Getting Around
The town is so small you can walk just about anywhere, except to the bus terminal. *Motokares* (motorcycle rickshaws) charge US$0.80 between the bus terminal and the center or ferry port. There are also motorcycle taxis which cost US$0.30 anywhere around town.

GUAPORÉ VALLEY
The Rio Guaporé forms the Brazil/Bolivia border for a stretch of 600km or more from its confluence with the Rio Mamoré, about 150km upstream of Guajará-Mirim.

Forte Príncipe da Beira & Costa Marques
☎ 0xx69 • postcode 78971-000
Remote Forte Príncipe da Beira, beside the Rio Guaporé 210km south of Guajará-Mirim, was constructed by the Portuguese between 1776 and 1783 to consolidate their hold on the lands east of the Guaporé and Mamoré against the Spanish. The star-

shaped fort, one of only two ever constructed by Portugal in the Brazilian interior, has 10m-high walls and four corner bastions, each of which held 14 cannons. Today just one cannon remains. The walls, nearly 1km around, are surrounded by a moat and enclose the ruins of a chapel, armory, officers' quarters, and prison cells in which bored convicts scrawled poetic graffiti. Underground passageways lead from the fortress to the river.

The fort was abandoned as a military post in 1889. Today Brazil maintains a garrison of around 70 soldiers beside the fort. There's also a village, Vila Príncipe da Beira, here.

Places to Stay & Eat In the town of Costa Marques (population 6600), 25km east of the fort, *Hotel Girassol Palácio (☎/fax 651-2215, Avenida Demétrio Melas 1796)* has air-conditioned apartamentos with TV costing US$13.50/23.50 for singles/doubles with breakfast. For meals, try *Peixaria do Reis (Avenida Demétrio Melas 1918),* which specializes in fish.

Getting There & Away In the past there have been planes flying to Costa Marques from Guajará-Mirim and Ji-Paraná. These were not operating at the time of research, but may start up again soon: Ask at a travel agency.

By bus, it's a long haul to the fort, and the Presidente Medici-Costa Marques road is impassable from about November to April. From Porto Velho, take a Eucatur/União Cascavel bus to Presidente Medici (US$41, around seven hours, four daily) and change there to a bus to Costa Marques (US$40, around 12 hours), a ride through a wild, severely deforested region. All being well, the 8 pm bus from Porto Velho gets you to Presidente Medici in time for the early morning bus to Costa Marques.

Two daily buses run from Costa Marques to the fort and back.

For information on boats to Forte Príncipe de Beira, see Getting There & Away in the Guajará-Mirim section earlier in this chapter.

Guaporé Valley Ecotourism Project

An interesting ecotourism program in the Guaporé valley, happening in various sites dotted between Costa Marques and the Reserva Extrativista Pedras Negras (20 hours upstream by boat), has been started by local rubber tappers' organizations with the help of NGOs.

Your visit can include an Amazon turtle conservation project, a nursery for Amazon plants, riverside villages, and extractive reserves; you can learn about the lives of rubber tappers and take walking, canoe and fishing trips.

The best months to go are August to November, when river beaches are exposed. From September, turtle nesting sites can be observed. You stand varying chances of seeing rare orchids, macaws, toucans, alligators, deer, river dolphins and jaguars.

The project's organizers envisage groups of between five and 12 people spending up to about a week in the area. Cost per person in the Reserva Extrativista Pedras Negras is US$65 a day. Two weeks' notice is needed. For further information contact the Brazil Eco Travel Center (see Organized Tours in the Natural Brazil chapter), which arranges visits, or the Organização dos Seringueiros de Rondônia (OSR, Rubber Tappers' Organization of Rondônia, ☎/fax 0xx69-224-1368, os.ro@bol.com.br), Rua Joaquim Nabuco 1215, Bairro Areal, Porto Velho, or visit the program's Web site (www.ronet.com.br/ecoturismo).

CENTRAL RONDÔNIA

The center of the state has, in general, suffered the severest deforestation, but it does contain a successful jungle-cum-ranch-hotel and Rondônia's only national park.

Hotel Fazenda Rancho Grande

The German-run *Hotel Fazenda Rancho Grande* (☎ 0xx69-535-4301, pousada@ ariquemes.com.br, Linha C 20, lote 23 – TB 65, Cacaulândia) is set amidst a tropical forest rich in wildlife, especially butterflies. Forest walks, swimming, horseback riding and meals are all included in the prices of US$65/90/120 for single/double/triple occupancy of the comfortable apartamentos. The host family, the Schmitzes, speak English and German. Rancho Grande is 162km southeast of Porto Velho on Hwy BR-364, then 26km south of the highway between Ariquemes and Jaru, near Cacaulândia. You can book on the fazenda's multilingual Web site, www.ariquemes.com.br/pousada.

Parque Nacional de Pacaás Novos

This remote and wild national park is currently only accessible on helicopter trips with IBAMA (see Information in the Porto Velho section), but IBAMA says it plans to construct a research and visitor center that might be operating by 2002. The 7648 sq km park's rugged relief encompasses Rondônia's highest peak, Pico do Tracoá (1230m), and lots of spectacular waterfalls. Fauna includes jaguars, tapirs, giant anteaters, howler monkeys and the rare blue macaw. The park lies inside an Indian reserve, Terra Indígena Uru-Eu-Wau-Wau.

Acre

The remote jungle state of Acre has seen not only some wanton environmental destruction and rampant high-level crime and corruption but also some of the most hope-generating movements against such horrors. As loggers and ranchers moved into Acre in the 1970s, Acre's rubber tappers, whose ancestors had started arriving in the 1870s, began to resist the destruction of the forests on which their livelihood depended. They formed human blockades against the chainsaws and opposed the paving of Hwy BR-364 into Acre. Their struggle received massive international attention in 1988 when their charismatic leader, Chico Mendes, was assassinated in his home town of Xapuri (see the boxed text 'Chico Mendes & His Legacy,' later in this chapter).

Partly thanks to the struggles of Mendes and others, today one-third of Acre's 153,000 sq km is under environmental protection or indigenous lands. This has not stopped deforestation, but the proportion of deforested land in Acre (9%) is below average for Brazilian Amazonia, and environmentalists have scored some political successes. In 1995 Marina Silva, a young unionist and former colleague of Mendes, was elected a federal senator for Acre as a member of the left-wing Partido dos Trabalhadores (PT, Workers' Party) and on a campaign focused on sustainable use of the forests. In 1998 Jorge Viana, another environmentalist and PT member, was elected state governor at the head of an anticorruption electoral coalition.

His predecessor Orleir Cameli, meanwhile, was under investigation for smuggling, enslaving Indians, encroaching on their land and logging illegally. Further revelations of the kinds of things that had gone on in Acre came in 2000 when Hildebrando Pascoal, formerly a deputy for Acre in Brazil's federal congress, was jailed for six years for corruption. Reportedly the head of a huge cocaine-smuggling operation from Bolivia, Pascoal was said to have run death squads responsible for dozens of murders and, according to a witness in a congressional drug inquiry, had personally cut off one live victim's arms and legs with a chainsaw. The same inquiry heard that Pascoal's gang of cocaine traffickers had allegedly included two Acre state governors, three state justices, half of Acre's top businessmen and hundreds of police officers.

Acre state is two hours behind Brazilian Standard Time.

RIO BRANCO
☎ 0xx68 • postcode 69900-000
• pop 226,000

Rio Branco, the capital of Acre, was founded in 1882 by rubber tappers on the banks of the Rio Acre.

Information
The Secretaria de Indústria, Comércio e Turismo (☎ 223-1390, 223-3994, fax 223-2699, seict@ac.gov.br), Rua Marechal Deodoro 219, 4th floor, can answer questions. It's open 7 am to 6 pm Monday to Friday.

The Banco do Brasil branch at Rua Porto Leal 85 exchanges cash US dollars, and trav-eler's checks if you're lucky. It's also worth trying for Visa-card cash advances (open 9 am to 2 pm Monday to Friday, 8 am to 1 pm from early October to mid-February). The ATMs at HSBC on Rua Rui Barbosa bear American Express, MasterCard, Maestro and Cirrus stickers and have been known to give cash on Cirrus or Maestro cards.

The central post office is at Rua Epaminondas Jácome 447. There's an open-air telephone office, open 7 am to 10 pm daily, outside Teleacre at Avenida Brasil 378. You can also make international calls (including collect calls) from card phones bearing the wording 'Chamadas Internacionais'. Razec Informática (☎ 223-2955), Rua Benjamin Constant 331, offers Internet access for US$1.75/3.50 per 30/60 minutes. It's open 8 am to noon and 2 to 5 pm Monday to Friday, and 8 am to noon Saturday.

Museums
At the small but interesting **Casa do Seringueiro**, Avenida Getúlio Vargas 309, there's a collection of photos, paintings and replicas of housing and utensils portraying the life of a typical *seringueiro* (rubber tapper). There's a small area devoted to Chico Mendes. The museum is open 8 am to 5:30 pm Monday to Friday (free).

The free **Museu da Borracha** (Rubber Museum), Avenida Ceará 1441, is divided into sections relating to archaeology, Indian artifacts, 19th-century Acre, rubber and the cult of Santo Daime (see Around Rio Branco later, for more about the cult). It's well organized, housed in a cute building, and well worth a visit – open 8 am to 6 pm Monday to Friday.

Places to Stay
If you're just passing through or have an early bus departure, the friendly *Hotel Chalé* (☎ 221-2293, Rua Palmeiral 334), just outside the bus station, has small single apartamentos with fan for US$8.50 and decent single/double apartamentos with air-con, TV and fridge for US$17/23. Prices include breakfast.

The *Albemar Hotel* (☎ 224-1938, fax 224-8965, Rua Franco Ribeiro 99) has clean,

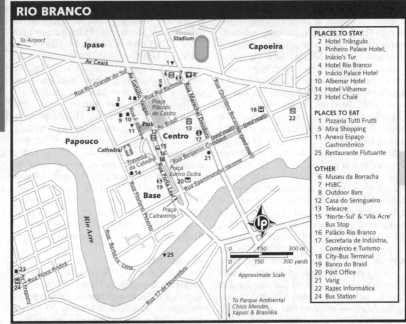

RIO BRANCO

PLACES TO STAY
2 Hotel Triângulo
3 Pinheiro Palace Hotel;
   Inácio's Tur
4 Hotel Rio Branco
9 Inácio Palace Hotel
10 Albemar Hotel
14 Hotel Vilhamor
23 Hotel Chalé

PLACES TO EAT
1 Pizzaria Tutti Frutti
5 Mira Shopping
11 Anexo Espaço
   Gastronômico
25 Restaurante Flutuante

OTHER
6 Museu da Borracha
7 HSBC
8 Outdoor Bars
12 Casa do Seringueiro
13 Teleacre
15 'Norte-Sul' & 'Vila Acre'
   Bus Stop
16 Palácio Rio Branco
17 Secretaria de Indústria,
   Comércio e Turismo
18 City-Bus Terminal
19 Banco do Brasil
20 Post Office
21 Varig
22 Razec Informática
24 Bus Station

small apartamentos with air-conditioning for US$17/21.

One of the best deals in town is the **Hotel Triângulo** (☎ 224-9206, *Rua Floriano Peixoto 727*), despite its parking-lot entrance. Good, clean apartamentos with TV and air-con cost US$21/27, with breakfast. More expensive versions, with fridge and phone, are US$27/33.

Hotel Vilhamor (☎/fax 223-2399, *Rua Floriano Peixoto 550*) offers clean, comfortable apartamentos for US$26/38 including breakfast (10% discount for cash). It's a popular place and it pays to book ahead.

Hotel Rio Branco (☎ 224-1785, *jbnunes@ mdnet.com.br, Rua Rui Barbosa 354*) is a long-established and dependable lodging with cheerful staff, a good breakfast and dated decor. Quite comfy air-conditioned apartamentos cost US$20/26 (cash).

Inácio Palace Hotel (☎ 223-6397, *Rua Rui Barbosa 469*) has very comfy new *luxo* apartamentos for US$50/70, adequate *supe-rior* ones for US$26/34, and old, small standard ones for US$20/26. All have air-con, TV, minibar and phone, and breakfast is included. The **Pinheiro Palace Hotel** (☎ 224-7191, *Rua Rui Barbosa 450*), across the street and under the same management, has a pool and good apartamentos for US$60/87 including breakfast. You can book both these hotels at www.irmaospinheiro.com.br.

Places to Eat

Rio Branco has a few excellent restaurants. The air-conditioned **Anexo Espaço Gastronômico** (*Rua Franco Ribeiro 99*) lives up to its ambitious name with the best per-kilo lunch we found in the north of Brazil. It's worth every centavo of US$8/kg, and the city's professional classes pack in for fresh and original salad combinations, tender meat and fish dishes, and irresistible desserts. At night there's à la carte fare.

Carnivores will definitely enjoy **Churrascaria Triângulo** at the Hotel Triângulo. The evening rodizio, for just US$5.50, comprises as much self-serve salad as you like and hot meats that keep arriving at your table until you just have to say 'No more.'

The open-air *Pizzaria Tutti Frutti (Avenida Ceará 1132)* does four sizes of good pizza from US$4.75 to US$17.50, and good and sizable chicken/meat/fish dishes for around US$10.

The food court of Mira Shopping, an air-conditioned oasis on Rua Rui Barbosa, contains *Café do Ponto*, excellent for coffee and pastries.

The *Restaurante Flutuante (☎ 224-7248)*, at the end of Rua Floriano Peixoto, is a pleasant floating restaurant on the Rio Acre. During the wet season, the water level raises the restaurant by 10m; they'll show photos if you should doubt it! Fish dishes start at US$11 and *tira-gostos* are around US$4.

Hungry, anyone?

Entertainment

The food court in the air-conditioned *Mira Shopping* is a popular place for a beer or three in the evening. The small triangle sandwiched between Avenida Ceará and Rua Rui Barbosa has a handful of *outdoor bars* that can get crowded at night.

Several central restaurants have live music a few nights a week. It's a matter of keeping your ears open as you head out for your evening meal.

Getting There & Away

The paved Hwy BR-364 runs to Rio Branco from Porto Velho. Beyond Rio Branco Hwy BR-364 is paved as far as Sena Madureira, 170km northwest. The road from Rio Branco to Brasiléia (235km southwest) is also paved, but Acre has few other paved roads. Except in the driest months (June/July to September), the unpaved roads are difficult and often impassable, leaving plane or boat as the only viable transportation options.

Varig (☎ 224-2226), Rua Marechal Deodoro 115, is the main airline flying interstate, with two flights daily to/from Porto Velho, Manaus (from US$195 one way), Brasília (from US$285) and São Paulo. The cheaper VASP also flies daily to Porto Velho, Manaus and Brasília. TAVAJ (☎ 226-1666) and Rico (☎ 223-5902) operate a number of regional flights.

Several travel agencies in central Rio Branco will book flights.

Acreana (☎ 221-1182) runs four buses daily to/from Brasiléia (US$9, 4½ hours, air-conditioned) and three to/from Xapuri (US$7, 3½ hours). Viação Rondônia runs four a day to/from Porto Velho (US$18, seven to eight hours) and one to/from Guajará-Mirim (US$17, seven to eight hours).

Açailândia (☎ 224-2746), Eucatur (☎ 221-4180) and the cheaper Rotas (☎ 221-1382) serve distant cities such as Cuiabá, Goiânia, Rio de Janeiro and São Paulo.

The Rio Acre is navigable all the way to the Peruvian border at Assis Brasil but there's little river traffic. From Boca do Acre in Amazonas state, a five-hour, US$12 bus ride from Rio Branco, there's river traffic along the Rio Purus as far as the Rio Amazonas and even Manaus.

Getting Around

The airport (☎ 211-1000) is about 20km west of town on Hwy BR-364. A taxi costs US$20 in either direction. City bus No 304 'Custódio Freire' (US$0.80) runs between the airport and the city-bus terminal on Rua Benjamin Constant about once an hour (last departure from the city is about 10:30 pm). Inácio's Tur (☎ 224-9626), Rua Rui Barbosa 450, runs a more commodious bus to (but not from) the airport four times daily for US$10 per person.

The bus station (☎ 221-1177) is on Avenida Uirapuru, 1.25km southwest of the center, across the Rio Acre. Bus 'Norte-Sul' (US$0.80) from outside the bus station runs to the city-bus terminal on Rua Benjamin Constant. Going to the bus station, you can catch it on Avenida Getúlio Vargas. A taxi to/from the city center is US$4.

AROUND RIO BRANCO
Parque Ambiental Chico Mendes
This is the Rio Branco area's most interesting park. About half of its 52 hectares is covered with native forest and there is some local fauna. The other half is regenerating.

A memorial to Chico Mendes stands near the entrance. The park also has a picnic area, a funny cast-iron treetop lookout, bike paths and a small zoo. Along the paths are theme huts representing different aspects of life in the region including rubber tappers, a *maloca* (Indian dwelling) and myths and legends.

You'll find the park at Km 3 on Hwy AC-040, about 10km south of Rio Branco. To get there take a 'Vila Acre' bus from Avenida Getúlio Vargas in the city center.

Santo Daime Centers
There are several centers of the Santo Daime religious cult in and around Rio Branco, where it was founded in 1930 by Raimundo Irineu Serra (1892-1971), also known as Mestre Irineu. The cult's practices revolve around a sacred hallucinogenic drink called *ayahuasca* (for more information see Religion in the Facts about Brazil chapter).

The ceremonial center at the cult's birthplace, called **Alto Santo**, is 7km from Rio Branco in Colônia Custódio Freire. You can reach it on an 'Irineu Serra' bus from the city-bus terminal. To get to the ceremonial center, ask anyone once you arrive.

Colônia Cinco Mil (Colony of the 5000), a community of Santo Daime followers, is 12km north of the city. If you wish to visit it, it's ideal to try to find somebody from the community to organize your visit, especially if you're thinking about participating in ceremonies. Ask around Rio Branco. You can reach the community by taxi (about US$10) or by catching a 'Porto Acre' bus along Hwy AC-010, which will drop you at the turnoff for Colônia Cinco Mil, from which it's a 2.5km walk.

Thursday is the cult's 'holy day,' and important ceremonies happen on the 15th and 30th of every month at Alto Santo and Colônia Cinco Mil.

XAPURI
☎ 0xx68 • pop 6000
This tidy little town of neat wooden houses along broad streets was home to environmental hero Chico Mendes. It is 12km north off Hwy BR-317, the road from Rio Branco to Brasiléia.

Fundação Chico Mendes
The Chico Mendes Foundation, one block southeast along Rua Dr Batista de Moraes from the bus station, is on the wide central plaza. Mendes' tomb is here, as well as photos, some of his many prizes, and personal effects (including the clothes he was wearing the night he was fatally shot). The Fundação is open 7 to 11 am and 1 to 5 pm Monday to Friday, and usually the same hours Saturday as well. Entry is free but a donation to the foundation will probably not be refused.

Chico Mendes' House
The house where Mendes and his wife and two children lived is just across the street from the Fundação, whose caretaker will open it for you as part of a visit. The simple house is maintained as it was when the Mendes family lived there. The caretaker will probably describe to you in graphic detail the fatal shooting at the kitchen door, where bloodstains remain on the wall.

Casa Branca
This large white wooden building overlooking the Rio Acre at the north end of town began life in the 19th century as the Intendencia Boliviana, a Bolivian government

post. It was here that the 'Acrean Revolution' of 1902 (a euphemism for Brazil's armed takeover of what had been part of Bolivia) started, when Xapuri townspeople joined Plácido de Castro's Brazilian force to capture this building. The Casa Branca houses a museum of historical memorabilia.

Places to Stay & Eat

There are decent air-conditioned apartamentos, with TV and minibar, at *Pousada das Chapurys* (☎ *542-2253, Rua Sadala Koury 1385)*, half a block off the central plaza. Singles/doubles cost from US$10/20 to US$16.50/30, including breakfast. Cheaper rooms are available at the *Santo Antônio Hotel* on Rua 6 de Agosto.

The airy *Restaurant Açai*, next door to Pousada das Chapurys and operating under the same management, offers a decent lunch for US$6.50.

Getting There & Away

Acreana buses leave Rio Branco for Xapuri at 7 am and 1:45 pm (US$7, 3½ hours), returning from Xapuri at 6 am and 1 pm. Buses leave Brasiléia for Xapuri at 10 am and 4:30 pm (US$3.50, two hours). There's a bus from Xapuri to Brasiléia at 1:30 pm.

Local hero: Chico Mendes

Going to Xapuri, a taxi from where the Rio Branco-Brasiléia buses stop on Hwy BR-317 and the town costs about US$9.

BRASILÉIA
☎ 0xx68 • postcode 69932-000 • pop 9000
The border town of Brasiléia is separated from Cobija, Bolivia, by the meandering Rio Acre and Igarapé Bahia.

Orientation & Information

Hwy BR-317 from Rio Branco approaches Brasiléia from the southeast, through the contiguous small town of Epitáciolândia. The Polícia Federal station (open 24 hours daily), where you need to obtain an exit/entry stamp if you're leaving/entering Brazil, is in Epitáciolândia. You can ask buses coming from the Rio Branco direction to drop you there.

To enter Bolivia by the international bridge across Igarapé Bahia, fork left (west) off Epitáciolândia's main street, Avenida Santos Dumont, by a gas station 500m from the Polícia Federal. It's only about 1km to the bridge.

The road into central Brasiléia continues past the above-mentioned fork and crosses the Rio Acre after 1km. Then it's 600m straight on to Brasiléia's main street, Avenida Prefeito Rolando Moreira. Buses head to the bus station on the north edge of town, 1km from the center.

See the Embassies & Consulates section of Facts for the Visitor for details of the Bolivian consulate in Brasiléia.

Places to Stay & Eat

Brasiléia's best lodging is *Pousada Las Palmeras* (☎ *546-3284, Avenida Geny Assis 425)*, near the church in the center. The apartamentos are air-conditioned and clean, with TV and minibar. The brighter, airier ones cost US$16.50/33/49.50 for singles/doubles/triples; dingier ones are US$13.50/27/40.50. All come with an excellent breakfast.

A few doors along the same street are two worthy alternatives: the friendly *Hotel Vitória Régia* (☎ *546-4743, Avenida Geny Assis 345)*, with more modern apartamentos for US$16.50/26.50/36.50, and *Hotel Fronteira* (☎ *546-4405, Avenida Geny Assis 347*) with ordinary apartamentos for US$12/16.50/23.50.

Brasiléia's best restaurant is *La Felicitá* (*Avenida Prefeito Rolando Moreira 361*), serving up a reasonably good buffet for US$5.75/kg.

Just 400m from the Polícia Federal in Epitáciolândia is *Hotel Kador* (☎ *546-3752, Avenida Santos Dumont 887*). Clean and adequate single/double apartamentos cost US$13.50/18.50 with air-con and breakfast. *Pizzaria Ribeira* across the road serves edible pizzas.

Getting There & Away

Bus & Jeep Four Acreana buses run daily to Rio Branco (US$9, 4½ hours), and two to Xapuri (US$3.50, two hours). In the dry season (roughly June to October), two daily buses take the unpaved road to Assis Brasil (US$6.75, about three hours). The rest of the year, Toyota 4WD vehicles make the trip from the bus station for US$13.50 per person (around four hours).

To/From Cobija A taxi from the Polícia Federal to Bolivian immigration on the international bridge then on to one of Cobija's bus terminals costs US$5 or so.

A rowboat ferry (US$0.30) crosses the Rio Acre from near the center of Brasiléia to near the center of Cobija. To find it take the short path down beside the Ministério de Fazenda building on Avenida Prefeito Rolando Moreira. It operates from about 5 am to 8:30 pm.

Chico Mendes & His Legacy

Chico Mendes was born in 1944 into a rubber-tapping family at Seringal Cachoeira, in the forests 35km from Xapuri. At an early age he became interested in improving the lot of the uneducated rubber tappers of the area.

In the 1970s the Plano de Integração Nacional, an ambitious military government plan to tame the Amazon, attracted developers, ranchers, logging companies and settlers into Acre. In 1977, Chico Mendes organized the Sindicato dos Trabalhadores Rurais de Xapuri (Xapuri Rural Workers' Union) to defy the violent intimidation and dispossession practiced by the newcomers, who were destroying the jungle, substituting cattle for people and robbing the forest workers of their livelihood. In the 8400 sq km of the Xapuri municipality between 1970 and 1976, Mendes later wrote, the ranchers destroyed by fire and power saw 180,000 rubber trees, 80,000 giant Brazil nut trees, and over a million other valuable trees.

Mendes organized large groups of rural workers to form nonviolent human blockades around forest areas threatened with clearance, and these actions soon attracted the wrath of developers, who were used to getting their way either through buying corrupt officials or by hiring *pistoleiros* to clear human impediments. These *empates,* or confrontational standoffs, proved effective in saving thousands of hectares of forest. Mendes also founded the Conselho Nacional de Seringueiros (National Council of Rubber Tappers) and launched the movement to set up extractive reserves – areas subject only to sustainable exploitation by their traditional 'extractive' populations (rubber tappers, nut collectors, fishers and so on).

International interest focused on Mendes as a defender of the forests. Among numerous honors, he was elected to the UN Environment Organization's Global 500 Honor Roll in 1987. But his role as a leader also made him a target for infuriated opponents at home, and he received numerous death threats. In December 1988 he moved to establish his birthplace, Seringal Cachoeira, as an extractive reserve, defying a local rancher and strongman, Darly Alves da Silva, who claimed the land. Mendes had already denounced da Silva to the police for threatening his life and for the murder of a union representative earlier that year.

See the Getting There & Away chapter for more on crossing the border into Bolivia.

COBIJA (BOLIVIA)

☎ 0842 • pop 15,000

The capital of Bolivia's Pando department is the wettest spot in Bolivia, with 1770mm of precipitation annually. Buses and flights head to/from many places in Bolivia.

Orientation & Information

From the international bridge over Igarapé Bahia (Arroyo Bahía to Bolivians), Avenida Internacional heads 600m uphill to a junction marked by a Christ statue. Turn right here along Avenida 9 de Febrero to Cobija's bus terminals and, a little over 1km away, the town center.

Bolivian immigration is on the international bridge. It's open 24 hours daily. The Brazilian consulate is on Avenida General Rene Barrientos (open 8 am to 1 pm Monday to Friday).

Casa de Cambio Cachito on Calle Teniente Coronel Cornejo, a block west of the central plaza, and Casa de Cambio Internacional, Avenida Internacional s/n, about 500m up from the international bridge, both exchange Bolivian, Brazilian and US currencies (cash) from 8 am to noon and 3 to 6 pm Monday to Friday, and 8 am to noon Saturday.

Places to Stay

These places are all within two blocks south of the central plaza. *Residencial Cocodrilo* (☎ 2215), on Avenida Fernández Molina,

---

Chico Mendes & His Legacy

On December 22, Mendes left the bodyguards in his house in Xapuri for just a moment and stepped onto the back porch. He was hit at close range by shots fired from the bushes and died shortly afterward.

His murderers gave themselves up to police, but they were considered beyond justice because of their connections with the influential landowners and corrupt officials – a common arrangement in Brazil's frontier lands. Intense national and international pressure finally brought the case to trial. In December 1990, Darly Alves da Silva received a 19-year prison term for ordering the assassination; his son, Darci Pereira da Silva, was given an identical sentence for pulling the trigger.

Of the many hundreds of murders of union leaders and land-rights campaigners in Brazil since the late 1970s, this was the first to be thoroughly investigated and prosecuted. Even this success looked to have been short-lived when both da Silvas escaped from jail in Rio Branco in 1993, apparently just walking free with the complicity of corrupt police. After another outcry, both were recaptured in 1996, but in 2000 they were granted day release, being required to spend only the nights in their prison in Brasília. We'd be surprised if they were still there by the time you read this.

The violent death of Chico Mendes – an environmentalist martyrdom – served to focus yet more attention on the fate of the Amazon rainforests. Ilzamar Mendes, his wife, was courted by numerous Hollywood producers to sell the film rights to the story of her husband's life. *(The Burning Season,* directed by John Frankenheimer and with Raul Julia playing Chico, was released in 1994.) Ilzamar Mendes and their two sons now live in Natal in the state of Rio Grande do Norte.

One lasting aspect of Chico Mendes' legacy is that there are now more than a dozen extractive reserves around Brazil, including the 9705-sq-km Reserva Extractivista Chico Mendes in southeast Acre, and a similar number are in the process of being created. But defending these and other protected areas against predatory loggers and ranchers remains a challenge.

AROUND BRASILÉIA

charges US$4.75/6.25 for clean (but far from opulent) singles/doubles, and US$8 for doubles with private bath. ***Residencial Frontera*** (☎ 2740), on Calle Beni, is clean but a bit overpriced, with fan-cooled rooms at US$9.50 with shared bath or US$11 with private bath. You might get a dollar or two off for single occupancy.

Hotel Nanijo's (☎ 2230, fax 2320, Avenida 9 de Febrero s/n) has nice breezy singles/doubles/triples with private bath and TV for US$16/22/33 (fan) or US$21/25/38 (air-con), including breakfast. The hotel is popular, so you need to try to get there early or book ahead.

Getting There & Away

Air Flights in June, July, August, December and January get heavily booked. Advertised schedules are not entirely reliable. TAM, the Bolivian military airline, is probably the most dependable. Many flights to La Paz and Santa Cruz connect with flights to other cities, but if you can't find any suitable flight, consider taking a bus to Riberalta and a flight from there.

TAM (☎ 2692), with an office at Avenida 9 de Febrero 59, flies Tuesday to Riberalta

(US$43), Guayaramerín (US$47) and Cochabamba (US$107), and Wednesday and Friday to/from La Paz (US$88).

AeroSur (☎ 3132), on Calle Teniente Coronel Cornejo just off the central plaza, flies Tuesday and Thursday to Trinidad and Santa Cruz, and on Sunday to/from La Paz.

LAB (☎ 2170), Avenida Fernández Molina s/n, about 400m past Residencial Cocodrilo (coming from the central plaza), has flights to La Paz on Friday and Sunday; to Riberalta, Guayaramerín and Trinidad on Wednesday and Sunday, continuing to Cochabamba, Sucre, Santa Cruz and Tarija on Wednesday.

One-way fares with AeroSur and LAB are US$135 to La Paz, Santa Cruz or Cochabamba, US$64 to Riberalta or Guayaramerín and US$111 to Trinidad.

The airport is 3km southeast of town on the Porvenir road. A taxi to/from the town center is US$2.25. Microbuses (US$0.25) stop on the airport approach road, 100m from the terminal.

Bus Bus companies are dotted along Avenida 9 de Febrero, between the town center and Avenida Internacional. The Guayaramerín company, nearest the center, goes to Riberalta (US$14, about 13 hours) and Guayaramerín (US$16, about 15 hours) on Tuesday, Thursday, Saturday and Sunday. At Riberalta you can connect to Trinidad. Transpando runs to Riberalta Sunday, Monday, Wednesday and Friday, and Flota Yungueña departs for La Paz (US$38, 48 hours) on Sunday.

All these buses leave early in the morning. The roads are nearly all gravel, and the Cobija-Riberalta stretch involves four river crossings. During the wettest season (roughly late December to late February), trips can take twice as long.

To/From Brasiléia A taxi from one of Cobija's bus terminals to the Bolivian immigration office then to the Brazilian Polícia Federal (with waiting time at each), then on to Brasiléia's bus station or town center, costs about US$2.50 to US$3.

To meet the rowboat ferry to Brasiléia (see the Brasiléia section), walk about five minutes north of Cobija's central plaza.

ASSIS BRASIL & IÑAPARI (PERU)

Access to Peru through the village of Assis Brasil, 110km west of Brasiléia, is reportedly possible for the adventurous traveler. Leaving Brazil, first complete Brazilian immigration procedures in Brasiléia. To cross to/from the muddy little Peruvian settlement of Iñapari (where you should be able to complete Peruvian immigration formalities), you have to wade the Rio Acre (knee-deep in July, travelers have reported).

Most days, minibuses, vans and trucks from Iñapari take passengers 70km south by

rough, unpaved road to Iberia (about US$9, five hours) and/or Puerto Maldonado (about US$22, 10 hours), a farther 170km south by a better track. Journey times can lengthen a great deal in the wet season. Puerto Maldonado has transportation to Cuzco and Lima and is a center for exploring part of Peruvian Amazonia. Occasional flights by Grupo Ocho, the Peruvian military airline, go from Iñapari airstrip (7km from the village) to Iberia, Puerto Maldonado and even Cuzco.

If you're planning on *entering* Brazil via Assis Brasil and need a Brazilian visa, get one in Lima or outside Peru.

Assis Brasil, Iñapari and Iberia all have some basic hotels.

Language

Viajando na maionese
'I'm traveling through the mayonnaise'
(colloquialism for 'I'm totally spaced out')

Portuguese is similar to Spanish on paper but sounds completely different. You will do quite well if you speak Spanish in Brazil. Brazilians will understand what you say, but you won't get much of what they say, so don't think studying Portuguese is a waste of time. Listen to language tapes and develop an ear for Portuguese – it's a beautiful-sounding language.

When they settled Brazil in the 16th century, the Portuguese encountered the diverse languages of the Indians. These, together with the various idioms and dialects spoken by the Africans brought in as slaves, extensively changed the Portuguese spoken by the early settlers.

Along with Portuguese, the Tupi-Guaraní language, written down and simplified by the Jesuits, became a common language that was understood by the majority of the population. It was spoken by the general public until the middle of the 18th century, but its usage diminished with the great number of Portuguese gold-rush immigrants and a royal proclamation in 1757 prohibiting its use. With the expulsion of the Jesuits in 1759, Portuguese was established as the national language.

Still, many words remain from Indian and African languages. From Tupi-Guaraní come lots of place names (such as Guanabara, Carioca, Tijuca and Niterói), animal names (such as piranha, capivara and urubu) and plant names (such as mandioca, abacaxí, caju and jacarandá). Words from the African dialects, mainly those from Nigeria and Angola, are used in Afro-Brazilian religious ceremonies (eg, Orixá, Exú and Iansã), cooking (eg, vatapá, acarajé and abará) and in general conversation (eg, samba, mocambo and moleque).

Brazilians are easy to befriend, but unfortunately the vast majority of them speak little or no English. This is changing, however, as practically all Brazilians in school are learning English. All the same, don't count on finding an English speaker, especially out of the cities. The more Portuguese you speak, the more you will get out of your trip.

Books

Most phrasebooks are not very helpful. The vocabulary is often dated and they often contain the Portuguese spoken in Portugal, rather than in Brazil. A notable exception is Lonely Planet's *Brazilian phrasebook*. Be certain that any English-Portuguese dictionary you use is a Brazilian Portuguese one. Wordsworth Reference publishes a handy one. If you're determined not to learn, get a copy of Jonathan Maeder's *The Wordless Travel Book* (Ten Speed Press), a collection of drawings of just about everything you'd need on a trip – point to what you want!

If you're more intent on learning the language, try the US Foreign Service Institute (FSI) tape series. It comes in two volumes. Volume 1, which includes 15 cassettes and accompanying text, costs US$225. It covers pronunciation, verb tenses and essential nouns and adjectives. Volume 2 includes 22 tapes with text, and includes some useful phrases and a travel vocabulary. Volume 2 costs US$285, or you can buy the set for US$395. The tapes are sold through Multilingual Books (☎ 800-218-2737) 1205 East Pike, Seattle, WA 91822.

For fluent Spanish speakers, FSI also has *From Spanish to Portuguese,* which explains the similarities and differences between these languages. This one costs US$45 for tapes, US$59 for CDs.

In Australia, most foreign-language and travel bookstores stock a range of material. The Foreign Language Bookshop (☎ 03-9654-2883), 259 Collins St, Melbourne, Victoria 3000, carries three types of learning kits: *Language 30: Portuguese* (booklet and cassette, A$35.95); Berlitz' *Portuguese for*

Travellers (booklet and cassette, A$30.95 or A$39.95 with CD); and HUGO's *Portuguese Travel Kit* (booklet & cassette, A$19.95).

Combine these with a few Brazilian samba tapes and some Jorge Amado novels and you're ready to begin the next level of instruction on the streets of Brazil.

Pronunciation

The big shocker is that generally, an 'r' is pronounced like an 'h': Rio becomes '**hee**-oh,' the currency is pronounced 'hay-**ow**' etc. In the same spirit of fun, a 't' (or 'd') followed by a vowel becomes a 'ch' (or 'dj'), so the word 'restaurante' is pronounced approximately 'hess-to-**roch**.' But wait – there's more! An 'lh' combination generally produces a 'ly-' sound, so 'Ilha Grande' sounds like 'eel-ya grunge.'

The 'ç' is pronounced like an English 's'; the letter 'x' as the 'sh' as in 'ship.' So 'Iguaçu' is 'ig-wa-**soo**' and 'Caxambu' 'ka-**sham**-boo.'

You'll know you've mastered Brazilian Portuguese pronunciation when you've successfully ordered one of the country's more popular beers, Antarctica (that's right, you say 'ant-**okt**-chee-kah'!).

Within Brazil, accents, dialects and slang (*gíria*) vary regionally. The Carioca inserts the 'sh' sound in place of 's.' The gaúcho speaks a Spanish-sounding Portuguese, the Baiano (from Bahia) speaks slowly, and the accents of the Cearense (from Ceará) are often incomprehensible to outsiders.

Basics

Portuguese has masculine and feminine forms of nouns and adjectives. Alternative gender endings to words appear separated by a slash, the masculine form first. Generally, 'o' indicates masculine and 'a' indicates feminine.

Greetings & Civilities

Hello.	*Oi.*
Good morning.	*Bom dia.*
Good afternoon.	*Boa tarde.*
Good evening.	*Boa noite.*
Good night.	*Boa noite.*
See you later.	*Até já.*
See you soon.	*Até logo.*

Goodbye.	*Adeus.* (polite)/ *Tchau.* (informal)
Yes.	*Sim.*
No.	*Não.*
Maybe.	*Talvez.*
Please.	*Por favor.*
Excuse me.	*Com licença.*
I'm sorry.	*Desculpe.* or *Me perdoe.* (lit: forgive me)
Thank you (very much).	*(Muito) obrigado/a.*
You're welcome.	*De nada.*

Small Talk

How are you?	*Como vai você?* or *Tudo bem?*
I'm fine.	*Vou bem* or *Tudo bem.*
What's your name?	*Qual é seu nome?*
My name is…	*Meu nome é…*
What country are you from?	*De onde você é?*
I'm from…	*Eu sou de…*
I'm a tourist/student.	*Eu sou um turista/ estudante.*
How old are you?	*Quantos anos você tem?*
I'm…years old.	*Eu tenho…anos.*
Are you married?	*Você é casado/a?*
Do you like…?	*Você gosta de…?*
I (don't) like..	*Eu (não) gosto de…*
I like…	*Gosto de…*
I like it very much.	*Eu gosto muito.*
May I?	*Posso?*
It's all right/ No problem.	*Está tudo bem/ Não há problema.*

Language Difficulties

Do you speak English?	*Você fala inglês?*
Does anyone speak English?	*Alguem fala inglês?*
I (don't) speak Portuguese.	*Eu (não) falo português.*
I (don't) understand.	*Eu (não) entendo.*
Please write it down.	*Escreva por favor.*
Please show me (on the map).	*Por favor, me mostre (no mapa).*
How do you say… in Portuguese?	*Como você fala… em português?*

Paperwork

I have a visa/ permit.	*Eu tenho um visto/ uma licença.*
Passport	*Passaporte*
Surname	*Sobrenome*
Given name	*Nome*
Date of birth	*Data de nascimento*
Place of birth	*Local de nascimento*
Nationality	*Nacionalidade*
Male/Female	*Masculino/ Feminino*

Getting Around

I want to go to…	*Eu quero ir para…*
I want to book a seat for…	*Eu quero reservar um assento para…*
What time does the…leave/arrive?	*A que horas o/a…sai/chega?*
Where does the… leave from?	*De onde o/a… sai?*
airplane	*avião*
boat	*barco*
bus	*ônibus*
ferry	*ferry/balsa*
train	*trem*
tram	*bonde*
Where is the…?	*Onde é o/a…?*
bus stop	*ponto de ônibus*
metro station	*estação do metrô*
tram stop	*ponto do bonde*
ticket office	*bilheteria*
timetable	*horário*
I want a one-way/ round-trip ticket.	*Eu quero uma passagem de ida/ ida e volta.*
How much is the fare?	*Quanto é a passagem?*
How long does the trip take?	*Quanto tempo a viagem demora?*
The (bus) is…	*O (ônibus) está…*
delayed	*atrasado*
cancelled	*cancelado*
on time	*na hora*
early	*adiantado*
I want to rent a…	*Eu quero alugar…*
bicycle	*uma bicicleta*
car	*um carro*
horse	*um cavalo*
motorcycle	*uma moto*

Directions

Where is…?	*Onde fica…?*
How do I get to…?	*Como eu chego a…?*
Is it near/far?	*É perto/longe?*
What…is this?	*O que…é isto?*
street/road	*rua/estrada*
suburb	*bairro*
town	*cidade*
Go straight ahead.	*Vá em frente.*
Turn left.	*Vire a esquerda.*
Turn right.	*Vire a direita.*
at the traffic lights	*no farol*
at the next corner	*na próxima esquina*
up/down	*acima/abaixo*
behind/opposite	*atrás/em frente*
here/there	*aqui/lá*
east/west	*este/oeste*
north/south	*norte/sul*

Around Town

Where is the…?	*Onde é o/a…?*
bank	*banco*
city center	*centro da cidade*
consulate	*consulado*
embassy	*embaixada*
exchange office	*casa de câmbio*
fort	*forte*
hospital	*hospital*
lake	*lago*
main square	*praça principal*
market	*mercado* or *feira*
old city	*cidade velha*
palace	*palácio*
post office	*correio*
public toilet	*banheiro público*
restaurant	*restaurante*
ruins	*ruínas*
square	*praça*
telephone office	*telefónica*
tourist office	*posto de infor- mações turísticas*
What time does it open/close?	*A que horas abre/ fecha?*
I'd like to change…	*Eu gostaria de trocar…*
money	*dinheiro*
traveler's checks	*cheques de viagem*
open/closed	*aberto/fechado*
entrance/exit	*entrada/saida*

Accommodations

I'm looking for the…	*Eu estou procurando o/a…*
campground	*camping*
guesthouse	*pousada*
hotel	*hotel*
manager	*gerente*
owner	*dono*
youth hostel	*albergue da juventude*
What is the address?	*Qual é o endereço?*
Do you have a…	*Você tem um…*
available?	*para alugar?*
cheap room	*quarto barato*
single room	*quarto de solteiro*
double room	*quarto de casado*
room with two beds	*quarto com duas camas*
room for rent	*quarto para alugar*
How much is it…?	*Quanto é…?*
per night	*por noite*
per person	*por pessoa*
Is breakfast included?	*O café da manhã está incluído?*
Can I see the room?	*Posso ver o quarto?*
Where is the toilet?	*Onde é o banheiro?*
It's very…	*É muito…*
dirty	*sujo*
noisy	*barulhento*
expensive	*caro*
Do you have…?	*Você tem…?*
a clean sheet	*um lençol limpo*
hot water	*água quente*
a key	*uma chave*
a shower	*um chuveiro*
I'm/We're leaving now.	*Eu estou/Nós estamos saindo agora.*

Food

breakfast	*café da manhã*
lunch	*almoço*
dinner	*jantar*
set menu	*refeição*
food stall	*barraca de comida*
grocery store	*mercearia*
delicatessen	*confeitaria*
restaurant	*restaurante*
I'm hungry/thirsty.	*Eu estou com fome/ sede.*
I'd like the set lunch please.	*Eu gostaria do prato feito por favor.*
Is the tip included in the bill?	*O serviço está incluído na conta?*
I'm a vegetarian.	*Eu sou vegetariano/a.*
I don't eat…	*Eu não como…*
I'd like some…	*Eu gostaria de…*
Another…, please.	*Outro/a…, por favor*
beer	*cerveja*
bread	*pão*
chicken	*frango*
coffee	*café*
eggs	*ovos*
fish	*peixe*
food	*comida*
fruit	*frutas*
meat	*carne*
milk	*leite*
mineral water	*água mineral*
pepper	*pimenta*
salt	*sal*
soup	*sopa*
sugar	*açucar*
tea	*chá*
vegetables	*verduras*
wine	*vinho*

Shopping

I'm looking for a…	*Estou procurando um/uma…*
bookshop	*livraria*
chemist	*farmácia*
clothing store	*loja de roupas*
laundry	*lavanderia*
market	*mercado (feira for fruits & vegetables)*
newsstand	*banca de jornal*
souvenirs	*lembranças*
stationery store	*papelaria*
Can I look at it?	*Posso ver?*
I'm just looking.	*Só estou olhando.*
I'd like to buy…	*Queria comprar…*
How much is it?	*Quanto custa?*
It's too expensive for me.	*É muito caro para mim.*
big/bigger	*grande/maior*

small/smaller	pequeno/menor
more/less	mais/menos
cheap/cheaper	barato/mais barato
Do you have…?	Você tem…?
another color	outra cor
another size	outro tamanho
Do you take…?	Você aceita…?
credit cards	cartões de crédito
traveller's checks	cheques de viagem

Times & Dates

What time is it?	Que horas são?
It's…	São…
1:15	uma e quinze
1:30	uma e meia
1:40	uma e quarenta
o'clock	horas
midnight	meia-noite
noon	meio-dia
in the morning	da manhã
in the afternoon	da tarde
in the evening	de noite
When?	Quando?
today	hoje
tonight	hoje a noite
tomorrow	amanhã
yesterday	ontem
morning	a manhã
afternoon	a tarde
night	a noite
all day	todo dia
every day	todos os dias
Monday	segunda-feira
Tuesday	terça-feira
Wednesday	quarta-feira
Thursday	quinta-feira
Friday	sexta-feira
Saturday	sábado
Sunday	domingo
January	janeiro
February	fevereiro
March	março
April	abril
May	maio
June	junho
July	julho
August	agosto
September	setembro
October	outubro
November	novembro
December	dezembro

Numbers

0	zero
1	um/uma
2	dois/duas
3	três
4	quatro
5	cinco
6	seis (meia is often used when quoting digits in phone numbers or addresses)
7	sete
8	oito
9	nove
10	dez
11	onze
12	doze
13	treze
14	catorze
15	quinze
16	dezesseis
17	dezessete
18	dezoito
19	dezenove
20	vinte
30	trinta
40	quarenta
50	cinqüenta
60	sessenta
70	setenta
80	oitenta
90	noventa
100	cem
1000	mil
one million	um milhão
first	primeiro/a
second	segundo/a
third	terceiro/a
last	último/a

Health

I need a doctor.	Eu preciso de um medico.
Where is the hospital?	Aonde é o hospital?
I'm…	Eu sou…
diabetic	diabético
epileptic	epilético
asthmatic	asmático
I'm allergic to…	Eu sou alérgico/a a…
penicillin	penicilina
antibiotics	antibióticos

antiseptic	*antiséptico*
aspirin	*aspirina*
condoms	*camisinhas* or *camisa de venus*
constipation	*prisão de ventre*
contraceptive	*contraceptivo*
diarrhea	*diarréia*
nausea	*nausea*
sunblock cream	*creme de proteção solar*
tampons	*absorventes internos*

Emergencies

Help!	*Socorro!*
Call the police!	*Chame a polícia!*
Call a doctor!	*Chame o médico!*
Where is the toilet?	*Onde é o banheiro?*
Go away!	*Va embora!*

Slang

Cariocas pepper their language with lots of strange oaths and odd expressions.

Everything OK?	*Tudo bem?*
Everything's OK.	*Tudo bom.*
That's great!/Cool!	*Chocante!*
That's bad!/Shit!	*Merda!*
Great!/Cool!/OK!	*'Ta lógico!/'Ta ótimo!/'Ta legal!*
You're crazy.	*'Ta louco.*
My God!	*Meu deus!*
Gosh!	*Nossa!* (lit: Our Lady!)
Whoops!	*Opa!*
Wow!	*Oba!*
You said it!	*Falou!*
shooting the breeze	*batendo um papo*
I'm mad at…	*Eu estou chateado com…*
Is there a way?	*Tem jeito?*
There's always a way.	*Sempre tem jeito.*
guy	*cara*
girl	*garota*
money	*grana*
bum	*bum-bum* or *bunda*
bald	*careca*
a fix/problem	*abacaxí*
a mess	*bagunça*
Brazilian thong bikini	*fio dental* (lit: dental floss)

marijuana	*fumo* (lit: smoke)
a mess	*bagunça*

Beach Talk

I can't swim.	*Eu não sei nadar.*
Can I swim here?	*Posso nadar aqui?*
Is it safe to swim here?	*É seguro nadar aqui?*
What time is high/low tide?	*A que horas será a maré alta/baixa?*
How's the surf?	*Como estão as ondas?*
Where's a good place to surf?	*Onde existe um bom lugar para surfar?*
beach	*praia*
beach towel	*toalha de praia*
coast	*costa*
lifeguard	*salva-vidas*
rock	*pedra*
sand	*areia*
sea	*mar*
sunblock	*creme de proteção solar*
wave	*onda*

Jungle Words

Does the tour include …?	*A excursão inclui…?*
Will we sleep in hammocks?	*Iremos dormir em redes?*
What is the breakdown of costs?	*Como é dividido o custo?*
Is the water level high or low?	*O nível das águas esta alto ou baixo?*
Does the boat have lifejackets?	*O barco tem coletes salva-vidas?*
How long does it take to get there?	*Quanto tempo leva para chegar lá?*
Can we shop for food together?	*Podemos ir comprar comida juntos?*
Do you have fishing gear?	*Você tem equipamento de pesca?*
Is it safe to go there?	*É seguro ir lá?*
Will we see animals?	*Iremos ver animais?*
Are there…?	*Existem lá…?*
dangerous animals	*animais perigosos*
spiders	*aranhas*
lots of mosquitos	*muitos mosquitos*

accommodations	*alojamento*
canoe	canoa
food/drinks	*comida/bebida*
fuel	*combustível*
guides	*guias*
jungle	*selva; mata; floresta*
tree	*arvore*

Body Language

Brazilians accompany their speech with a rich body language, a sort of parallel dialogue. The thumbs up of *tudo bem* is used as a greeting, or to signify 'OK' or 'Thank you.' The authoritative *não, não* finger-wagging is most intimidating when done right under someone's nose, but it's not a threat.

The sign of the *figa,* a thumb inserted between the first and second fingers of a clenched fist, is a symbol of good luck that has been derived from an African sexual charm. It's more commonly used as jewelry than in body language. To indicate *rápido* (speed and haste), thumb and middle finger snap while rapidly shaking the wrist – a gesture it often seems only Brazilians can make. If you don't want something (*não quero*), slap the back of your hands as if ridding yourself of the entire affair. Touching a finger to the lateral corner of the eye means 'I'm wise to you.'

Glossary

abandonados – abandoned children

abertura – opening; refers to the process, begun in the early 1980s, of returning to a civilian, democratic government

afoxé – music of Bahia with strong African rhythms and close ties to the Candomblé religion

aguardente – firewater, rotgut; any strong drink, but usually *cachaça*

albergue – lodging house or hostel

albergue da juventude – youth hostel

álcool – car fuel made from sugarcane

aldeia – originally a mission village built by Jesuits to convert Indians; now used for any small, usually Indian, village

andar – the verb 'to walk'; as a noun, a floor of a multistory building

apartamento – hotel room with a private bathroom

arara – macaw

artesanato – handcrafted workmanship

autódromo – racetrack; at Interlagos, São Paulo, the well-known location of the famous Brazilian Grand Prix

avelã – hazelnut

ayahuasca – hallucinogenic drink

azulejos – Portuguese ceramic tiles with a distinctive blue glaze; often seen in churches

babaçu – versatile palm tree that is the basis of the rural economy in Maranhão

bandeirantes – bands of *Paulistas* who explored the vast Brazilian interior while searching for gold and Indians to enslave; typically born of an Indian mother and a Portuguese father

banzo – a slave's profound longing for the African homeland, which often resulted in a 'slow withering away' and death

barraca – any stall or hut, including food and drink stands common at beaches, parks etc

bateria – any rhythm section, including the enormous ones in samba parades

beija-flor – hummingbird (literally 'flower kisser'); also the name of Rio's most famous samba school

berimbau – musical instrument that looks like a fishing rod and is used to accompany the martial art/dance of capoeira

bicho de pé – parasite, found near the beach and in some jungle areas, that burrows into the bottom of the foot and then grows until it is cut out

bloco – a large group, usually numbering in the hundreds, of singing or drumming Carnaval revelers in costume; organized around a neighborhood or theme

boate or **boîte** – a nightclub with a dance floor, sometimes with strippers

bogó – leather water pouch typical of the *sertão*

bonde – cable car, tram or trolley

bossa nova – music that mixes North American jazz with Brazilian influences

boto – freshwater dolphin of the Amazon; believed by Indians to have magical powers, including the ability to impregnate unmarried women

Brazilian Empire – the period from 1822 to 1889, when Brazil was independent of Portugal but was governed by monarchy

Bumba Meu Boi – the most important festival in Maranhão, a rich folkloric event that revolves around a Carnavalesque dance/procession

bunda – an African word for 'buttocks'

caatinga – scrub vegetation of the Northeast sertão

Cabanagem – the popular revolt that swept through Pará state in the 1830s

caboclo – person of mixed Caucasian and Indian ancestry (literally, 'copper-colored')

cachaça – a sugarcane spirit that is Brazil's national drink, also called *pinga* and *aguardente*; produced by hundreds of small distilleries throughout the country

cachoeira – waterfall

café – coffee, or the short term for *café da manha* (breakfast)

caipirinha – drink made from *cachaça* and crushed citrus fruit such as lemon, orange or *maracujá*

câmara – town council during colonial days

camisa-de-Vênus or **camisinha** – condom; literally, cover or shirt of Venus

Candomblé – Afro-Brazilian religion of Bahia

canga – wraparound fabric worn when going to and from the beach and for sitting on at the beach

cangaceiros – legendary bandits of the *sertão*

capanga – hired gunman, usually employed by rich landowners in the Northeast

capitania hereditária – hereditary province or estate

capivara – capybara; the world's largest rodent, which looks like a large guinea pig and lives in the waters of the Pantanal

capoeira – martial art/dance performed to the rhythms of an instrument called the *berimbau*; developed by the slaves of Bahia

capongas – a freshwater lagoon

Carioca – a native of Rio de Janeiro

casa grande – big house or plantation owner's mansion

casa de câmbio – money-exchange house

casal – married couple; also used for a double bed

castanha – brazil nut

cerveja – beer

chapada – tableland or plateau that divides a river basin

chopp – draft beer

churrascaria – restaurant featuring meat, which should be *churrasco* (barbecued)

Círio de Nazaré – Brazil's largest religious pilgrimage; takes place in Belém

cobra – any snake

comida caseira – home-style cooking

comida mineira – typical cuisine of Minas Gerais state

comida por quilo – pay-by-weight buffet

comunidade de base – neighborhood organization of the poor, involved in many struggles for social justice, led by the progressive Catholic Church and inspired by liberation theology

congelamento – freeze, as in a price freeze

coronel – literally, 'colonel'; a rural landowner who typically controlled the local political, judicial and police systems; refers to any powerful person

correio – post office

couvert – appetizer

delegacia – police station

dendê – palm oil; the main ingredient in the cuisine of Bahia

drogas do sertão – plants of the *sertão* such as cacao and cinnamon

Economic Miracle – period of double-digit economic growth while the military was in power during the late 1960s and early 1970s; now mentioned sarcastically to point to the failures of the military regime

embalagem – wrapping; a doggie bag of leftover food

embolada – a kind of Brazilian rap in which singers trade off performing verbal jests, teasing and joking with the audience; most common at Northeastern fairs

Embratur – federal government tourism agency

Empire – Brazilian Empire

ENASA – a decrepit government-run passenger-shipping line of the Amazon

engenho – sugar mill or sugar plantation

escolas de samba – large samba clubs that compete in the annual Carnaval parade

Estado Novo – literally, 'New State'; dictator Getúlio Vargas' quasi-fascist state, which lasted from 1937 until the end of WWII

estação ecológica – ecological station

estância hidromineral – spa, hot springs

Exú – spirit that serves as messenger between the gods and humans in Afro-Brazilian religions

facão – large knife or machete

fantasia – Carnavalesque costume

farinha – manioc flour; the staple food of Brazil's Indians before colonization and the staple for many Brazilians today, especially in the Northeast and Amazon

favela – slum, shantytown

fazenda – ranch or farm, usually a large landholding; also cloth, fabric

fazendeiro – estate owner

ferroviária – railway station

ficha – token; machines (eg, telephones) that take tokens, rather than coins

fidalgos – gentry

figa – good-luck charm representing a clenched fist with the thumb between the index and middle fingers; originated with Afro-Brazilian cults but now popular with all Brazilians

Filhos de Gandhi – Bahia's most famous Carnaval *bloco*

fio dental – literally, 'dental floss'; the term for Brazil's famous skimpy bikini

Flamengo – Rio's most popular football team; also one of Rio's most populated areas

Fluminense – native of Rio state; also the football team that is Flamengo's main rival

forró – the folk music of the Northeast, recently enjoying a wave of nationwide popularity

frevo – fast-paced, popular music that originated in Pernambuco

frigobar – minibar

FUNAI – Fundação Nacional do Indio; government Indian agency

Fusca – a Volkswagen Beetle, long Brazil's most popular car

futvolei – foot volleyball

garimpeiro – a prospector or miner; originally an illegal diamond prospector

gaúcho – pronounced 'gaoooshoo'; a cowboy of southern Brazil

gíria – slang

gringo – foreigner or person with light hair and complexion; can even refer to light-skinned Brazilians, not strictly a term for people from the US (not necessarily derogatory)

gruta – grotto or cavern

guaraná – an Amazonian shrub whose berry is a stimulant and is believed to have magical and medicinal powers; also, a popular soft drink

hospedagem – cheap boardinghouse used by locals

hidrovia – aquatic freeway

hidroviária – boat terminal

lemanjá – the Afro-Brazilian goddess of the sea

igapó – flooded Amazon forest

igarapé – creek or small river in Amazonia

ilha – island

INPA – Instituto Nacional de Pesquisas Amazonia; national agency for research on the Amazon

jaburú – jabiru; a giant white stork of the Pantanal with a black head and a red band on its neck

jacaré – an alligator or caiman

jagunço – the tough man of the *sertão*

jangada – beautiful sailboat of the Northeast, usually made by the people who fish themselves, with building techniques passed from generation to generation

jangadeiros – the crews who use *jangadas*

jeito – possibly the most Brazilian expression, both a feeling and a form of action; from *dar um jeito,* meaning 'to find a way to get something done,' no matter how seemingly impossible, even if the solution may not be completely orthodox or legal

jogo de bicho – a popular lottery in which each number is represented by an animal; technically illegal but played on every street corner by all Brazilians

jogo dos búzios – type of fortune-telling performed by a *pai* or *mãe de santo* by throwing shells

Labor Code – legislation designed to maintain government control over labor unions, modeled on Mussolini's system

ladrão – thief

lanchonete – snack bar

lavrador – peasant, small farmer or landless farmworker

leito – super-comfortable overnight express bus

liberation theology – movement within the Catholic Church that believes the struggle for social justice is part of Christ's teachings

literatura de cordel – literally, 'string literature'; popular literature of the Northeast, so named because pamphlets are typically hung on strings at markets, where authors read stories and poems

litoral – coastal region

maconha – type of marijuana

machista – male chauvinist

mãe de santo – female Afro-Brazilian spiritual leader

malandro do morro – vagabond; scoundrel from the hills; a popular figure in Rio's mythology

maloca – Indian dwelling

mameluco – offspring of a white father and an Indian mother

Manchete – a popular photo magazine

Maracanã – Rio's soccer stadium; considered the world's largest, allegedly holding 200,000 but remodeled to hold closer to 100,000

mate – popular tea of southern Brazil

mercado – market

mestiço – a person of mixed Indian and European parentage

Mineiro – a person from the state of Minas Gerais (literally, 'miner')

miúdo – change

mocambo – community of runaway slaves; small version of a *quilombo*

moço/a – waiter, waitress or other service industry worker

morro – hill; also used to indicate a person or culture of the *favelas*

motel – sex hotel with rooms to rent by the hour

mulato/a – person of mixed black and European parentage

novela – soap opera; Brazil's most popular TV shows

NS – *Nosso Senhor* (Our Lord) or *Nossa Senhora* (Our Lady)

O Globo – Brazil's number-one media empire, with the prime national TV station and several newspapers and magazines

Old Republic – period from the end of the Brazilian Empire in 1889 until the coup that put Getúlio Vargas in power in 1930

orixás – deities of the Afro-Brazilian religions

pagode – today's most popular samba music

pai de santo – male spiritual leader in Afro-Brazilian religions

pajé – shaman, witch doctor

palácio – palace or large government building

palafita – stilt or a house built on stilts

pampas – grassy plains of the interior of southern Brazil

papelaria – stationery shop

paroara – Amazon resident who came from the Northeast

parque nacional – national park

pau brasil – now-scarce brazilwood tree; a red dye made from the tree was the colony's first commodity

Paulista – native of São Paulo State

Paulistano – native of São Paulo city

PCB – Communist Party of Brazil

peixe-boi – manatee (literally, 'cowfish'); an endangered aquatic mammal that grows to 2m long

pelourinho – stone pillar that was used as a whipping post for slaves

pensão – guesthouse

Petrobras – Brazil's largest corporation, the government-owned oil company; referred to as a 'government within a government'

pinga – another name for *cachaça,* the sugarcane spirit

pistoleiro – gun-toting henchman

Planalto – enormous plateau that covers a part of almost every state in Brazil

Plano Real – financial plan introduced by finance minister Fernando Henrique Cardoso in 1994

por quilo – per kilo; used to describe self-serve buffet restaurants

posseiro – squatter

posto – post; the numbers of the lifeguard *postos* along Rio de Janeiro's beaches, used as shorthand names for different sections of beach

posto de gasolina – a gas (petrol) station

posto telefônico – a telephone office where you can make calls

pousada – guesthouse

praça – plaza or town square

praia – beach

prato feito- literally, 'made plate,' the plate of the day; typically, an enormous and incredibly cheap meal

prefeitura – city or town hall

PT – Worker's Party; Brazil's newest and most radical political party; came out of the strike waves of the early 1980's and is led by Luíz Inácio 'Lula' da Silva; has grown strongest in São Paulo and among the industrial workers and the Catholic base communities

puxar – means pull, not push

quarto – hotel room without a bathroom
quilombo – community of runaway slaves

rápido – fast
real – Brazil's unit of currency since 1994
rede – hammock
refeição – meal
refeição comercial – meal/serving of various dishes (normally comes with enough food for two to share)
reserva extravista – extractive reserve; an area dedicated to protecting the traditional extractive economy of human populations dependent on sustainable activities such as rubber tapping or fruit or nut collecting
reserva biológica – biological reserve
Revolution of '64 – the military takeover in 1964
rodízio – a smorgasbord, usually with lots of meat (similar to a *churrascaria)*
rodoferroviária – bus and train station
rodoviária – bus station

s/n – abbreviation for *sem número* (without number) used in some street addresses
salgadinhos – savory snacks
sambista – samba composer or dancer
sambódromo – street with tiers of seating built for samba parades
senzala – slave quarters
serra – mountain range
sertanejo – inhabitant of the *sertão*
sertão – the drought-prone backlands of the Northeast, with a dry, temperate climate and vegetation dominated by thorny shrubs
suco – juice

Terra da Vera Cruz – Land of the True Cross; the original Portuguese name for Brazil
terreiro – Afro-Brazilian house of worship
travesti – transvestite; a popular figure throughout Brazil, considered by some to be the national symbol
Treaty of Tordesillas – agreement signed in 1494 between Spain and Portugal, dividing Latin America
trio elétrico – literally, a three-pronged electrical outlet; also a musical style that is a sort of electrified *frevo* played on top of trucks, especially during Carnaval in Bahia
troco – change
tropicalismo – important cultural movement centered in Bahia in the late 1960s
Tupi – the Indian people and language that predominated along the Brazilian coast at the time of the European invasion

Umbanda – white magic, a mixture of Candomblé and spiritualism

vaqueiro – cowboy of the Northeast
várzea – Amazonian floodplain
Velho Chico – literally, 'Old Chico'; an affectionate nickname for the great Rio São Francisco ('Chico' is a nickname for 'Francisco')
violeiros – guitarists and guitar makers

zona da mata – bushland just inside the *litoral* in the Northeastern states

Thanks

Many thanks to the travelers who used the last edition and wrote to us with helpful hints, useful advice and interesting anecdotes:

Karin Ammeraal, Thomas Rude Andersen, Christine Arnold, Jeff Baer, Mike Babb, Nick Bailey, Mauricio Bergstein, Thaddeus G Blanchette, Jeohan Bonillo, Dirk Borowski, Stefan Braun, Robert J Brodey, Dr Olivier Brunel, Havelock Jimmy Campbell, Laura Cangas, Fernanda Cardoso de Almeida, Lars Clausen, Jean-Pierre Coens, Sophie & Mowgli Coyaud, Zita Crener, Koen De Rijcke, Guillermo Delfino, Rocio Diaz, Flavio Domingues, Michael & Chantal Donahue, Kristof Downer, Jean Marc Dugauquier, Laura Dunham, Yasmin Ebrahim, Tom Feehan, Judy Fennessy, Mirko Lerotic Filho, Pernille & Kennet Foh, Daniel Foster, James Fuhrman, Tomasz & Anna Galka, Pedro Villela Capanema Garcia, Jennifer Gongalves da Silva, Denise Gulshan, Peter Gustafsson, Susie Hanson, Paul Harker, Will Hegman, Jon Hepworth, Jim Hogan, Nadler Ishay, Valentina Jacome, Kalon Jelen, Sara Jones, Michael Kitzul, Lewis Kofsky, Leonhard Krause, Dolores Leao, Manfred Lenzen, Milton Lever, Lina Magni, Fernando Marins, Rebecca Martinsson, Nara Mattoso, Stephen McCurry, Bruce & Mathilde McGarvey, Marta Moe, Mark Mollet, Manoel da Silveira Netto, Gitte Nielsen, Klarissa Nienhuys, Hemal Parekh, Patrik Persson, Gonzalo Petracchi, Winfrid Rauch, Sofia Rehn, Loys Richards, Branden Rippey, Muriel Rive, Jeff Rothman, Christine Sadler, Urmimala Sarkar, Christien Scheepens, Mari Schmidt, Tracey Schmidt, Jamie Shand, Sabine Sibler, Pete Siegfried, Robert & Giselle Stride, Gillian Suss, Debora Tarantino, Martin Tremblay, David Tryhorn, Akira Umekawa, Marius Van Dam, Ruben van den Berg, Johan Veneman, Jadranka Vrsalovic, Colin Walker, Daniel Waterman, Dara and Jenne Wax, Susan Weber, Thomas Wilcke, Hanna Wilhelm, Jeroen Woesthuis.

LONELY PLANET

You already know that Lonely Planet produces more than this one guidebook, but you might not be aware of the other products we have on this region. Here is a selection of titles which you may want to check out as well:

Rio de Janeiro
ISBN 1 86450 306 8
US$14.99 • UK£8.99

Bolivia
ISBN 0 86442 668 2
US$21.99 • UK£13.99

Brazilian phrasebook
ISBN 1 864503 807
US$7.99 • UK£4.50

South America on a shoestring
ISBN 1 86450 283 5
US$29.99 • UK£17.99

Read this First: Central & South America
ISBN 1 86450 067 0
US$14.99 • UK£8.99

Peru
ISBN 0 86442 710 7
US$17.95 • UK£11.99

Available wherever books are sold.

Lonely Planet Guides by Region

Lonely Planet is known worldwide for publishing practical, reliable and no-nonsense travel information in our guides and on our Web site. The Lonely Planet list covers just about every accessible part of the world. Currently there are 16 series: Travel guides, Shoestring guides, Condensed guides, Phrasebooks, Read This First, Healthy Travel, Walking guides, Cycling guides, Watching Wildlife guides, Pisces Diving & Snorkeling guides, City Maps, Road Atlases, Out to Eat, World Food, Journeys travel literature and Pictorials.

AFRICA Africa on a shoestring • Botswana • Cairo • Cairo City Map • Cape Town • Cape Town City Map • East Africa • Egypt • Egyptian Arabic phrasebook • Ethiopia, Eritrea & Djibouti • Ethiopian Amharic phrasebook • The Gambia & Senegal • Healthy Travel Africa • Kenya • Malawi • Morocco • Moroccan Arabic phrasebook • Mozambique • Namibia • Read This First: Africa • South Africa, Lesotho & Swaziland • Southern Africa • Southern Africa Road Atlas • Swahili phrasebook • Tanzania, Zanzibar & Pemba • Trekking in East Africa • Tunisia • Watching Wildlife East Africa • Watching Wildlife Southern Africa • West Africa • World Food Morocco • Zambia • Zimbabwe, Botswana & Namibia
Travel Literature: Mali Blues: Traveling to an African Beat • The Rainbird: A Central African Journey • Songs to an African Sunset: A Zimbabwean Story

AUSTRALIA & THE PACIFIC Aboriginal Australia & the Torres Strait Islands • Auckland • Australia • Australian phrasebook • Australia Road Atlas • Cycling Australia • Cycling New Zealand • Fiji • Fijian phrasebook • Healthy Travel Australia, NZ and the Pacific • Islands of Australia's Great Barrier Reef • Melbourne • Melbourne City Map • Micronesia • New Caledonia • New South Wales • New Zealand • Northern Territory • Outback Australia • Out to Eat – Melbourne • Out to Eat – Sydney • Papua New Guinea • Pidgin phrasebook • Queensland • Rarotonga & the Cook Islands • Samoa • Solomon Islands • South Australia • South Pacific • South Pacific phrasebook • Sydney • Sydney City Map • Sydney Condensed • Tahiti & French Polynesia • Tasmania • Tonga • Tramping in New Zealand • Vanuatu • Victoria • Walking in Australia • Watching Wildlife Australia • Western Australia
Travel Literature: Islands in the Clouds: Travel in the Highlands of New Guinea • Kiwi Tracks: A New Zealand Journey • Sean & David's Long Drive

CENTRAL AMERICA & THE CARIBBEAN Bahamas, Turks & Caicos • Baja California • Belize, Guatemala & Yucatán • Bermuda • Central America on a shoestring • Costa Rica • Costa Rica Spanish phrasebook • Cuba • Cycling Cuba • Dominican Republic & Haiti • Eastern Caribbean • Guatemala • Havana • Healthy Travel Central & South America • Jamaica • Mexico • Mexico City • Panama • Puerto Rico • Read This First: Central & South America • Virgin Islands • World Food Caribbean • World Food Mexico • Yucatán
Travel Literature: Green Dreams: Travels in Central America

EUROPE Amsterdam • Amsterdam City Map • Amsterdam Condensed • Andalucía • Athens • Austria • Baltic States phrasebook • Barcelona • Barcelona City Map • Belgium & Luxembourg • Berlin • Berlin City Map • Britain • British phrasebook • Brussels, Bruges & Antwerp • Brussels City Map • Budapest • Budapest City Map • Canary Islands • Catalunya & the Costa Brava • Central Europe • Central Europe phrasebook • Copenhagen • Corfu & the Ionians • Corsica • Crete • Crete Condensed • Croatia • Cycling Britain • Cycling France • Cyprus • Czech & Slovak Republics • Czech phrasebook • Denmark • Dublin • Dublin City Map • Dublin Condensed • Eastern Europe • Eastern Europe phrasebook • Edinburgh • Edinburgh City Map • England • Estonia, Latvia & Lithuania • Europe on a shoestring • Europe phrasebook • Finland • Florence • Florence City Map • France • Frankfurt City Map • Frankfurt Condensed • French phrasebook • Georgia, Armenia & Azerbaijan • Germany • German phrasebook • Greece • Greek Islands • Greek phrasebook • Hungary • Iceland, Greenland & the Faroe Islands • Ireland • Italian phrasebook • Italy • Kraków • Lisbon • The Loire • London • London City Map • London Condensed • Madrid • Madrid City Map • Malta • Mediterranean Europe • Milan, Turin & Genoa • Moscow • Munich • Netherlands • Normandy • Norway • Out to Eat – London • Out to Eat – Paris • Paris • Paris City Map • Paris Condensed • Poland • Polish phrasebook • Portugal • Portuguese phrasebook • Prague • Prague City Map • Provence & the Côte d'Azur • Read This First: Europe • Rhodes & the Dodecanese • Romania & Moldova • Rome • Rome City Map • Rome Condensed • Russia, Ukraine & Belarus • Russian phrasebook • Scandinavian & Baltic Europe • Scandinavian phrasebook • Scotland • Sicily • Slovenia • South-West France • Spain • Spanish phrasebook • Stockholm • St Petersburg • St Petersburg City Map • Sweden • Switzerland • Tuscany • Ukrainian phrasebook • Venice • Vienna • Wales • Walking in Britain • Walking in France • Walking in Ireland • Walking in Italy • Walking in Scotland • Walking in Spain • Walking in Switzerland • Western Europe • World Food France • World Food Greece • World Food Ireland • World Food Italy • World Food Spain **Travel Literature:** After Yugoslavia • Love and War in the Apennines • The Olive Grove: Travels in Greece • On the Shores of the Mediterranean • Round Ireland in Low Gear • A Small Place in Italy

Mail Order

Lonely Planet products are distributed worldwide. They are also available by mail order from Lonely Planet, so if you have difficulty finding a title please write to us. North and South American residents should write to 150 Linden St, Oakland, CA 94607, USA; European and African residents should write to 10a Spring Place, London NW5 3BH, UK; and residents of other countries to Locked Bag 1, Footscray, Victoria 3011, Australia.

INDIAN SUBCONTINENT & THE INDIAN OCEAN Bangladesh • Bengali phrasebook • Bhutan • Delhi • Goa • Healthy Travel Asia & India • Hindi & Urdu phrasebook • India • India & Bangladesh City Map • Indian Himalaya • Karakoram Highway • Kathmandu City Map • Kerala • Madagascar • Maldives • Mauritius, Réunion & Seychelles • Mumbai (Bombay) • Nepal • Nepali phrasebook • North India • Pakistan • Rajasthan • Read This First: Asia & India • South India • Sri Lanka • Sri Lanka phrasebook • Tibet • Tibetan phrasebook • Trekking in the Indian Himalaya • Trekking in the Karakoram & Hindukush • Trekking in the Nepal Himalaya • World Food India **Travel Literature:** The Age of Kali: Indian Travels and Encounters • Hello Goodnight: A Life of Goa • In Rajasthan • Maverick in Madagascar • A Season in Heaven: True Tales from the Road to Kathmandu • Shopping for Buddhas • A Short Walk in the Hindu Kush • Slowly Down the Ganges

MIDDLE EAST & CENTRAL ASIA Bahrain, Kuwait & Qatar • Central Asia • Central Asia phrasebook • Dubai • Farsi (Persian) phrasebook • Hebrew phrasebook • Iran • Israel & the Palestinian Territories • Istanbul • Istanbul City Map • Istanbul to Cairo • Istanbul to Kathmandu • Jerusalem • Jerusalem City Map • Jordan • Lebanon • Middle East • Oman & the United Arab Emirates • Syria • Turkey • Turkish phrasebook • World Food Turkey • Yemen **Travel Literature**: Black on Black: Iran Revisited • Breaking Ranks: Turbulent Travels in the Promised Land • The Gates of Damascus • Kingdom of the Film Stars: Journey into Jordan

NORTH AMERICA Alaska • Boston • Boston City Map • Boston Condensed • British Columbia • California & Nevada • California Condensed • Canada • Chicago • Chicago City Map • Chicago Condensed • Florida • Georgia & the Carolinas • Great Lakes • Hawaii • Hiking in Alaska • Hiking in the USA • Honolulu & Oahu City Map • Las Vegas • Los Angeles • Los Angeles City Map • Louisiana & the Deep South • Miami • Miami City Map • Montréal • New England • New Orleans • New Orleans City Map • New York City • New York City City Map • New York City Condensed • New York, New Jersey & Pennsylvania • Oahu • Out to Eat – San Francisco • Pacific Northwest • Rocky Mountains • San Diego & Tijuana • San Francisco • San Francisco City Map • Seattle • Seattle City Map • Southwest • Texas • Toronto • USA • USA phrasebook • Vancouver • Vancouver City Map • Virginia & the Capital Region • Washington, DC • Washington, DC City Map • World Food New Orleans **Travel Literature**: Caught Inside: A Surfer's Year on the California Coast • Drive Thru America

NORTH-EAST ASIA Beijing • Beijing City Map • Cantonese phrasebook • China • Hiking in Japan • Hong Kong & Macau • Hong Kong City Map • Hong Kong Condensed • Japan • Japanese phrasebook • Korea • Korean phrasebook • Kyoto • Mandarin phrasebook • Mongolia • Mongolian phrasebook • Seoul • Shanghai • South-West China • Taiwan • Tokyo • World Food Hong Kong • World Food Japan **Travel Literature:** In Xanadu: A Quest • Lost Japan

SOUTH AMERICA Argentina, Uruguay & Paraguay • Bolivia • Brazil • Brazilian phrasebook • Buenos Aires • Buenos Aires City Map • Chile & Easter Island • Colombia • Ecuador & the Galápagos Islands • Healthy Travel Central & South America • Latin American Spanish phrasebook • Peru • Quechua phrasebook • Read This First: Central & South America • Rio de Janeiro • Rio de Janeiro City Map • Santiago de Chile • South America on a shoestring • Trekking in the Patagonian Andes • Venezuela **Travel Literature**: Full Circle: A South American Journey

SOUTH-EAST ASIA Bali & Lombok • Bangkok • Bangkok City Map • Burmese phrasebook • Cambodia • Cycling Vietnam, Laos & Cambodia • East Timor phrasebook • Hanoi • Healthy Travel Asia & India • Hill Tribes phrasebook • Ho Chi Minh City (Saigon) • Indonesia • Indonesian phrasebook • Indonesia's Eastern Islands • Java • Lao phrasebook • Laos • Malay phrasebook • Malaysia, Singapore & Brunei • Myanmar (Burma) • Philippines • Pilipino (Tagalog) phrasebook • Read This First: Asia & India • Singapore • Singapore City Map • South-East Asia on a shoestring • South-East Asia phrasebook • Thailand • Thailand's Islands & Beaches • Thailand, Vietnam, Laos & Cambodia Road Atlas • Thai phrasebook • Vietnam • Vietnamese phrasebook • World Food Indonesia • World Food Thailand • World Food Vietnam

ALSO AVAILABLE: Antarctica • The Arctic • The Blue Man: Tales of Travel, Love and Coffee • Brief Encounters: Stories of Love, Sex & Travel • Buddhist Stupas in Asia: The Shape of Perfection • Chasing Rickshaws • The Last Grain Race • Lonely Planet…On the Edge: Adventurous Escapades from Around the World • Lonely Planet Unpacked • Lonely Planet Unpacked Again • Not the Only Planet: Science Fiction Travel Stories • Ports of Call: A Journey by Sea • Sacred India • Travel Photography: A Guide to Taking Better Pictures • Travel with Children • Tuvalu: Portrait of an Island Nation

Index

Text

Bold indicates maps.

Bold indicates maps.

Bold indicates maps.

Boxed Text

MAP LEGEND

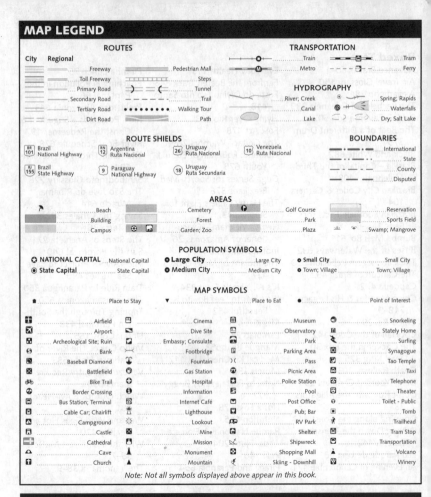

ROUTES

City	Regional	
		Freeway
		Toll Freeway
		Primary Road
		Secondary Road
		Tertiary Road
		Dirt Road

Pedestrian Mall
Steps
Tunnel
Trail
Walking Tour
Path

TRANSPORTATION

Train
Metro
Tram
Ferry

HYDROGRAPHY

River; Creek
Canal
Lake
Spring; Rapids
Waterfalls
Dry; Salt Lake

ROUTE SHIELDS

BR 101 Brazil National Highway
RN 12 Argentina Ruta Nacional
26 Uruguay Ruta Nacional
10 Venezuela Ruta Nacional
RJ 155 Brazil State Highway
9 Paraguay National Highway
18 Uruguay Ruta Secundaria

BOUNDARIES

International
State
County
Disputed

AREAS

Beach
Building
Campus
Cemetery
Forest
Garden; Zoo
Golf Course
Park
Plaza
Reservation
Sports Field
Swamp; Mangrove

POPULATION SYMBOLS

NATIONAL CAPITAL ... National Capital
State Capital ... State Capital
Large City ... Large City
Medium City ... Medium City
Small City ... Small City
Town; Village ... Town; Village

MAP SYMBOLS

Place to Stay
Place to Eat
Point of Interest

Airfield	Cinema	Museum
Airport	Dive Site	Observatory
Archeological Site; Ruin	Embassy; Consulate	Park
Bank	Footbridge	Parking Area
Baseball Diamond	Fountain	Pass
Battlefield	Gas Station	Picnic Area
Bike Trail	Hospital	Police Station
Border Crossing	Information	Pool
Bus Station; Terminal	Internet Café	Post Office
Cable Car; Chairlift	Lighthouse	Pub; Bar
Campground	Lookout	RV Park
Castle	Mine	Shelter
Cathedral	Mission	Shipwreck
Cave	Monument	Shopping Mall
Church	Mountain	Skiing - Downhill

Snorkeling
Stately Home
Surfing
Synagogue
Tao Temple
Taxi
Telephone
Theater
Toilet - Public
Tomb
Trailhead
Tram Stop
Transportation
Volcano
Winery

Note: Not all symbols displayed above appear in this book.

LONELY PLANET OFFICES

Australia
Locked Bag 1, Footscray, Victoria 3011
☎ 03 8379 8000 fax 03 8379 8111
email talk2us@lonelyplanet.com.au

USA
150 Linden Street, Oakland, California 94607
☎ 510 893 8555, TOLL FREE 800 275 8555
fax 510 893 8572
email info@lonelyplanet.com

UK
10a Spring Place, London NW5 3BH
☎ 020 7428 4800 fax 020 7428 4828
email go@lonelyplanet.co.uk

France
1 rue du Dahomey, 75011 Paris
☎ 01 55 25 33 00 fax 01 55 25 33 01
email bip@lonelyplanet.fr
www.lonelyplanet.fr

World Wide Web: www.lonelyplanet.com *or* AOL keyword: lp
Lonely Planet Images: lpi@lonelyplanet.com.au